Canadian
Tax
Principles

2001–2002

Edition

CLARENCE BYRD

Athabasca University

IDA CHEN

Clarence Byrd Inc.

Canadian
Tax
Principles
2001–2002
Edition

Prentice
Hall

Toronto

National Library of Canada Cataloguing in Publication Data

Canadian tax principles

Annual.
1988/89 ed.–
Some vols. include accompanying material in print and/or CD-ROM format.
Issues for 1994/95–   published: Scarborough, Ont.: Prentice-Hall Canada.
ISSN 1204-9174
ISBN 0-13-042510-9 (2001-2002 ed.)

1. Income tax – Canada.

HJ4661.B84   343.7105'2   C96-900996-8 rev

0-13-042510-9

Vice President, Editorial Director: Michael Young
Acquisitions Editor: Samantha Scully
Marketing Manager: Cas Shields
Associate Editor: Pamela Voves
Production Editor: Marisa D'Andrea
Production Coordinator: Patricia Ciardullo
Art Director: Mary Opper
Cover Design: Anthony Leung

1 2 3 4 5   06 05 04 03 02

Printed and bound in Canada.

Preface

Objectives

This book is designed to be used as a text in a comprehensive university or college course in taxation. The first 13 Chapters are largely concerned with personal taxation and could serve as a text for a one semester course in that subject. Chapters 14 through 21 emphasize corporate taxation, but also include material on the taxation of trusts and partnerships, as well as material on international taxation. These Chapters would provide the basis for a second one semester course in taxation. Note, however, that coverage of much of the material in the first 13 Chapters is essential to an understanding of this later material.

In terms of style, we have attempted to strike a medium ground between the kind of complete documentation that can render material on taxation totally incomprehensible, as opposed to the total elimination of references that would make it impossible for readers to expand their understanding of particular points. In those situations where we feel the issue is sufficiently complex that further investigation may be required, we have provided a reference to the relevant sections of the *Income Tax Act* or other related materials. In contrast, no direction has been provided when the material is either very straightforward or where the relevant parts of the *Act* would be obvious.

This book can be used with or without additional source material. Some instructors require students to acquire a copy of the *Income Tax Act* and permit its use as a reference during examinations. For instructors wishing to take this approach, we have included sufficient references to the *Act* that students will be able to use that reference. In addition, we have included an electronic version of the *Act* as part of the attached "Companion CD-ROM" (see later description).

For instructors not wishing to require the use of the *Income Tax Act*, we have designed the problem material so that students should be able to solve virtually all of the included problems relying solely on the text as a reference.

Companion CD-ROM

This edition of *Canadian Tax Principles* includes a Companion CD-ROM with an extensive tax research library, as well as a complete tax preparation software package. Thanks to our affiliations with the Canadian Institute Of Chartered Accountants (CICA) and Intuit Greenpoint, this Companion CD-ROM includes:

- The complete text of *Canadian Tax Principles*, presented in Folio Views software. This provides a powerful search engine for use with this text, as well as electronic jump links to other references on the CD-ROM (e.g., the *Income Tax Act*).
- The CICA's Federal Income Tax Collection (FITAC ^{Lite}). This includes the complete *Income Tax Act* and *Regulations,* as well as a complete set of Interpretation Bulletins and Information Circulars. These materials are also presented in Folio Views software, which provides for hypertext links for all references in the electronic version of *Canadian Tax Principles*.
- Intuit Greenpoint's T1 ProFile software for preparing 2000 personal tax returns (software for 2001 returns is not available at the time this book is published).
- Intuit Greenpoint's T2 ProFile software for preparing corporate tax returns.

The availability of these materials should allow you to provide a classroom setting that reflects the manner in which tax work is carried out in real world situations. To facilitate your use of these materials, each Chapter has an Electronic Library Research Problem that requires students to use the materials provided on this Companion CD-ROM.

Problem Material

There are five types of problem material included in this book. They can be described as follows:

Exercises   These are short problems that are generally focused on a single issue. This type of problem was first introduced three years ago and have been very favourably received by users of this text. New in this year's edition are boxes in the margins of the text indicating the point at which attempting the exercises would be appropriate.

Solutions to these problems are included in an Appendix which follows Chapter 21. We would suggest that students attempt these problems first, preferably as they are reading the related Chapter.

Self Study Problems   These problems are more complex than the exercises and often deal with more than one subject. As was the case with the exercises, solutions to these problems are included in the Appendix which follows Chapter 21. These problems are designed for students who wish to have more experience in solving problems. We have found that the more successful students in our courses have attempted the majority of these problems.

Assignment Problems   In general, these are the most difficult problems included in the text. They are often adapted from professional examinations and involve a number of different issues in each problem. Solutions to these problems are available only in a separate solutions manual that is provided to instructors. We do not make this solutions manual available to students.

Electronic Library Research Problems   The final assignment problem for each Chapter contains a group of questions that cannot be solved using the text. Solving these problems requires the use of the materials that have been provided on the Companion CD-ROM. As with other assignment problems, solutions to these problems are available only in a separate solutions manual that is provided to instructors.

Cases   In Chapters 13 and 15 there are cases designed to be solved using the Intuit Greenpoint software provided on the Companion CD-ROM. As with assignment problems, solutions to these cases are available only in a separate solutions manual that is provided to instructors.

We would note that the problem material in this text provides coverage of all of the issues that are specified in the Syllabuses of the CA, CGA, and CMA programs.

Using The Book

We have made every effort to enhance the usefulness of this book. There is a detailed table of contents which will direct you to the subject matter in each Chapter. In addition, to facilitate easy access to any subject being investigated, there is a comprehensive topical index at the end of the book. Finally, at the beginning of the book you will find a summary of tax rates and other data, including relevant web sites, that will be a convenient and useful reference when using the book.

The Federal Budget

The Process

One of the great difficulties in preparing a textbook on Canadian taxation is the fact that changes in the relevant legislation are made each year. The usual process has been for the Federal Government to have a budget statement in February that contains the changes that are applicable to that year. Complicating this process is the fact that draft legislation to implement this budget statement is usually not available until late in the year or, in many cases, the following year. As texts are generally made available for September classes, they must be prepared using the very general statements contained in the budget message.

This is not the case for 2001. There was a February 28, 2000 budget, followed by an October 18, 2000 Economic Statement and Budget Update. Given the extensive changes announced in these documents, no new budget statement was issued in February, 2001. The draft legislation to implement the February 28, 2000 budget and the October 18, 2000 Economic Statement and Budget Update, was issued on March 16, 2001. The content of this text is based on this draft legislation.

Recent Changes

Given the extent of the changes introduced in the February 28, 2000 budget and the October 18, 2000 economic statement, it is not surprising that the government chose not to introduce further modifications in a new budget for 2001. Among the major changes introduced for the years 2000 and 2001 were the following:

- A reduction in the inclusion rate for taxable capital gains and allowable capital losses. The rate was initially reduced to two-thirds but, in the October 2000 economic statement, there was a further reduction to one-half.

- The elimination of the federal surtax on individuals.

- The restoration of full indexing as opposed to indexing only for inflation in excess of three percent. This applies to both tax brackets and most tax credits.

- The deferral of recognition of the employment income inclusion on stock options issued by public companies from the time of exercise until the time the shares are sold.

- A new rollover provision for investments in small business corporations.

- Scheduled reductions in the effective tax rates on corporations. These reductions start at 1 percent for calendar 2001 and will increase to 7 percent for calendar 2004. This rate reduction process has been accelerated for an additional $100,000 of small business income so that the full 7 percent reduction is available in 2001 on Canadian active small business income between $200,000 and $300,000.

A further important change for 2001 is the fact that all of the provinces have switched from calculating their taxes payable as a percentage of basic federal tax payable, to a system where provincial taxes are calculated as a percentage of taxable income. This new approach has come to be referred to as a TONI (Tax ON Income) system.

As you can see from the list of changes, there is an effort at the federal government level to reduce both personal and corporate taxes. This has been combined with some significant reductions in provincial taxes, resulting in fairly dramatic reductions in taxes in certain situations. For 2001, the reductions are more significant for individuals. However, as the scheduled rate reductions in corporate taxes are phased in, corporate reductions will be similar to those that have been provided to individuals.

Acknowledgments

We would like to thank the many students that have used this book, the instructors that have adopted it at colleges and universities throughout Canada, as well as the assistants and tutors that have been involved in these courses. In particular, we would like to thank the following individuals who have reviewed the book and provided specific comments and suggestions that have enhanced the usefulness of it:

- Maria Bélanger of Algonquin College
- Ralph Gioia of the British Columbia Institute Of Technology
- Edward Gough of Centennial College
- Jane Kaake Nemeth of Durham College
- Alison Wiseman of Fanshawe College

Also essential to our efforts were the efforts of Diane Doyon. Mrs. Doyon was responsible for inputting the extensive changes in this year's problems, as well as compiling the problem material.

As always, we were greatly assisted by the staff at Prentice Hall Canada. Both Acquisitions Editor Samantha Scully and our Developmental Editor, Pamela Voves, made significant contributions to the success of this effort.

We would like to extend our thanks to Garth Steele of Welch & Company LLP. Mr. Steele has taken on the responsibility for reviewing the material on the GST. This includes Chapter 4, which is devoted entirely to GST considerations, as well as other material on this subject that is found in Chapters throughout the book. Garth has done an outstanding job in helping us with this material and we look forward to his continuing assistance in future years.

Finally, we would like to acknowledge the significant amount of work done by Mavis Jacobs in the development of Chapters 19, 20, and 21. For the past several years, Mrs. Jacobs has assumed responsibility for the material in these Chapters and has been listed as a co-author of the text. Unfortunately for us, her responsibilities as Director of the Centre For Commerce and Administrative Studies at Athabasca University have increased to the point where she is no longer able to participate in this year's edition of the text. Despite this year's lack of participation, the quality of these three Chapters will continue to reflect the efforts she made in the development of these Chapters.

As always, we have made every effort to accurately reflect appropriate tax rules. However, it is virtually certain that errors remain. These errors are solely the responsibility of the authors and we apologize for any confusion that they may cause you.

We welcome any corrections or suggestions for additions or improvements. These can be sent to us at:

Clarence Byrd Inc.
139 Musie Loop Road, Chelsea, Quebec   J9B 1Y6
e-mail address: byrddawg@passport.ca

July, 2001   Clarence Byrd, Athabasca University
                                                  Ida Chen, Clarence Byrd Inc.

2001 Rates And Other Data (Including Web Sites)

There are a number of tax rates and other statistics that are commonly used in solving tax problems. While most of the following can be found in various locations throughout this book, we are providing this summary list for your convenience.

Federal Tax Rates For Individuals

Taxable Income In Excess Of	Federal Tax	Marginal Rate On Excess
$ -0-	$ -0-	16%
30,754	4,921	22%
61,509	11,687	26%
100,000	21,695	29%

Surtax   For 2001, the federal surtax has been eliminated.

Federal Tax Credits   The following federal tax credits are applicable to 2001:

Personal Credits [ITA 118(1)]

Basic Personal   The basic personal credit is equal to 16% of $7,412 ($1,186).

Spousal   The spousal credit is equal to 16% of $6,294 ($1,007), less 16% of the spouse's net income in excess of $629. Not available when spouse's income is more than $6,922.

Equivalent To Spouse   The equivalent credit and supplement are the same here as for a spouse.

Infirm Dependants Who Have Attained The Age Of 18 Before The End Of 2001   16% of $3,500 ($560), less 16% of the dependant's Net Income in excess of $4,966. Not available when dependant's income is more than $8,465.

Caregiver   16% of $3,500 ($560), less 16% of the dependant's Net Income in excess of $11,953. Not available when dependant's income is more than $15,452.

Other Credits (Various ITA)

Age   16% of $3,619 ($579). The base for this credit is reduced by the lesser of $3,619 and 15% of the individual's net income in excess of $26,941. Not available when income is more than $51,067.

Canada Pension Plan   16% of amounts paid by employees up to the maximum Canada Pension Plan contribution of $1,496 [4.3% of ($38,300 less $3,500)]. This produces a maximum tax credit of $239 [(16%)($1,496)].

Employment Insurance   16% of amounts paid by employees up to the maximum Employment Insurance premium of $878 (2.25% of $39,000). This produces a maximum tax credit of $140 [(16%)($878)].

Pension   16% of the first $1,000 of eligible pension income.

Disability   16% of $6,000 ($960). If not used by the disabled individual, can be transferred to a person claiming that individual as a dependant.

Infirm Dependants Who Have Not Attained The Age Of 18 Before The End Of 2001 And Who Qualify For The Disability Tax Credit   16% of $3,500 ($560), reduced by child care and attendant care expenses in excess of $2,050.

Tuition Fees   16% of qualifying tuition fees.

Education   16% of $400 ($64) per month of full time attendance. 16% of $120 ($19) per month of part time attendance.

Transfer Of Tuition And Education   If the individual cannot use these credits, is not claimed as a dependant by his spouse, and does not transfer the unused credits to a spouse, then a parent or grandparent of the individual can claim up to $800 (16% of $5,000) of any unused tuition or education credits. The amount that can be transferred is reduced by any amounts of these credits claimed by the student for the year.

Interest On Student Loans   16% of interest paid on qualifying student loans.

Medical Expenses   16% of qualifying expenditures in excess of the lower of $1,678 and 3% of net income. When medical expenses claimed include those of dependent children, the taxpayer must deduct from the credit an amount equal to 68% of the dependant's Net Income in excess of $7,412.

Refundable Medical Expense Supplement   This amount is equal to the lesser of $520 and 25/16 of the medical expense tax credit. The refundable amount is then reduced by 5% of family Net Income in excess of $18,106.

Charitable Donations   The general limit on amounts for this credit is 75% of Net Income. There is an addition to this general limit equal to 25% of any taxable capital gains and 25% of any recapture of CCA resulting from a gift of capital property. In addition, the income inclusion on capital gains arising from a gift of some publicly traded shares is reduced from one-half to one-quarter. For individuals, the credit is 16% of the first $200 and 29% of the remainder. For corporations, charitable donations are a deduction from Net Income.

Political Donations   75% of the first $200, 50% of the next $350, one-third of the next $525 to a maximum credit of $500.

Dividend Tax Credit   Legislation specifies this credit to be two-thirds of the gross up. This can also be calculated as 13-1/3 percent of the grossed up dividends or 16-2/3 percent of the actual dividends received.

Other Data

Dividend Gross Up   Dividends from taxable Canadian corporations received by individuals are grossed up to 125% of the amount received.

Capital Gain Inclusion Rates   For individuals, the taxable portion of capital gains (deductible portion of capital losses) was one-half prior to 1988 and two-thirds for 1988 and 1989. Between 1990 and 1999, the taxable portion of capital gains was three-quarters for all taxpayers. This was reduced to two-thirds for capital gains realized after February 27, 2000 but before October 18, 2000. There was a further reduction in the inclusion rate to one-half for dispositions after October 17, 2000. This rate is in effect for the foreseeable future.

Clawback Limit   The repayment of social benefits is based on the lesser of 100% of such benefits and 15% of the amount of Division B Income in excess of $55,309 for Old Age Security. There is a similar clawback on Employment Insurance receipts once an individual's Net Income exceeds $48,750.

Provincial Tax Rates And Provincial Credits For Individuals   Provincial taxes are based on Taxable Income, with most provinces adopting a range of rates for various income levels (e.g., Ontario uses rates of 6.2%, 9.24%, and 11.16%). The exception to this is Alberta, which uses a single tax rate of 10.0 percent. Provincial tax credits are generally based on the minimum provincial rate applied to a credit base that is similar to that used for federal credits.

Corporate Tax Rates   The federal corporate tax rates for 2001 are as follows (federal tax abatement removed):

General Business	28%
General Rate Reduction	1%
Manufacturing Business	21%
Small Business:	
First $200,000 of Active Business Income	12%
Next $100,000 of Active Business Income	21%
Part IV Tax	33-1/3%
Part I Tax On Investment Income Of CCPC	6-2/3%

Provincial tax rates on corporations vary from a low of 5 percent on amounts eligible for the small business deduction in Newfoundland and Nova Scotia, to a high of 17 percent on other types of income in Manitoba, New Brunswick, and Saskatchewan.

Corporate Surtax   The corporate surtax rate is 4% for 2001.

Prescribed Rate (ITR 4301)   The following figures show the base rate that would be used in calculations such as imputed interest on loans. It also shows the rates applicable on amounts owing to and from the CCRA.   For recent quarters, the interest rates were as follows:

Quarter	Base Rate	Owing From	Owing To
First Quarter, 1999	5%	7%	9%
Second Quarter, 1999	5%	7%	9%
Third Quarter, 1999	5%	7%	9%
Fourth Quarter, 1999	5%	7%	9%
First Quarter, 2000	5%	7%	9%
Second Quarter, 2000	6%	8%	10%
Third Quarter, 2000	6%	8%	10%
Four Quarter, 2000	6%	8%	10%
First Quarter, 2001	6%	8%	10%
Second Quarter, 2001	6%	8%	10%
Third Quarter, 2001	5%	7%	9%

Tax Related Web Sites

Although by no means exhaustive, the following list contains web sites which provide useful tax resources.

GOVERNMENT

CCRA   http://www.ccra-adrc.gc.ca/menu-e.html
Department of Finance Canada   http://www.fin.gc.ca/

CHARTERED ACCOUNTING FIRMS

BDO Dunwoody   http://www.bdo.ca/
Deloitte & Touche   http://www.deloitte.ca/en/default.asp
Ernst & Young   http://www.ey.com/global/gcr.nsf/canada/tax_welcome
KPMG   http://www.kpmg.ca/english/services/tax/
PricewaterhouseCoopers   http://www.ca.taxnews.com/

OTHER

Canadian Tax Foundation   http://www.ctf.ca/
Canadian Institute of Chartered Accountants
    http://www.cica.ca/cica/cicawebsite.nsf/public/homepage
Intuit Greenpoint (Tax preparation software)   http://www.greenpointsoftware.com/

Table of Contents

Chapter 3
Liability For Tax

Chapter 4
Goods and Services Tax

Chapter 4 (continued)

Chapter 5
Income Or Loss From An Office Or Employment

Chapter 6
Retirement Savings And Other Special Income Arrangements

Chapter 6 (continued)

Chapter 7
Income Or Loss From A Business

Chapter 8
Capital Cost Allowances And Cumulative Eligible Capital

Chapter 9
Capital Gains And Capital Losses

Chapter 10
Non Arm's Length Transactions, Departures From Canada And Death Of A Taxpayer

Chapter 11
Income From Property, Other Income, And Other Deductions

Chapter 11 (continued)

Chapter 12
Taxable Income For Individuals

Chapter 13
Taxes Payable For Individuals

Chapter 14
Taxable Income And Taxes Payable For Corporations

(continued)

Chapter 14 (continued)

Chapter 15

Integration, Refundable Taxes, and Special Incentives For Corporations

Chapter 15 (continued)

Chapter 16
Corporate Taxation And Management Decisions

Chapter 17
Rollovers Under Section 85

Chapter 17 (continued)

Chapter 20
Partnerships

Chapter 21
Taxation Of International Income

Chapter 1

Introduction To Federal Taxation In Canada

The Canadian Tax System

Alternative Tax Bases

1-1. There are a variety of ways in which taxes can be classified. One possible basis of classification would be the economic feature or event that is to be taxed. Such features or events are referred to as the base for taxation and a large number of different bases are used in different tax systems throughout the world. Some of the more common tax bases are as follows:

Income Tax   A tax on the income of certain defined entities.

Property Tax   A tax on the ownership of some particular set of goods.

Consumption Tax   A tax levied on the consumption of some product or service. This type of tax is also called a sales tax.

Value Added Tax   A tax levied on the increase in value of a commodity or service that has been created by the taxpayer's stage of the production or distribution cycle.

Tariffs or Customs Duties   A tax imposed on the importation or exportation of certain goods or services.

Transfer Tax   A tax on the transfer of property from one owner to another.

User Tax   A tax levied on the user of some facility such as a road or airport.

Head Tax   A tax on the very existence of some classified group of individuals.

1-2. At one time or another, some level of government has used, or is still using, all of these bases for taxation. For example, the Canadian federal government currently has, in addition to income taxes on corporations, individuals and trusts, such taxes as the Goods and Services Tax (GST), an alcoholic beverages tax, special transaction taxes, a gasoline tax, as well as others. However, at the present time, the dominant form of Canadian taxation at the federal level is the income taxes levied on both corporations and individuals. This fact is reflected in Figure 1-1 (following page) which provides a percentage distribution of the $162 billion in revenues that the federal government expects to collect during fiscal 2000-2001.

1-3. Figure 1-1 makes it clear that personal income taxes constitute the most important source of federal government revenues. In actual fact, the share of government revenues from

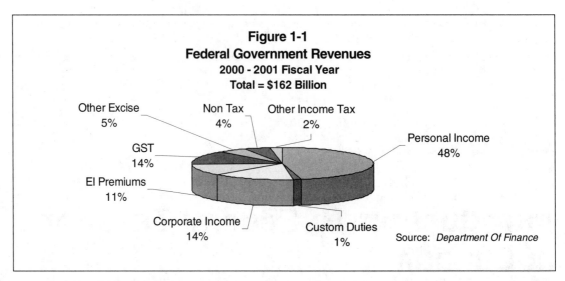

Figure 1-1
Federal Government Revenues
2000 - 2001 Fiscal Year
Total = $162 Billion

Other Excise 5%
Non Tax 4%
Other Income Tax 2%
Personal Income 48%
GST 14%
EI Premiums 11%
Corporate Income 14%
Custom Duties 1%
Source: *Department Of Finance*

this source has continued to grow. In 1997-1998, personal income taxes accounted for 46 percent of federal government revenues. For 2000-2001, this share has increased to 48 percent. However, recent budget changes appear to be reversing this trend. Current projections suggest that, in the 2001-2002 fiscal year, personal income tax revenues will drop to 46 percent of total federal government revenues.

1-4.   Other trends in recent years include the increasing importance of GST collections. They have increased from 12.7 percent of federal government revenues in 1997-1998, to 14.3 percent in 2000-2001. A further increase to 14.6 percent is expected in 2001-2002. The increasing importance of GST collections has been accompanied by a decreasing share of revenues being generated by employment insurance premiums. This source, which produced 12.3 percent of federal revenues in 1997-1998, has declined to 11.2 percent of this total in 2000-2001, and is expected to further decrease to 10.7 percent of the total in 2001-2002.

1-5.   Canada's heavy reliance on the taxation of personal income is not a universal phenomena. In other countries, indirect taxes and social security type taxes are much more important. Figure 1-2 shows the percentage of tax revenues generated by various types of taxes in the Group of Seven (G7) industrial countries. (Data for 1997 is the most recent available.) You will note that, in terms of the percentage of total tax revenues generated by personal income taxes, Canada, at 38.0 percent, is second only to the United States.

Figure 1 - 2
Types Of Taxes Used In Group Of Seven Countries

	Percent Of Total 1997 Tax Revenues				
Country	Personal Income Taxes	Corporate Income Taxes	Social Security Contributions	Taxes On Goods and Services	Payroll/ Property Taxes
Canada	38.0	10.3	13.4	24.4	12.1
France	14.0	5.8	40.6	27.8	7.8
Germany	23.9	4.0	41.6	27.7	2.7
Italy	25.3	9.5	33.5	25.9	5.2
Japan	20.5	15.0	36.9	16.5	10.6
United Kingdom	24.8	12.1	17.2	35.0	10.8
United States	39.0	9.4	24.2	16.7	10.7
OECD Average	26.6	8.8	24.9	32.1	6.4

1-6.   The 1991 introduction of the GST was intended to move Canada away from such heavy reliance on personal and corporate income taxation and towards greater reliance on taxing the sale of goods and services. While GST collections have become a somewhat more important component of total federal revenues, this appears to have been offset by declining employment insurance contributions, resulting in no reduction in the personal and corporate income tax share of these revenues.

1-7.   Canada's reliance on personal and corporate income taxes is implemented through the application of relatively high rates, a fact which has received much attention in the press in recent years. While Canadian rates are benefitting from changes introduced in the 2000 budgets, the maximum rate on individuals in Canada is about 50 percent. The corresponding figure for the U.S. is about 10 percentage points lower at 40 percent.

Taxable Entities In Canada
Income Taxes
1-8.   Three types of entities are subject to federal income taxation. The most obvious of entities would be individuals or persons. In addition to income taxes assessed on individuals, corporations and trusts are also treated as separate taxable entities. Note, however, that for income tax purposes, unincorporated businesses such as partnerships and proprietorships are not viewed as taxable entities. Rather, income earned by unincorporated business organizations is taxed in the hands of the partners and proprietors as individual persons. As will be seen in Chapter 2, all three types of taxable entities are required to file income tax returns. The returns for individuals, corporations, and trusts are referred to as T1s, T2s, and T3s, respectively.

1-9.   Tax courses are often described as either personal or corporate. While this may reflect the primary emphasis of the material in such courses, it does not reflect the realities of income tax legislation in Canada. The organization of this legislation is in terms of types of income (employment, business, property, and capital gains) rather than types of taxable entities. For example, most of the provisions related to business income apply equally to corporations, trusts, and individuals. A similar situation exists for property income and capital gains. Only employment income, earned exclusively by individuals, is associated with a single type of taxable entity.

GST
1-10.   The requirement to register to collect and remit GST generally extends to any person engaged in commercial activity in Canada. You should note that the definition of a person for GST purposes is different than that used in the *Income Tax Act*. For income tax purposes, "persons" are restricted to individuals, corporations, and trusts. Unincorporated businesses do not file separate income tax returns. Under GST legislation, the concept of a person is broader, including individuals, partnerships, corporations, estates of deceased individuals, trusts, societies, unions, clubs, associations, commissions, and other organizations.

Federal Taxation And The Provinces
Income Taxes
1-11.   Under the Constitution Act, the federal, provincial and territorial governments have the power to impose taxes. The provinces are limited to direct taxation as delegated in the Act, and this leaves all residual taxation powers to the federal government. The provinces are further limited to the taxation of income earned in the particular province and the income of persons resident in that province. Within these limitations, all of the provinces and territories impose both personal and corporate income taxes at the present time.

1-12.   Until 1999, the calculation of provincial taxes on individuals was simplified by the fact that provincial taxes were based on federal tax payable. This system was followed by all of the provinces except Quebec, resulting in a situation where a single taxable income figure was used at both the federal and provincial level. In addition, most tax credits had the same base at both levels of government. Once basic federal tax payable was determined, the basic provincial tax payable was simply this amount times a specified percentage. Most provinces then applied surtaxes at various levels of income.

1-13.   For 2001, there is a new system in place. (2000 was a transition year.) The provinces have negotiated a change in the federal provincial tax collection agreement so that personal provincial taxes will now be calculated on taxable income, as opposed to federal tax payable. The federal government will continue to administer the collection of federal and provincial taxes through a single tax return, except in Quebec which has always had its own tax system.

1-14.   All of the provinces (except Quebec) have adopted the tax on income system for 2001. This change introduces greater flexibility into the system in two ways:

- While it appears that most provinces will use federal taxable income as a starting point, each province will be able to make adjustments to this figure prior to the calculation of provincial taxes.
- Each province will be able to have different provincial credits apply against provincial taxes payable. Although the provinces cannot eliminate any credits available federally, they will be able to increase the value of the credits or create new provincial credits.

1-15.   As anyone who is familiar with the Quebec system is aware, these changes will complicate the preparation of personal tax returns. The level of complication will vary from province to province, depending on the degree to which provincial taxable income and provincial tax credits vary from those applicable at the federal level. However, filing personal tax returns will clearly be more difficult in 2001.

1-16.   Because of these additional complications, the problem material in this text will, in general, not require the calculation of provincial taxes for individuals. However, because the combined federal/provincial rate is important in many tax based decisions (e.g., selecting between alternative investments), we will continue to refer to overall combined rates, despite the fact that such figures are very specific to the province in which the income is taxed as well as the characteristics associated with the individual filing the return.

1-17.   This change in the calculation of personal taxes payable at the provincial level creates a system that is similar to the system that has been applicable to corporations for many years. Provincial corporate income tax is based on taxable income, not federal taxes payable. All provinces except Alberta, Ontario, and Quebec use the federal *Income Tax Act* to compute taxable income. Even in Alberta, Ontario, and Quebec, the respective provincial Tax Acts have many of the same features as the federal Act.

1-18.   With respect to the collection of income taxes, only Quebec collects its own personal income taxes and only Alberta, Ontario, and Quebec collect their own corporate income taxes. In all other cases, both personal and corporate income taxes are collected by the federal government on behalf of the provinces.

GST

1-19.   In making its 1987 proposals for sales tax reform, the federal government suggested a joint federal/provincial sales tax. Lack of interest by provincial governments meant the proposal was never implemented. Instead, the GST was introduced at the federal level and provincial sales taxes were left in place without significant alteration. With the exception of Alberta, where no provincial sales tax has ever been levied, there were two different sales taxes collected, accounted for, and remitted.

1-20.   This situation was very costly and time consuming for businesses. Not only were they faced with the costs of filing sales tax returns in multiple jurisdictions, but each jurisdiction also had its own rules for the goods or services on which the tax was applicable. This was clearly an inefficient approach to generating tax revenues and, not surprisingly, considerable pressure developed for the harmonization of the separate federal and provincial taxes.

1-21.   Despite the obvious efficiencies that would result from harmonization, progress has been slow. In 1992, Quebec began to operate under a harmonized system, with both the federal and provincial tax being collected by Quebec. Note, however, that while the Quebec and federal tax systems lay claim to being harmonized, there are differences between the two sets of tax rules.

1-22.   On April 1, 1997, New Brunswick, Nova Scotia, and Newfoundland harmonized their sales tax regimes with the GST. The resulting harmonized system is referred to as the Harmonized Sales Tax or HST. This leaves Ontario, Prince Edward Island, and the Western Provinces outside of the system. From the point of view of business, this is an unfortunate situation, resulting in millions of dollars being wasted in dealing with the inefficiencies of a dual system.

1-23.   The federal government continues to negotiate harmonization agreements with the other provinces. To date, all of the remaining provinces except Prince Edward Island have agreements with the federal government whereby their provincial taxes are collected along with the GST at border crossings, even though there is not yet harmonization of sales tax in those provinces.

Taxation And Economic Objectives

1-24.   The traditional economic objective of taxation policies has been to generate revenues for the relevant taxing authority. However, it is clear that today's approach to taxation objectives is multi faceted. We use taxation policy to effect resource allocation, to redistribute income and wealth among taxpayers with different economic resources and needs, to assist in keeping the economy stable, and to provide intergovernmental transfers. A brief description of how taxation deals with these economic objectives is as follows:

Resource Allocation   Tax revenues can be used to provide public goods and services. Pure public goods such as our national defense system are thought to benefit all taxpayers. As it is not possible to allocate costs to individuals on the basis of benefits received, such costs must be supported with general tax revenues. Similar allocations occur with such widely used public goods as education, health care, and pollution control. In some cases, the tax system also has an influence on the allocation of private goods. For example, excise taxes are used to discourage the consumption of alcohol and tobacco products.

Distribution Effects   Our tax system is also used to redistribute income and wealth among taxpayers. Such provisions as the federal GST tax credit and provincial sales tax exemptions on food and low priced clothing have the effect of taking taxes paid by higher income taxpayers and distributing them to lower income wage earners or taxpayers with higher basic living costs in proportion to their income.

Stabilization Effects   Taxes may also be used to achieve macro economic objectives. At various times, tax policy has been used to encourage economic expansion, increase employment, and to assist in holding inflation in check. An example of this is the emphasis placed on deficit reduction in recent federal budgets.

Fiscal Federalism   This term refers to the various procedures that are used to allocate resources among different levels of government. At present, about one-quarter of federal revenue is allocated to the provinces through grants and transfers. In the next step in the chain, a portion of provincial revenue is transferred to municipal governments.

Taxation And Income Levels

General Approaches

1-25.   Policy makers are concerned about the relationship between income levels and rates of taxation. Taxes can be proportional in that a constant rate is applied at all levels of income. In theory, this is our approach to taxing the income of corporations. For public companies, the system is based on a flat rate which is applicable to all income earned by the company. However, a wide variety of provisions act to modify the application of this rate, resulting in a situation where many Canadian companies are not subject to this notional flat rate.

1-26.   As an alternative, taxation can be regressive, resulting in lower effective rates of taxation as higher income levels are reached. Sales taxes generally fall into this regressive category as lower income individuals spend a larger portion of their total income and, as a consequence, pay a greater portion of their total income as sales taxes levied on their expenditures.

Consider the Werner sisters:

Gertrude Werner has income of $100,000 and spends $20,000 of this amount. She lives in a province with a 9 percent sales tax on all expenditures, resulting in the payment of $1,800 in provincial sales taxes. This represents a 1.8 percent tax rate on her $100,000 income.

Ingrid Werner has income of $20,000 and spends all of this amount. She lives in the same province as her sister, resulting in the payment of $1,800 in provincial sales taxes. This represents a 9 percent rate of taxation on her $20,000 income.

1-27.   In contrast to the regressive nature of sales taxes, the present system of personal income taxation is designed to be progressive since higher rates are applied to higher levels of income. For 2001, the federal rates range from a low of 16 percent on the first $30,754 of taxable income to a high of 29 percent on taxable income in excess of $100,000.

Progressive Vs. Regressive

1-28.   As personal income taxes are the major source of federal tax revenues under current Canadian legislation, the system can be described as predominantly progressive. The major arguments in favour of this approach can be described as follows:

Equity   Higher income individuals have a greater ability to pay taxes. As their income is above their basic consumption needs, the cost to the individual of having a portion of this income taxed away is less than the cost to the lower income individuals where additional taxation removes funds required for such essentials as food and clothing.

Stability   Progressive tax rates help maintain after tax income stability by shifting people to lower tax brackets in times of economic downturn and to higher brackets when there is economic expansion. The resulting decreases or increases in taxes serve to cushion the economic swings.

1-29.   There are, however, a number of problems that can be associated with progressive rates. These can be briefly described as follows:

Complexity   With progressive rates in place, efforts will be made to divide income among as many individuals (usually family members) as possible. These efforts to make maximum use of the lower tax brackets necessitate the use of complex anti-avoidance rules by taxation authorities.

Income Fluctuations   In the absence of relieving provisions, progressive rates discriminate against individuals with highly variable income streams. That is, under a progressive system, an individual with $1,000,000 in income in one year and no income for the next three years will pay substantially more in taxes than an individual with the same $1,000,000 total earned over four years at a rate of $250,000 per year.

Family Unit Problems   Progressive tax rates discriminate against single income family units. A family unit in which one spouse makes $100,000 and the other has no taxable income would pay significantly more in taxes than would be the case if each spouse earned $50,000.

Economic Growth   It is clear that the high tax brackets that are associated with a progressive system can discourage both employment and investment efforts. This will serve to limit economic growth and, as will be discussed later, it is possible for rates to reach a level that will actually result in less aggregate taxes being collected.

Tax Concessions   The high brackets associated with progressive systems lead to pressure for various types of tax concessions to be made available. Because high income individuals have a greater ability to effectively take advantage of favourable provisions in the income tax legislation, they may actually wind up paying taxes at lower effective rates. The fact that in extreme cases some high income individuals pay no income taxes at all led to the introduction of an alternative minimum income tax that is imposed on certain taxpayers.

Tax Evasion Progressive rates discourage income reporting and encourage the creation of various devices to evade taxation. Evasion strategies range from simple bartering, to cash only transactions, and finally to organized crime activities.

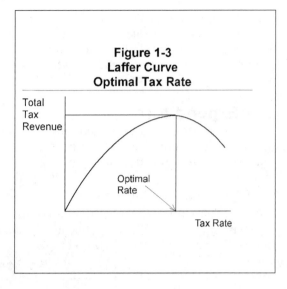

Figure 1-3
Laffer Curve
Optimal Tax Rate

Flat Tax Systems

1-30. While progressive tax systems continue to be pervasive, there has been a world wide trend towards flattening rate schedules. One of the reasons for this trend is the fact that effective tax rates are not as progressive as the rate schedules indicate. We have previously noted that high bracket taxpayers tend to have better access to various types of tax concessions, a fact which can significantly reduce the effective rates for these individuals. Given this situation, it has been suggested that we could achieve results similar to those which, in fact, prevail under the current system by applying a flat rate of tax to a broadened taxation base. In this context, the term base broadening refers to the elimination of tax concessions, with the result that tax rates are applied to a larger income figure.

1-31. In a 1988 study by Roger S. Smith of the University of Alberta, a flat 20 percent rate of tax was applied to a broadened base. This broadened base included the non taxable component of capital gains and did not permit deductions for such items as Registered Retirement Savings Plan contributions, the interest and dividend deduction (since repealed), or the pension income deduction. (This deduction has become a credit against taxes payable.) For those individuals with incomes below $4,500, a zero tax bracket was assumed. The results of this study indicated that, for the majority of taxpayers (i.e., those with incomes between $10,000 and $100,000), the application of a flat tax to a broadened base produces a tax liability that is only marginally different from the net tax liability under the present system of progressive rates accompanied by various tax concessions.

1-32. Canada's first flat tax system for individuals has now been implemented. Not surprisingly, it is in place in Alberta for 2001. Under this new system, all income is taxed at a flat provincial rate of 10.5 percent.

1-33. Another important factor that has encouraged the trend towards reduced progressivity is the fact that total tax revenues may actually decline if marginal tax rates are too high. This idea was developed by Professor Arthur Laffer and is often expressed in the Laffer Curve shown in Figure 1-3.

1-34. As can be seen in Figure 1-3, there is an optimal tax rate beyond which total tax revenues begin to decline. Major reasons for this would be the fact that high tax rates reduce the willingness to work and, at the same time, increase the willingness to evade taxes. While no hard evidence supports a particular rate as being the optimal rate, many experts believe that the maximum should be about 40 percent.

Tax Incidence

1-35. Tax incidence refers to the issue of who really pays a particular tax. While statutory incidence refers to the initial legal liability for tax payment, the actual economic burden may be passed on to a different group. For example, certain taxes on production might be the legal liability of the producer. However, they may be partly or entirely shifted to consumers through price increases on the goods produced.

1-36. Policy makers must be concerned with this to ensure that the system is working as intended. It is generally assumed that the incidence of personal income tax falls on individuals.

In addition, in their role as consumers, individuals also assume the responsibility for a large portion of the various sales taxes that are levied in Canada. The incidence of corporate taxes is more open to speculation. Shareholders may bear the burden of corporate taxes in the short run. However, most authorities believe that, in the long run, this burden is shared by employees and consumers.

Tax Expenditures

1-37.   In contrast to government funding programs which provide payments to various entities in the economy, a tax expenditure reflects revenues that have been given up by the government through the use of tax preferences, concessions, and other tax breaks. These expenditures may favour selected individuals or groups (senior citizens), certain kinds of income (capital gains), or certain characteristics of some taxpayers (the disabled).

1-38.   In an effort to quantify the importance of these expenditures, the Department Of Finance produces annually the publication, "Tax Expenditures". The 2000 edition contains estimates for 1995 to 1997 and projections for 1998 to 2002 of the costs of various income tax and GST expenditures. Examples of the 1997 estimates and 2002 projections of the cost of some of these expenditures include:

- The basic personal tax credit - $18.25 billion in 1997, $21.81 billion in 2002.

- The spousal tax credit - $1.15 billion in 1997, $1.49 billion in 2002.

- The treatment of private health and dental care as a non taxable employee benefit - $1.63 billion in 1997, $1.68 billion in 2002.

- The non taxation of capital gains on principal residences - $1.31 billion in 1997, $0.97 billion in 2002. (This decline does not reflect the reduction in the capital gains inclusion rate.)

- The deduction for RRSP contributions - $6.39 billion in 1997, $8.29 billion in 2002.

- The non taxation of lottery earnings - $1.34 billion in 1997, $1.76 billion in 2002.

- The provision of the small business deduction - $2.72 billion in 1997, $3.34 billion in 2002.

- The treatment of basic groceries as zero rated items for GST purposes - $2.89 billion in 1997, $3.63 billion in 2002.

1-39.   It is clear that such tax expenditures are of considerable significance in the management of federal finances. It is equally clear that the provision of this type of government benefit has become entrenched in our tax system. This situation can be explained by a number of factors:

- It is less costly to administer tax expenditures than it is to administer government funding programs.

- More decisions are left to the private sector so that funds may be allocated more efficiently.

- Tax expenditures reduce the visibility of certain government actions. This is particularly beneficial if some social stigma is attached to the programs. For example, a child tax benefit system is more acceptable than increasing social assistance payments.

- Tax expenditures reduce the progressivity of the tax system. As many of the tax expenditures, such as tax shelters, are more available to higher income taxpayers, they serve to reduce effective tax rates in the higher rate brackets.

1-40.   Tax expenditures are not only very substantial, they are also difficult to control. This was noted by Auditor General Kenneth Dye in his 1985 Annual Report as follows:

A cost conscious Parliament is in the position of a team of engineers trying to design a more fuel efficient automobile. They think they have succeeded, but the engine seems to go on consuming as much gas as it did before. They cannot understand the problem until they notice that, hidden from view, myriad small holes have been punched through the bottom of the gas tank. This is too often the way of tax expenditures. Revenue leaks away, and MPs do not know about it until it is too late.

Qualitative Characteristics Of Tax Systems

General Concepts

1-41.   In recent years, accounting standard setting bodies have established such concepts as relevance and reliability as being desirable qualitative characteristics of accounting information. While not established with the same degree of formality, it is clear that there are similar concepts that can be used to evaluate tax systems. Some of these desirable qualitative characteristics can be described as follows:

Equity Or Fairness   Horizontal equity entails similar levels of taxation for people in similar economic circumstances. In contrast, vertical equity means dissimilar tax treatment of people in different circumstances. Equity could be achieved by taxing individual taxpayers for the benefits that they receive from public services. In practice, medical and hospital premiums are sometimes levied on this basis. However, the costs of many public goods cannot be allocated on the basis of individual satisfaction and, as a result, equity is usually approached through the ability to pay principle. It is this principle that underlies the use of progressive tax rates in our system.

Neutrality   The concept of neutrality calls for a tax system which interferes as little as possible with decision making. An overriding economic assumption is that decisions are always made to maximize the use of resources. This may not be achieved when tax factors affect how taxpayers save, invest, or consume. Taxes, by influencing economic decisions, may cause a less than optimal allocation of resources.

Adequacy   A good tax system should meet the funding requirements of the taxing authority. It is also desirable that these revenues be produced in a fashion that is dependable and relatively predictable from year to year.

Elasticity   Tax revenues should be capable of being adjusted to meet changes in economic conditions, without necessitating tax rate changes.

Flexibility   This refers to the ease with which the tax system can be adjusted to meet changing economic or social conditions.

Simplicity And Ease Of Compliance   A good tax system is easy to comply with and does not present significant administrative problems for those charged with enforcing the system.

Certainty   Individual taxpayers should know how much tax they have to pay, the basis for payments, and the due date. Such certainty also helps taxing authorities estimate tax revenues and facilitates forecasting of budgetary expenditures.

Balance Between Sectors   A good tax system should not be overly reliant on either corporate or individual taxation. Attention should also be given to balance within these sectors, insuring that no type of business or type of individual is asked to assume a disproportionate share of the tax burden.

International Competitiveness   If an individual country's tax system has rates that are out of line with those that prevail in comparable countries, the result will be an outflow of both business and skilled individuals to those countries which have more favourable tax rates.

Conflicts Among Characteristics

1-42.   In designing a tax system, many compromises are required. Examples include the fact that flexibility is often in conflict with certainty, equity requires trade offs in simplicity and neutrality, and some taxes with very positive objectives are very non neutral in nature. An example of this last conflict is that rates to small business are very favourable because the government believes that this attracts investment to this sector, thereby encouraging employment and the development of active business efforts. However, this may not result in the optimal allocation of resources to the business sector as a whole.

Canadian Evaluation

1-43. Canadian policy makers often refer to the preceding qualitative characteristics in discussions involving taxation policies. This would make it appropriate to consider how the current system of federal taxation stacks up against these criteria. While any comprehensive evaluation of this question goes well beyond the objectives of this book, we offer the following brief comments:

- With respect to equity, Canada continues to have situations in which high income individuals pay little or no tax and relatively low income individuals are subjected to fairly high rates. While the alternative minimum tax was instituted to correct this problem, inequity is unlikely to be eliminated in a tax system which attempts to accomplish as many diverse objectives as does the current Canadian system.

- As noted previously, the Canadian system has a very heavy reliance on the taxation of personal income and receives a very low portion of its revenues from the corporate sector.

- The Canadian system has had problems with stability and dependability of revenues. The growing importance of the GST will probably act to alleviate this problem.

- The Canadian tax system is very complex, making compliance difficult for many taxpayers. In addition, administration of the legislation is made more difficult by the large number of provisions and the lack of clarity in in their content. The GST has clearly made this situation even worse for those individuals and businesses required to comply with its many complex requirements, particularly in those provinces where there is a non harmonized sales tax levied on a different group of items.

- Without question, Canada has a problem with the international competitiveness of its tax system. This is particularly true with respect to the United States. For both individuals and corporations, tax rates are lower in that country, a fact that has led to a significant loss to Canada of both business activity and skilled individuals. While Canada is in the process of lowering its personal and corporate tax rates, it appears that even larger reductions will be coming in the United States. This will likely maintain, or even increase, the differences in tax rates between the two countries.

Canadian Federal Income Tax Legislation

History Of The Federal Income Tax Act

1-44. The first Canadian income tax was imposed in 1917. This was the *Income War Tax Act* and it was needed as the more traditional custom and excise taxes were not capable of producing the revenues required by Canada's involvement in World War I. This Act persisted, with a large number of amendments, until 1949.

1-45. In 1948, the *Income War Tax Act* was merged into new legislation called the *Income Tax Act*. This Act was largely a rewording and codification of the *Income War Tax Act* with very few actual changes in policy. This new *Income Tax Act* was applicable to 1949 and subsequent years. In 1952, the 1949 version of the *Income Tax Act* was revised. However, except for transitional provisions and a complete renumbering of sections, the revision made few real changes and, as a consequence, legal decisions based on the provisions of the 1948 Act continued to be applicable.

1-46. In 1962, a major reform of federal income tax legislation began with the creation of a Royal Commission On Taxation under the chairmanship of Kenneth Carter. This Commission, subsequently designated the Carter Commission, presented its seven volume report in 1967. This report led to the November, 1969 White Paper On Tax Reform, followed on June 18, 1971 by Bill C-259. Bill C-259 was given Royal Assent on December 23, 1971 and became law on January 1, 1972.

1-47. Since January 1, 1972, every budget has presented a considerable number of amendments to fine tune existing legislation or to introduce new policies. For example, the amendments first presented in the November 12, 1981 budget appeared to many as another major reform of income tax legislation. The May 23, 1985 budget, with its introduction of the lifetime capital gains deduction, could be viewed as a major change in the approach to the taxation of individuals. The changes introduced in 1988 as the result of the June 18, 1987 White Paper on tax reform have also resulted in a significant overhaul of the taxation system. Despite all of these changes, the general approach to the taxation of income in Canada is still based on the reforms that were made effective beginning in 1972.

Structure Of The Federal Income Tax Act

1-48.   The fundamental source of federal income tax legislation is the federal *Income Tax Act*. The Act itself is an enormous document, with most paper editions approaching 2,500 pages. While we will not attempt to provide comprehensive coverage of the complete Act, frequent references will be made to various components of the document. Further, as with all other Canadian taxation texts, the basic organization of this book follows the structure of the *Income Tax Act*. As a consequence, it is desirable that you have some knowledge of the *Act's* basic structure.

Parts Of The Act

1-49.   The federal *Income Tax Act* is made up of Parts designated I through XVII. There are, in fact, more than seventeen parts because of the use of designations within a single roman numeral. Examples of this would be Parts X.1, X.2, X.3, X.4, and X.5. Within each of these Parts there are one or more Sections, with the total Section numbers in the *Act* running from 1 to 260 and cutting across the dividing lines between the various Parts. As was the case with Parts, the number of Sections in the Act exceeds 260 because of the use of designations within a single number. Examples of this would be Sections 80.1, 80.2, 80.3, and 80.4.

1-50.   About 70 percent of the Sections of the *Income Tax Act* are found in Part I which is titled "Income Tax". This Part contains Sections 1 through 180 of the Act and, because of its importance, we will subsequently provide a more detailed description of this Part.

1-51.   Parts I.1 through XVII cover a variety of special taxes as well as rules related to matters of administration, enforcement, and interpretation. The Parts, their titles, and the Section numbers which they contain are as follows.

- Part I.1 - Individual Surtax (Section 180.1)
- Part I.2 - Tax On Old Age Security Benefits (Section 180.2)
- Part I.3 - Tax On Large Corporations (Sections 181 through 181.9)
- Part II - Tobacco Manufacturers' Surtax (Section 182 and 183)
- Part II.1 - Tax On Corporate Distributions (Sections 183.1 and 183.2)
- Part III - Additional Tax On Excessive Election (Sections 184 and 185)
- Part IV - Tax On Taxable Dividend Received By Private Corporation (Sections 186 through 187)
- Part IV.1 - Taxes On Dividends On Certain Preferred Shares Received By Corporations (Sections 187.1 through 187.61)
- Part V - Tax In Respect Of Registered Charities (Sections 187.7 through 189)
- Part VI - Tax On Capital Of Financial Institutions (Sections 190 through 190.24)
- Part VI.1 - Tax On Corporation Paying Dividends On Taxable Preferred Shares (Sections 191 through 191.4)
- Part VII - Refundable Tax On Corporation Issuing Qualifying Shares (Sections 192 and 193)
- Part VIII - Refundable Tax On Corporation In Respect Of Scientific Research And Experimental Development Tax Credit (Sections 194 and 195)
- Part IX - Tax On Deduction Under Section 66.5 (Section 196)
- Part X - Taxes On Deferred Profit Sharing Plans And Revoked Plans (Sections 198 through 204)
- Part X.1 - Tax In Respect Of Over-Contributions To Deferred Income Plans (Sections 204.1 through 204.3)

- Part X.2 - Tax In Respect Of Registered Investments (Sections 204.4 through 204.7)
- Part X.3 - Registered Labour Sponsored Venture Capital Corporations (Sections 204.8 through 204.87)
- Part X.4 - Tax In Respect Of Overpayments To Registered Education Savings Plans (Sections 204.9 through 204.93)
- Part X.5 - Payments Under Registered Education Plans (Section 204.94)
- Part XI - Tax In Respect Of Certain Property Acquired By Trust Etc., Governed By Deferred Income Plans (Sections 205 through 207)
- Part XI.1 - Tax In Respect Of Certain Property Held By Trusts Governed By Deferred Income Plans (Sections 207.1 and 207.2)
- Part XI.2 - Tax In Respect Of Certain Property Disposed Of By Certain Public Authorities Or Institutions (Sections 207.3 and 207.4)
- Part XI.3 - Tax In Respect Of Retirement Compensation Arrangements (Sections 207.5 through 207.7)
- Part XII - Tax In Respect Of Certain Royalties, Taxes, Lease Rentals, Etc. Paid To A Government By A Tax Exempt Person (Section 208)
- Part XII.1 - Tax On Carved-Out Income (Section 209)
- Part XII.2 - Tax On Designated Income Of Certain Trusts (Sections 210 through 210.3)
- Part XII.3 - Tax On Investment Income Of Life Insurers (Sections 211 through 211.5)
- Part XII.4 - Tax On Qualifying Environmental Trusts (Section 211.6)
- Part XII.5 - Recovery Of Labour Sponsored Funds Tax Credit (Section 211.7 through 211.9)
- Part XII.6 - Tax On Flow Through Shares (Section 211.91)
- Part XIII - Tax On Income From Canada Of Non Resident Persons (Sections 212 through 218.1)
- Part XIV - Additional Tax On Corporations (Other Than Canadian Corporations) Carrying On Business In Canada (Sections 219 through 219.3)
- Part XV - Administration And Enforcement (Sections 220 through 244)
- Part XVI - Tax Avoidance (Sections 245 and 246)
- Part XVI.1 - Transfer Pricing (Section 247)
- Part XVII - Interpretation (Sections 248 through 260)

Divisions Of Part I

1-52.   As was previously noted, Part I is the largest and most important Part of the *Income Tax Act*. As a result, it will receive most of our attention in this text. To facilitate your comprehension of subsequent Chapters, some understanding of the structure of this Part is required.

1-53.   Part I is divided into the following eleven Divisions and some of these Divisions are further divided into Subdivisions. The Divisions and their more significant Subdivisions will be described in the following paragraphs:

Division A: "Liability For Tax" (Section 2)   This short Division is concerned with the question of what makes a legal or economic entity liable for payment of tax in Canada.

Division B: "Computation Of Income" (Section 3 through 108)   This is the longest Division in Part I and concerns itself with the determination of income from various sources. Its first five Subdivisions describe the major sources of income and deductions and are as follows:

- Subdivision a - "Income Or Loss From An Office Or Employment"   This Subdivision deals with the ordinary wages and salaries that are earned by individuals while an employee of a business entity.

- Subdivision b - "Income Or Loss From A Business Or Property"   This Subdivision deals with business income earned by proprietorships, partnerships, and corporations. Also covered in this subdivision is property income which includes rents, interest, dividends, and royalties.

- Subdivision c - "Taxable Capital Gains And Allowable Capital Losses"   This Subdivision deals with gains and losses resulting from the disposal of capital property.

- Subdivision d - "Other Sources Of Income"   Covered here are miscellaneous income sources, such as alimony received and various types of pension income, which do not fit into any of the major categories dealt with in Subdivisions a, b, and c.

- Subdivision e - "Deductions In Computing Income"   Covered here are miscellaneous deductions such as moving expenses, child care costs, and alimony paid. These are deductions that do not fit into any of the categories in Subdivisions a, b, and c.

Subdivisions a, b, and c each provide for both inclusions and deductions and, as a consequence, require the calculation of a net income figure. The deductions that are specified for each Subdivision can only be deducted from inclusions in that Subdivision. That is, deductions related to business income (Subdivision b) cannot be deducted from the inclusions for employment income (Subdivision a). This becomes a very important point when the inclusions in a particular Subdivision are not sufficient to support all of the available deductions in that Subdivision.

The remaining six Subdivisions of Division B do not provide new sources of income but, rather, provide rules which expand on the material in the first five Subdivisions. These remaining Subdivisions are as follows:

- Subdivision f - Rules Relating To Computation Of Income
- Subdivision g - Amounts Not Included In Computing Income
- Subdivision h - Corporations Resident In Canada And Their Shareholders
- Subdivision i - Shareholders Of Corporations Not Resident In Canada
- Subdivision j - Partnerships And Their Members
- Subdivision k - Trusts And Their Beneficiaries

Divisions C And D: "Computation Of Taxable Income and Taxable Income Earned In Canada By Non Residents" (Sections 109 through 116)   These two Divisions cover the conversion of Division B income (commonly referred to as Net Income For Tax Purposes or simply Net Income) into Taxable Income for residents and non residents.

Division E: "Computation Of Tax" (Sections 117 through 127.41)   This Division is concerned with determining the taxes that are payable on the taxable income determined in Divisions C and D. It has four Subdivisions as follows:

- Subdivision a - Rules Applicable To Individuals
- Subdivision a.1 - Child Tax Benefit
- Subdivision b - Rules Applicable To Corporations
- Subdivision c - Rules Applicable To All Taxpayers

Division E.1:   "Minimum Tax" (Sections 127.5 through 127.55)   This Division is concerned with the obligations of individuals to pay a minimum amount of tax, as well as the computation of this alternative minimum tax.

Division F: "Special Rules Applicable In Certain Circumstances" (Sections 128 through 143.2)   Covered here are rules related to transactions and organizations such as bankruptcies, private corporations, mutual funds, cooperative corporations, credit unions, and insurance companies.

Division G: "Deferred And Other Special Income Arrangements" (Sections 144 through 148.1)   Covered here are rules related to deferred income plans such as registered pension plans, registered retirement savings plans, and deferred profit sharing plans.

Division H: "Exemptions" (Sections 149 and 149.1)   Covered here are exemptions for individuals and organizations such as employees of foreign countries, pension trusts, and charitable organizations.

Division I: "Returns, Assessments, Payments And Appeals" (Sections 150 through 168)

Division J: "Appeals To Tax Court Of Canada And The Federal Court" (Sections 169 through 180)

1-54.   As this book progresses, references to the Divisions of Part I as well as many of its Subdivisions will become very familiar. However, you may find it helpful as you move to subsequent Chapters, to periodically review the preceding general outline as an aid to keeping some perspective on how the material you are reading fits into the bigger picture.

Other Income Tax Legislation

1-55.   While the *Income Tax Act* constitutes the major source of legislation relevant to the study of the federal income tax, there are three other sources of legislative materials which are relevant. These are the Income Tax Application Rules, 1971, the Income Tax Regulations, a group of International Tax Agreements between Canada and other countries, and draft legislation. A general description of these legislative materials follows.

Income Tax Application Rules, 1971

1-56.   When the *Income Tax Act* was heavily revised at the end of 1971, a large number of transitional rules were required, primarily to insure that the effects of the new legislation were not retroactive. These transitional rules are called the Income Tax Application Rules, 1971, and they continue to be of some significance in matters such as valuation day rules and the determination of tax free zones in calculating capital gains and losses. However, the significance of these rules declines with each passing year and, as a consequence, they will be given little attention in this text.

Income Tax Regulations

1-57.   Section 221 of the *Income Tax Act* allows the Governor In Council to make Regulations concerning the administration and enforcement of the *Income Tax Act*. Some of the items listed in this Section include:

* prescribing the evidence required to establish facts relevant to assessments under this Act;
* requiring any class of persons to make information returns respecting any class of information required in connection with assessments under this Act;
* prescribing anything that, by this Act, is to be prescribed or is to be determined or regulated by regulation; and
* defining the classes of persons who may be regarded as dependent for the purposes of this Act.

1-58.   While these Regulations cannot extend the limits of the law, they can serve to fill in details and, to some extent, modify the statutes. For example, most of the rules for determining the amount of Capital Cost Allowance that can be deducted are established in the Regulations. The Regulations provide an essential element of flexibility in the administration of the Act in that they can be issued without going through a more formal legislative process.

International Tax Agreements

1-59.   Canada currently has tax agreements with 79 countries. The most important of these are the Tax Conventions with the United States and the United Kingdom. While there is considerable variation in the agreements, most of them are based on the model Convention developed by the Organization For Economic Co-operation And Development. The purpose of these agreements is twofold. First, they attempt to avoid double taxation of taxpayers that may have reason to pay taxes in more than one jurisdiction and, second, they try to prevent international evasion of taxes. In situations where there is a conflict between the Canadian *Income Tax Act* and an international agreement, the terms of the agreement prevail.

Draft Legislation

1-60.   Budgets are typically presented each February (2001 was an exception, likely because of the October, 2000 budget update). However, the budget presentation is of a very general nature and does not contain the actual legislative provisions that are required to implement the proposals that are being put forward. The preparation of this legislation often takes a year or more and, when it is presented, it is referred to as draft legislation. For example, the draft legislation to implement the February, 2000 budget and the October, 2000 update was presented on December 21, 2000, with a revised and expanded version being presented as a Notice of Ways and Means Motion on March 16, 2001. As of May, 2001, the draft legislation has not received Royal Assent.

1-61. The problem with this schedule is that personal tax returns for the year 2000 must be filed on a basis that includes the proposals contained in the February, 2000 budget and October, 2000 budget update. This means that returns for 2000 had to rely on the draft legislation that first became available on December 21, 2000. This imparts a sort of quasi-legal status to draft legislation that has not yet passed into law.

Other Sources Of Income Tax Information
Internal Documents
1-62. As we have seen, the formal income tax legislation includes the Income Tax Act, Income Tax Application Rules, 1971, Income Tax Regulations, International Tax Agreements, as well as draft legislation. In addition, the Canada Customs and Revenue Agency (CCRA, formerly Revenue Canada) issues directives to its district offices in which interpretations and suggested procedures are set forth. However, these directives are not available to the public and their nature can only be determined by inference and experiences with assessments and court cases. To the public, the CCRA provides four other sources which, while they do not have the force of law, can be extremely helpful and influential in making decisions related to income taxes. These Interpretation Bulletins, Information Circulars, Technical Interpretations and Income Tax Technical Newsletters are described in the Paragraphs which follow.

Web Site
1-63. The CCRA has an extensive web site at http://www.ccra-adrc.gc.ca. Many of the forms, guides, Interpretation Bulletins and other documents provided by the CCRA are available on the web site. The forms and publications can be viewed and printed online or downloaded to a computer in one or more formats. There is also an online request available to have printed forms or publications mailed out. The web site is constantly being expanded to provide more forms and publications and more electronic services (such as EFILE and NETFILE).

Interpretation Bulletins
1-64. To date, over 530 Interpretation Bulletins have been issued by the CCRA. The objective of these Bulletins is to give the CCRA's interpretation of particular sections of the law that it administers and to announce significant changes in departmental interpretation along with the effective dates of any such changes. Examples of important Interpretation Bulletins include IT-63R5 dealing with an employee's personal use of an automobile supplied by an employer, and IT-221R2 which provides guidance on the determination of an individual's residence status. Note that the R5 and R2 in these Bulletin numbers refer to fifth and second revisions of the Bulletins.

Information Circulars
1-65. Of the more than 300 Information Circulars that have been issued, over 60 are currently in effect. The objective of these publications is to provide information regarding procedural matters which relate to both the *Income Tax Act* and the provisions of the Canada Pension Plan, and to announce changes in organization, personnel, operating programs, and other administrative developments. Subjects include such matters as how to establish a Registered Pension Plan, overpayments to the Canada Pension Plan, and guidelines for the preparation of tax returns by individuals.

Advance Tax Rulings And Technical Interpretations
1-66. In recognition of the considerable complexity involved in the interpretation of many portions of the *Income Tax Act*, the CCRA will, for a fee, provide an advance tax ruling on how it will tax a proposed transaction, subject to certain limitations and qualifications. Prior to 1997, it was the policy of the CCRA to publish selected Advance Tax Rulings that it considered to be of particular interest to taxpayers.

1-67. The last published Advanced Tax Ruling was issued in 1997. Since that time they have been replaced by Technical Interpretations. These are acquired by tax publishers (CCH, the Canadian Institute of Chartered Accountants and Carswell) and included in their tax libraries.

Income Tax Technical News

1-68.   The CCRA periodically issues a newsletter titled *Income Tax Technical News*. This newsletter provides up-to-date information on current tax issues. Two of the newsletters were published in 2000 (18 and 19) and in 1999 (16 and 17).

Guides And Pamphlets

1-69.   The CCRA publishes a large number of non technical Pamphlets and Guides which provide information on particular topics of interest to taxpayers. Examples of Pamphlets would be "Canadian Residents Going Down South" (P151) and "Tax Information For People With Disabilities" (P149). Examples of Guides would be "Business And Professional Income" (T4002), "Preparing Returns For Deceased Persons" (T4011), and "RRSPs And Other Registered Plans For Retirement" (T4040). These are available online on the CCRA web site, or, without charge, at district taxation offices.

Court Decisions

1-70.   Despite the huge volume of information available for dealing with income tax matters, disputes between taxpayers and the CCRA regularly find their way into the Canadian court system. Of the hundreds of tax cases that are reported each year, the great majority do not involve tax evasion or other criminal offences. Rather, they involve an honest difference of opinion between the taxpayer and the CCRA. Common areas of litigation include:

- establishing a property's fair market value;
- the question of whether a transaction took place at arm's length;
- distinguishing between profits which are capital in nature and those that are ordinary business income; and
- the deductibility of farm losses against other sources of income.

1-71.   Given the large number of cases and the fact that they cover the great majority of issues that might arise in the application of income tax legislation, attention must be given to the precedents that have been established in the court decisions. We will cite such cases as they apply to the various subjects that are being covered. A careful review of all relevant case material would be essential in providing advice to a client on any complex tax issue.

Abbreviations To Be Used

1-72.   In our writing we try to avoid using abbreviations because we believe that there is a tendency in accounting and tax literature to use such a plethora of them that the material sometimes becomes unreadable. However, in the tax area, some sources are so commonly cited that it is clearly inefficient to continue using their full description. Therefore, in the remainder of this book we will use the following abbreviations on a regular basis:

- CCRA - Canada Customs and Revenue Agency
- ITA - Federal *Income Tax Act*
- ITR - Federal Income Tax Regulations
- IT - Interpretation Bulletins
- IC - Information Circulars

1-73.   In addition to these abbreviations, there is a conventional manner in which components of the *Income Tax Act* are cited. The following represents a fairly complex citation of the Act:

$$115(1)(a)(i)(A)(I)$$

1-74.   This would be read as Section 115, Subsection (1), Paragraph (a), Subparagraph (i), Clause A, Subclause I.

References

1-75.   The material in this Introduction has been very general in nature. As a consequence, we have not included a listing of specific references to other sources. Subsequent Chapters will include a list of references for additional study.

Assignment Problems

(The solutions to these problem are only available in
the solutions manual that has been provided to your instructor.)

Assignment Problem One - 1

The principal source of Canadian income tax information is the *Income Tax Act*. There are, however, other sources that are of considerable significance in the application of these rules.

Required: List and briefly describe these other sources of information on Canadian income tax matters.

Assignment Problem One - 2

At a recent cocktail party, Mr. Right was heard complaining vehemently about the lack of progress towards tax simplification. He was tired of spending half of his time filling out various Revenue Canada forms and, if the matter were left to him, he could solve the problem in 10 minutes. "It is simply a matter of having one tax rate and applying that rate to 100 percent of income."

Required: Discuss Mr. Right's proposed flat rate tax system.

Assignment Problem One - 3

Many of the provisions of the *Income Tax Act* are written in very general terms. For example, ITA 18 lists a number of general characteristics that must apply before a particular expense can be deducted in the computation of business income.

Required: Indicate the situations in which such generally worded provisions of the *Income Tax Act* will be overridden.

Assignment Problem One - 4

A regressive tax can be described as one which is assessed at a lower rate as income levels increase. Despite the fact that the goods and services tax (GST) and provincial sales taxes are based on a single rate, they are referred to as a regressive form of taxation.

Required: Explain how a tax system with a single rate can be viewed as regressive.

Assignment Problem One - 5

The tax systems of various countries are designed to meet a variety of objectives. In addition to raising revenues, we call on our tax systems to provide fairness, to have the characteristic of simplicity, to meet social or economic goals, to balance regional disparities, and to be competitive on an international basis. While it would be a fairly simple matter to design a system that would meet any single one of these objectives, we frequently encounter conflicts when we attempt to create a system that meets several of these objectives.

Required: Discuss the possible conflicts that can arise when a tax system is designed to meet more than a single objective.

Assignment Problem One - 6

Discuss whether the following situations meet the objectives and match the characteristics of a good tax system. Identify any conflicts that exist and the probable economic incidence of the tax or tax expenditure.

A. Diamonds are South Africa's major export. Assume that a tax is levied on diamond production of Par Excellence Inc., which has a monopoly in the country. Movements of diamonds are closely monitored and accounted for.

B. Chimeree Inc. owns the largest diamond mine in Sierra Leone. A tax is levied on diamond production. Movements of diamonds are not closely controlled, and helicopters pick up shipments under the cover of darkness.

C. Gains on dispositions of principal residences are exempt from income tax in Canada.

D. A rule stipulates that only 50% of the cost of business meals can be deducted in calculating Canadian business income for personal and corporate taxable income.

E. A newly created country levies a head tax which requires every resident adult to pay an annual tax.

Assignment Problem One - 7

Concerned with her inability to control the deficit, the Minister Of Finance has indicated that she is considering the introduction of a head tax. This would be a tax of $200 per year, assessed on every living Canadian resident who, on December 31 of each year, has a head. In order to enforce the tax, all Canadian residents would be required to have a Head Administration Tax identification number (HAT, for short) tattooed in an inconspicuous location on their scalp. A newly formed special division of the RCMP, the Head Enforcement Administration Division (HEAD, for short), would run spot checks throughout the country in order to insure that everyone has registered and received their HAT.

The Minister is very enthusiastic about the plan, anticipating that it will produce additional revenues of $5 billion per year. It is also expected to spur economic growth though increased sales of Canadian made toques.

As the Minister's senior policy advisor, you have been asked to prepare a memorandum evaluating this proposed new head tax.

Required: Prepare the memorandum.

Assignment Problem One - 8 (Electronic Library Research Problem)

The *Income Tax Act* contains a number of definitions that are required in the application of tax legislation. Using the electronic tax library which accompanies this text, identify the appropriate provision of the *Act* where the following definitions can be found.

A. Spouse

B. Capital Gain and Capital Loss

C. Taxable Capital Gain and Allowable Capital Loss

D. Inter Vivos Trust

E. Canadian Newspaper or Periodical

F. Child Support Amount

G. Income Averaging Annuity Contract

H. Child Care Expense

I. Moving Expenses

J. Designated Educational Institution

Chapter 2

Procedures and Administration

Introduction

2-1.   On November 1, 1999, Revenue Canada became the Canada Customs and Revenue Agency (CCRA). The shift to Agency status was designed to give Canadians better service and to streamline tax, customs and trade administration in Canada. The CCRA assumed the full mandate of Revenue Canada, specifically the administration of tax, trade and customs programs, as well as the delivery of economic and social benefits. It administers the same provincial and territorial tax programs that Revenue Canada did. In addition, the CCRA has the authority to enter into new agreements with the provinces, territories, and other government bodies to administer non-harmonized taxes and other services, at their request and on a cost-recovery basis.

2-2.   This Chapter will begin with a brief overview of the administration of the CCRA. This will be followed by a description of filing and tax payment procedures for both individuals and corporations. A limited amount of attention will be given to these procedures as they relate to trusts.

2-3.   This material on filing and tax payment procedures will be followed by a description of the assessment and reassessment process, including the various avenues that can be followed in appealing unfavourable assessments. Attention will also be given to the collection procedures that are available to the CCRA in enforcing its claims against taxpayers. This Chapter concludes with a brief discussion of the general anti-avoidance rule (GAAR).

Administration Of The Department

2-4.   The CCRA has the responsibility for carrying out the tax policies that are formulated by the Department Of Finance. The chief executive officer of the CCRA is the Minister of National Revenue. His duties, as well as those of the Commissioner of Customs and Revenue, are described as follows:

ITA 220(1)   The Minister shall administer and enforce this Act and the Commissioner of Customs and Revenue may exercise all the powers and perform the duties of the Minister under this Act.

2-5.   The Minister of National Revenue is responsible for the CCRA and is accountable to Parliament for all of its activities, including the administration and enforcement of program legislation such as the *Income Tax Act* and the *Excise Tax Act*. The Minister has the authority to ensure that the CCRA operates within the overall government framework and treats its clients with fairness, integrity, and consistency.

2-6. The CCRA has a Board of Management consisting of 15 members appointed by the Governor in Council, 11 of whom have been nominated by the provinces and territories. The Board has the responsibility of overseeing the management of the CCRA, including the development of the Corporate Business Plan, and the management of policies related to resources, services, property, personnel, and contracts. The Commissioner of the CCRA, who is a member of the Board, is responsible for the CCRA's day-to-day operations.

2-7. Unlike the boards of Crown corporations, the Board is not involved in all the business activities of the CCRA. In particular, the CCRA Board has no authority in the administration and enforcement of legislation, which includes the *Income Tax Act* and the *Excise Tax Act*, for which the CCRA remains fully accountable to the Minister of National Revenue. The Board is denied access to confidential client information.

2-8. Following the ministerial mandate found in ITA 220(1), ITA 221(1) provides that the Governor In Council has the power to make Income Tax Regulations for various specific purposes or for the purpose of carrying out other provisions of the *Income Tax Act*. Unlike the provisions of the *Income Tax Act*, these Regulations may be passed by Order-In-Council without ratification by Parliament. They generally become effective when they are published in the Canada Gazette. Items that are set or established by regulation are generally referred to as prescribed (e.g., the prescribed rate of interest).

Source Deductions

Withholdings
Salaries And Wages
2-9. A large portion of the taxes paid by individuals working in Canada is collected through source deductions. Under ITA 153, any individual who earns employment income will have the estimated taxes on this income withheld from gross pay through payroll deductions made by their employer. The tax withheld is related to the amount of the individual's income and the required withholdings are intended to cover the taxes payable on this income. However, it would be unusual for such withholding to be exactly equal to the taxes payable for the year. As a consequence, most individuals will either owe taxes and be required to file a return or, alternatively, be entitled to a refund which can only be obtained by filing a return.

2-10. The amount withheld by the employer is based on a TD-1 form, filled out by the employee, which lists the personal credits and certain other deductible amounts that are available to the individual. The individual may elect to have the amount withheld increased and might choose to do so if, for example, the withholding is based on rates in a low tax rate province and the individual resides and pays taxes in a high tax rate province. This could allow the individual to avoid a large tax liability when his tax return is filed.

2-11. A different type of problem can arise when an employed individual who is subject to source deductions has significant losses or other deductions that can be used to offset employment income.

> **Example** Monica Kinney has 2001 employment income of $61,509 and lives in a Province with a 10.5 percent tax rate applied to all taxable income. She will owe combined federal and provincial taxes of $18,145 ($11,687 federal, plus $6,458 provincial, with all tax credits ignored) and will have approximately this amount withheld by her employer. If Ms. Kinney has annual deductible spousal support payments of $20,000, her actual 2001 basic federal and provincial taxes payable will only be $11,645 ($7,287 + $4,358), with the government paying no interest on the extra $6,500 in federal taxes withheld.

2-12. Under ITA 153(1.1), she can request a reduction in the amount of source deductions withheld by her employer. As long as the losses or deductions can be documented in a reasonable fashion, the CCRA will normally authorize the employer to reduce the amounts withheld from the employee's remuneration. There is no required form for making this request.

Other Payers

2-13.   In addition to requiring employers to withhold specified amounts from the salaries and wages of employees, ITA 153 contains a fairly long list of other types of payments from which the payer must withhold prescribed amounts. These include:

- Retiring Allowances
- Death Benefits
- Payments From Deferred Profit Sharing Plans
- Payments From Registered Retirement Savings Plans
- Payments From Registered Education Savings Plans

2-14.   In addition to payments listed in ITA 153, ITA 212 contains an additional list of payments from which the payer must withhold prescribed amounts. These rules apply to payments to non residents and include interest, rents, pension benefits, and spousal support payments.

Employer's Remittance Of Source Deductions

2-15.   The term source deductions covers amounts withheld from an employee's remuneration to cover:

- estimated income taxes;
- Canada or Quebec Pension Plan (CPP or QPP) contributions; and
- Employment Insurance (EI) premiums.

2-16.   These amounts are remitted to the Receiver General through a Tax Services Office, a Taxation Centre, or a financial institution belonging to the Canadian Payments Association. The amounts must actually be remitted by the due date in order to avoid a penalty. Postmarks do not count as a remittance date.

2-17.   The schedule for remitting these source deductions is based on the amounts involved. As described in the *Employers' Guide To Payroll Deductions (Basic Information)*, three classes of employers are identified. These classes, along with the related remittance requirements, are as follows:

Regular Remitters   These employers have average monthly withholdings in the preceding calendar year of less than $15,000 per month. Their remittances are due monthly on the 15th day of the month following the month in which the amounts were withheld.

Accelerated Remitters - Threshold 1   These employers have average monthly withholdings of $15,000 to $49,999.99 for the preceding calendar year. They are required to remit on a twice monthly basis. Payments are due on the 25th day of the month for remuneration paid during the first 15 days of the month, while payments due on the 10th day of the following month would be for remuneration paid during the remainder of the month.

Accelerated Remitters - Threshold 2   This class of employer has average monthly withholdings of $50,000 or more in the preceding year. For these employers, remittances are required four times per month. The schedule requires payments to be made within three working days (holidays are excluded) following pay periods ending on the 7th, 14th, 21st, and last days of a month.

2-18.   For employers with twice monthly pay periods ($15,000 to $49,999.99 in withholdings), it would be advantageous to establish pay dates on the 1st and 16th days of the month. This would provide for maximum deferral of source deduction remittances for semi monthly pay periods. Even more tax advantageous would be the establishment of monthly pay periods, which would reduce the frequency of the required remittances.

2-19. For very small employers, even the monthly remittance requirement can be burdensome. As a consequence, ITR 108(1.12) allows certain small employers to file on a quarterly basis. In order to qualify, employers must have a perfect compliance record for both filing and remitting source deductions and GST over the preceding 12 months. In addition, average monthly withholding must be less that $1,000 per month for either the first or second preceding year.

2-20. If a person required to withhold under ITA 153 fails to do so, there is a penalty equal to 10 percent of the amounts that should have been withheld. For a second offence within the same calendar year, the penalty can double to 20 percent.

2-21. Amounts withheld must be reported by the person or business entity making the payments on an annual information return, form T4. This T4 form must be filed no later than the last day of February of the following taxation year. Late remittances in excess of $500 are subject to a penalty of 10 percent on a first offence and 20 percent on additional offenses in the same year. Note that this is the same penalty that applies when there is a failure to make required withholdings. All late payments, whether or not the amounts have been withheld, are subject to interest at prescribed rates (prescribed rates are defined at a later point in this Chapter).

Returns And Payments - Individuals

Requirement To File

2-22. ITA 150(1.1) requires individuals to file a tax return if:

- they owe taxes for the year;
- they have a taxable capital gain for the year;
- they have disposed of a capital property during the year; or
- if they have an outstanding balance under the home buyers plan or lifelong learning plan legislation (see Chapter 6 for an explanation of these balances).

2-23. While there is no requirement for other individuals to file a tax return, if they are entitled to a refund it will only be available if a return is filed. In addition, it is advisable for others to file, especially low income taxpayers, in order to be eligible for income based benefits such as the child tax benefit, the GST credit and the Guaranteed Income Supplement. If they fail to file, they will not receive these amounts.

2-24. Individuals can either file a paper form or, alternatively, use an electronic or automated filing method. The advantage of electronic filing for the taxpayer, particularly if he is entitled to a refund, is that the return will be processed more quickly. For the CCRA, electronic filing eliminates the possibility of errors in the process of transferring information from paper forms to their computerized records. While documents (e.g., a receipt for a charitable donation) cannot be included with the electronic filing, the CCRA retains the right to request that such receipts be provided. EFILE is one electronic filing method. It must be done through a service provider approved by the CCRA.

2-25. A second alternative for filing is referred to as TELEFILE and is available to individuals with fairly simple returns who are provided with a TELEFILE Access Code by the CCRA. Under this system, returns are filed via a touch tone telephone on a seven day a week basis. There is no charge for this service.

2-26. The newest alternative for electronic filing, NETFILE, was introduced under a pilot program to selected individuals for the 1999 taxation year. Under the EFILE program, taxpayers are required to pay a preparer/transmitter in order to file their return on an electronic basis. Under NETFILE, the only filing requirements are that the taxpayer use a CCRA certified tax preparation software program and have internet access with an appropriate web browser.

2-27. For 1999, only 4 million Canadians were invited to use this system under the pilot program. For 2000, over 22 million Canadians were eligible to use this method. It is available to most taxpayers, with certain ineligible individuals specified. Examples of ineligible individuals are individuals in bankruptcy, non-resident individuals, individuals filing amended returns and deceased individuals. Although statistics are not yet available, it is anticipated that there was widespread use of this method for filing 2000 personal tax returns.

Due Date For Returns

General Rules

2-28.   For individuals, the income taxation year is defined as the calendar year and this means that, in general, a uniform filing date can be established for all individuals. This date is April 30th of the calendar year following the relevant taxation year.

2-29.   If an individual dies between January 1 and October 31, the due date of the return for the year of death (the final return) is the usual deadline of April 30 of the following calendar year. However, an extension is available when an individual dies between November 1 of a taxation year and April 30 of the following taxation year. If the death is in November or December, the representative of the deceased has up to six months following the date of death to file the final return for the year of death. If the death occurs between January 1 and April 30 and the prior year's return has not been filed, the due date for the prior year's return is extended to six months after the date of death.

> **Example**   An individual dies on March 1, 2002 without having filed a 2001 return. The due date of the 2001 return is September 1, 2002 and the due date of the 2002 final return is April 30, 2003.

Partners And Proprietors

2-30.   If an individual or his cohabiting spouse carried on business during the year, ITA 150(1) extends the due date for filing to June 15 of the calendar year following the relevant taxation year.

2-31.   The special six month rule for deceased individuals is also applicable here. If an individual partner or proprietor dies between December 16 (six months prior to the June 15 filing deadline) of a taxation year and June 15 of the following year, the filing deadline is six months after the date of death.

> **Example**   An individual earning business income dies on January 3, 2002 without having filed a 2001 tax return. The due date for the 2001 return is July 3, 2002. The due date for the 2002 tax return is June 15, 2003.

> Exercises 2-1 and 2-2 deal with filing dates. This would be an appropriate time to attempt these exercises.

Instalment Payments For Individuals

Basis For Requiring

2-32.   As we have noted, for many individuals the withholding of taxes constitutes the major form of tax payment in any taxation year. However, in situations where an individual has large amounts of income that are not subject to withholding, quarterly instalment payments may have to be made towards the current year's tax liability.

2-33.   The requirement for making instalments is stated in terms of when instalments are not required. Specifically, no instalments are required if:

> **ITA 156.1(2)(b)**   The individual's net tax owing for the particular year, or for each of the 2 preceding taxation years, does not exceed the individual's instalment threshold for that year.

2-34.   An individual's "instalment threshold" is defined in ITA 156.1(1) as $2,000 for all individuals except residents of Quebec where the federal instalment threshold is $1,200. "Net tax owing" is defined as the amount by which the total federal and provincial tax owing for a particular year, exceeds all tax deducted and withheld for that year.

2-35.   Stated in terms of when an individual will be required to make instalment payments, payments will be required if the difference between the combined federal and provincial tax payable and amounts withheld at source is greater than $2,000 in:

- the current year; and
- either of the two preceding years.

Due Dates For Individuals

2-36.   As noted, individuals are required to make quarterly instalments. These payments are due on March 15, June 15, September 15, and December 15.

Determining Amounts Of Instalments

2-37.   In simple terms, the required instalments will be based on the net tax owing, plus CPP contributions payable, divided by four. However, individuals are provided with alternatives with respect to which year's net tax owing should be used. ITA 156(1) describes three different approaches to calculating the required instalments for a particular quarter:

Approach 1   One-quarter of the estimated net tax owing for the current year [ITA 156(1)(a)(i)].

Approach 2   One-quarter of the net tax owing for the immediately preceding year [ITA 156(1)(a)(ii)].

Approach 3   The March and June instalments based on one-quarter of the net tax owing for the second preceding year. The September and December instalments based on one-half of the excess of the net tax owing for the preceding year over the amount paid for the first two instalments [ITA 156(1)(b)].

2-38.   In deciding which approach to use, there is a problem with the availability of the required information. With respect to the first instalment on March 15, it is unlikely that the taxpayer has prepared his tax return for the preceding year (which is not due until April 30 or June 15), so he will not know his net tax owing for the preceding year. Further, it is unlikely that he will know his net tax owing for the current year until sometime in the following year, subsequent to the due dates for all of the required instalments for the current year. As a consequence, if he uses either approach 1 or approach 2, some or all of his instalments will be based on estimates.

2-39.   Only the third alternative, where the first two instalments are based on the second preceding year and the second two are based on the preceding year, involves using net tax owing figures that are not estimates. (This statement assumes that the taxpayer has filed his second preceding year and preceding year tax return by the due dates.) As this net tax owing information is also available to the CCRA on the same timely basis, the CCRA uses this third approach to determine the amounts to be included in its quarterly Instalment Reminder notices to individuals. Note, however, the fact that the CCRA provides these amounts in its quarterly instalment notices does not mean that they must be paid by the taxpayer. The taxpayer can use any of the three approaches to calculate instalments. If the individual pays the amounts shown on the Instalment Reminders by the due date, no penalty or interest on deficient instalments will be assessed regardless of the actual tax liability for the year.

2-40.   If approach 1 or 2 is chosen and the resulting instalments are too small and less than the approach 3 amounts, non-deductible interest will be assessed on the deficiency. In contrast, if the estimates are too large and too much is paid, the CCRA does not pay interest on the excess. Although it is not clearly specified in the legislation, there is no requirement that the same approach be selected from quarter to quarter.

2-41.   As an example of these calculations, consider Mr. Hruba. He is not subject to any withholding and has the following amounts of net tax owing:

1999	$20,000
2000	32,000
2001 (Estimated)	24,000

2-42.   As the 1999 taxes payable of $20,000 are the lowest of the three years under consideration, approach 3 would result in payments on March 15, 2001 and June 15, 2001 of $5,000. If Mr. Hruba continues to use approach 3, payments on September 15, 2001 and December 15, 2001 would be based on the 2000 taxes payable of $32,000, less the $10,000 paid in March and June. Using these figures, the September and December payments would each be $11,000 [($32,000 - $10,000)(1/2)]. These would be the amounts shown on his Instalment Reminders. However, a better solution for the third and fourth instalments would be to switch to approach 1 under which instalments three and four would be based on the $24,000 estimated tax owing for 2001 and would only be $7,000 [($24,000 - $10,000)(1/2)]. If the 2001 estimate of taxes payable is too low, there could be a liability for interest on deficient instalments as his 2000 net tax owing is larger than the 2001 estimate.

2-43.   Note that following this approach would mean that the March and June instalments would be the amount suggested by the CCRA in the instalment notice. While the September and December payments would be less than the amount suggested by the CCRA, we stress that there is no need to use the numbers in the CCRA's instalment statement as long as each instalment is based on one of the three previously described approaches to calculating instalments.

Exercises 2-3 through 2-6 deal with instalment payments for individuals. This would be an appropriate time to attempt these exercises.

Interest

When Interest Will Be Charged

2-44.   A taxpayer will be charged interest on any unpaid amount of tax that is owing on May 1 that relates to the previous year. Interest is also charged if the taxpayer fails to pay any instalment when it is due, or if the amount paid is less than the amount required by the instalment base used.

2-45.   A further important point here is that interest accrued on late or deficient instalments can be offset by making instalment payments prior to their due date, or by paying an amount in excess of the amount required (creating contra interest). Note, however, if early or excess payments are made when there is no accrual of interest owed on late or deficient instalments, the government will not pay interest to the taxpayer on the excess.

Rate of Interest

2-46.   We will find that the implementation of several provisions in the *Income Tax Act* requires the use of an assumed rate of interest. Because the rates that must be used in these provisions are defined in the *Income Tax Regulations*, they are referred to as prescribed rates. Prior to 1995, ITR 4301 provided for a single prescribed rate of interest. This single rate, established on a quarterly basis, was based on the average rate paid on 90 day Treasury Bills during the first month of the preceding quarter. This average rate was then rounded to the next higher full percentage. Interest is calculated using daily compounding.

2-47.   However, for many taxpayers this rate was far below what was available on other types of debt. Particularly for individuals paying other amounts of non deductible interest (e.g., interest on credit card balances), there was a savings involved in paying off this higher rate debt as opposed to making instalment payments. The government has tried to discourage this approach by increasing the rate which is applicable to amounts owing for late or deficient tax payments and instalments. To this end, ITR 4301 adds additional percentage points to amounts owing to and from the Government. As a result, there are three different prescribed rates. They can be described as follows:

Regular Rate   This basic rate is still based on the Treasury Bill rate during the first month of the preceding quarter. It is applicable for all purposes except amounts owing to and from the Minister (e.g., the determination of the taxable benefit for an employee who receives an interest free loan from an employer). For the first quarter of 2001, this rate is 6 percent.

Regular Rate Plus Two Percent   This rate is applicable in calculating interest on refunds to the taxpayer. For the first quarter of 2001, this rate is 8 percent.

Regular Rate Plus Four Percent   This rate is applicable in calculating interest on late or deficient instalments, unpaid source deductions, and other amounts owing to the Minister. For the first quarter of 2001, this rate is 10 percent. Note that amounts paid to the Minister under this provision are not deductible for any taxpayer.

2-48.   Recent rates applicable to amounts owing to the Minister, including the extra four percentage points, are as follows:

Quarter	1999	2000	2001
First (Rates include extra 4 percent)	9%	9%	10%
Second	9%	10%	10%
Third	9%	10%	N/A
Fourth	9%	10%	N/A

2-49.   For the last three years, this rate has moved in the narrow range of eight to ten percent. This rate is higher than rates on some types of consumer debt (e.g., home mortgages), thereby reducing the incentive to use funds to pay off this type of debt in lieu of making instalment payments. In those cases where taxpayers are subject to high interest rates on other balances, making instalment payments will be less attractive. For example, interest charged on outstanding balances on some credit cards is calculated using rates as high as 18 percent.

Penalties
Late Or Deficient Instalments
2-50.   There is no penalty for late payment of income taxes or on moderate amounts of late or deficient instalments. However, there is a penalty when large amounts are involved. This penalty is specified in ITA 163.1 and is equal to 50 percent of the amount by which the interest owing on the late or deficient instalments exceeds the greater of $1,000 and 25 percent of the interest that would be owing if no instalments were made. As this penalty is based on the amount of interest owed, rather than the amount of late or deficient instalments, it would only apply to fairly large amounts of taxes payable.

Late Filing
2-51.   If the deadline for filing an income tax return is not met, a penalty is assessed under ITA 162(1). For a first offence, this penalty amounts to 5 percent of the tax which was unpaid at the filing due date, plus 1 percent per month of the unpaid tax for a maximum period of 12 months. This penalty would be in addition to interest on the amounts due. If there are no taxes owed on the due date, or the taxpayer is entitled to a refund, there is no late filing penalty. If the taxpayer has been charged a late filing penalty in the three preceding taxation years, ITA 162(2) doubles the penalty on the second offence to ten percent of the tax owing plus two percent per month for a maximum of 20 months.

2-52.   In terms of tax planning, the penalty for late filing is sufficiently severe that individuals should make every effort to file their income tax returns no later than the deadline of April 30 or June 15, even if all of the taxes owing cannot be paid at that time. This is of particular importance if they have filed late in one of the three preceding taxation years. This point is sometimes forgotten when the previous offence resulted in a negligible penalty. The penalty for a second offence will double, even if the amount involved in the first penalty was very small.

Due Date For Balance Owing
2-53.   If the combination of amounts withheld and instalments falls short of the total tax payable for the taxation year, there will be a balance owing. This balance is due on April 30 of the following year, regardless of whether the taxpayer qualifies for the June 15 filing due date. For a deceased taxpayer, the due date for the amount owing coincides with the due date for the return of the year of death and the preceding year. As with living individuals, the due date for the amount owing is not extended for deceased individuals with business income for whom the June 15 filing due date is relevant.

Returns And Payments - Corporations
Due Date For Corporate Returns
2-54.   Unlike the case with individuals, the taxation year of a corporation can end on any day of the calendar year. This makes it impossible to have a uniform filing date and as a consequence, the filing deadline for corporations is six months after the fiscal year end of the company. All corporations, except those that are registered charities throughout the year, are

required to file form T2 within this specified period. Financial statements must accompany this form, along with other required schedules and information.

Instalment Payments For Corporations

2-55.   Corporations are generally required to make monthly instalment payments throughout their taxation year. However, this requirement is eliminated if either the estimated taxes payable for the current year or the taxes paid for the preceding taxation year were less than $1,000. When instalments are required, they must be paid on or before the last day of each month, with the amount being calculated on the basis of one of three alternatives. As laid out in ITA 157(1)(a) these alternatives are as follows:

1.   Twelve instalments, each based on 1/12 of the estimated tax for the current year.

2.   Twelve instalments, each based on 1/12 of the tax that was payable in the immediately preceding year.

3.   Two instalments, each based on 1/12 of the tax that was payable in the second preceding year, followed by 10 instalments based on 1/10 of the amount by which the taxes paid in the immediately preceding year exceeds the sum of the first two instalments.

2-56.   Choosing between these alternatives is a relatively simple matter. The instalment base which provides the minimum cash outflow and the greatest amount of deferral should be the one selected. For businesses that are experiencing year to year increases in their taxes payable, the third alternative will generally meet this objective.

> **Example**   The Marshall Company estimates that its 2001 taxes payable will be $153,000. In 2000 the Company paid taxes of $126,000. The corresponding figure for 1999 was $96,000.
>
> **Example Solution**   Given the preceding information, the choices for instalment payments would be:
>
> 1.   Twelve instalments of $12,750 each ($153,000 ÷ 12)
> 2.   Twelve instalments of $10,500 each ($126,000 ÷ 12)
> 3.   Two instalments of $8,000 ($96,000 ÷ 12) and 10 instalments of $11,000 each [($126,000 - $16,000) ÷ 10]
>
> While the cash outflows under alternative 3 total the same amount as those under alternative 2, alternative 3 would be selected because it permits a somewhat greater deferral of the payments. Note that, similar to the situation for individuals, it is possible to switch between methods during the year if another method becomes more advantageous.

Due Date For Balance Owing

2-57.   Regardless of the instalment base selected, any remaining taxes are due within two months of the corporation's fiscal year end. An exception is made in the case of companies which claim the small business deduction and are a Canadian controlled private corporation throughout the year. For these corporations, the due date is three months after their fiscal year end. Note that the final due date for payment is earlier than the due date for filing returns. For example, a company with a March 31 year end which is not eligible for the small business deduction would not have to file its tax return until September 30. However, all of its taxes would be due on May 31. This means that this final payment will usually have to be based on an estimate of the total amount of taxes payable.

Exercises 2-7 through 2-9 deal with instalment payments for corporations. This would be an appropriate time to attempt these exercises.

Interest

2-58.   The rules for calculating and paying interest on late payments of corporate income taxes are the same as those that apply to individuals, including the fact that such interest payments are not deductible. These rules were covered previously. Note, however, that it is especially important that corporations avoid interest on late tax or instalment payments. Since corporations can generally deduct the interest that they accrue, the payment of non deductible interest on late tax payments represents an extremely high cost source of financing. For example, in the case of a corporation paying taxes at a rate of 40 percent, interest at a non deductible rate of 10 percent is the equivalent of a deductible rate of 16 percent.

Penalties

2-59.   The previously covered penalties applicable to individuals for late instalments and for late filing of returns are equally applicable to corporations. In addition to the penalties applicable to individuals, ITA 235 contains a further penalty applicable to large corporations. It calls for a penalty equal to one-quarter of one percent of the total amount of tax payable for the year under Parts I.3 (Tax On Large Corporations) and VI (Tax On Capital Of Financial Institutions) of the *Act* for each month the return is late. This is a fairly harsh penalty in that, unlike the usual penalties which are based on any additional tax payable at the time the return should have been filed, this penalty is based on a tax payable, without regard to instalments that have been made. This additional penalty was introduced in 1991 to deal with what the Department considered to be an excessive number of large corporations failing to file their returns by their due date.

Returns And Payments - Trusts

2-60.   As was the case with corporations, all trusts are required to file a return in each taxation year. This form T3 must be filed within 90 days of the end of the taxation year for the trust. Testamentary trusts can choose any fiscal year end and are not required to make instalment payments. In contrast, inter vivos trusts must use the calendar year for their taxation year and make instalment payments on the same quarterly basis as individuals (there appears to be an administrative exception to the instalment requirement). Interest and penalties for late payments and late returns follow the rules of those prescribed for individuals and corporations.

Income Tax Information Returns

2-61.   ITA 221(1)(d) gives the CCRA the right to require certain taxpayers to file information returns in addition to the returns in which they report their income. These information returns are detailed in Part II of the Income Tax Regulations and must be filed using a prescribed form. Common examples of these returns and the related prescribed form would be as follows:

T3   This form is used by trustees (which includes trustees of some mutual funds) and executors to report the allocation of the trust's income.

T4   This form is used by employers to report remuneration and taxable benefits paid to employees and the various amounts withheld for source deductions.

T5   This form is used by organizations to report interest, dividend, and royalty payments.

T4RSP   This form is used by trustees to report payments out of Registered Retirement Savings Plans.

Foreign Reporting Requirements

2-62.   As will be explained in Chapter 3, residents of Canada are liable for income taxes on their worldwide income. This means, for example, that if a Canadian resident has a bank account in the United Kingdom, any interest earned on that account should be reported in the appropriate Canadian tax return.

2-63.   For many years, the Department has been concerned that large amounts of such income were not being reported by Canadian residents. As a consequence, an information return for foreign income is now required. The filing requirement for the form is as follows:

Canadian resident individuals, corporations, and trusts, as well as partnerships, who held certain property outside Canada with a total cost amount of more than $100,000 at any time in the tax year, have to file Form T1135, "Foreign Income Verification Statement".

2-64. The reporting requirement is for specified foreign property which includes the following:

- Funds in foreign bank accounts.
- Shares of non resident corporations (even if held by a Canadian stockbroker).
- Land and buildings located outside Canada (other than personal use property).
- Interests in mutual funds that are organized in a foreign jurisdiction.
- Debts owed to residents by non residents.
- An interest in a partnership where non residents control more than 90 percent of the profit or loss.
- Patents, copyrights, or trademarks held outside Canada.

2-65. The following items are not included in the definition of specified foreign property:

- Property used to carry on an active business.
- Personal use property, such as a cottage.
- Shares or debt of a non resident corporation or trust that is a foreign affiliate.
- An interest in a U.S. Individual Retirement Account (IRA)
- Interests in Canadian based pension arrangements (e.g., RPPs or RRSPs) that hold foreign investments.
- An interest in a non resident trust that provides pension or other employee benefits, but that does not pay income tax in the jurisdiction where it is resident.

2-66. While there has been much weeping and gnashing of teeth over the introduction of this requirement, it is likely to result in a significant increase in the reporting of income on foreign property. This is particularly true in view of the harsh penalties associated with the requirement. A penalty of $500 per month for up to 24 months can be assessed for a failure to file. This will double if a demand to file is served. A further penalty of 5 percent of the cost of any unreported property, less other penalties assessed, may be applicable.

2-67. This filing requirement is applicable to taxation years that begin after 1997.

Refunds

2-68. When tax has been withheld from income and/or instalments have been paid, the CCRA's assessment may show that there has been an overpayment of income tax. In this situation, the taxpayer is entitled to a refund of any excess payments and, in the great majority of cases, such refunds are sent without any further action being taken. If for some reason the refund is not made, the taxpayer can apply for it in writing within four years from the end of the taxation year in question and the Minister must honour the request. However, if there are other tax liabilities outstanding, such as amounts from prior years, the Minister has the right to apply the refund against these liabilities.

2-69. Interest is paid at the rate prescribed in ITR 4301 (including an additional two percentage points) on overpayments of income tax. Two points should be made with respect to this interest. First, it begins to accrue 45 days after the date that the taxpayer's return was due for filing or, in those cases where the return is filed late, 45 days after the date on which it is filed. If, for example, an individual paid excessive income tax instalments during 2000, the excess would not begin to earn interest until June 15, 2001, even if the taxpayer filed a return prior to April 30, 2001. Also of note is the fact that interest is not paid on amounts claimed as the result of a loss carry back to previous taxation years.

Books And Records

2-70. For income tax purposes, every person carrying on a business, as well as every person who is required to pay or collect taxes, must keep adequate books and records. This requirement is found in ITA 230. Such records must be maintained at the taxpayer's place of business or at the individual's residence in Canada.

2-71.   Adequate record retention can become a cumbersome and costly process for taxpayers and, as a consequence, some limitations must be available. The general rules for retention of books and records are found in ITR 5800. Depending on the type of record and the class of taxpayer, these rules require retention for periods ranging from two years to six years. However, other provisions can extend this period for particular groups of taxpayers, or for taxpayers in specified circumstances. It is also possible to request permission for earlier disposal.

Assessments

Initial Assessment

2-72.   ITA 152(1) requires that the Minister shall, with all due dispatch, examine each return of income and assess the tax as well as the interest and penalties payable. After examining the return, the Minister is required to send a notice of assessment to the person who filed the income tax return. In the case of individuals, this notice of assessment is usually received within one or two months of filing, especially if the return was filed electronically. A somewhat longer period is normally required for corporate income tax assessments.

Reassessments

2-73.   The first notice of assessment is based on a quick pass through the data in the return to check for completeness and arithmetic accuracy. If no obvious errors are found, it will simply indicate that the Minister accepts the information that was included in the taxpayer's return. It does not, however, free the taxpayer from additional scrutiny of the return.

2-74.   In general, reassessments have to be made within three years for individuals and Canadian controlled private corporations, and within four years for other corporations. This is referred to in ITA 152(3.1) as the normal reassessment period. The time limit is measured from the day of mailing of a notice of an original assessment or of a notification that no tax is payable for a taxation year.

2-75.   As set out in ITA 152(4), the general time limits can be ignored and the Minister may reassess:

- At any time, if the taxpayer or person filing the return has made any misrepresentation that is attributable to neglect, carelessness or willful default or has committed any fraud in filing the return or in supplying information under the *Income Tax Act*.

- At any time, if the taxpayer has filed a waiver of the three year time limit. A taxpayer can revoke such a waiver on six months notice.

- An additional three years is added to the "normal reassessment period" if a reassessment is required under circumstances provided in ITA 152(6). The most common of these circumstances involves years in which a loss is being carried back in order to claim a refund of taxes paid. For example, if a loss incurred by an individual in 2001 was being carried back to 1998, this addition of three years means that the 1998 taxation year of that individual can be reassessed until 2004.

2-76.   When the date of the reassessment is beyond the three or four year limit, it can only apply to items which were misrepresented or to items covered by a waiver.

Adjustments to Income Tax Returns

2-77.   There is no general provision in the *Income Tax Act* for filing a complete and detailed amended return and, in fact, such returns are generally not filed. However, this does not mean that amounts included in the returns of previous years cannot be altered. It simply means that the adjustment process takes place through the use of a letter or a prescribed form, rather than the filing of a revised tax return for the year in question.

2-78. Statutory authority for such adjustments is found in ITA 152(6) which requires the Minister of Revenue to reassess certain specific changes in the returns of previous years. While several items are listed in this subsection, the most important of these items is loss carry backs. This provision requires reassessment for a previous year when a current year loss is carried back to that year. This carry back is implemented through form T1A (Individuals) or Form T2A (Corporations). This form should be filed with the income tax return for the year in which the loss was incurred.

2-79. IC 75-7R3, Reassessment of a Return of Income, provides an administrative solution to the problem of adjustments to returns. It permits such adjustments if the following conditions are met:

- the CCRA is satisfied that the previous assessment was incorrect;
- the reassessment can be made within the normal reassessment period (or the taxpayer has filed a waiver);
- the requested decrease in taxable income does not solely depend on an increase in a permissive deduction such as capital cost allowance; and
- the change is not based solely on a successful appeal to the courts by another taxpayer.

2-80. For individuals, this provision would be implemented by sending a letter detailing the adjustment requested or by filing Form T1-ADJ (T1 Adjustment Request), a one page form which allows the taxpayer to simply describe the requested change. It is also possible to request an adjustment through the CCRA web site. The calculations required to issue a reassessment are taken care of by the CCRA. This informal procedure can be used any time within the normal reassessment period.

2-81. IC 84-1 makes administrative provisions for situations where a business wishes to alter a permissive deduction. This could happen, for example, in a year in which the enterprise has a loss that it cannot carry back in full. This results in a carry forward which can be lost if the business does not produce sufficient taxable income to absorb it in the relevant carry forward period. In such a situation the enterprise may wish to minimize the loss carry forward amount by revising the capital cost allowance taken in the previous year. Such revisions are only permitted when they do not change the taxes payable for the previous year. In general, this will only happen when the downward revision in capital cost allowance is accompanied by an equivalent increase in the amount of loss being carried back to that year.

Appeals

Informal Request For Adjustments

2-82. If a taxpayer disagrees with an assessment or reassessment, the usual first step in the process of disputing the assessment is to contact the CCRA immediately. In many cases the proposed change or error can be corrected or resolved through telephone contact or by letter. To authorize a person or firm to act as a representative of the taxpayer, Consent Form T1013 must be signed and filed with the CCRA.

Notice Of Objection

General Rules

2-83. If the informal contact does not resolve the issue in question, ITA 165(1) gives the taxpayer the right to file a Notice of Objection. While its use is not required, Form T400A, Objection, can be used for this purpose. This form simply requires the facts and reasons for the objection. It is addressed to the Chief Of Appeals in the District Office, or to any Taxation Centre. While it can be sent by regular mail, registered mail provides third party evidence that the objection has been filed.

2-84. For corporations and inter vivos trusts, a notice of objection must be filed within 90 days of the date on which the notice of assessment was mailed. For individuals and testamentary trusts, the notice of objection must be filed before the later of:

- 90 days from the date of mailing of the notice of assessment or reassessment; or
- one year from the filing due date for the return under assessment or reassessment.

2-85.   For an individual required to file on April 30, 2001 who filed on April 26, 2001, a notice of assessment might be mailed about June 15, 2001. This means that, for this individual, a notice of objection could be filed up to the later of August 13, 2001 (90 days after the mailing) and April 30, 2002 (one year after the filing date). In this case the relevant date would be April 30, 2002, without regard to the actual filing date.

2-86.   When an individual dies after October of the assessment year and before May of the following year, you will recall that the filing date for the return is extended to six months after the date of death, thereby extending the date for filing a notice of objection by the same number of months.

2-87.   Under ITA 166.1(7), a taxpayer can request an extension of the filing deadline for the notice of objection. This is possible where:

    (a) the application is made within one year after the expiration of the time otherwise limited by this Act for serving a notice of objection or making a request, as the case may be; and

    (b) the taxpayer demonstrates that
        (i) within the time otherwise limited by this Act for serving such a notice or making such a request, as the case may be, the taxpayer
            (A) was unable to act or to instruct another to act in the taxpayer's name, or
            (B) had a bona fide intention to object to the assessment or make the request,
        (ii) given the reasons set out in the application and the circumstances of the case, it would be just and equitable to grant the application, and
        (iii) the application was made as soon as circumstances permitted.

2-88.   If the application for an extension is refused, the Minister's decision can be appealed to the Tax Court Of Canada.

2-89.   Once the notice of objection is filed, the Minister is required to reply to the taxpayer:

- vacating the assessment,
- confirming it (i.e., refusing to change it),
- varying the amount, or
- reassessing.

> Exercise 2-10 deals with filing a notice of objection. This would be an appropriate time to attempt this exercise.

2-90.   Unresolved objections will be subject to review by the Chief Of Appeals in each Tax Services Office. These appeals sections are instructed to operate independently of the assessing divisions and should provide an unbiased second opinion. If the matter remains unresolved after this review, the taxpayer must either accept the Minister's assessment or, alternatively, continue to pursue the matter to a higher level of appeal. The taxpayer has the right to bypass this notice of objection procedure and appeal directly to a higher level.

2-91.   The 1998 report of the Auditor General indicated that, in 1996-97, 53,407 notices of objection were filed. Of these, 63 percent were settled at the objection stage.

Rules For Large Corporations

2-92.   The Department Of Finance appears to believe that it has been the practice of certain corporate taxpayers to delay the dispute process by filing vague objections in the first instance, and subsequently bringing in fresh issues as the appeal process goes forward.

2-93.   To prevent this perceived abuse, the Department has issued ITA 165(1.11). This legislation requires that, in filing a notice of objection, a corporation must specify each issue to be decided, the dollar amount of relief sought for each particular issue, and the facts and reasons relied on by the corporation in respect of each issue. If the corporation objects to a reassessment or additional assessment made by the CCRA, or appeals to the Tax Court Of Canada, the objection or appeal can be only with respect to issues and dollar amounts properly dealt with in the original notice of objection. There is an exception to this general rule for new issues that are raised by the CCRA on assessment or reassessment. These limitations are only applicable to "large corporations", defined in terms of a liability to pay the Part I.3 tax on large corporations (see Chapter 14).

Tax Court Of Canada

2-94.   A taxpayer who does not find satisfaction through the notice of objection procedure may then proceed to the next level of the appeal procedure, the Tax Court of Canada. Appeals to the Tax Court of Canada can be made within 90 days of the mailing date of the Minister's response to the notice of objection which would confirm the assessment or reassessment, or 90 days after the notice of objection has been filed if the Minister has not replied. It is not possible to bypass the Tax Court of Canada and appeal directly to the Federal Court level.

2-95.   On appeal to the Tax Court of Canada, the taxpayer can elect to have his case heard under either the informal procedures or the general procedures. Informal procedures can be elected for appeals in which the total amount of tax and penalty involved for a given year is less than $12,000, or where the loss in question is less than $24,000. Cases involving larger amounts can use this informal procedure, provided the taxpayer restricts the appeal to these limits. While the appeal must be submitted in writing, rules of evidence remain fairly informal, allowing the taxpayer to represent himself or be represented by an agent other than a lawyer. A further advantage of this informal procedure is that, even if you are unsuccessful, you cannot be asked to pay court costs. The major disadvantage of the informal procedure is that the taxpayer gives up all rights to further appeals if the Court decision is unfavourable.

2-96.   If the taxpayer elects the general procedure, formal rules of evidence apply, resulting in a situation where the taxpayer must be represented by either himself or legal counsel. In practical terms this means that for cases involving substantial amounts, lawyers will have to be involved.

2-97.   Under the general procedure, if the taxpayer is unsuccessful, the court may require that costs be paid to the Minister. Under either procedure, if the taxpayer is more than 50 percent successful (e.g., if he is claiming $10,000 and is awarded more than $5,000), the judge can order the Minister to pay all or part of the taxpayer's costs.

2-98.   Prior to the hearing by the Tax Court Of Canada, discussions between the taxpayer and the Department are likely to continue. In some cases, the dispute will be resolved prior to the actual hearing. However, if a hearing proceeds, the Court may dispose of an appeal by:

• dismissing it; or
• allowing it and
  - vacating the assessment,
  - varying the assessment, or
  - referring the assessment back to the Minister for reconsideration and reassessment.

2-99.   Once again referring to the 1998 report of the Auditor General, in 1996-97, the Tax Court of Canada processed 4,014 cases. Of these, 36 percent were withdrawn by the taxpayer. Of the remaining 2,585 cases, 879 ended in consent judgments, with the remainder going to trial.

Federal Court And The Supreme Court Of Canada

2-100.   Either the Minister or the taxpayer can appeal a general procedure decision of the Tax Court of Canada to the Federal Court of Appeal. The appeal must be made within 30 days of the date on which the Tax Court Of Canada makes its decision.

2-101.   There are situations in which the Minister may pursue a matter because of its general implications for broad groups of taxpayers. The individual taxpayer is given protection from the costs associated with this type of appeal by the requirement that the Minister be responsible for the taxpayer's reasonable legal fees when the amount of taxes payable in question does not exceed $10,000 or the loss in dispute does not exceed $20,000. This is without regard to whether the appeal is successful.

2-102.   It is possible to pursue a matter beyond the Federal Court to the Supreme Court Of

Canada. This can be done if the Federal Court of Appeal refers the issue to the higher Court or if the Supreme Court authorizes the appeal. These things will generally not happen unless there are new issues or legal precedents to be dealt with and, as a result, such appeals are not common. However, when tax cases do reach the Supreme Court, they often attract a great deal of public attention. An example of this would be the Neuman v. Minister of National Revenue case, involving the discretionary payment of dividends to a related party.

2-103.   In 1996-97, the Federal Court Of Appeal disposed of 99 appeals by way of judgment. The CCRA succeeded in 20 of its 31 appeals, while taxpayers only succeeded in 8 of their 66 appeals. There were two consent judgments and a further 33 cases were discontinued.

Tax Evasion, Avoidance And Planning

Tax Evasion

2-104.   The concept of tax evasion is not difficult to understand. It is described in IC 73-10R3 as follows:

> Tax evasion is the *commission* or *omission* of an act knowingly, the conspiracy to commit such an act or involvement in the accommodation of such an act, which can result in a charge being laid in the Criminal Court under subsection 239(1) of the *Income Tax Act*.

2-105.   There is little ambiguity in this description as it involves deliberate attempts to deceive the taxation authorities. The most common of the offenses that fall under this description of tax evasion is probably unreported revenues of various types.

Avoidance And Planning

2-106.   When it comes to the question of tax avoidance, the issue becomes more difficult. The *Income Tax Act* contains a number of specific anti avoidance provisions. For example, ITA 69 has rules which deal with transfers of property between individuals that are not dealing at arm's length. However, at one time Section 246 of the Act contained a very broad statement on the subject of avoidance:

> **ITA 246 (Repealed Version)**   Where the Treasury Board has decided that one of the main purposes for a transaction or transactions effected before or after the coming into force of this Act was improper avoidance or reduction of taxes that might otherwise have become payable under this Act, the Treasury Board may give such directions as it considers appropriate to counteract the avoidance or reduction.

2-107.   The preceding provision did not clarify the exact nature of the difference between tax avoidance and tax planning. IC 73-10R (replaced by IC 73-10R3) attempted to help by describing tax avoidance and tax planning as follows:

> **Tax Avoidance**   The taxpayer has apparently circumvented the law, without giving rise to a criminal offence, by the use of a scheme, arrangement or device, often of a complex nature, whose main or sole purpose is to defer, reduce or completely avoid the tax payable under the law.

> **Tax Planning**   A taxpayer, in seeking a beneficial tax result, has merely selected a certain course of action that is either clearly provided for or not specifically prohibited in the law and has implemented that decision in a real way. Such planning consists of a genuine arranging of one's affairs openly and within the framework of the law so as to keep one's taxes to a minimum.

2-108.   From reading these descriptions, it is clear that the Minister had considerable discretion in applying ITA 246. As a consequence, ITA 246 was repealed in 1984, a decision which served to remove some of the uncertainty surrounding the concept of tax avoidance.

2-109.   However, the CCRA's interest in some type of general anti-avoidance provision was rekindled when a very important case related to tax avoidance was settled at the Supreme

Court level. For many years, the Department had assessed on the basis that a transaction which has no business purpose other than the avoidance or reduction of taxes is a sham and should not be considered acceptable for tax purposes. In Stubart Investments Ltd. v. The Queen, (84 DTC 6305) the Supreme Court rejected this doctrine, preferring the view that taxpayers have every right to order their affairs in such a fashion that the related tax under the appropriate legislation is as small as possible. The case involved a transfer of the assets of a profitable subsidiary to the books of a sister subsidiary which had large accumulated losses. There was no reason for the transaction other than the desire to have the losses of the latter subsidiary absorbed before their carry forward period expired. The Supreme Court upheld the right of Stubart Investments to undertake this transaction, thereby eliminating the judicial basis for a business purpose test.

General Anti-Avoidance Rule (GAAR)

2-110.   With the Supreme Court decision in the Stubart Investments case removing the CCRA's ability to assess general tax avoidance arrangements, the Department began to call for a new general anti-avoidance rule (GAAR). This was provided in the 1988 tax reform legislation in Section 245. Subsection 245(3) describes an avoidance transaction as follows:

ITA 245(3)   An avoidance transaction means any transaction

(a) that, but for this section, would result, directly or indirectly, in a tax benefit, unless the transaction may reasonably be considered to have been undertaken or arranged primarily for bona fide purposes other than to obtain the tax benefit; or

(b) that is part of a series of transactions, which series, but for this section, would result, directly or indirectly, in a tax benefit, unless the transaction may reasonably be considered to have been undertaken or arranged primarily for bona fide purposes other than to obtain the tax benefit.

2-111.   Note that the preceding provisions provide a basic defense against the GAAR in that it does not apply to transactions which have a bona fide non tax purpose. An additional line of defense is found in ITA 245(4) as follows:

ITA 245(4)   For greater certainty, subsection (2) does not apply to a transaction where it may reasonably be considered that the transaction would not result directly or indirectly in a misuse of the provisions of this Act or an abuse having regard to the provisions of this Act, other than this section, read as a whole.

2-112.   Taken together, these provisions mean that the GAAR will apply to any transaction other than those where there is a bona fide non tax purpose or where there is no misuse or abuse of the Act. If a transaction is judged to be an avoidance transaction, ITA 245(5) goes on to indicate the following possible outcomes:

(a) any deduction in computing income, taxable income, taxable income earned in Canada or tax payable or any part thereof may be allowed or disallowed in whole or in part,

(b) any such deduction, any income, loss or other amount or part thereof may be allocated to any person,

(c) the nature of any payment or other amount may be recharacterized, and

(d) the tax effects that would otherwise result from the application of other provisions of this Act may be ignored.

2-113.   The GAAR has been the most heavily criticized component of the tax reform agenda. The rule is so general that almost any transaction, including such everyday deductions as Registered Retirement Savings Plan contributions, could fall within its scope. While the CCRA has indicated that it intends to be reasonable in the application of this rule, such reasonableness will lie totally within the discretion of their assessors. This, in turn, introduces a large measure of uncertainty into almost all tax planning procedures.

2-114.   Some relief from this uncertainty was provided by the issuance of IC 88-2. This Information Circular was issued in 1988, with a Supplement 1 issued in 1990. These publications provide fairly detailed guidance with respect to the application of ITA 245. For example, they indicate that the following would not be considered avoidance transactions:

- The use of flow through shares.
- Gifts to adult children, except where the related income is given back to the parent.
- Most types of estate freezes.

2-115.   In contrast, the following transactions would fall under the provisions of ITA 245:

- Transitory arrangements (i.e., issuance and redemption of shares) not carried out for bona fide non tax purposes.
- Sale to an intermediary company to create a reserve, followed by a sale to a third party.
- Conversion of salary to capital gains by issuing preferred stock to employees entitled to profits, followed by a sale of the preferred stock.

2-116.   Other sources of guidance on this provision can be found in recent court cases.

Collection And Enforcement

Taxpayer Property
2-117.   At one time, the CCRA had very broad enforcement powers under the provisions of ITA 231.1 and 231.2. However, there was a general feeling that these powers could be abused and, as a consequence, amendments were adopted which provide judicial safeguards against any abuse.

2-118.   Tax officials have the right to enter a taxpayer's place of business, locations where anything is done in connection with the business, or any place where records related to the business are kept. However, in those cases where the place of business is also a dwelling, the officials must either gain the permission of the occupant or have a court issued warrant. In this process, the officials may audit the books and records, examine all property, and require that the taxpayer answer questions and provide assistance.

2-119.   Seizure of books and records requires a court issued warrant. If this occurs, taxpayers may apply to have the records returned. Also requiring judicial authorization is demands for information or documents from third parties. This could include information from the files of the taxpayer's lawyer or accountant. There are additional rules in this area which provide for professional/client confidentially with respect to such third party information.

Collections
2-120.   As noted previously, the final payment on personal taxes is due on April 30 of the following year and final payment on corporate taxes is due two months after the corporate year end (three months for Canadian controlled private corporations). Additional taxes may become due as a result of an assessment or reassessment. If this is the case, such taxes are due at the time the notice of assessment is mailed.

2-121.   Initial collection procedures will not normally extend beyond communicating with the taxpayer about his liability and the related interest which will be accrued. In the case of taxes resulting from an assessment or reassessment, the department cannot exercise its collection powers until:

- 90 days after the assessment or reassessment date when no objection is filed;
- 90 days after an assessment or reassessment is upheld when no appeal is made; or
- when an appeal is made, until the decision of the court is rendered.

2-122.   If informal procedures fail to result in payment of the tax owing, ITA 224 allows the CCRA to order a taxpayer owing money to the defaulter to make payments to the Department in settlement of the defaulter's liability. A common example of this would be garnishment of an individual's wages to pay income taxes owed. ITA 223 goes even further, allowing the

CCRA to obtain a judgment against a tax defaulter which can be enforced by seizure and sale of the taxpayer's property.

Penalties
Examples
2-123.   We have previously discussed the penalties associated with the late payment of taxes and the late filing of tax returns. There are a number of other penalties that are specified in tax legislation. Examples of such penalties would be as follows:

Failure To File An Information Return   Employers must file a T4 information return prior to the last day of February. If they fail to do this, the penalty for each failure is $25 a day, with a minimum penalty of $100 and a maximum of $2,500.

Failure To File A Partnership Information Return   If you file a partnership information return late, the partnership is liable in each case to a penalty of $25 per day, from a minimum of $100, to a maximum of $2,500. The partnership has to pay this penalty.

False Statements or Omissions   The greater of $100 and fifty percent of the understated tax. For a second or subsequent offence within three years, an additional penalty equal to 10 percent of the unreported income may be imposed.

Failure To Withhold At Source Or Remit Amounts Withheld   Ten percent of the amounts not withheld or remitted. This increases to 20 percent for a second or subsequent offence in any calendar year.

Evasion   Penalties here range from 50 percent to 200 percent of the relevant tax and, in addition, imprisonment for a period not exceeding two years.

Tax Advisers, Preparers and Promoters
2-124.   The February, 1999 budget proposed, for the first time, to assess civil penalties on tax advisers and preparers involved in encouraging or assisting clients with evasive practices. Subsequent to considerable discussion with the tax adviser community, proposals were codified in ITA 163.2.

2-125.   The first penalty, specified under ITA 163.2(2), is for misrepresentations in tax planning arrangements. It is applicable when a person makes a statement that they either know to be false or could be reasonably expected to know to be false unless they are involved in "culpable conduct". Culpable conduct is defined in the Section as follows:

Culpable Conduct means conduct, whether an act or a failure to act, that

(a)   is tantamount to intentional conduct;
(b)   shows an indifference as to whether the Act is complied with; or
(c)   shows a wilful, reckless or wanton disregard of the law.

2-126.   The Section makes it clear that "culpable conduct" does not generally arise when a tax adviser has relied, in good faith, on information provided by the taxpayer. However, this "good faith" defense does not apply to false statements made in the course of an excluded activity. These excluded activities are described as follows:

Excluded Activity in respect of a false statement means, generally, the activity of

(a)   promoting or selling (whether as principal or agent or directly or indirectly) an arrangement where it can reasonably be considered that the arrangement concerns a flow-through share or a tax shelter or is an arrangement one of the main purposes for a person's participation in which is to obtain a tax benefit; or
(b)   accepting (whether as principal or agent or directly or indirectly) consideration in respect of the sale of, or participation in, such an arrangement.

2-127.   When ITA 163.2(2) is applicable, the penalty is specified under ITA 163.2(3) as the greater of (1) $1,000 and (2) the total of the adviser's "gross entitlements" as determined at the time the notice of assessment of the penalty is sent to that person. Gross entitlements are defined as follows:

> **Gross Entitlements** of a person from a planning activity or a valuation activity, means all amounts to which the person is entitled, either absolutely or contingently, to receive or obtain.

2-128. ITA 163.2(4) applies a different penalty for participating in a misrepresentation in the preparation of a return. The penalty here is the greater of (1) $1,000 and (2) the penalty assessed against the tax preparer's client under ITA 163(2) for making the false statement or omission. The penalty on the client is equal to 50 percent of the amount of tax avoided as a result of the misrepresentation. The total amount of the penalty is capped at $100,000 plus the gross compensation to which the tax preparer is entitled to receive.

2-129. There is concern in the tax preparer community with respect to how the CCRA will apply these new rules. The January 12, 2001 IC-01-1 [Draft], "Third-Party Civil Penalties", is an extensive Information Circular which contains 17 examples of the application of third-party penalties. While the examples cited in the IC and the technical notes to the new ITA 163.2 illustrate clear cut abuses, there are many situations in which it is to the taxpayer's advantage to pursue a more aggressive stance in claiming deductions. It might be expected that these new penalties will inhibit tax preparers from suggesting this type of approach, out of fear that they may be liable for the suggested penalties due to the advice given. In addition, there is evidence that tax preparers will refuse to service certain types of high risk clients.

Fairness Package

2-130. There is a widespread perception that the application of some of the CCRA's rules on interest and penalties, as well as certain other rules, can result in individuals and other taxpayers being treated in an unfair manner. On May 24, 1991, the Minister Of Revenue introduced a "fairness package" to correct some of these problems. While the implementation of this package required a number of changes in the *Income Tax Act*, the guidelines for applying the rules were issued in three information Circulars, IC 92-1, IC 92-2, and IC 92-3. The content of these guidelines can be briefly described as follows:

> **IC 92-1** - *Guidelines For Accepting Late, Amended, Or Revoked Elections* While the *Act* contains numerous elections, there is rarely any provision for revoking, amending, or making them after the specified time period has passed. The Guideline identifies fourteen elections (for example, an election under ITA 73(1) not to have assets transferred to a spouse at tax cost) that can be revoked, amended, or filed late for taxation years after 1984. The request would not be accepted if the taxpayer had been negligent or if the request is retroactive tax planning.

> **IC 92-2** - *Guidelines For The Cancellation And Waiver Of Interest And Penalties* This Guideline indicates that, in certain circumstances, interest and penalties related to taxation years after 1984 can be waived. This can happen when they resulted from extraordinary circumstances beyond the taxpayer's control. Examples of this type of situation include:

- natural or human made disasters such as flood or fire;
- disruptions in civil services, such as a postal strike;
- a serious illness or accident; or
- serious emotional or mental distress, such as a death in the immediate family.

Interest and penalties may also be waived if they arose primarily because of the actions of the CCRA. Examples of this would include:

- processing delays that result in the taxpayer not being informed within a reasonable time that an amount was owing;
- material available to the public contains errors that leads the taxpayer to file returns or make payments based on incorrect information;
- errors in processing;

- delays in providing information; or
- the taxpayer receives incorrect advice, for example where the CCRA incorrectly advises that no instalment payments will be required for the current year.

IC 92-3 - *Guidelines For Refunds Beyond The Normal Three Year Period* This Guideline allows for refunds related to years back to 1985. It eliminates, in most cases, the normal three year limit on applying for a refund of taxes previously paid. Note, however, it does not apply if the refund relates to a permissive deduction such as capital cost allowance.

2-131.　The first two Guidelines are applicable to all taxpayers. In contrast, IC 92-3 is only applicable to individuals and testamentary trusts.

References

2-129.　For more detailed study of the material in this Chapter, we would refer you to the following:

ITA 150	Filing Returns Of Income - General Rule
ITA 151	Estimate Of Tax
ITA 152	Assessment
ITA 153	Withholding
ITA 161	Interest
ITA 162	Failure To File Return Of Income
ITA 163	Repeated Failures
ITA 163.1	Penalty For Late Or Deficient Instalments
ITA 163.2	Misrepresentation Of A Tax Matter By A Third Party
ITA 164	Refunds
ITA 165	Objections To Assessments
ITA 169-180	Appeal
ITA 220-244	Administration And Enforcement
ITA 245-246	Tax Avoidance
ITR Part II	Information Returns
ITR 4301	Prescribed Rate of Interest
ITR 5800	Retention Of Books And Records
IC 71-14R3	The Tax Audit
IC 73-10R3	Tax Evasion
IC 75-6R	Required Withholding From Amounts Paid To Non-Resident Persons Performing Services In Canada
IC 75-7R3	Reassessment Of A Return Of Income
IC 78-10R3	Books And Records Retention/Destruction
IC 81-11R3	Corporate Instalments
IC 84-1	Revision Of CCA Claims And Other Permissive Deductions
IC 88-2	General Anti Avoidance Rule (Also a Supplement 1 to this Information Circular)
IC 92-1	Guidelines For Accepting Late, Amended, Or Revoked Elections
IC 92-2	Guidelines For The Cancellation And Waiver Of Interest And Penalties
IC 92-3	Guidelines For Refunds Beyond The Normal Three Year Period
IC 00-1	Voluntary Disclosures Program
IC-01-1	Third-Party Civil Penalties [Draft]
IT-241	Reassessments Made After The Four Year Limit
IT-256R	Gains From Theft, Defalcation Or Embezzlement
IT-512	Determination And Redetermination Of Losses

Exercises

(The solutions for these exercises can be found following Chapter 21 of the text.)

Exercise Two - 1 (Deceased Taxpayer Filing Date)
Ms. Sally Cheung dies on February 15, 2002. Her 2001 Net Income included income from an unincorporated business. Her representatives must file her 2001 individual tax return by what date?

Exercise Two - 2 (Individual Tax Payment Date)
Mr. Brandon Katarski's 2001 Net Income includes business income. By what date must his 2001 tax liability be paid in order to avoid the assessment of interest on amounts due?

Exercise Two - 3 (Individual Instalments)
Mrs. Carter had net tax owing in 1999 of $3,500, net tax owing in 2000 of $4,000, and expects to have net tax owing in 2001 of $1,500. Is she required to make instalment payments for the 2001 taxation year? If so, what would be the minimum quarterly payment?

Exercise Two - 4 (Individual Instalments)
Mr. John Lee had net tax owing for 1999 of $3,500, net tax owing for 2000 of $1,500, and expects to have net tax owing for 2001 of $4,500. Is he required to make instalment payments for 2001? If so, what would be the minimum quarterly payment?

Exercise Two - 5 (Individual Instalments)
Mr. Farnsworth had net tax owing for 1999 of $25,000, net tax owing for 2000 of $37,000, and expects to have net tax owing for 2001 of $32,000. What would be his minimum quarterly instalments for 2001?

Exercise Two - 6 (Individual Instalments Penalty)
Despite the fact that her net tax owing has been between $3,000 and $4,000 in the two previous years, and is expected to be a similar amount during 2001, Mary Carlos has made no instalment payments for 2001. In addition, she is two months late in filing her 2001 tax return. What penalties will be assessed for the 2001 taxation year?

Exercise Two - 7 (Corporate Due Dates)
The taxation year end for Radco Inc. is January 31, 2001. Indicate the date on which the corporate tax return must be filed, as well as the date on which any final payment of taxes is due.

Exercise Two - 8 (Corporate Instalments)
Madco Ltd. has a December 31 year end. For 1999 its tax payable was $52,000, while for 2000 the amount was $89,000. For 2001, its estimated tax payable is $104,000. What would be the minimum monthly instalment payments for the 2001 taxation year?

Exercise Two - 9 (Corporate Instalments)
Fadco Inc. has a December 31 year end. For 1999 its tax payable was $152,000, while for 2000 the amount was $104,000. For 2001, its estimated tax payable is $67,000. What would be the minimum monthly instalment payments for the 2001 taxation year?

Exercise Two - 10 (Notice of Objection)
Mr. Jerry Fall filed his 2000 tax return as required on April 30, 2001. He receives his notice of assessment during June, 2001. However, on June 1, 2002, he receives a reassessment indicating that he owes additional taxes, as well as interest on the unpaid amounts. The reassessment was mailed on May 15, 2002. What is the due date for filing a notice of objection to this reassessment?

Problems For Self Study

(The solutions for these problems can be found following Chapter 21 of the text.)

Self Study Problem Two - 1

In January, 2001, you are asked to provide tax advice to Mr. Lester Gore. He has provided you with the following information about his combined federal and provincial tax liability and the amounts withheld by his employer for the 1999 and 2000 taxation years:

Year	Tax Liability	Amounts Withheld
1999	$14,000	$11,500
2000	10,800	11,750

For 2001, he estimates that his combined federal and provincial tax liability will be $17,000 and that his employer will withhold a total of $13,000.

He has asked you whether it will be necessary for him to pay instalments in 2001 and, if so, what the minimum amounts that should be paid are and when they should be paid.

Required: Provide the information requested by Mr. Gore.

Self Study Problem Two - 2

For its fiscal year ending December 31, 1999, Amalmor Inc. had taxable income of $250,000 and paid taxes of $62,500. In 2000, the corresponding figures were $320,000 and $80,000. It is estimated that for the current year ending December 31, 2001, the Company will have taxable income of $380,000 and taxes payable of $95,000.

Required: Determine the amount of the minimum monthly instalments that must be made by Amalmor Inc. during 2001.

Self Study Problem Two - 3

For the three years ending December 31, 2001, the taxpayer's combined federal and provincial taxes payable were as follows:

Year Ending December 31	Taxes Payable
1999	$23,540
2000	11,466
2001 (Estimated)	24,718

Case One   The taxpayer is an individual whose employer withholds combined federal and provincial taxes of $18,234 in 1999, $7,850 in 2000, and $27,346 in 2001.

Case Two   The taxpayer is an individual whose employer withholds combined federal and provincial taxes of $21,720 in 1999, $6,250 in 2000, and $21,833 in 2001.

Case Three   The taxpayer is a corporation with a taxation year that ends on December 31.

Case Four   The taxpayer is a corporation with a taxation year that ends on December 31. Assume that its combined federal and provincial taxes payable for the year ending December 31, 2000 were $32,560, instead of the $11,466 given in the problem.

Required: For each of the preceding independent cases:

A. Determine whether the taxpayer is required to make instalments payments for the year ending December 31, 2001 and explain your conclusion.

B. Indicate the minimum instalment payments that would be required and the due date for each instalment.

Self Study Problem Two - 4
The terms tax evasion, tax avoidance, and tax planning all refer to ways in which taxpayers can reduce their tax liabilities.

Required: Distinguish among these terms and provide an example of each.

Self Study Problem Two - 5
Mr. Coffee is one of your major clients. He is extremely wealthy and has paid his very sizable tax liability over the years without complaint.

On August 15th of the current year, Mr. Coffee receives a notice from the CCRA indicating that he is being reassessed for the preceding taxation year. The additional amount of taxes which is involved is $5,000 and he feels that the position of the CCRA is completely unjustified.

Mr. Coffee has approached you for advice on dealing with the matter.

Required: Indicate the procedures that may be used in dealing with this dispute between the CCRA and Mr. Coffee.

Self Study Problem Two - 6
List the three types of entities that are subject to federal income taxation in Canada and, for each, state:

A. the taxation year covered;
B. the filing deadlines for their respective income tax returns; and
C. how frequently income tax instalments must be made.

Assignment Problems

(The solutions for these problems are only available in
the solutions manual that has been provided to your instructor.)

Assignment Problem Two - 1

In January, 2001, you are asked to provide tax advice to Ms. Leslie Garond. She has provided
you with the following information about her combined federal and provincial tax liability
and the amounts withheld by her employer for the 1999 and 2000 taxation years:

Year	Tax Liability	Amounts Withheld
1999	$22,000	$9,500
2000	18,000	9,700

For 2001, she estimates that her combined federal and provincial tax liability will be $14,000
and that her employer will withhold a total of $9,850.

She has asked you whether it will be necessary for her to pay instalments in 2001 and, if so,
what the minimum amounts that should be paid are and when they are due.

Required: Provide the information requested by Ms. Garond.

Assignment Problem Two - 2

Because the majority of individual taxpayers have income taxes withheld at the source, not
everyone is required to make income tax instalment payments.

Required: Describe the circumstances under which an individual must make income tax instalment payments. In addition, describe the alternative methods that can be used to determine the amount of the instalment payments.

Assignment Problem Two - 3

The fiscal year of the Sloan Company ends on October 31. During the year ending October
31, 1999, its federal taxes payable amounted to $168,000, while for the year ending October
31, 2000, the amount payable was $153,000. It is estimated that federal taxes payable for the
year ending October 31, 2001 will be $144,000.

Required:

A. Calculate the instalment payments that are required for the year ending October 31, 2001
under the alternative methods available. Indicate which of the alternatives would be
preferable.

B. If the Company did not make any instalment payments towards its 2001 tax liabilities, indicate how the interest and penalty amounts assessed against it would be determined.

Assignment Problem Two - 4

For the year ending December 31, 1999, the taxpayer's combined federal and provincial
taxes payable amounted to $18,000, while for the year ending December 31, 2000 the
amount payable was $14,400. It is estimated that federal and provincial taxes payable for the
year ending December 31, 2001 is $12,500.

Required: For each of the following cases, calculate the minimum instalment payments that are required to be made towards the settlement of the tax liability for the year ending December 31, 2001. Included in your answer should be the date that each instalment is due to be paid.

A.   The taxpayer is an individual whose employer withholds combined federal and provincial taxes of $12,000 in 1999, $11,000 in 2000, and $10,000 in 2001.

B.   The taxpayer is an individual whose employer withholds combined federal and provincial taxes of $7,000 in 1999, $15,000 in 2000, and $9,000 in 2001.

C.   The taxpayer is a corporation.

D.   The taxpayer is a corporation. Assume that its combined federal and provincial taxes payable for the year ending December 31, 2001 are estimated to be $16,000, instead of the $12,500 given in the problem.

Assignment Problem Two - 5

In addition to interest charges on any late payment of taxes, penalties may be assessed for failure to file a return within the prescribed deadlines. These deadlines vary depending on the taxpayer.

Required: Indicate when income tax returns must be filed for each of the following types of taxpayers:

    A.   Trusts
    B.   Corporations
    C.   Living individuals
    D.   Final return for deceased individuals

Assignment Problem Two - 6

Mr. James Simon has asked for your services with respect to dealing with a reassessment notice requesting additional tax for the 1997 taxation year which he says he has just received. Your first interview takes place on March 15, 2001 and Mr. Simon informs you that he has had considerable difficulty with the CCRA in past years and, on two occasions in the past five years, he has been required to pay penalties as well as interest. With respect to the current reassessment, he assures you that he has complied with the law and that there is a misunderstanding on the part of the assessor. After listening to him describe the situation, it would appear that his analysis of the situation is probably correct.

Required: Indicate what additional information should be obtained during the interview with Mr. Simon and what steps should be taken if you decide to accept him as a client.

Assignment Problem Two - 7

For each of the following independent cases, indicate whether you believe a penalty would be assessed against the tax preparer under ITA 163.2. Explain your conclusion.

A.   Accountant X is asked by Client A to prepare a tax return including a business financial statement to be used in the return. In response to a request by Accountant X for business related documents, Client A supplies information to Accountant X, which includes a travel expense receipt. Accountant X relies on this information provided by Client A and prepares the business statement that is filed with the return. The CCRA conducts a compliance audit and determines that Client A's travel expense was a non-deductible personal expense.

B. Accountant X has several clients that have been reassessed in respect of a tax shelter. Accountant X knows that the CCRA is challenging the tax effects claimed in respect of the tax shelter on the basis that the shelter is not a business, is based on a significant overvaluation of the related property and, alternatively, is technically deficient. The Tax Court of Canada, in a test case (formal procedure), denies deductions claimed in respect of the tax shelter in a previous year by Client B (a client of Accountant X). Client B's appeal is dismissed. The case is not appealed and Accountant X is aware of the Court's decision. Accountant X prepares and files a tax return on behalf of Client C that includes a claim in respect of the same tax shelter that the Tax Court determined was ineffective.

C. Taxpayer Z approaches Tax-preparer X to prepare and e-file Z's tax return. Taxpayer Z provides X with a T4 slip indicating that Z has $32,000 of employment income. Taxpayer Z advises X that he made a charitable donation of $24,000 but forgot the receipt at home. Z asks that X prepare and e-file the tax return. In fact, Z never donated anything to a charity. X prepares Z's tax return without obtaining the receipt.

Assignment Problem Two - 8 (Electronic Library Research Problem)

Provide brief answers to the following questions. Your answers should be supported by references to materials found in your Electronic Library.

A. What is the policy of the CCRA with respect to taxpayers who voluntarily disclose the fact that they have been evading taxes?

B. The *Income Tax Act* requires the retention of books and records. Which persons are required to comply with these rules?

C. When a corporation is dissolved, what books and records must be retained and for what period of time?

D. What is the CCRA's view of treatment of stolen property?

Chapter 3

Liability For Tax

Liability For Income Tax

Charging Provisions

3-1.   The portion of any tax legislation which specifies who is liable to pay tax is called a charging provision. Section 2 of the *Income Tax Act* contains two Subsections dealing with this subject. ITA 2(1), the more important of these Subsections, establishes that, in general, Canadian income taxation is based on residence. This Subsection states the following:

> **ITA 2(1)**   An income tax shall be paid, as required by this *Act*, on the taxable income for each taxation year of every person resident in Canada at any time in the year.

3-2.   There are several terms used in this charging provision which require further explanation. These explanations are as follows:

Meaning Of Person   As used in the *Income Tax Act*, the term person refers not only to individuals, but to corporations and trusts as well. When a provision of the *Act* is directed at human taxpayers, the term individual is generally used.

Residence Vs. Citizenship   As is the case in the United Kingdom, Canadian taxation is based on the concept of residence. This differs from the situation in the United States where U.S. citizens are subject to taxation regardless of their place of residence.

Taxation Year   A taxation year is defined in ITA 249 as meaning the calendar year for individuals and inter vivos trusts. In contrast, taxation year means a fiscal year for both corporations and testamentary trusts.

Meaning Of Resident   While the concept of residence would seem to be self evident, at least for individuals, there are a number of difficulties associated with this idea that will be covered in detail in this Chapter.

Meaning Of Taxable Income   This is a technical term which is used to describe Net Income For Tax Purposes, less certain specific deductions. Examples of these deductions would include loss carry overs for all taxpayers, the lifetime capital gains deduction for individuals, and taxable dividends received by corporations. While the basic calculation of Net Income For Tax Purposes will be described in this Chapter, the calculation of Taxable Income for individuals will not be given any consideration until Chapter 12. Taxable Income for corporations will be covered in Chapter 14.

3-3.   The second charging provision in the *Income Tax Act* deals with the taxation of non-residents. It is as follows:

ITA 2(3)   Where a person who is not taxable under subsection (1) for a taxation year

(a) was employed in Canada,
(b) carried on a business in Canada, or
(c) disposed of a taxable Canadian property,

at any time in the year or a previous year, an income tax shall be paid, as required by this *Act*, on the person's taxable income earned in Canada for the year determined in accordance with Division D.

3-4.   This charging provision is directed at those situations in which non-residents are subject to Canadian income taxes. We will give less attention to this Subsection as it is not generally applicable to Canadian residents. We would note here, however, that there are difficulties associated with the meaning of the terms "employed in Canada", "carried on business in Canada", and "taxable Canadian property". These matters will be dealt with in detail in later Chapters.

Residence Of Individuals
General Concept
3-5.   The term residence is not specifically defined in the *Income Tax Act*. As a consequence, it becomes necessary to examine court decisions, Interpretation Bulletins, and other sources of guidance. In general, the courts have described residence by stating that persons are ordinarily resident where, in the settled routine of their regular life, they normally and customarily live. In addition, court decisions have taken the position that everyone is a resident of some country. However, they have also indicated that a single individual may, in certain circumstances, be considered to be a resident of more than one country.

3-6.   In the great majority of cases, the application of these general ideas does not present significant problems. For the average Canadian individual whose job, family, dwelling place, and other personal property are all in Canada, the concept of residence is not at all ambiguous. Such individuals would clearly be Canadian residents and, as a result, they would be liable for Canadian taxation on their worldwide income. Short departures from the country for holidays or business activities would not have any effect on this conclusion.

Temporary Absences
3-7.   Most of the problems associated with establishing residency involve situations where an individual leaves Canada for a temporary but extended period of time. The issue here is under what circumstances an individual should be viewed as having retained their Canadian residency status during the period of their absence from Canada. It is an important issue in that, if they are viewed as having retained their Canadian residency status, they will be subject to Canadian taxation on their worldwide income during the period of absence from Canada. While credits against Canadian income taxes payable would be available for any taxes paid in the foreign jurisdiction, they will often be insufficient to cover the full Canadian tax liability.

3-8.   IT-221R2 states that, if a person is out of the country for less than two years, that person will be presumed to have retained Canadian residency status unless it can be demonstrated that all residential ties have been severed at the time of the departure. The primary residential ties of an individual would be his dwelling place, his spouse and dependants, and his personal property and social ties. In addition, if there is evidence to suggest that, at the time of departure, the individual intended to return to Canada (e.g., an employment contract requiring such return), the CCRA will presume that the individual did not sever all residential ties.

3-9.   IT-221R2 also notes that, if the absence is in excess of two years, there will be a presumption that the individual has become a non resident provided the following tests are met:

• The individual did not leave a dwelling in Canada available to be reoccupied on return (IT-221R2 notes that retaining a property that is rented will not violate this test, provided the lease is with an arm's length party for a period of more than three months).

- The individual did not leave a spouse or other dependants in Canada.
- The individual did not leave personal property (furniture, cars, bank accounts) or social ties (club memberships) in Canada.
- The individual establishes a permanent residence in another jurisdiction.
- The individual does not return to visit Canada on a regular or frequent basis.

3-10. If an individual fails to meet one or more of these tests, the CCRA may attempt to assess him on the basis of continuing residency during the period of absence from Canada. As there are no fixed rules with respect to how many of these tests must be met to prove non residence, this issue periodically results in disputes between the CCRA and taxpayers.

Part Year Residence

3-11. In a year in which a person clearly terminates or establishes residency in Canada, they will be taxed in Canada on their worldwide income for the part of the year in which they are resident in Canada. While the date for the establishment of residency in Canada is based on the date of entry under immigration rules, the date on which an individual becomes a non resident is the latest of:

- The date they leave Canada.
- The date their spouse and other dependants leave Canada.
- The date they become residents of the country to which they are immigrating.

3-12. This part year residency requires a fairly complex prorating of income, deductions, and personal tax credits. For example, an individual who is a resident of Canada for only part of the year will not be entitled to a full personal tax credit. The process for prorating such deductions and credits is specified in ITA 114 and ITA 118.91.

Sojourners And Other Deemed Residents

3-13. ITA 250(1) extends the meaning of residents to include certain individuals as deemed residents. As deemed residents, the individuals listed in ITA 250(1) will be taxed as Canadian residents throughout the taxation year, without regard to where they live. In fact, it would be possible for such individuals to be taxed as Canadian residents even if they were never present in Canada during the taxation year in question. Included on this list of deemed residents of Canada are the following:

1. Sojourners in Canada for 183 days or more.
2. Members, at any time during the year, of the Canadian armed forces.
3. Ambassadors, ministers, high commissioners, officers or servants of Canada, as well as agents general, officers, or servants of a Province, provided they were Canadian residents at the time of their appointment.
4. An individual performing services, at any time in the year, in a country other than Canada under a prescribed international development assistance program of the Government of Canada, provided they were resident in Canada at any time in the 3 month period preceding the day on which those services commenced.
5. A child of a deemed resident, provided they are also a dependant whose net income for the year was less than the basic personal tax credit ($7,231 for 2000).
6. An individual who was at any time in the year, under an agreement or a convention with one or more other countries, entitled to an exemption from an income tax otherwise payable in any of those countries, because at that time the person was related to or a member of the family of an individual who was resident in Canada.

3-14. Of these items, numbers 1 and 6 require some further explanation. With respect to item 1, a sojourner is an individual who is temporarily present in Canada for a period of 183 days or more during any one calendar year. Because of ITA 250(1), this person is deemed to be a Canadian resident for the entire year.

3-15. For this sojourner rule to apply, the individual must be a resident of another country during the 183 days in question. This means that an individual who gives up their residence in another country and moves to Canada early in a taxation year will be considered a part year resident, not a sojourner. Correspondingly, a Canadian resident who leaves Canada to take up residence in another country, will not be a sojourner, despite the fact that they are in Canada for more than 183 days.

3-16.   This is an important distinction in that an individual establishing residence in Canada or departing from Canada during a given year will be treated as a resident only during the period subsequent to entry into Canada or prior to leaving Canada. In contrast, the sojourner will be taxed on his world income for the entire taxation year. This could result in situations where a sojourner is taxed on a greater proportion of his world income than a part time resident who actually spent a larger portion of the year in Canada.

3-17.   Item 6 refers to situations where someone is exempt from tax in a foreign country because they are related to an individual who is a Canadian resident. For example, the spouse of a Canadian diplomat working in the U.S. would be exempt from U.S. income taxes under the governing international tax treaty because she is the spouse of the diplomat. As the diplomat would be a deemed resident of Canada under item 3, the spouse would be a deemed resident of Canada under item 6.

Exercises Three-1 and Three-2 deal with the residence of individuals. This would be an appropriate time to attempt these exercises.

Residence Of Corporations

3-18.   Being an artificial legal entity, a corporation does not reside anywhere in the same physical sense that the term applies to an individual. To some extent, the jurisdiction of incorporation can assist in finding a solution to this problem. More specifically, ITA 250(4) indicates that all corporations which are incorporated in Canada after April 26, 1965 are deemed to be resident in Canada. For corporations chartered in Canada prior to April 27, 1965, the Act indicates that these organizations would also be treated as residents if they were resident in Canada (under the common law concept discussed in Paragraph 3-19 and 3-20) or carried on business in Canada in any taxation year ending after April 26, 1965.

3-19.   The location where the particular company was incorporated is not, however, the end of the story. If this were the case, it would be possible to escape Canadian taxation by the simple act of incorporating outside of the country. Beyond the rules described in the preceding Paragraph, a well established common law principle applies. This is the idea that a corporation is resident in the jurisdiction in which the mind and management of the company are located. Such factors as the location of the board of directors meetings and where day-to-day decisions are made, are used to determine the location of the mind and management of the corporation. If the conclusion is that the mind and management is in Canada, then a corporation that is not incorporated in Canada will be considered a resident for Canadian tax purposes.

3-20.   This "mind and management" criteria would also apply to a corporation that was incorporated in Canada prior to April 27, 1965. Such a corporation would become a resident if, after April 26, 1965, its operations were controlled within Canada. Unlike the foreign jurisdiction corporation, which would be considered to be a Canadian resident only as long as the mind and management remained in Canada, a pre April 27, 1965 Canadian corporation that became a resident because of the mind and management criteria, would remain a Canadian resident, even if the mind and management were moved to a different jurisdiction.

Exercises Three-3 and Three-4 deal with the residence of corporations. This would be an appropriate time to attempt these exercises.

3-21.   International tax treaties may also be influential in the determination of the residence of corporations. As noted previously, if there is a conflict between domestic legislation and the provisions of an international tax treaty, the treaty rules override the domestic legislation. For example, a situation might arise where a particular corporation is considered to be a resident of Canada under Canadian legislation and a resident of a foreign country under the legislation that prevails in that country. This is a situation which could result in the corporation being taxed in both jurisdictions. If Canada has a tax treaty with the foreign country, the treaty would prevent double taxation by providing provisions which would be used to determine the residency of the corporation.

Residence Of Trusts

3-22.   As with any other question of residence, establishing the residence of a trust is something that can only be determined by examining the circumstances involved in each case. In general, however, IT-447 indicates that a trust is considered to reside where the trustee, executor, administrator, heir or other legal representative who manages the trust or controls the trust assets resides. If this location is not clear, the same Interpretation Bulletin indicates that the authorities will look at the location where the legal rights with respect to the trust assets are enforceable and the location of the trust assets.

Taxation Of Non Residents

Employment Income, Business Income, and Capital Gains

3-23.   As we noted previously, under ITA 2(3), non residents are subject to taxation on Canadian employment income, income from carrying on a business in Canada, and on gains resulting from the disposal of "taxable Canadian property". As the term is used in ITA 2(3), Canadian employment income refers to income earned by a non resident while working as an employee in Canada. An example of this would be a U.S. citizen who is a resident of Detroit, Michigan, but is employed at an automobile plant in Windsor, Ontario. Such an individual would be subject to Canadian taxes on his employment income. However, as the individual is a non resident, his other sources of income would not be taxed in Canada.

3-24.   Many of the difficulties associated with the implementation of ITA 2(3) are related to determining what constitutes carrying on business in Canada. Under ITA 253, an extended meaning is given to this concept which provides for a very broad interpretation of this expression. More specifically, under ITA 253, carrying on business in Canada would apply not only to persons who produce or manufacture products in Canada, but also to persons who offer things for sale in Canada through an employee.

3-25.   This broad interpretation is, however, mitigated in those circumstances where the non resident is a resident of a country with which Canada has a tax treaty. For example, if a U.S. corporation had employees selling products in Canada, ITA 253 would suggest that it should be taxed as a non resident doing business in Canada. However, the Canada-U.S. tax treaty overrides ITA 253 in that this Agreement exempts a U.S. enterprise from Canadian taxation unless it is carrying on business through permanent establishments in this country.

3-26.   It is also important to distinguish between those situations in which a non resident is offering something for sale in Canada through an employee and those situations in which a non resident is selling to an independent contractor who resells the item. In the former case, the non resident person is carrying on business in Canada while in the latter case, the non resident is not.

3-27.   Finally, non residents are subject to Canadian taxation on gains resulting from the disposition of "taxable Canadian property". This concept will be discussed more completely in Chapter 10. However, you should note at this point that the major items in taxable Canadian property are real estate, capital property used to carry on a business in Canada, shares of private companies, and partnership interests in situations where more than 50 percent of the partnership's property is made up of taxable Canadian property. This provision means that, if a resident of the state of Washington disposes of a condominium that he owns in Whistler, British Columbia, any gain on that sale will be subject to Canadian taxation.

Property Income

3-28.   The charging provisions in ITA 2 do not cover Canadian source property income of non residents (rents, interest, or royalties). However, this type of income is covered in Part XIII of the Act which requires a flat 25 percent tax on this type of income (the rate is often reduced if the payment is going to a country with which Canada has a tax treaty). This tax is withheld at the source of income, is based on the gross amount of such income, and no provision is made for any expenses related to acquiring the income. Since this inability to deduct expenses could result in serious inequities, there are provisions which allow a non resident to elect to file a Canadian tax return under Part I of the Act. The Part XIII tax provisions are discussed more thoroughly in Chapter 21.

Exercise Three-5 deals with the taxation of non residents. This would be an appropriate time to attempt this exercise.

The Concept Of Income

The Economist's View

3-29.   Economists have traditionally viewed income as being limited to rents, profits and wages. In general, capital gains, gratuitous receipts, and other such increases in net worth were not included. However, most economists perceived income to be a net concept. That is, income is equal to gross revenues less any related expenses.

3-30.   In more recent times, the economist's concept of income has moved in the direction of including measures of net worth or capital maintenance. The oft cited quotation "Income is the amount that can be spent during the period and still be as well off at the end of the period as at the beginning" is perhaps as good a description of the current concept as any available.

3-31.   This broader concept of income is based on the idea that income should include all increases in net economic power that occur during the relevant measurement period.

The Accountant's View

3-32.   What we currently view as Net Income from an accounting point of view is the result of applying a fairly flexible group of rules that are referred to as generally accepted accounting principles (GAAP). In general, Net Income is determined by establishing the amount of revenue on the basis of point of sale revenue recognition. Then, by using a variety of cash flows, accruals, and allocations, the cost of assets used up in producing these revenues is matched against them and deducted to produce the accounting income for the period. If this same process is viewed from the perspective of the Balance Sheet, Net Income is measured as the increase in net assets for the period under consideration, plus any distributions that were made to the owners of the business during that period.

3-33.   Under historical cost measurement, the accountant's concept of income differs from that of the economist in that many changes in economic well being are not measured under generally accepted accounting principles. Increases in value associated with general or specific price level changes, as well as most internally developed intangibles, are not normally recorded by the accountant.

The Income Tax Act View

General Approach

3-34.   The *Income Tax Act* view of income, like that described under the accounting view, is the result of the application of a complex set of rules. With respect to business income, many of these rules are either identical or very similar to those contained in generally accepted accounting principles. For example, ordinary salaries to employees are a deduction in the computation of business income under both GAAP and the *Income Tax Act*. However, there are many differences between GAAP and tax rules, some of which are simply alternative approaches to allocation. An example of this would be the relationship between tax depreciation (capital cost allowance) and accounting depreciation. Other differences, such as the non taxable portion of capital gains, are included in accounting income although they will never be recognized for tax purposes. In accounting literature these two types of differences used to be referred to as timing differences and permanent differences, respectively. However, with the 1997 addition of Section 3465, "Income Taxes" to the *CICA Handbook*, the terminology has changed. Under Section 3465, differences between accounting and tax information are measured on the Balance Sheet, rather than on the Income Statement. Differences between the carrying value of an asset or liability and its tax basis are referred to as temporary differences. These amounts are multiplied by an appropriate tax rate to arrive at Future Income Tax Assets or, alternatively, Future Income Tax Liabilities.

ITA Division B - Computation Of Income

3-35.   Division B of Part I of the *Income Tax Act* is devoted to the computation of what is normally called Net Income For Tax Purposes. Note that, while this amount is sometimes referred to simply as Net Income, we will not use this designation in order to avoid confusion with the bottom line in the accounting Income Statement.

3-36. As was described in Chapter 1, Division B identifies and provides rules for the computation of three basic types of income:

- Income Or Loss From An Office Or Employment (Division B, Subdivision a)
- Income Or Loss From Business And Property (Division B, Subdivision b)
- Taxable Capital Gains And Allowable Capital Losses (Division B, Subdivision c)

3-37. Each of these Subdivisions specifies inclusions and deductions applicable to the particular type of income under consideration. In later Chapters, detailed attention will be given to each of these types of income (e.g., Chapter 5 covers employment income). However, at this point we would note that each of these types of income is calculated on a net basis (i.e., inclusions, less deductions).

3-38. In addition to these three basic components, two other Subdivisions often influence the calculation of Net Income For Tax Purposes. Division B, Subdivision d deals with miscellaneous inclusions in income. Examples of such miscellaneous inclusions would be spousal support received and various types of pension income. Division B, Subdivision e deals with miscellaneous deductions. Examples here would include Registered Retirement Savings Plan contributions, moving expenses, spousal support paid, and child care costs.

3-39. In somewhat simplified terms, Net Income For Tax Purposes (Division B Income) is calculated by adding net employment income, net business income, and the net of taxable capital gains less allowable capital losses. To this total we add the other inclusions from Subdivision d and subtract the other deductions from Subdivision e. While this description provides a general overview of the determination of Net Income For Tax Purposes, the actual calculation of this amount is subject to specific rules that are found in ITA 3. These rules will be covered in the next section of this Chapter.

Rules For Computing Net Income

ITA Section 3

3-40. As noted in the preceding Section, ITA 3 provides a set of rules for combining various types of income into Net Income For Tax Purposes. While some of the ideas involved in applying this formula will not be fully explained until later in the text, it is useful at this stage to provide the basic structure of this formula in order to enhance your understanding of how the material which follows is organized. The ITA 3 rules are presented graphically in Figure 3-1 (on the following page).

3-41. The process begins in ITA 3(a) with the addition of all positive sources of income other than capital gains. This includes positive amounts of employment income, business income, property income, and other miscellaneous non capital inclusions from subdivision d of Division B. Note that this is not a net calculation. For example, a business loss would not be deducted against a positive employment income under ITA 3(a). Rather, the loss would be deducted from the total carried forward to ITA 3(d).

3-42. To the ITA 3(a) total, ITA 3(b) requires the addition of the amount, if any, by which taxable capital gains exceed allowable capital losses. The wording of ITA 3(b) is that you "determine the amount, if any, by which" taxable capital gains exceed allowable capital losses. This phrase "if any" is commonly used in tax legislation to indicate that negative amounts are ignored. It is of particular importance here in that the fact that ITA 3(b) must be positive or nil establishes the rule that a particular year's allowable capital losses can only be deducted to the extent of taxable capital gains that have been recognized in that year.

3-43. Note, however, the excess allowable capital losses do not disappear. As will be explained in detail in Chapter 12, unused capital losses can be applied against taxable income in past or future years as net capital loss carry overs. More specifically, such losses can be carried back to the preceding three years, and forward indefinitely.

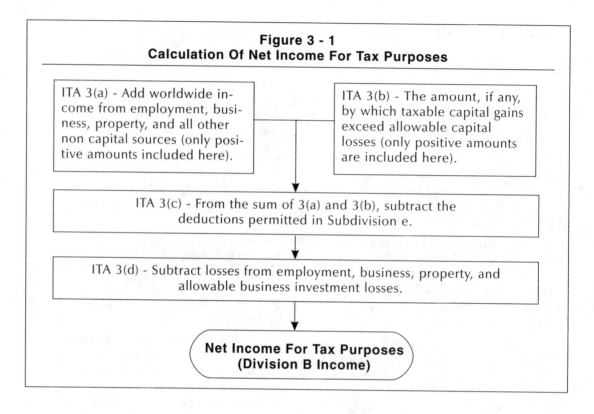

Figure 3 - 1
Calculation Of Net Income For Tax Purposes

| ITA 3(a) - Add worldwide income from employment, business, property, and all other non capital sources (only positive amounts included here). | ITA 3(b) - The amount, if any, by which taxable capital gains exceed allowable capital losses (only positive amounts are included here). |

ITA 3(c) - From the sum of 3(a) and 3(b), subtract the deductions permitted in Subdivision e.

ITA 3(d) - Subtract losses from employment, business, property, and allowable business investment losses.

Net Income For Tax Purposes (Division B Income)

3-44.   A further point here relates to capital gains terminology. The term "taxable capital gain" refers to the portion (generally one-half for 2001) of the gain that must be included in income. Correspondingly, the term "allowable capital loss" refers to the portion of the loss (generally one-half for 2001) that can be deducted. If the term used is capital gain or capital loss, it means the full amount of these items, before the removal of the non taxable or non deductible portion.

3-45.   Given the preceding definitions, the sum of ITA 3(a) and ITA 3(b) will either be positive or nil. If this total is nil, it means that the taxpayer's Division B Income is nil. Alternatively, if the total is positive, it is carried forward to ITA 3(c) where it will be reduced by any Subdivision e deductions that are available. These deductions, which will be covered in detail in Chapter 11, include payments for spousal support, moving expenses, child care costs, and contributions to Registered Retirement Savings Plans.

3-46.   If Subdivision e deductions exceed the total carried forward from ITA 3(a) and ITA 3(b), Division B Income is nil and some of the Subdivision e deductions may be lost. If, however, a positive balance remains, this balance is carried forward to ITA 3(d).

3-47.   Under ITA 3(d), the taxpayer can deduct various types of non capital losses. This would include the deduction of business losses, property losses, employment losses, and allowable business investment losses (allowable business investment losses are a special type of allowable capital loss that can be deducted against any type of income). If losses exceed the balance carried forward from ITA 3(c), Division B Income is nil. As was the case with non deductible allowable capital losses from ITA 3(b), any non deductible non capital losses here can be applied against taxable income in past or future years as non capital loss carry overs (the limits here are three years back and seven years forward).

Section 3 Example

3-48.   The following example provides an illustration of how the rules are applied.

Example   Jonathan Morley has the following income components for the year:

Employment Income	$17,000
Loss From Business	(21,000)
Income From Property	9,000
Taxable Capital Gains	14,000
Allowable Capital Losses	(19,000)
Subdivision e Deductions	(9,000)

3-49.   Mr. Morley's Division B Income would be calculated as follows:

Income Under ITA 3(a):		
Employment Income	$17,000	
Income From Property	9,000	$26,000
Income Under ITA 3(b):		
Taxable Capital Gains	$14,000	
Allowable Capital Losses	(19,000)	Nil
Balance From ITA 3(a) And (b)		$26,000
Subdivision e Deductions		(9,000)
Balance ITA 3(c)		$17,000
Deduction Under ITA 3(d):		
Loss From Business		(21,000)
Net Income For Tax Purposes (Division B Income)		Nil

3-50.   As Mr. Morley's Business Loss exceeds the amount carried forward from ITA 3(c), his Division B income is nil. However, there would be a carry over of non capital losses equal to $4,000 and of allowable capital losses in the amount of $5,000. As will be explained in Chapter 12, allowable capital loss carry overs can only be deducted to the extent that there are taxable capital gains in the carry over period. As a consequence, this type of loss carry over has to be segregated from non capital loss carry overs which can be deducted against any type of income in the carry over year.

3-51.   We would note here that, if this is your first exposure to income taxation, you should not expect to have a complete understanding of ITA 3 at this point. You should review this material and make an attempt to solve the relatively simple problems and exercises that are included in this Chapter. Rather, a periodic review of this set of rules as you proceed through Chapters 5 through 11 will enhance your understanding of the organization of that material as it is being covered.

> Exercises Three-6 through Three-8 deal with the calculation of Net Income for Tax Purposes. This would be an appropriate time to attempt these exercises.

Principles Of Tax Planning

Introduction

3-52.   Throughout this text, there will be a great deal of emphasis on tax planning and, while many of the specific techniques which are involved can only be fully explained after the more detailed provisions of tax legislation have been covered, there are some basic tax planning principles which can be described at this point. Our objective here is simply to provide a general understanding of the results that can be achieved through tax planning so that you will be able to recognize the goal of more specific tax planning techniques when they are examined. In addition, this general understanding should enable you to identify other opportunities for tax planning as you become more familiar with this material.

3-53.   The basic goals of tax planning can be summarized as follows:

- Tax Avoidance Or Reduction
- Tax Deferral
- Income Splitting

3-54.   While these classifications can be used to describe the goals of all tax planning arrangements, such arrangements seldom involve a clear cut attempt to achieve only one of these goals. For example, the principal reason for making contributions to a Registered Retirement Savings Plan is to defer taxes until later taxation years. However, such a deferral can result in the taxpayer avoiding some amount of taxes if he is taxed at a lower rate in those later years.

Tax Avoidance Or Reduction

3-55. The most desirable result of tax planning is to permanently avoid the payment of some amount of tax. This very desirability is probably the most important explanation for the scarcity of such arrangements and, while the number of possibilities in this area is limited, they do exist. An outstanding example of tax avoidance is the capital gains deduction that is available on the disposition of qualified farm property and qualified small business corporation shares. The first $500,000 of capital gains on such dispositions can be received by the taxpayer on a tax free basis. For individuals in a position to enjoy the benefits of this provision, it is one of the richest tax avoidance mechanism that is currently available.

3-56. Other forms of complete tax avoidance can be found in the employee benefits area in that some types of benefits can be given to employees without being considered taxable. These would include an employer's payments for disability and private health care insurance and the provision of discounts to employees on products or services normally sold by the employer.

3-57. Additional opportunities in this area require more complex arrangements. Such arrangements involve the use of trusts and private corporations and cannot be described in a meaningful manner at this stage.

Tax Deferral

3-58. The basic concept behind tax planning arrangements involving the deferral of tax payments is the very simple idea that it is better to pay taxes later than it is to pay them now. This is related to the time value of money and also involves the possibility that some permanent avoidance of taxes may result from the taxpayer being taxed at a lower marginal income tax rate at the time the deferred amounts are brought into taxable income.

3-59. Such deferral arrangements may involve either the delayed recognition of certain types of income or, alternatively, accelerated recognition of deductions. As an example of delayed recognition, an employer can make contributions to a registered pension plan on behalf of its employees without creating any taxable income for them until they actually receive retirement benefits. In other words, this arrangement allows employees to defer some of their compensation revenues both in terms of cash flows and in terms of taxable income.

3-60. As an example of expense acceleration, the ownership of a rental property may allow the owner to deduct its capital cost at a rate that is usually in excess of any decline in the physical or economic worth of the building. While this excess will normally be added back to the taxpayer's income when the building is sold, the payment of taxes on some part of the rental income from the property has been deferred.

3-61. Deferral arrangements are available in a number of different situations and currently represent one of the more prevalent forms of tax planning.

Income Splitting

General Idea

3-62. As we have previously noted, progressive rates are built into Canadian federal income tax legislation. This means that the taxes payable on a given amount of taxable income will be greater, if that amount accrues to one taxpayer, than would be the case if that same amount of taxable income is split between two or more people. Of course, this does not mean that it would be advantageous to give part of your income away to perfect strangers. What it does mean is that, within a family or other related group, it is desirable to have the group's aggregate taxable income allocated as evenly as possible among the members of the group.

Example

3-63.   The tax savings that can be achieved through income splitting are among the most dramatic examples of the effectiveness of tax planning. For example, if Mr. Jordan had taxable income of $400,000 (this is four times $100,000, the bottom of the highest federal tax bracket in 2001), his basic federal taxes payable in 2001 would be $108,695 (this does not take into consideration the various tax credits that would be available to Mr. Jordan). Alternatively, if Mr. Jordan was married and the $400,000 could be split on the basis of $200,000 to him and $200,000 to his wife, the federal taxes payable would total $101,390 [(2)($50,695)], a savings of $7,305.

3-64.   If we carry this one step further and assume that Mr. Jordan is married and has two children and that the $400,000 in taxable income can be allocated on the basis of $100,000 to each individual, the total federal taxes payable will be reduced to $86,780 [(4)($21,695)]. This represents a savings at the federal level of $21,915 when compared to the amount of taxes that would have been paid if Mr. Jordan had been taxed on the entire $400,000. When we add provincial effects, the potential savings could exceed $30,000, a substantial reduction on income of $400,000. Making this savings even more impressive is the fact that it is not a one shot phenomena but, rather, could occur in each year that the income splitting plan is in effect.

Problems

3-65.   Income splitting techniques can only be used with certain types of income and are not always capable of providing a uniform spread of income over all members of a family group. Further, the arrangements for implementing this form of tax planning tend to be fairly complex and, as a result, are expensive to implement. The situation can be complicated by the fact that parents often have strong emotional reactions to losing control over income. Even more difficult may be questions such as which members of the family group are more or less deserving of additional sources of income, and whether additional income should be allocated to a child with an unstable marriage. However, as the preceding example indicates, income splitting is one of the most powerful weapons in the tax planner's arsenal. For high income taxpayers with family members in different income tax brackets, a failure to make use of this tool can subject the family unit to a considerably higher tax liability.

1999 Budget Changes

3-66.   Income splitting is commonly implemented using private companies, partnerships, and trusts in a manner that allows income to be allocated to family members in lower tax brackets. While the income attribution rules (see Chapter 10) place significant limits on this process, the government did not feel that these rules were sufficiently effective. As a consequence, the February 16, 1999 budget introduced a significant change in the rules.

3-67.   Beginning in the year 2000, income received from certain sources by a minor child who is under 18 at the end of the calendar year, will be taxed at the top federal rate of 29 percent. As noted previously, the application of this rate does not normally begin until an individual's income is in excess of $100,000.

3-68.   The applicability of this special rule will be discussed more completely in Chapter 13 when we deal with the computation of taxes payable for individuals. However, we would note at this point that this change significantly restricts the ability of parents to implement income splitting arrangements with minor children. In fact, one article on this subject referred to the changes as the "death of income splitting".

> Exercises Three-9 and Three-10 deal with tax planning. This would be an appropriate time to attempt these exercises.

References

3-69. For more detailed study of the material in this Chapter, we would refer you to the following:

ITA 2	Tax Payable By Persons Resident In Canada
ITA 3	Income For Taxation Year
ITA 114	Individual Resident In Canada For Only Part Of Year
ITA 118.91	Part-Year Residents
ITA 249	Definition Of Taxation Year
ITA 250	Person Deemed Resident
ITA 253	Extended Meaning Of "Carrying On Business"
IT-163R2	Election By Non-Resident Individuals On Certain Canadian Source Income
IT-168R3	Athletes And Players Employed By Football, Hockey And Similar Clubs
IT-171R2	Non Resident Individuals - Computation Of Taxable Income Earned In Canada And Non Refundable Tax Credits
IT-193	Taxable Income Of Individuals Resident In Canada During Part Of A Year (Special Release)
IT-194	Foreign Tax Credit — Part-Time Residents
IT-221R2	Determination Of An Individual's Residence Status
IT-262R2	Losses Of Non-Residents And Part-Year Residents
IT-298	Canada-US Tax Convention - Number Of Days "Present" in Canada
IT-420R3	Non Residents - Income Earned In Canada
IT-447	Residence Of A Trust Or Estate
IT-451R	Deemed Disposition And Acquisition On Ceasing To Be Or Becoming Resident In Canada
IT-465R	Non Resident Beneficiaries Of Trusts
IT-497R3	Overseas Employment Tax Credit

Exercises

(The solutions for these exercises can be found following Chapter 21 of the text.)

Exercise Three - 1 (Individual Residency)
Mr. Jonathan Kirsh was born in Kansas and, until the current year, had lived in various parts of the United States. On September 1 of the current year he moves to Lethbridge, Alberta to begin work at a new job. He brings his family and all of his personal property with him. However, he continues to have both a chequing and a savings account in a U. S. financial institution. Explain how Mr. Kirsh will be taxed in Canada during the current taxation year.

Exercise Three - 2 (Individual Residency)
Ms. Suzanne Blakey was born 24 years ago in Paris, France. She is the daughter of a Canadian High Commissioner serving in that country. Her father still holds this position. However, Ms. Blakey is now working in London as a marketing consultant. She has never visited Canada. Determine the residency status of Suzanne Blakey.

Exercise Three - 3 (Corporate Residency)
Roswell Ltd. was incorporated in the State of New York in 1996. It carries on business in both the United States and Canada. However, all of the directors of the Company live in Kemptville, Ontario and, as a consequence, all of the director's meetings are held in Kemptville. Determine the residency status of Roswell Ltd.

Exercise Three - 4 (Corporate Residency)
Sateen Inc. was incorporated as a Manitoba corporation in 1995. However, since 1998, all of the Company's business has been carried on outside of Canada. Determine the residency status of Sateen Inc.

Exercise Three - 5 (Non Resident Liability For Tax)
Ms. Laurie Lacombe has Canadian employment income of $22,000. However, because she lives in Blaine, Washington and is a resident of the United States, she does not believe that she subject to taxation in Canada. Is her belief correct? Explain your conclusion.

Exercise Three - 6 (Net Income For Tax Purposes)
For the current year, Mr. Norris Blanton has employment income of $42,000, a business loss of $15,000, taxable capital gains of $24,000, and subdivision e deductions of $13,000. What is the amount of Mr. Blanton's Net Income For Tax Purposes for the current year?

Exercise Three - 7 (Net Income For Tax Purposes)
For the current year, Ms. Cheryl Stodard has interest income of $33,240, taxable capital gains of $24,750, allowable capital losses of $19,500, and a net rental loss of $48,970. What is the amount of Ms. Stodard's Net Income For Tax Purposes for the current year? Indicate the amount of any loss carry overs that would be available at the end of the current year.

Exercise Three - 8 (Net Income For Tax Purposes)
For the current year, Mrs. Marie Bergeron has employment income of $42,680, taxable capital gains of $27,400, allowable capital losses of $33,280, subdivision e deductions of $8,460, and a business loss of $26,326. What is the amount of Mrs. Bergeron's Net Income For Tax Purposes for the current year? Indicate the amount of any loss carry overs that would be available at the end of the current year.

Exercise Three - 9 (Tax Planning)
Mr. Stephen Chung has decided to make contributions to an RRSP in the name of his spouse, rather than making contributions to his own plan. What type of tax planning is involved in this decision? Explain your conclusion.

Exercise Three - 10 (Tax Planning)

Mr. Green's employer pays all of the premiums on a private dental plan which covers Mr. Green and his family. What type of tax planning is illustrated by this employee benefit? Explain your conclusion.

Problems For Self Study

(The solutions for these problems can be found following Chapter 21 of the text.)

Self Study Problem Three - 1

For Canadian income tax purposes, determine the residency of each of the following individuals for the current year. Explain the basis for your conclusion.

A. Jane Smith was born in Washington, D.C. where her father has been a Canadian ambassador for 15 years. She is 12 years old and has never been to Canada.

B. Marvin Black lives in Detroit, Michigan. He works on a full time basis in Windsor, Ontario.

C. John Leather was born in Canada and until September 12 of the current year, he has never been outside of the country. On this date he departed from Canada and established a home in Sante Fe, New Mexico.

D. Francine Donaire is a citizen of France and is married to a member of the Canadian armed forces stationed in France. She has been in Canada only on brief visits since she and her husband have been married and had never visited the country prior to that time. She is exempt from French taxation because she is the spouse of a member of the Canadian armed forces.

E. Robert Green lived most of his life in Texas. Early in the current year, he moved to Edmonton to take a job with a local oil exploration company. As he did not enjoy Edmonton, he resigned during the fall and returned to Texas.

F. Susan Allen is a Canadian citizen who has lived in New York City for the past seven years.

Self Study Problem Three - 2

For Canadian income tax purposes, determine the residency of each of the following corporations for the current year. Explain the basis for your conclusion.

A. AMT Ltd. was incorporated in New Brunswick in 1964. Until 1976, all of the directors' meetings were held in that province. However, since that time the directors have met on a regular basis in Portland, Maine.

B. UIF Inc. was incorporated in the state of Montana in 1968. However, until four years ago all of the directors' meetings were held in Vancouver, British Columbia. Four years ago, the President of the Company moved to Helena, Montana and since that time all of the directors' meetings have been held in that city.

C. BDT Ltd. was incorporated in Alberta in 1978. However, it is managed in Mexico where all directors' and shareholders' meetings have been held since incorporation.

D. QRS Inc. was incorporated in New York state. However, all of the directors are residents of Ontario and all meetings of the Board Of Directors have been held in that Province since incorporation.

Self Study Problem Three - 3

For Canadian income tax purposes, determine the residency for each of the following persons for the current year. Explain the basis for your conclusion.

A. Molly London was born in Salmon Arm, British Columbia. On October 31, after a very serious dispute with her fiancé, she left Salmon Arm and moved her belongings to San Diego, California. She has vowed to never set foot in Canada again.

B. Daryl Bennett is a Canadian citizen living in Sault Ste. Marie, Michigan. He has a summer cottage in Sault Ste. Marie, Ontario where he spent July and August. As his only sister lives in Sault Ste. Marie, Ontario, he spent a total of 27 days during the year staying with her in her home.

C. Tweeks Inc. was incorporated in Vermont in 1980 by two U.S. citizens who were residents of Quebec. All of the directors are residents of Quebec and all meetings of the Board Of Directors have been held in Montreal since incorporation.

D. Bordot Industries Ltd. was incorporated in British Columbia on September 29, 1973. However, the Directors of the corporation have always lived in Blaine, Washington. All of their meetings have been held at a large waterfront property just south of Blaine.

Self Study Problem Three - 4

The following facts relate to three individuals who spent a part of the current year in Canada:

Mr. Aiken   Mr. Aiken is a businessman and a U.S. citizen who moved to Canada in the middle of June. After the move, he spent the remaining 192 days of the year in Canada.

Mr. Baker   Mr. Baker is a businessman and a Canadian citizen who moved out of Canada in the middle of July. Prior to his move, he spent the preceding 192 days of the year in Canada.

Mr. Chase   Mr. Chase is a professional athlete and a U.S. citizen. His residence is located in Nashville, Tennessee and during most of the year his wife and children live in that city. Mr. Chase plays for a Canadian team and, during the current year, his work required him to be in Canada for a total of 192 days.

Required   All of the preceding individuals were in Canada for a total of 192 days. Explain their residence status for income tax purposes in the current year and their liability for Canadian income taxes.

Self Study Problem Three - 5

The following two cases make different assumptions with respect to the amounts of income and deductions of Miss Nora Bain for the current taxation year under the various Subdivisions of Division B of the *Income Tax Act*:

Case A

Employment Income	$34,000
Income (Loss) From Business	(36,000)
Income From Property	21,000
Taxable Capital Gains	42,000
Allowable Capital Losses	(57,000)
Subdivision e Deductions (Spousal Support)	(5,500)

Case B

Employment Income	$18,500
Income (Loss) From Business	(28,200)
Income From Property	12,000
Taxable Capital Gains	9,000
Allowable Capital Losses	(12,000)
Subdivision e Deductions (Spousal Support)	(10,500)

Required For both Cases, calculate Miss Bain's Net Income For Tax Purposes (Division B income) and indicate any possible loss carryovers from the current year.

Self Study Problem Three - 6

The following four cases make different assumptions with respect to the amounts of income and deductions of Mr. Knowlton Haynes for the current year under the various Subdivisions of Division B of the *Income Tax Act*:

	Case A	Case B	Case C	Case D
Employment Income	$45,000	17,000	$24,000	$18,000
Income (Loss) From Business	(20,000)	(42,000)	(48,000)	(20,000)
Income From Property	15,000	12,000	47,000	7,000
Taxable Capital Gains	25,000	22,000	22,000	13,000
Allowable Capital Losses	(10,000)	(8,000)	(73,000)	(18,000)
Subdivision e Deductions	(5,000)	(6,000)	(4,000)	(12,000)

Required For each Case, calculate Mr. Haynes' Division B income and any carry overs available to him. Ignore any carry over possibilities for losses to and from previous periods.

Assignment Problems

(The solutions for these problems are only available in
the solutions manual that has been provided to your instructor.)

Assignment Problem Three - 1

What are the general rules that determine whether a person is liable for the payment of taxes under Part I of the *Income Tax Act*?

Assignment Problem Three - 2

Explain the terms Net Income For Tax Purposes and Taxable Income.

Assignment Problem Three - 3

Distinguish between the accountant's, the economist's, and the *Income Tax Act* views of income.

Assignment Problem Three - 4

In most situations, residency is the factor that determines whether or not a person will be subject to Canadian income tax. As the term resident is not defined in the *Income Tax Act*, it becomes a question of fact as to whether certain individuals and corporations are considered residents subject to taxation.

Required:

A. What guidelines have been developed to determine Canadian residency in situations where an individual is present in Canada for only part of the year?

B. What approach is taken in determining the Canadian residency of corporations?

Assignment Problem Three - 5

Mr. Leduc is a U.S. citizen who has spent most of his working life in the employ of a Canadian subsidiary of a U.S. company. While he has been located in several Canadian cities where the subsidiary has offices, he has spent the last several years working in Vancouver.

Early in the current year, Mr. Leduc is offered an opportunity for advancement within the organization of the U.S. parent company. However, the opportunity is conditional on his moving to Chicago by no later than February 15. While moving on such short notice presents a considerable inconvenience to him, he concludes that the opportunity is too good to pass up and, as a consequence, he completes his move to Chicago by February 12.

Because of the short notice involved, Mr. Leduc's wife and children decide to remain in Vancouver until the end of the school term. Mr. Leduc also feels that this will provide a greater opportunity to sell the family residence at a reasonable price.

The family residence is not sold until June 20 at which time Mr. Leduc's wife and children depart from Canada and establish residency in Chicago.

Required For purposes of assessing Canadian income taxes, determine when Mr. Leduc ceased to be a Canadian resident and the portion of his annual income which would be assessed for Canadian taxes. Explain your conclusions.

Assignment Problem Three - 6

Mr. Desmond Morris is a U.S. citizen who has spent his entire working life with his current employer, the Alcorn Manufacturing Company. In his first years with the company, he was located in Grand Forks, North Dakota as a production supervisor. More recently, he was transferred to the Company's Calgary based subsidiary, where he has served as a manufacturing vice president until the current year.

Early in the current year, Mr. Morris was asked to return to the United States by April 1 to oversee the construction of a new manufacturing operation in Sarasota, Florida. It is expected that when the facility is completed, Mr. Morris will remain as the senior vice president in charge of all of the Florida operations. He does not have any intention of returning to live in Canada during the foreseeable future.

On April 1, Mr. Morris left Canada. In preparation for his departure, he had taken care to sell his residence, dispose of most of his personal property, and resign from all memberships in social and professional clubs. However, because Mr. Morris and his wife had three school age dependent children, it was decided that they would remain in Canada until the end of the current school year. As a consequence, Mrs. Morris and the children did not leave Canada until June 30. Until their departure, they resided in a small furnished apartment, rented on a month to month basis.

Required For purposes of assessing Canadian income taxes, determine when Mr. Morris ceased to be a Canadian resident and the portion of his annual income which would be assessed for Canadian taxes. Explain your conclusions.

Assignment Problem Three - 7

For each of the following persons, indicate how they would be taxed in Canada for the year ending December 31, 2001. Your answer should explain the person's status with respect to residency, what parts of their income would be subject to Canadian taxation, and the basis for your conclusions (including references to the *Income Tax Act*, when relevant to your conclusion).

A. Kole Ltd. was incorporated in Alberta in 1962 and, until December 31, 1996, carried on most of its business in that Province. However, on January 1, 1997 the head office of the corporation moved to Oregon and the Company ceased doing business in Canada in all subsequent years.

B. Forman Inc. was incorporated in Syracuse, New York during 1999. However, the head office of the corporation is in Smith Falls, Ontario and all meetings of the Board Of Directors have been held in that city.

C. Martin Judge was born in Kamloops, British Columbia in 1971. In 1973, Martin's family moved to southern California and, until October 1, 2001, Martin did not return to Canada. On October 1, 2001, Martin accepted a position with an accounting firm in London, Ontario. He returned to Canada and began working at his new job on this date.

D. Ms. Gloria Salinas is a Canadian citizen who, on November 1, 2001, is appointed as Canada's new ambassador to Mexico. While Ms. Salinas was born in and grew up in Nova Scotia, she has resided in Mexico for the last 15 years. She anticipates that she will continue to live in Mexico subsequent to her appointment as the Canadian ambassador.

E. Roberto Salinas is the 12 year old son of Ms. Gloria Salinas (see item D). Roberto has lived with his mother in Mexico since his birth.

Assignment Problem Three - 8

For Canadian income tax purposes, determine the residency of each of the following persons and briefly explain your conclusions.

A. Mr. Samuel Salazar lives in Detroit, Michigan and is a full time employee of a business in Windsor, Ontario. His responsibilities with the business in Windsor require him to be present for about eight hours per day, five days per week. He has no other source of income.

B. Mercer Ltd. was incorporated in British Columbia in 1963 and all of its directors' meetings were held in Vancouver until 1978. In 1978, all of the directors moved to Portland, Oregon and all subsequent meetings were held in Portland.

C. Joan Brothers was born in Livonia, Michigan. She is seven years old and has never visited Canada. Her father has been consul in the Canadian Consulate in Livonia for the past 15 years.

D. Brogan Inc. was incorporated in Montana in 1974, but until five years ago, all of the directors' meetings were held in Calgary, Alberta. Last year, the President of the Company moved to Butte, Montana and since that time all of the directors meetings have been held in Butte.

E. Mr. John Wills is a Canadian citizen who until September 1 of the current year had spent his entire life living in Regina. On September 1 of the current year, after disposing of all of his Canadian property, Mr. Wills moved his entire family to Bismark, North Dakota.

F. The Booker Manufacturing Company was incorporated in 1963 in Minnesota. All of the directors of the Company are residents of Winnipeg and, as a consequence, all meetings of the Board Of Directors have been held in Winnipeg since the Company was first incorporated.

Assignment Problem Three - 9

The following independent cases describe situations in which income has been earned by an individual or a corporation:

Required: In each of the cases, indicate whether the income amounts described would be subject to Canadian taxation. Explain the basis for your conclusions.

Case A   Martin Downs is a U.S. citizen who lives in Detroit, Michigan. He is employed two days each week in Windsor, Ontario and, during the current year, he is paid $10,000 (Canadian) for this work. In addition, he maintains a savings account at a bank in Windsor. This account earned interest of $1,500 during the current year.

Case B   Sarah Mennan is a Canadian citizen who lives in Syracuse, New York. She works as an accountant in that city and has professional income of $72,000. Ten years ago she left her husband at the end of the second period of the final game of the Stanley Cup Playoffs. She departed from Canada the following day, and has vowed to never set foot in Canada again. She is divorced from her husband and has no assets in Canada, other than a small savings account on which she earned interest of $150 during the current year.

Case C   Donald Plesser is a U.K. citizen who immigrated to Canada on July 1, of the current year. He immediately began employment as a retail clerk and, during the period July 1 through December 31, his employment income totaled $11,000. In addition, he has retained a large savings account in the U.K. Interest on this account, which was earned uniformly over the current year, totaled £11,000.

Case D   Uta Jurgens is the spouse of Colin Jurgens, a member of the Canadian armed forces stationed in Germany. Mrs. Jurgens is a German citizen and has never visited Canada. During the current year, she has employment income of DM28,000. She is exempt from German taxation because she is the spouse of a member of the Canadian armed forces.

Assignment Problem Three - 10

The following two cases make different assumptions with respect to the amounts of income and deductions of Mr. Morris Dorne for the current taxation year under the various Subdivisions of Division B of the *Income Tax Act:*

Case A   Mr. Dorne had employment income of $50,000 and interest income of $12,000. His unincorporated business lost $23,000 during this period. As the result of dispositions of capital property, he had taxable capital gains of $95,000 and allowable capital losses of $73,000. His subdivision e deductions for the year totalled $8,000. He also experienced a loss of $5,000 on a rental property that he has owned for several years.

Case B   Mr. Dorne had employment income of $45,000, net rental income of $23,000, and a loss from his unincorporated business of $51,000. As the result of dispositions of capital property, he had taxable capital gains of $25,000 and allowable capital losses of $46,000. His subdivision e deductions for the year amounted to $10,500. Fortunately for Mr. Dorne, he won $560,000 in a lottery on February 24.

Required: For both Cases, calculate Mr. Dorne's Net Income For Tax Purposes (Division B income) and indicate any possible loss carryovers from the current year.

Assignment Problem Three - 11

The following four cases make different assumptions with respect to the amounts of income and deductions of Ms. Sharon Barnes for the current year under the various Subdivisions of Division B of the *Income Tax Act:*

Case A

Employment Income	$35,000
Income (Loss) From Business	(10,000)
Income From Property	12,000
Taxable Capital Gains	42,000
Allowable Capital Losses	(18,000)
Subdivision e Deductions	(4,000)

Case B

Employment Income	$33,000
Income (Loss) From Business	(39,000)
Income From Property	14,000
Taxable Capital Gains	36,000
Allowable Capital Losses	(42,000)
Subdivision e Deductions	(7,000)

Case C

Employment Income	$16,000
Income (Loss) From Business	(21,000)
Income From Property	22,000
Taxable Capital Gains	32,000
Allowable Capital Losses	(69,000)
Subdivision e Deductions	(5,000)

Case D

Employment Income	$28,000
Income (Loss) From Business	(36,000)
Income From Property	15,000
Taxable Capital Gains	21,000
Allowable Capital Losses	(27,000)
Subdivision e Deductions	(11,000)

Required For each Case, calculate Ms. Barnes' Net Income For Tax Purposes (Division B income) and indicate any possible loss carryovers from the current year.

Assignment Problem Three - 12 (Electronic Library Research Problem)

Provide brief answers to the following questions. Your answers should be supported by references to materials found in your Electronic Library.

A. A deduction equal to one-half of any stock option benefit is generally available to residents of Canada in the calculation of taxable income. Would this deduction ever be available to a non resident?

B. Late in the current year, Jason Miculchuck has signed on to play for the Ottawa Senators. On signing, he received a $2 million bonus. He will not begin to play until next year, at which time he plans to move to Ottawa. He currently lives in the Ukraine. Would Mr. Miculchuck be subject to Canadian taxation on his signing bonus?

C. John Carter lives in Blaine, Washington, but is employed by a Vancouver transportation company. He spends about half of his working time in Canada and the other half in the United States. However, because the distances involved are longer, over 80 percent of the kilometers driven are in the U.S. Would Mr. Carter be subject to Canadian income taxes and, if so, would it be applied to all or part of his income?

Chapter 4

Goods and Services Tax

Introduction

4-1.   After significant controversy, a goods and services tax (GST, hereafter) was introduced in Canada on January 1, 1991. This broadly based, multi stage transaction tax replaced the more narrowly focused federal sales tax on manufactured goods, a widely criticized tax that had been in place for a number of years. To offset the regressive nature of the GST, an individual GST credit was also introduced.

4-2.   This Chapter will focus on the basic operations of the GST. In other Chapters, we have integrated coverage of the GST with the related income tax provisions. A summary of how the GST applies to employee benefits is included in Chapter 5. The application of the GST to capital acquisitions and dispositions is covered in Chapter 9. Some attention will also be given to the GST implications associated with the purchase and sale of a business in Chapter 18.

4-3.   We begin this Chapter with a brief consideration of some of the basic concepts that are involved in transaction taxes. The remainder of the Chapter will be devoted to the specific provisions of the GST. The GST affects virtually all individuals and organizations in Canada. It is also an increasingly important area of accounting and law practices.

Transaction Tax Concepts

General

4-4.   While taxes like the GST are often referred to as commodity taxes, the title is not appropriate as the term commodity does not include services. With the provision of services being taxed, what we are really concerned with here is the taxation of transactions as opposed to the taxation of income.

4-5.   In both Canada and the U.S., the bulk of federal tax revenues have been produced by taxes on personal and corporate income. However, transaction taxes are widely used in both countries at the provincial or state level. In addition, there has been a worldwide trend towards increased use of transaction taxes, with most industrialized countries now relying heavily on this type of taxation.

4-6.   Within Canada, there is continued movement towards harmonization of federal and provincial transaction taxes. On July 1, 1992, the Quebec government harmonized (although not completely) its provincial sales tax with the federal GST. On April 1, 1997, three of the Atlantic provinces fully harmonized their provincial sales taxes with the federal GST. As a result,

New Brunswick, Nova Scotia, and Newfoundland have what is referred to as a harmonized sales tax (HST).

4-7.   Some of the factors that support the increased use of transaction taxes are as follows:

- **Simplicity**   Transaction taxes are easy to administer and collect. No forms are required from individuals paying the tax and, if the individual wishes to acquire a particular good or service, it is difficult to evade payment.

- **Incentives To Work**   An often cited disadvantage of income taxes is that they can discourage individual initiative to work and invest. Transaction taxes do not have this characteristic.

- **Consistency**   Transaction taxes avoid the fluctuating income and family unit problems that are associated with progressive income tax systems.

4-8.   Given these advantages for transaction taxes, why is income taxation still used? The answer to this question largely involves the question of fairness. In general, transaction taxes relate to consumption. When this is combined with the fact that lower income individuals usually spend a larger portion of their total income on consumption, transaction taxes are assessed at higher effective rates on individuals with lower incomes. That is, transaction taxes are usually regressive. This conflicts with the widely held belief that individuals with higher incomes should have their income taxed at higher average rates. This goal is best accomplished through the continued use of a progressive income tax system.

4-9.   The government has compensated for the regressive nature of the GST by providing a GST tax credit that is available to low income individuals. Whether this is sufficient to offset the negative impact of the GST on the relative position of low income individuals is a matter that has been subject to debate.

Example
Basic Data
4-10.   In discussing the various approaches that can be used in the application of transaction taxes, a simple example is useful. Such an example is diagrammed in Figure 4-1. As can be seen in Figure 4-1, our example involves a manufacturer who produces goods that are sold to a wholesaler for $10,000. Note that, to simplify our example, we will make the unrealistic assumption that the manufacturer has no production costs. The wholesaler then sells the goods to a retailer for $25,000. The retailer, in turn, sells the goods to a consumer for $50,000.

Single Stage Transaction Tax - Retail Sales Tax

4-11.   A single stage transaction tax could be applied at any level in the preceding example. The most common type of single stage tax is applied at the consumer level. This would be the familiar retail sales tax that has been collected in every Canadian province except Alberta. For example, if the transactions depicted in Figure 4-1 took place in Ontario, an eight percent retail sales tax would be assessed on the $50,000 price that the retailer charged the consumer, resulting in a provincial sales tax of $4,000 being paid by the consumer.

4-12.   The consumer level is probably the most appropriate level to apply a single stage transaction tax. The tax is visible

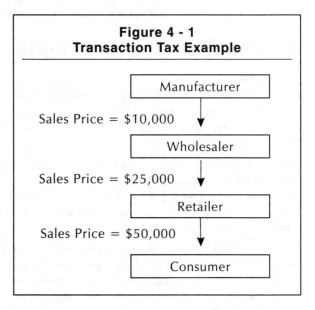

Figure 4 - 1
Transaction Tax Example

Manufacturer

Sales Price = $10,000

Wholesaler

Sales Price = $25,000

Retailer

Sales Price = $50,000

Consumer

and its incidence is relatively clear. In contrast, when a wholesale or manufacturer's tax is used, complications can arise when business relationships are formed that blur the lines between the manufacturing, wholesale, and retail levels. This can occur with vertical integration, and necessitates estimates or notional values for transfers between the manufacturing, wholesale, or retail levels of an organization.

Multi-Stage Transaction Taxes - Turnover Tax

4-13. Again referring to Figure 4-1, it would be possible to impose a multi stage transaction tax at any combination of the various levels depicted. For example, the tax could be applied at the wholesale and retail level, without application at the manufacturing level. Alternatively, the manufacturing and wholesale level could be taxed without application at the retail level. An extension of this taxation to all levels is sometimes referred to as a turnover tax, with transactions being taxed at all levels in the distribution chain.

4-14. The problem with such a turnover tax is that it involves the pyramiding of taxes when there is no credit for taxes paid earlier in the chain. For example, if there was a 7 percent turnover tax in place, the manufacturer in Figure 4-1 would charge the wholesaler $10,700 [($10,000)(1.07)]. When the wholesaler applies the normal markup to 250 percent of cost ($25,000 ÷ $10,000), the price would be $26,750, of which $1,750 [($700)(2.5)] represents the marked up value of the $700 in tax charged by the manufacturer. This $1,750 would then be subject to the 7 percent turnover tax when the wholesaler markets the goods at the retail level. Given this pyramiding problem, turnover taxes are not widely used.

Multi-Stage Transaction Taxes - Value Added Tax

4-15. Internationally, the most common type of multi stage transaction tax is the value added tax (VAT, hereafter). With a VAT, transactions are taxed at each level in the distribution chain. Using whatever rate is established, the VAT is applied to the value added by the business to goods and services, rather than to the gross sales of the business.

4-16. If we assume a 7 percent rate of tax and continue to use the example presented in Figure 4-1, a VAT would require the manufacturer to charge tax on the difference between the sale price of $10,000 and the related input costs which we have assumed to be zero. In corresponding fashion, the wholesaler would charge the 7 percent on the difference between the manufacturer's invoice of $10,000 and the wholesale price of $25,000 (i.e., the value added by the wholesaler). Finally, the retailer would charge the VAT on the difference between the retail price of $50,000 and the wholesaler's invoice for $25,000 before tax. The total tax calculation is as follows:

Manufacturer To Wholesaler [(7%)($10,000 - Nil)]	$ 700
Wholesaler To Retailer [(7%)($25,000 - $10,000)]	1,050
Retailer To Consumer [(7%)($50,000 - $25,000)]	1,750
Total Value Added Tax	$3,500

Multi-Stage Transaction Taxes - Goods And Services Tax

4-17. The Canadian GST represents something of a compromise between a straight turnover tax and a VAT. The net effect of the GST is similar to a VAT, but the calculations use turnover tax principles. An important component of the GST is the input tax credit (ITC) so that vendors, in many cases, may recover the GST paid on their business purchases. First, the GST is charged on the vendor's full selling price. Then, an input tax credit is available to offset the taxes charged on the goods that are being sold to the next level of the distribution chain.

4-18. Continuing to assume a 7 percent rate of tax is applied to our basic example from Figure 4-1, the GST calculations would be as follows:

Manufacturer

GST Collected [(7%)($10,000)]	$700
Input Tax Credits	Nil
Net Payable	$700

Wholesaler

GST Collected [(7%)($25,000)]	$1,750
Input Tax Credits [(7%)($10,000)]	(700)
Net Payable	$1,050

Retailer

GST Collected [(7%)($50,000)]	$3,500
Input Tax Credits [(7%)($25,000)]	(1,750)
Net Payable	$1,750

4-19.   Notice that the overall effect is the same under both the VAT and the GST approaches. That is, the total tax under either approach would amount to $3,500 or 7 percent of the $50,000 price to the consumer. Given this, and the fact that the GST approach appears to be more complex, there is some question as to why Canada did not adopt the more conventional VAT approach.

4-20.   While background documents on the GST do not provide a direct answer to this question, it would appear that the major advantage of the GST approach is that it does not rely on an accounting determination of value added. The tax is charged on all taxable goods sold, with input tax credits available for GST paid on all expenditures used in commercial activities. There is no requirement for matching of costs with revenues, or amortization of accounting costs over several fiscal periods. Also, full input tax credits can be claimed on capital purchases, unlike most other VAT systems that recognize credits over the life of the capital assets. Given these features, it appears that the Canadian GST system offers the advantage of less complex administration for the CCRA, and ease of compliance for taxpayers.

4-21.   With the GST, the ultimate result is to raise the same $3,500 that would result from the application of a 7 percent single stage tax at the retail level. This raises the question of why the government chose to use a multi stage tax, rather than implementing a less complex, single stage, federal sales tax at the retail level. An often cited reason is related to tighter administration and control. With the GST, a vendor does not have to determine whether or not customers of particular goods and services are exempt because they are one or more steps away from the retail or final consumption level. One of the main reasons for using a tax that is applied further up the distribution chain is that the tax revenues are received by the government more quickly.

> Exercise Four-1 deals with GST vs. VAT. This would be an appropriate time to attempt this exercise.

Definitions Of GST Terms

4-22.   The remainder of this Chapter outlines important features of the GST system. As the terminology is unique, we will first summarize definitions that are designed to explain technical GST terms in a non-technical manner. While they are not legal definitions as defined in the *Excise Tax Act*, they are "working definitions" that have appeared in "Tech Talk", a regular feature of the GST/HST News published by the Excise/GST Branch, National Revenue, Customs and Excise.

- **Business**, for GST purposes, is a very broad concept that includes a profession, trade, or undertaking of any kind, whether or not it is conducted for profit. "Business" also includes any activity engaged in on a continuous basis that involves the supply of property by way of lease or licence. However, "business" excludes employment (i.e., an employee), or an individual appointed or elected to an "office", such as a school board trustee.

- **Commercial Activity** means any business or trade carried on by a person, or any supply of real property made by a person. "Commercial activity" does not include any activity involving the making of an exempt supply (i.e., long-term residential rents, most health, medical and dental services, legal aid services, educational services), and any activity engaged in by an individual without a reasonable expectation of profit.

- **Consideration** is what a person gives to another person for the supply of property or a service. It can be money (i.e., the amount paid) or a good or a service given in exchange (i.e., barters or trades). GST is paid on the value of the consideration. If the consideration is monetary, the amount of money involved will be the basis of the GST calculation. If the consideration is non-monetary, the fair market value of the good or service given in exchange will be the basis of the GST calculation.

- **Input Tax Credit** means a credit claimable by a registrant for GST paid or payable on goods or services that were acquired or imported for consumption, use or supply in the course of the registrant's commercial activity.

- **Permanent Establishment** in Canada means that a person (an individual, company or partnership) has a fixed place of business in Canada and provides goods or services from that place. A fixed place of business is a place from which a person carries on a business on a regular basis.

- **Person** can be an individual, a partnership, a corporation, the estate of a deceased individual, a trust, or a body that is a society, union, club, association, commission or other organization of any kind.

- **Personal Property** refers to more than an individual's "personal belongings". It refers to any property that is not real property. Personal property can be both "tangible" (e.g., computers, cash registers, inventory for resale, etc.) or "intangible" (e.g., a patent, copyright, etc.).

- **Registrant** means a person who is registered, or who is required to apply to be registered, for the GST.

- **Service** means anything other than money or property. It does not include work provided to a business or organization by an employee or officer.

- **Short Term Accommodation**, in respect of the Visitor Rebate Program, means accommodation for less than one month per lodging establishment.

- **Supply** includes a broad range of transactions between persons. To "make a supply of property or a service" means to provide it in any way, including sale, transfer, barter, exchange, licence, rental, lease, gift or disposition.

- **Taxable** refers to most goods and services which are subject to the GST at a rate of 7 percent. Examples are clothing, furniture, taxi fares, restaurant meals and hotel accommodations. A zero rate of tax applies to a limited number of goods and services. These are called "zero-rated" supplies and include basic groceries (e.g., milk, bread and vegetables), prescription drugs and medical devices. Zero-rated goods and services are listed in Schedule VI of the *Excise Tax Act*. A registrant is entitled to claim input tax credits for GST paid on the business purchases acquired to provide taxable and zero-rated goods and services.

- **Tax Exempt** refers to property and services on which no GST is payable because they are listed in Schedule V of the *Excise Tax Act*. Examples include long-term residential rents, most health, medical and dental services, legal aid services and educational services. A person cannot claim input tax credits for the GST paid on purchases used to provide exempt goods and services. Qualifying public sector bodies may claim a GST rebate on purchases used in their exempt activities.

Commercial Activity

General Rules

4-23.   Just as the concept of "person" is broader than that used in the *Income Tax Act*, the concept of "commercial activity" is also broader than the definition of business for income tax purposes. In general terms, commercial activity includes all activities we identify as carrying on a business for income tax purposes. Except to the extent that any of these activities involve the making of exempt supplies, commercial activity includes:

1. any business carried on by a person,
2. an adventure or concern in the nature of trade carried on by a person, and
3. any activity a person engages in that involves the supply of real property.

4-24.   There are several exclusions from the definition of commercial activity. The provision of tax exempt supplies, as defined earlier, is excluded from the definition. Activities engaged in by an individual or a partnership without a reasonable expectation of profit are excluded. Therefore, hobbies are generally not considered to be the carrying on of commercial activities and sales are not subject to GST.

4-25.   Another important exclusion is employment activities. Salaries and wages are outside the scope of the GST. This means that employees do not register to collect and remit GST on employment income and employers do not pay GST on their payroll.

4-26.   Some activities are included in the tax base for GST which would not fall within the usual income tax concept of business income. These are:

- Activities of not-for-profit organizations that involve commercial components. An example of this would be a hospital that is involved in the operation of a parking facility.

- The provision of property under a lease or licence. For example, the lease of a commercial office building. This type of activity is generally classified as property income for income tax purposes.

Meaning of Carrying on a Business
4-27.   In the *Excise Tax Act*, "business" is defined to include a profession, calling, trade, manufacture or undertaking of any kind whatever, whether or not the activity or undertaking is engaged in for profit. The GST business test is much broader than that used for income tax purposes. Whereas a reasonable expectation of profit is required for individuals and partnerships to have their business considered a commercial activity, the GST business test does not require a profit motive for corporations. The business test is also broader because it is designed to encompass a range of activities carried on by governments, charities and not-for-profit organizations.

4-28.   "Carrying on a business" means that the business activity is regular or continuous. However, no set criteria or thresholds are used to establish how many activities constitute regular or how long a period is necessary to be continuous. To determine if a particular activity involves carrying on a business, reference should be made to the track record of the business and the intent of the entities involved in the business.

Adventure or Concern in the Nature of Trade
4-29.   We know that the GST applies to business that is carried on regularly and consistently, but what about infrequent or sporadic profit making activities? The *Excise Tax Act* includes "an adventure or concern in the nature of trade" in the definition of commercial activity. Accordingly, these trading activities would get caught in the GST net.

4-30.   The concept of an adventure or concern in the nature of trade is generally associated with the activity of buying and selling property for a gain or profit. The primary consideration is whether the taxpayer's actions are similar to those of a dealer in such property. If the actions are similar, then the trading activity is considered a commercial activity. As previously noted, an adventure or concern in the nature of trade carried on by an individual or a partnership must have a reasonable expectation of profit to be considered a commercial activity.

Liability for GST

Residence
4-31.   Residents of Canada must register to collect the GST if they are engaged in a commercial activity and make taxable supplies in Canada. To decide if a person is a resident, refer-

ence needs to be made to other jurisprudence, particularly to the *Income Tax Act* provisions which were outlined earlier in Chapter 3.

4-32. A corporation is deemed to be resident in Canada if it is incorporated in Canada. In addition, a corporation originally incorporated in a foreign jurisdiction that is continued in Canada is deemed to be resident in Canada. A corporation can also be deemed to be resident under the common law tests based on determining where the central management and control of the corporation is based.

4-33. Where a non resident person has a permanent establishment in Canada, the person is deemed to be resident in Canada with respect to the activities carried on through that particular establishment.

4-34. For other non residents, the residency test is based on the narrower concept of carrying on a business. The main difference is that for non residents, registration is only required if the activities undertaken constitute a business carried on in Canada. Non resident persons may also voluntarily register if they solicit orders, offer goods for supply or perform services in Canada.

Charging Provisions

4-35. Most businesses and organizations carrying on commercial activities in Canada have to register for and collect the GST. GST is levied on taxable supplies of goods and services provided by those businesses and organizations. While the concept of supplies is very similar to that of sales, it is a broader concept and includes the sale or rental of goods, gifting of goods, barters, the rendering of services, licensing arrangements, and the lease, sale, or other transfer of real property.

4-36. The legal liability for payment of the GST falls on the purchaser. Subsection 165(1) of the *Excise Tax Act* requires every recipient of a taxable supply made in Canada to pay a 7 percent GST based on the value of the supply. The liability to collect and remit the tax, however, lies with the supplier.

4-37. In some special circumstances, other persons must register for the GST. These include non residents who charge admissions in Canada to a place of amusement, a seminar, or an activity or event. Similarly, if a non resident holds a convention or conference in Canada, then GST must be charged on the convention or admission fees. Also, taxi and limousine operators are required to charge GST, regardless of their revenue level (i.e., even if total annual taxable sales are less than the $30,000 small suppliers threshold as discussed in Paragraph 4-41).

Requirement to Register

4-38. Under Subsection 240(1) of the *Excise Tax Act*, any person who makes a taxable supply in Canada in the course of commercial activities is required to register to collect the GST. As a result the term "registrant" is used to refer to a person who is registered or is required to register. Subsection 123(1) defines a "person" as "an individual, partnership, corporation, trust, estate of a deceased individual, trust or a body that is a society, union, club, association, commission or other organization of any kind." This definition is broader than the one used for income tax purposes where only individuals, corporations and trusts are required to file an income tax return. The rationale for the expanded coverage relates to the broader application of the GST to all types of transactions instead of the narrower application of income taxes to taxable income. For example, many not-for-profit organizations enter into commercial transactions which are taxable for GST purposes. However, these organizations are not usually required to file an income tax return.

> Exercises Four-2 and Four-3 deal with the requirement to register. This would be an appropriate time to attempt these exercises.

4-39. Ordinarily, a joint venture is not eligible to be registered separately from its co-venturers for the GST. However, joint ventures involved in oil and gas exploration, the development of real property and certain other activities can elect to appoint an operator to account for all GST transactions on behalf of the joint venture. Each investor is nevertheless jointly and severally liable for all GST obligations arising from the joint venture.

Associated Persons

4-40.   Two or more persons are associated for GST purposes where there is substantial common ownership. For example, where one corporation controls another, the two corporations are associated. An association may exist between two or more corporations, between an individual and a corporation, and among an individual, partnership, trust and corporation. While associated persons file separate GST returns, they must combine their total taxable sales of goods and services in certain situations, such as when determining:

- whether they qualify for the small supplier's exemption,
- whether they are eligible for the quick method of accounting,
- whether they are eligible for the simplified method of calculating input tax credits,
- the required filing frequency of their returns (i.e., monthly, quarterly or annual).

Small Suppliers Exemption

4-41.   As a concession to small business, persons whose revenues from taxable supplies do not exceed $30,000 in the previous four calendar quarters are not required to register or collect GST. When computing the sales figures, revenues from all associated businesses (i.e., generally businesses controlled by the same individual or group of individuals) must be used. A person qualifies as a small supplier throughout a calendar quarter, and the first month following, if total revenues from taxable supplies from it and any associated business in the four calendar quarters preceding the current quarter do not exceed $30,000. As a result, if the cumulative total of taxable supplies for four consecutive quarters exceeds $30,000, GST should be collected starting on the first day of the second month following the last quarter. This is sometimes referred to as the "last four calendar quarters test" for the small supplier exemption.

4-42.   An exception to the last four calendar quarters test exists where a person's total revenues from taxable supplies exceed $30,000 in a particular calendar quarter. When the $30,000 threshold is exceeded in a quarter, the person ceases to qualify as a small supplier and must register for and collect GST. The person is deemed to be a registrant beginning with the supply (sale) that caused the threshold to be exceeded. This test is referred to as the "calendar quarter test." The following examples will illustrate the application of the two small supplier tests.

Example One

4-43.   Supplier A opened for business on January 1, 2001, and earned the following revenues from taxable supplies during the year:

Quarter	Months	Taxable Supplies
One	January to March	$ 7,000
Two	April to June	8,000
Three	July to September	9,000
Four	October to December	20,000
Total		$44,000

4-44.   The small supplier threshold was not exceeded in any one of the calendar quarters for 2001, and Supplier A was eligible for the small supplier exemption in each quarter. However, the total taxable supplies for the four quarters was $44,000. This means that Supplier A is no longer eligible for the small supplier exemption and is required to collect the GST starting on February 1, 2002, which is the first day of the second month after December, 2001.

Example Two

4-45.   Supplier B also started in business on January 1, 2001. As the business is seasonal, Supplier B earned revenues from taxable supplies in only the second and third quarters of 2001, as follows:

Quarter	Months	Taxable Supplies
One	January to March	Nil
Two	April to June	$ 5,000
Three	July to September	39,000
Four	October to December	Nil
Total		$44,000

4-46.   Note that Suppliers A and B each earned taxable revenue of $44,000 in the four calendar quarters for 2001. Supplier B, however, exceeded the $30,000 threshold in Quarter Three. This results in Supplier B being deemed to be registered starting with the transaction on which the threshold was exceeded (sometime between July 1 and September 30, 2001). The day on which the transaction occurred is referred to as the deemed registration day. From that point, GST should have been collected on all taxable supplies made. While collection of tax revenue is required starting on the deemed registration day, Supplier B has 30 days in which to formally register.

4-47.   The small supplier exemption can represent a significant concession to persons with limited commercial activity. With some advance planning, the exemption can be extended within a family group provided members are not considered associated. For example, it may be desirable for individuals to undertake commercial activities on an individual basis rather than on a group basis to maximize any potential benefit from the small supplier exemption. In this scenario, however, the entities cannot be controlled by the same individual or group of individuals.

4-48.   The small supplier exemption is not always beneficial. If a person does not register, they cannot receive input tax credits for GST paid. They are effectively treated as the final consumer. This means that the business must either absorb these taxes or, alternatively, pass the GST paid on to its customers in the form of higher prices.

4-49.   For registered charities and other public service bodies, the small supplier threshold is increased to $50,000. Public service bodies include not-for-profit organizations, charities, schools, hospitals, public colleges and universities.

Voluntary Registration

4-50.   Any person engaged in commercial activity in Canada can apply to be registered, even if taxable sales are less than the $30,000 small supplier threshold. These registrants must be able to demonstrate that there is an intention to carry on a business or an intention to enter into an adventure or concern in the nature of trade. The reason for voluntarily registering is usually to claim input tax credits for the GST paid on purchases.

Accounting and the GST

4-51.   The concepts of generally accepted accounting principles and matching are integral to the determination of business income for both accounting and income tax purposes. For the GST, however, these concepts are less important because the tax is transaction based. That is, GST is collected on taxable supplies and input tax credits are refunded on purchase transactions. No attempt is made to match the costs on which input tax credits are claimed with the revenues generated by supply transactions. This means that most registrants will account for the GST on a transaction basis and accounting reports such as an Income Statement or Balance Sheet will not be used. However, the regular books of account will normally be used to track the GST transactions. This is to avoid setting up a separate set of books for GST purposes.

4-52.   Some of the more significant differences between information needs for GST purposes and information needs for accounting/income tax purposes are as follows:

• There is no need to match expenses with the resulting revenues. For example, input tax credits are available on purchases of inventory when purchased, without regard to when the items are actually sold.

- Most interperiod allocations, such as depreciation, amortization and CCA, are irrelevant for GST purposes. GST paid on capital expenditures can generally be claimed in the period in which the expenditure is made. This means there is no need to amortize the GST paid on the cost of the capital asset over the life of the capital asset.

- Many deductible expenses for income tax purposes do not affect the GST payable or receivable. For example, GST does not apply to employee wages, interest, property taxes, and educational services, which are usually fully deductible in the calculation of Net Income For Income Tax Purposes.

4-53. While there are differences between the accounting/income tax and GST procedures, there are some common features. For example, GST is normally collected and revenue is recognized for income tax purposes when an invoice is issued for the provision of goods or services. If an account receivable becomes uncollectible, an adjustment is required for both income tax and GST purposes.

4-54. For current expenses, input tax credits can be claimed in the period in which the expense is recognized for income tax purposes, regardless of when the account payable is paid. As well, some restrictions that apply in the deductibility of certain expenses for income tax purposes (e.g., 50 percent of business meals and entertainment and certain costs of owning or leasing automobiles) are also contained in the GST legislation.

4-55. With respect to dealing with GST collected and paid in the financial statements of enterprises which must comply with GAAP, the relevant issues are dealt with in Emerging Issues Committee Abstract No. 18, "Accounting For The Goods And Services Tax". This Abstract suggests that revenues should be reported net of GST collected. With respect to expenses, these amounts should also be reported net of GST to the extent that it is recoverable. Note, however, that even though the revenues and expenses are reported net of GST, the amounts due to and recoverable from the government must be included in the receivables and payables of the enterprises.

Concept Of Supply

General Rules

4-56. While many people think of the GST as a sales tax, the legislation is based on the provision of "supplies" in the course of commercial activities. The concept of supply is more comprehensive than sales or income, and includes all of the following:

- The sale, rental or transfer of goods.
- The rendering of services.
- Licensing arrangements for copyrights or patents.
- The lease, sale or other transfer of real property.
- Barter transactions or gifts.

4-57. As previously discussed, there are some important exclusions from the concept of commercial activity. The provision of supplies in the course of a commercial activity does not include an activity:

- connected to providing supplies of tax exempt goods or services, such as health care services and long-term residential rents;
- engaged in by an individual or partnership without a reasonable expectation of profit; or
- which earns employment income.

Supply Categories
Taxable Supplies - General Rules
4-58. The concept of a taxable supply is defined in terms of what is not included. More specifically, a taxable supply is any supply made by a person engaged in the course of commercial

activity in Canada. Taxable supplies include those taxed at 7 percent at the federal level only, those taxed at 15 percent in a province that participates in the harmonized sales tax (as explained at the end of this Chapter, Newfoundland, New Brunswick, and Nova Scotia have harmonized their sales tax with the GST, resulting in a combined HST rate of 15 percent), as well as those that are zero rated. Exempt supplies are excluded from the definition of commercial activity and are thus not taxable supplies. The majority of goods and services are subject to the GST at either the 7 percent rate or, where the HST is in effect, at the 15 percent rate.

4-59.   Some examples of goods and services taxable at 7 percent are:

- Transportation in Canada
- Restaurant meals and beverages
- Clothing and footwear
- Furniture
- Admissions to concerts, athletic and other events
- Contractors' services
- Legal and accounting fees
- Haircuts
- Cleaning services

Taxable Supplies - Zero-Rated

4-60.   Zero-rated supplies are taxable supplies, which are taxed at the rate of zero percent rather than 7 percent. At first glance, this concept seems a bit senseless in that there is no tax charged on either zero-rated supplies or exempt supplies. However, an important difference exists. Because zero-rated supplies are considered to be taxable supplies, the providers of such supplies can recover the GST paid on business purchases as input tax credits. In contrast, providers of exempt supplies are not eligible for input tax credits. Further, since zero-rated supplies are considered taxable at a rate of zero percent, they are included in the threshold amounts for determining the filing frequency of a registrant's GST returns.

4-61.   Major items that are included in the category of zero-rated supplies are as follows:

- Prescription drugs
- Medical devices such as wheelchairs, eye glasses, canes, hospital beds, and artificial limbs
- Basic groceries
- Most agricultural and fishing products
- Foreign travel and transportation services
- Goods and services exported from Canada

4-62.   Some elaboration is required for the meaning of foreign travel. Surface travel by ship, bus or train is zero-rated when the origin or termination point is outside Canada. Other surface travel is fully taxable at the 7 percent rate. In the case of air travel, the GST net is spread somewhat wider. Air travel is zero-rated only when the origin, stopover or termination point is outside North America. This broader definition makes transborder flights between Canada and the United States fully taxable at the 7 percent rate. Exceptions to this general rule apply when the flight is to Hawaii, there is a stopover outside North America or when the point of origin is outside Canada and the ticket is purchased outside Canada. When any of these conditions apply, the supply will be zero-rated.

Exempt Supplies

4-63.   No GST applies to the provision of exempt supplies. Persons supplying exempt items do not collect GST and are not eligible for input tax credits for GST paid on the related purchases. This means that suppliers of exempt supplies pay GST that is not refundable to them on goods and services required to operate their business. As a consequence, the non recoverable GST paid is a cost of doing business which is likely to be passed on to customers in the form of higher prices.

4-64.   The main items that are included in the category of exempt supplies are as follows:

- Most health care and dental services
- Financial services provided to Canadian residents (see later discussion)

- Sales of used residential housing and long term residential rents (e.g., apartment rentals for more than 30 days)
- Most land sold by individuals where the land was not used in a business
- Educational courses leading to certificates or diplomas, tutoring for credit courses, and music lessons
- Child or personal care services
- Recreational programs for children (less than 15 years old)
- Legal aid services provided by a legal aid administrator
- A wide variety of services provided by charities, not-for-profit, and government organizations (see later discussion)

Consideration

4-65. GST must be collected by registered suppliers at the rate of 7 percent of the consideration paid for taxable supplies. Consideration paid is usually monetary, but can also include the fair market value of goods or services bartered, or otherwise exchanged.

4-66. The consideration for a supply for purposes of calculating the GST includes all federal and provincial taxes, duties and fees that are imposed on either the supplier or recipient in respect of the property or services supplied. However, the general retail sales taxes of the provinces are excluded from the GST base. In calculating provincial sales taxes, Quebec and Prince Edward Island include GST in their sales tax base, while provinces west of Quebec exclude the GST from their sales tax base.

4-67. Where a good is traded in by a non registrant towards the supply of a new good, GST is only required to be levied on the net amount after the trade-in. These types of transactions are most often seen in the automotive business, where used cars are traded in when purchasing a newer automobile. The treatment of trade-ins for GST purposes is the same as their treatment under the provincial sales tax legislation in most provinces.

Input Tax Credits

Vendors Of Taxable Supplies (Fully Taxable And Zero Rated)
Current Expenditures

4-68. As noted, the Canadian GST system provides vendors of taxable supplies with credits for the GST incurred on their purchases. Input tax credits (i.e., recovery of GST paid) can be offset against the GST that such vendors have invoiced on their taxable revenues in a particular reporting period. If, in a given reporting period, the credits exceed the amount of GST collected or collectible by the vendor, a refund of the excess can be claimed.

4-69. To be eligible for treatment as an input tax credit, the expenditure must relate to goods or services that will be used in commercial activities. It is important to note, however, that no matching of expenses with revenues is required. For example, input tax credits on inventory purchases become available at the time the invoice for the inventory becomes payable, not when the goods are sold and charged to expense. Consistent with this approach, the supplier of the inventory becomes liable for payment of the GST when the invoice is issued.

4-70. If all or substantially all (generally understood to mean 90 percent or more) of a current expenditure is to be used for a commercial activity, then all of the GST can be claimed as an input tax credit. In contrast, if 10 percent or less of an expenditure is related to commercial activity, then no input tax credit can be claimed. If the percentage of the current expenditure used for commercial activities is between 10 and 90 percent, the input tax credit available is calculated by multiplying the total GST paid by the percentage of commercial activity usage.

Capital Costs

4-71. In line with the basic idea that input tax credits are not matched against amounts of GST collected on sales, the full amount of GST paid on purchases of all capital assets becomes eligible for treatment as an input tax credit at the time of purchase. There is no need to amortize the credit or to wait until the asset is actually paid for.

4-72. In order for the input tax credits to be available on capital assets other than real property (referred to in GST legislation as capital personal property), the assets must be used primarily in commercial activities (generally understood to be more than 50 percent). If this condition is not met, the GST paid on the capital asset's acquisition cannot be claimed as an input tax credit. Special rules apply to passenger vehicles. These rules are discussed in Chapter 7, "Income From A Business" in the Section on Restrictions on Claiming Input Tax Credits.

4-73. For real property (i.e., land and its appurtenances such as buildings and mineral rights), input tax credits are available even if commercial use is less than 50 percent. On these capital assets, input tax credits are available in proportion to the extent to which the property is used in commercial activities. That is, if the building is used 35 percent for commercial activities, the input tax credit will be equal to 35 percent of the GST paid on its acquisition.

Summary Of Rules

4-74. The rules for apportioning the maximum available input tax credits on purchases are summarized in Figure 4-2.

Figure 4 - 2 Maximum Input Tax Credits		
Taxable Purchase	**Percentage Used In Commercial Activities = X%**	**Input Tax Credit**
Current Expenditures and Real Property	X% ≤ 10%	Nil
	10% < X% < 90%	X%
	X% ≥ 90%	100%
Capital Personal Property (Except Automobiles*)	X% ≤ 50%	Nil
	X% > 50%	100%
*Special rules apply to automobiles. These rules are discussed in Chapter 7, "Income From A Business" in the Section on Restrictions on Claiming Input Tax Credits.		

Restrictions

4-75. Restrictions in the deductibility of certain costs for income tax purposes also apply to the GST. For example, no input tax credits are allowed for the costs of membership fees or dues to recreational or sporting facilities, personal or living expenses, 50 percent of business meals and entertainment, and the portion of the cost of a passenger vehicle that exceeds $30,000 (excluding GST and PST).

4-76. Restrictions apply to the time allowed for claiming input tax credits. For large businesses, whose sales are less than 90 percent taxable but in excess of $6 million, and listed financial institutions, the time limit is generally two years from the date the input tax credit was first available. For all other registrants the time limit is four years.

Example One - Vendor Of Taxable Supplies Only

4-77. As an example of the application of the GST provisions to a corporation that sells only taxable or zero-rated supplies, consider the GAAP based Income Statement of Marson Ltd. for the year ending December 31, 2001:

Sales	$9,500,000
Expenses:	
Cost Of Goods Sold	$6,500,000
Amortization Expense	900,000
Salaries And Wages	1,500,000
Other Expenses	200,000
Total Expenses Excluding GST and Income Taxes	$9,100,000
Net Income Before GST and Income Taxes	$ 400,000

Note   In accordance with the recommendations of the Canadian Institute Of Chartered Accountants, all of the items in the Income Statement are recorded net of any GST charged or paid.

Other Information:

1.   Of the total Sales, $6,800,000 were fully taxable supplies while the remainder were zero-rated supplies.

2.   Purchases of merchandise exceeded the Cost Of Goods Sold by $2,200,000, net of GST. GST was paid on all of the Other Expenses as well as on the merchandise acquired during the period.

3.   During the reporting period, capital expenditures totaled $7,500,000, net of GST, and the amounts have not been paid. All of the capital assets acquired will be used in commercial activities.

4.   Marson Ltd. operates solely in Alberta and has paid no provincial sales tax on its purchases.

4-78.   The GST refund for the year for Marson Ltd. is calculated as follows:

GST Collected [(7%)($6,800,000)]	$476,000
Input Tax Credits:	
Purchases [(7%)($6,500,000 + $2,200,000)]	(609,000)
Other Expenses [(7%)($200,000)]	(14,000)
Capital Expenditures [(7%)($7,500,000)]	(525,000)
GST Payable (Refund)	($672,000)

> Exercises Four-4 and Four-5 deal with GST calculations . This would be an appropriate time to attempt these exercises.

4-79.   You will note that, while Marson Ltd. is showing a positive net income for accounting purposes, the company is eligible for a GST refund. This example clearly illustrates the fact that GST reporting is not based on the matching principle. The full amount of input tax credits is available on all of the inventory purchases as well as on the unpaid capital expenditures. This is despite the fact that part of these items will not be charged to either accounting or taxable income until subsequent reporting periods.

Example Two - Vendor Of Exempt And Taxable Supplies

4-80.   In some situations, vendors are involved in making taxable or zero-rated supplies, as well as exempt supplies. These businesses can only recover GST paid on their taxable or zero-rated activities, and must therefore apportion their input tax credits on a "reasonable" basis. This applies to both current and capital expenditures that cannot be directly identified with particular exempt or taxable activities.

4-81.   To illustrate the allocation process, we will return to the Marson Ltd. example presented earlier. We will alter the example as follows:

• Sales consist of $2,375,000 in exempt supplies and $7,125,000 in fully taxable supplies.

• All of the merchandise purchased will be sold as taxable supplies. Eighty percent of the Other Expenses relate to the sale of taxable supplies.

• With respect to capital expenditures, $5,000,000 was for an office building that will be used 60 percent for activities related to taxable sales. The other $2,500,000 in capital expenditures is for furniture and fixtures that will be used 55 percent for functions related to taxable sales.

4-82.   Given these changes, the GST payable/refund calculation would be as follows:

GST Collected [(7%)($7,125,000)]	$498,750
Input Tax Credits:	
Purchases [(7%)($8,700,000)]	(609,000)
Other Expenses [(7%)(80%)($200,000)]	(11,200)
Building [(7%)($5,000,000)(60%)]	(210,000)
Furniture And Fixtures [(7%)($2,500,000)(100%)]	(175,000)
GST Payable (Refund)	($506,450)

4-83. As the furniture and fixtures were capital expenditures other than real property and used primarily for commercial activity (more than 50 percent), the full amount of the GST paid is eligible for an input tax credit. In contrast, the real property GST paid must be allocated on the basis of the expected use to produce taxable sales (60 percent). With respect to Other Expenses, only the 80 percent related to taxable supplies is eligible for an input tax credit.

> Exercise Four-6 deals with input tax credits. This would be an appropriate time to attempt this exercise.

Relief For Small Businesses

Small Suppliers Exemption

4-84. This provision was covered in detail beginning at Paragraph 4-41 and will not be repeated here.

Quick Method Of Accounting

4-85. Eligible businesses, defined as businesses with annual GST included taxable sales (including zero-rated sales) of $200,000 or less, can elect to use the Quick Method of determining the net GST remittance. Exempt supplies, supplies made outside of Canada, sales of real and capital property, and provincial sales taxes are excluded in calculating the $200,000 threshold. To determine eligibility, sales from associated businesses must be taken into consideration. Businesses involved in legal, accounting and financial consulting services are not eligible for the Quick Method.

4-86. Under this method, eligible businesses charge GST at the normal 7 percent rate on taxable sales. In order to streamline the accounting and filing procedures for these businesses, separate tracking of GST collections is not required, eliminating the need for special cash registers. Correspondingly, with the exception of GST paid on capital purchases, the business is not required to separately account for input tax credits on purchases.

4-87. In applying the Quick Method, a specified percentage is applied to the GST inclusive total of fully taxable sales to determine the amount of GST to be remitted. Note that the specified percentage is not an alternative GST rate. It is based on the estimated GST that would be remitted by a particular type of business, net of input tax credits that would be claimed. For example, if the specified rate for a particular business is five percent, this is based on the assumption that its available input tax credits on non capital expenditures, if they were tracked, would be equal to 1.65 percent of taxable sales [7% - (5%)(1.07)].

4-88. The remittance amount is arrived at by applying the specified percentage to total GST inclusive fully taxable sales, which is then reduced by input tax credits on qualifying capital expenditures. Thus, separate accounting is required for GST included sales and for input tax credits on capital expenditures to determine the GST remittance.

4-89. Different rates apply to different types of qualifying businesses. There are two business sectors, retailers and wholesalers who purchase goods to resell and service providers and small manufacturers. For each type of qualifying business, two different rates are used, with the rate on the first $30,000 of GST inclusive annual sales being one percent lower than the rate on any excess. The relevant percentages are shown in Figure 4-3 (on the following page).

Example of Quick Method

4-90. As an example of the application of the Quick Method, consider a quarterly filing hardware store with annual taxable sales of less than $200,000. Its first quarter taxable sales

---

Figure 4 - 3
Quick Method Percentages For Business Sectors

	Percentage on GST Included Sales	
Business Sectors	On First $30,000	On Excess
Retailers And Wholesalers (Note 1)	1.5%	2.5%
Service Providers and Manufacturers (Note 2)	4.0%	5.0%

Note 1 - Applies if purchases of goods for resale (excluding basic groceries) are 40 percent or more of total annual taxable sales. Examples of types of businesses eligible for the 2.5 percent rate include grocery and convenience stores, book stores, gas service stations, antique dealers and boutiques.

Note 2 - Applies to service businesses and small manufacturers such as consultants (other than financial), hair salons, restaurants, dry cleaners, travel agents, and taxi drivers. However, legal, accounting and financial consulting businesses are not eligible.

---

were $37,383 resulting in GST included sales of $40,000 [(107%)($37,383)]. Qualifying capital expenditures during the first quarter were $3,000 before GST. The required first quarter GST remittance, as determined by the Quick Method is calculated as follows:

First $30,000 at 1.5%	$450
Remaining $10,000 At 2.5%	250
Subtotal	$700
GST Paid On Capital Expenditures [(7%)($3,000)]	(210)
First Quarter GST Remittance	$490

> Exercises Four-7 and Four-8 deal with the quick method. This would be an appropriate time to attempt these exercises.

4-91.   The Quick Method approach can be preferable, even if adequate data is available to make the usual calculations. For example, an individual professional, operating out of a principal residence, might not have many input tax credits available. In this case, the Quick Method may result in a smaller net GST payment than the normal calculation of actual GST collected less input tax credits.

Simplified Input Tax Credits and Rebates

4-92.   A simplified method for claiming input tax credits and rebates is available to some registrants. Rather than tracking GST paid on each purchase, the simplified method bases input tax credits on GST-paid taxable inputs. Total taxable inputs are multiplied by 7/107 to arrive at the input tax credit for the GST return. This option is available to small businesses, charities, not-for-profit organizations, and selected public service bodies. As well, the organization must have annual GST taxable sales, including those of associated businesses, of $500,000 or less and annual GST taxable purchases of $2,000,000 or less.

4-93.   There is no election required to use this method. The input tax credit to be claimed is calculated as follows:

Total the GST included amounts of all GST fully taxable purchases and rentals for the reporting period. This should include:

- non-refundable provincial taxes
- tips
- capital expenditures that are not real property, such as equipment
- improvement expenses

It should not include:

- purchases of exempt and zero-rated supplies, such as salaries and interest payments
- purchases made outside Canada, which are not subject to GST

- purchases from non-registrants
- expenses not eligible for input tax credits (e.g., 50 percent of the cost of meals and entertainment)
- refundable or rebatable provincial sales taxes (e.g., reimbursable Quebec sales tax)
- real property purchases

Multiply the net amount by 7/107 or 0.0654. Add any input tax credit on real property purchases. The total is the Input Tax Credit that is included in the GST return.

4-94.   As under the regular rules, the simplified method may be used to claim an input tax credit only on the portion of purchases used to provide taxable goods and services. Where a supply is used to provide both taxable and exempt goods and services, or is used for personal consumption, the input tax credit claim must be pro-rated so that only the portion that applies to taxable goods and services is claimed. Similarly, the simplified method may be used to claim a rebate on the portion of purchases used to provide exempt goods and services.

Procedures And Administration

Returns And Payments
Timing Of Liability
4-95.   In general, the supplier becomes responsible for the tax at the earliest of when the invoice for goods or services is issued, when payment is received, and when payment is due under a written agreement. Following this rule, a registrant becomes responsible for remitting GST in the reporting period in which a customer is invoiced, even if this is not the same period in which the invoice is actually paid.

4-96.   Similarly, input tax credits for GST payable to suppliers can be claimed in the reporting period invoices are issued even if the supplier is paid in a later period. As discussed earlier in the chapter, registrants have an extended period of time in which to claim input tax credits for GST paid on qualifying purchases. For a particular business, these requirements may create a cash flow advantage or disadvantage, depending on how quickly receivables are collected and payables are settled.

Taxation Year For GST Registrants
4-97.   Every registrant is required to have a "fiscal year" for GST purposes. Normally, this fiscal year corresponds to the taxation year for income tax purposes. However, registrants have the option of using the calendar year or, alternatively, using their fiscal year. For example, a company with a fiscal year ending on January 31, 2001 and subject to quarterly filing requirements could choose a three month reporting period ending January 31, 2001, or a three month reporting period ending March 31, 2001. The GST fiscal year determines the reporting periods and filing deadlines for GST returns.

Filing
4-98.   All businesses and organizations that are required to register to collect GST are required to file a GST Return (Form GST34 E) on a periodic basis. Filing frequencies for the remittance of GST are determined by the total annual worldwide taxable supplies made by the registrant and its associated entities. If the annual taxable sales exceed $6,000,000, monthly filing and remittances are required. If annual taxable sales are less than $6,000,000, but greater than $500,000, quarterly filing is required. Annual filing applies if taxable sales are less than $500,000. A registrant may elect to have quarterly filing periods even if sales are less than $500,000. Similarly, a registrant with annual taxable supplies that are less than $6,000,000 may elect to file GST returns on a monthly basis. This may be advantageous for registrants who normally receive a GST refund, such as businesses with significant exports, or zero-rated sales (e.g., pharmacies and grocery stores).

4-99.   For monthly and quarterly filers, returns are due one month after the end of the filing period. In general, for annual filers, the return is due three months after the end of the reporting period. However, similar to the extension of the filing due date for income tax purposes to June 15 for certain taxpayers, qualifying GST registrants have an extended GST filing due date of June 15. To qualify, the registrant must be an individual with business income for income tax purposes who is an annual filer with a December 31 fiscal year end. Any GST owing for the year must be paid by April 30 (not June 15).

4-100.   If a registrant qualifies for the June 15 filing due date, the individual may be eligible to file his annual GST return with his income tax return by completing Form T1124, "GST/HST and Income Tax Reconciliation Form". This would permit an offset of a refund of one tax against a payable for the other. Any net amount owing would be due April 30.

Payments

4-101.   In general, payment of amounts owing are due when the GST returns are due. This is one month after the end of the reporting period for monthly and quarterly filers, and three months after the year end for annual filers (with the exception described in the preceding Paragraph). However, annual filers are required to make quarterly instalments if the net GST remitted for the previous fiscal year was more than $1,500. The instalments are based on the lesser of the previous year's remittances or an estimate of the current year's GST. These instalments are due one month after the end of each quarter. For example, calendar year filers are required to make instalments by April 30, July 31, October 31, and January 31. Annual filers below the $1,500 threshold can pay the net tax due when they file their GST return within three months of the end of their fiscal year or by April 30 if the June 15 filing due date is applicable.

Interest

4-102.   As with income tax payments and instalments, interest is payable on GST amounts not paid when due. The same prescribed rate is used for GST purposes as is used for late income taxes. On amounts owed to the government, the interest accrues from the date the taxes are due. By contrast, when amounts are owed to the taxpayer, interest accrues from 21 days after the registrant's return is filed. Unlike the situation with interest on late income tax instalments, interest charged on late GST payments is deductible for income tax purposes.

Penalties

4-103.   In contrast to late income tax payments, late GST payments and deficient instalments attract a six percent penalty in addition to interest charges. Also, other penalties can be assessed for the following:

> **Failure To Comply With Demand To File A GST Return**   A penalty of the greater of $250 and 5 percent of the tax payable may be assessed.

> **Failure To Provide Information Or Documentation**   A penalty of $100 may be assessed for each failure, unless a reasonable effort was made to obtain the information.

> **Gross Negligence**   If a person makes a false statement or knowingly omits to pay a GST amount, a penalty of the greater of $250 and 25 percent of the tax payable or rebate claimed may be assessed.

4-104.   Unlike penalties assessed under the *Income Tax Act*, these penalties may be deductible for income tax purposes, provided they are deductible under GAAP.

Refunds And Rebates

4-105.   If the net GST for a registrant's reporting period is a negative amount, a refund may be claimed in the return for that period. Interest on unpaid refunds starts accruing 21 days after the particular return is filed, provided all required returns have been filed and are up to date. Interest is payable at the prescribed rate.

4-106.   The *Excise Tax Act* also provides for a number of rebates of the GST paid by consumers under certain circumstances. For example, if a GST amount is paid in error or by a foreign diplomat, a rebate of the GST may be claimed on a General Rebate Application Form. Also, visitors to Canada can recover most of the GST they pay on goods that are acquired for use outside of Canada. This is accomplished by completing a Visitors' Rebate Application Form.

Books And Records

4-107.   For GST purposes, every registrant must keep adequate books and records. This requirement is found under Subsection 286(1) of the *Excise Tax Act*. Such records must be maintained at the taxpayer's place of business or at the individual's residence in Canada.

4-108.   All books and records, along with the accounts and vouchers necessary to verify them, must be kept for a period of six years from the end of the last taxation year to which they relate. This is the same record retention limit that is applicable for income tax purposes.

Appeals

Informal Procedures

4-109.   As is the case with income tax disputes, the usual first step in disputing an assessment or reassessment is to contact the CCRA. In many cases the proposed change or error can be corrected or resolved through telephone contact or by letter.

4-110.   In order to authorize a person or firm to represent a GST registrant in such disputes, a consent form must be signed and filed with the CCRA. For GST purposes the form is GST 153.

Notice Of Objection

4-111.   If the informal contact with the CCRA does not resolve the issue in question, the taxpayer should file a notice of objection. For GST purposes, a formal notice of objection procedure is required. Form GST 159 must be used for this purposes.

4-112. For GST disputes, the notice of objection must be filed within 90 days of the date on the notice of assessment. Unlike the situation with income tax objections, there is no general extension of this time period for GST registrants who are individuals, nor is there any special extension for individual GST registrants in the year of their death. Failure to meet the 90 day deadline may result in the taxpayer losing all rights to pursue the matter in question. However, it is possible to apply for an extension which can be granted at the Minister's discretion.

4-113.   On receiving the notice of objection, the Minister is required to reply to the GST registrant:

- vacating the assessment;
- confirming the assessment (refusing to change);
- varying the amount of the assessment; or
- reassessing.

4-114.   Unresolved objections will be subject to review by the Chief Of Appeals in each district office. These reviewers are instructed to operate independently of the assessing divisions and should provide an unbiased second opinion. If the matter remains unresolved after this review, the taxpayer must either accept the Minister's assessment or, alternatively, continue to pursue the matter to a higher level of appeal. The taxpayer has the right to bypass this notice of objection procedure and appeal directly to a higher level.

4-115.   As noted in Chapter 2, in income tax disputes, the Minister cannot institute collection procedures until after the notice of objection period has expired. When dealing with GST disputes, collection procedures are not delayed by the objection process.

4-116.   This more aggressive approach is allowed by GST legislation and probably reflects the fact that the government considers GST balances as amounts that are held in trust by the registrant on behalf of the government.

Tax Court Of Canada, Federal Court Of Appeal, And Supreme Court Of Canada

4-117.   Procedures for handling GST disputes in these courts are basically the same as the procedures for handling income tax disputes. These procedures were described in Chapter 2 and will not be repeated in this Chapter.

General Anti-Avoidance Rule

4-118.   The GST legislation includes a general anti-avoidance rule (GAAR). This rule is found under Section 274 of the *Excise Tax Act* and is very similar to the GAAR found in the *In-*

come Tax Act.

4-119.   While the GST GAAR is intended to prevent abusive tax avoidance transactions, it is not intended to interfere with legitimate commercial transactions. If a transaction is considered by the CCRA to be an avoidance transaction, the tax consequences of the transaction may be adjusted. This could involve denying an input tax credit, allocating an input tax credit to another person, or recharacterizing a payment. But, as with the application of the income tax GAAR, it does not apply if a transaction is undertaken primarily for bona fide purposes other than to obtain a tax benefit.

Specific Applications

4-120.   There are many GST procedures that are specific to certain types of transactions or organizations (e.g., imports or charities). We did not feel that this more detailed material was appropriate in a general tax text such as this. While we have not covered the detailed procedures related to these specific GST applications, we feel that you should be aware of the following general points related to this material:

- **Imports**   Imports are generally subject to GST.

- **Exports**   Exports of goods and services from Canada are generally zero-rated. This means that while no GST is charged on exports, input tax credits can be claimed by the exporter.

- **Charities**   In general, the revenues of registered charities are exempt from GST. However, revenues from commercial activities (e.g., museum gift shop revenues) are fully taxable. A special provision provides for a 50 percent rebate of GST paid on purchases related to exempt activities.

- **Not-For-Profit Organizations**   In contrast to the situation with registered charities, the revenues of not-for-profit organizations are generally fully taxable. However, exemptions are provided for such services as subsidized home care and meals on wheels. As was the case with registered charities, qualifying not-for-profit organizations receive a 50 percent rebate of GST paid on purchases related to their exempt activities.

- **Government Bodies**   All federal government departments receive a full rebate of the GST paid on purchases by means of a tax remission order. Each provincial and territorial government is registered as a separate entity for the GST, and uses "certificates" to receive point of purchase relief from the GST.

- **Crown Corporations**   Crown corporations are not included under the tax exempt government umbrella and are registered as separate persons for purposes of the GST.

- **Municipalities, Universities, Schools And Hospitals (MUSH)**   These organizations are classified as "Public Institutions" in the GST legislation and, except where there are specific exemptions, their revenues are fully taxable. Examples of exemptions include property taxes for municipalities, course fees for universities, and medical services for hospitals. Rebates for GST paid on purchases related to exempt activities are available, with the rates varying from 57.14 percent for municipalities to 83 percent for hospitals.

- **Financial Institutions**   The GST legislation defines financial institutions to include "listed" financial institutions, such as banks and insurance companies, as well as deemed financial institutions (e.g., businesses with financial revenues exceeding specified threshold levels). Revenues from providing financial services are designated as exempt. This means that, for those institutions where the bulk of revenues is from the provision of financial services, only limited input tax credits will be available.

4-121.   These brief comments serve only to give you a very general view of the approach taken to these specific types of transactions and organizations. If you are dealing with any of these applications you will, of course, have to consult a more specialized source of information.

Harmonized Sales Tax (HST)

4-122.   On April 1, 1997, the retail sales taxes in Nova Scotia, New Brunswick, and Newfoundland and Labrador, and the GST in those provinces were replaced by a single harmonized tax, the Harmonized Sales Tax (HST). The HST is governed by the *Excise Tax Act* and operates in the same manner as the GST. The HST and GST are effectively the same tax system except that two different rates are used. The HST rate is 15 percent, which applies to the same base of goods and services as the GST, and is made up of a 7 percent federal and an 8 percent provincial component.

4-123.   The HST represents a step towards the goal of a fully harmonized sales tax system in Canada. In the meantime, we have to deal with HST in the Maritime provinces (except for Prince Edward Island), Quebec Sales Tax in Quebec, and separate retail sales taxes for all the other provinces, except Alberta which has no sales tax.

4-124.   While the HST only applies in the participating provinces, it affects any GST registrant doing business there. Issues may arise relating to the "place of supply" of a particular good or service. The *Excise Tax Act* outlines the related rules, and should be referred to by all GST registrants. Whenever a taxable supply is deemed to take place in a participating province, the HST applies. Conversely, if a taxable supply is deemed to occur outside of a participating province, the GST applies.

4-125.   Any GST registrant providing taxable goods or services in Nova Scotia, New Brunswick, and Newfoundland and Labrador must collect HST at 15 percent rather than GST at 7 percent. For example, a furniture retail outlet operating in Halifax should collect only HST on its sales and no separate provincial sales tax. A clothing manufacturer with its head office in Ontario should charge HST on all goods it sells and ships to New Brunswick. Businesses engaged in commercial activities anywhere in Canada, that purchase goods and services in the participating provinces, are entitled to recover the HST as an input tax credit.

4-126.   The reporting requirements contained in the *Excise Tax Act* apply to both the GST and the HST and the same registration number is used to report both taxes. Registrants do not have to differentiate between the tax collected at 7 percent versus 15 percent. Similarly, no need exists to separately identify input tax credits claimed at 7 percent versus 15 percent.

Exercises

(The solutions for these exercises can be found following Chapter 21 of the text.)

Exercise Four - 1 (GST vs. VAT)

During a taxation period, Darvin Wholesalers purchases merchandise for $233,000. Merchandise sales during this period total $416,000 and the cost of the merchandise sold was $264,000. Ignoring all other costs incurred by Darvin and assuming a rate of five percent, how much tax would be paid by Darvin under a VAT system and under a GST system?

Exercise Four - 2 (Requirement To Register)

Ms. Sharron Salome begins her business on January 1 of the current year. Her quarterly sales of taxable items are as follows:

Calendar Quarter	Taxable Sales
One	$10,000
Two	4,000
Three	35,000
Four	40,000

At what point in time will Ms. Salome have to begin collecting GST?

Exercise Four - 3 (Requirement To Register)

Mr. Rock Laughton begins his business on January 1 of the current year. His quarterly sales of taxable items are as follows:

Calendar Quarter	Taxable Sales
One	$ 8,000
Two	23,000
Three	4,000
Four	17,000

At what point in time will Mr. Laughton have to begin collecting GST?

Exercise Four - 4 (GST Calculation)

During the current quarter, March Ltd. has taxable sales of $1,223,000 before GST. Its cost of sales for the period was $843,000 before GST and its merchandise inventories increased by $126,000, again before GST. Salaries and wages for the period totalled $87,000, interest expense was $16,000 and depreciation expense was $93,000. No capital expenditures were made during the period. Determine the amount of GST payable (refund) for the quarter.

Exercise Four - 5 (GST Calculation)

Ms. Marsha Stone, an accountant, delivers services that are billed at $124,000 during the current year. Rent for this period on her office premises totals $25,800 and she pays a clerical assistant an annual salary of $18,500. Her capital expenditures during the period are for new office furniture with a cost of $36,000 and computer hardware and software for $20,000. All amounts are before the addition of GST or PST. She files her GST return on an annual basis. Determine the amount of GST payable (refund) for the year.

Exercise Four - 6 (Input Tax Credits)

During its current quarter, Sodam Ltd. purchases an office building and land for a total of $1,200,000 before GST. The company spends an additional $226,000 (before GST) renovating the building to fit its business needs. The building will be used 40 percent for taxable supplies and 60 percent for exempt supplies. The renovations are to be allocated in the same ratio. For accounting purposes the building will be depreciated over 40 years, while the renovations will be written off over 10 years. Determine the input tax credits that Sodam Ltd. can claim as a result of these capital expenditures.

Exercise Four - 7 (Quick Method)
During the first quarter of the year, Robbins Hardware has taxable sales of $42,500, before the inclusion of GST. They have taxable purchases totalling $21,000 before GST and PST. They do not make any capital expenditures during the quarter. Using the quick method, determine the GST that is payable for the quarter.

Exercise Four - 8 (Quick Method)
During the first quarter of the year, Guy's Books has taxable sales of $56,100, before the inclusion of GST. Current expenses on which GST was paid total $23,400. Due to a major renovation of the store, Guy's Books has capital expenditures of $42,000. The store is used exclusively for the sale of taxable merchandise. Compare the use of the quick method and the regular method for this quarter.

Problems For Self Study

(The solutions for these problems can be found following Chapter 21 of the text.)

Self Study Problem Four - 1
Chantelle Chance is a hairdresser who started in business on October 1, 2000, and has not registered to collect the GST. Revenues from her business for last year were as follows:

First Quarter	$ 4,000
Second Quarter	6,500
Third Quarter	9,000
Fourth Quarter	9,500
Total Ending September 30, 2001	$29,000

For the quarter ending December 31, 2001, business revenues were $11,500.

Required: Advise Chantelle if she needs to register her business for the GST, and if so, state when collection should start.

Self Study Problem Four - 2
The government is considering introducing a pure turnover tax, so that businesses will only have to account for and remit tax collected on transactions. Assume goods normally move from the manufacturer, to wholesaler, to distributor, to retailer and finally to the consumer. There is a mark-up of 50 percent at each turnover and the tax applies to the selling price at each turnover.

Required: Calculate the transaction tax rate required to raise the same amount of tax as a 7 percent GST on consumer goods. In your calculations, assume a cost of $100 to manufacture a particular good.

Self Study Problem Four - 3
Just-In-Time Consulting started in business on September 1 of the current year and has a December 31 year end. It earned professional fees of $67,000, $78,000 and $89,000, respectively, in each of the first three months of operations. These fees would normally be taxable supplies if the business was registered for the GST. However, the principal consultants were too busy to register until the end of December.

Required: Explain whether input tax credits can be claimed for operating costs incurred in September, October and November. Also, discuss when GST should be collected and when it should be remitted.

Self Study Problem Four - 4

Quint Technics is a database management company, which is registered for GST purposes and files its GST returns on a calendar month basis. The company is installing a database retrieval system for a large national printing firm. The installation should have taken three months, but because of extensive custom work, the contract took from August to December to complete.

Quint normally invoices for its work for the previous month on the 10th day of each month. The August fees were invoiced on September 10, and the September fees were invoiced on October 10. Because of accounting delays, the October fees were invoiced on December 10. Then, to defer income to the following year, the November and December fees were invoiced on January 10. The invoices were paid by the customer within 21 days of receipt.

Required: Identify when the GST should be remitted for each month's fees.

Self Study Problem Four - 5

Bombardeaux provides commuter train plumbing services in Canada and France. The firm has offices in each country. Bombardeaux is registered for GST purposes, and files annually. The firm has elected to use the Quick Method for its GST remittances. It paid no GST installments for the current year as none were required. The following transactions occurred in the current year:

	Amount	GST	Total
Operating Revenue			
Canada	$70,000	$4,900	$74,900
France	43,000	0	43,000
Operating Expenses			
Canada - Taxable	22,000	1,540	23,540
Canada - Non-Taxable	15,000	0	15,000
France	21,000	0	21,000
Capital Purchases			
Canada	20,000	1,400	21,400
France	88,000	0	88,000

Required: Calculate the GST remittance (refund) for the current year.

Self Study Problem Four - 6

The Income Statement of Lassen Ltd. for the current fiscal year ending December 31 is as follows (all amounts as per generally accepted accounting principles with GST excluded):

Sales		$5,700,000
Less Expenses:		
Cost Of Goods Sold	$2,600,000	
Depreciation And Amortization	720,000	
Salaries And Wages	640,000	
Other Operating Expenses	370,000	
Accrued Interest	120,000	4,450,000
Income Before Taxes		$1,250,000
Less: Federal And Provincial Income Taxes		340,000
Net Income		$ 910,000

Other Information:

1. Sales included $1,200,000 in exempt supplies and $2,400,000 in zero rated supplies. The remaining sales were fully taxable for GST purposes, and included $1,000,000 of sales to customers in Nova Scotia.

2. All of the goods sold involved the provision of either fully taxable or zero rated supplies. During the year, inventories of these goods decreased by $200,000. GST was paid on all goods that were purchased for resale during the year.

3. Capital expenditures for the year amounted to $4,000,000, with GST being paid on all amounts. Of this total, $3,000,000 was for an office building that will be used 40 percent for the provision of fully taxable or zero rated supplies. The remaining $1,000,000 was for equipment that will be used 70 percent in the provision of exempt supplies. GST was paid on the acquisition of all assets on which depreciation and amortization is being taken during the year.

4. All of the Other Operating Expenses involved the acquisition of fully taxable supplies and were acquired to assist in the provision of fully taxable supplies. Included in other operating expenses is $100,000 of taxable supplies purchased in Nova Scotia.

5. Of the salaries and wages, 40 percent were paid to employees involved in providing exempt supplies.

Required: Calculate the total amount of GST that Lassen will pay or receive for the current year. Ignore the PST.

Assignment Problems

(The solutions for these problems are only available in
the solutions manual that has been provided to your instructor.)

Assignment Problem Four - 1

Fine Form Furniture Ltd. is a furniture distributor. The logging, sawmill, manufacturing, and retailing operations use separate companies for management control and limited liability purposes. As well, the companies are not closely related or associated. The raw materials for the desk cost $10, representing the cost of materials purchased from small suppliers. At each production step, $50 of business inputs (assume that these are wages only) are added and the desk is marked up by 50 percent of total cost. A seven percent GST is levied on each transfer.

Required: Calculate the GST on each transfer, the available input tax credit, and the net GST liability, as the desk moves through the manufacturing and distribution chain.

Assignment Problem Four - 2

The following is summary financial statement information for December for Bestomer's Best Balloons. The entity is a proprietorship registered to file a GST tax return on a monthly basis. GST was paid on purchases of balloons and operating costs. There were no capital purchases or dispositions in the month.

Sales	$69,000
Expenses:	
Cost Of Balloons Sold (Note)	$12,000
Salaries And Wages	19,000
Operating Costs	14,500
Amortization Expense	10,000
Total Expenses	$55,500
Income Before Income Taxes	$13,500
Less: Federal and Provincial Income Taxes	4,500
Net Income	$ 9,000

Note   The Inventory of balloons at the end of the month was $4,000. The corresponding figure at the beginning of the month was $3,000.

Required: Outline the GST treatment of each of the items presented and calculate the GST remittance for December.

Assignment Problem Four - 3

Rhapsody Music Supplies is a GST registrant, and reported the following sales and expenditures in October. All sales were cash sales, and all expenditures were invoiced for and paid in the month. An eight percent Provincial Sales Tax (PST) applied to some purchases.

	Amount	GST	PST	Total
Sales	$2,400	$168	$192	$2,760
Expenditures				
Capital Equipment	$ 400	$ 28	$ 32	$ 460
Interest	100	-0-	-0-	100
Purchases Of Inventory	600	42	-0-	642
Rent	400	28	-0-	428
Salaries	400	-0-	-0-	400
Supplies	200	14	16	230
Total Expenditures	$2,100	$112	$ 48	$2,260

Required: Using the simplified input tax credit calculation, determine the total input tax credit that can be claimed for the month and the required net GST remittance.

Assignment Problem Four - 4

Quarterhorse Saddles started operations in April, 2001 and has selected a September year end. Calendar quarters are selected for GST reporting. The business specializes in the custom manufacture of saddles for quarterhorses. All billings for a given month are billed on the last day of the month.

During the first year of operations, Quarterhorse Saddles provided the following services:

Month	Value Of Services
April 2001	$12,000
May	16,000
June	9,000
July	9,000
October	5,000
November	7,000
February 2002	4,000
March	10,000
April	in progress

Required:

A. Identify when Quarterhorse Saddles was required to register for and collect the GST.

B. Assume the GST is only applied to services after the $30,000 threshold is passed. Calculate the GST collectible for each quarter and specify the due date.

Assignment Problem Four - 5

Come-By-Chance operates white-water rafting trips along the Fraser River in British Columbia and is not registered for the GST. The business is seasonal, with the following trip fees received in 2000:

June	$ 5,200
July	13,400
August	9,500
Total 2000 Revenue	$28,100

To date, revenue received in 2001 is as follows:

May	$ 1,300
June	$ 6,200

Required: Come-By-Chance would like to know if, and when, the business needs to register for and collect GST.

Assignment Problem Four - 6

Claire, Nicole, Barbara and Elizabeth Sperry are sisters and each runs a separate unincorporated business. They provide you with the following annual information for their businesses. All amounts are reported inclusive of GST, and there were no zero rated or exempt sales or purchases.

	Type Of Business	Taxable Sales	Purchases
Claire	Lawn Maintenance	$150,000	$ 35,000
Barbara	Tennis Supplies	150,000	100,000
Nicole	Pro Golf Instruction	120,000	35,000
Elizabeth	Golf Watch Sales	120,000	75,000

Required: Recommend whether any of the businesses should use the Quick Method to calculate net GST remittances. Show your calculations.

Assignment Problem Four - 7

The Income Statement of Montagne Inc. for the current fiscal year ending December 31 is as follows (all amounts as per generally accepted accounting principles with GST excluded):

Sales And Other Revenues		$823,000
Less Expenses:		
Cost Of Goods Sold	$478,000	
Depreciation And Amortization	132,000	
Salaries And Wages	57,000	
Other Operating Expenses	32,000	
Accrued Interest	16,000	715,000
Income Before Taxes		$108,000
Less: Federal And Provincial Income Taxes		23,000
Net Income		$ 85,000

Other Information:

1. Sales And Other Revenues included $120,000 in exempt supplies and $116,000 in zero rated supplies. The remaining sales were fully taxable for GST purposes.

2. All of the goods sold involved the provision of either fully taxable or zero rated supplies. During the year, inventories of these goods decreased by $74,000. GST was paid on all goods that were purchased for resale during the year.

3. Capital expenditures for the year amounted to $1,200,000, with GST being paid on all amounts. Of this total, $800,000 was for an office building that will be used 85 percent for the provision of fully taxable or zero rated supplies. The remaining $400,000 was for equipment that will be used 27 percent in the provision of exempt supplies. GST was paid on the acquisition of all assets on which depreciation and amortization is being taken during the year.

4. All of the Other Operating Expenses involved the acquisition of fully taxable supplies and were acquired to assist in the provision of fully taxable supplies.

5. Of the salaries and wages, 32 percent were paid to employees involved in providing exempt supplies.

Required: Calculate the total amount of GST that Montagne Inc. will pay or receive for the current year. Ignore the PST.

Assignment Problem Four - 8

Norton's Variety is an unincorporated business owned by Sheila Norton. The business is a GST registrant that sells both fully taxable and zero rated goods. In addition, Norton's Variety provides exempt services. As Ms. Norton once dreamed of being a professional accountant, she has continued to prepare financial statements as per the requirements of the *CICA Handbook*. On this basis, her income statement for the relevant GST filing period is as follows:

Revenues:		
Fully Taxable Goods	$250,000	
Zero Rated Goods	100,000	
Exempt Services	150,000	$500,000
Less Expenses:		
Cost Of Fully Taxable Goods Sold	$175,000	
Cost Of Zero Rated Goods Sold	60,000	
Depreciation And Amortization	40,000	
Salaries And Wages	20,000	
Other Operating Expenses	10,000	
Accrued Interest	5,000	310,000
Income Before Taxes		$190,000
Less: Federal And Provincial Income Taxes		82,000
Net Income		$108,000

Other Information:

1. Inventories of fully taxable goods increased by $10,000 during this period, while inventories of zero-rated goods declined by $7,000. The zero-rated sales were generated by purchasing and selling zero-rated supplies.

2. Capital expenditures for this period amounted to $600,000, with GST being paid on all amounts. Of this total, $480,000 was for a building that will be used 40 percent for the provision of fully taxable or zero rated supplies. The remaining $120,000 was for equipment that will be used 70 percent in the provision of exempt supplies. GST was paid on the acquisition of all assets on which depreciation and amortization is being taken during this period.

3. Of the Other Operating Expenses, 91 percent were related to the provision of either fully taxable or zero rated supplies.

4. Of the salaries and wages, 40 percent were paid to employees involved in providing exempt supplies.

Required: Calculate the total amount of GST that Norton's Variety will pay or receive for the current period. Ignore the PST.

Assignment Problem Four - 9

Kole Ltd. is a retail business situated in Southern Manitoba. It has no associated businesses. Its Income Statement for the current year, prepared using generally accepted accounting principles, is as follows:

Revenues:		
Fully Taxable Goods	$175,000	
Exempt Services	50,000	$225,000
Less Expenses:		
Cost Of Goods Sold	$ 95,000	
Depreciation And Amortization	15,000	
Salaries And Wages	12,000	
Other Operating Expenses	35,000	
Accrued Interest	10,000	167,000
Income Before Taxes		$ 58,000
Less: Federal And Provincial Income Taxes		18,000
Net Income		$ 40,000

Other Information:

1. Inventories of taxable goods decreased by $10,000 during the year.

2. A capital expenditure was made during the year at a GST inclusive cost of $53,500. The expenditure was for equipment that will be used 60 percent for the provision of fully taxable goods. GST was paid on the acquisition of all assets on which depreciation and amortization is being taken during this period.

3. All of the Other Operating Expenses involved the acquisition of fully taxable supplies and were acquired to assist in the provision of fully taxable supplies.

4. Of the salaries and wages, 40 percent were paid to employees involved in providing exempt services.

Required:

A. Calculate the total amount of GST that Kole will pay or receive for the current year using regular GST calculations.

B. Determine if Kole is eligible to use the quick method.

C. Assume that Kole is eligible to use the quick method. Calculate the total amount of GST that Kole will pay or receive for the current year using the quick method.

Ignore the PST.

Chapter 5

Income Or Loss From An Office Or Employment

General Rules

Employment Income Defined

General Rules

5-1.   Income or loss from an office or employment (employment income, hereafter) is covered in Part I, Division B, Subdivision a of the *Income Tax Act*. This relatively short subdivision is made up of Sections 5 through 8, the general contents of which can be described as follows:

Section 5   contains a definition of employment income.

Section 6   provides detailed information on what amounts must be included in the determination of employment income.

Section 7   is a more specialized Section which provides the tax rules related to the issuance of stock options to employees.

Section 8   provides detailed information on what amounts can be deducted in the determination of employment income.

5-2.   The basic description of employment income is as follows:

ITA 5(1)   Subject to this Part, a taxpayer's income for a taxation year from an office or employment is the salary, wages and other remuneration, including gratuities, received by the taxpayer in the year.

5-3.   While ITA 5(2) contemplates the possibility of a loss from an office or employment, the limited amount of deductions that can be made against employment income inclusions would make such an event unusual.

5-4.   Employment is defined in ITA 248 as the position of an individual in the service of some other person and servant or employee means a person holding such a position. Similarly, office is defined as the position of an individual entitling him to a fixed or ascertainable stipend or remuneration. As will be discussed later, determining whether an individual is or is not an employee can be a contentious issue.

5-5.   As to what is included in employment income, the terms salary and wages generally refer to monetary amounts provided in return for employment services. However, the term remuneration is somewhat broader, bringing in any type of reward or benefit associated with employment services. With the specific inclusion of gratuities, it is clear that employment income includes not only payments from an employer but, in addition, includes any other payments that result from a taxpayer's position as an employee.

5-6.   As the preceding suggests, any benefit received by an employee that is related to the quantity or quality of services performed by the employee would constitute employment income, even if the amount was not received from the employer. While it would not be common, it is possible that an individual could receive a payment from an employer that is not related to the quantity or quality of services performed as an employee. For example, if the employee made a personal loan to the employer, any interest paid by the employer to the employee on the loan would not be considered employment income.

Bonus Arrangements

5-7.   As presented in Paragraph 5-2, the definition of an employee's income states that it is made up of amounts "received by the taxpayer in the year". This serves to establish that employment income must be reported on a cash rather than on an accrual basis.

5-8.   This fact, when combined with the fact that business income for tax purposes is on an accrual basis (see Chapter 7), provides a tax planning opportunity. A business can declare a bonus to one of its employees and, because it is on an accrual basis, deduct it for tax purposes by simply recognizing a firm obligation to pay the amount. In contrast, the employee who has earned the bonus will not have to include it in employment income until it is actually received.

> **Example**   A business with a December 31 year end declares a bonus in December, 2000, but stipulates that it will not be paid until January, 2001. This means that, while the business would get the deduction in 2000, the employee would not have to include the amount in income until the 2001 taxation year. If the bonus had been paid in December, 2000, the employee would have had to include it in income in 2000. In effect, this arrangement defers the taxation applicable to the employee by one taxation year.

5-9.   There are, however, limits to this procedure. ITA 78(4) indicates that, where such a bonus is not paid within 180 days of the employer's year end (note that this is not always December 31), the employer will not be able to deduct the amount until it is paid.

> **Example**   An employer with a June 30 year end declares a bonus for an employee on June 30, 2000 that is payable on January 1, 2001. As January 1, 2001 is more than 180 days after the employer's year end, no deduction would be available to the employer until the bonus is paid on January 1, 2001.

5-10.   A further problem arises when a "bonus" will not be paid until more than three years after the end of the calendar year in which the employee's services were rendered. In this case, the "bonus" would become a "salary deferral arrangement", resulting in the employee being taxed on the relevant amounts in the year in which the services were rendered. This type of arrangement is discussed more fully in Chapter 6.

5-11.   The tax consequences associated with these three types of arrangements are summarized in the following Figure 5-1:

Figure 5 - 1 Bonus Arrangements	
Type Of Bonus Arrangement	**Tax Consequences**
Standard Bonus (Paid within 180 days of business year end.)	The business deducts when declared. The employee includes when received.
Other Bonus (Paid more than 180 days after business year end but prior to three years after the end of the year in which the bonus was earned.)	The business deducts when paid. The employee includes when paid.
Salary Deferral Arrangement (Paid more than three years after the end of the year in which it was earned.)	The business deducts when earned. The employee includes when earned.

Exercise Five-1 deals with bonus arrangements. This would be an appropriate time to attempt this exercise.

Net Concept

5-12.   Employment income is a net income concept. That is, it is made up of both inclusions (e.g., salaries and wages) and deductions (e.g., registered pension plan contributions and union dues). In conjunction with this, we would point out that the deductions that are described in ITA 8 can only be deducted against employment income inclusions. Given the limited deductions available in the determination of employment income, it would be very rare for these deductions to exceed the inclusions. If this unusual result were to occur, the Section 8 deductions could not be applied against any other source of income. However, if other sources of income are available, the same result will be accomplished by deducting the net employment loss under ITA 3(d) as per the calculations for Net Income For Tax Purposes that were described in Chapter 3.

Employee Versus Self Employed

Introduction

5-13.   An individual doing work for an organization will be undertaking this activity in one of two possible roles. He may be working as an employee. If this is the case, he will be earning employment income and will be subject to the rules discussed in this Chapter. In contrast, he may be working as an independent contractor (from the point of view of the organization using the individual's services, this is often referred to as contracting out). The payments made to such self employed individuals will be classified as business income and will be subject to the rules that are covered in Chapter 7.

5-14.   This distinction is of considerable importance, both to the individual worker and to the organization using his services. Further, individuals and organizations can structure their arrangements in a manner that will provide the desired classification of the income that will be received by the individual. As a consequence, this Section will outline the tax features of these alternatives from the point of view of the worker and from the point of view of the organization using his services.

Employee Perspective

5-15.   As will be discussed later in this Chapter, the ability to deduct expenses from employment income is quite limited and may make it advantageous for tax purposes for an individual to avoid this classification and be considered self employed. The basis for this statement is that self employed individuals, commonly referred to as independent contractors, are taxed as businesses and, as a consequence, all reasonable expenses of doing business can be deducted from revenues generated by self employment. In addition, revenue is received by a self employed individual without any withholding for income tax, Canada Pension Plan contributions, or Employment Insurance premiums.

5-16.   The absence of income tax withholdings may offer some deferral of tax. This is not a clear cut conclusion, in that the self employed individual will generally be required to make instalment payments as described in Chapter 2. However, in practical terms, self employment income is sometimes received partially or wholly in cash in certain lines of work where the expenditure is not deductible for tax purposes and no receipt is issued (e.g., a self employed contractor working on private residences). If the individual is willing to evade taxes by not reporting these revenues, then the lack of withholding on self employment earnings becomes a permanent reduction in taxes. In reality, although clearly illegal, not reporting earnings received in cash is, for some individuals, one of the main motivations behind being self employed.

5-17.   The self employed individual has no liability for Employment Insurance (EI) premiums. For 2001, the employee's share of these contributions amounts to 2.25 percent of the first $39,000 in gross wages, with a maximum annual value of $878 (the individual's employer is assessed 1.4 times this amount, an effective rate of 3.15 percent). While a self employed individual is spared having to pay EI premiums, this may not be a completely desirable situation. The offsetting disadvantage is that self employed individuals are not eligible for the benefits that are provided by this program.

5-18.   With respect to Canada Pension Plan contributions, for 2001 both the employee and the employer are required to contribute 4.3 percent of gross wages in excess of a basic exemption of $3,500, and below a maximum of $38,300. This results in maximum contributions by both the employee and employer of $1,496, or a total of $2,992. While nothing is withheld from their revenues, self employed individuals are required to contribute to this program. In fact, self employed individuals have to make a double contribution, reflecting both the employee's share as well as what would have been the employer's share. The eventual pension benefits received by the self employed individual will be the same as would be available to an employed individual with the same earnings. Clearly, the self employed individual is worse off with respect to making contributions to the Canada Pension Plan.

5-19.   Another non tax disadvantage to self employment is that self employed individuals do not receive the various fringe benefits that many employers provide. An employee may receive a wide variety of benefits such as dental and drug plans, membership in a registered pension plan, or life insurance coverage. These benefits may, in some cases, add as much as 20 percent to an employee's remuneration. The fact that such benefits will not be extended to a self employed individual means that he will have to receive significantly higher basic remuneration to be in the same economic position as an individual working as an employee.

5-20.   As the preceding indicates, the desirability of self employed status is not clear cut. For an individual with limited deductible expenses, self employment may not be advantageous from an economic point of view. Alternatively, if the individual's work is such that a large amount of business expenses is generated, it is probably desirable to be taxed as a self employed contractor. Other possible advantages could include the ability to set work schedules and the freedom to choose the amount and type of work accepted. The added cost of accounting for the business and the implications of the GST should also be considered (as noted in Chapter 4, a self employed individual would have to charge GST if he was a registrant).

Employer Perspective

5-21.   There are several advantages to a business from using the services of self employed individuals as opposed to employees. One of the major advantages associated with the hiring of these independent contractors (a.k.a. contracting out) is that the employer avoids payments for Canada Pension Plan, Employment Insurance, Workers' Compensation and Provincial Health Care. The amounts involved here are consequential. Canada Pension Plan and Employment Insurance alone can add over seven percent to the wage costs. Provincial payroll taxes can push these costs above 10 percent of wage costs.

5-22.   Further savings result from the fact that the employer will avoid the administrative costs associated with having to withhold and remit income taxes, and the employee's share of Canada Pension Plan and Employment Insurance premiums. Also in favour of using independent contractors is the fact that the business will avoid the costs of any fringe benefits that it normally extends to its employees. A less measurable benefit is that employers are freed from ongoing commitments to individuals because there is generally no long term contract with self employed workers. Given these advantages, it is not surprising to find more businesses are contracting out in order to control labour costs.

Making The Distinction

5-23.   The general approach to distinguishing between an employee and an independent contractor is the question of whether an employer-employee relationship exists. As there is no clear definition of employer-employee relationships, disputes between taxpayers and the CCRA are not uncommon. To avoid such disputes and to assist taxpayers in determining whether or not a given individual is an employee, the CCRA has issued a pamphlet (RC4110) titled "Employee Or Self Employed". As described in this pamphlet, the major factors to be considered in this determination are as follows:

Control   Generally, in an employer-employee relationship, the employer controls, directly or not, the way the work is done and the work methods used. The employer assigns specific tasks that define the real framework within which the work is to be done.

Ownership Of Tools   In an employer-employee relationship, the employer generally supplies the equipment and tools required by the employee. In addition, the employer covers the following costs related to their use: repairs, insurance, transport, rental, and operations (e.g., fuel).

In some trades, however, it is customary for employees to supply their own tools. This is generally the case for garage mechanics, painters, and carpenters. Similarly, employed computer scientists, architects, and surveyors sometimes supply their own software and instruments.

Chance Of Profit/Risk Of Loss   Generally, in an employer-employee relationship, the employer alone assumes the risk of loss. The employer also generally covers operating costs, which may include office expenses, employee wages and benefits, insurance premiums, and delivery and shipping costs. The employee does not assume any financial risk, and is entitled to his full salary or wages regardless of the financial health of the business.

The income of an employee paid by the piece or on commission does not depend on the losses or profits of the employer's business. The employee is paid the same per unit amount no matter how many pieces the employer requires him to produce or sell.

Integration   Where the worker integrates his activities with the commercial activities of the payer, an employer-employee relationship probably exists. The worker is acting on behalf of the employer, he is connected with the employer's business and is dependent on it.

5-24.   The CCRA pamphlet includes a long list of questions that can be asked in making this determination (e.g., Who is responsible for planning the work to be done?). If you require more detailed information in this area, we would suggest that you consult this pamphlet.

5-25.   We would point out that it is extremely important for a business to be sure that any individual who is being treated as a self employed contractor qualifies for that status. If on review, the CCRA concludes that such an individual is, in fact, an employee, the business can be held responsible for unpaid source deductions. Actions that can be taken to ensure self employed status for the individual include:

• Having a lawyer prepare an independent contractor agreement.
• Having the individual work for other businesses.
• Having the individual advertise his services.
• To the extent possible, having the individual cover his own overhead, including phone service, letterhead, equipment, and supplies.
• Having the individual prepare periodic invoices, preferably on an irregular basis.
• If feasible, having the individual incorporate.
• Having the individual provide you with a GST number.

5-26.   A failure to take these steps could prove to be very costly to a business using the services of that individual. It is possible that, if the CCRA judges the individual to be an employee, the business could be held liable for CPP and EI amounts that should have been withheld from the individual's earnings, as well as the employer's share of these amounts.

Inclusions - Basic Provisions

Salaries And Wages

5-27.   We have noted that ITA 5 specifies that employment income includes salaries, wages and other remuneration. When only salaries or wages are involved, there is little need to elaborate on this point. Such amounts clearly must be included in the determination of employment income. However, for a variety of reasons, employers make use of a wide variety of benefits other than salaries or wages. These alternative forms of compensation are commonly referred to as fringe benefits and they create additional complexity in the determination of employment income for income tax purposes.

Fringe Benefits

ITA 6(1) - Amounts To Be Included In Income

5-28.   ITA 6(1)(a) is a general provision which states that all benefits received or enjoyed by an individual by virtue of an office or employment must be included in income. However, this same paragraph also notes a number of exceptions which can be left out. These include:

- employer's contributions to:
  - registered pension plans;
  - group sickness or accident insurance plans;
  - private health services plans;
  - supplementary unemployment benefit plans;
  - deferred profit sharing plans;
- benefits under a retirement compensation arrangement, some employee benefit plans (e.g. death benefit plans), and some employee trusts; and
- counseling services related to the mental or physical health of the employee or a related party, or related to re-employment or retirement of the employee.

5-29.   Other paragraphs under ITA 6(1) provide additional guidance in the form of specific items to be included in employment income. These are:

- 6(1)(b)   amounts received as personal or living expenses or as an allowance for any other purpose;
- 6(1)(c)   director's or other fees;
- 6(1)(d)   allocations under profit sharing plans;
- 6(1)(e)   standby charge for automobiles;
- 6(1)(f)   employment insurance benefits (e.g. disability insurance benefits);
- 6(1)(g)   employee benefit plan benefits (e.g. profit sharing plans);
- 6(1)(h)   allocations under some employee trusts;
- 6(1)(i)   salary deferral arrangement payments;
- 6(1)(j)   reimbursements and awards; and
- 6(1)(k)   automobile operating expense benefit.

IT-470R (Consolidated)

5-30.   At a less formal level, an important Interpretation Bulletin provides guidance with respect to other types of fringe benefits. This Bulletin, IT-470R (Consolidated), indicates that the following benefits should be considered as part of employment income:

- Board and lodging which is provided free or at an unreasonably low rate.
- Rent free and low rent housing.
- Travel benefits for the employee or the employee's family.
- Personal use of an automobile furnished by an employer.
- Gifts (with the exception of Christmas or wedding gifts with a value less than $100 and for which the employer does not claim the cost as an income tax deduction).
- Holiday trips, other prizes and incentive awards.
- Benefits earned in frequent flyer programs while traveling on employer paid business trips.
- Travel expenses of the employee's spouse.

- Premiums which are allocated to specific employees under provincial hospitalization and medical care insurance plans, and certain Government Of Canada plans.
- Tuition fees paid for or reimbursed by the employer during the year, for personal interest courses that are not related to the employer's business.
- Employer reimbursement for the cost of tools required to perform work.
- Payments related to wage loss replacement plans.
- Amounts related to interest free or low interest loans.
- Fees paid for employee counseling services. You will recall that ITA 6(1)(a) exempts two types of counseling services from this requirement. These are counseling in respect of the mental or physical health of the employee or a person related to the employee and counseling related to the re-employment or retirement of the employee.

5-31. Also found in IT-470R (Consolidated) is a list of non taxable benefits which are not included in employment income:

- Discounts on merchandise and the waiving of commissions on sales of merchandise or insurance for the personal use of the employee.
- Subsidized meals provided in employer facilities.
- Uniforms and special clothing.
- Subsidized school services in remote areas.
- Transportation to the job in employer vehicles.
- Use of employer recreational facilities and membership fees where it is an advantage to the employer for the employee to belong to a social or athletic club.
- Reimbursement of certain moving expenses. (See Chapter 11 for a detailed discussion of moving costs.)
- Premiums under private health services plans.
- Employer's required contributions under certain Provincial hospitalization and medical care insurance plans where remittances are based on some percentage of total payroll (e.g., Ontario Employer Health Levy).
- Transportation passes for employees of airline, bus, or rail companies.
- The costs of establishing, maintaining, or dismantling a blind trust when required by a public office holder.
- The costs of providing counseling services related to the mental or physical health of the employee, his re-employment, or his retirement [you will recall that this item was explicitly excluded under ITA 6(1)(a)].
- The cost of paying for an employee's professional membership fees.

Tax Planning Considerations

5-32. As described in the preceding Section, some benefits which can be provided to employees are fully taxable while other benefits can be extended without creating a taxable benefit. This has important implications in planning employee compensation.

5-33. As the bulk of employee compensation is in the form of wages or salaries, such payments provide the benchmark against which other types of compensation must be evaluated. From an income tax point of view, these benchmark payments are fully deductible to the employer in the year in which they are accrued and fully taxable to the employee in the year in which they are received. There is no valid tax reason for using a type of fringe benefit that has these same characteristics. For example, if an employer rewards a valued employee with a holiday trip, the cost of the trip will be fully deductible to the employer. However, the trip's cost will be fully taxable to the employee on the same basis as if the amount had been paid in the form of additional salary. This means that, while there may be a motivational reason for using a holiday trip as a form of compensation, there is no income tax advantage in doing so.

5-34. The most attractive form of employee compensation involves benefits that are deductible to the employer but are received tax free by the employee. Since IT-470R (Consolidated) indicates that private health care benefits are not taxable, an employer can provide employees with, for example, a dental plan without creating any additional tax liability. From a tax point of view, this type of compensation should be used whenever practical.

5-35.   Also attractive are those benefits which allow the employer to deduct the cost currently, with taxation of the employee deferred until a later period. An important example of this would be contributions to a registered pension plan. The employer will be able to deduct the contributions in the period in which they are made, while the employee will not be taxed until the benefits are received in the form of periodic pension income. This will usually involve a significant deferral of taxation for the employee.

5-36.   In the preceding cases, the tax planning considerations are very clear. There are no tax advantages associated with benefits that are fully and currently taxable to the employee. In contrast, advantages clearly arise when there is no taxation of the benefit or when the taxation is deferred until a later point in time. There is, however, a complication in the case of employer provided recreational facilities and employer payment of club dues. While IT-470R (Consolidated) indicates that such benefits are not taxable to the employee, we shall see in Chapter 7 that the employer is not allowed to deduct the cost of providing such benefits. This means that the advantage of no taxes on the employee benefit is offset by the employer's loss of deductibility. Whether this type of benefit is advantageous has to be evaluated on the basis of whether the tax savings to the employee are sufficient to offset the extra tax cost to the employer of providing a non deductible benefit. The decision will generally be based on the relative tax rates applicable to the employee and the employer. If the employee's rate is higher than the employer's, this form of compensation may be advantageous from a tax point of view.

GST On Taxable Benefits

5-37.   Many benefits included in employment income under ITA 6(1) are taxable supplies on which an employee would have to pay GST if he personally acquired the item. For example, if an employer provides a free domestic airline ticket to reward an employee for outstanding services, this is an item on which the employee would have to pay GST if he purchased the ticket on his own. This means that the benefit calculated should also include a GST component as the employee has received a benefit with a real value that includes both the price of the ticket and the related GST amount.

Exercise Five-2 deals with taxable benefits. This would be an appropriate time to attempt this exercise.

5-38.   Given this situation, ITA 6(7) requires the calculation of employee benefits on a basis that includes any provincial sales tax (PST) and GST (or HST) that were paid by the employer on goods or services that are included in the benefit. In situations where the employer is exempt from GST or PST, a notional amount is added to the benefit on the basis of the amounts that would have been paid had the employer not been exempt. Employers that are registered for the GST must actually remit the GST that is deemed to be included in the benefits allocated to their employees.

Inclusions - Detailed Considerations

Board And Lodging

5-39.   Two aspects of this fringe benefit require further explanation. The first relates to valuation. At one point in time, any board and/or lodging benefit received was valued at the lower of fair market value and the cost to the employer. However, under IT-470R (Consolidated) this benefit is now defined as fair market value less any amounts recovered from the employee. Also of note is that subsidized meals do not have to be included as long as the employee is required to pay a reasonable charge. This puts subsidized meals provided in conjunction with free or subsidized lodging on the same tax footing as subsidized meals in general.

5-40.   Under certain circumstances, board and lodging benefits will not be considered employment income. If an employee is required to work at a remote location some distance away from the employee's ordinary residence, the work is of a temporary nature such that establishment of a new residence would not be practical, and the benefits are provided for not less than 36 hours, then such benefits will not be considered taxable.

5-41.   In general, if an amount has to be included in income for board and/or lodging, the value of the benefit should be computed on a GST included basis. However, long term residential rents are GST exempt. As a result, the supply of a house, apartment, or similar accommodation to an employee is not subject to GST if the employee occupies it for at least one month and no GST amount would be associated with this type of employee benefit.

Employer Supplied Automobiles

Employees And Automobiles

5-42.   Automobiles have an influence on the determination of an individual's employment income in three different situations. The first situation arises when an employee is provided with an automobile by the employer. Under ITA 6, the benefits associated with any non business use of that vehicle must be included in the individual's employment income. The two types of taxable benefits associated with such personal use are referred to as a standby charge and an operating cost benefit. The calculation of these taxable benefits will be covered in detail in this Section.

5-43.   The other two situations in which automobiles influence employment income will be discussed in subsequent sections of this Chapter. While we are deferring the discussion of these situations, they are briefly described here in order to avoid possible confusion:

Allowances   As an alternative to providing an employee with an automobile, some employers pay an allowance to the employee for business use of his personally owned automobile. This allowance may be included in employment income and, when this is the case, the employee will be able to deduct some portion of the automobile's costs against such inclusions.

Deductible Travel Costs   Under certain circumstances, employees can deduct various travel costs. If the employee uses his personally owned automobile for travel related to his employment, a portion of the costs associated with this vehicle can be deducted in the determination of employment income.

5-44.   Both allowances and deductible travel costs involve the determination of amounts that can be deducted by an employee who owns or leases his own automobile. As you may be aware, tax legislation places limits on the amounts that can be deducted for automobile costs (e.g., for 2001, lease payments in excess of $800 per month are not deductible). As these limits are the same for an employee who owns or leases a vehicle that is used in employment activities, and for a business that owns or leases a vehicle that is used in business activities, they will be given detailed coverage in Chapter 7 on business income. However, it is important to note here that the limits that are placed on the deductibility of automobile costs have no influence on the amount of the taxable benefit that will be assessed to an employee who is provided with a vehicle by his employer. The taxable benefit to the employee will be the same, without regard to whether the employer can deduct the full costs of owning or leasing the vehicle.

General Approach

5-45.   Two types of benefits will be added to employment income when an employee makes any personal use of an employer supplied automobile. These benefits can be described as follows:

Standby Charge   This benefit could be thought of as relating to the fixed costs of having an automobile. If the employee owned the automobile, he would have to absorb the cost associated with depreciation on the vehicle. Within a broad range, this cost does not vary with the number of kilometers driven and, by having a car supplied by an employer, the employee avoids this cost. As a consequence, it would seem fair that some type of fixed cost benefit be allocated to the employee for those periods of time during which the automobile is available to him.

Operating Cost Benefit   Operating costs are other types of costs, some of which have a direct relationship to the number of kilometers the automobile is driven. Such costs as gasoline, oil, and maintenance costs are roughly proportional to usage of the vehicle. It would follow that, when an employer pays these costs and others such as license fees and insurance for an automobile that is available for an employee's personal use, a taxable benefit should be assessed to that employee. Given the nature of these costs, it would seem logical that the amount of this benefit should be calculated with reference to the personal use which the employee has made of the automobile.

Standby Charge

5-46.   In simplified terms, the standby charge for vehicles which the employer owns is 2 percent per month of the "cost" of the vehicle. For purposes of this calculation, "cost" includes both GST and Provincial Sales Tax (PST). Where the employer leases the vehicle, the charge is two-thirds of the total lease payments, also including GST and PST. This is expressed as a formula in ITA 6(2) but will be discussed in a somewhat less technical manner in the material which follows.

5-47.   **Employer Owns Automobile**   If the employer owns the automobile, the basic standby charge is determined by the following formula:

$$[(2\%)(\text{Cost Of Car})(\text{Periods Of Availability})]$$

5-48.   As noted earlier, the Cost Of Car includes both GST and PST. Periods Of Availability is roughly equal to months of availability. However, it is determined by dividing the number of days the automobile is "available for use" by 30 and rounding to the nearest whole number. Oddly, a ".5" amount is rounded down rather than up. The current administrative interpretation of "available for use" is that the automobile is "available for use" if the employee has the keys. This means that if, for example, an employee was hospitalized or out of the country for two months, these months would be considered part of the available for use period unless the car and its keys were returned to the employer. You should also note that the application of this formula can result in a situation where the cumulative standby charge will exceed the cost of the automobile. For example, if the employee were to have the automobile for 60 months, the standby charge would be 120 percent of the cost of the car.

5-49.   **Employer Leases Automobile**   When the employer leases the automobile, the basic standby charge is determined by the following formula:

$$[(2/3) (\text{Annual Lease Payments - Insurance Amounts})]$$

5-50.   The total annual lease payments include both GST and PST, and are reduced by any amounts that are included in the payment for liability or damage insurance. If the car is not available for the whole year, the standby charge is based on the fraction of the total that is determined by dividing the Periods Of Availability (roughly months of availability as described in Paragraph 5-48) by the total months covered by the lease payments.

5-51.   Unlike the situation with an employer owned vehicle, it is unlikely that the taxable benefit associated with a leased vehicle will exceed the value of the automobile. While we have seen no comprehensive analysis to support this view, it seems clear to us that, in most normal leasing situations, the taxable benefit on a leased vehicle will be significantly less than would be the case if the employer purchased the same vehicle. In a recent situation which came to our attention, a $55,000 (GST and PST inclusive) vehicle was leased for 48 months with a lease payment of $600 per month. If the car had been purchased, the standby charge would have been $13,200 per year [(2%)($55,000)(12)]. Alternatively, the standby charge on the leased vehicle was $4,800 per year [(2/3)(12)($600)]. It is our belief that this conclusion would only be altered if the lease was for a very short period (e.g., less than one year).

5-52.   **Reduced Standby Charge**   Whether the automobile is purchased or leased by the employer, IT-63R5 indicates that the standby charge can be reduced provided three conditions are met:

• The employee is required to use the automobile in his employment duties.

• "Substantially All" (defined as 90 percent or more) of the usage of the automobile is employment related.

• The total non employment use of the automobile is less than 12,000 kilometers for the year.

5-53.   The reduced amount is determined by multiplying the basic standby charge for either an owned or a leased vehicle by the following fraction:

$$\frac{\text{Non Employment Kilometers (Can' t Exceed Denominator)}}{\text{1,000 Kilometers Per Month Of Availability}}$$

5-54.   In applying this formula, the numerator is based on the number of kilometers driven for personal or non employment activities. To prevent the fraction from having a value in excess of one, the numerator is limited to the value in the denominator. The denominator is based on the idea that, if the employee uses the automobile for as much as 1,000 kilometers of personal activities in a month (12,000 kilometers per year), the vehicle has fully replaced the need for a personally owned vehicle. In technical terms, the number of months available in the denominator is calculated by dividing the available days by 30 and rounding to the nearest whole number.

Operating Cost Benefit

5-55.   An obvious approach to assessing an operating cost benefit would be to simply pro rate operating costs paid by the employer between personal vs. employment related usage. The problem with this, however, is that the employer would be required to keep detailed cost and milage records for each employee. This approach is further complicated by the fact that some operating costs incur GST (e.g., gasoline), while other operating costs are exempt from GST (e.g., insurance and licenses).

5-56.   Since 1993, ITA 6(1)(k) has provided an administratively simple solution to this problem. The operating cost benefit is determined by multiplying a prescribed amount by the number of personal kilometers driven. For 2001, this prescribed amount is $0.16 per kilometer ($0.15 per kilometer in 2000). This amount includes a notional GST component and, as a consequence, no further GST benefit has to be added to this amount. Note that this amount is applicable without regard to the level of the actual operating costs.

5-57.   There is an alternative calculation of the operating cost benefit. Employees who use an employer provided automobile "primarily" in the performance of the taxpayer's office or employment can elect to have the operating cost benefit calculated as one-half of the standby charge. In contrast to the 90 percent meaning which has been attached to the phrase "substantially all" in the calculation of the standby charge, the CCRA has indicated that "primarily" means more than 50 percent. This restricts the use of this elective alternative calculation to employees whose employment related use of the automobile is more than 50 percent. Employees wishing to use this method must notify the employer in writing before the end of the relevant year. This alternative calculation does not have to be used and, in most practical situations, it will not be a desirable alternative as it will produce a higher figure for the operating cost benefit.

5-58.   It should be noted that ITA 6(1.1) specifically excludes any benefit related to employer provided parking from the automobile benefit. This does not mean that employer provided parking is not a taxable benefit. While it is not considered to be a component of the automobile benefit calculation, it would still have to be included in the employee's income under ITA 6(1)(a). The logic of this is that parking may be provided to employees that are not provided with an automobile and, as a consequence, it should be separately accounted for in the employee benefit calculation.

Payments By Employee

5-59.   Under ITA 6(1)(e), the standby charge benefit can be reduced by payments made by the employee to the employer for the use of the automobile. In corresponding fashion under ITA 6(1)(k), the operating cost benefit can be reduced by such payments. Note, however, that if the employee pays any of the operating costs directly (e.g., the employee personally pays for gasoline), it does not reduce the basic $0.16 per kilometer benefit. This is not a desirable result and, if the employee is going to be required to pay a portion of the operating expenses, the employer should pay for all of the costs and have the employee reimburse the employer for the appropriate portion. Under this approach, the payments will reduce the operating cost benefit.

Example - Employer Owns Automobile

5-60. The following data will be used to illustrate the calculation of the taxable benefit where an employee is provided with a vehicle owned by an employer:

Cost Of The Automobile (Includes $1,600 PST and $1,400 GST)	$23,000
Months Available For Use (310 Days Rounded)	10
Months Owned By The Employer	12
Total Kilometers Driven	30,000
Personal Kilometers Driven	9,000

5-61. The standby charge benefit to be included in employment income would be calculated as follows:

$$\text{Standby Charge} = [(2\%)(\$23,000)(10)] = \underline{\$4,600}$$

5-62. In calculating the standby charge, no reduction based on actual personal kilometers is available. This reflects the fact that less than 90 percent (21,000 ÷ 30,000 = 70%) of the driving was for the employer's business. Also note that the cost figure used in the preceding calculation includes both PST and GST.

5-63. The operating cost benefit to be included in employment income is as follows:

$$\text{Operating Cost Benefit} = [(\$0.16)(9,000)] = \underline{\$1,440}$$

5-64. While the employee could have used the 50 percent of standby charge calculation of the operating cost benefit, it would have resulted in a benefit of $2,300. Employees eligible to use this calculation are not required to do so and, in this situation, it is clearly better to use the $0.16 per kilometer calculation.

5-65. As the employee does not make any payments to the employer for personal use of the automobile, the total taxable benefit to be included in employment income is as follows:

$$\text{Total Taxable Benefit} = (\$4,600 + \$1,440) = \underline{\$6,040}$$

Example - Employer Leases Automobile

5-66. To provide a direct comparison between the employer owned and employer leased cases, the example will be based on the same general facts. If the employer were to lease a $20,000 car with a 36 month lease term, the lease payment, calculated using normal lease terms, would be approximately $548 per month, including PST and GST. (This cannot be calculated with the information given.) With the exception of the fact that the car is leased rather than purchased by the employer, all of the other facts are the same as in the preceding example. The standby charge benefit would be calculated as follows:

$$\text{Standby Charge} = [(2/3)(12)(10/12)(\$548)] = \underline{\$3,653}$$

5-67. As was the case when the car was owned by the employer, there is no reduction for actual business kilometers driven because the car was driven less than 90 percent for employment related purposes. Also note that the benefit is based on the lease payment including both PST and GST.

5-68. The operating cost benefit is the same as the employer owned case and is as follows:

$$\text{Operating Cost Benefit} = [(\$0.16)(9,000)] = \underline{\$1,440}$$

5-69. As in the case where the employer owned the car, the employee is eligible for the alternative calculation of the operating cost benefit. However, one-half the standby charge is equal to $1,827, an amount that is in excess of that produced by the usual calculation.

5-70. As the employee does not make any payments to the employer for the personal use of the automobile, the total taxable benefit is as follows:

$$\text{Total Taxable Benefit} = (\$3,653 + \$1,440) = \underline{\$5,093}$$

5-71. Note that, as was discussed previously, the total benefit is significantly less ($5,093 as compared with $6,040) when the employer leases the car as opposed to purchasing it.

Company Cars And Tax Planning

5-72.   Providing employees with company cars was once a clearly desirable course of action. The costs of the car were fully deductible to the employer and the value of the benefit actually received was, in the great majority of situations, well in excess of the taxable benefit that was allocated to the employee. The situation is no longer so clear cut. Particularly when the car has a cost in excess of $30,000, it may be desirable to have the employee own the car and bill the employer for business usage. While a complete analysis of this issue goes beyond the scope of this book, some general tax planning points can be made.

Record Keeping   In the absence of detailed records, an employee can be charged with the full standby charge and 100 percent personal usage. To avoid this, it is essential that records be kept of both business and personal kilometers driven and of the actual number of months that the car was available for personal use.

Return The Keys   As the car will be considered to be available for the employee's use unless the keys are returned to the employer, the vehicle and its keys should be left with the employer during significant periods when the employee is not using it. This will not have any effect on the amounts that can be deducted for the car by the employer.

Leasing Vs. Buying   As was demonstrated in the preceding leased car example, in most cases a lower taxable benefit will result when the employer leases the car rather than purchases it. If employees are already using cars which have been purchased, it could be beneficial for the employer to sell the cars to a leasing company and reacquire them through a lease. One adverse aspect of leasing arrangements should be noted. Lease payments are made up of a combination of both interest and principal payments on the car. As the taxable benefit is based on the total lease payment, the interest portion becomes, in effect, a part of the taxable benefit.

Minimizing The Standby Charge   This can be accomplished in a variety of ways including longer lease terms, lower trade in values for old vehicles in purchase situations, larger deposits on leases, and the use of higher residual values in leasing arrangements. However, this minimization process is not without limits. As will be explained in Chapter 7, refundable deposits in excess of $1,000 on leases can reduce the deductible lease costs.

Cars Costing More Than $30,000   With the taxable benefit to the employee based on the full cost of the car and any portion of the cost in excess of $30,000 not being deductible to the employer (this limit on the deductibility of automobile expenses is discussed more completely in Chapter 7), it is difficult to imagine situations in which it would make economic sense for a profit oriented employer to provide any employee with a luxury car. As the taxable benefit to the employee is based on the actual cost of the car, while the deductible amount is limited to $30,000, a situation is created in which the employee is paying taxes on an amount which is larger than the amount that is deductible to the employer. The only winner in this type of situation is the CCRA.

Consider The Alternative   The alternative to the employer provided automobile is to have the employer compensate the employee for using his own automobile. In many cases this may be preferable to providing an automobile. For example, in those situations where business use is substantial but less than 90 percent, the provision of an automobile to an employee will result in a benefit assessment for the full standby charge. If business use were 80 percent, for example, it is almost certain that the amount assessed will far exceed the actual benefit associated with 20 percent personal use of the vehicle. If, alternatively, the employee is compensated for using his own personal vehicle, there may be no taxable benefit.

> Exercises Five-3 through Five-5 deal with automobile costs and benefits. This would be an appropriate time to attempt these exercises.

Allowances

General Rules

5-73.   The term allowance is used to refer to amounts received by employees from an employer other than salaries, wages, and benefits. In practice, allowances generally involve payments to employees to reimburse them for travel costs, use of their own automobile, or other costs that have been incurred by employees as part of their efforts on behalf of the employer. A milage allowance for a traveling salesperson or a technician who does service calls would be typical examples of such an allowance.

5-74. ITA 6(1)(b) provides a general rule which requires that allowances for personal or living expenses must be included in an employee's income. However, many of the items for which employees receive allowances are costs that an employee can deduct against employment income under ITA 8 (see the discussion of deductions later in this Chapter for a full explanation of these amounts). Examples of such deductible items are as follows:

- ITA 8(1)(f) - Salesperson's Expenses
- ITA 8(1)(h) - Traveling Expenses Other Than Motor Vehicle Expenses
- ITA 8(1)(h.1) - Motor Vehicle Traveling Expenses
- ITA 8(1)(i) - Professional Dues, Office Rent, Salaries, And Supply Costs
- ITA 8(1)(j) - Motor Vehicle Capital Costs (Interest And CCA)

5-75. If allowances for these items are included in the employee's income, a circular process is involved in which they are added under ITA 6(1)(b) and then subtracted under ITA 8. In view of this, ITA 6(1)(b) indicates that there are exceptions to the rule that allowances must be included in income. While there is a fairly long list of such items, the most important of these exceptions involve allowances paid for the types of costs that would be deductible under ITA 8. Specifically, the following allowances do not have to be included in an employee's income:

- ITA 6(1)(b)(v)   Reasonable allowances for traveling expenses paid during a period in which the employee was a salesperson (includes payments for use of a motor vehicle).

- ITA 6(1)(b)(vii)   Reasonable allowances for traveling expenses for any employee, not including payments for use of a motor vehicle.

- ITA 6(1)(b)(vii.1) Reasonable allowances for use of a motor vehicle.

5-76. ITA 6(1)(b) specifies two additional conditions that must be met by motor vehicle allowances before they can be excluded from an employee's income. First, they must be based solely on the number of kilometers for which the motor vehicle is used in the course of employment. In addition, there can be no additional reimbursement (except for specific outlays such as supplementary business insurance, toll, or parking charges) in addition to the allowance. If an allowance and additional reimbursement is paid, both amounts must be included in income.

5-77. These rules leave the employer with some discretion in dealing with allowances. Essentially the employer can structure the allowance in such a fashion that it is either a taxable allowance or a non taxable allowance. There is no GST benefit associated with either type of allowance. The alternatives can be described as follows:

Taxable Allowance An allowance can be paid to the employee and included in his employment income record (Information Return T4) for the period. To the extent the employee can qualify for the deduction of business travel or commission salespersons expenses, related expenses can be deducted by the employee in the determination of his net employment income. There are no restrictions on the employer's deduction of such allowances and the deductions taken by the employee could be more than, less than, or equal to the allowance. Assume, for example, that Ms. Scott uses her own automobile for 2001 employment related travel. The employment related kilometers for the year total 4,500. Her employer pays her an allowance of $100 per month ($1,200 for the year) to use her own vehicle, regardless of the actual employment related kilometers driven. As the allowance is not based on kilometers, it must be included in Ms. Scott's employment income. She will then be able to deduct an appropriate share (based on employment related milage) of the costs related to owning and operating her own automobile (for example, interest, capital cost allowance, gas, and maintenance).

Non Taxable Allowance This approach involves the payment of an allowance based on actual kilometers driven for employment related purposes. Referring to the example in the previous paragraph, Ms. Scott's employer could have paid her an allowance of $.30 per kilometer driven, or a total of $1,350 for the year. The employer will not include this allowance in the employee's income reported on the T4 and, as a consequence, the employee does not have to include the amount in income. However, if this allowance is not included in income, the employee is prohibited from deducting actual costs. In view of this, the employee can, if they believe the per kilometer amount they receive is not adequate, include the allowance in income and deduct the actual costs (subject to restrictions that will be described in our later discussion of deductions from employment income). In situations where the employee's actual deductible costs exceed the allowance paid by the employer, the employee may wish to take this approach. Alternatively, if the difference is fairly minor, the employee may prefer the administrative simplicity of excluding both amounts from employment income.

Employer's Perspective Of Allowances

5-78.   From the point of view of the employer, the payment of a taxable allowance has advantages. All amounts paid will be included in the employment income of the employees and, as a consequence, the amounts are fully deductible. Further, there is no necessity for the employer to keep detailed records of the employees' actual costs or milage.

5-79.   Alternatively, if the allowance or reimbursement of costs is not included in the income of the employees, the amount that can be deducted by the employer usually reflects actual costs. For travel costs such as food, lodging, or miscellaneous costs, the filing and compilation of actual receipts may be required. While it is administratively possible to use a reasonable per diem amount in lieu of actual costs and receipts for these purposes, this per diem approach would not cover the types of travel and entertainment costs that are incurred by more senior or experienced employees.

5-80.   The situation is even more complex with respect to amounts that an employer can deduct for automobile costs. As noted in Chapter 7 on business income, the 2001 amounts that can be deducted by an employer for automobile costs is limited to $0.41 per kilometer for the first 5,000 kilometers of use by a given employee and $0.35 per kilometer for subsequent kilometers. Allowances in excess of these limits are only deductible if they are reported on the employee's T4. Detailed employee-by-employee records are required to support even this limited deduction. The resulting record keeping is an additional factor weighing against the use of non taxable allowances based on actual costs or milage.

Employee's Perspective Of Allowances

5-81.   From the employee's point of view, the receipt of a non taxable allowance represents a very simple solution to the problem. While records will have to be kept for the information needs of the employer, the employee has the advantage of simply ignoring the allowance and the related costs when it comes time to file a tax return. In real terms, however, the non taxable allowance approach may or may not be advantageous. If the employee's actual deductible costs exceed the allowance, a failure to include the allowance in income eliminates the deductibility of the additional costs. Alternatively, if the actual costs are less than the allowance, the employee has, in effect, received a tax free benefit.

Employee Insurance Benefits

Life Insurance

5-82.   The cost of providing life insurance benefits to employees is a taxable benefit. This means that any premiums paid on a life insurance policy by the employer must be included in employment income. As insurance services are exempt from GST, no GST amount would be included in this benefit.

Disability Insurance (a.k.a. Group Sickness Or Accident Insurance Plan)

5-83.   The normal situation here is one in which an employer pays all or part of the premiums on a group sickness or accident insurance plan. The contributions made by the employer to such group plans are not treated as a taxable benefit to the employee at the time that they are made. This exclusion from treatment as a taxable benefit is found in ITA 6(1)(a)(i) and is only applicable to group plans. If the plan is not a group plan, contributions by the employer must be treated as a taxable benefit to the employee.

5-84.   Any contributions made by the employee towards the premiums on the sickness or accident insurance plan are not deductible at the time they are made. This would be the case regardless of whether the employee was sharing the cost of the premiums with an employer or paying the entire cost of the premiums.

5-85.   The tax status of benefits received from a disability plan will depend on whether or not the employer has contributed to the plan. If the employer has made any contributions to the plan, even if the contributions were treated as a taxable benefit when they were made, benefits received by an employee must be included in employment income under ITA 6(1)(f). However, at this point any of the cumulative contributions made by the employee to the particular plan that is paying the benefits can be used to reduce the amount of this inclusion. This, of course, compensates for the fact that such employee contributions were not deductible at the time they were made.

5-86.   If the employer has not made any contributions to the plan, it is an employee pay all plan. As the employee's contributions to such plans were not deductible when they were made, it is appropriate that the benefits received are not treated as taxable income. Note, however, if the employer makes any contribution to the plan, it will taint the plan in the sense that all of the benefits received, reduced by accumulated employee contributions, will become taxable.

> **Example**   During the current year, the premiums on Jane Forthy's disability insurance plan totalled $1,600. As in previous years, one-half of this cost was paid by Jane's employer, with the balance paid by Jane. As the result of a car accident during the current year, Jane received disability benefits of $16,000. In previous years, Jane has contributed a total of $3,600 towards the disability insurance premiums.
>
> **Tax Consequences**   Jane's income inclusion for the current year would be $11,600 [$16,000 - (1/2)($1,600) - $3,600].

5-87.   As noted previously, insurance services are exempt from GST and no GST amount is associated with taxable benefits related to disability insurance.

Health Care Insurance

5-88.   Where an employer pays the individual premiums on Provincial or Government Of Canada health care plans, the amounts are considered taxable benefits of the employees. Where provincial health care is funded by an employer payroll tax or other general levy (e.g., Manitoba, Quebec, and Ontario) and there are no individual premiums, these payments are not allocated to employees as a taxable benefit.

> Exercise Five-6 deals with insurance benefits. This would be an appropriate time to attempt this exercise.

5-89.   Payments made for private health care plans, for instance a dental plan, are specifically excluded from treatment as a taxable benefit under IT-470R (Consolidated). The benefits received under such plans are not taxable and, in addition, any contributions made by the employee to such private health care plans can be treated as a medical expense eligible for a credit against taxes payable.

5-90.   As was the case with other types of insurance benefits, there is no GST amount associated with taxable health care benefits.

Loans To Employees
General Rules

5-91.   If an employer extends a loan to an employee and the interest rate is below the going market rate, the employee is clearly receiving a benefit which should be taxed. This view is reflected in ITA 80.4(1) which requires the assessment of a taxable benefit on all interest free or low interest loans to employees. This provision applies whether the loan is made as a consequence of prior, current, or future employment. The taxable benefit would be the imputed interest calculated at the prescribed rate specified in Regulation 4301, less any interest paid on the loan by the employee during the year or within 30 days of the end of the year. (See Chapter 2 for a discussion of the prescribed rate.)

Example On January 1 of the current year, Ms. Brooks Arden borrows $50,000 from her employer at an annual rate of one percent. Assume that the prescribed rate is 6 percent during the first two quarters, and 7 percent during the last two quarters of the year. Ms. Arden pays the required one percent interest on December 31.

Tax Consequences The taxable benefit to be included in Ms. Arden's net Employment Income would be calculated as follows:

Imputed Interest:	
Quarters I and II [(6%)($50,000)(2/4)]	$1,500
Quarters III and IV [(7%)($50,000)(2/4)]	1,750
Interest Paid [(1%)($50,000)]	(500)
Taxable Benefit	**$2,750**

In calculating the imputed interest, we have used the approach illustrated in IT-421R2 and treated each calendar quarter as one-quarter of the year. Other approaches could be used. ITA 80.4(1) does not require the use of interest calculations prorated on the number of days the loan is outstanding.

5-92. Several additional points should be made with respect to these loans:

- In this application of the prescribed rate, it does not include the extra two percent applicable to amounts that are due from the CCRA or the extra four percent on amounts owed to the CCRA.

- ITA 80.4(2) contains a different set of rules that are applicable to loans made to certain shareholders of a company. The different rules that are applicable to shareholders will be described in Chapter 11 when we discuss property income.

- A loan may be made to an employee for the purpose of investing in assets that produce business or property income. While interest actually paid on such loans would normally be deductible against the income produced, there could be some question as to whether this applies to interest that was imputed rather than actually paid. ITA 80.5 resolves this issue in favour of taxpayers by clearly stating the imputed interest benefits assessed under ITA 80.4(1) or 80.4(2) are deemed to be interest paid for purposes of determining net business or property income. Referring to the example in Paragraph 5-91, if Ms. Arden had invested the $50,000 loan proceeds in income producing assets, her deductible interest would total $3,250, the $500 that she paid plus the assessed $2,750 taxable benefit.

- When the purpose of the loan is to assist an employee with a home purchase or home relocation, ITA 80.4(4) indicates that the amount of interest used in the benefit calculations cannot exceed the amount determined using the rate in effect when the loan was extended. This provides a ceiling for the benefit and, at the same time, allows the taxpayer to benefit if the prescribed rate becomes lower. This ceiling on the benefit is only available for the first five years such loans are outstanding. ITA 80.4(6) indicates that, after this period of time, the loan will be deemed to be a new loan, making the calculation of the benefit subject to the prescribed rate in effect at this point in time.

Home Relocation Loans

5-93. If an employer provides a home purchase loan when an employee moves to a new work location, it is referred to as a home relocation loan if certain conditions are met. If this is an interest free or low interest loan, the ITA 80.4(1) rules apply as outlined in the preceding Section. However, in the case of a home relocation loan, there is an offsetting deduction. This deduction is equal to the benefit associated with an interest free home relocation loan of up to $25,000. In effect, the usual ITA 80.4(1) imputed interest benefit will be included in employment income, with an offsetting deduction provided in the calculation of Taxable Income. The deduction from Taxable Income is covered in Chapter 12.

GST Benefit

5-94.   There is no GST benefit on imputed interest on a low or no interest loan as it is considered an exempt supply of a financial service.

Tax Planning For Interest Free Loans

5-95.   With the exception of the $25,000 home relocation loan, the current tax rules result in a taxable benefit to the employee if the interest rate on the loan is lower than the market rate. Given this, the question arises as to whether the use of employee loans is a tax effective form of employee compensation. As with other types of benefits, the question is whether it is better that the employer supply the benefit or, alternatively, provide sufficient additional salary to allow the employee to acquire the benefit directly. In the case of loans, this additional salary would have to be sufficient to allow the employee to carry a similar loan at commercial rates.

5-96.   The answer to the question of whether or not employee loans are a tax effective form of compensation depends on several factors:

- The employer's rate of return on alternative uses for the funds.
- The employer's tax rate.
- The prescribed rate.
- The rate available to the employee on a similar arm's length loan.
- The employee's tax rate.

5-97.   A simple example will illustrate the type of analysis that is required to make decisions regarding the use of employee loans.

Example   In 2001, a key executive asks for a $100,000 interest free housing loan which does not qualify as a home relocation loan. At this time the employer has investment opportunities involving a rate of return of 15 percent before taxes. The prescribed rate is 6 percent while the rate for home mortgages is 7 percent. The employee is subject to a marginal tax rate of 48 percent, while the employer pays corporate taxes at a marginal rate of 40 percent.

5-98.   In the absence of the interest free loan, the employee would borrow $100,000 at 7 percent, requiring an annual interest payment of $7,000. The after tax cash flow associated with providing sufficient additional salary to carry this loan would be calculated as follows:

Required Salary [$7,000 ÷ (1.00 - .48)]	$13,462
Reduction In Corporate Taxes At 40 Percent	(5,385)
After Tax Cash Flow - Additional Salary	$ 8,077

5-99.   Alternatively, if the loan is provided, the employee will have a taxable benefit of $6,000 [(6%)($100,000)], resulting in taxes payable of $2,880 [(48%)($6,000)]. To make this situation comparable to the straight salary alternative, the employer will have to provide the executive with both the loan amount and sufficient additional salary to pay the taxes on the imputed interest benefit. The amount of this additional salary would be $5,538 [$2,880 ÷ (1.00 - .48)]. The employer's after tax cash flow associated with providing the additional salary and the loan amount would be calculated as follows:

Required Salary [$2,880 ÷ (1.00 - .48)]	$ 5,538
Reduction In Corporate Taxes At 40 Percent	(2,215)
After Tax Cost Of Salary	$ 3,323
After Tax Lost Earnings [(15%)(1.00 - .40)($100,000)]	9,000
After Tax Cash Flow - Loan	$12,323

Exercise Five-7 deals with loans to employees. This would be an appropriate time to attempt this exercise.

5-100.   Given these results, payment of additional salary appears to be the better alternative. However, the preceding simple example is not a complete analysis of the situation. Other factors, such as the employee's ability to borrow at going rates or the ability to grant this salary increase in the context of other salary policies, would also have to be considered.

Stock Option Plans
Employment Income Inclusion

5-101.   A stock option is a contractual arrangement which allows the holder to acquire a specified number of shares for a specified period of time at a specified price. While corporations use them in a variety of ways, sometimes with different terminology (warrants and rights are essentially option arrangements), our concern here is with the options that are issued by corporations to their employees.

5-102.   A typical arrangement would be to grant options to some defined group of employees, allowing them to purchase the common shares of the company at a price of $10 per share. Normally, the fair market value of the shares at this time would be $10 or less, creating a situation in which the options will not be exercised unless the trading value of the common shares improves. The basic idea here is that the granting of the options provides an incentive to the employees to make efforts that will improve the share performance of the corporation. They will benefit from such activity through an enhanced value for the options which they hold while, at the same time, the shareholders of the corporation will benefit from higher market values for the shares.

5-103.   While options that are "not in the money" (i.e., the option price is equal to or greater than the market value of the shares) do, in fact, have value, neither accountants nor tax people have found an acceptable basis for measuring this value (for a more complete explanation of this point, see our discussion of the economics of option arrangements in Chapter 12). As a consequence, the granting of options is not recognized in the accounting records of the issuing corporation. Similarly, there are no tax consequences associated with the issuance of such options, either to the grantor or the employee.

5-104.   While there are not tax consequences associated with the granting of options, there is an employment income inclusion that is measured at the time the options are exercised. This inclusion is equal to the excess of the fair market value of the shares on the exercise date over the option price, multiplied by the number of shares acquired by the option holder.

> **Example**   On January 1, 2001, Notell Inc. grants options to buy 5,000 shares to Jean Rath. The option price is $15 per share and, at this time, the shares are trading at $15 per share. On December 1, 2001, when the shares are trading are $22 per share, Mr. Rath exercises all of the options.
>
> **Tax Consequences**   An employment income benefit will be measured at this point. The amount will be $35,000 [(5,000)($22 - $15)]. As per the discussion which follows, this may or may not have immediate tax consequences for Mr. Rath.

5-105.   You will have noticed that we have referred to the employment income inclusion being "measured" on the exercise date. It may or may not be included in the taxpayer's employment income at that time:

> **Canadian Controlled Private Corporation (CCPC)**   If the granting corporation is a CCPC, the employment income benefit will be measured at the exercise date. However, its inclusion in the employee's income will be deferred until such time as the shares are sold.
>
> **Public Corporation**   If the shares of the granting corporation are those of a publicly traded company, the general rule is that the employment income benefit will be measured and included in employment income at the time the options are exercised. However, new legislation provides for a deferral of the income inclusion on up to $100,000 of the shares, if the individual acquiring the shares makes the appropriate election. The $100,000 figure is based on the number of shares acquired, measured by their market value at the time the options were granted. The deferral is effective until such time as the shares are sold.

Other Factors

5-106.   The preceding paragraphs provide a description of the procedures required in dealing with the employment income inclusion resulting from the exercise of stock options. However, there are a number of complicating factors associated with these arrangements:

- There is a deduction that may be available in the calculation of Taxable Income. The amount of the deduction varies from one-quarter of the employment income inclusion to one-half of the employment income inclusion, depending on the year of exercise.

- The measurement of the employment income benefit changes the adjusted cost base of the shares, in turn influencing the measurement of future capital gains on the disposition of the shares.

- There are special rules related to the determination of the adjusted cost base on shares acquired through stock options.

5-107.　In previous editions of the text, we have tried to deal with these additional issues in this Chapter, despite the fact that some of the required concepts are not introduced until later Chapters. However, changes included in the 2000 budget have made the discussion of these matters much more complex. Given this, along with the problems we have experienced in teaching stock option material at this point in a course, we have concluded that it would be best to deal with this material comprehensively in Chapter 12, "Taxable Income For Individuals". As a result, our detailed treatment of stock options has been moved to Chapter 12.

> Exercises Five-8 and Five-9 deal with stock options. This would be an appropriate time to attempt these exercises.

5-108.　As a result of this change, the problem material in this Chapter will only deal with the calculation of the employment income inclusion. It will include examples of options granted by both CCPCs and publicly traded companies. However, the election to defer the employment income inclusion for publicly traded shares will not be dealt with in the problem material for this Chapter.

Other Inclusions

Payments By Employer To Employee

5-109.　ITA 6(3) covers any other form of payments from employer to employee. This includes payments for accepting employment, remuneration for services, and payments for work to be completed subsequent to the termination of employment. The Subsection requires that all such amounts be included in employment income.

Forgiveness Of Employee Loans

5-110.　There may be circumstances in which an employer decides to forgive a loan that has been extended to an employee. Not surprisingly, ITA 6(15) requires that the forgiven amount be included in the income of the employee in the year in which the forgiveness occurs. The forgiven amount is simply the amount due, less any payments that are made by the employee.

Housing Loss Reimbursement Under ITA 6(19)

5-111.　When an employee is required to move, employers often provide various types of financial assistance. As will be discussed in Chapter 11, an employer can pay for the usual costs of moving (e.g., shipping company costs) without tax consequence to the employee. In recent years, particularly when an employee is moved from an area with a weak housing market, it has become more common for employers to reimburse individuals for losses incurred in the disposition of their principal residence.

5-112.　Initially this type of reimbursement was allowed, with no limits on the amount that could be received by the employee on a tax free basis. However, the current rules limit the amount of housing loss that can be reimbursed without tax consequence. This is accomplished in ITA 6(20) by indicating that one-half of any amount received in excess of $15,000 must be included in the employee's income as a taxable benefit. Stated alternatively, the tax free amount is limited to the first $15,000, plus one-half of any amount paid in excess of $15,000. Note that, unless an eligible relocation is involved (see the rules for this in Chapter 11's discussion of moving expenses), any amount received as employer reimbursement for a housing loss will be treated as a taxable benefit.

Discounts On Employer's Merchandise

5-113.　When an employee is allowed to purchase merchandise which is ordinarily sold by an employer, any discount given to the employee is not generally considered to be a taxable benefit. If discounts are extended by a group of employers, or if an employer only extends the discounts to a particular group of employees, a taxable benefit may arise. This may also be true in the construction industry where attempts have been made to assess employees for the difference between their purchase price and the fair market value of houses purchased from employers who are builders. The CCRA has also indicated that, in the case of airline employees, a benefit is assessed if the employee travels on a space confirmed basis and pays less than 50 percent of the economy fare. The benefit is the difference between 50 percent of the economy fare and the amount paid.

5-114.   When a benefit must be included in income as the result of merchandise discounts, it will include any GST that is applicable to these amounts.

Club Dues And Recreational Facilities

5-115.   With respect to employer provided recreational facilities, IT-470R (Consolidated) notes that they are not considered a taxable benefit to the employee. In the case of employers paying membership fees in social or recreational clubs, the IT Bulletin indicates that as long as the facilities are used to the advantage of the employer, they would not be considered a taxable benefit to the employee. While this would seem to indicate that such fees do become a taxable benefit unless they are used primarily to further the business interests of the employer, the CCRA has not pursued this approach with any rigour. As a consequence, employer payments for social or recreational club memberships generally do not result in a taxable benefit to the employee. As noted previously, the attractiveness of this type of employee benefit is reduced by the fact that, in general, employers cannot deduct the cost of club dues or recreational facilities in the determination of business income.

Employer Paid Tuition Fees

5-116.   It would appear that the CCRA has not been consistent in its treatment of tuition fees paid by an employer. In some cases, particularly when the employer did not include the amount on the employee's T4, the amount was not treated as a taxable benefit to the employee. However, other cases were treated differently. In a situation which received considerable media attention, the Regina based steel maker IPSCO asked one of its employees to attend an executive MBA program at the University Of Pittsburgh. The CCRA assessed the employee, not only for the $30,000 course tuition, but for employer provided travel costs as well.

5-117.   As a result of this and other cases, the Department reviewed its guidelines in this area and published its conclusions in Technical News No. 13 (May 7, 1998). The guideline describes three situations as follows:

> **Specific Employer Related Training**   When it is reasonable to assume that the employee will resume his or her employment after completion of the courses, employer funded courses taken for maintenance or upgrading of employer related skills will not be viewed as a taxable benefit.

> **General Employment Related Training**   Courses which are business related, even through not specifically related to the employer's business, will not result in a taxable benefit. Examples provided include stress management, first aid, and language skills.

> **Personal Interest Training**   Employer funded courses that are not business related and taken primarily for the employee's personal interest will be treated as a taxable benefit to the employee.

5-118.   The Release also indicates that employees who have their tuition fees paid for or reimbursed by their employer will not be entitled to claim the tuition fee tax credit or the education amount credit.

Specific Deductions

General Approach

5-119.   The various classes of items that can be deducted in the determination of net employment income are listed in ITA 8. For many employees, the most important of these deductions is in ITA 8(1)(m), employee's registered pension plan contributions. These contributions are deducted in the determination of employment income as an individual must be an employee to be a member of such a plan. However, registered pension plans represent only one type of tax sheltered retirement savings. As a consequence, the discussion of this deduction under ITA 8(1)(m) will be deferred to the next Chapter which will give comprehensive coverage of all types of retirement savings vehicles.

5-120.   The other deductions in the determination of employment income that will be dealt with in this Chapter were listed in the discussion of allowances. Before proceeding to more detailed coverage of these items, we remind you that when any of these costs are covered by an allowance from an employer, the costs cannot be deducted by the employee unless the related allowance is included in the employee's income.

Salesperson's Expenses Under ITA 8(1)(f)

5-121.   Individual employees who are involved with the selling of property or the negotiation of contracts are permitted to deduct all expenses that can be considered necessary to the performance of their duties. Items that can be deducted under this provision include:

- Advertising and promotion
- Meals and entertainment (50 percent limit)
- Lodging
- Motor vehicle costs
- Parking (not a motor vehicle expense)
- Supplies (including long distance telephone calls and cellular phone airtime, but not the basic monthly charge for a telephone or amounts paid to connect or licence a cellular phone)
- Licences (e.g., for real estate sales)
- Bonding and liability insurance premiums
- Medical fees (life insurance sales)
- Computers and office equipment (leased only)
- Salary to assistant or substitute
- Office rent
- Training costs
- Transportation costs
- Work space in home (maintenance, property taxes, and insurance — no mortgage interest or depreciation)
- Legal fees to collect wages

5-122.   Except in the case of an automobile, aircraft or musical instrument, an employee cannot deduct capital cost allowances (i.e., tax depreciation). This means that if a salesperson purchases a computer to maintain sales records, he will not be able to deduct capital cost allowance on it. Alternatively, if the computer is leased, the lease payments can be deducted.

5-123.   In order to deduct the cost of meals, the salesperson must be away from the municipality or metropolitan area where the employer's establishment is located for at least 12 hours. As is the case in the determination of business income, no deduction is permitted for membership fees for clubs or recreational facilities. A salesperson is permitted to deduct motor vehicle costs and the cost of maintaining an office in his home. However, these costs can also be deducted by other types of employees and, as a consequence, will be dealt with in later sections of this Chapter.

5-124.   As stated in ITA 8(1)(f), to be eligible to deduct salesperson's expenses, all of the following conditions must be met:

1. The salesperson must be required to pay his own expenses. The employer must sign form T2200 certifying that this is the case. While the form does not have to be filed, it must be available if requested by the CCRA.

2. The salesperson must be ordinarily required to carry on his duties away from the employer's place of business.

3. The salesperson must not be in receipt of an expense allowance that was not included in income.

4. The salesperson must receive at least part of his remuneration in the form of commissions or by reference to the volume of sales.

5-125. The amount of qualifying expenses that can be deducted is limited to the commissions or other sales related revenues earned for the year. This limitation does not, however, apply to capital cost allowance or interest on a motor vehicle, aircraft or musical instrument which are deductible under ITA 8(1)(j). These costs can be deducted even when they exceed commission income and can be applied against other types of employment income.

5-126. When the expenses that are deductible under ITA 8(1)(f) exceed commission income, it may be advantageous for a salesperson to claim expenses under other provisions that are not subject to the commission income limitation. Traveling expenses are deductible for all employees under ITA 8(1)(h) and motor vehicle costs are deductible for all employees under ITA 8(1)(h.1). In addition, many of the other costs listed in Paragraph 5-140 can be deducted under ITA 8(1)(i). This would include legal fees to collect wages, supplies, salaries to an assistant or substitute, office rent, and the cost of a workspace in the home.

5-127. Note that all of these provisions cannot be used simultaneously to maximize the deductions. If a deduction is made under ITA 8(1)(f), no deduction can be made under ITA 8(1)(h) or (h.1) for travel or automobile expenses. However, deductions under ITA 8(1)(i) and (j) can be combined with deductions under ITA 8(1)(f).

5-128. This creates a fairly complex situation for commission salespeople. If they deduct under ITA 8(1)(f), the amount is limited to commissions earned. As this may be less than the amount that can be deducted using a combination of ITA 8(1)(h) and (h.1), they may wish to use this latter alternative. However, if they do choose this alternative, they will lose deductions for such things as advertising and entertainment costs that are deductible under ITA 8(1)(f). It is difficult to understand the need for such a complex solution to this problem.

Traveling Expenses And Motor Vehicle Costs

5-129. ITA 8(1)(h) provides for the deduction of such traveling costs as accommodation, airline or rail tickets, taxi fares, and meals. As was the case with salespersons' expenses, only 50 percent of the cost of meals is deductible. Here again, the deductibility of meals is conditional on being away from the municipality or metropolitan area in which the employer's establishment is located for at least 12 hours. ITA 8(1)(h.1) provides for the deduction of motor vehicle costs when an employee uses his own vehicle to carry out employment duties.

5-130. The availability of these deductions is not limited to salespersons. They can be claimed by any employee who meets specified criteria. Further, they are effectively not limited by employment income. They can be used to create a net employment loss which, if not usable against other types of income in the current year, is subject to the usual carry over provisions for non capital losses.

5-131. As we have noted, a salesperson can make deductions under these two paragraphs only if no deduction is made under ITA 8(1)(f). This means that a salesperson will have to determine whether the deduction will be greater under ITA 8(1)(f) where a wider range of items can be deducted, or under ITA 8(1)(h) and (h.1) where there is no overall limit on the amount that can be deducted.

5-132. The conditions for deducting expenses under ITA 8(1)(h) and (h.1) are similar to those for deductions under ITA 8(1)(f), except that there is no requirement that some part of the employee's remuneration be in the form of commissions. The conditions are as follows:

1. The person must be required to pay his own travel and motor vehicle costs. As was the case with commission salespersons, the employee must have form T2200, signed by the employer, certifying that this is the case.

2. The person must be ordinarily required to carry on his duties away from the employer's place of business.

3. The person must not be in receipt of an allowance for travel costs that was not included in income.

Automobile Expenses

5-133.   Under either ITA 8(1)(f) and ITA 8(1)(h.1) an employee can deduct the costs of an automobile used in employment duties. With respect to operating costs, this would include an appropriate share (based on the portion of employment related kilometers included in total kilometers driven) of such costs as fuel, maintenance, normal repair costs, insurance, and licensing fees.

5-134.   Unlike other capital assets used in employment activities, under ITA 8(1)(j) an employee can deduct capital cost allowance (tax depreciation) and interest costs on an automobile that is used in these activities (this provision also applies to aircraft). The deductible amounts are calculated in the same manner as they would be for a business. Capital cost allowance would be calculated on a 30 percent declining balance basis and interest would be based on actual amounts paid. However, there are limits on the amounts that can be deducted here for business purposes, and these limits are equally applicable to the calculation of employment income deductions.

5-135.   While these limits are discussed more completely in Chapter 7 on Business Income, we would note that for 2001 there is no deduction for capital cost allowance on the cost of an automobile in excess of $30,000 (up from $27,000 in 2000), that deductible interest is limited to $300 per month (up from $250 in 2000), and that deductible lease payments are limited to $800 per month (up from $700 per month in 2000). The employee's deduction would be based on the fraction of these costs, subject to the preceding limits, that reflects the portion of employment related kilometers included in total kilometers driven.

Other Expenses Of Performing Duties - ITA 8(1)(i)

5-136.   ITA 8(1)(i) contains a list of other items that can be deducted in the determination of employment income. The major items included here are as follows:

- Annual professional membership dues, the payment of which was necessary to maintain a professional status recognized by statute.

- Union dues that are paid pursuant to the provisions of a collective agreement.

- Office rent and salary paid to an assistant or a substitute. In order to deduct these amounts, the employee must be required to incur the costs under a contract of employment. This must be supported by form T2200, signed by the employer and certifying that the requirement exists. This would include deducting the costs associated with an office in the employee's home (see next section).

- The cost of supplies consumed in the performance of employment duties. Here again, the employee must be required to provide these supplies under his employment contract and this contract must be supported by form T2200.

Home Office Costs

5-137.   We have noted that salespersons can deduct the costs associated with an office in their home under ITA 8(1)(f), and that any employee who is required by his employment contract to maintain an office can make a similar deduction under ITA 8(1)(i). Because of the obvious potential for abuse in this area, ITA 8(13) establishes fairly restrictive conditions with respect to the availability of this deduction. Under the provisions of this Subsection, costs of a home office are only deductible when the work space is either:

- the place where the individual principally performs the duties of the office or employment, or

- used exclusively during the period in respect of which the amount relates for the purpose of earning income from the office or employment and used on a regular and continuous basis for meeting customers or other persons in the ordinary course of performing the duties of the office or employment.

5-138. Once it is established that home office costs are deductible, it becomes necessary to determine what kind of costs can be deducted. We have noted previously that, for employees, the only assets on which capital cost allowance and interest can be deducted are automobiles, aircraft and musical instruments. This means that no employee can deduct capital cost allowance or mortgage interest as it relates to an office that is maintained in their residence. With respect to other costs, IT-352R2 indicates that an employee making a deduction under ITA 8(1)(i) can deduct an appropriate portion (based on floor space used for the office) of maintenance costs such as fuel and electricity, light bulbs, cleaning materials, and minor repairs.

5-139. For salespersons making a deduction for a home office under ITA 8(1)(f), IT-352R2 indicates that they can deduct all of the preceding items, plus an appropriate portion of property taxes and house insurance premiums.

5-140. If the home office is in rented property, the percentage of rent and any maintenance costs paid related to the home office are deductible.

5-141. The amount deductible for home office costs is limited to employment income after the deduction of all other employment expenses. Stated alternatively, home office costs cannot be used to create or increase an employment loss. Only the income related to the use of the home office can be included in this calculation. Any home office costs that are not deductible in a year can be carried forward to the following year. They become part of the home office costs for that year and, to the extent that this total cannot be deducted in that year, the balance can be carried forward to the next following year. This, in effect, provides an indefinite carry over of these costs.

> Exercise Five-10 deals with employee expenses. This would be an appropriate time to attempt this exercise.

Employee And Partner GST Rebate

5-142. Many of the expenses employees can deduct against employment income include a GST component. If the individual was a GST registrant earning business income, these GST payments would generate input tax credits. However, employment is not considered to be a commercial activity and, as a consequence, employees who have no separate commercial activity cannot be registrants. This means that they will not be able to use the usual input tax credit procedure to obtain a refund of GST amounts paid with respect to their employment expenses . A similar analysis applies to partners who have partnership related expenses that are not included in partnership net income or loss.

5-143. The Employee and Partner GST Rebate allows employees and partners to recover the GST paid on their employment or partnership related expenses, including vehicles and musical instruments, in a way which is similar to the input tax credit that they would have received if they were GST registrants. Form GST370 is used to claim the GST rebate and is filed with the employee or partner's tax return.

5-144. To qualify for this rebate the individual must either be an employee of a GST registrant or a member of a partnership that is a GST registrant. Employees of financial institutions are not eligible for the rebate. However, employees of charities, not-for-profit organizations, universities, school boards, and municipalities are eligible as long as the organizations that they work for are registered. In addition, employees of provincial governments, Crown corporations, and the federal government qualify for the rebate. To claim the rebate the individual must have unreimbursed expenses that are eligible for income tax deductions against employment or partnership income.

5-145. The following simple example illustrates the calculation of the GST rebate for an employee:

Example Tanya Kucharik, a very successful sales manager, used her car 93 percent for employment related purposes during 2001. She claimed the following expenses on Form T777, Statement of Employment Expenses, for 2001:

Cellular phone charges	$ 1,200
Gas, maintenance and car repairs (93%)	17,500
Insurance on car (93%)	1,023
CCA on car (93%)	3,100

GST Consequences On Form GST370, her GST rebate would be as follows:

	Expenses	GST Rebate (7/107)
Eligible Expenses Other Than CCA	$18,700	$1,223
Eligible CCA On Which 7% GST Was Paid	3,100	203
Totals	$21,800	$1,426

5-146. Eligible expenses exclude expenses for which a non taxable allowance was received, zero-rated and exempt supplies, supplies acquired outside Canada, supplies acquired from non registrants and expenses incurred when the employer was a non registrant. In this example, the car insurance is excluded as it is an exempt supply on which no GST was charged. The expenses claimed are GST included amounts. The GST rebate is calculated by applying 7/107 to eligible expenses.

5-147. The related expenses that are listed in this calculation will be deducted in Ms. Kucharik's income tax return for 2001. As a consequence, the rebate is normally claimed in the return in which the expenses are deducted. The rebate can be claimed in any income tax return submitted within four years of the year in which the expenses are claimed. The rebate on expenses other than CCA will have to be included in income for income tax purposes in the year in which it is received. Any rebates related to CCA will be deducted from the capital cost of the relevant asset in the year in which it is received. This means that the rebate for 2001 expenses will be claimed in Ms. Kucharik's 2001 tax return. The amount claimed would normally be received in 2002 either as part of the 2001 refund or as a decrease in the amount owed for 2001. The amount received for expenses other than CCA ($1,223) will be included in other employment income on the 2002 tax return, and the amount received for CCA ($203), will be deducted from the undepreciated capital cost of the car in 2002.

References

5-148. For more detailed study of the material in this Chapter, we would refer you to the following:

ITA 5	Income From Office Or Employment
ITA 6	Amounts To Be Included As Income From Office Or Employment
ITA 7	Agreement To Issue Securities To Employees
ITA 8	Deductions Allowed
ITA 80.4	Loans
ITA 80.5	Deemed Interest
ITR 4301	Interest Rates [Prescribed Rate Of Interest]
IC 73-21R7	Away From Home Expenses
IT-63R5	Benefits, Including Standby Charge For An Automobile, From The Personal Use Of A Motor Vehicle Supplied By An Employer - After 1992
IT-85R2	Health And Welfare Trusts For Employees
IT-91R4	Employment At Special Or Remote Work Locations
IT-99R5	Legal And Accounting Fees
IT-103R	Dues Paid To A Union Or To A Parity Or Advisory Committee
IT-113R4	Benefits To Employees - Stock Options
IT-158R2	Employees' Professional Membership Dues
IT-196R2	Payments By Employer To Employee
IT-202R2	Employees' Or Workers' Compensation
IT-227R	Group Term Life Insurance Premiums
IT-316	Awards For Employees' Suggestions And Inventions
IT-352R2	Employee's Expenses, Including Work Space in Home Expenses
IT-377R	Director's, Executor's Or Juror's Fees
IT-389R	Vacation Pay Trusts Established Under Collective Agreements
IT-421R2	Benefits To Individuals, Corporations And Shareholders From Loans Or Debt
IT-428	Wage Loss Replacement Plans
IT-470R (Consolidated)	Employees' Fringe Benefits
IT-504R2	Visual Artists And Writers
IT-514	Work Space In Home Expenses
IT-518R	Food, Beverages And Entertainment Expenses
IT-522R	Vehicle, Travel and Sales Expenses of Employees
IT-525R	Performing Artists
RC4110	Tax Pamphlet - Employee Or Self Employed

Exercises

(The solutions for these exercises can be found following Chapter 21 of the text.)

Exercise Five - 1 (Bonus)
Neelson Inc. has a September 30 year end. On September 30, 2001, it declares a bonus of $100,000 payable to Mr. Sam Neelson, an executive of the Company. The bonus is payable on May 1, 2002. Describe the tax consequences of this bonus to both Neelson Inc. and Mr. Neelson.

Exercise Five - 2 (Taxable Benefits)
Ms. Vicki Correli, as the result of winning a sales contest with her organization, is awarded a two week vacation in the Bahamas. Her employer pays a travel agent $4,500 plus 7 percent GST for the trip. What is the amount of Ms. Correli's taxable benefit?

Exercise Five - 3 (Taxable Benefits - Automobile)
Mrs. Tanya Lee is provided with an automobile by her employer. The cost of the car to the employer was $25,000 plus $1,750 GST and $2,000 PST. During 2001, she drives the automobile a total of 28,000 kilometers, 24,000 of which were related to employment duties. The automobile is available to Mrs. Lee throughout the year. Calculate Mrs. Lee's 2001 taxable benefit for the use of the automobile.

Exercise Five - 4 (Taxable Benefits - Automobile)
Mr. Michael Forthwith is provided with an automobile that is leased by his employer. The lease payments for the year total $7,245 ($6,300 + $441 GST and $504 PST). During 2001, Mr. Forthwith drives the automobile a total of 40,000 kilometers, of which 37,000 kilometres are employment related. The automobile is available to him for 325 days during the year. Calculate Mr. Forthwith's 2001 taxable benefit for the use of the automobile.

Exercise Five - 5 (Deductible Automobile Costs)
Ms. Lauren Giacomo is required by her employer to use her own automobile in her work. To compensate her, she is paid an annual allowance of $3,600. During 2001, she drove her automobile a total of 24,000 kilometers, of which 6,500 were employment related. Her total automobile costs for the year, including capital cost allowance (i.e., tax depreciation), are $7,150. What amounts will Ms. Giacomo include and deduct from 2001 Employment Income?

Exercise Five - 6 (Disability Insurance Benefits)
Mr. Lance Bardwell is a member of a group disability plan sponsored by his employer. During 2001, his employer's share of the annual premium was $1,800. Beginning in 2000, Mr. Bardwell was required to contribute $300 per year to this plan. The 2000 and 2001 contributions were withheld from his wages by his employer. During 2001, Mr. Bardwell was incapacitated for a period of six weeks and received $5,250 in benefits under the plan. What amount will Mr. Bardwell include in his 2001 Employment Income?

Exercise Five - 7 (Housing Loan)
On January 1, 2001, Mrs. Caldwell receives a $25,000 loan from her employer to assist her in purchasing a home. The loan requires annual interest at a rate of 1 percent which she pays on December 31, 2001. Assume that the relevant prescribed rate is 4 percent during the first quarter of 2001, 5 percent during the second quarter and 3 percent during the remainder of the year. What is the amount of Mrs. Caldwell's taxable benefit on this loan for the year?

Exercise Five - 8 (Stock Option Benefits)

Ms. Meridee Masterson is employed by a large public company. In 1999, she was granted options to acquire 1,000 shares of her employer's common stock at a price of $23 per share. At the time the options were granted, the shares were trading at $20 per share. Early in 2001, when the shares are trading at $45 per share, she exercises her options and acquires 1,000 shares which she plans on holding for at least three years. As Ms. Masterson is taking unpaid leave for 10 months to pursue her passion for accounting courses, she does not make an election to defer the employment income benefit. Calculate the employment income that will be included in Ms. Masterson's Net Income for 2001 as a result of the stock options.

Exercise Five - 9 (Stock Option Benefits)

How would your answer to Exercise Five - 8 differ if Ms. Masterson's employer was a Canadian controlled private company?

Exercise Five - 10 (Commission Salesperson Expenses)

Mr. Morton McMaster is a commission salesperson. During 2001, his gross salary was $82,000 and he earned $12,200 in commissions. During the year he had advertising costs of $8,000 and expenditures for entertainment of clients of $12,000. His travel costs for the year totalled $13,100. He is required to pay his own expenses and does not receive any allowance from his employer. What is Mr. McMaster's maximum expense deduction for 2001?

Problems For Self Study

(The solutions for these problems can be found following Chapter 21 of the text.)

Self Study Problem Five - 1

Ms. Tamira Vines is a salesperson for Compudata Ltd., a Regina based software Company which is a GST registrant. As her work requires her to travel extensively throughout southern and central Saskatchewan, the Company provides her with an automobile.

From January 1, 2001 through May 31, 2001, the Company provided her with a Toyota Camry. This car was purchased by the Company on January 1, 2001 at a cost of $39,000 plus $3,120 in provincial sales tax and $2,730 in GST. During the period January 1, 2001 through May 31, 2001, the car was driven 38,800 kilometers for employment related purposes and 3,400 kilometers for personal use. The Company paid all operating costs during the period, an amount of $3,376 plus $160 in provincial sales tax and $140 in GST.

On June 1, 2001, following a late evening sales conference at the Shangri La Hotel in Moose Jaw, Ms. Vines was involved in an accident in which the Toyota was destroyed. Ms. Vines was hospitalized and was not able to return to work until July 1, 2001. Compudata's insurance company paid $27,500 to the Company for the loss of the car.

When she returned to work on July 1, 2001, the Company provided Ms. Vines with a Ford Taurus. The Company leased this vehicle at a monthly cost of $625 per month, plus provincial sales tax of $42 and $37 in GST. The total monthly charge of $704 includes a $100 per month charge for insurance. For the period July 1, 2001 through December 31, 2001, operating costs, other than insurance, totaled $3,456. These were paid for by the Company. During this period, Ms. Vines drove the car 15,600 kilometers for business and 14,600 kilometers for personal use.

Ms. Vines paid to the Company $0.10 per kilometer for the personal use of the cars owned or leased by the Company for the year.

Required: Calculate the taxable car benefit that will be included in Ms. Vines' employment income for the year ending December 31, 2001. Include any GST benefit in your calculations.

Self Study Problem Five - 2

During the current year, the Carstair Manufacturing Company provides automobiles for four of its senior executives with the value of the cars being in proportion to the salaries which they receive. While each of the individuals uses their car for employment related travel, they also have the vehicles available to them for personal use. The portion of personal use varies considerably among the four individuals. The details related to each of these cars, including the amount of personal and business travel recorded by the executives, is as follows:

Mr. Sam Stern Mr. Stern is the president of the Company and is provided with a Mercedes which has been purchased by the Company at a cost of $78,000. The car was new last year and, during the current year, it was driven a total of 38,000 kilometers. Of this total, only 6,000 kilometers were for employment related purposes while the remaining 32,000 were for personal travel. Operating costs totaled $.50 per kilometer and, because Mr. Stern made an extended trip outside of North America, the car was only available to Mr. Stern for eight months during the current year. The car and its keys were left with the Company during the duration of Mr. Stern's trip.

Ms. Sarah Blue Ms. Blue is the vice president in charge of marketing and has been provided with a Corvette. The Company leases this vehicle at a cost of $900 per month. During the current year, the car was driven a total of 60,000 kilometers with all but 5,000 of these kilometers being for employment related purposes. The car was available to Ms. Blue throughout the current year and total annual operating costs amount to $18,000.

Mr. John Stack Mr. Stack is the vice president in charge of finance and he has been provided with an Acura which was purchased by the Company in the preceding year at a cost of $48,000. During the current year, Mr. Stack drove the car 42,000 kilometers for employment related purposes and 10,000 kilometers for personal travel. Operating costs for the year were $20,800 and the car was available to Mr. Stack throughout the current year. In order to reduce his taxable benefit, Mr. Stack made a payment of $8,000 to the Company for the use of this car.

Mr. Alex Decker Mr. Decker, the Vice President in charge of industrial relations, chose to drive an Accord. This car was leased by the Company at a cost of $500 per month. The lease payment was significantly reduced by the fact that the Company made a refundable deposit of $10,000 to the leasing Company at the inception of the lease. During the current year, Mr. Decker drove the car 90,000 kilometers for employment related purposes and 8,500 kilometers for personal use. The operating costs were $0.35 per kilometer and, because of an extended illness, he was only able to use the car for the first 10 months during the year. He left the car and its keys with his employer during his illness.

Required: Calculate the minimum amount of the taxable benefit for the current year that will accrue to each of these executives as the result of having the cars supplied by the Company. In making these calculations, ignore GST and PST considerations. From the point of view of tax planning for management compensation, provide any suggestions for the Carstair Manufacturing Company with respect to these cars.

Self Study Problem Five - 3

Mr. Thomas Malone is employed by Technocratic Ltd. in a management position. Because of an outstanding performance in his division of the Company, he is about to receive a promotion accompanied by a large increase in compensation. He is discussing various possible ways in which his compensation might be increased without incurring the same amount of taxation as would be assessed on an increase in his salary. As he is currently in the process of acquiring a large new residence in a prestigious neighbourhood, he has suggested that it might be advantageous for the Company to provide him with a five year interest free loan in the amount of $200,000 as part of any increase in compensation. Other relevant information is as follows:

- Given Mr. Malone's present salary, any other income will be taxed at 45 percent.
- Technocratic Ltd. is able to invest funds at a before tax rate of 18 percent. It is subject to taxation at a 40 percent rate.
- Assume the current rate for five year mortgages on residential properties is 9 percent.
- Assume the current Regulation 4301 rate for imputing interest on various tax related balances is 7 percent.
- The loan would not qualify as a home relocation loan.

Required: Evaluate Mr. Malone's suggestion of providing him with an interest free loan in lieu of salary from the point of view of cost to the Company.

Self Study Problem Five - 4

For the last three years, Sam Jurgens has been employed in Halifax as a loan supervisor for Maritime Trust Inc. Maritime Trust is a large public company and, as a consequence, Mr. Jurgens felt that he did not have the opportunity to exhibit the full range of his abilities. To correct this situation, Sam decided to accept employment in Toronto effective July 1, 2001 as the general manager of Bolten Financial Services, a Canadian controlled private corporation specializing in providing financial advice to retired executives.

In January, 2001, prior to leaving Maritime Trust, Mr. Jurgens exercised options to purchase 5,000 shares of the public company's stock at a price of $15 per share. At the time that he exercised this option, the shares were trading at $16 per share. He did not make an election to defer the income inclusion. On February 10, 2002 he sold these shares at a price of $8 per share.

Mr. Jurgens had an annual salary at Maritime Trust of $65,000, while in his new position in Toronto, the salary was $50,000 per year. However, he has the option of acquiring 1,000 shares per year of Bolten stock at a price of $20 per share. On July 1, when he was granted the option, Bolten stock had a fair market value of $14 per share. On December 1, 2001, when the Bolten stock has a fair market value of $22 per share, Mr. Jurgens exercises this option and acquires 1,000 shares. It is his intent to hold these shares for an indefinite period of time.

Because there is extensive travel involved in the position with Bolten Financial Services, the Company has provided Mr. Jurgens with a $25,000 company car. Between July 1 and December 31, 2001, Mr. Jurgens drove this car a total of 25,000 km., of which 15,000 km. were clearly related to his work with Bolten Financial Services. The operating costs associated with the car for this period, all of which were paid for by the Company, amount to $5,000. Because of extensive repairs resulting from a manufacturer's recall, the car was not available to Mr. Jurgens during October and November of 2001.

At the time of his move to Toronto, Bolten Financial Services provided Mr. Jurgens with a $100,000 home relocation loan to purchase a personal residence near the center of town. No interest was charged on this loan.

During the year, Mr. Jurgens earned $15,000 in interest, and received $45,000 in dividends from taxable Canadian corporations.

Required: Compute Sam Jurgens' income from an office or employment for the year ending December 31, 2001. Assume the relevant Regulation 4301 rate (not including the extra two or four percent) is 6 percent.

Self Study Problem Five - 5

Mr. John Barth has been employed for many years as a graphic illustrator in Kamloops, British Columbia. His employer is a large publicly traded Canadian company. During 2001, his gross salary was $82,500. In addition, he was awarded a $20,000 bonus to reflect his outstanding performance during the year. As he was in no immediate need of additional income, he arranged with his employer that none of this bonus would be paid until 2006, the year of his expected retirement.

Other Information:

For the 2001 taxation year, the following items were relevant.

1. Mr. Barth's employer withheld the following amounts from his income:

Federal and provincial income taxes	$32,400
United Way donations	2,000
Registered pension plan contributions	3,200
Payments for personal use of company car	3,600

2. During the year, Mr. Barth is provided with an automobile owned by his employer. The cost of the automobile was $27,500. Mr. Barth drove the car a total of 10,000 kilometers during the year, of which only 4,000 kilometers related to the business of his employer. The automobile was available to Mr. Barth for 10 months of the year. During the other two months, he was out of the country and left the automobile with one of the other employees of the corporation.

3. During the year, the corporation paid Mega Financial Planners a total of $1,500 for providing counseling services to Mr. Barth with respect to his personal financial situation.

4. In order to assist Mr. Barth in diversifying his investment portfolio, the corporation provided him with a five year loan of $75,000. The loan was granted on October 1. Assume that, at the time the loan was granted, the relevant prescribed rate was 6 percent. Mr. Barth paid the corporation a total of $375 in interest during the year.

5. Mr. Barth was required to pay professional dues of $1,800 during the year.

Required: Calculate Mr. Barth's net employment income for the year ending December 31, 2001. Ignore GST and PST considerations.

Self Study Problem Five - 6

Ms. Sandra Firth is a commission salesperson who has been working for Hadley Enterprises, a Canadian public corporation for three years. During the year ending December 31, 2001, her gross salary, not including commissions or allowances was $72,000. Her commissions for the year totalled $14,000. The following amounts were withheld by Hadley Enterprises from Ms. Firth's gross salary:

Federal and provincial income taxes	$22,000
Registered Pension Plan contributions (Note One)	3,200
Payments for group disability insurance (Note Two)	250
Payments for personal use of company car (Note Three)	2,400
Payments for group term life insurance (Note Four)	450
Interest on home purchase loan (Note Five)	3,000
Purchase of Canada Savings Bonds	2,060

Note One Hadley Enterprises made a matching $3,200 contribution to Ms. Firth's Registered Pension Plan.

Note Two Ms. Firth is covered by a comprehensive disability plan which provides income benefits during any period of disability. Prior to 2001, Hadley Enterprises paid all of the $500 per year premium on this plan. However, as of 2001, Ms. Firth is required to pay one-half of this premium, the $250 amount withheld from her gross salary. During 2001, Ms. Firth was hospitalized for the month of March. For this period, the disability plan paid her $500 per week for a total of $2,000.

Note Three Hadley Enterprises provides Ms. Firth with a Lexus which was purchased in 2000 for $58,000. During 2001, she drove the car 92,000 kilometers, 7,000 of which were personal in nature. Ms. Firth paid all of the operating costs of the car, a total of $6,200 for the year ending December 31, 2001. However, the Company provides her with an allowance of $600 per month ($7,200 for the year) to compensate her for these costs. While Ms. Firth was hospitalized during the month of March (see Note Two), another unrelated employee of Hadley Enterprises had the use of the car.

Note Four   Ms. Firth is covered by a group term life insurance policy that pays her beneficiary $160,000 in the event of her death. The 2001 premium on the policy is $1,350, two-thirds of which is paid by her employer.

Note Five   On January 1, 2001, the Company provided Ms. Firth with a $200,000 loan to assist with the purchase of a new residence. The loan must be repaid by December 31, 2002. All of the interest that is due on the loan for 2001 is withheld from Ms. Firth's 2001 salary.

Other Information:

1. The Company gives all of its employees a Christmas gift of $200. The Company deducts this amount in full in its corporate tax return.

2. During 2000, Ms. Firth received stock options from Hadley to acquire 1,000 shares of its common stock. The option price is $5.00 per share and, at the time the options are issued, the shares are trading at $4.50 per share. In June, 2001, the shares have increased in value to $7.00 per share and Ms. Firth exercises her option to acquire 1,000 shares. She is still holding them at the end of the year and has no intention of selling them. Due to an extended vacation in the Galapagos Islands, Ms. Firth neglects to file the election with her employer to defer the employment income benefit on the exercise of the options.

3. The Company provides Ms. Firth with a membership in the Mountain Tennis Club. The cost of this membership for the year is $2,500. During the year, Ms. Firth spends $6,500 entertaining clients at this Club. The Company does not reimburse her for these entertainment costs.

4. Ms. Firth had travel costs related to her employment activities as follows:

Meals	$1,300
Lodging	3,500
Total	$4,800

    Her employer provides her with a travel allowance of $300 per month ($3,600 for the year) which is included on her T4 for the year.

5. Assume that the relevant prescribed rate for the entire year is 6 percent (not including the extra two or four percent applicable to payments that are due from or to the Minister).

Required: Calculate Ms. Firth's minimum net employment income for the year ending December 31, 2001. Ignore any GST or PST implications.

Assignment Problems

(The solutions for these problems are only available in
the solutions manual that has been provided to your instructor.)

Assignment Problem Five - 1

The Jareau Manufacturing Company owns a car with an original cost of $22,000. The car has been owned by the Company for two years. During the year, the car has been at the disposal of the Company's sales manager, Mr. Robert Stickler. During the year, Mr. Stickler drove the car 36,000 kilometers with all of the expenses being paid for by the Company. The operating costs paid for by the Company total $3,920. In addition, the Company deducted capital cost allowance of $5,610 related to this car for the current year.

Required: Ignore all GST and PST implications. Indicate the minimum taxable benefit that would be allocated to Mr. Stickler in each of the following cases:

Case A Mr. Stickler has the car available to him for the entire year and drives it a total of 7,200 kilometers for personal purposes.

Case B Mr. Stickler has the car available to him for 10 months of the year and drives it a total of 17,000 kilometers for personal purposes.

Case C Mr. Stickler has the car available to him for 6 months of the year and drives it a total of 25,200 kilometers for personal purposes.

Assignment Problem Five - 2

Mark DiSalvo is an employee of Noble Ltd., a GST registrant involved exclusively in making taxable supplies. The Company provides Mr. DiSalvo with an automobile which was acquired in 2000 at a cost of $40,250 (including $2,800 in provincial sales tax and $2,450 in GST). During 2001, Mr. DiSalvo drives the automobile a total of 50,000 kilometers, 35,000 of which were employment related.

During 2001, the Company paid for all of the costs of operating the automobile. These amounts were as follows:

Gas, Oil, And Maintenance (Includes $400 In Provincial Sales Tax and $350 In GST)	$5,750
Insurance And Licence Fees (No Provincial Sales Tax Or GST)	2,000
Total	$7,750

The Company also provides Mr. DiSalvo with group life insurance coverage in the amount of $250,000. The 2001 premium on this policy is $4,000.

As the result of winning a sales contest, the company gives Mr. DiSalvo a complete set of lawn and pool furniture. The furniture cost the Company $9,200, including $640 in provincial sales tax and $560 in GST.

Required: Determine the taxable benefits including GST effects that will be included in Mr. DiSalvo's 2001 income as a result of his employment by Noble Ltd.

Assignment Problem Five - 3

Three employees of the Cancar Company were given the use of company cars on January 1 of the current year. The three cars are identical. Each car was driven 16,000 kilometers during the year and the operating costs were $2,400 for each car during the year.

Required: Ignore all GST and PST implications. For each of the following cars, calculate the minimum taxable benefit to the employees for the current year ending December 31.

Car A is purchased for $30,000. It is available to Aaron Abbott for the whole year. He drives it for personal purposes for a total of 9,000 kilometers.

Car B is leased for $635 per month. It is available to Babs Bentley for 11 months of the year. She drives it for personal purposes for a total of 6,000 kilometers and pays Cancar Company $500 for the use of the car.

Car C is purchased for $30,000. It is available to Carole Cantin for 10 months of the year. She drives it for personal purposes for a total of 11,000 kilometers.

Assignment Problem Five - 4

The Martin Distributing Company provides cars for four of its senior executives. While the cars are used for employment related travel, the executives also use them for personal matters. The personal use varies considerably among the four individuals. The details related to each of these cars, including the amount of personal and employment related travel recorded by the executives, is as follows:

Mr. Joseph Martin   Mr. Martin is the President of the Company and is provided with a Mercedes which has been leased by the Company for $2,100 per month. During the current year, the car was driven a total of 42,000 kilometers, of which 19,000 could be considered employment related travel. Operating costs averaged $0.40 per kilometer. Because of an extended illness which required hospitalization, the car was only available to Mr. Martin for the first seven months of the year.

Mrs. Grace Martin   Mrs. Martin, the Vice President in charge of marketing, is provided with a Lexus which the Company has purchased for $78,000. During the current year, this car was driven a total of 15,000 kilometers of which all but 2,000 kilometers were employment related. Operating costs for the year amounted to $2,500 and the car was available to Mrs. Martin throughout the year.

Mr. William Martin   William Martin, the Vice President in charge of finance, is provided with a Ford Taurus which the Company leases for $600 per month. The total milage during the current year amounted to 38,000 kilometers of which 32,000 kilometers related to personal matters. Operating costs for the year were $5,400 and the car was available to Mr. Martin throughout the year. William Martin paid the Company $400 per month for the use of the car.

Mrs. Sharon Martin-Jones   Mrs. Martin-Jones, the Vice President in charge of industrial relations, is provided with a Nissan Maxima which the Company purchased for $39,000. During the current year, the car was driven 24,000 kilometers on employment related matters and 9,500 on personal matters. The operating costs average $0.20 per kilometer and, as the result of considerable travel outside of North America, the car was only available to Mrs. Martin-Jones for nine months of the year.

Required: Ignore all GST and PST implications. Calculate the minimum taxable benefit that will accrue to each of these executives as the result of having the cars supplied by the Company.

Assignment Problem Five - 5

Ms. Forest is employed by Noface Cosmetics to demonstrate a line of beauty products for women. While Ms. Forest lives in Burnaby, British Columbia, her employment contract requires her to travel extensively in all of the Western provinces. Ms. Forest is paid a generous salary but must pay for all of her own travel costs. As a consequence, she keeps very careful records of her expenses.

Required: Do you believe that Ms. Forest is entitled to deduct her travel expenses against her salary as an employee? Explain your position on this issue.

Assignment Problem Five - 6

Eileen Lee is an extremely successful computer salesperson living and working in Hearst, Ontario who is unhappy with her current employer. In October of 2001 she is discussing a compensation package with her future employer, HER Ltd., a Canadian controlled private company. As Ms. Lee's current and anticipated investment income place her in the 51 percent income tax bracket, she is very interested in finding ways in which she can be compensated without incurring the same amount of taxation as would be assessed on an equivalent amount of salary.

Ms. Lee is contemplating a major cash outlay. She plans to completely renovate her house. She had been planning to obtain a loan of $100,000 at a 9 percent rate in order to finance the renovations. She has suggested that it might be advantageous for the Company to provide her with an interest free loan of $100,000 as part of her compensation.

HER Ltd. is able to invest funds at a before tax rate of 20 percent. It is subject to taxation at a 28 percent rate. Assume that the current Regulation 4301 rate for imputing interest on various tax related balances is 7 percent.

Required: Evaluate Ms. Lee's suggestion of providing her with an interest free loan in lieu of sufficient salary to carry a commercial loan at the rate of 9 percent.

Assignment Problem Five - 7

Mr. Worthy is a commissioned salesman and has asked for your assistance in preparing his 2001 income tax return. He has provided you with the following information:

Employment Income		
Salary		$35,000
Commissions		$11,000
Cost Of Maintaining Home Office		
(Based On A Proportion Of Space Used)		
Utilities	$485	
House Insurance	70	
Maintenance	255	
Capital Cost Allowance - House	750	
Capital Cost Allowance - Office Furniture	475	
Mortgage Interest	940	
Property Taxes	265	$ 3,240
Telephone Charges		
Monthly Charge For Residential Line	$ 250	
Long Distance To Clients From Home Office	400	
Cellular Telephone Airtime To Clients	800	$ 1,450
Office Supplies And Postage At Home Office		$ 295
Traveling Expenses		
Car Operating Costs	$2,700	
Hotels And Deductible Portion Of Meals	3,300	$ 6,000
Capital Cost Allowance On Car (100%)		$ 2,450
Interest		
On Loan To Buy Office Furniture	$1,700	
On Loan To Buy Car	2,300	$ 4,000

Mr. Worthy's car was purchased, used, several years ago for $22,000. Twenty percent of the milage on the car is for personal matters. He is required by his employer to maintain an office in his home and is eligible to deduct home office costs. Mr. Worthy has received no reimbursement from his employer for any of the amounts listed.

Required: Calculate Mr. Worthy's net employment income for 2001. Ignore GST and PST implications.

Assignment Problem Five - 8

Mr. Jones is a salesman handling a line of computer software throughout Western Canada. During 2001, he is paid a salary of $25,800 and receives sales commissions of $47,700. He does not receive an allowance from his employer for any of his expenses. During the year, Mr. Jones made the following employment related expenditures:

Airline Tickets	$ 2,350
Office Supplies And Postage	415
Purchase of Laptop Computer	2,075
Client Entertainment	1,750
Cost Of New Car	24,000
Operating Costs Of Car	7,200

The new car was purchased on January 5, 2001, and replaced a car which Mr. Jones had leased for several years. During 2001, Mr. Jones drove the car a total of 50,000 kilometers of which 35,000 kilometers were for employment related purposes. The capital cost allowance for the car (100 percent) is $3,600.

In addition to expenditures to earn employment income, Mr. Jones has the following additional disbursements:

Blue Cross Payments	$435
Group Life Insurance Premiums	$665

Mr. Jones indicates that he regularly receives discounts on his employer's merchandise and during the current year he estimates the value of these discounts was $1,300.

One of the suppliers of his employer paid $2,450 to provide Mr. Jones with a one week vacation at a northern fishing lodge.

Required: Determine Mr. Jones' Net Income From Employment for the 2001 taxation year. Ignore all GST and PST implications.

Assignment Problem Five - 9

Ms. Marsh has been employed by the Ace Distributing Company for the past three years. During 2001 the following amounts were credited to Ms. Marsh's payroll account:

- Salary of $40,500 as per her employment contract.
- Reimbursement of business travel costs as per invoices supplied by Ms. Marsh totalling $4,250.
- Reimbursement of $1,100 in tuition fees for a work related course.
- A $1,560 dividend on Ace Distributing Company shares acquired through the employee purchase program.
- Fees of $1,200 for serving as the employee's representative on the company's board of directors.

From the preceding credits to Ms. Marsh's payroll account, the following amounts were withheld by the Company:

Income taxes	$6,423
Premiums on group medical insurance	342
Contributions to Registered Pension Plan	1,400

With respect to the Registered Pension Plan, the Company also made a $1,400 contribution on behalf of Ms. Marsh. In addition to the preceding, Ms. Marsh made the following payments during the year:

Dental expenses	$1,250
Charitable contributions	275
Costs of moving to a larger apartment	2,800
Tuition fees for work related course	1,100
Life insurance premiums	850
Cost of travel to and from place of employment	620
Cost of business travel	4,250

The dental expenses were not covered by her medical insurance. As the result of a job related injury during the current year, Ms. Marsh received $1,350 in worker's compensation payments.

Required: Determine Ms. Marsh's net employment income for the 2001 taxation year. Provide reasons for omitting items that you have not included in your calculations. Ignore all GST implications.

Assignment Problem Five - 10

Ms. Sarah Kline is a copy editor for a major Canadian publisher. Her gross salary for the year ending December 31, 2001 is $73,500. For the 2001 taxation year, Ms. Kline's employer withheld the following amounts from her income:

Federal And Provincial Income Taxes	$26,000
Registered Pension Plan Contributions	2,400
Contribution To Employee Stock Purchase Plan	800
Contributions To Group Disability Plan	200

Ms. Kline's employer made a $2,400 matching contribution to her registered pension plan and a $200 matching contribution for the group disability insurance.

Other Information:

1. During 2001, Ms. Kline is provided with an automobile that has been leased by her employer. The lease payments are $700 per month, an amount which includes a $50 per month payment for insurance. The car is available to her for 11 months of the year and she drives it a total of 40,000 kilometers. Of this total, 37,000 kilometers were for travel required in pursuing the business of her employer and the remainder was for personal use. The operating costs of the car totalled $5,200 for the year and were paid by her employer. She reimbursed her employer $.30 per kilometer for her personal use of the automobile.

2. During 2001, Ms. Kline was hospitalized for a period of three weeks. The disability plan provided her with benefits of $1,800 during this period. Ms. Kline began making contributions to this plan in 2000 at the rate of $200 per year.

3. Ms. Kline paid dues to her professional association in the amount of $1,650 for the year.

4. In 1999, Ms. Kline was given options to buy 200 shares of her employer's publicly traded stock at a price of $50 per share. At the time the options were issued, the shares were trading at $50 per share. On June 6, 2001, Ms. Kline exercises the options. At the time of exercise, the shares are trading at $70 per share. She does not file the election to defer the employment income inclusion. She sells the shares on May 6, 2002 for $95 per share.

Required: Calculate Ms. Kline's minimum net employment income for the year ending December 31, 2001. Ignore all GST and PST considerations.

Assignment Problem Five - 11

Mr. Brooks has lived and been employed in Winnipeg as a financial analyst by a large Canadian public company for the past five years. During 2001, his basic gross salary amounts to $53,000. In addition, he was awarded an $11,000 bonus based on the performance of his division. Of the total bonus, $6,500 was paid in 2001 and the remainder is to be paid on January 15, 2002.

During 2001, Mr. Brooks' employer withheld the following amounts from his gross wages:

Federal and provincial income taxes	$12,500
Donations to the United Way	480
Contributions to employee stock purchase plan	800
Payments for personal use of company car	2,000
Registered Pension Plan contributions	2,800

Other Information:

1. Due to an airplane accident while flying to Thunder Bay on business, Mr. Brooks was seriously injured and confined to a Thunder Bay hospital for two full months during 2001. As his employer provides complete group disability insurance coverage, he received a total of $4,200 in payments during this period. All of the premiums for this insurance plan are paid by the employer.

2. Mr. Brooks is provided with a car which the company leases at a rate of $600 per month plus provincial sales tax of $48 and $42 in GST. The Company also assumes all of the operating costs of the car and these amounted to $3,500 during 2001. Mr. Brooks drove the car a total of 35,000 kilometers during 2001, 30,000 kilometers of which was carefully documented as employment related travel. When he is out of town, the car and its keys are left with his employer.

3. On January 15, 2000, Mr. Brooks received options to buy 200 shares of his employer's common stock at a price of $23 per share. At this time the shares were trading at $20 per share. Mr. Brooks exercised these options on July 6, 2001 when the shares were trading at $28 per share. He does not plan to sell the shares for at least a year. He was not aware that there was an election to defer the income inclusion on stock options and did not file the required election.

4. In order to assist Mr. Brooks in acquiring a new personal residence in Winnipeg, his employer granted him a five year loan of $125,000 at an annual interest rate of two percent. The loan was granted on October 1, 2001 and, at this point in time the interest rate on open five year mortgages was 8 percent. Assume the relevant ITR 4301 rate was 5 percent on this date. The loan is not a home relocation loan.

5. In his 2000 income tax return, Mr. Brooks claimed a GST rebate of $100 for unreimbursed business travel costs. His 2000 income tax return was assessed as filed on June 1, 2001.

6. Other disbursements made by Mr. Brooks include the following:

Advanced financial accounting course tuition fees	$1,200
Fees paid to financial planner	300
Union dues	240
Payment of premiums on life insurance	642

Mr. Brooks' employer reimbursed him for the tuition fees.

Required: Calculate Mr. Brooks' net employment income including any GST benefit for the taxation year ending December 31, 2001. Provide reasons for omitting items that you have not included in your calculations.

Assignment Problem Five - 12 (Electronic Library Research Problem)

Provide brief answers to the following questions. Your answers should be supported by references to materials found in your Electronic Library.

A. Under what circumstances can an individual deduct legal costs against employment income?

B. ITA 6(6) allows the value of, or an allowance received in respect of expenses incurred by an employee for, board and lodging for a period at a remote work location to be excluded from employment income ("remote work location exclusion"). For the remote work location exclusion to apply, the employee must have worked at a remote work location, being a location at which, by virtue of its remoteness from any established community, the employee could not reasonably be expected to have established and maintained a self contained domestic establishment. What constitutes a remote work location? What circumstances would lead to the conclusion that the taxpayer could not reasonably be expected to establish and maintain a self contained domestic establishment?

C. ITA 8(1)(i)(i) provides for the deduction by an employee of annual professional dues. Under what circumstances can this deduction be made? Can a student deduct dues paid to a professional organization prior to becoming a full member of that organization?

D. What is the appropriate tax treatment by an employee for awards received from an employer for making suggestions or producing inventions? What is the appropriate tax treatment by an employer for the payment of such amounts?

Chapter 6

Retirement Savings And Other Special Income Arrangements

Planning For Retirement

Need For Planning

6-1. Increasing life expectancies and lower birth rates are creating a situation in which the portion of the Canadian population that is of retirement age has been increasing and will continue to do so. This in turn, leads to the need to allocate a growing proportion of our society's resources to caring for this older segment of the population. There are enormous social and economic considerations resulting from this trend and, given the growing political clout of the older portion of the Canadian population, it is not a situation that the government can ignore.

6-2. Minimal financial requirements for the retirement years are provided by the Canada Pension Plan system. However, this system is encountering financial strains and clearly does not provide for the lifestyle many individuals would like to enjoy during their retirement years. In response to this situation, the Canadian income tax system contains a number of provisions which encourage the development of various private retirement savings arrangements to supplement benefits provided under the Canada Pension Plan system. These include:

- Registered Pension Plans (RPPs)
- Registered Retirement Savings Plans (RRSPs)
- Registered Retirement Income Funds (RRIFs)
- Deferred Profit Sharing Plans (DPSPs)

6-3. The detailed provisions related to these various types of tax assisted retirement savings plans show considerable variation. For example, Registered Pension Plans and Deferred Profit Sharing Plans require employer sponsorship. In contrast, any Canadian resident can establish a Registered Retirement Savings Plan.

6-4. Despite such variations, the basic idea underlying all of these plans is the same. They allow individuals to invest a considerable amount of funds into a trusteed arrangement. The amounts invested are either deductible to the taxpayer (RRSP contributions and employee RPP contributions) or can be paid by an employer without creating a taxable benefit (employer RPP and DPSP contributions). Inside the trusteed arrangement, the invested funds earn income on a tax free basis for long periods of time. While all amounts will ultimately be subject to taxation, there is a substantial amount of tax deferral. This arrangement can be seen graphically in Figure 6-1.

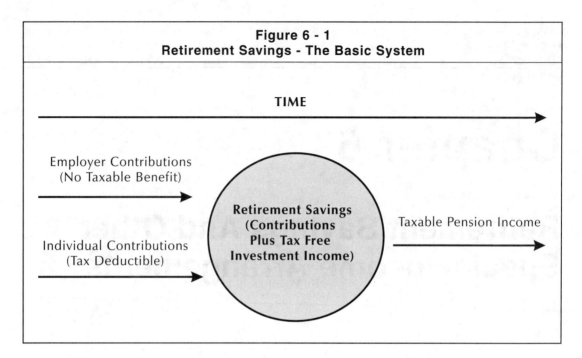

Figure 6 - 1
Retirement Savings - The Basic System

Tax Deferred Savings

6-5.   As shown in Figure 6-1, there are two sources for the investment funds going into retirement savings plans. First, for employed individuals, employers may make contributions to RPPs and DPSPs. As these contributions are not considered to be a taxable benefit until the funds are withdrawn from the plan, the employee has received a benefit on which the payment of tax has been deferred. The second source of investment funds is the contributions made by employed individuals to RPPs, and by all individuals to RRSPs. As the individual can deduct these contributions against certain types of income, they are the equivalent of receiving income on which the tax has been deferred. This means that, whether an employer has made contributions on behalf of the individual or the individual has personally made the contributions, the taxes on the amounts involved have been deferred from the year of contribution to the year of withdrawal from the plan. This period may exceed 45 years for contributions made at the beginning of an individual's working life.

6-6.   Also of great importance is the fact that the income earned by investments contained in these plans is not taxed until it is withdrawn. This allows earnings to accumulate at before tax rather than after tax rates and, given that such plans may extend over long periods of time, provides for a significantly larger accumulation of assets.

6-7.   The importance of this tax free accumulation cannot be overestimated. Consider, for example, Mr. Kerr, a 35 year old taxpayer who pays taxes at a marginal rate of 45 percent. Assume that for the next 30 years, he has $5,000 per year of pre tax earned income that he wishes to put aside for his anticipated retirement at age 65. If Mr. Kerr contributes this amount to an RRSP, it can be deducted and no taxes will be paid on the $5,000 per year of pre tax income. If this $5,000 per year is invested in an RRSP at a 10 percent per annum rate of return, it will accumulate to $822,470 at the end of 30 years. If the full amount is withdrawn when he reaches age 65 and he is still paying taxes at a marginal rate of 45 percent, he will be left with after tax funds of $452,359.

6-8.   If Mr. Kerr had not invested in the RRSP, taxes at 45 percent would have been paid on the $5,000, leaving only $2,750 per year to invest. If this $2,750 could be invested at an after tax rate of 10 percent outside of the RRSP, he would reach age 65 with the same after tax funds of $452,359 that were retained using the RRSP. However, the 10 percent rate used in the RRSP reflects the fact that investment income is not taxed while in the plan. If the same earnings stream were taxed at the individual's rate of 45 percent, the after tax return would only be

5.5 percent. At this after tax rate, the investment of $2,750 per year for 30 years would result in an accumulation at age 65 of only $199,198, less than half of the after tax accumulation resulting from using the RRSP approach. In effect, the deferral of taxes on the deductible contributions as well as on the income from fund investments, has allowed for an additional accumulation of income resulting from the investment of the amounts deferred. As this fairly realistic example illustrates, the amounts involved can be very substantial.

6-9.   The availability of tax free compounding in an RRSP makes it advantageous to contribute as early as possible. RRSP contributions for 2001 can be made as early as January 1, 2001 or, alternatively, as late as March 1, 2002. It can be demonstrated that, over a contribution period of 35 years, making contributions at the earliest date as opposed to the latest date can result in a 10 percent increase in the balance in the plan.

6-10.   The use of these tax deferred retirement savings plans may have additional advantages. There appears to be a trend towards lowering federal and provincial tax rates which could mean that overall tax rates will be lower in the future when the funds are paid out of the retirement savings plans. In addition, for some individuals, retirement may result in a sufficient reduction in income that they find themselves in a lower tax bracket. Someone who spends their working life subject to a 45 percent rate could find that, subsequent to retirement, they are subject to taxes at 25 percent. As this lower rate would apply to amounts withdrawn from a retirement savings plan, the deferral of taxation on contributions and investment earnings will result in an absolute reduction in taxes paid.

6-11.   Even if the individual is not paying taxes at a lower rate after retirement, there is an additional advantage associated with the funds taken out of these plans. The first $1,000 of pension income entitles the recipient to a credit against taxes payable each year equal to 16 percent of amounts received. Note that this $1,000 credit base is not subject to indexing and, as a consequence, has remained unchanged with the restoration of full indexing that was provided by the February 28, 2000 budget.

System Overview

Introduction

6-12.   The current retirement savings system was initiated in 1990 and is being phased in over a period that extends to 2005. Under the phase in plan, tax sheltered retirement savings will ultimately be limited to contributions of $15,500 per year (the limit for 2001 is $13,500). The major problem faced by the government in designing the current system was to insure that, despite the variety of retirement savings vehicles available, these limits were applied in a consistent manner to all individuals. In our view, an outstanding job was done in accomplishing this goal.

6-13.   Not surprisingly, the resulting system is quite complex, using dollar and benefit limits, carry over provisions for both contributions and deductions, pension adjustments, past service pension adjustments, and pension adjustment reversals. In this Section we will try to provide you with an overview of how these features serve to provide integrated limits for all types of retirement savings arrangements. However, before proceeding to a discussion of these items, we will provide you with a brief description of the difference between defined benefit and money purchase pension plans.

Defined Benefit Vs. Money Purchase Plans

6-14.   A major problem in the design of Canada's retirement savings system is the fact that, unlike RRSPs, DPSPs, and RRIFs, RPPs may be designed to provide a specified benefit after retirement. Such plans are normally referred to as defined benefit plans, while other types of RPPs are referred to as money purchase (a.k.a., defined contribution) plans. A basic understanding of the difference between these two types of plans is essential to the comprehension of the material in this Chapter. In view of this, the following brief descriptions are provided:

Defined Benefit Plans   In defined benefit plans, the plan sponsor undertakes to provide a specified benefit, usually expressed as a percentage of earnings, for each year of qualifying service. For example, such a plan might require an employer to provide a retirement benefit equal to 2 percent of an employee's average earnings for each year of service. Thus, if an employee worked for 20 years and earned an average salary of $50,000, the retirement benefit would be $20,000 per year [(2%)(20)($50,000)]. The employer has agreed to make whatever amount of contributions is required to provide these benefits. The required amount of contributions will vary depending on a number of factors, including earnings rates on fund assets, employee turnover, and employee life expectancy at retirement.

Money Purchase Plans   These plans are distinguished by the fact the employer agrees to make specified contributions for each plan participant. A typical plan might find an employer agreeing to contribute 3 percent of each employee's annual wages to a fund that would be established to provide retirement benefits. The employer would have no obligations beyond making the specified contributions and the employee would have no guarantee as to the amount of retirement benefit that is to be received.

6-15.   Before leaving these descriptions we would note that, while the term is not usually applied to them, RRSPs, DPSPs, and RRIFs are essentially money purchase plans. That is, the benefits to be received from such plans are based on the amounts transferred into the plan and the earnings resulting from the investment of these amounts. Such plans do not guarantee that the individual will receive a specified benefit after retirement. The only retirement savings arrangement that uses the defined benefit approach is the employer sponsored RPP. However, RPPs can take either form and, in an increasing number of cases, they are being established as money purchase plans.

Providing Consistency
RRSP Deduction Limit
6-16.   As noted in Paragraph 6-12, in implementing the overall limits on tax assisted retirement savings, the government's major problem was insuring that they were applied consistently, without regard to the types of retirement savings vehicles that were available to a given individual. The three major vehicles for the initial accumulation of retirement savings are RRSPs, RPPs, and DPSPs. Of these, only RRSPs are available to all individuals. Participation in an RPP or a DPSP is conditional on the individual being an employee of an employer who is a sponsor of such a plan. Given the universal availability of RRSPs, it is not surprising that limits on retirement savings use the RRSP Deduction Limit amount to calculate the limit for total tax deferred retirement savings.

6-17.   Although we will provide detailed coverage of RRSP calculations in a subsequent section, we will briefly describe the relevant components in this overview. The RRSP Deduction Limit is defined as the lesser of 18 percent of the individual's Earned Income for the previous year, and an absolute limit. For the years 1996 through 2002, the absolute limit is $13,500. Note that the limit is based on the individual's Earned Income for the previous year. This approach allows the individual to calculate his maximum contribution early in the current year. If the limit was based on the current year's earned income, the individual would not be able to calculate the maximum contribution for the current year until the following year.

Pension Adjustments (PAs)
6-18.   For many individuals, the RRSP deduction limit is the only determinate of retirement savings limits. However, if the individual participates in an RPP or a DPSP, his RRSP limit must be reduced to reflect retirement savings that are taking place in these plans. If this did not happen, individuals belonging to RPPs and DPSPs could have access to larger amounts of tax deferred retirement savings than would be the case for other individuals. Pension Adjustments (PAs) serve to integrate the limits of these various types of retirement savings.

6-19.   In simplified terms, an individual's PA reflects the value of all employer and employee contributions that have been allocated to that individual in the employer's RPP or DPSP for the current year. These PAs must be calculated each year by the individual's employer and reported on the T4 issued by that employer. This creates a problem in that the T4s are not issued until the year following that in which the RPP or DPSP contributions were allocated. That is, an employee's PA for any 2001 RPP or DPSP allocations will not be reported to the employee or the government until that employee's T4 information return is issued in January or February 2002. Reflecting this availability of data problem, the current year's RRSP Deduction Limit is reduced by the PA for the preceding year. Here again, the reason for this one year lag is that individuals need to know their 2001 maximum limit during 2001 in order to make appropriate contributions for 2001. If the 2001 deduction limit were based on the 2001 PA, individuals would not have the information required to calculate their maximum deductible contribution to an RRSP until February, 2002.

Past Service Pension Adjustments (PSPAs)

6-20.   A further problem can arise with defined benefit RPPs when past service benefits are granted. When, for example, a benefit formula is increased (e.g., from 1.75 percent per year of service to 2.0 percent per year of service) and the increased benefits are extended retroactively for earlier years of service, members of the RPP will receive a lump sum increase in their total benefits. As these benefits do not relate to current service, they will not be reflected in the PA for the year and, if a further adjustment was not required, individuals receiving past service benefits would be receiving additional retirement savings that would not be available to other individuals. To prevent this, Past Service Pension Adjustments (PSPAs) are subtracted from the deduction room of individuals receiving past service benefits.

Pension Adjustment Reversals (PARs)

6-21.   As a final point in this overview, we note that there are situations in which it is possible for an individual to lose their entitlement to pension benefits for which PAs have been issued. For example, if an individual belonged for some period of time to an RPP in which benefits were not vested, the employer would still be required to report PAs for the individual and this, in turn, would reduce this individual's ability to make deductible contributions to an RRSP. If the employee ceases to work for the employer prior to the benefits becoming vested, the benefits for which PAs were previously reported will not be transferred to the terminated employee. This means that there will be no retirement benefits corresponding to the previously reported PAs and, as a consequence, this individual will have permanently lost a portion of their entitlement to tax deferred retirement savings. When such amounts have been lost, they can be restored to the RRSP deduction limit through a mechanism called a pension adjustment reversal (PAR).

Exercise Six-1 relates to an overview of the system. This would be an appropriate time to attempt this exercise.

Registered Retirement Savings Plans (RRSPs)

Basic Operations

Establishment

6-22.   The general rules for Registered Retirement Savings Plans (RRSPs) are contained in ITA 146. Under these rules, an RRSP is simply a trust with the individual as the beneficiary and a financial institution acting as the administrator. Financial institutions offering such plans include Canadian chartered banks, Canadian mutual funds, Canadian trust companies, Canadian credit unions, Canadian brokerage firms and Canadian insurance companies. Registration of the plan results in the investor being able to deduct for income tax purposes a specified amount of contributions to the plan. Further, the individual is not subject to tax on the income earned by the assets in the plan until it is withdrawn.

Withdrawals

6-23.   Amounts that an individual withdraws from an RRSP must be included in income unless received under the Home Buyers' Plan or the Lifelong Learning Plan (these programs will be discussed later in this Section). Depending on the amount withdrawn, the trustee will be required to withhold a percentage of the amount withdrawn as a partial payment on the taxes that will be assessed on the withdrawal. Withdrawals are treated as an ordinary income inclusion under ITA 56(1)(h), even if they were earned as dividends or capital gains within the plan. This latter point is important in that dividends and capital gains are normally taxed at more favourable rates than other types of income. This favourable treatment is lost when the amounts are earned inside an RRSP.

Investment Options For An RRSP

6-24.   The Act is reasonably flexible with respect to the nature of RRSP investments. The basic choice to be made is whether the plan should be self administered by the individual taxpayer or managed by the financial institution which holds the fund assets. For individuals who prefer to make their own investment decisions with respect to the fund assets, the self administered type of plan is the obvious choice. An additional advantage of the self administered type of plan is that the taxpayer can transfer securities which he already owns into the plan. As the RRSP is a separate taxable entity, such transfers are dispositions and, any gains arising on the transfer will be subject to tax. Note, however, that ITA 40(2)(g) prevents the recognition of losses on such transfers.

6-25.   If the taxpayer's preference is to have a financial institution manage the plan, he will be confronted with a wide variety of choices. Managed funds include those that invest entirely in equity securities, funds that hold only long term bonds, funds with mixed portfolios, and funds that specialize in one type of asset such as Canada Savings Bonds or mortgages. Choosing between the many alternatives involves an assessment of their past performance, the fees charged by the various plans, as well as the investment goals of the individual taxpayer. With literally hundreds of choices available, the decision can be a very difficult one to make. However, considering the amount of financial resources that may eventually be involved in RRSP assets, it is not a decision that should be made without a thorough investigation of the alternatives.

6-26.   Since an individual can own any number of RRSPs, it is possible to have both a self administered and a managed plan. Further diversification could be achieved by having two or more types of managed plans.

6-27.   The Act is flexible with respect to the types of investments that can be included in either a self administered or a managed RRSP. ITR Part XLIX provides a detailed listing of the specific investment categories and includes publicly traded shares, mutual fund units, bonds, mortgages, warrants and rights. The only significant restrictions relate to investments in the shares of private companies, direct investments in real estate, and a limit on foreign property held in the plan. For many years this limit was set at 20 percent of the cost of the investments in the plan. This 20 percent limit was subject to heavy criticism as, in recent years, returns on foreign investments were often higher than those available on Canadian assets. In response to this criticism, the February 28, 2000 budget has increased this foreign property limit to 25 percent for 2000 and to 30 percent for 2001 and subsequent years. Note that, if the foreign content of an RRSP exceeds these limits, the excess is subject to a penalty of 1 percent for each month that it remains outstanding.

6-28.   It is interesting to note, however, that an RRSP can provide a mortgage on Canadian real property to the registrant of the plan, provided that the mortgage is insured under the National Housing Act or by some other company providing mortgage insurance. In addition, an individual can make a tax free withdrawal of funds from an RRSP for the purpose of purchasing a home (Home Buyers' Plan) or to finance full time training or education (Lifelong Learning Plan).

6-29.   As noted previously, capital gains and dividends that are earned within an RRSP are treated as ordinary income when they are withdrawn from the plan. As the favourable tax treatment that these two types of income normally receive is lost when they are earned in an RRSP, it would appear that it is better to earn capital gains or dividends outside an RRSP. This would suggest that, if an individual has investments both inside and outside an RRSP, it would be preferable to hold those investments that earn capital gains or dividends outside the plan.

6-30.   With the recent reduction of the capital gains inclusion rate from three-quarters to one-half, there has been some discussion of whether it makes sense to hold investments with potential capital gains inside an RRSP. The discussion is based on two considerations. First, with the inclusion rate reduced to 50 percent, the tax on capital gains earned inside an RRSP is essentially double the tax that would apply to capital gains earned outside of an RRSP. The other factor is that, in situations where investors hold securities for long periods of time, tax free earnings accumulation effectively occurs even when investments are held outside of an RRSP. The fact that capital gains are not taxed until there is a disposition of the investment significantly reduces the importance of the tax free deferral feature of RRSP investing.

6-31.   While a complete answer to this question goes beyond the scope of this text, we are convinced that RRSP arrangements are an advantageous vehicle, even for investments that earn capital gains. The fact that amounts invested in an RRSP are deductible means that, in effect, the government puts up as much as half of the required investment funds. For example, consider an individual in the 50 percent tax bracket with $10,000 in pre tax funds to invest. If this amount is invested in an RRSP it can be deducted and no taxes will currently be paid. Alternatively, if it is taxed, only $5,000 will be left for investments outside an RRSP. Under most realistic scenarios, this fact will more than offset the extra taxation that occurs when funds are withdrawn from the RRSP. Note, however, for individuals who have maximized their RRSP contributions and, as a consequence, have investments both inside and outside their RRSP, our original suggestion that investments with capital gains potential be held outside the plan is still appropriate.

Non Deductible Financing Costs

6-32.   As a final point it is important to note that interest paid on funds borrowed to finance RRSP contributions is not deductible. This suggests that it may not be desirable for an individual to borrow in order to make RRSP contributions. A complete analysis of this issue requires an estimate of how long the loan will be outstanding and a comparison of the individual's borrowing rate with his expected return on funds invested in the plan.

RRSP Deduction Limit

The Basic Formula

6-33.   At the heart of the retirement savings system is the RRSP Deduction Limit. It is this amount that indicates to the investor the maximum contributions to an RRSP that can be deducted in that year. While this amount is sometimes referred to as the contribution limit, this is not an accurate term. The RRSP Deduction Limit is neither a limit on contributions that can be made during the current year, nor a requirement that the contributions deducted in the current year be made in that year. Non deductible contributions can be made that are in excess of the RRSP Deduction Limit. Further, contributions made in earlier years that were not deducted in those years, or contributions made in the first 60 days of the following year, can be deducted under the RRSP Deduction Limit for the current year. For example, contributions made during the first 60 days of 2002 and undeducted contributions made in years prior to 2001, can be deducted against the RRSP Deduction Limit for 2001. Adding to the confusion is the fact that the RRSP Deduction Limit for 2001 is based on Earned Income for 2000, as well as the 2000 Money Purchase Limit.

6-34.   To assist taxpayers in dealing with this limit, the CCRA issues an RRSP Deduction Limit Statement to individuals who have filed income tax returns. It is attached to the Notice of Assessment and, assuming the return is filed on time, calculates the taxpayer's maximum RRSP deduction for the year after the assessed year. For example, the RRSP Statement included with the Notice of Assessment for the 2000 return, will normally be received during April or May, 2001, and will calculate the limit for 2001.

6-35.   The RRSP Deduction Limit is defined in ITA 146(1) and reproduced in Figure 6-2 (following page). In reading this definition, you will note that there are several technical terms included in this definition. These terms are indicated in Figure 6-2 with bold, italic type and each will be given separate attention in this section.

Unused RRSP Deduction Room

6-36.   As it is used in the Figure 6-2 formula, a taxpayer's Unused RRSP Deduction Room at the beginning of the current year is simply the cumulative total of all of the amounts determined under the formula for years prior to the current year, less any amounts that have been deducted in those years. As the current system for RRSP contributions was initiated in 1991,

---

Figure 6 - 2
RRSP Deduction Limit Formula - ITA 146(1)

"RRSP deduction limit" of a taxpayer for a taxation year means the amount determined by the formula

$$A + B + R - C$$

where

A   is the taxpayer's **unused RRSP deduction room** at the end of the preceding taxation year,

B   is the amount, if any, by which
   (a) the lesser of the **RRSP dollar limit** for the year and 18% of the taxpayer's **earned income** for the preceding taxation year,
   exceeds the total of all amounts each of which is
   (b) the taxpayer's **pension adjustment** for the preceding taxation year in respect of an employer, or
   (c) a **prescribed amount** in respect of the taxpayer for the year,

C   is the taxpayer's net **past service pension adjustment** for the year, and

R   is the taxpayer's total **pension adjustment reversal** for the year.

---

there is no carry forward for years prior to that date.

6-37.   This approach provides for an unlimited carry over of deduction room. As a consequence, taxpayers lacking the funds to make a deductible contribution in a particular year do not lose the deduction room applicable to that year. The deduction room is carried forward and provides the basis for a deductible contribution in any future year.

RRSP Dollar Limit

6-38.   As noted in our overview of the retirement savings system, the current year's RRSP Deduction Limit is reduced by the previous year's PA. For example, the 2001 RRSP Deduction Limit is reduced by the total PAs for 2000. With the same one year lag, the annual RRSP Deduction Limit is increased by 18 percent of the previous year's Earned Income. This means that the 2001 RRSP Deduction Limit is increased by 18 percent of 2000 Earned Income.

6-39.   The RRSP Dollar Limit is defined in terms of the Money Purchase Limit which is specified in quantitative terms in ITA 147.1(1). The Money Purchase Limit is the annual ceiling applicable to contributions made to RPPs. Because of the one year lag in the data used for the RRSP Deduction Limit, the RRSP Dollar Limit is defined as the Money Purchase Limit for the preceding year.

6-40.   The Money Purchase and RRSP Dollar Limits for the period beginning with 1996 and ending in 2005, the planned final year of the phase in, are as follows:

Exercise Six-2 deals with unused deduction room. This would be an appropriate time to attempt this exercise.

Year	Money Purchase Limit	RRSP Dollar Limit
1996 to 2002	13,500	13,500
2003	14,500	13,500
2004	15,500	14,500
2005	Indexed	15,500
2006	Indexed	Indexed

Earned Income

6-41.   Earned income is defined in ITA 146(1). The basic idea underlying this definition is that the income to be included in this designation is earned by the individual, rather than received as the result of owning property. This means that interest, dividends, and capital gains are excluded from the definition. Surprisingly, however, net rental income is included. Another unusual feature of the definition is that it does not include either net or gross employment income in unaltered form. Rather, the net employment income component of earned income is a hybrid concept that is not used anywhere else in the determination of Net Income For Tax Purposes.

6-42. As found in ITA 146(1), the basic components of earned income are as follows:

Additions
- Net employment income, computed without the deduction for RPP contributions
- Royalties, provided the recipient is the author, composer, or inventor of the work
- Taxable support payments received by a spouse (excludes non taxable child support payments - See Chapter 11 for a discussion of child support payments.)
- Supplementary unemployment benefit plan payments
- Income from carrying on a business
- Income earned as an active partner
- Net rental income from real property
- Research grants, net of certain related expenses
- Canada and Quebec Pension Plan disability benefits received

Deductions
- Losses from carrying on a business
- Losses accruing to an active partner
- Losses from the rental of real property
- Deductible support payments (excludes non deductible child support payments)

> Exercises Six-3 and Six-4 deal with earned income. This would be an appropriate time to attempt these exercises.

Pension Adjustments (PAs)

6-43. As explained in our overview of the retirement savings system, pension adjustments (PAs) are designed to reflect the benefits earned by an individual through defined benefit RPPs or contributions made to money purchase RPPs and DPSPs by an individual or his employer during a particular year. As RPPs and DPSPs are always sponsored by an employer, the CCRA requires the employer to calculate an annual PA for each employee who is a member of that employer's RPP or DPSP. This amount is reported on the employee's T4.

6-44. Because T4s are not issued until January or February of the year following that during which the RPP and DPSP contributions were made or RPP benefits were earned, it is deducted in the calculation of the taxpayer's RRSP Deduction Limit in the year the T4 is issued. More specifically, the 2001 RRSP Deduction Limit is reduced by PAs calculated with reference to 2000 benefits earned and contributions made. These PAs are reported to the CCRA and the taxpayer in the T4s that are issued in January or February of 2001. These PAs are also incorporated into the 2001 RRSP Deduction Limit Statements that the CCRA includes with Notices of Assessment for the 2000 taxation year.

6-45. **Money Purchase RPPs And DPSPs** The calculation of PAs for money purchase plans is relatively straightforward. As RRSPs operate in the same general format as money purchase plans (i.e., they do not promise a specific benefit), contributions to money purchase plans are directly comparable, on a dollar for dollar basis with contributions to an RRSP. As a consequence, the PA for a money purchase RPP is simply the sum of all employee and employer contributions for the year. Following the same reasoning, an employee's PA for a DPSP is simply the employer's contributions for the year that are allocated to the individual. A simple example will illustrate these calculations:

Example Ms. Jones' employer sponsors a money purchase RPP and a DPSP. Ms. Jones is a member of both. During 2000, she has earned income of $70,000 and contributes $2,000 to the RPP. Her employer contributes $2,000 to the RPP and $1,500 to the DPSP on her behalf. She has no Unused RRSP Deduction Room at the end of 2000. Calculate Ms. Jones' maximum deductible RRSP contribution for 2001.

Tax Consequences Ms. Jones' 2000 PA is $5,500 ($2,000 + $2,000 + $1,500), an amount that will be reported on the 2000 T4 that she will receive in early 2001. After filing her 2000 tax return, Ms. Jones will receive, attached to her Notice of Assessment, a statement from the CCRA which will calculate her RRSP Deduction Limit for

2001 to be $7,100. As she has no Unused RRSP Deduction Room at the end of 2000, this is calculated by comparing the $13,500 RRSP Dollar Limit for 2001 and $12,600 (18 percent of Ms. Jones' 2000 earned income), and subtracting her 2000 PA of $5,500 from the lesser amount of $12,600.

6-46. **Defined Benefit RPPs** As defined benefit plans guarantee the benefit to be provided, rather than specify the amount of contributions required, contributions made to these plans cannot be compared directly to contributions made to RRSPs, DPSPs, or money purchase RPPs. However, if retirement savings limits are to be applied equitably to all individuals, without regard to the type of arrangements available to them, it is necessary to equate the benefits earned under these plans with the contributions made to the other types of plans.

6-47. Unfortunately, there is no simple approach to converting a benefit earned into an equivalent amount of contributions. While there are a number of problems in dealing with this conversion, the most significant is the age of the employee. It costs an employer much less in the current year to provide a $1 retirement benefit to an individual who is 20 years old and 45 years away from receiving that benefit, than it does to provide the same retirement benefit to an individual who is 60 years old and only five years away from receiving the benefit. To have a completely equitable system for dealing with this problem, different values would have to be assigned to benefits that are earned by employees of different ages. Benefits earned by older employees would have to be assigned a higher value than those earned by younger employees.

6-48. In somewhat simplified terms, the solution to this problem that is incorporated into the retirement savings legislation is to equate $1 of benefits earned with $9 of contributions. That is, an individual receiving a $1 per year increase in his pension benefit at retirement, is viewed as having received the equivalent of $9 in contributions in the current year.

6-49. The use of the multiple nine is an arbitrary solution which fails to give any consideration to the age of the employee. It is systematically unfair to younger individuals as it overstates the cost of providing their pension benefits, thereby generating an excessive PA which, in turn, creates a corresponding reduction in their ability to contribute to their RRSP. For example if a 25 year old individual earned a pension benefit of $1,000 per year that was to be received at age 65, his pension adjustment and would be $9,000. If he had deposited this same $9,000 in his RRSP and made investments that earned 10 percent per annum, the balance after 40 years would be over $400,000, far in excess of the value of $1,000 per year benefit that would be received at age 65 under the defined benefit plan.

> Exercise Six-5 deals with pension adjustments. This would be an appropriate time to attempt this exercise.

6-50. While it was probably essential to the implementation of this system that some type of averaging process be used, it is unfortunate that the selected alternative has such a systematic bias against younger individuals. It is unlikely that the government could have arrived at any administratively convenient solution that would not appear inequitable to some individuals. However, it would have been more equitable to have used some type of age dependent sliding scale, as opposed to the inflexible application of the factor of 9.

Prescribed Amount

6-51. The Prescribed Amount is a deduction that may arise as the result of an individual transferring accumulated benefits from one RPP to a different RPP.

Past Service Pension Adjustments (PSPAs)

6-52. Past Service Pension Adjustments (PSPAs) are designed to deal with benefits under defined benefit RPPs related to credit for past service. They are far less common than PAs. Some of the events giving rise to PSPAs are as follows:

- A new RPP is implemented by an employer and benefits are extended retroactively for years of service prior to the plan initiation.

- The benefit formula is changed, increasing the percentage that is applied to pensionable earnings to determine benefits earned. Again, a PSPA is created only if the increased benefits are extended retroactively to years of service prior to the plan amendment.

• An individual, either voluntarily or because of terms contained in the plan, works for a number of years without being a member of the plan. On joining the plan, the employee is credited for the years of service prior to entry into the plan.

6-53. If an individual were to receive benefits such as those described in the preceding without experiencing any reduction in their RRSP Deduction Limit, they would have effectively beaten the system. The role of PSPAs is to make sure that this does not happen.

6-54. PSPAs are calculated on the basis of all of the PAs that would have applied in the previous years if the plan or improvement had been in effect, or if the individual had been a member in those years. From these "as if" PAs, the actual PAs reported would be deducted. The resulting difference is then reported as a PSPA for the current year. As would be expected, this process only applies to past service credits for years of service after 1989, the years that the current rules for retirement savings have been in effect. As with PAs, the employer is responsible for calculating and reporting PSPAs, normally within 60 days of the past service event. The amount will be reported on a PSPA information form (not on a T4) which will be sent to both the employee and the CCRA. Note that, unlike the one year lag in deducting PAs, PSPAs are deducted from the RRSP Deduction Room formula in the year in which they occur.

6-55. A simplified example will serve to illustrate the basic procedures involved in PSPA calculations:

Example Wally Oats has been a member of his employer's defined benefit RPP since 1995. Until 2001, the benefit formula provided a retirement benefit equal to 1.5 percent of pensionable earnings for each year of service. During 2001, the benefit formula was increased to 1.75 percent of pensionable earnings for each year of service, a change which is to be applied to all prior years of service. Mr. Oats has had $48,000 in pensionable earnings in each prior year. Calculate Mr. Oats' PSPA for 2001.

Tax Consequences The calculation of the PSPA would be based on the six years of service prior to the current year (1995 to 2000) as follows:

New Formula PAs [(1.75%)($48,000)(9)(6 Years)]	$45,360
Previously Reported PAs [(1.50%)($48,000)(9)(6 Years]	(38,880)
2001 PSPA	$ 6,480

6-56. Note that PSPAs only occur in the context of defined benefit plans. If additional contributions for past service are made to a money purchase plan, these amounts will be included in the regular pension adjustment for the year in which the contribution is made. This eliminates the need for any sort of catch up adjustment.

Pension Adjustment Reversals (PARs)

6-57. Employers are required to report PAs for all benefits or contributions earned by an employee during the year, regardless of when the employee receives the right to the benefits or pension. If an individual's employment is terminated before normal retirement age, it is possible that some of the benefits or contributions that were earned prior to the termination would be lost (e.g., non vested benefits are usually lost on termination of employment). As these lost benefits were included in the PAs that the employer reported during the years of employment, a portion of the RRSP Deduction Room that was eliminated by these PAs would also be lost. PARs were introduced in the 1997 budget to deal with this problem.

6-58. More specifically, PARs are calculated by the employer, after 1996, whenever an employee terminates membership in an RPP or DPSP and receives less from the plan than the total of the PAs and PSPAs reported for the employee. The amount will be reported to the CCRA and to the employee, and will be added to the individual's RRSP deduction room in the year of termination.

Examples

6-59. The following three examples illustrate the calculation of the RRSP Deduction Limit, Unused RRSP Deduction Room and the carryover of undeducted RRSP contributions.

Example A

Miss Brown has 2000 net employment income of $15,000, 2000 net rental income of $10,000, and 2000 interest income of $5,000. She is not a member of an RPP or a DPSP. During 2001, she contributes $5,000 to her RRSP and makes an RRSP deduction of $4,000 in her 2001 tax return. At the end of 2000, her Unused RRSP Deduction Room was nil and there were no undeducted contributions in her RRSP account.

Unused Deduction Room - End of 2000	Nil
Lesser of:	
• 2001 RRSP Dollar Limit = $13,500	
• 18% of 2000 Earned Income of $25,000 = $4,500	$4,500
2001 RRSP Deduction Limit	$4,500
RRSP Deduction ($5,000 Contributed)	(4,000)
Unused Deduction Room - End of 2001	$ 500

She has an undeducted RRSP contribution of $1,000 ($5,000 - $4,000) which can be carried forward and deducted in a subsequent year. The interest income is not Earned Income as defined in ITA 146(1).

Example B

After deducting an RPP contribution of $2,000, Mrs. Blue has 2000 net employment income of $34,000. In February, 2001, her employer reports a PA of $4,500 on Mrs. Blue's 2000 T4. Her 2001 RRSP contributions total $5,000 and she deducts $3,200 of this amount in her 2001 tax return. At the end of 2000, her Unused RRSP Deduction Room was $2,500 and there were no undeducted contributions in her RRSP account.

Unused Deduction Room - End of 2000	$2,500
Lesser of:	
• 2001 RRSP Dollar Limit = $13,500	
• 18% of 2000 Earned Income of $36,000 = $6,480	6,480
Less 2000 PA	(4,500)
2001 RRSP Deduction Limit	$4,480
RRSP Deduction ($5,000 Contributed)	(3,200)
Unused Deduction Room - End of 2001	$1,280

Mrs. Blue has 2000 Earned Income of $36,000 (net employment income of $34,000, plus her $2,000 RPP deduction). She has an undeducted RRSP contribution of $1,800 ($5,000 - $3,200).

Example C

Mr. Green receives taxable 2000 spousal support of $82,000, is not a member of an RPP or DPSP, and has no other source of income during 2000. In January, 2002, he contributes $11,500 to his RRSP. This full amount is deducted in his 2001 tax return. At the end of 2000, his Unused RRSP Deduction Room was $1,200 and there were no undeducted contributions in his RRSP account.

Unused Deduction Room - End of 2000	$ 1,200
Lesser of:	
• 2001 RRSP Dollar Limit = $13,500	
• 18% of 2000 Earned Income of $82,000 = $14,760	13,500
2001 RRSP Deduction Limit	$14,700
RRSP Deduction ($11,500 Contributed)	(11,500)
Unused Deduction Room - End of 2001	$ 3,200

Undeducted RRSP Contributions

General Rules

6-60.   There may be situations in which an individual makes a contribution which exceeds their RRSP Deduction Limit or, alternatively, chooses not to deduct all or part of an amount contributed that could be deducted. An example of the latter case would be a taxpayer who is currently in a low tax bracket and expects to be in a higher bracket in the future. Provided the amount was contributed after December 31, 1990, it can be deducted in any subsequent taxation year in which there is sufficient RRSP Deduction Room. There is no time limit applicable to this deduction and, in the event of death, it can be deducted in the taxpayer's final tax return for the year of death. Schedule 7, "RRSP Unused Contributions, Transfers, and HBP and LLP Activities" must be filed to report undeducted RRSP contributions.

Excess Contributions

6-61.   Given the desirability of having funds accumulate earnings on a tax free basis inside RRSPs, it is not surprising that rules have been developed to limit excess contributions. The basic limiting provision is found in ITA 204.1(2.1) which imposes a tax of one percent per month on the "cumulative excess amount for a year in respect of registered retirement savings plans". The "cumulative excess" is defined in ITA 204.2(1.1) as undeducted contributions in excess of the sum of the RRSP Deduction Limit plus a $2,000 cushion. This, in effect, means that the penalty applies to undeducted contributions that are $2,000 greater than the individual's RRSP Deduction Limit. This $2,000 cushion provides for a margin of error when a taxpayer makes contributions early in the taxation year on the basis of estimates of the amount that will be deductible. Note, however, the $2,000 cushion is only available to individuals who are 18 years of age or older in the year. This is to prevent parents from making undeducted contributions to an RRSP in the name of their children.

6-62.   The following simple example illustrates the application of this rule.

> **Example**   At the end of 1999, Mr. Woods has an RRSP Deduction Limit of nil and no undeducted contributions in his plan. During 2000, his RRSP Deduction Limit increases by $9,000. On April 1, 2000, Mr. Woods makes a contribution of $10,000 to the RRSP. No RRSP deduction is taken for 2000.
>
> During 2001, his RRSP Deduction Limit increases by $10,000. On July 1, 2001, $15,000 is contributed to the plan. No RRSP deduction is taken for 2001.
>
> **Tax Consequences**   There would be no penalty for 2000 as the excess of undeducted contributions over his ending 2000 Unused RRSP Deduction Room is $1,000 ($10,000 - $9,000), an amount less than the penalty free cushion of $2,000. There would, however, be a penalty in 2001. It would be calculated as follows:

	January To June	July To December
Undeducted RRSP Contributions	$10,000	$25,000
RRSP Deduction Limit	(19,000)	(19,000)
Cushion	(2,000)	(2,000)
Monthly Cumulative Excess Amount	$ Nil	$ 4,000
Penalty Rate	1%	1%
Monthly Penalty	$ Nil	$ 40

> Exercise Six-6 deals with excess RRSP contributions. This would be an appropriate time to attempt this exercise.

Tax Planning

6-63.   It is difficult to imagine an investment for which the elimination of tax effects would offset a penalty of 1 percent per month. Clearly, excess contributions that subject the taxpayer to this penalty should be avoided.

6-64.   This still leaves the question of whether it is worthwhile to make use of the $2,000 penalty free cushion. When the $2,000 is withdrawn from the RRSP, it will generally have to be included in the taxpayer's income whether or not it has been deducted. Mitigating this is the fact that, in those situations where the $2,000 is withdrawn from the RRSP prior to the end of the year following the year in which an assessment is received for the year in which the contribution is made, an offsetting deduction is available under ITA 146(8.2). If, however, any excess is not withdrawn within this specified time frame, it will be included in income and taxed on withdrawal even though it was never deducted from taxable income.

6-65. For individuals with a long term RRSP strategy, the benefits of tax free compounding inside the RRSP will offset the possible effects of having the $2,000 taxed on withdrawal, even if the amount is never deducted. A complete analysis of this issue would require consideration of different periods of time and different earnings rates. However, 15 or more years of earnings compounding on a tax free basis inside an RRSP will generally result in a balance which, even after being taxed at full rates on withdrawal, will exceed the balance resulting from after tax earnings compounding outside the RRSP. For example, if an individual in a 50 percent tax bracket puts $2,000 into an RRSP and it earns 10 percent compounded for 20 years, the individual would have a balance inside the RRSP of $13,455. If this balance is withdrawn and taxed at 50 percent, the individual will have after tax funds of $6,728. If the same $2,000 had been invested outside the RRSP, the after tax rate of return would have been five percent, resulting in a balance after 20 years of $5,307, nearly $1,500 less than the RRSP alternative. Longer periods of time would be even more favourable to the RRSP alternative.

6-66. More to the point, however, is the fact that undeducted contributions can be used in any subsequent year. Given this, making use of the $2,000 excess contribution cushion becomes a clearly desirable procedure for those with sufficient available funds. Whether the amount is left in the RRSP for a long or short period, it can be used as a deduction in any future year prior to the collapse of the plan. The only restriction on this procedure is that the taxpayer must have a sufficient RRSP Deduction Limit to be able to deduct the $2,000 in a future period. As this would apply to most working individuals, it is difficult to see any reason not to make use of the $2,000 cushion if the funds are available.

Spousal RRSP
Benefits
6-67. Under ITA 146(5.1), a taxpayer can deduct payments that are made to a plan which is registered in the name of a spouse. Any RRSP that is registered in the name of the taxpayer's spouse and to which the taxpayer has made a contribution, is considered to be a spousal RRSP. This means that, if an individual makes any contribution to his spouse's existing RRSP, that plan becomes a spousal RRSP, even if the great majority of the contributions were made by the individual's spouse.

6-68. A spousal RRSP is one of the few, relatively simple, income splitting devices that is generally available to all couples. In situations where one spouse is likely to have either no retirement income or a significantly lower amount, having the spouse with the higher expected retirement income make contributions to a plan in which the spouse is the annuitant will generally result in the income from the plan being taxed at lower rates. In addition, if one spouse has no potential retirement income, a spousal RRSP allows that individual to make use of the $160 annual pension income credit.

6-69. When an individual makes contributions to an RRSP in the name of his spouse, the contributions will be deductible in his tax return. However, the individual must have available deduction room and, as you would expect, contributions to a spousal plan erode this room in exactly the same manner as contributions to an RRSP in the individual's name.

Attribution Rules
6-70. The objective of all of the RRSP legislation is to encourage retirement savings. In the case of spousal RRSPs, the legislation also provides for an element of income splitting. However, as the Government does not want this element of income splitting to override the basic objective of retirement savings, there is an income attribution provision which discourages the use of spousal RRSPs to provide for an immediate transfer of income to a lower income spouse.

6-71. ITA 146(8.3) contains an income attribution provision which requires certain withdrawals from a spousal RRSP to be attributed back to the spouse who made contribution. Under this provision, if a taxpayer makes a contribution to a spousal RRSP and there is a withdrawal from any spousal RRSP before the January 1 following two calendar years after the end of the calendar year in which the taxpayer made the contribution, the withdrawal will be included in the income of the taxpayer making the contribution, not the income of the spouse. Note that, if the spouse has more than one spousal RRSP, the attribution applies to a withdrawal from any spousal plan, not just the RRSP to which the spousal contribution was made.

6-72. This attribution will apply to withdrawals up to the amount of the relevant contribution, but does not apply to withdrawals in excess of this amount. It also applies, whether or not the contributing spouse has deducted the contributions. In addition, it is applicable even when there are funds in the plan that were contributed prior to the attribution period. However, the rule does not apply when the taxpayer and spouse are living apart due to a marital breakdown at the time of the withdrawal.

6-73. When the taxpayer's spouse is eligible to make his or her own contributions to an RRSP, it can be useful to have these contributions made to a separate, non spousal RRSP. If there is a need to withdraw funds, this precaution allows the withdrawal to be made from a plan that has not received spousal contributions, thereby avoiding the possibility that the withdrawal will be attributed back to the taxpayer. However, if no withdrawals are anticipated in the foreseeable future, there is no real need to have a separate, non spousal plan.

> Exercise Six-7 deals with spousal RRSPs. This would be an appropriate time to attempt this exercise.

6-74. Contributions to a spousal RRSP can be made as long as the spouse is under 70. For example, if Mr. Gould is 73 and is unable to contribute to his own RRSP because he is over 69, he can still contribute to his wife's RRSP as long as she is under 70.

RRSP And RRIF Administration Fees

6-75. Administration fees for these plans, as well as investment counseling fees related to investments in these plans, cannot be deducted by an individual. As a consequence, such fees should be paid with funds that are in the plan. While there was some controversy associated with this issue, it has been concluded that such payments are not a withdrawal from the plan, nor do they create a taxable benefit for the taxpayer.

RRSP Withdrawals And Voluntary Conversions

6-76. A lump sum withdrawal from a Registered Retirement Savings Plan is possible at any point in time. The tax consequences of partial or complete withdrawals are very straightforward. In general, the amount withdrawn must be added to income in the year of withdrawal. Further, as a withdrawal does not result in an increase in the ability to make future contributions, such transactions result in a permanent reduction in the balances which will enjoy tax free earnings accumulation. Even when the individual is approaching retirement, a complete withdrawal of all funds would not be a reasonable alternative. This course of action would subject a large portion of the withdrawal to maximum rates at that time and, in the absence of other retirement income, would result in lost tax credits in subsequent years.

6-77. Besides lump sum withdrawals, the following options are available for converting an RRSP into an income stream:

Life Annuity A single life annuity or a joint life annuity with a spouse can be purchased. In this case, taxation occurs only as the payments are received.

Fixed Term Annuity A fixed term annuity can be purchased. As with the life annuity, taxation would occur as the annuity payments are received.

6-78. Note that these conversions can be made at any age and without regard to whether the taxpayer has retired. Further, there are no tax consequences resulting from the conversion. However, the resulting income stream will be fully taxable as it is received.

6-79. A final alternative for winding up an RRSP is as follows:

Registered Retirement Income Fund (RRIF) The funds can be transferred on a tax free basis to one or more Registered Retirement Income Funds (RRIFs). This arrangement will be described in a subsequent section of this Chapter.

Involuntary Termination Due To Age Limitation

6-80. The options for termination of an RRSP that were discussed in the preceding section are available at any age and without regard to whether the individual actually retires. However, government policy in this area takes the view that the tax sheltering features of RRSPs should not continue to be available to taxpayers in periods that are substantially beyond normal retirement age.

6-81. RRSPs must be terminated in the year in which the annuitant reaches age 69. If the individual taxpayer does not select one of the available options by the end of that year, the RRSP is automatically deregistered. For tax purposes, this deregistration is treated as if it was a lump sum withdrawal.

Other Plan Terminations
Departure From Canada

6-82. ITA 128.1(4)(b) requires a deemed disposition of most capital property when an individual departs from Canada (see coverage of this subject in Chapter 10). However, most pension benefits are exempt from these rules and, as a consequence, a departure from Canada will not automatically result in the collapse of an RRSP. Once the taxpayer has ceased to be a resident of Canada, he may find it desirable to collapse the plan. The collapse and subsequent payment to a non resident will result in taxation under ITA Part XIII. The Part XIII tax is a 25 percent tax on payments to a non resident and, for those countries with which Canada has a tax treaty, the rate can be as low as 10 percent. In addition, this lump sum payment will not be subject to any further taxation in most treaty countries. This places the RRSP registrant who becomes a non resident in a very favourable tax position relative to Canadian residents.

6-83. If the plan is not collapsed and payments are made to a non resident, such payments are also subject to Part XIII tax at a 10 percent or greater rate. In most treaty countries, only the interest component of such payments are subject to additional taxation at the local level.

Death Of The Registrant

6-84. The general rule here is that the fair market value of the assets in a deceased individual's RRSP are included in computing his income for the year of death. However, if the deceased has a surviving spouse, this income inclusion can be eliminated if the spouse is the beneficiary of the plan. Once this tax free rollover is accomplished, the surviving spouse has the usual types of alternatives. Part or all of the funds in the plan could be withdrawn, with the entire amount being taxable to the spouse. Alternatively, if the surviving spouse is less than the mandatory termination age, the plan can continue to operate with earnings accumulating free of tax. Additional alternatives that would continue to defer taxes would be the purchase of a life annuity or a transfer of funds to a Registered Retirement Income Fund.

6-85. A similar rollover is available if the RRSP assets are left to a financially dependent child or grandchild. Prior to 1999, this rollover was only available in cases where there was no surviving spouse. This restriction was removed by the 1999 budget, with the change being applicable to 1999 and subsequent years.

Home Buyers' Plan
Qualifying HBP Withdrawals

6-86. The Home Buyers' Plan (HBP) permits a withdrawal of up to $20,000 of "eligible amounts" from one or more of an individual's RRSPs. The "eligible amount" can be taken out on a tax free basis. Note that this provision would allow a married couple to make a total withdrawal of $40,000, provided they each have the required $20,000 in their RRSPs.

6-87. Prior to 1999, participation in the HBP was a once per lifetime privilege. That is, withdrawals could not be made under the HBP provisions if an HBP withdrawal had been made in any previous year. This restriction was removed by the 1998 budget and, provided all amounts previously withdrawn have been repaid, a qualifying individual can make multiple uses of the HBP legislation.

6-88.   In general, the HBP cannot be used by an individual if he or his spouse owned a home which he or she occupied during the preceding four years. However, the February 1998 budget created an exception to this constraint for disabled individuals. More specifically, if the home purchase is being made by or for the benefit of an individual who qualifies for the disability tax credit (see Chapter 13), and the home is more accessible for the individual or is better suited for the care of the individual, the HBP can be used even if the individual owned a home which was occupied during the specified four year period.

6-89.   The basic requirement for the tax free withdrawal is that the individual must have bought or built a "qualifying home" before October 1 of the year following the withdrawal. Extensions of the deadline are available where there is a written agreement to purchase a home or payments have been made towards the construction of a home by the October 1 deadline. A "qualifying home" is defined as a housing unit located in Canada, including a share of the capital stock of a cooperative housing corporation. Further, the definition of "eligible amounts" makes it clear that, within one year of the acquisition of this "qualifying home", the taxpayer must begin using it as a principal place of residence. Note, however, there is no minimum holding period for the home, provided that at some point it becomes a principal residence.

Restrictions On Withdrawals Of New RRSP Contributions

6-90.   The intent of this legislation is to allow individuals who have not recently owned a home to use accumulated RRSP contributions to acquire a residence. The government does not want to allow individuals to abuse the HBP by immediately withdrawing new contributions. To prevent this from happening, a special rule denies a tax deduction for contributions to an RRSP or a spousal RRSP that are withdrawn within 90 days under the Home Buyers' Plan. For this purpose, contributions to an RRSP within the 90 day period will not be considered to be withdrawn except to the extent that the RRSP balance after the withdrawal is less than the amount of the new contributions. This means that an individual can make the maximum $20,000 withdrawal and still make deductible contributions in the preceding 90 days, provided they have at least $20,000 in the RRSP prior to making the additional contributions.

> **Example**   Mr. Garth has an accumulated RRSP balance of $15,000. In order to make the maximum $20,000 withdrawal, he makes a $5,000 contribution to the RRSP. If he then withdraws the $20,000 within 90 days of making the $5,000 contribution, the resulting nil balance will be less than the amount of the contribution and no deduction will be allowed for the $5,000 contribution.

6-91.   As a final point you should note that this rule is applied on a plan by plan basis. If a withdrawal under the HBP serves to reduce the balance of a particular plan below the level of contributions made in the preceding 90 days, the contributions will not be deductible to the extent of this deficiency. This would be the case even if the taxpayer has balances in excess of $20,000 in other RRSPs.

Repayment of HBP

6-92.   Eligible amounts are not taxed when they are withdrawn from the RRSP and, if there was not a requirement for these funds to be returned to the plan at some point in time, they would constitute a significant tax free leakage from the retirement savings system. As a consequence, repayment of amounts withdrawn must begin in the second calendar year following the year of withdrawal. Any portion of an RRSP contribution made during the year or in the first 60 days of the following year can be designated an HBP repayment on Schedule 7 which is filed with the tax return. These repayments are not deductible in the determination of taxable income. Any amounts that are not returned to the plan as per the required schedule must be included in the taxpayer's income in the year in which they were scheduled to be returned.

6-93.   There is no upper limit on the amounts that can be repaid in any year subsequent to withdrawal. However, repayment must be made over a maximum period of 15 years. This is accomplished by requiring a minimum repayment based on the following calculation:

Eligible Amounts Withdrawn	$xx,xxx
Repayments In Previous Years	(xxx)
Amounts Included In Income In Previous Years	(xxx)
Balance	$ x,xxx

6-94. A fraction is then applied to this balance, beginning at 1/15 for the second year following the withdrawal. The denominator of the fraction is then reduced by one in each subsequent year, resulting in 1/14 for the third year after withdrawal, 1/13 for the fourth year after withdrawal, and so on, until the fraction reaches 1/1 in the sixteenth year following the withdrawal. These are minimum payments and, if they are made as per this schedule, there will be a fifteen year, straight line repayment of the eligible amounts. If payments are less than these minimum amounts, any deficiency must be included in that year's taxable income. As these income inclusions will be deducted from the balance to which the fraction is applied in the same manner as if they were payments made, this will not alter the schedule for the remaining payments. However, if payments are accelerated in any year, the schedule is changed. Further, these excess amounts do not count towards reducing subsequent deficiencies. A simple example will help clarify these points:

> **Example** Ms. Ritchie withdraws an eligible amount of $15,000 from her RRSP in July, 2001, and uses the funds for a down payment on a qualifying home. In 2003, a repayment of $2,400 is made and, in 2004, a repayment of $600 is made.

> **Tax Consequences** The minimum payment for 2003 is $1,000 [(1/15)($15,000)] and, since this is less then the actual payment, no income inclusion is required. The required payment for 2004 is $900 [(1/14)($15,000 - $2,400)]. As the actual payment is $600, an income inclusion of $300 will be required. Note that the required payment for 2005 is also $900 [(1/13)($15,000 - $2,400 - $600 - $300)].

Departures From Canada

6-95. If an individual ceases to be a resident of Canada, any unpaid balance under the HBP must be repaid before the date the tax return for the year should be filed, or no later than 60 days after becoming a non resident, whichever date is earlier. If this deadline is not met, the unpaid balance must be included in income.

Death Of The Registrant

> Exercise Six-8 deals with the home buyers' plan. This would be an appropriate time to attempt this exercise.

6-96. If a participant in the HBP dies prior to repaying all amounts to the RRSP, any unpaid balance will be included as income in the final tax return. However, a surviving spouse may elect with the legal representatives of the deceased to avoid the income inclusion. If this election is made, the surviving spouse assumes the position of the deceased by being treated as having received an eligible amount equal to the unpaid balance outstanding at the time of the deceased's death. This amount is added to any balance of eligible amounts received by the surviving spouse that have not been previously repaid to RRSPs.

Lifelong Learning Plan

General Format

6-97. Beginning in 1999, ITA 146.02 contains provisions which allow an individual to make tax free withdrawals from their RRSPs in order to finance the education of themselves or their spouse. Funds that have been withdrawn do not actually have to be used for education, they can be used for any purpose if the individual qualifies. Withdrawals under this Lifelong Learning Plan (LLP) must be repaid over a period of ten years. The repayment amounts are not deductible and, if they are not made as per the required schedule, deficiencies will be included in the individual's income.

Withdrawals

6-98. To qualify for the tax free withdrawals, the individual or his spouse must be enrolled as a full time student in a qualifying educational program at a designated educational institution. In general, a qualifying educational program is a post secondary program that requires students to spend 10 hours or more per week on courses or work in a program of at least three months duration. A designated educational institution is a university, college, or other educational institution that qualifies for the education amount (see Chapter 13).

6-99.   The maximum withdrawal is $10,000 in any one calendar year, to a maximum of $20,000 over a period of up to four calendar years. While the designated person for these withdrawals can be either the individual or his spouse, he cannot have a positive LLP balance (withdrawals, less repayments) for more than one person at any point in time. However, both an individual and his spouse can participate at the same time, provided they use funds from their own RRSPs.

6-100.   As was the case with HBPs, if an RRSP contribution is withdrawn within 90 days as a non taxable amount under the LLP provisions, it is not deductible in the calculation of the individual's Net Income For Tax Purposes.

Repayment of LLP

6-101.   Any RRSP contribution made during the year or in the first 60 days of the following year can be designated a LLP repayment on Schedule 7. Repayments must begin no later than the fifth year after the year of the first LLP withdrawal (actually the sixth year if payments are made in the first 60 days of following the fifth year).

> **Example**   Sarah makes LLP withdrawals from 2001 to 2004. She continues her education from 2001 to 2006, and is entitled to claim the education amount as a full-time student for at least three months on her return every year. Sarah's repayment period is from 2006 to 2015, since 2006 is the fifth year after the year of her first LLP withdrawal. The due date for her first repayment is March 1, 2007, which is 60 days after the end of 2006, her first repayment year.

6-102.   Repayments must begin earlier if the beneficiary of the program does not qualify for the full time education tax credit (see Chapter 13) for at least three months in each of two consecutive years. Specifically, repayment must begin in the second of the two non qualifying years (or the first 60 days of the following year).

> **Example**   Joseph makes an LLP withdrawal in 2002 for a qualifying educational program he is enrolled in during 2002. He is entitled to the education amount as a full-time student for five months of 2002. Joseph completes the educational program in 2003, and he is entitled to the education amount as a full-time student for five months on his return for 2003. He is not entitled to the education amount for 2004 or 2005. Joseph's repayment period begins in 2005.

6-103.   Minimum repayments must be made on a straight line basis over a period of ten years. As was the case with the HBPs, this is accomplished by using a formula in which 1/10 is repaid the first year, 1/9 the second year, 1/8 the third year, etc. Also in a manner similar to the HBPs, deficient repayments will be included in the taxpayer's income. Repayments in excess of the required minimum reduce the balance to which the fractions will be applied.

Other Considerations

6-104.   There is no limit on the number of times an individual can participate in the LLP. However, an individual may not participate in a new plan before the end of the year in which all repayments from any previous participation have been made.

6-105.   For a withdrawal to be eligible for tax free status, the designated person must complete the qualified educational program before April of the year following withdrawal or, alternatively, be enrolled in a qualified educational program at the end of March of the year following withdrawal. If this is not the case, the withdrawal will still be eligible for tax free treatment, provided less than 75 percent of the tuition paid for the program is refunded.

6-106.   Similar to the provisions under the HBP, if an individual ceases to be a resident of Canada, any unpaid balance under the LLP must be repaid before the date the tax return for the year should be filed, or no later than 60 days after becoming a non resident, whichever date is earlier. If this deadline is not met, the unpaid balance must be included in income.

Exercise Six-9 deals with the lifelong learning plan. This would be an appropriate time to attempt this exercise.

6-107. If an individual dies and has a positive LLP balance, this balance must be included in the individual's income for the year of death. As was the case with HBPs, there is an election which allows a spouse to make the repayments under the deceased's LLP terms.

Registered Pension Plans (RPPs)

Establishing An RPP

Types Of Plans

6-108. By far the most important type of Canadian pension arrangement is the Registered Pension Plan (RPP) provided by some employers for their employees. These plans have assets which are nearly double those of all other types of plans combined. Such plans are established by a contract between the employer and the employees and provide either for a pension benefit that is to be determined under a prescribed formula (a benefit based or defined benefit plan) or for a specified annual contribution by the employer which will provide a benefit that will be based on the funds available at the time of retirement (a contribution based or money purchase plan). An additional variable is the question of whether, in addition to the contributions made by the employer, the employees make contributions to the plan. If they do, it is referred to as a contributory plan. All contributions to the plan are normally deposited with a trustee who is responsible for safeguarding and managing the funds deposited.

Registration Of The Plan

6-109. It would be possible for an employer to have a pension plan which is not registered. However, such an arrangement would make very little sense. In order to deduct contributions for tax purposes, an employer sponsored pension plan must be registered with the CCRA. The basic requirements for registration are not difficult to meet in most situations. The plan must provide a definite arrangement established as a continuing policy by an employer under which benefits are provided to employees after their retirement. The terms and conditions must be set out in writing and the amounts of benefits to be provided must be reasonable in the circumstances.

Employer Contributions To The RPP

General Rules

6-110. ITA 20(1)(q) allows an employer to make a deduction for contributions to an RPP in the determination of Net Income. It indicates that such amounts can be deducted to the extent that they are provided for by ITA 147.2(1).

6-111. Turning to ITA 147.2(1), we find that contributions to money purchase plans are deductible as long as they are made in accordance with the plan as registered. For defined benefit plans there is a similar requirement. Contributions made during the year or within 120 days after the year end are deductible as long as they have not been deducted previously. Note that the reference is to contributions made, establishing the fact that the availability of deductions for pension costs is on a cash basis. As deductions under GAAP must be determined on an accrual basis, there may be differences between the accounting expense for the period and the tax deduction for the period.

Restrictions

6-112. The preceding general rules appear to provide for any level of deductions, as long as the amount is consistent with the plan as registered. As we have noted, however, the restrictions on contributions are implemented through the registration process. More specifically, ITA 147.1(8) indicates that RPPs become revocable in any year after 1990 where the PA of a member of the plan exceeds the lesser of:

- the money purchase limit for the year, and
- 18 percent of the member's compensation from the employer for the year.

6-113. Given the fact that the RRSP Deduction Limit is also based on these same factors (with a one year lag), this restriction means that an RPP cannot generally provide for more retirement savings than would be available to an individual whose only retirement savings vehicle is an RRSP. To illustrate this, consider an individual with 2001 earned income of $95,000 who is a member of a money purchase RPP. The RPP must be designed in such a fashion that it does not produce a combined employer/employee contribution that is in excess of the lesser of $13,500 (the money purchase limit for 2001) and $17,100 (18 percent of earned income of $95,000).

6-114.   With a one year lag, an individual with the same earned income who is not a member of an RPP or DPSP would be subject to the same limit. That is, in 2002, the maximum RRSP deduction for this individual would be the lesser of 18 percent of 2001 earned income of $95,000, and the 2002 RRSP Dollar Limit of $13,500. Until 2003, the money purchase limit and the RRSP dollar limit are both $13,500. An RPP that provides benefits to individuals in excess of this amount can have its registration revoked. Given that registration is required for RPP contributions to be deductible, this should insure that benefits are limited to the specified levels.

6-115.   Before leaving this discussion of employer contributions, you should note that this restriction on PAs would effectively restrict both employer and employee contributions to an RPP. Both types of contributions go into the PA calculation and, as a consequence, placing the limit on this measure of pension benefits insures that the combined employee/employer contributions will be restricted to the desired maximum level.

Employee Contributions To The RPP

6-116.   The basic provision here is ITA 8(1)(m) which indicates that, in the determination of employment income, individuals can deduct contributions to an employer's RPP as specified in ITA 147.2(4). Taking the same approach that was used for employer contributions, this subsection indicates that, for years after 1989, amounts contributed for current service are deductible if they are made in accordance with the terms of the plan. This places employee contributions under the same overall limit as employer contributions. That is, they must be made under the terms of a plan that does not produce a PA that exceeds the lesser of the money purchase limit for the year and 18 percent of the employee's compensation for the year.

6-117.   Additional amounts can also be contributed and deducted for service prior to the 1990 introduction of the current retirement savings legislation. However, such contributions are no longer sufficiently common to warrant coverage in a general taxation text.

Options At Retirement

6-118.   Individual RPPs generally involve rules which are applicable to the employee group in its entirety. As a consequence, the individual employee's options are usually limited to receiving the specified pension benefit. If the plan does permit a lump sum payment of benefits, it would become taxable on receipt by the employee. The plan might also permit transfers to other types of plans at or before retirement age. Such transfers are discussed in a later Section of this Chapter.

Registered Retirement Income Funds (RRIFs)

Establishment

6-119.   A RRIF is a trusteed arrangement, administered in much the same manner as an RRSP. A basic difference, however, is the fact that deductible contributions cannot be made to a RRIF. ITA 146.3(2)(f) makes it clear that the only types of property that can be accepted by the RRIF trustee is transfers for other types of retirement savings arrangements. The most common transfers would be the tax free rollover that can be made with respect to balances that are contained in RRSPs. As was indicated previously, this commonly occurs when an individual reaches age 69 and can no longer maintain an RRSP.

6-120.   There is no limit on the number of RRIFs that can be owned by a taxpayer and, in addition, the taxpayer has complete flexibility as to the number of RRSPs that can be transferred to a RRIF on a tax free basis. Further, the taxpayer is free to divide any RRSP and only transfer a portion of the funds to a RRIF. This in no way limits the options available for any remaining balance from the RRSP. You should also note that a lump sum payment from an RPP can be transferred to a RRIF.

6-121.   A RRIF can be established by an individual of any age and without regard to whether the individual is retiring. However, RRSPs have all of the same tax advantages as RRIFs, without the requirement that there be a minimum withdrawal in each year. Given this, there is no obvious advantage to establishing a RRIF prior to age 69.

6-122.   Any amount transferred from an RRSP to a RRIF is not subject to taxation until such time as it is received by the taxpayer from the RRIF. As was the case with RRSPs, withdrawals are taxed as ordinary income, without regard to how they were earned inside the RRIF (e.g., capital gains realized within the RRIF are taxed in full on withdrawal from the plan).

6-123.   Once inside the RRIF, the assets can be managed by the trustee of the plan according to the directions of the taxpayer. The list of qualified investments for RRIFs is similar to that for RRSPs and deferred profit sharing plans and allows for considerable latitude in investment policies. As is the case with RRSPs, fees paid by an individual for the administration of a RRIF are not deductible.

Minimum Withdrawals

6-124.   A significant difference between an RRSP and a RRIF is that a minimum annual withdrawal must be made from a RRIF beginning in the year following the year that the RRIF is established. If an individual is under the age of 71 at the beginning of the year, the minimum withdrawal is determined by dividing the fair market value of the RRIF assets at the beginning of the year by 90, minus the age of the individual at the beginning of the year. For example, a 65 year old individual with $1,000,000 in RRIF assets would have to withdraw a minimum of $40,000 [$1,000,000 ÷ (90 - 65)].

6-125.   Once an individual is 71 or over at the beginning of the year, the rules require a different calculation. A specified percentage [ITR 7308(4)] is applied to the fair market value of the RRIF assets at the beginning of the year. The percentage increases each year, starting at 7.38 percent at age 71, rising to 8.75 percent at age 80, and 13.62 percent at age 90. However, when it hits 20 percent at age 94, it remains at that level until the annuitant dies. This, of course, means that the RRIF balance will never reach zero if minimum withdrawals are made.

6-126.   It is possible to irrevocably elect to use a spouse's age to calculate the minimum RRIF withdrawal. If the spouse is younger, the minimum amount is lower and offers an opportunity to defer the tax effect of the withdrawals.

6-127.   While legislation establishes the minimum withdrawal from a RRIF, there is no maximum withdrawal. The entire balance in the RRIF can be withdrawn at any time. However, as was noted, any amounts removed from the RRIF must be included in Net Income For Tax Purposes in the year of withdrawal.

Death Of Registrant

6-128.   As was the case with RRSPs, when a RRIF registrant dies, his spouse can become the annuitant under the RRIF on a tax free basis. There is a similar rollover if the RRIF assets are left to a financially dependent child or grandchild. If the assets are left to any other beneficiary, their fair market value will have to be added to the decedent's income in the year of death. In some cases this will result in a very formidable tax liability.

Evaluation of RRIFs

6-129.   For individuals required by age to terminate their RRSP, lump sum withdrawals are usually not a good solution. This reflects the fact that such withdrawals can often result in a large portion of the income being taxed at the highest rate.

6-130.   This leaves individuals with a choice between using a RRIF and purchasing an annuity. The fact that life annuities are only available through life insurance companies means that the rates of return implicit in these financial instruments are often not competitive with other investments. Further, annuities lack flexibility. Once an individual has entered into an annuity contract, there is usually no possibility of acquiring larger payments if they are required due to some unforeseen event. In contrast, RRIFs offer some degree of flexibility with respect to amounts available to the taxpayer. In addition, the wide range of qualifying investments that can be acquired in RRIFs provide individuals with the opportunity to achieve better rates of return than those available through the purchase of annuities. It would appear that, for most individuals, the use of a RRIF is the most desirable option when the individual's age forces the collapse of an RRSP.

Exercise Six-10 deals with RRIFs. This would be an appropriate time to attempt this exercise.

Deferred Profit Sharing Plans

6-131.   ITA 147 provides for an arrangement where an employer can deduct contributions made to a trustee of a Deferred Profit Sharing Plan (DPSP, hereafter) for the benefit of the employees. Employees cannot make contributions to an employer sponsored DPSP. However, certain direct transfers of balances from other plans belonging to the employee can be made (see our Section on Transfers Between Plans).

6-132.   Amounts placed in the plan will be invested, with investment earnings accruing on a tax free basis. As with the other retirement savings vehicles, the beneficiary of the plan is taxed only when assets are distributed from the plan.

6-133.   As was the case with RPPs, the employer's contributions to these plans are limited by a maximum PA that must be complied with to avoid having the DPSP revoked. This is found in ITA 147(5.1) and is more restrictive than the corresponding limit for RPPs. Specifically, the PA for any individual with respect to benefits under a DPSP cannot exceed the lesser of:

  • one-half the money purchase limit for the year;
  • 18 percent of the beneficiary's compensation from the employer for the year.

6-134.   From the point of view of the employer, DPSPs are similar to RPPs. However, they have the advantage of providing greater flexibility in the scheduling of payments. Such plans are tied to the profits of the business and if the business has a bad year, it will normally result in a reduction of payments into the DPSP. Further, no specific benefits are promised to the employees. This relieves the employer from any responsibility for bad investment decisions by the fund trustee or estimation errors in the actuarial valuation process, factors that can cause significant uncertainty for the sponsors of benefit based RPPs.

6-135.   From the point of view of the employee, a DPSP operates in a manner similar to an RPP. The major difference is that employees are not permitted to contribute to DPSPs.

6-136.   DPSPs must invest in certain qualified investments and there are penalties for purchases of non qualified investments. A final important consideration is that DPSPs cannot be registered if the employer or a member of the employer's family is a beneficiary under the plan. This would include major shareholders if the employer is a corporation, individual owners if the employer is a proprietorship or partnership, and beneficiaries when the employer is a trust.

Profit Sharing Plans

6-137.   ITA 144 provides for Profit Sharing Plans. These plans are similar to DPSPs in that the employer can deduct contributions made on behalf of employees. Unlike the DPSPs, there are no specified limits on the employer's contributions as long as they are reasonable and are paid out of profits.

6-138.   However, these plans have not achieved the popularity of the DPSPs for a very simple reason. The employer's contributions to Profit Sharing Plans are taxable income to the employee in the year in which they are made. In addition, any income which accrues on the assets in the fund is allocated to the employee as it accrues. Although payments to the employees out of the fund are received on a tax free basis, this form of compensation offers no deferral of tax and requires the payment of taxes on amounts that have not been realized by the employee. Given these facts, it is not surprising that such Profit Sharing Plans have not been a popular compensation mechanism.

Retirement Compensation Arrangements

The Problem

6-139.   As we have seen throughout this Chapter, the rules related to maximum contributions by employers to the various available deferred income plans are very specific. However, it was once possible for employers to put aside additional amounts, particularly for employees currently receiving income that placed them in the maximum tax bracket, in plans that were not registered. Under such employee benefit arrangements, sometimes referred to as "off side" pension plans, the employee was not taxed until such amounts were actually received.

6-140.   While this could result in a substantial deferral of taxation for the employee, these arrangements were not widely used by taxable employers as the amounts contributed to such plans would not be deductible by them until the amounts became taxable to the employee. However, there was widespread use of such plans by non taxable entities as the lack of deductibility was of no consequence to them. This situation was viewed as an abuse of the system and, as a consequence, rules were introduced to remove the advantages associated with these "off side" plans.

Arrangements Defined

6-141.   These arrangement are defined in the *Income Tax Act* as follows:

> **ITA 248(1)   Retirement compensation arrangement** means a plan or arrangement under which contributions are made by an employer or former employer of a taxpayer, or by a person with whom the employer or former employer does not deal at arm's length, to another person or partnership in connection with benefits that are to be received or may be received or enjoyed by any person on, after or in contemplation of any substantial change in the services rendered by the taxpayer, the retirement of the taxpayer or the loss of an office or employment of the taxpayer.

6-142.   The definition goes on to indicate that the term retirement compensation arrangement does not include RPPs, DPSPs, RRSPs, profit sharing plans, supplementary unemployment benefit plans, or plans established for the purpose of deferring the salary or wages of a professional athlete.

Part XI.3 Refundable Tax

6-143.   Contributions made to retirement compensation arrangements can be deducted by the employer when they are made. However, they are subject to a 50 percent refundable tax under Part XI.3 of the *Income Tax Act*. The tax is paid on all contributions to the plan as well as on earnings on assets that are held by the plan. Refunds are available as payments are made to employees.

6-144.   For example, assume that during 2001 a non taxable entity contributes $50,000 to a plan established for several of its senior executives. The funds are used to purchase assets which earn interest of $4,500 and no payments are made to the executives during the year. This situation would result in the non taxable entity having to pay a Part XI.3 tax of $27,250 [(50%)($50,000 + $4,500)]. If, on January 1, 2002, this entire amount was distributed to the executives, the full amount of the Part XI.3 tax paid in 2001 would be refunded to the non taxable entity.

6-145.   The intent of this tax is clear. Before the establishment of these rules, non taxable entities could, without penalty to themselves, make contributions for the benefit of senior employees without any immediate tax consequences to these employees. Under the current rules, the non taxable entity will have to deposit the rough equivalent of the taxes that would have been paid by these employees had they received the amounts directly. Only when the amounts actually become taxable to the employees will the amounts be refunded to the non taxable entity. These rules, which effectively eliminate the tax advantages associated with such arrangements, have served to discourage the use of these plans.

Salary Deferral Arrangements

The Problem

6-146.   The fact that business income is on an accrual basis while employment income is on a cash basis has made it advantageous for employees to defer the receipt of salaries that can be accrued and deducted by employers. To the extent that these amounts are described as bonuses, ITA 78(4) has limited this deferral practice by deferring the deductibility of amounts that are not paid within 180 days of the employer's taxation year end. This still left open the possibility of employees voluntarily deferring some part of their regular salary to a later taxation year.

The Solution

6-147.   The *Act* defines a salary deferral arrangement as follows:

> **ITA 248(1)   Salary deferral arrangement**   A plan or arrangement, whether funded or not, under which any person has a right in a taxation year to receive an amount after the year where it is reasonable to consider that one of the main purposes for the creation or existence of the right is to postpone tax payable under this Act by the taxpayer in respect of an amount that is, or is on account or in lieu of, salary or wages of the taxpayer for services rendered by the taxpayer in the year or a preceding taxation year (including such a right that is subject to one or more conditions unless there is a substantial risk that any one of those conditions will not be satisfied).

6-148.   Converting this to everyday terms, a salary deferral arrangement involves an amount of salary which has been earned by an individual during the taxation year. However, the employee has made an arrangement with his employer to defer the actual receipt of the amount with the intent of postponing the payment of taxes. The definition of a salary deferral arrangement also contains a number of exclusions from its scope. These include RPPs, DPSPs, profit sharing plans, supplementary unemployment benefit plans, plans for providing education or training (sabbaticals), or plans established for the purpose of deferring the salary of a professional athlete.

6-149.   Employers can deduct amounts that fall within this definition, but employees cannot defer taxation on these amounts. They are required to include such amounts in their net income for tax purposes on an accrual basis, rather than on the cash basis that is the normal basis for employment income. In many cases, this will serve to remove any tax incentive from this type of arrangement and will discourage their continued use. Although the salary deferral rules do not apply to a bonus or similar payment that is to be paid within three years following the end of the year, if the bonus is not paid within 180 days of the employer's taxation year end, the employer cannot deduct the amount until it is paid. Despite these restrictions, certain salary deferral arrangements can be effective in that they do not fall within the ITA 248(1) definition. These include:

- Self funded leave of absence arrangements (sabbaticals).
- A bonus arrangement with payment deferred not more than three years, provided the employer is not concerned about the loss of deductibility that occurs after 180 days.
- Deferred compensation for professional athletes.
- Retiring allowances escape the salary deferral arrangement rules and, within limits, can be transferred on a tax free basis to an RRSP.

Transfers Between Plans

Accumulated Benefits

6-150.   As individuals may belong to several different retirement savings plans over their working lives, it is important that tax free transfers between different types of retirement savings plans can be made. For example, an individual who goes from a position where the employer provides RPP benefits, to a different position where no such benefits are provided, may wish to have his accumulated RPP benefits transferred to his RRSP. In the absence of a special provision to deal with this transfer, the benefits coming out of the RPP would have to be included in the individual's taxable income in the year of withdrawal. This, of course, would make such a transfer very unattractive.

6-151.   Fortunately, the *Act* provides great flexibility in this area. Provided the transfer is made directly between the relevant plans, the following transfers can be made on a tax free basis:

Registered Pension Plans   ITA 147.3 provides for the direct transfer of a lump sum amount from an RPP to a different RPP, to an RRSP and to a RRIF. The subsection also permits a transfer from a taxpayer's RPP to an RPP, RRSP or RRIF of his or her spouse or former spouse under a court order or written separation agreement in the event of a marriage breakdown.

Registered Retirement Savings Plans   ITA 146(16) provides for the transfer of lump sum amounts from an RRSP to a RRIF, an RPP, or to another RRSP. The subsection also permits a transfer from a taxpayer's RRSP to an RRSP or RRIF of his or her spouse or former spouse under a court order or written separation agreement in the event of a marriage breakdown.

Deferred Profit Sharing Plans   ITA 147(19) provides for the direct transfer of a lump sum amount from a DPSP to an RPP, an RRSP, or to a different DPSP.

Retiring Allowances

6-152.   The full amount of any retiring allowance, which includes amounts received for loss of office or employment and unused sick leave, must be included in the taxpayer's income in the year received. However, a deduction is available under ITA 60(j.1) for certain amounts transferred to either an RPP or an RRSP. This, in effect, creates a tax free transfer of all or part of a retiring allowance into an RRSP. The limit on this tax free transfer is as follows:

- $2,000 for each year or part year the taxpayer was employed by the employer prior to 1996.
- An additional $1,500 for each year or part year the taxpayer was employed by the employer prior to 1989 for which the employer's contributions to a RPP or DPSP had not vested by the time the retiring allowance was paid.

6-153.   This transfer does not have to be directly from the employer to the RRSP. The deduction is available if the taxpayer receives the funds and deposits the eligible amount into his RRSP within 60 days of the end of the year it is received. However, if a direct transfer is used, the taxpayer will avoid having income tax withheld on the retiring allowance. It should also be noted that, for the individual to deduct the amount transferred to his RRSP, the trustee must issue the usual RRSP contribution receipt.

> Exercise Six-11 deals with retiring allowances. This would be an appropriate time to attempt this exercise.

Example   Joan Marx retires at the end of 2001, receiving from her employer a retiring allowance of $150,000. She began working for this employer in 1982. The employer has never sponsored an RPP or a DPSP.

Tax Consequences   The entire $150,000 must be included in Ms. Marx's 2001 Net Income For Tax Purposes. Provided she makes a $38,500 [($2,000)(14 Years) + ($1,500)(7 Years)] contribution to her RRSP, she will be able to deduct the $38,500 RRSP contribution, without affecting her RRSP deduction room.

References

6-154.   For more detailed study of the material in this Chapter, we would refer you to the following:

ITA 144	Employees Profit Sharing Plans
ITA 146	Registered Retirement Savings Plans
ITA 146.01	Home Buyers' Plan
ITA 146.3	Registered Retirement Income Funds
ITA 147	Deferred Profit Sharing Plans
ITA 147.1	Registered Pension Plans
IC 72-13R8	Employees' Pension Plans
IC 72-22R9	Registered Retirement Savings Plans
IC 77-1R4	Deferred Profit Sharing Plans
IC 78-18R5	Registered Retirement Income Funds
IT-124R6	Contributions To Registered Retirement Savings Plans
IT-167R6	Registered Pension Plans — Employees' Contributions
IT-280R	Employees' Profit Sharing Plans — Payments Computed By Reference To Profits
IT-281R2	Elections On Single Payments From A Deferred Profit-sharing Plan
IT-307R3	Spousal Registered Retirement Savings Plans
IT-320R2	Registered Retirement Savings Plans — Qualified Investments
IT-337R3	Retiring Allowances
IT-363R2	Deferred Profit Sharing Plans — Deductibility Of Employer Contributions And Taxation Of Amounts Received By A Beneficiary
IT-379R	Employees Profit Sharing Plans — Allocations To Beneficiaries
IT-408R	Life Insurance Policies As Investments Of RRSPs and DPSPs
IT-415R2	Deregistration Of Registered Retirement Savings Plans
IT-500R	Registered Retirement Savings Plans — Death of An Annuitant

Exercises

(The solutions for these exercises can be found following Chapter 21 of the text.)

Exercise Six - 1 (Retirement Savings)
How does the Canadian retirement savings system prevent individuals who are a member of their employer's RPP or DPSP from being treated more favourably than individuals who can only use an RRSP for retirement savings?

Exercise Six - 2 (Unused RRSP Deduction Room)
Mr. Victor Haslich has 2000 Earned Income for RRSP purposes of $38,000. He is not a member of an RPP or a DPSP. At the end of 2000, his Unused RRSP Deduction Room was $4,800. During 2001, he contributes $6,000 to his RRSP and makes an RRSP deduction of $4,500. What is the amount of Mr. Haslich's Unused RRSP Deduction Room at the end of 2001?

Exercise Six - 3 (Earned Income)
Mr. Jarwhol Nacari has net employment income of $56,000 (he is not a member of an RPP), interest income of $22,000, net rental income of $2,500, and receives taxable support payments from his former spouse of $12,000 during the current year. What is Mr. Nacari's Earned Income for RRSP purposes for the current year?

Exercise Six - 4 (Earned Income)
Ms. Shelly Devine has net employment income of $82,000 (after the deduction of $3,000 in RPP contributions), a business loss of $12,500, dividend income of $4,200, and pays deductible support to her former spouse of $18,000 during the current year. What is Ms. Devine's Earned Income for RRSP purposes for the current year?

Exercise Six - 5 (Pension Adjustments)
Mr. Arnett's employer sponsors both a money purchase RPP and a DPSP. During the current year, his employer contributes $2,300 to the RPP and $1,800 to the DPSP on behalf of Mr. Arnett. Mr. Arnett contributes $2,300 to the RPP. Calculate the amount of the Pension Adjustment that will be included on Mr. Arnett's T4 for the current year.

Exercise Six - 6 (RRSP Excess Contributions)
Ms. Lucie Brownell is not a member of an RPP or a DPSP. At the beginning of 2000, Ms. Brownell has no Unused RRSP Deduction Room. During the year 2000 she has Earned Income of $120,000, makes a $14,500 RRSP contribution on July 1, but does not make any deduction for the year. In 2001, she has earned income of $120,000, makes a $16,500 contribution on May 1, but still does not make a deduction for the year. Determine any penalty that will be assessed to Ms. Brownell for excess contributions during either 2000 or 2001.

Exercise Six - 7 (Spousal RRSP)
During 1999, Mrs. Charron Garveau makes a $5,000 contribution to a new RRSP which has her husband as annuitant. He also makes a $5,000 contribution to this RRSP in that year. In 2000, Mrs. Garveau does not make any further contribution to her husband's RRSP. However, he makes a $6,500 contribution. During 2001, Mr. Garveau withdraws $9,000 from this RRSP. How will this withdrawal be taxed?

Exercise Six - 8 (Home Buyers' Plan)
During 1999, Ms. Farah DeBoo withdraws $18,000 from her RRSP under the provisions of the Home Buyers' Plan. Due to some unexpected income received during 2000, she repays $5,000 in that year. What is the amount of her minimum repayment during 2001?

Exercise Six - 9 (Lifelong Learning Plan)
Under the provisions of the Lifelong Learning Plan (LPP), Jean Paul Lee withdraws an eligible amount of $5,000 during July, 2001. This is subsequent to his acceptance in a community col-

lege program that runs from September to November, 2001. He completes the course.

On February 28 of each year from 2004 through 2013, he makes payments of $500 per year to his RRSP. These amounts are designated as LLP repayments in his tax returns for the years 2003 through 2012. Indicate the tax consequences to Jean Paul of these transactions.

Exercise Six - 10 (RRIF Calculations)
On January 1, 2001, Mr. Larry Harold transfers all of his RRSP funds into a RRIF. The fair market value of these assets on January 1, 2001 is $625,000. Mr. Harold is 65 years old on that date. What is the minimum withdrawal that Mr. Harold must make from the RRIF during 2001 and 2002?

Exercise Six - 11 (Retiring Allowance)
On December, 31, 2001, Mr. Giovanni Bartoli retires after 26 years of service with his present employer. In recognition of his outstanding service during these years, his employer pays him a retiring allowance of $100,000. His employer has never sponsored an RPP or a DPSP. What is the maximum deductible contribution that Mr. Bartoli can make to his RRSP as a result of receiving this retiring allowance?

Problems For Self Study

(The solutions for these problems can be found following Chapter 21 of the text.)

Self Study Problem Six - 1
During the calendar year 2000, Mr. Donald Barnes has the following income and loss data:

Gross Salary	$40,175
Taxable Benefits	1,150
Profit From Tax Advisory Service	4,150
Net Loss From Rental Property	(11,875)
Spousal Support Received From Former Wife	2,400
Dividends From Taxable Canadian Corporations	3,210
Interest On Government Bonds	3,640

In addition to the preceding information, Mr. Barnes paid union dues of $175, made Canada Pension Plan contributions of $1,496, and paid Employment Insurance premiums of $878. The total shown for dividends is the grossed up taxable amount.

At the end of 2000, Mr. Barnes had Unused RRSP Deduction Room of $700.

Required: For the calendar year 2001, determine Mr. Barnes' maximum allowable deduction for contributions to a Registered Retirement Savings Plan under the following assumptions:

A. During 2000, Mr. Barnes is not a member of a Registered Pension Plan or a Deferred Profit Sharing Plan.

B. Mr. Barnes is a member of a Registered Pension Plan, but not a member of a Deferred Profit Sharing Plan. His employer reports that his 2000 pension adjustment is $4,200.

Self Study Problem Six - 2
Mr. Jones is 62 years old and his wife is 58 years old. In January 2001, he agreed to undertake a special project for the Martin Manufacturing Company, a company which produces large industrial use motors. The project is expected to take three years to complete. Mr. Jones was previously employed by the Martin Manufacturing Company for a period of 11 years. However, for the last seven years, he has operated his own consulting organization in Vancouver. Accepting the special project for the Martin Manufacturing Company will require that Mr. Jones discontinue his consulting operation and move to Hamilton where the head offices of the Company are located. This does not concern Mr. Jones as he plans to retire in three years

under any circumstances. It will, however, require that he sell his home in Vancouver and acquire a new residence in Hamilton. Mr. Jones anticipates that he will require a mortgage of approximately $100,000 in order to purchase a residence.

Mr. Jones and the Company have agreed to a salary of $100,000 per year for the three year period with no additional benefits other than the required payments for employment insurance and the Canada Pension Plan. However, the Company has indicated that it is prepared to be flexible with respect to the type of compensation that is given to Mr. Jones, subject to the condition that the total cost of providing the compensation does not exceed $300,000 over the three year period.

The Martin Manufacturing Company is a Canadian controlled public Company and is subject to a combined federal and provincial tax rate of 50 percent. It currently has a registered pension plan for its employees. However, this plan was not in place during the earlier eleven year period in which Mr. Jones was employed by the Company.

Mr. Jones is concerned about the fact that his $100,000 per year salary will attract high levels of taxation. He is seeking your advice with respect to how his compensation arrangement with the Martin Manufacturing Company might be altered to provide some reduction or deferral of taxes. He indicates that, subsequent to retirement, his income is likely to be less than $40,000 per year.

Required: Advise Mr. Jones with respect to alternative forms of compensation that could reduce or defer taxes on the $300,000 that he is to receive from the Martin Manufacturing Company.

Self Study Problem Six - 3

Mr. Jonathan Beasley graduated from university in May, 2000. He immediately began work as an industrial designer, earning gross employment income of $24,000 during the calendar year ending December 31, 2000. Prior to 2000, Mr. Beasley had no earned income and had made no contributions to any type of retirement savings plan.

Up until May, 2000, Mr. Beasley had been supported by his spouse Samantha. However, they were separated on June 1, 2000. On July 1, 2000, Samantha was convicted of spouse abuse and was ordered by the court to pay spousal support to Jonathan in the amount of $1,500 per month (a total of $9,000 was received during 2000). In addition, she was required to pay damages to Jonathan in the amount of $100,000. Jonathan deposited this entire amount in his savings account, resulting in 2000 interest income of $1,500.

Jonathan did not contribute to an RRSP during 2000. However, his employer sponsored an RPP to which Jonathan contributed $1,300 during 2000. This contribution was matched by a $1,300 contribution by Jonathan's employer, resulting in a 2000 pension adjustment of $2,600.

During 2000, Jonathan received royalties of $500 on a song written by his mother, dividends from taxable Canadian corporations totalling $700, and a $5,000 gift from his parents. His parents also gave him a rental property in early 2000. This property experienced a net rental loss of $5,000 for the year ending December 31, 2000.

For 2000, Mr. Beasley's income places him in the lowest federal income tax bracket. Further, he anticipates that most of his 2001 income will also be taxed at this rate. However, he expects to receive a significant promotion at the end of 2001 and, as a consequence, he is likely to be in the maximum federal income tax bracket in 2002 and subsequent years.

Required:

A. Calculate Mr. Beasley's Net Employment Income for 2000.

B. Determine Mr. Beasley's maximum deductible RRSP contribution for 2001.

C. As Mr. Beasley's personal financial consultant, what advice would you give him regarding his RRSP contribution and deduction for 2001?

Self Study Problem Six - 4

Ms. Stratton has been the controller for a large publicly traded corporation for the last five years. The following information relates to the year ending December 31, 2001:

1. Ms. Stratton had a gross salary of $72,000 from which her employer made the following deductions:

Income taxes	$13,342
Registered Pension Plan contributions	2,390
Employment Insurance premiums	878
Canada Pension Plan contributions	1,496
Contributions to registered charities	1,600
Employee's portion of benefit plans (See Part 2 below)	1,436

2. It is the policy of the Company to pay one-half of the cost of certain benefit plans. The following amounts were paid by the Company for Ms. Stratton:

Group term life insurance	$ 96
Provincial health insurance plan	482
Dental plan	173
Major medical care (Private insurer)	396
Group income protection	289

3. Ms. Stratton's employer paid $2,300 for her annual membership in the Hot Rocks Curling Club. Ms. Stratton uses the Club largely for business related entertaining.

4. Because of assistance she provided with a difficult tax matter, Ms. Stratton was rewarded with a one week trip to Bermuda by one of her employer's major clients. The fair market value of this trip was $4,500.

5. Ms. Stratton is required to travel to the offices of her employer's clients on a regular and continuing basis. As a result, her employer paid her a monthly travel allowance based on actual milage and expenses. These payments totalled $8,462 for the year.

6. During the year, Ms. Stratton paid professional dues of $225 and made contributions to a Registered Retirement Savings Plan in the amount of $9,000. At the end of 2000, Ms. Stratton's unused RRSP Deduction Room was nil and she had no undeducted RRSP contributions. Her employer reported that she had a 2000 pension adjustment of $5,560. Her earned income for 2000 is equal to her 2001 earned income.

Required:

A. Calculate Ms. Stratton's net employment income for the year ending December 31, 2001. Ignore GST and PST implications.

B. Comment on the advisability of her $9,000 contribution to her Registered Retirement Savings Plan.

Self Study Problem Six - 5

Mr. Colt, an employee of Jeffco Ltd., has agreed to accept early retirement in 2001, in return for a retiring allowance of $125,000. Mr. Colt began working for Jeffco Ltd. in 1977. He has been a member of the company's registered pension plan for the last 10 years and his pension plan entitlement is vested.

At the beginning of 2001, Mr. Colt had unused RRSP deduction room of $32,000. His 2000 earned income was $46,000 and his 2000 T4 included a pension adjustment of $8,000.

Jeffco will transfer $50,000 of the retiring allowance into a registered retirement savings plan (RRSP) in Mr. Colt's name and the remainder into a spousal RRSP.

Required:

A. Determine the maximum RRSP deduction that Mr. Colt is allowed in 2001.

B. What are the tax implications in 2001 for Mr. Colt of the above payments ($50,000 payment to his RRSP and the remainder to a spousal RRSP)?

(Adapted from the 1992 UFE)

Assignment Problems

(The solutions for these problems are only available in
the solutions manual that has been provided to your instructor.)

Assignment Problem Six - 1

During 2000, in addition to employment income, Mr. Robert Sparks had the following amounts of income and deductions under the various Subdivisions of Division B of the *Income Tax Act:*

Income (Loss) from business	($16,000)
Income from property (Interest on term deposits)	6,000
Taxable capital gains	7,500
Allowable capital losses	(10,500)
Subdivision e deductions (Child care costs)	(3,000)

At the end of 2000, Mr. Sparks' Unused RRSP Deduction Room was nil and there were no undeducted contributions in his RRSP account.

Required:

A. Assume Mr. Sparks' net employment income is $30,000. Calculate his 2000 Net Income For Tax Purposes and any carryovers available to him. Ignore any carryover possibilities for losses of other years.

B. Calculate the maximum deductible registered retirement savings plan contribution Mr. Sparks can make to his RRSP for the 2001 taxation year for the following independent cases:

1. During 2000, he is a member of a money purchase registered pension plan in which he has contributed $1,000 and his employer has contributed $1,500. His net employment income is $30,000.

2. During 2000, he is a member of a deferred profit sharing plan in which his employer has contributed $1,500 per employee. His net employment income is $40,000.

3. During 2000, he is not a member of a registered pension plan or deferred profit sharing plan. His net employment income is $100,000. He has contributed $1,500 to his wife's registered retirement savings plan in August, 2001.

Assignment Problem Six - 2

After being unemployed for two years, Donald Parker found employment with a large, publicly traded corporation in early 2000. His gross 2000 salary was $40,000 and, in addition, he earned commissions of $20,000. The corresponding figures for 2001 were $53,000 and $32,000. Expenses related to the commission income were $3,000 in 2000 and $4,000 in 2001.

From his earnings, Donald's employer withheld the following:

	2001	2000
Federal And Provincial Income Taxes	$26,000	$18,000
CPP Contributions	1,496	1,330
EI Premiums	878	936
Disability Insurance Premiums	250	250
RPP Contributions	1,500	1,400

The employer makes RPP contributions and pays disability insurance premiums in an amount equal to the amounts withheld from employee earnings for these items. In addition, the employer provided Donald with a low interest loan. The taxable benefit on this loan was $2,750 in 2000 and $2,500 in 2001.

Other information for the years 2000 and 2001 is as follows:

	2001	2000
Net Rental Income (Loss)	$1,400	($2,500)
Taxable Spousal Support Received	2,600	2,400
Deductible Spousal Support Paid	(3,600)	(3,500)
Capital Gains (Losses)	(2,200)	1,750
Royalties*	875	920
Interest Income	273	496

*The royalties are on a song written by Donald's mother in 1962.

In 1998, just prior to losing his job, Donald contributed $7,500 to a self administered RRSP. As he realized he would be in the minimum tax bracket until he found work, Donald did not deduct this RRSP contribution prior to 2001. He has unused RRSP deduction room of $25,000 at the end of 2000.

In December, 2001, Donald wins $200,000 in a lottery. He would like to put as much of this amount as possible into his RRSP prior to the end of 2001.

Required:

A. Determine Donald's maximum RRSP deduction for 2001.

B. Calculate the amount you would recommend that Donald contribute to his RRSP in 2001.

Assignment Problem Six - 3

Mrs. Holly Goh is a graphic designer with two young children. Her current husband, a body builder, who once held the Mr. Alberta title, takes care of the children and the household and has no source of income. As this was also the situation with her former husband, she is required to pay him $200 per month in spousal support. In addition, she must pay $150 per month in child support for the child that is still in the custody of her former husband. These amounts were established in a December, 1999 court decree.

Mrs. Holly Goh has a self administered RRSP. At the end of 2000, Mrs. Goh has unused deduction room of $6,200. In addition, she has undeducted contributions in the plan of $5,500. As he has never earned any income, her current husband does not have an RRSP.

Mrs. Goh's 2000 salary is $75,000. Her only employment benefits are a dental plan which costs her employer $1,200 per year, $100,000 in group term life insurance for which her employer pays a premium of $850 per year, and a registered pension plan. During the 2000 year, her employer contributes $3,200 to this plan and Mrs. Goh contributes $2,500. The RPP is a money purchase (a.k.a., defined contribution plan).

During 2000, Mrs. Goh has various types of income as follows:

- Interest on term deposits of $4,600.
- Taxable capital gains of $14,500.
- A loss on a rental property of $8,000.
- Royalties of $4,800 on a design process that was invented by her father. (The patent for the process was awarded to Mrs. Goh's father and was left to Mrs. Goh in her father's will.)

Early in 2001, Mrs. Goh has indicated to you, her tax advisor, that she would like to maximize her RRSP deduction and contribution for 2001.

Required:

A. Determine Mrs. Goh's RRSP deduction limit for 2001.

B. Determine the maximum RRSP contribution that can be made by Mrs. Goh during 2001 without attracting the penalty for excess contributions.

C. Briefly explain to Mrs. Goh the advantages of making her 2001 contributions to a spousal RRSP.

Assignment Problem Six - 4

Mr. Frank Sabatini has been a salesman for a large, publicly traded Canadian corporation for the last fifteen years. During the year ending December 31, 2001 he earned a base salary of $58,000 and commissions of $74,000. In addition the corporation reimbursed him for invoiced travel costs of $12,300. Included in these travel costs was $5,600 in expenditures for business meals and entertainment.

Other Information:

1. The Corporation made a number of deductions from Mr. Sabatini's salary. The amounts were as follows:

Canada Pension Plan contributions	$ 1,496
Employment Insurance premiums	878
Income taxes	51,000
Registered Pension Plan contributions	3,500
Contributions to a registered charity	600
Parking fees - company garage	240
Employee share of life insurance premium	1,500
Employee share of sickness and accident insurance premium	550

2. Mr. Sabatini is covered by a group life insurance policy which pays $150,000 in the event of his death. The total annual premium on this policy is $3,000, with one-half of this amount paid by the employer.

3. Mr. Sabatini is covered by a group sickness and accident insurance plan which he joined on January 1, 2001. The premium on this plan is $100 per month, one-half of which is paid by Mr. Sabatini's employer. During 2001, Mr. Sabatini was hospitalized during all of June and received a benefit from the sickness and accident insurance plan in the amount of $4,500. Payment of the monthly premium was waived during the one month period of disability.

4. Mr. Sabatini's employer provides him with an automobile which was purchased in 2000 for $68,000. During 2001, Mr. Sabatini drives this automobile 99,000 kilometers, 92,000 of which are employment related. All operating costs are paid by the employer and for 2001 they amount to $16,300. During the period of his hospitalization, the automobile was returned to the employer's garage and was not available to Mr. Sabatini. Mr. Sabatini pays the company $1,000 for his personal use of the automobile during 2001.

5. As a result of his extensive business travel, Mr. Sabatini has accumulated over 300,000 points in a frequent flier program. All of this travel has been paid for by Mr. Sabatini's employer. On December 30, 2001, he uses 150,000 of these points for two first class tickets

to Cancun. Mr. Sabatini is accompanied on this one week trip by his secretary and, while there is some discussion of business matters, the trip is primarily for pleasure. At the same time, Mr. Sabatini uses another 30,000 of the points to provide his wife with an airline ticket to visit her mother in Leamington, Ontario. The normal cost of the Cancun tickets is $11,000 while the normal cost of the Leamington ticket is $600.

6. In 1998, Mr. Sabatini received options to purchase 1,000 shares of his employer's stock at a price of $12.50 per share. At the time the options were granted, the shares were trading at $10.00. During December, 2001, Mr. Sabatini exercises these options. At the time of exercise the stock is trading at $23.50 per share. Due to the Cancun trip and the resulting divorce proceedings, Mr. Sabatini neglects to file the election to defer the income inclusion related to the exercise of the stock options.

7. Mr. Sabatini's employer allows him to purchase merchandise at a discount of 30 percent off the normal retail prices. During 2001, Mr. Sabatini acquires such merchandise at a cost (after the applicable discount) of $6,790.

8. In addition to reimbursing him for invoiced travel costs, Mr. Sabatini's employer pays a $5,000 annual fee for his membership in a local golf and country club. During 2001, Mr. Sabatini spends $6,800 entertaining clients at this club. None of these costs are reimbursed by Mr. Sabatini's employer.

9. Mr. Sabatini's employer contributes $2,400 to the registered pension plan on his behalf and, in addition, contributes $2,000 in his name to the company's deferred profit sharing plan.

10. Mr. Sabatini has correctly calculated his 2000 Earned Income for RRSP purposes to be $111,000. At the end of 2000, Mr. Sabatini's unused RRSP Deduction Room was nil and he had no undeducted RRSP contributions. His employer reports that his pension adjustment for 2000 was $6,800.

11. On May 18, 2001, Mr. Sabatini contributes $2,600 into his wife's Registered Retirement Savings Plan. He contributed $10,000 to his own RRSP in February, 2001. This contribution was deducted in full on his 2000 tax return.

Required:

A. Determine Mr. Sabatini's minimum Net Employment Income for the year ending December 31, 2001 and indicate the reasons that you have not included items in your calculations. Ignore GST implications.

B. Calculate Mr. Sabatini's maximum RRSP deduction for the year ending December 31, 2001.

Assignment Problem Six - 5

On December 1, 2000, Mary Jo Bush, on the advice of her hairdresser, deposited her inheritance of $54,000 in her RRSP. She had made no RRSP contributions prior to this. Because she had very little taxable income in 2000, she did not deduct any portion of her RRSP contribution in that year.

She has provided you with the following information:

*   Her Unused RRSP Deduction Room is $10,000 at the end of 2000.
*   She made an additional RRSP contribution of $5,000 on February 1, 2001.
*   Mary Jo withdraws $35,000 from the RRSP on December 1, 2001.
*   For 2001, the annual increase in Mary Jo's RRSP Deduction Limit is $9,000 (18 percent of her 2000 Earned Income of $50,000).

Required: Determine the ITA 204.1 penalty (excess RRSP contributions), if any, that would be assessed to Mary Jo for the year ending December 31, 2001.

Assignment Problem Six - 6

Mr. White began working for Dynamics Inc. in 1984. The Company does not have either a registered pension plan or a deferred profit sharing plan.

Due to competitive pressures, Dynamics Inc. is attempting to reduce its overall work force. With this goal in mind, they have offered Mr. White a cash payment of $68,000 if he will immediately resign his position with the Company.

Required: Describe the tax consequences to Mr. White if he accepts this offer in 2001. Explain any alternatives that he might have in this regard and advise Mr. White as to an appropriate course of action.

Assignment Problem Six - 7

In each of the following independent Cases, calculate the Pension Adjustment (PA) or Past Service Pension Adjustment (PSPA) that would be reported by the employer:

Case A   Mrs. Anderson's employer sponsors both a money purchase RPP and a DPSP. She is a member of both. During 2000, the employer contributes, on her behalf, $2,200 to the RPP and $1,500 to the DPSP. Mrs. Anderson contributes $1,800 to the RPP. Mrs. Anderson's employment earnings for 2000 are $80,000. Calculate the 2000 PA.

Case B   Mr. Block's employer sponsors a defined benefit RPP and, during 2000, contributes $2,900 on Mr. Block's behalf. Mr. Block also contributes $2,900 to the plan in 2000. The plan provides a benefit equal to 1.75 percent of pensionable earnings for each year of service. Mr. Block's pensionable earnings for 2000 are $45,000. Calculate the 2000 PA.

Case C   Miss Carr has worked for her current employer since 1999. In January, 2001, this employer institutes a defined benefit RPP, with benefits extended for all years of service prior to the inception of the plan. The benefit formula calls for a retirement benefit equal to 1.25 percent of pensionable earnings for each year of service. In both of the previous years, Miss Carr's pensionable earnings were $38,000. Calculate the 2001 PSPA.

Case D   Ms. Dexter has worked for her current employer since 1999. She has been a member of her employer's defined benefit RPP during all of this period. In January, 2001, the employer agrees to retroactively increase the benefit formula from 1.6 percent of pensionable earnings for each year of service, to 1.8 percent of pensionable earnings for each year of service. In both of the previous years, Ms. Dexter's pensionable earnings were $59,000. Calculate the 2001 PSPA.

Assignment Problem Six - 8

Carla Goodman has been employed by Army Brake Products (ABP), a Canadian controlled private corporation, since 1999. The following information pertains to her income over the past two years:

	2001	2000
Salary Before Benefits	$70,000	$66,000
Employee Stock Option Benefit	8,000	5,000
Deemed Interest Benefit	6,000	5,000
Registered Pension Plan Contributions	(4,000)	(3,000)
Deductible Employment Expenses	(4,500)	(4,000)
Interest Income	1,800	1,600
Taxable Capital Gains	15,000	10,000
Business Income	34,000	35,000
Royalty Income	7,000	5,000
Rental Loss	(5,000)	(10,000)
Spousal Support Payments	(15,000)	(12,000)
Dividends On ABP Stock	900	1,000
Totals	$114,200	$99,600

Ms. Goodman had no earned income for RRSP purposes prior to 1998. While in 1998 and 1999, she had sufficient earned income to enable her to deduct the maximum allowable RRSP contribution for 1999 and 2000, she made no RRSP contributions in either of these years.

Beginning in 2000, Ms. Goodman participates in ABP's employee money purchase registered pension plan. ABP contributes two times the amount contributed by an employee to the plan. Her pension adjustment for 2000 is $9,000.

The royalty income listed above is 2 percent of the sales of the "Handy Shopper," a gadget Ms. Goodman invented three years ago. The business income listed above is earned from selling leather goods.

Required　Ignore all GST considerations.

Part A　Calculate Ms. Goodman's earned income for the purpose of determining her maximum 2001 RRSP contribution by listing the items and amounts that would be included in her earned income. List separately the items that are not included in the earned income calculation.

Part B　Based on the above information, calculate Ms. Goodman's maximum deductible RRSP contribution for 2001.

(Adapted from the 1993 UFE)

Assignment Problem Six - 9 (Electronic Library Research Problem)
Provide brief answers to the following questions. Your answers should be supported by references to materials found in your Electronic Library.

A. Some early retirement programs allow an employee to receive his retiring allowance in instalments over a period of years, as opposed to receiving a single lump sum at retirement. In some cases the total amount is larger than would be the case if a lump sum was received, reflecting an interest component on the deferred amount. How does this form of payment influence the ability of the taxpayer to make a deduction under ITA 60(j.1)?

B. ITA 146(8.3) contains an attribution rule for spousal RRSPs. Under certain circumstances this rule is not applicable. What are these circumstances?

C. Certain circumstances or events require that vested amounts contained in a DPSP must be paid to the entitled individual. What are these circumstances or events? When these circumstances or events apply, must the relevant amounts be paid as a single lump sum?

Chapter 7

Income Or Loss From A Business

Defining Business Income

The Nature Of Business Activity

7-1.   The subject of income or loss from a business is given coverage in ITA Division B, Subdivision b, Sections 9 through 37.3. Because of the many similarities in the procedures used to compute income from property, these ITA Sections also deal with property income. There are difference, however, in the treatment of these two types of income (e.g., a loss cannot be created through the deduction of capital cost allowance on property that is producing rental income). The provisions associated with property income will be given detailed coverage in Chapter 11.

7-2.   In very general terms, business activity involves organizations offering for sale merchandise which they have purchased, products which they have manufactured, or services which they have the ability to provide. A definition which is consistent with this view is as follows:

> **ITA 248(1)**   Business includes a profession, calling, trade, manufacture or undertaking of any kind whatever and, an adventure or concern in the nature of trade but does not include an office or employment.

7-3.   While this definition is fairly general in nature, its application in many situations is fairly straightforward (e.g., a retail store with all of its revenues from sales of merchandise is clearly earning business income). However, there are three areas in which distinguishing business income from other types of income is an important and sometimes controversial problem. Briefly described, these areas are as follows:

Business Income Vs. Employment Income   This distinction is important in that an individual earning business income is able to deduct more items than an individual earning employment income. This issue is discussed fully in Chapter 5.

Business Income Vs. Property Income   This distinction is important in that a corporation earning business income is eligible for the small business deduction. The availability of this deduction, along with a similar rate reduction at the provincial level, can reduce the corporation's combined federal/provincial tax rate by over 20 percentage points. This distinction is discussed fully in Chapter 14.

Business Income Vs. Capital Gains   On dispositions of property, it is sometimes difficult to establish whether the resulting gain is business income or, alternatively, a capital gain. This distinction is important because of the taxation of capital gains. When losses are involved, further importance attaches to this distinction in that capital losses can only be deducted against capital gains. The distinction between business income and capital gains is discussed fully in the next section of this Chapter.

7-4.   A final point here relates to what is referred to in the ITA 248(1) definition of business as an "adventure or concern in the nature of trade". There are situations in which a taxpayer engages in a single purchase and sale transaction, as opposed to carrying on a regular and continuous business activity. This, in effect, creates a third class of property in addition to business property and capital property. An example of this from a CCRA publication would be land purchased by an individual who is not in the land development business for eventual resale at a profit. Property such is this is treated in part like business income, in that profits or losses on the property are recognized in the income account and, in part like capital property, in that the profits or losses are recognized only on disposition.

Business Income Vs. Capital Gains

Importance of the Distinction

7-5.   When an asset is disposed of, there may be a question as to whether any resulting gain or loss should either be included in the income account (i.e., treated as business or property income) or included in the capital account (i.e., treated as a capital gain or loss). This distinction is important for two reasons:

- Only one-half of a capital gain is taxed and only one-half of a capital loss is deductible. If a gain transaction can be classified as capital in nature, the savings to the taxpayer can be very significant.

- Allowable capital losses (i.e., the deductible one-half) can only be deducted against taxable capital gains (i.e., the taxable one-half). This can be of great importance, particularly to individual taxpayers and smaller business enterprises. It many be years before such taxpayers realize taxable capital gains, resulting in a situation where there is significant deferral of the tax benefits associated with capital losses.

7-6.   This distinction is a source of much litigation. Those taxpayers experiencing gains will, of course, wish to have them classified as capital. Alternatively, those taxpayers who have incurred losses will wish to have them classified as on the income account. This makes it extremely important to understand the distinction between a capital asset and an asset whose disposition results in business or property income.

Capital Assets Defined

7-7.   The basic concept is a simple one — capital assets are held to produce income through their use, as opposed to producing income through being sold. Take, for example, the assets of a retail store. These will include inventories of purchased merchandise which are being held for resale. Such assets are not part of the capital of the business and any income related to their sale would be classified as business income. However, the building in which the merchandise is being offered for sale as well as the furniture and fixtures necessary to the operation of the business are capital assets. This would mean that if the operation were to sell these assets, any resulting gain or loss would be capital in nature. In general, capital assets are somewhat analogous to the accounting classification of non current assets. An additional analogy, sometimes applied in court cases, is with a fruit bearing tree. The tree itself is a capital asset and its sale would result in a capital gain or loss. In contrast, the sale of the fruit from the tree would generate business income.

7-8.   In general, it is the use of the asset that determines the appropriate classification. A particular type of asset can be classified as capital by one business and as inventory by another. Consider a piece of equipment such as a backhoe. For a construction company using this asset for excavating construction sites, it would clearly be a capital asset. Alternatively, if it were held for sale by a dealer in construction equipment, it would be classified as inventory, with any gain on its sale being taxed as business income.

Criteria For Identifying Capital Gains

7-9.   While in many situations the preceding distinction is clear, problems often arise, particularly with respect to investments in real estate and securities. In general, the courts have taken the position that for an investment to qualify as a capital asset it must be capable of earning income in the form of interest, dividends, royalties, or rents. Further, it must be the intent of the investor to hold the asset for its income producing capabilities, not simply for quick resale at a profit. Various criteria have been used in making this distinction, the most common of which are as follows:

Intent and Course of Conduct   This involves attempting to determine whether the investor intended to hold the investment as an income producing asset or to merely profit from a quick resale of the asset. In many cases this intent will be judged by the length of time the investment was held. The question of secondary intent would also apply here. If the investor made some effort to earn a return on the investment, but was clearly aware of an ability to sell at a profit if the investment return was inadequate, the investment might not qualify for capital gains treatment.

Number And Frequency Of Transactions   A large number of closely spaced transactions would be an indication that the investor was in the business of dealing in this type of asset.

Relationship To The Taxpayer's Business   If the transaction is related to the taxpayer's business, this may be sufficient to disqualify any gain or loss from capital gains treatment. For example, a gain on a mortgage transaction might be considered business income to a real estate broker.

Supplemental Work on the Property   Additional work on the property, directed at enhancing its value or marketability, would indicate an adventure in the nature of trade resulting in business income.

Nature Of The Assets   The conventional accounting distinction between fixed assets and working capital has been used in some cases to determine whether income was business or capital in nature. Note, however, the discussion in Paragraph 7-8 concerning this issue.

Objectives Declared In Articles Of Incorporation   Gains and losses on transactions which fall within the corporation's declared objectives may be considered business income. However, as most corporations state their objectives in a very broad manner, this criteria is not frequently used.

> Exercise Seven-1 deals with the identification of capital gains. This would be an appropriate time to attempt this exercise.

7-10   For more specific guidance in this area with respect to real estate transactions, IT-218R, "Profit, Capital Gains And Losses From The Sale of Real Estate, Including Farmland And Inherited Land And Conversion Of Real Estate From Capital Property To Inventory And Vice Versa", provides a check list of factors that the courts have considered in making the capital gains/business income distinction. A similar list for transactions in securities can be found in IT-479R, "Transactions In Securities".

Business Income And GAAP

7-11   Financial statements requiring audit opinions must be prepared in accordance with generally accepted accounting principles or GAAP. These principles have had a significant influence on the development of the tax concept of business income. This is reflected in the fact that, for tax purposes, business income is usually an accrual rather than a cash based calculation and it is a net rather than a gross concept. In addition, GAAP continues to be influential in that income as computed under these principles is usually required for tax purposes unless a particular provision of the *Act* specifies alternative requirements.

7-12.   This means that business income under the *Income Tax Act* will not be totally unfamiliar to anyone who has had experience in the application of GAAP. However, there are a number of differences between GAAP based income and taxable business income. While many of these will become apparent as we proceed through the discussion of the specific provisions of the *Act*, it is useful to note some of the more important differences at this point. They are as follows:

Amortization (Depreciation)   The amount that will be deducted to reflect the costs of capital assets used up during the period is referred to in tax practice as capital cost allowance (CCA) rather than amortization or depreciation expense. The *Act* and related Regulations specify the method for CCA calculations and the maximum amount of such allowances that may be deducted in a given taxation year. However, there is no requirement that this maximum amount be deducted, nor is there any requirement that a consistent policy be followed as long as the amount involved is less than the maximum specified in the Act. In contrast, GAAP allows management to choose from a variety of amortization methods. Further, once a method is adopted, it must be used consistently to deduct the full amount as calculated by that method. Because of these different approaches, capital cost allowance deducted will usually be different than the corresponding Amortization Expense under GAAP. This is the most common and, for most enterprises, the largest difference between accounting Net Income and Net Income For Tax Purposes.

Other Allocations   There are other items, similar to amortization charges, where the total cost to be deducted will be the same for tax and accounting purposes. However, they will be deducted using different allocation patterns. Examples would be pension costs (funding payments are deducted for tax purposes), warranty costs (cash payments are deducted for tax purposes), and scientific research and experimental development expenditures (some capital costs are fully deductible for tax purposes in the year of acquisition).

Permanent Differences   There are some differences between tax and accounting income that are permanent in nature. For example, 100 percent of capital gains are included in accounting Net Income, while only one-half of this income will be included in Net Income For Tax Purposes. Other examples of this type of difference would be the non deductible 50 percent of business meals and entertainment and the non deductible component of automobile lease payments in excess of the monthly limit (see discussion later in this Chapter).

Unreasonable Expenses   In applying GAAP, accountants are generally not required to distinguish between expenses which are reasonable and those which are not. If assets were used up in the production of revenues of the period, they are expenses of that period. This is not the case for tax purposes. ITA 67 indicates that only those expenditures which may be considered reasonable in the circumstances may be deducted in the computation of income. If, for example, a large salary was paid to a spouse or to a child that could not be justified on the basis of the services provided, the deduction of the amount involved could be disallowed under ITA 67. The fact that this salary could be deducted in the determination of accounting income would not alter this conclusion.

Non Arm's Length Transactions   ITA 69 deals with situations involving transactions between related parties and provides special rules when such non arm's length transactions take place at values other than fair market value. For example, if a taxpayer acquired something from a person with whom he was not dealing at arm's length at a value in excess of its fair market value, the transferee is deemed to have acquired it at fair market value while the transferor is taxed on the basis of the consideration received. If the transferee was a business, no value adjustment would be required under GAAP. Note, however, there are requirements under GAAP for disclosing related party transactions.

7-13.   As many of you are aware, the financial reporting rules applicable to accounting for taxes were significantly changed in 1997, with the addition of Section 3465 to the *CICA Handbook*. The now superseded Section 3470 divided accounting/tax differences into two categories — timing differences and permanent differences. These amounts were defined in terms of differences between accounting Net Income and Net Income For Tax Purposes. In contrast, Section 3465 focuses on temporary differences which are defined in terms of Balance Sheet items. However, in determining business income for tax purposes, the normal approach is to reconcile accounting Net Income with Net Income For Tax Purposes. As a consequence, individuals working in the tax area will continue to focus on Income Statement differences, as opposed to Balance Sheet differences. For a comprehensive discussion of these issues, we would refer you to our "A Self Study Course And Guide To CICA Handbook Section 3465 - Income Taxes", published in 1999 by the Canadian Institute Of Chartered Accountants.

> Exercises Seven-2 and Seven-3 deal with GAAP vs. tax issues. This would be an appropriate time to attempt these exercises.

Business Income - Inclusions (Revenues)

Amounts Received And Receivable

7-14. The most important inclusion in business income described in ITA 12(1) is amounts received and receivable for goods and services that have been or will be delivered. The wording used makes it clear that, in general, business income is on an accrual basis. However, the inclusion varies from the usual GAAP definition of a revenue in that it does not eliminate amounts received for goods and services that have not yet been delivered or rendered. Under GAAP, advances from customers are treated as a liability, rather than as a revenue. We will find that the tax treatment is, in fact, reconciled with GAAP through the use of a reserve.

7-15. In the next Section we will examine how reserves are used to modify the amount of revenues recorded under ITA 12(1). While these procedures appear to be somewhat different than those used under GAAP, they will generally result in a final inclusion that is identical to the amount of revenue that is recognized under GAAP.

Reserves

The General System

7-16. In tax work, the term reserve is used to refer to a group of specific items that can be deducted in the determination of net business income. Unlike most deductions which relate either to cash outflows or the incurrence of liabilities, these items are modifications of amounts received (reserve for undelivered goods) or amounts receivable (reserve for bad debts and reserve for uncollected amounts).

7-17. With respect to the use of such reserves, the basic rules are as follows:

- ITA 18(1)(e) indicates that a particular reserve cannot be deducted unless it is specifically provided for in the *Act*. This means that, for example, when estimated warranty costs are deducted as an accounting expense in the year in which the related product is sold, no reserve can be deducted for tax purposes as a reserve for estimated warranty costs is not specified in the *Act*. Note that while ITA 20(1)(m.1) does refer to a manufacturer's warranty reserve, careful reading will show amounts can be deducted under this provision only when the amounts are for an extended warranty covered by an insurance contract.

- When a reserve is deducted in a particular taxation year, it must be added back as an inclusion in the immediately following year. These additions are required under various paragraphs in ITA 12 (e.g., ITA 12(1)(g) requires the addition of reserves deducted for bad debts in the preceding year).

7-18. The most commonly encountered reserves to be deducted from business income are as follows:

- Reserve For Doubtful Accounts - ITA 20(1)(l)
- Reserve For Undelivered Goods And Services - ITA 20(1)(m)
- Reserve For Uncollected Amounts - ITA 20(1)(n)

7-19. The more specific details of these reserves will be covered in the sections which follow.

Bad Debts Reserve

7-20. While specific tax procedures for dealing with bad debts differ from those used under GAAP, the alternative procedures will generally produce identical results. Specifically, under ITA 20(1)(l), a year end deduction is permitted for anticipated bad debts. During the subsequent year, actual bad debts may be deducted under ITA 20(1)(p). Then, at the end of this subsequent year, the old reserve is included in business income under ITA 12(1)(d) and a new reserve is established under ITA 20(1)(l). The fact that this approach will generally produce the same results as the procedures used under GAAP can be illustrated with the following example:

Example On December 31, 2000, at the end of its first year of operations, Ken's Boutique estimates that $5,500 of its ending Accounts Receivable will be uncollectible. An Allowance For Bad Debts is established for this amount and a reserve is deducted under ITA 20(1)(l). During the year ending December 31, 2001, $6,800 in accounts are written off. At December 31, 2001, estimated uncollectible accounts total $4,800.

7-21. For accounting purposes, the $6,800 would be written off against the Allowance For Bad Debts account. This would leave a year end debit balance in this account of $1,300, reflecting the fact that last year's reserve was not adequate. This shortfall in last year's bad debt expense will be corrected by adding this debit balance to the Bad Debt Expense for 2001. This would mean that the Bad Debt Expense would total $6,100 ($6,800 - $5,500 + $4,800), an amount which reflects the new estimate of $4,800, plus the adjustment required to eliminate the debit balance in the Allowance For Bad Debts account. The resulting balance in the Allowance For Bad Debts would be $4,800, the new estimate as at December 31, 2001.

Exercise Seven-4 deals with bad debt procedures. This would be an appropriate time to attempt this exercise.

7-22. For tax purposes the total Bad Debt Expense would be the same $6,100. However, the calculation follows a different pattern:

Add: The 2000 Reserve		$ 5,500
Deduct:		
2001 Write Offs	($6,800)	
2001 Reserve	(4,800)	(11,600)
2001 Deduction For Tax Purposes		($ 6,100)

Reserve For Undelivered Goods

7-23. It was previously noted that, unlike the situation under GAAP, amounts received for goods or services to be delivered in the future must be included in tax revenues. However, this difference is offset by the ability to deduct, under ITA 20(1)(m), a reserve for goods and services to be delivered in the future. This means that, while the procedures are somewhat different, the treatment of amounts received for undelivered goods and services will be the same under both the *Income Tax Act* and GAAP.

Example During the taxation year ending December 31, 2001, Donna's Auto Parts has receipts of $275,000. Of this amount, $25,000 is for goods that will be delivered in 2002.

Tax Consequences While the $275,000 will be considered an inclusion in 2001 net business income, Donna will be able to deduct a reserve of $25,000 under ITA 20(1)(m). This $25,000 amount will have to be added back to her 2002 net business income, reflecting the fact that the goods have been delivered and the revenue realized.

Reserve For Unpaid Amounts

7-24. When a business sells goods with the amount being receivable over an extended period (i.e., instalment sales), ITA 20(1)(n) permits the deduction of a reasonable reserve. While this is analogous to the use of the cash basis of revenue recognition for instalment sales, its applicability in tax work is more restricted than it is in accounting. Specifically, a reserve can only be deducted under ITA 20(1)(n) if some of the proceeds are not receivable until two years after the property is sold. In addition, ITA 20(8) specifies that no reserve can be deducted in a year, if the sale took place more than 36 months before the end of that year.

7-25.   Because of the restrictions on the use of this reserve, it is of somewhat limited usefulness. Further, differences may arise between accounting income and business income for tax purposes, even when the cash basis of revenue recognition is being used in the accounting records.

Other Inclusions

7-26.   ITA 12 through ITA 17 contain a long list of other inclusions in the computation of income. Some of these, for example, interest and dividends, are property income and will not be considered until Chapter 11. Further, inclusions for recapture of capital cost allowance and amounts related to cumulative eligible capital cannot be covered until we deal with capital cost allowance concepts in Chapter 8. Other business income items include damage insurance proceeds, the taxpayer's share of any partnership income, bad debt recoveries, rebates from employees' profit sharing plans, tax credits for scientific research expenditures, grants under the Canadian Home Insulation Program, and tenant inducement receipts.

7-27.   Several additional points are relevant here:

Profits From Betting or Gambling   Generally speaking, these items are not included in net business income. However, if a taxpayer's gambling activities were so extensive as to constitute a business, such income could become taxable (e.g., a full time bookmaker). This would also suggest that losses would be fully deductible.

Profits From an Illegal Business   Many people are aware that the famous American gangster Al Capone was sent to jail, not for his illegal activities involving robbery and murder, but rather for his failure to pay taxes on the resulting profits. As illegal revenues must be included in business income, related expenses are generally deductible. This can lead to interesting conclusions as evidenced by a 1999 publication of the New Zealand Inland Revenue Department. This publication provided a detailed list of items that could be deducted by what was referred to as "sex workers". Without going into detail, we would note that see-through garments and whips were on the list, provided they were used in delivering services to a client.

Illegal Payments   Since 1994, payments made to government officials that constitute an offence under either the *Corruption of Foreign Officials Act* or Canada's *Criminal Code* are not deductible. This would be the case, even if the related income was taxable.

Debt Forgiveness   Situations arise in which outstanding debt is forgiven, often by a related taxpayer. When this happens, ITA 80 contains a complex set of rules which apply when a taxpayer has been able to deduct the interest expense on the forgiven debt. These rules may require the amount of debt forgiven to be applied to reduce loss carry over balances and, in some situations, to be included in income in the year of forgiveness. The details of the rules are beyond the scope of this text.

Restrictions On Deductions From Business And Property Income

General Approach

7-28.   It would be extremely difficult to provide a detailed list of all of the items that might possibly be considered a business expense. While ITA 20 spells out many such items, it is often necessary to have more general guidance when new items arise. ITA 18 through ITA 19.1 gives this guidance in a somewhat backwards fashion by providing guidelines on what should not be deducted in computing business income. However, this negative guidance frequently provides assistance in determining what should be deducted in computing business income.

7-29.   Note, however, that if an item is specifically listed in the *Act* as a deduction, the specific listing overrides the general limitation. For example, Section 18 prohibits the deduction of capital costs, thereby preventing the immediate write off of a capital asset. The fact that ITA 20(1)(aa) permits the deduction of landscaping costs, some of which would be capital expenditures, overrides the general prohibition found in Section 18.

7-30.   Note that the restrictions contained in ITA 18 apply only to deductions from business and property income. There are other restrictions, for example the cost of business meals and entertainment, that apply to deductions from either business and property income or employment income. Most of these more general restrictions are found in subdivision f, "Rules Relating To Computation Of Income", and will be discussed in the next Section of this Chapter. The more important of the ITA 18 through 19.1 limiting provisions will be discussed in this Section.

General Limitation

7-31.   One of the most important of the limiting provisions is as follows:

> **ITA 18(1)(a)**   No deduction shall be made in respect of an outlay or expense except to the extent that it was made or incurred by the taxpayer for the purpose of gaining or producing income from the business or property.

7-32.   When there is a question as to the deductibility of an item not covered by a particular provision of the Act, it is usually this general limitation provision that provides the basis for an answer. As a consequence, there are many Interpretation Bulletins dealing with such matters as legal and accounting fees (IT-99R5), deductibility of fines (IT-104R2), and motor vehicle expenses (IT-521R). In addition, there have been hundreds of court cases dealing with particular items. For example, with respect to insurance costs there have been cases in the following areas:

- Damage insurance on business assets (deductible)
- Life insurance when required by creditor (deductible if interest on loan is deductible)
- Life insurance in general (not deductible)
- Partnership insurance on partners' lives (not deductible)
- Insurance against competition (deductible)

7-33.   As can be seen from the preceding list, this is a complex area of tax practice. If there is doubt about a particular item's deductibility, it will sometimes be necessary to do considerable research to establish whether it is dealt with in either an Interpretation Bulletin or a court case.

7-34.   In applying this provision, it is not necessary to demonstrate that the expenditure actually produced income. It is generally sufficient to demonstrate that it was incurred with an intention and a reasonable expectation of making a profit.

Other Restrictions On
Business And Property Income Deductions

Capital Expenditures

7-35.   ITA 18(1)(b) prohibits the deduction of any expenditures which are designated as capital expenditures. However, deductions are permitted under ITA 20(1)(a) for capital cost allowances. The limitations on this deduction are discussed in detail in Chapter 8.

Appraisal Costs

7-36.   If appraisal costs are incurred on a capital property for the purpose of its acquisition or disposition, they are generally added to the adjusted cost base of the property. However, if such costs are incurred with respect to a proposed acquisition that does not take place, they should be treated as an eligible capital expenditure (See Chapter 8). Alternatively, if the appraisal costs are incurred for the purposes of gaining or producing income from a business (e.g., the cost of an appraisal required for insurance purposes), they are deductible in computing income for the year.

Exempt Income

7-37.   ITA 18(1)(c) prohibits the deduction of any expenditures that were incurred to produce income that is exempt from taxation. For a business this would have limited applicability as few sources of business income are tax exempt.

Personal And Living Expenses

7-38.   ITA 18(1)(h) prohibits the deduction of an expenditure that is a personal or living expense of the taxpayer. An example of this would be a situation where a business pays for the cost of travel for one of its employees or owners. If the travel is business related, the costs would be deductible. Alternatively, if no business purposes was involved, the travel would be classified as a non deductible personal or living expense. This can create a very unfortunate tax situation in that, not only will the costs of such travel be non deductible, the beneficiary of the trip may have to include the value of the trip in their income as a shareholder or employee benefit. Clearly, it would be preferable to simply pay additional salary equal to the value of the trip. Using this alternative, the tax consequences to the employee or owner would be the same. However, the business would benefit from being able to deduct the amount paid.

7-39.   Somewhat indirectly, ITA 18(1)(h) introduces an additional rule with respect to the deductibility of costs. The ITA 248(1) definition of "personal or living expenses" indicates that costs incurred will be considered personal or living expenses except when they are made in connection with a business that is carried on with a "reasonable expectation of profit". This definition has the effect of making business expense deductibility conditional on the business having a reasonable expectation of profit. Combining this with ITA 18(1)(a), it is clear that, in order to be deductible in the determination of business income, a cost must be made for the purpose of producing income for a business that has a reasonable expectation of profit. An important application of this concept is in the area of farm losses, a subject that will be discussed at a later point in this Chapter.

Recreational Facilities And Club Dues

7-40.   ITA 18(1)(l) prohibits the deduction of amounts that have been incurred to maintain a yacht, a camp, a lodge, a golf course, or similar recreational facilities, unless the taxpayer is in the business of providing such property for hire. A similar prohibition is made against the deduction of membership fees or dues to dining, sporting, or recreational facilities. Note, however, that there is no prohibition against deducting the cost of legitimate entertainment expenses incurred in such facilities, subject to the 50 percent limitation which will be described shortly.

Deferred Income Plans

7-41.   ITA 18(1)(i) restricts the deductibility of contributions under supplementary unemployment benefit plans to the amount specified in ITA 145. ITA 18(1)(j) and 18(1)(k) provide similar limitations for contributions to deferred profit sharing plans and profit sharing plans. ITA 18(1)(o) prohibits the deduction of contributions to an employee benefit plan. Finally, under ITA 18(1)(o.1) and (o.2), limits are placed on the deductibility of amounts paid to salary deferral arrangements and retirement compensation arrangements. These amounts are only deductible as specified under ITA 20(1)(r) and (oo). All of these provisions were discussed in detail in Chapter 6 under deferred compensation.

Expenses Of A Personal Services Business

7-42.   A personal services business is a corporation that has been set up by an individual to provide personal services that are, in effect, employment services. ITA 18(1)(p) restricts the deductible expenses of such a corporation to those that would normally be deductible against employment income. (Chapter 14 provides coverage of this subject.)

Automobile Mileage Payments

7-43.   As was discussed in Chapter 5, a business may pay their employees or shareholders a per kilometer fee for having them use their own automobile on behalf of the business. The amount of such payments that can be deducted by a business is limited by ITA 18(1)(r) to an amount prescribed in ITR 7306. For 2001, this amount is 41 cents for the first 5,000 kilometers and 35 cents for additional kilometers driven by an employee. Amounts paid in excess of these limits will not be deductible to the business. However, provided they are reasonable, such larger amounts will still not be considered a taxable benefit to the employee. As was noted in Chapter 5, if the reimbursement is paid on a tax free basis and not included on the employee's T4, it will be necessary for the employer to keep detailed records of each employee's mileage for the year.

Interest And Property Taxes On Land

7-44.   Many businesses pay interest and property taxes on land. To the extent that the primary purpose of holding this land is to produce income, these payments clearly represent amounts that can be deducted as part of the costs of carrying the land while it is producing income.

7-45.   When land is vacant or is not being held primarily to produce income, amounts paid for interest and property taxes may not satisfy the ITA 18(1)(a) condition that they be incurred to produce income. This is reflected in ITA 18(2) which, in general, limits the deductibility of interest and property taxes in these situations to the amount of any net revenues produced by the property. For example, if a parcel of land which is being held as a future plant site is producing some revenues by being rented for storage, interest and property taxes on the land can only be deducted to the extent of the net revenues from the rent. ITA 53(1)(h) allows the non deductible interest and tax costs to be added to the adjusted cost base of the property, thereby reducing any future capital gain resulting from the disposition of the property.

7-46.   The preceding general rules could be viewed as too restrictive for those companies whose "principal business is the leasing, rental or sale, or the development for lease, rental or sale, of real property". As a consequence, these real estate companies are allowed to deduct interest and property tax payments to the extent of net revenues from the property, plus a "base level deduction". This base level deduction is defined in ITA 18(2.2) as the amount that would be the amount of interest, computed at the prescribed rate, for the year in respect of a loan of $1,000,000 outstanding throughout the year. This means that, if the prescribed rate for the year was 6 percent, real estate companies could deduct interest and property taxes on the land that they are carrying to the extent of net revenues from the land, plus an additional $60,000 [(6%)($1,000,000)].

Soft Costs

7-47.   Costs that are attributable to the period of construction, renovation, or alteration of a building or in respect of the ownership of the related land are referred to as soft costs. These costs could include interest, legal and accounting fees, insurance, and property taxes. In general, ITA 18(3.1) indicates that such costs are not deductible and must be added to the adjusted cost base of the property.

Interest In Thin Capitalization Situations

7-48.   In general, interest paid on debt is deductible to a business, whereas dividends paid on outstanding shares are not. Given this, there is an incentive for a non resident owner of a Canadian resident corporation to take back debt rather than equity for the financing that he provides to the corporation. This could result in a situation where the interest on the debt reduces the profits of the Canadian corporation, without being subject to taxation in the hands of the non resident investor.

7-49.   To prevent this from happening, ITA 18(4) through (8) limit the deductibility of interest paid in such situations. Interest remitted to a non resident specified shareholder is disallowed if it is paid on amounts of debt in excess of two times the amount of the individual's share of paid up capital and retained earnings (this was reduced from three times by the 2000 budget). For this purpose, a specified shareholder is one who holds shares which give him 25 percent or more of the votes, or 25 percent or more of the fair market value of all shares. A simple example will serve to clarify these rules:

Example The capital structure of Thinly Ltd. is as follows:

Long Term Debt (11% Rate)	$5,000,000
Common Stock	200,000
Retained Earnings	300,000
Total Capital	$5,500,000

Mr. Lane, a resident of the U.S., owns 45 percent of the shares and holds $3,000,000 of the long term debt securities.

7-50.   Mr. Lane is clearly a specified shareholder, holding 45 percent of the equity investment with a book value of $225,000 [(45%)($200,000 + $300,000)]. His debt holding is clearly in excess of two times his equity holding, resulting in disallowed interest as follows:

Mr. Lane's Total Interest [(11%)($3,000,000)]	$330,000
Allowed Interest [(11%)(2)($225,000)]	(49,500)
Disallowed Interest	$280,500

Prepaid Expenses

7-51.   ITA 18(9) prevents the deduction of amounts that have been paid for goods or services that will be delivered after the end of the taxation year. This has the effect of reconciling the tax treatment of these items with their treatment under GAAP.

7-52.   With respect to interest, the normal calculation of interest involves multiplying a principal amount by an interest rate and then adjusting the product for the period of time that the principal amount is outstanding. Given this calculation, any payments over and above the calculated interest must be viewed as a reduction in the principal amount. Despite the clarity of this concept, we continue to see references to so called "prepaid interest".

7-53.   The most recent resurrection of this concept has been in a form that attempts to avoid the payment of taxes. This scheme involves designing a debt arrangement so that future interest payments are "prepaid" in order to create a larger current deduction in the calculation of taxable income for the payor. Consider the following example:

Example The Martian Company issues $1,000,000 in debt securities on January 1, 2001. The face amount of the securities must be repaid after five years on December 31, 2005. The securities pay interest at 10 percent with the $100,000 payments for 2001 and 2002 being made on December 31, 2001 and December 31, 2002. However, the discounted value of the 2003, 2004 and 2005 interest payments is also paid on December 31, 2001. The payment, equal to the present value of the three $100,000 payments, is $226,077. The Company's year ends on December 31.

7-54.   In the absence of a special provision, the full $226,077 would be deductible as interest expense for the year ending December 31, 2001. This situation is corrected by Sections ITA 18(9.2) through ITA 18(9.8) which require this "prepaid interest" to be treated as a reduction in the principal amount of the debt. Although the interest deducted over the life of the debt will still total $426,077 [($100,000)(2) + $226,077], the deductions will be allocated over the life of the debt. Given this, the deductible interest for the years 2001 through 2005 would be as follows:

Year		Deductible Interest
2001	[(10%)($1,000,000)]	$100,000
2002	[(10%)($1,000,000 - $226,077)]	77,392
2003	[(10%)($773,923 - $100,000 + $77,392)]	75,132
2004	[(10%)($751,315 + $75,132)]	82,644
2005	[(10%)($826,447 + $82,644)]	90,909
Total		$426,077

Home Office Costs

7-55.   Many self employed individuals maintain an office in their personal residence. Under certain circumstances, some of the costs associated with owning and maintaining this residence are deductible. ITA 18(12) restricts the deductibility of home office costs to those situations where:

• the work space is the individual's principal place of business; or
• the space is used exclusively for the purpose of earning income from business and is used on a regular and continuous basis for meeting clients, customers, or patients of the individual.

7-56.   If an individual qualifies for this deduction because it is his principal place of business, the space does not have to be used exclusively for business purposes. If, for example, a dining room table is used to run a mail order business and that room qualifies as the principal place of business for the operation, home office costs can be deducted for the dining room space. Note, however, that in determining the appropriate amount of costs, consideration would have to be given to any personal use of that space.

7-57.   If the work space is not the principal place of business, it must be used exclusively for the purposes of earning income. This requires that some part of the home must be designated as the home office and not used for any other purpose. In addition, this second provision requires that the space be used on a regular and continuous basis for meeting clients, customers, or patients. IT-514, "Work Space In Home Expense", indicates that a work space for a business which normally requires infrequent meetings or frequent meetings at irregular intervals would not meet this requirement.

7-58.   When the conditions for deductibility are met, expenses must be apportioned between business and non business use on a reasonable basis, usually on the basis of floor space used. Pro rata deductions can be made for rent, mortgage interest, property taxes, property insurance, utilities and various operating costs.

7-59.   You will recall that there is an equivalent deduction available to employees under ITA 8(13). As an employee, an individual cannot deduct the mortgage interest, property taxes, insurance or capital cost allowance on the property. However, as we are dealing with business income here, these deductions are available. While the interest deduction should be used, individuals are generally advised not to deduct capital cost allowance as this is likely to cause the business portion of the residence to lose its principal residence status (as explained in Chapter 9, capital gains on the disposition of a property that qualifies as a principal residence will generally not be subject to taxation).

7-60.   Regardless of the types of costs deducted, home office costs cannot create or increase a loss. As a result, the total deduction will be limited to the amount of net income from the business calculated without reference to the home office costs (IT-514). Any expenses which are not deductible in a given year because they exceed the business income in that year, can be carried forward and deducted in a subsequent year against income generated from the same business. In effect, there is an indefinite carry forward of unused home office costs.

Foreign Media Advertising

7-61.   In order to provide some protection to Canadian media, the *Act* places limitations on the deductibility of advertising expenditures in foreign media. For print media, this limitation is found in ITA 19, with ITA 19.1 containing a corresponding provision for broadcast media. In general, these provisions deny a deduction for expenditures made in print or broadcast foreign media in those cases where the advertising message is directed primarily at the Canadian market. It does not apply where such foreign media expenditures are focused on non Canadian markets.

7-62.   Amendments to ITA 19 have exempted foreign periodicals from the general non deductibility rule. Provided that 80 percent or more of the periodical's non advertising content is original, Canadian businesses will be able to deduct 100 percent of their advertising costs without regard to whether or not it is directed at the Canadian market. If the periodical cannot meet the 80 percent criteria, only 50 percent of such advertising costs will be deductible.

Provincial Capital and Payroll Taxes

7-63.   In the later 1980s and early 1990s, several provinces switched from having individual premiums for health care to a payroll tax applicable to all wages and salaries. This change had significant implications for the federal government because, as you may recall from Chapter 5, when an employer pays for individual provincial health care premiums, it is considered a taxable benefit to the employee. Given that many employers did, in fact, pay the individual provincial health care premiums, the switch to a non individualized payroll tax resulted in a significant loss of revenues for the federal government.

7-64.   In response to such changes, the February 27, 1991 federal budget proposed limiting the deduction of provincial capital and payroll taxes to an annual amount of $10,000. This proposal proved to be very controversial and, as a consequence, is still pending. While the government has indicated that, as an interim measure, it will deny deductibility to any increases in provincial payroll or capital taxes, at present these amounts continue to be fully deductible.

Restrictions On Deductions From Business, Property, Or Employment Income

Introduction

7-65.   The restrictions that are found in ITA 18 through ITA 19.1 are applicable only to business and property income. For the most part they involve expenses that would only be deductible against this type of income and so the restriction has no influence on the determination of other types of income. The exception to this is home office costs which can be deducted against either employment or business and property income. Note, however, that in this case a separate ITA Section is applicable to each type of income.

7-66.   Other types of expenses, for example business meals and entertainment, can be deducted against either employment or business income. The restrictions on deductions of this type are applicable to all types of income and, as a consequence, are found in other Sections of the *Act*. These more general restrictions will be discussed in the material which follows.

Meals And Entertainment

7-67.   It can be argued that business expenditures for food, beverages, or entertainment involve an element of personal living costs and, to the extent that this is true, such amounts should not be deductible in calculating taxable income. This idea is embodied in ITA 67.1(1) which restricts the amount that can be deducted for the human consumption of food or beverages or the enjoyment of entertainment. The amount of these costs that can be deducted is equal to 50 percent. The subsection makes it clear that this limit does not apply to meals related to moving costs, child care costs, or amounts eligible for the medical expense tax credit.

7-68.   ITA 67.1(2) provides for a number of exceptions to the general 50 percent limitation. They include:

- Hotels, restaurants, and airlines provide food, beverages, and entertainment in return for compensation from their customers. The costs incurred by these organizations in providing these goods and services continue to be deductible. However, when the employees of these organizations travel or entertain clients, their costs are subject to the 50 percent limitation.

- Meals and entertainment expenses relating to a fund raising event for a registered charity are fully deductible.

- Where the taxpayer is compensated by someone else for the costs of food, beverages, or entertainment, the amounts will be fully deductible against this compensation. For example, if Mr. Spinner was a management consultant whose client reimbursed all his travel costs, there would be no 50 percent limitation on meals and entertainment for Mr. Spinner. However, his client would only be able to deduct 50 percent of any reimbursements for meals and entertainment that are paid to Mr. Spinner.

- When amounts are paid for meals or entertainment for employees and, either the payments create a taxable benefit for the employee or the benefits do not create a taxable benefit because they are being provided at a remote work location, the amounts are fully deductible to the employer.

- When amounts are incurred by an employer for food, beverages or entertainment, that is generally available to all individuals employed by the taxpayer, the amounts are fully deductible.

7-69. In addition to the preceding exceptions, ITA 67.1(3) provides a special rule for meals that are included in conference or convention fees. When the amount included in the fee for meals and entertainment is not specified, the Subsection deems the amount to be $50 per day. In these circumstances, it is this $50 per day that is subject to the 50 percent limitation.

7-70. Airline, bus, and rail tickets often include meals in their price. It appears that the government views the value of such meals as being fairly immaterial. This is reflected in the fact that ITA 67.1(4) deems the food component of the ticket cost to be nil.

Costs Of Automobile Ownership And Leasing
Basic Concept
7-71. When a business provides an automobile to an employee or shareholder, it is clear that these individuals have received a taxable benefit to the extent that they make any personal use of the vehicle. This fact, along with the methods used to calculate the benefit, were covered in detail in Chapter 5. As you will recall, the amount of the benefit is based on the cost of cars purchased or, alternatively, the lease payments made on cars that are leased.

7-72. A different issue relates to the costs that can be deducted by the business in the determination of its business income for tax purposes. For a number of years, it has been the policy of the government to discourage business use of what it perceives to be luxury automobiles. This has been accomplished by limiting the amounts that can be deducted for CCA and interest on automobiles that are owned by the business, as well as by limiting the deductibility of payments made under leasing arrangements. Note that these same limitations apply to deductions against employment income that can be made by an employee in a position to deduct costs for using his own automobile in employment related activities.

7-73. We would again remind you that the taxable benefit resulting from a business providing an automobile to an employee or shareholder is calculated without regard to the deductibility limits that will be discussed here. That is, if an employee has the use of a $150,000 passenger vehicle that is owned by his employer, his taxable benefit will not be affected by the fact that the employer's deduction for CCA on this automobile is limited to $30,000.

CCA And Interest
7-74. With respect to cars that are owned by the business, ITA 13(7)(g) limits the deductibility of capital costs to a prescribed amount. For 2000, this prescribed amount was $27,000, plus GST/HST and PST. For 2001, this value has been increased to $30,000 plus GST/HST and PST. This amount would be reduced by any GST/HST and PST that was recoverable as input tax credits.

7-75. When the automobile is owned by the business, there may be interest costs associated with related financing. If this is the case, ITA 67.2 restricts the amount of interest that can be deducted on a loan to acquire an automobile to a prescribed amount. For 2001, this prescribed amount is $10 per day. Note that this amount is often expressed as $300 per month. While this is accurate for months with 30 days, the actual legislation is expressed as $300 ÷ 30, or $10 per day.

Lease Costs

7-76.   When a business leases a passenger vehicle, ITA 67.3 restricts the deductibility of the lease payments to a prescribed amount ($650 per 30 day period for 1999, $700 per 30 day period for 2000, and $800 per 30 day period for 2001). The basic formula that is used to implement this limitation is as follows:

$$\left[A \ X \ \frac{B}{30} \right] - C - D - E, \text{ where}$$

A   is a prescribed amount ($800 for 2001);
B   is the number of days from beginning of the term of the lease to the end of the taxation year (or end of lease if that occurs during the current year)
C   is the total of all amounts deducted in previous years for leasing the vehicle;
D   is a notional amount of interest since the inception of the lease, calculated at the prescribed rate on refundable amounts paid by the lessor in excess of $1,000;
E   is the total of all reimbursements that became receivable before the end of the year by the taxpayer in respect of the lease

7-77.   In simplified language, this Section restricts the deductibility of lease payments to $800 per 30 day period for leases entered into during 2001. However, it also contains provisions which:

- remove lease payments that were deducted in previous taxation years (Item C,);
- require the deduction of imputed interest on refundable deposits that could be used to reduce the basic lease payments (Item D);
- require the removal of amounts that are reimbursed to the taxpayer during the year (Item E).

7-78.   In applying this formula, you should note that all of the components are cumulative from the inception of the lease.

7-79.   While the basic concept of limiting the deductible amount to a prescribed figure is fairly straightforward, it would be very easy to avoid the intended purpose of the preceding formula. Almost any vehicle can be leased for less than $800 per 30 day period through such measures as extending the lease term or including a required purchase by the lessee at the end of the lease term at an inflated value. Because of this, a second formula is required. This second formula is based on the manufacturer's suggested list price for the vehicle, with the deductible amount being the lesser of the figures produced by the two formulas. This second formula is as follows:

$$\left[A \ X \ \frac{B}{.85 \ C} \right] - D - E, \text{ where}$$

A   is the total of the actual lease charges paid in the year;
B   is a prescribed amount ($30,000 for vehicles leased in 2001)
C   is the greater of a prescribed amount ($35,294 for vehicles leased in 2001) and the manufacturer's list price for the vehicle (note that this is the original value, even when a used vehicle is leased),
D   is a notional amount of interest for the current year, calculated at the prescribed rate on refundable amounts paid by the lessor in excess of $1,000;
E   is the total of all reimbursements that became receivable during the year by the taxpayer in respect of the lease.

7-80.   Note that, unlike the calculations in the basic formula, the components of this formula are for the current year only. Also note that the .85 in the denominator is based on the assumption of a standard discount off the manufacturers' list price of 15 percent. When the list price is $35,294, 85 percent of this amount is $30,000, leaving the (B ÷ .85C) component equal to one. This means that this component only kicks in when the list price exceeds $35,294, a vehicle that the formula assumes has been acquired for $30,000.

Example   A car with a manufacturer's list price of $60,000 is leased on December 1, 2001 by a company for $1,612 per month, payable on the first day of each month. The term of the lease is 24 months and a refundable deposit of $10,000 is made at the inception of the lease. In addition, the employee who drives the car pays the company $200 per month for personal use. Assume that the prescribed rate is 5 percent per annum for all periods under consideration. Ignoring GST and PST implications, determine the maximum deductible lease payments for 2001 and 2002.

2001 Solution   For 2001, the D component in the ITA 67.3 formula is $38 [(5%)($10,000 - $1,000)(31/365)] and the E component is $200 [($200)(1)]. The maximum deductible lease payment for 2001 is the lesser of:

- $$\left[\$800 \times \frac{31}{30} \right] - \$38 - \$200 = \underline{\$589}$$

- $$\left[\$1,612 \times \frac{\$30,000}{(85\%)(\$60,000)} \right] - \$38 - \$200 = \underline{\$710}$$

The lesser of these figures is $589 and that amount is the maximum deduction for lease payments for 2001.

2002 Solution   Because the lease was entered into during 2001, the 2001 limit of $800 applies for the life of the lease. For 2002, the D components in the ITA 67.3 formula are $488 [(5%)($10,000 - $1,000)(396/365)] in the cumulative formula and $450 [(5%)($10,000 - $1,000)(365/365)] in the non cumulative formula.

The 2002 E components are $2,600 [($200)(13)] in the cumulative formula, and $2,400 [($200)(12)] in the non cumulative formula.

Given these calculations, the maximum deductible lease payment for 2002 is the lesser of:

- $$\left[\$800 \times \frac{396}{30} \right] - \$589 - \$488 - \$2,600 = \underline{\$6,883}$$

- $$\left[\$19,344 \times \frac{\$30,000}{(85\%)(\$60,000)} \right] - \$450 - \$2,400 = \underline{\$8,529}$$

The lesser of these figures is $6,883 and this amount is the maximum deduction for lease payments for 2002.

> Exercises Seven-5 and Seven-6 deal with deductible automobile costs. This would be an appropriate time to attempt these exercises.

Leasing Property

7-81.   While from a legal perspective, leasing a property is a distinctly different transaction than purchasing the same property, the economic substance of many long term leases is that they are arrangements to finance the acquisition of assets. From the perspective of the CCRA, the problem with such long term leases is that they may be structured to provide the enterprise with accelerated deductions in comparison with the CCA schedule that is applicable to owners of those particular types of assets.

7-82.   In order to prevent abusive practices with respect to such arrangements, IT-233R provides rules which look through the legal form of certain long term leases. From the point of view of both the lessee and the lessor, this Bulletin requires that a lease be treated as a purchase and sale if any one of the following conditions is present:

- Title automatically passes to the lessee.
- The lessee is required to purchase the asset during or at the termination of the lease.
- The lessee is required to guarantee the residual value to the lessee.

- The lessee has the right to acquire the property at a price or under terms which, at the inception of the lease, are such that no reasonable person would refuse the option. This would involve what is normally referred to as a bargain purchase option or a bargain renewal option.

7-83. These guidelines require those leases in which title to the asset is certain to pass to the lessee, either with no consideration or under a bargain purchase option, to be treated as a purchase and sale. However, it is very easy for a lease to be structured in a manner that will avoid this requirement. For example, a lease for 95 percent of the asset's expected useful life, but with no bargain purchase option would not fall under the IT-233R rules. This creates a significant difference between the accounting and tax rules for dealing with leasing arrangements (e.g., Section 3065 of the *CICA Handbook* would require a lease which covered 95 percent of the life of the asset to be treated as a capital lease). The accounting rules focus on economic substance and, if the usual risks and rewards of ownership are transferred to the lessee, the lease must be treated as a sale and purchase. In contrast, the tax rules focus on legal form, requiring an actual transfer of title before the sale/purchase treatment is required.

Restrictions on Claiming Input Tax Credits

7-84. We have previously noted a number of restrictions related to the ability of a business to deduct certain types of costs in the calculation of income taxes payable. For many of these items, there is a corresponding restriction on the ability of the business to claim input tax credits for GST purposes. Some of the more common restrictions are as follows:

Club Memberships   No input tax credit is allowed for GST paid on membership fees or dues in any club whose main purpose is to provide dining, recreational or sporting facilities. Likewise, no credits are available for the GST costs of providing recreational facilities to employees, owners, or related parties.

Business Meals And Entertainment   The recovery of GST on meals and entertainment expenses is limited to 50 percent. There are two options available to claim input tax credits on meals and entertainment expenses. An input tax credit equal to 50 percent of the GST can be claimed in the reporting period the expense was incurred. Alternatively, the full input tax credit can be claimed in the reporting period incurred and, once a year, recapture of 50 percent of the total amount claimed is included in the registrant's GST return for the first reporting period of the next fiscal year.

Passenger Vehicles   No input tax credits are available for GST paid on the portion of the cost or lease payment of a passenger vehicle that is in excess of the deduction limits ($30,000 cost for cars acquired in 2001 and $800 monthly lease payments for leases entered into in 2001) plus the related provincial sales tax. Also, if the vehicle is owned by a registrant who is an individual or a partnership and the vehicle is used partly for business (less than 90 percent) and partly for personal use, the input tax credit is prorated based on the annual capital cost allowance claimed. As discussed in Chapter 8, Capital Cost Allowances, the input tax credit is deducted from the capital cost of the passenger vehicle in the year after the year the input tax credit was claimed.

Personal Or Living Expenses   Input tax credits cannot be claimed on costs associated with the personal or living expenses of any employee, owner, or related individual. An exception is available when GST is collected on the provision of the item to the employee, owner, or related party.

Reasonableness   Both the nature and value of a purchase must be reasonable in relation to the commercial activities of the registrant before an input tax credit can be claimed. This is similar to the test of reasonableness which is found in the *Income Tax Act*.

Business Income - Specific Deductions

Inventory Valuation (Cost Of Sales)
General Procedures

7-85.   IT-473R points out that ITA 10 and ITR 1801 allow two alternative methods of inventory valuation. They are:

- valuation at lower of cost or fair market value for each item (or class of items if specific items are not readily distinguishable) in the inventory;
- valuation of the entire inventory at fair market value.

7-86.   The selected method must be applied consistently from year to year, and cannot normally be changed. IT-473R indicates that, in exceptional circumstances, the Department will allow a change, provided it can be shown that the new method is more appropriate and the taxpayer uses the new method for financial statement purposes.

7-87.   In determining market value, the usual accounting definitions are acceptable. This means that market refers to either replacement cost or net realizable value. Cost can be determined through specific identification, an average cost assumption, a First In, First Out (FIFO) assumption, or through the use of the retail method. In IT-473R, the CCRA indicates that the use of a Last In, First Out (LIFO) assumption is not allowed and, while Interpretation Bulletins do not have the force of law, the prohibition against using LIFO has been tested in the courts (M.N.R. v. Anaconda American Brass, 55 DTC 1120) and it is unlikely that this decision will be reversed.

7-88.   Most of you will recognize that, with the exception of the CCRA's prohibition against LIFO, the tax rules for the valuation of inventory coincide with GAAP. This means that no adjustment will be required in converting accounting Net Income into Net Income for Tax Purposes.

Overhead Absorption

7-89.   While not discussed in ITA 10, IT-473R indicates that, in the case of the work in process and finished goods inventories of manufacturing enterprises, an applicable share of overhead should be included. The Department will accept either direct costing, in which only variable overhead is allocated to inventories, or absorption costing, in which both variable and fixed overhead is added to inventories. However, the Bulletin indicates that, if the method followed for financial statement purposes is one of these acceptable methods, the same method must be used for tax purposes. IT-473R also indicates that the Department will not accept prime costing, a method in which no overhead is allocated to inventories.

7-90.   Under absorption costing, amortization will generally be a component of the overhead included in beginning and ending inventories. In calculating business income for tax purposes, the amounts recorded as accounting amortization will be replaced by amounts available as capital cost allowance deductions. This process will require adjustments reflecting any amounts of amortization included in beginning and ending inventories. While these adjustments go beyond the scope of this text, interested readers will find that they are illustrated in an Appendix to IT-473R.

Special Rule For Artists

7-91.   When artists are required to apply normal inventory valuation procedures, it prevents them from writing off the cost of their various works until they are sold. Given the periods of time that such works are sometimes available for sale, this can result in hardship for some artists. As a consequence, ITA 10(6) allows artists to value their inventories at nil, thereby writing off the costs of producing a work prior to its actual sale.

Exercise Seven-7 deals with inventory costs. This would be an appropriate time to attempt this exercise.

Other Deductions

7-92.   The preceding material has described some of the many restrictions that the *Income Tax Act* places on the deduction of items in the determination of business income. In considering these restrictions it becomes clear that they also serve to provide general guidance on the items that are deductible. In addition to this general guidance, ITA 20 contains a detailed list of specific items which can be deducted in computing business income. If an item falls clearly into one of ITA 20's deduction categories, it is not subject to the restrictions listed in ITA 18. Some of the more important deductions described in ITA 20 are as follows:

- 20(1)(a) - **Capital Cost Of Property**   This paragraph provides for the deduction of a portion of the cost of capital assets. The detailed provisions related to this deduction are covered in Chapter 8, Capital Cost Allowances.

- 20(1)(b) - **Cumulative Eligible Capital Amount**   This relates to the write off of certain long lived assets, including goodwill and other intangibles as discussed in Chapter 8.

- 20(1)(c) and (d) - **Interest**   The two paragraphs cover both current and accrued interest, provided the borrowed money was used to earn business or property income. Chapter 11 contains a more detailed discussion of some of the problems that arise in this area.

- 20(1)(e) - **Expenses Re Financing**   In general, costs related to the issuance of shares or incurred on the borrowing of funds must be deducted on a straight line basis over five years. Any undeducted financing costs can be written off when the loan is repaid.

- 20(1)(f) - **Discount On Certain Obligations**   For tax purposes, bond discounts cannot be amortized over the life of the bonds, the normal accounting treatment. If the bonds are issued for not less than 97 percent of their maturity amount and, if the effective yield is not more than 4/3 of the coupon rate, the full amount of discount can be deducted when the bonds are retired. If these conditions are not met, the payment of the discount at maturity is treated as a capital loss, only one-half of which can be deducted.

- 20(1)(j) - **Repayment Of Loan By Shareholder**   As will be explained in Chapter 11, if a loan to a shareholder is carried on the Balance Sheet of a corporation for two consecutive year ends, the principal amount must be added to the income of the borrower. This paragraph provides for a deduction when such loans are repaid.

- 20(1)(l) - **Reserves For Doubtful Debts**

- 20(1)(m) - **Reserves For Goods And Services To Be Delivered In Future Taxation Years**

- 20(1)(m.1) - **Reserves For Warranties**   This provision only applies to amounts paid to third parties to provide warranty services. It does not apply to so-called "self warranty" situations where the business which sold the warrantied item assumes the risk of providing warranty services.

- 20(1)(p) - **Actual Write Offs Of Bad Debts**

- 20(1)(q) - **Employer's Contributions To Registered Pension Plans**   This deduction is subject to the limitations described in Chapter 6.

- 20(1)(y) - **Employer's Contributions Under A Deferred Profit Sharing Plan**

- 20(1)(z)and (z.1) - **Costs Of Cancellation Of A Lease**   This deduction, in effect, requires amounts paid by a lessor to cancel a lease to be treated as a prepaid expense. Such amounts can only be deducted on a pro rata per diem basis over the original term of the lease.

- 20(1)(aa) - **Costs For Landscaping Of Grounds**

- 20(1)(cc) - **Expenses Of Representation**

- 20(1)(dd) - **Costs Of Investigation Of A Site To Be Used In The Business**

- 20(1)(oo) - **Amounts Deferred Under A Salary Deferral Arrangement**

- 20(4) - **Uncollectible Portion Of Proceeds From Disposition Of A Depreciable Property**

- 20(10) - **Convention Expenses**   This allows the taxpayer to deduct the costs of attending no more than two conventions held during the year, provided they are in a location that is consistent with the territorial scope of the organization.

- 20(11) - **Foreign Taxes On Income From Property Exceeding 15 Percent**   This provision is only applicable to individuals and reflects the fact that their credit for foreign taxes paid is limited to 15 percent. This matter is discussed in Chapter 13.

- 20(16) - **Terminal Losses**   See Chapter 8 for an explanation of this deduction.

Reconciliation Schedule

7-93.   While it would be possible to calculate net business income for tax purposes starting with a blank page, adding inclusions, and subtracting deductions, this approach is rarely taken. Since most businesses have an accounting system that produces an accounting Net Income figure, the normal approach to determining net business income for tax purposes, is to start with accounting Net Income, then add and deduct various items that are different for tax purposes. Note, however, that some smaller businesses that do not require audited financial statements base their regular accounting system on tax rules. In such cases, no reconciliation is required.

7-94.   For those businesses that base their accounting system in whole or part on GAAP, a reconciliation is required. While there are many other items that could require adjustment, the items shown in the reconciliation schedule in Figure 7-1 are the common items for a taxpayer who is not a corporation.

Figure 7 - 1
Conversion Of Accounting Net Income To
Net Business Income For Tax Purposes

Additions To Accounting Income:	**Deductions From Accounting Income:**
• Income tax expense	• Capital cost allowances (CCA)
• Reserves deducted in the prior year	• Amortization of cumulative eligible
• Non deductible reserves in current	capital (CEC)
year (Accounting amounts)	• Gains on the disposal of capital assets
• Political contributions	(Accounting amounts)
• Charitable donations	• Allowable business investment losses
• Amortization, depreciation and	• Foreign non business tax deduction
depletion (Accounting amounts)	[ITA 20(11) and (12)]
• Scientific research expenditures	• Deductible scientific research
(Accounting amounts)	expenditures
• Resource amounts	• Deductible resource amounts
(Accounting amounts)	• Reserves claimed for the current year
• Excess of taxable capital gains	• Terminal losses
over allowable capital losses	
• Recapture of capital cost allowance	
• Interest and penalties on income tax	
assessments	
• Losses on the disposal of capital assets	
(Accounting amounts)	
• Foreign tax paid (Accounting amounts)	
• Non deductible automobile costs	
• Fifty percent of business meals and	
entertainment expenses	
• Club dues and cost of recreational	
facilities	

7-95.   Many of the items that are contained in this schedule have been explained in this Chapter. Others are explained in subsequent Chapters (e.g., capital cost allowances are given detailed consideration in Chapter 8). However, several general points can be made here:

- The income tax expense that is added back would include both the current tax expense and the future tax expense.

- The amounts deducted in the accounting records for amortization, scientific research, and resource amounts will generally be different from the amounts deducted for tax purposes. While it would be possible to simply deduct the net difference (the tax amount is normally larger than the accounting amount), the traditional practice here is to add back the accounting amount and subtract the tax amount.

- Accounting gains (losses) on the disposal of capital assets will be deducted (added) in this schedule. With these amounts removed, they will be replaced by the relevant tax amounts. As explained in Chapter 8, the disposal of capital assets can result in capital gains, recapture, or terminal losses. These amounts are listed in the Figure 7-1 schedule.

- As explained in more detail in Chapter 9, allowable capital losses can only be deducted against taxable capital gains. As a consequence, only the excess of taxable capital gains over allowable capital losses is included in this schedule. If there is an excess of allowable capital losses over taxable capital gains in the current year, the excess can be carried forward or carried back, but it cannot be deducted in the current year. As a consequence, such amounts are not included in this reconciliation schedule.

- Two major items in the GAAP based financial statements rarely require adjustments. These are Sales and Cost of Goods Sold. As noted previously in this Chapter, the various reserves that are associated with the sales figure (e.g., bad debts), generally produce tax results that are identical to those in the accounting records. Similarly, the inventory valuation methods that are available for tax purposes are, with the exception of the CCRA's refusal to accept LIFO, identical to those used in the GAAP based financial statements.

7-96.   With this reconciliation in mind, we will now turn our attention to a simple example of the calculation of business income.

Business Income - Example

Problem
7-97.   The Markee Company has a December 31 accounting and taxation year end and, for the year ending December 31, 2001, its GAAP determined income before taxes amounted to $1,263,000. You have been provided with the following additional information concerning the 2001 fiscal year:

1.   Accounting depreciation expense totalled $240,000. For tax purposes, the Company intends to deduct Capital Cost Allowance of $280,000.

2.   Accounting income includes a gain on the sale of land in the amount of $20,000. For tax purposes, one-half of this amount will be treated as a taxable capital gain.

3.   During December, the Company spent $35,000 on landscaping costs. These costs were capitalized in the Company's accounting records. As the expenditure was near the end of the year, no amortization was recorded.

4.   The Company's Interest Expense includes $5,000 in bond discount amortization.

5.   For accounting purposes the Company uses the LIFO approach to inventory cost determination. The opening Inventories would have been $22,000 higher using a FIFO approach, while the closing Inventories would have been $18,000 higher using FIFO.

6. Financing costs incurred to issue new common stock during the year totalled $60,000. The full amount of these costs was charged to expense in the accounting records.

7. Accounting expenses include $48,000 in business meals and entertainment.

8. During the year, the Company begins selling a product on which it provides a five year warranty. At the end of the year it recognizes a warranty liability of $20,000.

9. In the accounting records, the Company recognized a Pension Expense of $167,000. Contributions to the pension fund totalled $150,000.

10. The Company sponsors a Deferred Profit Sharing Plan for five of its senior executives, all of whom earn in excess of $50,000. During the year, the Company contributed $4,000 to the DPSP for each of these executives.

Required: Calculate the Company's 2001 Net Income For Tax Purposes.

Solution

7-98.   The following points are relevant to the Net Income calculation:

- Despite the fact that landscaping costs are usually capital costs, ITA 20(1)(aa) specifically permits their immediate deduction.

- As LIFO cannot be used for tax purposes, an adjustment to Cost Of Goods Sold is required. The LIFO adjustment to the opening inventories would increase Cost Of Goods Sold by $22,000, while the corresponding adjustment to the closing inventories would reduce Cost Of Goods Sold by $18,000. The net effect is an increase in Cost Of Goods Sold of $4,000 and a reduction in Net Income For Tax Purposes in the same amount.

- Financing costs must be amortized over five years on a straight line basis. As a result, only $12,000 is deductible in the current year and $48,000 must be added back to income.

- Only 50 percent of business meals and entertainment can be deducted.

- Warranty costs can only be deducted as incurred.

- Pension costs can only be deducted when they are funded.

- The Deferred Profit Sharing Plan contribution per executive is less than the $6,750 [($13,500)(50%)] limit. As a result the contributions are fully deductible.

7-99.   Taking into consideration the preceding points, the calculation of 2001 Net Income For Tax Purposes would be as follows:

Accounting Income Before Taxes		$1,263,000
Additions:		
Accounting depreciation	$240,000	
Taxable capital gain [(1/2)($20,000)]	10,000	
Bond discount amortization	5,000	
Financing costs [(80%)($60,000)]	48,000	
Meals and entertainment [(50%)($48,000)]	24,000	
Warranty liability	20,000	
Unfunded pension expense ($167,000 - $150,000)	17,000	364,000
Deductions:		
Capital Cost Allowance	($280,000)	
Accounting gain on sale of land	(20,000)	
Landscaping costs	(35,000)	
LIFO adjustment	(4,000)	(339,000)
Net Income For Tax Purposes		$1,288,000

Taxation Year

General Rules

7-100.   The *Act* defines a taxation year as follows:

ITA 249   For the purpose of this Act, a "taxation year" is

(a) in the case of a corporation, a fiscal period, and

(b) in the case of an individual, a calendar year, and when a taxation year is referred to by reference to a calendar year the reference is to the taxation year or years coinciding with, or ending in, that year.

7-101.   For corporations, ITA 249.1(1) defines a fiscal period as a period that does not exceed 53 weeks. The 53 week designation provides for situations where a corporation wishes to have a fiscal period which ends in a specified week within a month. For example, if the corporate year end is the last Friday in January, the fiscal year will periodically include 53 weeks.

7-102.   A new corporation can select any fiscal year end. However, subsequent changes require the approval of the Minister. In most situations, corporations will have a fiscal year for tax purposes that coincides with the fiscal period used in their financial statements.

Unincorporated Businesses

7-103.   Unincorporated businesses such as proprietorships and partnerships are not, for income tax purposes, separate taxable entities. The income of such businesses is included in the tax return of the individual proprietor or partner. As noted, the general rule applicable to individuals is that their taxation year is the calendar year.

7-104.   While not belabouring the history, a significant tax deferral was once available to unincorporated businesses that adopted a fiscal year that ended in the early part of the calendar year. Since ITA 11 indicates that the income from an unincorporated business accrues to the individual proprietor or partner on the last day of the business's fiscal year, if an unincorporated business had a January 1, 2001 year end, all of the income from that business would be included in the individual owner's 2001 tax return. This occurred despite the fact that virtually all of this income was earned by the business during 2000.

7-105.   Because of this fairly obvious loophole, the government initially attempted to eliminate the use of non calendar fiscal years by all unincorporated businesses. However, taxpayer response made it clear that there are significant non tax reasons for the use of non calendar fiscal years (e.g., having the year end at a low point in the activity of the business). As a consequence, unincorporated businesses can still have a year end that is not December 31.

7-106.   However, when a business does use a non calendar fiscal year, adjustments must be made which tend to eliminate any deferral benefit associated with this alternative. If, for example, a proprietorship had a January 31, 2001 year end, under ITA 34.1(1) they would have to proceed as follows:

- To the results for the 12 months ending January 31, 2001, they would have to add an estimate of the income for the stub period February 1, 2001 through December 31, 2001 ("additional business income").
- This estimate must be based on the income for the period ending January 31, 2001, multiplied by the number of days in calendar 2001 ending after January 31, 2001 (334), divided by the number of days in the fiscal period (365).
- This total is reduced by the stub period addition that was added to income for the period ending January 31, 2000.

7-107.   There are numerous complications in the implementation of this approach, particularly when the fiscal period is less than one year. As non calendar year ends are more commonly used by partnerships, the Appendix to Chapter 20, Partnerships, has further coverage of additional business income and stub period income.

Special Business Income Situations

Income For Farmers

Farm Losses

7-108. For an individual who looks to farming as his chief source of activity and income, farm losses are fully deductible against other types of income. The difficulty with farm losses is that there are various levels of interest in farming activity, ranging from a full time endeavour to produce profits from farming, through situations where an individual acquires a luxury home in a rural setting, allows three chickens to run loose in the backyard, and then tries to deduct all the costs of owning and operating the property as a "farm loss". In the latter case, the ownership of a "farm" is nothing more than a hobby or a means to enhance the individual's lifestyle.

7-109. For such hobby farmers, engaged in farming activity as merely an attractive addition to a lifestyle and with no serious intent to produce a profit from this type of activity, the costs of farming must be viewed as personal living expenses. This means that no portion of farm losses should be considered deductible by hobby farmers.

Restricted Farm Losses

7-110. The more complex situation is an individual who expects to make a profit from farming, but for whom farming is not his chief source of income. This individual is described in IT-322R, "Farm Losses", as:

> **Paragraph 1(b)** A taxpayer whose chief source of income is not farming or a combination of farming and some other source of income, but who still carries on a farming business. Such a taxpayer must operate the farm with a reasonable expectation of profit but devotes the major part of his or her time and effort to other business or employment.

7-111. In this situation ITA 31 comes into effect. This Section limits the amount of farming losses that can be deducted against other sources of income to the first $2,500 of such losses, plus one-half of the next $12,500, for a total deduction of $8,750 on the first $15,000 of farm losses.

7-112. Any amount that is not deductible in the current year is referred to as a "restricted farm loss" and is subject to carryover provisions. These carryover provisions are given detailed consideration in Chapter 12.

> Exercise Seven-8 deals with farm losses. This would be an appropriate time to attempt this exercise.

7-113. While the preceding distinctions between various types of farming activity may appear to be reasonably clear, this is not the case in actual practice. It is rare that a month goes by without a case involving these distinctions being heard at some stage of the assessment appeals process. In view of the amount of litigation involved, it seems obvious that some clarification of the distinctions between hobby farmers, farmers eligible for the deduction of all farm losses, and farmers whose losses are restricted under ITA 31, is badly needed.

Losses And Cash Basis Accounting

7-114. As previously noted in this Chapter, business income is generally computed on the basis of accrual accounting. A major exception to this applies to taxpayers engaged in a farming or fishing business. ITA 28 permits an election for a farming or fishing business to determine income on a cash basis. This is in contrast to the required use of accrual accounting in the computation of other types of business income.

7-115. As most farmers will have receivables and inventories in excess of their payables, the ability to calculate income on a cash basis has a general tendency to defer the payment of tax. While it is clear that the original intent of ITA 28 was to provide this form of relief to the farming industry, the government has become concerned that taxpayers were using even bona fide farms (in contrast to those described previously as hobby farms) as tax shelters, particularly in years when losses were incurred. The remedy to this problem that has evolved is to require an inventory adjustment in those cases where the use of the cash basis produces a loss. This requires the lesser of the amount of the cash basis loss and the value of purchased inventories to be added back to the cash basis income.

7-116.   Although the procedures involved are complicated by a number of factors such as transitional rules and the treatment of the preceding year's mandatory inventory adjustment, a simple example will illustrate some of the procedures:

> **Example**   Garfield Farms begins operations on January 1, 2001. At this time it has no Accounts Receivable, Accounts Payable, or Inventories. The Loss on a cash basis for the year ending December 31, 2001 amounted to $600,000. On December 31, 2001, Garfield Farms has the following:
>
> • Accounts Receivable of $2,000,000
> • Inventories which total $1,400,000
> • Accounts Payable of $750,000
>
> **Accrual Basis Income**   Accrual basis income for the year ending December 31, 2001 would amount to $2,050,000 (-$600,000 + $2,000,000 + $1,400,000 - $750,000).
>
> **Inventory Adjustment**   A mandatory inventory adjustment of $600,000 (lesser of the $600,000 loss and $1,400,000 in inventories) would be added to the loss of $600,000, resulting in a final income figure of nil.

Capital Gains Deduction

7-117.   While the general availability of the lifetime capital gains deduction ended in 1994, the $500,000 super deduction was retained for qualified farm property (see Chapter 12 for a more detailed description of this deduction). Qualified farm property includes real property used in a farming business by taxpayers or close family members, a share in a family farm corporation, or an interest in a family farm partnership.

Income For Professionals

7-118.   When a business involves the delivery of professional services, clients are billed on a periodic basis, normally after a block of work has been completed. This block of work may be task defined (e.g., billing when a client's tax return is completed), time defined (e.g., billing on a monthly basis), or on some other basis. However, in the majority of professional income situations, billing does not occur until after the work has been completed.

7-119.   If the normal accrual approach was applied to this type of business income, the inclusion in Net Income For Tax Purposes would be recorded at the time work is being done. This would require the inclusion of work in progress (i.e., unbilled receivables) in Net Income For Tax Purposes. However, ITA 34 contains a special rule that is applicable to accountants, dentists, lawyers, medical doctors, veterinarians, and chiropractors. These professionals can elect not to include unbilled work in progress in their income. This so-called billed basis of income recognition is not available to other professionals such as architects, engineers, and management consultants.

> **Example**   Ms. Shelly Hart begins her new accounting practice on January 1, 2001. During her first year of operation she records 2,050 billable hours. Her normal billing rate is $100 per hour and, at the end of her first year, she has billed 1,750 hours or a total of $175,000. Of this amount, $32,300 remains uncollected at the end of the year.
>
> **Tax Consequences**   As Ms. Hart is an accountant, she can elect the use of the billed basis. If she does so, her inclusion in Net Income For Tax Purposes will be $175,000. Alternatively, if she used the normal accrual approach, the inclusion would be $205,000 [($100)(2,050)]. It would clearly be to her advantage to use the billed basis.

Scientific Research And Experimental Development
General Rules

7-120.   In an effort to encourage expenditures in this area of business activity, special provisions for scientific research and experimental development (SR&ED) expenditures are provided in ITA 37 as well as other sections of the *Income Tax Act*. SR&ED is defined in ITA 248(1), with further guidance provided by IC 86-4R3 (a draft has been issued for a IC 86-4R4), "Scientific research and experimental development", and IT-151R4, "Scientific research and experimental development expenditures". The concepts involved are very technical in nature and, as a reflection of the value of the tax incentives associated with these expenditures, often the subject of dispute between taxpayers and the CCRA. Because of this, taxpayers intending to make claims in this area are well advised to seek specialized professional assistance.

7-121.   One of the advantages of SR&ED expenditures is that they, in effect, have an unlimited carry forward. Any expenditures that are not deducted in the current year are added to a pool and may be deducted in any future year.

7-122.   A second advantage associated with SR&ED expenditures is that, to the extent they involve capital assets other than buildings, the full cost of acquisition can be deducted in the year of acquisition. Even in the case of buildings, this immediate write off is available for those acquisitions that have a special SR&ED purpose (e.g., a wind tunnel). This provides for a much faster write off than the application of normal capital cost allowance rules.

7-123.   A further advantage associated with SR&ED expenditures is the fact that they generate some of the most generous investment tax credits that are available under today's tax legislation. As will be discussed in Chapter 15, if a Canadian Controlled Private Company can manage to spend $2 million on qualified SR&ED, the government may write that company a check for $700,000. At this point we would note that the use of such investment tax credits reduces the balance in the pool of deductible costs. Further, if the credits used exceed the balance in the pool, the negative amount must be taken into income.

Ceasing to Carry on a Business
General Rules
7-124.   ITA 22 through 25 contain a group of provisions which deal with situations where a person ceases to carry on business. Of particular importance are ITA 22, "Sale Of Accounts Receivable", and ITA 23, "Sale Of Inventory". These provisions apply to incorporated and unincorporated businesses.

7-125.   When a business ceases to operate, its assets are likely to be sold. As a business in its entirety is considered to be a capital asset, any resulting gains and losses would normally be considered to be capital gains and losses. While this may be appropriate with respect to many of the assets of a business, inventories and accounts receivable would generally not be viewed as capital assets if they were sold separately by a business that was continuing to operate. Given this, there are special provisions with respect to gains and losses on the disposition of inventories and accounts receivable that must be sold when a business ceases to operate.

Inventories
7-126.   ITA 23 provides that when inventories are included in the sale of a business, the sale will be viewed as being in the ordinary course of carrying on the business. This means that any gain or loss resulting from a sale of inventory will be treated as business income or loss. No election is required to produce this result.

Accounts Receivable
7-127.   In dealing with the sale of Accounts Receivable as part of a disposition of a business, there are two basic problems. The first is that, if the receivables are worth less than their carrying value, the difference will be considered to be a capital loss. This means that only one-half of the amount of the loss will be deductible and that the deduction can only be against taxable capital gains. The second problem is that bad debts cannot be deducted or a reserve established unless the receivables have been previously included in income. In the case of the sale of a business, this would create a problem for the purchaser in that the purchased receivables would not have been included in income. To deal with these two problems, ITA 22 provides for a joint election by the vendor and purchaser of the accounts receivable. The following example illustrates the application of this election.

Example   Mr. Whitney agrees to buy Mr. Blackmore's business. As part of the transaction Mr. Whitney acquires Mr. Blackmore's trade receivables for $25,000. These receivables have a face value of $30,000 and Mr. Blackmore has deducted a $5,000 reserve for bad debts with respect to these receivables.

7-128.   Whether or not the election is made under ITA 22, Mr. Blackmore will have to include the $5,000 reserve in income. If no election is made, he will then record an allowable capital loss of $2,500 [(1/2)($30,000 - $25,000)]. Even if Mr. Blackmore has taxable capital gains against which the $2,500 loss can be deducted, the transaction will result in a net inclusion in income of $2,500 ($5,000 - $2,500). In contrast, if the ITA 22 election is made, Mr. Blackmore would still have to include the $5,000 reserve in income. However, it will be exactly offset by a business loss of $5,000 on the sale of the receivables, a distinct improvement over the results with no election. Under this approach, there will be no net inclusion in income.

7-129.   From the point of view of Mr. Whitney, if no election is made he will record the receivables as a $25,000 capital asset. If more or less than $25,000 is actually collected, the difference will be a capital gain or a capital loss. If, however, the ITA 22 election is made, he will have to include the $5,000 difference between the face value and the price paid in income in the year the receivables are acquired. Subsequently, any difference between the $30,000 face value of the receivables and amounts actually collected will be fully deductible in the calculation of business income for tax purposes. If the amount collected is equal to $25,000, Mr. Whitney will be in exactly the same position, whether or not the election is made. If more than $25,000 is collected he will be worse off with the election because 100 percent rather than one-half of the excess will be taxable. Correspondingly, if less than $25,000 is collected, he will be better off as the shortfall will be fully deductible.

> Exercise Seven-9 deals with the ITA 22 election. This would be an appropriate time to attempt this exercise.

References

7-130.   For more detailed study of the material in this Chapter, we would refer you to the following:

ITA 10	Valuation Of Inventory
ITA 12	Income Inclusions
ITA 18	General Limitations [On Deductions]
ITA 20	Deductions Permitted In Computing Income From Business Or Property
ITA 22	Sale Of Accounts Receivable
ITA 23	Sale Of Inventory
ITA 24	Ceasing To Carry On Business
ITA 28	Farming Or Fishing Business
ITA 31	Loss From Farming Where Chief Source Of Income Not Farming
ITA 34	Professional Business
ITA 37	Scientific Research And Experimental Development
IC 86-4R3	Scientific Research and Experimental Development
IT-51R2	Supplies On Hand At The End Of A Fiscal Period
IT-80	Interest On Money Borrowed To Redeem Shares, Or To Pay Dividends
IT-99R5	Legal And Accounting Fees
IT-104R2	Deductibility Of Fines Or Penalties
IT-148R3	Recreational Properties and Club Dues
IT-151R4	Scientific Research and Experimental Development Expenditures
IT-154R	Special Reserves
IT-185R	Losses From Theft, Defalcation, Or Embezzlement
IT-188R	Sale Of Accounts Receivable
IT-218R	Profit, Capital Gains and Losses from the Sale of Real Estate, Including Farmland and Inherited Land and Conversion of Real Estate from Capital Property to Inventory and Vice Versa
IT-233R	Lease-Option Agreement - Sale-Leaseback Agreements
IT-256R	Gains From Theft, Defalcation Or Embezzlement
IT-287R2	Sale Of Inventory
IT-296	Landscaping Of Grounds
IT-322R	Farm Losses
IT-357R2	Expenses Of Training
IT-364	Commencement Of Business Operations
IT-417R2	Prepaid Expenses And Deferred Charges
IT-433R	Farming or Fishing - Use Of Cash Method
IT-442R	Bad Debts And Reserves For Doubtful Debts
IT-457R	Election By Professionals To Exclude Work In Progress From Income
IT-473R	Inventory Valuation
IT-475	Expenditures On Research And For Business Expansion
IT-479R	Transactions In Securities
IT-487	General Limitation On Deduction of Outlays or Expenses
IT-514	Work Space In Home Expenses
IT-518R	Food, Beverages And Entertainment Expenses
IT-521R	Motor Vehicle Expenses Claimed By Self-Employed Individuals
IT-525R	Performing Artists

Exercises

(The solutions for these exercises can be found following Chapter 21 of the text.)

Exercise Seven - 1 (Business vs. Capital Gain)
During 2001, Sandra VonArb acquired a four unit apartment building for $230,000. While it was her intention to operate the building as a rental property, one month after her purchase she received an offer to purchase the building for $280,000. She accepts the offer. Should the $50,000 be treated as a capital gain or as business income?

Exercise Seven - 2 (Cash To Accrual Basis)
During 2001, its first year of operation, Barbra's Boutique has cash sales of $53,400. At the end of the year, an additional $26,300 of revenues was receivable. Of the amounts received, $5,600 was for goods to be delivered during 2002. Barbra estimates that $425 of the end of year receivable amounts will be uncollectible. By what amount will the 2001 net business income of Barbra's Boutique be increased or decreased by the preceding information?

Exercise Seven - 3 (Tax vs. GAAP Treatment)
Markit Ltd. signs a 10 year lease for an asset with an economic life of 11 years. The lease payments are $23,000 per year and their present value is equal to 97 percent of the asset's fair value at the inception of the lease. There is no bargain purchase option and the title to the asset remains with the lessor at the end of the lease. Compare the tax treatment of the lease with its treatment under GAAP.

Exercise Seven - 4 (Bad Debts)
On December 31, 2000, Norman's Flowers estimates that $16,000 of its ending Accounts Receivable will be uncollectible. An Allowance For Bad Debts is established for this amount and a reserve is deducted under ITA 20(1)(l). During the year ending December 31, 2001, $17,200 in bad accounts are written off. At December 31, 2001, estimated uncollectible accounts total $18,400. By what amount will the 2001 net business income of Norman's Flowers be increased or decreased by the preceding information?

Exercise Seven - 5 (Deductible Automobile Costs)
On September 15, 2001, Ms. Vanessa Lord purchased an automobile to be used exclusively in her unincorporated business. She finances most of the purchase price and, as a consequence, has financing charges for the year of $1,200. How much of this total can be deducted in calculating her net business income for 2001? Ignore GST and PST considerations.

Exercise Seven - 6 (Deductible Automobile Costs)
On August 1, 2001, Mr. Sadim Humiz leases an automobile to be used 100 percent of the time in his unincorporated business. The lease cost is $985 per month. The manufacturer's suggested list price for the automobile is $78,000. Mr. Humiz makes no down payment and no refundable deposits. Determine the maximum lease payment that he can deduct for 2001. Ignore GST and PST considerations.

Exercise Seven - 7 (LIFO vs. FIFO)
Maxim Inc. uses LIFO to measure the costs of its merchandise inventories. On January 1, 2001, the LIFO value was $13,500 less than the FIFO value. On December 31, 2001, the LIFO figure was $11,200 less than the FIFO figure. Determine, for Maxim's 2001 taxation year, the amount of the adjustment required to convert accounting net income to tax net income with respect to cost of sales.

Exercise Seven - 8 (Farm Losses)
Ms. Suzanne Morph is a high school teacher. In her spare time she grows vegetables for sale in the local farmers' market. While in most years she has shown a profit, she incurred a loss in 2001 of $18,700. How much of this loss is deductible in her 2001 tax return?

Exercise Seven - 9 (Sale Of Receivables)

Mr. Donato Nero is selling his unincorporated business during 2001. Included in his assets are accounts receivable with a face value of $53,450. He and the purchaser of the business have agreed that the net realizable value of these receivables is $48,200. In 2000, he deducted a reserve for bad debts of $3,800. Determine the tax effect of selling these receivables, provided that he and the purchaser jointly elect under ITA 22.

Problems For Self Study

(The solutions for these problems can be found following Chapter 21 of the text.)

Self Study Problem Seven - 1

Ms. Wise is a very successful salesperson. She pays all of her own business expenses and provides the following information related to her taxation year ending December 31, 2001.

1. Travel costs, largely airline tickets, food and lodging on trips outside the area in which she resides totalled $23,000. Included in this amount is $8,000 of business meals.

2. During the year, she used 40 percent of her personal residence as an office. She has owned the property for two years. It is her principal place of business and it is used exclusively for meeting clients on a regular basis throughout the year. Interest payments on the mortgage on this property totalled $13,500 and property taxes for the year were $4,700. The undepreciated capital cost of the property is $120,000. Utilities paid for the house totalled $3,550 and house insurance paid for the year was $950. Other maintenance costs associated with the property amounted to $1,500.

3. For business travel, Ms. Wise drove a car which she purchased for $30,000 on October 15, 2000. During 2001, she drove a total of 50,000 kilometers, 35,000 of these being for business purposes. The business usage of her car varies from 60 to 80 percent each year. The total operating costs for the year were $8,500 which includes financing costs of $2,500 on a bank loan used to purchase the car. She has always taken maximum CCA on her car.

4. She paid dues to the Salesperson's Association (a trade union) of $600.

5. She was billed a total of $12,000 by a local country club. Of this amount, $2,500 was a payment for membership dues and the remaining $9,500 was for meals and drinks with clients.

Required:

A. Calculate the maximum amount of expenses that would be deductible by Ms. Wise for 2001 assuming:

    i.   She is an employee of a manufacturing company. Her employment income of $137,000 includes $15,000 in commissions.

    ii.   She represents a group of manufacturers with a diversified product line. During 2001 she earned total commissions of $137,000.

    In making these calculations, ignore GST and PST considerations.

B. Comment on the desirability of taking capital cost allowance on Ms. Wise's personal residence.

Self Study Problem Seven - 2

You have been engaged to calculate Net Income For Tax Purposes for Lawson Tools Ltd. for the year ending October 31, 2001. The president and founder of the Company is Mr. William Green. However, he is no longer a shareholder of the company.

The accounting records of the Company show a net income after taxes for this period of $298,000. An examination of the Company's records discloses the following information relative to this calculation:

1. The opening inventory for tax purposes amounts to $202,000. In the financial statements the closing inventory was determined to be $271,000 under a Last In, First Out (LIFO) cost flow assumption. The First In, First Out (FIFO) cost of this ending inventory would have been $296,000.

2. The increase in the Company's reserve for warranties during the year was $14,500. This amount is based on a self insurance warranty program.

3. The Company's income tax expense amounted to $158,000, of which $112,000 had been paid.

4. The Company paid $6,800 to its money purchase registered pension plan for Mr. Green, the President of the Company. In addition, the Company contributed $650 to a deferred profit sharing plan on his behalf. Mr. Green's salary for the fiscal year amounted to $135,000.

5. During the year, the Company spent $15,600 landscaping the premises of its office building. This amount was deducted as an expense in the determination of accounting net income.

6. Depreciation was deducted in the financial statements in the amount of $53,750.

7. Because of a failure to pay its municipal property taxes on their due date, the Company was charged interest of $975.

8. A contribution of $4,300 was made to a registered charity during the year.

9. Included in revenues was a payment of $31,200 from an insurance company to compensate for loss of profits when the Company was closed for two weeks because of a fire.

10. Dividends received from other Canadian companies during the year amounted to $1,675.

11. The Company follows a policy of providing various types of volume discounts to its regular customers. During the year, such discounts amounted to $21,250.

12. A life insurance premium in the amount of $3,100 was paid on the life of Mr. Green. The Company is the beneficiary of the policy and the policy was not part of a group life insurance plan for the employees of the Company.

13. During the fiscal year the Company amortized $5,900 in premiums on its outstanding bonds payable which decreased its interest expense.

14. The Company paid $1,400 for membership in a local golf and country club. The total of all meals charged at the club by Mr. Green and paid by the Company during the fiscal year was $3,400. These meals were all business related and his guests were always important clients or suppliers.

15. The Company paid $14,300 to amend its articles of incorporation prior to a reorganization of the Company's capital structure.

16. During the year, the Company deducted interest of $6,900 on a bank loan that was obtained to purchase shares in a dividend paying Canadian company.

17. The Company incurred and expensed appraisal costs of $7,400 in order to determine the current market value of certain assets that it intends to sell.

18. The Company paid legal and accounting fees of $15,600 in relation to a new issue of common shares during the year.

Required: Calculate Lawson Tools Ltd.'s Net Income For Tax Purposes for the year ending October 31, 2001. Ignore any deductions that might be made with respect to depreciable property or eligible capital property.

Self Study Problem Seven - 3

Barnes Industries Ltd. is a Canadian private company located in Nova Scotia. Mike Barnes, the majority shareholder of the Company, devotes all of his time to managing the operations of this enterprise. Over the years, the business has consistently shown a profit and, for the taxation year ending December 31, 2001, Mike has determined that the Company's income before income taxes is $426,000. In determining this income figure, Mike has used generally accepted accounting principles as specified in the *CICA Handbook*. (Mike is a Certified Management General Accountant who received his professional designation in 1977.) Other information with respect to the determination of accounting income before taxes for 2001 is as follows:

1. It is Mike's estimate that income tax expense for Barnes Industries Ltd. for the year will be $186,000, including $23,000 in future income taxes.

2. During the year, the Company has deducted contributions to various registered charities in the amount of $2,500. In addition, the Company has made and deducted a contribution to the registered federal Conservative New Liberal Reform party of $1,000.

3. For accounting purposes, the Company uses LIFO to determine the cost of its Inventory balances. The opening and closing figures under this method, as well as the corresponding figures using FIFO are as follows:

	January 1, 2001	December 31, 2001
LIFO	$346,000	$423,000
FIFO	366,000	447,000

4. The Company recorded Amortization Expense for the year of $241,000.

5. After attending a seminar on the tax advantages of income splitting among family members, Mike appoints his 6 month old son as a director of the Company. The son receives director's fees of $25,000 which are deducted in the accounting records of the company.

6. The maximum capital cost allowance for the year has been correctly determined to be $389,000.

7. The Company has deducted $23,000 for advertising in newspapers in the New England states. The advertising is directed towards selling the Company's products in that region.

8. The Company provides warranties on several of the products which it sells. For its accounting records it estimates the cost of providing these warranties and records a liability on the basis of these estimates. The liability at the beginning of the year was $18,000 and the corresponding figure at the end of the fiscal year was $27,000.

9. At the end of 2000, the Company estimated that its bad debts on ending Accounts Receivable would total $31,000. Actual write offs during 2001 amounted to $35,000. At the end of 2001, the estimate of bad debts on ending Accounts Receivable was $33,000. The accounting estimates are considered appropriate for tax purposes.

10. On December 31, 2001, the Company issued new common shares. The legal and accounting fees related to this issue of shares were $8,000. For accounting purposes, these costs were added to the intangible asset Organization Costs. As the issue of shares was on December 31, there was no 2001 amortization of this amount for accounting purposes.

11. In January, 2001, the Company incurred landscaping costs of $11,000 which were expected to have a useful life of 10 years. These costs were capitalized for accounting purposes and are being amortized on a straight line basis over a period of ten years. (This amortization is included in the Amortization Expense of $241,000 listed in Part 4.)

12. As a result of Mike's business travel, the Company incurred costs for meals and entertainment in the amount of $13,500. All of these costs were deducted in the determination of accounting income before taxes.

13. Amortization of bond discount for the year was $1,800.

14. On January 1, 2001, the Company leases a Mercedes for five years for Mike to use in his business travels. The total 2001 lease payments amount to $18,000 and, in addition, the Company pays all of the operating costs. These operating costs total $6,200 for the year. There are no refundable deposits associated with the lease and the lease payments do not include any amounts for insurance or licensing. All of these amounts are expensed in the determination of the Company's accounting income. The manufacturer's suggested list price for the car is $128,000. Mike has use of the car throughout the year. He drives it a total of 92,000 kilometers of which 38,000 kilometers were employment related.

Required: For Barnes Industries Ltd.'s 2001 taxation year, determine the minimum Income From Business Or Property (subdivision b income). Ignore any GST or PST implications.

Self Study Problem Seven - 4

Darby Inc. has just completed its fiscal year which ends December 31, 2001. The accountant has determined that, for financial statement purposes, the Company has experienced a Net Loss Before Taxes for the year of $113,000. The accountant provides the following information that was used in the determination of the Net Loss for accounting purposes:

1. The Company was forced to pay damages of $12,300 for failure to perform a service contract. The amount was paid when the client threatened to bring action for breach of contract and was expensed in the current year.

2. The Company's property tax expense of $19,500 includes an amount of $1,100 which was paid to a regional municipality in which the Company maintains a recreational facility for its employees.

3. The Company's expenses included the following donations:

Federal Conservative Party	$4,200
Registered Charities	9,500

4. The Company's expenses include costs of new landscaping at their administration building in the amount of $9,800.

5. The Company deducted interest expense of $42,000 on a bank loan, the proceeds of which were used to acquire 91 percent of the shares of another Canadian corporation.

6. With respect to executives and other salaried employees, the Company deducted the following contributions to its Registered Pension Plan:

President	$ 4,800
Administrative Assistant	3,820
Controller	2,950
Factory Supervision (Three employees at $2,700 each)	8,100
Other Employees (Less than $1,200 per employee)	11,100

   The President's salary was $176,000, that of the Administrative Assistant $86,000, and that of the Controller $77,500. None of these individuals owned shares in Darby Inc.

7. The Company also has a deferred profit sharing plan for some of its executives. The contributions for the year, all of which were deducted, were as follows:

President	$4,000
Administrative Assistant	$3,000
Controller	$2,000

8. The Company deducted a loss of $10,100 resulting from a theft by one of its clerical employees.

9. Effective December 31, 2001, as the result of a change in its distribution system, the Company was forced to cancel a tenant's lease that would have been in force until January 1, 2009. During the 2001 taxation year, it agreed to pay and deducted damages in the amount of $17,000. On December 31, 2001, $5,000 of this amount had not been paid.

10. The current salary expense included a bonus payable to the Company's President in the amount $14,500. It will be paid on February 1, 2002.

11. The insurance expense included the premium on a whole life policy on the life of the President's wife in the amount of $9,500. This was not a group life policy and the proceeds were payable to the Company.

12. During the year, the Company switched from a FIFO basis of inventory valuation to a LIFO basis. The opening inventories, valued on a FIFO basis, were recorded at $182,360. The ending inventories, valued on a LIFO basis, were $193,400, an amount which was $37,200 less than would have been recorded had the Company continued to use FIFO. In its accounting records the Company did not make a retroactive adjustment for this change.

13. As the Company changed property and casualty insurers during the year, all of its assets had to be appraised. The cost of this appraisal was $4,150 with the entire amount being expensed in the year.

14. The Company's revenues included dividends from a Canadian subsidiary in the amount of $79,500.

15. The Company's wage expense included $51,000 in management bonuses (other than that of the President described in item 10) which were not paid during 2001. In addition, $34,000 in unpaid bonuses, which were deducted for both tax and accounting purposes in 2000, were forfeited in 2001 as the result of various employees terminating their employment with the Company. These forfeited amounts were included in the determination of the Net Loss for the year.

16. Bad debt expense amounted to $11,000 and this amount included the write off of a $4,500 loan to a shareholder of a supplier.

17. Renovation costs in the amount of $153,000 were charged to expense during the year. This amount resulted from the need to completely renovate one of the Company's offices and involved the installation of plumbing and air conditioning systems, as well as rewiring and the installation of new concrete foundations.

18. The President and his wife attended a convention which resulted in $5,200 in travel expenses for the Company. Of this amount, $1,900 related to the fact that the President's wife chose to accompany him on this trip.

19. The Company's interest expense included bond discount amortization in the amount of $950.

20. The Company's legal expenses for the year amount to $10,500 and were related to the following transactions:

Defense of breach of contract (see item 1)	$2,450
Cost of amending articles of incorporation	3,600
Defense costs related to income tax reassessment	4,450

21. The Company's expenses included a total amount of $12,500 for business meals and entertainment.

Required: Compute the Company's income or loss from business or property for tax purposes for the year ending December 31, 2001. Ignore any tax deductions associated with depreciable assets or eligible capital property. Indicate why you have not included any of the preceding items in your calculations.

Self Study Problem Seven - 5

You have been engaged to calculate the Division B, Subdivision b income from a business or property for Norton Distribution Ltd. for the year ending December 31, 2001. The president and founder of the Company is Mr. Stanley Norton and, while the Company's shares are now publicly traded, Mr. Norton remains the largest single shareholder.

The accounting records of the Company show a net income before taxes for the year of $780,000. An examination of the Company's records discloses the following information relative to this calculation:

1. An insurance premium of $19,000 for coverage on the life of Mr. Norton was charged to expense. The proceeds of the policy are payable to the Company.

2. Interest expense included a $207,000 payment related to financing the acquisition of 95 percent of the shares of another Canadian corporation.

3. Included in traveling expenses was $4,500 which was the cost of having Mr. Norton's family accompany him to a convention where he finalized several important business contracts.

4. A $21,000 deduction was included for the cost of landscaping the grounds of the Company's headquarters.

5. An amount of $11,000, paid to an appraiser to determine asset values that were required for insurance purposes, was expensed.

6. A total of $23,000 was deducted for legal expenses. This amount included the following:
   - The $8,000 cost of defending against an action by a customer for the delivery of defective merchandise.
   - The $4,500 cost of issuing new shares.
   - The $10,500 cost of disputing an income tax assessment.

7. The Company deducted depreciation expense under generally accepted accounting principles in the amount of $275,000. You have been instructed to subtract maximum capital cost allowances and you determine that this amount is $410,000.

8. The Company deducted a total of $8,500 in contributions to registered charities and a total of $13,000 in contributions to federal political parties.

9. The revenues that were recorded included a dividend of $11,000 which was received from a Canadian subsidiary.

10. The bad debts expense included $8,500 on a loan that was made to the major shareholder of a supplier who had declared personal bankruptcy.

11. The salaries expense included the payment of a bonus of $28,000 to Mr. Norton. It also included a $17,000 amount which represented a dividend paid to him in his position as a shareholder of the Company.

12. Administrative expenses include an amount of $21,000 for the cost of property stolen by a trusted employee.

13. The amount charged for interest expense included a $14,000 charge for the amortization of a bond discount. The bonds mature in 2003.

14. On March 31, 2001, the Company as a lessor agreed to pay and deducted an amount of $28,000 in order to cancel a lease which had been scheduled to expire on March 31, 2008. Only $21,000 of this amount was paid to the tenant prior to December 31, 2001.

15. The salaries expense contains contributions to a registered pension plan totalling $140,800 for the current services of the 65 employees of Norton.

16. The December 31, 2000 inventories of the Company were valued on a first in, first out basis at $387,500. In view of the high increases in the cost of inventories which prevailed during the year, the Company changed to a last in, first out basis for inventory valuation for the 2001 year end. The last in, first out ending inventory figure was $72,000 less than the corresponding first in, first out calculation.

17. During the year, the Company deducted costs totalling $225,000 arising from a remodelling of its office space. These repairs included complete replacement of the heating, air conditioning, plumbing, and electrical systems that were contained in the building.

Required: Prepare the calculation of Division B, Subdivision b income for Norton Distribution Ltd. for the year ending December 31, 2001. As a part of your solution, provide a complete analysis of all of the preceding items, indicating the adjustment necessary or indicating no adjustment is necessary for each item in the calculation of Division B, Subdivision b income.

Assignment Problems

(The solutions for these problems are only available in
the solutions manual that has been provided to your instructor.)

Assignment Problem Seven - 1

Dr. Allworth is a dentist with an office in one of the less prosperous sections of Vancouver. While he has very large gross billings, his patients are such that he often has trouble collecting the amounts that are due to him. As a consequence, he takes great care in keeping track of outstanding balances in accounts receivable and in making estimates of the amounts that he expects will not be collectible.

At the end of the previous taxation year, his accounts receivable balance was $104,000 and he established an allowance for bad debts of $11,500. The corresponding balances at the end of the current year were $208,000 in total receivables with an allowance for bad debts of $15,900. Both of the bad debt estimates were established on the basis of a detailed aging schedule.

During the previous taxation year, there were recoveries of amounts written off as uncollectible in the amount of $190.

During the current taxation year, $8,800 in accounts were written off as bad. However, $700 of this amount related to a patient where there was some hope of collecting the amount due. As the patient was a personal friend of Dr. Allworth, no real effort had been made to collect the amount and further dental services had been extended on a credit basis. In addition, accounts totalling $1,500 which had been previously written off were recovered during the current taxation year.

Required: How would the preceding information affect the calculation of Dr. Allworth's business income for the current taxation year?

Assignment Problem Seven - 2

Jasper Retailers Inc. began business on January 1 of the current year and, at that point in time, purchased 15,000 units of merchandise at $10.00 per unit for a total cost of $150,000. During the year, the following additional purchases of the same type of merchandise were made.

Date	Purchases	Total Cost
March 1	35,000 @ $11.00	$385,000
June 15	42,000 @ $11.50	483,000
September 1	27,000 @ $12.00	324,000
October 1	17,000 @ $12.50	212,500

On December 31, the end of the Company's taxation year, the inventory on hand amounts to 22,000 units. It is estimated that these units have a net realizable value of $11.75 per unit.

Required: For purposes of calculating business income, what values would the CCRA accept for the value of the December 31 inventory?

Assignment Problem Seven - 3

Borris Industries is a Canadian controlled private corporation with a taxation year that ends on December 31. Mr. John Borris is the president of the Company and its only shareholder. He is also considered to be an employee of the Company.

On December 1, 2000, Borris Industries leases a new Mercedes to be used by Mr. Borris. The lease calls for monthly payments of $1,800 per month, payable on the first day of each month for a period of three years. At the time the lease is signed, the Company is required to make a refundable deposit of $10,000. The manufacturer's suggested list price for the car is $85,000. Mr. Borris will pay the Company $500 per month for his personal use of the car. This is the only automobile that is leased by Borris Industries.

During December, 2000, Mr. Borris drives the car a total of 2,500 kilometers, none of which are related to his Company's business activities. Operating costs for this period, all of which are paid by the Company, totaled $1,100.

During 2001, Mr. Borris drives the car 45,000 kilometers of which 40,000 were related to his Company's business. Operating costs for this period, all of which are paid by the Company, totaled $4,200.

During the period December 1, 2000 through December 31, 2001, the automobile was always available to Mr. Borris.

Required: Determine the following:

A. The maximum deduction for automobile lease payments that Borris Industries can take in each of the two years 2000 and 2001.

B. The minimum amount of the taxable benefit that Mr. Borris will have to include in his Net Income For Tax Purposes for each of the two years 2000 and 2001 as a result of having the Mercedes available for his personal use.

Show the details of all of your calculations and ignore GST and PST considerations. In making your calculations, assume that the prescribed rate is 6 percent (not including the extra four percent that is applicable for amounts owing to the Minister) for the period December 1, 2000 through December 31, 2001.

Assignment Problem Seven - 4

The Vernon Manufacturing Company, a Canadian controlled private company, has just ended its first fiscal year. During that year, a number of outlays were made for which the Company is uncertain as to the appropriate tax treatment. You have been asked to advise them in this matter and, to that end, you have been provided with the list of outlays and expenditures which follows:

1. A $275 speeding fine was incurred by one of the Company's sales representatives during the course of a business trip.

2. A part of the Company's raw materials had to be imported from Brazil. In order to obtain local financing for these inventories, the Company paid a $1,200 fee to a Brazilian financial consultant for assistance in locating the required financing.

3. Donations totalling $12,000 were given to various registered Canadian charities.

4. The Company paid $2,500 to the owner of a tract of land in return for an option to purchase the land for $950,000 for a period of 2 years. The land is adjacent to the Company's main factory and management believes it may be required for future expansion of the Company's manufacturing facilities.

5. Direct costs of $7,500, related to incorporating the Company, were incurred during the year.

6. An amount of $10,000 was paid for a franchise giving the Company the right to manufacture a Brazilian consumer product for a period of ten years.

7. Because of its rapid growth, the Company was forced to move into a building that they had originally leased to another company. In order to cancel the lease, it paid $8,000 to the tenant. In addition, $9,500 was spent to landscape the facilities and another $13,000 was spent to provide a parking lot for employees.

8. As some of its employees use public transportation, a pedestrian bridge over an adjacent

highway was required to allow these employees to reach the plant from the public transportation terminal. The cost of this bridge was $12,000.

Required: Indicate which of the preceding expenditures you feel that the Vernon Manufacturing Company will be able to deduct in the calculation of business income for the current year and the tax treatment of the non deductible expenditures. Explain your conclusions.

Assignment Problem Seven - 5

Dr. Sweet is a dentist with a well established practice in Smith Falls, Ontario. She has sought your advice regarding the deductibility of the following expenditures made during the current taxation year:

1. Insurance payments included a $680 premium for coverage of her office and contents, $1,800 for malpractice coverage, and $1,700 in life insurance premiums.

2. Payments were made to a collection agency in the amount of $1,250 for assistance in collecting past due amounts from patients.

3. Donations of $600 were made to the Liberal Party of Canada.

4. Dr. Sweet paid a total of $18,000 to her husband for his services as a full time bookkeeper and receptionist.

5. Dr. Sweet paid $5,000 for a painting by a Canadian artist which has been hung in her waiting room.

6. A total of $4,600 was spent to attend a dental convention in Phoenix, Arizona. Dr. Sweet was accompanied by her husband and $1,500 of the total cost of the trip relates directly to him.

7. An amount of $1,000 was paid for membership in a racquets club. In addition, $1,300 was spent for court time, approximately 40 percent of which was for time spent playing with patients.

8. Dr. Sweet paid $1,200 in legal and accounting fees. These fees related to fighting a personal income tax reassessment for a previous tax year. The fight was not successful and, as a consequence, Dr. Sweet was required to pay additional taxes of $13,000, plus $1,600 in interest on the late payments.

9. During the year, Dr. Sweet spent $3,200 purchasing provincial lottery tickets.

Required: Advise Dr. Sweet with respect to the deductibility of the preceding expenditures in the calculation of net income from a business. Explain your position on each expenditure.

Assignment Problem Seven - 6

The fiscal year for Morton Forms Ltd. has just ended and the accounting staff have prepared the following before tax Income Statement from information that will be included in its published financial statements:

Sales Revenue	$8,726,000
Cost Of Goods Sold	$4,253,000
Operating Expenses	1,785,000
Other Expenses (Not Including Income Taxes)	756,000
Total Expenses (Not Including Income Taxes)	$6,794,000
Income Before Taxes	$1,932,000

Other Information:

1. During the year, the Company spent $18,900 for landscaping the grounds around its Vancouver office. In accordance with generally accepted accounting principles, this amount

was treated as a capital expenditure. As the work was done late in the year, no depreciation was deducted for the current year.

2. Operating Expenses included contributions of $2,900 to the Company's Registered Pension Plan and $2,400 to the Company's Deferred Profit Sharing Plan for each of the Company's three top executives. None of these individuals is a shareholder of Morton Forms. Their salaries are as follows:

President	$95,000
Vice President	58,000
Controller	66,000

3. Operating Expenses also included the following amounts:

Depreciation expense	$693,000
Cost of sponsoring local baseball teams	7,200
Reserve for inventory obsolescence	15,000
Advertising on a foreign television station (Directed at Canadian market)	9,600
Advertising circulars (Only one-quarter distributed)	12,400
Business meals and entertainment	22,000

4. Maximum Capital Cost Allowance has been determined to be $942,000 for the fiscal year just ended.

5. Other Expenses (Not Including Income Taxes) contains the following amounts:

Charitable contributions	$21,500
Contributions to the federal Conservative party	16,300
Interest on late income tax instalments	2,000
Loss from theft	16,200
Interest paid on bonds issued	34,200
Amortization of bond discount	2,600
Appraisal costs on land to be sold	4,200
Damages resulting from breach of contract	3,800
Costs associated with the acquisition of a subsidiary's shares	10,400

Required: Calculate the minimum Net Income For Tax Purposes for the current year for Morton Forms Ltd.

Assignment Problem Seven - 7

Fairway Distribution Inc. is a Canadian controlled private corporation which provides for the distribution to retailers of a wide variety of health aid products. All of the shares of the Company are owned by Mr. John Fairway. His wife, Jane Fairway, is an avid golfer with no interest or experience in business matters.

During the taxation year ended December 31, 2001, the Company's financial statements, as prepared for the exclusive use of Mr. Fairway, reported a Net Income of $573,000. In preparing these statements, Mr. Fairway's accountant relied on generally accepted accounting principles except for the fact that no provision is made at the end of the year for anticipated bad debts. This variance from generally accepted accounting principles resulted from the accountant's belief that Mr. Fairway is a much more reasonable and pleasant person when he is presented with a higher net income figure.

Other Information Other information related to the 2001 taxation year is as follows:

1. The reported net income was after the deduction of $143,000 in Federal and Provincial income taxes.

2. In the previous year, a reserve for bad debts was deducted for tax purposes in the amount of $15,000. Actual bad debt write offs during 2001 amounted to $17,500 and the accountant felt that an appropriate reserve to be deducted for tax purposes at the end of

2001 would be $19,200.

3. Accounting income included a deduction for depreciation in the amount of $78,500. The accountant has determined that the maximum capital cost allowance for 2001 would be $123,600.

4. Mr. Fairway's accountant uses inventory valuation based on LIFO cost for accounting purposes. As this method is not allowed for tax purposes, he also calculates information based on FIFO cost. On December 31, 2000, the LIFO cost of inventories was $326,000 while the corresponding FIFO figure was $345,000. On December 31, 2001, the LIFO figure was $297,000 while the FIFO amount was $312,000.

5. The following items were included in the accounting expenses:

Cost of advertising in a foreign newspaper that is distributed in Canada	$ 3,500
Contributions to registered charities	1,260
Cost of appraisal on real estate to be sold	1,470
Costs of landscaping work done on the grounds of Mr. Fairway's personal estate	5,260
Management fee to Mrs. Jane Fairway	123,000

Required: Calculate the minimum 2001 business income for tax purposes for Fairway Distribution Inc.

Assignment Problem Seven - 8

Astrolab Industries has a taxation year which ends on December 31. For the year ending December 31, 2001, the Company's accounting statements prepared in accordance with generally accepted accounting principles showed a Net Income of $278,000. The accountant has provided the following other information that was used in the preparation of this Net Income figure:

1. A total of $123,000 was deducted as income tax expense. This amount included $16,000 in future income taxes.

2. As the Company was late in making its required income tax instalments, it was required to pay interest of $400.

3. The Company uses LIFO for the determination of Cost Of Goods Sold. Using this approach, the January 1, 2001 Inventories totaled $127,000 and the December 31, 2001 Inventories totaled $135,000. On a FIFO basis, the corresponding opening and closing Inventories were $112,000 and $122,000, respectively.

4. For the year ending December 31, 2001, the Company recorded $83,000 in Depreciation Expense. Maximum available CCA deductions for this period were $97,000.

5. The Company's accounting expenses included a payment of dues in a local golf club of $2,500. The cost of entertaining clients at this club during the year ending December 31, 2001 was $9,600.

6. For accounting purposes, no allowance for bad debts was established at either the beginning or the end of 2001. The $5,200 Bad Debt Expense which was included in the accounting records reflected only the amounts that were written off during the year. For tax purposes, the Company deducted a reserve of $3,400 for the taxation year ending December 31, 2000. An appropriate reserve for the year ending December 31, 2001 would be $4,200.

7. The 2001 accounting expenses include $1,500 for the premiums on a life insurance policy on the life of the Company president. The company is the beneficiary of this policy. One of the Company's major creditors requires that this policy be in force during all periods in which there are loan balances outstanding.

8. In order to be competitive, the Company's delivery trucks consistently violate load and speed restrictions, resulting in regular fines to its employees. It is the policy of the company to pay for these fines and, during the year ending December 31, 2001, they amounted to $12,000. These fines were deducted in the calculation of Net Income.

9. The 2001 accounting expenses included $37,000 in bonuses that were declared in favour of Company executives. Only $12,000 of these bonuses were paid in 2001, with the balance being payable in February, 2002.

10. The bond interest expense which is included in the accounting records includes $3,200 in discount amortization.

11. On December 31, 2001, the Company incurred landscaping costs of $27,000. These were treated as a capital expenditure for accounting purposes and, as the expenditure was made at the end of the year, no depreciation was recorded in the 2001 financial statements.

Required: For each of the preceding items, indicate the appropriate treatment in the tax records of Astrolab Industries Ltd. for the year ending December 31, 2001. For those items which require adjustments of accounting Net Income in order to arrive at Income From Business Or Property for tax purposes, indicate the specific adjustment that would be required. The calculation of Income From A Business Or Property for tax purposes is not required.

Assignment Problem Seven - 9

The Montpetit Fashion Group is a partnership that custom designs and retails high-fashion clothing in Calgary. The partnership commenced operations eleven months ago on February 1, 2001.

Part I   The three partners have sought your advice on a number of issues related to the tax procedures to be used by their business. Provide the requested advice on each of the following issues:

A. Explain to the partners how business income from partnerships is taxed in Canada.

B. The partners have not picked a partnership year end and would like to know what options they have.

C. The partnership has not made any income tax instalments. Will the partnership be penalized for this apparent oversight? To avoid the possibility in the future, how should instalments be calculated and when should they be paid?

D. Designer gowns, for which there are no production economies of scale, are designed and made by private seamstresses who work in their own homes. Montpetit supplies the fabric and accessories, and pays a previously agreed fixed amount upon satisfactory completion of each gown. The partners are uncertain as to the need for source deductions (income tax, EI and CPP contributions) on these amounts.

Part II   The partners would like you to review the following transactions which occurred during their first fiscal year of business ending on December 31, 2001. Advise the partners on the taxability of income amounts in the calculation of net business income for the year. Similarly, for expenditures, provide advice on the specific deductions (with amounts) that can be claimed. (Certain items require an understanding of eligible capital expenditures and capital cost allowances which are covered in Chapter 8.)

A. Legal fees of $800 were paid for the drafting of a partnership agreement.

B. Five industrial sewing machines were acquired at the beginning of the year at a cost of $1,100 each. Sewing accessories (thread, needles, scissors, etc.) were also acquired for a total of $850.

C. Each partner contributed $10,000 to get the business off the ground. Interest of 1% per month on the contributions was paid by the partnership for the last four months of the year. In addition, the partners are planning to deduct the $10,000 payments on their personal income tax returns for the current year.

D. At year-end, designer clothes with a retail price of $26,000 are held on consignment by boutiques throughout the city. The cost of making these clothes was $5,000 labour and $4,500 fabric. The partners consider that overhead is approximately 30% of the direct labour cost of making designer clothes.

E. All designer clothes not sold after six months of retail exposure can be sold to a Montreal Fashion House for 25% of their original selling price. The partners, however, can choose any of these clothes for their personal use, at no cost, before the clothes are parcelled for shipment to Montreal. The clothes retrieved had an average cost of $200 per partner per month. They claim that wearing clothes "By Montpetit" helps them in attracting new business.

F. Montpetit paid $15,000 for the exclusive right to distribute Dali sweaters for five years.

G. During 2001, payments totalling $3,250 were made to the Champs Elysee Club. Of this amount, $1,100 was for the annual membership fee and the remaining $2,150 was for charges in the Crepe Suzette Diner. Of the dining charges, $1,500 was spent for entertaining clients and the remainder was for the personal use of the three partners.

H. Montpetit paid $5,500 into registered retirement savings accounts for each of the three partners.

Assignment Problem Seven - 10

Christine Powell is a visual designer. Until May, 2001 she worked as an employee for a printing supply firm. In June, she became self employed when she started up "Design Power". Through this business, Christine works with several advertising agencies in the design and desktop publishing of promotional materials.

In January, 2002, she comes to you for tax advice. Being vaguely aware of the complexity of the tax laws, she has kept meticulous track of all business related costs for the period from June 1 to December 31, 2001.

Christine works out of her home. Her studio occupies 20 percent of the useable space in the house. The total operating costs related to the house during the period June 1, 2001 through December 31, 2001 are:

Utilities	$1,500
Home insurance	700
Mortgage interest	1,600
Property taxes	2,600
Total Home Operating Costs	$6,400

Christine does not want to claim any capital cost allowance on the house.

On June 1, 2001, Christine bought a used car for business and personal use. The total purchase price of the car was $18,000, financed with a $3,000 cash down-payment and a $15,000 term loan. Her detailed records show that she uses the car 70 percent for business. The motor vehicle costs include:

Down payment on car purchase	$3,000
Gasoline and oil	1,100
Licence and registration	200
Insurance	800
Interest on car loan	700
Total Motor Vehicle Costs	$5,800

On July 15, 2001, Christine purchased computer equipment for $5,000 and various applications software for $1,200. On August 1, she purchased several pieces of office furniture for $2,000. All of these assets were acquired solely for business use.

Her brother, an accounting student, has calculated the capital cost allowance for her business as her birthday present. His calculations show that the relevant capital cost allowance figure for June 1 to December 31, 2001 is equal to $4,200. [Unfortunately, this is not the correct figure.]

Her revenue and other costs for the period June 1, 2001 to December 31, 2001 were as follows:

Revenues

Collected	$22,000
Billed, but not collected	4,000
Unbilled work-in-progress	1,500

Costs

Legal and business license fees	$1,000
Meals and entertainment with clients	500
Office and computer supplies	650
Printing sub-contract fees	1,800

Christine's fiscal year end for the business is December 31.

Required:

A. Using her brother's capital cost allowance figure, calculate the minimum business income Christine would include in her 2001 personal income tax return.

B. Verify her brother's capital cost allowance calculation. (This part requires an understanding of capital cost allowance procedures, a subject which is not covered until Chapter 8.)

In preparing your solution, ignore PST and GST implications.

Assignment Problem Seven - 11

Beckett Enterprises is an unincorporated business that has operated successfully for a number of years under the direction of its owner, Ms. Joan Close. However, in early 2001, she decides to dispose of the business and retire. She will sell all of the assets of the business to an unrelated party, Mr. John Phar.

The date of the disposal is February 1, 2001 and, on that date, the business has Accounts Receivable with a face value of $120,000. Because of anticipated bad debts, the realizable value of these receivables is estimated to be $107,000. During the previous year, Ms. Close deducted a reserve for bad debts in the amount of $8,000.

Both Ms. Close and Mr. Phar have heard of an election under ITA 22 that may have some influence on the tax treatment of the transfer of Accounts Receivable. They would like to have your advice on this matter.

Beckett Enterprises has a December 31 year end. Mr. Phar will continue the business on an unincorporated basis and will also have a December 31 year end.

During the year ending December 31, 2001, $100,000 of the Accounts Receivable are collected, with the remainder being written off as non recoverable.

Required: Indicate the tax effects, for both Ms. Close and Mr. Phar, of the disposal of the Accounts Receivable and the subsequent 2001 collections and write offs, assuming:

A. that no election is made under ITA 22.

B. that they make an election under ITA 22.

Assignment Problem Seven - 12

Billy Jow is a music instructor at a local high school in your area. He is employed by the school board and earns approximately $50,000 annually. To supplement his income, Billy started to teach music on April 1, 2001, to a number of children in the neighbourhood in the evenings and on weekends.

Bill comes to you for advice on how he should report this supplementary teaching income and what expenses the CCRA would allow. Billy does not mind paying his fair share of income taxes, but he wants to pay no more than he has to. From discussions with friends, he understands that he may be entitled to claim a portion of the costs of his home.

Since he was not using the den in his home, he decided to use it for this supplementary teaching. He purchased his home a few years ago for about $250,000. The home is approximately 2,000 square feet in size. The den is approximately 200 square feet.

From April 1, 2001, to December 31, 2001, Billy earned $3,700 in music fees. He has chosen December 31 as his year end and has incurred the following costs since April 1:

Purchase Of Music Books	$ 250
Supplies (Paper, Pens, Etc.)	1,000
Tuxedo For Students' Performances	350
Snacks For Students (Pizza, Milk, Etc.)	250
Utilities For Home (Heat, Light, And Water)	3,500
Mortgage Interest Paid	25,000
Repairs And Maintenance For Home	2,600
Chair*	500
Piano And Bench*	5,000
Total	$38,450

*The maximum tax depreciation (a.k.a., capital cost allowance) on the chair, piano, and bench is $414.

Required:

A. When are expenses for work space in the home deductible? Explain.

B. Compute the business income or loss that Billy should report in his 2001 personal income tax return.

C. Briefly describe any issues that should be discussed with Billy concerning his home office costs.

Adapted From the 1994 UFE

Assignment Problem Seven - 13 (Electronic Library Research Problem)

Provide brief answers to the following questions. Your answers should be supported by references to materials found in your Electronic Library.

A. ITA 18(9) prohibits the deduction of prepaid expenses. How does the CCRA describe such items as prepaid expenses and deferred charges?

B. With respect to a merchandising enterprise, what guidelines are used by the CCRA to determine whether a business has commenced? What treatment is required for expenditures that are made prior to the commencement of the business?

C. During the current taxation year, an individual embezzled over $1 million from his employer. Should this individual include these amounts in his tax return for the current year? What are the tax consequences if he is required to repay these amounts in a subsequent year?

Chapter 8

Capital Cost Allowances And Cumulative Eligible Capital

Capital Cost Allowance System

General Rules

8-1.   ITA 18, in its general limitations on the deductibility of expenses, notes that a taxpayer cannot deduct capital outlays or an allowance in respect of amortization, obsolescence, or depletion, except as expressly permitted by the Act. However, ITA 20, in its list of specific deductions, states that a taxpayer can deduct that part of the capital cost of property that is permitted by Regulation. ITR Part XI lists the items to be included in the various classes and ITR Schedules II through VI provide the rates for all classes.

8-2.   The preceding means that, in computing income from business or property, a taxpayer is allowed to deduct something that is conceptually the equivalent of what is called amortization or depreciation in financial accounting. The basic format of this capital cost allowance system can be described as follows:

Acquisitions Of Capital Assets   The cost of additional capital assets is added to the undepreciated capital cost of the appropriate class as defined in the Regulations.

Disposals Of Capital Assets   The proceeds resulting from the disposal of a capital asset are deducted from the undepreciated capital cost of its class and, in the majority of situations, this procedure will have no immediate tax impact. However, if the proceeds exceed the balance in the class, the excess is called recapture and must be added to income. Further, if the last asset in the class is sold and a balance remains in the class, a terminal loss arises and is fully deductible. Both recapture and terminal losses will be explained more fully in this Chapter. Finally, the amount of proceeds to be deducted from the class is limited to the capital cost of the disposed asset. If there is an excess of proceeds over capital cost, the excess will be considered a capital gain. Such capital gains are explained in Chapter 9.

Capital Cost Allowance (CCA)   The maximum capital cost allowance is determined by applying the rate specified in the Regulations for that particular class to either the capital cost contained in that class at the end of the taxation year (like declining balance amortization) or, with some classes, to the original capital cost of the asset (like straight line amortization).

Tax And Accounting Procedures Compared

8-3. There are many similarities between the capital cost allowance system that is used for tax purposes and the amortization procedures that are used by financial accountants. In fact the general goal of both sets of procedures is to allocate the cost of a depreciable asset to the expenses (deductions) of periods subsequent to its acquisition. However, there are a number of differences that are generally described in the following material.

Terminology

8-4. The two sets of procedures use different terms to describe items that are basically analogous. While the amounts involved will be different, the underlying concepts are the same. For example, both Undepreciated Capital Cost and Net Book Value refer to the original cost of a depreciable asset, less amounts that have been charged to income to the present date. A comparison of these analogous terms is found in Figure 8-1.

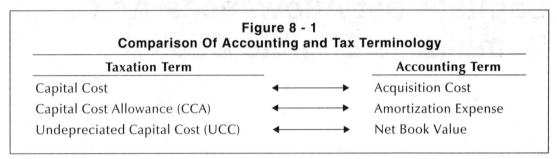

Figure 8 - 1
Comparison Of Accounting and Tax Terminology

Taxation Term		Accounting Term
Capital Cost	←——→	Acquisition Cost
Capital Cost Allowance (CCA)	←——→	Amortization Expense
Undepreciated Capital Cost (UCC)	←——→	Net Book Value

8-5. With respect to dispositions of depreciable assets, the accounting and tax procedures are very different and, as a consequence, the related terminology cannot be directly compared. For accounting purposes, a disposal will simply result in a gain or loss. For tax purposes, this transaction could result in a capital gain, recapture of capital cost allowance, a terminal loss, or no tax effect. There is no equivalency between these two sets of terminology.

Acquisitions

8-6. When capital assets are acquired, their costs are allocated to specific but, in general, broadly defined Classes for tax purposes. The total balance in the class (UCC) becomes the basis for future CCA. For accounting purposes, the cost of each individual asset is generally accounted for on a separate basis. In most cases, the amounts that will be added for tax purposes are the same as those used in accounting.

Capital Cost Allowance

8-7. Capital cost allowance calculations are based on either diminishing balance or straight line procedures. Further, the application of these methods is used to calculate a maximum charge and the taxpayer has complete discretion as to whether any or all of this amount is deducted in a particular year.

8-8. In contrast, accounting amortization is based on the consistent application of generally accepted accounting principles. These principles would encompass a wide variety of methods including those used for calculating the maximum charge for tax purposes. However, once a method is adopted, it must be applied consistently and the full amount calculated must be charged as an expense in the determination of accounting income in that period.

Disposals

8-9. For accounting purposes, the disposal of a depreciable asset will be accompanied by the recognition of a gain or loss based on the difference between the proceeds received and the net book value of the individual asset.

8-10. In contrast, tax procedures require that the lesser of the proceeds of disposal or the capital cost of the asset be deducted from the appropriate UCC class. This can result in capital gains, recapture, terminal losses or no immediate effect on taxable income. These more complex tax procedures will be explained in detail at a later point in this Chapter.

Additions To Capital Cost

Determination Of Amounts

General Rules

8-11. To be added to a CCA Class, an asset must be owned by the taxpayer and, in addition, it must be used for the purpose of producing income from business or property. To qualify for inclusion in a CCA Class, the asset must be a capital asset rather than inventory. This means that whether an asset should be added to a UCC class depends on the nature of the business. A drill press is a capital asset for a taxpayer using it in a manufacturing process. However, it would be treated as inventory by a taxpayer in the business of selling that type of equipment.

8-12. Capital cost means the full cost to the taxpayer of acquiring the property and would include all freight, installation costs, duties, most provincial sales taxes, legal, accounting, appraisal, engineering or other fees incurred to acquire the property. In the case of property constructed by the taxpayer for use by the taxpayer, it would include material, labour, and an appropriate allocation of overhead. If the property is paid for in a foreign currency, the Canadian dollar capital cost would be determined using the exchange rate on the date of acquisition.

Capitalization Of Interest

8-13. In addition to the direct costs described in the two preceding paragraphs, ITA 21(1) allows a taxpayer to elect to add the cost of money borrowed to acquire depreciable property to its capital cost. This election is in lieu of deducting the interest in the current taxation year and will usually be an undesirable choice. However, if the taxpayer does not have sufficient taxable income to use the interest deduction, this election may provide a useful way of deferring the deduction to an unlimited number of future years when it will become part of the capital cost allowances. If this election is not made in a loss year, the relevant interest will become part of the loss carry over for the year and would be subject to the time limits which are applicable to non capital loss carry forwards.

Government Assistance

8-14. Another consideration in determining the capital cost of an addition is government assistance. Under ITA 53(2)(k), any amounts received or receivable from any level of government for the purpose of acquiring depreciable assets must be deducted from the capital cost of those assets. This would include grants, subsidies, forgivable loans, tax deductions and investment tax credits. This tax requirement is consistent with the requirements of Sections 3800 and 3805 of the *CICA Handbook* which, in general, requires government assistance to be deducted from the cost of assets for accounting purposes (an alternative treatment using a deferred charge is also available).

Non Arm's Length Acquisitions

8-15. If transfers of depreciable property between persons not dealing at arm's length are not made at fair market value, they are subject to very unfavourable tax treatment. This may result in the capital cost of the asset not being equal to the amount of consideration given for the asset. This point is discussed in more detail in Chapter 10 under the heading "Inadequate Considerations".

GST Considerations

8-16. GST, PST (Provincial Sales Tax), or HST (Harmonized Sales Tax) may be paid on the acquisition of depreciable assets. As discussed in Chapter 4, GST and HST amounts paid on capital assets used primarily in commercial activities, as well as PST amounts paid in provinces where there is harmonization (e.g., Quebec), will usually be refunded to GST registrants through the input tax credit mechanism. Given this, these refunded amounts will be excluded from the capital cost of assets. This means that, with respect to PST, the capital cost of assets will include only those amounts that are paid in a province (e.g., Ontario) where the PST is not refundable. Capital cost will also include GST and HST when the amounts paid are not refundable (e.g., GST on assets used to produce exempt income such as medical fees).

8-17. The GST considerations for automobiles are complicated by special rules. In simple terms, the amount of GST/HST and PST paid on an automobile is added to the CCA Class in the year of acquisition, subject to the Class 10.1 limit ($30,000 for 2001). As described in Chapter 5, employees and partners who are eligible for the employee and partner GST rebate can claim a GST rebate on the automobile CCA deducted as an employment expense for the year. When this rebate is received, usually in the year following the year in which the expenses are deducted and the rebate claimed, it must deducted from the UCC of the automobile on which the CCA was taken. The GST procedures are similar for proprietors who use vehicles for both business and personal purposes. The input tax credit claimed on the automobile CCA deducted from business income reduces the UCC of the vehicle with a one year lag.

Available For Use Rules

8-18.   For many types of assets, the available for use rules do not present a problem. They are put into use when they are acquired and the acquirer is allowed to deduct CCA immediately. For other assets, the rules can make CCA calculations quite complicated. Real estate assets, especially those which require several years to develop, can be particularly hard hit by the fact that there can be a deferral of the right to deduct CCA for two years or until the structure is considered available for its income producing use.

8-19.   As found in ITA 13(26) through 13(32), the basic rules are as follows:

General Rules   Under ITA 13(27), properties other than buildings are considered to be available for use and, thereby, eligible for capital cost allowance deductions and investment tax credits, at the earliest of the following times:

- At the time the property is first used by the taxpayer.
- The second taxation year after the year in which the property is acquired. This maximum two year deferral rule is also referred to as the rolling start rule.
- For public companies, the year in which amortization is first recorded on the property under generally accepted accounting principles.
- In the case of motor vehicles and other transport equipment which require certificates or licences, when such certificates or licences are obtained.

Rules For Buildings   Buildings, including rental buildings, become eligible for capital cost allowance and/or investment tax credits at the earliest of:

- The time at which substantially all (usually 90%) of the building is used for the purpose for which it was acquired.
- The second taxation year after the building is acquired, the same rolling start rule that is applicable to other types of property.

8-20.   The preceding is a very incomplete description of the available for use rules. There are other special rules for particular assets, as well as significant complications in the area of rental properties. Detailed coverage of these rules goes beyond the scope of this text.

Segregation Into Classes

8-21.   Part XI and Schedules II through VI of the Income Tax Regulations provide a detailed listing of classes and rates for the determination of capital cost allowances. There are over 40 classes which vary from extremely narrow (Class 26 which contains only property that is a catalyst or deuterium enriched water) to extremely broad (Class 8 contains all property that is a tangible capital asset that is not included in another class). As the applicable rates vary from a low of four percent to a high of 100 percent, the appropriate classification can have a significant impact on the amount of capital cost allowance that can be taken in future years. This, in turn, has an impact on taxable income and taxes payable.

8-22.   Assets do not belong in a class unless they are specifically included in the ITR description of that class. However, there are a large number of classes and, in addition, Class 8 contains a provision for tangible property not listed elsewhere. This means that all tangible assets that have a limited life and are normally considered as capital assets would find an appropriate classification.

8-23.   For your convenience in working with capital cost allowance problems, the Appendix to this Chapter provides an alphabetical list of common assets, indicating the appropriate CCA class as well as the rate applicable to that class.

Separate Classes
Exceptions To General Rules
8-24.   The general rule is that all of a taxpayer's assets that belong in a particular class will be allocated to that class, resulting in a single class containing all of the assets of a particular type. There are, however, a number of exceptions to this general rule that are specified in ITR 1101. Some of these exceptions, for instance the requirement of a separate Class 30 for each tele-communication spacecraft, are not of general importance. However, other exceptions are applicable to a large number of taxpayers and will be considered in more detail.

Separate Businesses
8-25.   An individual may be involved in more than one unincorporated business. While the income of all of these businesses will be reported in the tax return of the individual, separate CCA classes will have to be maintained for each business. For example, an individual might own both an accounting practice and a coin laundry. Both of these unincorporated businesses would likely have Class 8 assets. However, a separate Class 8 would have to be maintained for each business.

Rental Properties
8-26.   Of particular significance in the tax planning process is the requirement that each rental property acquired after 1971 at a cost of $50,000 or more be placed in a separate CCA class. When the property is sold, the lesser of the proceeds of disposition and the cost of the asset will be removed from the particular Class. This will commonly result in a negative balance in the class and this amount will have to be taken into income by the taxpayer (see later discussion of recapture of CCA). If it were not for the separate class requirement, this result could be avoided by adding other properties to the class.

Luxury Cars
8-27.   The separate class rules apply to passenger vehicles that have a cost in excess of a pre-scribed amount. This prescribed amount changes periodically, being set at $30,000 for 2001 acquisitions. As will be noted subsequently, such vehicles are added to Class 10.1 and a sepa-rate Class 10.1 must be used for each vehicle.

Computers And Other Electronic Equipment
8-28.   There are a number of high tech or electronic products that are normally included in Class 8 (20 percent declining balance) or Class 10 (30 percent declining balance) that have ac-tual service lives that are significantly shorter than the rates applicable to those Classes would imply. For example, a computer might be disposed of after only one or two years of use. De-spite the fact that only 15 to 35 percent of its value has been deducted as CCA during this pe-riod, its disposal value has probably declined by 75 percent or more. However, in the usual situation, additional assets will be added to these broadly based Classes and, as a conse-quence, no loss can be recognized on the disposal.

8-29.   To correct this situation, ITR 1101(5p) allows taxpayers to allocate one or more assets to separate Class 8 or Class 10 balances. To be eligible, the assets must have a capital cost of $1,000 or more. The following electronic products are eligible for the separate class election:

- general purpose electronic data processing equipment and systems software therefor, in-cluding ancillary data processing equipment (Class 10)
- computer systems software (Class 10)
- photocopiers (Class 8)
- electronic communications equipment, such as a facsimile transmission device or tele-phone equipment, including related ancillary equipment (Class 8)

8-30.   At the end of five years in a separate class, any remaining balance must be transferred to the regular Class 10 or Class 8 balance. This does not present any real problem for the taxpayer in that it will generally be past the point in time where a disposition would result in a significant terminal loss.

Short Lived Manufacturing and Processing Assets

8-31. A further addition to the classes where separate balances can be maintained was added in the 2000 budget. In recognition of the fact that certain types of manufacturing equipment have unusually short economic lives, individual Class 43 items, provided they have a cost in excess of $1,000, can be allocated to separate classes. As was the case with the Class 10 and Class 8 balances discussed in the preceding Paragraphs 8-28 and 8-29, the goal here is to allow the recognition of terminal losses when there are dispositions of such assets.

8-32. As was the case with the separate classes for Class 8 and Class 10 assets, after five years any remaining balance in a separate Class 43 must be transferred to the aggregate Class 43 balance.

Capital Cost Allowances

General Overview

Methods

8-33. Once capital assets have been allocated to appropriate classes, these amounts form the base for the calculation of CCA. The maximum CCA is determined by applying a rate that is specified in the Regulations to either the original capital cost of the assets in the class (straight line classes), or more commonly, to the end of the period UCC for the class (diminishing balance classes). The following example will illustrate this difference:

> **Example** A particular CCA class contains assets with an original cost of $780,000 and an end of the period UCC balance of $460,000. There have been no additions to the class during the year. The rate for the class is 10 percent.

> **Diminishing Balance Class** If we assume that this is a diminishing balance class, the rate would be applied to the $460,000 end of the period UCC balance. This would result in a maximum CCA for this class of $46,000 [(10%)($460,000)].

> **Straight Line Class** If we assume that this is a straight line class, the rate would be applied to the $780,000 cost of the assets. This would result in a maximum CCA for this class of $78,000 [(10%)($780,000)].

8-34. This relatively simple process is complicated by the following:

> **Half Year (a.k.a. First Year) Rules** For most classes, one-half of any excess of additions for acquisitions over deductions for disposals to a class must be subtracted prior to the application of the appropriate CCA rate.

> **Class Changes** When the government wishes to change the rate applicable to certain types of assets, they normally implement this decision by allocating such assets to a new or different class. This means that the same type of asset may be found in more than one class, depending on the year in which it was acquired (e.g., buildings acquired before 1988 are in Class 3, while buildings acquired after 1987 are in Class 1).

> **Rental Property CCA Restriction** In general, taxpayers are not permitted to create or increase a net rental loss by claiming CCA on rental properties. This topic is covered in detail in Chapter 11.

Rates For Major Classes

8-35. The following is a brief description of the more commonly used CCA classes, including the items to be added, the applicable rates, and the method to be used:

> **Class 1 - Buildings (4%)** Class 1 is a four percent declining balance class. Most buildings acquired after 1987 are added to this class. If a rental building with a cost of $50,000 or more is involved, it must be allocated to a separate Class 1. This class also includes bridges, canals, culverts, roads, airport runways, parking areas, subways, tunnels, and

certain railway roadbeds.

Class 3 - Buildings Pre-1988 (5%)   Class 3 is a five percent declining balance class. It contains buildings acquired before 1988. As is the case for Class 1 rental properties, separate classes were required for each rental building with a cost of $50,000 or more. This class also includes breakwaters, docks, trestles, windmills, wharfs, jetties, and telephone poles.

The fact that there are two different classes for buildings provides a good example of the CCRA's approach to changing CCA rates. Prior to 1988, all buildings were included in Class 3 where they were subject to a five percent declining balance rate. The Department concluded that this rate was too high and that it should be lowered to four percent. Rather than change the rate on Class 3, they dealt with this problem by indicating that buildings acquired after 1987 should be allocated to Class 1, an existing class which had a rate of four percent. The advantage of this approach is that it avoided applying the new rate of four percent on a retroactive basis to buildings that were acquired before the change took place.

Class 8 - Various Machinery, Equipment and Furniture (20%)   Class 8 is a 20 percent declining balance class. It includes most machinery, equipment, and furniture not specifically included in another class, structures such as kilns, tanks and vats, electrical generating equipment, advertising posters, and bulletin boards. As previously noted, photocopiers, fax machines and telephone equipment purchased for $1,000 or more can be allocated to a separate Class 8.

Class 10 - Vehicles and Computers (30%)   Class 10 is a 30 percent declining balance class. It includes most vehicles (excluding certain passenger vehicles as described in Class 10.1), automotive equipment, trailers, wagons, contractors' movable equipment, mine railway equipment, various mining and logging equipment and TV channel converters and decoders acquired by a cable distribution system. Class 10 also contains computers (including minis and micros), computer hardware, and computer systems software (other software goes to Class 12). As previously noted, computer hardware and computer systems software purchased after April, 1993 for $1,000 or more can be allocated to a separate Class 10.

Class 10.1 - Luxury Cars   Class 10.1 is a class established for passenger vehicles with a cost in excess of an amount prescribed in ITR 7307(b). For cars acquired in 2001, the prescribed amount is $30,000 ($27,000 for 2000). Like Class 10, where most other vehicles remain, it is a 30 percent declining balance class. However, each vehicle must be allocated to a separate Class 10.1. Also important is that the amount of the addition is limited to the prescribed amount, thereby restricting the amount of CCA that can be deducted on the vehicle to this same amount. In the year in which the vehicle is retired, if it was owned at the end of the preceding year, one-half of the normal CCA for the year can be deducted, despite the fact that there will be no balance in the class at the end of the year. A further difference is that, in the year of retirement, no recapture is added to income nor any terminal loss allowed.

Class 12 - Computer Software and Small Assets (100%)   Class 12 includes computer software that is not systems software, books in a lending library, dishes, cutlery, jigs, dies, patterns, uniforms and costumes, linen, motion picture films, videotapes, dental and medical instruments, kitchen utensils, and tools costing less than $200. This Class is subject to a 100 percent write off in the year of acquisition.

Class 13 - Leasehold Improvements (Straight Line)   Class 13 contains leasehold improvements. In this case the Regulations specify that CCA must be calculated on a straight line basis for each capital expenditure incurred. The maximum deduction will be the lesser of:

- one-fifth of the capital cost of the improvement; and
- the capital cost of the lease, divided by the lease term (including the first renewal option, if any).

The lease term is calculated by taking the number of full 12 month periods from the beginning of the taxation year in which the particular leasehold improvement is made until the termination of the lease. For purposes of this calculation, the lease term is limited to 40 years. Note that, in the case of such straight line classes, the application of the half year rules (see later discussion) will mean that the maximum CCA in the first and last years will be based on one-half the straight line rate.

Class 14 - Limited Life Intangibles (Straight Line, No Half Year Rules Apply) Class 14 covers the cost of intangible assets with a limited life. These assets are subject to straight line amortization over their legal life. IT-477 indicates that CCA should be calculated on a pro rata per diem basis in the year of acquisition and the year of disposal. Because of this pro rata approach, the half year rules are not applicable to this Class. Unless the taxpayer elects to include them in this Class, patents are not included (see discussion of Class 44).

Class 43 - Manufacturing and Processing Assets (30%) While in previous years these assets have been included in other classes with different rates, they are currently included in Class 43 where the rate is 30 percent applied to a declining balance. As previously noted, certain manufacturing and processing assets purchased for $1,000 or more can be allocated to a separate Class 43.

Class 44 - Patents At one point in time, patents were allocated to Class 14 where there were amortized over their legal life of 20 years. This approach failed to recognize that the economic life of this type of asset was usually a much shorter period. To correct this problem, patents are now allocated to Class 44, where they are subject to write off at a 25 percent declining balance rate. Note, however, that a taxpayer can elect to have these assets allocated to Class 14. This would be a useful alternative if a patent were acquired near the end of its legal life.

Half Year Rules (a.k.a. First Year Rules)
General Rules
8-36. At one point in time, a taxpayer was permitted to take a full year's CCA on any asset acquired during a taxation year. This was true even if the asset was acquired on the last day of the year. Further, no CCA was allowed in the year of disposal even if the asset was held for most of that year. This was not an equitable situation and the most obvious solution would have been to base CCA calculations on the proportion of a taxation year that the asset was used. However, the CCRA decided that this would be too difficult to implement and an alternative approach was chosen.

8-37. The approach adopted is based on the arbitrary assumption that assets acquired during a particular taxation year were in use for one-half of that year. Stated simply, in determining end of the period UCC for the calculation of maximum CCA, one-half of the excess, if any, of the additions to UCC for acquisitions over the deductions from UCC for disposals is removed.

8-38. The following example is a simple illustration of the half year adjustment for additions to most CCA classes. It has not been complicated by the presence of capital gains, recapture of capital cost allowance, or terminal losses.

Example Radmore Ltd., with a taxation year which ends on December 31, has a Class 10 (30 percent) UCC balance on December 31, 2000 of $950,000. During 2001 it acquires 15 cars at a cost of $20,000 each for a total addition of $300,000. Also during 2001 it disposes of 18 cars for total proceeds of $144,000. In no case did the proceeds of disposition exceed the capital cost of the vehicle being retired. The maximum CCA for 2001 and the ending 2001 UCC is as follows:

December 31, 2000 UCC Balance	$ 950,000
Additions	300,000
Proceeds Of Disposal	(144,000)
One-Half Net Additions [(50%)($300,000 - $144,000)]	(78,000)
UCC Before CCA And Adjustment Reversal	$1,028,000
2001 CCA @ 30 Percent	(308,400)
One-Half Net Additions	78,000
December 31, 2001 UCC Balance	$ 797,600

Exceptions

8-39.   There are some classes or parts of classes to which the half year rules do not apply. For the classes that we have described in this Chapter, the exceptions are as follows:

- All assets included in Class 14.
- Some Class 12 assets such as medical or dental tools costing less than $200, uniforms and chinaware. Other Class 12 assets such as certified Canadian films, computer software, and rental video cassettes, are subject to the half year rules.

8-40.   A further exception is provided for some property transferred in non arm's length transactions. Specifically, property acquired in various non arm's length transactions is exempt from the half year rule if, prior to the transfer, the property was a depreciable property used in producing business income. The property remains in the CCA Class that it was in prior to its transfer. This prevents the double application of this rule in situations where there is no real change in the ownership of the property (e.g., the transfer of a depreciable asset from an unincorporated business to a corporation controlled by the owner of the unincorporated business).

Short Fiscal Periods

8-41.   The previous Section noted that a half year assumption has been built into the capital cost allowance system to deal with assets that are acquired or disposed of during a given taxation year. In contrast to this somewhat arbitrary provision for dealing with part year ownership, a more precise rule has been included in the Regulations for dealing with short fiscal periods.

8-42.   In the first or last years of operation of a business or in certain other types of situations (e.g., a deemed year end resulting from an acquisition of control), a taxation year with less than 365 days may occur. Under these circumstances, the maximum CCA deduction for most classes must be calculated on a proration based on the relationship between the days in the actual fiscal year and 365 days. For example, assume that a business with a taxation year which ends on December 31 begins operations on November 1. On December 1, $100,000 of Class 8 assets (20 percent declining balance) are purchased. There are no further additions or disposals in December. The CCA for the first fiscal year, taking into consideration the half year rules, would be calculated as follows:

$$[(1/2)(20\%)(\$100,000)(61/365)] = \underline{\$1,671}$$

8-43.   As is illustrated in the preceding calculation, the half year rules also apply in these short fiscal period situations. Note it is the period of operation for the business, not the period of ownership of the asset, which determines the proration.

8-44.   Two additional points are relevant here:

- As noted previously, Class 14 assets are subject to pro rata CCA calculations, based on the number of days of ownership in the year. This obviates the application of the short fiscal period rules.
- When an individual uses assets to produce property income (e.g., rental income), the full calendar year is considered to be the taxation year of the individual. This means that the short fiscal period rules are not applicable in these situations.

Tax Planning Considerations

8-45.   As previously noted, the tax rules on capital cost allowances are expressed in terms of maximum amounts that can be deducted. There is, however, no minimum amount that must be deducted and this leaves considerable discretion as to the amount of CCA to be taken in a particular year. In fact, under certain circumstances, a taxpayer is even allowed to revise the capital cost allowance for the previous taxation year. This can, in effect, create a negative capital cost allowance for the current year. The guidelines for this type of amendment are found in IC 84-1. Note, however, that a revision of capital cost allowance for a previous year is only permitted as long as there is no change in the taxes payable of any year.

8-46.   If the taxpayer has taxable income and does not anticipate a significant change in tax rates in future years, tax planning for capital cost allowance is very straightforward. The optimum strategy is to simply take the maximum allowance that is permitted in order to minimize the amount of taxes which must be paid.

8-47.   The situation becomes more complex in a loss year. If a taxpayer wishes to minimize a taxable loss, one approach is to reduce the amount of CCA taken for the year (whether or not the taxpayer will wish to minimize a loss is affected by carryover provisions that are discussed in Chapter 12). In these circumstances, it is necessary to decide on which Class or Classes the allowance reduction should be applied.

8-48.   The general rule is that CCA reductions should be allocated to the classes with the highest rates while taking full CCA on those classes with the lowest rates. For example, assume that a taxpayer wishes to reduce CCA by $100,000 in order to eliminate a loss and has the choice of reducing Class 1 CCA (4 percent) or Class 10 CCA (30 percent) by the required $100,000. If the full CCA is taken on Class 1, the following year's CCA will be reduced by only $4,000 (4 percent of $100,000). In contrast, taking the full $100,000 CCA on Class 10 would reduce the following year's CCA by $30,000 (30 percent of $100,000). It would clearly be preferable to take the full CCA on Class 1 and take $100,000 less CCA on Class 10, so that the following year's CCA can be maximized.

8-49.   Similar opportunities arise when current tax rates are below those expected in the future. For example, some Provinces institute periodic tax holidays for certain types of businesses. As taxes will be applied in future years, it may be advantageous to stop taking CCA in order to maximize taxable income during the years of tax exemption.

> Exercises Eight-1 through Eight-5 deal with the calculation of CCA. This would be an appropriate time to attempt these exercises.

Disposals Of Depreciable Assets

General Rules

8-50.   In previous Sections of this Chapter we have used terms such as recapture of capital cost allowance, capital gains, and terminal losses without providing a full explanation of their meaning. As these terms relate to the disposal of capital assets, a discussion of their meaning has been deferred until this Section which deals with the procedures related to such disposals.

8-51.   In most cases, when an enterprise disposes of a depreciable asset, the proceeds of disposition will be less than the original cost of the asset, and less than the UCC balance in the Class. Further, there will be other assets left in the class. In such situations, the rules related to disposals can be simply stated:

> **Simple Disposals**   The proceeds of disposition will be subtracted from the UCC of the Class, resulting in a reduction in this balance. This will, in turn, reduce the amount of CCA that can be taken for the year.

8-52.   In this simple type of disposal, there will be no immediate income inclusion or deduction for tax purposes. This is in contrast to the accounting procedures where net book value of the individual asset is subtracted from the proceeds of disposition, a process which will invariably result in an accounting gain or loss.

8-53.   There are situations, however, where the disposal of a depreciable asset will have immediate tax consequences. In terms of the resulting tax consequences, these situations can be described as follows:

Capital Gains   A capital gain will arise on the disposal of a depreciable asset if the proceeds of disposition exceed the capital cost of the asset.

Recapture Of CCA   Subtraction of the proceeds of disposition from the UCC may result in the creation of a negative balance in the Class. This can occur whether or not there are any assets left in the Class. If this negative balance is not eliminated by new acquisitions prior to the end of the taxation year, this negative amount must be included in income as recapture of CCA. The amount will also be added to the UCC for the Class, thereby restoring the end of year balance to nil.

Terminal Loss   This occurs only when there are no assets left in the Class at the end of the taxation year. If, when the proceeds from the disposal of the last asset(s) are deducted from the UCC for the Class, a positive balance remains, this balance can be deducted as a terminal loss. Note that it is not a capital loss. A terminal loss is 100 percent deductible against any other income. The amount of the terminal loss will also be deducted from the UCC for the Class, thereby restoring the end of year balance to nil.

8-54.   These situations will be described in more detail in the sections which follow.

Capital Gains

8-55.   If an asset is sold for more than its capital cost, the excess of the proceeds of disposition over the capital cost of the asset is a capital gain. As will be discussed in more detail in Chapter 9, only one-half of this gain will be included in the taxpayer's Net Income For Tax Purposes.

8-56.   The more important point in this Chapter is that this excess amount will not be deducted from the UCC. When the proceeds of disposition exceed the capital cost of the asset, the amount deducted from the UCC on the disposal is limited to its capital cost. This leads to a more general statement on the procedure to be used when there is a disposal of a depreciable asset:

General Rule For Disposals   When there is a disposal of a depreciable asset, the amount to be deducted from the UCC is the lesser of:

- the proceeds of disposition; and
- the capital cost of the individual asset.

8-57.   As an example of this type of situation, consider the disposal of a Class 8 asset with an original cost of $20,000. If it were sold for $25,000, only $20,000 would be deducted from the Class 8 UCC. The $5,000 excess would be treated as a capital gain. In the usual situation, there would be additional assets in Class 8 and the Class would continue to have a positive balance. This would mean that there would not be recapture of CCA or a terminal loss.

8-58.   You should note that, while CCA and UCC amounts are based on Class amounts rather than values for individual assets, it is still necessary to track the cost of individual assets so that the appropriate amount can be deducted from UCC when there is a disposal.

Recapture Of Capital Cost Allowance

8-59.   Recapture of capital cost allowance refers to situations in which a particular class contains a negative or credit balance at the end of the taxation year. As previously described, UCC for a particular class is calculated by starting with the opening balance of the Class, adding the cost of acquisitions, subtracting the lesser of the proceeds of disposition and the capital cost of any asset sold, and subtracting CCA. As the maximum CCA deduction can never exceed the balance in the UCC Class, negative balances can only arise when there is a disposal.

8-60.   Note, however, that a disposal which creates a temporary negative balance at some point during the year does not create recapture. If additions later in the year eliminate this negative balance prior to year end, no recapture would have to be included in income. A further point here is that, in those situations where each individual asset has to be allocated to a separate Class (e.g., rental buildings costing $50,000 or more), recapture cannot be eliminated by subsequent asset acquisitions.

8-61.   Recapture of CCA arises when deductions from the class exceed additions and this generally means that the proceeds of disposals when combined with the CCA taken exceeds the cost of assets added to the class. In effect, recapture is an indication that CCA has been deducted in excess of the real economic burden (cost minus disposal proceeds) of using the assets. As a reflection of this situation, ITA 13 requires that the recaptured CCA be added back to income. The recapture amount is also added to the UCC balance, thereby restoring the balance to nil.

Terminal Losses
General Provisions
8-62.   When the last asset in a class is sold, the proceeds are deducted from the class in the usual manner. If the resulting UCC balance is negative, the negative amount will be recapture. However, it is also possible for this final asset retirement to leave a positive balance in the class. Such a balance creates a terminal loss.

8-63.   The presence of a positive balance subsequent to the sale of the last asset in the class is an indication that the taxpayer has deducted less than the full cost of using the assets in this class. Under these circumstances, ITA 20(16) allows this terminal loss to be deducted in full. Note that this is not a capital loss. While it is possible to have capital gains on assets that are subject to CCA, it is not possible to have a capital loss on the disposition of a depreciable asset.

8-64.   A terminal loss occurs only when there are no assets in the Class at the end of the period. If there is a positive balance in the Class at some point during the year, but no assets in the Class, there is no terminal loss if additional assets are acquired prior to the end of the year.

Separate Class Election
8-65.   Earlier in this Chapter (Paragraphs 8-28 through 8-32), we noted that taxpayers could elect to have certain Class 8, Class 10, and Class 43 assets allocated to individual separate classes. Now that we have explained terminal losses, it is easier to understand the reason for making this allocation.

8-66.   Consider, for example, a $10,000 computer that would normally be allocated to Class 10. Over the first two years of the asset's life, CCA would be calculated as follows:

Year	CCA
One [(30%)(1/2)($10,000)]	$1,500
Two [(30%)($8,500)]	2,550
Total	$4,050

8-67.   Given the rate of technological change in this area, it is possible that this computer would be replaced after two years. Further, the value of the old computer would likely be very small. If this were the only computer owned by the taxpayer and it was disposed of for nil proceeds, there would be a terminal loss equal to $5,950 ($10,000 - $4,050).

8-68.   There are two problems with this analysis:

- Most businesses will own more than one computer and, if they are all included in a single Class 10, the disposition will leave other assets in the Class and no terminal loss can be recognized.
- Even if the business only owns one computer, a replacement will be acquired subsequent to the disposition, again resulting in a situation where no terminal loss can be recognized because there are remaining assets in the Class.

8-69.   The election to allocate this computer to a separate Class 10 balance alleviates these problems. When each individual computer is retired, a terminal loss can be recognized, even if the business replaces the computer or has other computers in use.

Special Rules For Buildings

8-70.   For dispositions of buildings, special rules apply. If a building is the last asset in its class and it is disposed of in conjunction with a sale of the land on which it is situated, any loss on the building is reduced to the extent of any gain on the land. The reason for this special rule is concern for the possibility that the total proceeds will be allocated in a manner that maximizes the terminal loss on the building (100 percent deductible), while minimizing the capital gain on the land (one-half taxable). The following simple example illustrates the rules.

Date of disposition	July 1, 2001
UCC Class 3 (Building - Only Asset In Class)	$150,000
Fair market value of building on July 1, 2001	110,000
Original cost of building	175,000
Adjusted cost base of land	200,000
Fair market value of land on July 1, 2001	300,000
Proceeds of disposition for land and buildings	410,000

8-71.   In the absence of the special rules, the $50,000 [(1/2)($300,000 - $200,000)] taxable capital gain on the land would be reduced by the $40,000 terminal loss on the building, resulting in a net inclusion of $10,000. ITA 13(21.1)(a) modifies the results in such situations by deeming the proceeds of disposition for the building to be the lesser of:

FMV Of Land And Building	$410,000	
Reduced By The Lesser Of The		
ACB And The FMV Of The Land	(200,000)	$210,000
The Greater Of:		
The FMV Of Building ($110,000)		
The Lesser Of Its Cost And UCC ($150,000)		$150,000

8-72.   The proceeds of disposition for the land is then deemed to be $260,000, the difference between the $410,000 proceeds of disposition and the $150,000 allocated to the building by the preceding formula.

8-73.   In situations where there is a terminal loss on a building combined with a capital gain on the related land, this formula has the effect of eliminating all or part of the terminal loss by shifting some amount of the building proceeds to the land. In our example, the net result is that the $40,000 terminal loss is completely eliminated and the capital gain is reduced by a corresponding amount to $60,000 ($260,000 - $200,000). The taxable amount of $30,000 would be included in the taxpayer's income.

8-74.   If the building had been disposed of for $110,000 while still retaining the land, under ITA 13(21.1)(b) the proceeds would be deemed to include one-half of the difference between the UCC of the Class and the fair market value of the building as evidenced by the actual proceeds. In this case, the deemed proceeds would be $130,000 [$110,000 + (1/2)($150,000 - $110,000)] and would result in a terminal loss of $20,000 ($150,000 - $130,000). This approach has the effect of treating the loss on the sale of the building as a capital loss, only one-half of which is deductible, rather than as a fully deductible terminal loss. If the land was subsequently sold for $300,000, there would be a taxable capital gain of $50,000 [(1/2)($300,000 - $200,000)]. This results in a net tax effect of $30,000 ($50,000 - $20,000) which is equal to the amount included in income in the preceding situation where the building and land were sold together.

> Exercises Eight-6 and Eight-7 deal with disposals. This would be an appropriate time to attempt these exercises.

CCA Schedule

8-75.   At this point, it is useful to summarize the CCA calculations in a schedule. A commonly used format is illustrated in the following example.

Example The fiscal year end of Blue Sky Rentals Ltd. is December 31. On January 1, 2001, the undepreciated capital cost balance for Class 8 is $155,000. During the year ending December 31, 2001, $27,000 was spent to acquire Class 8 assets. During the same period, used Class 8 assets were sold for $35,000. The capital cost of these assets was $22,000.

UCC Of The Class At The Beginning Of The Year	$155,000
Add: Acquisitions During The Year	27,000
Deduct: Dispositions During The Year - Lesser Of:	
• Capital cost = $22,000	
• Proceeds of disposition = $35,000	(22,000)
UCC Before Adjustment For The Half Year Rules	$160,000
Deduct: One-Half Net Additions [(1/2)($27,000 - $22,000)] (Note)	(2,500)
Base Amount For CCA Claim	$157,500
Deduct: CCA For The Year [(20%)($157,500)]	(31,500)
Add: One-Half Net Additions	2,500
UCC Of The Class At The End Of The Year	$128,500

Note The adjustment for the half year rule is equal to the cost of acquisitions during the year, less the proceeds of dispositions during the year. This net amount is then multiplied by one-half. Note that the adjustment is only made when this net amount is positive. No adjustment is made for a taxation year in a class for which the proceeds of dispositions exceed the costs of acquisitions.

CCA Determination - Special Situations

Deferral Provisions On Replacement Property
The Problem
8-76. The disposition of a capital property can give rise to capital gains and, in the case of depreciable capital property, recapture of CCA. In certain situations, such dispositions are unavoidable, with the related income inclusions creating significant financial problems for the taxpayer. For example, if an enterprise has its major plant building destroyed in a fire, the building will commonly be insured for its replacement cost. As this replacement cost will generally be higher than the original capital cost of the building, the disposition will result in both capital gains and recapture of CCA. Payment of taxes on these amounts can significantly erode the insurance proceeds, to the point where it may be difficult for the taxpayer to replace the destroyed property.

8-77. Given this situation, the government has concluded that it is appropriate to provide tax relief in such situations. In simple terms, any capital gain or recapture resulting from these dispositions can be, within certain limits, removed from income, provided the assets are replaced within a specified period of time. The removal of these items from income is accompanied by a corresponding reduction in the capital cost and UCC of the replacement assets. This, in effect, defers these income inclusions until the replacement assets are sold or used.

8-78. With respect to recapture of CCA, the relevant provisions are contained in ITA 13(4). These provisions will be discussed and illustrated in this Chapter. With respect to capital gains, the corresponding provisions are found in ITA 44. This material will be discussed in Chapter 9, after our more general discussion of taxable capital gains and allowable capital losses.

8-79. When the replacement of the assets takes place in the same taxation year as the disposition, the application of these provisions is relatively simple, with the elimination of income and the reduction of the cost and UCC of the replacement assets taking place within a single taxation year. In fact, in the case of recapture, no special provision is required. As the cost of the replacement assets will be added to the UCC of the Class before the end of the year in which the disposal took place, there will usually be a positive balance in the Class at this time.

8-80.   Alternatively, when the replacement takes place in a later year, the capital gain and recapture resulting from the disposition will have to be included in the current year's tax return. Provided, however, that the replacement takes place within a specified time period, these income inclusions can be eliminated through an amended return for the year of disposition. This amended return will normally result in a refund of taxes paid in the year of disposition.

8-81.   As a final point, it should be noted that both ITA 13(4) and ITA 44 provide for elections. They do not apply automatically and, if the taxpayer fails to the make the election, the result can be a significant increase in current taxes payable.

Voluntary And Involuntary Dispositions

8-82.   There are two types of situations for which ITA 13(4) and ITA 44 provide relief. They can be described as follows:

Involuntary Dispositions   This description is used to describe dispositions resulting from theft, destruction, expropriation, or loss. In the case of this type of disposition, the relieving provisions cover all types of capital property. In addition, these provisions are available as long as the replacement occurs before the end of the second taxation year following the year in which the proceeds of disposition were receivable.

Voluntary Dispositions   As the name implies, these are voluntary dispositions, usually involving the relocation of a business. As a relocation may involve a disposition, taxpayers undergoing a move may encounter problems similar to those experienced when there is an involuntary dispositions. In these voluntary dispositions, the applicability of ITA 13(4) and ITA 44 is more limited. Specifically, these provisions only apply to "former business property", a term that is defined in ITA 248 as real property. This means that assets other than land and buildings (e.g., equipment, furniture and fixtures) will not benefit from these provisions. A further difference here is that, for the relieving provisions to be available, the replacement must occur before the end of the first taxation year following the year in which the proceeds of disposition were receivable.

8-83.   For dispositions meeting the conditions described above, elections under ITA 13(4) and ITA 44 can provide a significant refund or reduction in taxes payable in the year in which the capital assets are replaced.

Example

8-84.   A simple example will serve to illustrate the application of ITA 13(4). ITA 44 is not relevant in this example as the insurance proceeds are less than the original cost of the building. This means that no capital gain arises on this disposition.

Example   A company's only building is destroyed in a fire in early 2000. The original cost of the building is $2,500,000, the fair market value is $2,225,000, and it is an older building with a UCC of only $275,000. The insurance proceeds, all of which are received in 2000, equal the fair market value of $2,225,000. The replacement building is completed in 2001 at a cost of $3,000,000.

8-85.   Deducting $2,225,000, the lesser of the proceeds of disposition and the capital cost of the building, from the UCC of $275,000 will leave a negative balance of $1,950,000. As there is no replacement of the asset during 2000, this negative balance will remain at the end of this year, resulting in recapture of CCA. This amount will have to be included in income for the 2000 taxation year and will be added back to the UCC to reduce the balance in the Class to nil.

8-86.   In the year in which the replacement occurs, the ITA 13(4) election provides for an alternative calculation of recapture as follows:

UCC Balance		$275,000
Deduction:		
Lesser Of:		
• Proceeds of Disposition = $2,225,000		
• Capital Cost = $2,500,000	$2,225,000	
Reduced By The Lesser Of:		
• Normal Recapture = $1,950,000		
• Replacement Cost = $3,000,000	(1,950,000)	(275,000)
Recapture Of CCA (Amended)		Nil

8-87.   This alternative calculation would have to be included in an amended return for the 2000 taxation year. It would result in a $1,950,000 reduction in the company's 2000 Net Income For Tax Purposes and, in most cases, would provide the basis for a tax refund. The $1,950,000 reduction of the deduction in the preceding calculation will have to be subtracted from the UCC of the replacement asset, leaving a balance of $1,050,000 ($3,000,000 - $1,950,000). This $1,050,000 balance reflects the economic substance of the events in that it is made up of the original UCC of $275,000, plus the $3,000,000 cost of the new building, less the $2,225,000 received from the Company's insurer.

> Exercise Eight-8 deals with involuntary dispositions. This would be an appropriate time to attempt this exercise.

8-88.   Note that the reversal of recapture is limited to the cost of the replacement property. In our example, if the cost of the replacement property had only been $1,800,000, this would have been the limit on the recapture reversal and the remaining $150,000 [$275,000 - ($2,225,000 - $1,800,000)] would have remained in 2000 income.

Change In Use
General Rules
8-89.   The basic idea here is that when a property used to produce income is converted to some other purpose or, alternatively, when a property that was acquired for some other purpose becomes an income producing property, ITA 13(7) requires that the change be treated as a deemed disposition combined with a deemed acquisition. If the conversion is from personal to business use, an amount will be added to the UCC of the appropriate Class. The amount to be added to UCC depends on the situation:

- If the fair market value of the property is less than its cost, the acquisition will be recorded at fair market value and this amount will be added to the UCC.

- If the fair market value exceeds the cost, there will be a capital gain on the disposition, one-half of which is taxable. In order to limit the increase in the depreciable portion of the property to the taxable portion of the capital gain, the new business property will be recorded, for CCA purposes only, at a value equal to its cost plus one-half of the excess of its fair market value over cost.

8-90.   Alternatively, a conversion from producing income to some other use is considered a disposal and acquisition with the fair market value being both the proceeds of disposition and the acquisition cost, regardless of the relation between cost and fair market value.

Example
8-91.   When the change is from business to personal use, ordinary disposal procedures for a business asset will apply. This could result in a capital gain, recapture of CCA, or a terminal loss. When the transfer is from personal use to business use, the only possible tax consequence would be a capital gain. The following example will serve to illustrate these procedures.

> **Data**   On January 1, 2000, Ms. Barker, a professional accountant, acquires a building at a cost of $500,000, $100,000 of which represents the fair market value of the land. During the entire year, 20 percent of the floor space was used for her accounting practice while the remainder was used as her principal residence.

On January 1, 2001, an additional 30 percent of the total floor space was converted to business use. On this date the fair market value of the asset had increased to $620,000 of which $140,000 could be allocated to the land.

On January 1, 2002, the entire building is converted to residential use as Ms. Barker's accounting practice has grown to the point where it must move to more extensive facilities. On this date the fair market value has increased to $700,000 of which $150,000 can be allocated to land.

Required: Calculate Ms. Barker's maximum capital cost allowance for each of the three years 2000, 2001, and 2002.

Solution To Example

8-92. **2000 CCA** The maximum 2000 CCA deduction for the business component of the property is calculated as follows:

January 1, 2000 UCC	$ -0-
Deemed Cost of Acquisition [(20%)($500,000 - $100,000)]	80,000
Deduct: One-Half Net Additions [(1/2)($80,000)]	(40,000)
Base Amount For CCA Claim	$40,000
Deduct: CCA For The Year [(4%)($40,000)]	(1,600)
Add: One-Half Net Additions	40,000
December 31, 2000 UCC	$78,400

8-93. **2001 CCA** The deemed cost of the additional 30 percent business floor space consists of 30 percent of the original cost of $400,000 plus 30 percent of one-half of the $80,000 ($480,000 - $400,000) increase in the fair market value of the building. The 2001 CCA is calculated as follows:

January 1, 2001 UCC		$ 78,400
Deemed Cost Of Increase:		
Cost [(30%)($400,000)]	$120,000	
Bump Up [(30%)(1/2)($480,000 - $400,000)]	12,000	132,000
Deduct: One-Half Net Additions [(1/2)($132,000)]		(66,000)
Base Amount For CCA Claim		$144,400
Deduct: CCA For The Year [(4%)($144,400)]		(5,776)
Add: One-Half Net Additions		66,000
December 31, 2001 UCC		$204,624

8-94. Note that we have applied the half year adjustment in this year. You will recall (Paragraph 8-40) that non arm's length transfers are exempt from this provision, provided the transferor used the property as a depreciable property prior to the transfer. The portion of the property being transferred was not previously used as a depreciable property.

8-95. **2002 CCA** As the asset is no longer being used for business purposes, there would be no 2002 CCA. The full deemed proceeds are $275,000 [(50%)($700,000 - $150,000)]. As noted previously, the one-half limitation on the increase in cost from a change in use disposition only applies for CCA purposes. For capital gains purposes, the cost of the 2001 transfer is $144,000 [$120,000 + (30%)(100%)($480,000 - $400,000)]. This means that the 2002 deemed disposition would result in a capital gain of $51,000 [$275,000 - ($80,000 + $144,000)]. In addition to the capital gain, there would be recapture of the CCA deducted in the previous two years. This totaled $7,376 ($1,600 + $5,776). The recapture of CCA can also be calculated as follows:

January 1, 2002 UCC	$204,624
Lesser of:	
• Cost for CCA Purposes ($80,000 + $132,000) = $212,000	
• Proceeds Of Deemed Disposition = $275,000	(212,000)
Recapture of CCA	($ 7,376)

8-96.   The change in use rules would also apply in cases where the use of an asset is split between business and personal usage. For example, if a taxpayer was using a $21,000 automobile on the basis of two-thirds for business use and one-third for personal purposes, CCA on two-thirds of the capital cost would be available as a deduction against business income. If, at a later point in time, the usage shifts to one-third business and two-thirds personal, a disposition of one-third of the car will be deemed to have occurred. The deemed proceeds will be one-third of the fair market value established at the time of the change in use. While this represents the tax law applicable to this situation, in practice, this procedure would not be followed. To avoid the complications of determining market values at the end of each year, it appears to be acceptable to simply adjust the portion of the CCA on the car that will be deducted.

> Exercise Eight-9 deals with the change in use rules. This would be an appropriate time to attempt this exercise.

8-97.   As will be discussed in detail in Chapter 11 under the Section, "Rental Income", taxpayers cannot create or increase a net rental loss by claiming CCA on rental properties. As a result, if the change in use involves a rental property, the CCA that can be deducted in a year may be restricted.

Damaged Property

8-98.   If compensation is received for damages to depreciable property, ITA 12(1)(f) requires that the amount be included in income to the extent that it is expended to repair the damages. This will, of course, be offset by the deduction for the repairs. If the amount of damages received exceeds the expenditures for the repairs, ITA 13(21) defines "proceeds of disposition" to include the excess. This means that this amount will be deducted from the UCC for the Class.

Cumulative Eligible Capital

Eligible Capital Expenditures Defined

8-99.   IT-123R6, "Transactions Involving Eligible Capital Property", describes eligible capital property as "intangible capital property, such as goodwill and other 'nothings', the cost of which neither qualifies for capital cost allowance nor is deductible in the year of its acquisition as a current expense". IT-143R2, "Meaning Of Eligible Capital Expenditures", lists the following items to be included in eligible capital expenditures:

- Goodwill purchased as one of the assets of a business.
- Customer lists purchased and not otherwise deductible.
- The cost of trademarks, patents, licences and franchises with unlimited lives. (In general, if these expenditures have a limited life they are Class 14 or Class 44 assets.)
- Expenses of incorporation, reorganization or amalgamation.
- Appraisal costs associated with valuing eligible capital property. Also appraisal costs on an anticipated property purchase which does not take place.
- The costs of government rights.
- Initiation or admission fees to professional or other organizations for which the annual maintenance fees are deductible.
- Payments made under non competition agreements.

8-100.   To clarify the matter further, IT-143R2 specifically excludes the following from the definition:

- The cost of non depreciable tangible assets (land).

- The cost of depreciable intangibles (such as Class 14 patents).
- Payments made to produce exempt income.
- Payments made to creditors for redemption or cancellation of bonds or other debt instruments.
- Payments by a corporation to a person as a shareholder of the corporation (dividends, payments to redeem shares, or for appropriations of property).
- The cost of acquiring or issuing shares, bonds, mortgages, notes, or an interest in a trust or partnership.
- Payments for fines or penalties.

Terminology

8-101.   While eligible capital expenditures are treated in much the same manner as expenditures for depreciable assets, the terminology is sufficiently different that some explanation would be useful. The term eligible capital expenditure is the equivalent of capital cost for depreciable capital assets. When these expenditures are made, three-quarters of the cost is added to a cumulative balance designated cumulative eligible capital (CEC). This CEC balance is the equivalent of the UCC balance for a particular class of depreciable capital assets. As such, it is reduced by amounts deducted as well as by three-quarters of the proceeds of any disposals.

8-102.   Amortization of depreciable capital assets is called capital cost allowance and is deducted under ITA 20(1)(a) at a variety of rates that are prescribed in the *Income Tax Regulations*.   Amortization of CEC is deducted under ITA 20(1)(b) at a rate specified in that paragraph. Since 1988, this rate has been set at seven percent. The term "CEC amount" is usually applied to this deduction.

8-103.   The terminology for disposals is more complex. We will find that there will be results that are similar to capital gains, recapture of CCA, and terminal losses on depreciable capital assets. However, there is no specific terminology that is consistently applied to these results.

Additions, Amortization, And Disposals

General Procedures

8-104.   All acquisitions and disposals of eligible capital expenditures are accounted for in the cumulative eligible capital account. The ending balance in this account is used to calculate the deductible amortization. The rules for dealing with eligible capital expenditures are similar to the procedures used for depreciable capital assets. There are, however, important differences which will be described in the following material.

Additions

8-105.   When an eligible capital expenditures is made, three-quarters of its cost is added to the CEC account. The probable reason for limiting the inclusion to three-quarters of the cost is the fact that the other party to the expenditure will often have a capital gain on the disposition. For example, when an individual sells a business including its goodwill, the goodwill will usually not have a tax value. This means that the total amount allocated to goodwill will be treated as a capital gain and, as you are aware, only a portion of such gains are subject to tax.

8-106.   In the past, the inclusion rate for CEC additions has been adjusted to reflect the capital gains inclusion rate. When the capital gains inclusion rate was changed from one-half to three-quarters in 1990, the inclusion rate for CEC additions was also increased from one-half to three-quarters. For reasons that have not been clearly explained by the Department of Finance, a similar adjustment did not accompany the changes in the capital gains inclusion rate that occurred in 2000. As a result of the February, 2000 budget and the October economic statement, the capital gains inclusion rate has gone from three-quarters at the beginning of 2000, to two-thirds for dispositions after February 27, 2000, to one-half for dispositions after October 17, 2000. No corresponding adjustment has been made to the inclusion rate for CEC additions.

Amortization

8-107.   Amortization is deducted under ITA 20(1)(b). The write off procedures for the cumulative eligible capital account are similar to those used for declining balance UCC classes. As noted previously, the rate is specified in ITA 20(1)(b) as 7 percent. This rate is applied to the end of the period balance in the cumulative eligible capital account.

8-108.   As with CCA, any amount up to the maximum can be claimed and deducted from the account. For CEC, there is no equivalent of the half year rules that can apply to CCA calculations.

8-109.   The 2000 budget made one change with respect to ITA 20(1)(b). In the past, the full 7 percent could be deducted, even in taxation years that were less than 12 months. Paragraph 20(1)(b) has now been modified to require that, when the taxation year is less than 12 months, a pro rata reduction is required based on the number of days in the short fiscal period. This puts the CEC deduction in line with the requirements for calculating the CCA deduction in short fiscal periods.

Disposals

8-110.   When there is a disposal of cumulative eligible capital, three-quarters of the proceeds of disposition are deducted from the CEC account. There are two things of note here. First, as was the case with the inclusion rate for additions to CEC, the amount to be deducted on a disposal was not changed by the 2000 budget. It remains at three-quarters of the proceeds of disposition as opposed to the one-half inclusion rate for capital gains. Also note that, unlike the situation with depreciable asset disposals, three-quarters will be deducted even in cases where this amount exceeds three-quarters of the original cost of the asset. This eliminates the need to track the cost of individual eligible capital expenditures. However, as will be discussed in the next section, a new election may make this cost information useful.

8-111.   If a positive CEC balance remains after making the deduction for the disposal, the business continues to deduct a CEC amount at the rate of 7 percent applied to the remaining balance.

8-112.   Alternatively, if the deduction creates a negative balance, we have a situation that is analogous to recapture. Prior to the 2000 budget, this negative balance was taken into income as an inclusion under ITA 14(1), and added back to the CEC balance to begin the next taxation year with a nil balance. As there was no need to limit the deduction from the CEC balance on the basis of the cost of the eligible capital expenditure, this ITA 14(1) income inclusion was made up of a combination of previously deducted CEC (the equivalent of recapture), as well as possible capital gains. As long as the capital gains inclusion rate was at three-quarters, this was an equitable situation. Additions, amortization, and disposals were all based on three-quarters of the CEC cost.

8-113.   However, we now have a situation where the CEC amounts have remained at the three-quarters level, while capital gains are being taxed at the lower one-half rate. As part of a negative CEC balance may reflect capital gains, following the pre 2000 budget procedures would result in capital gains being taxed on a three-quarters basis. To deal with this problem, ITA 14(1) has been modified to require that any negative balance be divided into two components. These components, along with their tax treatment, are as follows:

- To the extent that there have been CEC deductions in the past, the negative amount will be added to income under ITA 14(1), just as was the case prior to the February 28, 2000 budget. This is the equivalent of recapture for depreciable assets.

- Any excess of the negative amount over past CEC deductions will be viewed as similar to a capital gain. To give this excess treatment analogous to that given to capital gains , it will be multiplied by two-thirds prior to its inclusion in the taxpayer's income. This multiplication reduces the amount from a three-quarters inclusion to a one-half inclusion $[(3/4)(2/3) = 1/2]$. Note that the the multiplier would have been 8/9 for dispositions between February 27, 2000 and October 18, 2000, a short period during which the capital gains inclusion rate was two-thirds.

Example

8-114. The example which follows will be used to illustrate both the pre 2000 budget and the post 2000 budget procedures. The basic information is as follows:

Example A corporation begins operations on March 1, 2001 and acquires goodwill for $40,000 on May 24, 2001. In July, 2003, the goodwill is sold for $46,000. The company's fiscal year ends on December 31.

8-115. Based on this information, the analysis of the cumulative eligible capital account would be as follows:

	CEC Balance	CEC Deductions
Addition, May 24, 2001 [(3/4)($40,000)]	$30,000	
2001 Amortization [($30,000)(7%)(306/365)]	(1,761)	$1,761
Balance, January 1, 2002	$28,239	
2002 Amortization [($28,239)(7%)]	(1,977)	1,977
Balance, January 1, 2003	$26,262	
Proceeds Of 2003 Sale [(3/4)($46,000)]	(34,500)	
Balance After Sale	($ 8,238)	$3,738

8-116. Under the pre 2000 budget procedures, the full amount of the negative $8,238 CEC balance would be added back to income under ITA 14(1). It would also be added back to the CEC amount in order to restore its balance to nil. Note that under the pre 2000 budget procedures there would have been no proration in the year of acquisition for a short fiscal period.

8-117. Under the post 2000 budget procedures, an amount of $3,738 ($1,761 + $1,977) would be added to income as in the past. This amount represents recapture of previous CEC deductions and will be taxed on the same three-quarters basis on which these amounts were deducted. The $4,500 excess ($8,238 - $3,738) would be multiplied by two-thirds to arrive at an income inclusion of $3,000. The logic behind this approach becomes obvious when you recognize that $3,000 is one-half of the $6,000 ($46,000 - $40,000) capital like gain on the sale of the goodwill.

8-118. As a final point on disposals, an income inclusion under ITA 14(1) only occurs when the CEC balance is negative at the end of the year. As was the case with recapture, the income inclusion can be avoided if there are additions to the balance which eliminate the negative amount prior to the end of the taxation year.

A New Election

8-119. Prior to the 2000 budget, the entire proceeds from any disposal had to be deducted from the CEC balance. For companies with large CEC balances containing a number of different items, this was unlikely to result in a negative balance. Further, as this deduction was not limited to the cost of the inclusion, this requirement had the effect of deducting amounts which were, in effect, capital gains from the CEC balance. For companies that wished to recognize capital gains (e.g., companies with capital losses), this was not a totally equitable situation.

8-120. To correct this situation, a new ITA 14(1.01) provides for an election which effectively allows for separate treatment of individual disposals. Under this election, the amount deducted from the CEC balance is limited to the cost of the individual item being disposed of. The excess is then treated as an ordinary capital gain.

Example On January 1, 2001, Marq Ltd's CEC balance was nil. During 2001, Marq Ltd. acquires two eligible capital expenditures, one for $80,000, the other for $140,000. For the taxation year ending December 31, 2001, the Company deducts maximum CEC. In early 2002, the $80,000 item is sold for $120,000.

Tax Consequences. A total of $165,000 will be added to the CEC accounting [($80,00 + $140,000)(3/4)]. The CEC deduction for 2001 will be $11,550

[(7%)($165,000)], leaving a January 1, 2002 CEC balance of $153,450 ($165,000 - $11,550).

If no election is made, $90,000 [(3/4)($120,000)] will be subtracted from the CEC, leaving a balance of $63,450 ($153,450 - $90,000). There will be no income inclusion and the only tax consequence of the disposal is a reduction in the 2002 CEC deduction.

If an election is made under ITA 14(1.01), only $60,000 [(3/4)($80,000)] will be subtracted from the CEC, leaving a balance of $93,450 ($153,450 - $60,000). Under ITA 14(1.01)(b), the taxpayer is deemed to have disposed of a capital property with an adjusted cost base equal to the cost of $80,000 for proceeds of disposition equal to the actual proceeds of $120,000. This results in a capital gain of $40,000 with a taxable amount of $20,000 [(1/2)($40,000)].

8-121.   This election can only be used for eligible capital expenditures that have an identifiable cost. It could not be used, for example, to dispose of internally generated goodwill. In addition, the election cannot be used to recognize a loss.

Special Situations
Business Terminations
8-122.   When a business is terminated, a positive balance may remain in the CEC account. If this is the case, the situation is similar to that involving terminal losses on depreciable capital assets. As with such terminal losses, the balance remaining could be deducted in the computation of Net Income For Tax Purposes. In similar fashion, any CEC balance that is left when a business terminates can also be deducted. However, an important difference from the terminal loss situation on depreciable assets is that the deductible amount of any loss on CEC is only three-quarters of the actual amount of the loss. As is the case with terminal losses, any amount deducted from income is also deducted from the CEC balance in order to leave a balance of nil.

8-123.   A limitation on this involves situations where a taxpayer ceases doing business and the the property is transferred to a spouse or a corporation controlled by a spouse. In this situation ITA 24(2) prohibits the deduction of a loss, requiring that the balance must be transferred to the opening CEC balance for the continuing business.

Death Of A Taxpayer
8-124.   ITA 70(5.1) provides that when a taxpayer dies and the taxpayer's eligible capital property is acquired by some other person who continues to carry on the business, he is deemed to have disposed of it immediately before death at proceeds which are equal to the cumulative eligible capital balance. This would mean that no income inclusion or terminal loss occurs at this time.

Exercises Eight-10 and Eight-11 deal with CEC. This would be an appropriate time to attempt these exercises.

Replacement Properties
8-125.   As is the case with depreciable capital property, there are provisions which remove any ultimate tax liability associated with involuntary dispositions or certain voluntary dispositions, provided replacement occurs within a relatively short period of time. These rules, contained in ITA 14(6) and 14(7), indicate that, if replacement occurs prior to the end of the first taxation year after the taxation year in which the disposal took place, any income inclusion related to the disposal can be deferred.

References

8-126.   For more detailed study of the material in this Chapter, we would refer you to the following:

ITA 13	Recaptured Depreciation
ITA 14	Inclusion In Income From Business (Contains the "recapture" provision for cumulative eligible capital.)
ITA 20	Deductions Permitted In Computing Income From Business Or Property
ITR Part XI	Capital Cost Allowances
ITR II-VI (Schedules)	Capital Cost Allowances
IC-84-1	Revision Of Capital Cost Allowance Claims And Other Permissive Deductions
IT-79R3	Capital Cost Allowance - Buildings Or Other Structures
IT-123R6	Transactions Involving Eligible Capital Property
IT-128R	Capital Cost Allowance - Depreciable Property
IT-143R2	Meaning Of Eligible Capital Expenditure
IT-147R3	Capital Cost Allowance - Accelerated Write Off Of Manufacturing And Processing Machinery And Equipment
IT-172R	Capital Cost Allowance - Taxation Year Of Individual
IT-190R2	Capital Cost Allowance - Transferred And Misclassified Property
IT-195R4	Rental Property - Capital Cost Allowance Restrictions
IT-206R	Separate Businesses
IT-220R2	Capital Cost Allowance - Proceeds Of Disposition Of Depreciable Property
IT-259R3	Exchanges Of Property
IT-267R2	Capital Cost Allowance - Vessels
IT-285R2	Capital Cost Allowance - General Comments
IT-304R2	Capital Cost Allowance - Condominiums
IT-306R2	Capital Cost Allowance - Contractor's Movable Equipment
IT-313R2	Eligible Capital Property - Rules Where A Taxpayer Has Ceased Carrying On A Business Or Has Died
IT-317R	Capital Cost Allowance - Radio And Television Equipment
IT-336R	Capital Cost Allowance - Pollution Control Property
IT-386R	Eligible Capital Amounts
IT-418	Capital Cost Allowance - Partial Dispositions Of Property
IT-469R	Capital Cost Allowance - Earth-Moving Equipment
IT-472	Capital Cost Allowance - Class 8 Property
IT-476	Capital Cost Allowance - Gas and Oil Exploration and Production Equipment
IT-477	Capital Cost Allowance - Patents, Franchises, Concessions, And Licenses
IT-478R2	Capital Cost Allowance - Recapture And Terminal Loss
IT-482	Capital Cost Allowance - Pipelines
IT-492	Capital Cost Allowance - Industrial Mineral Mines
IT-501	Capital Cost Allowance - Logging Assets

Appendix - CCA Rates For Selected Assets

8-127.   This Appendix lists the CCA Class and rate for assets commonly used in business. Restrictions and transitional rules may apply in certain situations.   ITR Part XI contains detailed descriptions of the CCA Classes.

Asset	Class	Rate
Aircraft (Including Components)	9	25%
Airplane Runways	17	8%
Automobiles, Passenger (Purchased in 2000)		
Cost ≤ $30,000	10	30%
Cost > $30,000	10.1	30%
Automotive Equipment	10	30%
Billboards For Renting	**10**	**30%**
Boats, Canoes And Other Vessels	7	15%
Bridges, Canals, Culverts And Dams	1	4%
Buildings Acquired After 1987	1	4%
Buildings Acquired Before 1988	3	5%
Buses	10	30%
Calculators	**8**	**20%**
Cash Registers	8	20%
China, Cutlery And Tableware	12	100%
Computer Hardware	10	30%
Computer Software (Applications)	12	100%
Computer Software (Systems)	10	30%
Copyrights	14	Straight Line
Dies, Jigs, Patterns, And Moulds	**12**	**100%**
Docks, Breakwaters, And Trestles	3	5%
Electrical Advertising Billboards	**8**	**20%**
Electronic Point Of Sale Equipment	8	20%
Equipment (not specifically listed elsewhere)	8	20%
Fences	**6**	**10%**
Films, Certified Feature (Acquired Before 1996)	12	100%
Films (Other Than Certified Feature)	10	30%
Franchises (Limited Life)	14	Straight Line
Franchises (Unlimited Life)	CEC	N/A
Furniture And Fixtures	8	20%
Goodwill	**CEC**	**N/A**
Instruments, Dental Or Medical (Under $200)	**12**	**100%**
Kitchen Utensils (Under $200)	12	100%
Land	**N/A**	**N/A**
Leasehold Improvements	13	Straight Line
Licences (Limited Life)	14	Straight Line
Licences (Unlimited Life)	CEC	N/A
Linen	12	100%
Machinery And Equipment		
(not specifically listed elsewhere)	**8**	**20%**
Manufacturing And Processing Equipment	43	30%

Asset	Class	Rate
Office Equipment (not specifically listed elsewhere)	**8**	**20%**
Oil And Water Storage Tanks	6	10%
Other Tangible Property (Not Specifically Listed)	8	20%
Outdoor Advertising Billboards	8	20%
Parking Area And Similar Surfaces	**17**	**8%**
Patents (Limited Life)	44	25%
Patents (Unlimited Life)	CEC	N/A
Photocopy Machines	8	20%
Portable Buildings And Equipment	10	30%
Power Operated Movable Equipment	38	30%
Railway Cars	**35**	**7%**
Roads	17	8%
Sidewalks	**17**	**100%**
Software (Applications)	12	100%
Software (Systems)	10	30%
Taxicabs	**16**	**40%**
Telephone Systems	8	20%
Television Commercials	12	100%
Tools ($200 or Over)	8	20%
Tools (Under $200)	12	100%
Trucks And Trailers For Hauling Freight	16	40%
Trucks, Vans, Tractors, Wagons And Trailers	10	30%
Uniforms	**12**	**100%**
Video Games (Coin Operated)	**16**	**40%**
Video Tapes	10	30%
Video Tapes For Renting	12	100%

Exercises

(The solutions for these exercises can be found following Chapter 21 of the text.)

Exercise Eight - 1 (CCA Error)
During 2001, your company acquired a depreciable asset for $326,000 and your accountant included this asset in Class 1 at the end of the year. Early in 2002, you discover that the asset should have been allocated to Class 10. What was the impact of this error on your 2001 deductions from business income?

Exercise Eight - 2 (Separate CCA Classes)
In January, 2001, Edverness Inc. acquires 10 computer systems at a cost of $10,000 each. In December, 2001, two of these computers are traded in on faster machines. The new computers cost $11,000 each and the Company receives a trade in allowance for each old machine of $1,500. Indicate the amount(s) that would be deducted from 2001 business income if no election is made to put each computer in a separate class. Contrast this with the deduction(s) that would be available if the separate class election is used.

Exercise Eight - 3 (Class 13)
Vachon Ltd. leases its office space under a lease which was signed on January 1, 1996. The lease term is 10 years, with an option to renew at an increased rent for an additional five years. In 1996, the Company spends $52,000 renovating the premises. In 2001, changing needs require the Company to spend $31,000 renovating the space. Determine the amount of Class 13 CCA that the Company can deduct for 2001.

Exercise Eight - 4 (CCA Calculations)
Justin Enterprises, an unincorporated business, has a Class 8 UCC balance on December 31, 2000 of $212,000. During 2001 it acquires additional assets at a cost of $37,400. Also during 2001, it deducts $18,300 from UCC for disposals. Determine the maximum CCA for 2001 and the ending 2001 UCC Balance.

Exercise Eight - 5 (CCA Calculations)
Olander Inc. is incorporated on August 1, 2001. On September 15, 2001, the Company acquires $115,000 in Class 8 assets. The Company has a December 31 year end and no other depreciable assets are acquired before December 31, 2001. Determine the maximum CCA for the year ending December 31, 2001.

Exercise Eight - 6 (CCA Calculations - Disposals)
At the beginning of 2001, Codlin Inc. has two assets in Class 8. The cost of each asset was $27,000 and the balance in the Class 8 UCC was $24,883. On June 30, 2001, one of the assets was sold for $28,500. There are no other additions or disposals prior to the Company's December 31, 2001 year. What is the effect of the disposal on the Company's 2001 Net Business Income?

Exercise Eight - 7 (CCA Calculations - Disposals)
At the beginning of 2001, Codlin Inc. has two assets in Class 8. The cost of each asset was $27,000 and the balance in the Class 8 UCC was $24,883. On June 30, 2001, both of these assets are sold for $18,000. There are no other additions or disposals prior to the Company's December 31, 2001 year. What is the effect of the disposal on the Company's 2001 Net Business Income?

Exercise Eight - 8 (Involuntary Disposition)
During 2000, the only building owned by Foran Inc. is destroyed by a meteorite. Its original cost was $1,500,000, its fair market value was $1,400,000, and the Class 1 UCC was $650,000. The Company receives $1,400,000 in insurance proceeds during 2000 and replaces the building at a cost of $2,350,000 in 2001. The Company elects under ITA 13(4). What is the UCC of the new building?

Exercise Eight - 9 (Change In Use)

For a number of years, Ms. Mellisa Cornglow has owned a large sailboat that has been used for her personal enjoyment. The boat cost $111,000 in 1995 and, on May 1, 2001, it has a fair market value of $183,000. On this date she opens a chartering business with a December 31 year end in order to rent out her boat for the rest of the year. What is the maximum amount of CCA that she can deduct on the sailboat for 2001? The appropriate rate for sailboats is 15 percent of the declining balance (Class 7).

Exercise Eight - 10 (CEC)

During 1999, Keddy Inc. purchases another business and pays $85,600 for goodwill. At this time, the cumulative eligible capital of the company is nil. There are no additions to this balance in 2000 or 2001. On June 30, 2001, the business acquired in 1999 was sold and the sale price included a payment for goodwill of $93,400. The Company takes the maximum deduction for cumulative eligible capital in both 1999 and 2000. What amount, if any, will be included in the Company's 2001 income as a result of this sale?

Exercise Eight - 11 (CEC Election)

On January 1, 2001, Que Industries Ltd. has no CEC balance. During the taxation year ending December 31, 2001, it has the following expenditures:

Government License	$156,000
Payment for Non Competition Agreement	85,000
Customer List	223,000
Purchased Goodwill	50,000
Total	$514,000

The Company deducts the maximum amount of CEC for 2001. In November 2002, the customer list is sold for $296,000. Provided an election is made under ITA 14(1.01), what are the tax consequences associated with the 2002 sale of the customer list?

Problems For Self Study

(The solutions for these problems can be found following Chapter 21 of the text.)

Self Study Problem Eight - 1

Mr. Marker has been the sole proprietor of Marker Enterprises since its establishment in 1988. This business closes its books on December 31 and on December 31, 2000, the following information on its assets was contained in the records of the business:

Type Of Asset	Undepreciated Capital Cost	Original Capital Cost	CCA Rate
Equipment (Class 8)	$ 96,000	$130,000	20 Percent
Vehicles (Class 10)	$ 6,700	$ 30,000	30 Percent
Building (Class 3)	$115,000	$456,000	5 Percent

Other Information:

1. During the year ending December 31, 2001, Mr. Marker's business acquired additional Class 8 equipment at a total cost of $52,000. This new equipment replaced equipment which had an original cost of $75,000 and which was sold during the year for total proceeds of $35,000.

2. During the year ending December 31, 2001, Mr. Marker acquired a used automobile to be used in his business for a total cost of $8,000. Also during this year, Mr. Marker sold one of the trucks that was used in his business for proceeds of $25,000. This truck, which had an original capital cost of $20,000, had achieved a high value as the result of its extra features which were no longer available on late models.

3. As the result of a decision to lease its premises in future years, Mr. Marker sold his building for total proceeds of $110,000. Mr. Marker's business did not own any other buildings and this building was located on land which Mr. Marker had leased for a number of years. The lease terminated with the sale of the building.

Required: Calculate the effects of all of the preceding information on Mr. Marker's net income for tax purposes for the year ending December 31, 2001. Your answer should include the maximum capital cost allowance that can be deducted by Mr. Marker for this year. In addition, calculate the January 1, 2002 balance for the undepreciated capital cost of each of the three classes of depreciable assets.

Self Study Problem Eight - 2

The fiscal year of the Atlantic Manufacturing Company, a Canadian public company, ends on December 31. On January 1, 2001, the undepreciated capital cost balances for the various classes of assets owned by the Company are as follows:

Class 3 - Building	$625,000
Class 8 - Office Furniture And Equipment	155,000
Class 10 - Vehicles	118,000
Class 13 - Leasehold Improvements	61,750

During the year ending December 31, 2001, the following acquisitions of assets were made:

Class 8 - Office Furniture And Equipment	$ 27,000
Class 10 - Vehicles	33,000
Class 12 - Tools	34,000
Class 13 - Leasehold Improvements	45,000
Class 43 - Manufacturing Equipment	217,000

During this same period, the following disposals occurred:

Class 8   Used office furniture and equipment was sold for cash proceeds in the amount of $35,000. The original cost of these assets was $22,000.

Class 10   A delivery truck with an original cost of $23,000 was sold for $8,500.

Other Information:

1. The Company leases a building for $27,000 per year which houses a portion of its manufacturing operations. The lease was negotiated on January 1, 1998 and has an original term of 8 years. There are two renewal options on the lease. The term for each of these options is four years. The Company made $78,000 of leasehold improvements immediately after signing the lease. No further improvements were made until the current year.

2. On February 24, 2001, one of the Company's cars was totally destroyed in an accident. At the time of the accident, the fair market value of the car was $12,300. The proceeds from the Company's insurance policy amounted to only $8,000. The original cost of the car was $17,000.

3. The Class 10 vehicle purchased during the year was a delivery truck. The Class 12 tools purchased are not subject to the half year rule.

4. The Atlantic Manufacturing Company was organized in 1996 and has no balance in its cumulative eligible capital account on January 1, 2001. During March, 2001, the Company granted a manufacturing licence for one of its products to a company in southern Ontario. This licensee paid $87,000 for the right to manufacture this product.

5. It is the policy of the Company to deduct maximum CCA in all years.

Required: Calculate the maximum 2001 capital cost allowance that can be taken on each class of assets, the December 31, 2001 undepreciated capital cost for each class, and any other 2001 income inclusions or deductions resulting from the information provided in the problem.

Self Study Problem Eight - 3

Golden Dragon Ltd. begins operations in Vancouver on September 1, 1996. These operations include an elegant sit down restaurant specializing in northern Chinese cuisine, as well as a take out operation which provides home delivery throughout the city. To facilitate this latter operation, on October 12, 1996, the Company acquires 20 small cars to be used as delivery vehicles. The cost of these cars is $12,000 each and, for purposes of calculating Capital Cost Allowance, they are classified as Class 10 assets.

During the first year of operations, the Company establishes a fiscal year ending on December 31. In the fiscal periods 1997 through 2001, the following transactions take place with respect to the Company's fleet of delivery cars:

1997   The Company acquires five more cars at a cost of $12,500 each. In addition, three of the older cars are sold for total proceeds of $27,500.

1998   There are no new acquisitions of cars during this year. However, four cars are sold for total proceeds of $38,000.

1999   In December, 1999, 16 of the remaining 18 cars are sold for $128,000. It was the intent of the Company to replace these cars. However, because of a delay in delivery by the car dealer, the replacement did not occur until January, 2000.

2000   In January of 2000, the Company takes delivery of 25 new delivery cars at a cost of $16,000 each. No cars are disposed of during 2000.

2001   In March, 2001, there is a change in management at Golden Dragon Ltd. They conclude that the Company's take out operation is not in keeping with the more elegant image that the sit down restaurant is trying to maintain. As a consequence, the take out operation is closed and the 27 remaining delivery cars are sold. Because of the large number of cars being sold, the total proceeds are only $268,000.

Golden Dragon Ltd. takes maximum Capital Cost Allowances in each of the years under consideration.

Required: For each of the fiscal years 1996 through 2001, calculate capital cost allowance, recapture, or terminal loss with respect to the fleet of delivery cars owned by Golden Dragon Ltd.

Self Study Problem Eight - 4

For its taxation year ending December 31, 2001, Marion Enterprises has determined that its operating Net Income For Tax Purposes before any deduction for capital cost allowances amounts to $53,000. The Company does not have any Division C deductions so that whatever amount is determined as Net Income For Tax Purposes will also be the amount of Taxable Income for the taxation year.

On January 1, 2001, the Company has the following Undepreciated Capital Cost balances:

	Class 1	Class 8	Class 10
Undepreciated Capital Cost	$876,000	$220,000	$163,000

During 2001, the cost of additions to Class 10 amounted to $122,000 while the proceeds from disposals in this Class totalled $87,000. In no case did the proceeds of disposal exceed the Capital Cost of the assets retired and there were still assets in Class 10 on December 31, 2001.

There were no acquisitions or disposals in either Class 1 or Class 8 during 2001. During the preceding three taxation years, the Company reported taxable income totalling $46,000 for the three years. The Company anticipates that in the long run it will consistently produce large amounts of taxable income. However, it is faced with considerable uncertainty with respect to profits over the next eight to ten years.

Required:

A. Calculate the maximum Capital Cost Allowance that could be taken by Marion Enterprises for the taxation year ending December 31, 2001.

B. As Marion Enterprises' tax advisor, indicate how much Capital Cost Allowance you would advise the Company to take for the 2001 taxation year and the specific classes from which it should be deducted. Provide a brief explanation of the reasons for your recommendation.

Self Study Problem Eight - 5

During 1998, Miss Nash acquires an unincorporated business operation for a total price of $2,500,000. While most of this amount can be allocated to specific identifiable assets, an amount of $500,000 is left and must be allocated to goodwill.

Miss Nash operates the business until October 15, 2001. At that point she receives an offer of $3,800,000 for the business and decides to sell it. Of the total sales price, an amount of $780,000 is allocated to goodwill.

Required: Prepare a schedule showing the amount of amortization that can be deducted in each year of business and the tax effect related to the sale of goodwill by Miss Nash.

Self Study Problem Eight - 6

For the year ending December 31, 2001, the Income Statement of Markham Ltd., prepared in accordance with generally accepted accounting principles, is as follows:

Revenues		$973,000
Expenses:		
Cost Of Goods Sold	$272,000	
Selling And Administrative Costs	132,000	
Depreciation Expense	156,000	
Amortization Of Goodwill	7,000	
Other Expenses	137,000	704,000
Income Before Tax Provision		$269,000
Income Tax Expense:		
Current	$ 97,000	
Future	32,000	129,000
Net Income		$140,000

Other Information:

1. The Company spent $6,000 during the year on landscaping for its new building. For accounting purposes this was treated as an asset. The Company will not amortize this balance as it believes the work has an unlimited life.

2. The Company uses LIFO inventory valuation in its accounting records. On January 1, 2001, the LIFO value of Inventories was $4,000 below the FIFO value. On December 31, 2001, the LIFO value was $42,000 while the corresponding FIFO value was $45,000.

3. Selling And Administrative Costs include $15,000 in business meals and entertainment.

4. Other Expenses include contributions to registered charities of $2,500 and contributions to federal political parties of $1,200.

5. As the Company expects to issue more shares during 2002, it made a number of amendments to its articles of incorporation and included the legal costs in Other Expenses. These costs totalled $6,000.

6. During 2000, Markham Ltd. acquired a competing business at a price which included goodwill of $70,000. For accounting purposes, this amount is being amortized over 10 years on a straight line basis.

7. Other Expenses includes bond discount amortization of $2,500.

8. Selling And Administrative Costs include membership fees for several employees in a local golf and country club. These fees total $3,400.

9. On January 1, 2001, the Company had the following UCC balances:

Class 1	$400,000
Class 8	575,000
Class 10	45,000
Class 13	68,000

The Class 1 balance relates to a single building acquired in 1994 at a cost of $500,000. On February 1, 2001, this building is sold for $562,000, $105,000 more than its net book value of $457,000. This gain is included in the accounting revenues. The old building is replaced with a new building acquired at a cost of $623,000 on February 15, 2001. Both the old building and its replacement are located on land that is leased from the local municipality at very favorable rates. There was no penalty or other charges associated with the transfer of the land lease for the old building to its new owner. No election is made under either ITA 13(4) with respect to recapture or ITA 44(1) with respect to capital gains arising from this replacement of a business property.

There are no disposals of Class 8 assets during the year. However, there are acquisitions in the total amount of $126,000.

As the Company has decided to lease all of its vehicles in the future, all of the assets in Class 10 are sold during the year. The capital cost of these assets was $93,000 and the proceeds of disposal amounted to $37,000. The net book value of these assets was $52,000 and the resulting accounting loss of $15,000 was included in Other Expenses.

The Class 13 balance relates to a single lease which commenced on January 1, 1999. The lease has an initial term of seven years with two successive options to renew for three years each. Expenditures on this leasehold were $50,000 in 1999 and $27,000 in 2000. There were no further expenditures in 2001. The write off of these expenditures for accounting purposes is included in Depreciation Expense.

10. Other Expenses includes interest on late income tax instalments of $500 and on late municipal tax payments of $275.

11. Markham Ltd. deducts maximum capital cost allowance.

Required: Determine Markham Ltd.'s 2001 Net Income From Business. Indicate why you have excluded some items from your calculations. In addition, calculate the ending undepreciated capital cost for each CCA class.

Assignment Problems

(The solutions for these problems are only available in
the solutions manual that has been provided to your instructor.)

Assignment Problem Eight - 1
Global Manufacturing Ltd. has a taxation year which ends on December 31. On May 1, 2000, Global purchased equipment to be used in manufacturing and processing for $500,000. For 2000, it claimed $50,000 in capital cost allowance on this equipment. There are no other assets in this Capital Cost Allowance class.

During 2001, the Company received a government grant of $40,000 specifically for the equipment purchased in the previous year. In addition, one half of the equipment was sold for $275,000.

Required: Calculate the maximum amount of capital cost allowance that Global can deduct for 2001 and describe the tax effects of the equipment sale.

Assignment Problem Eight - 2
For a number of years, Mr. Stanton has invested his excess funds in various rental properties in Hearst, Ontario. At the beginning of 2001 he owned four properties as well as some furnishings used in one of the older buildings. The relevant information on these depreciable assets for 2001 is as follows:

Furniture   The furniture was used in the building at 18 Prince Street. It had a Capital Cost of $15,000, an Undepreciated Capital Cost of $8,000 at the end of 2000, and was sold during 2001 for $5,000.

18 Prince Street   This is a Class 3 building which had a Capital Cost of $42,000. Its Undepreciated Capital Cost at the end of 2000 was $18,000, and it was sold on August 1, 2001. Of the sale proceeds, $60,000 was allocated to the building. From January 1 to July 31, 2001, the building generated rents of $6,000 and incurred expenses (other than CCA) of $5,000.

4 McManus Street   This is a Class 3 building which had a capital cost of $45,000. Its Undepreciated Capital Cost at the end of 2000 was $32,000. During 2001 it generated rents of $6,000 and incurred expenses of $4,000.

94 George Street   This is a Class 3 building which has a capital cost of $850,000. Its Undepreciated Capital Cost at the end of 2000 was $550,000. During 2001 it generated rental income of $45,000 and incurred expenses of $34,000.

125 West Street   This Class 1 building has a capital cost of $102,000. Its Undepreciated Capital Cost at the end of 2000 was $98,000. During 2001 the unit generated rents of $13,000 and incurred expenses of $5,000.

Required: Calculate Mr. Stanton's net rental income for 2001. Specify how much CCA should be taken for each building.

Assignment Problem Eight - 3
Mr. Taylor bought a large triplex on January 1, 1999 for a total cost of $345,000. Of this amount, it is estimated that $255,000 should be allocated to the building and $90,000 to the land on which it is located. The three rental units in the triplex are identical in size and features and, for purposes of allocation to a CCA Class, the property is considered to be a single unit. At a bankruptcy sale in January, Mr. Taylor purchases furniture and appliances for one of the units at a total cost of $2,800.

Early in 1999, all three units are rented. Mr. Taylor's net rental income for 1999, before the deduction of any Capital Cost Allowance amounts to $10,200.

In November, 2000, the tenants in the furnished unit move out and purchase all the furniture and appliances from Mr. Taylor for $3,200. Mr. Taylor's net rental income for 2000, before consideration of Capital Cost Allowance is $12,600.

Early in 2001, Mr. Taylor decides to move into the empty unit. At this time, Mr. Taylor has no other personal residence and the market value of the triplex is estimated to be $315,000 for the building and $120,000 for the land. In March of 2001, one of the other tenants moves out. Because he cannot find another tenant, Mr. Taylor's net rental income for 2001, before consideration of Capital Cost Allowance is only $5,300. Mr. Taylor does not own any other rental properties.

Required:

A. Calculate the maximum Capital Cost Allowance that can be deducted by Mr. Taylor in each of the years 1999, 2000, and 2001. Include in your calculations his Undepreciated Capital Cost at the end of each year. In addition, indicate the amount of any recapture or terminal loss that occurs in any of the three years.

B. Indicate any tax consequences that may arise as a result of Mr. Taylor's decision to move into the building. (This part requires an understanding of capital gains and losses which is covered in detail in Chapter 9.)

Assignment Problem Eight - 4

Opening Balances   The taxation year of Burton Steel Ltd. ends on December 31. On January 1, 2001, the undepreciated capital cost balances for the various classes of assets owned by the Company are as follows:

Class 3 - Building	$1,562,000
Class 8 - Office Furniture And Equipment	278,000
Class 10 - Vehicles and Computers	204,000
Class 13 - Leasehold Improvements	106,250

Acquisitions   During the year ending December 31, 2001, the following acquisitions of assets were made:

Class 1 - Building	$258,000
Class 8 - Office Furniture And Equipment	72,000
Class 10 - Vehicles and Computers	63,000
Class 13 - Leasehold Improvements	58,000
Class 43 - Manufacturing Equipment	126,000

The addition to Class 10 was made up of one passenger vehicle, with a cost of $21,000, and $42,000 of computer equipment purchased in November, 2001.

Disposals   During this same period the following disposals occurred:

Class 8 - Office Furniture And Equipment was sold for cash proceeds of $42,000. The original cost of these assets totalled $38,000.

Class 10 - A delivery truck with an original cost of $37,000 was sold for $12,000.

Other Information:

1. The Company leases its main office building for $47,000 per year. The lease was negotiated on January 1, 1999 and had an original term of eight years. There are two renewal options on the lease, each for a period of two years. The Company made $125,000 of leasehold improvements immediately after signing the lease. No further improvements were made until the current year.

2. During the year ending December 31, 2001, some of the Company's Office Furniture And Fixtures were destroyed in a small fire. At the time of the accident the fair market value of

the destroyed property was $19,000. However, proceeds from the Company's insurance policy amounted to only $11,000. The original cost of the destroyed property was $18,000.

3. Maximum CCA has always been taken by Burton Steel.

Required: Calculate the maximum CCA that can be taken by Burton Steel Ltd. on each class of assets for the year ending December 31, 2001 and calculate the UCC for each class of assets on December 31, 2001. Indicate any other inclusions or deductions from taxable income resulting from the preceding information.

Assignment Problem Eight - 5

Sorrento Pizza begins operations in Ottawa on June 30, 1996. These operations include a formal dining room specializing in the cuisine of Northern Italy, as well as a take out operation which provides home delivery throughout the city. To facilitate this latter operation, on July 1, 1996, the Company acquires ten small cars to be used as delivery vehicles. The cost of these cars is $10,000 each and, for purposes of calculating Capital Cost Allowance, they are allocated to Class 10 (30 percent declining balance CCA). Sorrento Pizza takes maximum Capital Cost Allowances in each year of operation.

During the first year of operations, the Company establishes a fiscal year ending on December 31. In 1997 through 2001, the following transactions take place with respect to the Company's fleet of delivery cars:

1997   The Company acquires ten more cars at a cost of $10,500 each. In addition, three of the older cars are sold for total proceeds of $21,500.

1998   There are no new acquisitions of cars during this year. However, four cars are sold for total proceeds of $30,000.

1999   Near the end of 1999, 12 of the remaining 13 cars are sold for $84,000. It was the intent of the Company to replace these cars. However, because of a delay in delivery by the car dealer, the replacement did not occur until early 2000.

2000   In January of 2000, the Company receives 20 new delivery cars at a cost of $14,000 each. No cars are disposed of during the year.

2001   Early in this year, the management of Sorrento Pizza concludes that the take out operation is not profitable and is causing severe employee discipline problems. As a consequence, the take out operation is closed and the 21 remaining delivery cars are sold. Because of the large number of cars being sold, the total proceeds are only $174,000.

Required: For each of the fiscal years 1996 through 2001, calculate capital cost allowance, recapture, or terminal loss and the undepreciated capital cost with respect to the fleet of delivery cars owned by Sorrento Pizza.

Assignment Problem Eight - 6

For its taxation year ending December 31, 2001, Brownlee Inc. has determined that its Net Income For Tax Purposes before any deduction for capital cost allowances amounts to $23,500. The Company does not have any Division C deductions so that whatever amount is determined as Net Income For Tax Purposes will also be the amount of Taxable Income for the 2001 taxation year.

On January 1, 2001 the Company has the following Undepreciated Capital Cost balances:

Class 3	$263,000
Class 8	72,000
Class 10	52,000

During 2001, the cost of additions to Class 10 amounted to $38,000 while the proceeds from disposals in this Class totalled $23,000. In no case did the proceeds of disposal exceed the capital cost of the assets retired and there were still assets in the Class as of December 31, 2001.

There were no acquisitions or disposals in either Class 3 or Class 8 during 2001. The Company anticipates that its Taxable Income will exceed $500,000 per year in 2002 and subsequent years.

Required:

A. Calculate the maximum Capital Cost Allowance that could be taken by Brownlee Company for the taxation year ending December 31, 2001.

B. As Brownlee's tax advisor, indicate how much Capital Cost Allowance you would advise them to take for the 2001 taxation year and the specific classes from which it should be deducted. Provide a brief explanation of the reason for your recommendation. In providing this advice, do not take into consideration the possibility that losses can be carried either back or forward.

Assignment Problem Eight - 7

Miss Coos purchased a building to be used as her personal residence in 1999 at a cost of $90,000. On January 1, 2001, a portion of this residence was converted to an office and rented to a local accountant for $400 per month. At the time of the conversion the fair market value of the building was $120,000. Based on the amount of floor space allocated to the office, Miss Coos indicates that 30 percent of the building was converted into office space at this time.

On January 1, 2003, the office was rented by a new tenant who did not require the same amount of floor space as the previous tenant. As a result, one room was converted back to personal use. This room contained 10 percent of the total floor space and the fair market value of the building was $140,000 at this time.

Required: What is the maximum Capital Cost Allowance that can be deducted in 2001, 2002, and 2003? Ignore land values in calculating your solution.

Assignment Problem Eight - 8

Trail Resources Ltd. has a taxation year which ends on December 31. During 2000, its storage building was destroyed in a flash flood. This building was purchased in 1987 at a cost of $500,000 and, at the end of 1999, its undepreciated capital cost was $368,000. After negotiations with adjustors from the insurance company, a settlement of $490,000 was agreed upon and paid during 2000.

A replacement building was contracted for and started in September, 2000. It was completed in early 2001 for a cost of $650,000. Trail Resources Ltd. does not own any other buildings and always takes maximum CCA. The appropriate election is made by the company under ITA 13(4).

Required: Explain how the preceding transactions will affect the balance in the company's undepreciated capital cost at the end of each of the two years 2000 and 2001.

Assignment Problem Eight - 9

McLean Stores is a group of unincorporated retail stores, owned and operated by George McLean, specializing in the sale of bulk foods in Vancouver. In 1999, in order to expand his operations to Vancouver Island, he purchased 5 similar stores that were being operated as a group in the city of Victoria. The purchase price of these stores included a payment of $90,000 for the goodwill of the operation. The availability of this goodwill was insured by a long term no competition agreement signed by the former owner of the stores. The agreement covers all of Vancouver Island and is transferable.

In 2001, Mr. McLean sells McLean Stores at a price which includes a payment for goodwill of $300,000. It is estimated that $200,000 of this goodwill should be allocated to the Vancouver operations while the remaining $100,000 relates to the Victoria stores that were purchased in 1999.

The year end of the business is December 31. Mr. McLean has taken the maximum deductions for amortization of cumulative eligible capital in all years.

Required:

A. What is the maximum deduction that Mr. McLean can claim for amortization of cumulative eligible capital in 1999 and 2000?

B. What amounts will be included in Mr. McLean's 2001 Net Income For Tax Purposes as a result of the sale of McLean Stores?

Assignment Problem Eight - 10

The following information relates to Bartel Ltd. for its fiscal year which ends on December 31, 2001:

1. The Company has Undepreciated Capital Cost balances on December 31, 2000 for its tangible assets as follows:

Class 3	$590,000
Class 8	570,000
Class 10	61,000

2. During 2001, the Company purchased office furniture for $14,000.

3. During 2001, the Company purchased a truck from its majority shareholder for $22,000. The truck was four years old, had a fair market value of $36,000 and an undepreciated capital cost of $26,000.

4. On January 1, 1999, the Company expanded its operations by purchasing another business. The purchase price for this business included a payment of $92,000 for goodwill, $120,000 for a franchise with a six year life, and $28,000 for a franchise with an unlimited life.

5. During 1999, one of the Company's buildings was destroyed in a flood. The building was acquired in 1987 at a cost of $475,000 and had a fair market value of $440,000 at the time of the flood. The Company received $440,000 from its insurance company in 1999, signed a construction contract for replacement of the building on January 1, 2000, and saw the replacement building completed in early 2001. The replacement cost was $350,000. As the insurance proceeds did not create recapture for the class, no election was made under ITA 13(4).

6. During 2000, the Company sold part of its original operations. The proceeds of disposal included a payment for goodwill of $59,000.

7. Bartel Ltd. has always deducted the maximum Capital Cost Allowance and the maximum write off of cumulative eligible capital allowable in each year of operation.

Required: Calculate the maximum Capital Cost Allowance and the maximum write off of cumulative eligible capital that can be deducted for 2001.

Assignment Problem Eight - 11

Darlington Inc. has a fiscal year which ends on December 31. For the year ending December 31, 2001, the Company's accounting income, determined in accordance with generally accepted accounting principles, was $596,000. Other information related to the preparation of its 2001 tax return is as follows:

1. The Tax Expense was $55,000, including $7,000 in future tax expense.

2. The Company uses a LIFO assumption for inventory valuation purposes. The January 1, 2001 LIFO inventory was $15,000 less than it would have been under a FIFO assumption, while the December 31, 2001 LIFO inventory was $20,000 less than the corresponding FIFO value.

3. The Company spent $95,000 on landscaping for its main office building. This amount was recorded as an asset in the accounting records and, because the work has an unlimited life, no amortization was recorded on this asset.

4. The Company spent $17,000 on advertisements in *Fortune* Magazine, a U.S. based publication. Approximately 90 percent of its non advertising content is original editorial content. The advertisements were designed to promote sales in Canadian cities located on the U.S. border.

5. The Depreciation Expense was $623,000. At the beginning of 2001, the Company has a balance in Class 3 of $1,000,000, representing the UCC of its headquarters buildings. In general, other buildings are leased. However, in 2001 a policy change results in the acquisition of a new store building at a cost of $650,000 of which $125,000 is allocated to land.

    The January 1, 2001 balance in Class 8 was $4,200,000. During 2001, there were additions to this Class in the total amount of $700,000. In addition, Class 8 assets with a cost of $400,000 were sold for proceeds of $550,000. The net book value of these assets in the accounting records was $325,000 and the resulting gain of $225,000 was included in the accounting income for the year. There are numerous assets remaining in the Class at the end of the 2001 taxation year.

    At the beginning of 2001, the UCC in Class 10 was $800,000, reflecting the Company's fleet of cars. As the Company is changing to a policy of leasing its cars, all of these cars were sold during the year for $687,000. The capital cost of the cars was $1,200,000 and their net book value in the accounting records was equal to the sale proceeds of $687,000.

6. Included in travel costs deducted in 2001 for accounting purposes was $12,000 for airline tickets and $41,400 of business meals and entertainment.

7. The Company paid and deducted for accounting purposes a $2,500 initiation fee for a corporate membership in the Highland Golf And Country Club.

8. The Company paid and deducted property taxes of $15,000 on vacant land that was being held for possible future expansion of its headquarters site.

Required: Calculate Darlington Inc.'s minimum Net Income For Tax Purposes for the 2001 taxation year. In addition, calculate the ending undepreciated capital cost balances for each capital cost allowance class.

Assignment Problem Eight - 12

Ms. Georgia Valentine is an employee of Peach Ltd., a public corporation and GST registrant. She is required to travel as part of her job. She uses a car which she owns for this travel and pays all other costs out of her own funds. The car is used 100 percent for employment related purposes. The car was purchased in 2000 for a total of $23,000 which includes $1,600 in provincial sales tax and GST of $1,400. She claimed the maximum CCA on the car and the related GST rebate in her 2000 tax return. Her Notice of Assessment received in June, 2001 indicated that her 2000 return was accepted as filed. She does not receive any reimbursement or allowance from her employer.

In her 2001 tax return, she deducts the following amounts in the calculation of employment income:

Accommodation (Includes Provincial Sales Tax Of $240 And GST Of $210)	$ 3,450
Deductible Portion Of Meals And Entertainment (Includes Provincial Sales Tax Of $160 And GST Of $140)	2,300
Automobile Costs:	
Gas And Maintenance (Includes Provincial Sales Tax Of $400 And GST Of $350)	4,750
Interest On Automobile Loan	1,800
Insurance	800
Total Deductions Excluding CCA	$13,100

Ms. Valentine intends to claim the maximum CCA on her car as she has always done in the past.

Required: Calculate the maximum CCA that Ms. Valentine can claim on her car for 2001. In addition, calculate the 2001 GST rebate that Ms. Valentine will claim as a result of her deductible expenses.

Assignment Problem Eight - 13 (Electronic Library Research Problem)

Provide brief answers to the following questions. Your answers should be supported by references to materials found in your Electronic Library.

A. If a building is erected on leased land, would it be included in Class 1 (buildings) or Class 13 (leasehold improvements)?

B. Various types of portable buildings are used by organizations to solve their immediate need for additional space. Would such structures be included in Class 1 (buildings) or Class 8 (miscellaneous tangible property)?

C. Depreciable assets are sometimes sold with a portion of the consideration being made up of amounts that will be receivable in the future. In some instances, all or part of this amount receivable may have to be written off as a bad debt. What is the appropriate tax treatment of this bad debt?

D. Indicate the appropriate CCA Class and its rate for each of the following items:
   1. A Windmill
   2. A Marine Railway
   3. Deuterium Enriched Water
   4. Fibre Optic Cable
   5. Chemical Pulp Mill
   6. Electrical Advertising Signs Offered For Rent
   7. Dental Instruments Costing Less Than $200
   8. Electrical Generating Equipment

Chapter 9

Capital Gains And Capital Losses

Economic Background

Capital Assets And Income Taxation Policy

9-1.   The discussion of business income in Chapter 7 stated that capital gains and losses arise on the disposition of assets that are earning business or property income. In general, the income from the sale of such assets will be incidental to the ongoing activities which produce business income and, as a consequence, a case can be made for exempting any resulting capital gains and losses from income taxation.

9-2.   This case is reinforced during periods of high inflation. If a business is going to continue operating as a going concern, it will usually have to replace any capital assets that are sold. As gains on the sale of capital assets often reflect nothing more than inflationary price increases, such gains cannot be distributed to the owners of the business as they must be used to finance the replacement of the assets sold.

9-3.   Until 1972, Canadian tax legislation did not levy any income tax on capital gains. This left Canada as one of the few industrial nations which imposed no tax on these gains. Further, there was some feeling that, despite the arguments against taxing capital gains, the ability to completely escape taxation on this type of income was creating severe inequities in the taxation system. As a result, one of the more significant changes in the 1972 tax reform legislation was the introduction of taxation on capital gains.

9-4.   The capital gains taxation which became effective January 1, 1972, represented a compromise between the view that capital gains should be exempt from tax and the position that such freedom from taxation creates serious inequities among various classes of taxpayers. Taxation of capital gains was introduced, but on a basis that was very favourable to the taxpayer.

9-5.   In simple terms, the 1972 rules indicated that one-half of a capital gain would be treated as a taxable capital gain and, similarly, one-half of a capital loss would be deductible against capital gains as an allowable capital loss. This meant that for a taxpayer in the 50 percent tax bracket, the effective tax rate on capital gains was an attractive 25 percent.

Lifetime Capital Gains Deduction

9-6.   In 1985, the government introduced one of the most complex and controversial provisions ever added to the *Income Tax Act*. In simple terms, this legislation provided that every resident Canadian could enjoy over their lifetime up to $500,000 in capital gains on a tax free basis. This provision was heavily criticized as a gift to higher income Canadians, particularly in view of the fact that it was available on any type of capital gain. It was difficult for many analysts to see the economic justification for providing favourable tax treatment of gains on the sale of a wealthy Canadian's Florida condominium.

9-7.   As a result of such criticism, this deduction is no longer available on a general basis. However, a $500,000 "super " deduction continues to be available on gains resulting from the disposition of shares or debt of a qualified small business corporation or a qualified farm property.

9-8.   It should be noted here that the provisions related to the lifetime capital gains deduction do not affect any of the material in this Chapter. The lifetime capital gains legislation did not alter the determination of the amount of taxable capital gains to be included in Net Income For Tax Purposes. Rather, the legislation provided for a deduction in the determination of Taxable Income for all or part of the taxable capital gains included in Net Income For Tax Purposes. This material is covered in Chapter 12, Taxable Income For Individuals.

Changes In The Inclusion Rate

9-9.   As we noted, the 1972 tax reform concluded that it was appropriate to tax only a portion of capital gains, resulting in the concept of a "taxable" capital gain. A similar approach was taken with capital losses, with the deductible portion being referred to as an "allowable" capital loss. From the introduction of this approach in 1972 through the changes introduced with the 1988 tax reform, the inclusion rate for determining taxable capital gains was one-half.

9-10.   The 1988 tax reform brought a change in this inclusion rate for capital gains. It was decided to increase the taxable portion of the gain to three-quarters of the total amount. This was phased in over three years, taxing two-thirds of capital gains in 1988 and 1989, and increasing the rate to three-quarters for gains realized in 1990 and subsequent years.

9-11.   An inclusion rate of three-quarters created a situation where the effective rate of tax on capital gains in Canada was significantly higher than the rates applicable to this type of income in the U.S. This led to considerable pressure from the business community to make Canadian rates competitive with the lower rates which prevailed in the U.S. This pressure, combined with an improved federal financial picture, led to a complete reversal of the 1988 reform changes.

9-12.   This was accomplished in two stages. The February 28, 2000 budget reduced the inclusion rate for capital gains and losses from three-quarters to two-thirds. A further, largely unexpected change, took place when the Minister of Finance issued an *Economic Statement and Budget Update* on October 18, 2000. This further reduced the inclusion rate from two-thirds to one-half. In effect, we were back where we started in 1972.

9-13.   These changes created a fairly complex situation for the year 2000. Depending on when the relevant disposition occurred, the inclusion rate for the gain or loss could be three-quarters (dispositions prior to February 28), two-thirds (dispositions after February 27 but prior to October 18), or one-half (dispositions after October 17). This was further complicated by the need to deal with situations where there were gains in one of these periods and losses in others. Clearly, the calculation of the amount of taxable capital gain or allowable capital loss to be included in 2000 tax returns could have been a fairly complex exercise.

9-14.   At first glance, it would appear that we could ignore these complications. The focus of this text is on the 2001 taxation year and dispositions during this year will consistently result in the inclusion of one-half the gain or loss. While this suggests that we could ignore the multiple inclusion rates applicable to the year 2000, this is not the case. In Chapter 12 we give detailed attention to the carry back and carry forward of allowable capital losses that cannot be deducted in the year of disposition. We will find that, in situations where a capital loss is carried over to an earlier or later year, it will be deducted at the inclusion rate applicable to that year. This means that, if a capital loss is carried back to 2000, we will have to be able to deal with the determination of the inclusion rate applicable to gains for that year. This becomes particularly complex when the gains have been included in 2000 income at more than one inclusion rate. In this type of situation, the capital loss will have to be deducted using an average rate for the gains.

9-15. Given this situation, we will have to give some attention to the multiple inclusion rates applicable to the year 2000. However, our major focus will be on the capital gains rules as they apply in 2001 and subsequent years where the inclusion rate for both gains and losses is one-half.

General Rules

Capital Gains In The Income Tax Act

9-16. This material is a continuation of our discussion of the calculation of Net Income For Tax Purposes. In Chapters 5 and 6, detailed attention was given to employment income and related matters involving deferred income. This discussion was largely a reflection of Subdivision a of Division B of the *Income Tax Act*. Chapters 7 and 8 dealt with Subdivision b of Division B and provided a comprehensive consideration of business income, including the calculations related to capital cost allowance. We will return to Subdivision b in Chapter 11 in the material related to property income.

9-17. Capital gains and losses are the third major component of Net Income For Tax Purposes. This subject is covered in Subdivision c of Division B, Sections 38 through 55. Sections 38 and 39 define capital gains, capital losses, and other items which relate to the calculation of these amounts. Section 40 provides the general tax rules for computing these amounts. The remaining Sections 41 through 55 deal with more specific matters such as identical properties (Section 47), adjustments to the cost base (Section 53), and various additional definitions (Section 54).

Capital Gains Defined
Capital Assets

9-18. In general, capital gains occur when a taxpayer disposes of a capital asset. You will recall that capital assets were described in Chapter 7 as being those assets which are capable of earning income in the form of business profits, interest, dividends, royalties, or rents. Further, the assets must be held for this income producing purpose, rather than for a quick resale at a profit. It was also noted in Chapter 7 that, in making the determination as to whether a particular amount of income was capital in nature, the courts would take into consideration the intent and course of the taxpayer's conduct, the number and frequency of transactions involving the type of asset under consideration, the nature of the asset, the relationship of the asset to the business of the taxpayer, and the objectives set out in the articles of incorporation.

9-19. Despite these guidelines, the fact that capital gains receive favourable income tax treatment has led to much controversy and litigation with respect to the distinction between capital and other assets. Until 1977, this was particularly true with respect to holdings of securities. It was often difficult to distinguish between those situations where a taxpayer was holding securities for their income producing ability and those situations where the goal was to generate profits on trading activities. In 1977, the CCRA offered taxpayers an election to alleviate this problem.

Capital Gains Election On Canadian Securities
9-20. ITA 39(4) allows taxpayers, including corporations and trusts, to elect to have all Canadian securities which they own deemed to be capital property and all sales of such securities deemed to be dispositions of capital property. Once this election is made, it applies to all future dispositions of Canadian securities by the taxpayer, thus assuring the taxpayer that all gains and losses will be treated as capital. ITA 39(5) indicates that this election is not available to traders or dealers in securities, banks, trustees, credit unions, insurance companies, or non residents.

Dispositions

9-21.   As defined in ITA 54, a disposition is any transaction or event which entitles the taxpayer to proceeds of disposition of property. In addition to sales of property, the definition of a disposition includes redemptions, cancellations, expiries, expropriations, and conversions resulting from an amalgamation or merger (the exercise of a conversion option on a convertible bond or preferred share would not be considered to be a disposition).

9-22.   The definition also refers to situations where there is a change in legal ownership without a change in beneficial ownership. In general, transactions such as transfers between two trusts with the same beneficiary are not considered to be dispositions. However, the definition specifically notes that transfers to RRSPs, DPSPs, and RRIFs are not covered by this exception. This means that if an individual transfers assets to an RRSP, DPSP, or RRIF, the transfer will be viewed as a disposition, despite the fact that there is no change in beneficial ownership.

9-23.   In addition to actual dispositions of capital property, there are a number of situations in which a disposition is deemed to have occurred. These would include changes in use as discussed in Chapter 8. Other deemed disposition situations such as the death of a taxpayer, certain gifts by taxpayers, and the taxpayer ceasing to be a resident of Canada, will be given consideration in Chapter 10.

Proceeds Of Disposition

9-24.   The term proceeds of disposition is defined in ITA 54. Included in this definition are the following:

- The sale price of property sold.
- Compensation for property unlawfully taken or for property destroyed, including related proceeds from insurance policies.
- Compensation for property that has been appropriated or injuriously affected whether lawfully or unlawfully.
- Compensation for damaged property, including amounts payable under insurance policies.

9-25.   You will recall from our discussion of property damages in Chapter 8 that special rules apply to involuntary and certain voluntary dispositions of assets. These rules have the effect of reversing any recapture of CCA associated with the disposition of one asset by deducting such amounts against the cost of its replacement. Similar rules exist with respect to capital gains which may arise on these transactions and they will be discussed later in this Chapter.

Adjusted Cost Base

Definition

9-26.   The adjusted cost base of an asset is defined in ITA 54 as follows:

(i) where the property is depreciable property of the taxpayer, the capital cost to him of the property as of that time, and

(ii) in any other case, the cost to the taxpayer of the property adjusted, as of that time, in accordance with section 53.

9-27.   This definition means that, in general, the adjusted cost base of a capital asset is analogous to the accounting concept of historical cost. As with the historical cost concept, it includes the invoice cost, delivery and setup charges, non refundable provincial sales taxes, and any other costs associated with acquiring the asset or putting it into use.

9-28.   As indicated in the definition, ITA 53 specifies a number of adjustments to the cost base. Some of the more important of these adjustments can be described as follows:

Government Grants And Assistance   When a taxpayer receives government grants or other types of assistance, these amounts are deducted from the adjusted cost base of the related asset. This is consistent with the accounting treatment of government grants specified in Section 3800 of the *CICA Handbook*.

Superficial Losses   A superficial loss occurs when a taxpayer, his spouse, or a corporation controlled by the taxpayer disposes of a property and, within the period of 30 days before the disposition and 30 days after the disposition, one of the cited taxpayers acquires the same or identical property. The identical property is referred to as the substitute property and any loss on the disposal of the original property is called a superficial loss. Such losses cannot be deducted but must be added to the adjusted cost base of the substitute property.

As an example, assume that in 1998 Ms. Deffett acquires 100 shares of Norton Limited for $75 per share. On December 27, 2001 the shares are trading at $60 and, because she has realized capital gains in 2001, Ms. Deffett sells the shares on this date in order to realize a loss that can be used to offset the capital gains. One-half of the capital loss of $15 per share on the December 27, 2001 sale would be deductible, provided no Norton Limited shares are purchased between November 27, 2001 and January 26, 2002. If, however, she were to purchase 100 Norton shares on December 15, 2001 or January 15, 2002 for $65 per share, the December, 2001 loss would be disallowed. The disallowed loss would be added to the adjusted cost base of the new shares, giving these shares an adjusted cost base of $80 ($65 + $15) per share. This amount would be appropriate in that it reflects her net cash outlay per share ($75 - $60 + $65).

> Exercise Nine-1 deals with superficial losses. This would be an appropriate time to attempt this exercise.

Stock Dividends   When an investor receives a stock dividend, it will be taxed in the same manner as a cash dividend (see Chapter 11). As a consequence, the fair market value of the shares received is added to the adjusted cost base of the group of shares.

Other Adjustments To The Cost Base   Other important adjustments would include the addition of interest and property taxes on holdings of undeveloped land to the adjusted cost base, the addition of subsequent contributions by a shareholder to a corporation to the cost base of the shares, and the requirement that under certain circumstances forgiveness of debts on property must be deducted from the cost base of that property. There are several other such adjustments in ITA 53. You should note, however, that in the case of depreciable property, any deductions taken for CCA do not change the adjusted cost base of the property. Capital gains are determined on the basis of the original capital cost of the asset, not the UCC.

Negative Adjusted Cost Base

9-29.   It is possible that sufficient adjustments could be made to an adjusted cost base that its balance will become negative. When this occurs, ITA 40(3) requires that the deficiency be treated as a capital gain and the adjusted cost base of the asset be adjusted to zero. Note that, unlike the situation with recapture of CCA, this would apply even if additions to the cost base prior to the end of the taxation year were sufficient to eliminate the deficit balance.

9-30.   Also note that ITA 40(3) is not applicable to most partnership interests. That is, a negative adjusted cost base for a partnership interest does not automatically trigger a capital gain and can be carried forward indefinitely. However, this exemption from ITA 40(3) does not apply to certain limited partnership interests. For more details on this point, see Chapter 20.

GST Considerations

9-31.   When capital assets are used in commercial activities, all or part of the GST paid on their acquisition can be recovered as input tax credits. When this is the case, the GST amount recovered would not be included in the adjusted cost base of the asset. There are, however, situations in which there will be no input tax credits available for GST paid on the acquisition of capital assets. Examples of this would be acquisitions of capital assets that will be used in providing exempt services or that will not be used primarily for commercial activities. In these situations the GST payment on the asset acquisition is a permanent outflow of enterprise resources and must be added to the adjusted cost base of the asset. A more complete discussion of the GST implications associated with capital assets will be found at the end of this Chapter.

Calculating The Capital Gain Or Loss

9-32. The general formula for determining the amount of a capital gain or loss can be described very simply. The calculation, using assumed data, is as follows:

Proceeds Of Disposition		$4,750
Less - The Aggregate Of:		
Adjusted Cost Base	($3,890)	
Expenses Of Disposition	(560)	(4,450)
Capital Gain (Loss)		$ 300
Inclusion Rate		1/2
Taxable Capital Gain		$ 150

9-33. If, as in the preceding example, there is a capital gain, one-half of the amount will be treated as a taxable capital gain. The adjective taxable is consistently used to indicate the portion of the total gain that will be included in income. Similarly, one-half of a negative amount (a capital loss) resulting from the application of the preceding formula would be treated as an allowable capital loss. The adjective allowable is consistently used to indicate the deductible portion of the total amount of the loss. As was noted in Chapter 3, allowable capital losses can only be deducted against taxable capital gains.

Year 2000 Complications

9-34. As noted in the section on Changes in the Inclusion Rate (Paragraph 9-9), the year 2000 saw the inclusion rate for capital gains reduced, first to two-thirds on February 28, followed by a further reduction on October 18 to one-half. The one-half rate is applicable for all of 2001, as well as subsequent years and will be used in most of the material in this Chapter. However, capital loss carry overs to the year 2000 will require establishing an appropriate inclusion rate to be used for their deduction. While it appears that the CCRA will provide this rate to taxpayers based on the return that they filed for 2000, some familiarity with the procedures used to arrive at these rates is useful and will be provided in this section. Note, however, that a comprehensive treatment of this issue goes beyond the scope of this text.

9-35. With respect to inclusion rates, there are three relevant periods in 2000. The following table provides four independent cases which serve to illustrate some of the calculations used in determining the capital gains inclusion rate applicable to the year 2000.

	2000 Capital Gain (Loss)			
	Before February 28 (3/4 Rate)	After Feb. 27 Before Oct. 18 (2/3 Rate)	After October 17 (1/2 Rate)	Total
Case One	$60,000	$33,000	$10,000	$103,000
Case Two	72,000	(42,000)	(10,000)	20,000
Case Three	(42,000)	72,000	10,000	40,000
Case Four	(36,000)	27,000	(10,000)	(18,000)

9-36. The analysis of these four cases is as follows:

Case One In this situation, where the taxpayer only experiences capital gains in the three periods, there is no real problem. The taxable capital gain for the year 2000 will be $72,000 [(3/4)($60,000) + (2/3)($33,000) + (1/2)($10,000)]. This creates an effective capital gains inclusion rate for 2000 of 69.9 percent ($72,000 ÷ $103,000). This would be the rate that would be applicable to any carry over to the year 2000 from a previous or subsequent year.

Case Two In this Case the first period capital gain exceeds the sum of the capital losses in periods two and three. The three-quarters rate would be applicable here, resulting in a net taxable capital gain of $15,000 [(3/4)($72,000 - $52,000)]. Capital loss carry overs from previous or subsequent years would be deducted using this rate.

Case Three   In this case, the capital gain in the second period exceeds the capital loss in the first period. The net gain for the first two periods, or the interim net gain, is $30,000 and the interim inclusion rate is 2/3. The rate that will be applied to the net gain for the year of $40,000 is a weighted average of the interim inclusion rate and the third period rate. It would be calculated as follows:

$$[(2/3)(\$72,000 - \$42,000) + (1/2)(\$10,000)] \div (\$30,000 + \$10,000) = 62.5\%$$

This give a taxable capital gain for the year of $25,000 [($40,000)(62.5%)]. The 62.5 percent rate would also be applicable to capital losses carried over to the 2000 taxation year.

Case Four   In this case the capital loss in the first period exceeds the capital gain in the second period. The net loss for the first two periods, or the interim net loss, is $9,000 and the interim inclusion rate is 3/4. The rate that will be applied to the net loss for the year of $19,000 is a weighted average of the interim inclusion rate and the third period rate. It would be calculated as follows:

$$[(3/4)(\$36,000 - \$27,000) + (1/2)(\$10,000)] \div (\$9,000 + \$10,000) = 61.8\%$$

This gives a deductible loss for the year of $17,742 [($19,000)(61.8%)]. As it cannot be deducted during the current year, this amount will be added to the "net capital loss balance". (This is the balance that reflects capital losses that can be carried over to other years. As will be discussed in Chapter 12, additions to this balance are not adjusted for changes in the capital gains inclusion rate.)

9-37.   The preceding cases, while not comprehensive in their coverage, provide an indication of the types of calculations that are required for carry over purposes. Throughout the remainder of this Chapter, we will generally use the one-half rate in our examples. However, we will have to return to this issue in Chapter 12 when we present the material on capital loss carry overs.

Assets Acquired Before 1972
Concept Of Valuation Day (V-Day)
9-38.   Prior to 1972 there was no taxation of capital gains. However, there was a problem with the introduction of capital gains taxation in that many taxpayers were holding assets which had already experienced accrued capital gains prior to the end of 1971. As an example, assume that Mr. Munro purchased a piece of land in 1965 for $15,000 and sold it on January 1, 1972 for $25,000. As it is clear that the resulting gain of $10,000 accrued prior to the introduction of capital gains taxation, it would not be equitable to assess Mr. Munro for taxes on this $10,000 capital gain. In order to avoid retroactive application of taxation on capital gains which occurred prior to 1972, the CCRA established the concept of valuation day (V-Day). For publicly traded securities, V-Day was December 22, 1971. For other types of capital property, V-Day is specified to be December 31, 1971.

Application Of The Median Rule
9-39.   For non depreciable capital assets that were owned by a taxpayer on December 31, 1971, ITAR 26(3) states that the adjusted cost base for the asset will be the median value of three amounts:

- The proceeds of disposition
- The actual cost of the asset
- The valuation day value of the asset

9-40.   Consider an asset acquired on December 31, 1968 at a cost of $500. As of V-Day its value has increased to $700 and, during 2001, it is sold for $2,000. The capital gain would be calculated as follows:

Proceeds Of Disposition	$2,000
Adjusted Cost Base (Median of $500, $700, And $2,000)	(700)
Capital Gain	$1,300

9-41.   As this simple example illustrates, the median rule limits the gain to the amount which accrued after the introduction of capital gains taxation in Canada. The pre V-Day accrual of $200 ($700 - $500) is realized on a tax free basis. Similar results will be achieved when capital losses are involved, so that only the capital loss accruing after V-Day is deductible.

Exercise Nine-2 deals with pre 1972 assets. This would be an appropriate time to attempt this problem.

9-42.   For many years after 1971, an understanding of such transitional rules was essential for tax practitioners. However, at this point in time, pre 1972 asset dispositions are no longer common. As a consequence, we will devote no further attention to these once important transitional rules.

Detailed Application Of The Rules

Identical Properties

Basic Rules

9-43.   A taxpayer can own a group of identical properties which have been acquired over a period of time at different capital costs. This would arise most commonly with holdings of securities such as common stock in a particular corporation. If part of such a group of assets is disposed of, ITA 47 requires that the adjusted cost base for the assets being disposed of be based on the average cost of the entire group.

9-44.   The following example illustrates the application of this idea:

Example   An individual has engaged in the following transactions involving Gower Company common stock:

Year	Shares Purchased (Sold)	Cost (Proceeds) Per Share	Total Cost (Proceeds)
1986	4,000	$10	$40,000
1988	3,000	12	36,000
1993	(2,000)	(10)	(20,000)
1997	2,500	11	27,500
1999	3,000	10	30,000
2001	(1,500)	(13)	(19,500)

Tax Consequences   The average cost for the first two purchases was $10.86 [($40,000 + $36,000) ÷ (4,000 + 3,000)]. This means that the loss to be recorded on the 1993 sale would be as follows:

Proceeds Of Disposition [(2,000)($10)]	$20,000
Adjusted Cost Base [(2,000)($10.86)]	(21,720)
Capital Loss	($ 1,720)
1993 Inclusion Rate	3/4
Allowable Capital Loss	($ 1,290)

This sale would leave the remaining 5,000 at $54,280 ($76,000 - $21,720). The new average cost for the 2001 sale would be $10.65 [($54,280 + $27,500 + $30,000) ÷ (5,000 + 2,500 + 3,000)]. Given this, the gain on the 2001 sale would be calculated as follows:

Proceeds Of Disposition [(1,500)($13)]	$19,500
Adjusted Cost Base [(1,500)($10.65)]	(15,975)
Capital Gain	$ 3,525
Inclusion Rate	1/2
Taxable Capital Gain	$ 1,762

2000 Budget Changes

9-45.   The procedures illustrated in the preceding example are still applicable in most situations. However, legislation flowing from the February 28, 2000 budget added a new ITA 47(3) which exempts certain securities from inclusion in the weighted average calculations. Without going into detail, the adjusted cost base of certain shares that have been acquired through stock option arrangements or withdrawals from deferred profit sharing plans, will now be calculated independently of adjusted cost base of any other identical shares held by the individual. Stated alternatively, the adjusted cost base of these option shares will not be based on the average cost of all such shares owned by the taxpayer.

> Exercise Nine-3 deals with identical properties. This would be an appropriate time to attempt this exercise.

9-46.   While these provisions could be covered at this point, they are complex and involve a detailed understanding of stock option arrangements. Given this, we will defer coverage of the new ITA 47(3) until Chapter 12, where you will find our comprehensive coverage of stock option arrangements.

Partial Dispositions

9-47.   In those situations where a taxpayer disposes of part of a property, ITA 43 requires that a portion of the total adjusted cost base be allocated to the disposal on a reasonable basis. For example, if a 500 hectare tract of land had an adjusted cost base of $6,000,000 and 200 hectares of the tract were sold, it would seem reasonable to allocate $2,400,000 or 40 percent (200 hectares ÷ 500 hectares) of the total adjusted cost base to the land which was sold. If, however, there was some reason to believe that the part of the tract sold had a value that was not proportionate to the total tract, some alternative basis of allocation could be used.

Warranties

9-48.   If a taxpayer disposes of capital property and the proceeds include some payment for a warranty or other contingent obligation, ITA 42 requires that the full proceeds must be used in determining the capital gain. Stated alternatively, no reserve can be established to provide for any future obligations. However, one-half of any outlays related to such contingent obligations which are made in a subsequent year can be deducted as capital losses, provided the taxpayer has past or present capital gains which can absorb them.

> Exercise Nine-4 deals with warranties on capital assets. This would be an appropriate time to attempt this exercise.

Bad Debts On Sales Of Capital Property

9-49.   When an amount receivable results from the disposition of a capital property, the possibility arises that some of the proceeds of disposition will have to be written off as a bad debt. When this occurs, ITA 50(1) deems the seller to have disposed of the receivable and immediately reacquired it at a proceeds and cost of zero. Consider the following:

Example During 2001, a capital property with a cost of $500,000 is sold for $510,000. The proceeds are made up of $360,000 in cash, plus the purchaser's note for $150,000.

9-50.   If the vendor of the land does not choose to deduct a reserve for the uncollected amount, a capital gain of $10,000 would be recognized in 2001. If, during 2001, the note received from the purchaser turns out to be uncollectible, the deemed disposal and reacquisition would result in a capital loss of $150,000, more than offsetting the $10,000 capital gain on the disposal. If, at a later point in time, some amount of debt were recovered, any excess over the deemed nil proceeds would be considered a capital gain.

Capital Gains Reserves
General Principles

9-51.   In some instances, all of the proceeds from the disposition will not be received in cash in the year of disposal. If, for example, Mr. Filoso were to sell a piece of land for a capital gain and collect only 10 percent of the total proceeds in the year of sale, it would seem reasonable to allow him to defer recognition of a part of the capital gain. This deferral can be accomplished through the establishment of a capital gains reserve.

9-52.   The general idea is that a reserve can be deducted from the total gain when the total proceeds are not receivable in the year of the sale. The reserve would reflect the portion of the gain that is contained in the uncollected proceeds. As with other reserves, this amount must be added back to the following year's income, with a new reserve deducted to reflect any remaining uncollected proceeds.

9-53.   At one point in time, the deductible reserve was simply based on the portion of the proceeds of disposition not yet received. If, as in the previous example, a taxpayer collected only 10 percent of the proceeds, the reserve could be equal to 90 percent of the gain. It appears that this provision was being used for what the government viewed as excessive deferrals and, as a consequence, ITA 40(1)(a)(iii) limits the reserve to the lesser of:

- [(the total gain)(the proceeds not receivable until after December 31 of the current year ÷ the total proceeds)]
- [(20% of the total gain)(4, less the number of preceding taxation years ending after the disposition)].

9-54.   This has the effect of permitting a maximum reserve of 80 percent in the year of disposition, 60 percent in the following year, 40 percent in the second year after the disposition, 20 percent in the third year, and nil in the fourth. Stated alternatively, a minimum of 20 percent of the gain must be recognized in each year. If the proceeds are collected faster than 20 percent per year, the reserve will be based on the actual uncollected proceeds and the total gain will be recognized more quickly.

Example - Cash Received Is Less Than 20 Percent Of Total Proceeds

9-55.   Assume that during 2001, Mr. Filoso sells a piece of land with an adjusted cost base of $340,000, for total proceeds of $1,000,000, resulting in a capital gain of $660,000 ($1,000,000 - $340,000) and a taxable capital gain of $330,000 [(1/2)($660,000)]. He received only $100,000 of the total amount in cash in 2001 and accepted a $900,000 note payable for the balance. The note is payable at the rate of $100,000 per year beginning in 2002.

9-56.   The maximum reserve for 2001 is $528,000, the lesser of:

- $594,000 [($660,000)($900,000 ÷ $1,000,000)]
- $528,000 [(20%)($660,000)(4 - 0)]

9-57.   This means that $132,000 ($660,000 - $528,000) of the capital gain would be recognized in 2001 even though only $66,000 [($100,000 ÷ $1,000,000)($660,000)] of the total capital gain was realized in terms of cash collected. The taxable amount of the 2001 gain would be $66,000 [(1/2)($132,000)].

9-58.   In 2002, the $528,000 reserve would have to be added back to income. The new reserve for 2002 would be $396,000, the lesser of:

- $528,000 [($660,000)($800,000 ÷ $1,000,000)]
- $396,000 [(20%)($660,000)(4 - 1)]

9-59.   For the year 2002, this would leave a net addition to income of $66,000 [(1/2)($528,000 - $396,000)], or 20 percent of the $330,000 taxable capital gain. Based on similar calculations, the maximum reserve in 2003 would be $264,000. This would decline to $132,000 in 2004 and, at the end of 2005, no reserve would be available. This would result in $66,000 [(1/2)($132,000)] being added to income each year. The entire $330,000 of the taxable capital gain will have been included in income by the end of 2005. This is despite the fact that, at the end of this five year period, $500,000 of the initial proceeds remains uncollected.

Example - Cash Received Exceeds Minimum Reserve Levels

9-60.   In the preceding example, collections of cash were less than 20 percent in all years under consideration. As a result, the use of the maximum reserve resulted in the recognition of the minimum 20 percent per year of the gain.

9-61.   Before leaving this subject, you should consider situations in which the proportion of the proceeds of disposition received in cash exceeds minimum recognition requirements. As an illustration of this possibility, assume that in the preceding example, Mr. Filoso collected $250,000 in the year of the disposition and that the required payments were $75,000 per year for the following ten years.

9-62.   Based on this information, the maximum reserve for 2001 would be the lesser of:

- $495,000 [($660,000)($750,000 ÷ $1,000,000)]
- $528,000 [(20%)($660,000)(4 - 0)]

9-63.   This means that a taxable capital gain of $82,500 [(1/2)($660,000 - $495,000)] would be recognized in 2001.

9-64.   In 2002, the $495,000 reserve would be added back to income. The new reserve for 2002 would be $396,000, the lesser of:

- $445,500 [($660,000)($675,000 ÷ $1,000,000)]
- $396,000 [(20%)($660,000)(4 - 1)]

9-65.   This results in the recognition of a $49,500 [(1/2)($495,000 - $396,000)] taxable capital gain in 2002. At this point, the minimum 20 percent per year recognition requirement has become the determining factor in calculating the capital gain to be included in income. As a consequence, the amount to be included in income in the years 2003, 2004, and 2005 would be as presented in Paragraph 9-59.

> Exercise Nine-5 deals with capital gains reserves. This would be an appropriate time to attempt this exercise.

Deferral Provisions On Small Business Investments

2000 Budget Changes

9-66.   Legislation resulting from the February 28, 2000 budget introduces a new ITA 44.1 which provides for the deferral of capital gains resulting from the the disposition of an "eligible small business investment". The deferral is conditional on reinvestment of some or all of the proceeds of disposition in "replacement shares". As you would expect, the adjusted cost base of these replacement shares will be reduced by the capital gain that is eliminated in the current year. In effect, this defers the gain until such time as the new investment is sold.

9-67.   There are some special rules for dispositions made after February 27, 2000 and before October 18, 2000. However, we do not feel that these warrant consideration in this text and, as a consequence, we will focus on the rules applicable to dispositions made after October 17, 2000.

Definitions

9-68.   ITA 44.1 is a very technical Section of the *Act* and, as such, requires a number of definitions. The most important of these are as follows:

Eligible Small Business Corporation   This is a Canadian controlled private corporation that has substantially all (meaning more that 90 percent) of the fair market value of its assets devoted principally to an active business carried on primarily (meaning 50 percent or more) in Canada. The corporation can include in the qualifying assets its holdings of shares or debt in other eligible small business corporations.

Qualifying Disposition   To qualify for the deferral, the gain must result from the sale of common shares in an eligible small business corporation that was owned by the investor throughout the 185 day period that preceded the disposition.

Qualifying Portion of a Capital Gain   This is an amount determined by the following formula:

$$J \times [1 - (K/L)]$$

Where:

    J   is the capital gain on the qualifying disposition.

    K   is the amount, if any, by which the adjusted cost base of the shares sold exceeds $2,000,000.

    L   is the adjusted cost base of the shares sold.

If an individual sold eligible shares with an adjusted cost base of $2,600,000 for $3,000,000, the qualifying portion of the gain would be $320,000 {[$400,000][1 - ($600,000/$3,000,000)]}.

Qualifying Portion of the Proceeds of Disposition   This is an amount determined by the following formula:

$$M \times (N/O)$$

Where:

    M is the proceeds of disposition.

    N is the qualifying portion of the capital gain from the disposition.

    O is the capital gain from the disposition.

Using the example in the preceding definition, the qualifying portion of the proceeds of disposition would be $2,400,000 [($3,000,000)($320,000/$400,000)]

Replacement Shares   These are shares of an eligible small business corporation that are acquired within 60 days after the end of the year, but not later than 120 days after the qualifying disposition. They must be designated as replacement shares in the individual's return of income.

Qualifying Cost   The qualifying cost of replacement shares is the lesser of (1) their actual cost and (2) the amount by which $2,000,000 exceeds the total of the cost of all other replacement shares. This, in effect, limits the qualifying cost of each group of replacement shares to $2,000,000.

Permitted Deferral   This is an amount determined by the following formula:

$$(G/H) \times I$$

Where:

    G is the lesser of the cost of the replacement shares and amount included in H.

    H is the qualifying portion of the proceeds of disposition.

    I is the qualifying portion of the capital gain.

Continuing with the example from the preceding definitions, assume that $1,800,000 of the proceeds of disposition is invested in replacement shares. The qualifying cost would be $1,800,000 and the permitted deferral would be $240,000 [($1,800,000/$2,400,000)($320,000)].

Adjusted Cost Base Reduction   This is the reduction in the adjusted cost base of each of the blocks of replacement shares resulting from the application of ITA 44.1. The amount is determined by the following formula:

$$D \times (E/F)$$

Where:

    D is the permitted deferral.

    E is the qualifying cost of each block of the replacement shares.

    F is the cost of all of the replacement shares.

In our example, the adjusted cost base reduction would be $240,000 [($240,000)($1,800,000/$1,800,000)]. This would leave an adjusted cost base for these shares of $1,560,000 ($1,800,000 - $240,000).

Example

9-69.   The technical notes provided with the March 16, 2001 Notice of Ways and Means motion included the following example of the application of ITA 44.1:

> **Example**   An individual makes a qualifying disposition of shares of Corporation A with an adjusted cost base of $3,000,000 for proceeds of disposition of $4,500,000.
>
> The individual purchases replacement shares in Corporation B with a cost of $2,200,000 and in Corporation C with a cost of $2,300,000.
>
> **Tax Consequences**   The qualifying portion of the capital gain would be $1,000,000 [$1,500,000][1 - ($1,000,000/$3,000,000)]. This represents the limit on the amount of the capital gain that can be deferred, essentially the amount related to the first $2,000,000 of the proceeds of disposition.
>
> The qualifying portion of the proceeds of disposition is $3,000,000 [($4,500,000)($1,000,000/$1,500,000)].   This represents the maximum replacement shares that can be used to determine the maximum permitted deferral.
>
> The qualifying cost of the replacement shares is $2,000,000 for Corporation B and $2,000,000 for Corporation C, a total of $4,000,000.
>
> The permitted deferral of $1,000,000 [($3,000,000/$3,000,000)($1,000,000)] would leave a capital gain from the disposition, after deducting the permitted deferral, of $500,000 ($1,500,000 - $1,000,000).
>
> The adjusted cost base reduction for each block of replacement shares would be determined by the same calculation.   The amount would be $500,000 [($1,000,000)($2,000,000/$4,000,000)]. This would leave the adjusted cost base of Corporation B at $1,700,000 ($2,200,000 - $500,000) and the Corporation C adjusted cost base at $1,800,000 ($2,300,000 - $500,000).

> Exercise Nine-6 deals with capital gains deferral small business shares. This would be an appropriate time to attempt this exercise.

Deferral Provisions On Replacement Property
Basic Rules
9-70.   As indicated in Chapter 8, the ITA 13(4) and ITA 44 replacement property rules apply when there is a replacement related to certain types of dispositions. For all types of capital property, the special rules apply to involuntary dispositions where capital property is lost, stolen, destroyed, or expropriated. When the disposition is voluntary, the rules are only applicable to real property (i.e., land and buildings). The applicability of the rules is also limited by the timing of the replacement. For involuntary dispositions, the replacement must occur before the end of the second taxation year after the year in which the proceeds of disposition become receivable. This period is reduced to one year for voluntary dispositions.

9-71.   The ITA 13(4) rules related to recapture of CCA were discussed and illustrated in Chapter 8. Our concern here is with the ITA 44 rules related to capital gains. If a qualifying property is disposed of and replaced within the required time frame, ITA 44 allows a taxpayer to elect to reduce the capital gain on the disposition to the lesser of:

- an amount calculated by the usual approach (proceeds of disposition, less adjusted cost base); and

- the excess, if there is any, of the proceeds of disposition of the old property over the cost of the replacement property.

9-72.   In effect, if the cost of the replacement property is greater than the proceeds of disposition for the replaced property, no capital gain will be recorded. We would remind you that, in those cases where the replacement occurs in a period subsequent to the disposition, this election will have to be applied in an amended return for the year of disposition.

Example

9-73.   The following example will serve to illustrate the election under both ITA 13(4) and ITA 44:

Example During its 2001 taxation year, the Martin Company decides to change the location of its operations. Its current property consists of Land with an adjusted cost base of $500,000, as well as a building with a capital cost of $1,500,000 and a UCC of $340,000. These assets are sold for a total price of $2,400,000, of which $600,000 is allocated to the land and $1,800,000 is allocated to the building. During January, 2002, property is acquired at a new location at a cost of $2,800,000, of which $700,000 is allocated to the land and $2,100,000 is allocated to the building.

9-74. As a result of the disposition, the Martin Company will include the following amounts in its 2001 Net Income For Tax Purposes:

	Land	Building
Proceeds Of Dispositions	$600,000	$1,800,000
Adjusted Cost Base	(500,000)	(1,500,000)
Capital Gain	$100,000	$ 300,000
Inclusion Rate	1/2	1/2
Taxable Capital Gain	$ 50,000	$ 150,000
Recapture of CCA ($340,000 - $1,500,000)	N/A	$1,160,000

9-75. When the replacement occurs in 2002, the cost allocated to land and building exceeds the proceeds of disposition from these assets. As a consequence, the revised capital gain for the year will be nil, a fact that would be reflected in an amended 2001 tax return. However, the capital cost of the replacement assets would be reduced as follows:

	Land	Buildings
Actual Capital Cost	$700,000	$2,100,000
Capital Gain Removed By Election	(100,000)	(300,000)
Adjusted Capital Cost	$600,000	$1,800,000

9-76. With respect to the recapture of CCA, the replacement cost of the new building exceeded the recapture on the disposition of the old. This means that all of the recapture can be removed from the amended tax return. However, this amount will also have to be removed from the UCC of the replacement building, leaving a balance of $640,000 ($2,100,000 - $300,000 - $1,160,000). This amount can also be derived by noting that the old UCC was $340,000 and an additional $300,000 ($2,100,000 - $1,800,000) of the Company's funds were required to acquire the building, a total of $640,000.

Replacement Cost Less Than Old Capital Cost

9-77. In the preceding example, we are able to remove 100 percent of the capital gain through the application of the ITA 44 election. This resulted from the fact that the cost of the replacement property exceeded the proceeds of disposition for the old property. If this is not the case, some of the capital gain will have to remain in income. This point can be illustrated by making a small change in our example:

Example This example is the same as the one presented in Paragraph 9-73, except that we will assume that the cost of the replacement property was $2,650,000, with $550,000 allocated to land and $2,100,000 allocated to the building.

9-78. The capital gains and recapture on the disposition will be as presented in Paragraph 9-74. However, in the 2001 amended return, a taxable capital gain equal to one-half of the excess of the proceeds of disposition of the old land, over the cost of the replacement land will have to remain in 2001 income. This amount is $25,000 [(1/2)($600,000 - $550,000)]. The relevant tax values for the replacement assets are as follows:

	Land	Building
Actual Cost	$550,000	$2,100,000
Capital Gain Removed By Election	(50,000)	(300,000)
Adjusted Capital Cost	$500,000	$1,800,000
Recapture Removed By Election	N/A	(1,160,000)
Adjusted UCC	N/A	$ 640,000

ITA 44(6) Election

9-79.   In the preceding example, the fact that the replacement cost of the land was less than the proceeds of disposition of the previously owned land, resulted in a situation where a portion of the capital gain on this disposition had to remain in the 2001 tax return. Fortunately, a further election contained in ITA 44 provides, in many cases, a solution to this problem.

9-80.   Under ITA 44(6), the taxpayer is allowed to reallocate the total proceeds of disposition on the sale of a former business property, without regard to the respective market values of the land and building. If, in the example presented in Paragraph 9-77, the total proceeds of $2,400,000 are allocated on the basis of $550,000 to the land and $1,850,000 to the building, the 2001 taxable capital gains will be as follows:

	Land	Building
Proceeds Of Dispositions	$550,000	$1,850,000
Adjusted Cost Base	(500,000)	(1,500,000)
Capital Gain	$ 50,000	$ 350,000
Inclusion Rate	1/2	1/2
Taxable Capital Gain	$ 25,000	$ 175,000

9-81.   While the total taxable capital gain remains the same, this reallocation of the total proceeds of disposition results in a situation where the replacement cost of both the land and building exceed the proceeds of disposition. This, in turn, means that all of the capital gains on both of these capital assets will be removed from the 2001 amended tax return. Under this scenario, the tax values for the replacement assets would be as follows:

	Land	Building
Actual Cost	$550,000	$2,100,000
Capital Gain Removed By Election	(50,000)	(350,000)
Adjusted Capital Cost	$500,000	$1,750,000
Recapture Removed By Election	N/A	(1,160,000)
Adjusted UCC	N/A	$ 590,000

9-82.   Note that this election is not made without a cost. Had the $50,000 been left as a capital gain, tax would have applied on only one-half of the total. While we have eliminated this $25,000 in income, we have given up future capital cost allowance for the full amount of the $50,000. In other words we have given up $50,000 in future deductions in return for eliminating $25,000 of income in 2001. As explained in our Chapters 14 and 15 on corporate taxation, for some corporations, taxable capital gains are initially taxed at higher rates than business income which could be a factor in this decision. In addition, anticipated future tax rates could be a consideration. In situations where the reallocation process shifts proceeds from the building to the land, the results can be reversed. However, as the preceding examples illustrate, the combination of ITA 13(4) and ITA 44 elections can provide significant tax relief in situations where a business is relocating. Similar advantages are available for involuntary distributions.

Exercise Nine-7 deals with replacement properties. This would be an appropriate time to attempt this exercise.

Changes In Use

9-83.   In Chapter 8 we noted that when an asset's use is changed from personal to business or from business to personal, it is considered to be a deemed disposition and reacquisition of the asset. ITA 13(7) specifies that, in general, the proceeds of the disposition are equal to the fair market value of the asset and the capital cost of the reacquisition is equal to the same value. An exception occurs when:

- the change is from personal use to business use; and
- the fair market value of the asset exceeds its original capital cost.

9-84.   In this case, the capital cost for UCC purposes of the reacquisition is deemed to be equal to the original capital cost, plus one-half of the excess of the current fair market value over the original capital cost. This procedure reflects the fact that the gain on the deemed disposition will be a capital gain, only one-half of which will be taxed. In order to prevent a partially taxed capital gain from being converted to a fully deductible UCC balance, the addition to this balance is limited to one-half of the excess of fair market value over the original capital cost.

9-85.   There is no similar limit on the capital cost to be recognized in the new use. In all cases the capital cost of the reacquisition will be equal to the fair market value of the asset. A simple example will illustrate these procedures:

> **Example**   On September 1, 2001, Mr. Reid converts his summer cottage to a rental property. He has owned two other rental properties for three years. The cost of the building was $100,000, its fair market value is $130,000, and it has not been designated as his principal residence.
>
> As the change is from personal to business use and the fair market value exceeds the cost, the deemed reacquisition value for purposes of calculating CCA or recapture would be $115,000 {$100,000 + [(1/2)($130,000 - $100,000)]}.   Given this value, the resulting CCA for 2001 is $2,300 [($115,000)(4%)(1/2)].
>
> In contrast, the deemed reacquisition value for capital gains purposes is the fair market value of $130,000. If the cottage was later sold for $150,000, there would be a capital gain of $20,000 ($150,000 - $130,000). However, only $115,000 would be subtracted from the UCC, thereby limiting recapture to the amount of CCA taken since the change in use.

9-86.   As a final point, when the change is from personal to business use, ITA 45(2) allows the taxpayer to elect not to have the deemed disposition rules from ITA 13(7) and ITA 45(1) apply. This would eliminate the recognition of capital gains and possible recapture at the time of the change. However, the election requires the taxpayer to assume that he has not started to use the property for business purposes. This means that no deduction for CCA will be available on the property. This provision is of particular importance when a principal residence is converted to a rental property and, as a consequence, it will be given further attention in the next section of this Chapter.

> Exercise Nine-8 deals with changes in use. This would be an appropriate time to attempt this exercise.

Provisions For Special Assets

Principal Residences
Principal Residence Defined

9-87.   For many individuals resident in Canada, one of the most attractive features of our tax system is the fact that, in general, there is no taxation of capital gains arising on the disposal of a principal residence. Before 1982, this situation was even more attractive since both spouses were allowed to have a principal residence. This meant that a second property which was owned by a married couple could also escape capital gains taxation. Under current rules, only one taxpayer in a family unit can designate a property as a principal residence for a particular year. For these purposes, a family unit includes a spouse, as well as children unless they are married or over 18 during the year.

9-88.   ITA 54 defines principal residence as any accommodation owned by the taxpayer that was ordinarily inhabited in the year by the taxpayer, his spouse, a former spouse, or a dependent child and is designated by the taxpayer as a principal residence. The definition notes that this would include land up to a limit of one-half hectare as well as a building. If the property includes additional land, it will be subject to capital gains taxation unless the taxpayer can demonstrate that the additional land was necessary for the enjoyment of the property.

9-89.   If a taxpayer owns more than one property which might qualify as a residence, only one property can be designated as a principal residence in any given year. From an administrative point of view, however, the CCRA does not require that such a designation be made from year to year. Rather, the filing of form T2091, *Designation Of A Principal Residence,* is only required when a property is disposed of and a taxable capital gain remains after applying the reduction formula described in the following material. From an administrative point of view, this requirement is often ignored, reflecting its irrelevance in situations where the family has only one property that could be designated as a principal residence.

Gain Reduction Formula
9-90.   Technically speaking, capital gains on a principal residence are taxable. However, ITA 40(2)(b) provides a formula for reducing such gains. The formula calculates the taxable portion, which is based on the relationship between the number of years the property has been designated a principal residence and the number of taxation years ending after the acquisition date (since 1971) during which the property was owned. It is as follows:

$$A - \left[A \times \frac{B}{C}\right] \text{ where}$$

A   is the total capital gain on the disposition of the principal residence;
B   is one plus the number of years the property is designated as the taxpayer's principal residence;
C   is the number of years since 1971 that the taxpayer has owned the property.

9-91.   The formula in Paragraph 9-90 is applied to any capital gain resulting from the disposition of a principal residence in order to determine the amount which will be subject to taxation. For example, a property was purchased in 1993, was sold in 2001 for an amount which resulted in a capital gain of $100,000. If it was designated as a principal residence for six of the nine years of ownership, the calculation of the taxable portion of the capital gain would be as follows:

$$\left[\$100,000 - (\$100,000)\left(\frac{(1+6)}{9}\right)\right]\left[\frac{1}{2}\right] = \$11,111$$

9-92.   If a taxpayer has only a single property which could qualify as a principal residence, that property can be designated as the principal residence for all years owned. In such situations, the use of this formula will then completely eliminate any capital gains on the disposition of that property. Further, the additional year in the numerator of the formula will permit a taxpayer to sell one principal residence and buy and sell a second property in the same year. This latter point can be illustrated with the following example:

> **Example**   During 1996, Mr. Fodor acquires a principal residence at a cost of $130,000. The residence is sold in 1999 for $150,000. A replacement residence is acquired in 1999 at a cost of $170,000. In 2001 the second residence is sold for $200,000, with Mr. Fodor moving to an apartment.

9-93.   During 1999, Mr. Fodor owns two properties, only one of which can be designated as a principal residence for that year. If there were no extra year in the numerator of the reduction formula, Mr. Fodor would be taxed on a portion of one of the gains. For example, assume Mr. Fodor allocates 1996 through 1998 to the first property and 1999 through 2001 to the second. All of the $30,000 gain on the second property would be eliminated. Since the first property was sold in 1999, the denominator in the reduction formula is 4 (1996 to 1999). Without the extra year, only three-quarters of the $20,000 gain would be eliminated, leaving a capital gain of $5,000 [(1/4)($150,000 - $130,000)]. However, with the addition of the plus one to the numerator of the reduction formula, the fraction on the first property becomes four-fourths and the remaining $5,000 capital gain is eliminated.

Change In Use - Residence To Rental

9-94.   We have previously noted that when the use of a property is changed from personal to business, ITA 45(1) requires that this change be treated as a deemed disposition at fair market value. The conversion of a principal residence to a rental property is a common example of this type of situation and, in the absence of any election, the fair market value at the time of the change will become the adjusted cost base of the rental property. As was previously discussed, if the fair market value exceeds the cost, a different value will be used for the calculation of CCA.

9-95.   An alternative to this treatment is provided under ITA 45(2). Under this subsection, the taxpayer can make an election under which he will be deemed not to have commenced using the property for producing income. If this election is made, the taxpayer will still have to include the rents from the property as rental income. The taxpayer will be able to deduct all of the expenses associated with the property other than CCA. However, use of the ITA 45(2) election prevents the taxpayer from deducting any amounts for CCA on this property.

9-96.   While this inability to deduct CCA can be viewed as a disadvantage associated with the election, the election does, in fact, have an offsetting advantage. The property can continue to be designated as a principal residence for up to four years while the election is in effect. This would appear to be the case even in situations where the individual does not return to live in the property.

9-97.   In practical terms, the preceding means that an individual who moves out of a principal residence can retain principal residence treatment for the property for up to four years. This allows the individual to enjoy any capital gains that accrue on that property on a tax free basis. This would be of particular importance to an individual who moves to a rental property and does not have an alternative principal residence during this period. Even if the individual purchases an alternative residential property, the election can be helpful as it allows a choice as to which property will be designated as the principal residence during the relevant years. If one of the properties experiences a significantly larger capital gain during this period, the use of this election could produce a large savings in taxes.

9-98.   Also of interest is the fact that the four year election period can be extended without limit under the following circumstances as specified in ITA 54.1:

- you leave the residence because the employer of you or your spouse requires you to relocate;
- you return to the original residence while still with the same employer or before the end of the year following the year you leave that employer, or you die before such employment terminates; and
- the original residence is at least 40 kilometers further from your or your spouse's new place of employment than your temporary residence.

Change In Use - Rental To Residential

9-99.   Here again, unless an election is made, this change in use will be treated as a deemed disposition at fair market value, with possible results including both capital gains and recapture. In this case, ITA 45(3) allows you to elect out of the deemed disposition for capital gains purposes as long as no CCA has been taken on the property. The election must be made by April 30 of the year following the disposition.

9-100.   When the ITA 45(3) election is used, it is possible to designate the property as your principal residence for up to four years prior to the time it stopped being used as a rental property. This can be beneficial both to individuals who did not own another residential property during this four year period and to individuals with an alternative residential property that experiences capital gains at a lower annual rate.

Non Residential Usage

9-101.   A complication arises when a taxpayer either rents a part of his principal residence or uses it for non residential purposes (e.g., a self employed individual who maintains an office at home). In this situation, the portion of the principal residence that is used for non residential purposes may be subject to tax on any gain that arises on the disposition of the property. However, it is not common for such gains to be assessed except in situations where the taxpayer deducted CCA on the portion of the principal residence used for earning business or property income. Given this, the standard tax planning advice to taxpayers who use a portion of their principal residence for business purposes is not to deduct CCA on this property.

Transitional Election - Pre-1982 Two Principal Residences

9-102.   As previously noted, it is no longer possible to have more than one principal residence per family unit. When this change was introduced in 1982, it was recognized that it could have some retroactive effect on real estate purchases made in earlier years on the assumption that they would always be treated as principal residences. To mitigate this effect, ITA 40(6) contains a transitional provision. It provides an election which allows the taxpayer to calculate his gain on the actual sale of a principal residence on the assumption that there was a deemed sale and reacquisition of the residence on December 31, 1981 at fair market value. This allows the gain to be split into two components — a pre 1982 component and a post 1981 component. Note, however, there is no plus one in the reduction formula for the post 1981 component of the gain.

9-103.   When a taxpayer owns more than one property that could qualify as a principal residence (e.g., a city home and a cottage), this election may help minimize the portion of capital gains on the properties that will have to be taken into income. The following example serves to illustrate this point:

Example   Ms. Jones acquired both a cottage and a city home on June 30, 1976. Both properties are sold on July 1, 2001. Relevant information is as follows:

	Cottage	City Home
Cost - June 30, 1976	$ 50,000	$110,000
Fair Market Value - December 31, 1981	80,000	120,000
Proceeds of Disposition - July 1, 2001	120,000	240,000
Selling Costs	7,200	13,200

9-104.   If one only considers the full 26 year period from 1976 through 2001 and applies ITA 40(2)(b), the city home experiences the larger gain and would be designated the principal residence for 25 of the 26 years. The result of this designation would be as follows:

Capital Gain Without ITA 40(6) Election

	Cottage	City Home
Proceeds of Disposition	$120,000	$240,000
Adjusted Cost Base	(50,000)	(110,000)
Selling Costs	(7,200)	(13,200)
Total Capital Gain	$ 62,800	$116,800
Reduction:		
$62,800 [(1 + 1) ÷ 26)]	(4,831)	
$116,800 [(1 + 25) ÷ 26)]		(116,800)
Capital Gain After Reduction	$57,969	Nil

9-105.   While the use of ITA 40(2)(b) has eliminated a significant part of the capital gains resulting from the disposition of the two properties, a better solution can be achieved using the election under ITA 40(6). This is because the cottage experienced the larger gain during the pre 1982 period and the city home experienced the larger gain after 1981. The ITA 40(6) election allows the taxpayer to take advantage of this difference. With this election, the results would be as follows:

Capital Gain With ITA 40(6) Election

1976 Through 1981	Cottage	City Home
Fair Market Value - December 31, 1981	$ 80,000	$120,000
Adjusted Cost Base	(50,000)	(110,000)
Total Capital Gain	$ 30,000	$ 10,000
Reduction:		
$30,000 [(5 + 1) ÷ 6)]	(30,000)	
$10,000 [(1 + 1) ÷ 6)]		(3,333)
Capital Gain After Reduction	Nil	$ 6,667

1982 Through 2001	Cottage	City Home
Proceeds of Disposition - July 1, 2001	$120,000	$240,000
Adjusted Cost Base (Deemed)	(80,000)	(120,000)
Selling Costs	(7,200)	(13,200)
Total Capital Gain	$ 32,800	$106,800
Reduction = $106,800 (20 ÷ 20) (Note)	Nil	(106,800)
Capital Gain After Reduction	$ 32,800	Nil

Note When the ITA 40(6) election is used, the plus one year rule does not apply to the post 1981 period.

9-106. Using this approach, the non exempt portion of the capital gain is reduced from $57,969 to $39,467 ($6,667 + $32,800). For someone in a combined federal/provincial tax bracket of 45 percent, this $18,502 reduction will generate a tax savings of $4,163 [($18,502)(1/2)(45%)].

Farm Properties

9-107. Many farmers have a principal residence which is a part of their farm property. This means that when the farm is sold, the farmer's principal residence will generally be included in the package which is sold. In this situation, ITA 40(2)(c) identifies two approaches that can be used in this situation. The first approach requires that the land be divided into two components — the portion used for farming and the portion used for the enjoyment of the principal residence. Separate capital gains are calculated for each, with the gain on the principal residence portion being eligible for the principal residence reduction. Note that IT-120R5 indicates that, as a general guideline, the land required for the enjoyment of the principal residence is limited to one-half hectare.

9-108. As an alternative, a farmer can elect to be taxed on the capital gain from the sale of the entire property, reduced by $1,000 plus an additional $1,000 per year for every year for which the property was a principal residence.

> Exercises Nine-9 and Nine-10 deal with principal residence issues. This would be an appropriate time to attempt these exercises.

Personal Use Property

Definition

9-109. ITA 54 defines personal use property as any property that is owned by the taxpayer and used primarily for his enjoyment or for the enjoyment of one or more individuals related to the taxpayer. In non technical terms, we are talking about any significant asset owned by a taxpayer that is not used for earning business or property income. This would include personal use automobiles, principal residences, vacation homes, boats, furniture, and many other items.

Capital Gains And Losses

9-110.   In general, gains on the disposals of personal use property are taxed in the same manner as gains on other capital assets. However, there is an important difference. While capital gains on personal use property are taxable, losses on such property are generally not deductible. The reason for this is that most types of personal use property depreciate over time and to allow capital losses or capital cost allowance on the property to be deductible would, in effect, permit a write off of the cost of normal wear and tear.

9-111.   To simplify the enforcement of capital gains taxation on personal use property, ITA 46(1) provides a $1,000 floor rule. In using this rule to calculate capital gains on personal use property, the proceeds are deemed to be the greater of $1,000 and the actual proceeds. In a similar fashion, the adjusted cost base is deemed to be the greater of $1,000 and the actual cost base. This rule is illustrated in the following example which uses four cases involving dispositions of personal use property.

Capital Gains (Losses) On Personal Use Property

	Case A	Case B	Case C	Case D
Proceeds Of Disposition (POD)	$300	$850	$ 500	$1,500
Adjusted Cost Base (ACB)	800	400	1,300	900
Using the $1,000 floor rule results in the following capital gain or loss:				
Greater of Actual POD or $1,000	$1,000	$1,000	$1,000	$1,500
Greater Of ACB Or $1,000	(1,000)	(1,000)	(1,300)	(1,000)
Gain (Loss - Not Deductible)	$ -0-	$ -0-	($ 300)	$ 500

9-112.   In situations where a taxpayer disposes of a part of an item of personal use property while retaining the remainder, the taxpayer must establish the ratio of the adjusted cost base of the part disposed of to the total adjusted cost base of the property. Then, in applying the $1,000 floor rule, the adjusted cost base is deemed to be the greater of the portion of the adjusted cost base associated with the part disposed of, or the same portion of $1,000. In the same fashion, the proceeds would be deemed to be the greater of the actual proceeds and the appropriate portion of $1,000.

9-113.   The CCRA has perceived an abuse of this $1,000 floor rule in the case of gifts of personal use property to charities. The feeling is that it was being used to get a donation tax credit based on $1,000 in return for donating art and other personal use property of fairly trivial value. As a result, when there is a donation of personal use property after February, 2000, the ITA 46(1) $1,000 deemed adjusted cost base rule will not be applicable.

Listed Personal Property

9-114.   Listed personal property consists of certain specified items of personal use property. The specified items are found in ITA 54 as follows:

> Listed personal property of a taxpayer means his personal use property that is all or any portion of, or any interest in or right to, any

> (i)   print, etching, drawing, painting, sculpture, or other similar work of art,
> (ii)   jewelry,
> (iii)   rare folio, rare manuscript, or rare book,
> (iv)   stamp, or
> (v)   coin.

9-115.   In general, listed personal property is subject to the same capital gains rules as would apply to other personal use property. This would include the applicability of the $1,000 floor rule. However, there is a very important difference. While any losses on personal use property cannot be deducted, allowable capital losses on listed personal property can be deducted subject to a significant restriction.

9-116. The restriction is that allowable capital losses on listed personal property can only be deducted against taxable capital gains on listed personal property. In the absence of such taxable capital gains, the listed personal property losses cannot be deducted. However, any undeducted losses are subject to carry over provisions which will be described in Chapter 12.

Gains And Losses On Foreign Currency

Income Transactions

9-117. When a business buys or sells goods or services with the amounts denominated in a foreign currency, the resulting payable or receivable is normally not settled immediately. As foreign exchange rates are subject to constant change, gains and losses will be recorded on these foreign exchange payables and receivables. As these gains and losses are related to operating transactions, they will be treated as business gains or losses, as opposed to capital gains or losses.

9-118. IT-95R indicates that, with respect to such income transactions, the taxpayer can use any method that is in accordance with generally accepted accounting principles. Under Section 1650 of the *CICA Handbook*, "Foreign Currency Translation", current payables and receivables must be recorded at current rates of exchange as at each Balance Sheet date. The resulting changes in value must be recorded as gains or losses at the time they are measured. This would suggest that, for tax purposes, foreign exchange gains and losses on income transactions should be taken into income on an accrual basis, rather than waiting until the foreign exchange balance is settled in Canadian dollars.

Capital Transactions

9-119. Some foreign exchange gains and losses relate to capital transactions. For example, long term debt denominated in a foreign currency might be used to finance the acquisition of capital assets. In this type of situation, any change in the value of the long term liability will be treated as a capital gain or loss.

9-120. Under generally accepted accounting principles, exchange gains and losses on long term balances are recognized at the time the exchange rate changes. While the current version of Section 1650 requires that the resulting gain or loss be amortized over the life of the related item, this approach is certain to be changed in the near future to a new rule which will require the full amount of the exchange gain or loss to be taken into income at the time that it is recognized.

9-121. Despite the fact that it is the approach required under generally accepted accounting principles, the CCRA does not permit the accrual of exchange gains or losses on foreign exchange balances related to capital transactions. More specifically, IT-95R indicates that exchange gains and losses on capital transactions should be recognized:

(a) at the time of conversion of funds in a foreign currency into another foreign currency or into Canadian dollars,

(b) at the time funds in a foreign currency are used to make a purchase or a payment (in such a case the gain or loss would be the difference between the value of the foreign currency expressed in Canadian dollars when it arose and its value expressed in Canadian dollars when the purchase or payment was made), and

(c) at the time of repayment of part or all of a capital debt obligation.

9-122. This means that, if a Canadian company has used long term foreign currency debt to finance capital assets, no exchange gain or loss will be included in the determination of Net Income For Tax Purposes until the debt matures and is paid off in Canadian dollars. This will result in significant differences between accounting Net Income and Net Income For Tax Purposes.

9-123. IT-95R also notes that foreign currency funds on deposit are not considered to be disposed of until they are converted into another currency or are used to purchase a negotiable instrument or some other asset. This means that foreign funds on deposit may be moved from one form of deposit to another as long as such funds can continue to be viewed as "on deposit".

Individuals

9-124.   Individuals will most commonly encounter foreign exchange gains or losses when they purchase or sell securities in a foreign currency either through a Canadian dollar transaction or through a brokerage account maintained in that foreign currency. Under the IT-95R rules, exchange gains and losses will be recognized at the time of each purchase and each sale of securities. A simple example will illustrate this point:

> **Example**   On August 1, 1998, Mr. Joseph Bolero uses $210,000 to open a Deutsch Mark (DM) account with his broker. At this time, DM1 = $.70, so that his $210,000 is converted to DM300,000.
>
> On December 31, 1998, he uses his entire Deutsch Mark balance to acquire 10,000 shares in a German company, Widmung Inc. at a cost of DM30 per share. At this time, DM1 = $0.72.
>
> On July 1, 2001, the shares are sold for DM62 per share. On this date, DM1 = $0.86.
>
> **Tax Consequences**   As a result of his December 31, 1998 purchase, he will have to report an exchange gain of $6,000 [(DM300,000)($.72 - $.70)]. When he sells the shares for DM62, his total gain will be $317,200 [(DM620,000)($.86) - (DM300,000)($.72)]. From a technical perspective, this total is made up of an exchange gain of $42,000 [(DM300,000)($.86 - $.72)], combined with a capital gain of $275,200 [(DM620,000 - DM300,000)($.86)]. However, as the exchange gain is related to capital assets, it will also be treated as a capital gain for tax purposes.

9-125.   A further point with respect to exchange gains is that, for individuals, ITA 39(2) requires that only those exchange gains in excess of $200 be included in income. This allows individuals to avoid the complications associated with the determination of exchange gains or losses on relatively small balances. In the preceding example, Mr. Bolero's foreign exchange gain would be reduced by $200 in both years when calculating the capital gain to be reported. Note that this provision is only applicable to exchange gains associated with capital transactions.

Exercise Nine-11 deals with exchange gains and losses. This would be an appropriate time to attempt this exercise.

Gains and Losses on Weak Currency Debt

9-126.   There are additional complications associated with exchange gains and losses on so-called weak currency debt. New rules in this area are found in ITA 20.3 which was added by the February 28, 2000 budget. Because this legislation also involves the deductibility of interest, this new section will be covered in Chapter 11 as part of our general discussion of interest deductibility.

Options

9-127.   The term options would include stock rights, warrants, options to purchase capital assets, as well as stock options granted to executives and other employees. From the point of view of the taxpayer acquiring these options, they are treated as capital property. If they are sold before their expiry date, a capital gain or loss will usually arise. However, if they are exercised, the cost of acquiring the options will be added to the adjusted cost base of the assets acquired. If the options expire before they are either sold or exercised, a capital loss equal to the cost of the options will be incurred. Note that there are many special rules associated with those options granted to employees. The issues associated with this specific type of option were introduced in Chapter 5 and will be given comprehensive treatment in Chapter 12.

9-128.   From the point of view of the issuer of the option, any proceeds from the sale of the option will be treated as a capital gain at the time the option is issued. If the holder decides to exercise the option, the sale price of the option becomes part of the proceeds of disposition to the issuer and the original gain on the sale of the option is eliminated. If the sale of the option occurs in a different taxation year than the exercise of the option, the issuer is permitted to file an amended return for the year of sale.

9-129.   An example will serve to illustrate the preceding rules.

> **Example**   John Powers has a capital property with an adjusted cost base of $250,000.   During 2001, he sells an option on this property to Sarah Myers for $18,000. This option allows her to acquire the capital property for $300,000 at any time prior to December 31, 2004.
>
> **Tax Consequences - Option Expires**   Mr. Powers, as a result of selling the option in 2001, will have to record a capital gain of $18,000 in that year. If the option expires, there will be no further tax consequences to Mr. Powers as he has already recognized the $18,000 option proceeds in 2001. For Ms. Myers, the expiry of the option will allow her to recognize a capital loss of $18,000, the cost of acquiring the option.
>
> **Tax Consequences - Option Is Exercised**   If the option is exercised in 2004, Mr. Powers can file an amended return for 2001, removing the capital gain that was recognized in that year. However, he will have to include the $18,000 in the proceeds of disposition from the sale of the asset, thereby recording a capital gain of $68,000 ($18,000 + $300,000 - $250,000). Ms. Myers will have acquired a capital property at a cost of $318,000 ($300,000 + $18,000).

9-130.   There are two exceptions to the preceding general rules for vendors of options. The first of these is an exemption from taxation on the proceeds of any options sold on a taxpayer's principal residence. The second involves options sold by a corporation on its capital stock or debt securities. In this situation, the corporation will not be taxed on the proceeds at the time the options are sold. Rather, the proceeds will be treated as part of the consideration for the securities issued if the options are exercised. However, if the options expire without being exercised, the corporation will have a capital gain equal to the amount of the proceeds.

Capital Gains And Tax Planning

9-131.   The capital gains area offers many opportunities for effective tax planning since the realization of capital gains or losses is largely at the discretion of the taxpayer. If the taxpayer desires that gains or losses fall into a particular taxation year, this can often be accomplished by deferring the disposition of the relevant asset until that period. This means that gains can often be deferred until, perhaps, retirement when the taxpayer may be in a lower tax bracket. Other examples of tax planning would include selling securities with accrued losses in order to offset gains realized earlier in the taxation year and deferring until after the end of the year the sale of any asset on which there is a significant capital gain.

9-132.   Tax planning for capital gains is more complex if an individual owns small business corporation shares or a farm property. This is due to the fact that such properties may be eligible for the $500,000 lifetime capital gains deduction. Additional complications result from the application of capital losses, particularly with respect to carry overs of such amounts. These problems will be discussed in Chapter 12.

Capital Property And The GST

GST Definition

9-133.   For GST purposes, capital property includes any property that is capital property for income tax purposes. This includes any property on which capital cost allowance may be claimed as well as any property that, if disposed of, would result in a capital gain or loss. Excluded from the definition of capital property is property included in CCA Classes 12, 14 and 44. Class 12 includes assets such as small tools, dishes, cutlery, software and video tapes, while Class 14 includes patents, franchises, concessions and licenses with a limited life. Class 44 includes property that is a patent or right to use patented information for a limited or unlimited period.

9-134.   Capital property is divided into two principal groups for purposes of the GST — capital real property and capital personal property. Different rules apply to each group of property with respect to the collection of GST by the vendor and to the availability of input tax credits to the purchaser.

9-135.   Capital real property includes land, buildings, mobile homes and interests therein. Capital personal property includes all other capital properties. Examples of capital personal property include the following assets used in a business, provided they are not being held for resale:

- store fixtures, display shelving, and shopping carts
- office furniture
- refrigerators, freezers and ovens used by restaurants and grocery stores
- computers, cash registers and cellular phones
- photocopiers, laser printers and offset presses
- machinery and equipment used in production processes

9-136.   We will begin by considering the availability of input tax credits when capital property is purchased. This will be followed by an explanation of how the GST applies to sales of capital personal property. Finally, we will review the more complicated application of GST to sales of capital real properties.

Input Tax Credits On Capital Personal Property
9-137.   When capital property is purchased for use in a commercial activity, input tax credits can be claimed for any GST paid on the purchase. As input tax credits are not matched against amounts of GST collected on the purchaser's revenues, the full amount of GST paid on purchases of capital assets, including real property, becomes an input tax credit at the time of purchase. There is no need to amortize the credit or to wait until such time as the asset is actually paid for.

9-138.   Input tax credits on capital personal property are restricted in that the assets must be used primarily (defined as more than 50 percent) for commercial activity, including fully taxable or zero rated activities. If this condition is met, all of the GST paid on acquisition can be claimed as an input tax credit. If this condition is not met, no part of the GST paid on the acquisition of capital personal property can be claimed as an input tax credit. If, in a particular reporting period, the asset ceases to meet this test, there will be a deemed disposition at the fair market value to which the GST will be applied.

9-139.   If an existing asset, which did not meet the criteria of primary use for commercial activity in earlier periods, meets it in the current period, an input tax credit will be available based on the lesser of the GST paid at acquisition and the GST on the fair market value of the asset at the time of its change in use.

Input Tax Credits On Capital Real Property
9-140.   The rules governing how input tax credits can be claimed on the purchase of capital real property depend on whether the registrant is an individual, a partner, or another business. Input tax credits on real property purchases can usually be claimed in proportion to the business use of the asset.

9-141.   For corporations, input tax credits are available on the purchase of real property in proportion to its use for commercial activity. While the property must be used at least 10 percent for commercial purposes, there is no "primary use" test as there is for capital personal property.

9-142.   For individuals and partners, however, capital real property must not be used primarily (at least 50 percent) for personal use and enjoyment to be eligible to claim an input tax credit.

9-143.   Assuming the overall business use tests are met, when there is a significant (defined as 10 percent or more) increase in commercial use, an input tax credit will be available on the new portion. It will be based essentially on a pro rata share of the lesser of the GST paid at the time of acquisition and the GST that would be paid on the asset's current fair market value.

Similarly, if the proportion of use decreases by 10 percent or more, there will be a deemed disposition with GST applicable on a pro rata share of the lesser of the asset's original cost and its value at the time of the change.

Sales Of Capital Personal Property

General Rules

9-144.   The sale or resale of capital personal property is generally subject to GST. Tax applies regardless of whether the asset is sold outright or is traded in. Sale of equipment that was used in zero-rated activities, such as in a grocery, prescription drug or agricultural business, is also subject to GST on resale or trade-in. There are some exceptions for large equipment used in farming and fishing, which may be sold on a zero-rated basis.

9-145.   When capital property is sold that was previously used in taxable activities for less than 50 percent of the time, the vendor is not required to collect GST as the vendor would not have been entitled to an input tax credit at the time of purchase. For example, if a computer was used 30 percent of the time to provide taxable supplies and 70 percent of the time to provide tax exempt supplies, GST would not be applicable when it is sold.

Vehicle Sales

9-146.   The GST treatment of vehicle sales requires clarification when there is a trade-in associated with the sale of a vehicle. In most provinces, the trade-in and purchase of a vehicle are considered to be a single transaction for provincial sales tax (PST) purposes. The PST is applied to the difference between the selling price of the new vehicle and the trade-in. Effectively, PST applies only on the net amount after the trade-in.

9-147.   For vehicles traded in by non-registrants, or registrants who are not required to charge the GST on the trade-in because they engage in a combination of taxable and exempt activities, the tax is applied in a fashion similar to PST. That is, GST is charged on the difference between the selling price of the new vehicle and the value of the trade-in.

9-148.   When a registrant who claimed input tax credits on the initial vehicle purchase trades it in on the purchase of another vehicle, the trade-in and purchase are viewed as two separate transactions. In effect, the registrant sells the trade-in vehicle to the dealer, collecting the applicable GST. He then purchases a vehicle from the dealer, paying applicable GST.

9-149.   When a GST registrant trades in a vehicle as part of a new vehicle purchase and charges GST on the trade-in, GST will be charged by the dealer on the full price of the vehicle purchased. The dealer does not deduct the GST amount related to the trade-in from the GST payable on the purchase price of the vehicle. Both the purchaser and dealer are generally eligible to claim input tax credits for the GST paid.

9-150.   A final point on vehicle transactions relates to trade-ins of Class 10.1 vehicles (cars costing more than a prescribed amount — $30,000 for 2001). When such vehicles are purchased, input tax credits are not available on any portion of the cost of the vehicle that exceeds the prescribed amount. If, for example, a business purchased a $100,000 passenger vehicle in 2001, $7,000 in GST would be paid. However, the input tax credit would be limited to $2,100 [(7%)($30,000)]. When such vehicles are traded in, a special rule provides for an input tax credit for the trade-in amount in excess of the prescribed amount. Continuing our example, if the business received a trade-in allowance of $50,000 on the $100,000 vehicle, an input tax credit of $1,400 would be available [(7%)($50,000 - $30,000)].

Sale Of All Capital Assets Of A Business

9-151.   If a person is selling a business, and all or substantially all of the assets that are necessary to carry on that business are being transferred, then an election can be filed to not collect the GST on the sale of the assets. The details of this election will be covered when we review how the GST affects the sale of assets or shares of a business in Chapter 18.

Sales of Capital Real Property
Exemptions
9-152.   Special rules apply to the collection and remittance of GST when real property (i.e., land and buildings) is sold. The special treatment begins with a number of exemptions for particular types of transactions. These include:

- **Sale Of Used Residential Units**   These sales are exempt from GST. By contrast, the sale of new residential housing is taxable. There is, however, a partial rebate on new housing which will be explained later.

- **Sale Of Personal Use Real Property**   Included in this category are cottages and other vacation or recreational properties. The sale of personal use property is exempt from GST when it was not used in a business of the vendor.

- **Certain Sales Of Farmland**   Sales of farmland to related individuals or family farm corporations are often not taxable.

- **Sales And Rentals Of Real Property By Charities, NPOs And Other Public Service Bodies**   Usually, sales of real property by these organizations are exempt. However, if the property has been used in a commercial activity, then its resale is taxable.

Responsibility For GST Payment
9-153.   As a general rule, vendors are required to collect GST on behalf of the government. However, for certain real property transactions, the purchaser rather than the vendor is responsible for remitting the related GST directly to the Receiver General. This occurs when:

- the vendor is a non resident of Canada or,
- the purchaser is registered for the GST and the sale does not involve a residential complex being sold to an individual.

9-154.   If the above conditions are met and the purchaser is registered for GST, the purchaser is responsible for determining and remitting the net GST owing on any taxable real property transaction. For example, if a registered corporation purchases a warehouse from another registered corporation, the purchaser self assesses the GST owing on the purchase. If the purchaser can claim an offsetting input tax credit, there will effectively be no GST outlay on the purchase as the purchase and corresponding input tax credits are reflected on the same GST return. It is necessary to determine who is responsible for reporting the tax payable before the closing of a transaction.

9-155.   If the conditions specified above are not met (e.g., the purchaser is not registered for the GST) the vendor will be required to collect the GST on a taxable sale of real property, even if the vendor is not registered.

Timing Of Liability
9-156.   When there is a sale of capital real property, GST is generally payable on the earlier of the day the purchaser of the taxable property is required, under a written agreement, to pay the vendor for the property, and the date of payment.

Other Taxable Supplies
9-157.   Payments required under commercial rental or leasing agreements are also dealt with as a taxable supply. In addition, the GST applies to commissions or fees charged by real estate brokers, lawyers and appraisers for services provided when property is bought or sold.

9-158.   If the vendor is a registrant who uses the Quick Method, the assigned percentage rate does not apply to tax collected on the sale of real property. Instead, the full 7 percent GST on the sale should be remitted.

Residential Property And The New Housing Rebate
9-159.   Residential real estate is an area of considerable importance to most Canadians. Given this, as well as the fact that lower federal sales tax rates were traditionally available on building materials, it is not surprising that residential real estate is provided special treatment under the GST legislation.

9-160.   In somewhat simplified terms, GST applies to residential property only on the first sale of a new home. If this new home is resold in substantially unaltered condition, no GST will apply on this later transaction. If the owner undertakes renovations, GST will be charged on the materials and other costs going into the renovation. By contrast, if a used home is acquired and substantial renovations are made before the home is lived in by the purchaser, the acquisition will be treated as a new home purchase and the transaction will be taxable for GST purposes.

9-161.   While the sale of new homes attracts the full 7 percent GST, a new housing rebate is available which, in effect, reduces the GST rate to 4.48 percent on homes that cost less than $347,223. The rebate decreases until, for homes over $450,000, the sale is subject to the full 7 percent GST. The rebate schedule is as follows:

House Price	Rebate Amount
Under $347,223	2.52% Of House Price
$347,223 - $350,000	$8,750
> $350,000 < $450,000	$8,750, Less 8.75% Of Excess Over $350,000
Over $450,000	Nil

9-162.   The GST can be included in the selling price of a residence in two ways. The most straightforward way is to include the full 7 percent GST, in which case the purchaser would file for a new housing rebate equal to 2.52 percent of the GST excluded purchase price (100/107 of the total price). If GST is included in the purchase price, but is net of the new housing rebate, the calculation to determine the GST rebate needs to remove the GST component from the total price. This calculation requires multiplying the total, not by the usual factor of (100/107), but rather by [100/(107 - 2.52)] to arrive at the GST excluded purchase price. Again, the amount of the new housing rebate would be calculated by multiplying the GST excluded price by 2.52 percent. The new housing rebate is claimed by the purchaser of the residence, but can be assigned to the builder which is a common practice.

9-163.   Improvements subsequent to the purchase of a new residence will generally be taxed at the full 7 percent GST rate. To be eligible for the new residence rebate, the improvements must be done by the builder and be included in the overall price of the residence.

9-164.   After February, 2000, builders of long-term rental properties, for example apartment buildings or multi-unit retirement homes, qualify for a "New Residential Rental Property Rebate" which is similar to the GST new housing rebate.

References

9-165.   For more detailed study of the material in this Chapter, we would refer you to the following:

ITA 38	Taxable Capital Gain And Allowable Capital Loss
ITA 39	Meaning Of Capital Gain And Capital Loss
ITA 40	General Rules
ITA 41	Taxable Net Gain From Disposition Of Listed Personal Property
ITA 43	Part Dispositions
ITA 44	Exchanges Of Property
ITA 45	Property With More Than One Use
ITA 46	Personal Use Property
ITA 47	Identical Properties
ITA 53	Adjustments To Cost Base
ITA 54	Definitions
IC 88-2	General Anti-Avoidance Rule — Section 245 Of The Income Tax Act
IT-66R6	Capital Dividends
IT-84	Capital Property Owned On December 31, 1971 - Median Rule
IT-88R2	Stock Dividends
IT-95R	Foreign Exchange Gains And Losses
IT-96R6	Options Granted By Corporations To Acquire Shares, Bonds Or Debentures And By Trusts To Acquire Trust Units
IT-102R2	Conversion Of Property, Other Than Real Property, From Or To Inventory
IT-104R2	Deductibility Of Fines Or Penalties
IT-120R5	Principal Residence
IT-159R3	Capital Debts Established To Be Bad Debts
IT-199	Identical Properties Acquired In Non-Arm's Length Transactions
IT-236R4	Reserves - Disposition Of Capital Property
IT-259R3	Exchanges Of Property
IT-262R2	Losses Of Non-Residents And Part-Year Residents
IT-264R	Part Dispositions
IT-268R4	Inter Vivos Transfer Of Farm Property To A Child
IT-297R2	Gifts In Kind To Charity And Others
IT-330R	Dispositions Of Capital Property Subject To Warranty, Covenant, Or Other Conditional or Contingent Obligations
IT-332R	Personal Use Property
IT-381R3	Trusts — Capital Gains And Losses And The Flow Through Of Taxable Capital Gains To Beneficiaries
IT-387R2	Meaning Of Identical Properties
IT-403R	Options On Real Estate
IT-418	Capital Cost Allowance — Partial Dispositions Of Property
IT-437R	Ownership Of Property (Principal Residence)
IT-456R	Capital Property — Some Adjustments To Cost Base
IT-479R	Transactions In Securities
IT-484R2	Business investment losses
IT-491	Former Business Property

Exercises

(The solutions for these exercises can be found following Chapter 21 of the text.)

Exercise Nine - 1 (Superficial Loss)
Ms. Nadia Kinski owns 1,000 shares of Bord Ltd. They have an adjusted cost base of $23 per share. On August 20, 2001, she sells all of these shares at $14.50 per share. On August 25, she acquires 500 shares of Bord Ltd. at a cost of $13.75 per share. What are the tax consequences of these transactions?

Exercise Nine - 2 (Pre-1972 Capital Assets)
Mr. Jerome Detwiler acquires 1,000 shares of General Rotors on January 1, 1967 at a cost of $43.50 per share. The V-day value of the shares was $37.75. On June 30, 2001, he sells the 1,000 shares for $92.25 per share. If he uses the median rule, what will be the amount of Mr. Detwiler's taxable capital gain?

Exercise Nine - 3 (Identical Properties)
Ms. Chantal Montrose makes frequent purchases of the common shares of Comco Inc. During 2000, she purchased 650 at $23.50 per share on January 15, and 345 shares at $24.25 on March 12. She sold 210 shares on September 15, 2000 at $25.50 per share. On February 14, 2001 she purchases an additional 875 shares at $26.75 and, on October 1, 2001, she sells 340 shares at $29.50. Determine Ms. Montrose's taxable capital gains for 2000 and 2001.

Exercise Nine - 4 (Warranties)
During December, 2000, Vivid Ltd. sells a capital asset with an adjusted cost base of $237,000 for proceeds of $292,000. The Company provides the purchaser with a one year warranty and the Company estimates that it will cost $4,500 to fulfill the warranty provisions. During July, 2001, the Company spends $4,800 to fulfill the warranty provisions. Determine the effect of these transactions on Net Income For Tax Purposes for 2000 and 2001.

Exercise Nine - 5 (Capital Gains Reserves)
During December 2000, Mr. Gerry Goodson sells a capital property with an adjusted cost base of $293,000 for proceeds of disposition of $382,000. Selling costs total $17,200. In the year of sale, he receives $82,000 in cash, along with the purchaser's note for the balance of the proceeds. The note is to be repaid at the rate of $60,000 per year beginning in 2001. He receives the 2001 payment in full. Determine the maximum capital gains reserve that Mr. Goodson can deduct in 2000 and in 2001.

Exercise Nine - 6 (Deferral Of Small Business Gains)
On July 1, 2001, Jerri Hamilton sells all of her shares of Hamilton Ltd., an eligible small business corporation. The adjusted cost base of these shares is $750,000 and they are sold for proceeds of disposition of $1,350,000. On August 15, 2001, all of these proceeds are invested in the common shares of JH Inc., a new small business corporation. How much of the $600,000 capital gain arising on the sale of the Hamilton Ltd. shares can be deferred by the investment in JH Inc.? If the maximum deferral is elected, what will be the adjusted cost base of JH Inc. shares?

Exercise Nine - 7 (Involuntary Dispositions)
Hadfeld Ltd., a Company with a December 31 year end, operates out of a single building that cost $725,000 in 1994. At the beginning of 2001, the UCC for its Class 1 was $623,150. On June 30, 2001, the building was completely destroyed in a fire. The building was insured for its fair market value of $950,000 and this amount was received in September, 2001. The building is replaced in 2002 at a cost of $980,000. Describe the 2001 and 2002 tax consequences of these events, including the capital cost and UCC for the new building, assuming Hadfeld Ltd. wishes to minimize taxes.

Exercise Nine - 8 (Change In Use)

During July, 2001, Ms. Lynn Larson decides to use her summer cottage as a rental property. It has an original cost of $23,000 and its current fair market value is $111,000. It has never been designated as her principal residence. Describe the 2001 tax consequences of this change in use, including the capital cost and UCC that will be applicable to the rental property.

Exercise Nine - 9 (Principal Residence Rules)

Mr. Norm Craft purchases his first home in 1992 at a cost of $89,000. In 1997, this home is sold for $109,500 and a second home is purchased for $152,000. In 2001, this second home is sold for $178,000 and Mr. Craft moves to a rental property. Determine the minimum tax consequences of the two property sales.

Exercise Nine - 10 (Principal Residence Rules)

Ms. Jan Sadat owns a house in Ottawa, as well as a cottage in Westport. She purchased the house in 1990 for $126,000. The cottage was gifted to her in 1993 by her parents. At the time of the gift, the fair market value of the cottage was $85,000. During June, 2001, both properties are sold, the house for $198,000 and the cottage for $143,500. She has lived in the Ottawa house during the year, but has spent her summers in the Westport cottage. Determine the minimum capital gain that she can report on the 2001 sale of the two properties.

Exercise Nine - 11 (Foreign Currency Gains And Losses)

During 1998, Mr. Michel Pratt acquires 450 shares of a French company, Matim Inc., at a price of 68 French Francs (FF) per share. He paid for the shares with French Francs purchased at a rate of FF1 = $0.30. During September, 2001, the shares are sold for FF96 per share. The French Francs are immediately converted into Canadian dollars at a rate of FF1 = $0.32. What amounts will be included in Mr. Pratt's Net Income For Tax Purposes as a result of these transactions?

Problems For Self Study

(The solutions for these problems can be found following Chapter 21 of the text.)

Self Study Problem Nine - 1

For over 20 years, Mr. Hall has taken a sporadic interest in the common shares of Clarkson Industries Ltd., a Canadian public company. As he is approaching retirement age and anticipates moving to Florida, he sold his total holding of Clarkson shares on March 15, 2001, when the shares were trading at $174 per share. Over the years, Mr. Hall has had the following transactions in the shares of Clarkson Industries:

- On October 15, 1977, he purchases 5,500 share at $40 per share.

- On May 8, 1979, he sells 1,500 shares at $52.

- On December 12, 1983, he purchases 3,200 shares at $79 per share.

- On February 3, 1984, he sells 2,600 shares at $94 per share.

- On January 15, 1988, he receives a 10 percent stock dividend that has been paid by Clarkson Industries. As part of this transaction, the Company transfers Retained Earnings of $99 per share to contributed capital.

- On June 15, 1992, he acquires 3,800 shares at $104 per share.

- On December 23, 1994, he receives a 10 percent stock dividend that has been paid by Clarkson Industries. As part of this transaction, the Company transfers $125 per share from Retained Earnings to contributed capital.

Required:

A. Determine the amount of the taxable capital gain or allowable capital loss which would arise on the sale of 1,500 shares on May 8, 1979, and the 2,600 shares on February 3, 1984.

B.   Indicate the amount of the taxable capital gain that would be included in Mr. Hall's 2001 Net Income For Tax Purposes.

Ignore transaction costs in all of your calculations.

Self Study Problem Nine - 2

On November 1, 2001, Miss Stevens sells a capital property for $500,000. The adjusted cost base of the property is $230,000 and she incurs selling costs in the amount of $20,000. She receives an immediate cash payment of $200,000 on November 1, 2001, with the balance of the $500,000 to be paid on June 1, 2007.

Required: Calculate the taxable capital gain that would be included in Miss Stevens' Net Income For Tax Purposes for each of the years 2001 through 2007.

Self Study Problem Nine - 3

On May 1, 2001, a fire completely destroys Fraser Industries Ltd.'s Edmonton office building and all of its contents. An immediate settlement is negotiated with the Company's fire and casualty insurer. The insurer agrees to pay $4,800,000 for the building and an additional $1,256,000 for the contents of the building. These amounts represent the estimated fair market values of the destroyed assets and become receivable to Fraser Industries Ltd. on June 15, 2001. A cheque is received for these amounts on August 15, 2001.

As the City has been acquiring adjacent land for the development of a park, the Company is notified on May 15, 2001 that the land on which the building was located will be expropriated in order to expand the park area. The expropriation takes place on November 30, 2001, with the City paying an amount of $723,000 which is the estimated fair market value of the land.

Other information on the Edmonton property is as follows:

Land   The land was acquired in 1982 at a cost of $256,000.

Building   The building was constructed during 1983 and 1984 at a total cost of $3,700,000. It is the only building owned by Fraser Industries Ltd. and, at the beginning of 2001, the undepreciated capital cost in Class 3 was $1,856,000.

Building Contents   The contents of the building consisted entirely of Class 8 assets. These assets had an original cost in 1983 of $972,000 and the undepreciated capital cost balance in Class 8 is $72,000 at the beginning of 2001. Fraser Industries Ltd. does not own any other Class 8 assets.

In replacing the destroyed property, the Company decides to relocate to an area which has lower land costs. As a consequence, a replacement property is found in Hinton at a cost of $6,200,000. It is estimated that the fair market value of the land on which the building is located is $500,000. The remaining $5,700,000 is allocated to the building. The acquisition closes on January 31, 2002 and, during the following month, contents are acquired at a cost of $1,233,000. All of the contents are Class 8 assets.

The Company has a taxation year which ends on December 31. The replacement of the land, building, and building contents was completed prior to the filing date for the Company's 2001 tax return.

Required:

A.   Assume that the 2001 tax return is prepared without making any election under ITA 13(4), ITA 44(1), or ITA 44(6). Determine the amounts that would be included in Fraser Industries Ltd.'s 2001 Net Income For Tax Purposes as a result of receiving the insurance and expropriation proceeds.

B. Assume that the 2001 tax return is prepared making an election under ITA 13(4) and ITA 44(1), but not under ITA 44(6). Determine the amounts that would be included in Fraser Industries Ltd.'s 2001 Net Income For Tax Purposes as a result of receiving the insurance and expropriation proceeds. Indicate the adjusted cost base and, where appropriate, the undepreciated capital cost of the new items of property.

C. Indicate the maximum amount of any reduction in 2001 Net Income For Tax Purposes that could result from the use of the ITA 44(6) election, in addition to the elections under ITA 13(4) and ITA 44(1). Should the Company make the election? Explain your conclusion.

Self Study Problem Nine - 4

Mr. Larson, the President of Larson Distributing Inc., was offered $1,875,000 for the land, building, and equipment used by his business at its suburban Toronto location. As he believed that his business could be operated at a less valuable rural location, he accepts the offer and sells the business property on October 15, 2001. The details relating to this property are as follows:

Land The land was acquired in 1986 at a cost of $137,000. At the time of the sale it was estimated that the fair market value of the land was $772,000.

Building The building was constructed in 1987 at a total cost of $605,000. At the time of the sale its undepreciated capital cost was $342,000 while its estimated fair market value was $989,000.

Equipment The equipment had an original cost of $452,000. On October 15, 2001, its undepreciated capital cost was $127,000 and its estimated fair market value $114,000.

On January 5, 2002, (prior to the filing date for the 2001 tax return), Mr. Larson acquires a replacement property in Barry's Bay at a total cost of $1,500,000. This cost is allocated as follows:

Land	$ 253,000
Building	1,042,000
Equipment	205,000
Total	$1,500,000

The Company would like to defer any capital gains or recapture resulting from the sale of the Toronto property. The Company's tax year ends on December 31, 2001 and it does not own any buildings or equipment on this date.

Required:

A. Indicate the 2001 tax effects related to the sale of the Toronto property, assuming maximum deferrals under ITA 44(1) and 13(4) but no use of the ITA 44(6) election to transfer proceeds between land and building. Indicate the adjusted cost base and, where appropriate, the undepreciated capital cost of the three new items of property at the time of acquisition.

B. Indicate the maximum amount of any reduction in Net Income For Tax Purposes that could result from the use of the ITA 44(6) election.

Self Study Problem Nine - 5

Mr. Simms has lived most of his life in Vancouver. In 1972, he purchased a three bedroom home near English Bay for $125,000. In 1977, he acquired a cottage in the Whistler ski area at a cost of $40,000. In all subsequent years, he has spent at least a portion of the year living in each of the two locations. When he is not residing in these properties they are left vacant.

On December 31, 1981, as the result of an appraisal undertaken by Mr. Simms, it was determined that the value of the English Bay property was $335,000 and that of the cottage at Whistler was $205,000. On October 1, 2001, Mr. Simms sells the English Bay property for $515,000 and the cottage at Whistler for $320,000.

Required: Calculate the minimum capital gain that Mr. Simms would be required to report as a result of selling the two properties in 2001 under the following alternative assumptions:

A. He uses ITA 40(2)(b) on both properties.

B. He uses ITA 40(6) on both properties.

Self Study Problem Nine - 6

Quincy Corporation is not registered for GST purposes as its business is in the start-up phase. Construction costs of a building are capitalized, along with some legal and engineering fees. Other costs incurred are expensed for income tax purposes. GST is paid on all costs.

Required: When Quincy Corporation registers for the GST, explain if it will be entitled to claim input tax credits on any of these costs?

Self Study Problem Nine - 7

Vivian Driver is planning to purchase a home, and she is considering three properties. The prices of the homes and the costs of any improvements planned, all before GST, commissions and transfer fees, are as follows:

Property	Purchase Price	Improvements
Shuswap Cedar A-Frame - Used	$120,000	None
Millcreek Bi-Level - New (Note 1)	90,000	$24,000
Sunset Beach Cottage - Used (Note 2)	60,000	56,000

Note 1 As the Millcreek Bi-level is under construction, $14,000 of the improvements would be made by the contractor at the same time as the house is being finished. Then, as a winter project, Vivian would finish the fireplace with a materials cost of $10,000.

Note 2 The Sunset Beach cottage needs to be winterized, requiring the replacement of electrical wiring, wall and roof insulation, and new inside walls. The improvements would be made by a home renovation firm, and require $26,000 of labour and $30,000 of materials.

Required: Before making any offer to purchase, Vivian has asked you to determine what the GST and total out-of-pocket costs of each purchase would be.

Self Study Problem Nine - 8

Tiffany Inc. is a registrant for GST purposes. Tiffany plans to purchase a commercial property in Saskatoon for $10,000,000, before GST. Tiffany will occupy 40 percent of the floor space and 60 percent will be leased to commercial tenants. Tiffany provides taxable and exempt supplies. For general administrative expenses, Tiffany recovers 20 percent of GST paid as input tax credits.

Required: Tiffany Inc. has asked for your advice on:

A. How the GST will apply to the proposed purchase.

B. Whether any special elections can be made to minimize the GST cash outlays to the company.

C. Whether Tiffany will have to charge GST on the lease.

Assignment Problems

(The solutions for these problems are only available in
the solutions manual that has been provided to your instructor.)

Assignment Problem Nine - 1

For the year 2000, the following table gives information with respect to the capital gains
(losses) experienced by four different individuals:

	2000 Capital Gain (Loss)		
	Before February 28	After Feb. 27 Before Oct. 18	After October 17
Sam Spencer	($ 96,000)	$120,000	$ 24,000
Sally Smooth	220,000	145,000	(55,000)
Sheaei Sayers	(42,000)	(9,000)	16,000
Saul Sinkley	180,000	(45,000)	32,000

Required: For each of these individuals indicate the amount of any taxable capital gain that
will be included in their 2000 tax return, the amount of any allowable loss carry over from the
2000 taxation year, and the effective capital gains inclusion rate applicable to the year 2000.

Assignment Problem Nine - 2

Ms. Browning has followed the stock market with great interest for a number of years. While
she trades the shares of some Companies fairly actively, there are three companies whose
shares she has held since becoming interested in the market in the late 1960s. During November 2001, Ms. Browning decided to sell these three blocks of shares. The relevant data on
these share holdings and their disposal is as follows:

	Domtar	Inco	Stelco
Acquisition Cost	$76,000	$20,000	$ 92,000
V-Day Value	91,000	14,000	62,000
Proceeds Of Sale	4,900	17,000	176,000
Selling Costs	300	1,400	1,500

Required: Determine the taxable capital gain or allowable capital loss resulting from the
2001 sale of each block of shares. Make comparative calculations using both the valuation
day election and the median rule approaches.

Assignment Problem Nine - 3

Miss Wells has purchased the shares of two Companies over the years. Purchases and sales of
shares in the first of these Companies, Memo Inc., are as follows:

February, 1997 purchase	60 @ $24
November, 1998 purchase	90 @ 28
April, 1999 purchase	45 @ 30
October, 1999 sale	(68) @ 36
September, 2001 purchase	22 @ 26
November, 2001 sale	(53) @ 40

Purchases and sales of shares in the second Company, Demo Ltd., are as follows:

April, 2000 purchase	200 @ $24
December, 2000 purchase	160 @ 33
July, 2001 sale	(260) @ 36

Required:

A. Determine the cost to Miss Wells of the Memo Inc. shares that are still being held on December 31, 2001.

B. Determine the taxable capital gain resulting from the July, 2001 disposition of the Demo Ltd. shares.

Assignment Problem Nine - 4

On May 1, 2001, Mr. Rowe sold a parcel of suburban land to a developer for $2,600,000. The land had cost Mr. Rowe $1,400,000 in 1987 and no additions or improvements had been made to the land. He classifies any gain on the land sale as a capital gain. In order to convince the purchaser that he should pay the full $2,600,000 in cash, Mr. Rowe has agreed to refund a part of the purchase price if less than 100 lots are sold by December 1, 2002. The agreement calls for a refund of $26,000 for each of the 100 lots that is not sold within the specified period. At the time of the sale, Mr. Rowe estimates that he will probably have to pay $104,000 to the purchaser on December 1, 2002.

Over the next two years a number of plants in the area are closed, substantially reducing the demand for the lots in the development. By December 1, 2002, only 60 lots have been sold and Mr. Rowe is obliged to pay the purchaser $1,040,000 [($26,000)(40 Lots)] as agreed.

Required: Describe the tax effects associated with the guarantee provided by Mr. Rowe at the time the land is sold and with the payment that he is required to make on December 1, 2002.

Assignment Problem Nine - 5

During July, 2001, Mrs. Simpkins sold a painting to a friend for $25,000. She had purchased the painting in 1990 at a cost of $15,000. As her friend was short of cash, Mrs. Simpkins accepted a down payment of $15,000 and a note which required the friend to make a payment of $10,000 at the end of 2002. No interest payments were required on the note and, because Mrs. Simpkins had no other income during 2001, she did not establish a capital gains reserve.

Shortly before the end of 2002, Mrs. Simpkins tried to locate her friend. She was not successful and it appeared that the friend, along with the painting, had disappeared without a trace. As a reflection of this fact, Mrs. Simpkins wishes to write off the bad debt in 2002.

Required: Determine the 2001 and 2002 tax effects resulting from the preceding transactions.

Assignment Problem Nine - 6

Mr. Rhodes purchased a large tract of land on the edge of Edmonton in 1978 for $750,000. It was sold during April, 2001 to a developer for $2,500,000. He receives a down payment of $625,000 and accepts a 25 year 8 percent mortgage for the balance of $1,875,000. The payments on this mortgage begin in the second year and require the repayment of $75,000 per year in capital.

Mr. Rhodes wishes to use reserves to defer the payment of capital gains taxes for as long as possible. He classifies any gain on the land sale as a capital gain.

Required: Calculate the capital gains taxation effects of this sale assuming that Mr. Rhodes deducts the maximum capital gains reserve in 2001 and subsequent years.

Assignment Problem Nine - 7

In 1978, Ms. Gerhardt purchased a substantial parcel of land in Northern Ontario at a cost of $600,000. During May, 2001, she sells it for $1,350,000.

The terms of the sale call for a down payment at the time of closing, with Ms. Gerhardt accepting a 9 percent mortgage for the balance of the $1,350,000. The terms of the mortgage require annual payments beginning in the year subsequent to the sale. The payments are designed to include principal payments of 5 percent of the sales price or $67,500 per year.

Ms. Gerhardt wishes to use reserves to defer the payment of capital gains taxes for as long as possible.

Required: Compare the capital gains taxation effects of this sale assuming:

A. The down payment was 15 percent of the sales price.

B. The down payment was 45 percent of the sales price.

Assignment Problem Nine - 8
The following two independent cases involve dispositions of eligible small business corporation shares, with the proceeds being invested in replacement shares.

Case A On March 31, 2001 Harold sells his shares in Corporation A which are eligible small business investments. His proceeds of disposition are $100,000 and his capital gain is $60,000. On July 1, 2001, Harold invests $90,000 in shares of Corporation B which are new eligible small business investments.

Case B On November 6, 2001, Kate disposes of shares in Corporation C which are eligible small business investments. Her proceeds of disposition are $1,000,000 and she realizes a capital gain of $600,000. On February 1, 2002, Kate acquires shares in Corporation D at a cost of $1,000,000 which are new eligible small business investments.

Required: For each case, determine the maximum permitted capital gains deferral, as well as the adjusted cost base of the replacement shares.

Assignment Problem Nine - 9
You are the tax consultant for Leblanc Ltd. The Company has a December 31 year end. The sole shareholder of Leblanc Ltd. wants to minimize the Company's taxes payable. You are given the following information.

In 2001 LL replaced a Class 8 asset destroyed by a fire in May 2000 with another Class 8 asset that cost $500,000. Insurance proceeds of $300,000 were received in December 2000. The original cost in 1988 of the destroyed asset was $250,000. This was the only Class 8 transaction in either 2000 or 2001. The undepreciated capital cost of Class 8 at the beginning of 2000 was $175,000.

Required:

A. Indicate the tax consequences of the involuntary disposition which occurred in 2000.

B Calculate the maximum capital cost allowance that Leblanc Ltd. will be able to claim for Class 8 assets for the years 2000 and 2001.

(Adapted from the 1994 UFE))

Assignment Problem Nine - 10
On July 1, 1999, the manufacturing plant of Janchek Ltd. was expropriated by the provincial government in order to make way for a new expressway. It is the only building that Janchek Ltd. owns. The land on which the plant was situated was purchased in 1988 for $88,000. The building, a Class 1 asset, was erected in 1989 at a cost of $290,000. The Company's year end is December 31.

On November 23, 2000, after extended negotiations between Janchek and the provincial government, the Company received compensation in the amount of $130,000 for the land and $430,000 for the building. On January 1, 1999, the Undepreciated Capital Cost balance in Class 1 was $248,000. Janchek took no Capital Cost Allowance on the building in either 1999 or 2000.

On June 20, 2001, a new manufacturing plant was purchased for a total cost of $1,050,000. Of this amount $210,000 was allocated to the land with the remaining $840,000 going to the building.

Janchek Ltd. will make any available elections in order to reduce the tax effects of the replacement of the expropriated property.

Required:

A. Explain the tax effects of the receipt of compensation resulting from the expropriation.

B. Calculate the adjusted cost base for the land and the building and the Undepreciated Capital Cost of the building after the 2001 replacement occurs, but before the deduction of CCA for the year.

Assignment Problem Nine - 11

Mr. Blake purchased a house on June 30, 1983 at a total cost of $176,000. Mr. and Mrs. Blake and their two teenaged children moved in during the next month. On January 1, 2001, a portion of this property was converted to an apartment and rented to a tenant at a rate of $850 per month for a term of eighteen months. At the time of this conversion the fair market value of the total property was $253,000. The apartment was located in the back of the house, faced a busy parking lot and occupied 32 percent of the total floor space of the property.

On June 30, 2002, at the end of the lease term, Mr. Blake and the tenant agree to reduce the size of the area rented to 21 percent of the total floor space of the property. A new lease is signed with a reduced rent of $750 per month and a new term of 30 months. On June 30, 2002, the fair market value of the property is $278,000. Two months after the new lease is signed, Mr. Blake makes improvements in the rented area of the property at a cost of $12,350.

On June 30, 1983 the fair market value of the land on which the property is situated is $83,000. By January 1, 2001 it has increased to $106,000 and on June 30, 2002, it is estimated to be $110,000. During the year ending December 31, 2001, Mr. Blake made payments for insurance, hydro and property taxes on his property in the amount of $5,600. The corresponding figure for the period January 1, 2002 through June 30, 2002 was $2,900. For the period July 1, 2002 through December 31, 2002, this amount was $3,200. There were no repair costs during either 2001 or 2002.

Mr. Blake does not make an election under ITA 45(2) with respect to his change in use.

Required: For each of the two taxation years 2001 and 2002, indicate the amounts that would be included in Mr. Blake's Net Income For Tax Purposes as the result of the preceding transactions and events.

Assignment Problem Nine - 12

At the end of 2001, Mr. Vaughn sold both his city home and his summer cottage. Relevant information on the two properties is as follows:

	City Home	Cottage
Date acquired	1967	1968
Original cost	$120,000	$ 30,000
Market Value, December 31, 1971	264,000	36,000
Market Value, December 31, 1981	432,000	180,000
Gross proceeds from sale	528,000	330,000
Real estate commissions	32,000	16,000

Required: Mr. Vaughn wishes to minimize any capital gains resulting from the sale of the two properties. How should the residences be designated in order to accomplish this goal? In addition, calculate the amount of the gain that would arise under the designation that you have recommended.

Assignment Problem Nine - 13

At August 1, 2001, Mrs. Vargo sold a number of personal assets, all of which she had acquired in the last five years. The relevant information on these sales is as follows:

	Cost	Proceeds	Selling Costs
Automobile	$25,000	$27,000	$150
Coin Collection	1,600	1,300	50
Rare Manuscript	1,700	800	30
Boat	4,500	3,500	175
Painting	700	1,100	50
Antique Clock	800	1,700	50

Required: Determine the net taxable capital gain that Mrs. Vargo will have to include in her income for the current year. Indicate any amounts that may be available for carry over to other years.

Assignment Problem Nine - 14

Ms. Rodeway is a Canadian resident who, on occasion, purchases securities in the over the counter market in the United States. In September of 1996 she acquired a large block of shares of Comweb for US$53,000. She purchased these shares with U.S. dollars acquired at a rate of C$1.00 = US$1.10. These shares were held until March of the current year.

In March, 2001, the Comweb shares were sold for US$97,000 with the funds remaining in a U.S. bank account until September. In September, the US$97,000 was converted into Canadian dollars and transferred to her Canadian bank account.

Assume relevant exchange rates between the U.S. and Canadian dollar are as follows:

September, 1996	US$1.00 = C$1.10
March, 2001	US$1.00 = C$1.45
September, 2001	US$1.00 = C$1.50

Required: Calculate the amount of taxable capital gains that will have to be included in Ms. Rodeway's Net Income For Tax Purposes for the current year.

Assignment Problem Nine - 15

Each of the following independent cases describes a situation with a proposed tax treatment.

1. Mr. Acker has owned a small triplex for a number of years and, throughout this period, all three of the units have been rented. During the current year, Mr. Acker has moved into one of the three units and, as a result, will be reporting reduced rental revenues in his tax return. As he has not sold any property, he will not report any capital gains or losses during the current year.

2. Mr. Jones has sold a property with an adjusted cost base of $72,000 for total proceeds of $105,000. He is providing a warranty on the property that he estimates will cost him $6,000 to service. As a consequence, he is recognizing a capital gain of $27,000.

3. Ms. Turner sold her dining room table to her daughter for $400 and a painting to her brother for $900. These prices equalled their estimated fair market value. She purchased the table several years ago for $950 at the same time she purchased the painting for $667. She does not plan to report any capital gain or loss.

4. Mrs. Brown purchased corporate bonds for $11,200 of which $800 was accrued interest and $10,400 represented the principal. The bonds were later sold for $11,600 which includes $200 for accrued interest. Mrs. Brown recognizes a taxable capital gain of $500.

5. A corporation has owned all of the shares in a subsidiary company since 1968. The cost of these shares was $750,000 and their V-day value was $1,250,000. During the current year the corporation has sold the shares for $1,000,000. It recognizes a capital loss of $250,000.

6. Several years ago, Miss Lee transferred three sports cars with a total value of $182,000 to a corporation in return for all of the shares of the company. The cars are profitably used in her personal escort business. During the current year, all of the cars are destroyed in a fire on her estate. Unfortunately, Miss Lee did not believe that people in her financial position needed insurance and, as a consequence, no compensation was available for the loss. As the corporation had no assets other than the cars, there was no reason for her to continue to hold the shares. In view of this situation, she sells the shares to a friend who requires a corporate shell for some business operations. The sale price is $500 and Miss Lee uses the allowable capital loss of $90,750 [(1/2)($182,000 - $500)] to offset taxable capital gains resulting from real estate transactions.

Required: In each of the preceding cases, indicate whether or not you believe that the tax treatment being proposed is the correct one. Explain your conclusion.

Assignment Problem Nine - 16

All of the following independent Cases involve the purchase of a new house for $200,000. Varying assumptions are made with respect to what is included in the $200,000.

Case A   The price includes GST at 7 percent.

Case B   The price includes GST, net of the new housing rebate.

Case C   The price does not include any GST.

Required: For each Case, determine the GST rebate that can be claimed on the purchase.

Assignment Problem Nine - 17

A house renovator purchases a used house in 2001 from a private individual for upgrading and resale. The purchase price of the house is $85,000. The renovator, a GST registrant, makes substantial renovations including an addition to the house that includes a country kitchen, jacuzzi room, and art studio. The electrical wiring is replaced and a new roof is installed. As a result of the renovations, the renovator sells the house for $200,000 before consideration of commissions and transfer fees.

The costs associated with the house and its renovation are as follows:

Purchase Price		$ 85,000
Renovation costs:		
Subcontractors - No GST Included	$10,700	
Subcontractors - GST Included	21,400	
Materials - GST Included	32,100	
Employee Wages	6,000	70,200
Total Costs		$155,200

Required: What are the GST consequences of this undertaking for the renovator and the purchaser of the renovated house? Calculate the cost of the house to the purchaser and the net profit on the sale for the renovator, ignoring the effect of commissions and transfer fees. Include a calculation of the GST remittance of the renovator in your solution.

Assignment Problem Nine - 18
A new building is purchased for $5,000,000, before GST. The purchaser, Total Health Inc., is a GST registrant who provides all types of health care services and products. Sixty percent of the building will be used by Total Health Inc. employees as medical and dental offices. The remaining 40 percent will be used to house a pharmacy run and managed by Total Health Inc. staff.

Required:

A. How much GST will be payable on the purchase?

B. Explain who will be responsible for payment of the GST?

C. Can an input tax credit be claimed, and if so, for how much?

Assignment Problem Nine - 19 (Electronic Library Research Problem)
Provide brief answers to the following questions. Your answers should be supported by references to materials found in your Electronic Library.

A. In some circumstances, shareholders of a corporation may be required to make additional capital contributions. Do such contributions have any influence on the adjusted cost base of the shares?

B. ITA 47 provides rules for determining gains on "identical properties". How does the CCRA interpret the phrase "identical properties"? Would two classes of shares of the same corporation, that differed only in that one had voting rights and the other did not have such rights, be considered to be identical properties?

C. Car leasing companies normally remove vehicles from the leasing fleet when the milage on the individual units is relatively low. The vehicles are then offered for sale, a process which means that most of these companies are also running a fairly significant used car business. What are the tax consequences of removing a vehicle from the leasing fleet with a view to selling it to the public? How would any gain or loss on the sale of the vehicle be taxed?

Chapter 10

Non Arm's Length Transactions, Departures From Canada And Death Of A Taxpayer

Introduction

10-1.   As is apparent from the title, this Chapter is something of a potpourri. It contains a discussion of several aspects of Canadian income taxation that are more or less related but do not conveniently fit under any single description. One of these subjects is non arm's length transfers of property for inadequate consideration. This relates to the previous Chapter since there may be complications in the calculation of capital gains and losses. We will also cover transfers to spouses and minors which result in the application of income attribution rules. This material may involve both the previous Chapter on capital gains and the following Chapter 11 which deals with income from property. Attention will also be given to those deemed dispositions which arise when a taxpayer leaves Canada or dies. This will usually involve the calculation of capital gains and losses.

Non Arm's Length Transfers Of Property

Inadequate Considerations
The Problem
10-2.   When a transfer of property takes place between taxpayers who are dealing with each other at arm's length, there is usually no reason to assume that the transfer took place at a value which was significantly different from the fair market value of the property transferred. As a consequence, the consideration given for the property would normally be used as both the proceeds of the disposition and the adjusted cost base for the new owner. However, when a transfer takes place between taxpayers who are not dealing at arm's length, there is the possibility that the consideration can be established at a level which will allow one or both taxpayers to avoid taxes. For example, an individual could sell a capital asset to a related individual at a price well below fair market value. If this related individual was in a lower tax bracket, there could be a significant tax savings if the asset was subsequently sold on an arm's length basis at its real value. To prevent tax avoidance in such situations, ITA 69 provides rules for dealing with inadequate considerations (i.e., the transfer of property for consideration that is not equal to the fair market value of that property).

10-3.   ITA 251(1), in effect, defines the term arm's length by noting that for purposes of the Act:

(a) related persons shall be deemed not to deal with each other at arm's length; and

(b) it is a question of fact whether persons not related to each other were at a particular time dealing with each other at arm's length.

10-4.   With respect to individuals, ITA 251(2)(a) points out that they are related if they are connected by blood relationship, marriage or adoption. With respect to the question of whether corporations are related, ITA 251(2)(b) and (c) have a fairly long list of possibilities, for example, a corporation is related to the person who controls it, and two corporations are related if they are both controlled by the same person. There are, of course, many complications in this area. However, the examples used in this Chapter and its accompanying problems involve situations in which the taxpayers are obviously related and, as a consequence, not at arm's length.

General Rules

10-5.   When there is a non arm's length transfer between persons, ITA 69 requires that the transferor is deemed to have received proceeds equal to either the fair market value of the property at the time of the transfer or, in those situations in which the consideration received is greater than the fair market value of the property being sold, the actual amount received becomes the proceeds. The situation is more complex for the transferee. The transferee's adjusted cost base will be depend on the transfer price. The applicable rules are as follows:

- If the transfer price is greater than fair market value,
    the fair market value becomes the adjusted cost base.
- If the transfer price is less than fair market value,
    the transfer price becomes the adjusted cost base.
- If the transfer is a gift, bequest or inheritance,
    the fair market value becomes the adjusted cost base.

Example

10-6.   In order to illustrate the preceding general rules, assume that John Brown has a capital asset with an adjusted cost base of $50,000 and a fair market value of $75,000. If the asset is sold for consideration equal to its fair market value of $75,000, the result will be a capital gain of $25,000 for John Brown and an adjusted cost base for the new owner of $75,000. This would be result without regard to whether the purchaser was related to John Brown.

10-7.   If the asset is transferred to a non arm's length party, and the consideration provided is not equal to fair market value, ITA 69 becomes applicable. The following three cases illustrate the various possible alternatives. In each case we will assume the transfer is to John Brown's brother, Sam Brown.

Case A - Transfer At $100,000 (Greater Than Fair Market Value) The proceeds to John Brown will be the actual amount of $100,000, while the adjusted cost base to Sam Brown will be limited by ITA 69(1)(a) to the $75,000 fair market value. This will result in an immediate capital gain to John Brown of $50,000 ($100,000 - $50,000), an amount which includes the difference between the fair market value of $75,000 and the transfer price of $100,000. Since the adjusted cost base to Sam Brown will only be $75,000, he will have to record a capital gain if there is a later sale at a value above $75,000. As John Brown has already been taxed on the difference between $75,000 and $100,000, this will result in this amount being, in effect, taxed twice.

Case B - Transfer At $60,000 (Less Than Fair Market Value)   If the transfer took place at a price of $60,000, ITA 69(1)(b) would deem John Brown to have received the fair market value of $75,000. As there is no special rule applicable to the purchaser in this case, the adjusted cost base to Sam Brown would be the actual transfer price of $60,000. Here again, double taxation could arise, this time on the difference between the transfer price of $60,000 and the fair market value of $75,000.

Case C - Gift, Bequest, Or Inheritance   In this Case, ITA 69(1)(a) would deem the proceeds of disposition to be the fair market value of $75,000, and ITA 69(1)(c) would deem Sam Brown's adjusted cost base to be the same value. Note that this is the same result that would be achieved if the asset were sold to Sam Brown at its fair market value of $75,000. There is no double taxation involved in this case.

10-8.   Given the presence of ITA 69, the rules for transferring property to related parties are very clear. Either transfer the property at a consideration which is equal to fair market value or, alternatively, give the property away. A non arm's length transfer at a value that is either above or below the fair market value of the property will result in double taxation on some part of any gain recognized when there is a later sale of the property by the transferee.

Applicability Of ITA 69

10-9.   The inadequate consideration rules in Section 69 are prefaced by the phrase "except as expressly otherwise provided in this Act". This means that if there is a provision which deals with a particular non arm's length transfer, that provision takes precedence over the general provisions of Section 69. For example, as covered later in this Chapter, ITA 73(1) indicates that a non depreciable capital property that is gifted to a spouse will be transferred at its adjusted cost base. This provision overrides the general requirement under ITA 69 that gifted property be transferred at fair market value.

Avoidance

10-10.   In recent years there has been some avoidance of the provisions of Section 69 through the use of leasing arrangements. These arrangements involved the rental of a property to a person with whom the owner/lessor was not dealing at arm's length. The required lease payment was set at a sufficiently low level that the fair market value of the property was significantly reduced. This would allow a sale or gift to be made with the deemed proceeds of disposition being based on this lower value.

10-11.   As an example of this arrangement, consider a situation where an individual has a property with a fair market value of $100,000. If this property were leased on a long term basis to a spouse for an unrealistically low value, say $2,000 per year, the fair market value of the property might be reduced to about $20,000. If there were no restrictions, it could then be gifted or sold for $20,000 to a child and there would be no double taxation under the provisions of ITA 69.

10-12.   ITA 69(1.2) is designed to make this an unattractive strategy. Under the provisions of this Subsection, the taxpayer's proceeds of disposition on the gift or sale will be the greater of the actual fair market value at the time of the disposition ($20,000) and the fair market value determined without consideration of the non arm's length lease ($100,000). This means the transferor will be taxed on the basis of having received the full $100,000 and, under the usual provisions of Section 69, the transferee will have an adjusted cost base of $20,000. This will result in double taxation of the difference between $100,000 and $20,000 and should serve to discourage this type of avoidance strategy.

> Exercises Ten-1 through Ten-3 deal with inadequate considerations. This would be an appropriate time to attempt these exercises.

Inter Vivos Transfers To A Spouse And Others

Capital Property To A Spouse

10-13.   An inter vivos transfer is one that occurs while the transferor is still alive, rather than at the time of, or subsequent to, that individual's death. ITA 73 deals with the treatment of a number of different inter vivos transfers of capital property, the most important of which is transfers of capital property to a spouse. With respect to this type of transfer, ITA 73(1) provides that, where a capital property is transferred to a spouse, a former spouse in settlement of rights arising out of their marriage, or to a trust in favour of a spouse, the deemed proceeds of disposition to the transferor and the capital cost to the transferee will be as follows:

Non Depreciable Capital Property   The proceeds will be deemed to be the adjusted cost base of the property transferred.

Depreciable Capital Property   The proceeds will be deemed to be the UCC of the Class or, in cases where only part of a Class is transferred, an appropriate portion of the Class.

10-14.   From the point of view of the transferee, his values will be as follows:

Non Depreciable Capital Property   The capital cost to the transferee will be deemed to be the old capital cost to the transferor.

Depreciable Capital Property   The UCC to the transferee will be the old UCC to the transferor. In addition, the old capital cost will also be retained by the transferee, with the difference between this and his UCC being considered to be deemed CCA.

10-15. These rules mean that the transfer will have no tax consequences for the transferor and that the transferee will retain the same tax values that were contained in the transferor's records. This is illustrated by the following example:

> **Example** A wife gifts land with an adjusted cost base of $100,000 and a fair market value of $250,000 to her husband. At the same time, three-quarters (based on fair market values) of her Class 10 assets are also given to her husband. The specific Class 10 assets transferred have a capital cost of $225,000 and a fair market value of $310,000. The UCC for the entire Class 10 prior to the gift is $260,000.

10-16. The wife would be deemed to have received $100,000 for the disposition of the land and $195,000 [(3/4)($260,000)] for the Class 10 assets. Given these values, the transactions would have no tax consequences for the wife. For the husband, the land would have an adjusted cost base of $100,000. The transferred Class 10 assets would have a UCC of $195,000, combined with a capital cost of $225,000. This means that, if the husband sold all the transferred assets immediately for their fair market value of $560,000 ($250,000 + $310,000), there would be a capital gain of $235,000 ($560,000 - $100,000 - $225,000) and recapture of CCA of $30,000 ($195,000 - $225,000).

10-17. Before leaving this example, we would note that tax rules such as ITA 73(1) are referred to as rollover provisions. They allow taxpayers to transfer assets to other parties without incurring any current taxes payable. In addition, the property transferred retains the transferor's tax values (i.e., adjusted cost base or UCC) in the hands of the transferee. We will encounter an additional rollover in this Chapter when we discuss transfers to a spouse at death. Other rollovers applicable to corporations will be given attention in Chapters 17 and 18.

Electing Out Of Spousal Rollover

10-18. While the ITA 73(1) rollover automatically applies to spousal rollovers, the taxpayer can elect out of this approach if he wishes to recognize capital gains or recapture at the time of the transfer. For example, if the transferor incurred capital losses during the current year, he might wish to recognize capital gains so that these amounts could be deducted during the current year. Note, however, if the taxpayer elects out of ITA 73(1), ITA 69 becomes applicable. This means that, in these situations, care should be taken to ensure that the transfer is either a gift or is made in return for consideration equal to the fair market value of the property. If this is not done, the ITA 69 provisions will result in double taxation as was discussed previously.

10-19. ITA 73(1) uses the phrase "elects in his return of income". This means that, if the taxpayer wishes to avoid the normal application of ITA 73(1), the only required action is to include the income resulting from the transfer in his return of income in the year of disposition.

> **Example Continued** In the preceding example, the wife could have elected to record the land transaction at the fair market value of $250,000, resulting in a $150,000 capital gain being recorded at the time of transfer. In this case, the adjusted cost base to her husband would be $250,000. The election would be made by simply including the taxable portion of the $150,000 gain in the wife's tax return.

10-20. You might note at this point that, when a phrase such as "elects in his return of income" is used, no official tax form is required to make the election. In contrast, if an official form is required, a phrase such as "elects in the prescribed manner" will be used. For example, at a later point in this Chapter, we will find that an individual departing from Canada can elect to have all of his property treated as taxable Canadian property. The relevant legislation for making this election, ITA 128.1(4)(b)(iv), uses the phrase "elects in prescribed manner" meaning an official form is required to make the election.

Farm Property To A Child

10-21. ITA 73(3) and (4) provide for inter vivos transfers of farm property, including unincorporated farms, farm corporations and farm partnerships, to a child on a tax free basis. As was the case with ITA 73(1), the provisions of ITA 73(3) and (4) take precedence over the provisions of ITA 69. For purposes of this Section, "child" refers to children and their spouses, grandchildren, great grandchildren, and any other person that prior to their attaining the age of 19 were dependent on the taxpayer and under his custody or control. To qualify, the child must be a resident of Canada at the time of the transfer. In addition, the property must be in use in a farming business operated by the taxpayer, the taxpayer's spouse, or any of their children.

10-22. The transfer is deemed to have taken place at the actual proceeds of disposition, restricted by floor and ceiling amounts. For depreciable property, the floor is the property's UCC while the ceiling is its fair market value. For non depreciable property, including shares in a farm corporation, the floor is the adjusted cost base while the ceiling is fair market value. If the transfer is made to a child who disposes of the property before reaching 18, all capital gains, both those existing at transfer and those accruing subsequently, are attributed back to the transferor. To illustrate the transfer values, assume that a farm consists of land with an adjusted cost base of $200,000 and a fair market value of $350,000 and depreciable assets with a UCC of $400,000, a capital cost of $550,000, and a fair market value of $675,000. If the properties were transferred to a child, the appropriate treatment would be as follows:

Land　If the transfer is for proceeds of disposition below $200,000 (this includes gifts), the deemed proceeds of disposition and adjusted cost base to the child would be $200,000. If the transfer is for an amount in excess of $350,000, the deemed proceeds of disposition and adjusted cost base to the child would be limited to $350,000. For transfers between $200,000 and $350,000, the actual proceeds of disposition would be used.

Depreciable Property　For transfers below $400,000, the deemed proceeds of disposition and transfer price to the child would be $400,000. Correspondingly, for transfers above $675,000, the deemed proceeds of disposition and adjusted cost base to the child would be $675,000. For transfers between $400,000 and $675,000, the actual proceeds of disposition would be used. Note, that when the transfer price for the child is less than the taxpayer's capital cost of $550,000, the difference is deemed to be CCA taken by the child. This means that the $550,000 value will be retained as the capital cost to the child, and that this value will be used to determine capital gains or recapture on any subsequent disposition by the child.

Income Attribution

The Problem

10-23. In the general discussion of tax planning in Chapter 3, it was noted that income splitting can be the most powerful tool available to individuals wishing to reduce their tax burden. The basic goal is to redistribute income from an individual in a high tax bracket to related individuals, usually a spouse or children, in lower tax brackets. When such redistribution can be achieved, it can produce very dramatic reductions in the aggregate tax liability of the family unit.

10-24. It is obvious that, if there were no restrictions associated with transfers of property to related persons, there would be little standing in the way of a complete equalization of tax rates within a family unit and the achievement of maximum income splitting benefits. For many years, it has been the policy of the Government to limit access to the tax benefits of income splitting and, as a consequence, we have a group of legislative provisions which are commonly referred to as the income attribution rules.

Basic Rules

Applicable Individuals

10-25. The income tax application rules are applicable to situations where an individual has transferred capital property to:

- a spouse [ITA 74.1(1)]; or
- an individual who is under the age of 18 and does not deal with the individual at arm's length [ITA 74.1(2)].

10-26.   Note that the rules are applicable, not just to children or grandchildren under the age of 18, but to any non arm's length individual who is under the age of 18, except nieces and nephews.

10-27.   The general idea here is that, unless certain conditions are met, income associated with holding or disposing of a transferred property may be attributed back to the transferor of the property (i.e., included in the Net Income For Tax Purposes of the transferor).

Types Of Income

10-28.   There are two types of income that may be attributed back under these rules. The first type would be property income while the capital property is held by the transferee. This would include interest, dividends, rents, and royalties. This type of income is attributed back to the transferor without regard to whether the transferee is a spouse or a related individual under the age of 18.

10-29.   The second type of income that may be subject to the attribution rules is capital gains resulting from a disposition of the transferred property. Whether or not this type of income is subject to the attribution rules will depend on the relationship of the transferee to the transferor:

Transferee Is A Spouse   When property is transferred to a spouse, the application of ITA 73(1) generally means that the property is transferred at the transferor's tax cost, with no taxation at the time of transfer. This means that the transferred property will be recorded at the adjusted cost base value for non depreciable assets and at UCC for depreciable assets. Given this, it seems logical that any capital gain or recaptured CCA on a subsequent sale by the spouse would be measured from that tax cost and attributed back to the transferor. This approach is, in fact, required under ITA 74.2(1).

Transferee Is A Related Individual Under 18   There is no rollover provision for related minors that corresponds to ITA 73(1) for a spouse. This means that when property is transferred to a related minor, the transfer will normally take place at the fair market value of the property, resulting in the transferor recognizing any capital gains or recaptured CCA that have accrued to the time of transfer. Reflecting this fact, any gain on a subsequent sale by the related minor would be measured using the fair market value at the time of transfer. Further, such gains are not attributed back to the transferor but are taxed in the hands of the related minor.

10-30.   Note that some capital property may earn business income while it is held (e.g., profits resulting from the sale of goods or services). This type of income is not attributed back to the transferor.

Applicable Transfers

10-31.   The basic idea behind the income attribution rules is to restrict an individual's ability to simply give a source of income to a related individual for income splitting purposes. Avoiding these rules for transfers to related minors is a fairly simple process:

Transfers To Related Minors   In this case, ITA 74.5(1)(a) indicates that the income attribution rules are not applicable if the related minor provides, from his own resources, consideration equal to the fair market value of the asset transferred. ITA 74.5(1)(b) indicates that where such consideration includes debt payable by the related minor, it is acceptable only if it requires interest based on the prescribed rate at the time of the transfer.

10-32.   The avoidance of the income attribution rules on transfers to a spouse is complicated by the presence of ITA 73(1):

Transfers To A Spouse   The provisions of ITA 74.5(1)(a) provides that the income attribution rules are not applicable if the spouse provides, from his/her own resources, consideration equal to the fair market value of the asset transferred. ITA 74.5(1)(b) indicates that where such consideration includes debt payable by the related spouse, it is acceptable only if it requires interest based on the prescribed rate at the time of the transfer.

In addition, in the case of transfers to a spouse, ITA 74.5(1)(c) indicates that avoidance of the attribution rules requires that the transferor must elect out of ITA 73(1) by including any gain on the transfer in his/her income tax return for the year of transfer.

The wording of ITA 74.5(1) is such that, in order for an individual making a transfer to a spouse to avoid the income attribution rules, that individual must elect out of ITA 73(1) and transfer the property for consideration equal to fair market value.

Consider a situation in which John Doan has a capital property with an adjusted cost base of $100,000 and a fair market value of $150,000. If he sells this property to his spouse for consideration equal to the fair market value of $150,000, the income attribution rules will apply unless he elects out of ITA 73(1) by recognizing the $50,000 capital gain in his income. Note that, if he fails to elect out of ITA 73(1), the adjusted cost base to his spouse will be John's adjusted cost base of $100,000, not the price she paid of $150,000. This means that any capital gains attribution will be measured from this $100,000 value.

Alternatively, if he gifts the property to his spouse and elects out of ITA 73(1) by recording a $50,000 capital gain, the income attribution rules will apply because she did not give consideration equal to $150,000. Note that, in this case, because ITA 69 applies to spousal transfers when the transferor elects out of ITA 73(1), any subsequent capital gain attribution would be measured from the $150,000 fair market value at the time of transfer.

10-33.   The following example will illustrate the provisions that we have just discussed.

Example   Mrs. Blaine owns a group of equity securities with an adjusted cost base of $200,000. On December 31, 2000 the fair market value of these securities is $300,000. On this date she gives one-half of the securities to her unemployed husband Mark and the other one-half to her five year old daughter Belinda.

Both Mark and Belinda hold the securities until December 31, 2001 at which point they are sold for a total of $350,000 ($175,000 each). During 2001, the securities paid $37,500 in dividends ($18,750 each to Mark and Belinda).

Transfer To Spouse   Assuming that Mrs. Blaine has not elected out of the ITA 73(1) rules, the transfer would take place at the adjusted cost base of $100,000 [(1/2)($200,000)] and she would not record a 2000 gain. However, the adjusted cost base of the shares to Mr. Blaine would be Mrs. Blaine's adjusted cost base of $100,000. This means that when Mr. Blaine sells the shares, the capital gain will be $75,000 ($175,000 - $100,000), all of which will be attributed back to Mrs. Blaine in 2001. In addition, the $18,750 in dividends received by Mr. Blaine in 2001 would also be attributed to Mrs. Blaine.

Transfer To Minor   As indicated previously, the rules for minors are somewhat different. In the absence of a rollover provision for minor children, the gift would be treated as a disposition at fair market value, resulting in a 2000 capital gain for Mrs. Blaine of $50,000 [(1/2)($300,000 - $200,000)]. Belinda's adjusted cost base for the shares would then be $150,000. When the shares are sold by Belinda, the additional capital gain of $25,000 ($175,000 - $150,000) would be taxed in the daughter's hands and would not be attributed back to Mrs. Blaine. The treatment of the dividends is the same as with Mr. Blaine, resulting in an additional $18,750 in dividends being attributed back to Mrs. Blaine for 2001.

10-34.   If either Mr. Blaine or Belinda reinvest the proceeds from selling the shares, dividend or interest income resulting from the reinvestment will also be attributed back to Mrs. Blaine. Any capital gains on new investments that are realized by Mr. Blaine will also be attributed back to Mrs. Blaine. This will not be the case with capital gains realized by Belinda. Note, however, that the compound earnings resulting from the reinvestment of the dividends received is not subject to the attribution rules.

Anti-Avoidance Provisions

10-35.   Given the attractiveness of income splitting, it is not surprising that tax planners have shown considerable ingenuity in devising procedures to avoid these attribution rules. It is equally unsurprising that the CCRA has continued to come up with new rules to deal with these procedures.

10-36.   Current legislation contains a number of provisions directed at preventing the use of indirect transfers, corporations, or trusts to circumvent the attribution rules. Complete coverage of these anti-avoidance rules is beyond the scope of this book. However, some of the more important anti-avoidance rules can be described as follows:

* Subsection 74.1(3) prevents the substitution of a new low rate or interest free loan for an existing commercial rate loan.

* Subsection 74.5(6) prevents a loan from being made to a person not subject to the attribution rules who then makes a similar loan to a person who would be subject to the attribution rules. The use of the intermediary would be disregarded and indirect attribution would apply.

* Subsection 74.5(7) prevents the use of loan guarantees to avoid the attribution rules. That is, a higher income spouse cannot get around the attribution rules by providing a guarantee on a low rate or interest free loan to a spouse.

* Sections 74.3 and 74.4 contain a variety of rules designed to prevent the avoidance of attribution rules through the use of a trust (74.3) or a corporation (74.4).

Tax Planning

10-37.   In recent years it has become increasingly difficult to avoid the income attribution rules. Further, many of the plans that are available for this purpose involve corporations and trusts and, for the purposes of this book, are too complex to be dealt with in detail. However, there are a number of relatively simple points that can be helpful:

Detailed Records   In order to have low income family members acquire investment income, it is necessary for them to have funds to invest. Having the higher income spouse pay for non deductible expenditures such as household expenses, clothing, vacations and the lower income spouse's income tax liability can help provide for this. Although tuition fees can be eligible for a tax credit (see Chapter 13), they do not have to be paid by the student to be eligible for the credit. It may be desirable to maintain separate bank accounts and relatively detailed records to ensure that it is clear the lower income family member's funds are being used for investment purposes.

Gifts To Spouses And Minors   If a spouse or minor child receives a gift or inheritance from a source to which attribution would not apply, the funds should be segregated for investment and, if possible, should not be used for such non deductible purposes as vacations, reducing the mortgage on the family home or purchases of personal effects.

New Businesses   When a new business is started, low income family members should be allowed to acquire an equity position, particularly if the capital requirements are small. Note, however, if the business experiences losses in its first years of operation, this may not be the best alternative.

Salaries To Family Members   When business income is earned in the family unit, or through a related corporation, the lower income spouse and any children should be paid reasonable salaries for any activity that can be justified as business related. Examples would include bookkeeping, filing and other clerical or administrative work.

Spousal RRSPs   As was discussed in Chapter 6, the spousal Registered Retirement Savings Plan is a readily available device for a limited amount of income splitting.

Loans   As noted previously, the prescribed rate is currently six percent. Given this rate, making a loan at this low prescribed rate with the proceeds to be reinvested at a higher rate may be a useful strategy.

Assets With Capital Gains Potential   As there is no attribution of capital gains on transfers to related minors, assets with capital gains potential should be given to children rather than to a spouse.

Income Attribution - Other Related Parties

10-38.   The applicability of the income attribution provisions that were discussed in the preceding Section is limited to transfers and loans to spouses and other related individuals under the age of 18 at the end of the taxation year. There is a further income attribution provision that applies to a broader group of individuals. This is found in ITA 56(4.1) and indicates that, if an interest free or low rate loan is made to a related party for the purpose of producing property income, the income can be attributed back to the individual making the loan. A further condition for this attribution is that one of the main reasons for making the loan is to reduce or avoid tax.

10-39.   The most important application of this provision is with loans made by parents to their adult children. For children 18 or over, the general income attribution rules do not apply. Although there are no tax consequences associated with cash gifts to adult children, parents interested in providing some financial assistance to their children can be reluctant to completely lose control over the resources involved. As an example, a parent might extend an interest free loan to an adult child to assist with the purchase of a property. If the child decides to live in the property, there is no attribution related to the interest free loan used to purchase the principal residence. However, if the child uses the property to produce rental income, this income can be attributed back to the parent making the loan.

10-40.   The tax planning conclusion in this situation is obvious. If a parent wishes to provide financial assistance to an adult child to earn property income, the appropriate route is to use an outright gift. While an interest free loan can accomplish the goal of providing financial assistance to the child, ITA 56(4.1) can eliminate the potential tax savings associated with this form of income splitting.

Tax On Split Income

10-41.   The 1999 budget introduced a new tax on split income, sometimes referred to a the "kiddy tax". As laid out in ITA 120.4, this tax is assessed at the top marginal rate on taxable dividends and other shareholder benefits on unlisted shares of Canadian and foreign companies, as well as on income from a partnership or trust where the income of the partnership or trust is derived from a business carried on by a relative. The specified types of split income will not be eligible for any deductions or credits other than related dividend tax credits and foreign tax credits. This change is expected to significantly reduce income splitting with related minors and it is discussed in Chapter 13, Taxes Payable For Individuals.

10-42.   This new tax has no direct effect on the income attribution rules. However, it is mentioned in this section as the budget proposals indicate that, if income is to be taxed under this new measure, it will not be subject to the income attribution rules. However, with the applicable tax on such income being assessed at the top marginal rate, removal of the attribution rules will not be of any great benefit to taxpayers.

Exercises Ten-4 through Ten-6 deal with income attribution. This would be an appropriate time to attempt these exercises.

Leaving Or Entering Canada

A Note On Legislation

10-43.   Since 1998, the government has been attempting to revise the rules related to tax-payer migration. Draft legislation has been released on several occasions, with the latest being the inclusion in the 2000 budget materials that were released on March 16, 2001. The material which follows will be based on information contained in the March 16, 2001 Notice of Ways and Means, with occasional references to earlier legislation.

Taxable Canadian Property

10-44.   We have previously encountered the concept of Taxable Canadian Property in Chapter 3. In our discussion of the liability for Canadian income tax, we noted that one of the instances in which non residents were subject to Canadian tax was when they disposed of a "taxable Canadian property". As a result, the tax effect of capital gains or losses arising on the disposition of Taxable Canadian Property is not changed by the taxpayer leaving or entering Canada.

10-45.   Taxable Canadian Property is defined in ITA 248. The main categories listed in that definition are as follows:

* real property situated in Canada;
* property used or held by the taxpayer in carrying on a business in Canada (including eligible capital property), or inventory of such a business;
* unlisted shares of Canadian resident corporations;
* unlisted shares of non resident corporations if, at any time during the preceding 60 month period, the fair market value of the company's Canadian real and resource properties made up more than half the fair market value of all of its properties;
* listed shares if, at any time during the preceding 60 month period, the taxpayer owned 25 percent or more of the issued shares of any class of stock;
* a partnership interest if, at any time in the preceding 60 month period, more than 50 percent of the partnership's value is attributable to Taxable Canadian Property.

10-46.   The actual definitions contained in ITA 248 are somewhat more complex than those presented here. However, the preceding will suffice for our purposes.

Entering Canada - Immigration
General Rules

10-47.   The rules related to entering Canada are found in ITA 128.1(1). ITA 128.1(1)(b) indicates that, with certain exceptions, a taxpayer is deemed to have disposed of all of their property immediately before entering Canada for proceeds equal to fair market value. ITA 128.1(1)(c) calls for a deemed re-acquisition of the property at the same fair market value figure. This process establishes a new cost basis for the taxpayer's property, as at the time of entering Canada. The goal here is to avoid having Canadian taxation apply to gains which accrued prior to the individual's immigration. For example, consider an individual entering Canada with securities which cost $100,000 and have a current fair market value of $150,000. In the absence of these deeming provisions, a subsequent sale of these securities would result in the $50,000 accrued gain being taxed in Canada, despite the fact that it accrued prior to the individual becoming a Canadian resident.

10-48.   The properties that are excluded from the deemed disposition/re-acquisition are listed in ITA 128.1(1)(b) and are essentially those properties that are already subject to tax in Canada. While there are some other more technical items, the basic exclusion is for Taxable Canadian Property as defined in ITA 248.

Departures From Canada - Emigration
Problem With The Current System

10-49.   Taxpayer emigration is a problem area for those in charge of Canadian tax policy. To begin, Canada is significantly out of line with all of its trading partners in the manner in which it deals with the accrued capital gains of emigrants. As an illustration of this problem, consider an individual who departs from Canada at a time when he owns capital assets with an adjusted cost base of $80,000 and a fair market value of $120,000. On departure from Canada, this individual will be deemed to have disposed of these assets at their fair market value of $120,000, resulting in an assessment for a capital gain of $40,000. In the great majority of other countries, in particular the United States, this would not occur. The individual could leave the country, taking the capital assets to a new country of residence, without incurring any taxation in his former country of residence. It would be assumed that, when the assets are ultimately disposed of, all of the gain on the assets will be taxed in the new country of residence. This situation clearly raises the possibility of double taxation for individuals emigrating from Canada.

10-50. A further problem in this area is the ability of some taxpayers to avoid the Canadian emigration tax rules, resulting in large sums of money being removed from Canada on a tax free basis. Some types of assets can be removed tax free on the assumption that they will be subject to Canadian taxation at a later point in time. This might not happen if one of Canada's bilateral tax treaties prohibits Canadian taxation after an individual has been a non resident for a specified period of time. Other leakages can occur when assets are bumped up in value for foreign tax purposes, with no corresponding change in the Canadian tax base. This is essentially what happened in the Bronfman trust case in which several billion dollars in assets were removed from Canada without being subject to Canadian income taxes.

10-51. As noted in Paragraph 10-43, new legislation has been introduced to deal with some of these problems. It will be the basis for the discussion which follows and, when the legislation is passed, it will be effective from October 1, 1996.

Deemed Disposition On Leaving Canada

10-52. When a taxpayer leaves Canada, ITA 128.1(4)(b) calls for a deemed disposition of all property owned at the time of departure. The disposition is deemed to occur at fair market value. If the taxpayer is an individual, certain types of property are exempted from this deemed disposition rule. The major categories of exempted property are as follows:

- Real property situated in Canada, Canadian resource properties, and timber resource properties.
- Property of a business carried on in Canada through a permanent establishment. This would include capital property, eligible capital property, and inventories.
- "Excluded Right or Interest" - This concept is defined in ITA 128.1(10). The definition includes registered pension plan balances, registered retirement savings plan balances, deferred profit sharing plan balances, stock options, death benefits, retiring allowances, as well as other rights of individuals in trusts or other similar arrangements.

10-53. This list of exempted property is significantly different than the previous legislation which simply exempted Taxable Canadian Property. Without going into a detailed analysis, the major difference is the fact that the designation Taxable Canadian Property included shares of private companies, an asset that is no longer included in the exempted list. This means that a departure from Canada will now trigger taxation on gains that have accrued on the shares of Canadian controlled private companies owned by an emigrant.

Elective Dispositions

10-54. As noted in the preceding Paragraphs, certain types of property are exempted from the ITA 128.1(4)(b) deemed disposition rules. There may, however, be circumstances in which an individual wishes to override these exemptions and trigger capital gains at the time of departure. Under the old rules, which exempted shares of unlisted companies, the most important example of this was situations in which the lifetime capital gains deduction was available on shares of a qualified small business corporation. The new legislation does not exempt unlisted shares from the deemed disposition rules and, as a consequence, no election is required in these circumstances.

10-55. However, an individual may still wish to trigger capital gains on the exempted property at the time of departure for other reasons. An example of this would be an immigrant who wants to realize a loss on exempt property in order to offset a gain on non exempt property. This situation in provided for in ITA 128.1(4)(d) which allows an individual to elect to have a deemed disposition on certain of the properties that are exempted from the general deemed disposition rule. The properties on which the election can be made include real property situated in Canada, Canadian resource and timber resource properties, as well as property of a business carried on in Canada through a permanent establishment. Note that, if this election results in losses, they can only be used to offset gains resulting from other deemed dispositions. They cannot be applied against other sources of income, including capital gains, for the taxation year.

Stock Options

10-56. There are new rules related to the treatment of stock options at the time of emigration. You may recall from Chapter 5 that the increasing complexity of the rules related to stock option arrangements led us to conclude that this subject should be covered in Chapter 12. Consistent with that decision, the stock option rules that related to emigration will also be deferred to be included in our comprehensive treatment of stock options in Chapter 12.

Security For Departure Tax

10-57. The preceding deemed disposition rules can be very burdensome for an emigrating individual. If that individual has substantial amounts of property on which gains have accrued, the deemed disposition rule can result in an enormous tax bill. This is further complicated by the fact that there are no real dispositions to provide funds for paying this assessment.

10-58. In recognition of this problem, new subsections 220 (4.5) through (4.54) allow the taxpayer to provide security in lieu of paying the tax that results from the application of ITA 128.1(4)(b). Similar provisions have been added as ITA 220(4.6) through (4.63) for dealing with trusts distributing Taxable Canadian Property to non residents.

10-59. ITA 220(4.5) requires the Minister Of National Revenue to accept "adequate security". While the exact meaning of this phrase is not entirely clear, it is understood that, in the case of a gain on shares, the Minister will not exclude the possibility of accepting some or all of the shares as security.

10-60. If the taxpayer elects under ITA 220(4.5), interest does not accrue on the tax that has been deferred until such time as the amount becomes unsecured. This will usually be at the time when there is an actual disposition of the property which was subject to the deemed disposition.

10-61. A final point here is that ITA 220(4.5) creates deemed security on an amount that is the total amount of taxes under Parts I and I.1 that would be payable, at the highest tax rate that applies to individuals, on taxable income of $50,000. This amount is one-half of a $100,000 capital gain and the effect of this provision is to exempt emigrants from the requirement to provide security on the first $100,000 in capital gains resulting from their departure.

Unwinding The Deemed Disposition

10-62. A potential problem can arise when an individual departs from Canada and, at a later point in time, returns. A simple example will serve to illustrate this difficulty:

Example John Fuller emigrates from Canada on June 1, 2001. At that time he owns shares of a private company with a fair market value of $200,000 and an adjusted cost base of $125,000. As a result of the deemed disposition/re-acquisition of these shares, he has a taxable capital gain of $37,500 [(1/2)($200,000 - $125,000)]. In 2003, he returns to Canada. At the time of immigration, he still owns the shares and they have a fair market value of $260,000.

10-63. In the absence of any special provision, Mr. Fuller's departure from Canada would cost him the taxes paid on the $37,500 taxable capital gain arising on the deemed disposition at emigration. While on his return, the adjusted cost base of his property has been increased to $200,000, the fact remains that his temporary absence has resulted in an out-of-pocket tax cost on a $37,500 taxable capital gain.

10-64.   A new ITA 128.1(6) provides relief from this type of situation. With respect to Taxable Canadian Property such as Mr. Fuller's, ITA 128.1(6)(a) allows a returning individual to make an election with respect to property that was Taxable Canadian Property at the time of emigration. The effect of making this election is that the deemed disposition that was required under ITA 128.1(b) at the time of departure, is reversed when the individual returns to Canada. Returning to our example from Paragraph 10-62, if this election is made, the tax that was assessed when Mr. Fuller left Canada would be reversed through an amended return and, as there was no disposition at the time of emigration, there would be no need for a disposition/re-acquisition when he returns to Canada. This means that after the appropriate election and amended return are filed, Mr. Fuller would wind up in the same tax position as when he departed from Canada. That is, he would own securities with an adjusted cost base of $125,000 and no net taxes paid as a result of his departure and return.

10-65.   There are several points relevant to the provisions in the new ITA 128.1(6):

- As there is no real basis for establishing whether an emigrant will eventually return as an immigrant, ITA 128.1(6) has no influence on the tax consequences resulting at the time of emigration.
- ITA 128.1(6)(b) contains a fairly complex provision related to situations in which dividends are paid on shares while the individual is absent from Canada. Coverage of this topic goes beyond the scope of this text.
- ITA 128.1(6)(c) contains a further provision dealing with property other than Taxable Canadian Property. This includes an election which allows the emigrant to partially reverse the tax effects resulting from his deemed disposition on departure. Coverage of this topic goes beyond the scope of this text.
- ITA 128.1(7) contains a provision which deals with situations where there is a loss on the property while the individual is absent from Canada. Once again, coverage of this topic goes beyond the scope of this text.

Short Term Residents

10-66.   With the increasing presence of multinational firms in the Canadian business environment, it has become common for executives and other employees to find themselves resident in Canada for only a small portion of their total working lives. In the absence of some special provision, the deemed disposition rules could be a significant hardship to employees who are in this position. For example, if Ms. Eng was transferred from Hong Kong to work in Canada for three years, she could become liable on departure for capital gains taxation on all of her capital property owned at the time that she ceases to be a resident of Canada. The liability could put a severe drain on her available liquid assets and could result in taxation on personal items such as paintings and furniture. This would not be an equitable situation and could discourage the free movement of employees to and from Canada.

10-67.   In recognition of the preceding problem, ITA 128.1(4)(b)(v) provides special rules for short term residents. The rules apply to taxpayers who, during the ten years preceding departure, have been resident in Canada for a total of 60 months or less. For such taxpayers, the deemed disposition rules do not apply to any property that was owned immediately before the taxpayer last became resident in Canada or was acquired by inheritance or bequest during the period after he last became resident in Canada. However, the rules still apply to property acquired other than by inheritance or bequest during the period of residency.

> Exercises Ten-7 through Ten-8 deal with taxpayer emigration. This would be an appropriate time to attempt these exercises.

Death Of A Taxpayer

Representation

10-68.   The deceased do not, of course, file tax returns. However, a considerable amount of filing and other tax work may need to be done by the legal representative of the deceased. This legal representative may be an executor. This is an individual appointed in the will to act as the legal representative of the deceased in handling his estate. In the absence of a will, or in situations where an executor is not appointed in the will, a court will generally appoint an administrator as legal representative of the deceased. This administrator will normally be the spouse or next of kin of the deceased.

10-69.   With respect to the *Income Tax Act*, the basic responsibilities of the legal representative of an estate are as follows:

- filing all necessary tax returns;
- paying all taxes owing;
- obtaining a clearance certificate from the CCRA for all tax years before property under his control is distributed to the beneficiaries (a failure to do this can result in personal liability for taxes owing); and
- advising beneficiaries of the income from the estate that will be taxable in their hands.

10-70.   In order to deal with the CCRA in these matters, the legal representative will have to provide a copy of the deceased person's death certificate, as well as a copy of the will or other document identifying him as the legal representative of the deceased. Without this documentation, the CCRA will not provide any of the deceased person's income tax information.

Deemed Disposition Of Capital Property
General Rules
10-71.   ITA 70(5) provides the following general rules for capital property of a deceased taxpayer:

Capital Property Other Than Depreciable Property   The deceased taxpayer is deemed to have disposed of the property at fair market value immediately before his death. The person receiving the property is deemed to have acquired the property at this time at a value equal to its fair market value.

Depreciable Property   The basic rules for this type of property are the same. That is there is a disposition of the property by the deceased taxpayer at fair market value, combined with an acquisition of the property at the same value by the beneficiary. When the capital cost of the property in the hands of the deceased exceeds this fair market value, the beneficiary is required to retain the original capital cost, with the difference being treated as deemed CCA.

10-72.   A simple example will serve to illustrate the rule for depreciable property:

Example   Eric Nadon dies leaving a depreciable property to his son that has a capital cost of $100,000, a fair market value of $60,000, and a UCC of $50,000.

Tax Consequences   Under ITA 70(5), the transfer will take place at the fair market value of $60,000. This means that Mr. Nadon's final tax return will include recaptured CCA of $10,000 ($60,000 - $50,000). While the son's UCC will be the $60,000 transfer price, the capital cost of the asset will remain at Mr. Nadon's old value of $100,000. This means that, if the asset is later sold for a value between $60,000 and $100,000, the resulting gain will be treated as recaptured CCA, rather than as a more favourably taxed capital gain.

10-73.   The transfer of non capital property (i.e., property not used to produce income) at the time of death has no federal tax implications. This reflects the fact that items such as cash or term deposits represent after tax amounts of funds which should not be taxed a second time. Note, however, that the taxpayer's final tax return will have to include any amounts of income that have been earned in the taxation year prior to the date of death.

Rollover To A Spouse Or A Spousal Trust
10-74.   ITA 70(6) provides an exception to the general rules contained in ITA 70(5) in situations where the transfer is to a spouse or a spousal trust. This is a rollover provision which allows the transfer of non depreciable property at its adjusted cost base and depreciable property at its UCC. This means that the transfer does not generate a capital gain or loss or recapture and that the surviving spouse will assume the same property values as those carried by

the deceased. This has the effect of deferring any capital gains or recapture until the surviving spouse disposes of the property or dies.

10-75.   It is possible for the legal representative of the deceased to elect in the final return to have one or all asset transfers take place at fair market value. This election could be used to take advantage of charitable donations, medical expenses, unused loss carry forwards, and, in the case of qualified farm property or the shares of a qualified small business corporation, an unused lifetime capital gains deduction.

10-76.   To qualify as a spousal trust, ITA 70(6) indicates that the spouse must be entitled to receive all of the income of the trust that arises before the death of the surviving spouse. In addition, no person other than the spouse may, prior to the death of this spouse, receive the use of any of the income or capital of the trust.

10-77.   There are at least two advantages to using a spousal trust. First, this arrangement allows the deceased to determine the ultimate disposition of any property. For example, if after his death, Mr. Hall wishes his property to go only to his children, this can be specified in the trust arrangement and avoid the possibility that property could be redirected to any additional children that his wife might have on remarrying, or to her new husband. In addition, a spousal trust can also provide for the administration of the assets of the deceased in those situations where the surviving spouse is not experienced in business or financial matters.

Tax Free Transfers Other Than To A Spouse

10-78.   As we have seen, the most common situation in which capital property can be transferred at the time of death on a tax free basis is when the transfer is to a spouse or a spousal trust. However, ITA 70 provides for other tax free transfers involving specific types of farm assets. These are similar to the inter vivos transfers of farm property to a child which were previously covered. For each of the following types of transfers, the legal representatives of the deceased can elect to transfer the property at any value between its adjusted cost base and its fair market value. These elections can be used to utilize any accumulated losses of the deceased, or any unused lifetime capital gains deduction.

- **Farm Property**   When farm property has been used by a taxpayer or the taxpayer's family, it can be transferred on a tax free basis to a resident child, grandchild, or great grandchild at the time of the taxpayer's death. These provisions can also be used to transfer farm property from a child to a parent in situations where the child dies before the parent.

- **Family Farm Corporation**   A family farm corporation can be transferred on a tax free basis to a resident child, grandchild, or great grandchild at the time of a taxpayer's death. It is possible to have tax free transfers of farm corporation shares from a child to a parent and, in addition, the rules provide for the rollover of shares in a family farm holding company.

- **Family Farm Partnerships**   Rules similar to those described in the two preceding situations allow for the tax free transfer of family farm partnerships to resident children at the time of the taxpayer's death.

Filing Returns

Multiple Returns

10-79.   Filing the appropriate tax returns in the most advantageous manner for a deceased taxpayer can be complicated as there are a number of exceptions to the normal rules as well as special rules for final returns. As we have not yet covered some of the topics, such as personal credits, medical expenses and charitable donations, this material may not be fully understood at this point. In some situations, more than one return will be filed on behalf of a deceased individual. Some of these are required by the ordinary provisions of the *Income Tax Act*. Other returns can be filed on the basis of an election and may or may not be filed in particular cases. The potential returns and their deadlines can be described as follows:

- **Prior Year Return** As discussed in Chapter 2, if an individual dies between January 1 and his usual filing date for the preceding year, he will often not have filed his tax return for the preceding year. In this situation, the filing deadline for the preceding year is the later of six months after the date of death, or the due date of the return (April 30 or, if the individual or his spouse has business income, June 15). For example, if a taxpayer died on January 10, 2001, his representative would have until July 10, 2001 to file his 2000 tax return.

- **Ordinary Return - Year Of Death** The ordinary return for the year of death, also referred to as the final or terminal return, will be due on April 30 or June 15 of the subsequent year. However, if the death occurs between November 1 and December 31 of the current year, the deceased taxpayer's representative has until the later of the normal filing date and six months after the date of death to file the current year's return. For example, if a taxpayer died on December 1, 2000 and his normal filing date was April 30, his representative would have until June 1, 2001 to file his 2000 tax return. Alternatively, if his return contained business income, his normal filing date of June 15, 2001 would be applicable.

- **Elective Return - Rights Or Things** Under ITA 70(2), this special return is due the later of one year from the date of death or 90 days after the mailing date of the notice of assessment of the final return. (See subsequent section which explains rights and things.)

- **Elective Return - Unincorporated Business** If the deceased had business income from a partnership or proprietorship with a non calendar fiscal year, his death creates a deemed year end for the business. If the death occurred after the fiscal year end, but before the end of the calendar year in which the fiscal period ended, the representative of the deceased can elect to file a separate return for the income earned by the business between the end of the fiscal year and the date of death. This allows the legal representative to choose to limit the business income (or loss) reported in the final return to that related to only 12 months. The filing deadline is the same as the one applicable to the final return.

- **Elective Return - Testamentary Trust Beneficiary** Under ITA 104(23)(d), if the deceased is an income beneficiary of a testamentary trust, the representative may elect to file a separate return for the period between the end of the trust's fiscal year and the date of the taxpayer's death. The filing deadline is the same as the one applicable to the final return.

- **Amended Prior Year Return** Under ITA 111(2), a deceased taxpayer is allowed to deduct unused capital losses against other sources of income in the year of death and the immediately preceding year. Charitable donations can also be carried back to the preceding year if not needed on the final return. If either item is applied to the preceding year, the prior year's return should be amended.

10-80. There are two basic reasons for filing as many tax returns as possible. The first relates to the fact that the income tax rates are progressive and income starts at nil in each return. This means that the first $30,754 in each return has the advantage of being taxed at the lowest federal rate of 16 percent. If multiple returns are not filed, there may be amounts taxed at the higher rates of 22, 26, or 29 percent that would have been eligible for this lower rate if multiple returns had been filed.

10-81. The second advantage of filing multiple returns is that some personal tax credits can be deducted in each return. As will be discussed in the next section, this could save the deceased taxpayer's estate more than $4,000 for each tax return filed.

Deductions And Credits

10-82. As noted in the preceding section, one of the major advantages of being able to file multiple returns is that some personal tax credits can be used in all returns filed (these various tax credits are discussed more fully in Chapter 13). More specifically, the following non refundable credits can be claimed in each of the tax returns filed:

- basic personal amount [$1,186 (16%)($7,412) for 2001]
- age [$579 (16%)($3,619) for 2001]
- spousal or equivalent to spouse amount [$1,007 (16%)($6,294) for 2001]
- amounts for infirm dependents [$560 (16%)($3,500) for 2001]

10-83.   The combined value of these federal tax credits is $3,332. When combined with similar credits in the various provinces, the total value is between $4,000 and $5,000. This represents a significant tax savings that becomes available in each tax return filed. Achieving these savings is, of course, conditional on each of the individual returns having sufficient taxes payable to make use of the credits.

10-84.   Other non refundable credits can be split between or deducted in full in any of the returns filed. However, the total claimed cannot exceed the amount that would be included in the ordinary return for the year of death. These credits include the following:

- disability amount for the deceased person
- disability amount for a dependant other than a spouse
- interest paid on certain student loans
- tuition fees and education amount for the deceased person
- tuition fees and education amount transferred from a child
- medical expenses (note that the total expenses must be reduced by the lesser of $1,637 and 3 percent of the net income shown in all returns)
- charitable donations including amounts gifted in will (limited to 100 percent of net income)
- cultural, ecological and government (to Canada or a province) gifts

10-85.   With respect to the following deductions and non refundable credits, they can only be claimed in the return in which the related income is reported:

- registered pension plan deduction
- registered retirement savings plan deduction
- annual union or professional dues
- other employment expenses
- Canada or Quebec Pension Plan contributions credit
- Employment Insurance premiums credit
- pension income credit
- employee home relocation loan deduction
- stock option deduction
- social benefits repayment (clawback)

10-86.   Finally, there is a group of deductions and non refundable credits which can only be claimed in the deceased's ordinary return. These include the following:

- amounts transferred from a spouse
- child care expenses
- attendant care expenses
- business investment losses
- moving expenses
- support payments made
- losses from other years
- capital gains deduction
- northern residents deduction
- caregiver amount

Ordinary Return(s)

10-87.   As noted previously, the legal representative of the deceased will be responsible for filing a return for the year of death and, in some cases, a return for the previous year. This return would contain the usual sources of income including employment income, business income, property income, and taxable capital gains. With respect to employment income, it would include salary or wages from the end of the last pay period to the date of death.

10-88. For example, if the last pay period is May 16 through 31, the payment date for this period is June 5, and the taxpayer dies on June 4, the accrual for the period June 1 through June 4 would be included in the ordinary return. In contrast, salary or wages for a pay period completed before the date of death but paid after death can either be included in this return or, alternatively, included in a separate return for rights or things. In the preceding example, the May 16 through 31 accrual could be included in a separate return for rights or things as described in the following material.

Rights Or Things Return

10-89. Rights or things are defined as unpaid amounts that would have been included in the deceased's income when they were realized or disposed of, had the taxpayer not died. Included would be unpaid salaries, commissions, and vacation pay for pay periods completed before the date of death. Also included would be:

- uncashed matured bond coupons
- interest accrued before the most recent payment date
- harvested farm crops and livestock on hand
- inventory and accounts receivable of taxpayers using the cash method
- declared but unpaid dividends

10-90. While all of these amounts could be included in the ordinary return of the taxpayer, it is generally advisable to file this separate return as it permits a doubling up of certain tax credits and, in many cases, will result in additional amounts being taxed at the lowest federal rate.

10-91. As a final point, note that rights or things can be transferred to a beneficiary, provided this is done within the time limit for filing a separate rights or things return. If this election is made, the amounts will be included in the beneficiary's income when they are realized and should not be included in either the ordinary or the rights or things return of the deceased.

Other Elective Returns

10-92. None of the other elective returns warrant discussion beyond that previously provided. We would note, however, that it is normally advisable to file these returns, both for the additional credits that can be claimed and for the additional amounts that will be allocated to the lowest federal tax bracket.

Payment Of Taxes

10-93. Regardless of the extension of filing dates for the final and elective returns, the tax owing is due on April 30 of the year following the year of death unless the death occurs between November 1 and December 31. If this is the case, the due date for the payment of taxes is six months after the date of death.

10-94. With respect to income from the value of rights or things and from deemed dispositions of capital property at death, the legal representative for the deceased individual can elect to defer taxes payable. Under ITA 159(5), payment can be made in ten equal annual instalments, with the first payment due on the regular payment due date of the final return. Security acceptable to the Minister must be furnished to guarantee payment of the deferred taxes. Interest will be charged on amounts outstanding and, as is the usual case, such interest is not deductible.

Allowable Capital Losses

10-95. One of the difficulties with allowable capital losses is that, in general, they can only be deducted against taxable capital gains. As there is no time limit on the carry forward of such undeducted losses, an individual can die with a substantial balance of these amounts on hand. Losses may also arise in the year of death, either through a disposition prior to death or through a deemed disposition at death. ITA 111(2) contains a special provision with respect to both undeducted allowable capital losses from years prior to death and to additional amounts of such losses arising in the year of death. Essentially, this provision allows these accumulated losses to be applied against any type of income in the year of death or the immediately preceding year.

10-96. Two points should be noted with respect to the application of this provision. First, the ability to use this provision is reduced by the previous deduction of amounts under the lifetime capital gains provision. This reduction reflects the actual amount of the lifetime capital gains deduction made, without regard to the capital gains inclusion rate that was applicable at the time. (See Chapter 12 for coverage of the lifetime capital gains deduction.)

10-97. The second point is that, unlike the usual procedure with capital loss carry overs, this carry over deduction is applied at the capital gain/loss inclusion rate which prevailed in the year in which the capital loss was realized. To illustrate this provision, consider the following example:

> **Example** Ms. Vincent has an undeducted net capital loss of $22,500 [(3/4)($30,000)] which has been carried forward from 1990. She dies in December, 2001 and, as the result of a deemed disposition in June of that year, has a taxable capital gain of $4,500 [(1/2)($9,000)]. Under the provisions of the lifetime capital gains deduction, she has deducted $8,000 [(1/2)($16,000)] in 1987.

> **Tax Consequences** The amount of the 1990 carry forward, adjusted to the 1/2 inclusion rate, is $15,000 [(2/3)($22,500) or (1/2)($30,000)]. Of this amount, $4,500 will be deducted against the 2001 taxable capital gain. This will leave a balance of $10,500 which, in order to use the ITA 111(2) provision, must be adjusted back to the 3/4 inclusion rate for 1990. This will leave $15,750 [(3/2)($10,500)]. This can be verified using the 100 percent figures which gives the same $15,750 [(3/4)($30,000 - $9,000)] amount. The $8,000 lifetime capital gains deduction will be removed from this balance, leaving $7,750 which can be applied against any type of income in 2001. If there is not enough income to fully utilize the loss, it can be carried back to 2000 in an amended return. Note that the $8,000 amount is based on one-half of the gain and it is not adjusted for the fact that the $15,750 is based on a three-quarters inclusion.

10-98. Capital losses realized by the estate on disposals of an individual's property in the first year after his death can be included in the final tax return of the deceased. Note, however, that these losses cannot be carried back to the immediately preceding year.

Deferred Income Plans At Death

Matured RRSPs

10-99. A matured RRSP is one which has begun to pay income in the form of an annuity. The taxation of these payments will be determined by the identity of the beneficiary. The possible outcomes are as follows:

> **Spouse Is Beneficiary** If a surviving spouse is the beneficiary in the RRSP contract, the ongoing payments will be taxed in his or her hands.

> **Estate Is Beneficiary** If the estate, spouse, and legal representative jointly elect, the ongoing payments will be taxed in the hands of the surviving spouse. Otherwise, the commuted value (lump sum fair market value) of the remaining payments will be included in the deceased's income. However, the amount to be included can be reduced if some amount is payable from the estate to a surviving spouse or to a financially dependent child or grandchild.

> **Other Beneficiaries** In general, the commuted value (i.e., lump sum fair market value) of the payments will be included in the deceased's final return. However, the amount to be included can be reduced if a financially dependent child or grandchild is a beneficiary.

Unmatured RRSP

10-100. With unmatured RRSPs, the issue is, who will be taxed on the fair market value of the total assets in the plan at the time of the taxpayer's death? Here again, the taxation will be determined by the identity of the beneficiary. The possibilities are as follows:

Spouse Is Beneficiary   If a spouse is the beneficiary of the plan, the fair market value of the assets will be taxable in his or her hands. However, if the balance is transferred to an RRSP, a RRIF, or to an issuer to buy an eligible annuity, an offsetting deduction is available to the spouse. This, in effect, provides for a tax free rollover of an RRSP to a spouse at death.

Estate Is Beneficiary   In general, the fair market value of the assets will have to be included in the deceased taxpayer's income. However, the amount to be included can be reduced if some amount is payable from the estate to a surviving spouse or to a financially dependent child or grandchild.

Other Beneficiaries   In general, the fair market value of the assets will have to be included in the deceased taxpayer's income. However, the amount to be included can be reduced if a deceased taxpayer has a financially dependent child or grandchild as a beneficiary.

RRIFs

10-101. As with an unmatured RRSP, there is a tax sheltered group of assets in a RRIF and, in the absence of some alternative provision, the fair market value of these assets would be included in the deceased taxpayer's final tax return. Here again, there are alternative provisions for transfers to a spouse or a financially dependent child or grandchild. They can be described as follows:

Spouse Is RRIF Annuitant   If the surviving spouse receives the ongoing payments from the RRIF, the payments will be taxed in his or her hands.

Spouse Is RRIF Beneficiary   If all of the RRIF property is paid to the surviving spouse, it will be included in his or her income. In general, if this amount is transferred to an RRSP, a RRIF, or used to purchase an eligible annuity, the surviving spouse will have an offsetting deduction. This, in effect, provides for a tax free rollover of the RRIF balance.

Other Beneficiaries   In all other cases, including situations where the deceased's estate is the beneficiary, the fair market value of the RRIF property will be included in the deceased taxpayer's final return. The amount to be included can be reduced if a surviving spouse or a financially dependent child or grandchild is a beneficiary of the estate or a direct beneficiary of the RRIF.

Charitable Donations - Special Rules

10-102.   Charitable donations made in the year of death or through bequests in the will can be claimed for tax credit purposes subject to a limit of 100 percent of net income as opposed to the normal limit of 75 percent. Any charitable donations that are not claimed in the final return can be carried back to the immediately preceding year subject to the 100 percent of net income limit.

Exercises Ten-9 through Ten-10 deal with death of a taxpayer. This would be an appropriate time to attempt these exercises.

Medical Expenses - Special Rules

10-103.   Medical expenses paid can normally be claimed for any 12 month period ending in the year to the extent they exceed a threshold amount (see Chapter 13). In the year of death the time period is extended to the 24 month period prior to death.

References

10-104.   For more detailed study of the material in this Chapter, we would refer you to the following:

ITA 56(4.1)	Interest Free Or Low Interest Loans
ITA 69	Inadequate Considerations
ITA 70	Death Of A Taxpayer
ITA 73	Inter Vivos Transfer Of Property To Spouse, Etc., Or Trust
ITA 74.1	Transfers And Loans To Spouse And To Minors
ITA 74.2	Gain Or Loss Deemed That Of Lender Or Transferor
ITA 74.5	Transfers For Fair Market Consideration
ITA 128.1	Immigration
IC- 72-17R4	Procedures Concerning The Disposition Of Taxable Canadian Property By Non Residents Of Canada - Section 116
IT-209R	Inter Vivos Gifts Of Capital Property To Individuals Directly or Through Trusts
IT-210R2	Income Of Deceased Persons - Periodic Payments And Investment Tax Credits
IT-212R3	Income Of Deceased Persons - Rights Or Things
IT-226R	Gift To A Charity Of A Residual Interest In Real Property Or An Equitable Interest In A Trust
IT-268R4	Inter Vivos Transfer Of Farm Property To A Child
IT-278R2	Death Of A Partner Or Of A Retired Partner
IT-295R4	Taxable Dividends Received After 1987 By A Spouse
IT-325R2	Property Transfers After Separation, Divorce And Annulment
IT-326R3	Returns Of Deceased Persons As "Another Person"
IT-349R3	Intergenerational Transfers Of Farm Property On Death
IT-385R2	Disposition Of An Income Interest In A Trust
IT-405	Inadequate Considerations - Acquisitions And Dispositions
IT-419R	Meaning Of Arm's Length
IT-451R	Deemed Disposition And Acquisition On Ceasing To Be Or Becoming Resident In Canada
IT-490	Barter Transactions
IT-510	Transfers And Loans Of Property Made After May 22, 1985 To A Related Minor
IT-511R	Interspousal And Certain Other Transfers And Loans Of Property

Exercises

(The solutions for these exercises can be found following Chapter 21 of the text.)

Exercise Ten - 1 (Inadequate Consideration)
Mr. Cal Lipky owns a piece of land with an adjusted cost base of $100,000 and a fair market value of $75,000. He sells the land to his brother for $95,000. Determine the amount of capital gain or loss to be recorded by Mr. Lipky as a result of the sale to his brother, as well as the adjusted cost base of the land to his brother.

Exercise Ten - 2 (Inadequate Consideration)
Ms. Jennifer Lee owns a depreciable asset which she has used in her unincorporated business. It has a cost of $53,000 and a fair market value of $56,600. It is the only asset in its UCC class and the balance in the Class is $37,200. On October 1, 2001 Ms. Lee sells the asset to her father for $37,200. Determine the amount of income to be recorded by Ms. Lee as a result of the sale to her father, as well as the capital cost of the asset to her father.

Exercise Ten - 3 (Inadequate Consideration)
Mr. Ned Bates has land with an adjusted cost base of $33,000 and an unencumbered fair market value of $211,000. He leases this land to his wife for $3,300 per year for a period of 35 years. Similar leases are based on 10 percent of the value of the property and, as a consequence, the fair market value of the land with the lease in place falls to $33,000. He sells the land to a corporation controlled by his wife for this reduced value. Determine the amount of capital gain or loss to be recorded by Mr. Bates as a result of this sale, as well as the adjusted cost base of the land to the corporation.

Exercise Ten - 4 (Income Attribution)
On December 31, 2000, Ms. Norah Moreau gives shares with an adjusted cost base of $23,000 and a fair market value of $37,000 to her husband, Nick Moreau. On February 24, 2001, the shares pay dividends of $2,500 ($3,125 taxable amount) and, on August 31, 2001, Mr. Moreau sells the shares for $42,000. What are the tax consequences for Mr. and Mrs. Moreau for the 2000 and 2001 taxation years?

Exercise Ten - 5 (Income Attribution)
On December 31, 2000, Ms. Norah Moreau gives shares with an adjusted cost base of $23,000 and a fair market value of $37,000 to her 12 year old daughter, Nicki Moreau. On February 24, 2001, the shares pay dividends of $2,500 ($3,125 taxable amount) and, on August 31, 2001, Nicki sells the shares for $42,000. What are the tax consequences for Mrs. Moreau and Nicki for the 2000 and 2001 taxation years?

Exercise Ten - 6 (Income Attribution)
On December 31, 2000, Mr. Nadeem Bronski gives corporate bonds to his wife in exchange for a note with a face value of $122,000. The corporate bonds have an adjusted cost base of $115,000 and a fair market value of $122,000. The note from his wife does not pay interest and has no specific maturity date. During 2001, the bonds pay interest to Mrs. Bronski in the amount of $6,100. On October 1, 2001, immediately after an interest payment, Mrs. Bronski sells the bonds for $129,000. She uses $122,000 of the proceeds to pay off the loan to her husband. What are the tax consequences for both Mr. Bronski and Mrs. Bronski in the 2000 and 2001 taxation years?

Exercise Ten - 7 (Emigration)
Ms. Gloria Martell owns publicly traded securities with an adjusted cost base of $28,000 and a fair market value of $49,000. On April 21, 2001, she permanently departs from Canada. What would be the tax consequences of her departure with respect to these securities?

Exercise Ten - 8 (Emigration)
Mr. Harrison Chrysler owns a rental property in Nanaimo, B.C. with a capital cost of $190,000 and a fair market value of $295,000. The land values included in these figures are $45,000 and $62,000 respectively. The UCC of the building is $82,600. On December 31, 2001, Mr. Chrysler permanently departs from Canada. What are the tax consequences of his departure with respect to this rental property?

Exercise Ten - 9 (Death Of A Taxpayer)
Ms. Cheryl Lardner, who owns two trucks that were used in her business, dies in July, 2001. Her will transferred truck A to her husband Michel and truck B to her daughter Melinda. Each of the trucks cost $42,000 and had a fair market value at the time of her death of $33,000. The balance in the UCC Class for the trucks is $51,000. What are the tax consequences resulting from Ms. Lardner's death with respect to these two trucks? Your answer should include the capital cost and the UCC for the trucks in the hands of Michel and Melinda.

Exercise Ten - 10 (Death Of A Taxpayer)
Mr. Derek Barnes has an undeducted net capital loss from 1990 of $7,500 [(3/4)($10,000)]. He dies during June, 2001 and, as the result of a deemed disposition on death, he has a taxable capital gain of $2,000 [(1/2)($4,000)]. He has made no use of his lifetime capital gains deduction in any previous year. Describe the tax treatment of these two items in his final tax return.

Problems For Self Study

(The solutions for these problems can be found following Chapter 21 of the text.)

Self Study Problem Ten - 1
Mr. John Bolton owns 5,000 shares of Marker Manufacturing Ltd., a Canadian public company. These shares were purchased in 2000 at a price of $45 per share. On July 20, 2001, they are trading at $105 per share.

Consider the following four independent assumptions with respect to the transfer of these shares on July 20, 2001 to Mr. Alex Bolton, John's 35 year old brother:

Case A The 5,000 shares are sold to Alex Bolton at a price of $75 per share.

Case B The 5,000 shares are sold to Alex Bolton at a price of $125 per share.

Case C The 5,000 shares are sold to Alex Bolton at a price of $105 per share.

Case D The 5,000 shares are given to Alex Bolton as a gift.

Required: For each of these four cases, determine the effect on John Bolton's 2001 Taxable Income and the adjusted cost base that will apply for Alex Bolton on any future sale of the Marker Manufacturing Ltd. shares.

Self Study Problem Ten - 2
During 2001, Mr. Langdon makes a non interest bearing loan of $100,000 to his wife who acquires a $100,000 bond with the proceeds. He also makes a non interest bearing loan of $100,000 to both of his children:

• Pat, aged 15, who acquires a $100,000 bond, and

• Heather, aged 23, who uses the funds as a down payment on her principal residence. Without this loan she would have paid mortgage interest of $6,000 during the year.

During the year, both bonds pay interest of $5,000.

Required: Determine the amount of income that will be attributed to Mr. Langdon for the 2001 taxation year as the result of the non interest bearing loans.

Self Study Problem Ten - 3

Dr. Sandra Bolt is 49 years of age and an extremely successful physician in Halifax, Nova Scotia. She is married to Tod Bolt and has two children. On December 31, 2001, her son Dirk is 20 years old and her daughter Dolly is 15 years old. Each of the children earns about $10,000 per year in income from part time acting jobs. While her husband Tod qualified as a professional accountant, he did not enjoy the work and, for the last ten years, he has assumed the role of house parent. As a consequence, his only current source of income is the interest on $335,000 that he has in his personal savings account. This interest amounts to about $20,000 per year and all of the savings were accumulated from amounts that he earned while working as a professional accountant.

On December 28, 2001, Dr. Bolt is holding equity securities with an adjusted cost base of $185,000 and a fair market value of $225,000. She is considering transferring these securities to either her husband or to one of her two children. She seeks your advice as to the tax consequences, both to herself and to the transferee, that would result from such a transfer.

During your discussions, Dr. Bolt has indicated the following:

- The transfer will take place on December 31, 2001.
- Any proceeds she receives from her family on the share transfer will not be invested in income producing assets.
- She wishes you to assume that the securities would pay dividends during 2002 of $18,500 ($23,125 taxable amount) and that the transferee would sell the securities on January 1, 2003 for $260,000.

Required: Each of the following independent cases involves a transfer by Dr. Bolt to a member of her family. Indicate, with respect to the Net Income For Tax Purposes of both Dr. Bolt and the transferee, the 2001, 2002, and 2003 tax effects of the transfer, the assumed 2002 receipt of dividends, and the assumed 2003 disposition by the transferee. Note that some of the cases have been included to illustrate specific provisions of the relevant legislation and do not necessarily represent a reasonable course of action on the part of Dr. Bolt.

Case A   Dr. Bolt gives the securities to her husband and does not elect out of the provisions of ITA 73(1).

Case B   Dr. Bolt's husband uses money from his savings account to purchase the securities for their fair market value of $225,000. Dr. Bolt does not elect out of the provisions of ITA 73(1).

Case C   Dr. Bolt's husband uses money from his savings account to purchase the securities for their fair market value of $225,000. Dr. Bolt elects out of the provisions of ITA 73(1).

Case D   Dr. Bolt's husband uses money from his savings account to purchase the securities for $140,000. Dr. Bolt does not elect out of the provisions of ITA 73(1).

Case E   Dr. Bolt's husband uses money from his savings account to purchase the securities for $140,000. Dr. Bolt elects out of the provisions of ITA 73(1).

Case F   Dr. Bolt gives the securities to her daughter Dolly.

Case G   Dr. Bolt gives her daughter Dolly a $225,000 loan. The loan requires interest to be paid at commercial rates and Dolly uses the proceeds of the loan to purchase her mother's securities at fair market value. Dr. Bolt believes that the combination of dividends on the securities and Dolly's income from part time jobs will be sufficient to pay the interest on the loan.

Case H   Dr. Bolt gives her son Dirk a $225,000 interest free loan. Dirk uses the proceeds to purchase his mother's securities at their fair market value of $225,000.

Self Study Problem Ten - 4

Mrs. Sarah Long, a management consultant, is married with two children. Her son Barry is 27 years old and her daughter Mary is 13. Mrs. Long has not previously gifted or sold property to her husband or either of her children.

On April 1, 2001, Mrs. Long owns the following properties:

Long Consulting Ltd. Mrs. Long owns 100 percent of the voting shares of Long Consulting Ltd., a Canadian controlled private company. These shares have a cost of $210,000, and a current fair market value of $475,000.

Rental Property Mrs. Long owns a rental building which is located on leased land. The building was acquired at a cost of $190,000. On April 1, 2001, its undepreciated capital cost is $125,000 and its fair market value is estimated to be $275,000.

Dynamics Inc. Mrs. Long owns 4,000 shares of Dynamics Inc., a Canadian public company. These shares have a cost of $212,000, and a current fair market value of $384,000.

Farm Land Mrs. Long owns farm land with a cost of $80,000, and a current fair market value of $175,000. Mrs. Long's son Barry uses the farm land on a full time basis to grow various crops.

Mrs. Long is considering giving all or part of the properties to her spouse and/or her two children.

Required: You have been hired as a tax consultant to Mrs. Long. She would like a report which would detail, for each of the four properties, the tax consequences to her of making a gift of the item to her husband or to either of her children. Your report should include the resulting tax position of the beneficiary of the gift and some indication of the tax effects that might arise if the beneficiary later sold the gifted property for its current fair market value.

Self Study Problem Ten - 5

Mr. Howard Caswell is 67 years of age and his spouse Charlene is 58. They have one son John who is 36 years of age. On September 1, 2001, Mr. Howard Caswell owns the following properties:

Rental Property Mr. Caswell owns a rental building which is located on leased land. The building was acquired at a cost of $95,000. As at September 1, 2001, its undepreciated capital cost is $67,000 and its fair market value is estimated to be $133,000.

General Industries Ltd. Mr. Caswell owns 5,000 shares of General Industries Ltd., a Canadian public company. These shares have a cost of $200,000, and a current fair market value of $350,000. Mr. Caswell has never owned more than 3 percent of the outstanding shares of this Company.

Farm Land Mr. Caswell owns farm land with a cost of $325,000, and a current fair market value of $550,000. The land is farmed on a full time basis by Mr. Caswell's son, John.

Caswell Enterprises Mr. Caswell owns 100 percent of the voting shares of Caswell Enterprises, a Canadian controlled private company. The company was established with an investment of $275,000 and it is estimated that the current fair market value of the shares is $426,000.

Required: Explain the tax consequences that would result in each of the following Cases:

A. Mr. Caswell dies on September 1, 2001, leaving all of his property to his spouse Charlene.
B. Mr. Caswell dies on September 1, 2001, leaving all of his property to his son John.
C. Mr. Caswell departs from Canada and ceases to be a resident on September 1, 2001.

Assignment Problems

(The solutions for these problems are only available in
the solutions manual that has been provided to your instructor.)

Assignment Problem Ten - 1

In 1981, Mr. Lowrey established an unincorporated retail business which now operates in a number of cities in central and southern Alberta. In 2001, a series of health problems force Mr. Lowrey to retire from active participation in the business. In view of this situation he decides to sell the business to his younger brother for a consideration that includes a $562,000 payment for goodwill. An independent appraisal of the business indicates that the goodwill is actually worth $900,000.

Required: Describe the tax effects of the sale of goodwill for both Mr. Lowrey and his younger brother for the year ending December 31, 2001.

Assignment Problem Ten - 2

Ms. Carmen Bryers owns 1,000 shares of Karmac Distributing Company, a Canadian public company. These shares were purchased four years ago at a price of $20 per share. On December 31 of the current year they are trading at $80 per share.

Ms. Bryers transfers these shares on December 31 to Marcello Bryers, her 35 year old brother.

Required: For each of the following four cases, determine the effect on Carmen Bryers' Net Income For Tax Purposes for the current year and the adjusted cost base that will apply for Marcello Bryers on any future sale of the Karmac Distributing Company shares.

A. The 1,000 shares are sold to Marcello Bryers at a price of $60 per share.

B. The 1,000 shares are sold to Marcello Bryers at a price of $95 per share.

C. The 1,000 shares are sold to Marcello Bryers at a price of $80 per share.

D. The 1,000 shares are given to Marcello Bryers as a gift.

Assignment Problem Ten - 3

On February 1, 1998, Mrs. Morris used her own funds to acquire 10,000 shares of Merryweather Farms, a Canadian public company. The cost of these shares was $150,000 and Mrs. Morris holds the shares until August 31, 2001.

On August 31, 2001, Mrs. Morris gives 5,000 of the shares to her husband and 5,000 shares to her 15 year old daughter Martha. The fair market value of the shares at the time of the gift is $20 per share. Merryweather Farms declares taxable dividends of $1 per share on September 30, 2001 which are paid on October 15, 2001. On December 1, 2001, Mr. Morris sells his 5,000 shares at $22 per share and on December 15, 2001, Martha sells her 5,000 shares for $25 per share.

Required: Determine the total net income to be recorded for the 2001 taxation year by Mrs. Morris, her husband, and her daughter, on the preceding transactions.

Assignment Problem Ten - 4

Mr. Goodby, a self employed contractor, is married and has two children. His son Harry is 25 years old and his daughter Martha is 14. Mr. Goodby has not previously gifted or sold property to his spouse or either of his children.

At the end of the current year, Mr. Goodby owns the following property:

Farm land   Mr. Goodby owns farm land which cost $160,000 and has a current fair market value of $350,000. Mr. Goodby's son Harry uses the farm land on a full time basis to grow various crops.

DRC Ltd.   Mr. Goodby owns 5,000 shares of DRC Ltd., a Canadian public company. These shares have a cost of $320,000 and a current fair market value of $573,000.

Rental property   Mr. Goodby owns an apartment building which is located on leased land. The building was acquired at a cost of $256,000. At the end of the current year, its undepreciated capital cost is $178,000 and its fair market value is $386,000.

Goodby Construction Company   Mr. Goodby owns 100 percent of the voting shares of Goodby Construction Company, a Canadian controlled private company. These shares have a cost of $227,000 and a current fair market value of $452,000.

Mr. Goodby is in poor health and is considering giving all or part of the properties to his spouse and/or his two children. He has fully utilized his lifetime capital gains deduction.

Required: You have been hired as a tax consultant to Mr. Goodby. He would like a report which would detail, for each of the four properties, the tax consequences to him of making a gift of the item to his wife or to either one of his children. Your report should include the resulting tax position of the beneficiary of the gift and some indication of the tax effects that might arise if the beneficiary sold the gifted property for its current fair market value later in the year.

Assignment Problem Ten - 5

After an extensive period of marital counselling, Mr. and Mrs. Hadley agree to a separation in June of the current year. Mr. Hadley has owned two small rental properties for many years and these properties are still in his name at the time of the separation. On June 1 of the current year, Mr. Hadley agrees to transfer one of these properties to Mrs. Hadley. The relevant information on the property at the time of its transfer is as follows:

	Land	Building
Original Cost	$26,000	$ 85,000
Market Value - Date Of Transfer	51,000	107,000
Undepreciated Capital Cost - Date Of Transfer	N/A	48,500

Prior to the end of the current year, as the result of a decision to move to another province, Mrs. Hadley sells the property for $165,000. Of this total $55,000 is allocated to the land and the remaining $110,000 to the building. During the period that the property was in her name, the net rental income was zero. Mr. and Mrs. Hadley were formally divorced the following year.

Required: Determine the tax effects associated with the transfer and subsequent sale of the property for both Mr. Hadley and Mrs. Hadley assuming:

A. In keeping with a verbal understanding reached in negotiating the separation, Mr. Hadley gives Mrs. Hadley the building in lieu of any support payments.

B. Mr. Hadley agrees to pay spousal support and Mrs. Hadley agrees to purchase the property at its fair market value on June 1.

Assignment Problem Ten - 6

For all of his adult life, Mr. Lange has been a resident of Canada. However, in recent years the severity of the climate has begun to have an adverse influence on his health. As a consequence, on June 15 of the current year he is planning to move to Sarasota, Florida. On this date he owns the following assets:

	Adjusted Cost Base	Fair Market Value
Vacant land	$15,000	$ 46,000
Automobile	31,000	18,000
Coin collection	5,000	11,000
Inco Ltd. shares	24,000	38,000
Alcan shares	42,000	35,000
Toronto Dominion Bank shares	15,000	23,000
Nal Enterprises Ltd. shares	26,000	153,000

Mr. Lange has come to you for advice just prior to moving to Florida.

Required:

A. What elections with respect to his assets would you recommend that he consider before leaving Canada? Explain your recommendations.

B. Assume he has made no elections regarding his assets. Determine the amount of the taxable capital gain or allowable capital loss which Mr. Lange will report in his Canadian income tax return for the current year.

Assignment Problem Ten - 7

In 1991, Mr. Forsyth purchased a small apartment building at a cost of $350,000. Of the total cost, $100,000 was allocated to land with the $250,000 balance going to the cost of the building. For Capital Cost Allowance purposes, the building was included in Class 1.

During the years 1991 through 2000, the building was usually fully occupied. At the end of 2000 the Undepreciated Capital Cost for the building was $170,000.

On October 10, 2001, Mr. Forsyth is killed in an automobile accident and his will leaves the apartment building to his 23 year old daughter. At the time of his death, the fair market value of the land was $212,000 and the fair market value of the building was $325,000.

His daughter, a busy executive with an advertising agency, makes an immediate effort to sell the apartment. During 2001, she continues to operate the building and takes maximum Capital Cost Allowance for that year. In February of 2002 it is sold for a total price of $600,000, of which $225,000 is allocated to the land and $375,000 to the building.

Required:

A. Indicate the tax effects to be included in Mr. Forsyth's tax return as a result of the 2001 deemed disposition at his death and calculate the tax effects associated with the 2002 sale of the building for Mr. Forsyth's daughter.

B. Assume Mr. Forsyth had willed the building to his wife rather than to his daughter and his wife took maximum CCA in 2001 before selling the building for $600,000 in 2002. Indicate the tax effects to be included in Mr. Forsyth's tax return as a result of the 2001 deemed disposition at his death and calculate the tax effects associated with the 2001 sale of the building for Mrs. Forsyth.

Assignment Problem Ten - 8

Mr. Cheever is 66 years of age and his wife Doreen is 56. They have one daughter Mary who is 32 years of age. On July 1, 2001, Mr. Cheever owns the following properties:

Rental property   Mr. Cheever owns a rental building which is located on leased land. The building was acquired at a cost of $45,000. On July 1, 2001 its undepreciated capital cost is $27,000 and its fair market value is estimated to be $87,000.

Brazeway Dynamics   Mr. Cheever owns 2,500 shares of Brazeway Dynamics, a Canadian public company. These shares have a cost of $275,000 and a current fair market value of $425,000. Mr. Cheever has never owned more than 1 percent of the outstanding shares of this Company.

Farm land   Mr. Cheever owns farm land with a cost of $525,000, and a current fair market value of $750,000. The land is farmed on a full time basis by Mr. Cheever's daughter, Mary.

Cheever Inc.   Mr. Cheever owns 100 percent of the voting shares of Cheever Inc., a Canadian controlled private company. The company was established with an investment of $155,000 and it is estimated that the current fair market value of the shares is $227,000.

Required: Explain the tax consequences to Mr. Cheever for 2001 in each of the following Cases:

A. Mr. Cheever dies on July 1, 2001, leaving all of his property to his spouse Doreen.

B. Mr. Cheever dies on July 1, 2001, leaving all of his property to his daughter Mary.

C. Mr. Cheever departs from Canada and ceases to be a resident on July 1, 2001.

Assignment Problem Ten - 9 (Electronic Library Research Problem)

Provide brief answers to the following questions. Your answers should be supported by references to materials found in your Electronic Library.

A. Investment tax credits earned on depreciable assets are applied against an individual's taxes payable in the current year, but are deducted from the capital cost of the asset in the following year. What is the appropriate treatment of these amounts when a taxpayer dies after deducting the credits from taxes payable, but prior to removing them from the capital cost of the asset?

B. ITA 69 contains rules for dealing with transactions between taxpayers who are dealing at "arm's length". Do members of a partnership deal with each other at "arm's length"? Can individual partners be considered to be dealing with the partnership at "arm's length"?

C. In 1997, the taxpayer transferred capital property with a fair market value of $50,000 to the taxpayer's spouse at the taxpayer's adjusted cost base of $20,000. In 1998, the spouse sold the transferred property for $80,000 and acquired a substituted property with the proceeds from the sale. In 2000, the spouse disposed of the substituted property for $120,000 and acquired substituted property with the proceeds from the disposition. In 2002, the spouse disposed of the substituted property for $150,000. Would the income attribution rules apply to the spouse's sale of the two substituted properties?

Chapter 11

Income From Property, Other Income, And Other Deductions

Introduction

11-1.   Subdivision b of Division B of the *Income Tax Act* provides simultaneous coverage of both income from business and income from property. The parts of these Sections relating to business income were covered in Chapter 7 and many of these provisions are equally applicable to income from property. However, there are sufficient features that are unique to income from property that separate coverage of this subject is warranted and is provided in this Chapter.

11-2.   In addition to property income, this Chapter also covers Other Sources Of Income (Division B, subdivision d) and Deductions In Computing Income (Division B, subdivision e). With the discussion of property income in this Chapter, we have now completed our coverage of the basic types of income included in a taxpayer's Net Income For Tax Purposes. There are, however, certain inclusions and deductions that do not fit into any of the categories that we have described. For example, the receipt of a pension benefit cannot be categorized as employment income, business or property income, or a taxable capital gain. Correspondingly, an RRSP deduction can be related to any type of earned income and, as a consequence, cannot be specifically allocated to any of the previously described income categories. These miscellaneous inclusions and deductions will be given detailed attention in the latter part of this Chapter.

Property Income: General Concept

11-3.   Income from property is thought of as the return on invested capital in those situations where little or no effort is expended by the investor to produce the return. Falling into this category would be rents, interest, dividends, and royalties paid for the use of purchased property. In general, capital gains are not treated as a component of property income even in cases where they arise on investments being held to produce property income (e.g., capital gains on dividend paying shares).

11-4.   In cases where a great deal of time and effort is directed at producing interest or rents, such returns can become business income. For example, the rents earned by a large property management company would be treated as a component of business income. As explained in a later Chapter, this is an important distinction for corporations since business income qualifies for the small business deduction while property income generally does not.

11-5.   The primary characteristic which distinguishes property income from business income is the lack of effort directed towards its production. However, in some circumstances, other factors must also be considered. Some examples of why the correct classification is important are as follows:

- With respect to rental properties, the deduction of capital cost allowance is not permitted to create or increase a net loss for the period.
- The income attribution rules that were discussed in Chapter 10 apply to property income, but not to business income.
- Certain expenses can be deducted against business income but not property income. These include write offs of cumulative eligible capital and convention expenses. In contrast, there is a deduction for foreign taxes on property income in excess of 15 percent that is not available against foreign business income.

Interest Income

General Provision

11-6.   ITA 12(1) lists inclusions in business and property income. Paragraph (c) of this subsection is as follows:

> **Interest**   ... any amount received or receivable by the taxpayer in the year (depending on the method regularly followed by the taxpayer in computing the taxpayer's income) as, on account of, in lieu of payment of or in satisfaction of, interest to the extent that the interest was not included in computing the taxpayer's income for a preceding taxation year;

11-7.   Note that, while ITA 12(1)(c) generally requires the inclusion of interest received or receivable, ITA 12(3) and (4) exclude amounts that have previously been included in income.

11-8.   The wording of ITA 12(1)(c) suggests that taxpayers can use the cash basis to recognize interest income (amounts received or receivable). This is not the case. ITA 12(3) and 12(4) requires the use of an accrual approach by all taxpayers. As will be discussed in the following material, the accrual approach used by individuals differs from that used by corporations and partnerships.

Corporations and Partnerships

11-9.   ITA 12(3) requires that corporations, partnerships, and some trusts use accrual accounting. The concept of accrual accounting that is applied to these taxpayers is the conventional one in which interest income is recorded as a direct function of the passage of time. As a result, interest income for tax purposes is, generally speaking, identical to that required under the application of generally accepted accounting principles and, as a consequence, no further explanation is required.

Individuals

11-10.   While ITA 12(3) requires conventional accrual accounting for corporations and partnerships, ITA 12(4) provides for a less familiar version of this concept for individuals. Under this modified version of accrual accounting, interest is not accrued on a continuous basis. Rather, ITA 12(4) requires the accrual of interest on each anniversary date of an investment contract. ITA 12(11) defines "investment contracts" to include most debt obligations and "anniversary date" to be that date that is one year after the day before the date of issue of the obligation and every successive one year interval. This would mean that, for a five year contract issued on July 1, 2001, the anniversary dates would be June 30 of each of the five years 2002 through 2006.

11-11.   To the extent that the income accrued on the anniversary date has not been previously included in income, it must then be included in the individual's income, regardless of whether the amount has been received or is receivable.

11-12.   The following example is an illustration of the annual accrual rule.

> **Example**   An investment contract with a maturity value of $100,000 and an annual interest rate of 10 percent is issued on July 1, 2001. The $100,000 maturity amount is due on June 30, 2006. An interest payment for the first 2.5 years of interest ($25,000) is due on December 31, 2003. The remaining interest ($25,000) is due with the principal payment on June 30, 2006. The contract is purchased by an individual at the time that it is issued.

> **Tax Consequences**   Annual interest of $10,000 would have to be accrued on the first two anniversary dates of the contract, June 30, 2002 and June 30, 2003. This means that $10,000 would be included in Net Income For Tax Purposes for each of these two years. When the $25,000 payment is received on December 31, 2003, an additional $5,000 would be subject to taxation for that year because it has been received and not previously accrued. This results in taxation of $15,000 in 2003. For 2004, the June 30, 2004 anniversary date would require the accrual of $10,000. However, as $5,000 of this amount was already included in income during 2003, only $5,000 of this amount would be subject to taxation in 2004. There would be a further accrual of $10,000 on each of the anniversary dates in the years 2005 and 2006.

11-13.   Note that the anniversary date is established by the date on which the investment contract is issued. It is not influenced by the date on which the individual investor acquires the contract.

Discount And Premium On Long Term Debt Obligations
Economic Background
11-14.   When a debt obligation is issued with an interest rate below the current rate, investors will react by offering a price that is less than the maturity value of the obligation. Such obligations are said to sell at a discount and, in economic terms, this discount generally represents an additional interest charge to be recognized over the life of the obligation. For example, a 10 year obligation with a maturity value of $100,000 and a 10 percent stated interest rate would sell to investors expecting a 12 percent interest rate for $88,700. The discount of $11,300 would then be added to interest expense at the rate of $1,130 per year for the ten year period (to simplify the presentation, we are using the straight line approach to amortizing discount). In a corresponding fashion, a debt obligation which offered an interest rate above that currently expected by investors would command a premium. Such a premium would then be treated as a reduction in interest expense over the remaining life of the debt obligation.

11-15.   The procedures described in the preceding paragraph are, of course, well known to anyone familiar with generally accepted accounting principles. Surprisingly, the applicable tax rules do not reflect these principles and take an approach to this situation that is totally lacking in conceptual support.

Tax Procedures
11-16.   Tax procedures take the view that the taxable amount of interest is based on the accrual of the coupon or stated rate, without consideration of any discount or premium arising on issue. If the investor holds the bonds to maturity, any difference between the amount originally paid and the amount received at that time will generally be treated as a capital gain (discount case) or capital loss (premium case).

Prescribed Debt Obligations
11-17.   Over the last two decades, a number of financial instruments have been developed to provide a return to investors in a less conventional manner. For example, debt obligations were developed which specified low interest payments during the early years of issue, followed by compensation in the form of higher rates during the later years. Other instruments, such as the principal component of strip bonds and zero coupon bonds, provided for no payment of interest. Investors were compensated for this lack of "interest" by maturity payments

in excess of the initial issue price of the securities.

11-18.   The Government responded to this situation with the issuance of more sophisticated regulations. Specifically, ITR 7000(1) identifies four types of prescribed debt obligations and indicates their required tax treatment as follows:

ITR 7000(1)(a) describes obligations which only pay a specified sum at maturity, with no interim interest payments. In the case of these obligations, referred to as zero coupon bonds, interest must be accrued by the effective rate method at the rate which will equate the original cost of the obligation to the present value of its maturity value.

ITR 7000(1)(b) describes stripped bonds in which the maturity value and the interest payments are sold separately.   Interest on the maturity value component will be determined as per ITR 7000(1)(a). The interest to be recognized on the interest payment component will be based on the yield that equates the cost of that component with the present value of all future payments.

ITR 7000(1)(c) describes debt obligations that contain variable interest rate provisions. Here the interest to be accrued will be based on the greater of the maximum interest rate stipulated for the year or the accrued interest based on the yield that equates the principal amount of the debt to the present value of the maximum future payments.

ITR 7000(1)(d) describes debt obligations in which the interest rate to be paid is contingent on a future event. In this case, the interest to be recognized must be based on the maximum rate potentially payable.   For example, if an extra one percent interest was added to the investment's return if the obligation is held to maturity, the annual accrual would have to include this extra one percent.

11-19.   A comprehensive treatment of these obligations goes beyond the scope of this book. However, an example of the types of calculations that are involved would be as follows:

Example   On January 1, 2001, Albert Litton purchases a zero coupon bond with a maturity value of $10,000. The bond is issued on this date and the maturity value is due on December 31, 2003. The price paid by Mr. Litton is $7,312, providing an effective annual yield of 11 percent.

Tax Consequences   The total interest income of $2,688 ($10,000 - $7,312) would have to be reported by Mr. Litton as follows:

Year	Opening Balance	Interest At 11%	Closing Balance
2001	$7,312	$804	$ 8,116
2002	8,116	893	9,009
2003	9,009	991	10,000

Indexed Debt Obligations

11-20.   Debt obligations are sometimes issued with the amount of interest and principal to be paid determined by reference to a change in the purchasing power of money. ITR 7001 requires that indexed amounts be included in income, even when the amounts are not actually received by the investor. An example will serve to illustrate this provision:

Example   On November 1, 2001, an individual acquires at par a $1,000 bond issued on that date. The bond is indexed to the Consumer Price Index (CPI) and on maturity will be redeemed for $1,000 plus an amount that reflects the increase in the CPI while the bond was outstanding. The bond also pays interest each November 1 of 4 percent based on the indexed principal. Assume that from November 1, 2001 to October 31, 2002, the CPI increases by 5 percent and from November 1, 2002 to October 31, 2003 it increases a further 3 percent.

Given the preceding, the amounts that would be included in the taxpayer's income for 2001, 2002, and 2003 would be calculated as follows:

Year		Amount
2001		Nil
2002:		
Interest [($1,000)(1.05)(4%)]	$42.00	
Inflation Adjustment [($1,000)(5%)]	50.00	$ 92.00
2003:		
Interest [($1,000)(1.05)(1.03)(4%)]	$43.26	
Inflation Adjustment [($1,050)(3%)]	31.50	74.76
Three Year Total		$166.76

11-21.   While the inflation adjustment amounts will have to be included in the taxpayer's income in the years indicated in the preceding table, these amounts will not be received until the bond matures. Also note that, under the provisions of this regulation, the amounts that have to be included in the income of the purchaser of the bond would also be deductible to the issuer.

Accrued Interest At Transfer

11-22.   Publicly traded debt obligations are exchanged on a day-to-day basis, without regard to the specific date on which interest payments are due. To accommodate this situation, accrued interest from the date of the last interest payment date will be added to the purchase price of the security. Consider, for example, a 10 percent coupon, $1,000 face value bond with semi-annual interest payments of $50 on June 30 and December 31 of each year. If we assume that the market value of the bond is equal to its face value and it is purchased on October 1, 2001, the price would be $1,025, including $25 of interest for the three month period from June 30, 2001 through October 1, 2001.

> Exercises Eleven-1 through Eleven-3 deal with interest income. This would be an appropriate time to attempt these exercises.

11-23.   In the absence of a special provision dealing with this situation, the $25 would have to be included in the income of the purchaser when it is received as part of the $50 December 31, 2001 interest payment. Further, the extra $25 received by the seller would receive favourable treatment as a capital gain. To prevent this result, ITA 20(14) indicates that the seller must include the accrued interest in income and the purchaser can deduct a corresponding amount from the interest received on the bonds.

Interest As A Deduction

The Problem

11-24.   There are differing views as to the extent to which interest costs should be considered a deductible item for various classes of taxpayers. At one extreme we have the situation which existed in the United States at one point in time where all interest costs, without regard to the purpose of the borrowing, could be deducted by individual taxpayers. In contrast, there are tax regimes where the deductibility of interest is restricted to certain very specific types of transactions.

11-25.   From a conceptual point of view, it can be argued that interest should only be deductible to the extent it is paid on funds that are borrowed to produce income that is fully taxable in the period in which the interest is deducted. This would clearly disallow the deduction of interest related to the acquisition of items for personal consumption. In accordance with this view, it would not be equitable to allow the full deduction of interest costs against income, such as dividends or capital gains, that is only partially taxed. It would be equally unfair to allow a current deduction for interest when any related income will not be taxed until a later taxation year.

11-26.   To some extent, the preceding view is incorporated into the current legislation. The real problem, however, is that there are such a multitude of provisions related to the special treatment of certain types of income and to the deferral of income, that the application of these fairly straightforward principles becomes very complex. This has been further complicated by an important court case in this area. This case, which involved the Bronfman Trust, will be considered later in this Section.

11-27.   As was noted in Chapter 7, the general provision for the deduction of interest is found in ITA 20(1)(c). This provision basically provides for the deduction of interest only if it relates to the production of business or property income. This means that, in general, interest cannot be deducted if it relates to such other sources of income as employment income or capital gains. Note, however, that the deduction is available to all types of taxpayers, including corporations, individuals and trusts.

11-28.   You will recall that, when an employee receives an interest free or low interest loan from an employer, imputed interest on the loan will be included in employment income as a taxable benefit. Under ITA 80.5, this imputed interest is deemed to be interest paid and, if the loan is used to produce business or property income, the amount will be deductible under ITA 20(1)(c).

Non Deductible Interest

11-29.   Both the general limitation found in ITA 18(1)(a) and the conditions related to the specific deduction of interest in ITA 20(1)(c) make it clear that, for interest to be deductible, it must be on borrowings that relate to the production of business or property income. This means that, if an individual borrows to invest in a 180 day term deposit that pays fully taxable interest, the interest paid on the borrowed funds is clearly deductible. Further, interest on borrowing to make investments in dividend paying shares is also deductible, despite the fact that dividends will be taxed at less than full rates and that dividends may not be declared in a particular year. However, if the borrowing were for the acquisition of idle land, the interest would not generally be deductible. This reflects the fact that idle land cannot produce business or property income. Other situations where interest is not deductible because there is no related business or property income include the following:

*   Interest on loans to make contributions to an RRSP.
*   Interest on loans used to acquire personal property or listed personal property, including a principal residence.
*   Interest on loans used to make interest free loans to family members.
*   Interest on loans used to pay tax instalments.
*   Interest paid on late or deficient tax instalments.
*   Interest on loans to pay for personal living expenses.

11-30.   Note that the deductibility of the interest relates to the purpose of the loan and not to its collateral. For example, if an individual assumes a mortgage in order to acquire a principal residence, the interest is clearly not deductible. However, when the mortgage has been paid off, the investor may use the residence as collateral for a new loan, the proceeds of which are to be invested in income producing shares. While the collateral for the loan is the same under both the original and the new loan, the purpose is different and the interest on the new loan will be deductible.

11-31.   As can be seen in the preceding example, for interest to be deductible, there must be documentation to establish the purpose of the borrowing. If debt arrangements cannot be traced to the production of business or property income, interest deductibility is lost. An interesting case in this area involved an individual who used his personal residence as collateral for a loan to purchase income producing investments. He then proceeded to deduct the interest on this loan against the income produced by the securities. Later, he was required to move and, because there was a delay in selling his old residence, a mortgage was assumed on his new principal residence. A short time later, when the old residence was sold, the proceeds were used to pay off the mortgage on the old residence. Due to his inability to purchase his new house without a mortgage, he was not allowed to deduct the interest on his new mortgage as the loan proceeds using his new house as collateral went directly towards the acquisition of the new residence.

The Disappearing Source Problem

11-32. Until recently, a major source of unfairness was generally referred to as the disappearing source problem. This problem can be illustrated by the following example:

Example Mr. Patek borrows $100,000 which he invests in securities which cost $100,000 but are later sold for $25,000. This results in a loss of $75,000. If the remaining $25,000 is then used to acquire new securities, only the interest on the reinvested $25,000 is deductible under the usual rules for interest deductibility. This is despite the fact that he still owes the full $100,000 that was borrowed on the original investment.

11-33. ITA 20.1 deals with this problem. Under the provisions of this Section, interest on the borrowed funds that are lost through the disposition of a property will continue to be deductible. This means that in our example, interest on the full $100,000 in borrowings would continue to be deductible. The interest on the $25,000 would be deductible under the usual rules because it has been reinvested to produce income, while the interest on the remaining $75,000 would be deductible under the provisions of ITA 20.1.

Bronfman Trust Case

11-34. In the case, Bronfman Trust vs. the Queen, the trustees wished to make a capital distribution to the beneficiaries of the trust. While they could have sold some of the investments in the trust in order to finance the distribution, they chose not to do so and financed the distribution with borrowed funds. The trustees believed that the interest would be deductible as there was indirect production of income through the retention of trust investments. This position was supported by past precedents and by IT-80 which specifically provided for the deduction of interest in the similar situation where funds are borrowed to pay dividends.

11-35. This case eventually reached the Supreme Court Of Canada and, at this level, the deduction was disallowed on the grounds that the funds borrowed were not directly related to the production of income. The result engendered considerable uncertainty in this area and, as a consequence, on December 20, 1991, the Department Of Finance issued a set of new proposals on the deductibility of interest.

Proposed Legislation

11-36. Surprisingly, the 1991 draft legislation has still not become law (May, 2001). However, it appears that assessments are being made on the basis of these proposals and, as a consequence, they will be reviewed here. The issues dealt with in this draft legislation, along with the conclusions reached, can be described as follows:

Borrowings To Make Loans To Employees And Shareholders The issue here is whether interest paid on money borrowed to make loans to employees and shareholders should be deductible to the business. A proposed ITA 20(1)(c)(v) indicates that all such interest is deductible with respect to amounts borrowed to make loans to employees. When the borrowing is to make loans to shareholders, deductible interest is limited to the amount of interest income recorded by the corporation on the loan.

Borrowings To Acquire Preferred Shares The problem here is that the interest on the loan may exceed the grossed up dividends on the preferred shares. A proposed ITA 20(1)(qq) would limit the deduction of interest in this situation to the amount of grossed up dividends on the preferred shares. Any excess interest can be carried over and deducted in the following year, subject to the same grossed up dividends limitation. Note that this proposed rule does not apply to common shares as they may have additional income in the form of capital gains.

Borrowings Related To Business Interests If the proceeds of the borrowing is used to make an interest free or low interest loan to a business in which the borrower has an interest, or to acquire preferred shares with little or no dividend entitlement, than there is no reasonable expectation of a profit on the loan. However, a proposed ITA

20(3.1) and 20(3.2) deem the borrowing to have been made for the purposes of producing income, provided two conditions are met:

- The proceeds of the loan must be used by the business to produce Canadian source income.
- There must be an indication that the business could not have borrowed the funds on comparable terms.

Funds Borrowed By A Business To Make A Distribution   This, of course, was the issue addressed in the Bronfman case, where the Supreme Court Of Canada found that such borrowings were not directed towards the production of income. Under a proposed ITA 20.1 and 20.2, such borrowings will be deemed to have been made for the purpose of producing income. However, the applicable amount will be limited to equity (assets, less liabilities as specifically defined for this purpose) of the business. Interest on amounts borrowed within this limit will be deductible.

Weak Currency Debt

11-37.   An interesting case involving the deductibility of interest on weak currency debt reached the Supreme Court Of Canada during 1999 (*Shell Canada vs. The Queen*). In order to raise approximately US$100 million, Shell Canada borrowed the funds in New Zealand dollars. As the New Zealand dollar was considered to be a weak currency, the rate on the borrowing was 15.4 percent, much higher than the 9.1 percent rate that was available if they had borrowed in U.S. dollars. As was expected, the New Zealand dollar declined over the period the debt was outstanding and, as a consequence, Shell experienced a significant gain on the maturity value of the debt. As the borrowing was for capital expenditures, the gain was capital in nature, with only three-quarters (the inclusion rate on capital gains at the time of the borrowing) of the total amount being included in Shell's income.

11-38.   In effect, Shell traded higher interest payments (fully deductible) for a capital gain (three-quarters taxable). The CCRA found this favourable tax outcome to be unpalatable and attempted to disallow the deduction for interest in excess of the 9.1 percent rate that would have been paid on U. S. dollar borrowings. The Agency also attempted to have the foreign currency gain taxed as business income rather than as a capital gain. While they were successful in the lower courts, the Supreme Court ruled in favour of Shell, allowing the deduction of the full amount of interest and permitting the foreign currency gain to be treated as a capital item.

11-39.   On this issue, the CCRA turned out to be a sore loser. Not liking the outcome resulting from the Supreme Court decision, they have proposed new legislation which will achieve their desired goal. A new ITA 20.3 defines weak currency debt in terms of three characteristics:

1.   The proceeds of the borrowing are in a currency other than the currency where it will be used for income producing purposes (referred to as the final currency). An example of this would be funds borrowed in U.K. pounds sterling, converted to Canadian dollars, and invested in Canadian assets. The Canadian dollar is the final currency in this example.

2.   The amount has to exceed $500,000. This, in effect, exempts debt issues below this threshold from the provisions of ITA 20.3.

3.   The interest rate on the debt has to be more than two percentage points (200 basis points) greater than the interest that would have been paid on a similar issue of debt in the final currency.

11-40.   If a debt issue has these characteristics, the following tax consequences will follow:

1.   Under ITA 20.3(2)(a), interest on the debt will only be deductible to the extent of the amount of interest that would have been paid on a similar borrowing in the final currency. The excess interest, by definition two percent or more, will be disallowed.

2.   Under ITA 20.3(2)(b), any exchange gain or loss arising on the settlement of the debt

will be on income account. Regardless of whether it relates to a capital transaction or an income transaction, capital gains treatment will be denied.

3. While the exchange gain or loss arising on the settlement of the debt must be treated as ordinary income, ITA 20.3(2)(c) indicates any interest that was disallowed because of ITA 20.3(2)(a) is deemed to b an amount paid to settle the debt. This will serve to reduce any exchange gain or increase any exchange loss which arises on the settlement of the debt.

11-41.   There are a number of other provisions contained in ITA 20.3 related to identification of the final currency and to situations where the debt is hedged. Coverage of these provisions goes beyond the scope of this text.

11-42.   It is likely that this proposed legislation will serve to eliminate this type of borrowing arrangement, a goal which could not be achieved by the CCRA through the courts.

Exercise Eleven-4 deals with weak currency debt. This would be an appropriate time to attempt this exercise.

Royalties And Payments Based On Production Or Use

11-43.   ITA 12(1)(g) requires that any amount received by a taxpayer that was dependent on the production from property or the use of property, be included in income. The property involved would include real and personal property as well as intangibles such as patents, franchises, and copyrights.

11-44.   The provision also requires that, except in the case of agricultural land, payments that represent instalments on the sale price of the property must also be included if their payment is related to production or use. An example will serve to illustrate this provision:

> **Example**   The owner of a mineral deposit sells the asset with the proceeds to be paid on the basis of $2 per ton of ore removed. The total amount to be paid is not fixed by the sales agreement.

11-45.   In this situation, the original owner of the property would have to include in income the full amount received in subsequent years, even though a portion of the payment may be of a capital nature.

Rental Income

General Rules

11-46.   Rental income is not specifically mentioned in the ITA Sections which deal with income from property. There is some merit in the view that rental receipts fall into the category of payments for production or use. However, rents are generally payable without regard to whether or not the property is used and, as a consequence, this view may not be appropriate. In any case, it is clear that rental receipts must be included in income and, given this fact, income from property would appear to be the most logical classification.

11-47.   Once the rental revenues are included in income, a variety of expenses become deductible against them. These would include heat, light, power, repairs, maintenance, interest, property taxes, payments for management, and fees to rental agents for locating tenants.

Capital Cost Allowances

11-48.   In addition to other expenses, capital cost allowance on rental properties can be claimed. For individuals, the fiscal year is the calendar year so there is no proration of CCA for a short fiscal year in the first year a rental property is acquired. (See IT-172R, "Capital cost allowance — Taxation year of individual"). However, the first year one-half rule is applicable to rental properties.

11-49.   Rental properties acquired after 1987 will generally fall into Class 1 where they are eligible for CCA calculated on a declining balance basis at a rate of four percent. As mentioned in Chapter 8, rental properties acquired prior to 1988 were allocated to Class 3 where the rate was five percent. This rate is still available on properties that were allocated to that Class prior to 1988. Note, however, that in both Classes the rate is applied to the UCC of the building only. Some part of the value of the total cost of the property must be allocated to land and this amount is not subject to CCA.

11-50. Since the introduction of capital gains taxation in 1972, two special rules have been applied to CCA calculations on rental properties. These two rules, along with a brief explanation of the reason that each was introduced, are as follows:

Rental Property CCA Restriction In general, taxpayers are not permitted to create or increase a net rental loss by claiming CCA on rental properties. For this purpose, rental income is the total rental income or loss from all properties owned by the taxpayer. The amount includes any recapture, but does not include terminal losses. The reason for this restriction is a desire to limit the use of rental losses for purposes of sheltering other types of income (e.g., applying rental losses against employment income). The fact that CCA is the only restricted deduction is probably based on the fact that, unlike most depreciable assets, the value of rental properties does not usually decline over time. This restriction does not apply to a corporation or a corporate partnership whose principal business throughout the year is the rental or sale of real property. Also note that this restriction, unlike the separate class restriction, applies to any property that is leased or rented, not just real estate.

Separate Classes Each rental building that is acquired after 1971 at a cost of $50,000 or more must be placed in a separate class for calculating capital cost allowances, recapture, and terminal losses. In most situations, the amount of CCA that can be deducted on a rental property exceeds any decline in the value of the building. In fact, it is not uncommon for the value of such properties to increase over time. This means that, if an investor is required to account for each rental property as a separate item, a disposition is likely to result in recapture of CCA and an increase in taxes payable. In the absence of this special rule, all rental properties would be allocated to a single class. This would mean that the investor could avoid recapture for long periods of time by simply adding new properties to the class. This separate class rule prevents this from happening.

11-51. Without question, these special rules make real estate less attractive as an investment. However, a number of advantages remain:

- taxation on a positive cash flow can be eliminated through the use of CCA;
- some part of the capital cost of an asset can be deducted despite the fact that real estate assets are generally not decreasing in value;
- increases in the value of the property are not taxed until the property is sold; and
- any gain resulting from a sale is taxed as a capital gain, only one-half of which is taxable.

11-52. These factors continue to make the tax features of investments in rental properties attractive to many individuals.

Rental Income Example

11-53. An example will serve to illustrate the basic features involved in determining net rental income.

Example Mr. Bratton owns two rental properties on January 1, 2001. They can be described as follows:

Property A was acquired prior to 1988 at a cost of $120,000 of which $20,000 was allocated to land. It has a current UCC of $78,000.

Property B was acquired prior to 1988 at a cost of $90,000. It is situated on land which Mr. Bratton leases and has a current UCC of $74,200. On August 28, 2001, Property B is sold for $125,000.

On December 1, 2001, Mr. Bratton acquires Property C at a cost of $200,000 of which $50,000 is allocated to land. Rents on all of the properties totaled $35,000 during 2001 and the cost of maintenance, property taxes, and mortgage interest totaled $45,400.

Net Rental Income Calculation   The maximum available CCA on the three properties would be as follows:

- Property A (Class 3) = $3,900 [(5%)($78,000)]
- Property B (Class 3) = Nil (The property was sold during the year.)
- Property C (Class 1) = $3,000 [($150,000)(1/2)(4%)]

Since a rental loss cannot be created by claiming CCA, the net rental income would be calculated as follows:

Gross Rents	$35,000
Recapture Of CCA On Property B ($90,000 - $74,200)	15,800
Expenses Other Than CCA	(45,400)
Income Before CCA	$ 5,400
CCA Class 1 (Maximum)	(3,000)
CCA Class 3 (Limited)	(2,400)
Net Rental Income	Nil

11-54.   Note that the maximum CCA was taken on Class 1, the four percent class, leaving the limited CCA deduction for Class 3 which has the higher rate of five percent. This follows the general tax planning rule that suggests that, when less than the maximum allowable CCA is taken, the CCA that is deducted should be taken from the Classes with the lowest rates. Also note that there would be a taxable capital gain of $17,500 [(1/2)($125,000 - $90,000)] on the sale of Property B.

> Exercise Eleven-5 deals with rental properties. This would be an appropriate time to attempt this exercise.

Dividends From Canadian Corporations

Cash Dividends

The Concept of Integration

11-55.   While this concept will be given much more detailed attention in the Chapters dealing with corporate taxation, it is impossible to understand the tax procedures associated with dividends without some elementary understanding of the concept of integration. It is fundamental, both to the procedures associated with the taxation of dividends, as well as to many other provisions related to the taxation of corporations.

11-56.   An individual who controls a source of business or property income can choose to receive that income directly or, alternatively, have the income source owned by a corporation. If the individual receives the income directly, it will be subject to tax only once. Alternatively, if the income source is owned by a corporation, the resulting income will be subject to taxation at the corporate level and, if the remainder is distributed to the individual as dividends, the residual amount will be subject to tax a second time in the hands of the individual.

11-57. It is a general objective of Canadian income tax legislation to attempt to neutralize the presence of the corporation in the taxation process. Stated alternatively, an effort is made to ensure that the after tax amount received by an individual from an income source is the same, without regard to whether the income is received directly or, alternatively, channeled through a corporation. This is referred to as integration of corporate and personal taxes.

11-58.   In attempting to achieve this goal of integration, the most important procedures are those associated with the taxation of dividends. These procedures involve a gross up of dividends received, combined with an individual tax credit for taxes that were paid at the corporate level. These dividend gross up and credit procedures will be described in the next section.

Gross Up and Credit Procedures

11-59.   The current version of the gross up and credit procedures is based on the assumption that a corporation is taxed at a rate of 20 percent. This means that, if a corporation earned $10,000 and distributed all of the after tax income to its shareholders, the resulting Income Statement would appear as follows:

Pre Tax Income	$10,000
Income Taxes (At 20 Percent)	(2,000)
Net Income	$ 8,000
Dividends Declared	(8,000)
Increase in Retained Earnings	$ Nil

11-60.   Under ITA 12(1)(j), dividends received from corporations resident in Canada must be included in the income of taxpayers. When the taxpayer is an individual, ITA 82(1) requires that the income inclusion be 125 percent of the amount actually received. This means that the individual who received the $8,000 of dividends in the example would have to include $10,000 [(125%)($8,000)] in his Net Income For Tax Purposes. The purpose of this gross up, as is evident from the preceding Income Statement, is to restore the individual's income to the same $10,000 amount that was earned by the corporation. Note, however, that this only works when the corporate tax rate is 20 percent. If the rate was below 20 percent, the grossed up amount would be too large and, alternatively, if the corporate rate exceeds 20 percent, the grossed up amount would be too small.

11-61.   Since the individual receiving dividends will have the amount grossed up to reflect the pre tax amount earned by the corporation, it seems fair that the individual would be eligible for a tax credit to compensate for the taxes paid by the corporation. This, in fact, is the case. Under ITA 121, the individual will receive a credit against taxes payable that is equal to two-thirds of the gross up. This credit can also be expressed as 16-2/3 percent of dividends received or as 13-1/3 percent of taxable (i.e., grossed up) dividends. In our example, this amount would be $1,333 [(66-2/3%)($2,000) or (16-2/3%)($8,000) or (13-1/3%)($10,000)].

11-62.   You will note that this tax credit is less than the $2,000 in taxes that were paid by the corporation. This is because we have only calculated the federal component of the dividend tax credit. While the focus of this text is on federal income taxation, some discussion of provincial taxes is required here in order to complete our elementary discussion of integration.

11-63.   You may recall from Chapter 1 that, until recently, most provincial taxes payable were calculated as a percentage of federal taxes payable. This meant that, if a federal tax credit reduced the federal tax payable, there was an implicit provincial tax credit equal to the provincial tax rate times the federal tax credit. Using our dividend tax credit example, if the individual lived in a province with a tax rate equal to 50 percent of federal tax payable, the $1,333 federal dividend tax credit would result in a $667 [(50%)($1,333)] provincial dividend tax credit. Note that the sum of these two credits is equal to $2,000, the amount of income taxes paid by the corporation in our example.

11-64.   Again referring to Chapter 1, we pointed out that as of this year, all of the provinces have moved to a system whereby the provincial tax is calculated on taxable income, as opposed to being calculated on federal taxes payable. This does not really change our analysis of integration. The difference is that, under this new system, each province will have to provide an explicit dividend tax credit. It appears that all of the provinces will follow the federal pattern by requiring a 25 percent gross up of dividends received, accompanied by a dividend tax credit based either on a percentage of the federal dividend tax credit or, alternatively, on the 25 percent gross up. In those cases where the provincial credit is equal to 33-1/3 percent of the gross up, the combined federal/provincial tax credit will be the same as it was for those provinces that had a 50 percent rate applied to federal taxes payable. That is, the combined credit would be $2,000 [($2,000)(66-2/3% + 33-1/3%)].

Example

11-65. The following example illustrates the gross up and tax credit procedures associated with the taxation of dividends:

Example During 2001, Mr. Plummer and Ms. Black each receive $8,000 in dividends from taxable Canadian corporations. They both live in the same province. Mr. Plummer's income is subject to a 16 percent federal tax rate and an 8 percent provincial tax rate. Ms. Black's income is subject to a 29 percent federal tax rate and and a 14.5 percent provincial tax rate. The provincial dividend tax credit is equal to one-third of the gross up.

Tax Consequences The taxes payable and after tax amount of the dividends received by the two individuals would be calculated as follows:

	Mr. Plummer	Ms. Black
Dividends Received	$ 8,000	$ 8,000
Gross Up Of 25 Percent	2,000	2,000
Taxable Dividends	$10,000	$10,000
Federal Tax At 16% or 29%	$1,600	$2,900
Provincial Tax At 8% or 14.5%	800	1,450
Federal Dividend Tax Credit (2/3 of Gross Up)	(1,333)	(1,333)
Provincial Dividend Tax Credit (1/3 of Gross Up)	(667)	(667)
Total Tax Payable	$ 400	$2,350
Dividends Received	$8,000	$8,000
Total Tax Payable	(400)	(2,350)
After Tax Dividend	$7,600	$5,650

11-66. Notice in this example that the combined federal/provincial dividend tax credit ($1,333 + $667) is equal to the gross up ($2,000). This occurs only when the provincial credit is equal to one-third of the gross up. The actual combined value will vary from province to province. For example, the dividend tax credit in Ontario has been set at 26.67 percent of the gross up, giving a combined federal/provincial value for the dividend tax credit that is significantly less than the gross up. In contrast, Alberta has set the provincial credit at 32 percent of the gross up, resulting in a combined credit that is nearly equal to the gross up.

Investment Returns

11-67. Using the numbers in the preceding example, we can see that for an individual such as Ms. Black who is in the maximum federal tax bracket of 29 percent, the combined federal/provincial rate of taxation on dividends is only 29.4 percent ($2,350 ÷ $8,000). If instead of being dividends, the $8,000 had been interest income, Ms. Black would have been taxed at a combined rate of 43.5 percent (29% + 14.5%), retaining only $4,520 of the $8,000 in interest received. This means that, in order to provide the same after tax return to an investor in the maximum federal tax bracket, an interest bearing investment has to provide a return that is about 25 percent higher than the rate on an alternative dividend paying investment. For example, in 2001, for an investor in Ms. Black's position, a 7 percent rate on an interest bearing bond will provide about the same after tax return to an investor in the maximum federal tax bracket as a 5.6 percent dividend rate on a preferred share issue.

11-68. Prior to the February 28, 2000 budget, dividends provided better after tax returns than capital gains. If Ms. Black had an $8,000 capital gain prior to the budget date, three-quarters of the amount would be taxable and the taxes would be $2,610 [($8,000)(3/4)(29% + 14.5%)]. This represents a combined federal/provincial levy of 32.6 percent, somewhat higher than the 29.4 percent rate applicable to dividends. However, with the post budget inclusion rate of one-half, the taxes on an $8,000 capital gain would be $1,740 [($8,000)(1/2)(29% + 14.5%)]. This gives a rate of 21.8 percent, significantly lower than the rate on dividends.

11-69. The analysis would be different for an individual such as Mr. Plummer. His taxes on an $8,000 capital gain would be $960 [($8,000)(1/2)(16% + 8%)], reflecting a rate of 12 percent [($960 ÷ $8,000)]. This is significantly higher than the 5 percent rate [($400 ÷ $8,000)] that Mr. Plummer paid on dividends. For individuals in lower tax brackets, dividends continue to be attractive, despite the lower inclusion rate that is now available on capital gains.

11-70. The relationship between the rate on dividends and the rate on capital gains is also influenced by the provincial dividend tax credit rate. The rates illustrated by our example were based on the fact that the provincial dividend tax credit was equal to one-third of the gross up. When the provincial credit is higher than one-third, this credit increases in value, thereby improving the after tax rate on dividends. In contrast, when the provincial credit is below one-third, the credit declines in value, resulting in a lower after tax rate on dividends. However, for individuals in the top tax bracket, it is unlikely that any provincial dividend tax credit rate will bring the after tax rate on dividends anywhere close to the after tax rate on capital gains.

Stock Dividends

11-71. A stock dividend involves a pro rata distribution of additional shares to the existing shareholders of a company. For example, if the XYZ Company had 1,000,000 shares outstanding and it declared a 10 percent stock dividend, the Company would be distributing 100,000 new shares to its present shareholders on the basis of one new share for each ten of the old shares held. While there is no real change in anyone's financial position as a result of this transaction, it is usually accompanied by a transfer from the Company's Retained Earnings to contributed or paid up capital. The amount of this transfer is normally the fair market value of the shares to be issued, determined on the date of the dividend declaration.

11-72. While the tax treatment of stock dividends has varied over the years, stock dividends must currently be dealt with on the same basis as cash dividends. The value of the dividend is based on the amount of the increase in the paid up capital of the payor, usually the fair market value of the shares issued. This amount is subject to the usual gross up and tax credit procedures and is added to the adjusted cost base of all of the shares owned by the investor. However, this approach places the investor in the position of having to pay taxes on an amount of dividends that has not been received in cash, an unfavourable situation with respect to the investor's cash flows. As a consequence, the use of stock dividends is much less common than the use of cash dividends.

Capital Dividends

11-73. Most dividends paid by corporations will be taxable in the hands of individuals. However, ITA 83(2) provides an exception to this when the dividend is a capital dividend. The tax free portion (one-half, one-third, or one-quarter, depending on the year) of capital gains realized by a private corporation is allocated to a special "capital dividend account" (as will be explained in Chapter 15, other amounts are allocated to this account as well). When these amounts are paid out to shareholders and the corporation elects to have it treated as a capital dividend under ITA 83(2), it will be received by investors on a totally tax free basis. Also to be noted here is that such capital dividends do not have to be deducted from the adjusted cost base of the investor's shares. The procedures associated with these dividends will be covered in Chapter 15.

Mutual Fund Dividends

11-74. In Canada, most mutual funds are organized as trusts. As long as its income and most of its realized capital gains are passed through to the unit holders (investors), trusts are exempt from tax. This means that there is a strong incentive for such funds to distribute their income to the investors. In addition, the by-laws of most mutual funds require such distributions, without regard to tax incentives.

11-75. It is important to note that the income earned by mutual fund trusts retains its character through this distribution process. That is, if the mutual fund has a capital gain, the distribution of that gain will be a capital gain to the investor in the mutual fund. This means that, when a mutual fund provides an investor with an information return (T3 Supplementary if the fund is organized as a trust), it will indicate the various types of income that are included in its dividend distribution. These types will include:

- **Canadian Net Interest Income** These amounts will be taxed as ordinary interest income.

- **Foreign Interest And Dividend (Non Business) Income** These amounts are taxable on the same basis as domestic interest. As will be discussed in the next Section of this Chapter, the gross amount of this income will be included in income, with amounts withheld at the foreign source being eligible for tax credit treatment.

- **Dividends From Taxable Canadian Corporations** These amounts will be subject to the gross up and credit procedures that were previously discussed in this Chapter.

- **Capital Gains** As with capital gains earned directly by the individual, only one-half of these amounts will be subject to taxes.

- **Capital Distributions** A fund can make a distribution that exceeds its income for the year. These are identified as returns of capital and are received tax free. They do, however, reduce the adjusted cost base of the investment.

11-76. Mutual fund corporations are less common than mutual fund trusts. While these funds typically pay out all of their income, the income is subject to taxation prior to being distributed to investors. However, since distributions are from tax paid funds, all dividend distributions are eligible for the usual gross up and tax credit procedures. There are other complications here involving capital dividends and refundable taxes on investment income that go beyond the scope of this book.

11-77. When a mutual fund trust makes a distribution, the Net Asset Value Per Share (NAVPS) will drop by the amount of the distribution. This drop, when combined with the fact that most investors have these distributions reinvested in additional units, is a source of some confusion. A simple example will clarify this situation:

> **Example** On July 20, 2001, CIC Growth Fund has a distribution of $.50 per unit. Martin Diaz, who holds 1,000 units purchased at $7.30 per unit (total value $7,300) would, on that date, see his NAVPS drop by exactly that amount to $6.80. If Mr. Diaz chooses not to reinvest the distribution, he will receive $500 [(1,000 units)($0.50)] in cash. He would then have 1,000 units with a total value of $6,800, plus $500 in cash, an amount equal to his original $7,300. Alternatively, if the distribution is reinvested, which is normally the case with mutual funds, he will receive 73.53 ($500 ÷ $6.80) additional units with a total value of $500 [($73.53)($6.80)]. This will leave him with a holding of 1,073.53 units with total value of $7,300 [(1,073.53 units)($6.80)].

11-78. Without regard to whether the distribution is received in cash or reinvested, there will be an income inclusion. The amount of the income inclusion would depend on the type of income included in the distribution. If the distribution was interest, the increase in income would be $500. If the distribution was dividends from taxable Canadian corporations, it would be subject to the same gross up and tax credit procedures as other dividends. If the distribution was capital gains, the taxable capital gain would be $250 [(1/2)($500)].

> Exercise Eleven-6 deals with dividend income. This would be an appropriate time to attempt this exercise.

Foreign Source Income

General Rules

11-79. As Canadian taxation is based on residency, income that has a foreign source must be included in full in the calculation of Net Income For Tax Purposes. This is complicated by the fact that most foreign jurisdictions levy some form of withholding tax on such income. The general approach is to require Canadian residents to include 100 percent of any foreign income earned in their Net Income For Tax Purposes and to provide a credit against taxes payable for any taxes withheld in the foreign jurisdiction.

11-80.   The basic idea behind this approach is to have the combined foreign and Canadian tax on this income be the same as that which would be levied on the same amount of income earned in Canada. If, for example, an individual earned $1,000 in a foreign jurisdiction, with the taxation authorities in that jurisdiction withholding $100, the full $1,000 would be included in the taxpayer's Canadian taxable income. If we assume that this individual is taxed at a combined federal/provincial rate of 45 percent, the $450 in taxes on this $1,000 would be reduced by a $100 credit for foreign taxes paid. The balance of $350 in Canadian taxes, when combined with the $100 paid in the foreign jurisdiction, would be equal to the $450 that would be paid on the receipt of $1,000 in Canadian source income.

Foreign Non Business Income (Property Income)

11-81.   Following the general rule, 100 percent of foreign source non business income is included in Net Income For Tax Purposes. However, for individuals, the credit against taxes payable which is provided under ITA 126(1) is limited to a maximum of 15 percent of the foreign source non business income. If the withheld amounts exceed 15 percent, the excess can be deducted under ITA 20(11). For example, if Mr. Grant earns foreign source property income of $1,000 and the foreign government withholds 40 percent or $400, the $1,000 will be included in income, the $250 of withholding in excess of 15 percent will be a deduction against this amount, and the $150 of withholding that is within the 15 percent limit will be used to calculate a credit against taxes payable. The detailed procedures for the calculation of foreign tax credits will be covered in Chapter 13.

Foreign Business Income

11-82.   In the case of foreign source business income, there is no direct limitation on the use of the amounts withheld as a credit against taxes payable and, correspondingly, no deduction in the calculation of Net Income For Tax Purposes for any part of the amount withheld by the foreign jurisdiction. Assume that in contrast to the preceding example, Mr. Grant is allocated $1,000 of foreign source business income that is subject to the same foreign jurisdiction withholding of 40 percent. In this case, he would include the full $1,000 in his Net Income For Tax Purposes with no deduction for any withholding in excess of 15 percent and the $400 in withholding would be used to calculate a credit against taxes payable.

Shareholder Benefits

Appropriations

11-83.   ITA 15(1) deals with situations where a corporation has made payments to a shareholder, where corporate property has been appropriated for the benefit of a shareholder, or where a corporation has conferred a benefit on a shareholder. Examples of this type of situation would include a corporation providing a shareholder with a jet for personal use, a corporation building a swimming pool at a shareholder's personal residence, or a corporation selling assets to a shareholder at prices that are substantially below fair market value.

11-84.   When any of these events occur, the shareholder is required to include the value of these benefits or appropriations in his income. In most cases, such amounts will not be considered dividends and, as a consequence, they will not be eligible for the dividend tax credit.

11-85.   A further point here is that when an amount is included in a shareholder's income under ITA 15(1), IT-432R2 indicates that the corporation is not allowed to deduct the amount that has been included in the shareholders' income. If, for example, a corporation provides a shareholder with a holiday trip to Italy, ITA 15(1) would require the inclusion of the cost of the trip in the income of the shareholder. Despite the fact that this amount is being taxed in the hands of the shareholder, the corporation would not be able to deduct the cost of the trip. It would seem clear, given this non deductibility, that corporations should avoid providing benefits that will be assessed to shareholders under ITA 15(1).

Shareholder Loans

General Rule

11-86.   ITA 15(2) is applicable when a corporation makes a loan to a shareholder or an individual connected to a shareholder. Under ITA 15(2.1), persons are connected for this purpose if they do not deal with each other at arm's length. When such loans are made, this general rule requires that the full principal amount of the loan be included in the Net Income For Tax Purposes of the shareholder in the taxation year in which the loan is made. This general rule applies without regard to the level of interest paid on the loan. Note, however, in periods subsequent to the inclusion of the principal amount of the loan in the income of the shareholder, there is no imputed interest benefit, even in cases where the loan is on an interest free basis.

11-87.   Under this general rule, the granting of the loan to a shareholder has the same tax consequences as the payment of an equivalent amount of salary to the shareholder. However, there is an important difference. Taxes paid on salary cannot be recovered by repaying the salary. In contrast, when all or part of a shareholder loan which has been included in the taxpayer's income under ITA 15(2) is repaid, the amount of the repayment can be deducted from Net Income For Tax Purposes under ITA 20(1)(j).

11-88.   You should contrast this general rule on loans to shareholders with the treatment of loans to employees which are discussed in Chapter 5. Under no circumstances will the principal amount of a loan to an employee be included in that employee's income. If the employee pays interest on the loan at a rate equal to the prescribed rate or higher, there will be no tax consequences associated with the receipt of the loan. If the loan is interest free, or has an interest rate below the prescribed rate, the individual will be assessed a taxable benefit for imputed interest calculated as the difference between interest on the loan at the prescribed rate and the amount of interest actually paid on the loan.

Exceptions To The General Rule

11-89.   There are three exceptions to this general rule that are available to shareholders, without regard to whether or not they are also employees of the corporation. They can be described as follows:

Non Resident Persons   ITA 15(2.2) indicates that the general rule does not apply to indebtedness between non resident persons. This means that, if both the corporation and the shareholder receiving the loan were non residents, the principal amount of any loan would not have to be included in income.

Ordinary Lending Business   ITA 15(2.3) indicates that the general rule does not apply when the corporation is in the business of making loans, provided bona fide arrangements are made to repay the loan. This covers situations where, for example, an individual happens to be a shareholder of the bank which provides him with a personal loan.

Repayment Within One Year   ITA 15(2.6) indicates that the general rule does not apply when the loan is repaid within one year after the end of the taxation year of the lender or creditor in which the loan was made or the indebtedness arose. If, for example, a corporation with a June 30 year end extended a $100,000 loan to a shareholder on January 1, 2001, the $100,000 would not have to be included in income if it is repaid prior to June 30, 2002.

A further point with respect to this exception is that IT-119R4 indicates that this exception is not available when the repayment is part of a series of loans and repayments. The primary evidence of this type of situation would be a repayment near the end of a corporate taxation year, followed by a loan for a similar amount early in the following corporate taxation year.

11-90.   Additional exceptions to the general rule requiring the principal of shareholder loans to be included in income involve situations where the shareholder is also an employee of the corporation making the loan. These exceptions are found in ITA 15(2.4) and can be described as follows:

Not Specified Employee ITA 15(2.4)(a) indicates that loans made to shareholders who are employees are not subject to the general rule if they are not a specified employee. A specified employee is one who owns 10 percent or more of the shares of the corporation or who does not deal at arm's length with the corporation. This exception applies without regard to the purpose of the loan.

Dwelling Loans ITA 15(2.4)(b) indicates that loans made to a shareholder who is an employee to acquire a dwelling are not subject to the general rule.

Stock Acquisition Loans ITA 15(2.4)(c) indicates that loans made to a shareholder who is an employee to acquire shares in the lending corporation are not subject to the general rule.

Motor Vehicle Loans ITA 15(2.4)(d) indicates that loans made to a shareholder who is an employee to acquire a motor vehicle to be used in employment duties are not subject to the general rule.

11-91. In order for these exceptions to apply, the following conditions must be met:

- the loan must be made to the individual because he is an employee, not because he is a shareholder; and
- at the time the loan is made, bona fide arrangements must be made to repay the loan within a reasonable period of time.

11-92. The first of these conditions is likely to create significant problems for owner-managers of private corporations wishing to give themselves loans. In order to avoid having the principal amount of the loan included in Net Income For Tax Purposes, the owner-manager must demonstrate that he received the loan because of his role as an employee. To demonstrate that he has received the loan in his role as an employee, the owner-manager will likely have to make similar loans available to all employees. That is, if the company gives the owner-manager a $100,000, low interest loan to purchase a residence, such loans would have to be made available to all employees. If this is not the case, the CCRA is likely to conclude that the owner-manager received the loan because of his role as a shareholder.

11-93. A further problem would arise if, as would not be uncommon in owner-managed situations, there are no other employees of the business. It is not clear in this case whether the owner-manager would be able to demonstrate that he received a loan in his capacity as an employee.

Imputed Interest Benefit
11-94. It was previously noted that, if the principal amount of a shareholder loan is included in the taxpayer's income, there is no additional benefit related to deficient interest payments on the loan. However, if the loan is exempted from the general inclusion in income rule by one of the exceptions described in the preceding section, ITA 80.4(2) is applicable and a benefit may be assessed [the analogous benefit for employees is assessed under ITA 80.4(1)].

Example On July 1, 2001, Andros Ltd. extends a $100,000 loan to its only shareholder, George Andros. The loan bears interest at 1 percent and, because it will be repaid in January, 2002, the $100,000 principal amount does not have to be included in his income. Assume the prescribed rate throughout 2001 is 6 percent.

Tax Consequences For 2001, Mr. Andros will be assessed a taxable benefit under ITA 80.4(2) equal to $2,500 [(6% - 1%)($100,000)(6/12)]*. We would remind you that, if the loan proceeds are invested in income producing assets, the imputed interest will be deductible under ITA 80.5.

*In the examples in IT-421R2, "Benefits To Individuals, Corporations, And Shareholders From Loans Or Debt", interest is calculated on the basis of number of months the loan is outstanding. While not illustrated, calculations could also be based on the number of days the loan is outstanding.

11-95.   In the fairly common situation where the shareholder also works as an employee of the business, the benefit may be assessed under either ITA 80.4(1) or 80.4(2). As far as the calculation of the benefit is concerned, this distinction makes no difference. However, if the purpose of the loan is to acquire a home, there is a significant difference. In the case of a benefit assessed under ITA 80.4(1), for the first five years of the loan, the benefit calculation will use a rate no higher than the rate that prevailed when the loan was made. Should the rate go down, the employee is entitled to use the lower rate for the benefit calculation. Alternatively, in the case of a home purchase loan to a shareholder, the ITA 80.4(2) benefit must be calculated using the actual rates which prevail over the term of the loan.

> Exercise Eleven-7 deals with shareholder loans. This would be an appropriate time to attempt this exercise.

11-96.   A further difference between home purchase loans to employees and home purchase loans to shareholders relates to a provision which is discussed in Chapter 5. If the home purchase loan is related to a relocation, an employee can deduct from any calculated benefit on the loan, an amount that is the equivalent to the benefit on a $25,000 interest free home purchase loan. This deduction is not available to shareholders.

Securities Lending Arrangements

11-97.   When an investor believes that the price of a security is going to decline, he may try to take advantage of the decline by selling it short. This process involves selling a security that the investor does not own, borrowing the security from another investor during the short period, acquiring the security after the price has fallen, and using the new security to replace the borrowed security. If a dividend is declared on the borrowed security during the short period, the borrower must compensate the lender for the amount involved.

11-98.   Section 260 of the *Income Tax Act* deals with this type of situation. ITA 260(2) states that the loan of securities is not considered to be a disposition and its replacement with an identical security is not considered an acquisition. Consistent with this position, ITA 260(5) allows the lender to treat compensation received from the borrower for dividends paid on the security as an ordinary dividend received from a taxable Canadian corporation. This means that such amounts, even though they are received from an individual rather than a corporation, will be eligible for the dividend gross up and tax credit procedures if the lender is an individual. As the payment is being given dividend treatment, ITA 260(6) prohibits the deduction of such payments by the borrower of the securities.

Other Sources Of Income

Pension Benefits

11-99.   ITA 56(1)(a)(i) requires that payments received from certain types of pension plans be included in the income of individuals. For many individuals, the major item here would be amounts received under the provisions of Registered Pension Plans. Also included would be pension amounts received under the *Old Age Security Act* (OAS), as well as any similar payments received from a province. In addition, benefits received under the Canada Pension Plan or a provincial pension plan would also become part of the individual's net income for tax purposes.

11-100.   With respect to Canada Pension Plan receipts, you should note that the relevant legislation allows this income to be shared with a spouse. The amount that can be shared is based on the length of time the individuals have been living together relative to the length of the contributory period. The assignment of CPP benefits can be a useful form of income splitting in situations where one spouse is subject to a lower tax rate.

Employment Insurance Benefits

11-101.   ITA 56(1)(a)(iv) requires that Employment Insurance or EI benefits received be included in income, even if they are subsequently repaid. Repayment of these benefits can be required if an individual has Net Income in excess of a specified level. If such repayment is required, the repayment can be deducted under ITA 60(n).

Retiring Allowances

11-102.   ITA 56(1)(a)(ii) requires that retiring allowances be included in an individual's net income for tax purposes. ITA 248 defines these payments as follows:

> **"retiring allowance"** means an amount (other than a superannuation or pension benefit, an amount received as a consequence of the death of an employee or a benefit described in subparagraph 6(1)(a)(iv)) received
>
> (a) on or after retirement of a taxpayer from an office or employment in recognition of the taxpayer's long service, or
> (b) in respect of a loss of an office or employment of a taxpayer, whether or not received as, on account or in lieu of payment of, damages or pursuant to an order or judgment of a competent tribunal,
>
> by the taxpayer or, after the taxpayer's death, by a dependant or a relation of the taxpayer or by the legal representative of the taxpayer.

11-103.   The term retiring allowance covers all payments on termination of employment. This includes rewards given for good service, payments related to early retirement (e.g., federal government buyout provisions) at either the request of the employee or the employer, as well as damages related to wrongful dismissal actions.

11-104.   Within specified limits, amounts received as a retiring allowance for service prior to 1996 can be deducted if they are transferred to either a Registered Pension Plan or a Registered Retirement Savings Plan within 60 days of the end of the year in which it is received. (See Chapter 6). This serves to defer the taxation on amounts transferred until the funds are withdrawn from the registered plan. For individuals who are retiring, this can be an important component of their tax planning.

Lump Sum Payments
The Problem

11-105.   For individuals, such income receipts as wages and salaries, pension income, and spousal support are taxed on a cash basis. As a consequence, retroactive lump sum payments are taxable when they are received, even though a significant portion of the amount normally relates to prior years.

11-106.   There is an advantage in that there has been some deferral of the tax on these amounts. However, because of the presence of progressive rates in the Canadian tax system, the tax liability on such lump sum payments may be higher than would have been the case had the payments been received and taxed year by year. Because of this problem, the 1999 budget introduced tax relief in this area.

Qualifying Amounts

11-107.   The relief will be available on payments that are referred to as "qualifying amounts". These are given a technical definition in ITA 110.2(1). In the Explanatory Notes which accompany the proposed legislation, the following more general description is found:

> A qualifying amount is the principal portion of certain amounts included in income. Those amounts are: spousal or child support amounts, superannuation or pension benefits otherwise payable on a periodic basis, employment insurance benefits and benefits paid under wage loss replacement plans. Also included is the income received from an office or employment (or because of a termination of an office or employment under the terms of a court order or judgment), an arbitration award or in settlement of a lawsuit.

Relief Mechanism

11-108.   ITA 110.2(2) provides a deduction for the "specified portion" of a "qualifying amount" that was received by an individual during a particular taxation year. The "specified portion" is the fraction of the qualifying amount that relates to an "eligible year". An "eligible year" is any prior year after 1977 in which the individual was a resident of Canada throughout the year and during which the individual did not become a bankrupt. No deduction is available if the qualifying amount is less than $3,000. In somewhat simplified terms, this means that an individual can remove from the current year's income, the types of payments described as qualifying amounts to the extent that they relate to prior years.

11-109.　ITA 120.31 describes an alternative tax that will be payable on the amounts that are deducted under ITA 110.2(2). This tax is the total of the additional taxes that would have been triggered for each relevant preceding year if the portion of the qualifying amount that relates to that preceding year were added to the individual's taxable income for that year.

11-110.　In addition to the tax for those years, a notional amount of interest is added to reflect the fact that the tax was not paid in the relevant years. This interest is accrued from May 1 of the year following the relevant preceding year, through the end of the year prior to the receipt of the lump sum payment.

11-111.　The goal of these procedures is to spread the lump sum payment over earlier tax years, thereby eliminating the influence of progressive rates on the total tax bill. For example, if a 2001 court settlement reflected a wage adjustment for the years 1996 through 2000, the recipient would pay the amount of taxes that would have been due if he had received the amounts in the years 1996 through 2000. In many cases this will provide significant tax relief. However, if the individual is in the maximum bracket for all years under consideration, using this approach could result in higher taxes because of the addition of the notional amount of interest. In such cases, the taxpayer would not make the deduction under ITA 110.2(2).

11-112.　In recomputing the tax liability for prior years, no adjustments will be allowed for items such as RRSP contributions based on the new information. Further, the government will not recapture income tested benefits paid in those years (e.g., goods and services tax credit).

Death Benefits

11-113.　Death benefits are included in income under ITA 56(1)(a)(iii). ITA 248 defines these death benefits as follows:

> **"death benefit"** means the total of all amounts received by a taxpayer in a taxation year on or after the death of an employee in recognition of the employee's service in an office or employment ....

11-114.　When death benefits are received by a surviving spouse from the deceased taxpayer's employer, the definition goes on to indicate that only amounts in excess of an exclusion of $10,000 are considered to be a death benefit for purposes of ITA 56(1)(a)(iii). This $10,000 exclusion would be available even if the benefit were payable over a period of several years. A CPP death benefit is not eligible for the $10,000 exemption as it is not a death benefit paid in recognition of the employee's service.

11-115.　The $10,000 exclusion is also available on payments to individuals other than a spouse, with the amount being reduced to the extent it has been used by the spouse. For example, if Ms. Reid dies and her employer pays a death benefit of $8,000 to her husband and an additional $8,000 to her adult son, the husband could exclude the entire $8,000 from income and the son could use the remaining $2,000 of the exclusion to reduce his income inclusion to $6,000.

11-116.　Although death benefits are normally paid to the family of the deceased, it would appear that the $10,000 exclusion is available without regard to whom the death benefit is paid. This would suggest that an employer could pay himself a $10,000 tax free death benefit on the death of any employee. Further, it would seem that an employer could repeatedly make such payments on the death of each of his employees.

Spousal Support And Child Support Received
Introduction

11-117.　For many years, no tax distinction was made between payments made by an individual for child support and payments made for spousal support. These amounts were referred to in earlier legislation as alimony or maintenance and, provided they were paid to a former spouse on a periodic basis under the terms of a formal agreement, they were fully deductible to the payor and fully taxable to the recipient.

11-118. This approach was challenged in a highly publicized case which reached the Supreme Court of Canada. Ms. Thibaudeau claimed that being taxed on child support payments violated her constitutional rights. As the Supreme Court rejected her arguments, this left in place a system in which such payments were deductible to the payor and taxable to the recipient.

11-119. Provided tax considerations are included in the determination of the amounts that must be paid, this arrangement is clearly in the best interests of the family unit. The fact that the person paying child support is usually in a higher tax bracket than the recipient of such payments provides for a significant form of income splitting. There is no question that when these payments are deductible to the payor and taxable to the recipient, less money will be paid to the government and more will be retained by the parties to the support agreement.

11-120. Despite the income splitting benefits of the old system, Ms. Thibaudeau's arguments had wide support, particularly among women. In short, the government was placed in a situation where it could change the tax rules in what appeared to be a response to the needs of women and, at the same time, increase aggregate tax revenues. It is hardly surprising that they took advantage of this opportunity.

11-121. Changes were introduced which, in effect, implemented the view of Ms. Thibaudeau. The terms alimony and maintenance were replaced by the more general term, support. To the extent this support is for a child, as opposed to a spouse, the payments are no longer deductible to the payor or taxable to the recipient.

11-122. The new rules are applicable to agreements made after April, 1997 and, in certain circumstances, to agreements made before that time. In general, however, agreements made before May, 1997 and any amounts paid for spousal, as opposed to child, support will continue to operate under the old rules. This dual system is reflected in ITA 56(1)(b) for inclusions and ITA 60(b) for deductions.

General Conditions For Inclusion And Deduction

11-123. While the amounts that are potentially deductible and taxable vary with the date of the agreement and the type of support payment made, certain conditions must be met for this deductibility and inclusion to occur. The specific conditions which have to be met are set out in ITA 56.1 as follows:

- the amount is paid as alimony or an allowance for the maintenance of the spouse (which includes a common law spouse) or former spouse, children of the marriage, or both;
- the spouses or former spouses are living apart at the time the payment is made and throughout the remainder of the year and were separated pursuant to a divorce, judicial separation, or written separation agreement;
- the amount is paid pursuant to a decree, order, or judgment of a competent tribunal or pursuant to a written agreement; and
- the amount is payable on a periodic basis.

11-124. If all of these conditions are met, the payments are deductible to the payor and taxed in the hands of the recipient. If one or more of these conditions is not met, the payor will not receive a deduction for the payments and the recipient will not be taxed on the receipts.

11-125. The reasons for most of these conditions are fairly obvious. For example, without the condition that the spouses are living apart, a couple could effectively split income by getting a written separation agreement and having the spouse with the higher income make payments to the spouse with the lower income.

11-126. While payments prior to the date of a court decree cannot technically be made pursuant to that decree, ITA 56.1(3) and ITA 60.1(3) deem that payments made in the year of the decree or the preceding year will be considered paid pursuant to the decree, provided that the order or agreement specifies that they are to be so considered. This provision is unchanged by the 1998 legislation.

11-127.   Problems often arise with respect to the requirement that payments be made on a periodic basis. Clearly, a single lump sum payment does not qualify, nor does a payment which releases the payor from future obligations. Payments that are in excess of amounts required to maintain the spouse and/or children in the manner to which they were accustomed are also likely to be disallowed. Other factors that will be considered is the interval at which the payments are made and whether the payments are for an indefinite period or a fixed term.

11-128.   Under some circumstances, a person who receives support payments and includes the amount received in income may be required to repay some portion of these amounts. In these circumstances, ITA 60(c.2) allows the person making the repayment to deduct the amount repaid. Correspondingly, ITA 56(1)(c.2) requires the recipient to include a corresponding amount in income. These provisions are unchanged by the new legislation.

Rules For Agreements Made Before May 1, 1997
11-129.   Under the revised provisions, the old rules on support are still in effect for agreements that were made before May 1, 1997, provided that they have not been altered since that date. This means that both child and spousal support payments are treated as income to the recipient under ITA 60(b), and are deductible to the individual making the payments under ITA 56(1)(b).

Agreements Made After April, 1997
11-130.   For agreements made after April, 1997, support payments for child support will not be deductible to the payor under ITA 60(b) nor taxable to the recipient under ITA 56(1)(b). The ITA definition of child support payments is such that any amount that is not clearly identified as being for the benefit of the spouse will be considered child support. This makes it extremely important for the written agreement which describes the payments to clearly specify any amounts that are to be designated spousal support.

11-131.   A further problem relates to situations where less than the full amount of required payments is made. If the required payments include both child support and spousal support, the formula used in ITA 56(1)(b) and 60(b) is such that only payments in excess of the required child support will be deductible/taxable. Consider an individual required to pay $4,000 in child support and $12,000 in spousal support. If a total of $7,000 is paid during the year, only $3,000 of that amount will be deductible/taxable.

11-132.   Under some circumstances, the current rules with respect to child support become applicable to agreements made before May, 1997. These circumstances are as follows:

1.   Where the payor and recipient file a joint election with the CCRA that the payor will not, for income tax purposes, deduct from income and the recipient will not include in income payments in respect of child support obligations that arise on or after a specified commencement day.

2.   Where the agreement or order is changed or varied after April, 1997 to change the amount of child support.

3.   Where a new commencement day is specified in an agreement or order.

11-133.   A number of additional points are relevant here as follows:

• Under the old rules, payments to third parties for the benefit of a spouse or children (e.g., mortgage payments on a residence) were deductible to the payor and taxable to the recipient. To the extent that payments are clearly for the benefit of the spouse, they will continue to be deductible/taxable.

• Under the current rules, child support payments will not reduce the payor's earned income for RRSP purposes, nor increase the recipient's earned income for tax purposes (see Chapter 6).

• The recipient of child support payments will continue to be eligible for the equivalent to spouse tax credit (see Chapter 13).

Exercise Eleven-8 deals with support payments. This would be an appropriate time to attempt this exercise.

- ITA 118(5) prevents an individual from taking a tax credit for a spouse and, at the same time, deducting support payments to that spouse. This rule is unchanged.

- While it is not part of the legislation, the Government of Canada has published an extensive, province by province list of guidelines for child support. These guidelines are dependent on the number of children involved and the income of the payor. For example, an individual with a gross income of $82,000, supporting five children in New Brunswick, would be expected to pay $1,840 per month in child support. These guidelines are very influential in shaping support agreements.

Income Inclusions From Deferred Income Plans

11-134. Income inclusions from deferred income plans such as Registered Retirement Savings Plans, Registered Retirement Income Funds and Deferred Profit Sharing Plans do not fall into any of the major categories of income. Such amounts do not directly relate to employment efforts, business activity, ownership of property, or the disposition of capital assets. However, they clearly constitute income and, as a consequence, ITA 56 requires that income inclusions from these various deferred income plans be included in the taxpayer's income. A brief description of the various provisions in this area is as follows:

Payments From RRSPs All amounts that are removed from a Registered Retirement Savings Plan must be included in income under ITA 56(1)(h).

Payments From DPSPs Under ITA 56(1)(i), all amounts removed from a Deferred Profit Sharing Plan must be included in income.

RRIF Withdrawals The required minimum withdrawal, plus any additional withdrawals from Registered Retirement Income Funds, must be included in income under ITA 56(1)(h) and (t). Note that ITA 56(1)(t) would require the inclusion of the minimum withdrawal amount in income, even if the amount were not actually withdrawn.

Income Inclusions From Home Buyers' And Lifelong Learning Plans You will recall from Chapter 6 that, if repayments to these plans are not made as per the required schedule, the specified amounts must be included in income. These amounts would be included in income under ITA 56(1)(h.1) and (h.2), respectively.

Annuity Payments

11-135. ITA 248 defines an annuity as an amount payable on a periodic basis, without regard to whether it is payable at intervals longer or shorter than a year. As the term is generally applied, it refers to the investment contracts that are generally sold by insurance companies, either directly to individuals or to trustees administering RPPs, RRSPs, or DPSPs. In simple terms, the investor pays a lump sum to the insurance company in return for the promise of a periodic payment over either a fixed term or for the individual's life. The payments are designed to return the purchaser's capital and to provide a rate of return on the funds held.

11-136. As an example, assume that the Secure Insurance Company is using an interest rate of 5 percent. Given this, $10,000 would buy a five year ordinary annuity of $2,309 per year. The total payments would amount to $11,545, of which $10,000 would represent a return of capital and the $1,545 balance would represent interest earned. If an individual had used $10,000 from an ordinary savings account to purchase this annuity, only $1,545 of the annuity payments should be taxed, with the balance of the payments being treated as a tax free return of capital.

11-137. In contrast, a common approach to getting retirement benefits out of an RRSP is to have the trustee use the funds in the plan to purchase an annuity that is payable to the beneficiary of the plan. In this situation, the $10,000 required to purchase the annuity has been removed from a tax deferred balance and, because an eligible annuity has been purchased, there are no immediate tax consequences to the beneficiary. As a consequence, the annuity payments received by the beneficiary should be taxed in full.

11-138. Despite a somewhat indirect approach to this situation, the tax legislation produces results that are consistent with the preceding analysis. ITA 56(1)(d) requires the inclusion of all annuity payments that are not "otherwise required to be included" in computing income. As payments out of RPPs, RRSPs, and DPSPs are "otherwise required to be included", this means that only the payments from annuities that were purchased with after tax funds will be included under ITA 56(1)(d).

11-139. To reflect the fact that a portion of these annuity payments represents a return of capital, ITA 60(a) allows a deduction for the capital amount of such payments. However, this deduction is only available for payments that are included in income under ITA 56(1)(d). This means that in the case of annuities purchased through RPPs, RRSPs, and DPSPs, this deduction will not be available as these payments will be included in income under provisions other than ITA 56(1)(d). This, in effect, means that annuity payments resulting from purchases of these arrangements through RPPs, RRSPs, and DPSPs will be taxed in full.

11-140. As presented in ITR 300, the formula for calculating the capital element of a fixed term annuity payment is as follows:

$$\frac{\text{Capital Outlay To Buy The Annuity}}{\text{Total Payments To Be Received Under The Contract}}$$

11-141. This ratio would be multiplied by the annuity payment which was included in income for the year to provide the capital element which is eligible for deduction. To illustrate this procedure, refer to the Secure Insurance Company example in Paragraph 11-136. If this annuity had been purchased with $10,000 in after tax funds, the entire annual payment of $2,309 would be included in income under ITA 56(1)(d). However, this would be offset by a deduction under ITA 60(a) which is calculated as follows:

$$\left(\frac{\$10,000}{\$11,545}\right)(\$2,309) = \$2,000$$

> Exercise Eleven-9 deals with annuity payments. This would be an appropriate time to attempt this exercise.

Education Assistance Payments
Scholarships And Bursaries
11-142. ITA 56(1)(n) requires that all amounts received as scholarships, bursaries, grants, and prizes, to the extent that these amounts exceed $500. This, in effect, exempts the first $500 of such amounts from taxation. As of 2000, an additional exemption of $2,500 is available when the individual is eligible for the education tax credit, bringing the total to $3,000 for those in qualifying programs. It should also be noted that any work related or business related awards do not qualify for the $3,000 exemption for scholarships, bursaries, grants, or other prizes.

Research Grants
11-143. Payments that represent grants for doing research are treated somewhat differently. While there is no exemption that can be applied, the unreimbursed costs incurred in carrying out the research can be deducted from the grant. This means that only the amount of the payment that is in excess of such unreimbursed costs is included in income.

Registered Education Savings Plans (RESPs)
Contributions
11-144. The contribution rules for Registered Education Savings Plans (RESPs) are found in ITA 146.1. Under these rules, the payments made to an RESP are not deductible to the contributor. The maximum contribution to these plans is limited to $4,000 per year per beneficiary. While such contributions can be made for a period of 21 years, the lifetime limit for a single beneficiary is restricted to $42,000. The fact that the annual limit would, over a period of 21 years, exceed this overall limit, reflects a desire to allow contributors who do not begin such plans when their children are young to make catch up contributions in later years. Excess contributions, either on an annual basis or on a cumulative basis, are subject to a penalty of

one percent per month. Also note that these limits apply on a per beneficiary basis. If several individuals are contributing to plans with the same beneficiary (e.g., Joan's father and her grandmother are both contributing to a plan on her behalf), the sum of their contributions cannot exceed the specified limits.

11-145.   The major tax benefit of RESPs occurs after the contributions have been made. Earnings are allowed to accumulate on the assets acquired with the contributions on a tax free basis. As was pointed out in Chapter 6 in the discussion of tax assisted retirement savings, the tax free accumulation of investment earnings can produce dramatic increases in rates of return. This tax free accumulation is limited to 25 years after the plan is established. At the end of that period, the plan is automatically deregistered.

Canada Education Savings Grants

11-146.   Under the Canada Education Savings Grant (CESG) program, the government will make additional contributions to an RESP to supplement those being made by the contributor. More specifically, each child under age 18 will accumulate CESG contribution room of $2,000 per year, up to and including the year in which they attain age 17. The CESG will be payable at a rate of 20 percent on contributions made in the year to the extent that the contributions in respect of the child do not exceed the lesser of $4,000 and the unused CESG contribution room available in the year. While unused CESG contribution room will be carried forward for use in future years, contributions made in one year that exceed the amount of available CESG contribution room cannot be carried forward for purposes of attracting a CESG payment in a subsequent year. Contributions made by any subscriber in respect of a beneficiary can qualify for the CESG. The maximum total amount of CESG that can be paid in respect of any individual is $7,200 [(20%)($2,000)(18 years)]. As an example, consider the following:

> **Example**   Tom is born in February, 2001. Tom's CESG contribution room for 2001 is $2,000. In March, 2001, Tom's father makes an RESP contribution of $800 for Tom. A CESG of $160 [(20%)($800)] is paid to the plan trustee. In November of 2001, Tom's grandmother makes a $2,500 contribution to another RESP for Tom. Since only $1,200 of Tom's CESG contribution room is available at the time of his grandmother's contribution, only $1,200 of his grandmother's contribution qualifies for a CESG of $240 [(20%)($1,200)]. The remaining $1,300 will not qualify for a CESG in the following year. If no contributions other than the father's contribution were made, the remaining $1,200 worth of CESG contribution room would be carried forward for use in the future.

11-147.   CESG payments will not be paid for RESP beneficiaries for years in which they are age 18 or older. In addition, in a year in which the beneficiary is 16 or 17, CESG payments will be made only where:

- a minimum of $2,000 of RESP contributions was made in respect of the beneficiary before the year in which the beneficiary attains 16 years of age; or
- a minimum of $100 in annual RESP contributions was made in respect of the beneficiary in any four years before the year in which the beneficiary attains 16 years of age.

Distributions

11-148.   The tax deferred earnings from the plan are distributed to a beneficiary of the plan when they become a full time student at an institution that would qualify for the education tax credit (i.e., college or university courses, as well as other courses designated by the Minister of Human Resources). The contributions to the plan are distributed on a tax free basis. The rate at which this distribution will occur is determined by the provisions of the plan and is not limited by tax legislation.

11-149.   This arrangement has two significant tax advantages:

- The parent has been able to allocate resources to a child while they were under 18 years of age without the income attribution rules being applicable.
- If the child is attending college or university on a full time basis, his income will often be sufficiently low that little or no tax will be paid on the income received.

11-150.   If the intended beneficiary is not pursuing higher education by age 21, and the plan has been running for at least ten years, a contributor who is a Canadian resident will be able to withdraw both principal and accumulated earnings from the plan. The principal will be received tax free. With respect to the distribution of the earnings, there are two possibilities:

- Up to $50,000 of such receipts can be transferred to an RRSP, provided the contributor has sufficient contribution room. The distribution that will be included in income will be offset, in this case by the RRSP deduction. Note that this is not an addition to the RRSP contribution room. The transfer has to be within the existing RRSP contribution limit for the plan.

- To the extent that a transfer to an RRSP as described in the preceding paragraph cannot be made, the earnings distribution will be subject to both regular tax, as well as a special 20 percent additional tax at the federal level. This additional tax is a sort of catch up mechanism for the tax that was deferred while the funds were in the plan. It should serve to discourage the use of RESPs for tax deferral that is unrelated to funding education.

11-151.   Distributions for non educational purposes are complicated by the fact that some of the assets in the plan may reflect CESG contributions. As these contributions were intended to assist with the cost of post secondary education, they should not be available for non educational purposes. As a reflection of this, when CESG assisted contributions are withdrawn for non educational purposes, the RESP trustee will be required to make a CESG repayment equal to 20 percent of the withdrawal. Where a plan also contains unassisted contributions, assisted contributions will be considered to be withdrawn before unassisted contributions. A simple example will clarify these rules:

> **Example**   A father establishes an RESP for his daughter in 2001 and contributes $1,500 a year for six years. CESGs paid to the plan total $1,800 [(6)($1,500)(20%)]. In 2016, after his daughter has turned 21 and made it clear she has no interest in attending university, her father withdraws $3,000 of contributions from the plan for non educational purposes. In this situation, the RESP trustee is required to make a $600 CESG repayment to the government (20 percent of $3,000).

11-152.   An RESP trustee will also be required to repay CESG money in certain other situations:

- when the plan is terminated or revoked;
- when a beneficiary under the plan is replaced, except where the new beneficiary is under 21 years of age and either the new beneficiary is a brother or sister of the former beneficiary or both beneficiaries are related to the subscriber by blood or adoption; and
- when there is a transfer from the plan to another RESP involving either a change of beneficiaries or a partial transfer of funds.

11-153.   Repayment will not be required when an RESP beneficiary does not pursue post secondary education, provided the RESP is a group plan in which earnings are allocated to other beneficiaries.

Type Of Plans
11-154.   RESP legislation provides for "family plans" in which each of the beneficiaries is related to the subscriber by blood or adoption. Family plans, which are typically established for several siblings under age 18, are subject to the same contribution limits per beneficiary, but provide additional flexibility for the contributor because educational assistance payments need not be limited to the proportion of each child's "share" of the contributions. For example, this allows a contributor who has named his three children as beneficiaries to direct the entire income to the two children pursuing education if the third child is not eligible. To ensure that family plans do not provide unintended benefits, no beneficiaries 21 years of age or older can be added to a family plan that is submitted for registration after 1998.

11-155.   There are basically two types of RESPs available. They can be described as follows:

Scholarship Plans are available through "scholarship trust companies" such as the Canadian Scholarship Trust Plan. These plans are distinguished by the fact that all of their funds must be invested in government guaranteed investments. These companies offer group plans (earnings are allocated only to those children who attend college or university) as well as individual plans (contributors can recover their share of the investment earnings)

Self Directed Plans allow investors to choose their own investments. The list of qualified investments is similar to that applicable to self directed RRSPs. For example, publicly traded stocks are eligible but income producing real estate is not. Note, however, there is no foreign content limit for self directed RESPs.

Evaluation

11-156.   For families who manage their resources in a manner that permits taking full advantage of all types of tax deferred investment, there is little question that such plans should be established for children that may attend post secondary education.

11-157.   However, in the real world, many families expend all of their resources on current consumption and have few funds left for any type of tax deferred investment. For example, only a fraction of the deductible contributions that could be made to RRSPs are, in fact, actually made.

11-158.   In situations where there are sufficient resources to contribute to either an RRSP or a RESP, but not to both, there is the question of how to determine which of these two vehicles is more advantageous. A rigorous analysis of this question is dependent on a large number of assumptions and goes beyond the scope of this text. However, several relevant points can be made:

- A major advantage of RESPs relative to RRSPs is the fact that contributions can be eligible for a Canada Education Savings Grant, within certain limits.

- A major advantage of RRSPs relative to RESPs is the fact that the contributions are deductible against current taxable income. Given a particular before tax amount available, this allows for larger contributions to be made in the case of RRSPs.

- Offsetting the deductibility of RRSP contributions, payments out of these plans will likely be taxed. While some individuals may be in a lower tax bracket in the period of payment, many individuals will be taxed at the same rates at which their contributions were deductible. In contrast, a distribution of RESP earnings to a student attending university or college may be received on a tax free basis. With personal, education, and tuition tax credits available, a student can receive a significant amount of income before having to pay any taxes. Even when taxes must be paid, all amounts are likely to be taxed in the minimum tax bracket.

- Both RRSPs and RESPs offer the advantage of having earnings compound on a tax free basis. As was illustrated in Chapter 6, this is a very powerful mechanism for tax deferral. In this area, an advantage for RRSPs is that the tax free compounding period is likely to be longer.

11-159.   Given these offsetting advantages, the choice between contributing to an RRSP and contributing to an RESP can be a very difficult decision.

Social Assistance and Workers' Compensation Payments

11-160.   Payments received under various social assistance programs must be included in income under ITA 56(1)(u) while workers' compensation payments are included under ITA 56(1)(v). It is not, however, the intent of the government to tax these amounts. They are sometimes referred to as exempt income as they have no net effect on taxable income. However, they are included in Net Income For Tax Purposes, a figure that is used in a variety of eligibility tests. For example, to get the full tax credit for a spouse, the spouse's income must be less than a threshold amount ($629 for 2001). Since the policy is to reduce this credit in proportion to the spouse's income in excess of that amount, it is important that all types of income be included in the Net Income For Tax Purposes calculation. To accomplish this goal without actually taxing social assistance and worker's compensation payments, they are included in the calculation of Net Income For Tax Purposes and then deducted in the calculation of Taxable Income.

Other Deductions

Spousal Support And Child Support Paid

11-161.   As noted in our discussion of other sources of income, under certain specific conditions, child and spousal support payments that are paid under agreements made before May, 1997 must be included in the income of the recipient. When these conditions are met, the individual paying the support is allowed to deduct the equivalent amounts. The same situation applies to spousal support payments under agreements made after April, 1997. As these conditions were discussed earlier, there is no need for further elaboration at this point.

Capital Element Of An Annuity

11-162.   As explained in our discussion of other inclusions, there is a deduction for the capital element of an annuity payment when the annuity is purchased with tax paid funds. As this deduction was illustrated as part of the consideration of the related inclusion, no further comment is required here.

Moving Expenses

General Rules

11-163.   ITA 62, read in conjunction with IT-178R3 (Consolidated), allows a deduction for moving expenses for four distinct categories of taxpayers. These are as follows:

- Taxpayers who move to a new work location, either as employees or as independent contractors (a new work location may not involve a new employer).
- Taxpayers who move in order to commence full time attendance at a post secondary institution.
- Taxpayers who move to a new work location after ceasing to be a full time student at a post secondary institution.
- An unemployed taxpayer who moves to a new location in Canada to take up employment at that new location.

11-164.   The new home must be at least 40 kilometers closer to the new work location or post secondary institution than the previous home. This distance is measured using the routes that would normally be traveled by an individual rather than "as the crow flies".

11-165.   Moving expenses can only be deducted against income, including scholarships and research grants, received in the new work location or institution. If the moving expenses exceed the income earned at the new location during the year of the move, the *Act* provides for a one year carry over and deduction against the following year's income at the new location. To the extent that the moving expenses are reimbursed by the employer, they cannot be claimed by the taxpayer.

11-166.   As described in ITA 62(3), moving expenses include:

- Traveling costs (including a reasonable amount expended for meals and lodging), in the course of moving the taxpayer and members of the household from the old residence to the new residence.
- The cost of transporting or storing household effects.
- The cost of meals and lodging near either the old or new residence for a period not exceeding 15 days. Note that, in measuring the 15 days, days spent while en route to the new location are not included.
- The cost of canceling a lease on the old residence.
- The selling costs on the old residence.
- The legal and other costs associated with the acquisition of the new residence, provided

an old residence was sold in conjunction with the move. Note that this does not include any GST paid on the new residence.

- Up to $5,000 of interest, property taxes, insurance, and heating and utilities costs on the old residence, subsequent to the time when the individual has moved out and during which reasonable efforts are being made to sell the property.

- Costs of revising legal documents to reflect a new address, replacing drivers licenses and non commercial vehicle permits, and connecting and disconnecting utilities.

11-167. Any costs associated with decorating or improving the new residence would not be included in the definition of moving expenses, nor would any loss on the sale of the old residence. Also note that any costs associated with trips to find accommodation at the new location are not included in the definition.

Simplified Method Of Calculating Vehicle and Meal Expenses

11-168. In an effort to simplify claiming vehicle and meal expenses, the CCRA permits the optional use of pre-established flat rates. Receipts are not needed to claim these amounts. The flat rate for meals is $11 per meal, to a daily maximum of $33, per person, per day. The flat rate for vehicle expenses depends on the province from which the move begins and ranges from $0.36 per kilometer for Saskatchewan to $0.44 per kilometer for the Northwest Territories for 2001. The vehicle claim is calculated by multiplying the total kilometers driven during the year related to the move by the rate of the originating province.

Employer Reimbursements

11-169. As noted in Chapter 5, an employer can reimburse an employee's moving expenses without creating a taxable benefit. It would appear that, for this purpose, the definition of moving expenses is broader than that which applies when an employee is deducting such expenses directly. For example, if an employee incurs costs to visit a new work location in order to find housing or evaluate local schools, he cannot deduct these costs. Despite the fact that the employee would not be able to deduct such a cost, the reimbursement by the employer does not appear to create a taxable benefit.

11-170. Another example of this situation involves employer reimbursement for a loss on the sale of a residence at the old work location. ITA 6(20) indicates that one-half of any reimbursement in excess of $15,000 will be included in the employee's income as a taxable benefit. This means, for example, if an employer provided a $40,000 reimbursement for a loss on an old residence, the employee would be assessed a taxable benefit of $12,500 [(1/2)($40,000 - $15,000)]. Note that, unless the loss is related to an eligible relocation (i.e., 40 kilometers closer to a new work location), the full amount of any loss reimbursement would be considered to be a taxable benefit.

11-171. Employers have also attempted to compensate employees for being required to move to a new work location where housing costs are significantly higher. While there has been a considerable amount of litigation in this area, the issues now seem to be clarified:

Lump Sum Payments In those situations where an employer provides an employee with a lump sum payment to cover the increased cost of equivalent housing at the new work location, the decision in *The Queen v. Phillips* (94 DTC) has established that such amounts will be treated as taxable benefits to the employee.

Interest Subsidies Other efforts to compensate employees for higher housing costs involved low rate or interest free loans. While several court cases [*A. G. of Canada v. Hoefele et al* (95 DTC) and *Siwik v. The Queen* (96 DTC)] indicated that such subsidies were not taxable benefits to the employee, the 1998 budget effectively overturned these decisions. ITA 6(23) clarifies that an amount paid or assistance provided in respect of an individual's office or employment in respect of the acquisition or use of a residence is an employment benefit.

Tax Planning

11-172.   In those cases where the employer does not reimburse 100 percent of an employee's moving expenses, the fact that employers can reimburse certain costs that would not be deductible to the employee can be of some tax planning importance. In such partial reimbursement cases, it is to the advantage of the employee to have the employer's reimbursements specifically directed towards those moving costs which the employee would not be able to deduct from Net Income For Tax Purposes. This procedure costs the employer nothing and, at the same time, it permits the employee to maximize the deduction for moving expenses.

> **Example**   An employee has total moving expenses, including an $8,000 loss on his old residence, of $22,000. All of the costs, other than the loss on the old residence, are deductible to the employee. His employer has agreed to pay one-half of all moving costs.

> **Tax Consequences**   Of the $11,000 that will be paid by the employer, $8,000 should be earmarked for the loss on the old residence. This will allow the employee to deduct the full $11,000 that he must pay out of personal funds.

> Exercise Eleven-10 deals with moving expenses. This would be an appropriate time to attempt this exercise.

Attendant Care Expenses

11-173.   For an individual who is eligible for the disability tax credit and who is in need of attendant care, the *Income Tax Act* provides two alternative approaches to claim the costs associated with such care. Under ITA 118.2(2)(b.2), such costs can be included in the base for determining the medical expense tax credit (see Chapter 13 for a more complete explanation of the disability tax credit and the medical expense tax credit). This use of the attendant care expenses does not require the individual to be involved in any particular type of activity.

11-174.   Alternatively, if the attendant care will allow the disabled person to do certain types of activities, the related expenses can be deducted under ITA 64. As the medical expense tax credit is based on the lowest federal tax bracket of 16 percent, this approach will be beneficial to disabled individuals with sufficient income to be taxed in a higher bracket. The specified activities are as follows:

- carrying on a business;
- working as an employee;
- carrying on research; or
- attending a designated educational institution or secondary school.

11-175.   In general, the amount that can be deducted is limited to the lesser of:

1. the amount paid to the attendant; and
2. 2/3 of the sum of:
   - employment income;
   - business income; and
   - training allowances, the taxable portion of scholarships, and net research grants.

11-176.   A further limit applies when the disabled individual qualifies for this deduction because he is attending a designated educational institution or secondary school. In this case the maximum deduction is two-thirds of the total of:

1. the individual's earned income for the year, and
2. the least of:
   - the amount by which the individual's total income for the year exceeds the individual's earned income for the year;
   - $15,000; and
   - $375 multiplied by the number of weeks in the year during which the individual attends the institution or school.

11-177.   To qualify for either of the preceding tax benefits, the attendant care expenses must be paid to an individual who is neither the taxpayer's spouse nor under 18 years of age.

Child Care Expenses
Basic Definitions
11-178.   The basic idea here is that a taxpayer is permitted to deduct the cost of caring for children if such costs were incurred in order to produce taxable income. However, it is the policy of the government to place limits on the amount that can be deducted and, in the process of setting these limits, the rules related to child care costs have become quite complex. In applying these rules, a number of definitions are relevant:

Eligible Child   An eligible child is defined in ITA 63(3) to include a child of the taxpayer or his spouse, or a child that is dependent on the taxpayer or his spouse and whose income does not exceed the basic personal credit amount ($7,412 for 2001). In addition, the child must be under 16 years of age at some time during the year or dependent on the taxpayer or his spouse by reason of physical or mental infirmity.

There are different limits for disabled children who are eligible to claim the disability tax credit and those who are not (see following paragraph). To be defined as an eligible child simply requires that they be dependent as the result of some form of mental or physical disability (a mature child with Down's Syndrome would qualify here, despite the fact that the child would not likely qualify for the disability tax credit).

Annual Child Care Expense Amount   There are three annual limits. For a dependent child of any age who is eligible for the disability tax credit (e.g., a blind child), the amount is $10,000. For a child under 7 years of age at the end of the year, the amount is $7,000. For a child aged 7 to 16, or a dependent child over 16 who has a mental or physical infirmity, but is not eligible for the disability tax credit, the amount is $4,000.

Periodic Child Care Expense Amount   This weekly amount is defined as being equal to 1/40 of the annual child care expense amount applicable to the particular child. Depending on the child, the value will be $250 [(1/40)($10,000)], $175 [(1/40)($7,000)], or $100 [(1/40)($4,000)].

Earned Income   For use in determining deductible child care expenses, earned income is defined as employment income, business income, and income from scholarships, training allowances, and research grants.

11-179.   Using the definitions, we can now give attention to the rules applicable to determining the deductible child care expenses.

Lower Income Spouse Or Single Parent
11-180. There is an implicit assumption in the child care cost legislation that two parent families with a single bread winner should not be able to deduct child care costs. This assumption is implemented through the requirement that, in general, only the spouse (or "supporting person") with lower income can deduct child care costs. This means that in families that have a house parent earning no outside income, child care costs cannot be deducted.

11-181.   The amount that can be deducted by the lower income spouse in a two parent family, or by the single parent when there is no other supporting person, is the least of three amounts:

1. The amount actually paid for child care services plus limited amounts (see later discussion) paid for lodging at boarding schools and camps.

2. The sum of the **Annual Child Care Expense Amounts** for the taxpayer's eligible children ($10,000, $7,000, of $4,000 per child).

3. 2/3 of the taxpayer's **Earned Income**.

11-182.   Note that there is no requirement that these amounts be spent on individual children. For example, a couple with three qualifying children under the age of seven would have an overall amount under limit 3 of $21,000 [(3)($7,000)]. This $21,000 amount would be the applicable limit even if all of it was spent on care for one child and nothing was spent for the other children.

11-183.   Actual costs include amounts incurred for care for an eligible child in order that the taxpayer may earn employment income, carry on a business, or attend a designated educational institution or a secondary school. In order to be deductible, amounts paid for child care must be supported by receipts issued by the payee and, where the payee is an individual, the social insurance number of the payee must be provided. Any payments that are made to the mother or father of the child, as well as any payments made to a related party under the age of 18, are not deductible (see IT-495R2, "Child Care Expenses").

11-184.   A further limitation on actual costs involves situations where one or more children are attending a boarding school or an overnight camp. Since the CCRA does not wish to provide tax assistance for facilities that might be considered luxurious, when the actual costs involve overnight camps or boarding school fees, the deductible costs are limited to the **Periodic Child Care Expense Amount** ($250, $175, or $100 per week per child). Amounts paid to the camp or boarding school in excess of these amounts would not be deductible. Note that this weekly limit does not apply to fees paid to day camps or sports camps that do not include overnight stays.

Higher Income Spouse

11-185.   In the preceding section, we noted the general rule that child care costs must be deducted by the lower income spouse. There are however, a number of exceptions to this general rule. Specifically, the higher income spouse is allowed to make the deduction if:

- the lower income spouse is a student in attendance at a designated educational institution (i.e., an institution which qualifies the individual for the education credit) or a secondary school and enrolled in a program of the institution or school of not less than 3 consecutive weeks duration that provides that each student in the program spend not less than 10 hours per week on courses or work in the program (i.e., full time attendance);

- the lower income spouse is a student in attendance at a designated educational institution or a secondary school and enrolled in a program of the institution or school that is not less than 3 consecutive weeks duration and that provides that each student in the program spend not less than 12 hours in the month on courses in the program (i.e., part time attendance);

- the lower income spouse is infirm and incapable of caring for the children for at least 2 weeks;

- the lower income spouse is a person confined to a prison or similar institution throughout a period of not less than 2 weeks in the year; or

- the spouses are separated for more than 90 days beginning in the year.

11-186.   In situations where the higher income spouse is making the deduction, the amount of the deduction would be subject to the same limitations that were described for situations where the deduction is being made by the lower income spouse. However, in these situations, there is a further limitation. This further limit is calculated by multiplying the sum of the **Periodic Child Care Expense Amounts** for all eligible children, by the number of weeks that the lower income spouse is infirm, in prison, attending an educational institution, or separated from the higher income spouse. In most situations, this will provide the applicable limit on the amount to be deducted by the higher income spouse.

11-187.   ITA 63(2.2) allows a taxpayer who is attending a designated educational institution on a full or part time basis to deduct child care costs if there is no supporting person of an eligible child of the taxpayer for the year or, alternatively, the income of the taxpayer for the year exceeds the income for the year of a supporting person of the child. The calculation of the deductible amount is specified under ITA 63(2.3) and generally follows the rules for deductibility by the higher income spouse. That is, the amount deductible is limited to the sum of the **Periodic Child Care Expense Amounts** for all eligible children. There is a difference, however, in that for this type of situation, the income limitation is based on total Net Income For Tax Purposes, not just Earned Income as defined in ITA 63(3).

Example

11-188.   The following example will serve to clarify some of the general rules for child care costs.

Example   Jack and Joanna Morris have three children. At the end of 2001, Bruce is aged 18 and, while he is physically disabled, his disability is not severe enough that he qualifies for the disability tax credit. With respect to their other children, Bobby is aged 6 and Betty is aged 2 at the end of the year. Jack has 2001 earned income of $45,000 while Joanna has 2001 earned income of $63,000. The couple has full time help to care for their children during 49 weeks of the year. The cost of this help is $210 per week ($10,290 for the year). During July, the children are sent to camp for three weeks. The camp fees total $3,500 for this period for all three children. As the result of a substance abuse conviction, Jack spends seven weeks in November and December in prison.

The general limits on deductible child care costs would give the following amounts:

	Joanna	Jack
Actual child care costs plus maximum deductible camp fees {$10,290 + [($175)(2)(3 weeks)] + [($100)(1)(3 weeks)]}	$11,640	$11,640
2/3 of earned income	42,000	30,000
Annual Child Care Expense Amount [($7,000)(2) + ($4,000)(1)]	18,000	18,000
Periodic Child Care Expense Amounts [($175)(7 Weeks)(2) + ($100)(7 Weeks)(1)]	3,150	N/A

> **Exercise Eleven-11** deals with child care costs. This would be an appropriate time to attempt this exercise

While Joanna is the higher income spouse, she will be able to deduct child care costs during the seven weeks that Jack is in prison. Her maximum deduction is $3,150. As the lower income spouse, Jack will deduct additional child care costs of $8,490 ($11,640 − $3,150). Note that, while Bruce is an eligible child because of his disability, the fact that the disability is not severe enough to qualify for the disability tax credit means that his annual limit is $4,000 rather than $10,000, and that the periodic limit for Joanna and for the camp fees is $100 rather than $250.

References

11-189.   For more detailed study of the material in this Chapter, we refer you to the following:

ITA 15	Benefit Conferred On Shareholder
ITA 56	Amounts To Be Included In Income For Year
ITA 60	Other Deductions
ITA 62	Moving Expenses
ITA 63	Child Care Expenses
ITA 80.4(2)	Loans
ITA 146.1	Registered Education Savings Plans
ITA 260(1)	Securities Lending Arrangements
ITR 300	Capital Element Of Annuity Payments
IC 93-3	Registered Education Savings Plans
IT-67R3	Taxable Dividends From Corporations Resident In Canada
IT-75R3	Scholarships, Fellowships, Bursaries, Prizes And Research Grants
IT-119R4	Debts of Shareholders And Certain Persons Connected With Shareholders
IT-172R	Capital Cost Allowance — Taxation Year Of Individual
IT-178R3 (Consolidated)	Moving Expenses

Exercises

(The solutions for these exercises can be found following Chapter 21 of the text.)

Exercise Eleven - 1 (Interest Income)
On October 1, 2001, Ms. Diane Dumont acquires an investment contract with a maturity value of $60,000. It matures on September 30, 2007 and pays interest at an annual rate of 8 percent. Payment for the first three and one-quarter years of interest is on December 31, 2004, with interest for the remaining two and three-quarters years payable on the maturity date. What amount of interest will Ms. Dumont have to include in her tax returns for each of the years 2001 through 2007?

Exercise Eleven - 2 (Interest Income)
On January 1, 2001, a debt obligation is issued with a coupon interest rate of 7 percent, a maturity value of $250,000, and a maturity date of December 31, 2003. The interest coupons and the maturity amount are sold separately at prices which provide an effective yield of 7 percent. The price of the maturity payment is $204,075, while the price of the interest coupons is $45,925. Calculate the amount of interest that the purchasers of these two financial instruments will have to include in their tax returns in each of the three years.

Exercise Eleven - 3 (Interest Income)
On May 1, 2001, Mr. Milford Lay purchases bonds with a face value of $50,000. These bonds pay semi annual interest of $3,000 on June 30 and December 31 of each year. He purchases the bonds for $52,000, including interest accrued to the purchase date. He holds the bonds for the remainder of the year, receiving both the June 30 and December 31 interest payments. What amount of interest will be included in Mr. Milford's 2001 tax return?

Exercise Eleven - 4 (Weak Currency Debt)
On January 1, 2001, Kanadian Ltd. issues debt securities in the amount of 40,000,000 Malyasian Ringgits (R). At this time the exchange rate is R1 = $0.40. The proceeds are converted to $16,000,000 for investment in capital assets in Canada. As there is concern with respect to the stability of the Ringgit, the interest rate on the debt is 20 percent, a rate that is 12 percentage points higher than that being paid on similar debt issued by the company in Canada. Interest is payable on December 31 of each year. The debt is repaid on December 31, 2003. Relevant exchange rates are as follows:

December 31, 2001	R1 = $0.35
December 31, 2002	R1 = $0.25
December 31, 2003	R1 = $0.18

What are the tax consequences for Kanadian Ltd. in each of the three years 2001 through 2003?

Exercise Eleven - 5 (Rental Income)
Ms. Sheela Horne acquires a rental property in September, 2001 at a total cost of $185,000. Of this total, $42,000 can be allocated to the value of the land. She immediately spends $35,000 to make major improvements in the property. Rents for the year total $7,200, while rental expenses other than CCA total $5,100. This is the only rental property owned by Ms. Horne. Determine the maximum CCA that Ms. Horne can deduct in calculating her 2001 rental income.

Exercise Eleven - 6 (Dividend Income)
Mr. John Johns receives $17,000 in dividends from a taxable Canadian corporation. His income is such that all additional amounts will be taxed at a 29 percent federal rate and a 12 percent provincial rate. He lives in a province with a dividend tax credit equal to 30 percent of the 25 percent gross up. Determine the total federal and provincial tax that will be payable on these dividends.

Exercise Eleven - 7 (Shareholder Loans)

Ms. Martha Rourke is an employee of Rourke Inc., a Company in which her husband owns 70 percent of the outstanding shares. Ms. Rourke owns the remaining 30 percent of the shares. On July 1 of the current year, she receives a $50,000 interest free loan that will be used to purchase an automobile to be used in her employment duties. The loan is to be repaid in four annual instalments to be made on June 30 of each year. The prescribed rate for the current year is six percent. What are the current year tax implications of this loan for Ms. Rourke?

Exercise Eleven - 8 (Support Payments)

On July 1, 2001, Sandra and Jerry Groom sign a separation agreement which calls for Sandra to pay Jerry $1,500 per month in child support (Jerry will have custody of their five children) and $2,500 per month in spousal support. To the end of 2001, Sandra's payments total only $11,000. How will these payments be dealt with in Sandra and Jerry's 2001 tax returns?

Exercise Eleven - 9 (Annuity Payments)

On January 1 of the current year, Barry Hollock uses $55,000 of his savings to acquire a fixed term annuity. The term of the annuity is four years, the annual payments are $15,873, the payments are received on December 31 of each year, and the rate inherent in the annuity is six percent. How much of the $15,873 annual payment should Mr. Hollock include in his annual tax return?

Exercise Eleven - 10 (Moving Expenses)

On December 20, 2001, at the request of her employer, Ms. Martinova Chevlak moves from Edmonton to Regina. She has always lived in a rented apartment and will continue to do so in Regina. The total cost of the actual move, including the costs of moving her personal possessions, is $6,400. In addition, she spent $1,300 on a visit to Regina in a search for appropriate accommodation and $1,200 as a penalty for breaking her lease in Edmonton. During the year, her salary totalled $64,000, of which $2,000 can be allocated to the period after December 20, 2001. Her employer is prepared to pay up to $6,000 towards the cost of her move. Determine Ms. Chevlak's maximum moving expense deduction for 2001.

Exercise Eleven - 11 (Child Care Expenses)

Mr. and Mrs. Sampras have 3 children. The ages of the children are 4, 9, and 14, and they are all in good mental and physical health. During the current year, Mr. Sampras has employment income of $36,000. Mrs. Sampras has business income during this period of $78,000. The child care costs for the current year, all paid for by cheque and properly documented for tax purposes are $10,500. Determine the maximum deduction for child care costs during the current year.

Problems For Self Study

(The solutions for these problems can be found following Chapter 21 of the text.)

Self Study Problem Eleven - 1

Mr. James Loyt is in the middle of the 26 percent federal tax bracket and the 12 percent provincial tax bracket. The province requires a 25 percent gross up on dividends received and provides a dividend tax credit equal to 30 percent of this gross up. He has $20,000 in cash to invest for a period of one year and is considering the following two investments:

- Bonds issued by Faxtext Ltd., a taxable Canadian corporation. These bonds pay interest at an annual rate of 7.75 percent.

- Preferred Shares issued by the same corporation. These shares pay an annual dividend of 5 percent on all amounts invested.

Required: Based on your calculations, advise Mr. Loyt as to which investment he should make.

Self Study Problem Eleven - 2

During December, 2000, Ms. Holmes reaches a settlement with her former husband which requires him to make a lump sum payment to her of $100,000 on January 1, 2001. While Ms. Holmes has no immediate need for the funds, she will require them on January 1, 2002 in order to finance a new business venture that she plans to launch. As a consequence, she would like to invest the funds for the year ending December 31, 2001. She is considering the following alternatives:

- Investment of the full $100,000 in a one year, guaranteed investment certificate which pays annual interest of 5.5 percent.

- Investment of the full $100,000 in a rental property with a cost of $165,000. The property currently has a tenant whose lease calls for rental payments during 2001 of $13,200. Cash expenses for the year (interest, taxes, and condominium fees) are expected to be $9,600. Of the total cost of $165,000, an amount of $15,000 can be allocated to the land on which the building is situated. Ms. Holmes believes that the property can be sold on December 31, 2001 to net her $175,000.

- Investment of the full $100,000 in the shares of Norton Ltd., a publicly traded Canadian company. Ms. Holmes expects that the Company will pay dividends on these shares during 2001 of $5,000. She anticipates that by the end of 2001 the shares will be worth at least $106,000.

Ms. Holmes expects to have employment income in excess of $100,000 during 2001. Her provincial tax rate is equal to 15 percent of taxable income. The province requires dividends to be grossed up by 25 percent and provides a dividend tax credit equal to 35 percent of the gross up.

Required:

A. Would Ms. Holmes be subject to any taxes on the $100,000 she received from her former husband? Explain your conclusion.

B. Write a brief memorandum providing investment advice to Ms. Holmes on the three alternatives.

Self Study Problem Eleven - 3

In May of the current year, following a dispute with her immediate superior, Ms. Elaine Fox resigned from her present job in Halifax and began to look for other employment. She was not able to find suitable work in Halifax. However, she did locate another job in Regina and was expected to report for work on October 1.

After locating the new job, Ms. Fox flew to Regina to find living quarters for herself. After two days of searching, Ms. Fox was able to locate a suitable house. Subsequent to purchasing her new home, Ms. Fox remained in Regina for an additional four days in order to purchase various furnishings for this residence. Her expenses for this trip were as follows:

Air Fare (Halifax - Regina, Return)	$ 689
Car Rental (6 Days At $35)	210
Hotel (6 Days At $110)	660
Food (6 Days At $40)	240
Total Expenses	$1,799

On her return to Halifax, she received the following statements from her attorneys:

Real Estate Commission - Old Home	$ 9,500
Legal Fees - Old Home	1,400
Unpaid Taxes On Old Home To Date Of Sale	800
Legal Fees - New Home	1,850
Transfer Tax On New Home	600
Total	$14,150

On August 31 of the current year, after supervising the final packing of her property and its removal from the old house, Ms. Fox spent three days in a Halifax hotel while she finalized arrangements for her departure. Expenses during this period were as follows:

Hotel (Three Days At $95)	$285
Food (Three Days At $45)	135
Total	$420

On September 3, she leaves Halifax by automobile, arriving in Regina on September 10. As her new residence is not yet available, she is forced to continue living in a Regina hotel until September 26. Her expenses for the period September 3 through September 26 are as follows:

Gasoline	$ 350
Hotels (23 Days At $95)	2,185
Food (23 Days At $45)	1,035
Total	$3,570

On moving into the new residence, she is required to pay the moving company a total of $3,800. This fee includes $675 for the 16 days of storage required because the new home was not available when the furnishings arrived.

Ms. Fox's only income for the current year was employment income and the net amounts to be included in her Net Income For Tax Purposes are as follows:

Old Job (5 Months)	$15,000
New Job (3 Months)	10,500
Total Net Employment Income	$25,500

Ms. Fox's new employer did not provide any reimbursement for moving expenses.

Required: Calculate the maximum allowable moving expenses that Ms. Fox can deduct from her Net Income For Tax Purposes for the current year and any amount that can be carried over to the subsequent year.

Self Study Problem Eleven - 4

Mr. and Mrs. Pleasant have three children who are eight, ten and fifteen years of age and live at home. In order to keep up with the costs of a family of this size, both Mr. Pleasant and Mrs. Pleasant are employed. However, this requires that a considerable amount be spent on care for their children.

During 2001, Mr. Pleasant had earned income of $33,000 while Mrs. Pleasant had earned income of $18,000. Payments for child care amounted to $100 per week for a total of 48 weeks.

Also during 2001, there was a period of 6 weeks during which Mrs. Pleasant was hospitalized for injuries suffered in a fall while rock climbing. This period was part of the 48 weeks for which child care payments were made.

Required: Determine the amount that can be deducted by Mr. Pleasant and by Mrs. Pleasant during the year ending December 31, 2001, for child care expenses.

Assignment Problems

(The solutions for these problems are only available in
the solutions manual that has been provided to your instructor.)

Assignment Problem Eleven - 1

Bill Martin, Dave Martin, and Charles Martin are three brothers living in the same province. They each have $20,000 which they wish to invest. Because of differences in their current employment situations, they are in different tax brackets. These brackets are as follows:

	Federal Tax Bracket	Provincial Tax Bracket
Bill Martin	16 Percent	6 Percent
Dave Martin	22 Percent	9 Percent
Charles Martin	29 Percent	14 Percent

The provincial dividend tax credit is equal to one-third of the dividend gross up.

For a number of years they have been interested in the securities of Moland Industries and, at the present time, they are considering two securities of the Company which are currently outstanding. These securities and their investment characteristics are as follows:

Bonds   The Company has a large issue of debenture bonds which has a coupon interest rate of 6 percent. They are selling at par value and mature in 18 years.

Preferred Stock   The company has an issue of preferred shares which is offering a dividend of 4 percent based on the current market price. The dividend is cumulative, but not participating.

The income from these investments would not move Bill or Dave Martin to a higher tax bracket.

Required:

A. Calculate the after tax income that would be generated for each of the three brothers assuming that they invested their $20,000 in the Moland Industries bonds.

B. Calculate the after tax income that would be generated for each of the three brothers assuming that they invested their $20,000 in the Moland Industries Preferred Stock.

Assignment Problem Eleven - 2

Mr. Arthur Blaine is President and sole shareholder of Blaine Enterprises, a Canadian controlled private company involved in manufacturing. He is also employed by the Company at a salary of $57,000 per year. Since arriving at his office this morning two things have come to Mr. Blaine's attention. They are as follows:

1. Mr. Blaine's accountant has submitted financial statements indicating that his Company has income before taxes of $195,000 for the current year. As the Company is eligible for the small business deduction, this income is taxed at a rate of about 20 percent, leaving an after tax profit in excess of $150,000.

2. Mr. Blaine has a $125,000 mortgage on his personal residence and it must be renewed within the next month.

Putting these two items of information together, Mr. Blaine concludes that it would make sense for his corporation to lend him the required $125,000 on an interest free basis for a period of ten years. He believes that there should be no problem with this action in that he is the sole shareholder of the Company and the Company has sufficient extra cash to make the loan without interfering with its basic business operations.

Required: As Mr. Blaine's personal and corporate tax advisor, give your advice on Mr. Blaine's solution to his mortgage refinancing problem.

Assignment Problem Eleven - 3

For the last 12 years, Miss Stone has been the president and only shareholder of Stone Enterprises, a Canadian controlled private company. She handles all marketing and oversees the day to day operations of the business. Her annual salary is $80,000.

The Company has a December 31 year end. During the four year period, January 1, 1998 through December 31, 2001, there were a number of transactions between Miss Stone and her Company. They can be described as follows:

1998 Stone Enterprises loaned $28,000 on an interest free basis to Miss Stone for various personal expenditures.

1999 The Company loaned an amount of $40,000 to Miss Stone in her capacity as an employee to assist her with the acquisition of a new car. The loan calls for payments of $10,000 per year for the next four years but does not require the payment of any interest. Payments have been made in 2000 and 2001. The car is to be used solely for Company business. Stone Enterprises makes car loans available to all employees with at least five years of service with the company.

2000 The Company provided Miss Stone with a $90,000 loan to assist her in purchasing a new home. The loan is to be paid off at the rate of $6,000 per year with interest at 2 percent per annum. Stone Enterprises makes housing loans available to all employees with at least five years of service with the company.

Also in 2000, the Company declared dividends of $22,000 and accrued a bonus to Miss Stone in the amount $32,000. While the dividends were paid in 2000, Miss Stone did not receive the bonus until March, 2001. All of the dividends and $10,000 of the bonus were redeposited in the Company on March 31, 2001 and used by the Company for purchasing inventories. The Company considered $28,000 of these redeposited funds a repayment of the 1998 loan to Miss Stone.

2001 Miss Stone has only one competitor in her region and, in order to diminish the effectiveness of this company, Miss Stone purchases 40 percent of its outstanding shares for $72,000. Stone Enterprises loans her the entire $72,000 on an interest free basis and Miss Stone anticipates that she will repay the loan in 2004.

Required: Discuss, without showing any numerical calculations, the tax effects of the transactions described in the preceding paragraphs.

Assignment Problem Eleven - 4

Mrs. Norton is a lawyer with a well established practice located in Regina. During the taxation year ending December 31, 2001, she had professional fees of $169,500 and operating expenses associated with running her practice of $42,800. In addition to these operating expenses, Mrs. Norton spent $1,500 for accommodations and seminar fees attending a convention in Saskatoon and $5,400 in travel costs (air fare, accommodations and 50 percent of meals) attending a convention in Singapore on doing business in Asia.

In addition to her professional income, Mrs. Norton received $1,000 in dividends from a Canadian public company and $1,250 in interest on Canada Savings Bonds. Mrs. Norton also owns a rental property which generated revenues of $6,000 and cash expenses of $4,000. The Undepreciated Capital Cost of this property at the beginning of the current year was $55,000 and it is subject to Capital Cost Allowance at a rate of five percent.

Mrs. Norton paid rent of $9,600 for the house in which she and her family reside. Mrs. Norton is married and her husband had no income during 2001. They have two children, aged 8 and 12.

During 2001, Mrs. Norton contributed $4,200 to an RRSP. Her 2000 earned income was $95,000. At the end of 2000, she has no unused RRSP deduction room or undeducted RRSP contributions.

Required: Determine Mrs. Norton's minimum Net Income For Tax Purposes for the year ending December 31, 2001.

Assignment Problem Eleven - 5

On January 1, 2001, Miss Heather Plant receives a $50,000 cheque from an attorney representing the estate of her recently deceased aunt, Mildred. The money was bequeathed by Miss Plant's aunt without any conditions and is not subject to any form of taxes at the time that it is received.

In anticipation of this bequest, Miss Plant has purchased a condominium which will be available for occupancy on January 1, 2002. As she has no need for the $50,000 until the condominium becomes available, she would like to invest the funds for the year ending December 31, 2001. She is considering the following two alternatives:

- Investment of the full $50,000 in a guaranteed investment certificate which will pay annual interest at the rate of 6 percent for the year ending December 31, 2001.

- Investment of the full $50,000 in 1,000 shares of a common stock of a public company which is selling for $50 per share on January 1, 2001. For a number of years, this stock has paid an annual dividend of $1 per share. In addition, Miss Plant is advised that the price of the shares is likely to increase to at least $55 by December 31, 2001.

Miss Plant has sufficient employment income that she is in the 29 percent federal tax bracket and the 14 percent provincial tax bracket. The provincial dividend tax credit is equal to 25 percent of the gross up.

Required: Write a brief memorandum providing investment advice to Miss Plant.

Assignment Problem Eleven - 6

On January 1 of the current year, Mr. Drake owns a total of four rental properties. All of the properties were acquired after 1972 and before 1988 and are of brick construction. The cost and undepreciated capital cost for the properties as at January 1 of the current year are as follows:

	Original Cost	UCC
Property A	$36,000	$21,500
Property B	48,000	43,000
Property C	63,000	46,000
Property D	90,000	64,000

During the year, rental revenues and cash expenses on the four properties are as follows:

	Rental Revenue	Property Taxes	Interest	Other Expenses
Property A	$ 5,200	$ 1,200	$ 1,750	$ 500
Property B	6,700	1,550	-0-	1,800
Property C	12,200	2,750	7,800	1,700
Property D	15,300	3,750	13,500	3,900

Other transactions which occurred during the year are as follows:

1. Property A was sold for cash proceeds of $72,000 on July 20.

2. Property C was sold for $61,000 in cash on August 24.

3. A new rental property, Property E was acquired at a cost of $192,000. It was acquired late in the year and as a result, rents for the year total only $2,000, interest charges $2,300, property taxes $275, and other expenses $325.

Mr. Drake wants to take the maximum capital cost allowances permitted on all of his properties and owns no other properties.

Required: Calculate Mr. Drake's income from property, taxable net capital gains, and recapture for the current taxation year.

Assignment Problem Eleven - 7

On January 2, 2001, Mrs. Long died in an automobile crash. Mrs. Long was 55 years old and, at the time of her death, was a full time employee of Apex Distribution Systems. During 2000, Mrs. Long earned $47,000 in employment income.

Because of her years of faithful service, Apex decides to pay a death benefit to Mrs. Long's surviving spouse in the amount of $24,000. The amount is to be paid in annual instalments of $6,000 per year with the first instalment being paid in 2001.

Required: What effect will this death benefit have on the Net Income For Tax Purposes of Mrs. Long's spouse in 2001 and in subsequent years?

Assignment Problem Eleven - 8

Arthur Madison, Jules Madison, and Stanley Madison are brothers and they have asked you to assist them in preparing their tax returns for the 2001 taxation year. They have provided you with the following information:

	Arthur	Jules	Stanley
Net employment income	$6,000	$18,000	$23,000
Net business income (Loss)	-0-	5,000	(12,000)
Net property income (Loss)	8,000	(4,000)	11,000
Capital gains	5,625	14,000	-0-
Capital losses	-0-	(17,000)	(10,000)
Employment insurance received	3,000	-0-	-0-
Pension benefits received	-0-	3,000	-0-
Charitable donations	(4,000)	(2,000)	(1,000)
Tuition fees paid	-0-	-0-	(800)
Spousal support payments made	-0-	-0-	(4,800)

Required: Determine the 2001 Net Income For Tax Purposes for each of the Madison brothers and indicate any losses that can be carried over to other years.

Assignment Problem Eleven - 9

Mr. Plate's earned income for 2000 was $32,000. During the year ending December 31, 2000, Mr. Plate's records indicate that he contributed $2,500 to a money purchase RPP sponsored by his employer. His employer contributed the same amount on his behalf during this period. At the end of 2000, he had no unused RRSP deduction room or undeducted RRSP contributions.

Mr. Plate's 2001 earned income for RRSP purposes was $35,000. During the year ending December 31, 2001, Mr. Plate's records indicate that he contributed $2,800 to a money purchase RPP sponsored by his employer. His employer again matched his contribution to his RPP during 2001.

Mr. Plate made a $2,000 payment on April 30, 2001 to his RRSP. On September 1, 2001, he contributed $5,300 to his 8 year old son's Registered Education Savings Plan.

Required: Indicate which of the contributions that have been made by Mr. Plate can be deducted in calculating his Net Income For Tax Purposes for the 2001 taxation year and any carry overs available to him at the end of 2001. Provide any advice you feel would assist him in planning future actions concerning his son's RESP.

Assignment Problem Eleven - 10

Mr. Masters entered the University of Manitoba as a freshman on September 1, 2001. His tuition fees for the period September 1, 2001 through April 30, 2002 were $3,000 and his textbook purchases totalled $640. One-half of the tuition fees and textbook purchases were for the September to December, 2001 semester. The remainder related to the January to April, 2002 semester. All of these amounts were paid by Mr. Masters' father.

During 2001, Mr. Masters received the following amounts:

Wages from part time employment	$ 2,400
Scholarship granted by university	3,500
Dividends from taxable Canadian corporations	2,000

Required: Determine the minimum Net Income For Tax Purposes that Mr. Masters will have to report for his 2001 taxation year.

Assignment Problem Eleven - 11

In September of the current year, following a dispute with his immediate superior, Mr. Tully resigned from his job in Calgary and began to look for other employment. He was not able to find suitable work in Calgary. However, he did locate another job in Ottawa and was expected to report for work on December 1.

After locating the new job, Mr. Tully flew to Ottawa to find a new home for himself and his family. While he located a desirable house and signed the purchase agreement after four days in the city, finalizing all of the details associated with the purchase required him to remain in Ottawa for another three days. His expenses for this trip were as follows:

Air fare (Calgary - Ottawa, Return)	$ 675
Car rental (7 days at $30)	210
Hotel (7 days at $90)	630
Food (7 days at $30)	210
Total Expenses	$ 1,725

On his return to Calgary, he received the following information from his lawyer:

Real estate commission - old home	$ 9,000
Legal fees - old home	1,500
Unpaid taxes on old home to date of sale	1,200
Legal fees - new home	1,750
Transfer tax on new home	1,100
Total	$14,550

On November 14 of the current year, after supervising the final packing of their property and its removal from the old house, Mr. Tully and his family leave Calgary by automobile. They arrive in Ottawa on November 20th. However, because of some delays in the completion of their new home, they are unable to move in until November 30. Their expenses during the period November 14 through November 30 are as follows:

Gasoline	$ 415
Hotels (16 days at $75)	1,200
Food (16 days at $60)	960
Total	$2,575

On moving into the new residence, they are required to pay the moving company a total of $4,500. This fee includes $450 for the 9 days of storage required because their new home was not completed when they arrived.

Mr. Tully's only income for the current year was employment income and the net amounts to be included in his Net Income For Tax Purposes are as follows:

Old job (9 months)	$54,000
New job (1 month)	8,000
Total Net Employment Income	$62,000

Mr. Tully's new employer did not provide any reimbursement for moving expenses.

Required: Calculate the maximum allowable moving expenses that Mr. Tully can deduct from his Net Income For Tax Purposes for the current year and any amount that can be carried over to the subsequent year.

Assignment Problem Eleven - 12

Mr. and Mrs. Harris have four children and, at the end of 2001, their ages are 6, 10, 12, and 15. The 15 year old child has a prolonged physical handicap which qualifies him for the disability tax credit.

Mrs. Harris is a stock broker and had 2001 salary and commissions of $63,500. Mr. Harris is involved in a travel business and, due to some bad strategic decisions, his share of the earnings of this business for the year ending December 31, 2001 amounts to only $4,200. In addition to his business earnings, Mr. Harris has interest income for 2001 of $12,500.

As both spouses must spend considerable time at work, full time child care is required. As a consequence, their payments for child care amount to $250 per week for 49 weeks of the year. With respect to the other three weeks, all of the children attend a prestigious music camp during the month of June. The cost of this camp is $3,000 per child, or a total of $12,000 for the three weeks.

In February, 2001, Mr. Harris fell off a chair lift while skiing and was in the hospital for a period of four weeks.

In late September, 2001, Mrs. Harris is convicted of insider trading activities and sentenced to 6 months in prison. She immediately begins serving the sentence and spends the last 12 weeks of 2001 in jail.

Required: Determine the maximum amount that can be deducted by Mr. Harris and by Mrs. Harris for child care costs with respect to the 2001 taxation year.

Assignment Problem Eleven - 13 (Electronic Library Research Problem)

Provide brief answers to the following questions. Your answers should be supported by references to materials found in your Electronic Library.

A. For the year 2001, the first $3,000 of scholarships, fellowships, and bursaries, can be excluded from the recipient's income. Would income from a student assistanceship, paid for marking exams or staffing tutorials, qualify for this exemption?

B. Youngman Inc. provides its only shareholder, Ms. Helena Youngman, with a residence that cost the corporation $450,000. Ms. Youngman does not use the property for corporate entertaining, nor does she maintain an office in the property. Ms. Youngman would like your advice on the value of the shareholder benefit that she should include in income as a result of having the use of this property. What advice would you give Ms. Youngman?

C. An individual owns a large apartment building. He is aware that, if the rentals from this building are considered to be business income as opposed to property income, he will be able to deduct maximum capital cost allowance, even if the result is a loss on the property. What factors would be considered in deciding whether the rents on this building are business income or property income?

Chapter 12

Taxable Income For Individuals

Introduction

12-1.   Chapters 5 through 11 have dealt largely with the determination of income from various sources. The specific sources discussed were income from employment, income from business or property, taxable capital gains and allowable capital losses, other miscellaneous sources of income, and other miscellaneous deductions from income. While the term is not used in the usual accounting sense, the sum of all of these items is generally referred to as Net Income or Net Income For Tax Purposes. Since all of the components of this figure, including the rules for combining the components, are found in Division B of the *Income Tax Act*, this total is also referred to as Division B Income.

12-2.   This Chapter will cover converting Net Income For Tax Purposes (Division B Income) to Taxable Income (Division C Income). For individuals, this process begins with combining the various components that have been determined under Division B. Note that three of these components of Net Income For Tax Purposes (employment income, business and property income, and net taxable capital gains) are net figures themselves. That is, they consist of a combination of inclusions and deductions that are specific to that type of income.

12-3.   When the Net Income For Tax Purposes figure is completed, Division C specifies a number of deductions that can be made by residents of Canada (Taxable Income for non residents is covered in Division D). The major deductions in the calculation of taxable income for an individual are as follows:

- Employee Stock Options Deduction - ITA 110(1)(d) and (d.1)
- Deductions For Payments (Social Assistance And Workers' Compensation Received) - ITA 110(1)(f)
- Home Relocation Loan Deduction - ITA 110(1)(j)
- Lifetime Capital Gains Deduction - ITA 110.6
- Northern Residents Deductions - ITA 110.7
- Loss Carry Over Deductions - ITA 111

12-4.   With respect to the stock option deduction, you may recall mention of stock options in several earlier Chapters. In previous editions of this text, we provided fairly comprehensive coverage of stock options in our discussion of employment income in Chapter 5. As was noted in that Chapter, recent changes have added considerable complexity to the taxation of stock options and, in order to deal with this, we have moved our in-depth coverage of stock options to this Chapter. This includes the employment income inclusion (Chapter 5), the treatment of identical properties at time of disposition (Chapter 9), and the treatment of options and shares acquired through options at the time of emigration (Chapter 11).

12-5.   As an additional point, we would note that this Chapter is only concerned with the calculation of taxable income for individuals. Of the deductions listed, only loss carry overs are available to corporations. However, corporations have additional deductions for charitable contributions and for dividends received from other taxable Canadian corporations. These deductions are covered in Chapter 14.

Stock Option Plans

The Economics of Stock Option Arrangements

12-6.   Stock options allow, but do not require, the holder to purchase a specified number of shares for a specified period of time at a specified acquisition price. At the time of issue, the option price is usually at or above the market price of the shares. For example, options might be issued to acquire shares at a price of $10 at a time when the shares are trading at that same $10 value. At first glance, such an option would appear to have no value as it simply allows the holder to acquire a share for $10, at a time when that share is only worth that amount. In reality, however, this option could have significant value in that it allows the holder to participate in any upward price movement in the shares without any obligation to exercise the option if the price stays at or falls below $10. Stated alternatively, the option provides full participation in gains on the option shares, with no downside risk. Further, for an employee receiving such options, they provide this participation with no real investment cost until such time as the options are exercised.

12-7.   Stock options are used as a form of compensation in the belief that, by giving the employee an interest in the stock of the company, he has an incentive to make a greater effort on behalf of the enterprise. In recent years, this form of employee compensation has become more widely used, both in terms of the number of companies issuing such options and in terms of the types of employees to which this type of compensation is granted. The use of options is particularly common in the high tech sector though the recent fall in high tech stock prices has seriously affected the exercise of stock options.

12-8.   Another hidden, but clearly significant advantage to the use of stock options, is that the cost of issuing such options is not recorded in the financial statements of the issuing corporation. Because of an inability of accountants to agree on the appropriate value for options that are not "in the money" (i.e., options are referred to as in the money if the market price of the shares exceeds the option price), corporations are generally able to issue huge quantities of stock options without recording any compensation expense. As tax legislation discourages the issuance of options with an exercise price that is less than the fair market value of the option shares, in the money options are rarely issued by public companies. Given this, the inability of accountants to agree on a valuation method for options that are out of the money results in no accounting entry being made when options are issued. This means that, from the point of view of the issuing corporation, the use of options systematically understates compensation expense and overstates income.

12-9.   While accountants do not recognize any employment compensation expense in the accounting records, tax legislation has taken the position that there is employment income, not at the time the options are issued but, rather, at the time the options are exercised. This employment income is measured as the excess of the fair market value of the shares at the time of exercise over the option price paid for the shares. Note that, in the absence of an excess, the options would not be exercised and, as a consequence, there will always be employment income when options are exercised.

> **Example**   An executive receives options to acquire 1,000 of his employer's common shares at an option price of $25 per share when the common shares are trading at $25 per share. He exercises the options when the shares are trading at $40 per share.

Employment Income At the time of exercise, tax legislation will require the measurement of an employment income benefit. In this case, the amount will be $15,000 [(1,000)($40 - $25)]. As we shall see later in this section, this benefit may be recognized at this time or, alternatively, deferred until the shares are sold.

12-10. If the executive had simply purchased the shares for $25 without the use of an option arrangement, this $15,000 would be considered a capital gain, rather than employment income. In view of this, the treatment of this amount as employment income creates an inequity in that only one-half of capital gains are subject to tax. In order to correct this inequity, tax legislation permits a deduction in the calculation of Taxable Income equal to the non taxable one-half of the employment income inclusion. This puts the taxation of this employment income inclusion on the same footing as capital gains on the equivalent share values.

12-11. Applying this to our example, at the time the options are exercised, the Taxable Income of the executive would be measured as follows:

Employment Income	$15,000
Deduction (One-Half of Inclusion)	(7,500)
Taxable Income	$ 7,500

12-12. There are several relevant points with respect to the employment income inclusion and the related deduction from Taxable Income:

- The employment income inclusion will always be measured at the time the options are exercised. However, its recognition for tax purposes may be deferred until the acquired shares are sold. This will be discussed in detail in the material which follows.

- The $7,500 deduction is from Taxable Income, not employment income. The net employment income figure that will be included in the executive's current or future Net Income for Tax Purposes is $15,000.

- The availability of the $7,500 deduction is conditional. For options involving public company shares, it is only available when, at the time the options are issued, the fair market value of the shares to be acquired is equal to or less than the option price. It is this rule that discourages public companies from issuing options that are "in the money".

  For options involving the shares of private companies, the availability of the deduction is also available when the fair market value of the shares at the time the options were issued was equal to or less than the option price. If this condition is not met, the deduction is still available, provided the shares have been held at least two years after acquisition.

- As a final point in this section you should note that, because the increase in value from $25 to $40 will be taxed as employment income, the $40 value becomes the new adjusted cost base of the shares for purposes of determining capital gain and losses on their subsequent sale. If, at a later point in time, the shares were sold for $60, the taxable capital gain would be $10,000 [(1,000)(1/2)($60 - $40)].

Relevant Dates

12-13. In turning to the more detailed rules related to the taxation of stock options, there are four dates that are relevant to understanding the required procedures. They can be described as follows:

- **Issue Date (a.k.a. Grant Date)** The date on which the corporation commits to providing the options and specifies the terms under which they are available to the employee.

- **Vesting Date** The date on which the employee earns the irrevocable right to have the options, without regard to whether he continues in the employ of the corporation. Typically, but not necessarily, this is also the date on which the options become exercisable.

- **Exercise Date** The date on which the employee exercises the option and actually acquires the shares.

- **Disposal Date** The date on which the shares acquired under the option arrangement are sold.

Private vs. Public Companies

12-14. Tax legislation makes distinction between public and private companies in its approach to recognizing the employment income resulting from stock options. In very simplified terms, when options are issued by public companies, the employment income inclusion is taxed when the options are exercised. In contrast, when options are issued by Canadian controlled private companies, the employment income inclusion is deferred until the shares are actually sold.

12-15. This approach was viewed as problematical in that, for public companies, taxation at the time of exercise often forced the employee to sell a portion of their shares in order to pay the taxes due on the employment income inclusion. As a consequence, there has been considerable lobbying for some modification of the system as it applies to public companies. The government responded to this lobbying with changes in the February 28, 2000 budget.

12-16. These changes did not alter the basic rules for public companies. The employment income inclusion is still measured and, in general, included in employment income as at the exercise date. However, the new legislation provides for an election that allows an individual who has exercised stock options to defer recognition of all or part of the employment income inclusion until such time as the acquired shares are sold. In somewhat simplified terms, the election provides the individual with an annual deferral of the employment income inclusion on options that become vested during the year for up to $100,000 of the "specified value" of the shares. As will be discussed in more detail, the specified value is the market value of the option shares at the time the options are granted.

12-17. Note carefully that the general approach (i.e., taxation at time of exercise) applies unless the individual files an election. Further, it is also applicable to amounts in excess of the $100,000 deferral amount. This means that it will provide only limited benefits to those high-level executives who receive millions of dollars worth of options. However, significant benefits will be provided to lower and middle management recipients of options.

General Rules for Public Companies

12-18. Under ITA 7(1), when options to acquire the shares of a publicly traded company are exercised, there is an employment income inclusion equal to the excess of the fair market value of shares acquired over the price paid to acquire them. A deduction, equal to one-half of the employment income inclusion under ITA 7(1), is available under ITA 110(1)(d). As was noted in Paragraph 12-12, this ITA 110(1)(d) deduction in the calculation of Taxable Income is only available when, at the time the options are issued, the fair market value of the shares to be acquired is equal to or less than the option price. If this is not the case, the deduction will not be available and the individual will be subject to tax on the full amount of the employment income inclusion.

> **Example** On December 31, 1999, John Due receives options to buy 10,000 shares of his employer's common stock at a price of $25 per share. The employer is a publicly traded company and the options are vested and exercisable as of their issue date. At this time, the shares are trading at $25 per share.
>
> On July 31, 2001, Mr. Due exercises all of these options. At this time, the shares are trading at $43 per share. Mr. Due does not make an election to defer the employment income inclusion.
>
> On September 30, 2002, Mr. Due sells the shares that he acquired with his options. The proceeds from the sale are $45 per share.

Tax Consequences

- Issue Date (December 31, 1999)   Despite the fact that the options clearly have a positive value at this point in time, there are no tax consequences resulting from the issuance of the options.

- Exercise Date (July 31, 2001)   The tax consequences resulting from the exercise of the options would be as follows:

Fair Market Value Of Shares Acquired [(10,000)($43)]	$430,000
Cost Of Shares [(10,000)($25)]	(250,000)
ITA 7(1) Employment Income Inclusion	$180,000
ITA 110(1)(d) Deduction [(1/2)($180,000)]	(90,000)
Increase in Taxable Income	$ 90,000

- Disposal Date (September 30, 2002)   The tax consequences resulting from the disposal of the shares would be as follows:

Proceeds Of Disposition [($45)(10,000)]	$450,000
Adjusted Cost Base [($43)(10,000)]	(430,000)
Capital Gain	$ 20,000
Inclusion Rate	1/2
Taxable Capital Gain	$ 10,000

Canadian Controlled Private Companies

12-19.   The public company rules that we have just described require the recognition of a taxable benefit when the options are exercised, prior to the realization in cash of any benefit from the options granted. This may not be an insurmountable problem for employees of publicly traded companies in that they can sell part of the shares or use them as loan collateral if they need to raise the cash to pay the taxes on the benefit. However, for employees of Canadian Controlled Private Companies (CCPCs), a requirement to pay taxes at the time an option is exercised could create severe cash flow problems. As a consequence, a different treatment is permitted for stock options issued by CCPCs. The employment income inclusion is still measured at the time the options are exercised, but it is not taxed at the exercise date.

12-20.   For CCPCs, the employment income inclusion is specified under ITA 7(1.1). The ITA 110(1)(d) deduction from Taxable Income is also available to CCPCs provided the option price was equal to or more than the fair market value of the shares at the option grant date. However, if this condition is not met, an additional provision under ITA 110(1)(d.1) which allows the taxpayer to deduct one-half of the income inclusion under ITA 7(1.1), provided the shares are held for at least two years after their acquisition.

12-21.   Using the same information that was contained in the example in Paragraph 12-18, altered only so that the employer is a CCPC, the revised tax consequences would be as follows:

- Issue Date (December 31, 1999)   Despite the fact that the options clearly have a positive value at this point in time, there are no tax consequences resulting from the issuance of the options.

- Exercise Date (July 31, 2001)   While the amount of the employment income inclusions and related Taxable Income deduction would be measured at this point, they would not be included in income at this point. The $90,000 addition to Taxable Income would be deferred until such time as the shares are sold. This process would also increase the adjusted cost base of the shares to $43, the market value of the shares at this time.

- Disposal Date (September 30, 2002)   The tax consequences resulting from the disposal of the shares would be as follows:

Deferred Employment Income		$180,000
Proceeds Of Disposition [($45)(10,000)]	$450,000	
Adjusted Cost Base [($43)(10,000)]	(430,000)	
Capital Gain	$ 20,000	
Non Taxable One-Half	(10,000)	10,000
Increase in Net Income for Tax Purposes		$190,000
ITA 110(1)(d) Deduction [(1/2)($180,000)]		(90,000)
Increase in Taxable Income		$100,000

12-22.   Note that this is the total increase in Taxable Income that would have resulted from simply purchasing the shares at $25 and later selling them for $45 [(10,000)(1/2)($45 - $25) = $100,000]. The structuring of this increase is different and, in some circumstances, the difference could be significant. For example, the fact that the $180,000 increase in value has been classified as employment income rather than capital gains means that it is not eligible for the lifetime capital gains deduction.

Deferral on Publicly Traded Shares

12-23.   As noted earlier, when options are exercised to acquire the shares of a publicly traded company, there is a general requirement to include in employment income the difference between the fair market value of the share and the option price, as measured on that date. Also as described previously, the February 28, 2000 budget introduced a limited deferral of this employment income inclusion. This deferral is available under ITA 7(8) provided two general conditions are met:

1.   The acquisition must be a "qualifying acquisition".

2.   The taxpayer must make an election under ITA 7(10) in order to have subsection 7(8) apply.

12-24.   "Qualifying acquisition" is defined in ITA 7(9). This subsection indicates that the exercise of options involves a qualifying acquisition if:

- The acquisition occurs after February 27, 2000.
- The employee is entitled to a deduction under ITA 110(1)(d). This requires that the option price be not less than the fair market value of the shares at the time the options were granted, that the acquired shares be common shares, and that the employee must be dealing at arm's length with the employer.
- The employee must not be a specified shareholder of the employer. A specified shareholder is an individual who owns at least 10 percent of the shares of a corporation.
- The acquired shares must be listed on a Canadian or foreign stock exchange.

12-25.   The election to have the deferral provision apply must be made no later than January 15th of the year following the year in which the securities are acquired. In general, the election will be filed with the employer. The employer then has the responsibility for reporting the information to the Minister of National Revenue and including the amount deferred as a special item on the employee's T4.

12-26.   The election can only be filed by an individual who is a resident of Canada when the relevant securities are acquired. Further, the amount elected cannot exceed the lesser of $100,000 and the "specified value" of the securities acquired. This limit is an annual amount and is based on the securities that are available on options that vest during the year. It is not affected by the shares that are acquired during the year or by the options that are granted which do not vest during the year.

12-27.   The term specified value is defined in ITA 7(11). In general, this amount is the fair market value of the securities acquired, measured at the time the options were granted. As the definition is in terms of a single security, there is a mechanism for adjusting this value for stock splits, stock dividends, and exchanges of shares.

12-28. Examples will serve to illustrate the application of these rules. These examples are adapted from the technical notes provided with the March 16, 2001 Notice of Ways and Means Motion.

Example 1 In January, 2001, Suzanne's corporate employer grants her options to acquire 16,000 of the company's publicly traded shares. The exercise price is $10 a share, which is the fair market value of the shares at the time the options are granted. Half of the options vest in 2001, the other half in 2002. Suzanne exercises all of the options in 2004, at which time the shares have a fair market value of $100 each. Suzanne wishes to take maximum advantage of the deferral that is available under ITA 7(8).

Tax Consequences As the annual $100,000 limit on the deferral is based on the year in which the options vest, the total number of options granted in 2001 can be divided into two blocks of 8,000 shares each. Both of these blocks have a specified value of $80,000 [(8,000)($10)] and, as a consequence, all of the employment income measured in 2004 can be deferred.

The total amount of employment income measured on the exercise date is $1,440,000 [(16,000)($100 - $10)]. While Suzanne's employer will have to report this amount as a special item on her 2004 T4, it will not become taxable until Suzanne disposes of the shares. Note that the related ITA 110(1)(d) deduction will also be deferred until this later point in time.

If all 16,000 of the options had vested in the same year, the total specified value would have been $160,000 [(16,000)($10)]. In this case the employment income deferral would have been limited to $900,000 [(10,000)($100 - $10)], with the remaining $540,000 [(6,000)($100 - $10)] being taken into income in 2004. An ITA 110(1)(d) deduction of $270,000 [(1/2)($540,000)] would also be available in that year.

Example 2 On January 1, 2001, Mario's corporate employer grants him options to acquire 10,000 of the company's publicly traded shares. The exercise price is $10 per share, which is the fair market value of the shares at the time the options are granted. The options vest on January 1, 2003. On July 1, 2002, his employer grants him options on another 10,000 shares. The exercise price is $5 per share, which is the fair market value of the shares at that time. These options vest on July 1, 2003. Mario exercises all of the $10 options on January 1, 2003, when the shares have a fair market value of $100. He exercises all of the $5 options on July 1, 2003, when the shares have a fair market value of $150.

Tax Consequences The specified value of the options that vested in January, 2003 is $100,000 [(10,000)($10)]. The specified value of the options that vested in July 2003 is $50,000 [(10,000)($5)]. As this total exceeds the $100,000 annual limit, he cannot defer the total employment income generated by the exercise of the options. His goal is to defer on the options that will maximize his employment income deferral.

The per share benefit on the options exercised in January, 2003 is $90 per share ($100 - $10). The corresponding benefit on the options exercised in July, 2003 is $145 ($150 - $5). Given this, Mario elects to defer on all of the options exercised in July, 2003. The specified value of these shares is $50,000 [(10,000)($5)] and the deferred employment income is $1,450,000 [(10,000)($150 - $5)]. As $50,000 of the $100,000 annual limit remains, he can also elect to defer on half of the options exercised in January, 2003. These shares have a specified value of $50,000 [(5,000)($10)] and provide an employment income deferral of $450,000 [(5,000)($100 - $10)]. The $450,000 of employment income on the other half of the options exercised in January, 2003 cannot be deferred.

On Mario's T4 for 2003, his employer will report a deferred employment income of $1,900,000 ($1,450,000 + $450,000), as well as an employment income inclusion of $450,000. An ITA 110(1)(d) deduction of $225,000 [(1/2)($450,000)] will also be available in 2003.

Revoked Election

12-29. As we have noted, the employment income deferral requires an election on the part of the taxpayer, an action which absorbs all or part of the $100,000 limit available for that year. There may be situations where, at a later point in time, the individual may wish to restore the limit in order to use it on options that involve a larger deferral. In such circumstances, ITA 7(13) provides for the revocation of an election. An example will serve to clarify this procedure.

Example On April 30, 2001, Francine's employer grants her options to acquire 10,000 of the publicly traded shares of the company. The exercise price is $10 per share, which is the fair market value of the shares at that time. The options vest immediately, are exercisable immediately, and expire on April 30, 2005. On September 30, 2001, Francine's employer grants her option to acquire another 5,000 of its publicly traded shares. The exercise price is $15 per share, which is the fair market value of the shares at that time. The options vest immediately and expire on September 30, 2005.

Francine exercises all of the $10 options on April 30, 2005, when the fair market value is $100 per share. She files an election at that time to defer, under subsection 7(8), recognition of the employment benefit of $900,000 [(10,000)($100 - $10)]. Since the total specified value of the shares in respect of which the election is made is $100,000 [(10,000)($10)], the election fully utilizes the deferral limit for the 2005 year.

Francine exercises the remaining options on September 30, 2005, when the fair market value is $295 per share. She wishes to defer recognition of as much of the employment benefit of $1,400,000 [(5,000)($295 - $15)] as possible. However, because of the previous election on the $10 options, she has no deferral room available. Since she needs $75,000 [(5,000)($15)] of deferral room she immediately files with the employer a written request to revoke the election previously made on 7,500 of the $10 options. This provides her with sufficient room to make an election to defer the employment benefit on all of the $15 options.

On Francine's T4 slip for 2005, the employment benefit of $675,000 [(7,500)($100 - $10)] associated with the revoked election will be included as income for the year. The remaining benefit of $1,625,000 [(2,500)($100 - $10) + (5,000)($295 - $15)] will be reported as a deferred amount which will be taxed in the year in which Francine disposes of the shares.

12-30. The revocation must be filed in writing with the employer with whom the election was originally filed. This must take place no later than January 15 of the year following the year in which the securities on which the election was made were acquired.

Disposals

12-31. In Chapter 9, we noted the general rule under ITA 47(1), the adjusted cost base for identical properties is equal to the average cost of all such properties that have been acquired. For example, if Mark acquired 50 common shares of Quron Ltd. for $45 and another 75 shares of the company for $58, the adjusted cost base of all of these shares would be $52.80 {[(50)($45) + (75)($58)] ÷ (75 + 50)}. This is the value that would be used in determining the amount of any capital gain or loss on a subsequent disposition of all or part of the 125 shares acquired.

12-32. This creates a problem in situations where an employment income inclusion has been deferred from the time an option has been exercised until the time when the acquired shares are sold. In situations such as this, the disposition not only triggers a capital gain, it also ends the deferral of the employment income inclusion.

12-33.   To deal with this problem, a new ITA 47(3) deems the deferral shares not to be identical properties under ITA 47(1). This means that the cost averaging rule is no longer applicable and each block of deferral shares can be separately identified and will have a unique adjusted cost base. This unique adjusted cost basis will be used to determine any capital gain or loss on the disposition of the shares. While there are other more technical applications, the most important deferral securities to which the new ITA 47(3) applies are:

- Shares of a CCPC acquired through options. While the employment income benefit has always been deferred on these shares, they were subject to the average cost rules under ITA 47(1).
- Shares of a public company acquired through options and an election has been filed to defer the employment income inclusion.

12-34.   Given this change, a new rule is required establishing the order in which deferral and non deferral shares are sold. This rule is found in an amended ITA 7(1.3) which specifies the following:

- When there is a disposition by a taxpayer holding both deferral and non deferral shares, the non deferral shares are considered to be sold first. This rule applies even in situations where the non deferral shares were acquired after the deferral shares.

- After all non deferral shares have been disposed of, if the taxpayer has deferral shares that were acquired at different points in time, the assumption for subsequent dispositions is that the shares will be sold in the order they were acquired (First-In, First-Out).

- In situations where the taxpayer has acquired identical deferral shares at a single point in time but under different option arrangements, subsequent dispositions will be based on the assumption that the sales occur in the order the options were granted.

12-35.   An example can be used to illustrate the preceding rules.

Example   Mark is an employee of Quron Ltd., a Canadian public company. During 1998, he acquires 50 shares of the Company for $45 per share and during 1999 he acquire an additional 75 shares for $58. This provides an average cost for these shares of $52.80 {[(50)($45) + (75)($58)] ÷ (75 + 50)}.

During 1999, Mark becomes a member of his employer's stock option plan. In April of that year, he is granted options to buy 10 shares at $50 per share. In October, 1999, he is granted additional options for 15 shares at $58 per share. In March, 2000, he is granted options to acquire a further 25 shares at $40 per share. In all cases, the option price was equal to the fair market value of the shares at the time the options were granted.

On July 1, 2001 Mark exercises the March, 2000 options. At this time the shares are selling for $45 per share. On December 1, 2001, he exercises both the April 1999 options and the October, 1999 options. At this time the shares are selling for $85 per share. Mark files an election with his employer to defer all of the employment income related to the exercise of the options. The total amount deferred by the election would be as follows:

April, 1999 Options [(10)($85 - $50)]	$350
October, 1999 Options [(15)($85 - $58)]	405
March, 2000 Options [(25)($45 - $40)]	125
Total Deferral	$880

During 2002, Mark sells 100 of his Quron Ltd. shares for $110 per share. During 2003, he sells a further 35 shares for $120 per share. During 2004, he sells 25 shares for $95 per share. During 2005, he sells his remaining 15 shares for $32 per share.

Tax Consequences 2001   Other than the fact that his T4 will indicate a deferral of $880 of employment income, there are no tax consequences for Mark in 2001.

Tax Consequences 2002   As required under ITA 7(1.3), the 100 shares sold during 2002 would be from the 125 non deferral shares that were purchased in the open market. This would result in a taxable capital gain of $2,860 [(100)($110.00 - $52.80)(1/2)].

Tax Consequences 2003   The 35 shares sold in 2003 would consist of the remaining 25 that were acquired in the open market, plus 10 of the 25 shares acquired through the use of the options granted in March, 2000. While these options were granted at a later date than those issued in 1999, they were exercised sooner and, under the ordering rules found in ITA 7(1.3), they would be considered the first sold. The tax consequences of the sale of 35 shares is as follows:

Taxable Capital Gains:	
Open Market Shares [(25)($120.00 - $52.80)(1/2)]	$ 840
March, 2000 Option Shares [(10)($120.00 - $45.00)(1/2)]	375
Employment Income [(10)($45.00 - $40.00)]	50
ITA 110(1)(d) Deduction [(1/2)($50)]	(25)
Increase In Taxable Income	$1,240

Tax Consequences 2004   The 25 shares sold in 2004 would consist of the remaining 15 shares from the March 2000 options, plus the 15 shares from the April, 1999 options. As the April, and October, 1999 options were exercised on the same date, the choice of the shares from the April options is based on the fact that they were granted at an earlier date. The tax consequences of the sale of the 25 shares would be as follows:

Taxable Capital Gains:	
March, 2000 Options [(15)($95.00 - $45.00)(1/2)]	$375
April, 1999 Options [(10)($95.00 - $85.00)(1/2)]	50
Employment Income:	
March, 2000 Options [(15)($45.00 - $40.00)]	75
April, 1999 Options [(10)($85.00 - $50.00)]	350
ITA 110(1)(d) Deduction [(1/2)($75 + $350)]	(213)
Increase In Taxable Income	$637

Tax Consequences 2005   When the remaining 15 shares are sold, they would all be from the October, 1999 options. The tax consequences of the sale would be as follows:

Allowable Capital Loss [(15)($32.00 - $85.00)(1/2)]	($397.50)

Employment Income [(15)($85.00 - $58.00)]	$405.00
ITA 110(1)(d) Deduction [(1/2)($405)]	(202.50)
Increase In Taxable Income	$202.50

Note that we have not netted these two amounts. This reflects the fact that the allowable capital loss cannot be deducted against employment income.

Emigration And Stock Options

12-36.   You may recall from our discussion of emigration in Chapter 10 that, when an individual emigrates from Canada, there is a deemed disposition of most of the assets he owns at that time. While there are a few exceptions to this rule (e.g., real property), this deemed disposition rule applies to the shares of both public and private corporations. To understand the consequences of this provision, consider the following example:

Example Joan Martin holds options to buy 1,000 shares of Dermo Ltd., a Canadian Controlled Private Corporation (CCPC), at a price of $50 per share. When the options were issued, the fair market value of the shares was equal to the option price of $50 per share. On May 1, 2001, Joan exercises the options and, at this time, the shares are trading at $71 per share. On December 1, 2001, when the shares are trading at $80, Joan emigrates from Canada.

12-37. While the benefit is deferred, it is measured at the exercise date. This means that, in the absence of any special provision, the deemed disposition resulting from Joan's emigration would have the following tax consequences:

Employment Income Inclusion [($71 - $50)(1,000)]	$21,000
ITA 110(1) Deduction [(1/2)($21,000)]	(10,500)
Balance	$10,500
Taxable Capital Gain [($80 - $71)(1,000)(1/2)]	4,500
Increase In Taxable Income	$15,000

12-38. However, there are new provisions which deal with this situation. A new ITA 7(1.6) indicates that, when an individual emigrates from Canada while holding shares of a CCPC acquired through a stock option arrangement, the usual deemed disposition on departure from Canada is not considered to be a disposition for the purposes of the employment income inclusion under ITA 7(1.1) or the related deduction under ITA 110(1)(d) or (d.1).

12-39. Unfortunately, this unwinding of the deemed disposition creates a different problem. ITA 53(1)(j) is written in such a fashion that the adjusted cost base of the shares is increased by the amount of the employment income inclusion only at the time this inclusion is recognized. This means that, in the absence of a further provision, the capital gain at emigration time would be based on a cost of $50, a situation that would ultimately result in double taxation of the difference between $71 and $50. A second new provision, ITA 128.1(4)(d.1), deals with this situation by indicating that the taxpayer can deduct from the proceeds of disposition the amount of the benefit that would have been recognized in the absence of ITA 7(1.6). Overall, the tax consequences of Joan's emigration would be as follows:

Proceeds Of Disposition [$80 - ($71 - $50)][1,000]	$59,000
Adjusted Cost Base [($50)(1,000)]	(50,000)
Capital Gain	$ 9,000
Inclusion Rate	1/2
Taxable Capital Gain	$ 4,500

12-40. This somewhat circuitous process, while continuing to defer the employment income inclusion and related ITA 110(1) deduction, results in the same taxable capital gain that would have been recorded on an actual disposition of the shares (See Paragraph 12-37). The employment income inclusion will be subject to tax when the shares are eventually sold.

12-41. Note that these provisions apply only to the shares of a CCPC. If an individual departs Canada while holding option acquired shares of a public company, any employment income benefit that has been deferred under ITA 7(8) will have to be recognized at that time.

A Final Note on Stock Options

12-42. We would note that the preceding discussion of stock options, while fairly extensive, is less than complete. There are other more detailed provisions which go beyond the scope of this text, an indication that this is becoming a fairly complex area of tax practice.

Exercises Twelve-1 through Twelve-5 deal with stock options. This would be an appropriate time to attempt these exercises.

12-43.   For those of you who keep up with financial reporting, you are likely aware that an equally complex set of rules are being put forward by the Accounting Standards Board with respect to accounting for stock options.

12-44.   All of these new rules probably reflect the fact that the use of stock options has dramatically increased during the last ten to fifteen years. As noted earlier, this has been particularly true in the high tech sector of the economy. It is somewhat ironic that these new rules coming into force just as a major downturn is being experienced in that sector, an event that is likely to result in a significant drop in the use of stock options.

Treatment Of Losses

Carry Over Provisions

12-45.   In earlier Chapters there have been references to a taxpayer's ability to carry back or carry forward losses. Before reviewing the carry over rules related to specific types of losses, some additional consideration needs to be given to the general procedures associated with these carry overs.

12-46.   If a taxpayer experiences a loss in the current year with respect to a particular type of income, it must be used, to the extent possible, to offset other types of income in the current year. However, if other sources of income are not sufficient for this purpose (e.g., a business loss is greater than all other sources of income) or, if the other income sources are not of the right type (e.g., capital losses cannot be used to offset employment income), then the loss can be used to reduce the Taxable Income of other years.

12-47.   If the taxpayer has income in the three preceding years, he can apply the loss against the income that was included in his tax return for the relevant earlier year. This will result in a refund of the taxes that were paid in that year on the loss carried back. As you would expect, the refund will be based on the rate(s) applicable to the carry back year.

12-48.   Note that, with respect to some types of losses, they can only be applied against income of the same type. For example, capital losses can only be applied against capital gains earned in the previous year or years. Correspondingly, losses on listed personal property can only be carried over and applied against gains on listed personal property, and restricted farm losses can only be carried over and applied against farm income.

12-49.   If there is not sufficient income of the appropriate type in any of the three preceding years, any unused portion of the loss becomes part of a loss carry forward balance. While the carry back period for all types of losses is three years, the carry forward period varies with the type of loss (e.g., ten years for farm losses, seven years for other non capital losses, and an unlimited period for capital losses). Because of these differing time periods, as well as restrictions on the type of income to which certain types of losses can be applied, loss carry forward balances must be segregated by type. The separate balances which must be tracked are:

- Listed Personal Property Losses
- Non Capital Losses
- Net Capital Losses (As this term is used in the *Income Tax Act*, it refers to the allowable fraction of these losses which will be 1/2, 2/3, or 3/4, depending on the year in which the disposition which gave rise to the loss occurred.)
- Allowable Business Investment Losses
- Regular Farm Losses
- Restricted Farm Losses

12-50.   Once the current year losses are allocated to a carry forward balance, they can be used to reduce taxable income in future years. As was the case with loss carry backs, listed personal property losses, net capital losses, and restricted farm losses can only be applied against future income of the same type.

12-51.   In general, both loss carry backs and loss carry forwards are a deduction from Net Income For Tax Purposes in the calculation of Taxable Income. The exception to this is losses on listed personal property. When there is a carry over of a loss on listed personal property, it is deducted from the current year's gains on listed personal property, with the net amount being shown as an inclusion in Net Income For Tax Purposes.

Personal Use Property

12-52.   As covered in the discussion of personal use property in Chapter 9, taxable capital gains on personal use property, determined on the assumption that both the proceeds of disposition and the adjusted cost base are at least $1,000, are included in the calculation of Net Income For Tax Purposes. However, losses on such property are not deductible under any circumstances.

Listed Personal Property Losses
General Rules
12-53.   As defined in ITA 54, listed personal property includes:

- works of art;
- stamps;
- coins;
- rare books; and
- jewelry.

12-54.   As was the case with personal use property, taxable capital gains on listed personal property are included in Net Income For Tax Purposes and are also calculated on the assumption that both the proceeds of disposition and the adjusted cost base are at least $1,000 (as noted in Chapter 9, this rule may not be applicable when a charitable donation is involved). The difference here is that allowable capital losses on listed personal property can be deducted. However, they can only be deducted against taxable capital gains on listed personal property and cannot be used to reduce taxes on any other type of income, including taxable capital gains on other types of property.

Carry Over Provisions
12-55.   In some years, a taxpayer may have capital losses on listed personal property without having capital gains on such property. This means that the losses cannot be used in the current year and will become subject to carry over rules. The carry back period for these losses is three years and the carry forward period is seven years. If the losses are not used to offset capital gains on listed personal property within the carry over periods, they will expire without providing any benefits to the taxpayer.

12-56.   When the losses on listed personal property are carried over to a preceding or subsequent year, they can only be used to offset capital gains on listed personal property in that year and, as a consequence, they do not enter into the computation of Taxable Income under Division C. Under ITA 41(2), carry overs of allowable losses on listed personal property are deducted from the current year's taxable gains on listed personal property, with the net amount added under ITA 3(b) in the calculation of Net Income For Tax Purposes. This is in contrast to other types of deductible loss carry overs which are treated as ITA 111 deductions from Net Income For Tax Purposes in the computation of Taxable Income.

Non Capital Losses
General Rules
12-57.   As their name implies, non capital losses are losses other than those on dispositions of capital assets. They can result from the calculation of income from employment, income from a business, or income from property. However, given the limited number of deductions from employment income, it is very unlikely that they will occur in that context. Normally, non capital losses would result from the operation of a business or the ownership of property. For example, a non capital loss on rental property could occur when expenses associated with the property exceed the rental revenues. Non capital losses include terminal losses on the sale of depreciable assets.

Carry Over Provisions

12-58.   Non capital losses for the current year are deducted under ITA 3(d) in the calculation of Net Income For Tax Purposes and must be used to offset all other types of income including net taxable capital gains. If current year non capital losses remain after Net Income For Tax Purposes has been reduced to nil, these amounts can be carried over to other years. Such losses may be carried back three years and applied against any type of income in those years. If there is not sufficient income in those years to absorb the full amount of these non capital losses, any remaining balance can be carried forward for a period of seven years. Whether the amounts are carried back or forward, they will be a deduction in the computation of Taxable Income under ITA 111(1)(a).

12-59.   Non capital losses are defined in ITA 111(8) in such a fashion that a carry over is only available after the current year's income is reduced to nil. Stated alternatively, the current year's non capital losses become available for carry over only after they have been applied to the maximum extent possible against the current year's income. If they are available for carry over, they can be applied, at the taxpayer's discretion, to any of the eligible carry over years. However, ITA 111(3) indicates that a non capital loss carry over for a particular year cannot be used until the available non capital loss carry overs from all preceding years have been exhausted.

Net Capital Losses
General Rules

12-60.   The term "Net Capital Loss" is defined in ITA 111(8) as the excess of allowable capital losses over taxable capital gains for the current taxation year. Note carefully that, as the term is used in the *Act*, "Net Capital Loss" refers to the deductible portion of capital losses, not to the 100 percent amounts. This is somewhat confusing in that this deductible portion is generally referred to as an allowable capital loss in the year it occurs. A further complication is that amounts are included in this balance without adjustment for changing inclusion rates on capital gains.

Changing Inclusion Rates

12-61.   As covered in Chapter 9, the capital gains inclusion rate for individuals has changed over the years as follows:

1972 to 1987	1/2
1988 and 1989	2/3
1990 to February 27, 2000	3/4
After February 27, 2000 before October 18, 2000	2/3
After October 17, 2000	1/2

Carry Over Provisions

12-62.   While Net Capital Losses cannot be deducted in the calculation of the current year's Net Income For Tax Purposes, they are available for carry over to other years. Such losses may be carried back three years and forward to any subsequent year. When they are carried forward or back, they will be deducted under ITA 111(1)(b) in the calculation of Taxable Income. However, ITA 111(1.1) restricts the deduction of such carry over amounts to the amount included in Net Income For Tax Purposes under ITA 3(b) (net taxable capital gains).

12-63.   When Net Capital Losses are carried over they must be deducted at the rate that is applicable to the carry over year. For example, if an individual experienced a $20,000 capital loss in 1990, it would be carried forward as a Net Capital Loss of $15,000 [(3/4)($20,000)]. If this $15,000 net capital loss was carried forward to 2001, when the capital loss inclusion rate is one-half, it would have to be adjusted to $10,000 to reflect the applicable rate for the carry forward year. The required adjustment will multiply the net capital loss that is being claimed by the current inclusion rate of one-half, divided by the inclusion rate in the year in which the loss was realized. The two examples in Figure 12-1 (following page) illustrate this process.

12-64.   As was noted in Chapter 9, there is an additional complication for carry overs to the year 2000. As documented in Paragraph 12-61, there were three different inclusion rates for

---

Figure 12 - 1
Capital Gain and Loss Inclusion Rates

Example One An individual has a capital loss in 1990 of $60 (allowable amount $45) and a capital gain in 2001 of $120 (taxable amount $60). The 1990 loss is carried forward and deducted in 2001. The deduction for 2001 is calculated as follows:

$$[\$45]\left[\frac{\frac{1}{2}}{\frac{3}{4}}\right] = \$30$$

Example Two An individual has a capital loss in 1989 of $90 (allowable amount $60) and a capital gain in 2001 of $120 (taxable amount $60). The 1989 loss is carried forward and deducted in 2001. The deduction for 2001 is calculated as follows:

$$[\$60]\left[\frac{\frac{1}{2}}{\frac{2}{3}}\right] = \$45$$

---

capital gains during 2000. This means that any carry over to that year will have to be converted to the inclusion rate at which capital gains were recognized during that year.

Example Jill Clawson has a Net Capital Loss balance from 1995 of $33,750 [(75%)($45,000)]. During the year 2000 she has a capital gain of $60,000 resulting from a July disposition (inclusion rate = two-thirds), and a further capital gain of $75,000 resulting from a December disposition (inclusion rate = one-half).

Tax Consequences Ms. Clawson's taxable capital gain for the year is equal to $77,500 [($60,000)(2/3) + ($75,000)(1/2)]. This provides an effective inclusion rate of 57.4 percent [$77,500 ÷ ($60,000 + $75,000)]. This means that the deduction amount for the loss carry forward will be $25,830 [($33,750)(57.4% ÷ 75%)].

12-65. This type of calculation is, of course, a transitional problem which only affects the year 2000. As a consequence, in our examples which involve 2000, we will generally use the one-half inclusion rate that applies after October 17 of 2000. As this appears to be the applicable rate for future years, this will simplify the analysis of these examples.

Conversion of Net Capital Loss To Non Capital Loss Carry Over

12-66. A problem can arise when a taxpayer has a net capital loss balance, taxable capital gains in the current year, and a non capital loss that is large enough to reduce his Net Income to nil. As net capital losses can only be deducted against taxable capital gains, the taxpayer is usually anxious to use such carry overs whenever taxable capital gains are available. A simple example will illustrate this problem.

Example For 2001, Mr. Waring has property income of $25,000, taxable capital gains of $45,000 [(1/2)($90,000)], and a business loss of $150,000. He also has a net capital loss from 1999 of $90,000 [(3/4)($120,000)]. He does not anticipate having any taxable capital gains in the foreseeable future.

12-67. The usual ITA 3 calculation of Net Income For Tax Purposes would be as follows:

ITA 3(a) Non Capital Positive Sources	$ 25,000
ITA 3(b) Net Taxable Capital Gains	45,000
ITA 3(c) - Sum of ITA 3(a) and 3(b)	$ 70,000
ITA 3(d) Non Capital Losses	(150,000)
Net Income For Tax Purposes	$ Nil

12-68. The business loss reduced Net Income to nil and this is a problem for Mr. Waring in that he does not anticipate having further taxable capital gains in the near future. Given this, it would appear that he has lost the ability to use this year's net taxable capital gains to absorb the net capital loss balance. Fortunately, this is not the case. The ITA 111(8) definition of the non capital loss is such that, if the taxpayer wishes, net capital losses can be added to this balance to the extent that there are taxable capital gains that have been realized during the year. In simplified terms, this definition for an individual taxpayer is as follows:

Non Capital Loss Available For Carry Over = E - F, where,

E = The sum of non capital losses for the year, plus any amount of Net Capital Loss that the taxpayer wishes to deduct (can't exceed the net taxable capital gains for the year).

F = The amount of income determined under ITA 3(c).

12-69.   If we assume that Mr. Waring wishes to deduct the maximum amount of net capital loss in 2001, the non capital loss definition would be applied as follows:

Non Capital Loss For Year	$150,000
Net Capital Loss Deducted (Limited To Taxable Capital Gains)	45,000
Total For E	$195,000
F = Income Under ITA 3(c)	(70,000)
Non Capital Loss Available For Carry Over	$125,000

12-70.   There are three points that should be made with respect to this solution:

- The amount of net capital loss deducted is limited to the $45,000 in net taxable capital gains that were realized during the year. As a result he has utilized $67,500 [($45,000)(3/4) ÷ 1/2] of his 1999 net capital loss.

- The deduction of the net capital loss is discretionary. That is, the taxpayer can deduct any amount between nil and the maximum value of $45,000. In the solution presented, he has deducted the maximum amount, which results in a non capital loss carry over of $125,000 and a net capital loss of $22,500 ($90,000 - $67,500). An alternative would have been to deduct the minimum amount of nil. This would have left a non capital loss of $80,000 ($150,000 - $70,000) and a net capital loss of $90,000 [(3/4)($120,000)]. A tax-payer might choose this latter alternative if he were more concerned about the seven year time limit on the non capital loss balance, and less concerned about having sufficient future taxable capital gains to absorb the net capital loss balance.

- With the confusion arising from the different inclusion rates, we have found it useful to verify calculations using the 100 percent figures. For example, the $22,500 net capital loss can be verified as [($120,000 - $90,000)(3/4)], or 100% of the 1999 loss less 100% of the 2001 capital gain at the 1999 inclusion rate.

Allowable Business Investment Losses
Defined
12-71.   A Business Investment Loss (BIL), as defined in ITA 39(1)(c), is a special type of capital loss resulting from the disposition of shares or debt of a "small business corporation". In addition to losses on arm's length sales, business investment losses can be incurred when there is a deemed disposition for nil proceeds. This could occur for shares of a small business corporation due to bankruptcy or insolvency or if the debt is considered uncollectible. A small business corporation is defined in ITA 248(1) as a Canadian controlled private corporation of which all or "substantially all" of the fair market value of its assets are used in an active business carried on "primarily" in Canada. In tax work, the term "substantially all" generally means 90 percent or more, while "primarily" is generally interpreted to mean more than 50 percent.

12-72.   In making this determination, shares or debt of a connected small business corporation would count towards the required 90 percent. A connected corporation is one which the potential small business corporation either controls or owns more than 10 percent of all of the outstanding shares. As you would expect, an Allowable Business Investment Loss (ABIL) is the deductible one-half of a BIL.

Special Treatment
12-73.   In general, allowable capital losses can only be deducted against taxable capital gains. However, ABILs are given special treatment in that the taxpayer is permitted to deduct

these amounts from any source of income. For example, an individual with net employment income of $50,000 and an ABIL of $10,500 [(1/2)($21,000)] would be able to deduct the loss against the employment income, resulting in a Net Income For Tax Purposes of $39,500. If this had been an ordinary allowable capital loss, the taxpayer's Net Income For Tax Purposes would be $50,000 and the loss would be added to the carry over balance.

12-74.   If there is sufficient income, the ABIL must be deducted in the year in which it is realized. However, if other sources of income are not sufficient for deducting all or part of an ABIL under ITA 3(d) in the current year, it becomes a part of the non capital loss carry over balance. This permits this special type of allowable capital loss to be deducted against any type of income in either the three year carry back or the seven year carry forward period. Note that, because they are being carried over as part of the non capital loss balance, ABILs are not adjusted if the capital gains inclusion rate is different in the carry over year. If the ABIL has not been used by the end of the normal seven year carry forward period, it reverts to its original status as an allowable capital loss and becomes a component of the net capital loss carry over balance. While this restricts the types of income that the loss can be applied against, it gives the loss an unlimited carry forward period.

Effect Of The Lifetime Capital Gains Deduction

12-75.   As we shall see in our discussion of the lifetime capital gains deduction, the realization of a business investment loss reduces the taxpayer's ability to take advantage of this deduction. Of note here, however, is the fact that under ITA 39(9), Business Investment Losses are reduced by the use of the ITA 110.6 lifetime capital gains deduction. Note that, because the Business Investment Loss is a 100 percent figure and the ITA 110.6 deduction is based on the capital gains inclusion rate for the year deducted, ITA 39(9) requires that the disallowed amount must be based on the actual ITA 110.6 deduction multiplied by an appropriate number or fraction. For deductions at the one-half inclusion rate, the multiplier is 2; for deductions at the two-thirds inclusion rate, the multiplier is 3/2; and for deductions at the three-quarters inclusion rate, the multiplier is 4/3.

> **Example**   In 1990, Mr. Mercer has a taxable capital gain of $12,000 ($16,000 capital gain) and deducts this amount under the provisions of ITA 110.6 lifetime capital gains deduction. In July, 2001, he has a $60,000 loss on the sale of shares of a small business corporation. Mr. Mercer has no capital gains or losses in any other year.

12-76.   If Mr. Mercer had made no use of ITA 110.6, he would have an allowable business investment loss of $30,000 [(1/2)($60,000)] in 2001. However, since he has made a deduction under ITA 110.6, the business investment loss would be reduced as follows:

Actual Loss On Disposition	$60,000
Disallowed Portion [(4/3)($12,000)]	(16,000)
Business Investment Loss	$44,000
Inclusion Rate	1/2
Allowable Business Investment Loss (ABIL)	$22,000

12-77.   The disallowed $16,000 does not disappear. It becomes an ordinary capital loss subject to the usual restriction that it can only be deducted against capital gains. The remaining $22,000 ABIL can be deducted in 2001 against any source of income. As noted previously, if it is not deducted in that year, it becomes part of the non capital loss carry over for seven years. If still not used after seven years, it becomes part of the net capital loss carry over.

Farm Losses

Restricted Farm Losses

12-78.   As covered in Chapter 7, restricted farm losses arise when there is a reasonable expectation of a profit, but a taxpayer's chief source of income is neither farming nor a combination of farming and something else. The deduction of such farm losses from any source of income in a year is restricted to all of the first $2,500, plus one-half of the next $12,500, to a maximum of $8,750 [$2,500 + (1/2)($12,500)] on an actual loss of $15,000 ($2,500 +

$12,500). The loss in excess of the deductible limit is the restricted farm loss.

12-79.   Restricted farm losses are eligible for a carry over provision. Such losses can be carried back three years and forward for a maximum of 10 years. In carry over periods, restricted farm losses can only be deducted to the extent that income from farming has been included in Net Income For Tax Purposes. For example, if a restricted farm loss carry forward of $15,000 was available at the beginning of 2001 and 2001 farming income totaled $12,000, only $12,000 of the carry forward could be deducted in calculating 2001 taxable income.

12-80.   If a farm property is disposed of before the taxpayer has an opportunity to fully utilize restricted farm losses carried forward, a part of the undeducted losses can be used to increase the adjusted cost base of the property. This would have the effect of reducing any capital gains arising on the disposition of the property. This treatment is only possible to the extent that the loss was created by real estate taxes or interest payments on the farm property. The same provision would be available for regular farm losses as well.

Regular Farm Losses

12-81.   For full time farmers, all losses can be deducted against any source of income. When they cannot be used during the current year, they can be carried over on the same basis as restricted farm losses. That is, they can be carried back three years and forward for ten years. Unlike restricted farm losses, when they are deducted on a carry over basis, regular farm losses can be applied against any type of income.

> Exercises Twelve-6 through Twelve-9 deal with losses. This would be an appropriate time to attempt these exercises.

Lifetime Capital Gains Deduction

Background
The General Provision

12-82.   The legislation providing for the lifetime capital gains deduction has been, since the time that it was introduced, the subject of intense criticism. At the time of its initial introduction, it was the intent of the government to allow every individual resident in Canada to enjoy up to $500,000 in tax free capital gains during their lifetime. This privilege was available without regard to the type of property on which the gain accrued.

12-83.   Considering the magnitude of the benefits involved, it is not surprising that the relevant legislation was extremely complex. Further, this new tax privilege created serious distortions in the allocation of economic resources, and it appeared to have little economic justification other than providing a near outright gift to wealthy Canadians. Given this effect, it is not surprising that it survives today only in a very limited form.

12-84.   The demise of the general lifetime capital gains deduction took place in two steps:

- In 1992, the deduction was eliminated for gains resulting from the disposition of most real property (a.k.a., non qualifying real estate). This was accomplished in a fairly complex manner that served to apply the change only to gains that accrued subsequent to February, 1992.

- In 1994, the deduction was eliminated with respect to all dispositions other than those involving qualified farm property and shares or debt of qualified small business corporations.

12-85.   The 1994 change was accompanied by an election which allowed holders of capital assets with accrued gains to have a deemed disposition in order to make use of all or part of any remaining lifetime amount that was available to them. The election created a new adjusted cost base which would be used to calculate a capital gain or loss on the future disposition of the asset.

12-85.   These changes left a very complex legacy with respect to the determination of the adjusted cost base of either non qualifying real estate held at the time of the 1992 change, or other assets on which the 1994 election was made. While tax practitioners will have to deal with this problem for many years to come, we do not believe that it is of interest to most users of this material and, as result, no longer provide coverage of these issues.

The $500,000 Lifetime Capital Gains Deduction

12-87.   At this point in time, the $500,000 deduction on qualified farm property and qualified small business corporation shares is the only type of lifetime capital gains deduction that is available. While there have been periodic rumors that this tax privilege would also be dropped, it has not happened yet. When it can be used, it is one of the most significant tax breaks available to Canadian individuals.

Qualifying Property

12-88.   Only gains on the disposition of either qualified farm property or shares of a qualified small business corporation are eligible for the lifetime capital gains deduction. Note that the $500,000 limit is not available on each type of asset. Rather, it is a total amount that must be shared on dispositions of both types.

12-89.   Qualified farm property is defined in ITA 110.6(1) and includes not only property used for farming by a taxpayer, the taxpayer's spouse, or their children, it also includes a share of a family farm corporation, an interest in a family farm partnership, real property used in a farming business, and eligible capital property used in a farming business. To qualify for this deduction, the farm property must be owned for at least 24 months prior to its disposition.

12-90.   ITA 248(1) defines a small business corporation as a Canadian controlled private corporation (CCPC) of which all or substantially all (90 percent or more) of the fair market value of its assets are used in an active business carried on primarily (more than 50 percent) in Canada. In order to be a qualified small business corporation for the purposes of the lifetime capital gains deduction, the corporation must meet this definition of a small business corporation at the time of the disposal of shares or debt.

12-91.   This is not a difficult criteria to satisfy. Whether or not a particular CCPC is a small business corporation is measured at a specific point in time. If less than 90 percent of the corporation's assets are involved in producing active business income, it is usually a simple matter to sell some of the non qualifying assets and distribute the proceeds to the shareholders. This process, commonly referred to as the "purification of a small business corporation", can normally be carried out in a short period of time, thereby satisfying the small business corporation criteria.

12-92.   However, not all small business corporations are qualified small business corporations. To achieve this stature, ITA 110.6(1) requires two other conditions to be met. In somewhat simplified terms, they are:

- the shares must not be owned by anyone other than the taxpayer or a related person for at least 24 months preceding the disposition; and

- throughout this 24 month period, more than 50 percent of the fair market value of the corporation's assets must be used in an active business carried on primarily in Canada.

12-93.   There are additional rules that are applicable when intercorporate investments are involved in the preceding determinations. More specifically, additional requirements apply when the condition that 50 percent of the assets must be used in active business for a 24 month period can only be met by adding in the shares or debt of another small business corporation. These special rules go beyond the scope of this text and, as a consequence, will not be covered here.

12-94.   A failure to meet these criteria is more difficult to correct. As they involve measurements made over a period of time, a failure to satisfy them can only be corrected by the passage of time. For example, if the 50 percent for 24 months criteria is not met, the problem cannot be solved by current dispositions of non qualifying assets.

Determining The Deductible Amount

General Rules

12-95.   The determination of the amount of the lifetime capital gains deduction that can be deducted in a year involves some reasonably complex calculations. In general terms, the available deduction is the least of the following three items:

- Capital Gains Deduction Available
- Annual Gains Limit
- Cumulative Gains Limit

12-96.   These items will be explained in detail in the sections which follow.

Capital Gains Deduction Available

12-97.   The "capital gains deduction available" is the maximum capital gains deduction for the year, less any amounts that have been used up in preceding years. The lifetime maximum for both qualified farm property and qualified small business corporation shares or debt is $250,000 [(1/2)($500,000)].

12-98.   A problem arises in determining the amounts used up in previous years. Clearly, it would not be appropriate to subtract an $12,000 deduction made in 1990 when it represented the taxable portion of a $16,000 capital gain, from the 2001 limit of $250,000 which is based on one-half of the gain. Amounts used up in earlier years have to be adjusted to the current inclusion rate of one-half. Specifically, gains deducted at a one-half inclusion rate require no adjustment, gains deducted at a two-thirds inclusion rate have to be multiplied by 3/4 [(1/2) ÷ (2/3)], and gains deducted at a three-quarters inclusion rate have to be multiplied by 2/3 [(1/2) ÷ (3/4)].

> **Example**   Mr. Little realizes capital gains on sales of qualified small business corporation shares of $24,000 in each of 1987, 1998, and 2001. He has not claimed a capital gains deduction prior to 1987 and he has no other capital gains in the period 1987 through 2000. He used his lifetime capital gains deduction to eliminate the 1987 and 1998 gains. Determine the amount of lifetime capital gains deduction that is available for use in 2001.
>
> **Tax Consequences**   As the $12,000 that was deducted in 1987 was at the one-half inclusion rate, no adjustment is required for the purpose of determining the available deduction for 2001. He would have deducted $18,000 [(3/4)($24,000)] in 1998. This amount will have to be converted to $12,000 {[$18,000][(1/2) ÷ (3/4)]}. This means that the available deduction remaining for 2001 would be $226,000 ($250,000 - $12,000 - $12,000). If he also deducts the taxable amount of the 2001 gain, the remaining amount available will be $214,000 ($226,000 - $12,000).

12-99.   This result can be verified using the full capital gain figures, usually the simpler approach. The $500,000 limit is reduced by $72,000 ($24,000 for three years) and, when the remaining $428,000 is multiplied by the current inclusion rate of one-half, it gives the balance of $214,000 as previously calculated.

Annual Gains Limit

12-100.   The annual gains limit is calculated as follows:

Net taxable capital gains for the year [ITA 3(b)]
Less:
   - Allowable business investment losses realized during the year; and
   - Net capital losses (carry overs) deducted during the year.

12-101.   With respect to the allowable business investment losses realized, the full amount is subtracted in the preceding formula, without regard to whether they have been deducted in the calculation of Net Income For Tax Purposes. Keep in mind that the amount of allowable business investment losses realized is based only on those amounts that have not been disallowed by the previous use of the lifetime capital gains deduction.

12-102.   The second item reducing the annual gains limit is the amount of net capital loss carry overs that are deducted during the current year. If the net capital loss is a carry forward from a year where the inclusion rate was not one-half, it will have to be converted to that rate before it can be deducted.

12-103.   As a further point here, the deduction of net capital losses is discretionary. This means that in cases where there is the possibility of using either the lifetime capital gains deduction or a net capital loss balance due to the presence of a capital gain, the individual must choose between the two alternatives. This is inherent in the annual gains limit formula which reduces the limit on a dollar for dollar basis for net capital losses deducted. While this choice between the two alternatives will have no influence on the current year's taxable income, we would suggest a preference for not deducting the net capital loss and making maximum use of the lifetime capital gains deduction. There is no time limit on using the net capital loss balance and, more importantly, it can be used when any type of taxable capital gain is realized. In contrast, the lifetime capital gains deduction can only be used for particular types of capital gains. In addition, there is the ongoing possibility that the availability of this deduction will be eliminated.

Cumulative Net Investment Loss (CNIL)

12-104.   Cumulative Net Investment Loss (CNIL), is a restriction introduced in the 1988 tax reform legislation. The problem, as perceived by the government, was that it was inequitable for individuals to simultaneously deduct investment losses while sheltering investment income through the use of the lifetime capital gains deduction. As a consequence, legislation was introduced which, in simple terms, restricts the use of the lifetime capital gains deduction in a given year by the cumulative amount of post 1987 investment losses.

12-105.   CNIL is defined as the amount by which the aggregate of investment expenses for the current year and prior years ending after 1987, exceeds the aggregate of investment income for that period. That is, the CNIL consists of post-1987 investment expenses minus investment income.

12-106.   As will be explained in the next Section, individuals who have a CNIL will have their ability to use their lifetime capital gains deduction reduced. Therefore, if eligible capital gains are anticipated, it is important to minimize the CNIL. Some examples of ways in which the impact of CNIL can be reduced are as follows:

- Delay disposing of a qualifying asset with accrued capital gains until the CNIL has been eliminated.
- Consider realizing capital gains on qualifying assets early if cumulative net investment losses may be incurred in future years.
- For owner/managers, consider having the business pay interest on shareholder loan accounts or pay dividends rather than salaries to increase investment income.
- Maximize investment income by investing in securities with high yields.

Cumulative Gains Limit

12-107.   In conceptual terms, the cumulative gains limit is simply the sum of all of the annual gains limits from previous years, less the amounts that have been deducted under the lifetime capital gains provisions. In those cases where maximum amounts have been deducted, the cumulative gains limit will usually equal the annual gains limit for the current year. A further complication is that the cumulative gains limit is reduced by any CNIL balance. A simple example will illustrate the calculation:

> **Example**   In 2001, Ms. Nolan has $5,600 of deductible interest on loans for investment purposes, and $2,600 of net rental income. She has had no other investment income or losses in years prior to 2001, so her cumulative net investment loss (CNIL) is $3,000 ($5,600 - $2,600). During 2001, she has a $60,000 taxable capital gain on the sale of qualified small business shares. As she has made no previous use of her lifetime capital gains deduction, her unused lifetime limit is $250,000. While her annual gains limit would be $60,000, the amount of the taxable capital gain, her ability to use the lifetime capital gains deduction would be limited to her cumulative gains limit of $57,000 ($60,000 - $3,000).

12-108.   If you are working on figures for the current year, you will not necessarily have the annual gains limits for earlier years. This means that you will be calculating this cumulative gains limit directly. The calculation is as follows:

Total net taxable capital gains realized since 1984
Less:
- The total of all net capital loss carry overs deducted after 1984.
- The total of all allowable business investment losses realized after 1984.
- The total of all capital gains deductions claimed in previous taxation years.
- The cumulative net investment loss at the end of the year.

12-109.   All of the items are included in this calculation without adjustment for changing capital gains inclusion rates. This means that, depending on the year in which the gain, loss, or deduction occurred, there may be a mix of items included on the basis of one-half, two-thirds, or three-quarters of their full amounts.

Example

12-110.   The example which follows illustrates the basic rules involved in the application of the lifetime capital gains deduction.

Example   In 1987, Dwight Treadway realized a $20,000 taxable capital gain ($40,000 capital gain) from the sale of publicly traded shares and claimed a deduction for this amount. In 1990, he realized an allowable capital loss of $13,500 (three-quarters of $18,000) which is deducted as a loss carry forward from Taxable Income in 2001. Mr. Treadway's 2001 Net Income is as follows:

Employment Income	$ 60,000
Taxable Capital Gain On Disposition Of Qualified Farm Property	200,000
Net Income For Tax Purposes	$260,000

Other than the 1987 taxable capital gain of $20,000 and the 1990 allowable capital loss of $13,500, Dwight Treadway had no capital gains, capital losses, loss carry overs, or allowable business investment losses in 1985 through 2000. The farm property was purchased in 1980.

Required: Determine the maximum capital gains deduction that Mr. Treadway can claim in 2001.

12-111.   For 2001, the maximum deduction under ITA 110.6 would be the least of the:

Capital Gains Deduction Available   The maximum available deduction is $230,000 [(1/2)($500,000 - $40,000)].

Annual Gains Limit   This would be the $200,000 net taxable capital gain for the year, less the $9,000 [($13,500)(2/3)] loss carry forward deducted under ITA 111(1)(b), an amount of $191,000.

Cumulative Gains Limit   This would be the $211,000 sum of the annual gains limits for 1987 and 2001 ($20,000 + $191,000), less the $20,000 in taxable capital gains that were deducted in 1987, an amount of $191,000.

12-112.   Given these calculations, the maximum deduction for 2001 would be $191,000, the amount of both the annual gains limit and the cumulative gains limit. The full gain on the farm could have been deducted if Mr. Treadway had not chosen to deduct the $9,000 net capital loss balance. The deduction of this amount reduced both the annual gains limit and the cumulative gains limit.

> Exercise Twelve-10 deals with the lifetime capital gains deduction. This would be an appropriate time to attempt this exercise.

Other Deductions And Inclusions In Taxable Income

12-113.   In the calculation of Taxable Income, there are a few more Division C deductions that have not yet been covered in this Chapter. These can be described as follows:

Deduction For Certain Payments   ITA 110(1)(f) provides for the deduction of certain amounts that have been included in the calculation of Net Income For Tax Purposes. The items listed here are amounts that are exempt from tax in Canada by virtue of a provision in a tax convention or agreement with another country, workers' compensation payments received as a result of injury or death, income from employment with a prescribed international organization, and social assistance payments made by a registered charity or by the government on the basis of a means or income test.

Home Relocation Loans   As noted in Chapter 5, an employer can provide up to the equivalent of an interest free $25,000 home relocation loan without it becoming a taxable benefit to the employee. Technically, however, the total loan benefit must be included in employment income, with the allowable amount deducted under ITA 110(1)(j). This has the desired effect of removing the allowable amount from taxable income. Note that this deduction, which is calculated independently of the benefit, cannot exceed the benefit.

Northern Residents Deductions   ITA 110.7 provides a deduction for individuals residing in certain prescribed northern and isolated areas for a continuous period of six months beginning or ending in the taxation year. This deduction is designed to compensate individuals for the high costs that are associated with living in such areas.

> Exercise Twelve-11 deals with home relocation loans. This would be an appropriate time to attempt this exercise.

Ordering Of Deductions And Losses

Significance Of Ordering

12-114.   If an individual has sufficient income to absorb all of the losses and deductions that are available in the calculation of taxable income, the question of ordering is not important. The real significance of provisions covering the ordering of losses and other deductions is in the determination of the amounts and types of items that can be carried over into previous or subsequent years.

12-115.   For example, assume that a taxpayer has taxable capital gains of $25,000, non capital losses of $25,000, and allowable capital losses of $25,000. No matter how these items are ordered, the Net Income For Tax Purposes will be zero. However, it does make a difference whether the loss carry over is for the non capital losses or for the allowable capital losses. The non capital losses can only be used for a limited period of time while, by contrast, the allowable capital losses can be carried forward indefinitely. On the other hand, the timing of the realization of future capital gains must be considered as allowable capital losses can only be deducted from taxable capital gains, while non capital losses can be deducted from other types of income. The *Income Tax Act* appears to put more emphasis on this latter consideration in that ITA 3 requires that capital losses be netted against capital gains [ITA 3(b)] before non capital losses can be deducted [ITA 3(d)].

Ordering In Computing Net Income

12-116.   The basic rules for the computation of Net Income under Division B are found in ITA 3. In computing Net Income For Tax Purposes, ITA 3 indicates that we begin by adding together positive amounts of income from non capital sources, plus net taxable capital gains. Net taxable capital gains are defined as the amount, if any, by which the current year's taxable capital gains exceed the current year's allowable capital losses. This, in effect, requires that capital losses be deducted prior to the deduction of non capital losses. From this total we subtract the various deductions available under Subdivision e (spousal support paid, child care costs, moving expenses, etc.). If a positive balance remains, the final step in computing Net Income For Tax Purposes is to subtract any non capital losses that have been incurred during the year.

Ordering In Computing Taxable Income

12-117.   With respect to the computation of taxable income for individuals, the Act is much more specific. Under ITA 111.1, the order in which individuals must deduct Division C items is as follows:

- Various deductions provided by ITA 110 (stock options, home relocation loans)
- Loss carry overs under ITA 111
- Lifetime capital gains under ITA 110.6
- Northern residents deductions under ITA 110.7

12-118.   Within ITA 111, available loss carry overs can be deducted in any order the tax-payer wishes. The only constraint is the ITA 111(3) requirement that, within a particular type of loss (e.g., non capital losses), the oldest losses have to be used first.

12-119.   When several different types of loss carry overs are available, decisions in this area can be difficult. On the one hand, certain types of carry overs have a limited period of availability (i.e., non capital losses can be carried forward seven years and regular farm losses can be carried forward ten years). In contrast, net capital losses have no time limit, but can only be deducted to the extent of taxable capital gains that have been realized in the year. Restricted farm loss carry overs and carry overs of losses on listed personal property represent the worst case scenario. These losses are restricted with respect to both time and type of income (e.g., restricted farm loss carry forwards are only available for ten years and can only be deducted to the extent of farm income earned in the year.)

12-120.   Decisions in this area will involve a careful weighing of which type of loss carry over is most likely to have continued usefulness in future years. For example, if a non capital loss carry forward is six years old and the business is expecting no taxable income in the following year, then use of this carry forward would appear to be a prudent course of action. An additional consideration is that any tax credits available (see Chapter 13) should be fully utilized before applying loss carry overs. The amount of loss carry over that is claimed should not be more than is needed to reduce taxes payable (not taxable income) to nil.

Example

12-121.   The following is an example of the ordering rules used in computing taxable income for individuals:

Example   At the beginning of 2001, Miss Farnum had unused loss carry forwards as follows:

Non Capital Losses	$24,000
Net Capital Losses From 1994 [(3/4)($20,000)]	15,000
Restricted Farm Losses From 1993	5,000

During 2001, she had the following income as calculated under Division B rules:

Employment Income	$15,000
Property Income (Interest)	4,000
Farming Income	2,000
Income From Sole Proprietorship	15,000
Capital Gains	12,000

Required: Calculate Miss Farnum's minimum net and taxable income for 2001 and the amount of any losses that will be carried forward to later years.

12-122.   Miss Farnum's 2001 Net Income For Tax Purposes would be calculated as follows:

Income Under ITA 3(a):	
Employment Income	$15,000
Property Income	4,000
Farming Income	2,000
Business Income (Proprietorship)	15,000
Income Under ITA 3(b):	
Taxable Capital Gain [(1/2)($12,000)]	6,000
Net Income For Tax Purposes	$42,000

12-123.   Miss Farnum's 2001 Taxable Income is as follows:

Net Income For Tax Purposes	$42,000
Loss Carry Overs:	
Restricted Farm Losses (Limited to farming income)	(2,000)
Net Capital Losses (Limited to taxable capital gains)	(6,000)
Non Capital Losses	(24,000)
Taxable Income	$10,000

12-124.   The remaining loss carry forwards consist of the $3,000 balance in the restricted farm loss and a net capital loss of $6,000 [(3/4)($20,000 - $12,000)]. Note that, in this example, the amount of capital and farm losses deducted was restricted by the availability of capital gains and farm income. However, there was sufficient overall income that the taxpayer did not have to make a choice as to which type of loss to deduct.

References

12-125.   For more detailed study of the material in this Chapter, we would refer you to the following:

ITA 110	Deductions Permitted
ITA 110.6	Capital Gains Exemption
ITA 111	Losses Deductible
ITA 111.1	Order Of Applying Provisions
IT-113R4	Benefits To Employees — Stock Options
IT-232R3	Losses - Their Deductibility In The Loss Years Or In Other Years
IT-322R	Farm Losses
IT-523	Order Of Provisions Applicable In Computing An Individual's Taxable Income And Tax Payable

Exercises

(The solutions for these exercises can be found following Chapter 21 of the text.)

Exercise Twelve - 1 (Stock Options)

During 1999, Mr. Gordon Guise was granted options to buy 2,500 of his employer's shares at a price of $23.00 per share. At this time the shares are trading at $20.00 per share. His employer is a large publicly traded company. During July, 2001, he exercises all of the options at a point in time when the shares are trading at $31.50 per share. The shares are sold immediately at that price. What is the effect of the exercise of the options and the sale of the shares on Mr. Guise's 2001 Taxable Income?

Exercise Twelve - 2 (Stock Options)

In 1997, Ms. Milli Van was granted options to buy 1,800 of her employer's shares at a price of $42.50 per share. At this time the shares have a fair market value of $45.00 per share. Her employer is a Canadian controlled private company. In June, 2001, at a time when the shares have a fair market value of $75.00 per share, she exercises all of her options. She used funds received from the sale of a rental property which resulted in a capital gain of $100,000. In September, 2001 Ms. Van sells her shares for $88,200 ($49 per share). What is the effect of the exercise of the options and the sale of the shares on Ms. Van's 2001 Taxable Income?

Exercise Twelve - 3 (Stock Options)

Ms. Meridee Masterson is employed by a large public company. In 1999, she was granted options to acquire 1,000 shares of her employer's common stock at a price of $23 per share. At the time the options were granted, the shares were trading at $20 per share. In 2001, when the shares are trading at $45 per share, she exercises her options and acquires 1,000 shares. At the end of 2001 she makes an election to defer the maximum amount of any employment income benefit. In 2002, she sells these shares for $42 per share. What is the effect of these transactions on Ms. Masterson's 2001 and 2002 Taxable Income?

Exercise Twelve - 4 (Stock Options)

How would your answer to Exercise Twelve - 3 differ if Ms. Masterson's employer was a Canadian controlled private company?

Exercise Twelve - 5 (Stock Option Deferral)

In March, 2001, John Traverse is granted options to acquire 25,000 shares of his employer's publicly traded common stock at a price of $12 per share. At this time the shares were trading at $12 per share. The option arrangement is such that options for 10,000 shares vest in 2002, with the remaining options vesting in 2003. All of the options are exercised during 2004, at which time the shares are trading at $32 per share. Mr. Traverse makes the election required to defer the maximum amount of employment income in 2004. How will these transactions be reflected on Mr. Traverse's 2004 T4 slip?

Exercise Twelve - 6 (Capital Losses)

During 2000, Mr. Ronald Smothers was unemployed and had no income of any kind. In order to survive, he sold a painting on December 1, 2000 for $89,000. This painting had been left to Mr. Smothers by his mother and, at the time of her death, it had a fair market value of $100,000. During 2001, Mr. Smothers finds a job and has employment income of $62,000. In addition, during June he sells a second painting for $53,000. He had purchased this painting several years ago for $49,000. Determine Mr. Smothers' Net Income For Tax Purposes and Taxable Income for 2001.

Exercise Twelve - 7 (Loss Carry Forwards)

During 1999, Ms. Laura Macky had an allowable capital loss of $22,500. Prior to 2001, she has had no taxable capital gains and, as a consequence, she has not been able to deduct this loss. In 2001, her income consists of a taxable capital gain of $40,000 [(1/2)($80,000)] and a net rental loss of $30,000. She does not anticipate any future capital gains. Determine Ms.

Macky's minimum 2001 Net Income For Tax Purposes and the amounts of any capital or non capital loss carry forwards.

Exercise Twelve - 8 (Business Investment Losses)
During 1986, Mr. Lawrence Latvik used his lifetime capital gains deduction to eliminate a taxable capital gain of $13,000 [(1/2)($26,000)]. During 2001, he has capital gains on publicly traded securities of $18,000, and a business investment loss of $50,000. His employment income for 2001 is over $100,000. Determine the amount of the business investment loss that can be deducted in 2001, as well as any capital or non capital loss carry over that will be available at the end of the year.

Exercise Twelve - 9 (Farm Losses)
Ms. Elena Bodkin has a full time appointment as a professor at a Canadian university. As she has considerable free time, she is developing an organic vegetable farm. In 2000, the first year of operation, she had a loss of $16,000. In 2001, in addition to her employment income of $85,000, her farming operation showed a profit of $3,500. Determine Ms. Bodkin's 2001 Taxable Income, as well as any loss carry overs that are available at the end of the year.

Exercise Twelve - 10 (Lifetime Capital Gains Deduction)
Mr. Edwin Loussier had a 1986 capital gain of $10,000 and a 1989 capital gain of $26,000. He used his lifetime capital gains deduction to eliminate both of these gains. He has no other capital gains or business investment losses in the period 1985 through 2000. In December, 2000 he has a $63,000 capital loss which he cannot deduct. In July, 2001, he has a $510,000 gain on the sale of a qualified farm property. In addition, he deducts the $63,000 2000 capital loss. Mr. Loussier does not have a CNIL balance. Determine Mr. Loussier's maximum lifetime capital gains deduction for 2001.

Exercise Twelve - 11 (Relocation Loan)
On January 1, 2001, in order to facilitate an employee's relocation, Lee Ltd. provides her with a five year, $82,000 loan. Annual interest at the rate of two percent must be paid on December 31 of each year. Assume that at the time the loan is granted the prescribed rate is 5 percent. What is the effect of this loan on the employee's 2001 Taxable Income?

Problems For Self Study

(The solutions for these problems can be found following Chapter 21 of the text.)

Self Study Problem Twelve - 1
During 2001, Ms. Sara Wu's employer, Imports Ltd., granted her stock options which allowed her to acquire 12,000 shares of the Company's common stock at a price of $22 per share. At this time, the shares have a fair market value of $20 per share.

On June, 1, 2002, Ms. Wu exercises all of these options. At this time, Imports Ltd. shares have a fair market value of $31 per share. Ms. Wu makes any available elections to defer employment income.

On January 31, 2003, Ms. Wu sells the 12,000 Imports Ltd. shares at a price of $28 per share.

Required   For each of the following cases, determine the 2001, 2002, and 2003 tax consequences for Ms. Wu, resulting from the receipt and exercise of the options, as well as the sale of the shares.

   Case A   Imports Ltd. is a public company and Ms. Wu is a specified shareholder (i.e., she owns more than 10 percent of the outstanding shares of the corporation).

   Case B   Imports Ltd. is a public company and Ms. Wu is not a specified shareholder.

   Case C   Imports Ltd. is a Canadian controlled private company.

Self Study Problem Twelve - 2

Over a four year period ending on December 31, 2001, Mr. Edward Fox experienced the following income and losses:

	1998	1999	2000	2001
Employment Income	$18,000	$15,000	$19,000	$12,000
Business Income (Loss)	14,500	(39,000)	34,000	(52,000)
Farming Income (Loss)	(6,000)	1,000	8,000	(2,000)
Capital Gains	-0-	7,400	6,300	-0-
Capital Losses	(3,600)	-0-	-0-	(15,000)
Dividends (Amount Received)	5,000	6,525	8,000	10,125

Both the business operation and the farming operation began in 1998. With respect to the farming operation, Mr. Fox expects to make some profit on this operation even though it is not a full time occupation for him. All of the dividends are from taxable Canadian corporations. The 2000 capital gain resulted from a December disposition.

None of Mr. Fox's losses can be carried back before 1998.

Required: For each of the four years, calculate the minimum net income and taxable income for Mr. Fox. Indicate the amended figures for any years to which losses are carried back. Also indicate the amount and types of loss carry overs that would be available to Mr. Fox at the end of each year.

Self Study Problem Twelve - 3

At the beginning of 2001, Harold Borgen had $19,800 (100%) of unused capital loss carry forwards from 1994. His net employment income amounted to $36,000 in 2001.

During 2001, Mr. Borgen realized a taxable capital gain of $37,500 (1/2 of $75,000) on the sale of shares of a qualified small business corporation and an allowable capital loss of $9,000 (1/2 of $18,000) on the sale of a video business.

Mr. Borgen paid interest of $17,000 in 2001 on a loan for the investment in the shares of a Canadian controlled private corporation. These shares paid no dividends in 2001. His investment expenses and investment income prior to 2001 were nil.

As of the beginning of 2001, Mr. Borgen had made no deduction under ITA 110.6 (lifetime capital gains deduction) in any previous year. His only prior sale of capital assets created the capital loss carryforward.

Required: Calculate Mr. Borgen's minimum Taxable Income for 2001.

Self Study Problem Twelve - 4

Mr. Joe Shipley is a construction worker employed by the Urban Construction Company, a Canadian controlled private company. During 2001, his salary from the Company was $44,000. The Company provides no retirement or other employee benefits for its employees. However, it does have a fairly generous stock option plan. Under the terms of this plan, Mr. Shipley purchased 400 shares of the Urban Construction Company common stock on March 1, 2001 at a price of $10.50 per share. The fair market value of the shares was $10 per share when the options were issued. At the time of this purchase, the shares had a fair market value of $15.00 per share. No dividends were declared on this stock during 2001 and he does not sell any of the shares in 2001.

Other Information:

1. Mr. Shipley owned 460 shares of CDC Industries, a Canadian public company which were purchased in 1999 for $9.50 per share. On January 1, 2001, CDC Industries declared a cash dividend of $1.10 per share and, on January 15, 2001, a 15 percent stock dividend

was declared and paid. In conjunction with this stock dividend, the Company increased its paid up capital by $10.00 per share. On October 31, 2001, Mr. Shipley sold all of his CDC Industries shares at a price of $12.75 per share.

2. Mr. Shipley has a 25 percent income interest in a partnership that has a fiscal year ending on December 31. On July 1, 2001, the partners decide to terminate the business. Between January 1, 2001 and July 1, 2001, the partnership earned $4,500. The assets are sold for total proceeds of $32,000 and Mr. Shipley receives his proportionate share. His cost base for the partnership interest at the time of its termination was $5,500.

3. During January, 2002, Mr. Shipley contributed $7,500 to his Registered Retirement Savings Plan. To calculate the maximum RRSP deduction, assume that his 2000 earned income equals his 2001 earned income. At the end of 2000, he has no unused RRSP deduction room or undeducted RRSP contributions.

4. For a number of years, Mr. Shipley has supplemented his employment income by stealing building materials from his employer's work sites and selling them to a local contractor. Mr. Shipley estimates that his 2001 profits from this activity amount to $18,000.

5. In September of 2001, after a period of separation, Mr. and Mrs. Shipley were divorced. The terms of the divorce decree required Mr. Shipley to make spousal support payments of $325 per month commencing on October 1. On October 1, Mr. Shipley paid a lump sum of $25,000 to Mrs. Shipley as a privately negotiated settlement for giving up her share of their car and furnishings. As a result, he did not have sufficient cash to make the monthly support payments until 2002.

Required: Calculate Mr. Shipley's minimum taxable income for the year ending December 31, 2001.

Self Study Problem Twelve - 5

Mr. Frank Bubel works as a computer software salesman for a publicly traded company with which he has been associated for five years. He is remunerated solely through commissions and stock options. His employment contract requires that he pay all of his own expenses. The only employee benefits the company offers besides the stock options are the standard statutory benefits. During 2001 Mr. Bubel earned commissions of $61,200 and had the following related expenditures:

Hotels And Deductible Portion Of Meals	$4,100
Airline Tickets	3,800
Automobile Operating Costs	4,700
Cost Of Attending Sales Convention for Mr. and Mrs. Bubel	2,900
Telephone Answering Service	2,400
Purchase Of Demonstration Software	6,800

Mr. Bubel has owned the car that he uses for business purposes for two years. At the beginning of 2001, it had an undepreciated capital cost of $15,100. The car was driven a total of 35,000 kilometers during the current year, of which 60 percent was for business purposes.

On April 24, 2000, Mr. Bubel was granted stock options which would permit him to purchase 1,000 shares at a cost of $22 per share after April 30, 2001. The stock was trading at $20 on the grant date and $25 on the vesting date. He exercised his options on June 18, 2001 when the stock was trading at $28. On December 28, 2001, he sells the shares at a price of $18 per share.

Mr. Bubel is married and has two children aged 3 and 5. During June, 2001, his wife received proceeds of $12,800 from the sale of shares. These shares had been inherited by Mr. Bubel with a $2,000 adjusted cost base and he gave them to his wife at the time of inheritance.

The children's income for 2001 consisted of interest on Canada Savings Bonds which had been given to them at their birth by their father. The amounts were $500 for the older child and $300 for the younger.

In April 2001, Mr. Bubel contributed $5,500 to a spousal RRSP and, in February of 2002, he contributed $4,000 to his own RRSP. Assume that Mr. Bubel's 2000 earned income is equal to his 2001 earned income. At the end of 2000, Mr. Bubel has no unused RRSP deduction room or undeducted RRSP contributions.

On March 22, 2001, Mr. Bubel sold 100 shares of common stock for $75 per share. These shares had been purchased in 1998 at a cost of $89 per share. On April 10, 2001, the price of the shares had fallen to $62.50 per share, so Mr. Bubel acquired 50 shares in hopes of recovering part of his losses.

Mr. Bubel had other income and receipts during 2001 as follows:

Dividends From Taxable Canadian Corporations	$ 1,800
Interest On Kentucky State Bonds	
(Net of a withholding tax of 25 percent)	945
Workers' Compensation Board Payment	
(from previous employment injury)	10,000
Net Race Track Winnings	2,700

Required: For the 2001 taxation year, calculate Mr. Bubel's minimum Net Income For Tax Purposes and Taxable Income. In addition, indicate any carry overs that would be available to Mr. Bubel at the end of the taxation year. Ignore GST and PST considerations.

Assignment Problems

(The solutions for these problems are only available in the solutions manual that has been provided to your instructor.)

Assignment Problem Twelve - 1

On February 24, 1999, during her first year as an employee of Hardin Weaving Ltd., Ms. Jones was granted options to purchase 5,000 shares of the Company's stock at a price of $20 per share.

When Ms. Jones paid the Company $100,000 in order to exercise the options and acquire the 5,000 shares, the shares had a fair market value of $28 per share. Ms. Jones makes any available elections to defer employment income.

On October 3, 2001, Ms. Jones sells all of her 5,000 Hardin Weaving Ltd. shares at a price of $32 per share.

Required: Indicate the tax effect on Ms. Jones with respect to the granting of the options, their exercise, and the sale of the shares under each of the following independent assumptions:

A. Hardin Weaving Ltd. is a Canadian controlled private company. At the time the options were granted, the Company's shares had a fair market value of $18. The options were exercised on December 1, 2000.

B. Hardin Weaving Ltd. is a Canadian public company. At the time the options were granted, the shares were trading at $18. The options were exercised on December 1, 2000.

C. Hardin Weaving Ltd. is a Canadian public company. At the time the options were granted, the shares were trading at $22. The options were exercised on December 1, 2000.

D. Hardin Weaving Ltd. is a Canadian controlled private company. At the time the options were granted, the Company's shares had a fair market value of $22. The options were exercised on October 1, 1999.

Assignment Problem Twelve - 2

During 1997, Miss Lynn Atwater invested $170,000 to acquire 100 percent of the common shares of a corporation specializing in pet food products. The company was a Canadian controlled private company with a fiscal year ending on January 31. All of its assets were used to produce active business income.

In 1998 and 1999, the company operated successfully but did not pay any dividends. In 2000, it began to experience serious financial difficulties. On July 15, 2001, the company was forced into bankruptcy by its creditors and it is clear to Miss Atwater that, after the claims of the creditors have been dealt with, her investment will be worthless.

Other financial data for Miss Atwater for the years ending December 31, 2000 and December 31, 2001, is as follows:

	2000	2001
Net employment income	$34,200	$35,200
Interest income	4,000	4,200
Basic personal amount	7,231	7,412

The basic personal amount is used to calculate the non refundable tax credit available to each individual. The only tax credit available to Miss Atwater in either year is the basic personal credit. Miss Atwater had no Taxable Income or Loss for 1998 and 1999. At the beginning of 2000, she did not have any loss carry overs from previous years.

Required: Determine Miss Atwater's optimum taxable income for the years ending December 31, 2000 and December 31, 2001. Indicate any loss carry over that is present at the end of either year and the rules applicable to claiming the loss carry over.

Assignment Problem Twelve - 3

During the four year period 1998 through 2001, Ms. Brenda Breau had the following financial data:

	1998	1999	2000	2001
Business income (Loss)	$18,000	($14,000)	$28,000	($20,000)
Farming income (Loss)	(6,000)	2,000	3,150	(2,000)
Dividends from taxable				
Canadian corporations	1,888	2,360	3,170	5,160
Capital gains (Losses)	(3,000)	2,000	4,000	(10,000)

Because of the nature of her farming activities, Ms. Breau's farm losses are restricted.

At the beginning of 1998, Ms. Breau had no loss carry overs from previous years. None of her losses can be carried back before 1998. The 2000 capital gain resulted from a disposition in December of that year.

Required: Calculate Ms. Breau's minimum Net Income For Tax Purposes and Taxable Income for each of the four years. Indicate the amount and types of loss carry overs that would be available at the end of each year.

Assignment Problem Twelve - 4

At the beginning of 2001, Mr. Lindon had a $10,250 [(2/3)($15,375)] net capital loss carry forward from 1988. His net employment income amounted to $21,300 in 2001.

During October, 2001, Mr. Lindon realized a taxable capital gain of $18,300 on the sale of shares in a qualified small business corporation and an allowable capital loss of $4,800 on the sale of shares of a public company.

In 1994, Mr. Lindon used the lifetime capital gains deduction election to fully utilize his $100,000 general lifetime capital gains deduction. He has made no other deduction under

ITA 110.6 (lifetime capital gains deduction). As of the end of 2001, he has no cumulative net investment loss.

Required: Calculate Mr. Lindon's minimum Taxable Income for 2001.

Assignment Problem Twelve - 5

Mr. Andrew Fine is a lawyer with an established practice in Prince Edward Island. The following represents a summary of the operating figures for his practice for the taxation year which ends December 31, 2001:

Gross Billings	$162,000
Salaries For Staff	42,900
Office Rent	12,000
Allowance For Bad Debts:	
Opening Balance	2,500
Closing Balance	1,800
Bad Debts Written Off During Year	1,300
Bad Debts From Previous Year Recovered In Current Year	300
Cost Of Attending Legal Convention	800
Office Expenses	33,700

In addition to his law practice, Mr. Fine operates a small farm which experienced a $4,500 loss during the year. While Mr. Fine views the farm as a sideline, he anticipates that it will become profitable within two years.

Mr. Fine has been married for several years and has two children under the age of 18. During 2001, Mr. Fine made charitable contributions of $515.

Required: Calculate Mr. Fine's minimum Net Income For Tax Purposes and Taxable Income for the year ending December 31, 2001.

Assignment Problem Twelve - 6

Mr. Charles Brookings was divorced from his wife in 1995. Under the terms of the settlement, he is required to pay child support to his former spouse in the amount of $600 per month. The former spouse has custody of their two children, both of whom are under 13 years of age.

For 2001, Mr. Brookings has provided you with the following financial data:

1. Mr. Brookings' salary for the year is $50,000. In addition, his employer provides him with a car which was purchased for $24,000. Operating costs for the car totalled $5,200 during the current year and it was driven a total of 35,000 kilometers. While Mr. Brookings had the use of the car for the whole year, only 8,000 kilometers of the distance driven was for personal matters.

2. Mr. Brookings is a member of his employer's registered pension plan, but made no contributions for 2001 and his Pension Adjustment was nil for 2000. His 2000 earned income was $30,931. At the end of 2000, Mr. Brookings' Unused RRSP Deduction Room was nil and he had no undeducted RRSP contributions.

3. Mr. Brookings received pension income from a former employer in the amount of $6,000.

4. Mr. Brookings had investment income which consisted of $1,800 in interest on corporate bonds, $2,500 in dividends on Canadian public company shares, capital gains resulting from stock exchange transactions in the amount of $4,500, and an $8,000 loss on the sale of shares of a small business corporation.

5. During the year, Mr. Brookings made contributions to registered Canadian charities in the amount of $1,200, paid private health care plan premiums of $475, and, in October, contributed $2,800 to an RRSP.

Required: Determine Mr. Brookings' minimum Net Income and Taxable Income for 2001.

Assignment Problem Twelve - 7

The following information relates to Mr. Randy Delorme for the year ending December 31, 2001:

1. Mr. Delorme's gross salary was $50,000. His employer deducted Canada Pension Plan contributions of $1,496, Employment Insurance premiums of $878, registered pension plan contributions of $2,100, union dues of $220, and income taxes of $11,400. His employer paid $750 for Mr. Delorme's membership in a country club.

2. On May 1, Mr. Delorme received a $30,000 interest free home relocation loan from his employer. This loan was associated with a promotion and move to a new city.

3. In May, Mr. Delorme incurred $900 of moving costs that were not reimbursed by his employer.

4. Mr. Delorme received dividends from taxable Canadian corporations in the amount of $1,500, interest on corporate bonds of $2,000, and dividends from a private company in which he is the sole shareholder of $1,000.

5. Mr. Delorme has a farm which he operates on a part time basis. While he anticipates that the farm operation will soon be profitable, the farm lost $12,000 during the year.

6. With respect to listed personal property, Mr. Delorme had a gain of $10,000 on the sale of one item, and a loss of $11,000 on the sale of another.

7. On his personal use property, he experienced a gain on the sale of one item in the amount of $4,500, and realized a loss on the sale of another item in the amount of $6,000. In all sales transactions involving personal use and listed personal property, the sales proceeds and the adjusted cost base of the properties exceeded $1,000.

8. Mr. Delorme paid spousal support of $500 per month to his former wife.

9. Mr. Delorme borrowed to purchase shares of a company in which he is a minority shareholder. Interest on this loan amounted to $2,800.

10. Mr. Delorme paid life insurance premiums of $2,300.

11. Early in the year, Mr. Delorme purchased a lake lot. Due to his contacts, he knew that a road would be built to provide access to the lake. On October 3, after the road was completed, it was sold for a gain of $7,800.

12. Mr. Delorme contributed $2,500 to his registered retirement savings plan during the year. His Pension Adjustment on his 2000 T4 is $5,300. Assume that his 2000 earned income equals his 2001 earned income. At the end of 2000, Mr. Delorme has no unused RRSP deduction room or undeducted RRSP contributions.

13. Assume that the prescribed interest rate was 6% for all of 2001.

Required: Calculate Mr. Delorme's minimum Net Income For Tax Purposes and Taxable Income for the year ending December 31, 2001. In addition, indicate any carry overs that would be available to Mr. Delorme at the end of the 2001 taxation year.

Assignment Problem Twelve - 8

On December 31, 2001, Mr. Marvin Hathway retires after 35 consecutive years of service with the same employer. He is 63 years of age, in good health, and plans to spend his retirement years in Northern Ontario.

During 2001, Mr. Hathway had the following receipts:

Gross Salary	$65,900
Gambling Profits	6,500
Dividends From Taxable Canadian Corporations	2,300
Dividends From British Companies (Net Of 15 Percent Withholding Tax)	765
Proceeds From May 20 Sale Of Budd Ltd. Shares (110 Shares At $115)	12,650
Proceeds From Sale Of Painting	33,000
Retiring Allowance	80,000
Interest On Federal Government Bonds	1,800

On January 5, 2002 he received a bonus and vacation pay totalling $8,300 related to 2001.

With respect to the shares of Budd Ltd., a Canadian public company, the number of shares purchased and sold, and the total cost or selling price was as follows:

September 23, 1999 - 40 Purchased	$ 3,100
October, 11, 1999 - 60 Purchased	5,300
March 3, 1999 - 20 Sold	(2,000)
April 4, 2000 - 60 Purchased	6,100
November 12, 2000 - 120 Purchased	15,400

The painting that was sold by Mr. Hathway was inherited in 1990 when its fair market value was $25,000. The painting was sold for a total price of $45,000, with $33,000 being received in 2001 and the balance of $12,000 to be paid in 2002.

Mr. Hathway has contributed to his employer's registered pension plan in each of the 35 years that he has worked for the company. The Pension Adjustment reported on Mr. Hathway's 2000 T4 slip was $5,400. Mr. Hathway has a 2001 Past Service Pension Adjustment of $2,000. With respect to the retiring allowance received, Mr. Hathway transferred the entire amount to his RRSP on December 31, 2001.

At the end of 2000, Mr. Hathway has no unused RRSP deduction room or undeducted RRSP contributions. Assume his 2000 earned income was equal to his 2001 earned income for RRSP purposes.

During 2001, Mr. Hathway's employer withheld the following from his salary:

Canada Pension Plan Contributions	$ 1,496
Employment Insurance Premiums	878
Registered Pension Plan contribution	2,800
Income taxes	18,000
Private health care (40 percent of the total cost)	400

At the time of his retirement, Mr. Hathway was required to return his company car. The car was leased by the company for $480 per month and the company paid the 2001 operating expenses of $4,700. Mr. Hathway drove the car 32,000 kilometers during 2001, of which 10,000 were for personal matters. The car was available to him during the whole year.

During 2001, Mr. Hathway rented a safety deposit box for $180 and paid accountant fees of $1,400 for the appeal of a 1998 income tax reassessment.

Required: Calculate Mr. Hathway's minimum Net Income For Tax Purposes and Taxable Income for the year ending December 31, 2001.

Assignment Problem Twelve - 9

Mrs. Cynthia Shields is the chief executive officer of a large publicly traded Canadian corporation, the Milword Group Ltd. She was promoted to this position early in 2001 and the promotion involved a significant increase in her salary. She is aware that this may result in a large increase in taxes payable and has approached you, in January, 2002, for advice regarding her taxes payable. Through the course of an extended interview, you accumulate the following information:

Salary   Her salary for the year ending December 31, 2001 amounted to $225,000. In addition she earned a bonus of $16,200 which was based on her outstanding performance with the Company. This bonus was paid in January of 2002.

Other Benefits   During 2001, the Company provided a number of other benefits. She described them as follows:

1. Contributions by the Company to its money purchase Registered Pension Plan for Mrs. Shields totalled $5,645.

2. The Company paid provincial health care premiums on her behalf which totalled $196. The Company also provided a private supplementary health care plan at a cost of $275.

3. Throughout the year, the Company provided her with a car which it had purchased for her at a cost of $45,000. During the year she drove the car 40,000 kilometers, only 8,000 of which could be justified as employment related travel. The Company paid for all operating costs which totalled $6,200 during the year. To avoid being taxed on this benefit, Mrs. Shields took the advice of a friend and has been paying the Company $100 per month. Total payments for the year amount to $1,200.

4. The Company paid her membership fees in the local golf and country club. These totalled $2,600 for the year. In addition, Mrs. Shields was reimbursed for $8,900 in expenses related to entertaining clients at this club.

5. When she had to be out of town on Company business, the Company paid a flat rate of $150 per day for food and lodging. Such travel during the year amounted to 31 days and she was paid a total of $4,650 for her travel costs. The rate was considered reasonable and the amount paid was not included on her T4.

6. The Company has a stock option plan for its senior executives. During September, 2001, Mrs. Shields purchased 8,500 shares of the Company's stock under the provisions of this plan. The price paid for the shares was $7.00 per share and, at the time of purchase, the per share fair market value was $11.00. In 2000, when the options were granted, the market price of the shares was $6.50. Ms. Shields makes an election with her employer to have the employment income inclusion on these shares deferred until they are sold.

7. During the year, the Company made the following payroll deductions from Mrs. Shields' salary:

Income Taxes Withheld	$97,000
Contributions To Registered Pension Plan	5,000
United Way Fund Contributions	650
Employment Insurance Premiums	878
Canada Pension Plan Contributions	1,496

Royalties   Mrs. Shields writes a column in her industry's trade journal. During 2001 she received royalties of $12,200 for this work.

Investment Income   During 2001, the following amounts were received on various investments that have been made by Mrs. Shields:

Dividends Received From Canadian Public Companies	$ 950
Foreign Dividends (Net Of 30 Percent Withholding Tax)	3,500
Canadian Source Interest	340
Life Annuity (Capital Portion of $650)	1,450

Payments From Former Employer   When she left her previous employer in 2000, she was entitled to a number of benefit transfers. During 2001 she received a retiring allowance of $30,000 and notification that she would be entitled to a payment of $53,000 from the Deferred Profit Sharing Plan in 2002. She transfers the entire $30,000 retiring allowance into a newly established RRSP. She was with this former employer for 23 years and was a member of its registered pension plan in all of these years.

Dispositions Of Assets   During 2001, Mrs. Shields disposed of two assets. The relevant facts are as follows:

1. On June 15, a David Milne painting which she had purchased in 1975 for $500 was sold for $63,000.

2. On August 31, her 39 foot sailboat was sold for $73,000. This boat was purchased by Mrs. Shields in 1988 for $25,000. The terms of sale required the purchaser to pay $13,000 at the time of the sale, followed by payments of $20,000 in 2002, 2003, and 2004.

Income Protection Payments   During the month of July, Mrs. Shields was hospitalized for minor surgery. While away from her job she received $2,000 in income protection payments under a plan provided for her by the Company.

Required: Using the information provided by Mrs. Shields, calculate her minimum 2001 Net Income and Taxable Income. In making these calculations, ignore GST and PST considerations. Provide any suggestions that might assist Mrs. Shields in reducing the amount of her taxes payable for 2001 and future years.

Assignment Problem Twelve - 10 (Electronic Library Research Problem)

Provide brief answers to the following questions. Your answers should be supported by references to materials found in your Electronic Library.

A. An individual has options to acquire convertible preferred shares at a price of $100 per share. This was the fair market value of the shares at the time the options were issued. What event will give rise to an employment income benefit under ITA 7(1) with respect to these options?

B. In order for a farming activity to be considered a source of income it must be a business carried on with a reasonable expectation of profit. What are the criteria used by the CCRA to determine whether or not a farm operation is a business?

Chapter 13

Taxes Payable For Individuals

Calculation Of Taxes Payable

The Basic System

13-1.   For individuals, the basic system for calculating taxes payable is relatively straightforward. At the federal level for 2001 there is a schedule of four rates, 16 percent, 22 percent, 26 percent, and 29 percent. The 16 percent rate applies to Taxable Income between nil and $30,754, the 22 percent rate applies to Taxable Income between $30,755 and $61,509, and the 26 percent rate applies to amounts between $61,510 and $100,000. The high rate of 29 percent applies to amounts in excess of $100,000. In order to maintain the fairness of the tax system, these threshold income levels should be indexed to reflect inflation. In the absence of such indexation, taxpayers could find themselves subject to higher rates without having an increased level of real, inflation adjusted, income.

13-2.   ITA 117.1 does, in fact, require indexing of these amounts for the effects of inflation as measured by the Consumer Price Index (CPI). However, until the issuance of the February 28, 2000 budget, indexing was limited to amounts of inflation in excess of three percent and, because the movements of the CPI have been less than that in recent years, there was no indexing of these three federal tax brackets in the years 1993 through 1999. The February 28, 2000 federal budget proposals have changed this situation. As of January 1, 2000, full indexing was restored to the personal income tax system. The adjustment is based on the 12 month period ending September 30 of the previous year and, for 2001, it amounts to 1.25 percent.

13-3.   Until recently, all of the provinces with the exception of Quebec have applied flat rates to graduated amounts of basic federal tax in order to determine the provincial taxes payable. As of 2001, all of the provinces have switched to a system of calculating their taxes on the basis of a Taxable Income figure. This alternative approach has come to be referred to as the TONI (Tax ON Income) system.

13-4.   It is believed that the TONI system eliminates the impact of changes to federal tax rates and credits on provincial-territorial revenues. At the same time, the Federal Government's willingness to continue administering provincial taxes under this system serves to maintain a common federal/provincial taxable income base. This has a number of benefits including:

- uniformity across provinces and territories with respect to what income should be taxed by both levels of government;

- a single form for taxpayers;
- a single tax collection agency; and
- substantial cost savings for the provinces and territories as a result of the federal government collecting their taxes generally free of charge. It is claimed that, over the past five years, the provinces have saved some $1.5 billion as a result of the federal government administering their taxes.

13-5.   In implementing the TONI system, it appears that most provinces will use the same Taxable Income figure that is used for the calculation of federal taxes payable. However, flexibility is available in this area and, with the passage of time, it is likely that variations from the federal figure will be introduced. The Quebec experience certainly suggests that this will be the case. Quebec has been using this type of system for many years and, at this point in time, the Quebec Taxable Income figure can be significantly different than the federal figure.

13-6.   With respect to rates, it appears that most provinces will use graduated rates applied to brackets that are the same or similar to those used at the federal level. Ontario, for example, uses three rates. A rate of 6.2 percent on Taxable Income up to $30,814, 9.24 percent on additional Taxable income up to $61,629, and 11.16 percent on Taxable Income over $61,629 (the top rate here is somewhat deceptive in that Taxable Income over $68,360 will attract a 56 percent surtax, bringing the real top rate to 17.41 percent). There are, however, exceptions to this graduated rate approach. Alberta is calculating provincial taxes at a flat 10 percent of Taxable Income, without regard to the individual's level of income.

Federal Taxes Payable Before Credits

13-7.   The calculation of Federal Taxes Payable for individuals begins with Taxable Income as determined using the procedures discussed in the previous Chapter. As the Canadian system is progressive in nature, higher rates are applied to higher levels of Taxable Income. The Taxable Income segments to which the various rates apply are referred to as tax brackets and, for 2001, Canada will use four tax brackets (in previous years, only three brackets were used). The four brackets and their rates are as follows:

Taxable Income	Basic Federal Tax	Marginal Rate On Excess
$ -0-	$ -0-	16%
30,754	4,921	22%
61,509	11,687	26%
100,000	21,695	29%

13-8.   Note that the average rate for someone just entering the highest 29 percent bracket is 21.7 percent ($21,695 ÷ $100,000). This points out the importance of keeping an annual income level within this bracket. To this point, the average rate is 21.7 percent. For all income that exceeds this level, the federal rate goes to 29 percent.

13-9.   The preceding table suggests that individuals are taxed on their first dollar of income. While the 16 percent rate is, in fact, applied to all of the first $30,754 of Taxable Income, a portion of this amount is not really subject to taxes. As will be discussed later in this Chapter, every individual resident in Canada is entitled to a personal tax credit. For 2001, this tax credit is $1,186 [(16%)($7,412)]. In effect, this means that no taxes will be paid on at least the first $7,412 of an individual's Taxable Income. This tax free amount would be even higher for individuals with additional tax credits (e.g., age credit).

13-10.   As an example of the calculation of Federal Tax Payable Before Credits, consider an individual with Taxable Income of $82,300. The calculation would be as follows:

Tax On First $61,509	$11,687
Tax On Next $20,791 At 26%	5,406
Federal Tax Before Credits	$17,093

Tax On Split Income

13-11.   A number of arrangements have been used to channel business and property income into the hands of related individuals with little or no other source of income. If, for example, the owner of a corporation can arrange his affairs so that corporate income is paid out as dividends to his children, each child can receive over $25,000 per year of such income on a tax free basis. As is discussed in Chapter 20, family trusts were once also widely used for this purpose.

13-12.   As the government has had little success in attacking these arrangements through the courts, it has decided to solve the problem through legislation. Beginning in 2000, ITA 120.4 imposes a new tax (referred to by some writers as the "kiddie tax") on the "split income" of specified individuals. This tax is assessed at the maximum federal rate of 29 percent. The tax is applied to all such income, beginning with the first dollar received. Further, the only tax credit that can be applied against this income is the dividend tax credit.

13-13.   For the purposes of this Section, a specified individual is anyone who has not attained the age of 17 years before the taxation year end, is a resident of Canada throughout the year, and has a parent who is a resident of Canada at any time in the year.

13-14.   As indicated, the tax on "split income" which is defined in ITA 120.4 includes the following:

(a) taxable dividends from private companies received directly, or through a trust or partnership;
(b) shareholder benefits under ITA 15 received from a private corporation; and
(c) income from a partnership or trust if the income is derived from the provision of goods or services to a business:
  - carried on by a person related to the individual,
  - carried on by a corporation of which a person related to the individual is a specified shareholder (i.e., owns 10 percent or more of the shares), or
  - carried on by a professional corporation of which a person related to the individual is a shareholder.

13-15.   To avoid double taxation of this block of income subject to the high 29 percent rate, it is deductible in calculating the individual's regular Taxable Income.

Example   A 15 year old individual receives dividends from a private company in the amount of $20,000. In addition she has employment income from her summer job of $5,500. She has no deductions in the calculation of Taxable Income.

Tax Consequences   Her Taxable Income will be calculated as follows:

Taxable Dividends [(125%)($20,000)]	$25,000
Employment Income	5,500
Taxable Income	$30,500

Her federal tax payable before credits would be calculated as follows:

Income Splitting Tax [(29%)($25,000)]	$7,250
Regular Tax [(16%)($30,500 - $25,000)]	880
Federal Tax Payable Before Credits	$8,130

She is eligible for a federal dividend tax credit of $3,333 [(2/3)(25%)($20,000)] as well as other possible tax credits against the tax payable on the employment income.

13-16.   Two other aspects of this new tax should be noted:

- To insure that this new tax is paid, the budget proposes that the parents of the child be held jointly and severally liable for its remittance.

- The tax is not applicable to an individual who has no parent who is resident in Canada, to income from property inherited by the individual from a parent, nor to income from any inherited property if the minor is either in full time attendance at a post secondary educational institution or eligible for the disability tax credit.

13-17. While this proposal has been met with howls of outrage from many in the tax community, in our view it is an appropriate modification of the existing system. There has been widespread use of vehicles such as family trusts to shelter income from taxes. In effect, it was possible to pay for a large portion of the expenses of raising children on a tax advantaged basis. This type of benefit is clearly not available to the majority of Canadians and it would be difficult to describe our tax system as fair and equitable if such arrangements were allowed to continue.

Basic Federal Tax Payable
Credits To Be Deducted
13-18. The major subject matter of this Chapter is a detailed consideration of the various credits that are available to reduce Taxes Payable (e.g., medical expense tax credit). Using some of these tax credits, Basic Federal Tax Payable is calculated as follows:

Federal Tax Before Credits	$xx,xxx
Specified Tax Credits (e.g., Medical Expense Credit)	(x,xxx)
Basic Federal Tax Payable	$xx,xxx

13-19. Until this year, Basic Federal Tax Payable was an important concept. This was because most provinces calculated their tax payable on the basis of this number. Further, implicit provincial tax credits were created by any federal tax credit that was deducted in the computation of this number. As of this year, however, all of the provinces are using a TONI system, thereby diminishing the importance of this Basic Federal Tax Payable concept.

13-20. The credits which are deducted in the calculation of Basic Federal Tax are listed in ITA 118.92. This Section also contains an ordering provision, specifying the sequence in which these federal tax credits must be deducted. Figure 13-1 lists the federal tax credits that go into the determination of Basic Federal Tax Payable in the order required by ITA 118.92.

Figure 13 - 1
Calculation of Basic Federal Tax Payable

Gross Federal Tax Payable (Taxable Income times the appropriate rates)
Less The:
- basic, spousal, equivalent-to-spouse, and infirm dependant tax credits
- caregiver credit
- age credit
- Canada (Quebec) pension plan credit
- employment insurance credit
- pension income credit
- disability credit
- tuition fee credit
- education credit
- transfer of tuition fee and education credits
- transfer of spouse's credits
- medical expenses credit
- charitable donations credit
- interest on student loans credit
- dividend tax credit

Equals: Basic Federal Tax Payable

13-21.   Additional federal tax credits are available to reduce the total tax payable. These additional federal tax credits are as follows:

- foreign tax credits
- federal political contributions tax credit
- investment tax credits
- labour sponsored funds tax credit
- employee and partner GST rebate

Federal Surtax Payable

13-22.   With all of the provinces now using a TONI system, the only remaining reason for a separate calculation of Basic Federal Tax Payable was for the calculation of surtaxes. In recent years, the federal government has assessed surtaxes as high as 8 percent, with the rate being applied to Basic Federal Tax Payable.

13-23.   In its February, 2000 budget, the government indicated that, while a surtax on high incomes would remain, it would be reduced in 2001. However, as a reflection of the government's improving fiscal situation, the October, 2000 budget update announced the complete elimination of the federal surtax for 2001 and subsequent years.

13-24.   With the elimination of the federal surtax, there is no current reason for distinguishing between credits that are deducted in the calculation of Basic Federal Tax Payable and those that are deducted from this figure. However, the legislation for this concept is still in place and could become relevant again if federal surtaxes are brought back into the system.

Provincial Taxes Payable

TONI

13-25.   For 2001, all of the provinces are using a Tax On Income (TONI) system to calculate provincial taxes payable. With the exception of Alberta, they are using a graduated range of rates applied to brackets that appear to be similar but not identical to those used at the federal level. As noted earlier, Alberta is using a flat rate applied to all levels of income. Adding further complexity to these new approach is the fact that several provinces are using surtaxes, sometimes at very formidable levels. For example, Ontario adds a surtax of 56 percent to its taxes payable for income levels in excess of $68,360.

13-26.   To give you some idea of the range of provincial rates, the 2001 minimum and maximum rates, along with applicable surtaxes are as found in the following table:

Province/Territory	Minimum Tax Rate	Maximum Tax Rate	Applicable Surtax
Alberta	10.00%	10.00%	N/A
British Columbia	8.40%	19.70%	N/A
Manitoba	10.90%	17.50%	N/A
New Brunswick	9.68%	17.84%	N/A
Newfoundland	10.57%	18.02%	9%
Nova Scotia	9.77%	16.67%	10%
Ontario	6.20%	11.16%	20% and 56%
Prince Edward Island	9.80%	16.7%	10%
Québec	18.0%	25.0%	N/A
Saskatchewan	11.50%	16.0%	N/A

13-27.   Given the large differences in brackets and surtaxes, it is not immediately apparent from the preceding table how the real rates of taxation in the various provinces compare. Real comparisons require further calculations in order to give consideration to the manner in which these various components of provincial taxation work together. Further, different effective rates apply depending on the type of income. The following table indicates the maximum effective combined federal/provincial rates that are applicable to ordinary income, dividend income and capital gains (data from the PricewaterhouseCoopers web site):

Province	Ordinary Income	Capital Gains	Canadian Dividends
Alberta	39.00%	19.50%	24.08%
British Columbia	45.70%	22.85%	32.21%
Manitoba	46.40%	23.20%	33.83%
New Brunswick	46.84%	23.42%	32.38%
Newfoundland	48.64%	24.32%	31.87%
Nova Scotia	47.34%	23.67%	31.92%
Ontario	46.41%	23.21%	31.34%
Prince Edward Island	47.37%	23.69%	31.96%
Québec	48.72%	24.36%	33.44%
Saskatchewan	45.00%	23.20%	29.58%
Non Residents	42.92%	21.46%	28.98%

13-28.   You should note the significant differences in rates between the provinces. An individual making amounts in excess of the threshold of the maximum bracket is almost ten percentage points better off living in Alberta as opposed to Québec. This amounts to $10,000 on each additional $100,000 of income. Provincial tax differences could be a major consideration when deciding whether or where to move or relocate.

13-29.   A further important point is the different rates on alternative sources of income. Both dividends and capital gains have always received favourable tax treatment. However, until 2001, these two types of income enjoyed a similar status with respect to effective rates of taxation. However, with the reduction in the capital gains inclusion rate to one-half, capital gains are now subject to much lower rates of taxation than is the case with dividends.

13-30.   It is clear from the preceding table, that there are significant differences in provincial tax rates. Given this, it is a bit surprising that the rules related to where an individual will be taxed are fairly simple. With respect to an individual's income other than business income, it is deemed to have been earned in the province in which he resides on the last day of the taxation year. This means that, if an individual moves to Ontario from Nova Scotia on December 30 of the current year, any income for the year other than business income, will be deemed to have been earned in Ontario.

Taxes On Income Not Earned In A Province

13-31.   It is possible for an individual to be considered a resident of Canada for tax purposes without being a resident of a particular province or territory. For example, members of the Canadian Armed Forces are taxed as Canadian residents even if they do not set foot in Canada during the relevant taxation year. Such individuals will not be taxed by a Province. However, they will be subject to an equivalent amount of taxation at the federal level. In addition to their regular federal taxes, under ITA 120(1) there is a further non resident federal tax equal to 48 percent of basic federal tax. Note that this tax is still calculated on federal tax payable, not taxable income.

Tax Credits

Calculating Credits

Federal Tax Credits

13-32.   The most direct way of applying a tax credit system is to simply specify the amount of each tax credit available. In 2001, for example, the basic personal tax credit could have been specified to be $1,186. However, the Canadian system is based on a less direct approach. Rather than specifying the amount of each credit, a base amount is provided, to which the minimum federal tax rate (16 percent) is applied. This means that for 2001, the basic personal tax credit is calculated by taking 16 percent of $7,412 (we will refer to this number as the tax credit base), resulting in a credit against taxes payable of $1,186. Note that the legislation is such that, if the minimum federal tax rate of 16 percent is changed, the new rate will be used in determining individual tax credits. This, in fact, happened for 2001. The minimum rate was reduced from 17 percent to 16 percent. As a result, the rate used to calculate the tax credits was also reduced in order to maintain the value of the base amounts.

13-33. As was the case with the tax rate brackets, the base used for tax credits must be indexed to offset the effects of inflation. As was the case with tax brackets, prior to 2000, this adjustment was limited to inflation in excess of three percent. Because of low rates of inflation during the 1990s, no adjustments were made in the years 1993 through 1997. A limited increase in credits was provided in both the 1998 and 1999 budgets, though the amount fell short of full indexation. However, as of 2001, full indexation has been restored to the system.

13-34. A technical problem in calculating credits will arise in the year a person becomes a Canadian resident or ceases to be a Canadian resident. As discussed in Chapter 3, such individuals will only be subject to Canadian taxation for a part of the year. Given this, it would not be appropriate for them to receive the same credits as an individual who is subject to Canadian taxation for a full year. This view is reflected in ITA 118.91 which requires a pro rata calculation for personal tax credits, the disability tax credit, and tax credits transferred from a spouse or a person supported by the taxpayer. Other tax credits, for example the charitable donations tax credit, are not reduced because of part year residence.

Provincial Tax Credits

13-35. In the past, there was little need to discuss provincial tax credits. With provincial taxes payable being based on Federal Basic Taxes Payable, provincial tax credits were implicit in the calculation of this figure and required no further discussion. One of the problems with this approach is that it did not leave the provinces any flexibility with respect to types or amounts of credits to be provided.

13-36. With the universal adoption of the TONI system, this situation is changed. Provincial tax credits must now be made explicit. While there is considerable variation from province to province, the basic system now seems to be one which follows the federal pattern. That is, the minimum tax rate for the province is applied to an indexed tax credit base.

13-37. While we will not pursue this issue in detail, a simple example is appropriate. In our discussion of the calculation of federal tax credits, we noted that for 2001, individuals are entitled to a credit of $1,186, a base amount of $7,412 multiplied by the lowest federal rate of 16 percent. Ontario is calculating their credit on a slightly higher base ($7,426) multiplied by their lowest rate of 6.2 percent, producing a credit against provincial taxes payable of $460. In contrast, Alberta is considerably more generous. Their individual tax credit is based on an amount of $12,900, multiplied by their flat tax rate of 10 percent. The result is a credit of $1,290, larger than the federal credit and almost triple the size of the Ontario credit.

Personal Tax Credits - ITA 118
Basic Concepts

13-38. ITA 118 is titled Personal Credits and, under the rules provided, all taxpaying individuals are divided into three categories as follows:

Individual With a Spouse or a Common-Law Partner   ITA 118(1)(a) provides the two credits available to an individual taxpayer who has either a spouse or a common-law partner at any time during the year. This includes what is generally referred to as the basic personal credit, as well as an income tested credit for the individual's spouse or common-law partner.

Supporter of Wholly Dependent Person (Equivalent to Spouse)   ITA 118(1)(b) provides the two credits available to an individual taxpayer who is not married, but maintains a self contained domestic establishment and supports a dependant who lives in that establishment. Individuals in this category receive credits for the same basic personal amount as individuals with a spouse or common-law partner, as well as the same income tested credit that was provided for the spouse or common-law partner.

Single Individuals   ITA 118(1)(c) provides the credit available to an individual who does not qualify for a deduction under ITA 118(1)(a) or (b). This remaining category would be made up of those single individuals who are not supporting a dependant in a self contained domestic establishment. These individuals receive a credit only for the basic personal amount.

13-39.   All individual taxpayers are eligible for a credit based on the basic personal amount under one of these provisions and, under the first two, they may receive an additional credit for a spouse or a dependant. ITA 118 also contains four other credits which individuals may receive in addition to those cited above. These are for in home care of a relative [ITA 118(1)(c.1)], infirm dependants 18 or over [ITA 118(1)(d)], age [ITA 118(2)], and pension income [ITA 118(3)]. These credits will be explained in detail in this section.

Married Persons

13-40.   For married persons filing tax returns in 2001, ITA 118(1)(a) provides for two tax credits, with each one being calculated on a different base. The first amount is calculated as 16 percent of the basic personal amount, which for the 2001 taxation year is equal to $7,412. This provides for a credit against taxes payable of $1,186.

13-41.   The second amount available to a married person is usually referred to as the spousal amount. For 2001, the available credit is equal to 16 percent of $6,294, an amount of $1,007. However, this amount is reduced by the Net Income For Tax Purposes of the spouse in excess of $629. This limiting amount is generally referred to as the income threshold for the credit. The complete expression for the credit is as follows:

$$[16\%][\$6,294 - (\text{Spouse's Net Income} - \$629)]$$

13-42.   As an example, if an individual had a spouse with Net Income of $5,200, the total credit under ITA 118(1)(a) would be equal to:

$$\{16\%\}\{\$7,412 + [\$6,294 - (\$5,200 - \$629)]\} = \underline{\$1,462}$$

13-43.   There are several other points to be made with respect to the credits for married individuals:

- **Spouse's Income**   The income figure that is used for limiting the spousal amount is Net Income For Tax Purposes, with no adjustments of any sort. Note that when this figure reaches $6,923 ($6,294 + $629), the spousal amount will be nil and the married individual's credit will be calculated using only the basic personal amount.

- **Applicability To Either Spouse**   The ITA 118(1)(a) provision is applicable to both spouses and, while each is eligible to claim the basic amount of $7,412, IT-513R specifies that only one of the spouses may claim the additional spousal amount. IT-513R indicates that the spouse making the claim should be the one that supports the other, a fairly vague concept.

- **Eligibility**   As recently as 1992, the only basis for claiming the ITA 118(1)(a) credit was a legally recognized marriage. Starting in 1993, the definition of spouse was extended to cover common-law relationships, but only with an individual of the opposite sex. A further liberalization is applicable for 2001 and subsequent years. While the definition of spouse has been altered to refer only to legally recognized marriages, the new concept of a common-law partner has been added to ITA 118(1)(a). As defined in ITA 248, a common-law partner is a person who cohabits with the taxpayer in a conjugal relationship for a continuous period of one year, or is the parent of a child of whom the taxpayer is also a parent. There is no longer a requirement that the cohabiting person be of the opposite sex.

- **Multiple Spouses**   Based on the preceding definition, it would be possible for an individual to have more than one spouse. ITA 118(4)(a) makes it clear that, if this is the case, a credit can only be claimed for one of these individuals.

• **Year Of Separation Or Divorce** In general, ITA 118(5) does not allow a tax credit based on the spousal amount in situations where the individual is making a deduction for spousal support. However, IT-513R indicates that, in the year of separation or divorce, an individual can either deduct amounts paid for spousal support or claim the additional tax credit for a spouse. The taxpayer can select the most advantageous alternative, but cannot claim both the deduction and the credit.

Transfer of Dividends to a Spouse or Common-Law Partner

13-44. There may be situations in which a taxpayer's spousal credit has been reduced or eliminated by dividends received by that spouse. ITA 82(3) permits all of the dividends to be transferred from the spouse's income to that of the taxpayer if it creates or increases the spousal credit. Consider the following example:

Example Mrs. Albert's total income consisted of $6,200 in dividends received from taxable Canadian corporations. Mrs. Albert's basic personal tax credit, along with part of the dividend tax credit, eliminate all taxation on the grossed up amount of $7,750 [(125%)($6,200)]. However, because she has this income receipt, Mr. Albert is not able to claim a spousal tax credit.

Tax Consequences In this situation, the transfer of dividends under ITA 82(3) would eliminate all of Mrs. Albert's income and Mr. Albert would be able to claim the full spousal credit of $1,007. Mr. Albert would then be taxed on the $7,750 [(125%)($6,200)] of grossed up dividends . He would, however, be eligible for the dividend tax credit associated with these dividends. Whether this is a good alternative or not depends on Mr. Albert's marginal tax rate as can be seen in the following calculations:

	16%	29%
Increase In Taxable Income [(125%)($6,200)]	$7,750	$7,750
Tax on $7,750	$1,240	$2,248
Increase In Spousal Credit	(1,007)	(1,007)
Dividend Tax Credit [(2/3)($1,550)]	(1,033)	(1,033)
Increase (Decrease) In Taxes Payable	($ 800)	$ 208

As can be seen in the table, if Mr. Albert is in the low 16 percent federal tax bracket, his taxes would be reduced by $800. Alternatively, if he is in the top 29 percent bracket, the transfer would not be desirable as federal taxes would be increased by $208.

> Exercise Thirteen-1 deals with dividend transfers. This would be an appropriate time to attempt this exercise.

Equivalent To Spouse Tax Credit

13-45. For a single individual supporting a dependant in a self contained domestic establishment, ITA 118(1)(b) allows for tax credits based on the same two amounts that are used under ITA 118(1)(a) for married individuals. The only difference is that the reduction in the $6,294 amount is based on the Net Income of a supported individual other than a spouse.

13-46. The most common beneficiaries of this credit are probably single parents who are supporting a minor child. More generally, this credit is available to individuals who are single, widowed, divorced, or separated and supporting a dependant who is:

• under 18, or the individual's parent or grandparent, or mentally or physically infirm;
• related to the individual by blood, marriage, or adoption;
• living with the individual in a home that the individual maintains; and
• residing in Canada.

13-47. The residence requirement is not applicable to the individual's children. However, the child must still be living with the individual. This would be applicable, for example, to an individual who is a deemed resident (e.g., a member of the Canadian Armed Forces) and living with their child outside of Canada.

13-48. You will note that, while there is no general tax credit for dependent children under age 18, the equivalent to spouse credit can still be claimed for dependants in this age group.

13-49. The equivalent to spouse credit cannot be claimed:

- if the dependant's Net Income exceeds $6,923 ($6,294 + $629);
- if the individual is claiming the spousal credit;
- if the individual has a spouse throughout the year (the claim is for someone who is single at any time in the year);
- for a common-law spouse (the spousal credit may be available);
- if someone other than the individual is making this claim for the same individual; or
- for the individual's child if the individual is making child support payments to another individual for that child. As noted in Chapter 11, when child support is being paid, only the recipient of such payments can claim this tax credit. This is the case without regard to whether or not the individual making the payments is able to deduct them in determining Net Income For Tax Purposes.

Single Persons

13-50. As noted in our categorization of individual taxpayers, ITA 118(1)(c) entitles single individuals who do not qualify for the equivalent to spouse tax credit, a tax credit calculated as 16 percent of the basic personal amount of $7,412. As noted previously, for 2001 the amount of this credit is $1,186 [(16%)($7,412)].

Dependants

13-51. A dependant is defined in ITA 118(6) as a person who, at any time in the year, is dependent on the individual for support and includes a child or grandchild of an individual or of his spouse and, if resident in Canada, a parent, grandparent, brother, sister, uncle, aunt, niece or nephew of the individual or the individual's spouse.

13-52. In view of today's less stable family arrangements, the question of exactly who is considered a child for tax purposes requires some elaboration. As explained in IT-513R, the credit may be taken for natural children, children who have been formally adopted, as well as for natural and adopted children of a spouse.

13-53. ITA 118(1)(d) specifies a credit for dependants who attain the age of 18 prior to the end of the year, provided they are dependent by reason of mental or physical infirmity. For 2001, the credit is 16 percent of $3,500 or $560. This credit is reduced by 16 percent of the dependant's income in excess of $4,966.

13-54. This credit should not be confused with the mental and physical impairment credit that is available to individuals under ITA 118.3(1). The credit here under ITA 118(1)(d) is for an individual with sufficient infirmity that they cannot be gainfully employed and, as a result, they are a dependant of the supporting person claiming the credit. For example, a supporting mother would be eligible for this credit if her adult son suffered from a physical handicap severe enough to prevent him from working. A doctor's certification of this type of mental or physical infirmity is not required. In contrast, the credit under ITA 118.3(1) requires a doctor to certify on form T2201 that there is a prolonged impairment that severely restricts basic living activities. Note, however, because this latter credit can be transferred to a supporting person, one individual may be able to claim both of these credits.

13-55. The credit for an infirm dependant cannot be taken if an equivalent to spouse credit is being taken for the same dependant. In addition, if an individual is making deductible support payments for a child, he cannot claim this credit for that child.

Caregiver Tax Credit

13-56. ITA 118(1)(c.1) provides a caregiver tax credit to an individual who provides in home care for an adult (18 years or older) relative. To be eligible for this credit, the individual has to maintain a dwelling in which the individual and the relative ordinarily reside, and the relative has to be the individual's or the individual's spouse's child, grandchild, parent, grandparent, brother, sister, aunt, uncle, nephew or niece. Except where the relative is the individual's child or grandchild, the relative must be resident in Canada. Also, except where the relative is the individual's parent or grandparent who is 65 years old or over, the relative must be dependent on the individual because of the relative's mental or physical infirmity.

13-57.   The credit has a value of $560 [(16%)($3,500]. It is reduced by 16 percent of the amount by which the dependant's Net Income for the year exceeds $11,953. This means that it will disappear when the dependant's Net Income reaches $15,453.

13-58.   The credit is not available to an individual with respect to a dependant for whom anyone is claiming the equivalent to spouse credit [ITA 118(1)(b)] or the 18 or over and infirm credit [ITA 118(1)(d)]. As these credits are worth $1,007 and $560 respectively, the caregiver credit is of no value with respect to a dependant who is fully eligible for one of these claims. The value of the caregiver credit lies in its higher income threshold ($11,953 vs. $629 or $4,966). This makes it clear that this credit is largely targeted at individuals providing care for an infirm parent or grandparent whose income level is above the ITA 118(1)(b) or (d) threshold levels and below $15,453.

Age Tax Credit

13-59.   For individuals who attain the age of 65 prior to the end of the year, ITA 118(2) provides an additional tax credit of 16 percent of $3,619 or $579. However, the base for this credit is reduced by 15 percent of the individual's Net Income For Tax Purposes in excess of $26,941. This means that, at an income level of $51,068, the reduction will be equal to $3,619 [(15%)($51,068 - $26,941) = $3,619] and the individual will no longer receive an age credit. As an example, a 67 year old individual with 2001 Net Income of $35,000 will have an age credit of $386 {[16%][$3,619 - (15%)($35,000 - $26,941)]}.

13-60.   As we shall see when we consider the transfer of credits to a spouse, if an individual does not have sufficient taxes payable to use this credit, it can be transferred to a spouse.

Pension Income Tax Credit

13-61.   ITA 118(3) provides for a credit equal to 16 percent of the first $1,000 of eligible pension income. This results in a maximum credit of $160. There is no provision for indexing this amount and, as a result, the real value of this credit declines each year, without regard to the level of inflation. Not all types of pension income are eligible for this credit. ITA 118(8) specifically excludes payments under the Old Age Security Act, the Canada Pension Plan, a provincial pension plan, a salary deferral arrangement, a retirement compensation arrangement, an employee benefit plan, and death benefits.

13-62.   For individuals who have reached age 65 before the end of the year, this credit is available on "pension income" as defined in ITA 118(7). This includes pension payments that are:

- a life annuity out of or under a pension plan;
- an annuity payment under an RRSP;
- a payment out of a RRIF;
- an annuity payment from a DPSP; and
- the interest component of other annuities.

13-63.   For an individual who has not reached age 65 before the end of the year, the credit is based on "qualified pension income", also defined in ITA 118(7). This includes the life annuities out of or under a pension plan and, in situations where such amounts are received as a consequence of the death of a spouse, the other types of pension income described in the preceding paragraph. However, this means that, in ordinary circumstances, individuals who have not reached age 65 will only be eligible for the pension tax credit to the extent their pension income is made up of life annuity payments.

Summary of Tax Credits

13-64.   This completes the discussion of the personal tax credits listed in ITA 118. The base amounts, credits, and applicable income thresholds are summarized in the following table:

Exercises Thirteen-2 and Thirteen-3 deal with personal tax credits. This would be an appropriate time to attempt these exercises.

	Base	Credit	Income Threshold
Basic Personal	$7,412	$1,186	N/A
Spouse And Equivalent To Spouse	6,294	1,007	$ 629
Dependants (Over 17 And Infirm)	3,500	560	4,966
Caregiver	3,500	560	11,661
Age 65 And Over (Maximum)	3,619	579	26,941
Pension Income	1,000	160	N/A

Charitable Donations Credit - ITA 118.1
Eligible Contributions
13-65.   ITA 118.1 defines four types of charitable donations:

1. **Total Charitable Gifts** is defined as the aggregate of all amounts donated by an individual to a registered charity, a registered Canadian amateur athletic association, a housing corporation resident in Canada that is exempt from tax under ITA 149(1)(i), a Canadian municipality, the United Nations or an agency thereof, a university outside of Canada which normally enrolls Canadian students, and a charitable organization outside of Canada to which Her Majesty in right of Canada has made a gift.

2. **Total Crown Gifts** is defined as the aggregate of all gifts made to Her Majesty in right of Canada or to Her Majesty in right of a province.

3. **Total Cultural Gifts** is defined as the aggregate of all gifts of objects that the Canadian Cultural Property Export Review Board has determined meet the criteria of the *Cultural Property And Import Act*.

4. **Total Ecological Gifts** is defined as a gift of land certified by the Minister of the Environment to be ecologically sensitive land, the conservation and protection of which is important to the preservation of Canada's environmental heritage. The beneficiary of the gift must be a Canadian municipality or a registered charity, the primary purpose of which is the conservation and protection of Canada's environmental heritage.

13-66.   In addition to these items specified in the *Act*, the U. S./Canada Tax Treaty provides for claiming any deductions that would be allowed on a U.S. tax return.

Limits On Amount Claimed
13-67.   It is the policy of the government to limit charitable donations that are eligible for the tax credit to a portion of a taxpayer's Net Income For Tax Purposes. Note that, while corporations deduct their donations as opposed to receiving a credit against taxes payable, the limits on the amount of eligible donations are the same for corporations as they are for individuals.

13-68.   The limit on eligible amounts of Charitable Gifts and Crown Gifts is 75 percent of Net Income For Tax Purposes. For individuals, this limit is increased to 100 percent of Net Income For Tax Purposes in the year of death and the preceding year. In those situations where a gift of capital property resulted in a capital gain, the overall limit is increased by 25 percent of the taxable capital gain. In the case of gifts of depreciable capital property, 25 percent of any recaptured CCA resulting from such gifts is also added to the limit. The reasons for these additions to the limit will be explained in the section on gifts of capital property. There is no income limit on the amount of eligible Cultural Gifts or Ecological Gifts. Credits can be claimed for these gifts up to 100 percent of Net Income For Tax Purposes.

Gifts Of Publicly Traded Securities
13-69.   A special rule applies to gifts of publicly traded shares made before January 1, 2002. (Although the deadline may be extended, no extension has been announced at the time of writing.) For capital gains arising on the disposition of the shares, only one-half of the usual capital gains inclusion rate will apply. This means that, for donations made during 2001, the inclusion rate will be 25 percent [(1/2)(1/2)].

13-70.   There was a potential problem for donations of publicly traded shares purchased through stock options which was corrected in the 2000 budget. To illustrate the problem, consider the following example:

Example   An individual has options to acquire 100 shares of Donner Ltd., a Canadian public company, at $50 per share. On July 1, 2001, the shares are trading at $80 per and, at this time the individual exercises all of his options. He immediately donates the shares to a registered charity.

13-71.   The problem here is that, the deemed disposition which results from the donation of the shares creates an employment income inclusion of $30 per share, as opposed to a capital gain. This means that, in the absence of some special provision, the donation of shares that have been acquired with options and donated immediately, will not receive the same treatment as publicly traded shares that have been purchased and donated.

13-72.   In order to correct this situation, individuals who acquire shares through stock options and, in the year shares are acquired and not more than 30 days after that acquisition date, donate those shares to a qualified donee, will be allowed to deduct an additional one-quarter of the employment income benefit resulting from the exercise of the options. In our example, the results would be as follows:

Employment Income [($80 - $50)(100]	$3,000
One-Half Deduction Under ITA 110(1)(d)	(1,500)
One-Quarter Deduction From 2000 Budget	(750)
Increase In Taxable Income	$ 750

13-73.   This procedure levels the playing field between donations of publicly traded shares acquired through stock options and donations of publicly traded shares acquired through other means. Note that this extra deduction is only available in the case of publicly traded shares and is only applicable to donations made before January 1, 2002.

Calculating The Credit

13-74.   Once the contribution basis is established, the credit is equal to 16 percent of the first $200 and 29 percent of any additional donations. The charitable donation credit is the only credit that features two rates for determining the allowable credit. The reason for this approach was concern that, because charitable donations are voluntary, an overall credit at the lowest bracket rate of 16 percent would have resulted in a decline in donations. The 29 percent credit on larger donations was added to avoid this result.

13-75.   While the same level of total giving could probably have been achieved with a compromise rate somewhere between 16 and 29 percent, this would have changed the composition of sources for giving. Such a compromise rate would have been an incentive for low income contributors and would have increased donations to organizations such as churches that rely on this sector of the population. In contrast, high income givers would have less incentive to contribute and this would have reduced donations to such beneficiaries as educational institutions. This was not viewed by the government as a desirable result and, as a consequence, we have a two rate system for charitable donations.

13-76.   The following example illustrates the calculation of the charitable donations tax credit, including the determination of eligible amounts:

Example   Nancy Hart has a 2001 Net Income For Tax Purposes of $100,000. On the receipt of a large inheritance, she makes total charitable gifts of $52,000 and total crown gifts of $31,000.

Tax Consequences   The total for all eligible gifts is limited to 75 percent of her Net Income For Tax Purposes or $75,000. As her total gifts amount to $83,000 ($52,000 + $31,000), the $75,000 limit applies and $8,000 in contributions are carried forward. Given this, her tax credit would be calculated as follows:

16 Percent Of $200	$ 32
29 Percent Of $74,800	21,692
Total Credit	$21,724

13-77. For married couples, the CCRA's administrative practices permit either spouse to claim all of the donations made by both spouses. Given the dual rates on the credit, there is a small advantage in combining the donations. In addition, this may be an important consideration when one spouse has a sufficiently low income that it is limiting the use of his or her donations.

Carry Over

13-78. The claim for charitable donations is optional. Unused charitable donations can be carried forward for five years to be used as a basis for credits in those years. Except in the year preceding death, the 75 percent of Net Income limitation applies to the amounts deducted in the carry over year.

Gifts Of Capital Property

13-79. When an individual makes a charitable gift, a crown gift, or an ecological gift of capital property, an election is available under ITA 118.1(6). On such properties there will usually be a difference between the adjusted cost base of the property and its current fair market value. If the fair market value is the higher value, the taxpayer can elect to transfer the property at any value between the adjusted cost base and the fair market value. For example, a property with an adjusted cost base of $100,000 and a fair market value of $150,000 could be transferred at any value between these two figures. The elected value will then become both the value of the donation for purposes of determining the tax credit, as well as the proceeds of disposition. If a value higher than the adjusted cost base is elected, a taxable capital gain will be triggered. In the case of depreciable assets, there may also be recaptured CCA.

13-80. Generally, it will be advisable to elect the highest possible figure, reflecting the fact that any amount of elected value in excess of $200 will be eligible for a tax credit on the full amount at the maximum federal tax rate of 29 percent. In contrast, only one-half of any capital gain that results from the increase will be subject to tax. In fact, if publicly traded shares are involved, only one-quarter of the capital gain will be subject to tax. A simple example will serve to illustrate this point:

Example Mr. Vignesh Menan has a non depreciable capital asset with an adjusted cost base of $100,000 and a fair market value of $150,000. In July, 2001 he intends to gift this asset to a registered charity and would like to know whether he should elect to make the donation at $100,000 or alternatively, at $150,000. He has other income which puts him in the 29 percent federal tax bracket, without considering any gain resulting from this disposition.

Tax Consequences The tax consequences of the two alternatives are as follows:

Mr. Menan Elects $100,000

Tax Credit [(16%)($200) + (29%)($99,800)]	$28,974

Mr. Menan Elects $150,000

Tax Credit [(16%)($200) + (29%)($149,800)]	$43,474
Tax On Gain [(1/2)($50,000)(29%)]	(7,250)
Credit Net Of Tax	$36,224

As expected, Mr. Menan is better off electing the $150,000. The tax benefit associated with this choice is $7,250 higher than with the $100,000 election. The results would be even more favourable to the $150,000 if the donated property consisted of shares of a listed company.

13-81. A potential problem here is that, if an individual's eligible donations are restricted to 75 percent of net income for the year, making a gift and electing to use fair market value may result in income that cannot be eliminated with the related tax credit. In other words, making a gift could result in the payment of taxes. To avoid this problem, two other components are added to the base for charitable donations, resulting in a total base equal to:

- 75 percent of all Net Income for the year; plus
- 25 percent of any taxable capital gain resulting from a gift; plus
- 25 percent of any recaptured CCA resulting from a gift.

13-82. A simple example will serve to illustrate the importance of these additions to the overall limit:

> **Example** In July, 2001, Mr. Jonas Anderson gifts a depreciable capital asset to a registered charity. The asset has a fair market value of $130,000, a capital cost of $100,000 and a UCC of $65,000. He elects to make the gift at the fair market value of $130,000. He has no other source of income, other than amounts arising as a result of the gift.

13-83. The election to make the gift at the fair market value of $130,000 will result in total Net Income of $50,000. This is comprised of a taxable capital gain of $15,000 [(1/2)($130,000 - $100,000)] and recaptured CCA of $35,000 ($100,000 - $65,000). As Mr. Anderson has no other source of income, his basic limit for charitable donations would be $37,500 [(75%)($50,000)]. If his eligible gifts were limited to $37,500, he would be faced with paying taxes on $12,500 ($50,000 - $37,500), simply as a result of his generosity in making the gift. However, with the additions to the limit, his overall limit is as follows:

75 Percent Of Net Income	$37,500
25 Percent Of Taxable Capital Gain	3,750
25 Percent Of Recaptured CCA	8,750
Total Limit	$50,000

13-84. As you can see, the additions to the limit serve the purpose of creating a base for charitable donations that includes 100 percent of any income resulting from gifts of capital property. Note, however, this does not insure that the actual credit is equal to the taxes paid. In this case, with Mr. Anderson having no other source of income, his actual taxes payable will be based on 16 percent and 22 percent. In contrast, except for the first $200, the credit will be based on 29 percent. Even in cases where the individual has other income sources which push him into the 29 percent bracket prior to including income on a gift, the fact that the first $200 of the credit is based on 16 percent will result in a small amount of tax being paid as a result of making the gift.

Canadian Cultural Property

13-85. We have noted that, when an individual makes a charitable gift, crown gift, or ecological gift of capital property, they can elect to have the proceeds be any value between the adjusted cost base of the property and the fair market value. In the case of cultural gifts of capital property, ITA 118.1(10.1) deems the proceeds of disposition to be the fair market value of the property in all cases. This rule must be considered in conjunction with the fact that a provision in ITA 39(1)(a)(i.1) indicates that, with respect to gifts of Canadian cultural property, the difference between the fair market value and the adjusted cost base of the asset does not fall within the meaning of capital gain. As a consequence, any gain on a gift of cultural property is not subject to tax. Given this, it is not unreasonable to require that the proceeds of disposition on cultural gifts of capital property be equal to the fair market value of the property.

Exercise Thirteen-4 deals with donations. This would be an appropriate time to attempt this exercise.

Medical Expense Credit - ITA 118.2
General Rules
13-86.   Under ITA 118.2, individuals can deduct a credit equal to 16 percent of medical expenses paid and not reimbursed in excess of the lower of $1,678 and three percent of Net Income. For individuals with Net Income in excess of $55,933, the $1,678 figure is the relevant floor for these expenditures.

Qualifying Expenses
13-87.   Medical expenses can be claimed for any 12 month period ending in the year and must be documented by receipts. The ability to claim expenses for a 12 month period ending in the year is advantageous for individuals with large expenses in a 12 month period other than a calendar year. If, for example, an individual who had a Net Income For Tax Purposes of $60,000 in 2000 and 2001, had $10,000 in medical expenses in the period July to December, 2000, and a further $12,000 in the period January to June, 2001, the $22,000 total could be claimed in full in the 2001 taxation year. The advantage of doing this is that the $1,678 threshold amount would be applied only once in 2001. If medical expenses had to be claimed in the year in which they were incurred, this individual would have had to apply the $1,637 reduction in 2000 and $1,678 in 2001. Deducting the full amount in 2001 involves a savings in federal taxes of $278 [(17%)($1,637)].

13-88.   Qualifying items, as described in ITA 118.2(2), include amounts paid to doctors and dentists, to full time home attendants, for full time nursing home care, to institutions for the disabled, for ambulance transportation, for reasonable travel expenses for medical care, for artificial limbs, for prescription eyeglasses or contact lenses, for oxygen, for seeing eye dogs, for any device prescribed by a medical practitioner, for drugs or medicine, for laboratory work, or as a premium for private health services plans.

13-89.   This definition has been repeatedly extended in various budgets. Recent additions include the costs of arranging a bone marrow or organ transplant, the costs of home modifications for those with severe mobility restrictions and to allow individuals confined to a wheelchair to be mobile within their home, costs of up to $10,000 in a year for a part time attendant to help a person with a severe and prolonged mental or physical impairment, the costs for a specially trained animal to help persons with restricted use of arms and legs, products for the incontinent and the cost of rehabilitative therapy to adjust for speech or hearing loss. The new item introduced in the February 28, 2000 budget was costs incurred, in the process of constructing a principal residence for a disabled person, to improve access or mobility within that residence.

Spouse And Dependant Expenses
13-90.   ITA 118.2(2) defines the medical expenses of an individual to include those of the individual, the individual's spouse or common-law partner, and other individuals who meet the definition in ITA 118(6) of a dependant. Note carefully that, in the case of dependants, there is no requirement that the individual claiming the medical expenses be able to claim a tax credit for the dependant. In practical terms, this means that a parent can claim the medical expenses of dependent children of any age, despite the fact that no tax credit is available for the dependants.

13-91.   There is, however, a limiting factor on the deduction of a dependant's medical expenses. This is that, in situations where a claim is being made for medical expenses of a dependant other than a spouse, the total medical expense credit must be reduced by 68 percent of the dependant's income in excess of the basic personal amount found in ITA 118(1)(c). For 2001, that amount equals $7,412.

> **Example**   Mr. Fowles and his spouse have medical expenses which total $12,500. In addition, Mr. Fowles paid qualifying dental expenses of $5,000 for his dependent 20 year old daughter. Mr. Fowles' daughter had Net Income For Tax Purposes of $7,800. Mr. Fowles' Taxable Income exceeds $100,000 while Mrs. Fowles has no Taxable Income.

13-92.   The credit that would be available to Mr. Fowles would be calculated as follows:

Total Medical Expenses (Spouse And Daughter)	$17,500
Threshold Amount (Maximum)	(1,678)
Eligible For Credit	$15,822
Rate	16%
Credit Before Reduction	$ 2,532
Reduction [(68%)($7,800 - $7,412)]	(264)
Benefit To Mr. Fowles	$ 2,268

13-93.   As his daughter falls within the definition of a dependant, Mr. Fowles is able to use her medical expenses in calculating his credit. This is clearly beneficial to Mr. Fowles in that his additional credit of $800 [(16%)($5,000)] is acquired at a cost of only $264. While the medical expenses are no longer available to his daughter, this is not a significant consideration in that her total federal tax payable will only be $62 [(16%)($7,800 - $7,412)] if she cannot claim other credits.

Refundable Medical Expense Supplement

13-94.   The government recognizes that there has been a loss of subsidies for disability related support under provincial social assistance programs. This can be an important barrier to participation in the labour force by Canadians with disabilities and, to address this problem, the government introduced a refundable tax credit (ITA 122.51) for low income working Canadians with above average medical expenses. As this is a refundable supplement, it will be paid even if the taxpayer has no tax liability.

13-95.   To be eligible for the medical expense supplement, the individual must have earned income (employment and business) of at least $2,598. The credit is the lesser of $520 and 25/16 of the medical expense tax credit that can be claimed for the year (this can also be described as 25 percent of the expenses eligible for the medical expense tax credit). This amount is reduced by 5 percent of family Net Income For Tax Purposes in excess of an indexed threshold amount. For 2001, the amount is $18,106. The credit is completely eliminated when family Net Income For Tax Purposes reaches $28,506. A simple example will serve to illustrate this provision:

Example   Mr. Larry Futon and his spouse have medical expenses which total $3,250. His Net Income For Tax Purposes is $18,460, all of which qualifies as earned income. His spouse has no income of her own.

Tax Consequences   Mr. Futon's allowable medical expenses for tax credit purposes would be $2,696 [$3,250 - (3%)($18,460)], resulting in a tax credit of $431 [(16%)($2,696)]. 25/16 of this amount would be $673. This means that his credit would be based on $520, less a reduction of $18 [(5%)($18,460 - $18,106)], a balance of $502.

13-96.   The receipt of this refundable credit does not affect an individual's ability to claim a tax credit for the same medical expenses that are used to calculate the refundable credit. Assuming he has no tax credits other than the individual, the spousal, and medical expense, his Basic Federal Tax Payable would be reduced to $329 [(16%)($18,460 - $7,412 - $6,294 - $2,696)]. When this result is combined with the refundable credit of $502, Mr. Futon winds up with a negative tax position for the year.

> Exercise Thirteen-5 deals with medical expenses. This would be an appropriate time to attempt this exercise.

Disability Credit - ITA 118.3

13-97.   This credit is available under ITA 118.3 and, for 2001, it is equal to 16 percent of $6,000 or $960. In addition, as of 2000, there is a supplement to this amount for a disabled child who is under the age of 18 at the end of the year. For 2001, the base for the supplement is $3,500, providing a total credit for such a child of $1,520 [(16%)($6,000 + $3,500)]. Note, however, that the supplement amount of $3,500 is reduced by child care and attendant care costs in excess of $2,050. This means that once such costs reach $5,550, the supplement is completely eliminated.

13-98.   An individual qualifies for the disability credit when a medical doctor or optometrist certifies on form T2201 that a severe physical or mental impairment exists. The impairment must be such that there is a marked restriction of the activities of daily living and has lasted or can be expected to last for at least 12 months.

13-99.   ITA 118.4(1) tries to make the conditions for qualifying for this credit as clear as possible. This subsection points out that an individual clearly qualifies if they are blind. They also qualify if 90 percent of the time they cannot perform, or take an inordinate amount of time to perform, a basic activity of daily living. The following are listed as basic activities:

- perceiving, thinking and remembering;
- feeding and dressing oneself;
- speaking such that the individual can be understood in a quiet setting by someone familiar with the individual;
- hearing such that the individual can, in a quiet setting, understand someone familiar with the individual;
- bowel or bladder functions; or
- walking.

13-100.   Despite what was intended to be clear guidance in this area, reassessments appear to be common. Many practitioners feel that the CCRA is, perhaps, overly aggressive in its interpretation of the terms "markedly restricted" and an "inordinate amount of time" (e.g., the credit was denied for a cerebral palsy victim because he was able to walk with braces).

13-101.   Perhaps reflecting the public's dissatisfaction with the CCRA's policies in this area, the February 28, 2000 budget extends the availability of the credit to individuals who must undergo therapy at least three times a week for a total period averaging not less than 14 hours a week in order to sustain a vital function. This is likely to make this credit available to a large number of individuals that were not able to qualify under the pre budget rules.

Disability Credit Transfer To A Supporting Person

13-102.   In many cases, an individual who is sufficiently infirm to qualify for this credit will not have sufficient taxes payable to use it. In these situations, all or the unused part of the credit may be transferred to a spouse or a supporting person who claimed the disabled individual as a dependant under the equivalent to spouse provision or as a disabled dependant over 17. The list of potential transferees includes parents, grandparents, children, grandchildren, brothers, sisters, aunts, uncles, nieces, and nephews.

13-103.   In order to make the disability credit transfer available in most situations where a disabled child, parent or grandparent is dependent on a taxpayer for support, the transfer is extended by a somewhat awkward measure to situations in which the supporting person:

- could have made the equivalent to spouse claim if neither the supporting person nor the disabled dependant were married;
- could have made the disabled dependant over 17 claim if the dependant had been 18 years of age or older; and
- could have made the equivalent to spouse or disabled dependant over 17 claim if the dependant had no income.

13-104.   The amount that can be transferred is the same $960 (or $1,520 if the supplement is available) that could be claimed by the impaired individual. However, if the disabled individual has taxes payable in excess of his ITA 118 personal credits, pension credit, and CPP and EI credits, the credit must first be applied to reduce the disabled individual's taxes payable to nil. If a balance remains after all taxes payable have been eliminated, it can be transferred to the supporting person.

Other Credits and Deductions

13-105.   Disabled individuals or a supporting person may have medical expenses that are eligible for tax credits, including attendant care and nursing home care. Further, individuals who qualify for the disability tax credit can deduct from Net Income For Tax Purposes the full amount of any costs for attendant care that facilitates their ability to earn income. Finally, a supporting person may be in a position to deduct child care costs for a disabled individual. There is a fairly complex interplay among these provisions with respect to which of them can be used for a given individual. While a full discussion of this point goes beyond the scope of this book, the following points are relevant:

- Neither the individual nor a supporting person can claim the disability credit if a medical expense credit is claimed for a full time attendant or for full time care in a nursing home. However, the individual or supporting person can claim either of the two amounts.
- The disability credit can be claimed if a medical expense credit is claimed for a part time attendant. Part time is defined as expenses of less than $10,000 for the year ($20,000 in the year of death). Note that, if this type of medical expense credit is claimed for an individual, no deduction can be made for child care costs or for attendant care required to produce income.
- Amounts deducted for an attendant required to facilitate earning income cannot also be claimed as a medical expense.

Education Related Credits - ITA 118.5, 118.6, 118.61, 118.62
Tuition Credit
13-106. Under ITA 118.5, individuals receive a credit against taxes payable equal to 16 percent of qualifying tuition fees paid for the calendar year, regardless of the year in which they are actually paid. There is no upper limit on this credit. To qualify, the fees must be paid to:

- a university, college, or other institution for post secondary courses;
- an institution certified by the Minister of Human Resource Development for a course that developed or improved skills in an occupation (individual must be 16 or older);
- a university outside Canada, if enrolled full time in a course that was at least 13 consecutive weeks long; or
- for individuals who live near the U.S. border, a U.S. college or university for part time studies.

13-107. It has been noted that universities are placing greater reliance on various ancillary fees for such items as health services, athletics, and various other services. As a reflection of this situation, ITA 118.5(3) extends the tuition tax credit to cover all mandatory ancillary fees that are imposed by universities on all of their full time or all of their part time students. In addition, ITA 118.5(3)(d) allows up to $250 in such ancillary fees to be added to the total, even if they do not meet the condition of being required for all full or part time students.

Education Credit
13-108. Under ITA 118.6(2), there is a credit for 2001 equal to $64 [(16%)($400)] per month of full time attendance at a designated educational institution or enrollment in a qualifying educational program. For this purpose, designated educational institutions include universities, colleges, and institutions certified by the Minister of Human Resource Development for a course that develops or improves skills in an occupation. Enrollment in a qualifying educational program is described in IT-515R2 as a program that must run for at least three consecutive weeks and must require instruction or work in the program of at least 10 hours a week throughout its duration. Both of these descriptions can be thought of as full time pursuit of educational activities.

13-109. An alternative education credit of $19 [(16%)($120)] per month is available for attendance in a specified educational program. In general terms this is defined as a program that, were it not for the requirement that at least 10 hours per week be devoted to its requirements, would be a qualifying educational program. In fairly simple terms, this credit is available to individuals pursuing part time studies, defined in terms of a minimum of 12 hours per month of course work.

13-110. A further modification of the general rules for the education credit is available to individuals that either qualify for the disability tax credit or, because of a mental or physical disability, cannot pursue educational activities on a full time basis. The full education credit of $64 per month is available to such individuals without regard to whether their attendance is full or part time.

Carry Forward Of Tuition And Education Credits

13-111. There are situations in which a student does not have sufficient Taxable Income to use their tuition and education credits and has not transferred them to a supporting person (see subsequent section on Transfers). To deal with this type of situation, ITA 118.61 allows a carry forward of unused tuition and education credits. The amount is determined by, first, adding to the student's unused tuition and education tax credits from the previous year, the portion of the tuition and education credits for the current year that is not needed to eliminate the student's tax payable for the current year. This total is then reduced by the amount of the tuition and education tax credits carry forward that is claimed for the current year, which is equal to the lesser of the previous year's carry forward and the tax that would be payable for the current year by the student if no tuition and education tax credits were allowed. Finally, this total is further reduced by any tuition and education tax credits transferred for the year by the student to the student's spouse, parent or grandparent.

13-112. Unused amounts that are carried forward will be available for the student's personal use in any subsequent year, but cannot be transferred. While students will have to provide the required information, the CCRA will track the carry forward amounts. Note that, because, starting in 2001, the minimum tax rate was reduced to 16 percent from 17 percent, any carry forward from 2000 will have to be multiplied by the fraction 16/17.

Interest On Student Loans Credit

13-113. A further provision in ITA 118.62 relates to interest on student loans. Under this provision, an individual will be entitled to deduct 16 percent of amounts paid in the year, or in any of the five preceding years ending after 1997, on account of interest on a loan under the *Canada Student Loans Act*, the *Canada Student Financial Assistance Act*, or a provincial statute governing the granting of financial assistance to students at the post secondary school level.

Employment Insurance (EI) And Canada Pension Plan Credits (CPP) - ITA 118.7

13-114. ITA 118.7 provides a tax credit equal to 16 percent of an individual's Employment Insurance (EI) premiums and Canada Pension Plan (CPP) contributions. Note that only the premiums and contributions paid by the individual are used to determine these credits.

13-115. For 2001, CPP contributions are based on maximum pensionable earnings of $38,300, less a basic exemption of $3,500. The rate for 2001 is 4.3 percent, resulting in a maximum contribution of $1,496. This provides for a maximum 2001 credit against federal taxes payable of $239. For employed individuals, the employer pays an amount which matches the employee's CPP contributions.

13-116. In contrast, a self employed individual earning business income as opposed to employment income must make a matching CPP contribution for himself. Self employment earnings equal to or greater than the maximum pensionable earnings of $38,300 require CPP contributions of $2,992 [(4.3%)(2)($38,300 - $3,500)]. The maximum CPP credit on self employed earnings is equal to $479 [(16%)($2,992)].

13-117. For 2001, EI premiums are based on maximum insurable earnings of $39,000. The employee's rate is 2.25 percent, resulting in a maximum annual premium of $878. This results in a maximum credit against federal taxes payable of $140.

13-118. Employers are also required to make EI contributions, the amount being 1.4 times the contributions made by the employee. However, these premiums do not provide the employee with a tax credit. Further, self employed individuals are not eligible to participate in the EI program and, as a consequence, they will not make contributions and will not be eligible for any EI tax credit.

Overpayment of Employment Insurance Premiums and Canada Pension Plan Contributions

13-119. It is not uncommon for employers to withhold EI and CPP amounts that are in excess of the amounts required. This can happen through an error on the part of the employer's payroll system. Even in the absence of errors, overpayments can arise when an individual changes employers.

13-120. A refund of these excess amounts is available on an individual's tax return. While any CPP or EI overpayment is not a tax credit, it will increase the refund available or decrease the tax liability that is calculated in the return. As an example, assume that Jerry Weist changed employers during 2001 and, as a consequence, the total amount of EI premiums withheld during the year was $1,050. In a similar fashion, the total amount of CPP contributions withheld by the two employers was $1,625. His employment income was well in excess of the maximum insurable and pensionable earnings. Given this, Jerry will claim a refund of $57 calculated as follows:

EI Premiums Withheld	$1,050
CPP Contributions Withheld	1,625
Total Withheld	$2,675
2001 Maximum ($1,496 + $878)	(2,374)
Refund Due	$ 301

Transfers To A Spouse Or Common-Law Partner - ITA 118.8

13-121. ITA 118.8 permits the transfer of five specific tax credits to a spouse or common-law partner. The credits that are eligible for transfer are:

- the age credit,
- the disability credit,
- the pension income credit, and
- the unused portion of the tuition fee and education credits (see following section for rules and limits)

13-122. The transferable amount is the excess of these credits over the spouse's taxes payable after applying the personal credits under ITA 118(1), as well as the EI and CPP credits. A further point here is that no transfer of these credits is available if the spouses were separated for a period of 90 days or more that included December 31 of the taxation year.

> Exercise Thirteen-6 deals with transfers from a spouse. This would be an appropriate time to attempt this exercise.

Transfer Of Tuition Fee And Education Credits - ITA 118.9
Basic Rules

13-123. ITA 118.9 provides for the transfer of current year unused education credits and tuition fee credits to a supporting parent or grandparent of a student or the student's spouse. The interest on student loans credit cannot be transferred.

13-124. The maximum transfer that can be made by a student is equal to $800 [(16%)($5,000)]. However, this must be reduced by any amount claimed by the student. Further, the student must use these credits in calculating his taxes payable in the order specified under ITA 118.92 (e.g., he cannot deduct a dividend tax credit prior to deducting the tuition/education credit).

Example Megan Doxy has 2001 Taxable Income of $11,000. She attends university full time for 8 months of the year, paying a total amount for tuition of $9,000. This gives her a potential tax credit of $1,952 [(16%)(8)($400) + (16%)($9,000)]. Her only other tax credit is her personal amount of $1,186.

Tax Consequences Her tax payable before credits would be $1,760 [(16%)($11,000)]. This amount would be reduced by her personal credit of $1,186 to $574. She would then be required to use $574 of her tuition/education credit to reduce her tax payable to nil, leaving an unused amount of $1,378. The amount of the available transfer would be $226 ($800 - $574), leaving an unused credit to be carried forward of $1,152. Note that Megan would have to claim the carry forward in a subsequent year as it cannot be transferred to a spouse or supporting person.

13-125.   It is the transferor who is subject to the $800 limit. A parent or grandparent could have $800 transfers from any number of children or grandchildren. For obvious reasons, transfers from more than one spouse would not be acceptable for tax purposes (tax considerations might be the least of such an individual's problems). If the individual is married, the supporting parent or grandparent can make the claim only if the student's spouse did not claim the spousal credit or any unused credits transferred by the student.

Dividend Tax Credit

13-126.   As is covered in Chapter 11, dividends received from taxable Canadian corporations are subject to a gross up and tax credit system. To determine the taxable amount of dividends, the dividends received must be increased by 25 percent, referred to as the gross up. The dividend tax credit is then calculated as two-thirds of the gross up. While ITA 121 expresses the credit in this fashion, it can also be expressed as 13-1/3 percent of the grossed up dividends or as 16-2/3 percent of the dividends received.

Foreign Tax Credits

Rules For Corporations

13-127.   Corporations are allowed to use foreign non business income and foreign business income taxes paid as a basis for a credit against Canadian taxes payable. The rules for corporations are somewhat different from those for individuals and, in addition, require an understanding of some concepts that have not been introduced at this stage in the text. As a consequence, the foreign tax credit rules applicable to corporations are discussed in Chapter 14.

Foreign Non Business (Property) Income Tax Credit For Individuals

13-128.   ITA 126(1) provides for a tax credit in situations where a Canadian resident has paid foreign taxes on non business income. As was noted in Chapter 11, the full amount of foreign non business income earned, including amounts withheld for taxes in the foreign jurisdiction, must be added to the taxpayer's Net Income For Tax Purposes. This 100 percent amount is then subject to Canadian taxes, with the amount withheld in the foreign jurisdiction being allowed as a credit against Canadian taxes payable. The objective of this procedure is to tax non business income earned in a foreign jurisdiction at the same overall rate as would apply to non business income earned in Canada.

13-129.   There are a number of complications with this procedure. The first of these is that, for individuals, amounts withheld that exceed 15 percent of the total foreign non business income must be deducted under ITA 20(11). Foreign taxes deducted under this provision cannot be used as a credit against Canadian taxes payable, thereby limiting the amount of the foreign tax credit for taxes on non business income to 15 percent of the total income.

13-130.   A further problem is that the government wants to ensure that taxpayers do not receive a credit that is greater than the Canadian taxes that would have been paid on the foreign non business income. This is accomplished by limiting the foreign non business tax credit to the lesser of the amount withheld and the amount determined by multiplying the ratio of foreign non business income to total income by Canadian taxes payable. This approach is reflected in the following calculation:

The Foreign Non Business Income Tax Credit is the lesser of:

- The tax paid to the foreign government. For individuals, this is limited to 15 percent of foreign non business taxes paid, and

- An amount determined by the following formula:

$$\left[\frac{\text{Foreign Non Business Income}}{\text{Adjusted Division B Income}}\right][\text{Tax Otherwise Payable}]$$

13-131.   The "Adjusted Division B Income" in this formula is defined as follows:

Division B Income, less:
- net capital loss carry overs deducted under ITA 111(1)(b);
- any lifetime capital gains deduction taken;
- any amounts deductible for stock options under ITA 110(1)(d) and (d.1);
- any amounts deductible under ITA 110(1)(f) for workers' compensation or social assistance;
- any amounts deductible under ITA 110(1)(j) for a home relocation loan.

13-132. "Tax Otherwise Payable" in this calculation consists of:

Part I taxes payable before the deduction of:
- dividend tax credits;
- employment outside of Canada tax credits;
- political contributions tax credits;
- investment tax credits;
- labour sponsored funds tax credits.

13-133. You should note that the preceding definition of Adjusted Division B Income is unique to the calculation of foreign tax credits. It starts with Net Income For Tax Purposes (Division B Income), and proceeds to deduct some, but not all, of an individual's available Division C deductions. For example, if the individual has non capital loss carry overs, they are not deducted in this calculation. As a result, "Adjusted Division B Income" is a figure that is neither Net Income For Tax Purposes nor Taxable Income.

13-134. The preceding rules would have to be applied on a country by country basis if non business income was received from more than one foreign source. If the result is that the amount of foreign non business taxes withheld exceeds the amount determined by the formula, there is no carryover of the unused amount. However, ITA 20(12) allows a taxpayer to deduct such unused amounts in the determination of Net Income For Tax Purposes.

Foreign Business Income Tax Credit For Individuals

13-135. If a Canadian resident has income from an unincorporated business in a foreign country, ITA 126(2) provides for a credit for foreign taxes paid that is similar to that for non business income. As is the case with foreign non business income tax credits, individuals must include 100 percent of the foreign business income in their Net Income For Tax Purposes, with foreign taxes withheld being allowed as a credit against taxes payable. While the amount of the credit that can be used does not have the 15 percent limit that is applicable to foreign non business credits, it is limited by a formula that is similar to that applicable to the non business income credit. The only difference between these two formulas is that, with respect to the foreign business income credit, there is an additional limit based on the tax otherwise payable for the year, reduced by any foreign non business tax credit deducted. The calculation of the foreign business income tax credit is as follows:

The Foreign Business Income Tax Credit is the least of:

- The tax paid to the foreign government
- An amount determined by the following formula:

$$\left[\frac{\text{Foreign Non Business Income}}{\text{Adjusted Division B Income}}\right][\text{Tax Otherwise Payable}]$$

- Tax Otherwise Payable for the year, less any foreign tax credit taken on non business income under ITA 126(1).

13-136. A further important difference between the two foreign tax credits is that, when foreign business income taxes paid exceed the amount that can be used as a credit during the current year, there is a three year carry back and seven year carry forward available. That is, if a taxpayer does not have sufficient taxes payable to use all of the foreign business income tax credits during the current year, it can be treated as a credit against taxes payable in any of the three preceding years or in any of the seven subsequent years. Note, however, that it can only be used in those years within the constraints provided by the formula in Paragraph 13-135.

Political Contributions Tax Credits

13-137.   A tax credit is available on political contributions made to a registered federal political party, or to candidates at the time of a federal general election or by-election. The maximum value is $500 and it is available to both individuals and corporations. The credit is calculated as follows:

Contributions	Credit Rate	Tax Credit
First $200	75 Percent	$150
Next $350	50 Percent	175
Next $525	One-Third	175
Maximum Credit		$500

Exercise Thirteen-7 deals with political contributions. This would be an appropriate time to attempt this exercise.

13-138.   The $500 credit is achieved when contributions total $1,075. Contributions in excess of this amount do not generate additional credits. Also note that most provinces have a similar credit. There is a difference, however, in that the eligible contributions must be made to a registered provincial political party.

Investment Tax Credits

13-139.   When taxpayers make certain types of expenditures, they become eligible for investment tax credits. These credits reduce the total federal tax payable after arriving at Basic Federal Tax. While these credits can be claimed by individuals as well as corporations, they are more commonly used by corporations and, as a consequence, we will defer the discussion of eligibility for investment tax credits to Chapter 14.

Labour Sponsored Funds Tax Credit

Exercise Thirteen-8 deals with labour sponsored funds. This would be an appropriate time to attempt this exercise.

13-140.   The government wishes to encourage investment in small and medium sized enterprises. To that end, ITA 127.4 provides a credit for individuals investing in the shares of prescribed labour sponsored venture capital corporations. For purposes of this Section, these corporations must be set up under provincial legislation and managed by a labour organization. The assets of the corporation must be invested in small and medium sized businesses. In many cases, there will be a corresponding credit at the provincial level. The credit is based on the cost of the shares purchased by the individual.

13-141.   The federal credit is equal to 15 percent of the net cost of the labour sponsored venture capital corporation (LSVCC) shares. To be eligible for the credit, the investor must be the first registered holder of the LSVCC shares. In addition, the maximum credit for a year is $750. This limits the net cost of eligible investments to $5,000.

Refundable GST Credit

13-142.   One of the major problems with the goods and services tax (GST) is the fact that it is a regressive tax. In order to provide some relief from the impact of this characteristic on low income families, there is a refundable GST credit available under ITA 122.5. A feature that makes this credit different from other types of credits is that the CCRA calculates it for the individual. Unlike other tax credits, where the relevant calculations are included in the individual's tax return, the GST credit is determined by the CCRA on the basis of eligibility information supplied in the individual's tax return.

13-143.   For 2001, the system provides for a total credit that is calculated as follows:

- $207 for the "eligible individual". An eligible individual is a Canadian resident who is married, a parent, or 19 years of age or over on December 31 of the taxation year. In the case of a married couple, only one spouse can be an eligible individual.

- $207 for a "qualified relation". A qualified relation is defined as a cohabiting spouse. If the eligible individual does not have a qualified relation, he is entitled to an additional credit that is the lesser of $107 and two percent of the individual's Net Income in excess of

$6,710.

- $207 for a dependant eligible for the equivalent to spouse tax credit.

- $105 for each "qualified dependant". A "qualified dependant" is defined as a person for whom the individual or his qualified relation are claiming a dependency tax credit or a child of the individual who is residing with the individual at the end of the year. In the case of a child, the qualified dependant cannot be either an eligible individual or a qualified relation. Further, this credit cannot be claimed for a dependant if the $207 was claimed for that dependant because he or she was eligible for the equivalent to spouse tax credit.

13-144.   The total of these amounts must be reduced by five percent of the excess of the individual's "adjusted income" over an indexed threshold amount. For 2001, this threshold amount is $26,941. "Adjusted Income" is defined as total Net Income of the individual and his qualified relation, if any.

13-145.   The refundable GST credit is available to all eligible individuals, without regard to whether they have taxes payable. The amount of the credit is calculated on the basis of information included in the individual's tax return for a particular year, and the amounts are automatically paid to the taxpayer in subsequent years. Taxpayers cannot calculate this credit for themselves, nor do they have the option of applying this credit against the current year's taxes payable.

Canada Child Tax Benefit System

13-146.   The Child Tax Benefit is in the form of a non taxable monthly payment. As is the case with the refundable GST credit, the amount of this benefit is calculated by the CCRA. The benefits under this program have been significantly enhanced in recent years and proposals contained in the February 28, 2000 budget make it clear that this process will continue. This budget introduces increased benefits as of July 1, 2000, as well as scheduled further increases as of July 1, 2001. The current benefits are as follows:

- $1,117 for each qualified dependant, basically a child who is under 18;

- an additional $78 for each dependant in excess of two;

- an additional $221 for each dependant under age seven, with this amount being reduced by 25 percent of all child care expenses claimed; and

- a National Child Benefit (NCB) supplement. The amount of the NCB supplement is $1,255 for the first child, $1,055 for the second, and $980 for the third and subsequent. The benefit is phased out based on family net income in excess of $21,744 (the phase out rate is 12.2 percent for a one child family, 22.5 percent for a two child family, and 32.1 percent for larger families).

- The total of the preceding amounts is reduced by five percent (two and one-half percent when there is only one qualified dependant) of family Net Income in excess of $32,000.

13-147.   Given that the CCRA will be doing the calculations associated with the benefits, the payment is not taxable and will not be included in tax returns, and the fact that its complex data requirements make a realistic calculation extremely difficult, we have not included specific calculations of the child tax benefit in any of the problem material in this book.

Social Benefits Repayment (OAS and EI)

OAS Clawback

13-148.   For many years, one of the cornerstones of Canadian tax and economic policy was that social assistance programs should be provided on a universal basis, without regard to income level or financial need. This is, of course, a very expensive policy. Further, there was some question as to whether providing Old Age Security (OAS) benefits to wealthy individuals was in keeping with such tax policy goals as fairness and equity.

13-149.   Whether the decision was based on tax policy goals or simply reflected a need for additional revenues, the concept of universality is no longer being applied. Starting in 1989, the government began to require a repayment of some portion of old age security benefits received by individuals with Net Income above a threshold amount. The recovery of old age security and employment insurance benefits is called the Social Benefits Repayment in the tax return and is commonly referred to as the clawback.

13-150.   ITA 180.2 requires repayment of OAS benefits up to an amount equal to 15 percent of the taxpayer's Net Income in excess of $55,309. This Net Income figure includes all of the OAS benefits received and, as a consequence, ITA 60(w) provides a deduction from Net Income for amounts that are repaid.

13-151.   Since 1996, amounts that the government estimates that the taxpayer will have to repay are withheld at the time the payments are made. Note that, even in cases where no payments are made, the individual will receive an information slip [T4A(OAS)] indicating that they were entitled to the amount of the benefit, with the same amount being shown as taxes withheld from the payment.

113-152.   The government withholds on the basis of estimates made on a "base taxation year". For OAS payments made during the first six months of a year, the base taxation year will be the second preceding year and for OAS payments made during the last six months of the year, the base taxation year will be the immediately preceding year. For individuals with consistently high levels of income, this withholding procedure will result in the full amount of the OAS payments being withheld. For 2001, OAS payments will total about $5,200 per individual. This means that that the benefit will disappear completely at an income level of about $90,000.

> Exercise Thirteen-9 deals with the OAS clawback. This would be an appropriate time to attempt this exercise.

Employment Insurance Benefits Clawback

13-153.   The *Employment Insurance Act* requires the partial repayment of benefits received if the recipient's Net Income For Tax Purposes is greater than an income threshold of $48,750. An individual must determine the lesser of EI benefits included in income and Net Income in excess of $48,750 for the year. The CCRA collects 30 percent of this amount as a clawback of EI benefits through the recipient's tax return as part of the Social Benefits Repayment. Like the OAS benefits clawback, the repayment is a deduction in the calculation of Net Income For Tax Purposes.

Comprehensive Example

13-154.   While this Chapter has provided a reasonably detailed description of the determination of taxes payable for individuals, including small examples of some of the issues that arise in this process, a more comprehensive example is appropriate at this point. We have used provincial rates that are based on the federal brackets and provincial credits that use the same base as the federal credits. At the end of this Chapter, there is an additional example containing a filled in tax return.

> **Example**   Mr. Thomas Baxter is 66 years of age and his 2001 income is made up of net employment income of $73,800, eligible pension income of $10,000, dividends from taxable Canadian corporations of $8,200 and Old Age Security benefits of $5,200 (because of large business losses during the previous two years, no amount was withheld from these payments). For 2001, Mr. Baxter's employer withheld maximum CPP and EI contributions and a total of $20,000 in income tax. Other information pertaining to 2001 is as follows:
>
> 1.   Mr. Baxter's spouse is 49 years old and is physically disabled. Her only 2001 income is $5,000 in Canadian source interest. The investment funds were inherited from her father at the time of his death.
>
> 2.   Mr. and Mrs. Baxter have two daughters and, on December 31, 2001 their ages were 14 and 17. Kim, the younger daughter, earned $2,700 with her summer job in 2001.

Lori, the older daughter, earned income of $2,000 through part time work in 2001. In September, 2001, Lori began full time attendance at a Canadian university. Mr. Baxter paid her tuition fees of $3,800 of which $1,900 was for the fall semester.

3. The 2001 family medical expenses, all of which are claimed by Mr. Baxter, totalled $2,843.

4. During 2001, Mr. Baxter made donations to registered Canadian charities in the amount of $3,000.

5. Mr. Baxter made contributions to federal political parties totalling $1,500 which enabled him to claim the maximum political donations tax credit of $500.

6. Tax rates used in his province are 8 percent on the first $30,754 of Taxable Income, 10 percent on amounts between $30,755 and $61,509, and 13 percent on any amounts in excess of $61,509. Provincial credits use the same base as the federal credits, with the 8 percent lowest rate generally applied to this base. The exception is charitable donations in excess of $200, where the highest rate of 13 percent is used. The provincial dividend tax credit is equal to one-third of the dividend gross up. The province does not have a political contributions tax credit.

Required: Calculate Mr. Baxter's minimum federal and provincial tax payable for the year ending December 31, 2001.

Solution   Mr. Baxter's Net and Taxable Income would be calculated as follows:

Net Employment Income	$73,800
Eligible Pension Income	10,000
OAS Benefits	5,200
Dividends Received	8,200
Dividend Gross Up	2,050
Income Before Clawback	$99,250
OAS Clawback	(5,200)
Net And Taxable Income	$94,050

The required repayment of OAS is the lesser of the actual OAS payments of $5,200 and $6,591 [(15%)($99,250 - $55,309)].

The following notes are relevant to the calculation of Mr. Baxter's tax payable:

Note One   Mr. Baxter's age credit would be calculated as follows:

Full Base Amount	$3,619
Reduction - Lesser Of:	
• $10,066 [(15%)($94,050 - $26,941)]	
• $3,619 The Full Base Amount	(3,619)
Age Credit	Nil

Note Two   Since Lori had insufficient income to use her tuition fees and education credits, the solution assumes they are transferred to her supporting parent. She could choose to carry forward these credits to apply against her own taxes payable in a subsequent year. The total credit is calculated as follows:

Education (Four Months At $400)	$1,600
Tuition ($3,800 - $1,900)	1,900
Total Credit Available For Transfer Or Carry Forward	$3,500

Note Three   Medical expenses eligible for the credit are the actual expenditures of $2,843, less the maximum of $1,678 as this limit is less than three percent of Mr.

Baxter's Net Income. Since the income of both of Mr. Baxter's daughters is below the basic personal tax credit base of $7,412, there is no need for a reduction in this amount.

Using the preceding Taxable Income and Notes, Taxes Payable would be calculated as follows:

Tax On First $30,754 At 24 Percent (16% + 8%)		$ 7,381
Tax On Next $30,755 ($61,509 - $30,754)		
At 32 Percent (22% + 10%)		9,842
Tax On Next $32,541 ($94,050 - $61,509)		
At 39 Percent (26% + 13%)		12,691
Gross Tax		$29,914
Tax Credits:		
Individual	$ 7,412	
Mr. Baxter's Age (Note One)	Nil	
Spouse [$6,294 - ($5,000 - $629)]	1,923	
Mrs. Baxter's Disability	6,000	
Lori's Education And Tuition (Note Two)	3,500	
Pension Income	1,000	
CPP Contributions (Maximum)	1,496	
EI Premiums (Maximum)	878	
Medical Expenses (Note Three)		
($2,843 - $1,678)	1,165	
Total	$23,374	
Rate (16% + 8%)	24%	(5,610)
Charitable Donations - {[(16% + 8%)($200)]		
+ [(29% + 13%)($3,000 - $200)]}		(1,224)
Dividend Tax Credit [(2/3 + 1/3)($2,050)]		(2,050)
Federal Political Contributions Tax Credit		(500)
Basic Federal Tax		$20,530
Social Benefits Repayment (OAS)		5,200
Total Payable		$25,730
Income Tax Withheld		(20,000)
Total Due		$ 5,730

Alternative Minimum Tax

General Concept

13-155.   For many years, a common complaint about the Canadian tax system was that an individual could have a six figure income and still pay only minimal income taxes. While such cases involve no more than taking full advantage of the various provisions in the Act that allow individuals to reduce their taxes payable, there was a strong public feeling that allowing wealthy individuals with high levels of economic income to pay little or no taxes is not an equitable situation. To deal with this, an alternative minimum tax (AMT) was introduced in 1986.

13-156.   This tax is directed at individuals who take advantage of tax shelters and other "tax preference" items. The basic idea is that individuals who have certain types of income, deductions or credits must calculate an adjusted taxable income by adding back all of the "tax preferences" that have been used in the calculation of regular taxable income. After deducting a basic $40,000 exemption, a flat rate of 16 percent is applied to the remaining net adjusted taxable income. The resulting taxes payable is reduced by some, but not all, of the individual's regular tax credits to arrive at a minimum tax. The taxpayer must pay the greater of the regular taxes payable and the minimum tax.

Minimum Tax

Definition

13-157.   The minimum tax is specified in ITA 127.51 as follows:

An individual's minimum amount for a taxation year is the amount determined by the formula

$$A(B - C) - D, \text{ where}$$

A is the appropriate percentage for the year (currently 16 percent);

B is his adjusted taxable income for the year determined under section 127.52;

C is his basic exemption for the year determined under section 127.53 (currently $40,000); and

D is his basic minimum tax credit for the year determined under section 127.531.

13-158.   The calculation of adjusted taxable income that is described in ITA 127.52 is illustrated in a somewhat more comprehensible fashion in Form T691. The basic idea behind this adjusted taxable income is to put back into regular taxable income those items that are felt to be "tax preferences". Examples of such preference items would be losses on tax shelters, and the non taxable portion of capital gains.

Adjusted Taxable Income

13-159.   The required calculation of adjusted taxable income is as follows:

Regular Taxable Income

Plus Additions:
- The non taxable one-half of the excess of capital gains over capital losses.
- The employee stock option deduction under ITA 110(1)(d) and (d.1).
- The relocation housing loan deduction.
- Losses arising through the deduction of capital cost allowances on Certified Canadian Films.
- The excess of capital cost allowance and interest charges claimed on rental and leasing property, over the net income reported for such property.
- Losses arising as a result of Canadian Exploration Expense (CEE), Canadian Development Expense (CDE), or depletion.
- Losses deducted by limited partners, and members of a partnership who have been specified members at all times since becoming partners, in respect of their partnership interests.
- Losses deducted in respect of investments identified or required to be identified under the tax shelter identification rules.

Less Deductions:
- The gross up of Canadian dividends.
- The non deductible one-half of allowable business investment losses claimed in the year.

Equals: Adjusted Taxable Income For Minimum Tax Purposes

Tax Payable Before Credits

13-160.   A basic exemption is subtracted from the adjusted taxable income figure. This basic exemption is specified in ITA 127.53. Since the introduction of the AMT, this amount has been $40,000.

13-161.   After subtraction of the basic exemption, a flat rate is applied to the resulting balance. This rate is referred to in the ITA 127.51 formula as the "appropriate percentage". Appropriate percentage is defined in ITA 248 as the lowest percentage applicable in calculating federal tax payable. For 2001 this rate is 16 percent. The resulting figure could be described as the alternative minimum tax before the deduction of tax credits.

Tax Credits For AMT

13-162.   ITA 127.531 specifies the tax credits, as calculated for the determination of regular taxes payable, which can be applied against the alternative minimum tax. The credits specified are as follows:

- Personal credits under ITA 118(1).
- Age credit under ITA 118(2), but not the transfer from a spouse.
- Charitable donations credit under ITA 118.1.
- Medical expense credit under ITA 118.2.
- Disability credit under ITA 118.3, but not the transfer from a spouse or other dependant.
- Education, tuition fee, and interest on student loans credits under ITA 118.5, 118.6 and 118.62, but not the transfer from a spouse or other dependant.
- CPP and EI credits under ITA 118.7.

13-163.   While ITA 127.531 is written in terms of credits that can be claimed, an easier approach to the calculation of available credits is taken in Form T691. This form, which is used for the calculation of minimum tax, starts with the sum of all of the non refundable credits from the regular tax calculation and removes those that cannot be used for minimum tax purposes. These include the dividend tax credit, pension income credit, all transfers from a spouse or other dependant (disability, pension, age, tuition, or education credits), investment tax credits, the political contribution tax credit, and the labour sponsored funds tax credit.

Exercise Thirteen-10 deals with the alternative minimum tax. This would be an appropriate time to attempt this exercise.

Carry Over

13-164.   The deduction of these credits will produce the alternative minimum tax payable. If this amount exceeds the regular taxes that are payable on the regular taxable income, the amount of alternative tax must be paid. There will be individuals that become subject to this alternative tax in only some taxation years. The most common example of this situation is the realization of a large capital gain during the year. To provide for this, an excess of alternative minimum tax over regular taxes payable can be carried forward for up to seven years to be applied against any future excess of regular taxes payable over the alternative minimum tax.

References

13-166.   For more detailed study of the material in this Chapter, we would refer you to the following:

ITA 117	Tax Payable Under This Part
ITA 117.1	Annual Adjustment
ITA 118	Personal Credits
ITA 118.1	Charitable Gifts
ITA 118.2	Medical Expense Credit
ITA 118.3	Credit For Mental Or Physical Impairment
ITA 118.5	Tuition Credit
ITA 118.6(2)	Education Credit
ITA 118.7	Credit For UI Premium And CPP Contribution
ITA 118.8	Transfer Of Unused Credits To Spouse Of Common-Law Partner
ITA 118.9	Transfer To Parent Or Grandparent
ITA 122.5	Definitions (GST Credit)
ITA 122.6 To 122.64	Canada Child Tax Benefit
ITA 127(3)	Contributions To Registered Parties And Candidates
ITA 127.4	Definitions (Labour Sponsored Funds Tax Credit)
ITA 127.5 To 127.55	Obligation To Pay Minimum Tax
IC 75-2R4	Contributions To A Registered Political Party Or To A Candidate At A Federal Election
IC 75-23	Tuition Fees And Charitable Donations Paid To Privately Supported Secular and Religious Schools
IC 80-10R	Operating A Registered Charity
IC 84-3R5	Gifts In Right Of Canada
IC 92-3	Guidelines For Refunds Beyond The Normal Three Year Period
IT-110R3	Gifts And Official Donation Receipts
IT-226R	Gift To A Charity Of A Residual Interest In Real Property Or An Equitable Interest In A Trust
IT-244R3	Gifts By Individuals Of Life Insurance Policies As Charitable Donations
IT-270R2	Foreign Tax Credit
IT-288R2	Gifts Of Capital Properties To A Charity And Others
IT-295R4	Taxable Dividends Received After 1987 By A Spouse
IT-407R4	Dispositions Of Cultural Property To Designated Canadian Institutions
IT-513R	Personal Tax Credits
IT-515R2	Education Tax Credit
IT-516R2	Tuition Tax Credit
IT-517R	Pension Tax Credit
IT-519R2 (Consolidated)	Medical Expense And Disability Tax Credits And Attendant Care Expense Deduction
IT-520	Unused Foreign Tax Credits - Carry Forward And Carry Back

Sample Personal Tax Return

This text has presented the material on personal taxation in a technically correct manner, following the various provisions for inclusions and deductions as they are laid out in the *Income Tax Act*. The actual tax return for individuals, the T1 General, modifies this approach in order to make certain items easier for individuals to deal with. For example, RPP and RRSP contributions are technically different deductions. RPP contributions must be deducted against employment income while RRSP contributions are deducted against all types of income. However, the T1 General deducts both of these items against total income. This does not make any real difference as it would be virtually impossible to have a deduction of RPP contributions without a positive employment income.

To illustrate some of the differences, the following simplified example contains a four page T1 individual income tax return completed using the ProFile T1 Personal Income Tax Program for 2000 tax returns from GreenPoint software.

Sample File on CD-ROM

The complete sample tax return is available on the CD-ROM included with this book in two versions, a .PDF file and a T1 ProFile return file.

GreenPoint ProFile Version

After starting the 2000 ProFile T1 program, open the file "Sample T1 Personal Tax Return.00T" in the subdirectory \Greenpoint\Sample Canadian Tax Principles tax return files.

To get the maximum benefit from using the program, we strongly advise that you do the tutorials "Getting Started" and "Using the Form Explorer" that are included with the program. A Quick Reference Card, as well as complete manuals, are available on the CD-ROM in .PDF format. To view .PDF files, you will need to have Adobe Acrobat installed on your system and this program is also included on the CD-ROM.

When viewing the sample return file we offer the following suggestions:

- By pressing <F4> you can view the Form Explorer. Under each of the tabs, double clicking on the column title "Used", will sort the list so that the forms that have been used in the return are at the top. You can then double click on the form itself to view it.

- Right clicking on a number in a field shows a variety of options, including the form or schedule where the amount originated from.

PDF File Version

To view the complete return, including schedules, as a .PDF file, start the Adobe Acrobat program and open the file "PDF Sample T1 Return.pdf" in the subdirectory \Greenpoint\Sample Canadian Tax Principles tax return files.

Sample Problem Data

George Kercher is a divorced, semi-retired air force pilot living in Banff, Alberta. He has been your client for a number of years. George was born on February 24, 1950 and is in good health.

George supports his two daughters. Willa (SIN 527-000-228) was born on July 22, 1982 and is attending university in Alberta. Willa had Net Income of $3,300 during 2000. Janice (SIN 527-000-269), born June 6, 1987, is in high school and she had no earnings during the year.

George needs to supplement his pension, so for the last two years he has been flying fire bombers June 1 to September 30 for the provincial forest service fire control squad which is located in Banff.

He brings you the following receipts and documents.

1. A T4, T4A and T5. These receipts are included as Exhibit 1.

2. His 1999 Notice of Assessment which shows that his 2000 RRSP Deduction Limit is $3,979. He has no undeducted RRSP contributions from previous years.

3. An RRSP contribution receipt for $2,000 from Bull & Bear Inc. dated February 20, 2001.

4. A T2202 "Education Amount Certificate" for Willa from the University of Alberta. It showed she had 4 months of full time credit and paid $2,100 in tuition for 2000. She had signed the certificate authorizing the transfer of all tuition and education amounts to her father.

5. A receipt for $2,000 from George's sister, Shirley Burns (SIN 527-000-582) for child care. She took care of Janice after school during 2000.

6. A receipt for Janice from the MI2 Rock Climbing Camp. The receipt for two weeks at the camp was $1,600.

7. A receipt for $1,000 from the Canadian Wildlife Federation dated December, 2000.

8. An agreement of purchase and sale for the purchase of a house at 69 Beaver St. in Banff. The deal closed March 31, 2000. His new home is 5 kilometers from the Alberta Fire Control offices.

9. A receipt for $2,148 from the Mountain Moving Company dated April 1, 2000. The invoice showed that the fee was charged to pack and move George's household effects from Calgary to Banff, a total of 125 kilometers.

10. An instalment reminder for 2000 that showed that George had paid instalments of $2,500 on September 15 and December 15 ($5,000 in total). These were the instalments requested by the CCRA for the year.

Other Information

After some discussion with George, you note the following information.

1. On February 12, 2000, George received $200,000 from his mother's estate. Using some of these funds, George bought the house in Banff. The remainder of the funds were invested with his stockbroker, Bull & Bear Inc. He had been living in a rented townhouse in Calgary prior to the move.

2. He paid $6,000 in spousal support to his ex-wife, Marilyn (SIN 527-000-103), pursuant to a written agreement.

3. On January 8, 2000, George sold a B26 bomber for $45,000. The bomber used to be contracted out to Montana Airspray. Its original price in 1985 was $6,000, and George reconditioned it over the years at a cost of $12,000. He had not taken any capital cost allowance on the plane.

4. In the winter months, George gives private flying lessons. His statement of income of this unincorporated business, Kercher's Flying School, for the fiscal year ended December 31, 2000 is as follows:

Kercher's Flying School

Lesson fees	$30,200
Plane rentals	$ 9,600
Business meals and entertainment	3,250
Licenses and fees	1,650
Office expenses	550
Accounting fees	300
Total expenses	$ 15,350
Net Income	$ 14,850

5. George is also a 20 percent partner in an elk ranch, Alberta Elk Ranch, established in 1998. His cousin, Leo Lane, holds the remaining 80 percent and lives on the farm that is located at 100 Moose Road in Athabasca, Alberta T9S 1S2. Of the 100 acres that are owned, 50 are farmed. The farm was profitable for the first time this year. The statement of income of this partnership, for the fiscal year ended December 31, 2000 is as follows:

Alberta Elk Ranch Partnership

Farm Revenue	$125,000
Salaries	$ 50,000
Feed	13,750
Livestock purchased	40,000
Office expenses	10,000
Accounting fees	4,000
Total expenses	$117,750
Net Income	$ 7,250

6. At the beginning of 2000, George has a $13,300 restricted farm loss carry forward from 1998 and a net capital loss carry forward of $2,580 from 1997.

7. George authorizes the CCRA to provide information to Elections Canada and he does not own foreign property of more than $100,000 Canadian.

Required: With the objective of minimizing George's taxes payable, complete his 2000 tax return. Include the calculation of his maximum deductible RRSP contribution for 2001. Ignore any GST implications.

Notes To The Return

1. On the T2032, Statement of Professional Activities, the non deductible portion of business meals and entertainment of $1,625 (50% of $3,250) has been excluded.

2. George has claimed his net capital loss carry forward of $2,580 as his taxable capital gains were well in excess of this amount. He can only deduct his restricted farm loss carry forward to the extent of farm income for the year. His restricted farm loss carry forward at the end of 2000 is $11,850 ($13,300 - $1,450).

3. Janice has been claimed under the equivalent to spouse amount on Schedule 5. Since Willa had Net Income of $3,300, and Janice had no income, if Willa had been claimed for the equivalent to spouse credit, it would have resulted in a reduced claim.

4. The deduction for child care costs is limited to $100 per week for overnight camp fees. The $2,000 paid to Shirley Burns is totally deductible.

5. Form T1M, Claim For Moving Expenses should be filled out to calculate the deductible moving expenses. This form should be retained, but does not have to be submitted to the CCRA. George cannot deduct the costs of purchasing his new home because he had been living in a rented townhouse in Calgary.

6. George should consider opening an RESP for Janice if he has not already. She can still benefit from the Canada Education Savings Grant program.

Exhibit 1

Sample Personal Tax Return **447**

T4 — STATEMENT OF REMUNERATION PAID / ÉTAT DE LA RÉMUNÉRATION PAYÉE

Employer's name - Nom de l'employeur: **Alberta Fire Control**

Canada Customs and Revenue Agency / Agence des douanes et du revenu du Canada

Year / Année: **2000**

14 Employment Income / Revenus d'emploi	18,000 00
22 Income tax deducted / Impôt sur le revenu retenu	4,500 00
54 Business Number / Numéro d'entreprise	RP
10 Province of employment / Province d'emploi	AB
16 Employee's CPP contributions - line 308 / Cotisations de l'employé au RPC - ligne 308	565 50
24 EI insurable earnings / Gains assurables d'AE	
12 Social insurance number / Numéro d'assurance sociale	527 000 145
29 Employment code / Code d'emploi	
17 Employee's QPP contributions - line 308 / Cotisations de l'employé au RRQ - ligne 308	
26 CPP/QPP pensionable earnings / Gains donnant droit à pension - RPC/RRQ	
18 Employee's EI premiums - line 312 / Cotisations de l'employé à l'AE - ligne 312	440 00
44 Union Dues - line 212 / Cotisations syndicales - ligne 212	75 00
20 RPP contributions - line 207 / Cotisations à un RPA - ligne 207	900 00
46 Charitable donations - Schedule 9 / Dons de bienfaisance - Annexe 9	
52 Pension adjustment - line 206 / Facteur d'équivalence - ligne 206	1,800 00
50 RPP or DPSP registration number / No d'agrément d'un RPA ou d'un RPDB	

VOID ANNULE ☐

Exempt-Exemption CPP/QPP / EI — 28 RPC/RRQ / EI

Employee's name and address - Nom et adresse de l'employé
Last name - Nom de famille: **Kercher**
First name - Prénom: **George**
Initials - Initiales:
69 Beaver Street
Banff AB CAN   T0L 0C0

1

RC-00-599

Other Information / Autres renseignements:
N/A | N/A | N/A | N/A | N/A | N/A
Box/Case — Amount/Montant

T4 (00)

T4A — STATEMENT OF PENSION, RETIREMENT, ANNUITY, AND OTHER INCOME / ÉTAT DU REVENU DE PENSION, DE RETRAITE, DE RENTE OU D'AUTRES SOURCES

Canada Customs and Revenue Agency / Agence des douanes et du revenu du Canada

Year / Année: **2000**

Box	Description	Amount
16	Pension or superannuation / Prestations de retraite ou autres pensions	27,000 00
18	Lump-sum payments / Paiements forfaitaires	0 00
20	Self-employed commissions / Commissions d'un travail indépendant	0 00
22	Income tax deducted / Impôt sur le revenu retenu	6,000 00
24	Annuities / Rentes	0 00
26	Eligible retiring allowances / Allocations de retraite admissibles	0 00
27	Non-eligible retiring allowances / Allocations de retraite non admissibles	0 00
28	Other income / Autres revenus	0 00
30	Patronage allocations / Répartitions selon l'apport commercial	0 00
32	Registered pension plan contributions (past service) / Cotisations à un régime de pension agréé (services passés)	0 00
34	Pension adjustment / Facteur d'équivalence	0 00
36	Pension plan registration number / Numéro d'agrément du régime de pension	
40	RESP accumulated income payments / Paiements de revenu accumulé d'un REEE	0 00
42	RESP education assistance payments / Paiements d'aide aux études d'un REEE	0 00
46	Charitable donations / Dons de bienfaisance	0 00
12	Social insurance number / Numéro d'assurance sociale	527 000 145
38	Footnote codes / Codes de notes	
39	Government use only / Réservé au gouvernement	
14	Recipient's number / Numéro du bénéficiaire	
61	Business Number - Numéro d'entreprise	R

Employer's or payer's name - Nom de l'employeur ou du payeur: **Canadian Armed Forces**

Recipient's name and address - Nom et adresse du bénéficiaire
Last name - Nom de famille: **Kercher**
First name - Prénom: **George**
Initials - Initiales:
Address - Adresse: 69 Beaver Street
Banff AB CAN   Postal code - Code postal: T0L 0C0

Footnote codes and explanation - Explication des codes de notes

1

T4A (00)   RC-00-599

T5 — STATEMENT OF INVESTMENT INCOME / ÉTAT DES REVENUS DE PLACEMENTS

Canada Customs and Revenue Agency / Agence des douanes et du revenu du Canada

Year / Année: **2000**

Dividends from Canadian corporations - Dividendes de sociétés canadiennes

Box	Description	Amount
10	Actual amount of dividends / Montant réel des dividendes	4,200.00
11	Taxable amount of dividends / Montant imposable des dividendes	5,250.00
12	Federal dividend tax credit / Crédit d'impôt fédéral pour dividendes	700.00
13	Interest from Canadian sources / Intérêts de source canadienne	832.00
14	Other income from Canadian sources / Autres revenus de source canadienne	
15	Foreign income / Revenus étrangers	
16	Foreign tax paid / Impôt étranger payé	
17	Royalties from Canadian sources / Redevances de source canadienne	
18	Capital gains dividends - Period 3 / Dividendes sur gains en capital - Période 3	
19	Accrued income: Annuities / Revenus accumulés: Rentes	
40	Capital gains dividends - Period 1 / Dividendes sur gains en capital - Période 1	
41	Capital gains dividends - Period 2 / Dividendes sur gains en capital - Période 2	
20	Amount eligible for resource allowance deduction / Montant donnant droit à la déduction relative aux ressources	
21	Report code / Code du feuillet	0
22	Recipient identification number / Numéro d'identification du bénéficiaire	527 000 145
23	Recipient type / Type de bénéficiaire	1

VOID ANNULÉ

Recipient's name and address - Nom et prenom et adresse du bénéficiaire
KERCHER GEORGE
69 BEAVER STREET
BANFF AB CAN   T0L 0C0

Payer's name and address - Nom et adresse du payeur
BULL & BEAR INC.
1 MONEY PLACE, SUITE 1
CALGARY   AB

Currency and identification codes / Codes de devise et d'identification
27 Foreign currency / Devises étrangères
28 Transit - Succursale
29 Recipient account / Numéro de compte du bénéficiaire

1

T5 (00)   RC-00-599

Canada Customs
and Revenue Agency

Agence des douanes
et du revenu du Canada

T1 GENERAL 2000

Income Tax and Benefit Return

Identification

| 7 |

First name and initial
George

Last name
Kercher

Care of

Address
69 Beaver Street

Apt. or unit no.

City
Banff

Province or territory
Alberta

Postal Code
T0L 0C0

Enter your province or territory of residence on
December 31, 2000:   Alberta

If you were self-employed in 2000, enter the province or territory of
self-employment: Alberta

If you became or ceased to be a resident of Canada **in 2000**, give:
Month/Day   Month/Day
entry date   or departure date

Enter your social insurance number: 527 000 145

Enter your date of birth:

Year/Month/Day
1950-02-24

Your language of correspondence:
Votre langue de correspondance :English

☒ Francais ☐

If this return is for a deceased
person, enter the date of death:

Year/Month/Day

Marital status on December 31, 2000
(see the "Marital status" section in the guide for details)

1 ☐ Married   2 ☐ Living common law   3 ☐ Widowed
4 ☒ Divorced   5 ☐ Separated   6 ☐ Single

If box 1 or 2 applies, enter your spouse's social
insurance number:

Enter the first name of your
spouse:

Check if your spouse was self-employed in 2000:   1 ☐

Do not use this area

Elections Canada (see the guide for details)

Do you authorize the Canada Customs and Revenue Agency to provide your name, address, and
date of birth to Elections Canada to update your information on the **National Register of Electors**?
Yes   ☒ 1   No ☐ 2
Your authorization is needed each year. This information can be used for electoral purposes only.

Goods and services tax / Harmonized sales tax (GST/HST) credit application

Are you applying for the GST/HST credit? (see the guide for details)   Yes ☐ 1   No ☒ 2
If *yes*, enter the number of children under age 19 on December 31, 2000 (if applicable)
If *yes*, enter your spouse's net income from line 236 of your spouse's return (if applicable)

Foreign income

As a Canadian resident, you have to report your income from all sources both inside and outside Canada.

Please answer the following question

Did you own or hold foreign property at any time in 2000 with a total cost of more than CAN$100,000?
(read the "Foreign income" section in the guide for details)   **266** Yes ☐ 1   No ☒ 2
If *yes*, attach a completed Form T1135.

If you had certain dealings with a non-resident trust or corporation in 2000, see the "Foreign income" section in the guide.

Do not use this area	172				171					

Complete tax return available on the CD-ROM

Total income

Employment income (box 14 on all T4 slips)	**101**	18,000 00
Commissions included on line 101 (box 42 on all T4 slips) **102**		
Other employment income (see line 104 in the guide)	**104**	
Old Age Security pension (box 18 on the T4A(OAS) slip)	**113**	
Canada or Quebec Pension Plan benefits (box 20 on the T4A(P) slip)	**114**	
Disability benefits included on line 114 (box 16 on T4A(P) slip) **152**		
Other pensions or superannuation (see line 115 in the guide)	**115**	27,000 00
Employment Insurance benefits (box 14 on the T4E slip)	**119**	
Taxable amount of dividends from taxable Canadian corporations (see line 120 in guide)	**120**	5,250 00
Interest and other investment income (attach Schedule 4)	**121**	832 00
Net partnership income: limited or non-active partners only (attach Schedule 4)	**122**	
Rental income Gross **160** Net **126**		
Taxable capital gains (attach Schedule 3)	**127**	20,250 00
Support payments received Total **156** Taxable amount **128**		
RRSP income (from all T4RSP slips)	**129**	
Other income (see line 130 in the guide) Specify:	**130**	

Self-employment income (see lines 135 to 143 in the guide)

	Gross		Net	
Business income	**162**		**135**	
Professional income	**164**	30,200 00	**137**	16,475 00
Commission income	**166**		**139**	
Farming income	**168**	125,000 00	**141**	1,450 00
Fishing income	**170**		**143**	

Workers' Compensation benefits (box 10 on the T5007 slip) **144**		
Social assistance payments (see line 145 in the guide) **145**		
Net federal supplements (box 21 on the T4A(OAS) slip) **146**		
Add lines 144, 145, and 146 ▸ 147		
Add lines 101, 104 to 143, and 147		
This is your **total income**. **150**	89,257 00 ▸	89,257 00

Net income

Pension adjustment (box 52 on all T4 slips and box 34 on all T4A slips) **206**	1,800 00	
Registered pension plan deduction (box 20 on T4 slips and box 32 on T4A slips)	**207**	900 00
RRSP deduction (see Schedule 7; attach receipts)	**208**	2,000 00
Saskatchewan Pension Plan deduction (see line 209 in the guide)	**209**	
Annual union, professional, or like dues (box 44 on T4 slips, or from receipts)	**212**	75 00
Child care expenses (attach Form T778)	**214**	2,200 00
Attendant care expenses (see line 215 in the guide)	**215**	
Business investment loss (see line 217 in the guide) Allowable		
Gross (before) **227** Gross (after) **228** deduction **217**		
Moving expenses (see line 219 in the guide)	**219**	2,148 00
Support payments made Total **230** 6,000 00 Allowable deduction **220**		6,000 00
Carrying charges and interest expenses (attach Schedule 4)	**221**	
Exploration and development expenses (attach Schedule 4)	**224**	
Other employment expenses (see line 229 in the guide)	**229**	
Cleric's residence deduction (see line 231 in the guide)	**231**	
Other deductions (see line 232 in the guide)Specify:	**232**	
Add lines 207 to 224, 229, 231 and 232. 233	13,323 00 ▸	13,323 00
Line 150 minus line 233 (if negative, enter "0"). This is your **net income before adjustments**. 234		75,934 00
Social benefits repayment (if you reported income on line 113, 119, or 146, see line 235 in the guide) **235**		•
Line 234 minus line 235 (if negative, enter "0") This is your **net income**. 236		75,934 00

Before you mail your return, make sure you have attached here all completed schedules, required information slips, receipts, and corresponding statements.

Taxable Income

Enter your **net income** from line 236		**236**	75,934 00

Employee home relocation loan deduction (box 37 on all T4 slips)	**248**		
Stock option and shares deductions (box 39, 41, 98 and 99 on all T4 slips)	**249**		
Other payments deduction (if you reported income on line 147, see line 250 in the guide)	**250**		
Limited partnership losses of other years	**251**		
Non-capital losses of other years	**252**	1,450 00	
Net capital losses of other years	**253**	2,580 00	
Capital gains deduction (see line 254 in the guide)	**254**		
Northern residents deductions (attach Form T2222)	**255**		
Additional deductions Specify:	**256**		

Add lines 248 to 256. **257**	4,030 00 ▶	4,030 00
Line 236 minus line 257 (if negative, enter "0")		
This is your **taxable income. 260**		71,904 00

Non-refundable tax credits

Basic personal amount (see line 300 in the guide) claim $7,231.00	**300**	7,231 00	
Age amount (if you were born in 1935 or earlier, see line 301 in the guide)	**301**		
Spousal amount (see line 303 in the guide)			
Base amount	6,754 00		
Minus: Your spouse's net income	0 00		
Spousal amount (if negative, enter "0")**(maximum $6,140)**	▶ **303**		
Equivalent-to-spouse amount (see line 305 in the guide) **(maximum claim $6,140)**	**305**	6,140 00	
Amount for infirm dependants age 18 or older (see line 306 in the guide)	**306**		
Canada or Quebec Pension Plan contributions			
Contributions through employment from box 16 and 17 on T4 slips (maximum $1,329.90)	**308**	565 50 ●	
Contributions payable on self-employment and other earnings (Schedule 8)	**310**	1,398 15 ●	
Employment Insurance premiums from box 18 on T4 slips (line 312 in guide)	**312**	432 00 ●	
Pension income amount (maximum $1,000; see line 314 in the guide)	**314**	1,000 00	
Caregiver amount (see line 315 in the guide)	**315**		
Disability amount (see line 316 in the guide)	**316**		
Disability amount transferred from a dependant other than your spouse	**318**		
Interest paid on your student loans (see line 319 in the guide)	**319**		
Tuition and education amounts (attach Schedule 11)	**323**		
Tuition and education amounts transferred from a child (see line 324 in the guide)	**324**	2,900 00	
Amounts transferred from your spouse (attach Schedule 2)	**326**		

Medical expenses (line 330 in guide; attach receipts)	**330**	
Minus: $1,637, or 3% of line 236, whichever is **less**	1,637 00	
Subtotal		
Minus: Medical expenses adjustment (line 331 in guide)	**331**	
Allowable portion of medical expenses (if negative, enter "0")	▶ **332**	

Add lines 300, 301, 303 to 326, and 332 (if this total is more than line 260, see line 338 in the guide) **335**	19,666 65	

Multiply the amount on line 335 by 17% = 338		3,343 33
Donations and gifts Complete Schedule 9 to calculate your tax credit for donations and gifts. Enter the amount from line 9 of Schedule 9 and attach a copy to your return. **349**		266 00
Add lines 338 and 349. Use this amount to determine your federal tax on Schedule 1. These are your **total non-refundable tax credits. 350**		3,609 33

File: Kercher, George SIN: 527000145 Printed: 2001-06-28 10:57

Refund or Balance owing

4

Federal tax: Complete Schedule 1 and enter the amount from line 25.	406	11,742	22
Total federal political contributions (attach receipts) **409**			
Federal political contribution tax credit (see lines 409 and 410 in the guide) **410**		•	
Investment tax credit (attach Form T2038 (IND)) **412**		•	
Labour-sponsored funds tax credit Net cost **413** Allowable credit **414**		•	
Add lines 410, 412, and 414. 416	▶		
Line 406 minus line 416 (if you have an amount on line 16 of Schedule 1, see Form T1206) 417		11,742	22
Additional tax on RESP accumulated income payments (attach form T1172)	418		
Federal individual surtax (line 32 of Schedule 1)	419		
Add lines 417, 418, and 419. This is your **net federal tax**. 420		11,742	22
Canada Pension Plan contributions payable on self-employment and other earnings (from Schedule 8)	421	1,398	15
Social benefits repayment (enter the amount from line 235)	422		
Provincial or territorial tax (see line 428 in the guide)	428	5,526	10
Add lines 420 to 428. This is your **total payable**. 435		18,666	47 •

Total income tax deducted (from all information slips) **437**	10,500 00 •		
Tax transfer for residents of Québec (see line 438 in the guide) **438**	•		
Line 437 minus line 438	10,500 00 ▶ 439	10,500	00
Refundable Québec abatement (see line 440 in the guide) **440**		•	
Canada Pension Plan overpayment (see line 448 in the guide) **448**		•	
Employment Insurance overpayment (see line 450 in the guide) **450**	8 00	•	
Refundable medical expense supplement (attach Schedule 10) **452**		•	
Refund of investment tax credit (attach Form T2038 (IND)) **454**		•	
Part XII.2 trust tax credit (box 38 on all T3 slips) **456**		•	
Employee and partner GST/HST rebate (attach Form GST 370) **457**		•	
Tax paid by instalments (see line 476 in the guide) **476**	5,000 00	•	
Provincial or territorial credits (see line 479 in the guide) **479**		•	
Add lines 439 to 479. These are your **total credits**. 482	15,508 00 ▶	15,508	00
Line 435 minus line 482		3,158	47

If the result is negative, you have a **refund**. If it is positive, you have a **balance owing**.
Enter the amount below on whichever line applies. We do not charge or refund a difference of less than $2.

Refund **484**   •   Balance owing **485**   3,158 47 •

Direct Deposit Request - Start or Change (see line 484 in the guide)

You do not have to complete this area every year. Do not complete it this year if your direct deposit information for your refund has not changed.

Refund and GST/HST credit - To start direct deposit, or to change account information only, attach a "void" cheque or complete lines 460, 461, and 462.

Note: To deposit your **CCTB** payments (including certain related provincial or territorial payments) into the **same** account, also check box 463.

Branch number	Institution number	Account number	CCTB
460	**461**	**462**	**463**

Amount enclosed **486**   •

Attach to page 1, a **cheque** or **money order** payable to the Receiver General. Your payment is due no later than April 30, 2001.

I certify that the information given on this return and in any documents attached is correct, complete, and fully discloses all my income.

Sign here _____

It is a serious offence to make a false return.

Telephone (111) 111-1111 Date 2000-04-10

490 [X] **For professional tax preparers only.**

Name _____

Address _____

Telephone (   )   -

Do not use this area	487	488

RC-00-148

Prepared without audit based on information provided by the taxpayer.

Exercises

(The solutions for these exercises can be found following Chapter 21 of the text.)

Exercise Thirteen - 1 (Transfer Of Dividends To A Spouse)

Mr. Albert Ho is 38 years old and has over $100,000 in Taxable Income. His provincial tax rate is 14.5% of Taxable Income and the provincial dividend tax credit is equal to one-third of the dividend gross up. His wife's only source of income is $5,700 in dividends received from taxable Canadian corporations. Would Mr. Ho benefit from the use of the ITA 82(3) election to include the dividends received by his spouse in his Net Income For Tax Purposes?

Exercise Thirteen - 2 (Personal Tax Credits)

Mr. Johan Sprinkle is married but has no dependants. His 2001 Net Income For Tax Purposes is $25,450. His spouse has 2001 Net Income For Tax Purposes of $2,600. Determine Mr. Sprinkle's personal tax credits for 2001.

Exercise Thirteen - 3 (Equivalent To Spouse Tax Credit)

Ms. Jane Forest is 48 years old and divorced from her husband. Her Net Income For Tax Purposes for 2001 is $43,000. She has retained the family home and has custody of both of the children of the marriage. Her son is 20 years old and suffers from Down syndrome. He does not qualify for the disability tax credit. Her daughter is 16 years old and in good health. Her son has no income during 2001 while her daughter has Net Income For Tax Purposes of $1,800. Based on this information, determine Ms. Forest's federal tax credits for 2001.

Exercise Thirteen - 4 (Donation of Listed Shares)

Mr. Saheed Radeem has employment income of $70,000. He owns shares that are listed on the Toronto Stock Exchange. These shares have a fair market value of $110,000 and an adjusted cost base of $30,000. During July, 2001, these shares are given to a registered Canadian charity. He has no deductions in the calculation of Taxable Income (i.e., his Taxable Income is equal to his Net Income For Tax Purposes). His tax credits, other than the charitable donations credit, total $4,000. Determine Mr. Radeem's maximum federal charitable donations tax credit for 2001. Indicate any carry over of unused amounts that will be available in future years.

Exercise Thirteen - 5 (Dependant Medical Expenses)

Ms. Maxine Davies and her spouse have medical expenses of $4,330. Ms. Davies has Net Income For Tax Purposes in excess of $150,000, her spouse has no income, and her son has Net Income For Tax Purposes of $7,460. Ms. Davies paid for $8,425 of medical expenses incurred by her son. Based on this information, determine Ms. Davies' federal medical expenses tax credit for 2001.

Exercise Thirteen - 6 (Transfer Of Credits From A Spouse)

Mr. Martin Levee is 68 years old and has Net Income For Tax Purposes of $42,000. Of this total, $24,000 was from a life annuity that he purchased with RRSP funds. His spouse is 66 years old, has no income of her own (she is ineligible for OAS), and is attending university on a full time basis. Her tuition fees for the year were $2,200 and she was in full time attendance for 4 months of the year. Based on this information, determine Mr. Levee's federal tax credits for 2001.

Exercise Thirteen - 7 (Political Contribution Tax Credit)

Ms. Vivacia Unger contributes $785 to the Liberal New Conservative Reform Party, a registered federal political party. Determine the amount of her federal political contributions tax credit.

Exercise Thirteen - 8 (Labour Sponsored Funds Credit)

On June 30, 2001, Mr. Brad Clintor purchases newly issued shares in a prescribed labour sponsored venture capital corporation at a cost of $3,000. Determine the amount of the federal tax credit that will result from this purchase.

Exercise Thirteen - 9 (OAS Clawback)

For 2001, Ms. Marilyn Jacobi has received $5,200 in Old Age Security (OAS) payments. No amount was withheld from these payments because she had a very low income in the previous two years. Due to the success of her new business, her Net Income For Tax Purposes for the current year, including the OAS payments, is $75,400. How much of the $5,200 that she has received during the year will have to be repaid?

Exercise Thirteen - 10 (Alternative Minimum Tax)

Mr. Norton Blouson has Taxable Income for 2001 of $85,000. This includes taxable capital gains of $22,500 [(1/2)($45,000)] and taxable dividends of $25,000 [(125%)($20,000)]. In addition, he received a $50,000 retiring allowance that was contributed to his RRSP. The full contribution was deductible. His only tax credits are the basic personal credit and the dividend tax credit. Determine Mr. Blouson's federal liability for alternative minimum tax.

Problems For Self Study

(The solutions for these problems can be found following Chapter 21 of the text.)

Self Study Problem Thirteen - 1

Mr. and Mrs. Bahry have been retired for several years. They are both in their early seventies, residents of Canada, and rely on pension income to provide for most of their needs. More specifically, the components of their income for the year ending December 31, 2001 are as follows:

	Mr. Bahry	Mrs. Bahry
Old Age Security Pension	$ 5,200	$5,200
Receipts From Registered Pension Plan	12,340	820
Received From Registered Retirement Income Fund	N/A	700
Canada Pension Plan	3,690	830
Dividends Received From Taxable Canadian Companies	1,600	336
Interest On Savings Accounts	1,239	443
Charitable Donations	1,510	N/A
Capital Gain On Sale Of Painting	N/A	500
Capital Loss On Sale Of Shares	3,975	820

Required: Determine the minimum Taxable Income for both Mr. and Mrs. Bahry and the maximum federal tax credits that will be available to Mr. Bahry for the 2001 taxation year.

Self Study Problem Thirteen - 2

The following five independent cases make varying assumptions with respect to Mr. Stanley Murphy and his 2001 tax status.

Case A Mr. Murphy is 30 years of age and unmarried. Mr. Murphy provides home care for his 68 year old father. His father's 2001 Net Income is $7,200. In June of last year, Stanley graduated from a Canadian University with a degree in mathematics. In January 2001, Stanley began to repay his student loan of $25,000 in monthly installments of $325. Stanley paid $375 in interest related to his student loans in 2001. His only income is $41,000 in net employment income.

Case B Mr. Murphy is 48 years of age and has income from employment of $41,000.

His wife, Helen Murphy, is 43 years of age and has employment income of $4,650. They have one child, Eileen, who is 11 years of age. During the year, the family had eligible medical expenses of $1,050 for Stanley, $1,800 for Helen and $300 for Eileen. Eileen has no income in 2001.

Case C Mr. Murphy is 48 years of age and his wife, Helen, is 43. Mr. Murphy has income from employment of $41,000. Helen has employment income of $5,050. They have a son, Albert, who is 19 years old and lives at home. He attends university on a full time basis during 8 months of the year. Stanley pays $3,400 for Albert's tuition for two semesters during the calendar year 2001 and $525 for required textbooks. Albert had employment income of $3,000 that he earned during the summer.

Case D Mr. Murphy is 67 and his wife Helen is 68. Helen has been completely disabled for a number of years. The components of Stanley and Helen's income are as follows:

	Stanley	Helen
Interest	$ 300	$ 50
Canada Pension Plan	4,400	200
Old Age Security Pension	5,200	5,200
Income From Registered Pension Plan	30,750	500
Taxable Dividends (125%)	600	150
Total Net Income	$41,250	$6,100

The Murphys use the ITA 82(3) election to transfer Helen's dividends to Stanley.

Case E Stanley is 48 years of age and his income is made up of business income of $37,400, $3,000 in taxable dividends from a company in which he has a controlling interest, and $600 [(125%)($480)] in taxable dividends from portfolio investments. In addition, he makes contributions to federal political parties in the amount of $1,000. Mr. Murphy is not married and has no dependants.

Required: In each Case, calculate Mr. Murphy's Taxable Income and minimum federal taxes payable. To concentrate on the differences generated by the varying assumptions, ignore any amounts Mr. Murphy might have had withheld or paid in instalments, and any EI or CPP contributions.

Self Study Problem Thirteen - 3
The following information relates to Mr. Michael Slater for the year ending December 31, 2001:

Receipts

Revenue From Farming		$ 36,000
Drawings From Proprietorship		9,000
Interest On Savings Account		4,600
Gross Salary From Employer		35,000
Gambling Income		1,600
Canada Pension Plan Benefits		5,100
Loans To Friends:		
Interest Received	$12,000	
Principal Repaid	21,000	33,000
Cash Inheritance From Deceased Aunt		25,000
Dividends From Taxable Canadian Corporations (100%)		44,000
Dividends From U.S. Corporations -		
Net Of 15 Percent Withholding		8,500
Proceeds From Sale of Land		111,500
Total Receipts		$313,300

Disbursements

Contributions To Federal Conservative Party	$ 500
Interest On Bank Loan	2,300
Farm Expenses	45,000
Life Insurance Premiums	11,000
Mortgage Payments On Personal Residence	15,000
Personal Funds Invested In Proprietorship	42,000
Charitable Donations	2,700
Safety Deposit Rental (For Securities)	150
Total Disbursements	$118,650

Other Information:

1. Mr. Slater's farm is operated on a part time basis. While the operating results are highly variable, the overall profit picture has been favourable.

2. The proprietorship began operations on May 1, 2001 and has a fiscal year end of December 31. The proprietorship had income of $28,300 for the period May 1 to December 31, 2001.

3. The land that was sold during 2001 was purchased at a cost of $23,000 three years ago. Mr. Slater had intended to build a cottage on it.

4. The bank loan on which interest was paid was used to finance the establishment of the proprietorship.

5. Mr. Slater is 71 years old. His wife is 61 and has no income of her own. She has been blind for several years.

6. Mr. Slater's employer has withheld a total of $9,000 in income taxes from his gross salary of $35,000 during 2001. In addition, Mr. Slater has made instalment payments totalling $2,500. This is sufficient to bring his total tax payments up to the level of his 2000 taxes payable.

7. As Mr. Slater has had consistently high levels of income, the full $5,200 of Old Age Security benefits has been withheld.

8. Mr. Slater files his 2001 return on July 15, 2002.

Required: Calculate Mr. Slater's minimum income federal taxes payable for the year ending December 31, 2001. Ignore any alternative minimum tax that might be payable. Include in your solution any penalties, interest or other amounts that are payable on federal balances, as well as any carry overs that are available at the end of the year. Assume that the prescribed rate, including the extra 4 percent on amounts owing to the Minister, for all relevant periods is 9 percent compounded on an annual basis.

Self Study Problem Thirteen - 4

Ms. Linda Worthmore is employed by Intra Graphics Inc. and, for the year ending December 31, 2001, she has a gross salary of $72,476. The following amounts were withheld by her employer during the year:

Canada Pension Plan Contributions	$1,496
Employment Insurance Premiums	878
Registered Pension Plan Contributions	1,233
Donations To Registered Charities	342

During 2001, Intra Graphics Inc. paid the following amounts on behalf of Ms. Worthmore:

Premium For Private Drug Plan	$ 115
Premium For Private Extended Health Care	235
Premium For Provincial Health Care Plan	413

Ms. Worthmore is married and lives with her husband, Mr. John Dalton. During 2001, her husband received $750 in interest on a five year term deposit. In 2000, Ms. Worthmore gave her husband 52 shares of a publicly traded Canadian company. Ms. Worthmore had acquired the shares at $12 per share and, at the time of the gift, the shares were trading at $32 per share. On August 31, 2001, Mr. Dalton sold these shares for $56 per share. On June 15, 2001, the shares paid a dividend of $3.50 per share.

Mr. Dalton was a full time student at a designated educational institution during four months of the year. His tuition fees, which were paid by Ms. Worthmore, were $2,300. During the remainder of the year he had additional earnings from part time employment of $2,475. No CPP or EI payments were deducted from this income.

Ms. Worthmore and her husband have three children, all of whom live at home. Relevant information on these children is as follows:

Joyce   Joyce is six years of age and has no income of her own. During 2001, Ms. Worthmore was required to pay $2,200 in medical expenses for Joyce.

Jayne   Jayne is fourteen years of age and had earnings from part time employment of $1,225. On March 15, 2001, Ms. Worthmore gave her daughter 27 shares of a publicly traded Canadian company. The shares had cost Ms. Worthmore $18 per share and, at the time of the gift, they were trading at $27 per share. The shares paid no dividends during 2001 and are still held by Jayne on December 31, 2001.

June   June is seventeen years of age and, during 2001, had income of $7,500. In July, 2001, June was involved in a serious accident. As a result of the accident, Ms. Worthmore was required to pay $9,850 of medical expenses on June's behalf.

Other Information:

1. Ms. Worthmore is the sole shareholder of Lindworth Inc. This Canadian controlled private company has a December 31 year end and, during 2001 paid dividends in the total amount of $4,325 to Ms. Worthmore. As an employee of this Company she received a salary of $2,500 for the year. No CPP or EI payments were deducted from the salary. On January 1, 2001, the Company loaned Ms. Worthmore an amount of $5,000 to help finance an extended vacation for her husband. The loan is interest free and must be repaid in 2006. Ms. Worthmore has no intention of repaying it before that time.

2. During 2001, Ms. Worthmore made contributions to a Registered Retirement Savings Plan in the amount of $7,500. A pension adjustment of $6,161 was reported on her 2000 T4. Assume that her 2000 Earned Income equals her 2001 Earned Income. At the end of 2000, she has no unused RRSP deduction room or undeducted RRSP contributions.

3. Under the provisions of a court decree, Ms. Worthmore pays spousal support to her former husband in the amount of $225 per month.

4. During 2001, Ms. Worthmore sold 122 shares of Lackmere Ltd. at a price of $86 per share. Ms. Worthmore owned a total of 300 shares of this Company, having acquired 122 at a price of $92 in 1999 and the other 178 at a price of $71 per share in 2000. Lackmere is not a qualified small business corporation.

5. During 2001, Ms. Worthmore sold land to her older brother for $10,000. The land had a fair market value of $28,000 and had been acquired by Ms. Worthmore on January 1, 1996 for $10,000. The land had been rented out to local farmers for agricultural use. The land is not a qualified farm property.

6. During 2001, Ms. Worthmore makes contributions to the Federal Liberal Party in the amount of $100.

Required: Calculate, for the 2001 taxation year, Ms. Worthmore's minimum Taxable Income, and Federal Taxes Payable. Ignore GST and PST considerations, as well as payments that were made by Ms. Worthmore through instalments or withholding.

Self Study Problem Thirteen - 5

Cheryl Delancey, a tax consultant, has provided tax assistance on a regular basis to her two aunts, Alma and Irene Delancey. For the 2001 taxation year, Cheryl and her aunts are concerned about the impact of the Alternative Minimum Tax on the amount of taxes they will have to pay. In order to estimate the taxes that will be payable, they each have estimated the amounts and types of income they expect to earn and deductions to claim for 2001. These estimates are as follows:

	Cheryl	Alma	Irene
Employment And Business Income	$60,800	$36,000	$ 22,900
Dividends Received			
From Canadian Corporations	26,300	-0-	29,400
Taxable Capital Gains	9,100	-0-	300,000
Retiring Allowance	-0-	58,000	-0-
RRSP Contributions	3,500	58,000	-0-
Lifetime Capital Gains			
Deduction Claimed	9,100	-0-	250,000

On Cheryl's 2000 T4, a Pension Adjustment of $8,600 was reported. Assume that her 2000 Earned Income equals her 2001 Earned Income. She has no Unused RRSP Deduction Room or Undeducted RRSP Contributions at the end of 2000.

As Alma had worked for her present employer for over 36 years, she is eligible for a tax free rollover of the entire retiring allowance to an RRSP.

All taxable capital gains relate to the sale of shares of qualified small business corporations.

None of the Delancey women have ever married and they have no dependants. All three women are under 65 years of age and are in good health.

Required: Calculate the minimum regular 2001 federal Taxes Payable for each of the three women, as well as the alternative minimum tax amount. Ignore any EI and CPP contributions.

Assignment Problems

(The solutions for these problems are only available in
the solutions manual that has been provided to your instructor.)

Assignment Problem Thirteen - 1

All of the following cases are independent and involve the determination of personal tax credits for the 2001 taxation year:

1. Mr. Hanson is single, has Net Income of $40,000 and provides support for his mother. His mother is a widow who lives in England and has an income of $700 per year.

2. Mr. Johnson earns $250,000 per year and was married on December 1, 2001. His wife is an accounting student with a salary of $2,500 per month.

3. Mr. Massey has Net Income of $60,000 and provides full support for his common-law wife and her two children from a previous marriage. The two children are both under ten years of age and neither his wife nor the children have any other source of income.

4. Mr. Jones is married and has Net Income of $70,000. His 19 year old dependent son attends university. His wife has Net Income of $1,200 and his son has Net Income of $2,900.

5. Ms. Morrison is divorced, maintains a residence far from her former spouse, and receives $1,000 per month in child support payments. She has custody of the two children from the marriage. They are aged seven and ten and have no income of their own. Her Net Income is $50,000.

6. Mrs. Olsen's husband died on January 1, 2001. During 2001, semi-annual interest of $16,000 was paid on bonds that he owned when he died. This interest was paid on April 30 and October 31. Interest income had been accrued and reported on his 2000 tax return. The bonds were left to his wife in his will. Mrs. Olsen earned $62,000 in employment income during the year.

7. Mr. Bagley is 68 years old and has Net Income of $26,000 which is comprised of OAS of $5,200 and $20,800 of pension income. His wife is 52 years old and is blind. She has no income of her own.

Required: In each of the preceding independent cases, determine the maximum amount of 2001 personal tax credits, including transfers from a spouse or dependant, that can be applied against federal taxes payable by the taxpayer.

Assignment Problem Thirteen - 2

Mr. and Mrs. Hanson have been retired for several years. They are both in their early seventies, residents of Canada, and rely on pension income to provide for most of their needs. More specifically, the components of their income for the year ending December 31, 2001 are as follows:

	Mr. Hanson	Mrs. Hanson
Old Age Security Pension	$ 5,200	$5,200
RRSP Income	30,000	-0-
Receipts From Registered Pension Plan	15,380	1,330
Dividends Received From Taxable Canadian Companies	800	180
Interest On Government Bonds	500	525
Charitable Donations	600	200
Capital Gain On Sale Of Shares	N/A	375
Capital Loss On Sale Of Shares	N/A	725

Required: Determine the Taxable Income for both Mr. and Mrs. Hanson and the maximum federal tax credits that will be available to Mr. Hanson for the 2001 taxation year.

Assignment Problem Thirteen - 3

Mr. William Norris is 45 years old. The following five independent cases make varying assumptions for the 2001 taxation year with respect to Mr. Norris' marital status, number of dependants, and type of income received. Where employment income is involved, assume his employer has withheld EI premiums of $878 and CPP contributions of $1,496.

Case A Mr. Norris is unmarried and provides in home care for his 73 year old mother, Bernice. Bernice had Net Income of $12,000 for the year. Mr. Norris earned employment income of $46,000.

Case B Mr. Norris earned employment income of $46,000. His wife, Susan, has interest income of $4,410. They have one child, Martha, who is 10 years of age. During the year, the family had medical expenses as follows:

William	$1,200
Susan	1,600
Martha	350
Total	$3,150

Case C Mr. Norris earned employment income of $46,000. His wife, Susan, has employment income of $4,500. They have a son, Allen, who is 19 years old and lives at home. He attends university on a full time basis during 8 months of the year. Mr. Norris pays $4,000 for Allen's tuition and $900 for required textbooks. Allen had employment income during the summer months of $2,200. He will transfer any unused credits to his father.

Case D Mr. Norris is not married and has no dependants. His income is made up of rental income of $42,400, dividends of $3,100 (taxable amount) from a company in which he has a controlling interest, and dividends of $500 (taxable amount) from portfolio investments. On receipt of a $300,000 inheritance in December, he donates $50,000 to his local hospital. In addition, he makes contributions to federal political parties in the amount of $1,000.

Case E Mr. Norris is a single father. He has a daughter, Mary, who is 8 years old and lives with him. Mary had no income for the year. Two years ago, Mr. Norris graduated from a Canadian University. He currently has $12,000 outstanding in Canada Student Loans. Mr. Norris pays back these loans in monthly instalments of $125. During the year, he paid $250 in interest on these loans. Mr. Norris earned employment income of $46,000.

Required: In each Case, calculate Mr. Norris' minimum federal taxes payable. In making this calculation, ignore any tax amounts that Mr. Norris might have had withheld or paid in instalments. Indicate any carry overs available to him.

Assignment Problem Thirteen - 4

Mr. Jack Leonard has asked you to assist him in preparing his 2001 tax return. To this end, he provides you with the following information.

He is married and has one 16 year old son. Mr. Leonard's employer is a large, publicly traded corporation. During 2001, Mr. Leonard received a gross annual salary of $58,000, living accommodation having a fair market value of $1,000 per month, and an award of $2,100 in recognition of outstanding job performance. Awards for performance are paid instead of investing in employee benefits, so there is no pension plan and Mr. Leonard's 2000 Pension Adjustment amount is nil. Assume his 2000 earned income was equal to his 2001 earned income for RRSP purposes.

On August 1, 2001, his employer granted him an option to purchase 100 of its shares at a price of $7 per share. The market price of the shares at that time was $7 per share. On December 1, 2001, the market price of the shares had increased to $16 per share. On that date, Mr. Leonard exercises his option and purchases the 100 shares, filing with his employer the election to defer the employment income inclusion. He is still holding the shares on December 31, 2001.

Mr. Leonard provides the following list of receipts and disbursements:

Receipts	
Director's Fees	$ 1,300
Royalties On Patent Purchased In 1993	23,370
Bond Interest	430

Disbursements	
RRSP Contribution	$3,600
Rent Paid To Employer For Living Accommodation	1,200
Financial Support Of His Aunt	3,100

You ascertain that his aunt is physically infirm, is wholly dependent upon Jack Leonard for support, had income of $3,000 during the year, and lives in Florida for health reasons.

Mr. Leonard provides you with the following information on his disposals of property during the year:

	Proceeds	Cost
Diamond Ring	$1,200	$ 950
Painting	1,100	1,800
Pistol Collection	2,000	1,400

On further enquiry, you learn that Mr. Leonard's wife had income of $2,990 during the year. His son, who lives at home, was employed during 12 weeks of the summer at a golf course as a greens keeper at a salary of $250 per week. In September, he left his employment to commence full time studies at university. Tuition fees paid for the 2001 calendar year amounted to $3,000 and were paid by Mr. Leonard. The son's only other source of income was $700 in interest on bonds received from his father as a birthday gift in 1992. He will transfer any unused credits to his father.

Required: For 2001, compute the following amounts for Mr. Leonard in accordance with the provisions of the *Income Tax Act*. Indicate any available loss carry over amounts and the applicable loss carry over provisions. In making your calculations, ignore CPP and EI contributions.

- A. Employment Income
- B. Income From Property
- C. Taxable Capital Gain Or Allowable Capital Loss
- D. Net Income, Including Other Sources And Deductions
- E. Taxable Income
- F. Federal Tax Payable

Assignment Problem Thirteen - 5

Mr. Dennis Lane has been a widower for several years. For 2001, both his Net and Taxable Income totaled $65,000.

Other Information:

1. Net Income includes dividends received from taxable Canadian corporations in the amount of $1,440 (taxable dividends of $1,800). Net Income also includes $1,100 (Canadian dollars) in dividends from U.S. corporations. He received $935 after the 15 percent U.S. withholding tax.

2. Mr. Lane made political contributions to Federal political parties in the amount of $450.

3. Mr. Lane's employer withheld $12,100 in income taxes, $878 for Employment Insurance premiums and $1,531 in Canada Pension Plan contributions. Because of an error by his employer, an overcontribution of $35 was made for the Canada Pension Plan.

4. Due to an extensive business trip, Mr. Lane did not file his 2001 return until June 1, 2002.

5. Mr. Lane has three children age 10, 12, and 15. They all live with him in his principal residence and, other than his 15 year old son, have no income of their own. Mr. Lane paid no medical expenses other than $4,400 for hospital care for his 15 year old son. His son had 2001 income of $7,700. His son did not use the medical expense credit as he had no taxes payable.

6. Mr. Lane's provincial tax payable, net of all applicable credits, has been correctly calculated to be $4,250.

Required: Calculate Mr. Lane's minimum 2001 federal taxes payable. Include in your solution any penalties and interest that will result from the late filing. Assume that the prescribed interest rate for all relevant periods, including the extra four percent on amounts owing to the Minister, is 9 percent compounded on an annual basis.

Assignment Problem Thirteen - 6

On January 10, 2001, Ms. Marcia Klaus formally separated from her husband and retained custody of her 15 year old son, Martin. Martin has no income during 2001. She is also responsible for her 20 year old daughter Louise who has a severe and prolonged disability (a medical doctor has certified her disability on Form T2201). Louise has 2001 income of $6,000 resulting from income on investments that were left to her by her grandmother.

In order to get a fresh start in life, Ms. Klaus found a new job. She resigned from her position in Ottawa and moved to a similar position in Toronto. The move took place on October 31, 2001. She has asked for your assistance in preparing an estimate of her 2001 personal tax liability and, in order to assist you with your calculations, she has prepared the following list of transactions that occurred during 2001:

1. Her gross salary from her Ottawa employer, a large public company, for the first 10 months was $62,000. Her employer withheld from this amount CPP contributions of $1,496, EI premiums of $878, RPP contributions of $2,500, and income tax of $18,000. The employer also contributed $2,500 to the RPP on her behalf. She was a member of her employer's money purchase RPP during all of her years of employment.

   In appreciation of her 25 years of excellent service, the Ottawa employer paid her a retiring allowance of $30,000.

   Before leaving her Ottawa employer, she exercised stock options to acquire 2,000 of the Company's shares at a price of $15 per share. The options were issued in 1999 when the market price of the shares was $12 per share. On August 12, 2001, the day that she exercised the options, the shares were trading at $20 per share. Ms. Klaus sells the shares as soon as she acquires them. Brokerage fees totalled $350 on the sale.

2. During November and December, her gross wages with her Toronto employer amounted to $13,000. Her new employer withheld CPP contributions of $500, EI premiums of $390, $650 in RPP contributions, and $4,000 in income taxes. Her Toronto employer also contributed $650 to the money purchase RPP on her behalf.

   Ms. Klaus found a new home in Toronto during her September house hunting trip there. The legal arrangements for the house purchase were finalized on October 10. In Ottawa, she and her husband had lived in a home which they rented. Her agreement with her new employer requires that they pay her moving costs. In order to simplify the record keeping, the employer paid her an allowance of $7,500 and did not require a detailed accounting of expenses. Her actual expenses were as follows:

Moving company charges	$3,800
Airfare for September Toronto trip to acquire new home	350
Meals and lodging on September Toronto trip	275
Gas for October 31 move to Toronto	65
Lodging in Ottawa on October 30	110
Meals on October 30 and October 31	85
Charges for cancellation of lease on Ottawa apartment	1,100
Legal and other fees on acquisition of Toronto home	1,500
Total	$7,285

3. In 1998, the mother of Ms. Klaus died, leaving her 5,000 shares of Lintz Industries. These shares had cost her mother $50,000 and had a fair market value at the time of her death of $95,000. Ms. Klaus received dividends of $7,500 on these shares in May and, in December, she sells the shares for $105,000. Selling costs were $1,050.

4. Ms. Klaus made $1,500 in donations to a registered Canadian charity and $900 in contributions to the Libcon Rebloc Party, a registered federal political party.

5. Ms. Klaus incurred the following child care costs:

Payments To Individuals For Martin And Louise	$7,160
Fees For Martin To Attend Camp (4 Weeks At $200 Per Week)	800
Food And Clothing For The Children	6,400
Total	$14,360

6. Ms. Klaus paid the following medical expenses:

For Herself	$ 9,700
Martin	900
Louise	7,250
Total	$17,850

7. In previous years, Ms. Klaus' husband took care of her financial affairs. She has no under-standing of either RPPs or RRSPs but will make the maximum deductible RRSP contribution for 2001 as soon as you have calculated it. Her RRSP Deduction Limit State-ment from the CCRA states that her 2000 Earned Income was $61,100 and that, at the end of 2000, she had no unused RRSP Deduction Room. Her 2000 T4 from her employer indi-cates a pension adjustment of $4,500. There are no undeducted contributions in her RRSP.

8. During the year, Ms. Klaus paid legal fees of $2,500 in connection with her separation agreement. This settlement requires her husband to make a lump sum payment of $25,000 on March 1, 2001, as well as child support payments of $4,000 at the end of each month beginning on January 31, 2001. All required payments were received for the year.

9. In addition to her employment income, Ms. Klaus operates an unincorporated mail order business with a December 31 year end. Her husband has dealt with the records of this business in the past. However, he is no longer willing to handle this responsibility. She knows that net cash receipts for the year ending December 31, 2001 totaled $22,000. All sales are for cash and she does not maintain an office in her home. However, she must purchase inventories in advance and on account. Her husband has indicated that on Jan-uary 1, 2001 she had inventories that cost $8,000 and owed suppliers a total of $6,000. She has determined that on December 31, 2001, she has inventories with a cost of $7,000 and owes suppliers a total of $4,500. During the year ending December 31, 2001, Ms. Klaus withdraws $27,000 from the bank account maintained by the business.

10. Assume that the Ontario provincial tax payable, net of all provincial credits, has been cor-rectly calculated to be $6,250.

Required: Calculate Ms. Klaus' minimum Net Income, minimum Taxable Income, and mini-mum Taxes Payable for 2001. In the minimum Net Income calculation, provide separate dis-closure of:

- Net Employment Income,
- Net Income From Business Or Property,
- Taxable Capital Gains less Allowable Capital Losses,
- Other Sources Of Income, and
- Other Deductions From Income.

Ignore all GST and PST considerations. Explain why you omitted any amounts from your cal-culations.

Assignment Problem Thirteen - 7
On June 3, 2001, Mrs. Steele unexpectedly died of complications associated with minor sur-gery. Her husband, a man with little experience in financial matters, has asked you to assist him with the administration of Mrs. Steele's estate. After working with her records for several days, you have accumulated the following information:

1. Mrs. Steele's tax return for the year ending December 31, 2000 indicated a net capital loss of $76,500 from a disposition that occurred in 1996.

2. Prior to the date of her death, Mrs. Steele's investments paid 2001 cash dividends in the amount of $1,090. In addition, she had Canadian source interest income of $2,025 dur-ing this period.

3. Mrs. Steele's office desk contained a number of uncashed bond coupons which were dated for payment in 2000. The total amount was $3,270 and none of this amount had been included in her 2000 tax return.

4. Mrs. Steele was the proprietor of a successful boutique which had been in operation for eight years. The fiscal year of this unincorporated business ends on December 31. From January 1, 2001 until the date of Mrs. Steele's death, the income of this business totalled $55,200. The fair market value of the assets of the boutique at the time of Mrs. Steele's

death was $4,800 greater than their UCC.

5. In connection with the boutique, Mrs. Steele paid Mr. Steele wages of $425 during the period January 1, 2001 through June 3, 2001. This money was paid for assistance in handling the inventories of the operation. Mr. Steele's only other income for the year was $2,100 in interest on a group of mortgages that had been given to him as a gift by Mrs. Steele three years ago.

6. Mrs. Steele had a rental property which she had owned for a number of years. Rents received in 2001 prior to her death amount to $41,200 while cash expenses totalled $24,650. The undepreciated capital cost of the building was $144,800 on January 1, 2001. The building had been purchased for $183,000. At the time of her death, an appraisal indicated that the fair market value of the building was $235,000. The land on which the building is situated has a cost of $92,000, and a fair market value at the time of her death which is estimated to be $164,000.

7. Other assets which were owned by Mrs. Steele at the time of her death are as follows:

Shares In AGF Industries   AGF Industries is a Canadian public company and Mrs. Steele purchased common shares at a cost of $10,600. Their value at the time of Mrs. Steele's death was $7,900.

Shares In Rolston Inc.   Rolston Inc. is also a Canadian public company and Mrs. Steele purchased shares at a cost of $36,800. Their value at the time of Mrs. Steele's death was $169,400.

Painting   The painting Mrs. Steele had purchased for $8,000 had a fair market value at the time of her death of $37,000.

Residence   Mrs. Steele owned the family home. It had been purchased at a cost of $109,400. At the time of her death the appraised value of the property was $144,000.

8. The terms of Mrs. Steele's will provide that the shares in AGF Industries and Rolston Inc., the painting and the assets of the boutique be left to Mr. Steele. The family home and the rental property are to be left to Mrs. Steele's 27 year old daughter.

Required: Calculate Mrs. Steele's minimum 2001 federal taxes payable for the year of her death.

Assignment Problem Thirteen - 8

Wanda Lanson, an established tax professional, has provided tax assistance on a regular basis to her two brothers, Wally and Wesley Lanson. For the 2001 taxation year they are both concerned about the impact of the Alternative Minimum Tax on the amount of taxes they will have to pay. In order to help them prepare for any additional tax payments that they encounter, she has asked them to estimate the amount of various types of income and deductions they expect to record for 2001. These estimates, along with the similar figures for herself, are as follows:

	Wanda	Wally	Wesley
Employment And Business Income	$39,500	$32,800	$ 18,250
Dividends Received			
From Taxable Canadian Corporations	60,500	-0-	62,000
Taxable Capital Gains	24,500	-0-	267,750
Retiring Allowance	-0-	50,000	-0-
RRSP Contributions	-0-	50,000	-0-
Lifetime Capital Gains Deduction Claimed	24,500	-0-	250,000

As Wally had worked for his present employer for over 40 years, he was eligible for a tax free rollover of the entire retiring allowance to an RRSP. All disposals resulting in taxable capital gains were of shares of qualified small business corporations.

None of the Lansons have ever married, they have no dependants, they are under 65 years of age, and they are not disabled.

Required: Calculate the regular 2001 federal Tax Payable for each of the three Lansons, as well as the federal alternative minimum tax amount. Ignore EI and CPP contributions in your calculations.

Assignment Problem Thirteen - 9 (Electronic Library Research Problem)

Provide brief answers to the following questions. Your answers should be supported by references to materials found in your Electronic Library.

A. When an individual makes a donation of Canadian cultural property, he may incur significant appraisal costs in establishing a fair market value for the gift. How should these costs be dealt with for tax purposes?

B. Individuals sometimes contribute services to a registered charity and, in many cases, the services have a significant market value. Is it ever possible for the charity to issue an official donation receipt which reflects the fair market value of these services?

C. The education tax credit is available to students enrolled in a "qualifying education program". Would an individual be eligible for this credit if his employer required him to take an appropriate program as part of his employment duties? Would an individual be eligible for this credit if he was taking an appropriate program during a leave of absence that was financed by his employer? Would an individual be eligible for this credit if he was taking an appropriate program and has received financing from a business that is conditional on his becoming an employee of that business on completion of his studies?

D. For purposes of the medical expense tax credit, ITA 118.2(2) refer to amounts paid to "medical practitioners".   Which of the following would qualify for this designation:

   1. A chiropractor
   2. A naturopath
   3. A massage therapist
   4. An acupuncturist
   5. A faith healer
   6. A dietician
   7. A Christian Science practitioner
   8. A psychologist

Cases - Using ProFile T1 Software For 2000 Tax Returns

Case Thirteen - 1 (Using ProFile T1 Software For 2000 Tax Returns)

Mr. Buddy Cole (SIN 527-000-061) was born on August 28, 1933. He has spent most of his working life as a pianist and song writer. He and his family live at 1166 West Pender Street, Vancouver, B.C. V6E 3H8, phone (604) 669-7815. His income during 2000 consisted of:

Employment Income   Mr. Cole earned $16,500 for work as the house pianist at the Loose Moose Pub. His T4 showed that his employer withheld $4,200 for income taxes and $436 for EI. Due to an error on the part of the payroll accountant, he overpaid his EI by $40. No CPP was withheld as he is receiving CPP benefits.

OAS And CPP Receipts   Mr. Cole receives $5,040 in Old Age Security payments and $5,500 in Canada Pension Plan payments. There was no tax shown as withheld on his T4A(OAS) or his T4A(P).

Royalty Payments   Several of Mr. Cole's songs, including his outstanding hit, "Drop Kick Me Jesus Through The Goal Posts Of Life", are still providing him with royalty payments. He received $78,000 in royalty payments from the Never Say Die Record Company. No withholdings were shown on the T5.

RRSP Payments   Mr. Cole received $52,000 in payments from a life annuity purchased with funds accumulated in his RRSP. His T4RSP showed that total tax of $28,000 was deducted from these payments.

Other Information:

1. Mr. Cole's wife Natasha (SIN 527-000-129) was born on June 6, 1975 and was a professional singer prior to her marriage to Mr. Cole. She still enjoys singing and gave a few weekend performances during 2000 at the Loose Moose Pub. She earned $3,200 for these performances. She and Mr. Cole have four children. Each child was born on April 1 in the following years, Linda; 1995, Larry; 1996, Donna; 1997, and Donald; 1998. She has never filed a tax return before and does not plan on filing one this year.

2. Buddy and Natasha Cole have two adopted children. Richard (SIN 527-000-285) was born on March 15, 1983, has income of $2,800, and started full time attendance at university in September of 2000. His first semester tuition fee is $2,000 and he requires books with a total cost of $375. These amounts are paid by Mr. Cole. The other adopted child, Sarah, was born on September 2, 1980 and is in full time attendance at university for all of 2000 (including a four month summer session). Her tuition is $5,600 and she requires textbooks which cost $750. These amounts are also paid by Mr. Cole. Sarah has no income during the year. Any unused credits of either child will be transferred to their father.

3. Mr. Cole's mother, Eunice was born on April 10, 1913 and his father, Earl was born on November 16, 1911. They both live with Mr. Cole and his wife. While his father is still physically active, his mother is blind. Eunice Cole had income of $7,500 for the year, while Earl Cole had income of $5,500.

4. Mr. Cole has been married before and is required by a court order to pay spousal support of $400 per month to his former spouse, Lori Cole (SIN 527-000-319). Lori is 52 years old and lives in Fort Erie, Ontario. Mr. Cole made spousal support payments of $4,800 during 2000.

5. Mr. Cole has two additional children who live with their mother, Ms. Dolly Holt (SIN 527-000-582), in Burnaby, British Columbia. The children are age 15 and 16 and, while Ms. Holt and Mr. Cole were never married, Mr. Cole acknowledges that he is the father of both children. As a consequence, he is required by a 1994 court order to make child support payments of $350 per month. A total of $4,200 was paid during 2000.

6. During 2000, Mr. Cole made $3,000 in donations to Planned Parenthood Of Canada, a registered Canadian charity.

7. On December 2, 2000, Mr. Cole paid dental expenses to Canada Wide Dental Clinics for the following individuals:

Himself	$1,200
His Wife, Natasha	700
His Son, Richard	800
His Daughter, Sarah	300
His Daughter, Linda	100
His Father	1,050
His Former Wife, Lori	300
Ms. Dolly Holt	675
The Children Of Ms. Holt And Himself	550
Total	$5,675

8. Mr. Cole makes 2000 contributions to the Federal Liberal party in the amount of $610.

9. As Mr. Cole had large business losses in the previous two years, he paid quarterly instalments totalling only $4,000 for 2000 as requested on his Instalment Reminders from the CCRA.

Required: Prepare Mr. Cole's 2000 income tax return using the GreenPoint ProFile software program.

Case Thirteen - 2 *(Using ProFile T1 Software For 2000 Tax Returns)*

Ms. Eleanor Trubey's husband died two years ago. In addition to her employment income she receives a pension from his previous employer and CPP survivor benefits. After her husband died, she moved from her house in Prince George, B.C. to a rented house in Victoria, B.C. She did not sell her house as it is her intention to move back into it within a year. It is currently rented on a month to month lease.

Ms. Trubey's widowed mother, Marjorie Takarabe, had extremely bad luck last year in a visit to Las Vegas. She lost all of her life savings and her house. As a result, she has moved in with Ms. Trubey and takes care of the house, Ms. Trubey's daughter, Amy and all of the cooking.

Diane Trubey, her daughter, is studying psychology at McGill University in Montreal. Her field is addiction research with a special emphasis on gambling. She does volunteer work at a gambling addiction treatment centre in Montreal in the summers. As Eleanor has paid for her tuition and living costs, Diane has agreed that any credits available should be transferred to her mother.

Diane has decided not to file a tax return this year as she is too busy with her studies and volunteer work. Her income was earned driving for a client of the addiction treatment centre who had lost his licence after being charged with impaired driving.

Information concerning Ms. Trubey for 2000 is given on the following pages.

Required: Prepare the 2000 income tax return of Eleanor Trubey using the GreenPoint Pro-File software. List any assumptions you have made and any notes and tax planning issues you feel should be placed in the file.

Personal Information	
Title	Ms.
First Name	Eleanor
Last Name	Trubey
SIN	527-000-087
Date of birth (Y/M/D)	1952-05-15
Marital Status	Widowed
Provide information to Elections Canada?	Yes
Own foreign property of more than $100,000 Canadian?	No
Instalments paid for the year	$7,528

Taxpayer's Address
1415 Vancouver St., Victoria, B.C. V8V 3W4
Phone number (250) 363-0120

Dependants	Child 1	Child 2	Mother
First Name	Diane	Amy	Marjorie
Last Name	Trubey	Trubey	Takarabe
SIN	527-000-293		
Date of birth (Y/M/D)	1980-05-14	1988-10-11	1920-05-21
Net income	$2,300	Nil	$5,079.51

T3	Box	Amount
Issuer - Global Strategy Financial		
Foreign country - United States		
Capital gains - first period	21	198.60
Capital gains - second period	21	625.28
Capital gains - third period	21	158.34
Foreign non business income	25	310.94

T4	Box	Amount
Issuer - 1750 Canada Inc.		
Employment income	14	60,201.80
Employee's CPP contributions	16	1,329.90
Employee's EI premiums	18	936.00
RPP contributions	20	2,406.16
Pension adjustment	52	7,829.00
Income tax deducted	22	19,408.00
Union dues	44	748.59
Charitable donations	46	200.00

T4A	Box	Amount
Issuer - 3601 Canada Inc.		
Pension	16	22,249.44
Income tax deducted	22	3,510.78

T4A(P)	Box	Amount
Survivor benefit	14	4,823.28
Income tax deducted	22	Nil

T5	Box	Slip 1	Slip 2
Issuer		Scotia Bank	Bank of Montreal
Actual amount of dividends	10		1,859.32
Taxable amount of dividends	11		2,324.15
Interest from Canadian sources	13	509.45	

T2202	Box	Amount
Tuition fees - for Diane Trubey (daughter)	A	4,414.56
Number of months in school - part-time	B	2
Number of months in school - full-time	C	8

RRSP information	(Y/M/D)	Amount
Issuer of receipt - Scotia Bank	2001-02-10	2,620.00
Contributions made prior to 2001/03/02 and not deducted	2000-01-25	1,665.51
Unused deduction room at the end of 1999		Nil
Earned income for 1999		38,873.00
Pension adjustment for 1999		4,376.00

Patient	(Y/M/D)	Medical Expenses	Description	Am't
Amy	2000-05-11	Walk Right Foot Clinic	Orthodics	450
Marjorie	2000-01-23	Dr. Tamo	Dental	1,120
Marjorie	2000-05-20	Dr. Zhang	Acupuncture	50
Marjorie	2000-07-06	Pharmacy	Prescription	75
Diane	2000-09-01	Dr. Glassman	Physiotherapist	100
Eleanor	2000-08-15	Grace Hospital	Ambulance charge	392
Eleanor	2000-08-18	Paramed Home Health	Nursing care	1,350

Donor	Charitable Donation Receipts	Am't
Eleanor	Heart and Stroke	300
Eleanor	Terry Fox Foundation	50
Diane	Addiction Research Council of Canada	100

Child	Child Care Expenses (Organization or Name and SIN)	No. of weeks	Amount
Amy	Croft Computer Camp (14 days overnight)	2	1,000
Amy	F.I.S. Ski Camp (8 Saturdays)		400

Real Estate Rental	Amount
Address - 280 Victoria St., Prince George, B.C. V2L 4X3	
Gross rents	15,600.00
Property taxes	2,190.73
Insurance	1,093.27
Interest on mortgage	5,377.58
Payment on principal	3,688.95
Plumbing repairs	290.94
Snow plow annual contract	300.00
Lawyer's fees for new lease	172.54
Hydro (during vacancy)	288.34
UCC of building - beginning of year	168,900.00
UCC of appliances - beginning of year	421.00
Purchase of stove and refrigerator during year (old appliances were traded-in)	1,500.00

Case Thirteen - 3 (Using ProFile T1 Software For 2000 Tax Returns)

Seymour Gravel and Mary Walford have been married for more than 10 years. Seymour does business writing and editing on a contract basis for six different clients under the business name Crystal Clear Communications. He operates this business out of his home. To help him deal with his son who has been refusing to go to school and is displaying hostile tendencies, he enrolled in a three month course on child psychology at Dalhousie University.

Mary had been working with him in the business until three years ago when she was hired by one of their clients as an employee. Due to her writing skills and strong accounting background she has progressed quickly in the firm and has been rewarded with large bonuses each year.

Mary has invested a portion of her bonuses in the stock market and has done well. She plans to continue investing in growth stocks. The securities dispositions for the year are from her stock portfolio.

Mary's parents have established an RESP for William, their grandson, and are the sole contributors. They have contributed $300 per year since his birth in lieu of Christmas and birthday presents.

Information concerning Seymour and Mary for 2000 is given on the following pages.

Required: Prepare the 2000 income tax returns of Seymour Gravel and Mary Walford using the GreenPoint ProFile software. List any assumptions you have made and any notes and tax planning issues you feel should be placed in the files.

Personal Information	Taxpayer	Spouse
Title	Mr.	Ms.
First Name	Seymour	Mary
Last Name	Gravel	Walford
SIN	527-000-079	527-000-129
Date of birth (Y/M/D)	1941-01-29	1962-12-08
Marital Status	Married	Married
Provide information to Elections Canada?	Yes	Yes
Own foreign property of more than $100,000 Cdn?	No	No
Instalments paid for the year	$2,748	Nil

Taxpayer's Address
126 Prince William Street, Saint John, N.B.   E2L 4H9
Phone number (506) 636-5997
Spouse's address same as taxpayer? Yes

Dependants	Child
First Name	William
Last Name	Gravel
SIN	527-000-319
Date of birth (Y/M/D)	1993-02-24
Net income	Nil

T4 - Mary	Box	Amount
Issuer - 3600 Canada Inc.		
Employment income	14	152,866.08
Employee's CPP contributions	16	1,359.90
Employee's EI premiums	18	936.00
RPP contributions	20	Nil
Income tax deducted	22	52,265.11
Charitable donations	46	1,000.00

T4A - Seymour	Box	Amount
Issuer - 3065 Canada Inc.		
Contract payment	28	20,000.00
Income tax deducted	22	Nil

Securities Dispositions	Security 1	Security 2	Security 3
Description (All owned by Mary)	Fidelity Small Cap Fund	Mosaid Technologies	Mosaid Technologies
Number of units	258.92	800	600
Year of acquisition	1995	1998	1998
Date of disposition	2000-02-17	2000-01-06	2000-03-14
Proceeds of disposition	5,300.00	11,845.80	13,489.44
Adjusted cost base	2,892.31	3,973.44	2,980.08
Outlays and expenses	Nil	29.00	29.00

T2202 - Seymour	Box	Amount
Tuition fees	A	2,200
Number of months in school - part-time	B	0
Number of months in school - full-time	C	3

RRSP information - Mary	(Y/M/D)	Amount
Issuer of receipt - Royal Bank Action Direct	2000-12-10	5,400
Issuer of receipt - Royal Bank Action Direct	2001-02-28	16,800
Contributions made prior to 2001/03/02 and not deducted		Nil
Unused deduction room at the end of 1999		19,762
Earned income for 1999		80,000

RRSP information - Seymour	(Y/M/D)	Amount
Issuer of receipt - Royal Bank Action Direct	2001-02-28	4,000
Contributions made prior to 2001/03/02 and not deducted		Nil
Unused deduction room at the end of 1999		14,091
Earned income for 1999		47,068

Donor	Charitable Donation Receipts	Amount
Seymour	Canadian Cancer Foundation	500
Seymour	Salvation Army	250

Child	Child Care Expenses (Organization or Name and SIN)	No. of weeks	Amount
William	Gaye Normandin SIN 527-000-392		3,100
	(after school and summer)		
William	Da Vinci Institute - private tutoring @ $25/hour		2,750

Business or Professional Income - Seymour	
Revenues without T4A	41,603.17
T4A's issued (see T4A information)	20,000.00
Membership dues - Business Writers Association	231.00
Business Insurance	126.16
Interest on demand loan	527.27
Interest on late payment of 1999 income tax	233.72
Interest on insufficient tax instalments for 1999	52.81
Interest on late GST payments	204.24
Penalty for late filing of 1999 tax return	303.92
Bank service charges	156.20
Cell phone air time	485.27
Postage and courier charges	110.00
Office supplies	2,982.17
Separate business phone line charge and long distance charges	577.86
Fees for accounting and tax advice	500.00
Air fare (business travel)	526.97
Hotels (business travel)	1,240.91
Meals when traveling on business	607.14
Meals and drinks when entertaining clients	887.12
UCC of furniture- beginning of year	2,254.94
UCC of software - beginning of year	219.15
UCC of computer hardware - beginning of year	1,101.58
Software purchased during year	525.00
Laptop computer purchased during year	2,048.00

Car Costs - Seymour	
Description - Subaru, cost = $35,000, bought 1997-02-15	
January 1 odometer	89,726
December 31 odometer	124,701
Business km driven	8,412
Parking	321.71
Gas	582.12
Maintenance and repairs	458.63
Insurance	779.00
Licence and registration fees	49.87
Interest on car loan	597.89
UCC of Class 10.1 - beginning of year	15,470.00

House Costs	
Area of home used for business (square feet)	160
Total area of home (square feet)	1,500
Gas for heating	1,712.86
Hydro	1,641.18
Insurance - house	757.55
Snow plowing contract	450.00
Installation of new gas furnace	3,675.00
Painting of kitchen and dining room	548.05
Mortgage interest	8,456.22
Mortgage life insurance premiums	375.00
Mortgage principal paid	1,279.58
Property taxes	1,533.01
Interest on late property taxes	122.52

Chapter 14

Taxable Income And Taxes Payable For Corporations

Computation Of Net Income

14-1.   The day to day records of most corporations are kept in terms of accounting procedures and policies that are normally designated as generally accepted accounting principles (GAAP). As noted in Chapter 7 on business income, many of the rules for computing business income under Division B of the *Income Tax Act* are identical to those under generally accepted accounting principles. However, there are a number of differences that are specifically provided for and, as a result, the first step in the computation of Taxable Income for a corporation is to convert accounting Net Income as determined under generally accepted accounting principles into Net Income For Tax Purposes. Only then can we move from Division B's Net Income For Tax Purposes to Division C's Taxable Income.

14-2.   In making this conversion, there are many adjustments that could be required in particular circumstances. Some adjustments are necessary because of different allocation patterns that result in timing differences between accounting and tax income. Examples of this would be differences between amortization and CCA as well as alternative approaches to the determination of pension cost deductions. Other adjustments involve permanent differences between accounting and tax amounts. An example of this type of difference would be the non taxable one-half of capital gains. As was noted in Chapter 7, a reconciliation between accounting Net Income and Net Income For Tax Purposes is a required part of the corporate tax return. The form that the CCRA provides for this reconciliation is designated Schedule 1. The most common adjustments from this Schedule are listed in Figure 14-1 (following page).

14-3.   Chapter 7 on business income provided a detailed discussion of the conversion of GAAP Net Income into Net Income For Tax Purposes. As that discussion was equally applicable to corporations and unincorporated businesses, it will not be repeated here. However, if it has been some time since you covered the material in Chapter 7, we suggest that you review it before proceeding with these Chapters on corporate taxation.

Figure 14 - 1
Conversion Of Accounting Net Income To Net Income For Tax Purposes

Accounting Net Income (Loss)

Plus:
- Provision for income tax (including current, future and large corporations tax)
- Interest and penalties on federal income taxes
- Amortization, depreciation and depletion (Accounting amounts)
- Recapture of capital cost allowance
- Gains resulting from the sale of eligible capital property
- Losses on the disposal of capital assets (Accounting amounts)
- Charitable donations
- Excess of taxable capital gains over allowable capital losses
- Political donations
- Scientific research expenditures (Accounting amounts)
- Club dues and fees
- Fifty percent of business meals and entertainment
- Non deductible automobile costs
- Tax deductible reserves from previous year
- Non deductible reserves at end of current year (Accounting amounts)
- Foreign taxes withheld on foreign business and non business income

Less:
- Gains on the disposal of capital assets (Accounting amounts)
- Dividends not taxable under ITA 83 (Capital dividends)
- Capital cost allowances and CEC deductions
- Terminal losses
- Allowable business investment losses
- Scientific research expenditures (Deductible amounts)
- Tax deductible reserves for the current year
- Non deductible reserves at beginning of current year (Accounting amounts)
- Landscaping costs

Equals Net Income (Loss) For Tax Purposes

Exercise Fourteen-1 deals with the Schedule 1 reconciliation. This would be an appropriate time to attempt this exercise.

Computation of Taxable Income

Deductions Available To Corporations

14-4.   The reconciliation schedule illustrated in Figure 14-1 is used to establish a corporation's Net Income For Tax Purposes. When this task is completed, certain specified items are deducted from the resulting Net Income figure in order to arrive at Taxable Income. These deductions are specified in Division C of the *Income Tax Act* and the relevant items for individuals were given detailed coverage in Chapter 12. However, there are significant differences in the Division C deductions available to individuals and those available to corporations.

14-5.   With respect to the Division C items that are available to individuals, the following are not available to corporations:

- Lifetime capital gains deduction
- Employee stock option deduction
- Home relocation loan deduction
- Northern residents deduction
- Social assistance and workers' compensation benefits deduction

14-6.   A further significant difference relates to two items that, with respect to individuals, serve as a base for credits against taxes payable. While these items are not available as a base for credits against corporate taxes payable, they are available as deductions in the calculation of corporate taxes payable. These items are:

Charitable Donations   Unlike the situation for individuals where charitable donations are the basis for a tax credit, corporations deduct charitable donations from Net Income For Tax Purposes in the determination of Taxable Income. While corporations have a deduction rather than a tax credit, the rules for determining which donations can be deducted by a corporation are essentially the same as the rules for determining which donations qualify for the tax credit for individuals. Further, corporations are subject to the same 75 percent of Net Income limit that applies with respect to individuals. The five year carry forward provision is also available to corporations. These matters were covered in Chapter 13 and will not be repeated here.

Dividends   As noted in previous Chapters, individuals must gross up dividends received by 25 percent. This is accompanied by a dividend tax credit equal to two-thirds of the gross up at the federal level. There is no corresponding gross up or tax credit with respect to dividends received by a corporation. However, a corporation is permitted to deduct the full amount of such dividends in the calculation of Taxable Income. Note that, while this deduction removes dividends from Taxable Income and the Taxes Payable calculation, they must be included in Net Income For Tax Purposes.

14-7.   In addition to the two preceding deductions, corporations are allowed to deduct loss carry overs from previous or subsequent years in the calculation of Taxable Income. Other than in situations where a corporation has been the subject of an acquisition of control, the rules related to the deduction of corporate loss carry overs are basically the same as those applicable to individuals. These general rules were covered in Chapter 12 and that coverage will not be repeated here. Note, however, that this Chapter will contain coverage of the special rules that apply to loss carry-overs subsequent to an acquisition of control.

> Exercise Fourteen-2 deals with taxable income. This would be an appropriate time to attempt this exercise.

14-8.   The calculation of corporate Taxable Income is outlined in Figure 14-2.

Figure 14 - 2
Conversion Of Corporate Net Income To Taxable Income

Net Income (Loss) For Tax Purposes

Less:
- Charitable donations (Limited to 75 percent of net income with a five year carry forward of unused amounts)
- Loss carry overs from subsequent or prior taxation years
- Dividends received from taxable Canadian corporations

Equals Taxable Income (Loss)

Dividends From Other Corporations
Deduction From Taxable Income

14-9.   In the calculation of Taxable Income, ITA 112(1) permits a corporation to deduct from Net Income, dividends that are received from taxable Canadian corporations. The reason for this deduction is fairly obvious. If taxes were levied on transfers of dividends between companies, it could result in taxes being repeatedly assessed on the same diminishing stream of income. That is, the paying corporation would be taxed on the income that provided the dividend and if, in addition, the receiving corporation had to include the amount received in its taxable income, double taxation of the same income would result.

Example   Mr. X owns 100 percent of the shares of Company X, and Company X owns 100 percent of the common shares of Company Y. Both Company X and Company Y are subject to a combined federal/provincial tax rate of 40 percent. Mr. X is subject to a combined federal/provincial tax rate on dividends of 34 percent (this is approximately the average various combined rates that would be applicable in the ten provinces). Both Companies pay out all of their after tax income as dividends.

Tax Consequences   A comparison of the after tax flow through, without the intercompany dividend deduction and with the intercompany dividend deduction, would be as follows:

	No Deduction	Deduction
Company Y Income	$1,000	$1,000
Corporate Taxes At 40 Percent	(400)	(400)
Dividends To Company X	$ 600	$ 600
Corporate Taxes At 40 Percent	(240)	Nil
Dividends To Mr. X	$ 360	$ 600
Individual Taxes At 34 Percent	(122)	(204)
After Tax Retention	$ 238	$ 396

14-10.   Without the deduction, the after tax retention is only $238. This means that the total tax rate on the $1,000 of income earned by Company Y is an almost confiscatory 76.2 percent. While the application of the dividend deduction provides a more reasonable level of taxation, you should note that the combined corporate and personal tax on the $1,000 income stream is $604 ($400 + $204). This heavy level of taxation reflects the fact that, with a corporate tax rate of 40 percent, flowing income through a corporation can result in the payment of higher taxes than would be the case with the direct receipt of income. This point will be discussed more fully in the following Chapter which provides detailed coverage of the concept of integration.

Dividends From Untaxed Income
14-11.   While the preceding justifications for not taxing intercorporate dividends make sense in the majority of situations, problems can arise. One problem involves situations in which the corporation paying the dividend was not taxed on the funds prior to their distribution. Given the fact that, for most companies, accounting income is higher than taxable income, it would not be surprising to find cases where there is sufficient accounting income to warrant a dividend payment combined with a tax loss for the period.

14-12.   In this case, there will be no taxation of the original income at the corporate level. This means that only personal taxes will be paid on the income stream and, as a consequence, the use of a corporation will result in a significantly lower level of taxation than would be the case if the income were received directly by the individual. In addition, because no tax will be assessed until the income is paid out in dividends, this situation may result in a significant deferral of the taxation that is applicable to the income stream.

Term Preferred Shares
14-13.   A further problem arises when corporations attempt to achieve what is sometimes referred to as "after tax financing". Because of the favourable tax treatment given to both individual and corporate recipients of dividend income, rates that corporations will have to pay on preferred shares will generally be somewhat lower than rates paid on debt securities. For most corporations, debt securities will continue to remain attractive because the tax deductibility of interest payments provides a lower after tax cost of funds than would be the case with the use of preferred shares. However, this is not the case when the corporation is in a loss position and, as a consequence, such companies have often used preferred shares.

14-14.   To make these preferred shares more attractive to investors, issuers add features such as redemption provisions. These features produce a preferred share that has most of the characteristics of debt. In fact, Section 3860 of the *CICA Handbook* may require that such preferred shares be treated as debt for accounting purposes. Despite many debt like features, the payments made on such preferred shares are, for tax purposes, dividend income. As previously discussed, this type of income is taxed very favourably in the hands of individual investors and is not taxed at all in the hands of corporate investors.

14-15.   The lost tax revenues on this type of security could be very high. To prevent this loss, Part IV.1 and Part VI.1 taxes alter the tax treatment of dividends on term preferred shares. However, these provisions go beyond the scope of this book.

Dividends On Shares Sold For Loss (Stop Loss Rules)

14-16.   As the declaration and payment of dividends by a corporation reduces the corporation's net assets, it would be expected that the value of the shares would fall by approximately the amount of any dividend declared and paid. Given this, it would be possible for one corporation to acquire an influential interest in another corporation and have the acquired corporation pay a large dividend which would be non taxable to the recipient corporation. If the value of the acquired company's shares declined by a proportional amount, the acquiring company could then sell the shares to create a deductible loss. To illustrate this point, consider the following example:

> **Example**   On June 30, 2001, Brian Company acquires 1,000 shares of Leader Company at a cost of $20 per share. On July 1, 2001, the Leader Company declares and pays its regular $3 per share dividend. Because this dividend had been anticipated by the market, the price of the Leader Company stock falls $3 per share to $17 dollars. On July 15, 2001, Brian Company sells all of its Leader Company shares at a price of $17 per share.

14-17.   In the absence of a special rule, the preceding situation would provide very favourable results for Brian Company. They would have received $3,000 in dividends which, because of the deduction for intercorporate dividends, would not be included in their taxable income. In addition, they would have a potentially deductible capital loss of $3,000 on the disposition of the shares.

14-18.   To prevent this from happening, ITA 112(3) and (4) contain a "stop loss" rule applicable to shares held as either capital or non capital property. Under these rules, any capital or non capital loss resulting from a disposition of shares by a corporation must be reduced by the amount of dividends received that are eligible for deduction under ITA 112(1). The rules are applicable unless:

- the corporation owned the shares for more than 365 days prior to the disposition date, and
- the corporation and persons with whom the corporation was not dealing at arm's length, did not, at the time the dividend was received, own more than 5 percent of the outstanding shares of any class of stock of the corporation paying the dividend.

14-19.   In the preceding example Brian Company had owned the Leader Company shares for less than 365 days prior to the disposition. As a consequence, the $3,000 capital loss would be eliminated by the $3,000 non taxable dividend received.

> Exercise Fourteen-3 deals with stop loss rules. This would be an appropriate time to attempt this exercise.

Foreign Source Dividends Received

14-20.   The situation for dividends received from non resident corporations is more complex. The general rules were discussed in Chapter 11 which noted that foreign source dividends are included in income on a gross basis, before the deduction of any foreign taxes withheld. However, in Chapter 13 we introduced the foreign non business tax credit provisions. These credits against Canadian federal tax payable are designed to compensate the recipient of foreign source non business income for foreign taxes withheld at source, provided the income has been subject to a reasonable amount of Canadian taxation. You will recall that, in most situations, the credit against Canadian taxes payable will be equal to the amount of foreign taxes withheld at source.

Loss Carry Overs And Acquisition Of Control

Economic Background

14-21.   Over a period of years, some corporations may experience sufficiently large losses that they have no hope of recovering their economic health. While they may have accumulated large amounts of capital or non capital loss carry forwards, they have no real prospect of being able to use these amounts. Such companies become attractive takeover targets for profitable corporations that are in a position to structure their affairs in a manner that will make use of the tax benefits associated with these losses.

14-22.   This situation is of concern to the government in that there are billions of dollars of such benefits available in the economy at any point in time. As of 1995, it is estimated that accumulated loss carry forwards amount to $108 billion, an enormous increase from the $40 billion estimate for 1985. The 1995 figure represents 2.5 times the aggregate income of Canadian corporations for that year (David Perry, *Canadian Tax Highlights*, April 22, 1997). If access to these benefits were relatively trouble free, the cost to the government could be enormous. As a consequence, the government has enacted increasingly restrictive legislation with respect to the use of loss carry overs in situations where there has been an acquisition of control.

Acquisition Of Control

14-23.   IT-302R3, which deals with restrictions on loss carry overs, indicates that control has the usual meaning in this context. That is, ownership of a majority of the company's voting shares. In many instances, an acquisition of control also involves a change in control and this explains why the rules restricting the use of loss carry overs are sometimes referred to as the "change in control" rules. This designation is not, however, appropriate in all situations. For example, if ownership of a corporation's voting shares by investors A, B, and C was changed from 70 percent, 15 percent, and 15 percent, respectively, to 40 percent, 30 percent, and 30 percent, there would be a change in control. However, as no one investor is in control after this change, there has been no acquisition of control and the rules restricting loss carry overs would not be applicable.

Deemed Year End

14-24.   At one point in time, losses could be used without restriction prior to the end of the first taxation year ending after the acquisition of control took place. To prevent this, ITA 249(4) requires that, when there is an acquisition of control, the corporation is deemed to have an immediate year end.

14-25.   If the acquisition of control is prior to the corporation's normal year end, this will create a short fiscal period. For example, if the corporation's normal year end was December 31 and the acquisition of control took place on January 31, 2001, the deemed year end would create a year with only one month (January 1 through January 31, 2001). Further, if the corporation retains its old year end after the acquisition of control, there will be a second short year which runs from February 1, 2001 through December 31, 2001. Note, however, ITA 249(4) allows the corporation to change its year end when there is an acquisition of control. This means that the corporation could have extended its first year after the acquisition of control to January 31, 2002.

14-26.   The extra year end is of importance in that the non capital losses which may be available after the acquisition of control are time limited. In our example, the deemed year end creates, in effect, an extra year end which shortens the period during which available losses can be used. Other implications of such short fiscal periods include the need to base CCA calculations on a fraction of the year, as well as a need to pro rate the $200,000 annual business limit for the small business deduction (the annual business limit will be discussed in a later section of this Chapter).

Restrictions On Losses

14-27.   The acquisition of control rules apply to any losses that have not been deducted at the deemed year end. This would include losses that have been carried forward from prior years, as well as any additional losses which accrue in the taxation year that is created by the deemed year end. As will be explained later, the losses in this deemed taxation year can be increased by provisions which require the recognition of unrealized losses on the capital assets of the corporation. They can also be reduced by an election to have one or more deemed dispositions.

14-28. The acquisition of control rules are particularly harsh in their treatment of capital losses. ITA 111(4)(a) indicates that any unused capital losses that are present at the deemed year end are simply lost. They cannot be carried forward to future years and, as a consequence, they will be of no benefit to the corporation subsequent to the acquisition of control. Note that this would include any unused business investment losses that are present at the deemed year end. In addition, if there are capital gains in the three years before the deemed year end, ITA 111(4)(b) prevents capital losses from years subsequent to the deemed year end from being carried back to those years.

14-29. While non capital losses can be carried forward, they too are subject to restrictions. These restrictions, found in ITA 111(5), are that:

- after the acquisition of control has taken place, the corporation must carry on the same or a similar line of business to that in which the losses occurred;
- there must be a reasonable expectation of profit in that line of business; and
- the losses can only be applied against future income generated by the same or a similar line of business.

14-30. A brief example can be used to illustrate these provisions:

Example Bostox Ltd. has two lines of business, manufacturing cameras and the sale of specialty food products. During the year ending December 31, 2001, the camera business experienced a loss for tax purposes of $5 million while the food products business had zero taxable income. The $5 million loss could not be carried back and, as a result, it became a loss carry forward. On December 31, 2001, Bostox Ltd. is acquired by another company. During the year ending December 31, 2002, the camera business lost an additional $1 million while the food products business earned $7 million.

Tax Consequences If there was no acquisition of control, both the current 2002 loss of $1 million and the $5 million loss carry forward resulting from the camera business could be deducted against the income of the specialty food products division. This would have resulted in a 2002 Net Income of $1 million ($7 million profit on food products, offset by a current loss of $1 million on cameras and a loss carry forward of $5 million).

However, with the acquisition of control at the end of 2001, the loss carry forward can only be used against profits produced by the camera business. This would mean that none of the loss carry forward could be used in 2002. However, the $1 million 2002 camera business loss could be netted against the $7 million food products profits, resulting in a 2002 Net Income of $6 million.

Unrecognized Losses At Deemed Year End

14-31. As previously indicated, the acquisition of control restrictions apply to losses which accrue in the taxation year which has been created by the deemed year end. As there has been a deemed year end, there may be a loss from normal operations for the fiscal period that has ended. In addition, there may be losses resulting from actual disposals of capital assets during the period.

14-32. However, the acquisition of control rules are also concerned with accrued losses that have not been recognized at the deemed year end. The problem is that, if such accrued losses are realized after that time, they will not be subject to the acquisition of control restrictions. Assume, for example, that at the deemed year end the corporation owned a parcel of land with an adjusted cost base of $200,000 and a fair market value of $150,000. If the land were to be disposed of subsequent to the acquisition of control, the result would be a deductible capital loss. This could be viewed as a way of avoiding the restrictions imposed by the acquisition of control.

14-33. As a reflection of this view, the acquisition of control rules require a number of special procedures at the deemed year end. They are as follows:

Accounts Receivable   ITA 111(5.3) does not permit the deduction of a reserve for doubtful accounts under ITA 20(1)(l). Rather, amounts must be written off as specific bad debts on the basis of the largest possible amount. If a doubtful account is not written off at the time when an acquisition of control occurs, no deduction is available if the account subsequently becomes uncollectible. This procedure will generally result in a larger deduction and, if the corporation already has a non capital loss for the year, it will increase the amount of that loss.

Depreciable Capital Property   ITA 111(5.1) requires that depreciable capital property be written down to fair market value if that value is below the UCC. The write down amount is treated as CCA and will be added to any non capital loss for the deemed taxation year. The property will retain the same capital cost and, as the write down is on depreciable capital property, there can be no capital losses.

Eligible Capital Property   ITA 111(5.2) requires that eligible capital property be written down to three-quarters of fair market value if that value is below the cumulative eligible capital balance. The write down is a deduction under ITA 20(1)(b) and will add to any non capital loss for the deemed taxation year.

Non Depreciable Capital Property   ITA 111(4)(c) requires that non depreciable capital property be written down to its fair market value if that value is below its adjusted cost base. ITA 111(4)(d) requires that the amount of the write down be treated as a capital loss. The new lower value becomes the adjusted cost base of the property. The resulting allowable capital loss can be applied against available taxable capital gains. However, if it is not used at the deemed year end, it is lost forever.

Deemed Disposition Election

14-34.   The requirement that non depreciable capital property be written down to fair market value at the deemed year end is particularly onerous in that the resulting capital losses may simply disappear. To offset the harshness of this requirement, ITA 111(4)(e) allows the corporation to elect, at the time of the deemed year end, to have a deemed disposition/reacquisition of any depreciable or non depreciable capital property. This election can be used to trigger capital gains to offset unused capital losses of the current period or unused capital loss carry forwards from earlier periods.

14-35.   The election can also be used to trigger recapture which can absorb non capital losses from the current or previous years. This is a less important application in most situations as non capital losses do not disappear at the deemed year end. However, as noted in Paragraph 14-29, there are restrictions on the use of such losses after the deemed year end and, as a consequence, it may be desirable to minimize non capital losses when an acquisition of control occurs.

14-36.   The elected value, which will serve as the deemed proceeds of disposition, cannot exceed the fair market value of the asset at the time of the disposition. The minimum value for the election is the adjusted cost base of the property. The elected value can be any amount between the minimum and maximum. This means that, in the case of property on which CCA has been taken, any election that will create a capital gain will also create recapture of CCA.

14-37.   If the corporation has unused capital losses and there are non depreciable properties with accrued gains, this election is clearly desirable in that it will generate capital gains that can be used to offset the capital losses which are about to disappear as a result of the acquisition of control. The situation is less clear cut when the gains are on depreciable capital property. While the deemed disposition will create the needed capital gains, in many situations it will also result in recapture of CCA. This may or may not be a desirable situation. A simple example will illustrate these points:

Example   Burkey Ltd. has a December 31 year end. On June 1, 2001, a new investor acquires control of the Company. While its basic operations have been profitable for many years, it has a net capital loss carry forward from 1997 of $300,000 [(3/4)($400,000)]. At June 1, 2001, the Company has non depreciable capital assets with a fair market value of $800,000 and an adjusted cost base of $500,000. Its depreciable capital assets have a fair market value of $1,200,000, a capital cost of $1,100,000, and a UCC of $600,000.

Tax Consequences   The ITA 111(4)(e) election is clearly desirable with respect to the non depreciable capital property. It generates a taxable capital gain of $150,000 [(1/2)($800,000 - $500,000)]. Deducting a $150,000 carry forward against this 2001 gain will use up $225,000 [($150,000)(3/2)] from the 1997 net capital loss balance. This will leave an unused amount of $75,000 ($300,000 - $225,000).

Using the ITA 111(4)(e) election on the depreciable capital property will create a $50,000 [(1/2)($1,200,000 - $1,100,000)] taxable capital gain. Deducting a $50,000 loss carry forward against this amount will use up the remaining $75,000 [($50,000)(3/2)] of the net capital loss balance. However, the election will also recapture CCA of $500,000 ($1,100,000 - $600,000), an amount on which it appears that taxes would have to be currently paid. Given that, in the absence of this election, taxation on the recapture could be deferred indefinitely, the election may not be desirable with respect to the depreciable capital property.

14-38.   In addition to serving as the deemed proceeds of disposition, the elected value also becomes the capital cost of the deemed reacquisition of the asset. If the election were made at fair market value on both properties described in the preceding example, the new adjusted cost base of the non depreciable assets would be $800,000 and the capital cost of the depreciable assets would be $1,200,000. However, if this value were also used for CCA purposes, the Company would be allowed to deduct 100 percent of the $100,000 difference between the $1,200,000 elected value and the old capital cost of $1,100,000, despite the fact that they have, in effect, paid taxes on only one-half of this amount.

14-39.   To prevent this from happening, ITA 13(7)(f) specifies that, when an election is made under ITA 111(4)(e), the capital cost of the property for CCA purposes is equal to the old capital cost of the asset, plus one-half of the excess of the elected value over the old capital cost of the asset. In our example this value would be $1,150,000 [$1,100,000 + (1/2)($1,200,000 - $1,100,000)]. Future CCA would be based on this figure and, in addition, if the assets were sold for more than $1,150,000, this value would be subtracted from the UCC to determine recapture. However, any future capital gain would be based on the elected value of $1,200,000.

> Exercise Fourteen-4 deals with the acquisition of control rules. This would be an appropriate time to attempt this exercise.

Non Capital Loss Carry Over For A Corporation

14-40.   As the general rules for loss carry overs are the same for all taxpayers, most of the relevant material on this subject was dealt with in Chapter 12 when we discussed the determination of Taxable Income for individuals. There is, however, an additional problem in calculating the amount of the current year's non capital loss carry over for a corporation. This problem relates to the fact that dividends from other taxable Canadian corporations can be deducted by a corporation in the determination of its Taxable Income. To illustrate this problem, consider the following:

Example   During 2001, Marco Inc. has net taxable capital gains of $30,000 [(1/2)($60,000)], dividends from other taxable Canadian corporations of $25,000, and an operating loss of $60,000. The Company also has a net capital loss from 1995 of $75,000 [(3/4)($100,000)].

14-41.   Using the ITA 3 rules for calculating Net Income For Tax Purposes, the result would be as follows:

ITA 3(a)	Dividends Received	$25,000
ITA 3(b)	Net Taxable Capital Gains	30,000
ITA 3(c)	Subtotal	$55,000
ITA 3(d)	Operating Loss	(60,000)
Net And Taxable Income		Nil

14-42. From an intuitive point of view, it would appear that the non capital loss for the year is $5,000, the ITA 3(c) subtotal less the operating loss. Further, as Net Income is nil, it appears that none of the net capital loss can be deducted, despite the presence of a $30,000 taxable capital gain. In addition, it does not appear that the Company will get any benefit from the potential deduction of the $25,000 in dividends that were received during the year. Fortunately, the ITA 111(8) definition of non capital loss solves both of these problems.

14-43. You may recall that this formula was discussed previously in Chapter 12 (see the material starting at Paragraph 12-66). In that Chapter we noted that when Net Income was nil, it was still possible, to the extent that there were taxable capital gains during the year, to deduct net capital losses. This was accomplished through the definition of non capital loss that was presented in Paragraph 12-68. Now that we are dealing with corporations, we can present the more complete definition as follows:

Non Capital Loss For The Year = E - F, where,

E = The sum of non capital losses for the year, net capital losses deducted during the year, and deductible dividends received by a corporation.

F = The amount of income determined under ITA 3(c).

14-44. Assuming that Marco Inc. wishes to deduct the maximum amount of net capital loss in 2001, the non capital loss for the year would be calculated as follows:

Amount E ($60,000 + $30,000* + $25,000)	$115,000
Amount F - ITA 3(c) Balance	(55,000)
Non Capital Loss For The Year	$ 60,000

*The net capital loss deduction is limited to $30,000 [($45,000)(1/2 ÷ 3/4)], the amount of taxable capital gains realized during the year. This leaves a net capital loss balance of $30,000 ($75,000 - $45,000).

> Exercises Fourteen-5 and Fourteen-6 deal with non capital losses. This would be an appropriate time to attempt these exercises.

14-45. Note the results of applying the non capital loss definition. In effect, if there is not sufficient Net Income to allow their deduction in the calculation of Taxable Income, both dividends and net capital loss amounts deducted are added to the non capital loss carry over balance and become subject to a three year carry back, seven year carry forward limit.

Ordering Of Deductions

14-46. Chapter 12 covered the specific ordering rules in ITA 111.1 for claiming deductions in the calculation of taxable income. However, these rules are directed at individuals and they do not apply to corporations. The Act does not contain an equivalent provision for corporations and, as a consequence, there is a question as to how deductions should be ordered for a corporation.

14-47. Charitable donations in excess of 75 percent of Net Income For Tax Purposes are not deductible in the current year but can be carried forward for five years, subject to the same 75 percent limitation in those years. As this is shorter than the carry forward period for any type of loss, this would suggest using these amounts prior to claiming loss carry forwards.

14-48. Turning to the deduction of loss carry overs, ITA 111(3) requires that losses within any single category must be deducted in chronological order. That is, if a corporation chooses to deduct a portion of its non capital loss balance during the current year, the oldest losses of this type must be deducted first. However, there are no rules with respect to the order in which the individual types of loss carry forwards must be deducted.

14-49. Non capital and farm loss carry forwards have restrictions on the time for which they are available. This would suggest that they be deducted first. However, while there is no restriction on the period of availability for capital loss carry forwards, these amounts can only be used to the extent that there are capital gains during the period. A similar restriction is applicable to carry overs of restricted farm losses. For a corporation that experiences only limited capital gains or farming income, these restrictions may be a more important consideration than the period of time during which the loss will be available.

14-50.   An additional factor in making decisions on whether to deduct non capital or farm losses is the period left to their expiry. Clearly, items which expire in the current year should be deducted immediately, with additional consideration given to items near the end of their carry forward period.

Geographical Allocation Of Income

Permanent Establishments

14-51.   After taxable income is calculated, in order to determine the amount of provincial taxes that are payable and the province to which they are due, it is necessary to allocate the income of the business to the various provinces. Given the variations in provincial tax rates on corporations, this can be a matter of considerable significance.

14-52.   The key concept here is the idea of a "permanent establishment". This concept is defined as follows:

> **ITR 400(2)**   Permanent establishment means a fixed place of business of the corporation, including an office, a branch, a mine, an oil well, a farm, a timberland, a factory, a workshop or a warehouse.

14-53.   This meaning has been extended to include having an agent or employee in a province, if that agent has the authority to contract for a corporation or carries a stock of merchandise from which orders are regularly filled. The mere presence of a commission salesperson or an independent agent is not considered evidence of a permanent establishment. In addition, the presence of a controlled subsidiary in a province is not necessarily indicative of a permanent establishment. However, ITR 400(2)(d) indicates that where a corporation that has a permanent establishment anywhere in Canada owns land in a province, such land will be deemed to be a permanent establishment. In addition, ITR 400(2)(e) indicates that where a corporation uses substantial machinery or equipment in a particular place, that corporation shall be deemed to have a permanent establishment in that place.

Activity At Permanent Establishments

14-54.   Once the location of permanent establishments has been determined, income will be allocated on the basis of two variables. These are sales from the permanent establishment and salaries and wages paid by the establishment. ITR 402(3) provides rules for allocating these two variables to permanent establishments.

14-55.   Once these values are established, the next step is to calculate, for each province, that province's sales as a percentage of total corporate sales and that province's salaries and wages as a percentage of total corporate salaries and wages. A simple average of these two percentages, without regard to the relative dollar values associated with the corporate totals, is then applied to corporate taxable income to determine the amount of taxable income which will be taxed in that province.

Example - Permanent Establishments

14-56.   The following example illustrates the process of allocating taxable income on a geographic basis:

> **Example**   The Linford Company has permanent establishments in Alberta, Manitoba, and Ontario. The Company's taxable income for this year totaled $100,000, with gross revenues of $1,000,000 and salaries and wages of $500,000.

14-57.   The following allocation of the gross revenues and the salaries and wages among the provinces occurred this year:

Province	Gross Revenues		Salaries And Wages	
	Amount	Percent	Amount	Percent
Alberta	$ 250,000	25.0	$100,000	20.0
Manitoba	400,000	40.0	200,000	40.0
Ontario	350,000	35.0	200,000	40.0
Totals	$1,000,000	100.0	$500,000	100.0

14-58.   Using the average of the two percentages for each province, the Linford Company's taxable income would be allocated to the three provinces as follows:

Province	Average Percent	Taxable Income	Amount Allocated
Alberta	22.5	$100,000	$ 22,500
Manitoba	40.0	100,000	40,000
Ontario	37.5	100,000	37,500
Totals	100.0	N/A	$100,000

> Exercise Fourteen-7 deals with geographical allocation of income. This would be an appropriate time to attempt this exercise.

14-59.   If the corporation has operations outside of Canada, the total allocated to the provinces will be less than 100 percent. This will be taken into consideration when the federal tax abatement is calculated (see Paragraph 14-67).

Types Of Corporations

14-60.   The type and status of a corporation is important in determining how its income will be taxed. As a consequence, before moving to the calculation of corporate taxes payable, we need to describe the three different types of corporations that the *Income Tax Act* identifies:

Public Corporations   ITA 89(1) states that a public corporation is a corporation that is resident in Canada and has its shares traded on a prescribed stock exchange in Canada. In situations where a corporation's shares are widely held, an election can be made for it to be taxed as if it were a public corporation even if the shares are not listed on an exchange. This latter provision would generally apply only to companies whose shares are traded in the over the counter markets.

Private Corporations   Under ITA 89(1), a private corporation is any corporation that does not fall within the definition of public corporation and is not controlled by a public corporation. This means that controlled investees of public companies would be taxed as public corporations, not as private corporations.

Canadian Controlled Private Corporations   This designation, found in ITA 125(7), is used for private corporations that are not controlled, directly or indirectly, by one or more non resident individuals.

14-61.   In Section 1590, "Subsidiaries", the *CICA Handbook* defines control in such a way that it can exist when there is less than 50 percent ownership of the outstanding voting shares of a corporation. In general, this is not the case for tax purposes. In this area, control is usually defined in terms of majority ownership. The basic definition is found in ITA 256(1.2)(c) which indicates that a corporation is controlled when another corporation, a person, or group of persons owns:

- shares of the capital stock of the corporation having a fair market value of more than 50% of the fair market value of all the issued and outstanding shares of the capital stock of the corporation, or

- common shares of the capital stock of the corporation having a fair market value of more than 50% of the fair market value of all the issued and outstanding common shares of the capital stock of the corporation.

Federal Taxes Payable

Federal Corporate Rate

14-62.   All corporations are initially subject to the same basic tax rate. This rate is specified in ITA 123 and, for many years, has been set at 38 percent (as will be seen in the next section, this rate is reduced by 10 percentage points for income earned in a province, leaving an effective federal rate on Canadian income of 28 percent). A plan to reduced this rate by 7 percentage points was outlined in the February 28, 2000 budget, with a detailed plan for implementation provided in the the October 18, 2000 Economic Statement.

14-63.   With the issuance of draft legislation on March 16, 2001, we find that the government has chosen a somewhat indirect approach to this reduction. Instead of lowering the 38 percent rate specified in ITA 123, they have introduced a new ITA 123.4(2) which provides for a deduction based on multiplying the corporation's "general rate reduction percentage" by its "full rate taxable income" for the year. The reduction will be phased in on the basis of calendar years as follows:

2001	1 Percent
2002	3 Percent
2003	5 Percent
2004 And Subsequent	7 Percent

14-64.   For non calendar fiscal years, an average rate will be calculated based on the number of days in each year. For example, the general rate reduction percentage for a corporation with a January 31, 2002 year end would be:

$$[(1\%)(334/365) + (3\%)(31/365)] = 1.08\%$$

14-65.   This "general rate reduction percentage" must be applied to "full rate taxable income". This new income concept is, in fairly simple terms, income that does not benefit from either the small business deduction or the manufacturing and processing profits deduction. As will be discussed later in this Chapter, as well as in Chapter 15, these two deductions reduce the amount of taxes that must be paid by a corporation. In introducing this corporate rate reduction, the government concluded that it should not be available on income that already benefits from the special rates applicable to small businesses and businesses engaged in manufacturing and processing. To implement this view, the general rate reduction is only applicable to income that is taxed at "full rate".

14-66.   The actual calculation of "full rate taxable income" is somewhat complex. However, we will deal with these complications at a later point, when consideration is given to the small business deduction and the manufacturing and processing profits deduction. We would also note that there is a further complication here in that there is an additional rate reduction available to CCPCs. This reduction of 7 percentage points is available on amounts of active business income between $200,000 and $300,000. This accelerated reduction will be discussed at a later point in this Chapter.

Federal Tax Abatement

14-67.   ITA 124(1) provides a reduction of 10 percentage points in the federal tax rate. This is normally referred to as the federal tax abatement and it is designed to leave room for the provinces to apply their respective tax rates. This reduces the federal tax rate from 38 percent to 28 percent, before the application of the corporate surtax.

14-68.   Note that this 10 percentage point reduction in the federal tax rate is only applicable to income earned in a Canadian jurisdiction. When a corporation has foreign operations, less than 100 percent of its income will be allocated to the various provinces. When this is the case, the amount of abatement to be deducted is reduced by multiplying the 10 percent by the total percentage of taxable income that was allocated to the provinces. For example, if only 80 percent of a corporation's Taxable Income was allocated to one or more Provinces, the abatement would be reduced to eight percent [(10%)(80%)].

Surtax

14-69.   While the surtax on individuals has been eliminated, a corporate surtax remains. Since 1995, the rate has been four percent of tax otherwise payable. The tax otherwise payable is defined as being after the federal tax abatement, but before the additional refundable tax on investment income, the small business deduction, foreign tax credits, investment tax credits, political contributions tax credits, as well as any deduction under the new ITA 123.4. Another way of describing this calculation is to indicate that the rate is applied to taxes payable after the deduction of the federal tax abatement. However, even this is complicated by the fact that, for purposes of this calculation only, the abatement is calculated without regard to the percentage of Taxable Income earned in a Province. This means that, in cases where the abatement has been reduced to reflect income earned outside Canada, a different abatement calculation is required in order to determine the surtax. This would suggest that a more straight forward way to calculate the surtax is to take 4 percent of 28 percent of Taxable Income. We will generally use this approach in our examples and problems.

> **Example**   Borders Inc. has full rate Taxable Income of $146,000 for the year ended December 31, 2001. Based on the ITR 402 formula, 83 percent of this income has been earned in a Canadian province. Determine federal corporate taxes payable, including the applicable surtax.

Basic Tax [(38%)($146,000)]	$55,480
Federal Tax Abatement [(10%)(83%)($146,000)]	(12,118)
General Rate Reduction [(1%)($146,000)]	(1,460)
Federal Tax Before Surtax	$41,902
Surtax [(4%)(28%)($146,000)]	1,635
Federal Tax After Surtax	$43,537

Provincial Income Tax Payable

General Rules

14-70.   In calculating taxes payable for individuals, a graduated rate structure is involved at both the federal and provincial levels. While limits on the brackets may differ from those used at the federal level, all of the provinces except Alberta assess taxes on individuals using graduated rates applied to Taxable Income. In contrast, provincial corporate taxes are based on a flat rate applied to a Taxable Income figure. With the exception of Alberta, Ontario, and Quebec, the federal Taxable Income figure is used. While these three provinces administer their own corporate taxes, the taxable income figure that they use is normally similar to that used at the federal level.

14-71.   All provinces have at least two basic rates for corporations — a low rate for the first $200,000 of Canadian active business income earned by a Canadian controlled private corporation, and a high rate that is generally applicable to other income earned by a Canadian controlled private corporation, and to all of the income of other types of corporations. Several provinces have a different rate for manufacturing and processing income that is not eligible for the small business deduction. A further complication is that some provinces, following the federal lead (see Paragraph 14-66), have extended their lower small business rate to an additional $100,000 of income.

14-72.   In Figure 14-3 (following page), we have shown the three basic provincial tax rates for corporations. The Small Business Rate in this table is applicable to the first $200,000 of active business income. In some provinces (e.g., Alberta) this rate is applicable to an additional $100,000 of income. In others (e.g., British Columbia), it is not applicable to this amount.

Figure 14 - 3
Provincial Corporate Rates As At January 1, 2001

Province Or Territory	General Rate	M&P Rate	Small Business Rate
Alberta	13.99%	13.75%	5.25%
British Columbia	16.50%	16.50%	4.75%
Manitoba	17.00%	17.00%	6.00%
New Brunswick	17.00%	17.00%	4.50%
Newfoundland	14.00%	5.00%	5.00%
Northwest Territories	14.00%	14.00%	5.00%
Nova Scotia	16.00%	16.00%	5.00%
Ontario	14.00%	12.00%	6.50%
Prince Edward Island	16.00%	7.50%	7.50%
Quebec	9.04%	9.04%	9.04%
Saskatchewan	17.00%	10.00%	8.00%
Yukon Territories	15.00%	2.50%	6.00%

The general rate applies to corporations that are not Canadian controlled private corporations. In some Provinces, there is a reduced rate for corporations involved in manufacturing and processing (M&P). The small business rate is applicable to the first $200,000 of active business income earned by a Canadian controlled private corporation. However, in some provinces it is extended to the first $300,000.

Example

14-73.   The following example illustrates the use of the basic corporate rules.

Example   A corporation has taxable income of $100,000 for the year ending December 31, 2001. All of this income can be allocated to a province. The corporation's shares are publicly traded and it is not involved in manufacturing. The applicable provincial corporate tax rate is 15 percent of taxable income as determined at the federal level. The taxes payable for the year are as follows:

Federal Taxes [(38%)($100,000)]	$38,000
General Rate Reduction [(1%)($100,000)]	(1,000)
Federal Tax Abatement [(10%)($100,000)]	(10,000)
Net Federal Tax For Surtax	$27,000
Federal Surtax [(4%)(28%)($100,000)]	1,120
Total Federal Tax	$28,120
Provincial Tax [(15%)($100,000)]	15,000
Total Taxes Payable	$43,120

14-74.   As can be seen in the preceding calculations, the general rate of corporate taxation at the federal level is 28.12 percent. When combined with a provincial rate of 15 percent, the overall rate is 43.12 percent. This rate is applicable to the non manufacturing income of public companies, as well as to certain types of income earned by private corporations. Note, however, that the federal rate will be reduced by a further 6 percentage points by 2004, providing a federal rate of 22.12 percent and, continuing to assume a provincial rate of 15 percent, a combined rate of 37.12 percent.

Other Provincial Taxes

14-75.   In addition to their basic corporate taxes, most provinces also levy capital and payroll taxes on corporations. Unlike provincial income taxes on corporations, these taxes are treated as deductions in the calculation of taxable income, a situation which lowers the amount of federal taxes that can be collected on that corporation's income. This, in effect, reduces the cost of these capital and payroll taxes to the paying corporation.

14-76.   However, the use of such taxes also reduces federal tax revenues and, as a consequence, the federal government has threatened to eliminate the deductibility of capital and payroll taxes. At present, there is an interim measure which, since March, 1993, has denied deductibility to any increases in these taxes after that date. This "interim" measure is still on the books.

Other Goals Of The Corporate Tax System

14-77.   If raising revenues was the only goal of the corporate taxation system, there would be nothing much to discuss with respect to this matter and there would be little need for the Chapters on corporate taxation that follow. However, in addition to raising revenues, the Canadian corporate taxation system has been structured to accomplish a number of other objectives. These can be briefly described as follows:

- **Incentives For Small Business**   While there are several features of the tax system directed at encouraging small businesses, the major tax incentive for these organizations is the small business deduction.

- **Incentives For Certain Business Activities**   The Canadian tax system encourages scientific research through a generous system of tax credits and a liberal policy towards deductible amounts. Support is also provided to the natural resource industries through a variety of programs. Support for manufacturing activity is given through the manufacturing and processing profits deduction.

- **Incentives For Certain Regions**   While less common than in the past, certain regions of Canada are given assistance through investment tax credits and other programs.

- **Integration**   The Canadian tax system is designed to keep the level of taxes paid on a given stream of income the same, regardless of whether or not a corporation is placed between the original source of the income and the ultimate recipient.

14-78.   The small business deduction, the manufacturing and processing deduction and investment tax credits will be examined in this Chapter. Integration will be dealt with in detail in Chapter 15.

Large Corporations Tax

General Provisions

14-79.   The preceding discussion of the basic Canadian tax system and its various modifications was restricted to the taxation of income under Part I of the *Income Tax Act*. In order to raise additional revenues and to ensure that large corporations pay a minimum tax without regard to their income level, Part I.3 of the *Income Tax Act* was introduced in 1989. Part I.3 levies a tax on the capital of large corporations. This tax is similar in nature to the capital taxes that are used in most Provinces.

14-80.   The federal large corporations tax is, in effect, a corporate minimum tax in that it is calculated without reference to corporate taxable income. A corporation would be liable for this tax, even in years in which it has losses for tax purposes.

Basic Calculation Illustrated

Components

14-81.   The components of the amount that will be subject to the large corporations tax can be described as follows:

Total Capital   Total Capital includes all of the corporation's contributed capital for all classes of shares, as well as its retained earnings balance. In addition, loans, advances and other indebtedness that is outstanding for more than 365 days before the year end is included. Future Income Tax Liabilities and Deferred Exchange Gains are added to the total. Deferred Exchange Losses are subtracted from the total. While current legislation refers specifically to subtracting Deferred Tax Assets, it is not clear whether Future Income Tax Assets will be subtracted when a company is applying Section 3465 of the *CICA Handbook*, "Income Taxes".

Most of the amounts used in this calculation will be GAAP based. However, the tax rules require that the figures used in this calculation be based on single entity rather than consolidated financial statements. In addition, any difference resulting from the application of the equity method as opposed to the cost method for long term investments must be removed from retained earnings. For example, if a long term investment with a cost of $2,300,000 had been written up to $2,500,000 through the application of the equity method, the Retained Earnings figure used here would have to be reduced by $200,000.

Taxable Capital   The total capital figure is reduced by an "Investment Allowance" to arrive at taxable capital. The investment allowance is based on all of the corporation's investments, including both debt and equity, in other corporations. As these investments will be part of the investee corporation's capital, a failure to provide for this allowance could result in these amounts being subject to a double application of the large corporations tax.

Taxable Capital Employed In Canada   In the case of corporations where some part of their income is not earned in a province, an appropriate percentage is applied to Taxable Capital to arrive at Taxable Capital Employed In Canada. The percentage used is the same as that used to calculate the ITA 124(1) federal tax abatement.

Capital Deduction   From Taxable Capital Employed In Canada, a basic deduction of $10 million is subtracted. This $10 million deduction must be shared among any associated corporations in the same way in which associated corporations share the $200,000 annual small business limit. (See the material on associated corporations later in this Chapter.) The appropriate tax rate is then applied to this balance.

Rate   The Part 1.3 Tax Payable is calculated by applying a rate of .225 percent (.00225) to the balance after the subtraction of the capital deduction of $10 million.

Credit For Canadian Surtax Paid

14-82.   The goal of any minimum tax is to insure that all taxpayers of a particular category pay at least some amount of tax. In general, such taxes are not intended to increase the tax burden of taxpayers that are already paying an appropriate amount of tax. In the case of the alternative minimum tax on individuals (see Chapter 13), this is accomplished by requiring payment only when the amount of the minimum tax exceeds the regular tax payable for the taxation year.

14-83.   In the case of the corporate minimum tax, this goal is accomplished by allowing taxpayers to credit "Canadian" surtax paid against the liability for Part I.3 tax payable. In addition, any Canadian surtax in excess of the Part I.3 liability for the current year can be credited against the Part I.3 liability for the three preceding and seven subsequent taxation years.

14-84.   Note that only "Canadian surtax" can be used in this process. Canadian surtax is the total surtax multiplied by the ratio of Taxable Capital Employed In Canada to Taxable Capital. This ratio would be based on the allocation of income which was earned in a Canadian jurisdiction as calculated for the federal tax abatement. We would stress that this "Canadian surtax" is not the amount of surtax that will be paid. It is a notional number that is used only in this particular application. There are no other applications of this number.

Short Fiscal Periods

14-85.   The large corporations tax is assessed on an annual basis, without regard to the amount of income earned. As you would expect given this taxation basis, when a corporation has a taxation year of less than 51 weeks, the amount of Part I.3 taxes payable will be prorated on the basis of the number of days in the year divided by 365.

Acquisition Of Control

14-86. There are restrictions on the ability to apply Canadian surtax against Part I.3 tax in situations where there has been an acquisition of control. In a manner analogous to the restrictions on the use of non capital loss carry forwards in such circumstances, surtax paid prior to the acquisition of control can be deducted against Part I.3 tax arising in periods after the acquisition of control only if the business to which the tax relates is carried on throughout that later year and only against the portion of the corporation's Part I.3 taxes payable for the later year which relates to that business or similar businesses.

Example

14-87. The following example illustrates the calculation of the Part I.3 large corporations tax in a fairly simple situation:

Share Capital		$25,000,000
Plus:		
Contributed Surplus	$12,000,000	
Retained Earnings	22,000,000	
Loans, Advances, And Other Indebtedness		
Outstanding For More Than 365 Days	33,000,000	67,000,000
Total Capital		$92,000,000
Less: Investments In Other Corporations		(7,000,000)
Taxable Capital		$85,000,000
Percentage Employed In Canada		92%
Taxable Capital Employed In Canada		$78,200,000
Capital Deduction		(10,000,000)
Amount Subject To Tax		$68,200,000
Part I.3 Rate of .225%		.00225
Part I.3 Tax Payable Before Surtax		$ 153,450
Canadian Surtax Paid [($1,000,000)(4%)(28%)(92%)]		(10,304)
Part I.3 Tax Payable		$ 143,146

> Exercise Fourteen-8 deals with calculation of the large corporations tax. This would be an appropriate time to attempt this exercise.

Tax Planning

14-88. There are a number of actions that can be taken by a corporation to minimize its large corporations tax payable. This is of particular importance in view of the fact that these actions will generally serve to also reduce provincial capital taxes payable. Some of the possibilities in this area include:

- **Reduce Equity** Actions in this area include paying dividends, maximizing discretionary deductions, and paying out paid up capital (PUC) amounts to shareholders.

- **Reduce Debt** Actions here include paying off as much debt as possible, deferring new financing until after the year end, stretching the payment of short term accounts in order to delay the need for financing, withdrawing shareholders' loans, and using off balance sheet financing.

- **Increase Investment Allowance** Appropriate actions might include making only eligible investments (e.g., commercial paper as opposed to treasury bills), converting some accounts receivables to loans, and advancing funds to an associated company with a different year end or one that operates in a jurisdiction with no capital tax.

- **Reduce Total Assets** This can be accomplished by factoring trade receivables, paying dividends, or transferring non corporate investments to other affiliates. In addition, several *CICA Handbook* Sections (e.g., Section 3060 on capital assets) provide for asset write downs in certain circumstances. As capital is defined in terms of GAAP values for purposes of this tax, such write downs could reduce the amount of tax paid.

- **Allocation Of $10 Million Deduction**   If a group of associated corporations is involved, the $10 million deduction should be allocated to less profitable members of the group. This is based on the probability that the more profitable members will be able to use their Canadian surtax to decrease or eliminate their large corporations tax.

- **Interprovincial Planning**   With respect to provincial capital taxes, attempts should be made to locate permanent establishments in provinces with low or no capital tax.

Manufacturing And Processing Profits (M&P) Deduction

Introduction

14-89.   The manufacturing and processing sector of the Canadian economy accounts for almost 20 percent of both Gross Domestic Product and employment. Given this importance, it is not surprising that the government has consistently provided tax assistance to enterprises that are involved in manufacturing and processing. We noted in Chapter 8 that increased rates of CCA deductions are available for assets used in this type of activity. A further important incentive is the deduction available to some corporations for their manufacturing and processing profits. This manufacturing and processing profits (M&P) deduction has the effect of significantly reducing the rate of federal taxation for some corporations involved in this type of activity. In addition, some provinces also provide a lower rate of taxation on M&P income.

Calculating The Deduction

Rate

14-90.   ITA 125.1 provides for a deduction from taxes payable equal to 7 percent of a company's M&P profits. Given that this amount is deducted from taxes payable, it would be more consistent to refer to this "deduction" as a tax credit. However, ITA 125.1 uses the term deduction and, as a consequence, we will use this terminology throughout this section.

14-91.   Before illustrating the calculation of this deduction, we must return to our discussion of the general corporate rate reduction that was introduced in the February, 2000 budget. We noted previously that this reduction under ITA 123.4 was calculated by applying the general rate reduction percentage to "full rate taxable income". To arrive at this full rate taxable income figure, a number of adjustments are required. The one that is relevant here is that regular taxable income must be reduced by 100/7 of the amount deducted under ITA 125.1. In effect, we are required to remove any amounts of income that are eligible for the M&P deduction before we calculate the reduction.

> **Example**   Sadley Inc. has Taxable Income equal to $150,000 for the year ending December 31, 2001, with $100,000 of this amount eligible for the M&P deduction.

> **Tax Consequences**   As the M&P deduction is equal to $7,000 [(7%)($100,000)], full rate taxable income would be equal to $50,000 [$150,000 - (100/7)($7,000)]. This means that the general rate reduction would be $500 [(1%)($50,000)].

14-92.   For a corporation with income consisting entirely of M&P profits, there is no general rate reduction. This is illustrated in the following example:

> **Example**   For the year ending December 31, 2001, Daren Ltd., a Canadian public company, has Taxable Income equal to $100,000, all of which has been generated by M&P activity. It is subject to a provincial tax rate on M&P profits of 12 percent.

> **Tax Consequences**   Taxes Payable for Daren Ltd. would be calculated as follows:

Federal Taxes [(38%)($100,000)]	$38,000
General Rate Reduction [1%][$100,000 - (100/7)($7,000)]	Nil
Federal Tax Abatement [(10%)($100,000)]	(10,000)
Net Federal Tax For Surtax	$28,000
Federal Surtax [(4%)(28%)($100,000)]	1,120
M&P Deduction	(7,000)
Total Federal Tax	$22,120
Provincial Tax [(12%)($100,000)]	12,000
Total Taxes Payable	$34,120

14-93.   This calculation illustrates the fact that the general federal rate on income that is eligible for the M&P deduction is 22.12 percent. Depending on the Province, the combined federal/provincial rate ranges from a low of 27 percent in Newfoundland, to a high of 39 percent in New Brunswick.

14-94.   As a final point here, you might note that, when it is fully phased in in 2004, the general rate reduction will be equal to 7 percentage points, the same amount as the M&P deduction. It would suggest that it is the goal of the government to reduce the general rate for all corporations to the same rate that is available on M&P profits.

Constraints On The Amount
General Formula

14-95.   We have noted that using the M&P deduction reduces the availability of the general rate reduction. Working from the other direction, there are a number of limits on the amount of the M&P deduction. While the basic idea is that the deduction is equal to 7 percent of M&P profits, there are a number of other constraints (explained in the material that follows) as reflected in the general M&P deduction formula found in ITA 125.1(1). This subsection specifies that the deduction will be equal to seven percent of the lesser of:

A. manufacturing and processing profits, less amount eligible for the small business deduction (this amount will be discussed in the next section of this Chapter but, in general, is limited to $200,000); and

B. taxable income, less the sum of:
1. amount eligible for the small business deduction;
2. 10/4 of the foreign tax credit for business income (for this purpose only, the foreign tax credit is calculated without consideration of the ITA 123.4 general rate reduction); and
3. where the corporation is a Canadian controlled private corporation throughout the year, aggregate investment income as defined in ITA 129(4).

14-96.   Part A of this formula provides a basic limit based on the amount of M&P profits earned during the year. As will be explained subsequently, Part A's manufacturing and processing profits must be calculated by a formula established in ITR 5200. In many cases, particularly for public companies, this will be the factor that limits the amount of the M&P deduction.

Small Business Deduction

14-97.   As will be discussed in the next section, the small business deduction provides certain corporations with a deduction equal to 16 percent of the first $200,000 of their active business income. It appears that the government believes that granting both the M&P deduction and the small business deduction on the same income would be too generous. As a consequence, any amounts of income that are eligible for the small business deduction are not eligible for the M&P deduction. In the preceding ITA 125.1(1) formula, this is accomplished by removing amounts eligible for the small business deduction from both the A and B components.

Taxable Income Constraint

14-98.   The M&P deduction is a credit against Canadian federal taxes payable. Given this, it would not be appropriate to provide this credit on income which has not been subject to Canadian taxes. Component B of the ITA 125.1(1) formula is a check to make sure that this does not happen.

14-99.   M&P profits are included in Net Income For Tax Purposes and, in many cases, this amount will also be included in full in Taxable Income. However, it is possible that large Division C deductions could eliminate all or part of this income from the Taxable Income total. Examples of Division C deductions that could reduce or eliminate M&P profits included in Net Income would be:

• Non Capital Loss Carry Overs
• Charitable Contributions
• Farm Loss Carry Overs

14-100.   You will notice that neither Dividends nor Net Capital Losses are included on this list. This reflects the fact that these amounts can only be deducted to the extent that either dividends or taxable capital gains are included in Net Income. Given this, they cannot serve to offset amounts of active business income that are included in Net Income.

14-101.   A simple example will illustrate the need for this constraint on the M&P deduction:

Example   During the current year, Allard Ltd. has M&P profits of $123,000, taxable capital gains of $15,000, and dividends received from taxable Canadian corporations of $50,000. At the beginning of the year, Allard Ltd. has a net capital loss of $35,000 and a non capital loss carry over of $105,000. The Company intends to use the loss carry overs to the extent possible during the current year.

The calculation of Allard's Net Income For Tax Purposes and Taxable Income would be as follows:

Net Income ($123,000 + $15,000 + $50,000)	$188,000
Dividends	(50,000)
Net Capital Loss (Restricted To Taxable Capital Gains)	(15,000)
Non Capital Loss	(105,000)
Taxable Income	$ 18,000

14-102.   Note that, if only the net capital loss and dividends were deducted, Taxable Income would have been equal to the $123,000 in M&P profits. The problem is the non capital loss carry over. It has further reduced Taxable Income to $18,000, an amount well below the amount of M&P profits. It would make no sense in this situation to provide a deduction against Taxes Payable based on the $123,000 of M&P profits as only a fraction of this income would be subject to tax. This example clearly illustrates the need for the Taxable Income constraint on the M&P profits deduction.

Foreign Tax Credit Constraint

14-103.   The government is also concerned that the M&P deduction not be provided against taxes that have not been paid in Canada. To prevent this from happening, in the B component of the ITA 125.1(1) formula, Taxable Income is further reduced by 10/4 of any credit against Canadian taxes payable for foreign taxes that have been paid. The 10/4 is based on the notional assumption that foreign business income will be subject to a federal tax rate of about 40 percent. This is roughly equal to the basic federal rate of 38 percent plus the surtax but, reflecting the fact that foreign business income is not taxed in a province, there is no reduction for the federal tax abatement.

14-104.   Given these assumptions, the subtraction of 10/4 of any foreign tax credit given has the effect of removing from Taxable Income the amounts of foreign income on which the foreign tax credits have eliminated Canadian taxation at the assumed rate of 40 percent. An example will serve to clarify this point:

Example   Consider a situation in which a corporation earns $100,000 in foreign business income, with $15,000 being withheld by the foreign government.

If this income had been received from a domestic source, the taxes would be $40,000 (using the notional rate of 40 percent). Being received from a foreign source, the $40,000 in Canadian taxes will be offset by the $15,000 foreign tax credit, leaving a net Canadian Tax Payable of $25,000.

If we use the formula to remove $37,500 [(10/4)($15,000)] from Taxable Income, we are left with $62,500 ($100,000 - $37,500). Taxes at 40 percent on this amount would be $25,000, thereby demonstrating that the formula has served to remove the portion of Taxable Income on which the foreign tax credit has eliminated Canadian taxation.

Aggregate Investment Income Constraint

14-105.   This constraint is more difficult to explain at this stage. It is based on the fact that a part of federal taxes paid on the "aggregate investment income" of a Canadian controlled private corporation can be refunded to the corporation (this procedure will be discussed in detail in Chapter 15). As it would not appear to be appropriate to provide a tax credit against taxes that may eventually be refunded, these amounts are removed from the Taxable Income that is eligible for the M&P deduction.

14-106.   Note the reference to "aggregate investment income as defined in ITA 129(4)" in the formula in Paragraph 14-95. This somewhat unusual concept of investment income includes taxable capital gains, interest, rents, and royalties, but does not include dividends that a corporation can deduct in the calculation of Taxable Income. It includes both foreign and Canadian amounts for these items, and is reduced by net capital losses deducted under the ITA 111(1)(b) provision for net capital loss carry overs.

Eligibility

14-107.   On the surface, eligibility for the M&P deduction appears to be easily determinable. Any corporation that derives more than 10 percent of its gross revenues from Canadian manufacturing or processing is eligible. The problem with this rule, however, is the determination of what constitutes M&P activity.

14-108.   The *Act* does not define the terms manufacturing or processing. However, ITA 125.1(3) specifically excludes several types of activity from the designation of manufacturing or processing. These include logging, farming and fishing, construction, producing industrial minerals, and processing mineral resources. To find more guidance on the nature of manufacturing and processing, it is necessary to turn to IT-145R (Consolidated). This IT Bulletin notes that manufacturing generally involves the creation of something or the shaping, stamping or forming of an object from something. Correspondingly, processing is described as techniques of preparation, handling or other activity designed to effect a physical or chemical change in an article or substance. Needless to say, these descriptions have not settled the issue and, as a consequence, the distinction between qualified and non qualified activity has been the subject of numerous court cases. In fact, there is often a very fine line between qualified and non qualified activities. For example, for the owner of a pub, IT-145R (Consolidated) advises that the mixing of a drink is a qualified processing activity, whereas serving that same drink is a non qualifying service activity.

M&P Profits Defined

Basic Formula

14-109.   We have previously noted that the amount of the M & P deduction is usually calculated as seven percent of a company's Canadian M&P profits for the year. Since many businesses will have other types of income in addition to M&P profits, it is necessary to have a method for determining what portion of total income can be classified as M&P profits. This is accomplished through the use of the following formula which is described in ITR 5200:

$$
\begin{bmatrix} \text{Adjusted} \\ \text{Active} \\ \text{Business} \\ \text{Income} \end{bmatrix} \left[\frac{\left(\begin{array}{c} [^{100}\!/_{75}] \text{ of Canadian} \\ \text{M\&P Labour Costs} \end{array} \right) + \left(\begin{array}{c} [^{100}\!/_{85}] \text{ of Canadian} \\ \text{M\&P Capital Costs} \end{array} \right)}{\left(\begin{array}{c} \text{Total Canadian} \\ \text{Labour Costs} \end{array} \right) + \left(\begin{array}{c} \text{Total Canadian Active Business} \\ \text{Income Capital Costs} \end{array} \right)} \right]
$$

14-110.   The application of this formula requires an understanding of the meaning of each of the components of the formula. These components are defined in ITR 5202 and discussed in the material which follows.

Adjusted Active Business Income

14-111.   In simplified terms, active business income is the income that results from carrying on business activity. It can be contrasted with property income, which is earned without active effort on the part of the recipient. This distinction is extremely important in that, as we shall discuss in detail later in this Chapter, only active business income is eligible for the small business deduction.

14-112.   As defined in ITR 5202, "adjusted active business income" simply means the corporation's income for the year from active business carried on in Canada, less the corporation's losses for the year from active business carried on in Canada.

14-113.   It is clear from this formula that M&P profits are a subset of active business income. Stated alternatively, all M&P profits are active business income, but not all types of active business income come from M&P activities.

Qualified Activities

14-114.   The ITR 5202 definitions provide guidance with respect to what activities qualify for the deduction. Specifically listed as qualifying activities are the following:

- engineering design of products and production facilities;
- receiving and storing of raw materials;
- producing, assembling and handling of goods in process;
- inspecting and packaging of finished goods;
- line supervision;
- production support activities including security, cleaning, heating, and factory maintenance;
- quality and production control;
- repair of production facilities; and
- pollution control.

14-115.   Also included are all other activities that are performed in Canada directly in connection with non excluded manufacturing or processing, as well as scientific research and experimental development.

14-116.   Specifically excluded by the definition of qualified activities are the following:

- storing, shipping, selling and leasing of finished goods;
- purchasing of raw materials;
- administration, including clerical and personnel activities;
- purchase and resale operations;
- data processing; and
- providing facilities for employees, including cafeterias, clinics, and recreational facilities.

Cost Of Labour

14-117.   As defined in ITR 5202, the "cost of labour" includes salaries, wages and commissions paid to employees of the company. In general, fringe benefits are excluded. In addition to salaries and wages paid to employees of the corporation, the cost of labour includes amounts paid to non employees for management and administration, scientific research, and other services that would normally be performed by an employee. This brings into the calculation employee services that have, in effect, been contracted out.

14-118.   Excluded from this total would be labour costs that have been added to the cost of capital assets (e.g., labour costs added to the costs of self constructed assets) and any labour costs related to foreign active business income. Note, however, that no attempt is made to segregate and remove labour costs associated with property or investment income.

Cost Of Manufacturing And Processing Labour

14-119.   ITR 5202 defines "manufacturing and processing labour" as 100/75 of that portion of the "cost of labour" that was engaged in "qualified activities" (see preceding definitions). The 100/75 gross up factor reflects the fact that even a company that is completely engaged in qualified activities will require some non qualifying labour to administer M&P activities. The gross up provides for such administrative labour without eroding the availability of the M&P deduction.

14-120.   You should also note that the definition restricts the cost of manufacturing and processing labour to a maximum value equal to the total cost of labour. For example, if the "cost of labour" was $1,200,000 and the amount of this labour involved in qualifying activities was $1,000,000, the "cost of manufacturing and processing labour" in the definition would be $1,333,333 [($1,000,000)(100/75)]. However, the amount used in the M&P formula would be limited to $1,200,000, the "cost of labour".

Cost Of Capital

14-121.   A basic problem here is the need to deal with both assets owned by the corporation and assets leased (rented) by the corporation. The solution is a fairly arbitrary one. For depreciable assets owned by the corporation, the included amount is 10 percent of the gross cost of the asset. To be included, the property must be owned by the corporation at the end of the year and used by the corporation at any time during the year. "Gross cost" in this situation would be the cost before any deduction for government grants and investment tax credits that relate to the capital assets. As these amounts are usually deducted for accounting and tax (UCC) purposes, they will have to be added back to asset values used for other purposes. The cost of land is not included in the cost of capital.

14-122.   In addition to 10 percent of the gross cost of depreciable assets owned, the cost of capital includes payments made to lease or rent assets during the year. This allocation equates 10 percent of the cost of the asset with the value of leasing that asset. While this is an arbitrary rule, it is certainly preferable to ignoring the fact that leased assets constitute a major part of the physical plant of many Canadian businesses. Where the rent is for property which is comprised of land and a building, only the rent that can be reasonably allocated to the building is included. This is consistent with the exclusion of the cost of land from the cost of capital.

14-123.   As was the case with the cost of labour, the cost of capital excludes assets used to produce foreign active business income. Unlike the determination of the cost of labour, the cost of capital excludes assets that are used to produce investment income as defined in ITA 129(4).

Cost Of Manufacturing And Processing Capital

14-124.   As defined in ITR 5202, "manufacturing and processing capital" is equal to 100/85 of the portion of the total cost of capital that is devoted to qualified activities (see previous definition). As was the case with the cost of M&P labour, this amount is grossed up to reflect the fact that, even if a company is completely engaged in M&P activity, some non manufacturing assets will be required for administrative purposes.

14-125.   Like the limit placed on manufacturing and processing labour, manufacturing and processing capital cannot exceed the total cost of capital. As before, this means that if the application of the gross up factor to the capital cost of assets related to qualifying activities produces a number that is larger than the total cost of capital, the cost of manufacturing and processing capital is limited to the total cost of capital.

Applying The Formula
Example
14-126. To illustrate the application of the preceding formula, a simple example will be used.

> **Example** The following information has been provided by the Narder Company, a Canadian public company, for its current taxation year:
>
> | | |
> |---|---|
> | Adjusted Active Business Income | $2,500,000 |
> | Manufacturing And Processing Labour Costs | 3,700,000 |
> | Manufacturing And Processing Capital Costs | 6,500,000 |
> | Total Labour Costs | 5,200,000 |
> | Total Capital Costs | 8,000,000 |

Based on this information, the calculation of M&P profits for the current year is as follows:

$$[\$2,500,000]\left[\frac{\left(\frac{100}{75}\right)(\$3,700,000) + \left(\frac{100}{85}\right)(\$6,500,000)}{(\$5,200,000 + \$8,000,000)}\right]$$

$$= [(\$2,500,000)(.95306)] = \underline{\$2,382,650}$$

This calculation indicates that Narder Company's M&P profits, as determined by the ITR 5200 formula, amount to $2,382,650. Provided Taxable Income, as adjusted by the requirements of the ITA 125.1(1) formula, exceeds this amount, the Company will be eligible for a deduction from federal tax payable of $166,786 [($2,382,650)(7%)].

> Exercise Fourteen-9 deals with the M&P deduction. This would be an appropriate time to attempt this exercise.

Tax Planning Opportunity
14-127. In calculating the amount eligible for the M&P deduction, you will notice that the calculation is based on the relative amounts of labour and capital that are used in qualified activities and not on the amounts of profits that might be allocated. This means that non qualifying business activities that are labour or capital intensive will reduce the amount of profits that qualify for this deduction, even if those activities make no contribution to a company's profits. In such a situation, a company that has non qualifying activity that is only marginally profitable might find it worthwhile to spin off this activity into a separate company. As an example of this, consider the following:

> **Example** Spiral Inc. uses the following information in calculating its manufacturing and processing profits:
>
> | | |
> |---|---|
> | Adjusted Active Business Income | $ 450,000 |
> | Manufacturing And Processing Labour Costs | 800,000 |
> | Total Labour Costs | 1,600,000 |
> | Manufacturing And Processing Capital Costs | 1,500,000 |
> | Total Capital Costs | 2,500,000 |

The M&P profits of Spiral Inc. would be calculated as follows:

$$[\$450,000]\left[\frac{\left(\frac{100}{75}\right)(\$800,000) + \left(\frac{100}{85}\right)(\$1,500,000)}{(\$1,600,000 + \$2,500,000)}\right]$$

$$= [(\$450,000)(.69058] = \underline{\$310,761}$$

Assume these figures include a division which has a loss of $200,000, labour costs of $500,000, capital costs of $600,000, and that none of the labour or capital costs are involved in manufacturing activities. If this division were removed and set up as a separate corporation, the total eligible M&P profits would be increased to $613,464, as shown in the following calculation, resulting in a significantly larger amount of profits eligible for the M&P deduction.

$$[\$650,000]\left[\frac{\left(\frac{100}{75}\right)(\$800,000) + \left(\frac{100}{85}\right)(\$1,500,000)}{(\$1,100,000 + \$1,900,000)}\right]$$

$$= ([\$650,000][.94379]) = \underline{\$613,464}$$

14-128   This change would increase the amount eligible for the M&P deduction by $302,703. As the 1 percent general tax reduction will be lost on any amounts for which the M&P deduction is claimed, the net tax savings for 2001 would be $18,162 [(7% - 1%)($302,703)] at the federal level alone. This approach could also be used if an investor controls several companies and one of them is involved in a marginally profitable business that qualifies for the deduction. In this situation, it could be worthwhile to combine this manufacturing business with a more profitable non qualifying business in order to be able to bring some non qualifying profits into the calculation. This, in effect, would make some part of these profits eligible for the M&P deduction.

14-129.   It is interesting to note that the value of this type of change will decline as the general rate reduction increases. When the general rate reduction reaches 7 percent in 2004, there will no longer be any advantage to such tax planning procedures.

Small Business Deduction

Introduction

14-130.   It has been a long standing goal of the Canadian taxation system to provide incentives to small business. The underlying assumption is that, particularly during their formative years, these businesses need some degree of tax relief in order to allow them to accumulate the capital required for expansion. In order to provide this relief, the small business deduction was introduced in 1972. In somewhat simplified terms, it provides a deduction against the tax payable of a Canadian Controlled Private Corporation (CCPC) that is equal to 16 percent of the first $200,000 of active business income earned in Canada. Further enhancing this deduction is that all of the provinces except Quebec have reduced rates of taxation on this same income (see Figure 14-3).

Example   A corporation has taxable income of $100,000 for the current taxation year. All of this income is eligible for the small business deduction. The provincial tax rate applicable to income eligible for the small business deduction is 6 percent.

Tax Consequences   Given the preceding, the corporation's taxes payable for this year would be calculated as follows:

Federal Taxes [(38%)($100,000)]	$38,000
Federal Tax Abatement [(10%)($100,000)]	(10,000)
Federal Tax Before Surtax	$28,000
Federal Surtax [(4%)(28%)($100,000)]	1,120
Federal Tax Before Small Business Deduction	$29,120
Small Business Deduction [(16%)($100,000)]	(16,000)
Federal Tax	$13,120
Provincial Tax [(6%)($100,000)]	6,000
Total Taxes Payable	$19,120

The ITA 123.4 general rate reduction has implications for CCPCs which will be considered when we examine the detailed calculation of the small business deduction. It has no influence, however, in this particular example because the active business income is under $200,000.

14-131.   Note that the overall tax rate here is under 20 percent, a level that should provide a significant incentive to businesses that qualify for this rate. Only certain types of corporations qualify for this deduction and, in addition, it is only available on certain amounts and types of income. The criteria for qualification can be described as follows:

Type Of Corporation   The availability of the small business deduction is restricted to Canadian controlled private corporations (CCPCs).

Type Of Income   The deduction is only available on income earned in Canada that qualifies as "active business income". This would include the income of professional corporations and management companies, provided they are private and Canadian controlled. However, the income of specified investment businesses and personal service companies (see definitions later in this Chapter) does not qualify.

Limit On Amount   The deduction is only available on the first $200,000 per year of active business income. This amount is referred to as the annual business limit and, in some circumstances, it is subject to a reduction formula.

Associated Corporations   The annual business limit of $200,000 must be shared among associated corporations.

14-132.   The issues associated with these criteria are discussed in the material which follows.

Canadian Controlled Private Corporations (CCPCs)

14-133.   As was noted previously in this Chapter, CCPCs are defined in ITA 125(7) as private corporations that are not controlled, directly or indirectly, by one or more non resident individuals. Also as noted, a private corporation is defined in ITA 89(1) as a corporation that does not fall within the definition of a public corporation and is not controlled by a public corporation. This would mean that to qualify as a CCPC, shares of the company must not be traded on a prescribed stock exchange in Canada. It should also be noted that, in order to qualify for the small business deduction, the corporation must be a CCPC through the taxation year.

Active Business Income
The General Idea
14-134.   ITA 125(7) contains the following definition of active business:

"active business carried on by a corporation" means any business carried on by the corporation other than a specified investment business or a personal services business and includes an adventure or concern in the nature of trade.

14-135.   While the preceding defines active business, a further definition in ITA 125(7) defines income from an active business as:

"Income of the corporation for the year from an active business" means the total of

(i)   the income of the corporation for the year from an active business carried on by it including any income for the year pertaining to or incident to that business, other than income for the year from a source in Canada that is a property, and

(ii)   the amount, if any, included under subsection 12 (10.2) in computing the income of the corporation for the year. [The reference to 12(10.2) involves an income stabilization account for agricultural products and is of no interest in a text such as this.]

14-136.   While these definitions are not models of clarity, they express the basic idea that active business income involves "doing something" to produce income. The concept excludes what we generally refer to as property income. Property income is distinguished by the fact that it generally becomes available with little or no effort on the part of the recipient (e.g., interest earned on long term bonds).

The Problem With Property Income
14-137.   As noted, the preceding definitions of active business and active business income are largely directed towards excluding property income, such as interest, dividends, and rents

from eligibility for the small business deduction. The federal government does not wish to allow individuals to have access to the small business deduction by simply placing their passive investments in the shelter of a Canadian controlled private corporation. However, a blanket exclusion of property income is inappropriate since there are corporations that are "actively" involved in earning such income.

14-138.   The difficulty is in finding a way to distinguish between corporations that are simply being used as tax shelters for property or passive income and corporations that engage in active property management. For example, if a corporation has a single residential rental property, the rents from this property would undoubtedly be viewed as passive income. Alternatively, a corporation that owns a chain of hotels with more than 10,000 rooms would certainly be entitled to view the rentals from these properties as an active business. The question is at what point the corporation crosses the line between passive and active business activity.

14-139.   Similar, but less obvious, problems arise with interest income. If a corporation has no activity other than collecting interest on term deposits, the amounts that it earns would almost certainly be viewed as passive income. Alternatively, interest earned by a company actively involved in providing mortgage financing to corporate clients, could be viewed as business income. Again, a problem exists in finding the point at which a crossover is made between the two situations.

Specified Investment Business

14-140.   A somewhat arbitrary solution to these problems was introduced in 1980. This is the concept of a "specified investment business" which is defined in ITA 125(7) as follows:

> "specified investment business" carried on by a corporation in a taxation year means a business (other than a business carried on by a credit union or a business of leasing property other than real property) the principal purposes of which is to derive income from property (including interest, dividends, rents or royalties), unless
>
> (i)   the corporation employs in the business throughout the year more than five full-time employees, or
>
> (ii) in the course of carrying on an active business, any other corporation associated with it provides managerial, administrative, financial, maintenance or other similar services to the corporation in the year and the corporation could reasonably be expected to require more than five full time employees if those services had not been provided.

14-141.   As these specified investment businesses are excluded from the definition of active business, it means that property income generated by such businesses is not eligible for the small business deduction. Stated alternatively, for corporations that are primarily engaged in earning property income, the Act specifies that only those with more than five full time employees involved in earning such income are considered active businesses and eligible for the small business deduction.

14-142.   While this is an arbitrary solution to the problem of distinguishing between active and passive property income, it does serve to resolve most of the uncertainty in this area. You should also note that to count as one employee, the employee must be directing his efforts toward managing the property income on a full time basis. It is interesting to note, however, that a recent court decision ruled that five full time employees plus additional part time help would qualify as "more than five".

Incidental Property Income

14-143.   The definition of active business income includes incidental property income that is earned by a corporation engaged in an active business. In this regard, many corporations experience temporary excess cash balances and these balances will usually be invested in interest bearing assets. Within reasonable limits, such interest can be included as a component of active business income. In similar fashion, revenues resulting from temporary rentals of excess space usually qualify for this treatment as well.

Non Qualifying Property Income

14-144.   Property income of specified investment businesses and non incidental property income earned by active businesses do not qualify for the small business deduction. However, when a corporation derives income from holding property and the income is received from an associated company that deducted the amounts in computing active business income, ITA 129(6)(b) deems the income to be active business income to the recipient. There are some additional rules that partially eliminate the double taxation that occurs when property income is earned in a corporation. These special rules will be covered in the next Chapter when we deal with refundable taxes on property income.

Annual Business Limit
14-145.　As indicated previously, the maximum amount of income that is eligible for the small business deduction in a single taxation year is the annual business limit of $200,000. Further, as described in detail in the next section of this Chapter, this amount must be reduced by any portion that is allocated to associated companies.

Associated Companies
The Problem
14-146.　In the absence of special rules it would be very easy to avoid the annual limit that applies to the small business deduction. This could be accomplished by dividing a single corporation's activities between two separate corporations, thereby doubling up on the annual $200,000 limit. However, the Act prevents this by requiring that associated companies share their annual business limit.

14-147.　For example, assume that Mr. Robards owns all of the outstanding voting shares of both the Mark Company and the Grand Company. These two companies would be considered to be associated and, as a consequence, would have to share the $200,000 annual business limit. They can elect to allocate the annual limit in any proportion they wish as long as the total does not exceed $200,000. If the Mark Company has active business income and the Grand Company does not, it would be most advantageous to allocate the annual limit only to the Mark Company so that it could claim the maximum small business deduction.

14-148.　The preceding example is very clear cut and results in an allocation of the small business deduction that reflects the goals of the relevant legislation. However, with a deduction that can be worth over $40,000 per year in federal and provincial taxes, there is a significant incentive to develop arrangements that will avoid the intent of the legislation. Correspondingly, there is a need to have legislation that is sophisticated enough to frustrate these arrangements. As a consequence, the identification of associated companies can be very complex.

Definitions
14-149.　Associated companies are defined in ITA 256(1). However, there are a number of definitions and rules that are used in the provisions related to identifying associated corporations. The most important of these are as follows:

> **ITA 251(2) - Related Persons**　With respect to individuals, paragraph (a) notes that individuals are related if they are connected by blood relationship, marriage or adoption. Various other subsections in ITA 251 and 252 elaborate on this statement to point out that all of the following individuals would be "related" to the taxpayer:
>
> * Parents and grandparents, as well as the parents and grandparents of the taxpayer's spouse.
> * The taxpayer's spouse, as well as the spouse's siblings and their spouses.
> * Siblings of the taxpayer, as well as spouses of the taxpayer's siblings.
> * Children, including those that are adopted or born outside of marriage. Also included here would be spouses of children and children of the taxpayer's spouse.
>
> **ITA 251(2)(b)** indicates that a corporation is related to:
>
> * a person who controls it, if it is controlled by one person;
> * a person who is a member of a related group that controls it; or

- any person related to a person who controls it or who is a member of a related group that controls it.

ITA 251(2)(c) indicates that two corporations are related if:
- they are controlled by the same person or group of persons;
- each of the corporations is controlled by one person and the person who controls one of the corporations is related to the person who controls the other corporation;
- one of the corporations is controlled by one person and that person is related to any member of a related group that controls the other corporation;
- one of the corporations is controlled by one person and that person is related to each member of an unrelated group that controls the other corporation;
- any member of a related group that controls one of the corporations is related to each member of an unrelated group that controls the other corporation; or
- each member of an unrelated group that controls one of the corporation is related to at least one member of an unrelated group that controls the other corporation.

ITA 256(1.2)(c) - Control   The definition of associated companies also involves the concept of control. While there may be complications in the application of this concept, it generally means ownership of a majority of the voting shares of the corporation in question.

ITA 256(1.2)(a) - Definition Of Group   For purposes of defining associated companies, a group is two or more persons, each of whom owns shares in the corporation in question. A related group involves a group of persons, each member of which is related to every other member. An unrelated group is any group, other than a related group.

ITA 256(1.1) - Specified Class, Shares Of   This term refers to non voting shares that have a fixed dividend rate and redemption amount. Such shares are normally designated preferred shares. As they do not normally have voting rights, specified class shares are generally ignored in the determination of associated companies.

Deeming Rules   The most relevant deeming (a.k.a. look through) rules can be described as follows:

- **ITA 256(1.2)(d) - Holding Companies**   This provision indicates that where shares of a corporation are held by another corporation, a shareholder of the holding corporation is deemed to own the shares of the held corporation in proportion to their interest in the holding corporation. Similar provisions apply to shares held by partnerships and trusts.

- **ITA 256 (1.3) - Children Under 18**   This provision requires that shares owned at any time during the year by a child under 18 are deemed to be shares owned by each parent for purposes of determining associated companies.

- **ITA 256(1.4) - Rights And Options**   This provision requires that rights to acquire shares be treated as though they were exercised for purposes of determining associated companies. This subsection also indicates that, where a person has a right to require a shareholder to redeem, cancel, or acquire its own shares, for purposes of determining association, the corporation is deemed to have carried out the redemption, cancellation, or acquisition.

- **ITA 256(2) - Association With Third Corporation**   This provision indicates that two corporations, both of which are associated with a third corporation, are deemed to be associated with each other. This subsection also includes an election which can mitigate this rule. The third corporation can elect on Schedule 28 not to be associated with the other two corporations. A consequence of this is that the third corporation's annual business limit will be set at nil. However, the election will allow the other two corporations to be exempt from the association rules under ITA 256(2).

14-150.   Given these definitions and rules, we are now in a position to look at the definition of associated companies as it is found in ITA 256(1).

Examples - Associated Company Rules

14-151.   The preceding definitions are essential to the understanding of the associated corporation rules from ITA 256(1). This subsection contains five paragraphs designated (a) through (e), with each paragraph describing a relationship involving association. These five paragraphs will be given individual attention in the material which follows.

14-152.   The first of the paragraphs which define association states the following:

> **ITA 256(1)(a)**   One of the corporations controlled, directly or indirectly in any manner whatever, the other.

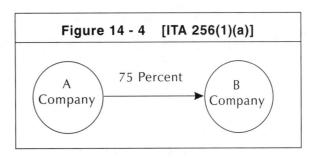

Figure 14 - 4   [ITA 256(1)(a)]

14-153.   This type of association can be illustrated by the situation shown in Figure 14-4 in which A Company owns 75 percent of the outstanding voting shares of B Company. In this situation, Company A and Company B are associated by virtue of ITA 256(1)(a).

14-154.   The second paragraph in the ITA 256 definition of associated companies is as follows:

> **ITA 256(1)(b)**   Both of the corporations were controlled, directly or indirectly in any manner whatever, by the same person or group of persons.

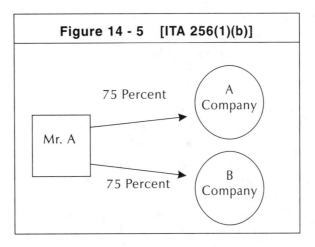

Figure 14 - 5   [ITA 256(1)(b)]

14-155.   This type of association can be illustrated by the situation shown in Figure 14-5. In this situation, Mr. A owns 75 percent of the shares in both A Company and B Company. As a consequence, these two Companies are associated by virtue of ITA 256 (1)(b), in that they are both controlled by the same person.

14-156.   The third paragraph in the ITA 256 definition of associated companies is as follows:

> **ITA 256(1)(c)**   Each of the corporations was controlled, directly or indirectly in any manner whatever, by a person and the person who so controlled one of the corporations was related to the person who so controlled the other, and either of those persons owned, in respect of each corporation, not less than 25 percent of the issued shares of any class, other than a specified class, of the capital stock thereof.

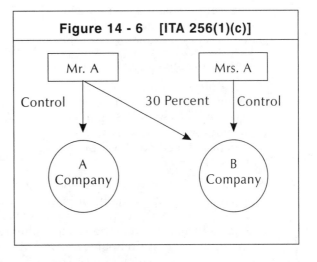

Figure 14 - 6   [ITA 256(1)(c)]

14-157.   This type of association can be illustrated by the situation shown in Figure 14-6. In this situation, Mr. A owns 70 percent of A Company and his spouse, Mrs. A, owns 70 percent of B Company. In addition, Mr. A owns not less than 25 percent of the shares of B Company. Provided that the B Company shares owned by Mr. A are not of a specified class, Companies A and B are associated under ITA 256(1)(c). As the required cross ownership can be in either direction, the two companies would also be associated if the cross ownership was by Mrs. A in A Company.

14-158.   A fourth paragraph in ITA 256(1) defining association is as follows:

ITA 256(1)(d)   One of the corporations was controlled, directly or indirectly in any manner whatever, by a person and that person was related to each member of a group of persons that so controlled the other corporation, and that person owned, in respect of the other corporation, not less than 25 percent of the issued shares of any class, other than a specified class, of the capital stock thereof.

14-159.   This type of association can be illustrated by the situation in Figure 14-7. In this situation, Mr. A owns 80 percent of the shares of A Company, while Mrs. A, and Mr. A's brother each own 35 percent of the shares of B Company. This means that Mr. A is related to each member of a group that controls B Company. Mr. A also has the required cross ownership in that he owns 30 percent of the shares of B Company. Provided that the shares of B Company owned by Mr. A are not of a specified class, A Company and B Company are associated by virtue of ITA 256(1)(d). Note that, under paragraph ITA 256(1)(d), the cross ownership has to be by Mr. A in B Company. If the cross ownership was in the other direction (e.g., Mrs. A owns 30 percent of A Company), the two Companies would not be associated.

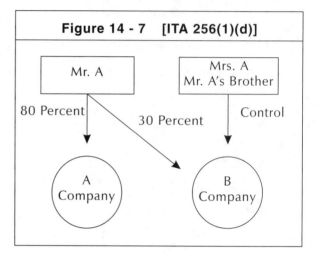

Figure 14 - 7   [ITA 256(1)(d)]

14-160.   The final paragraph in ITA 256(1) describing associated companies is as follows:

ITA 256(1)(e)   Each of the corporations was controlled, directly or indirectly in any manner whatever, by a related group and each of the members of one of the related groups was related to all of the members of the other related group, and one or more persons who were members of both related groups, either alone or together, owned, in respect of each corporation, not less than 25 percent of the issued shares of any class, other than a specified class, of the capital stock thereof.

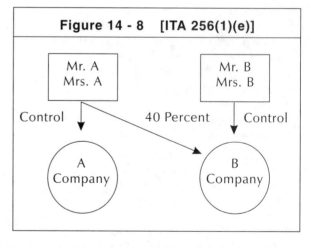

Figure 14 - 8   [ITA 256(1)(e)]

Exercise Fourteen-10 deals with associated companies. This would be an appropriate time to attempt this exercise.

14-161.   This type of association can be illustrated by the situation in Figure 14-8. Mr. and Mrs. A are a related group that control A Company and Mr. and Mrs. B are a related group that control B Company. If we assume that Mrs. B is Mr. A's sister, then each member of one related group is related to all of the members of the other related group. Mr. and Mrs. A each own 50 percent of the shares of A Company, Mr. and Mrs. B each own 30 percent of the shares of B Company. Mr. A owns the remaining 40 percent of the shares of B Company. In this situation, A Company and B Company are associated under ITA 256(1)(e). Once again, Mr. A's cross ownership has to be other than a specified class of shares. However, if A Company shares were available, the cross ownership could be in the other direction (e.g., Mrs. B owns not less than 25 percent of Company A).

Calculating The Small Business Deduction
The General Formula
14-162.   In our discussion of the M&P deduction, we noted that there were a number of constraints which served to limit this tax credit (see Paragraph 14-95). These were expressed in a formula under which the maximum deduction was the lesser of two amounts. A similar formula serves to limit the small business deduction. After noting that to qualify for this deduction, a corporation must be a CCPC throughout the year, ITA 125(1) specifies that the deduction from federal taxes payable is equal to 16 percent of the least of three figures:

A. Net Canadian active business income.
B. Taxable income, less:
  1. 10/3 of the aggregate of the foreign tax credit on foreign non business income (for this purpose only, the non business foreign tax credit is calculated without consideration of the additional refundable tax under ITA 123.3 or the general rate reduction under ITA 123.4); and
  2. 10/4 of the foreign tax credit on foreign business income (for this purpose only, the business income tax credit is calculated without consideration of the general rate reduction under ITA 123.4).
C. The annual business limit of $200,000, less any portion allocated to associated corporations.

Constraints On The Amount
14-163.   We have already noted that the deduction is only available on active business income earned in Canada, the item A constraint. We have also discussed possible problems with allocating the annual business limit of $200,000. These largely involve identification of associated companies and the allocation of this amount to the companies so identified.

14-164.   With respect to the constraints in item B, the reasons for their being listed here are basically the same as was the case when they were part of the formula for limiting the M&P deduction. As was the case with M&P profits, amounts eligible for the small business deduction may be eliminated in the process of converting Net Income For Tax Purposes into Taxable Income. This could happen, for example, if the company deducted a large non capital loss carry over. The Taxable Income constraint is included in order to insure that the small business deduction is not provided on income which is not part of Taxable Income. This point is illustrated in detail starting in Paragraph 14-98.

14-165.   The reason for removing a multiple of the foreign tax credits on non business and business income is also the same here as was the case with the M&P deduction. By removing 10/4 of any foreign tax credit on business income, the intent is to remove the income on which Canadian taxation was eliminated by the use of the credit. The fact that a different fraction is used for non business income is based on the assumption that this income is taxed at a 30 percent notional rate in Canada. The difference from the 40 percent rate is that, unlike business income, non business income is taxed in a province, making it eligible for the 10 percent federal tax abatement. A more complete discussion of this procedure was presented starting at Paragraph 14-103.

ITA 123.4 General Rate Reduction For CCPCs
Deduction Under ITA 123.4(2) - Available To Public Corporations
14-166.   The general rate reduction, as it applies to Canadian public companies, was considered in our discussion of the the federal corporate tax rate (see Paragraph 14-62). As noted in that discussion, this reduction is being accomplished through a deduction from tax payable under ITA 123.4 (2). This deduction is being phased in over four years, beginning at 1 percent in 2001 and increasing to 7 percent in 2004.

14-167.   The application of this deduction was subsequently illustrated in our discussion of the M&P deduction, where we noted that this general reduction would not be available on income which benefits from the 7 percent M&P deduction. This was implemented by requiring that the ITA 123.4(2) reduction be calculated as the "general rate reduction" percentage multiplied by "full rate taxable income". We note that, in order to avoid a corporation benefitting from both the general rate reduction and the M & P deduction, full rate taxable income was defined as regular taxable income, less 100/7 of the M & P deduction.

14-168.   Similar to the situation with the M&P deduction, the government has concluded that the deduction under ITA 123.4(2) should not be available on an income stream that has benefitted from the small business deduction or the preferential tax treatment of investment income that is available to CCPCs. This goal is implemented by defining full rate taxable income for a CCPC as follows:

Taxable Income, Reduced By:

1. 100/7 of any M&P deduction taken
    (To remove income that benefits from the M&P deduction);

2. 100/16 of any small business deduction taken
    (To remove income that benefits from the small business deduction);

3. The corporation's aggregate investment income for the year as defined in ITA 129(4); and

4. 100/7 of any Accelerated Deduction under ITA 123.4(3) - See following Section.

14-169.   You may recall from Paragraph 14-106 that the definition of aggregate investment income in ITA 129(4) includes net taxable capital gains, interest, rents, and royalties, but not dividends. It includes both domestic and foreign amounts of such income and the balance is reduced by net capital losses deducted during the year.

14-170.   As is covered in Chapter 15, a portion of the Part I tax paid by CCPCs on their aggregate investment income is refunded when dividends are paid. Since this type of income is already taxed advantageously when it is flowed through a CCPC, it does not receive the 1 percent general rate reduction or the accelerated deduction.

Accelerated Deduction Under ITA 123.4(3) - Available To CCPCs

14-171.   There is a further provision applicable to CCPCs in the new general rate reduction legislation. The government concluded that, while it would not provide the general reduction on the $200,000 of income that was eligible for the small business deduction, it would like to accelerate the phase in of the general reduction on an additional $100,000 of Canadian active business income. In effect, a reduction of 7 percent is provided under ITA 123.4(3) on the Canadian active business income of a CCPC between $200,000 and $300,000 beginning in 2001.

14-172.   In technical terms, this is accomplished by applying the 7 percent reduction to an amount that is determined first by selecting the least of the following three amounts:

1. 3/2 of the corporation's annual business limit. If the annual business limit for the corporation limit was not reduced (e.g., by sharing with an associated corporation), this amount would be $300,000 [(3/2)($200,000)].

2. Active business income for the year.

3. Taxable income used in the small business deduction calculation as specified in ITA 125(1) (see our Paragraph 14-162, part B), reduced by aggregate investment income as defined in ITA 129(4).

14-173.   The least of the preceding three amounts is reduced by the total of:

1. 100/7 of any M&P deduction taken; and

2. 100/16 of any small business deduction taken.

14-174.   Also note that on amounts that benefit from this accelerated deduction, the general ITA 123.4(2) rate reduction is not available. This is accomplished by further expanding the definition of full rate taxable income of a CCPC. As can be seen in Paragraph 14-168, one of the deductions from this figure is 100/7 of amounts deducted under ITA 123.4(3).

Example A CCPC has $150,000 in taxable income, made up entirely of active business income earned in Canada for the year ending December 31, 2001. It is associated with another company and, as per the agreement with that company, it is entitled to 40 percent of the annual business limit.

Tax Consequences This CCPC has a business limit of $80,000 [(40%)($200,000)] and a small business deduction of $12,800 [(16%)($80,000)]. Since its Taxable Income and Active Business Income are less than $120,000 [(3/2)($80,000)], it would have an additional deduction of $2,800 {[7%][(3/2)($80,000) - (100/16)($12,800)]} under ITA 123.4(3).

For purposes of the ITA 123.4(2) deduction from taxes payable, full rate taxable income would be $30,000 [$150,000 - (100/16)($12,800) - (100/7)($2,800)]. This would result in a deduction under ITA 123.4(2) of $300 [(1%)($30,000)].

14-175. This creates the potential for three different rates of federal corporate taxation on the active business income of a CCPC. On the first $200,000 of active business income, the rate is 13.12 percent [(38% - 10%)(1.04) - 16%], for amounts between $200,000 and $300,000, the rate is 22.12 percent [(38% - 10%)(1.04) - 7%], and for amounts in excess of $300,000, the rate is the full corporate rate of 28.12 percent [(38% - 10%)(1.04) - 1%]. Bringing in provincial corporate taxes results in a great variety of applicable rates, particularly since some provinces provide a special rate on small business income between $200,000 and $300,000 (e.g., Alberta), while others do not (e.g., Nova Scotia).

14-176. As active business income may also be M&P income, the question arises as to whether the 7 percent general rate reduction under ITA 123.4(3) is available on income that gets the 7 percent M&P deduction. The answer to this is negative. The amount eligible for this deduction must be reduced by 100/7 of any M&P deduction taken. As both deductions are equal to 7 percent, the order in which they are claimed does not appear to make any difference. However, the legislation is such that the M&P amount must be claimed first.

14-177. The example which follows incorporates most of the ideas discussed in this section.

Example For the year ending December 31, 2001, Kleen Ltd., a Canadian Controlled Private Corporation, has Taxable Income of $340,000, all of which is active business income. Of this total, $225,000 results from M&P activity. All income is earned in a province with a 6 percent rate on the first $200,000 of a CCPC's active business income and 15 percent on all other income. It is not associated with any other corporation.

Tax Consequences Tax Payable for Kleen Ltd. would be calculated as follows:

Base Amount of Part I Tax [(38%)($340,000)]	$129,200
Federal Surtax [(4%)(28%)($340,000)]	3,808
Federal Tax Abatement [(10%)($340,000)]	(34,000)
Small Business Deduction [(16%)($200,000)]	(32,000)
M&P Deduction [(7%)($225,000 - $200,000)]	(1,750)
ITA 123.4 Rate Reduction (Note)	(5,650)
Total Federal Tax Payable	$ 59,608
Provincial Tax Payable:	
[(6%)($200,000)]	12,000
[(15%)($340,000 - $200,000)]	21,000
Total Tax Payable	$ 92,608

Note The ITA 123.4(3) accelerated rate reduction must be calculated prior to the calculation of the ITA 123.4(2) general rate reduction. The calculation is as follows:

Enhanced Small Business Amount [(3/2)($200,000)]		$300,000
Amount Eligible For M&P [(100/7)($1,750)]	($ 25,000)	
Amount Eligible For SBD [(100/16)($32,000)]	(200,000)	(225,000)
Base For ITA 123.4(3)		$ 75,000
Rate		7%
ITA 123.4(3) Reduction		$ 5,250

Given the preceding, the ITA 123.4(2) reduction would be calculated as follows:

Taxable Income		$340,000
Amount Eligible For M&P [(100/7)($1,750)]	($ 25,000)	
Amount Eligible For SBD [(100/16)($32,000)]	(200,000)	
Amount Eligible For ITA 123.4(3) Reduction [(100/7)($5,250)]	(75,000)	(300,000)
Base For ITA 123.4(2)		$ 40,000
Rate		1%
ITA 123.4(2) Reduction		$ 400

Combining these figures gives the total reduction of $5,650 ($5,250 + $400).

14-178.   You will note that this results in a combined tax rate of 27.2 percent ($92,608 ÷ $340,000). This is higher than the 19.12 percent rate [(28%)(1.04) - 16% + 6%] that would apply if the company's Taxable Income had been below $200,000. However, it is significantly lower than the 43.12 percent rate [(28%)(1.04) - 1% + 15%] that would have applied if this had been a public company with no M&P profits.

Elimination Of Small Business Deduction For Large CCPCs
The Problem
14-179.   As the name implies, the small business deduction was designed to provide assistance to small corporations. For a variety of reasons, including the belief that such corporations have a positive impact on employment growth and the fact that small corporations often experience financing difficulties in their formative years, the generous tax advantages provided by this deduction were thought to be appropriate.

14-180.   However, in designing the provisions, eligibility was based on the type of income earned (active business income) and the type of corporation (CCPCs). No consideration was given to the size of the corporation's income or assets. As a consequence, some very large private corporations were receiving the benefit of the small business deduction on the first $200,000 of their active business income each year. This was clearly not in keeping with the intent of this legislation.

The Solution
14-181.   This problem has been resolved by phasing out the amount of income on which the small business deduction is available on the basis of the size of the corporation's liability to pay the Large Corporations Tax. The phase out begins when the corporation has Taxable Capital Employed In Canada (TCEC) of $10 million. The reduction increases on a straight line basis until the corporation has TCEC In Canada of $15 million and a Large Corporations Tax liability of $11,250. The ITA 125(5.1) formula for the reduction is as follows:

$$A \times \frac{B}{\$11,250} \text{ where,}$$

A   is the amount of the corporation's annual business limit for the year (if it is shared with associated corporations, it will be less than $200,000).

B   is the corporation's large corporations tax liability for the preceding year, without consideration of any reduction resulting from surtax paid.

14-182.   Note carefully that this formula calculates the **reduction** in the business limit, not the limit after the reduction. Recall that there is a basic exemption from the Large Corporations Tax for the first $10 million of TCEC. This means that for corporations with less than $10 million in TCEC, the Large Corporations tax liability will be nil, B in the above formula will be nil, and there will be no reduction in the amount eligible for the small business deduction.

14-183.   When the amount of TCEC reaches $15 million, the Large Corporations Tax liability will be $11,250 [(.00225)($15,000,000 - $10,000,000)] and the formula will produce an amount equal to the annual business limit. This means corporations with $15 million or more in TCEC will not benefit from the small business deduction.

14-184.   Not surprisingly, a CCPC that is associated with one or more other corporations in a taxation year ending in a given calendar year will be required to take into account its own as well as the large corporations tax liability of associated corporations for their last taxation year ending in the preceding calendar year.

14-185.   There are also provisions to negate the effect of short taxation years on the application of this formula. Specifically:

- the large corporations tax payable for previous years of less than 365 days will be increased to reflect a full year's tax liability; and

- the amount that would otherwise be deducted from a corporation's business limit for a taxation year of less than 365 days in length will be reduced in accordance with the rules that currently reduce the business limit for short taxation years.

Example
14-186.   The example which follows will illustrate the provisions discussed in the preceding section:

> **Example**   Largess Inc. is a CCPC with a December 31 year end. All of its income is earned in Canada and it is not associated with any other corporation. At December 31, 2001, the following information is available:
>
> | | |
> |---|---:|
> | 2001 Active Business Income | $ 423,000 |
> | 2001 Taxable Income | 550,000 |
> | Taxable Capital Employed In Canada During 2000 | 13,700,000 |

14-187.   For 2000, the actual Large Corporations Tax liability would be $8,325 [(.225%)($13,700,000 - $10,000,000)]. Using this in the ITA 125(5.1) formula would produce the following reduction in the annual business limit:

$$\$200,000 \times \frac{\$8,325}{\$11,250} = \$148,000$$

14-188.   Given this, the reduced annual business limit would be $52,000 ($200,000 - $148,000) and the small business deduction for 2001 would be 16 percent of the least of:

Active Business Income	$423,000
Taxable Income	550,000
Reduced Annual Business Limit ($200,000 - $148,000)	52,000

14-189.   The reduced annual business limit is the least of the three figures and the 2001 small business deduction would be $8,320 [(16%)($52,000)], a significant reduction from the $32,000 [(16%)($200,000)] that would have been available in the absence of ITA 125(5.1) and its requirement for reducing the annual business limit for large CCPCs.

Personal Services Corporations

14-190.   The small business deduction represents a very significant reduction in corporate taxes and, as a consequence, taxpayers have a strong incentive to channel income into a corporation qualifying for this benefit. At one point in time, this could be accomplished by having an executive of a corporation resign, establish a company, and immediately have this company sign a contract with his former employer to provide the same services as the individual was previously performing as an employee. Since this new corporation could then qualify for a small business deduction, the use of such personal services corporations could have provided significant tax savings for individuals such as executives, professional athletes, and entertainers.

14-191.   Under the current rules, such blatant tax avoidance schemes are no longer possible. To begin, ITA 125(7) defines a personal services business as follows:

> ... a business of providing services where
>
> (a) an individual who performs services on behalf of the corporation (referred to as an incorporated employee), or
> (b) any person related to the incorporated employee
>
> is a specified shareholder of the corporation and the incorporated employee would reasonably be regarded as an officer or employee of the person or partnership to whom or to which the services were provided but for the existence of the corporation, unless
>
> (c) the corporation employs in the business throughout the year more than five full time employees, or
> (d) the amount paid or payable to the corporation in the year for the services is received or receivable by it from a corporation with which it was associated in the year.

14-192.   In somewhat less technical language, a corporation will be classified as a personal services business where a specified shareholder of the corporation is providing services to another business and the individual who is performing the services can reasonably be regarded as an officer or employee of the entity for which the services are performed. As the term is used in this definition, specified shareholder refers to situations in which an individual owns, directly or indirectly, not less than a 10 percent interest in the company under consideration.

14-193.   If a corporation falls under the preceding definition, it is not eligible for the small business deduction on any of its income and, as a consequence, it is subject to tax at full corporate rates. In addition, no deduction is permitted to the corporation for any expenses other than:

- salary, wages, other remuneration, and benefits paid in the year to the individual who performed the services on behalf of the corporation; and

- other expenses that would normally be deductible against employment income. For example, travel expenses incurred to earn employment income.

14-194.   These rules are designed to remove the availability of the small business deduction in certain situations when a corporation is being used as a device to channel an individual's income from performing services into a less heavily taxed classification. With respect to personal services corporations established to replace an executive's personal employment arrangements, these rules have served to eliminate most of the tax incentives for such arrangements. However, athletes, entertainers and consultants may still find it attractive to incorporate. In many cases, they will either have sufficient diversity of income or a sufficient number of full time employees to qualify for the small business deduction.

Professional Corporations And Management Companies

14-195.   In general terms, these two types of corporations can be described as follows:

Professional Corporations   This term is used where a corporation is established to carry on the practice of a specified profession. These situations include the professional practice of an accountant, dentist, lawyer, medical doctor, veterinarian, or chiropractor. At one time, very few provinces permitted the incorporation of a professional practice. However, this is gradually changing as several provinces, including both Alberta and Ontario, now permit this practice.

Management Companies This is a term that refers to corporations established to provide various management services primarily to an unincorporated business. The unincorporated business is usually a professional practice, such as that of a doctor or dentist, which is not permitted to incorporate because of provincial legislation. The services provided by this type of company include various personnel functions such as payroll and accounting services, purchasing all supplies and equipment necessary to carry on the business, and providing the necessary office space required by the professional practice. The unincorporated business pays fees to the company to cover the cost of providing management services and to provide for some income. A 15 percent mark up for profit is usually allowed. The fees paid are deductible from the revenues of the professional practice. These companies are often used to transfer a portion of a professional's income to a lower income spouse or other related parties.

> Exercises Fourteen-11 and Fourteen-12 deal with calculating the small business deduction. This would be an appropriate time to attempt these exercises.

14-196. Both types of companies are eligible for the small business deduction. However, the fact that medical services are exempt goods under the GST legislation has resulted in a reduced attractiveness for management companies. While GST must be paid on services billed by the management company, these amounts cannot be recovered by such professionals as doctors and dentists because their services are GST exempt. Given this situation, management companies for medical professionals delivering GST exempt services are not as common as they once were.

Foreign Tax Credits For Corporations

Introduction

14-197. The foreign tax credits that are available to individuals earning foreign business or non business income were discussed in detail in Chapter 13. Under rules that are very similar to those applicable to individuals, corporations are also allowed to use foreign taxes paid on business and non business income as credits against Canadian taxes payable. While the rules are similar to those for individuals, there are differences that will be discussed in this Section.

Foreign Non Business (Property) Income Tax Credit

14-198. The formula which limits the Canadian tax credit for foreign taxes paid on foreign source non business income appears to be the same as that applicable to individuals. It is as follows:

The Foreign Non Business Income Tax Credit is the lesser of:

- The tax paid to the foreign government (for corporations, there is no 15 percent limit on the foreign non business taxes paid); and

- An amount determined by the following formula:

$$\left[\frac{\text{Foreign Non Business Income}}{\text{Adjusted Division B Income}} \right] [\text{Tax Otherwise Payable}]$$

14-199. While the general descriptions in the formula (e.g., Adjusted Division B Income and Tax Otherwise Payable) are the same as those applicable to individuals, their meaning is somewhat different. More specifically, for a corporation, "Adjusted Division B Income" is defined as follows:

Division B Income, less:
- net capital loss carry overs deducted under ITA 111(1)(b);
- taxable dividends received that are deductible under ITA 112; and
- dividends received from a foreign affiliate that are deductible under ITA 113.

14-200. Also for a corporation, "Tax Otherwise Payable" means Part I tax, after deducting the 10 percent federal tax abatement and the general rate reduction under ITA 123.4(2), but before deducting:

- the small business deduction;

- the M&P deduction;
- foreign tax credits, or investment tax credits; or
- in the case of a CCPC, the general rate reduction under ITA 123.4.

14-201. It includes both the surtax and the ITA 123.3 additional refundable tax on investment income (see Chapter 15 for a discussion of this tax).

14-202. You will recall that the purpose of the 10 percent federal tax abatement is to leave room for the provinces to tax corporations. It is deducted in the formula for determining foreign non business tax credits because non business income will, in general, be taxed in a province. As a consequence, it is appropriate to deduct this abatement in determining the limit on the foreign non business tax credit. You will note in the following discussion of the foreign business income tax credit, the abatement is not deducted from "Tax Otherwise Payable" in the formula which limits that credit. This reflects the fact that, in general, foreign business income will not be taxed in a province and no abatement will be available on such amounts.

14-203. Foreign non business income taxes paid in excess of the amount that can be applied as a credit against federal taxes payable can usually be claimed against provincial taxes payable. There is no carry over of unclaimed amounts to previous or subsequent years. As noted in Chapter 13, amounts that are not claimed against federal or provincial taxes payable can generally be deducted by a taxpayer under ITA 20(12). An exception to this is when the amount relates to a dividend paid to a corporation by an incorporated foreign affiliate.

Foreign Business Income Tax Credit

14-204. The formula which limits the amount of foreign business income taxes paid that can be used as a foreign tax credit is as follows:

The Foreign Business Income Tax Credit is the least of:

- The tax paid to the foreign government
- An amount determined by the following formula:

$$\left[\frac{\text{Foreign Non Business Income}}{\text{Adjusted Division B Income}} \right] [\text{Tax Otherwise Payable}]$$

- Tax Otherwise Payable for the year, less any foreign tax credit taken on non business income under ITA 126(1).

14-205. As was the case with individuals, there is an additional factor to consider in the case of foreign business income tax credits. This is the "Tax Otherwise Payable", reduced by any foreign non business income tax credit deducted under ITA 126(1).

14-206. The other difference in the calculation of the foreign non business and foreign business income tax credit is the composition of the "Tax Otherwise Payable". As was noted previously, this figure is not reduced by the 10 percent federal tax abatement, reflecting the fact that foreign business income will not be taxed in a Province. Also different is the fact that this version of "Tax Otherwise Payable" does not include the additional refundable tax on investment income under ITA 123.3. (See Chapter 15.)

14-207. Unlike the case with the foreign non business income taxes paid in excess of amounts used as tax credits, unused foreign business taxes can be carried back to the three preceding taxation years and forward to the seven subsequent taxation years. In calculating the allowable tax credit for such carry overs, these unused amounts will be added to the foreign tax paid factor in the calculation of the foreign business income tax credit.

Investment Tax Credits

General Rules

14-208. Investment tax credits are tax incentives that are available to Canadian taxpayers who are earning business income. They are available, on basically the same terms, to both individuals and corporations.

14-209. These credits have been used to provide specific direction to the allocation of economic resources in several areas, including manufacturing and processing, scientific research, as well as to particular regions of the country. In recent years, there has been a reduction in the general availability of these credits. More specifically, there has been a tendency to restrict their availability to certain regions of the country and to scientific research expenditures.

14-210. In general terms, the procedures for investment tax credits, which are contained in ITA 127(5) through ITA 127.41, allow the taxpayer to deduct a specified percentage of the cost of certain types of current and capital expenditures from taxes payable. The credits provide for a direct reduction in the amount of taxes that are payable.

14-211. When capital expenditures are involved, the amount of the investment tax credit must be removed from the capital cost of the asset so that only the net capital cost is deductible through capital cost allowances. The deduction from UCC will occur in the year after the claim is made. The capital cost must also be reduced by any government or non government assistance received for the property such as grants or subsidies. However, the reduction for these other types of assistance is made in the year in which the assistance is received.

14-212. When the investment tax credits are earned by making deductible current expenditures, the deductible amount of the expenditures is reduced by the amount of the investment tax credits. In general, this reduction takes place in the taxation year in which the current expenditure is made. An exception to this is when the credits are for current scientific research and experimental development expenditures. Like investment tax credits related to capital expenditures, investment tax credits related to current scientific research and experimental development expenditures are deducted in the year following their incurrence.

14-213. In effect, the tax mechanism that is involved with investment tax credits is that the enterprise gives up $1 of current or future tax deductions, in return for a $1 reduction in the amount of tax payable. This is clearly beneficial in that the cost of losing a $1 deduction is only $1 times the company's tax rate. By contrast, $1 of reduced taxes is a cash flow savings of $1.

Eligible Expenditures

14-214. To provide a general picture of the types of assets that are eligible for investment tax credits, brief descriptions are provided of expenditures that qualify for these credits:

Qualified Property is defined in ITA 127(9) with further elaboration provided in ITR 4600 and 4601. As presented in this material, qualified property must be newly acquired for use in Canada and it must be used in specified activities. These activities include manufacturing and processing, operating an oil or gas well, extracting minerals, logging, farming or fishing, storing grain and producing industrial minerals.

Qualified Scientific Research And Experimental Development Expenditures (SR&ED) include amounts spent for basic or applied research and for the development of new products and processes. Expenditures may be current, if they relate to administration or maintenance of related facilities or equipment, or they may be capital in nature. This is discussed more fully in the next section of this Chapter on scientific research and experimental development.

Other As discussed in Chapter 13, for individuals there is an investment tax credit for investments made in labour sponsored venture capital corporations set up by a province. This credit is provided under ITA 127.4 and is based on a percentage of the investment made.

Rates
General

14-215. The rates for various types of expenditures are generally found under the definition of "specified percentage" in ITA 127(9). While there have been a number of changes in recent years, the current rates are as follows:

Type Of Expenditure	Rate
Qualified Property	
In Gaspe And Atlantic Provinces	10%
Prescribed Offshore Regions (East Coast)	10%
Rest Of Canada	Nil
Scientific Research And Experimental Development	
Incurred By Any Taxpayers	20%
Incurred By Some Canadian Controlled Private Corporation (CCPCs)	35%

CCPCs Rate On SR&ED

14-216.   Note that there is an additional 15 percent credit on the SR&ED of some CCPCs. This rate, which is provided for in ITA 127(10.1), is only available on the first $2 million of qualified expenditures, a limit which must be shared by associated corporations.

14-217.   To qualify for this special rate on the full $2 million, the company must be a "qualifying corporation". For this purpose, a "qualifying corporation" is a corporation that is a CCPCs throughout the year, with Taxable Income in the immediately preceding year that is no more than $200,000. If the corporation's Taxable Income in the preceding year exceeds the $200,000 limit, the corporation is no longer a qualifying corporation and the eligible amount is reduced. More specifically, under ITA 127(10.2) the $2 million limit for eligibility must be reduced by $10 for each $1 of the corporation's taxable income in excess of $200,000. This means that when the corporation's taxable income in the previous year reaches $400,000, the eligible limit is reduced by the full $2,000,000 [($10)($400,000 - $200,000)] to nil. In applying this limit, associated corporations have to be considered.

Refundable Investment Tax Credits

General Rules - 40 Percent Refund

14-218.   A problem with tax credits is that, in general, they have value only when the taxpayer has a tax liability. To deal with this problem, some tax credits are "refundable". What this means is that, when a taxpayer has earned a tax credit and does not have sufficient Taxes Payable to use it in full, the government will pay ("refund") all or part of the unused amount to the taxpayer. We have encountered this type of situation previously for individuals with respect to the GST tax credit, as well as the refundable medical expense tax credit (see Chapter 13).

14-219.   A refund can be made for up to 40 percent of the refundable investment tax credits earned by a taxpayer, provided the taxpayer is:

- an individual;
- a qualifying corporation (i.e., a Canadian controlled private corporation with Taxable Income in the previous year of $200,000 or less); or
- a trust where the beneficiary is an individual or a qualifying corporation.

14-220.   This means that if, for example, an individual had $1,000,000 in SR&ED current expenditures, he would be eligible for a $200,000 [(20%)($1,000,000)] investment tax credit. If the individual did not have sufficient Taxes Payable to use this credit, the government would provide a refund (payment) of up to $80,000 [(40%)($200,000)].

Additional Refund - 100 Percent Refund

14-221.   In the case of a qualifying corporation (a CCPC with Taxable Income of $200,000 or less for the previous year), additional amounts are refundable. To the extent that current SR&ED expenditures are eligible for the additional 15 percent investment tax credit (total credit of 35 percent), the resulting credit is eligible for a 100 percent refund. This means that a qualifying corporation that spends $2,000,000 on current SR&ED expenditures is eligible for a refund payment of up to $700,000 [(35%)($2,000,000)] from the government. This is, of course, an extremely rich tax benefit for corporations that qualify.

14-222.   The 100 percent refund is only available on the first $2,000,000 of current expenditures that qualify for the additional 15 percent investment tax credit. Capital expenditures that qualify for this additional 15 percent are refundable at a lower rate of 40 percent. An example will clarify this point:

> **Example**   Research Inc., a Canadian controlled private company, has current SR&ED expenditures of $750,000 and capital SR&ED expenditures of $600,000. The Company has no Taxable Income in the current or the preceding year.

> **Tax Consequences**   The Company's total investment tax credit will be $472,500 [(35%)($750,000 + $600,000)].   The refundable portion will be $346,500 [(100%)(35%)($750,000) + (40%)(35%)($600,000)].

14-223.   When the CCPC's Taxable Income for the preceding year is more than $200,000, the amount eligible for the 15 percent additional credit is reduced in the manner described in Paragraph 14-214. As the 100 percent refund is only available on amounts that qualify for this additional credit, there is a corresponding reduction in the ability of the corporation to claim such a refund.

> Exercise Fourteen-13 deals with refundable investment tax credits. This would be an appropriate time to attempt this exercise.

Carry Overs Of Investment Tax Credits

14-224.   Under the definition of investment tax credit in ITA 127(9), unused investment tax credits may be carried back for up to three years and forward for up to ten years. Note that this carry forward provision is more generous than the seven year period that is available for non capital loss carry forwards. A taxpayer is required to claim all other available tax credits before calculating and claiming the investment tax credit for the year. Also, a taxpayer must reduce, to the fullest extent possible, federal taxes payable for a current year before using investment tax credits to reduce previous years' federal taxes payable.

Acquisition Of Control

14-225.   As was the case with companies having accumulated loss carry forwards, the government is concerned about the large amount of unused investment tax credits that are being carried forward in the tax records of Canadian corporations. The carry forwards reflect the fact that these corporations have experienced losses and, as a consequence, have not had a tax liability to which the credits could be applied. While the government does not object to these credits being used against taxes payable resulting from improved profitability for the corporations that have experienced losses, there is concern that these loss corporations will be acquired by profitable corporations in order to make use of these credits. As a consequence, there are acquisition of control rules that apply to the carry forward of investment tax credits in a manner similar to the acquisition of control rules that apply to the carry forward of non capital losses.

14-226.   These rules are found in ITA 127(9.1) and (9.2). They state that when there is an acquisition of control, investment tax credits earned prior to the change may be used:

• to obtain a refund, to the extent that the unused investment tax credit is included in refundable investment tax credits for the period;

• for the taxation year in which an acquisition of control occurs, to offset the corporation's Part I tax liability for the period, on income from a business that was carried on before the acquisition of control, on income from a similar business subsequent to the acquisition of control, or on net taxable capital gains from the disposition of property owned at the time control was acquired;

• for taxation years after the year in which the acquisition of control occurred, to offset that portion of the Part I tax liability on income from the same or similar business in respect of which the investment tax credit was earned, or to net taxable capital gains from the disposition of property owned before the time control was acquired.

14-227.   The effect of these provisions is to put investment tax credits on a footing similar to that given to non capital loss carry overs when there is an acquisition of control.

Special Incentives For SR&ED Expenditures

General Rules

14-228.   There is a well established belief that SR&ED expenditures are vital to the continued growth and prosperity of the Canadian economy. As a consequence, a generous system of tax incentives is available to businesses that make such expenditures. For example, under these programs, it is possible for a corporation to receive a cash payment (refundable investment tax credit) of up to $700,000 for a single year. It is recognized that Canada's system for encouraging SR&ED expenditures is one of the most generous in the world.

14-229.   Given the magnitude of the potential benefits associated with SR&ED expenditures, it is not surprising the rules and regulations incorporated into these programs are very complex. While it would not be difficult to devote an entire Chapter to this subject, that would not be in keeping with the objectives of this text. What follows is a broad overview of the provisions associated with SR&ED costs.

14-230.   The rules for the deduction of SR&ED expenditures are found in ITA 37 and in Part XXIX of the *Income Tax Regulations*. As specified in these sources, the treatment of SR&ED has the following special features:

- All qualifying SR&ED costs are allocated to a special SR&ED pool. Amounts included in this pool can be deducted in the current or any subsequent year. There is no time limit on their deductibility as would be the case if they simply contributed to a non capital loss carry forward balance.

- In general, capital expenditures other than real property can be deducted, in full, in the year that the assets become available for use. There are exceptions to this which will be described in the subsequent material.

- The amounts added to the SR&ED cost pool are eligible for investment tax credits ranging from 20 percent to 35 percent, depending on the type of taxpayer making the expenditures and the amount of the expenditures.

14-231.   To be eligible for this treatment, expenditures must qualify as SR&ED expenditures, and they must be related to a business carried on by the taxpayer making the expenditures. Further, the expenditures are only deductible from income of a business carried on in Canada.

Qualifying Expenditures

Basic Definition

14-232.   ITR 2900 defines scientific research and experimental development as follows:

.... the systematic investigation or search carried out in a field of science or technology by means of experiment or analysis, that is to say,

(a) basic research, namely, work undertaken for the advancement of scientific knowledge without a specific practical application in view,

(b) applied research, namely, work undertaken for the advancement of scientific knowledge with a specific practical application in view,

(c) experimental development, namely, work undertaken for the purposes of achieving technological advancement for the purposes of creating new, or improving existing, materials, devices, products or processes, including incremental improvements thereto, or

(d) work with respect to engineering, design, operations research, mathematical analysis, computer programming, data collection, testing and psychological research where such work is commensurate with the needs, and directly in support, of the work described in paragraphs (a), (b), or (c),

but does not include work with respect to

(e) market research or sales promotion;

(f) quality control or routine testing of materials, devices, products or processes;

(g) research in the social sciences or the humanities;

(h) prospecting, exploring or drilling for or producing minerals, petroleum, or natural gas;

(i) the commercial production of a new or improved material, device or product or the commercial use of a new or improved process;

(j) style changes; or

(k) routine data collection.

Rules For Current Expenditures

14-233. To qualify for SR&ED treatment, the current expenditure must be incurred for this purpose and must relate to the business of the taxpayer. This would include expenditures made for SR&ED outside of Canada on behalf of the taxpayer.

14-234. As described in IT-151R5, one category of current expenditures includes:

> expenditures of a current (or capital) nature incurred for and **all or substantially all** of which were attributable to the prosecution, or to the provision of premises, facilities, or equipment for the prosecution, of SR&ED in Canada.

14-235. The IT Bulletin points out that, in this context, all or substantially all means 90 percent or more. If this test is met, 100 percent of the expenditure goes into the SR&ED pool. If the usage is less than 90 percent for SR&ED, the expenditure will still be deductible, but not as an SR&ED expenditure.

14-236. A second category of current SR&ED expenditures is described in the Bulletin as follows:

> expenditures of a current nature that were directly attributable to the prosecution of SR&ED in Canada, or expenditures of a current nature that were directly attributable to the provision of premises, facilities or equipment for the prosecution of SR&ED in Canada.

14-237. In somewhat simplified terms, this is a reference to SR&ED related overhead. Such costs could include labour, general and administrative costs, the cost of heat and light, and long distance telephone charges. Note that, for these overhead type expenditures, there is no 90 percent test. These expenditures will be allocated on a pro rata basis, without the application of any minimum threshold.

14-238. For the costs of material and labour, qualification for inclusion in the SR&ED pool as an overhead cost requires only that they be directly attributable to the prosecution of SR&ED. With respect to other types of overhead costs, the taxpayer must be able to demonstrate that they would not have been incurred if the SR&ED activities were not being carried out.

Rules For Capital Expenditures

14-239. As previously noted, capital expenditures can be allocated to the SR&ED pool and written off in the year of acquisition, subject to the available for use rules. Assets excluded from this treatment are land and most buildings acquired after 1987. However, a building that has a special SR&ED purpose (e.g., a wind tunnel) does qualify. This same approach applies to rents for buildings. That is, the rents qualify for SR&ED treatment only if a special purpose building is involved.

14-240. Unlike current expenditures, capital expenditures must be for SR&ED carried on in Canada in order to qualify for inclusion in the pool. In addition, capital expenditures must meet the 90 percent (all or substantially all) threshold in order to be included in the SR&ED pool. If they do not meet this test, they will be allocated to the appropriate CCA Class.

14-241. Capital assets that are allocated to the SR&ED pool cannot be allocated to a CCA Class. Further, within the SR&ED pool, each asset must be in a separate Class. The deduction of its cost will be considered deemed CCA, and its disposal may result in recapture or capital gains.

Shared Use Capital Equipment

14-242.   We noted previously that there is no provision for pro rating the cost of capital expenditures where the use for SR&ED purposes is less than 90 percent. The costs of such assets are not eligible for inclusion in the SR&ED pool or, in general, for the special SR&ED investment tax credit rate.

14-243.   While this 90 percent rule continues in place with respect to adding the cost of shared use capital assets to the SR&ED pool, a different investment tax credit rule applies to capital equipment acquired after 1992 that does not meet the 90 percent test, but is used primarily (more than 50 percent) for SR&ED purposes. One-half of the cost of such shared use equipment is eligible for a special investment tax credit that becomes available over a two year period. In general terms, the credit is based on one-half the cost of the equipment and becomes available over the first two years of the asset's use.

14-244.   More specifically, after the shared use equipment has been used for 12 months, an investment tax credit becomes available. It is calculated at one of the usual rates for SR&ED credits (20 percent or 35 percent) on one-quarter of the cost of the equipment. After 24 months of usage, a second investment tax credit becomes available with respect to this equipment. It is also calculated on one-quarter of the cost of the equipment.

14-245.   Note, however, that none of the cost of such assets are allocated to the SR&ED pool. Rather, the full cost is allocated to the appropriate CCA class. It would appear to follow that the investment tax credits on these assets are deducted from the relevant CCA classes and not from the SR&ED pool.

Prescribed Proxy Amount

14-246.   We have previously noted that current expenditures of an overhead nature could be allocated to the SR&ED pool, provided they are directly attributable to SR&ED activities. This allocation process can be difficult and time consuming in that the taxpayer has to be able to demonstrate that the costs are directly attributable to SR&ED activities, that they are pro rated to SR&ED and other activities on a reasonable basis, and, except in the case of materials or labour, that they would not have been incurred in the absence of SR&ED activity. To simplify this situation, an alternative approach can be elected.

14-247.   This election would not change the treatment of current or capital SR&ED expenditures that meet the all or substantially all test. These costs, which meet the test of being at least 90 percent attributable to SR&ED, will continue to be allocated to the SR&ED pool and will be eligible for the usual SR&ED tax credits.

14-248.   However, all other current expenditures, including those that are directly attributable to SR&ED and could be allocated to the pool as overhead costs, must be deducted as ordinary expenditures. The only effect of this change is that those expenditures that could have been included in the SR&ED pool lose their right to an unlimited carry forward period. In the absence of taxable income, they will contribute to the non capital loss carry forward balance that is subject to a seven year limitation.

14-249.   In exchange for giving up SR&ED treatment of these SR&ED overhead amounts, the taxpayer would be allowed to establish what is referred to as a "prescribed proxy amount". This amount would be calculated as 65 percent of salaries and wages of employees that are directly engaged in SR&ED carried on in Canada.

14-250.   The resulting prescribed proxy amount would not be added to the SR&ED pool nor would it be deductible as an ordinary business expense. However, it would be eligible for investment tax credits at the usual SR&ED rates. In addition, the value of any investment tax credits earned on the prescribed proxy amount must be deducted from the SR&ED pool in the year following their use.

14-251.   Whether or not this election is desirable will depend on whether actual SR&ED overhead costs are more or less than 65 percent of SR&ED labour costs. However, since the use of the election is much simpler than going through the detailed overhead allocation process, it is likely that many taxpayers will use the election and not make any effort to answer this question.

References

14-252.   For more detailed study of the material in this Chapter, we refer you to the following:

ITA 37(1)	Scientific Research And Experimental Development
ITA 82(1)	Taxable Dividends Received
ITA 89(1)	Definitions (Private Corporation And Public Corporation)
ITA 110	Deductions Permitted
ITA 111	Losses Deductible
ITA 112	Deduction Of Taxable Dividends Received By Corporations Resident In Canada
ITA 113	Deduction In Respect Of Dividend Received From Foreign Affiliate
ITA 121	Deduction For Taxable Dividends
ITA 123	Rate For Corporations
ITA 123.1	Corporation Surtax
ITA 124	Deduction From Corporation Tax
ITA 125	Small Business Deduction
ITA 125.1(1)	Manufacturing And Processing Profits Deductions
ITA 127 to 127.41	Investment Tax Credits
ITA 256	Associated Corporations
ITA Part I.3	Tax On Large Corporations
ITR 2900	Scientific Research And Experimental Development
ITR 4600	Investment Tax Credit - Qualified Property
ITR 4601	Investment Tax Credit - Qualified Transportation Equipment
ITR 4602	Certified Property
ITR 5200	Canadian Manufacturing And Processing Profits - Basic Formula
ITR 5201	Canadian Manufacturing And Processing Profits - Small Manufacturers' Rule
ITR 5202	Canadian Manufacturing And Processing Profits - Interpretation
ITR Part IV	Taxable Income Earned In A Province By A Corporation
IC 78-4R3	Investment Tax Credit Rates
IC 86-4R3	Scientific Research And Experimental Development
IT-64R4	Corporations: Association And Control
IT-67R3	Taxable Dividends From Corporations Resident In Canada
IT-73R5	The Small Business Deduction
IT-98R2	Investment Corporations
IT-145R (Consolidated)	Canadian Manufacturing And Processing Profits — Reduced Rate Of Corporate Tax
IT-151R5	Scientific Research And Experimental Development Expenditures
IT-177R2	Permanent Establishment Of A Corporation In A Province And Of A Foreign Enterprise In Canada
IT-189R2	Corporations Used By Practising Members Of Professions
IT-232R3	Losses — Their Deductibility In The Loss Year Or In Other Years
IT-302R3	Losses Of A Corporation — The Effect That Acquisition Of Control, Amalgamations, And Wind Ups Have On Their Deductibility — After January 15, 1987
IT-391R	Status Of Corporations
IT-458R2	Canadian Controlled Private Corporation

Exercises

(The solutions for these exercises can be found following Chapter 21 of the text.)

Exercise Fourteen - 1 (Schedule 1 Reconciliation)

You have been asked to prepare a Schedule 1 reconciliation of accounting and tax net income for the year ending December 31. Available information includes the following:

1. A capital asset was sold for $48,300. It had a cost of $120,700 and had a net book value of $53,900. It was the last asset in its CCA Class and the balance in this Class was $34,600 before the disposal. There were no other additions or disposals during the year.

2. On January 1 of the current year, the company acquired goodwill at a cost of $180,000. For accounting purposes it is being amortized over a period of 10 years on a straight line basis.

3. During the year, the company has expensed estimated warranty costs of $15,000.

4. Premium amortization on the company's bonds payable was $4,500 for the current year.

Required: Determine the addition and/or deduction that would be made in Schedule 1 for each of the preceding items.

Exercise Fourteen - 2 (Taxable Income)

The Chapman Company had Net Income For Tax Purposes for the taxation year ending December 31, 2001 of $263,000. This amount included $14,250 in taxable capital gains. During the year, the Company received dividends from taxable Canadian corporations in the amount of $14,200, made donations to registered charities of $8,600, and made contributions to a federal political party of $4,300. At the beginning of the year, the company had a non capital loss carry over from 1997 of $82,000, as well as a net capital loss from 1995 of $27,000. Determine the Company's minimum Taxable Income for the year ending December 31, 2001.

Exercise Fourteen - 3 (Stop Loss Rules)

On June 16, 2001, Loren Ltd. acquires 1,000 shares of Manon Inc. at a cost of $25.30 per share. On July 1, 2001, these shares pay a dividend of $2.16 per share. Loren sells the shares on July 29, 2001 for $21.15 per share. Assuming adequate taxable capital gains, what is the amount of the allowable capital loss, if any, that Loren Ltd. will include in its tax return for the taxation year ending December 31, 2001?

Exercise Fourteen - 4 (Acquisition Of Control)

India Inc. has two divisions, one of which sells fountain pens, the other provides professional accounting services. In the taxation year ending December 31, 2000, the pen division had a Net Loss For Tax Purposes of $192,000, and the accounting division showed Net Income For Tax Purposes of $57,000. For the taxation year ending December 31, 2001, the pen division had Net Income For Tax Purposes of $42,000 and the accounting division had Net Income For Tax Purposes of $247,000. Determine taxable income for each of the two years, assuming that there was no acquisition of control in either year. How would your answer be different if there was an acquisition of control on January 1, 2001?

Exercise Fourteen - 5 (Non Capital Losses)

The following information is for Loser Ltd., a Canadian public company, for the taxation year ending December 31, 2001:

Capital Gains	$111,000
Capital Losses	(84,000)
Allowable Business Investment Loss	(5,250)
Dividends Received	48,000
Canadian Source Interest Income	27,200
Business Loss	(273,000)

The Company also has a net capital loss from the 1997 taxation year of $28,500. It would like to deduct this loss during the current year. Determine the non capital loss balance [ITA 111(8)(b)] for Loser Ltd. at the end of the 2001 taxation year.

Exercise Fourteen - 6 (Net Income With Losses)
For the taxation year ending December 31, 2001, Hacker Inc. has business and property income of $63,500. Also during this year, capital asset dispositions result in capital gains of $23,100 and capital losses of $38,400. The Company experiences a further loss on the sale of shares of a small business corporation in the amount of $151,500. Determine Hacker Inc.'s Net Income For Tax Purposes, any non capital loss at the end of the year, and any net capital loss at the end of the year.

Exercise Fourteen - 7 (Geographical Allocation)
Sundown Ltd., a Canadian public company, has Taxable Income for the taxation year ending December 31, 2001 in the amount of $226,000. It has Canadian permanent establishments in Ontario and Manitoba. The Company's gross revenues for the 2001 taxation year are $2,923,000, with $1,303,000 of this accruing at the permanent establishment in Ontario, and $896,000 accruing at the permanent establishment in Manitoba. Wages and salaries total $165,000 for the year. Of this total, $52,000 is at the permanent establishment in Ontario and $94,000 is at the permanent establishment in Manitoba. Based on this information, calculate federal tax payable for the taxation year ending December 31, 2001.

Exercise Fourteen - 8 (Part I.3 Tax)
Big Ltd., a Canadian public company, has Taxable Capital of $27,900,000. Its Taxable Income for the current year is $623,000, of which 78 percent is earned in a province. It is not associated with any other company. Determine the amount of Part I.3 tax that is payable by Big Ltd. for the current taxation year.

Exercise Fourteen - 9 (M&P Deduction)
Glass Formers Ltd., a corporation involved in the manufacture of various glass products, has active business income which totals $333,000. It owns $1,432,000 in depreciable capital assets, and leases additional capital assets at an annual cost of $26,000. All of the leased capital assets are used in producing glass products. With respect to the assets owned, they are used as follows:

Production And Handling	45%
Storing Finished Goods	12%
Storing Raw Materials	15%
Purchasing Operations	10%
Quality And Pollution Control	8%
Employee Cafeteria And Recreational Facilities	10%

The company's total salaries and wages for the current year are $987,000. All of this labour was directed at qualified M&P activities. In addition, $45,000 is spent on contract workers involved in administration of the corporation.

Based on the preceding information, determine the company's manufacturing and processing profits for the current year.

Exercise Fourteen - 10 (Associated Companies)
The Top Company owns 65 percent of the shares of Middle Company, as well as 10 percent of the shares of Bottom Company. Middle Company owns 22 percent of the shares of Bottom Company. Mr. Top, who owns all of the shares of Top Company, also owns 5 percent of the shares of Bottom Company. Mr. Top's 12 year old son owns a further 15 percent of the Bottom Company shares. Mr. Top has options to acquire another 10 percent of Bottom Company's shares. Indicate which of these Companies are associated, citing the relevant provisions of the *Income Tax Act*.

Exercise Fourteen - 11 (Small Business Deduction Reduction)

Largely Small Inc. is a Canadian controlled private corporation. Its Net Income For Tax Purposes is $1,233,000 for the year ending December 31, 2001, all of which is active business income except for $36,000 in foreign source non business income. Fifteen percent of this amount was withheld in the foreign jurisdiction and the corporation receives a foreign tax credit against federal taxes payable that is equal to the amount withheld. The corporation's only deduction in the calculation of Taxable Income is for a non capital loss carryover of $914,000. The corporation had Taxable Capital Employed In Canada of $11,300,000 for the year ending December 31, 2000 and $11,600,000 for the year ending December 31, 2001. It is not associated with any other corporation. Determine the amount of Largely Small Inc.'s small business deduction for the year ending December 31, 2001.

Exercise Fourteen - 12 (Small Business and M&P Deductions)

Marion Manufacturing is a Canadian controlled private corporation throughout the current taxation year. It has Net Income For Tax Purposes of $362,000, a figure which includes $311,000 in manufacturing and processing profits (as per ITR 5200). The $362,000 also included foreign source business income of $21,000 and taxable capital gains of $30,000. Because of withholding on the foreign source business income, the Company is entitled to a foreign tax credit of $3,150. The Company's only deduction in the calculation of Taxable Income is donations to registered charities in the amount of $210,000. Marion is not associated with any other Company. Determine the amount of Marion's small business deduction and Marion's manufacturing and processing deduction. Include in your answer any alternatives that could be used to save taxes.

Exercise Fourteen - 13 (Refundable Investment Tax Credits)

Sci-Tech Inc. has made a number of expenditures that qualify for investment tax credits. They have invested $123,000 in Qualified Property in the Province of Nova Scotia. In addition they have $1,200,000 in current expenditures for Scientific Research And Experimental Development, as well as $1,500,000 in capital expenditures for Scientific Research And Experimental Development. The Company is a Canadian controlled private company and its Taxable Income for the previous year was $176,000. As the Company has no Taxable Income for the current year, its taxes payable are nil. Determine the amount of the refund that Sci-Tech will receive as a result of earning these investment tax credits.

Problems For Self Study

(The solutions for these problems can be found following Chapter 21 of the text.)

Self Study Problem Fourteen - 1

The Income Statement that has been prepared by Margo Ltd.'s accountant for the year ending December 31, 2001, is as follows:

Sales Revenue		$925,000
Cost Of Goods Sold (Note 1)		(717,000)
Gross Profit		$208,000
Operating Expenses:		
Salaries And Wages	$40,200	
Rents	22,200	
Property Taxes (Note 2)	8,800	
Depreciation	35,600	
Amortization Of Goodwill (Note 3)	1,700	
Charitable Contributions	19,800	
Legal Fees (Note 4)	2,220	
Bad Debt Expense	7,100	
Warranty Provision	5,500	
Social Club Membership Fees	7,210	
Other Operating Expenses	39,870	(190,200)
Operating Income		$ 17,800
Other Revenues (Expenses):		
Gain On Sale Of Investments (Note 5)	$9,500	
Interest Revenue	2,110	
Interest On Late Income Tax Instalments	(1,020)	
Investment Counsellor Fees	(500)	
Foreign Interest Income (Note 6)	1,530	
Dividends From Taxable Canadian Corporations	3,000	
Premium On Redemption Of Preferred Shares	(480)	14,140
Income Before Taxes		$ 31,940

Notes And Other Information:

1. The calculation of cost of goods sold was based on an opening inventory of $225,000 and a closing inventory of $198,600. In addition, the closing inventory was reduced $15,000 by a reserve for future declines in value. This is the first year the Company has used an inventory reserve.

2. Property taxes include $1,200 for taxes paid on vacant land. The company has held this land since 1994 in anticipation of relocating its head office.

3. As the result of a business combination during the year, Margo Ltd. acquired $34,000 in goodwill. For accounting purposes, this balance is being amortized on a straight line basis over 20 years. The goodwill qualifies as an eligible capital expenditure for tax purposes. At the beginning of the year, there is no balance in the cumulative eligible capital account.

4. The legal fees are made up of $1,200 paid to appeal an income tax assessment and $1,020 paid for general corporate matters.

5. The gain on the sale of investments involved marketable securities with a cost of $21,000. The securities were sold for $30,500.

6. The gross foreign interest of $1,800 was received net of $270 in foreign withholding taxes.

7. The maximum capital cost allowance for the current year is $78,000.

Required: Determine the minimum Net Income For Tax Purposes and Taxable Income of Margo Ltd. for the year ending December 31, 2001.

Self Study Problem Fourteen - 2

Linden Industries Inc. began operations in 1998 and has a December 31 fiscal year end. While it was fairly successful in its first year of operation, excessive production of an unmarketable product resulted in a large operating loss for 1999. Profits have come back in 2000 and 2001.

The relevant Division B income and loss figures, along with charitable donations during the years under consideration are as follows:

	1998	1999	2000	2001
Business Income (Loss)	$95,000	($205,000)	$69,500	$90,000
Capital Gains	-0-	-0-	9,000	10,000
Capital Losses	(10,000)	(14,000)	-0-	-0-
Dividends Received	12,000	42,000	28,000	32,000
Charitable Donations	21,400	4,600	8,000	22,000

All of the dividends have been received from taxable Canadian corporations. The 2000 capital gains resulted from dispositions which occurred in December, 2000.

Required: Compute the minimum Net Income and Taxable Income that would be reported for Linden Industries in each of the four years under consideration. Also indicate the amended figures for any years to which losses are carried back. Provide an analysis of the amount and type of carry overs that would be available at the end of each of the four years.

Self Study Problem Fourteen - 3

On May 1, 2001, Ontario Lawn Care Ltd. (OLC), which provides gardening and lawn services for the southern Ontario market, purchased, from an arm's length party, all of the shares of Lawn Fertilizer Inc. (LF), a company in the business of manufacturing lawn fertilizers. LF has a December 31 year end.

A highly competitive fertilizer market gas resulted in the following losses for LF:

	Non Capital Loss	Net Capital Loss
1999	$180,000	$75,000
2000	140,000	Nil

It is estimated that business losses of $125,000 for the 2001 year will be experienced. This is made up of an actual loss of $55,000 up to May 1, 2001 and an estimated loss of $70,000 for the remainder of the year.

Relevant values for LF's assets at May 1, 2001 were as follows:

	Cost	UCC	FMV
Inventory	$100,000	N/A	$105,000
Land	450,000	N/A	925,000
Class 3 - Building	675,000	$515,000	650,000
Class 8 - Furniture	25,000	10,000	15,000
Class 43 - Manufacturing Equipment	415,000	375,000	285,000

Required: Describe the tax implications to LF of OLC acquiring its shares. Your answer should include a description of the elections that are available to LF and a recommendation as to which elections should be made. If any assumptions are made in arriving at your answer, specifically indicate what they are.

(ICAO Adapted)

Self Study Problem Fourteen - 4

The Sundean Company has its national headquarters in Toronto and all of its senior management people have their offices at this location. The Company also has operations in Vancouver, Calgary, Saskatoon, and Halifax. In each of these cities, warehouse space is maintained and orders are filled. In addition, a sales staff operates out of each office, taking orders throughout the Province in which the office is located.

For the current taxation year, the Company's taxable income totalled $1,546,000 on gross revenues of $10,483,000. Also during the current year, the Company had salaries and wages totalling $1,247,000. These gross revenues and expenses were distributed among the Provinces where the Company has operations in the following manner:

	Gross Revenues	Wages And Salaries Accrued
Alberta	$ 1,873,000	$ 264,000
British Columbia	2,246,000	273,000
Nova Scotia	1,397,000	179,000
Saskatchewan	1,298,000	104,000
Ontario	3,669,000	427,000
Total	$10,483,000	$1,247,000

Required: Calculate the amount of the Sundean Company's taxable income for the current year that would be allocated to each of the five Provinces.

Self Study Problem Fourteen - 5

Max Inc. is a public corporation involved in retailing. On December 31, 2001, the Company had the following Balance Sheet:

Cash	$ 23,000,000
Accounts Receivable	47,000,000
Inventory	126,000,000
Investment In Mini Ltd. (Carried At Equity)	63,000,000
Loan To Mini Ltd.	14,000,000
Loan To Ms. Mini (President Of Mini Ltd.)	3,000,000
Plant And Equipment (Net)	456,000,000
Total Assets	$732,000,000
Accounts Payable	$ 31,000,000
Mortgage Payable	97,000,000
Bank Debt (Due On Demand)	106,000,000
Future Income Taxes	242,000,000
Common Stock - No Par	60,000,000
Retained Earnings	196,000,000
Total Equities	$732,000,000

Other Information:

1. Max Inc. owns 25 percent of the outstanding voting shares of Mini Ltd. As this gives Max Inc. significant influence, the investment is carried at equity. The original cost of this investment was $59,000,000.

2. Taxable Income for the taxation year ending December 31, 2001 for Max Inc. was $42,000,000. Based on the relevant calculations, 73 percent of this amount was earned in a province.

3. Max Inc. had Taxable Income of nil in 1998, 1999, and 2000.

4. Max Inc. paid no Part I.3 (Large Corporations) tax in 1998 or 1999. However, in 2000, the Company paid Part I.3 tax of $475,000.

5. In its related group of corporations, Max Inc. is allocated $6,500,000 of the group's capital deduction.

Required: Determine Max Inc.'s Part I.3 tax liability, net of Canadian surtax paid, for the taxation year ending December 31, 2001. Indicate any surtax carry over that can be used to offset Part I.3 tax paid in previous years or payable in subsequent years.

Self Study Problem Fourteen - 6

The Gladstone Company is a diversified public company involved in both manufacturing and other types of operations. The following information relates to the Company's income for the taxation year ending on June 30, 2001:

Canadian active business income	$2,353,000
Canadian investment income	726,000
Active business income of U.S. subsidiary	1,402,000

Other information pertaining to the Canadian operations of the Gladstone Company for the year ending June 30, 2001 is as follows:

Total Canadian labour costs	$4,618,000
Total Canadian active business income capital costs	4,923,000
Manufacturing and processing labour costs	2,986,000
Manufacturing and processing capital costs	4,127,000

The capital cost figures provided in the preceding schedule are 10 percent of the gross cost of the relevant capital assets owned plus 100 percent of the annual lease payments on capital assets that are leased.

Required: Calculate the amount of Gladstone Company profits that would be eligible for the manufacturing and processing profits deduction in the year ending on June 30, 2001.

Self Study Problem Fourteen - 7

Mason Industries is a Canadian controlled public company, involved in the manufacture of component parts used in the production of automobiles. The Company's only operation is in Regina and it has a fiscal year which ends on December 31. The building which houses its operations is rented under a long term arrangement at an annual rent of $375,000. Of this amount, $50,000 is applicable to the land. Because of the size of the facility, Mason Industries normally sublets 25 percent of the available space to an unrelated wholesaler. The annual net rental income from this arrangement is $106,000. In addition to the rental operation, approximately 20 percent of the floor space in the building is used as administrative offices.

Other Information:

1. Mason Industries' Taxable Income for 2001 is $1,556,000. With the exception of the net rental income, this entire amount would be considered active business income.

2. During 2001, the Company's total labour costs amounted to $1,940,000. Of this total, $30,000 was required as the result of responsibilities associated with the rental of the excess space in the warehouse and the remainder of $1,910,000 was related to the production of active business income. Of the $1,910,000 related to active business income, $1,270,000 was direct manufacturing labour.

3. During 2001, the Company owned depreciable assets which cost $6,850,000. Of this total, assets with a cost of $5,560,000 were used directly in the manufacturing operations of the business. Other than the building, Mason Industries did not use any leased assets.

Required: Calculate federal income taxes payable for Mason Industries Ltd. for the year ending December 31, 2001.

Self Study Problem Fourteen - 8

The Mercury Manufacturing Company is a private corporation with two shareholders. Jennifer Mercury owns 47 percent of the voting shares and lives in Hamilton, Ontario. She is in charge of the Canadian operations which are located in Hamilton. John Mason owns 53 percent of the voting shares and lives in Rochester, New York. He is in charge of the U.S. operations which are located in Rochester. The Company's fiscal year ends on December 31.

All money amounts are expressed in Canadian dollars.

For the year ending December 31, 2001, the Company had accounting income before any provision for income taxes of $523,000. This amount included the following:

Dividends From Taxable Canadian Corporations	$ 9,400
Gain On Sale Of A Long Term Investment In Shares	22,900
Interest Income From Canadian Sources	7,800
Donations To Registered Canadian Charity	18,700
Contributions To Registered Federal Political Party	7,400
Dividends From U.S. Portfolio Investments	
(Before $4,845 Of Taxes Withheld In U.S.)	32,300
U.S. Business Income (Before $20,700 Of Taxes Withheld In U.S.)	64,200

The Company has a non capital loss of $21,950 available for carry forward to 2001. In addition, there is a net capital loss carry forward from 2000 of $13,500 [(1/2)($27,000)].

The Company sells its products in Canada in the provinces of Ontario and Manitoba. U.S. sales are all in the state of New York. Its head office and manufacturing operations are in Ontario. However, the Company has warehouses and sales people in Ontario and New York. Manitoba customers are serviced through Ontario warehouses and sales people. Sales, manufacturing salaries and wages, and non manufacturing salaries and wages for these locations are as follows:

	Ontario	Manitoba	New York	Total
Sales	$3,850,000	$1,875,000	$565,000	$6,290,000
Salaries And Wages:				
Manufacturing	$3,250,000	Nil	$380,000	$3,630,000
Non Manufacturing	290,000	Nil	58,000	348,000
Total Salaries And Wages	$3,540,000	Nil	$438,000	$3,978,000

With respect to the Company's property, gross costs are as follows:

Canadian Investment Property (This Property Had No	
Income Or Loss During 2001)	$ 472,000
Business Property In Canada (75% Used For Manufacturing)	2,680,000
Business Property In U.S. (85% Used For Manufacturing)	487,000
Total	$3,639,000

In addition to the preceding property, the Company's manufacturing operations use space in Canada that was rented at a cost of $67,200 for the year ending December 31, 2001.

All property costs and rent amounts given are only for the portions related to the buildings.

Required: Calculate the Federal Part I tax payable for the taxation year ending December 31, 2001. Show all calculations, whether or not they are necessary to the final solution.

Self Study Problem Fourteen - 9

The following situations are independent of each other. All of the corporations involved are Canadian controlled private corporations.

A.   John Fleming and Eric Flame are married to women who are sisters. John Fleming owns 100 percent of the outstanding common shares of Fleming Ltd. and 32 percent of the outstanding common shares of Lartch Inc. Eric Flame owns 100 percent of the outstanding common shares of Flame Ltd. and 28 percent of the outstanding common shares of Lartch Inc. The remaining common shares of Lartch Inc. are owned by an unrelated party.

B. Mr. Cuso owns 80 percent of the outstanding common shares of Male Ltd. The remaining 20 percent of the Male Ltd. shares are owned by his spouse, Mrs. Cuso. Mrs. Cuso owns 82 percent of the outstanding common shares of Female Inc. Her spouse owns the remaining 18 percent of the shares in this Company.

C. Ms. Jones, Mrs. Kelly, and Miss Lange are unrelated individuals. Ms. Jones owns 50 percent of the outstanding common shares of Alliance Ltd. and 25 percent of the outstanding voting shares of Breaker Inc. Mrs. Kelly does not own any of the Alliance Ltd. shares but owns 50 percent of Breaker Inc.'s outstanding voting shares. Miss Lange owns 50 percent of the outstanding common shares of Alliance Ltd. and 25 percent of the outstanding voting shares of Breaker Inc.

D. Mr. Martin owns 60 percent of the outstanding voting shares of Martin Inc. and 50 percent of the outstanding voting shares of Oakley Ltd. Mr. Oakley, who is not related to Mr. Martin, owns 50 percent of the outstanding voting shares of Oakley Ltd. and 40 percent of the outstanding voting shares of Martin Inc.

Required: For each of these situations, indicate which of the involved corporations would be associated under the rules established in ITA 256(1) and related sections of the *Act*. You should provide complete support for your conclusion, including references to appropriate provisions in the *Act*.

Self Study Problem Fourteen - 10

The Serendipity Shop Corp. sells art works on consignment in Winnipeg. The shares of Serendipity Shop Corp. are all owned by Elizabeth Montgomery, a Canadian, resident in Winnipeg.

The Serendipity Shop Corp. has net income for tax purposes of $240,000 for the year ending December 31, 2001. The net income is comprised of $220,000 from business activity and $20,000 in dividends from various investments in public companies. In May 2001, the Serendipity Shop Corp. donated $48,000 to the Canadian Indigenous Art Foundation, a registered Canadian charity. There are no carry forwards of donations or losses, and the corporation paid no dividends in the year.

Because Serendipity is associated with another corporation, its annual business limit is reduced to $135,000.

Required: Determine taxable income and Part I federal taxes payable for the Serendipity Shop Corp. for the year ending December 31, 2001.

Self Study Problem Fourteen - 11

During the taxation year ending December 31, 2001, the condensed Income Statement of Borscan Inc. was prepared in accordance with the requirements of the *CICA Handbook*. In condensed form it is as follows:

Borscan Inc.
Income Statement
Year Ending December 31, 2001

Revenues	$2,800,000
Expenses (Excluding Taxes)	(1,550,000)
Income Before Extraordinary Items And Taxes	$1,250,000
Extraordinary Gain (Before Income Tax Effects)	125,000
Income Before Taxes	$1,375,000

Other Information:

1. The Extraordinary Gain resulted from the expropriation of a building for proceeds of $525,000. The building had a capital cost of $500,000 and was acquired in 1984. As the Company leases all of its other assets, the building was the only asset in Class 3. The undepreciated capital cost of this class prior to the disposal of the building was $350,000. The land on which the building is situated was leased and the government entity expropriating the building has assumed Borscan's responsibilities under the lease.

2. Amortization included in the accounting expenses amounts to $255,000. Maximum available deductions for capital cost allowance amount to $287,000, without consideration of the building that was expropriated.

3. Expenses include a contribution to federal political parties in the amount of $1,500.

4. Expenses include interest and penalties of $500 resulting from a failure to file the last year's tax return on time.

5. Revenues include dividends from taxable Canadian corporations in the amount of $25,000.

6. Expenses include a deduction for charitable contributions in the amount of $12,000.

7. Prior to the deduction of any 2001 amortization, the ending balance in the Company's cumulative eligible capital account is $85,000. The items reflected in this balance have been charged to expense in previous years for accounting purposes.

8. The Company has available non capital loss carry overs from previous years that total $35,000. Net capital loss carry overs from 1995 amount to $30,000 [(3/4)($40,000)].

9. The Company's shares are publicly traded and none of its income is from manufacturing or processing.

Required:

A. Calculate the minimum Net Income For Tax Purposes for Borscan Inc. for the 2001 taxation year.

B. Calculate the minimum Taxable Income for Borscan Inc. for the 2001 taxation year. Indicate the amount and type of carry overs that are available at the end of the year.

C. Calculate minimum Federal Tax Payable for Borscan Inc. for the 2001 taxation year.

Assignment Problems

(The solutions for these problems are only available in
the solutions manual that has been provided to your instructor.)

Assignment Problem Fourteen - 1

It has been determined that, for the current year, the accounting net income, determined in accordance with generally accepted accounting principles, of Heather's Inc. is $456,000. Additional information was available for preparing the corporation's Schedule 1. For each of the following pieces of information, indicate the adjustment(s) that would be required to convert the Company's $456,000 accounting net income to minimum Net Income For Tax Purposes. Explanations are not required.

A. Accounting depreciation expense for the year was $28,000. Maximum CCA for the year is $22,500.

B. For accounting purposes, the Company deducted $4,800 in estimated warranty costs during the year. Actual expenditures for providing warranties during the year totalled $5,100.

C. During the year, the Company's bonds payable premium account declined by $2,400. Cash payment for interest on the relevant bonds amounted to $34,000.

D. During the year, the Company sold depreciable assets with a net book value of $87,000 for cash proceeds of $56,000. These assets were the last assets in their CCA class and there were no additions to the class during the year. At the beginning of the current year, the balance in the CCA class was $62,000.

E. Accounting net income for the year was reduced by the deduction of $3,700 in charitable donations.

F. During the year, the Company sold temporary investments for proceeds of $14,000. The cost of these investments was $16,000. The Company did not have any taxable capital gains during the current year.

Assignment Problem Fourteen - 2

The following information relates to the operations of Notem Inc. for the taxation year ended December 31, 2001:

Dividends From Taxable Canadian Corporations	$ 33,500
Taxable Capital Gains	9,600
Allowable Capital Losses	(4,425)
Charitable Donations	(5,400)
Business Loss	(141,800)

At the beginning of the taxation year, the Company had a carry forward of unused charitable donations of $1,350, and a net capital loss carry forward from 1995 of $15,750.

Required: Compute the corporation's Net Income For Tax Purposes and Taxable Income for its 2001 taxation year. Indicate any balance available for carry forward to 2002 and subsequent years.

Assignment Problem Fourteen - 3

One of your assistants has been calculating Net Income For Tax Purposes for the Sanklee Company. For both accounting and tax purposes, the Company uses a December 31 year end. Your assistant has been able to complete most of the required Schedule 1. However, there are a number of items that he would like you to review. The items are as follows:

1. The Company has recorded Depreciation Expense in its accounting records of $254,000. The maximum deductible CCA for the taxation year is $223,000.

2. The Company has recorded Interest Expense of $57,000. The accounting Balance Sheet indicates that the Bonds Payable - Premium account declined by $2,000 during the year.

3. On January 1 of the current year, the Company acquired a franchise with an unlimited life at a cost of $120,000. Despite its unlimited life, it is being amortized in the accounting records over ten years on a straight line basis.

4. During the last half of the year, the Company sold for $120,000 an asset with an original cost of $80,000. In the accounting records, the asset had a net book value of $53,000. It was a Class 43 asset and, at the end of the year, there is a positive balance in this Class and the Company still owns other Class 43 assets. Only one-half of the $120,000 proceeds is received in cash, with the remainder to be paid at the end of the following taxation year.

5. During the year, the Company paid $8,000 for two memberships in the Ottawa Ritz Golf And Country Club. The two Company executives that hold the memberships billed the Company $12,000 for entertainment of clients at this Club. Both of these amounts were deducted in the Company's accounting records.

6. During the year, the Company made charitable donations of $11,000. This amount was deducted in their accounting records.

7. During the year, the Company sold a Class 10 asset for $23,000. The original cost of the asset was $50,000 and its net book value at the time of sale was $39,000. This was the last asset in Class 10 and, at the end of the preceding year, the balance in Class 10 was nil. No Class 10 assets were acquired during the current year.

Required: For each of the items listed, indicate the addition to and/or deduction from accounting Net Income that would be required in the calculation of the minimum Net Income For Tax Purposes.

Assignment Problem Fourteen - 4

The following information on Dunway Ltd., a Canadian public company, is applicable to the year ending June 30, 2001:

Active Business Income (Does Not Include Any Dividends Or Capital Gains)	$192,000
Dividends From Controlled Subsidiary	37,500
Dividends From Non Controlled Public Companies	15,000
Capital Gain On Investment Sale	222,000
Dividends Paid	182,000
Donation To Canadian Government	26,000
Purchase Of Local Church Raffle Tickets	5,000
Donations To Registered Charities	141,000

At the beginning of this fiscal year, the Company has a net capital loss balance from 1998 of $222,000 and a non capital loss carry forward of $137,000.

Required: Calculate the minimum Taxable Income for Dunway Ltd. for the year ending June 30, 2001. Indicate the amount of any carry overs that will be available in future years.

Assignment Problem Fourteen - 5

Fortan Ltd. has normally had a fiscal year that ended on April 30. However, for 2001 and subsequent taxation years, the Company has requested and received permission from the CCRA to switch its year end to December 31. Its Income Statement, before consideration of income taxes, for the period May 1, 2001 to December 31, 2001 is as follows:

Sales		$465,000
Cost Of Sales		267,000
Gross Margin		$198,000
Operating Expenses (Excluding Taxes):		
Wages And Salaries	$73,600	
Office Rent	17,600	
Bad Debt Expense	1,800	
Promotion Expense	3,405	
Warranty Reserve	4,440	
Depreciation Expense	12,384	
Charitable Contributions	2,160	
Foreign Exchange Loss	4,080	
Reserve For Self Insurance	2,322	
Interest Expense	1,974	
Other Operating Expenses	14,400	138,165
Income Before Taxes		$ 59,835

Other Information:

1. As of April 30, 2001, the Undepreciated Capital Cost of the Company's office furniture was $32,500. During the eight month period ending December 31, 2001, a new conference table and chairs were acquired at a cost of $2,000. There were no disposals during this year.

2. On May 1, 2001, the Company has a non capital loss carry forward of $10,800.

3. The interest expense relates to a bank loan that was incurred to acquire shares of a Canadian corporation. This investee corporation did not declare any dividends during the year.

4. On September 1, 2001, Fortan Ltd. declared common stock dividends of $7,200.

5. The Foreign Exchange Loss resulted from the purchase of merchandise in Germany.

6. Other than setting up reserves for self insurance, the Company makes no provision for insuring its fixed assets.

7. The bad debt expense includes a loss of $1,000 resulting from the bankruptcy of a major customer.

8. On September 1, 2001, the Company purchased a delivery van for $18,000. All other vehicles used by the Company are leased.

9. Promotion expense includes a golf club membership fee of $1,080 and $1,500 in airfare and accommodation that was incurred by the sales manager in attending a sales convention in Denver. The golf club is used exclusively for entertaining clients. The remaining balance in the Promotion Expense account of $820 is the total reimbursement paid to the President of the Company for amounts spent on meals and refreshments while entertaining clients at the club.

10. Charitable contributions include $1,680 for the United Way Appeal and $480 that was paid to the United States Organ Transplant Association.

11. This is the first year that the Company has established a warranty reserve.

Required: Calculate the minimum Net Income For Tax Purposes and Taxable Income for Fortan Ltd. for the taxation year ending December 31, 2001.

Assignment Problem Fourteen - 6

Rodem Inc. is a Canadian controlled private corporation. The Company began operations on January 1, 1998 and uses a taxation year that ends on December 31. Its income (loss) before taxes, calculated using generally accepted accounting principles and amounts included in the GAAP income figures, for the four years 1998 through 2001 are as follows:

	1998	1999	2000	2001
Income Before Taxes (GAAP)	$110,000	($180,000)	$85,000	($42,000)
Charitable Contributions	3,200	5,800	4,100	2,900
Capital Gains (Losses)*	18,000	(9,000)	12,000	2,000
Dividends From Taxable				
Canadian Corporations	11,000	19,000	18,000	12,000

*All gains and losses are on the disposition of land. As a consequence, the capital gains and losses for tax purposes are equal to the accounting gains and losses. The 2000 disposition took place in November.

It is the policy of the Company to deduct charitable contributions prior to any loss carry overs. They also have a policy of minimizing non capital loss carry overs, as opposed to net capital loss carry overs.

Required: Calculate the minimum Net Income For Tax Purposes and Taxable Income for each of the four years and indicate the amount and type of carry overs that are available at the end of each year.

Assignment Problem Fourteen - 7

Lockwood Industries is a Canadian controlled private corporation that qualifies for the small business deduction on its active business income. It began operations in 1998 and during that year experienced a modest loss. During 1999 and 2000 its basic operations moved into the black. However, in 2001, strong competition from offshore companies severely eroded the Company's competitive position and, as a consequence, a large loss was experienced. The loss has encouraged the owners to make significant changes in their operations and they anticipate profits will be restored in 2002. The fiscal year end of Lockwood Industries is December 31.

The various components of Division B income, along with the charitable contributions made by the Company during the period January 1, 1998 through December 31, 2001 are as follows:

	1998	1999	2000	2001
Business Income (Loss)	($22,000)	$78,000	$95,000	($176,000)
Capital Gains*	-0-	-0-	24,000	21,938
Capital Losses	(66,000)	-0-	-0-	-0-
Dividends Received	4,000	6,000	6,000	5,000
Charitable Contributions	-0-	12,000	23,800	1,200

*The 2000 capital gain resulted from a disposition made on December 1, 2000.

All of the dividends have been received from taxable Canadian corporations. It is the policy of the Company to minimize its net capital loss balance.

Required: Compute the minimum net income and taxable income for Lockwood Industries in each of the four years under consideration. Also indicate the amended figures for any years to which losses are carried back. Provide an analysis of the amount and type of carry overs that would be available at the end of each of the four years.

Assignment Problem Fourteen - 8

Tasty Bread Inc. opened a large bakery operation on January 1, 1999. At this time the Company's year end was established as December 31. In addition to baking bread, the Company was in charge of the wholesale distribution of its products and operated a large retail outlet on the bakery premises.

The owners of the corporation had little experience in any aspect of baking or selling bread and, as a consequence, during the first two years they experienced the following losses:

	1999	2000
Non Capital Losses	$63,500	$78,500
Capital Losses (100%)*	68,000	85,000

*The 2000 capital losses occurred during December of that year.

At the beginning of 2001, the owners did not see any real hope for improved results under their own management and they began looking for new investors with more experience in the bakery industry. Their efforts met with success when, on March 31, 2001, Dough Products Ltd. acquired 72 percent of the outstanding shares of Tasty Bread Inc. Dough Products is a large Canadian public company with a December 31 year end and many years of successful operation in the industry. It is the intent of the new owners to inject additional capital and management expertise with a view to making Tasty's operations profitable within two years.

As this acquisition of control will result in a deemed year end, Tasty prepared an Income Statement for the period January 1, 2001 through March 31, 2001. This three month Income Statement showed an additional non capital loss of $23,000 for the period, but no further capital losses.

On March 31, 2001, the values of the Company's assets were as follows:

	Cost	UCC	Fair Market Value
Temporary Investments	$ 53,000	N/A	$ 23,000
Inventories	45,000	N/A	33,000
Land	275,000	N/A	420,000
Building	285,000	$270,000	320,000
Fixtures And Equipment	120,000	95,000	90,000
Vehicles	110,000	80,000	87,000

Shortly after taking over Tasty Bread Inc., Dough Products Ltd. decided that some of the extra space in Tasty's facilities could be used for manufacturing illuminated glass figurines. Tasty's income (loss) in the two lines of business for the period April 1, 2001, through December 31, 2001, was as follows:

Line Of Business	Income (Loss)
Figurines	$123,000
Bread Operations	(45,000)

For 2002, the income (loss) figures for the two lines of business were as follows:

Line Of Business	Income (Loss)
Figurines	($ 40,000)
Bread Operations	211,000

Required:

A. If Tasty Bread Inc. makes all possible elections to minimize the unused net capital and non capital loss balances, determine the amount of the non capital loss balance that will be carried forward after the acquisition of control by Dough Products Ltd., and the amount of the capital loss balance that will be lost as a result of this change in ownership.

B. Indicate the maximum amount of non capital loss carry forward that can be used during the period April 1 through December 31, 2001, and the amount remaining at December 31, 2001.

C. Indicate the maximum amount of non capital loss carry forward that can be used during 2002, and the amount remaining at December 31, 2002.

Assignment Problem Fourteen - 9

Fortunato Ltd. was incorporated in 1987 in Calgary. All of the shares were issued to Mr. Salvatore Fortunato. The corporation operated a bakery and for several years it enjoyed satisfactory profits. The Company has a December 31 year end.

In 1997, Mr. Fortunato retired and turned the management of the business over to his daughter, Angela Fortunato. Mr. Fortunato retained ownership of all of the Company's shares.

Unfortunately, Angela demonstrated considerably more interest in fast cars and handsome men than she did in running the business. As a consequence, Fortunato Ltd. has experienced losses in every year since 1997. As of December 31, 2000, it has a non capital loss carry forward of $225,000, as well as a net capital loss carry forward of $39,000. The net capital loss carry forward was realized in 1998.

On March 1, 2001, after a lengthy and heated discussion on the merits of various life styles, Mr. Fortunato fires his daughter and sells all of the shares in Fortunato Ltd. to Foodland Inc., a large public company involved in the production and distribution of a variety of food products.

For the period January 1, 2001 through March 1, 2001, Fortunato Ltd. experienced a business loss of $26,000. This figure includes a write down of inventories to their fair market values on March 1, 2001, and a deduction for uncollectible receivables calculated as per the provisions of ITA 111(5.3). It does not include any taxable capital gains, allowable capital losses, allowable business investment losses, or property losses.

On March 1, 2001, Fortunato Ltd.'s assets had the following values:

	Cost	UCC	Fair Market Value
Long Term Investments*	$ 32,000	N/A	$ 90,000
Land	140,000	N/A	225,000
Building	426,000	$320,000	426,000
Equipment	250,000	120,000	100,000

*Foodland Inc. intends to sell these Investments as soon as possible.

Required:

A. Indicate the amount of any non capital and net capital loss carry forwards that would remain after the March 1, 2001 acquisition of control, using the assumption that Foodland Inc. makes all elections required to minimize these amounts. Indicate the March 1, 2001 adjusted cost base and, where appropriate, UCC, for each of the assets listed.

B. If Foodland Inc. decides to only use the election(s) required to eliminate those losses which would expire at the acquisition of control, indicate the assets on which the election should be made and the amount that should be elected.

C. Advise Foodland Inc. as to which course of action (Part A or B) they should take.

Assignment Problem Fourteen - 10

Borodin Ltd. has its national headquarters in Halifax and all of its senior management people have their offices at this location. The Company also has operations in Victoria, Edmonton, Regina, and Toronto. In each of these cities, warehouse space is maintained and orders are filled. In addition, a sales staff operates out of each office, taking orders throughout the Province in which the office is located.

During the current year, the Company had salaries and wages totalling $5,800,000. The Company's gross revenues for the current year were $20,865,000. These were distributed among the Provinces where the Company has operations in the following manner:

Province	Wages And Salaries Accrued	Gross Revenues
Alberta	$ 946,000	$ 3,426,000
British Columbia	1,143,000	4,727,000
Nova Scotia	746,000	2,843,000
Saskatchewan	492,000	2,626,000
Ontario	2,473,000	7,243,000
Total	$5,800,000	$20,865,000

For the current taxation year, the Company's taxable income totalled $2,983,000.

Required: Calculate the amount of the Borodin Ltd.'s taxable income for the current year that would be allocated to each of the five Provinces.

Assignment Problem Fourteen - 11

Mega Enterprises (ME) is a public corporation involved in wholesale distribution of a variety of products. On December 31, 2001, the Company had the following Balance Sheet:

Cash	$ 2,600,000
Accounts Receivable	5,400,000
Inventory	10,300,000
Investment In Multi Ltd. (Carried At Cost)	16,700,000
Loan To Multi Ltd.	2,100,000
Loan To Halton Partnership	3,000,000
Plant And Equipment (Net)	25,700,000
Future Income Tax Asset	2,000,000
Total Assets	$67,800,000

Accounts Payable	$ 1,200,000
Other Current Liabilities	2,400,000
Mortgage Payable	4,600,000
Bank Debt (Due On Demand)	10,900,000
Common Stock - Stated Value	19,000,000
Contributed Surplus	15,600,000
Retained Earnings	14,100,000
Total Equities	$67,800,000

Other Information:

1. ME owns 15 percent of the outstanding voting shares of Multi Ltd. As this does not give Max Inc. significant influence, the investment is carried at cost. Halton Partnership is a partnership that sells products that are acquired from ME.

2. Taxable Income for the taxation year ending December 31, 2001 for ME was $9,200,000. Based on the relevant calculations, 14 percent of this amount was earned outside of Canada.

3. ME had Taxable Income of nil in 1998, 1999, and 2000.

4. ME paid no Part I.3 (Large Corporations) tax in 1998 or 1999. However, in 2000, the Company paid Part I.3 tax of $67,200.

5. In its related group of corporations, ME is allocated $9,000,000 of the group's capital deduction.

Required: Determine ME's Part I.3 tax liability, net of Canadian surtax paid, for the taxation year ending December 31, 2001. Indicate any surtax carry over that can be used to offset Part I.3 tax paid in previous years or payable in subsequent years.

Assignment Problem Fourteen - 12

Galoshes Galore Ltd. is a wholly-owned subsidiary of a U.S. corporation that manufactures and sells galoshes in Canada. For its first taxation period ended December 31, 2000, the company reported a non capital loss for tax purposes of $325,000.

Galoshes Galore Ltd. reported net income for tax purposes of $550,000 for the 2001 taxation year. For the manufacturing and processing profits tax deduction calculation, the adjusted active business income is $350,000, the cost of manufacturing and processing capital equals the cost of capital, and the cost of the manufacturing and processing labour equals the cost of labour.

Required: Compute the manufacturing and processing profits deduction for the 2001 taxation year. Comment on any tax planning issues that should be reviewed.

Assignment Problem Fourteen - 13

Facturing Ltd. is a Canadian controlled public company. In order to assist you in calculating their manufacturing and processing deduction for the current taxation year, they have provided you with the following information:

1. Taxable Income, all of which is earned in Canada, is made up of:

Investment Income	$ 93,500
Manufacturing Income	523,000
Net Income For Tax Purposes	$616,500
Contributions To Registered Charities	(20,700)
Taxable Income	$595,800

2. Facturing Ltd. owns the following assets:

Manufacturing Equipment	$1,275,000
Data Processing Equipment	69,300
Office Furniture And Equipment	141,400
Equipment For Employee Cafeteria	13,800
Total	$1,499,500

3. Wage and salary costs are as follows:

Plant Employees	$1,132,000
Accounting Employees	277,300
Quality Control Employees	211,200
Plant Supervision And Maintenance Employees	127,300
Distribution Employees (Finished Goods)	91,700
Receiving Employees (Receiving And Storing Raw Materials)	62,800
Purchasing Employees (Raw Materials)	49,600
Total	$1,951,900

Required: Calculate Facturing Ltd.'s manufacturing and processing profits deduction for the current year.

Assignment Problem Fourteen - 14

Each of the following is an independent case involving the ownership of voting shares of Canadian controlled private corporations. All of the corporations have taxation years that end on December 31.

1. Mr. Jones owns 35 percent of the shares of Jones Ltd. and 20 percent of the shares of Twitty Inc. Mr. Twitty owns 20 percent of the shares of Jones Ltd. and 40 percent of the shares of Twitty Inc. Mr. Jones and Mr. Twitty are not related.

2. Ms. Wynette owns 60 percent of the shares of Wynette Enterprises Ltd. and 30 percent of the shares of Lynn Inc. The remaining 70 percent of the shares of Lynn Inc. are held by Ms. Wynette's sister and her spouse.

3. Mr. Travis, Mr. Jennings, and Mr. Cash, three unrelated individuals, each hold one third of

the shares of Cowboys Ltd. In addition, Mr. Travis and Mr. Cash each hold 50 percent of the shares of Horses Inc.

4. Mr. Nelson owns 100 percent of the shares of Willie's Hits Ltd. and 30 percent of the shares of Randy's Boots Inc. The remaining 70 percent of the shares of Randy's Boots Inc. is owned by Mr. Nelson's brother.

5. Ms. Parton owns 90 percent of the shares of Alpha Company and her spouse owns 100 percent of the shares of Centra Company. Ms. Parton and her spouse each own 40 percent of the shares of Beta Company.

6. Ms. Gale owns 90 percent of the shares of Kristal Enterprises Ltd. and 10 percent of the shares of Norton Music Inc. Her 12 year old son owns 30 percent of the shares of Norton Music Inc. and Ms. Gale holds an option to buy 20 percent of the shares of Norton Music Inc. from an unrelated shareholder.

Required: For each of the preceding cases, determine whether the corporations are associated. Support your conclusions with references to specific provisions of ITA 256.

Assignment Problem Fourteen - 15
The following situations are independent of each other. All of the corporations involved are Canadian controlled private corporations.

A. Barton Ltd. owns 51 percent of the shares of Norton Inc.

B. Thomas Boulding owns 60 percent of the shares of Boulding Ltd. and 70 percent of the shares of Boulding Inc.

C. Mary Cunningham and Brenda Parton each own 50 percent of the shares of Elm Ltd. In addition, they each own 50 percent of the shares of Maple Inc. Mary and Brenda are not related.

D. Alice Fielding owns 100 percent of the shares of Fielding Inc. and 40 percent of the shares of Lawson Ltd. Betty Falcon owns 100 percent of the shares of Falcon Inc. and 40 percent of the shares of Lawson Ltd. Alice is the sister of Betty's husband. The remaining 20 percent of the shares of Lawson Ltd. are owned by strangers.

E. Michael Forbes owns 70 percent of the shares of Forbes Ltd. and 30 percent of the shares of Malcom Inc. Forbes Ltd. also owns 30 percent of the shares of Malcom Inc.

F. Richard Barnes, Susan Firth, and Terry Anson each own one-third of the shares of Rastau Ltd. In addition, Richard and Susan each own 50 percent of the shares of Sucrol Inc.

Required: For each of these situations, indicate which of the involved corporations would be associated under the rules established in ITA 256(1) and related Sections of the *Act*. You should provide complete support for your conclusion, including references to appropriate provisions in the *Act*.

Assignment Problem Fourteen - 16
Worldwide Enterprises was established in 1986 and has been, since its incorporation under the Canada Business Corporations Act, a Canadian controlled private company. Its head office is located in Vancouver and it has branches in both Seattle, Washington and Portland, Oregon. Its taxation year ends on December 31. All income of the company is derived from the sale of seafood in local markets.

During the 2001 taxation year, the Company's Net Income For Tax Purposes and Taxable Income amount to $219,000. This amount includes $32,000 (Canadian) that was earned by the two branches operating in the United States. The $32,000 earned by these branches is before the deduction of any U.S. or Canadian income taxes. As a result of earning this amount in the

United States, the Company was required to pay $6,200 (Canadian) in U.S. federal income taxes and $3,400 (Canadian) in state income taxes.

Required: Determine the amount of Canadian federal income taxes that must be paid by Worldwide Enterprises for the 2001 taxation year.

Assignment Problem Fourteen - 17

During its taxation year ending December 31, 2001, the condensed Income Statement of Industrial Tools Ltd. was prepared in accordance with the requirements of the *CICA Handbook*. In condensed form it is as follows:

Industrial Tools Ltd.
Condensed Income Statement
For The Year Ending December 31, 2001

Revenues	$6,585,000
Expenses (Excluding Taxes)	(4,280,000)
Net Income Before Taxes	$2,305,000

Other Information:

1. The Company's shares are publicly traded and none of its income is from manufacturing or processing.

2. The January 1, 2001 balance in the Company's cumulative eligible capital account is $115,000.

3. The Company's expenses include a contribution to a federal political party in the amount of $5,000.

4. Revenues include an accounting gain of $225,000, resulting from the sale of a building for $950,000 in cash. The building had a capital cost of $875,000 and was acquired in 1994. It is the only asset in Class 1 and the Undepreciated Capital Cost balance in this Class prior to the sale was $625,000. The land on which the building is situated was leased and the purchaser of the building has assumed Industrial Tool's obligations under the lease.

5. There is a Net Capital Loss carry over from 1998 of $90,000.

6. Expenses included a deduction for charitable contributions in the amount of $23,000.

7. The expenses include interest and penalties of $2,500 resulting from a failure to file last year's tax return within the prescribed time period.

8. Expenses include a warranty reserve of $20,000. This is the first year that the Company has deducted such a reserve.

9. Revenues include dividends from taxable Canadian corporations of $42,000.

10. Amortization included in the accounting expenses amounts to $478,000. Maximum available deductions for Capital Cost Allowance, without consideration of the building that was sold, amount to $523,000.

Required:

A. Calculate minimum Net Income For Tax Purposes for Industrial Tools Ltd. for the year ending December 31, 2001.

B. Calculate Taxable Income for Industrial Tools Ltd. for the year ending December 31, 2001. Indicate the amount of any loss carry overs that are still available for use in subsequent years.

C. Calculate Federal Taxes Payable for Industrial Tools Ltd. for the year ending December 31, 2001.

Assignment Problem Fourteen - 18 (Electronic Library Research Problem)

Provide brief answers to the following questions. Your answers should be supported by references to materials found in your Electronic Library.

A. What is the difference between "adjusted business income" as used in the ITR 5200 formula for calculating M & P profits, and "active business income" as defined in ITA 125(7)?

B. Does income produced by a restaurant qualify for the manufacturing and processing profits deduction?

C. There may be situations where two corporations, as a result of the death of their controlling shareholders, come under the common control of a trustee or executor. Would these two companies be associated?

D. Marston Ltd. is a corporation that, for tax purposes, is resident in Canada. It controls Larch Inc., a second corporation that is resident in Canada. However, Marston Ltd. is controlled by an American company. Can Larch Inc. qualify as a Canadian controlled private company?

E. In the definitions contained in ITA 125(7), a personal services business is described as a corporation that provides services and:

> an individual who performs the services provided to another person or partnership on behalf of the corporation (referred to as an incorporated employee) would, if it were not for the existence of the corporation, reasonably be regarded as an officer or employee of the entity to which the services were provided.

What factors does the CCRA consider in the determination of whether this part of the definition of a personal services business is applicable?

F. Corporate gifts to Universities are sometimes directed at projects which would qualify as scientific research and experimental development. Can the corporation deduct such amounts as both a scientific research and experimental development expenditure in the calculation of Net Income, and as a charitable contribution in the calculation of Taxable Income?

Chapter 15

Integration, Refundable Taxes, and Special Incentives For Corporations

Integration

The Basic Concept

15-1.   In designing a system for assessing taxes on business income, there are two theories or perspectives as to the appropriate treatment of corporations. These two perspectives are referred to as the entity view and the integration view. They can be described as follows:

Entity View   The entity view holds that corporations have a perpetual life of their own, that they are independent of their shareholders, and that they are legal entities. As such, they should pay tax separately on their earnings.

Integration View   Under the integration approach to the taxation of business income, corporations are viewed as simply the legal form through which one or more individuals (shareholders) carry on business. Therefore, business income that flows through a corporation to an individual should not be taxed differently, in total, from business income earned directly by that individual as a proprietor or partner.

15-2.   In practice, we find a variety of relationships between corporations and their shareholders. Given this situation, it would not be reasonable to apply either of these views to all Canadian corporations. For large corporations, where the shares are widely held and publicly traded, the entity theory seems appropriate. Management of the corporation is separate from its ownership, with income allocation and distribution decisions being made without directly consulting these shareholders. Not all corporate profits are paid out to the shareholders. In addition, some of these amounts are paid to foreign shareholders, subject only to the non resident withholding tax. In this type of situation, the entity view's treatment of the corporation as a separate taxable unit appears to be an equitable way to tax business income.

15-3.   This would not be the case for small corporations where the shares are privately held, either by a single individual or a small group of related individuals. With these owner managed businesses, the affairs of the shareholders and the business are closely related. Tax planning decisions involving salaries, dividends, or capital gains, affect both personal and corporate taxes and the line between the corporation and its owners is often faint. This would lead to the conclusion that the taxation of business income in these situations should not be influenced by the presence of the corporation. This conclusion is consistent with the integration view of business income taxation.

15-4. In a strict legal sense, the *Income Tax Act* reflects the entity view in that corporations are considered to be taxable units that are separate from their owners. Both the corporation and the owners are subject to taxation and this, in effect, involves double taxation of the income earned initially by the corporation. In the absence of special provisions, there would be a significantly higher level of taxation on income earned by a corporation and paid out as dividends, than there would be on income earned directly, either through a proprietorship or partnership.

15-5. Such higher levels of taxation do, in fact, occur with respect to income earned by publicly traded companies. We have noted previously that dividend gross up/tax credit procedures are an integration measure designed to compensate shareholders for taxes paid at the corporate level. While these procedures are generally available to all shareholders who are individuals, they are based on the assumption that the combined federal/provincial corporate tax rate is 20 percent. As the combined tax rate for publicly traded corporations is generally above 40 percent, dividend tax credits do not offset the corporate taxes paid by these corporations and, as a consequence, there is a significant degree of double taxation. In other words, the CCRA's approach to the taxation of business income earned by publicly traded companies, despite the presence of the dividend gross up and tax credit procedures, produces results that are consistent with the entity view of corporate taxation.

15-6. A near full implementation of the integration view of corporate taxation only occurs when the dividend gross up and tax credit procedures are applied to a corporation that is eligible for the small business deduction. For 2001, the combined federal/provincial tax rate on the first $200,000 of income eligible for the small business deduction ranges from a low of 15.62 percent (Yukon) to a high of 22.16 (Quebec). With the average of these rates around 20 percent, the combined dividend tax credit, when calculated as 25 percent of dividends received, is approximately equal to the amount of corporate taxes paid. This means, that with respect to total taxes paid, it makes little difference whether this type of income is flowed through a corporation or received directly by the individual.

15-7. Note, however, this full implementation of the integration view is dependent on the presence of a combined federal/provincial corporate tax rate of 20 percent. Even when the small business deduction is available, a combined federal/provincial rate in excess of 20 percent results in what analysts refer to as under integration (i.e., the use of a corporation results in higher total tax payments). When the combined federal/provincial corporate rate is less than 20 percent, for example when a province has a tax holiday, over integration occurs (i.e., the use of a corporation results in lower total tax payments).

15-8. An additional problem here is related to provincial tax rates on individuals. When a corporation is used, integration procedures compensate for corporate taxes paid by providing a dividend tax credit. This, in effect, requires that the combined federal/provincial dividend tax credit be equal to the 25 percent gross up, which in turn is equal to corporate taxes paid at a 20 percent rate. Prior to this year, with provincial tax payable based on federal tax payable, provincial tax credits were implicitly calculated as the federal credit multiplied by the provincial tax rate on individuals. As the federal dividend tax credit is defined as two-thirds of the dividend gross up, having the combined federal/provincial dividend credit equal to the gross up required that the provincial tax rate on individuals be set at 50 percent of basic federal tax. With this rate, the provincial dividend tax credit would be equal to 50 percent of the federal dividend tax credit and, with the federal dividend tax credit set at two-thirds of the gross up, the provincial credit would be equal to one-third of the gross up.

15-9. With the adoption of TONI (Tax ON Income) procedures, the provincial tax rate on individuals is no longer an issue with respect to the total amount of taxes paid when a corporation is used. Under this system, the provincial dividend tax credit is not consistently tied to the provincial tax rate on individuals. This now means that, for the combined federal/provincial dividend tax credit to be equal to the gross up, the provincial dividend tax credit must be equal to one-third of the gross up. This could be expressed directly as one-third of the gross up or, alternatively, as 50 percent of the federal credit. While the provincial dividend tax credit may be tied in some manner to provincial rates, this is not necessarily the case.

Dividend Gross Up And Tax Credit

15-10.   An example will be used to illustrate the dividend gross up and tax credit procedures that are central to the Canadian approach to integration. We will consider a corporation with taxable income of $10,000 and, in order to show the full implementation of the integration system, we will assume that the corporate income is subject to a combined federal and provincial rate of 20 percent, ignoring the corporate surtax. The corporation pays out any after tax earnings as dividends. This results in the following data at the corporate level:

Corporate Taxable Income	$10,000
Corporate Taxes (20%)	(2,000)
Dividends Paid (After Tax Earnings)	$ 8,000

15-11.   We will consider two cases illustrating the taxation of individuals receiving the dividends. Mr. A is in the 16 percent federal tax bracket and the 6 percent provincial tax bracket. Ms. B is in the 29 percent federal tax bracket and 16 percent provincial tax bracket (note that the provincial rates used are not equal to 50 percent of the federal rates). They both live in a province where the provincial dividend tax credit is equal to one-third of the gross up. Their tax calculations are as follows:

	Mr. A	Ms. B
Dividends Received	$ 8,000	$ 8,000
Gross Up of 25%	2,000	2,000
Taxable Dividends	$10,000	$10,000
Tax Rate:		
(16% + 6%)	22%	
(29% + 16%)		45%
Gross Federal Taxes	$ 2,200	$ 4,500
Less: Dividend Tax Credit		
[(2/3)($2,000) + (1/3)($2,000)]	(2,000)	(2,000)
Personal Taxes Payable	$ 200	$ 2,500

15-12.   When the provincial dividend tax credit is equal to one-third of the gross up, the total dividend tax credit is equal to the gross up. Given our corporate tax rate of 20 percent, the corporate dividends equal 80 percent of corporate income, with the gross up being equal to 25 percent of this amount. This 25 percent gross, when based on 80 percent of corporate income, is equal to 20 percent of corporate income. This is in turn equal to the corporate taxes paid at the 20 percent rate. Further, when the provincial dividend tax credit is equal to one-third of the gross up, the combined federal/provincial dividend tax credit is equal to the gross up. With the dividend tax credit equal to the gross up, which in turn is equal to corporate taxes paid, the $2,000 dividend tax credit received by the individual just exactly compensates for the $2,000 in taxes that were paid at the corporate level.

15-13.   Given this relationship, it is not surprising that the after tax retention for either Mr. A or Ms. B is not altered by the use of a corporation. If a corporation is used, the after tax dividends retained by Mr. A and Ms. B can be calculated as follows:

	Mr. A	Ms. B
Dividends Received	$8,000	$8,000
Personal Taxes Payable (Preceding Calculation)	(200)	(2,500)
After Tax Dividends	$7,800	$5,500

15-14.   Alternatively, if Mr. A or Ms. B had earned the $10,000 in income directly, without having it channeled through a corporation, the after tax retention would be identical:

	Mr. A	Ms. B
Pre Tax Income	$10,000	$10,000
Taxes At Personal Rates (22% and 45%)	(2,200)	(4,500)
After Tax Income	$ 7,800	$ 5,500

15-15.   This example illustrates that, given our particular assumptions about federal and provincial tax rates and dividend tax credits, we have perfect integration, with the amount of total taxes paid not being influenced in either direction by the use of a corporation. As will be discussed in the next section, this is rarely the outcome that we encounter in the real world.

Integration And Business Income

15-16.   As the preceding example illustrates, the question of whether the use of a corporation will increase or decrease taxes paid is dependent on two major considerations:

- The combined federal/provincial rate on corporate income. Given a combined federal/provincial dividend tax rate equal to the gross up, corporate rates in excess of 20 percent will result in higher taxes when a corporation is used, while rates below 20 percent creates a situation where the use of a corporation can create a tax savings.

- The provincial dividend tax credit. Given a combined federal/provincial tax rate on corporations of 20 percent, a provincial dividend tax credit that exceeds one-third of the gross up provides a combined credit that exceeds corporate taxes paid. In contrast, if the provincial credit is less than one-third of the gross up, the result will be higher taxes when a corporation is used.

15-17.   With respect to the first of these considerations, real world tax rates are generally above 20 percent. However, with several different rates applicable at the federal level and additional differences being added by variations in provincial rates, there are many different effective corporate tax rates, ranging from a low of 15.62 percent for the first $200,000 of income eligible for the small business deduction in the Yukon, to a high of 45.12 percent for public companies in New Brunswick and Saskatchewan. Figure 15-1 (following page) illustrates the calculation of some fairly typical rates for three different types of corporations.

15-18.   We will provide a more detailed analysis of the other variables in Chapter 16, where you will find a comprehensive discussion of the issues associated with the incorporation of an income source.

Tax Basis Shareholders' Equity

Shareholders' Equity Under GAAP

15-19.   In this Chapter we will be considering various distributions to shareholders and the fact that, in some circumstances, such distributions will trigger refunds of taxes that have been previously paid by the corporation. In order to comprehend this material, some understanding of the tax basis components of shareholders' equity is required.

15-20.   You are all familiar with the components of Shareholders' Equity as they appear in a Balance Sheet prepared using generally accepted accounting principles (GAAP). The two basic components of the total balance disclosed are:

- **Contributed Capital**   This is the amount that has been paid by investors in return for shares issued. In jurisdictions where par value shares can still be used, this balance may be divided into par value amounts and an excess over par amount, commonly designated contributed surplus.

- **Earned Capital (Retained Earnings)**   This component reflects amounts that have been earned by the corporation and retained in the business. While this balance is sometimes

---

Figure 15 - 1
Example Of Federal/Provincial Tax Rates On Corporations

Three companies each have $100,000 of taxable income for the year ending December 31, 2001.

- Company A is a Canadian controlled private company and all of its income is from manufacturing and processing. Since its income is eligible for the small business deduction, it is not eligible for the general rate reduction or the M&P deduction. It is subject to a provincial rate of 7 percent on this income.
- Company B is a public company and all of its income is eligible for the M&P deduction. It is not eligible for the general rate reduction and is subject to a provincial rate of 10 percent.
- Company C is a public company and none of its income is eligible for the M&P deduction. It is eligible for the general rate reduction and is subject to provincial taxes at a rate of 14 percent.

	Company A	Company B	Company C
Base Amount of Part I Tax (38%)	$38,000	$38,000	$38,000
Surtax [(4%)(28%)($100,000)]	1,120	1,120	1,120
Federal Tax Abatement (10%)	(10,000)	(10,000)	(10,000)
Small Business Deduction (16%)	(16,000)	(-0-)	(-0-)
M&P Deduction (7%)	(-0-)	(7,000)	(-0-)
General Rate Reduction (1%)	N/A	N/A	(1,000)
Total Federal Tax	$13,120	$22,120	$28,120
Provincial Tax	7,000	10,000	14,000
Taxes Payable	$20,120	$32,120	$42,120
Effective Tax Rate	20.12%	32.12%	42.12%

referred to as earned surplus, the more common designation is retained earnings. In some situations, parts of this balance may be disclosed as separate reserves.

15-21. This segregation is based on the legal requirement that dividends cannot be paid out of contributed capital. Therefore, this disclosure informs investors as to the legal basis for payment of dividends by the corporation. However, this legal basis may not be supported by the cash resources that would be needed to, in fact, pay dividends.

Paid Up Capital (Tax Basis Contributed Capital)

15-22. ITA 89(1) defines paid up capital, normally referred to as "PUC". The paragraph indicates that the amount should be calculated without reference to the *Income Tax Act*, telling us that PUC should be based on legal stated capital as determined under the legislation governing the particular corporation (*Canada Business Corporations Act* or relevant provincial legislation). As contributed capital under GAAP is also based on legal stated capital, the initial PUC for shares issued will be equal to contributed capital under GAAP. However, as will be discussed in this and subsequent Chapters, there will be adjustments to PUC which have no equivalent under GAAP.

15-23. PUC is applied on an average per share basis. This means, for example, that if a corporation sells 100,000 shares at $10 per share and sells an additional 100,000 shares at $15 per share, the per share PUC will be $12.50 for all shares. For purposes of determining capital gains, the adjusted cost base of the shares will not necessarily be equal to the per share PUC. The taxpayers acquiring the first issue will have an adjusted cost base of $10, while the purchasers of the second issue will have an adjusted cost base of $15. If, however, all 200,000 of

Exercise Fifteen-1 deals with PUC. This would be an appropriate time to attempt this exercise.

the shares were acquired by the same taxpayer, under the identical property rules in ITA 47, that taxpayer's adjusted cost base would be the average cost of $12.50.

15-24. PUC is a capital contribution and does not reflect accumulated earnings. Therefore, it can be returned to investors without tax consequences for either the corporation or the shareholder.

Tax Basis Retained Earnings

Amount

15-25. The situation with respect to Retained Earnings is much more complex. To begin, we will be dealing with a different total for tax purposes. There are significant differences between accounting income and tax income. While the accounting literature now defines accounting/tax differences as temporary differences with reference to Balance Sheet accounts (e.g., the difference between the Net Book Value and the UCC of a depreciable asset), most of these Balance Sheet differences are created by Income Statement differences (e.g., the difference between Amortization Expense and CCA). As a result, total retained earnings as determined under GAAP will, in most cases, be a significantly different number than the corresponding tax figure. Reflecting the fact that most corporations attempt to minimize their Taxable Income, the tax figure will generally be lower than the accounting figure.

15-26. A further point here relates to terminology. In general, the term Retained Earnings has replaced Earned Surplus in accounting literature and in published financial statements. However, the term surplus is still alive and well in tax work. As evidence we would note that the *Income Tax Act* contains only 8 references to Retained Earnings, in contrast to 89 references to Surplus.

Basic Components

15-27. Moving beyond the differences in the total amount, we encounter further problems in relating tax and GAAP figures. Under GAAP, retained earnings is generally a single homogenous balance, all of which has the same significance for financial statement users. This is not the case with the corresponding tax figure. It is made up of four different categories which can be described as follows:

- Pre 1972 Undistributed Surplus
- Post 1971 Undistributed Surplus
- Pre-1972 Capital Surplus On Hand (CSOH)
- Capital Dividend Account

15-28. Pre 1972 Undistributed Surplus, sometimes referred to as Surplus Nothings, is simply earnings that accrued prior to 1972 and were retained in the corporation. Correspondingly, "Post 1971 Undistributed Surplus" is used for earnings retained after 1971 that do not have any special tax status. The distinction between these two balances is sometimes of importance. For an example of this, see the material on capital gains stripping in Chapter 17. When there is a distribution to shareholders related to the disposition of shares in another corporation, its treatment will depend on whether the distribution is made from the pre 1972 undistributed surplus or, alternatively from post 1971 undistributed surplus.

Pre-1972 Capital Surplus On Hand (CSOH)

15-29. This balance reflects capital gains and capital losses which accrued prior to 1972, but were realized subsequent to that date. As you may recall from Chapter 9, there was no taxation of capital gains in Canada prior to 1972. However, capital gains are not recognized until there is a disposition of a capital asset and, as a consequence, pre 1972 gains can be recorded when there is a post 1971 disposition of an asset that was acquired prior to 1972.

15-30. From the point of view of the corporation disposing of such assets, the median rule (see Chapter 9) will prevent taxation of this type of gain at the corporate level. However, the corporation still has the funds from the disposition and, in the absence of a special provision for such amounts, their distribution would result in a taxable dividend to shareholders.

15-31. To prevent this from happening, such gains and losses are accumulated in a Pre-1972 CSOH balance. As you would expect, this balance can be paid out to shareholders on a tax free basis. It should be noted, however, that such tax free distributions can only occur as part of an ITA 88(2) windup of the corporation. Procedures for such windups are discussed in Chapter 18.

15-32. The components of this account are calculated as follows:

Additions When the proceeds of disposition exceed the original cost of the asset, an addition is calculated by subtracting the original cost of the asset from the lesser of its V-Day value and the proceeds of disposition. For example, if an asset which cost $100,000 in 1968, had a V-Day value of $120,000, and was sold in 2001 for $150,000, the addition to Pre-1972 CSOH would be $20,000 ($120,000, less $100,000). The 2001 capital gain would be $30,000 ($150,000 - $120,000). One-half of this amount would be taxable in 2001, with the remaining one-half added to the capital dividend account (see next section).

Deductions When the proceeds of disposition are less than the original cost of the asset, a deduction is calculated by subtracting the greater of its V-Day value and the proceeds of disposition from the original cost of the asset. For example, if a non depreciable asset cost $200,000 in 1968, had a V-Day value of $190,000, and was sold in 2001 for $140,000, the deduction from the Pre-1972 CSOH would be $10,000 ($200,000 - $190,000). The 2001 capital loss would be $50,000 ($140,000 - $190,000). One-half of this amount would be allowable in 2001, with the remaining one-half deducted from the capital dividend account (see next section).

15-33. We would also note, as we did in our brief Chapter 9 presentation of the median rule, V-Day occurred nearly 30 years ago. As a consequence, this material declines in importance with each passing year. Given this, only very limited coverage of this subject will be found in the problem material.

Capital Dividend Account

15-34. When capital gains taxation was introduced in 1972, it was decided that a portion of realized capital gains should be received by taxpayers on a tax free basis (this was an alternative to having special lower rates on these gains as is the case in the U.S.). For many years, this tax free portion was one-half of the total capital gain. It was reduced to one-third for 1988 and 1989, and was further reduced to one-quarter for 1990 and subsequent years. Reflecting a total reversal of policy, the non taxable component reverted to one-third for dispositions after February 27, 2000, and returned to the pre-1988 level of one-half for dispositions after October 17, 2000.

15-35. When a corporation records a gain on the disposition of a capital asset, there is no tax at the corporate level on the non taxable portion of this gain. However, the cash which reflects this gain is still inside the corporation and, as a consequence, some mechanism is needed to ensure that this portion of the gain remains untaxed when it is distributed to the corporation's shareholders. The capital dividend account is that mechanism.

15-36. The non taxable portion of capital gains realized since 1972 are added to this account and can be distributed at any subsequent time as a tax free capital dividend under ITA 83(2). These dividends will be discussed more completely in the next section which deals with distributions of corporate surplus.

15-37. When a capital asset that was acquired before 1972, is sold after 1971, both the Pre-1972 CSOH and the capital dividend account can be affected. Consider the following:

Example Norquay Ltd. acquires a capital asset in 1965 at a cost of $250,000. On V-day, the fair market value of this asset is $350,000 and, during June, 2001, it is sold for $600,000.

Tax Consequences The $350,000 ($600,000 - $250,000) difference between the asset's cost and its ultimate sale price can be analyzed as follows:

Addition To Pre-1972 CSOH ($350,000 - $250,000)	$100,000
Addition To Capital Dividend Account [(1/2)($600,000 - $350,000)]	125,000
Taxable Capital Gain [(1/2)($600,000 - $350,000)]	125,000
Total Difference	$350,000

15-38.   The preceding discussion emphasizes the allocation of the non taxable portion of capital gains to the capital dividend account. However, there are other items that the concept of integration suggests should flow through the corporation and into the hands of shareholders on a tax free basis. The capital dividend account is used for several of these items.

15-39.   The complete definition of the capital dividend account is found in ITA 89(1) and is very complex. Without becoming involved in a variety of complicating factors which influence this account, its basic components can be described as follows:

1. The non taxable portion of net capital gains realized during the year are added to the account (the non taxable portion of capital gains, less the non deductible portion of capital losses). Note that the amounts are added at the fraction (one-half, one-third, or one-quarter) that is appropriate for the year in which the gains are realized. The amounts are not subsequently adjusted for changes in this fraction.

2. Capital dividends received from other corporations are added. This preserves the tax free status of non taxable amounts that pass through more than one corporation.

3. The non taxable portion of gains on the sale of eligible capital property is added to the account. If, for example, a corporation has acquired goodwill for $100,000, three-quarters of this amount or $75,000 would be added to the cumulative eligible capital balance. This would be amortized at a seven percent rate, leaving a balance after two years of $64,868.

    If the goodwill were then sold during 2001 for $150,000, three-quarters of the proceeds or $112,500 would be subtracted from the account. This would leave a negative balance of $47,632, an amount which reflects the $10,132 write off of cumulative eligible capital, plus $37,500. This latter amount is three-quarters of the $50,000 ($150,000 - $100,000) economic gain resulting from the sale of the goodwill and, prior to the February 28, 2000 budget, this amount would have been added to the taxpayer's income, with the other $12,500 (one-quarter of the gain) going to the capital dividend account.

    As discussed in Chapter 8, while the capital gains inclusion rate was reduced from three-quarters to two-thirds and subsequently to one-half, the inclusion rate for cumulative eligible capital has remained unchanged at three-quarters. This created a need to adjust some part of the ITA 14(1) income inclusion resulting from negative cumulative eligible capital balances. For dispositions after October 17, 2000, any negative amount in excess of amounts deducted in previous years would be multiplied by two-thirds in order to reduce the inclusion rate for the economic gain from three-quarters to one-half. In our example, the income inclusion would be $25,000 [(2/3)($37,500)]. Consistent with this approach, the addition to the capital dividend account would also be $25,000.

4. Life insurance proceeds received by the corporation are added to the account, net of the adjusted cost base of the policy. This can be an important addition when the company insures the life of one or more of its shareholders. This is a common procedure in owner/managed businesses, where life insurance proceeds are sometimes used to finance the buy out of the estate of a deceased shareholder.

5. The account is reduced by capital dividends paid under ITA 83(2).

15-40.   A further aspect of the complete definition of the capital dividend account is that it is a cumulative total beginning with the 1972 introduction of capital gains taxation in Canada. However, since only private corporations have a capital dividend account, the definition has to deal with companies that were not private companies at that point in time. This could involve either corporations that have been established since that date or, alternatively, companies that have gone private since that date.

Exercise Fifteen-2 deals with the capital dividend account. This would be an appropriate time to attempt this exercise.

Distributions Of Corporate Surplus

Introduction

15-41. Corporate surplus, also known to accountants as retained earnings, is periodically distributed to shareholders of the corporation. This happens most commonly through the regular cash dividends that are paid by most Canadian companies. Less commonly, we encounter stock dividends and dividends in kind (corporate assets other than cash). These fairly routine types of dividends were given coverage in Chapter 12 in our material on property income. However, they will be reviewed at this point as an introduction to the various types of deemed dividends that are under consideration here.

15-42. In addition to the following types of deemed dividends, we will also give attention in this Section to ITA 83(2) capital dividends.

15-43. The basic types of deemed dividends are as follows:

- ITA 84(1) Deemed Dividend on Increase of PUC
- ITA 84(2) Deemed Dividend on Winding Up
- ITA 84(3) Deemed Dividend on Redemption, Acquisition, or Cancellation of Shares
- ITA 84(4) Deemed Dividend on Reduction of PUC

15-44. You should note that, when such deemed dividends are received by an individual, they are treated in the same manner as cash dividends and are subject to the usual gross up and tax credit procedures.

Regular Cash Dividends

15-45. Regular cash dividends are paid out of a corporation's unrestricted surplus balances. The payment of cash dividends serves to reduce these balances. Unlike the payment of interest on debt, the payment of cash dividends does not create a tax deduction for the corporation.

15-46. If cash dividends are received by an individual, they are subject to the usual gross up and tax credit procedures. In contrast, if they are paid to another corporation, they are received on a tax free basis.

15-47. A further point here relates to dividends on certain types of preferred shares. Section 3860 of the *CICA Handbook*, "Financial Instruments - Disclosure And Presentation", Recommends that shares which require mandatory redemption by the issuer be classified as liabilities. Consistent with this, the dividend payments on these shares must be disclosed as interest, resulting in the amount of the distribution being deducted in the determination of accounting net income. To date, this treatment has not been recognized by the CCRA. From a tax point of view, the dividends paid on preferred shares with mandatory redemption provisions will be given the same treatment as any other dividend.

Stock Dividends

15-48. A stock dividend is a pro rata distribution of new shares to the existing shareholder group of the corporation, accompanied by a capitalization of Retained Earnings. Consider the following simple example:

Example The stock of Fergis Ltd. is trading at $30 per share. Its shareholders' equity is as follows:

No Par Common Stock (1,000,000 Shares)	$ 7,500,000
Retained Earnings	12,500,000
Total Shareholders' Equity	$20,000,000

15-49.   If Fergis Ltd. were to declare a 10 percent stock dividend, it would distribute 100,000 shares on a pro rata basis to its existing shareholders. At the same time, it would transfer an amount equal to the $3,000,000 [($30)(100,000)] market value of these shares from Retained Earnings to the contributed capital account, resulting in the following new shareholders' equity:

No Par Common Stock (1,100,000 Shares)	$10,500,000
Retained Earnings	9,500,000
Total Shareholders' Equity	$20,000,000

15-50.   From a tax point of view, the $3,000,000 increase in contributed capital would be an increase in PUC, reflecting an increase in the amount that could be distributed to the shareholders of the company on a tax free basis. Because of this, shareholders are viewed as having received a dividend equal to the fair market value of the new shares received.

15-51.   Consider an individual holding 100 shares of this corporation, with an adjusted cost base of $25 per share, or $2,500 in total. As a result of the stock dividend, he would receive 10 shares of stock worth $300 [($30)(10)]. For tax purposes, this would be a fully taxable dividend, subject to the usual gross up and tax credit procedures. Given that this $300 amount has been taxed, it will be added to the shareholder's adjusted cost base, leaving an adjusted cost base for his 110 shares of $2,800 ($2,500 + $300), or $25.45 per share.

15-52.   These rules create an unfortunate situation for the taxpayer. An individual receiving stock dividends will require a cash outflow (taxes on the dividend received) with no corresponding cash inflows (the dividends are not received in cash). This approach to the taxation of stock dividends serves to significantly discourage their use in Canada.

Dividends In Kind

15-53.   While somewhat unusual, corporations do sometimes declare dividends that are payable in assets other than cash or the corporation's own shares. An example of this might be a situation in which a corporation has a major holding of another corporation's shares and wishes to dispose of them. If the block is large, sale on the open market could significantly depress the proceeds received. A possible alternative is to distribute the shares on a pro rata basis to the corporation's existing shareholders.

15-54.   The tax effect of declaring such a dividend is that it is a disposition of the shares. Under ITA 52(2), the proceeds will be deemed to be the fair market value of the property distributed. This will usually result in a capital gain or loss for the corporation.

15-55.   Also under ITA 52(2), the shareholders are deemed to have acquired the assets at their fair market value. Further, this amount is considered to be a taxable dividend subject to the usual gross up and tax credit procedures.

15-56.   As an example, consider the following:

Example   Hold Ltd. owns share in Bold Inc. These shares have an adjusted cost base of $800,000 and a fair market value of $3,500,000. Hold Ltd. declares a dividend on these shares that will be paid to the existing shareholders of Hold Ltd. in July, 2001.

Tax Consequences   The tax consequences of this dividend are as follows:

- Based on deemed proceeds of $3,500,000, Hold Ltd. will have a taxable capital gain of $1,350,000 [(1/2)($3,500,000 - $800,000)].

- Hold Ltd. will have declared a dividend of $3,500,000, resulting in a decrease in their undistributed surplus by this amount.

- The shareholders will be deemed to have received a taxable dividend of $3,500,000, subject to the usual gross up and tax credit procedures.

- The adjusted cost base of the Bold Inc. shares to the Hold Ltd. shareholders will be $3,500,000.

Capital Dividends Under ITA 83(2)

15-57.   As we have previously indicated, the balance in the capital dividend account reflects amounts that can be distributed tax free to the shareholders of the corporation. This, however, does not happen automatically.

15-58.   When a corporation makes a distribution, an amount not in excess of the balance in the capital dividend account can be designated as a capital dividend. This is accomplished through an election under ITA 83(2), using Form T2054.

15-59.   Electing to distribute a capital dividend reduces the balance in the capital dividend account. It will be received by the taxpayer, whether the taxpayer is a corporation or an individual, on a tax free basis with no reduction in the adjusted cost base. Note that, if the recipient of the capital dividend is a private corporation, the amount of the dividend will be added to the recipient corporation's capital dividend account.

15-60.   A final point with respect to capital dividends is that the election should be made with care. If an election is made for an amount in excess of the balance in the capital dividend account, a penalty equal to 75 percent of the excess will be assessed under Part III of the *Income Tax Act*. In some circumstances, an excess election can occur inadvertently. For example, the non taxable portion of a capital gain may be added to the capital dividend account and, at a subsequent point in time, a reassessment will cause the gain to be reclassified as business rather than capital. This in turn means that the capital dividend account will be reduced through the reassessment process. If this happens, ITA 184(3) contains a provision which allows for a revision of the election to avoid the 75 percent penalty.

Deemed Dividends Under ITA 84(1) - Increase in PUC

15-61.   ITA 84(1) dividends involve a situation where there has been an increase in the corporation's PUC, accompanied by a smaller increase in the net assets of the corporation.

15-62.   This type of deemed dividend usually occurs when the corporation issues additional shares. For example, if a corporation were to issue shares with a PUC of $500,000 to a creditor, in settlement of debt with a carrying value of $450,000, there would be an ITA 84(1) deemed dividend of $50,000 ($500,000 - $450,000). The reason for treating this $50,000 as dividend income to the shareholders is that, while it represents an amount that can be distributed to shareholders on a tax free basis, no corresponding amount was invested in the corporation's net assets.

15-63.   Continuing with the example from the previous paragraph, the creditor's claim is for $450,000. However, this creditor, along with the other shareholders will pay tax on a deemed dividend of $50,000, despite the fact that they have not currently received any assets from the corporation. To provide equity in this situation, the creditor's share of the $50,000 ITA 84(1) deemed dividend is added to the adjusted cost base of the shares that were issued to him, resulting in an adjusted cost base for these shares of $450,000 plus his share of the deemed dividend. Note that this will not be the PUC of these shares as PUC is calculated as an average value for all of the outstanding shares.

15-64.   There are a number of transactions involving increases in PUC which are specifically excluded from this deemed dividend treatment under ITA 84(1). The most important of these are:

- **Stock Dividends**   While there will be an increase in PUC in excess of the increase in net assets when a stock dividend is declared, such dividends are not considered to be an ITA 84(1) deemed dividend. Rather, they are taxed under ITA 82(1) as regular dividends. From the point of view of the recipient of the dividend, this distinction is of no consequence.

- **Shifts Between Classes**   When the PUC of one class of shares is decreased and, at the same, the PUC of a different class is increased by a corresponding amount, there is no ITA 84(1) deemed dividend.

• **Conversion Of Contributed Surplus**   In situations where the consideration received for shares issued is in excess of the amount added to PUC, a contributed surplus balance is created. This contributed surplus balance can be converted to PUC, without the increase in PUC being treated as a deemed dividend under ITA 84(1).

Deemed Dividends Under ITA 84(2) - On Winding Up

15-65.   When there is a winding up of a Canadian corporation under the provisions of ITA 88(2), the corporate assets will be sold and the liabilities, including taxes on the various types of income created by the sale of the assets, will be paid. The remaining cash will then be distributed to the shareholders of the corporation. Subsequent to this distribution, the shares of the corporation will be canceled. This process will be covered in more detail in Chapter 18.

15-66.   In this Chapter we would note that ITA 84(2) indicates that the excess of the amount distributed over the PUC of the shares that are canceled is considered to be a deemed dividend. While ITA 84(2) defines this entire amount as a deemed dividend, some components of this total are, in effect, redefined under ITA 88(2)(b). Specifically ITA 88(2)(b) indicates that the ITA 84(2) dividend will be dealt with as follows:

Distribution Of Pre-1972 CSOH   To the extent the corporation has a balance here, the distribution of this amount will be deemed not to be a dividend. Mere mortals may have trouble grasping the awkward manner in which this balance has been dealt with. It was deemed to be a dividend by ITA 84(2). Now we find that ITA 88(2)(b) has deemed this deemed dividend not to be a deemed dividend.

Capital Dividend   To the extent that the corporation has a balance in its capital dividend account, ITA 88(2)(b) indicates that this amount of the distribution will be considered a separate dividend that will be received on a tax free basis under ITA 83(2). As will be noted in our discussion of capital dividends, this treatment will only apply if an appropriate election is made.

Taxable Dividend   Any remaining distribution will be treated as a taxable dividend, subject to the usual gross up and tax credit procedures.

15-67.   To illustrate these provisions, consider the following:

Example   After selling its assets and paying all of its liabilities, a corporation has cash of $1,200,000 available for distribution to its only shareholder. The PUC of the company's shares is $100,000 and it has a pre-1972 CSOH balance of $250,000. The adjusted cost base of the shares is equal to their PUC of $100,000. The V-Day value of the shares is $225,000. The balance in the capital dividend account is $175,000. The company makes the appropriate election to have the distribution of the $175,000 treated as a capital dividend under ITA 83(2).

15-68.   The analysis of the $1,200,000 distribution would be as follows:

Cash Distributed	$1,200,000
PUC Of Shares	(100,000)
ITA 84(2) Deemed Dividend	$1,100,000
Pre-1972 CSOH Balance - Deemed Not A Dividend	(250,000)
Remaining ITA 84(2) Deemed Dividend	$ 850,000
ITA 83(2) Capital Dividend	(175,000)
ITA 88(2)(b) Taxable Dividend	$ 675,000

15-69.   From the point of view of the shareholder, there has been a disposition of his shares. This creates a problem in that the amount received as proceeds for the shares includes taxable dividends as indicated in the preceding example. However, this problem is resolved by the ITA 54 definition of "proceeds of disposition". This definition indicates that, to the extent that an amount received is considered to be a deemed dividend under ITA 84(2), it is excluded from the proceeds of disposition. This means that the capital gain on the disposition of shares in the example would be calculated as follows:

Proceeds For Shares	$1,200,000
ITA 84(2) Deemed Dividend [Not Including The Portion Deemed By ITA 88(2)(b) Not To Be A Dividend]	(850,000)
ITA 54 Proceeds Of Disposition	$ 350,000
Adjusted Cost Base (Median Value)	(225,000)
Capital Gain	$ 125,000

15-70.   The taxable capital gain would be $62,500 [(1/2)($125,000)].

Deemed Dividends Under ITA 84(3) - On Redemption, Acquisition Or Cancellation Of Shares

15-71.   An ITA 84(3) deemed dividend occurs most commonly when a corporation redeems a part of its outstanding shares. Such dividends can also occur when the corporation acquires or cancels a part of its outstanding shares. To the extent that the redemption amount paid by the corporation exceeds the PUC of the shares redeemed, a deemed dividend is assessed under ITA 84(3). For the corporation, this is a distribution of their unrestricted surplus balance.

15-72.   From the point of view of the person receiving the redemption proceeds, the deemed dividend component of the proceeds will be treated as an ordinary taxable dividend, subject to the usual gross up and tax credit procedures. However, the transaction also involves a disposition of the shares being redeemed, with the redemption proceeds being the amount received from the corporation. The problem with this is that, unlike the proceeds of disposition in an ordinary capital asset disposal, a portion of the amount received here is subject to tax as a deemed dividend. As was the case with ITA 84(2) dividends, this problem is resolved by the ITA 54 definition of proceeds of disposition. This definition excludes any amounts received that are deemed to be ITA 84(3) dividends.

Example   Mr. Jonas owns all of the preferred shares of Jonas Ltd. They were issued with a PUC of $75,000. However, their adjusted cost base to Mr. Jonas is $25,000. They are redeemed in July, 2001 by the corporation for $200,000.

Tax Consequences   The required analysis of this transaction is as follows:

Redemption Proceeds	$200,000
PUC Of Shares Redeemed	(75,000)
ITA 84(3) Deemed Dividend	$125,000
Redemption Proceeds	$200,000
Less: ITA 84(3) Deemed Dividend	(125,000)
ITA 54 Proceeds Of Disposition	$ 75,000
Adjusted Cost Base	(25,000)
Capital Gain	$ 50,000
Inclusion Rate	1/2
Taxable Capital Gains	$ 25,000

Deemed Dividends Under ITA 84(4) And ITA 84(4.1)

15-73.   This type of dividend is not as common as the others we have discussed in this section. It arises when a corporation resident in Canada distributes a part of its invested capital to its shareholders, without redeeming or canceling any of its shares. It might occur, for example, if a corporation divested itself of a major division and did not wish to reinvest the proceeds from the sale in other corporate assets. In this type of situation, the proceeds may be distributed to shareholders. Such distributions are commonly referred to as liquidating dividends.

15-74.   In order to make all or part of the distribution tax free, it is usually accompanied by a reduction in PUC. If the reduction in PUC is equal to the amount distributed, no dividend arises. However, if the distribution exceeds the PUC reduction, an ITA 84(4) deemed dividend is created. The rules for determining this dividend depend on whether or not the shares of the company are publicly traded.

> **Example**   Jong Ltd. has shares with a PUC of $5,000,000. As it has disposed of a major division of the Company, it would like to distribute $1,000,000 to its existing shareholders. In order to limit the tax effects of this distribution, the PUC of the shares will be reduced by $700,000.

15-75.   Under ITA 84(4), $700,000 of the total distribution will be a tax free distribution of PUC. Under ITA 84(4), the remaining $300,000 is treated as a deemed dividend, subject to the usual gross up and tax credit procedures. The adjusted cost base of the shares would be reduced by $700,000, the amount of the tax free distribution to shareholders. However, there would be no reduction in the adjusted cost base for the $300,000 distribution as it would be subject to tax as a deemed dividend.

Exercises Fifteen-3 and Fifteen-4 deal with deemed dividends. This would be an appropriate time to attempt these exercises.

15-76.   ITA 84(4.1) provides a different rule which overrides ITA 84(4) in the case of public companies. For these companies, if a payment is made in conjunction with a reduction of PUC, and there is no redemption, acquisition, or cancellation of shares, the entire distribution is treated as a deemed dividend. With respect to our example, this means that, if Jong Ltd., is a public company, the entire $1,000,000 distribution will be considered to be a deemed dividend under ITA 84(4.1). As the $1,000,000 amount will be subject to tax, the adjusted cost base of the shares will not be reduced in conjunction with this distribution.

Refundable Taxes On Investment Income

Meaning Of Aggregate Investment Income

15-77.   In the following material on refundable taxes, we will be using the term "investment income". For purposes of determining the amount of refundable taxes available, this term has a very specific meaning. Further, it is not the usual meaning that we associate with this term. Under ITA 129(4), the relevant "aggregate investment income" is defined as follows:

- Net taxable capital gains for the year, reduced by any net capital loss carry over deducted during the year.
- Property income including interest, rents, and royalties, but excluding dividends that are deductible in computing taxable income. Note that foreign dividends are not deductible and would be included in aggregate investment income.

15-78.   Note carefully the differences between this "aggregate investment income" and what we normally think of as property or investment income. Unlike the normal definition of property or investment income, this concept includes net taxable capital gains, reduced by net capital loss carry overs deducted during the year. In addition, it excludes most dividends from other Canadian corporations. This reflects the fact that dividends generally flow through a corporation without being subject to corporate taxes. You should also note that aggregate investment income includes income from both domestic and foreign sources.

Basic Concepts

15-79.   As shown in Figure 15-2 (following page), when income is flowed through a corporation, it is subject to two levels of taxation. It is taxed first at the corporate level and, if the after tax corporate amount is distributed to the individual shareholder, it will be taxed again in the hands of that individual. If we assume that the corporate tax rate on the investment income of a CCPC is 45 percent and that the individual shareholder is taxed at a rate of 30 percent on dividend income, the overall rate of taxation on investment income flowed through a corporation would be 61.5 percent [45% + (1 - 45%)(30%)]. If the same individual had received the

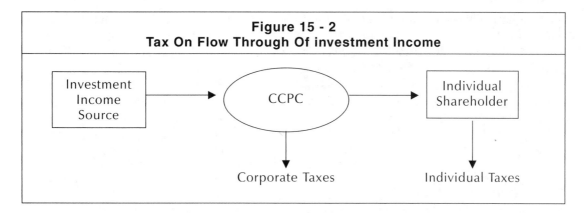

Figure 15 - 2
Tax On Flow Through Of investment Income

investment income directly, without it having been flowed through a corporation, the individual's tax rate on investment income would have been about 45 percent. This difference is clearly not consistent with the concept of integration which attempts to neutralize the influence of using a corporation on the after tax amount of income received by an individual.

15-80.   A possible solution to this problem would be to lower the rate of corporate taxation on the investment income of a CCPC. For example, if the corporate rate were lowered to 21 percent, the overall rate on the flow through of income would be the same 45 percent [21% + (1 - 21%)(30%)] that is applicable to the direct receipt of income by the individual.

15-81.   The problem with this solution is that it would provide for a significant deferral of taxes on investment income. If an individual received the investment income directly, the full amount of taxes must be paid when the income is earned. In contrast, when a corporation is used, only the first or corporate level of taxation is assessed when the income is earned. If the after tax amount is left in the corporation, the assessment of the individual level of tax can be deferred indefinitely. For higher income individuals not requiring their investment income for current consumption, this would present an outstanding opportunity for tax deferral. This would be the case whenever the corporate tax on investment income was below the rate applicable to the individual on the direct receipt of income.

15-82.   Given the opportunity for tax deferral that would result from the use of lower corporate tax rates, it is not surprising that a different solution to the problem of excessive tax rates on the flow through of a CCPC's investment income has been adopted. This solution involves leaving the corporate tax rate at a high level, but having a portion of the tax being designated as refundable. The refund of this portion of the corporate tax occurs when the income is distributed in the form of dividends that will be subject to the second level of taxation in the hands of the shareholders.

15-83.   While the detailed procedures related to these refundable taxes are complex, the basic concept is not. Some part of taxes paid on investment income at the corporate level are refunded when the income is distributed to investors in the form of dividends. This keeps the corporate tax rate in line with the rate that would be applicable to an individual on the direct receipt of income. This rate of corporate tax prevents tax deferral, while at the same time, the refund procedures avoids the excessive rate of taxation that would occur if a high corporate tax rate was combined with individual taxes on the same income stream. Stated simply, the use of a refundable tax allows the government to charge a corporate tax rate that is high enough to remove the incentive for accumulating investment income in a corporation, while at the same time providing a reasonable overall rate of taxation when the income is flowed through the corporation to the individual shareholder.

15-84.   In implementing this refundable tax approach, the *Income Tax Act* designates three different components of total taxes paid that can be refunded on the payment of dividends. They can be described as follows:

Ordinary Part I Tax   At this point you are all familiar with the calculation of the regular Part I tax that is assessed on the Taxable Income of a corporation. A portion of this tax, basically the part that is applicable to investment income, will be designated as refundable when the corporation pays dividends. Note the fact that a portion of the Part I tax will be designated as refundable does not change, in any way, the manner in which the Part I tax is calculated.

Additional Refundable Tax On Investment Income (ART) In the early 1990s, the provincial tax rates applicable to individuals had increased to the point that leaving investment income in a corporation was attractive, despite the fairly high combined rate of federal/provincial taxes on this type of income earned by a corporation. In order to discourage the use of corporations to defer tax on investment income, it was felt that a higher rate of corporate taxation was required. To implement this view, an addition Part I tax was added under ITA 123.3, applicable only to the investment income of CCPCs. This tax, normally referred to by the acronym ART, is assessed at a rate of 6-2/3 percent on the investment income of CCPCs and is refundable when the corporation pays dividends. As we have not previously discussed this tax, it will be given detailed consideration in this Chapter. It might be noted that this tax has been left in place, despite the fact that, in more recent years, provincial tax rates on individuals have fallen, in some cases fairly dramatically (e.g., Ontario and Alberta).

Part IV Tax There is still the possibility of using a related group of corporations to attempt to defer taxation on investment income. The Part IV refundable tax is a 33-1/3 percent tax on certain intercorporate dividends that is designed to prevent this from happening. As was the case with the ART, we have not previously discussed this tax and, as a consequence, it will be given detailed consideration in this Chapter.

15-85.   In dealing with this material, we will first consider the issues involved with a single corporation. Only the refundable components of Part I tax are relevant here and, as a part of this material, we will give detailed consideration to the ART.

15-86.   A subsequent section will discuss the Refundable Dividend Tax On Hand account (RDTOH). This is a balance which allows us to track the various components of taxes paid that are eligible for refund, as well as the amount of refunds that have been made.

Refundable Part I Tax On Income From Investments

Additional Refundable Tax On Investment Income (ART)
Basic Calculations
15-87.   As was noted previously, tax legislation contains a refundable tax on the investment income of a Canadian Controlled Private Corporation (CCPC). This additional refundable tax (ART) is assessed under ITA 123.3, with the amount payable equal to 6-2/3 percent of the lesser of:

- the corporation's "aggregate investment income" for the year [as defined in ITA 129(4)]; and

- the amount, if any, by which the corporation's taxable income for the year exceeds the amount that is eligible for the small business deduction.

15-88.   The basic objective of this tax is to make it less attractive to shelter investment income within a corporate structure in order to defer full taxation of the amounts earned. When this additional 6-2/3 percent is added to the usual rates applicable to a CCPC's investment income, the total rate is in the 45 percent [(38% - 10%)(104%) + 9% (lowest provincial rate) + 6-2/3%] to 53 percent [(38% - 10%)(104%) + 17% (highest provincial rate) + 6-2/3%] range, depending on the applicable provincial rate on corporations. As noted in Chapter 13, the combined federal/provincial maximum rates on individuals range from 39 to 49 percent. This means that, with the addition of the ART, rates on the investment income of a CCPC will generally be higher than the rates applicable to an individual receiving the same income. Given this, there is little or no incentive to use a corporation to defer taxation on this type of income.

15-89. As described in Paragraph 15-87, the ART is based on the lesser of investment income and the amount of taxable income that is not eligible for the small business deduction. The reason for the latter limit is to ensure that such deductions as charitable contributions or non capital loss carry overs have not eliminated all or part of the investment income from the amount flowing through to Taxable Income. The goal is to prevent the ART from being inappropriately applied to active business income.

ART And Foreign Tax Credits

15-90. As discussed in Chapter 14, the use of foreign taxes paid as credits against Canadian taxes payable is limited by a formula that includes the "tax otherwise payable". In the case of foreign taxes paid on non business income, the "tax otherwise payable" in the formula includes the ART that is assessed under ITA 123.3. This creates a problem in that the calculation of ART includes the amount eligible for the small business deduction [ITA 123.3(b)]. In turn, the determination of the amount eligible for the small business deduction requires the use of the foreign tax credits for foreign taxes paid on non business and business income [ITA 125(1)(b)(i) and (ii)].

15-91. This would have created an insolvable circular calculation were it not for the fact that ITA 125(1)(b)(i) was modified in a manner that, for the purpose of calculating the small business deduction, permits the foreign tax credit for taxes paid on non business income to be calculated using a "tax otherwise payable" figure that does not include the ART under ITA 123.3. This means that in situations where both the small business deduction and the ART are involved, the following procedures should be used:

1. Calculate the foreign non business tax credit using a "tax otherwise payable" that excludes the ART. This initial version of the foreign non business tax credit will be used only for determining the small business deduction, with the actual credit to be applied calculated after the ART has been determined.

2. The foreign business tax credit uses a "tax otherwise payable" figure that, by definition, excludes the ART. However, this credit is limited by the amount of tax otherwise payable, reduced by the foreign non business tax credit. As a consequence, it will be necessary to calculate an initial version of this foreign business tax credit, using the initial version of the foreign non business tax credit. This initial version will be used only for the purpose of determining the small business deduction.

3. Calculate the amount eligible for the small business deduction using the numbers determined in steps 1 and 2.

4. Calculate the ART, using the amount eligible for the small business deduction determined in step 3.

5. Calculate the actual foreign non business tax credit using a "tax otherwise payable" figure which includes the ART.

6. Calculate the actual foreign business tax credit using the actual foreign non business tax credit determined in step 5.

Problem One: Excessive Tax Rates on the Flow Through of a CCPC's Investment Income

15-92. With the addition of the 6-2/3 percent ART on the investment income of a Canadian controlled private corporation, this investment income will be taxed at an overall federal rate of just under 36 percent [(38% - 10%)(104%) + 6-2/3%]. With the addition of provincial taxes at corporate rates ranging from 9 percent to 17 percent, the combined federal/provincial rate on this income will range from 45 percent to 53 percent. All of these combined rates are more than double the 20 percent rate required for perfect integration. In the absence of some type of relieving mechanism, the objective of integrating corporate and individual tax rates would not be met.

15-93. The problem of excessive rates of tax on investment income flowed through a corporation was discussed previously in Paragraph 15-79. A more complete example will be presented here.

Example Mr. Monroe is subject to a combined federal/provincial tax rate of 43.5 percent. The dividend tax credit in his province of residence is equal to one-third of the gross up. He earns $100,000 in interest income during the year. Calculate Mr. Monroe's after tax cash flows resulting from this investment income under the following alternative assumptions:

Case A He receives the $100,000 in interest income directly.

Case B Mr. Monroe is the sole shareholder of a Canadian controlled private corporation that earns the $100,000 of investment income. The corporation is subject to a combined federal/provincial tax rate, including the ITA 123.3 tax on investment income, of 50 percent. The corporation pays out all of its after tax earnings as dividends, resulting in a dividend to Mr. Monroe of $50,000. Ignore any refund of Part I taxes paid.

15-94. The calculations comparing investment income if it was received directly (Case A) and if it was earned in a corporation (Case B), are as follows:

Case A - Income Received Directly

Investment Income	$100,000
Taxes At 43.5%	(43,500)
After Tax Cash Flow	$ 56,500

Case B - Income Flowed Through Corporation

Corporate Income	$100,000
Corporate Taxes At 50%	(50,000)
Available For Dividends	$ 50,000

Dividends Received	$ 50,000
Gross Up (25%)	12,500
Personal Taxable Income	$ 62,500
Tax Rate	43.5%
Taxes	$ 27,188
Dividend Tax Credit [(2/3 + 1/3)(Gross Up)]	(12,500)
Personal Taxes Payable	$ 14,688

Dividends Received	$ 50,000
Personal Taxes Payable	(14,688)
After Tax Cash Flow	$ 35,312

Savings - Direct Receipt

Income received directly	$ 56,500
Income flowed through corporation	35,312
Net savings on direct receipt	$ 21,188

15-95. The results show that when the income is flowed through a corporation, the result is an effective tax rate of nearly 65 percent [($100,000 - $35,312) ÷ $100,000]. This is significantly higher than the 43.5 percent rate that is applicable to the direct receipt of the investment income, an outcome that would represent a major failure in the government's attempt to achieve integration.

15-96.   Before leaving this example you should note that, with the inclusion of the ART on investment income, there is no longer a deferral advantage associated with using a corporation. Prior to the introduction of this tax, in some situations, the amount of tax paid at the corporate level on investment income was less than the amount that would be paid by an individual receiving the income directly. This is no longer the case. In our example, corporate taxes alone are $50,000, well in excess of the $43,500 that would be paid if Mr. Monroe had received the income directly.

15-97.   Even if we use the highest provincial rates on individuals in effect in Canada, taxes at the corporate level would only be marginally lower than taxes on the direct receipt of the income. As was the intent of the government, the ART has eliminated any significant tax advantage associated with using a corporation to defer taxes on investment income. In fact, in view of the recent reductions in provincial rates on individuals, a 6-2/3 percent ART may constitute overkill.

Solution To Problem One: Refundable Portion Of Part I Tax
Basic Concepts
15-98.   The preceding example makes it clear that taxes on investment income earned by a corporation and flowed through to its shareholders are potentially much higher than would be the case if the shareholders received the income directly. This major imperfection in the system of integration results from a federal/provincial tax rate on the investment income of CCPCs that is generally over 50 percent.

15-99.   In those cases where the income is retained in the corporation, this is an equitable arrangement in that this high rate discourages the use of a CCPC to temporarily shelter passive income from a portion of the taxes that would be assessed on the direct receipt of the income by the individual. However, when the property income is flowed through a CCPC and paid as dividends, the result is not consistent with the government's desire to tax CCPCs under the integration view of corporate taxation.

15-100.   As noted previously, the government could have dealt with this problem by reducing the corporate tax rate on the investment income of CCPCs, but this would have allowed the owners of CCPCs to defer personal taxes on this income by leaving the investment income in the corporation. To avoid this, the refundable tax approach is used. Under this approach, the investment income of Canadian controlled private corporations is taxed at the usual high rates, including the ART on investment income. However, when the corporation distributes its after tax income in the form of dividends, a part of this tax is refunded. The refund is based on the amount of dividends paid by the corporation, with the refund being equal to $1 for each $3 of dividends paid.

Concepts Illustrated
15-101.   In order to give you a better understanding of how the concepts associated with the refund of Part I tax work, we will use an example based on the corporate tax rates that are inherent in the integration procedures contained in the *Income Tax Act*. You will recall that the dividend gross up and tax credit procedures are based on an assumed rate of corporate tax of 20 percent. In our example, we will assume that this is the combined federal/provincial rate applicable to income eligible for the small business deduction. For income that is not eligible for the small business deduction, we will assume a combined federal/provincial rate of 40 percent, before the addition of the ART. While this is somewhat lower than most of the combined rates, the use of these notional rates will permit us to illustrate how integration is supposed to work in this situation. We will subsequently present a second example which uses more realistic rates.

15-102.   The basic idea here is that the investment income of a Canadian controlled private corporation will be taxed at a rate of 46-2/3 percent (the 40 percent described in the preceding Paragraph, plus the ART of 6-2/3 percent). When the residual after tax income is paid out in dividends, a refund of the tax in excess of 20 percent will be provided. This can be accomplished by providing a dividend refund equal to $1 for each $3 of dividends paid. These ideas can be illustrated with the following example:

Example Ms. Banardi has investments which generate income of $100,000 per year. You have been asked to advise her as to whether there would be any benefits associated with transferring these investments to her Canadian controlled private corporation. Ms. Banardi is subject to a combined federal/provincial tax rate of 43.5 percent on her individual taxable income and the dividend tax credit in her province is equal to one-third of the gross up. Her corporation would be taxed on this income at a combined federal/provincial rate of 46-2/3 percent, including the ART on investment income.

15-103. If the income is received directly, Ms. Banardi will pay taxes of $43,500 and retain cash of $56,500. Alternatively, if the investments are transferred to a corporation, the after tax retention will be calculated as follows:

Corporate Investment Income	$100,000
Basic Corporate Tax At 40%	(40,000)
ART At 6-2/3%	(6,667)
Income Before Dividends	$ 53,333
Dividend Refund*	26,667
Dividends Paid To Ms. Banardi	$ 80,000

*In these somewhat academic examples of the dividend refund mechanism, it is assumed that all of the after tax income of the corporation will be paid out as dividends. As this will trigger a $1 for $3 refund ($26,667 ÷ $80,000), the after tax balance represents two-thirds of the dividend ($53,333 ÷ $80,000). This means that the amount of the refund will be calculated as one-half (1/3 ÷ 2/3) of the after tax balance of corporate income. This is not consistent with the real world approach in which the amount of the dividend is determined by a variety of factors (e.g., alternative investment opportunities) and the refund is calculated as one-third of the amount paid.

Dividends Received	$ 80,000
Gross Up Of 25%	20,000
Taxable Dividends	$100,000

Individual Tax At 43.5%	$ 43,500
Dividend Tax Credit [(2/3 + 1/3)(Gross Up)]	(20,000)
Individual Taxes Payable	$ 23,500

Dividends Received	$ 80,000
Individual Taxes Payable	(23,500)
After Tax Cash Retained	$ 56,500

15-104. This is the same amount of after tax cash that would have been retained if Ms. Banardi had received the $100,000 in investment income directly, thereby demonstrating that this refundable tax restores integration to the system with respect to total taxes paid. Also of importance is the fact that the use of a corporation has not provided any tax deferral. Corporate taxes total $46,667, an amount that is in excess of the $43,500 in taxes that would be paid if the investment income had been received directly by Ms. Banardi.

Use Of Other Rates In Refundable Part I Tax Example
15-105. The preceding example is useful in that it illustrates how perfectly integration can work if the appropriate rates are used. As has been discussed in Chapters 13 and 14, there is considerable variance in provincial rates for both corporations and individuals. Not surprisingly, these variations will influence how well these integration measures succeed. In order to illustrate this effect, we will present the following second example using different rates.

Example Mr. Leoni has investments which generate income of $100,000 per year. You have been asked to advise as to whether there would be any benefits associated with transferring these investments to his Canadian controlled private corporation. Mr. Leoni has over $200,000 in other income and, as a consequence, he is in the top tax bracket. This means that, in his province, he is subject to a combined federal/provincial tax rate of 47 percent. The provincial dividend tax credit is equal to 40 percent of the gross up. His corporation would be taxed on this income at a combined federal/provincial rate of 51.8 percent, including the ART on investment income [(38% - 10%)(104%) + 16% + 6-2/3%].

15-106. If the income is received directly, Mr. Leoni will pay taxes of $47,000 and retain cash of $53,000. Alternatively, if the investments are transferred to his corporation, the after tax retention will be calculated as follows:

Corporate Investment Income	$100,000
Corporate Tax At 51.8% (Includes ART)	(51,800)
Income Before Dividends	$ 48,200
Dividend Refund ($1 For Each $3 Of Dividends Paid)	24,100
Dividends Paid To Mr. Leoni	$ 72,300
Dividends Received	$ 72,300
Gross Up Of 25%	18,075
Taxable Dividends	$ 90,375
Individual Tax At 47%	$ 42,476
Dividend Tax Credit [(2/3 + 40%)($18,075)]	(19,280)
Individual Taxes Payable	$ 23,196
Dividends Received	$ 72,300
Individual Taxes Payable	(23,196)
After Tax Cash Retained	$ 49,104

15-107. While there are differences, the results here are similar to those produced by the example in 15-102 for income retained in the corporation. Corporate taxes before the refund ($51,800) are higher than those applicable to the direct receipt of income ($47,000). Clearly, the use of a corporation when the applicable tax rates are as per the example does not produce any tax deferral. Note however, that in this example the after tax retention when the income is flowed through a corporation is much less than the amount retained through direct receipt of the income ($49,104 vs. $53,000). The high corporate tax rate tends to reduce the amount retained via the corporate route. Although the high provincial rate on the individual and the large provincial dividend tax credit (more than one-third of the gross up) serves to make the use of a corporation more attractive, there is clearly a tax disadvantage in flowing investment income through a CCPC. Given the ART and the fact that provincial tax rates on individuals have been declining, this will be a fairly common result in real world situations.

Refundable Part IV Tax On Dividends Received

Problem Two: Use Of Multi Level Affiliations To Defer Taxes On Investment Income

15-108. In the preceding section, we demonstrated how refund procedures applicable to Part I taxes payable are used to lower the overall rate of taxation on the investment income of a CCPC, while at the same time preventing the use of a corporation to defer a portion of the overall taxation on such income. While varying provincial tax rates on corporations and indi-

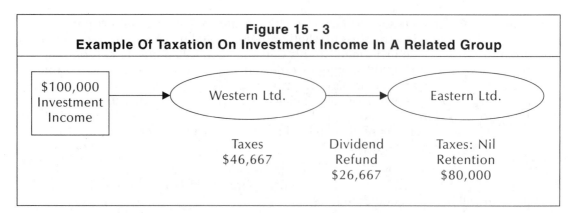

Figure 15 - 3
Example Of Taxation On Investment Income In A Related Group

viduals prevent these procedures from providing perfect results, they appear to produce results that come close to achieving the goal of integration of personal and corporate taxes.

15-109. As was noted earlier, the situation becomes more complex when a related group of companies is involved. The refundable tax procedures that were described in the previous section are not effective in such situations and, as a consequence, there is a need for additional procedures.

Example

15-110. As an example of this type of situation, Eastern Inc. has a 100 percent owned subsidiary, Western Ltd. Both Companies are Canadian controlled private corporations and have a December 31 year end. During the year ending December 31, 2001, Western has income of $100,000, made up entirely of interest and taxable capital gains. The provincial tax rate for both companies is 12 percent, resulting in a combined federal/provincial rate of 40 percent. Western pays out all of its income in dividends to Eastern Ltd. This situation is illustrated in Figure 15-3.

15-111. On receipt of the $100,000 of investment income, Western would pay taxes of $46,667, including the ART. However, when the remaining $53,333 is paid out in dividends, a refund of $26,667 (one-third of the $80,000 total dividend) becomes available, resulting in a total dividend of $80,000 as shown in the following calculation:

Investment Income		$100,000
Basic Corporate Tax At 40%	($40,000)	
ART At 6-2/3%	(6,667)	(46,667)
Income Before Dividends		$ 53,333
Dividend Refund ($1 For Each $3 Of Dividends Paid)		26,667
Dividends Paid To Eastern		$ 80,000

15-112. As the dividends from Western will be received tax free by Eastern, they will have after tax retention of $80,000. Until such time as Eastern pays out taxable dividends to its shareholders, no additional Part I tax will be assessed. This means that, in the absence of additional procedures for dealing with this type of situation, there would be a significant deferral of taxes on investment income resulting from the use of two related corporations.

Solution To Problem Two: Refundable Part IV Tax
Corporations Subject To Part IV Tax

15-113. To eliminate this potential flaw in the integration system, a Part IV tax is assessed on dividends received by a private corporation from certain other types of corporations. Note that this tax is assessed on all private corporations, without regard to whether or not they are Canadian controlled.

15-114. In general, only private corporations are liable for Part IV tax. However, there remains the possibility that a company that is controlled largely for the benefit of an individual or a related group of individuals might use a small issue of shares to the public in order to avoid this tax. Such corporations are referred to as subject corporations and they are defined in ITA 186(3) as follows:

> **Subject Corporation** means a corporation (other than a private corporation) resident in Canada and controlled, whether because of a beneficial interest in one or more trusts or otherwise, by or for the benefit of an individual (other than a trust) or a related group of individuals (other than trusts).

15-115. ITA 186(1) indicates that, for purposes of Part IV tax, subject corporations will be treated as private corporations. This means that both private corporations, as well as those public corporations that fall within the definition of subject corporations, will be liable for the payment of Part IV tax.

Rates
15-116. The Part IV tax is assessed at a rate of 33-1/3 percent. It is applicable, as will be discussed in the material which follows, to portfolio dividends as well as some dividends from connected corporations (both of these terms will be subsequently explained). The rate at which this tax is refunded is the same as the rate for refunds of Part I taxes. Refunds of Part IV tax are equal to $1 for each $3 of dividends paid. Corporate income tax instalment calculations do not take into consideration the Part IV tax liability.

Applicable Dividends
15-117. The Part IV tax is not applicable to all of the dividends received by a private corporation. Specifically, Part IV tax is payable on dividends received by private or subject corporations in the following circumstances:

- The dividend is received from a connected company and the company paying the dividend received a refund as a result of its payment.
- The dividend is received from an unconnected company (referred to as portfolio dividends).

15-118. Each of these types of dividends will be given separate attention in the two sections which follow.

Dividends Paid Out Of A Connected Corporation's Investment Income
15-119. Connected companies are defined in ITA 186(4) as follows:

- a controlled corporation, where control represents ownership of more than 50 percent of the voting shares by any combination of the other corporation and persons with whom it does not deal at arm's length, or
- a corporation in which the other corporation has more than 10 percent of the voting shares and more than 10 percent of the fair market value of all of the issued shares of the corporation.

15-120. It is the intent of the government to allow a Canadian controlled private corporation to be used to defer taxes on active business income. Earning such income entitles the corporation to the use of the small business deduction and this, in most situations, provides a rate of corporate taxation that will effectively defer taxes on income left in the corporation. To the extent the connected corporation is paying dividends out of such income, there will be no dividend refund and no Part IV tax to be paid by the recipient corporation. This maintains the tax deferral on active business income as it moves between corporations.

15-121. However, when the connected corporation is a private company (whether or not it is Canadian controlled) and the dividends are paid out of investment income, a problem arises. This problem was illustrated by the example presented in Paragraph 15-110.

15-122. In that example, Western paid an $80,000 dividend to Eastern, a payment which included a $26,667 refund of taxes previously paid by Western. Under the general rules for dividends, the $80,000 dividend paid by Western would be included in the calculation of Eastern's Net Income and deducted in the determination of its Taxable Income, with the net result that no taxes would be paid on the $80,000. This would, in effect, allow retention of 80 percent of the investment income within the corporate group, a result that is contrary to the general concept of integration. In order to correct this situation, a Part IV tax is required as follows:

Part IV Tax - Connected Companies   When a private corporation receives dividends from a connected private corporation that has received a dividend refund under ITA 129(1) as a result of paying dividends, the recipient company is liable for a Part IV tax equal to its share of the refund received by the paying corporation. If the dividend paid is eligible for a full $1 refund on each $3 paid, the Part IV tax can also be expressed as 33-1/3 percent of the dividends received. However, the payor corporation may be earning both active business income and investment income.

In such situations, dividends may reflect a distribution of both types of income, resulting in a situation where a dividend refund is not likely to be at the full $1 for $3 rate. This is why the Part IV tax on dividends received from a connected corporation is expressed in terms of the recipient's share of the refund received by the paying corporation, not in terms of a specific rate.

This Part IV tax is refundable, on the basis of $1 for each $3 of dividends paid, when such dividends are passed on to the shareholders of the recipient corporation.

15-123.   Returning to the example presented in Paragraph 15-110, the results for Eastern, assuming that all amounts of after tax income are paid out as dividends, would be as follows:

Investment Income (Dividends Received From Western)	$80,000
Part IV Taxes Payable (100% Of Western's Refund*)	(26,667)
Available Before Refund	$53,333
Dividend Refund ($1 For Each $3 Of Dividends Paid)	26,667
Total Dividends Paid	$80,000

*Because all of Western's income was from investments, the dividend refund to Western is the full $1 for each $3 of dividends. This means that Eastern's Part IV tax can also be calculated as 33-1/3% of the $80,000 in dividends received from Western.

15-124.   As this simple example shows, the purpose of the Part IV refundable tax in this situation is to ensure that full corporate tax rates are charged on any undistributed investment income that is earned within a group of private companies. In the absence of this provision, an individual subject to a personal tax rate of 50 percent could transfer investment income into a group of private companies where it might only be taxed at a rate of 20 percent. This would result in a significant deferral of taxes until such time as the income was distributed out of the corporate group.

15-125.   When Eastern pays dividends to its shareholders, the total is the same as the amount received from Western. This illustrates the fact that the Part IV procedures achieve their goal of preventing tax deferral, yet allow the dividends to flow through Eastern without additional taxation.

15-126.   We would remind you again that the Part IV tax on dividends from a connected company is only applicable when the paying corporation has received a dividend refund. This means that only those dividends that are paid out of the corporation's investment income will be subject to Part IV tax. If the paying corporation was earning active business income, it would be taxed at the low small business rate and no refund would be available when this after tax income was paid out as dividends. As a consequence, no Part IV tax would be assessed on the corporation receiving the dividend.

15-127.   This result is consistent with the goals of integration in that, when a corporation is earning active business income, tax deferral is permitted on income that is retained in the corporation and not paid out in dividends.

15-128. In many cases, a corporation will be earning both investment income and active business income. This will result in a situation, unlike the example previously presented, where some part of the dividends paid by the corporation will be eligible for a refund and the remainder will not. In this type of situation, the Part IV tax will not be equal to 33-1/3 percent of the dividends received. An example will make this point clear:

> **Example** On December 1, 2001, Lower Ltd. declares and pays a dividend of $45,000. As a result of paying this dividend, the Company receives a dividend refund of $8,000 (as will be shown later in this Chapter, the limiting factor would be the balance in the Refundable Dividend Tax On Hand account). This would suggest that Lower Ltd. received a refund on only $24,000 of the dividends paid. Upper Inc. owns 60 percent of the outstanding shares of Lower Ltd.

> **Tax Consequences** As the $8,000 refund was less than one-third of the $45,000 in dividends paid by Lower Ltd., it is clear that a dividend refund was received on only part of the dividends paid. In this situation, Upper Inc.'s Part IV tax payable would be equal to $4,800 [(60%)($8,000)]. This is not equal to 33-1/3 percent of the $27,000 [(60%)($45,000)] in dividends received by Upper. The Part IV tax payable can also be calculated by taking 60 percent of one-third of the $24,000 in dividends on which Lower Ltd. received a dividend.

Part IV Tax On Portfolio Dividends Received

15-129. A portfolio dividend is one that is received from a company to which the recipient of the dividend is not connected. This means that a dividend would be considered a portfolio dividend unless it is received from a company which is controlled or in which the recipient owns more than 10 percent of the outstanding voting shares and more than 10 percent of the total market value of all shares. In more practical terms, what we are talking about here is an intercorporate investment in which the investor company does not have the ability to exercise significant control or influence over the investee.

15-130. An example of a portfolio dividend would be a dividend received on an investment made by a private company in 500 shares of a large publicly traded company. The 500 shares would be significantly less than 10 percent of the total outstanding and would not constitute control of the company. As a consequence, the dividends would be considered a portfolio dividend and Part IV taxes would be applicable.

15-131. The problem here again relates to integration. If such dividends are received by an individual, they are generally subject to taxation. For example, assume that the $80,000 in dividends received by Eastern in our example from Paragraph 15-110 are, alternatively received by an individual. This individual is subject to a combined federal/provincial tax rate of 43.5 percent and lives in a province with a dividend tax credit equal to one-third of the gross up. The resulting taxes payable would be calculated as follows:

Dividends Received	$ 80,000
Gross Up (25%)	20,000
Taxable Income	$100,000
Marginal Tax Rate	43.5%
Taxes	$ 43,500
Dividend Tax Credit [(2/3 + 1/3)(Gross Up)]	(20,000)
Taxes Payable	$ 23,500

15-132. As an alternative, consider what would happen if the same $80,000 in dividends had been received by a corporation. Under the general rules for intercorporate dividends, no taxes would be paid by the corporation and, in view of the fact that such portfolio dividends are little different than other types of investment income that might be earned by an investor, this would appear to be a significant flaw in the integration system.

15-133. In order to correct this flaw, there is a second application of Part IV tax as follows:

Part IV Tax - Portfolio Dividends When a private corporation receives a dividend on shares that are being held as a portfolio investment, the recipient company is liable for a Part IV tax of 33-1/3 percent of the dividends received. Note that, in this case, the 33-1/3 percent rate is always applicable. This Part IV tax is refundable, on the basis of $1 for each $3 of dividends paid, when such dividends are passed on to the shareholders of the recipient corporation.

15-134. We can see the reasoning behind the rate of this tax by referring back to the preceding example in Paragraph 15-131. You will notice that the effective tax rate on the dividends received by the individual is just over 29 percent ($23,500 ÷ $80,000). By charging a Part IV tax of 33-1/3 percent at the corporate level, the tax paid by the corporation is in excess of the 29 percent effective tax rate that would apply to dividends received by an individual with a marginal tax rate of 43.5 percent. This makes it disadvantageous to use a private corporation as a shelter to defer the payment of taxes on dividend income. Again, however, by making the tax refundable, it allows the dividends to flow through the recipient corporation without a permanent increase in taxes.

Other Considerations
15-135. The preceding material has dealt with the basic features of the Part IV tax on dividends received by private corporations. There are a few additional points to be made. First, you should note what kinds of dividends are not subject to Part IV taxes. For a private company or a subject company, the only dividends that will not be subject to Part IV tax are those received from a connected corporation that does not get a dividend refund as a result of paying the dividend.

15-136. A second point is that ITA 186(1) allows a corporation to use unabsorbed non capital losses to reduce any Part IV tax. One-third of any non capital or farm losses claimed for this purpose is deducted from the Part IV tax otherwise payable. However, if this option is chosen, the corporation has effectively used a possible permanent reduction in future taxes to acquire a reduction of taxes payable that would otherwise ultimately be refunded. This would only make sense in situations where the non capital loss carry forward was about to expire or where the company did not expect to have taxable income in the carry forward period.

Refundable Dividend Tax On Hand (RDTOH)

Basic Concepts
15-137. In the simple examples we used to illustrate refundable taxes, it was easy to see the direct connection between amounts of investment income and the amount of the refund that could be made on payment of dividends. In the real world, such direct relationships do not exist. Corporations generally earn a combination of investment and business income, they seldom pay out all of their earnings in the form of dividends, and there are usually lags between the period in which income is earned and the period in which dividends are paid. As a consequence, some mechanism is needed to keep track of amounts of taxes that have been paid that are eligible for the refund treatment. This mechanism is the Refundable Dividend Tax On Hand (RDTOH, hereafter).

15-138. This RDTOH is defined in ITA 129(3) and we will give detailed consideration to that subsection. However, before getting into this detailed consideration, a general overview of the RDTOH may be helpful.

15-139. The RDTOH will normally start with an opening balance, reflecting amounts carried over from the previous year. This balance will be increased by the payment of the various types of refundable taxes. In somewhat simplified terms, these additions will be:

- The refundable portion of Part I tax paid, calculated as 26-2/3 percent of aggregate investment income.

- Part IV tax on dividends received, calculated at a rate of 33-1/3 percent of portfolio dividends, plus an amount equal to the recipient's share of the dividend refund received by the connected corporation paying the dividend.

15-140.   After these amounts are added, the total is then reduced by the dividend refund received by the corporation for the preceding year.

15-141.   The dividend refund for the current year will be limited by the balance in this account. That is, the dividend refund for the current year will be equal to the lesser of the balance in the RDTOH, and one-third of the dividends paid for the year. These ideas will be presented in a more technical form in the next Section.

RDTOH Defined
Basic Definition
15-142.   ITA 129(3) defines the RDTOH at the end of a taxation year as the aggregate of four items. The first three are additions and can be described as follows:

ITA 129(3)(a)   Refundable Part I taxes for the year.

ITA 129(3)(b)   The total of the taxes under Part IV for the year.

ITA 129(3)(c)   The corporation's RDTOH at the end of the preceding year.

15-143.   The fourth item, the corporation's dividend refund for its preceding taxation year, is subtracted from the total of the first three under **ITA 129(3)(d)**.

15-144.   The only one of these four items that requires further elaboration is ITA 129(3)(a), the refundable portion of Part I taxes for the year. This will be provided in the section which follows.

Part I Taxes Paid
15-145.   The situation here is made complex by the fact that in calculating a corporation's taxable income and Part I Taxes Payable, there is no segregation of taxes on investment income from taxes on other types of income. This means that there is no direct measure of what portion of the regular Part I Tax Payable should be refunded. To deal with this situation, the RDTOH definition limits this addition to the least of three amounts. These are specified under ITA 129(3)(a)(i), (ii), and (iii).

15-146.   The first of these amounts is determined as follows:

ITA 129(3)(a)(i)   the amount determined by the formula

$$A - B, \text{ where}$$

A   is 26-2/3 percent of the corporation's aggregate investment income for the year, and

B   is the amount, if any, by which the foreign investment income tax credit exceeds 9-1/3 percent of its foreign investment income for the year.

15-147.   Aggregate investment income is as defined in ITA 129(4). As previously indicated, the components of aggregate investment income are:

• Taxable capital gains in excess of the sum of allowable capital losses of the current year plus net capital losses from other years deducted during the current year.

• Property income except for dividends that are deductible in computing the corporation's taxable income.

15-148.   These amounts do not include interest or rents that are incidental to the corporation's efforts to produce active business income. As noted in Chapter 14, these amounts would be considered active business income.

15-149.   If the corporation has no foreign source investment income, this amount is simply 26-2/3 percent of investment income. This rate reflects a portion (20 percentage points) of the regular Part I taxes payable, as well as the 6-2/3 percent tax on investment income under ITA 123.3.

15-150.   The aggregate investment income definition includes both Canadian and foreign source income of the types specified. The legislation assumes that foreign investment income pays Canadian tax at a rate of 36 percent before any foreign tax credit. If the foreign tax credit on this income reduces the level of taxation on this income below 26-2/3 percent, the government does not want to give a refund based on this rate. In our comprehensive example which follows, we will find that the corporation earns $20,000 in foreign investment income and receives a foreign non business tax credit of $3,000. At a 36 percent rate, Canadian taxes on this income would be $7,200, with the foreign tax credit of $3,000 reducing this to $4,200. The refundable taxes on this $20,000 at 26-2/3 percent would be $5,333. This means that if a refund is based on 26-2/3 percent, the refund will be $1,133 ($5,333 - $4,200) larger than the Canadian taxes paid on the foreign income.

15-151.   To deal with this problem, the formula requires that the available refund be reduced by the amount by which the foreign investment income tax credit exceeds 9-1/3 percent (36 percent, less 26-2/3 percent) of the foreign investment income. For the example described in the preceding Paragraph, this would be the appropriate $1,133 [$3,000 - (9-1/3%)($20,000)].

15-152.   A further problem with respect to determining the refundable portion of Part I taxes payable is that the corporation's taxable income may include amounts that are not taxed at full corporate rates (e.g., amounts eligible for the small business deduction). Further, taxable income may be reduced by such things as non capital loss carry overs to a level that is less than the amount of investment income on which ITA 129(3)(a)(i) would provide a refund. To deal with this, the refundable portion of the Part I tax is limited as follows:

> **ITA 129(3)(a)(ii)**   26-2/3 percent of the amount, if any, by which the corporation's taxable income for the year exceeds the total of
>
> A   amount eligible for the small business deduction;
> B   25/9 of the tax credit for foreign investment income; and
> C   10/4 of the tax credit for foreign business income.

15-153.   Item B is designed to remove foreign investment income which is not taxed because of the foreign investment income tax credit. The elimination is based on the notional assumption that it is taxed at 36 percent (9/25). In similar fashion, Item C is designed to remove foreign business income that is not taxed because of the foreign business income tax credit. The elimination here is based on the notional assumption that this type of income is taxed at 40 percent.

15-154.   A final problem here relates to the fact that the refund could exceed the corporation's actual taxes payable for the year. This could happen if, for example, the company had large amounts of tax credits for scientific research and experimental development. To deal with this problem, the refundable portion of Part I tax paid is limited as follows:

> **ITA 129(3)(a)(iii)**   the corporation's tax for the year payable under this Part [Part I] determined without reference to section 123.2 [the 4 percent corporate surtax].

15-155.   Taking all of these items into consideration, the addition to the RDTOH for Part I taxes is the least of:

> **ITA 129(3)(a)(i)**   26-2/3 percent of Canadian and foreign investment income, reduced by the excess of foreign non business income tax credits over 9-1/3 percent of foreign investment income.
>
> **ITA 129(3)(a)(ii)**   26-2/3 percent of the amount, if any, by which Taxable Income exceeds the sum of amounts eligible for the small business deduction, 25/9 of the foreign non business tax credit, and 10/4 of the foreign business tax credit.
>
> **ITA 129(3)(a)(iii)**   Part I taxes payable, calculated without the inclusion of the surtax.

The Dividend Refund

15-156.   While in theory, dividend refunds should only be available when dividends are paid out of investment income, corporate tax records do not provide a basis for tracking the income source of a particular dividend payment. As a consequence, a dividend refund is available on any dividend that is paid by the corporation as long as there is a balance in the

RDTOH. Given this, the dividend refund will be equal to the lesser of:

- the balance in the RDTOH account; and
- 1/3 of all dividends paid.

Example

15-157. The following example illustrates the calculations discussed in this Section.

Basic Data Fortune Ltd. is a Canadian controlled private corporation. Based on the formula in ITR 402, 90 percent of the Company's income is earned in a province. The following information is available for the year ending December 31, 2001:

Canadian Source Investment Income (Includes $25,000 in Taxable Capital Gains)	$100,000
Gross Foreign Business Income (15 Percent Withheld)	10,000
Gross Foreign Investment Income (15 Percent Withheld)	20,000
Active Business Income (No Associated Companies)	150,000
Portfolio Dividends Received	30,000
Net Income	$310,000
Portfolio Dividends	(30,000)
Net Capital Loss From Preceding Year Deducted	(15,000)
Taxable Income	$265,000

Tax Payable in this situation would be calculated as follows:

Base Amount of Part I Tax [(38%)($265,000)]	$100,700
Surtax [(4%)(28%)($265,000)]	2,968
ART: Equal To The Lesser Of:	
• [($265,000 - $150,000)(6-2/3%)] = $7,667	
• [($100,000 + $20,000 - $15,000)(6-2/3%)] = $7,000	7,000
Federal Tax Abatement [(10%)(90%)($265,000)]*	(23,850)
Foreign Non Business Tax Credit (Note 1)	(3,000)
Foreign Business Tax Credit (Note 1)	(1,500)
Small Business Deduction (Note 2)	(24,000)
Accelerated Tax Reduction (Note 3)	Nil
General Rate Reduction (Note 3)	(100)
Part I Taxes Payable	$ 58,218

RDTOH - December 31, 2000	$110,000
Dividend Refund For 2000	20,000
Taxable Dividends Paid During 2001	40,000

Note 1 The foreign tax credits are assumed to be equal to the amounts withheld. Additional calculations would be required to support this conclusion.

Note 2 The small business deduction would be equal to 16 percent of the least of:

1.	Active business income	$150,000
2.	Taxable Income	$265,000
	Less 10/3 Of Foreign Non Business Tax Credit	(10,000)
	Less 10/4 Of Foreign Business Income Tax Credit	(3,750)
	Total	$251,250
3.	Annual Business Limit	$200,000

The least of these figures is $150,000, providing for a small business deduction of $24,000 [(16%)($150,000)].

Note 3   Aggregate Investment Income is equal to $105,000 ($100,000 + $20,000 - $15,000). The base for the ITA 123.4(3) accelerated rate reduction would be the least of:

1. 3/2 the annual business limit	$300,000
2. Active business income	$150,000
3. Taxable income, less aggregate investment income ($265,000 - $105,000)	$160,000

This gives an accelerated reduction of Nil {[7%][$150,000 - (100/16)($24,000)]}.

The general reduction under ITA 123.4(3) would be calculated as follows:

Taxable Income	$265,000
SBD Amount [(100/16)($24,000)]	(150,000)
Aggregate Investment Income	(105,000)
Full Rate Taxable Income	$ 10,000
Rate	1%
ITA 123.4(2) Reduction	$ 100

15-158.   Based on the preceding information, the refundable portion of Part I tax would be the least of:

26-2/3 Percent Of Aggregate Investment Income [(26-2/3%)($100,000 + $20,000 - $15,000)]	$28,000
Less: Foreign Non Business Tax Credit, Reduced By 9-1/3% Of Foreign Investment Income [$3,000 - (9-1/3%)($20,000)]	(1,133)
ITA 129(3)(a)(i)	$26,867

Taxable Income		$265,000
Deduct:		
Amount Eligible For Small Business Deduction	($150,000)	
25/9 Foreign Non Business Income Tax Credit	(8,333)	
10/4 Foreign Business Income Tax Credit	(3,750)	(162,083)
Total		$102,917
Rate		26-2/3%
ITA 129(3)(a)(ii)		$ 27,445

ITA 129(3)(a)(iii) Adjusted Part I Taxes Payable ($58,218 - $2,968)	$ 55,250

The Refundable Portion Of Part I Tax is equal to $26,867 which is the least of the preceding three amounts.

15-159.   The Part IV tax would be $10,000, one-third of the $30,000 in portfolio dividends received. Given this, the balance in the RDTOH account at the end of the year is as follows:

RDTOH - End Of Preceding Year	$110,000
Deduct: Dividend Refund For The Preceding Year	(20,000)
Refundable Portion Of Part I Tax	26,867
Part IV Tax Payable [(33-1/3%)($30,000)]	10,000
RDTOH - End Of Current Year	$126,867

15-160.   The dividend refund for the year would be $13,333, the lesser of:

- One-Third Of Taxable Dividends Paid ($40,000 ÷ 3) = $13,333
- RDTOH Balance - December 31, 2001 = $126,867

15-161.   Using the preceding information, the total federal Taxes Payable for Fortune Ltd. is calculated as follows:

Part I Tax Payable	$58,218
Part IV Tax Payable	10,000
Dividend Refund	(13,333)
Federal Taxes Payable	$54,885

Exercises Fifteen-5 through Fifteen-7 deal with refundable taxes. This would be an appropriate time to attempt these exercises.

Accounting For The RDTOH

15-162.   As described in the preceding material, the RDTOH balance contains taxes which have been paid by the corporation that will be refunded when dividends are distributed to shareholders. Tax practitioners tend to think of this balance as an asset that can be distributed to shareholders as a component of dividends declared and paid. Further, in most tax texts, when a tax Balance Sheet is presented, the RDTOH balance is normally presented as an asset. While we will follow this tradition in this text, you should be aware that, in general, this is not the appropriate treatment in GAAP based financial statements. Section 3465 of the *CICA Handbook* requires that, in most circumstances, refundable taxes paid should be charged to Retained Earnings. In the unusual situation where recovery of the amounts is unlikely, the amounts should be charged to income. The only time that refundable taxes would be treated as an asset is when they relate to those redeemable preferred shares that must, under the provisions of Section 3860, "Financial Instruments - Disclosure And Presentation", be classified as a liability.

References

15-163.   For more detailed study of the material in this Chapter, we refer you to the following:

ITA 82(1)	Taxable Dividends Received
ITA 89(1)	Definitions (Canadian Corporations)
ITA 129(1)	Dividend Refund To Private Corporation
ITA 186	Tax On Taxable Dividends Received By Private Corporations
ITA 251(1)	Arm's Length
IT-67R3	Taxable Dividends From Corporations Resident In Canada
IT-98R2	Investment Corporations
IT-243R4	Dividend Refund To Private Corporations
IT-269R3	Part IV Tax On Taxable Dividends Received By a Private Corporation Or A Subject Corporation
IT-328R3	Losses On Shares On Which Dividends Have Been Received
IT-419R	Meaning Of Arm's Length
IT-432R2	Benefits Conferred On Shareholders
IT-458R2	Canadian Controlled Private Corporation

Sample Corporate Tax Return

The following simplified example contains a T2 corporate income tax return jacket and Schedule 1, completed using the ProFile T2 corporate tax preparation program from GreenPoint software. As this sample is designed to illustrate the corporate tax return calculations, no GIFI (General Index of Financial Information) data has been included.

Sample File on CD-ROM

The complete sample tax return is available on the CD-ROM included with this book in two versions, a .PDF file and a T2 ProFile return file.

GreenPoint ProFile Version

After starting the ProFile T2 program, open the file "Sample T2 Corporate Tax Return.GT2" in the subdirectory \Greenpoint\Sample Canadian Tax Principles tax return files.

To get the maximum benefit from using the program, we strongly advise that you do the tutorials "Getting Started" and "Using the Form Explorer" that are included with the program. A Quick Reference Card, as well as complete manuals, are available on the CD-ROM in .PDF format. To view .PDF files, you will need to have Adobe Acrobat installed on your system and this program is also included on the CD-ROM.

When viewing the sample return file we offer the following suggestions:

- By pressing <F4> you can view the Form Explorer. Under each of the tabs, double clicking on the column title "Used", will sort the list so that the forms that have been used in the return are at the top. You can then double click on the form itself to view it.

- Right clicking on a number in a field shows a variety of options, including the form or schedule where the amount originated from.

PDF File Version

To view the complete return, including schedules, as a .PDF file, start the Adobe Acrobat program and open the file "PDF Sample T2 Return.pdf" in the subdirectory \Greenpoint\Sample Canadian Tax Principles tax return files.

Sample Problem Data

Metro Inc. is a Canadian controlled private corporation based in Saskatoon which manufactures furniture. Most of its income is earned from active business in Canada. The Company has no associated corporations. Its Business Number is 123456789 0001.

During the taxation year ending December 31, 2001, the condensed before tax Income Statement of Metro Inc. was prepared in accordance with the requirements of the *CICA Handbook*. In condensed form it is as follows:

Metro Inc.
Condensed Income Statement
Year Ending December 31, 2001

Revenues	$3,980,000
Expenses (Excluding Taxes)	(2,380,000)
Income Before Extraordinary Items And Taxes	$1,600,000
Extraordinary Gain (Before Tax Effects)	160,000
Accounting Income Before Taxes	$1,760,000

Other Information:

1. The Extraordinary Gain resulted from the expropriation of a building by the municipal government for proceeds of $692,000. The building has an adjusted cost base of $664,000 and was acquired in 1986. As the Company leases all of its other buildings and equipment, the building is the only asset in Class 3. The undepreciated capital cost of this class prior to the disposal of the building was $514,000. The land on which the building is situated was leased. The municipal government has assumed Metro's responsibilities under the lease.

2. Depreciation included in the accounting expenses amounts to $407,000. The opening UCC balance was $905,000 for Class 8 and $800,000 for Class 10. The only fixed asset acquisition was $200,000 in Class 8 assets. There were no dispositions in either Class 8 or 10.

3. Expenses include interest and penalties of $2,300 resulting from late installments and a failure to file the 1999 tax return within the prescribed time period.

4. Revenues include dividends of $36,000 from Canadian Tax Save Inc., a taxable Canadian corporation.

5. Expenses include a deduction for charitable contributions to the Cancer Research Society in the amount of $15,000.

6. The Company has available a non capital loss carry over from the previous year of $56,000. The net capital loss carry over from 1998 is $33,750 (3/4 of $45,000).

7. Information related to Canadian manufacturing and processing activities for the year is as follows:

Cost of Capital (10% of $8,000,000)	$ 800,000
Portion of capital used in M&P activities	500,000
Cost of Labour	1,000,000
Portion of labour used in M&P activities	760,000

8. During 2001, the Company earned $97,000 of interest income on bonds purchased in 2000 and which mature in 2005.

9. The beginning balance in the Company's cumulative eligible capital account is $90,000. There were no acquisitions or dispositions that affected this account during the year.

10. The beginning balance in the Company's capital dividend account is nil.

11. The Company paid $100,000 in taxable dividends during the year. There was no balance in the refundable dividend tax on hand at December 31, 2000 and there was no dividend refund for 2000.

12. All of the common shares of Metro Inc. are held by Jack Brown (SIN 527-000-582), a resident of Dundas, Ontario.

13. The Saskatchewan provincial taxes for the year ending December 31, 2001 total $255,384.

Required: Prepare the corporate tax return for Metro Inc. for the 2001 taxation year. Ignore the GIFI requirements.

Notes On Metro Inc. Sample Tax Return

Capital Dividend Account
The balance in the Capital Dividend Account is $14,000 [(1/2)($692,000 - $664,000)]. A tax free capital dividend of $14,000 could have been paid if form T2054 had been filed.

General Rate Reduction
Metro Inc. is not eligible for the accelerated rate reduction due to the size of its claim for both the small business deduction and the M&P deduction. However, it is eligible for the general rate reduction for CCPCs.

Building Expropriation
The $160,000 extraordinary gain is deducted on Schedule 1 as the tax effects of the disposition are included in Net Income For Tax Purposes. As calculated on Schedule 6, the taxable capital gain on the building expropriation is $14,000 [(1/2)($692,000 - $664,000)].

As calculated on Schedule 8, the recapture of CCA on the building is equal to $150,000 ($664,000 - $514,000). This is shown as an addition on Schedule 1.

Loss Carry Forwards
The losses of prior taxation years deducted in the calculation of taxable income consist of the non capital loss of $56,000 and a $28,000 capital loss. As calculated on Schedule 4, the capital loss deduction is limited by the $28,000 capital gain for the year and leaves a capital loss carry forward of $17,000 ($45,000 - $28,000). There is no non capital loss carry forward remaining.

Active Business Income
As calculated on Schedule 7, active business income of $1,594,000 ($1,741,000 - $36,000 - $97,000 - $14,000) is Net Income less:

- dividends received,
- interest income and
- taxable capital gains

This figure is used in the small business deduction calculation.

Investment Income
In calculating the refundable portion of the Part I tax, the investment income of $97,000 consists of $97,000 in interest income, plus the $14,000 taxable capital gain, less the $14,000 net capital loss claimed. This calculation is on Schedule 7.

M&P Labour
As the grossed up M&P Labour of $1,013,333 ([100/75][$760,000]) is greater than the $1,000,000 Cost of Labour, M&P Labour in the Schedule 27 calculation is limited to $1,000,000.

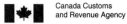 Canada Customs   Agence des douanes
and Revenue Agency   et du revenu du Canada

T2 CORPORATION INCOME TAX RETURN   **Schedule 200**
(1998 and later taxation years)

This form serves as a federal, provincial, and territorial corporation income tax return, unless the corporation is located in Quebec, Ontario or Alberta. If the corporation is located in one of these provinces, you have to file a separate provincial corporate return.

Parts, sections, subsections, and paragraphs mentioned on this return refer to the *Income Tax Act*. This return may contain changes that had not yet become law at the time of printing. If you need more information about items on the return, including proposed legislation, see the corresponding items in the 2000 T2 Corporation Income Tax Guide.

Send one completed copy of this return, including schedules, and the *General Index of Financial Information (GIFI)* to your tax services office or to the tax centre that serves the corporation. You have to file the return within six months after the end of the corporation's taxation year. For more information on when and how to file T2 returns, see items 1 to 5 in the guide.

055	Do not use this area

─── Identification ───

Business number (BN) (item 11)   **001** 12345 6789 RC 0001
Name of corporation (item 12)
002

Metro Inc.

Has the corporation changed its name since the last time we were notified?   **003** ☐ Yes ☒ No

If *yes*, do you have a copy of the articles of amendment?   **004** ☐ Yes ☐ No

Address of head office (item 13)
Has the address changed since the last time we were notified?   **010** ☒ Yes ☐ No
011 340 - 3rd Avenue North
012

City	Province
015 Saskatoon	**016** SK

Country (other than Canada)	Postal code
017	**018** S7K 0A8

Mailing address (if different from head office address) (item 14)
Has the address changed since the last time we were notified?
020 Yes ☒ No ☐
021 C/o
022 340 - 3rd Avenue North
023

City	Province
025 Saskatoon	**026** SK

Country (other than Canada)	Postal code
027	**028** S7K 0A8

Location of books and records (item 15)
031 340 - 3rd Avenue North
032

City	Province
035 Saskatoon	**036** SK

Country (other than Canada)	Postal code
037	**038** S7K 0A8

040 Type of corporation at end of taxation year (item 16)
1 ☒ Canadian controlled private corporation (CCPC)
2 ☐ Other private corporation
3 ☐ Public corporation
4 ☐ Corporation controlled by a public corporation
5 ☐ Other corporation (please specify, below)
_____

If the type of corporation changed during the taxation year, provide the effective date of the change   **043** _____

To which taxation year does this return apply? (item 17)
From   **060** 2001-01-01 ____ to   **061** 2001-12-31

Has there been an acquisition of control to which subsection 249(4) applies since the previous taxation year?   **063** ☐ Yes ☒ No

If *yes*, provide date control was acquired   **065** _____

Is the corporation a professional corporation that is a member of a partnership? (item 18)   **067** ☐ Yes ☒ No

Is this the first year of filing after:
Incorporation? (item 19)   **070** ☐ Yes ☒ No
Amalgamation? (item 20)   **071** ☐ Yes ☒ No
If *yes*, please provide Schedule 24

Has there been a wind-up of a subsidiary under section 88 during the current taxation year? (item 21)
If *yes*, please provide Schedule 24   **072** ☐ Yes ☒ No

Is this the final taxation year before amalgamation? (item 22)   **076** ☐ Yes ☒ No

Is this the final return up to dissolution? (item 23)   **078** ☐ Yes ☒ No

Is the corporation a resident of Canada? (item 24)   **080** ☒ Yes ☐ No
If *no*, give the country of residence.   **081** _____

Is the non-resident corporation claiming an exemption under an Income Tax treaty? (item 24)
If *yes*, please provide Schedule 91   **082** ☐ Yes ☒ No

If the corporation is exempt from tax under section 149, tick one of the following boxes: (item 25)
085 1 ☐ Exempt under 149(1)(e) or (l)
2 ☐ Exempt under 149(1)(j)
3 ☐ Exempt under 149(1)(t)
4 ☐ Exempt under other paragraphs of section 149

Do not use this area

091	092	093	094	095	096
097					

Complete tax return available on the CD-ROM

Metro Inc. CCRA Business # 123456789 Year-end: 2001-12-31 Printed: 2001-07-14 22:27

Attachments

Guide	item		Yes	No	Schedule
27	Is the corporation related to any other corporations?	**150**	☐	☒	9
28	Does the corporation have any non-resident shareholders?	**151**	☐	☒	19
29	Is the corporation an associated Canadian-controlled private corporation (CCPC)?	**160**	☐	☒	23
30	Is the corporation an associated CCPC that is claiming the expenditure limit?	**161**	☐	☒	49
32	Has the corporation had any transactions, including section 85 transfers, with its shareholders, officers, or employees, other than transactions in the ordinary course of business? Exclude non-arm's length transactions with non-residents	**162**	☐	☒	11
33	If you answered *yes* to the above question, and the transaction was between corporations not dealing at arm's length, were all or substantially all of the assets of the transferor disposed of to the transferee?	**163**	☐	☒	44
34	Has the corporation paid any royalties, management fees, or other similar payments to residents of Canada?	**164**	☐	☒	14
35	Is the corporation claiming a deduction for payments to a type of employee benefit plan?	**165**	☐	☒	15
37	Is the corporation claiming a loss or deduction from a tax shelter acquired after August 31, 1989?	**166**	☐	☒	T5004
38	Is the corporation a member of a partnership for which an identification number has been assigned?	**167**	☐	☒	T5013
40	Did the corporation, a foreign affiliate controlled by the corporation, or any other corporation or trust that did not deal at arm's length with the corporation have a beneficial interest in a non-resident discretionary trust?	**168**	☐	☒	22
41	Did the corporation have any foreign affiliates during the year?	**169**	☐	☒	25
42	Has the corporation made any payments to non-residents of Canada under subsections 202(1) and 105(1) of the federal *Income Tax Regulations*?	**170**	☐	☒	29
43	Has the corporation had any non-arm's length transactions with a non-resident?	**171**	☐	☒	T106
47	Has the corporation made payments to, or received amounts from a retirement compensation arrangement?	**172**	☐	☒	-----
46	Does the corporation (private corporations only) have any shareholders who own 10% or more of the corporation's common and/or preferred shares?	**173**	☒	☐	50
53	Is the net income/loss shown on financial statements different from the net income for income tax purposes?	**201**	☒	☐	1
76-79	Has the corporation made any charitable donations or gifts of cultural or ecological property?	**202**	☒	☐	2
80,102	Has the corporation received dividends or paid taxable dividends for purposes of the dividend refund?	**203**	☒	☐	3
67-74	Is the corporation claiming any type of losses?	**204**	☒	☐	4
128	Is the corporation claiming a provincial tax credit or does it have a permanent establishment in more than one jurisdiction?	**205**	☐	☒	5
54	Has the corporation realized any capital gains or incurred any capital losses during the taxation year?	**206**	☒	☐	6
100	(i) Is the corporation claiming the small business deduction and reporting income from : (a) property (other than dividends), (b) a partnership, (c) a foreign business, or (d) a personal services business; or (ii) is the corporation claiming the refundable portion of Part I tax?	**207**	☒	☐	7
55	Does the corporation have any property that is eligible for capital cost allowance?	**208**	☒	☐	8
56	Does the corporation have any property that is eligible capital property?	**210**	☒	☐	10
57	Does the corporation have any resource-related deductions?	**212**	☐	☒	12
58	Is the corporation claiming reserves of any kind?	**213**	☐	☒	13
59	Is the corporation claiming a patronage dividend deduction?	**216**	☐	☒	16
60	Is the corporation a credit union claiming a deduction for allocations in proportion to borrowing?	**217**	☐	☒	17
146	is the corporation an investment corporation or a mutual fund corporation?	**218**	☐	☒	18
127	Is the corporation carrying on business in Canada while not a Canadian corporation?	**220**	☐	☒	20 *
115	Is the corporation claiming any federal or provincial foreign tax credits, or logging tax credits?	**221**	☐	☒	21
151	Is the corporation a non-resident-owned investment corporation claiming an allowable refund?	**226**	☐	☒	26 *
108	Does the corporation have any Canadian manufacturing and processing profits?	**227**	☒	☐	27
118	Is the corporation claiming an investment tax credit?	**231**	☐	☒	31
61	Is the corporation claiming any scientific research and experimental development expenditures?	**232**	☐	☒	T661/T665
121	Is the corporation subject to Part 1.3 tax?	**233**	☐	☒	33/34/35
121	Is the corporation a member of a related group with one or more members subject to gross Part 1.3 tax?	**236**	☐	☒	36
121	Is the corporation claiming a surtax credit?	**237**	☐	☒	37
125	Is the corporation subject to gross Part VI tax on capital of financial institutions?	**238**	☐	☒	38
125	Is the corporation claiming a Part I tax credit?	**242**	☐	☒	42
126	Is the corporation subject to Part IV.1 tax on dividends received on taxable preferred shares or Part VI.1 tax on dividends paid?	**243**	☐	☒	43
126	Is the corporation agreeing to a transfer of the liability for Part VI.1 tax?	**244**	☐	☒	45
122	Is the corporation subject to Part II - Tobacco Manufacturers' surtax?	**249**	☐	☒	46
125	For financial institutions: Is the corporation a member of a related group of financial institutions with one or more members subject to gross Part VI tax?	**250**	☐	☒	39
125	For life insurance corporations: Is the corporation a member of a related group of insurance corporations with one or more members subject to the additional gross Part VI tax?	**251**	☐	☒	40
125	For deposit-taking institutions: Is the corporation a member of a related group of financial institutions (other than life insurance corporations) with one or more members subject to the additional Part VI tax?	**252**	☐	☒	41
148	Is the corporation claiming a Canadian film or video production tax credit refund?	**253**	☐	☒	T1131

Metro Inc.   CCRA Business # 123456789   Year-end: 2001-12-31   Printed: 2001-07-14 22:27

Attachments - Continued from page 2

Guide item	Yes Schedule
149 Is the corporation claiming a film or video production services tax credit refund?	☐ T1177
44 Did the corporation have any foreign affiliates that are not controlled foreign affiliates?	☐ T1134-A
44 Did the corporation have any controlled foreign affiliates?	☐ T1134-B
44 Did the corporation own specified foreign property in the year with a cost amount over $100,000	☐ T1135
44 Did the corporation transfer or loan property to a non-resident trust?	☐ T1141
44 Did the corporation receive a distribution from or was it indebted to a non-resident trust in the year?	☐ T1142
- Has the corporation entered into an agreement to allocate assistance for SR&ED carried out in Canada?	☐ T1145
- Has the corporation entered into an agreement to transfer qualified expenditures incurred in respect of SR&ED contracts?	☐ T1146
- Has the corporation entered into an agreement with other associated corporations for salary or wages of specified employees for SR&ED?	☐ T1174

Additional information

Is the corporation inactive? (item 48)	**280**	1 Yes ☐	2 No ☒
Has the major business activity changed since the last return was filed? (enter yes for first time filers) (item 49)	**281**	1 Yes ☐	2 No ☒

What is the corporation's major business activity? (item 50)   **282** _____
(Only complete if *yes* was entered at line 281.)

If the major activity involves the resale of goods, indicate whether is is wholesale or retail (item 51)   **283** 1 Wholesale ☐   2 Retail ☐

Specify the principal product(s) mined, manufactured, sold, constructed, or service provided, giving the approximate percentage of the total revenue that each product or service represents. (item 52)

284 Furniture manufacturer	**285**	100.000	%
286 _____	**287**		%
288 _____	**289**		%

Taxable income

Net income or (loss) for income tax purposes from Schedule 1, financial statements or GIFI (item 75)	**300**	1,741,000	A
Deduct: Charitable donations from Schedule 2 (item 76)	**311**	15,000	
Gifts to Canada or a province from Schedule 2 (item 77)	**312**		
Cultural gifts from Schedule 2 (item 78)	**313**		
Ecological gifts from Schedule 2 (item 79)	**314**		
Taxable dividends deductible under section 112 or 113, or subsection 138(6) from Schedule 3 (item 80)	**320**	36,000	
Part VI.1 tax deduction from Schedule 43 (item 81)	**325**		
Non-capital losses of preceding taxation years from Schedule 4 (item 82)	**331**	56,000	
Net capital losses of preceding taxation years from Schedule 4 (item 83)	**332**	14,000	
Restricted farm losses of prior taxation years from Schedule 4 (item 84)	**333**		
Farm losses of prior taxation years from Schedule 4 (item 85)	**334**		
Limited partnership losses of prior years from Schedule 4 (item 86)	**335**		
Taxable capital gains or taxable dividends allocated from a central credit union (item 87)	**340**		
Prospector's and grubstaker's shares (item 88)	**350**		
Subtotal		121,000	121,000 B
Subtotal			1,620,000 C
Add: Section 110.5 additions (item 89)	**355**		D
Taxable income (amount C plus amount D) (item 90)	**360**		1,620,000
Income exempt under paragraph 149(1)(t) (item 91)	**370**		
Taxable income for a corporation with exempt income under paragraph 149(1)(t) (line 360 minus line 370) (item 92)			Z

Metro Inc.   CCRA Business # 123456789   Year-end: 2001-12-31   Printed: 2001-07-14 22:27

Small business deduction

Canadian-controlled private corporations throughout the taxation year

Income from active business carried on in Canada from Schedule 7 (item 93)	**400**	1,594,000 A
Taxable income from line 360 or amount Z above, whichever applies, **minus** 10/3 of the amount that would be deductible at line 632*, and 10/4 of line 636 on page 7, and **minus** any amount that, because of federal law, is exempt from Part I tax (item 94)	**405**	1,620,000 B
Business limit (for associated corporations, enter business limit from Schedule 23) (item 95)	**410**	200,000 C

Reduction to business limit: (item 96)

Amount C _____200,000__ X __**415** **__ _____ D
                                            11,250   = _____ E

Reduced business limit (amount C minus amount E) (if negative, enter "0")	**425**	200,000 F
Small business deduction - 16% of the least of amounts A, B, C, and F	**430**	32,000 G

(enter amount G of line 9 on page 7)

* Calculate the amount of foreign non-business income tax credit deductible at line 632 without reference to the refundable tax on CCPC's investment income (line 604).

** **Large corporation tax for preceding year** - Enter the total gross Part I.3 tax for the corporation for its preceding taxation year, before deducting the surtax credits, increased to reflect a full-year tax liability if the previous year is less than 51 weeks. For associated corporations, see Schedule 23 for the special rules that apply.

Accelerated tax reduction

Canadian-controlled private corporations throughout the taxation year that claimed the small business deduction

Reduced business limit (amount from line 425)	200,000 x 3/2 =	300,000 A
Net active business income (amount from line 400)*		1,594,000 B
Taxable income used for the small business deduction (amount from line 405)	1,620,000 C	

Deduct:

Aggregate investment income (amount from line 440)	97,000 D	
Amount C minus amount D (if negative, enter "0")	1,523,000 ▶	1,523,000 E
The least of amounts A, B, or E above		300,000 F
Amount Z from Part 9 of Schedule 27	84,453 x 100 / 7 =	1,206,471 G
Amount QQ from Part 13 of Schedule 27		H
Resource allowance (amount from line 346 of Schedule 1) _____ x 3 =		I
Amount used to calculate the credit union deduction (amount E in Part 3 of Schedule 17)		J
Least of amounts on lines 400, 405, 410, and 425 of the small business deduction	200,000 K	
Total of amounts G, H, I, J, and K	1,406,471 ▶	1,406,471 L
Amount F minus amount L (if negative, enter "0")		M

Amount M_____ x Days in the taxation year after December 31, 2000 ____365____ = _____ N
                              Days in the taxation year   365

Accelerated tax reduction - 7% of amount N _____ O

(Enter amount O on line 637 of page 7)

* Specified partnerships need to use Schedule 70 to calculate net active business income, if the amount at line 450 of Schedule 7 is positive.

Metro Inc. CCRA Business # 123456789 Year-end: 2001-12-31 Printed: 2001-07-14 22:27

General tax reduction for Canadian-controlled private corporations

Canadian-controlled private corporations throughout taxation year

Taxable income from line 360 or amount Z of page 3			1,620,000	A
Amount Z from Part 9 of Schedule 27	84,453 x 100 / 7 =	1,206,471	B	
Amount QQ from Part 13 of Schedule 27			C	
Resource allowance (amount from line 346 of Schedule 1)	x 3 =		D	
Amount used to calculate the credit union deduction (amount E in Part 3 of Schedule 17)			E	
Least of amounts on lines 400, 405, 410, and 425 of the small business deduction		200,000	F	
Aggregate investment income from line 440 of page 6		97,000	G	
Amount used to calculate the accelerated tax reduction (amount M on page 4)			H	
Total of amounts B, C, D, E, F, G, and H		1,503,471 ▶	1,503,471	I
Amount A minus amount I (if negative, enter "0")			116,529	J

Amount J ___116,529___ x $\dfrac{\text{Days in the taxation year after December 31, 2000} \quad 365}{\text{Days in the taxation year} \quad 365}$ = ___116,529___ K

General tax reduction for Canadian-controlled private corporations - 1% of amount K   1,165 L

(Enter amount L on line 638 of page 7)

General tax reduction

Corporations other than a Canadian-controlled private corporation, an investment corporation, a mortgage investment corporation, a mutual fund corporation, or a non-resident-owned investment corporation

Taxable income from line 360 or amount Z of page 3				A
Amount Z from Part 9 of Schedule 27	x 100 / 7 =		B	
Amount QQ from Part 13 of Schedule 27			C	
Resource allowance (amount from line 346 of Schedule 1)	x 3 =		D	
Amount used to calculate the credit union deduction (amount E in Part 3 of Schedule 17)			E	
Total of amounts B, C, D, and E		▶		F
Amount A minus amount F (if negative, enter "0")				G

Amount G _____ x $\dfrac{\text{Days in the taxation year after December 31, 2000}}{\text{Days in the taxation year}}$ = _____ H

General tax reduction - 1% of amount H   I

(Enter amount I on line 639 of page 7)

T2 E (00)

Metro Inc. CCRA Business # 123456789 Year-end: 2001-12-31 Printed: 2001-07-14 22:27

Refundable portion of Part I tax (item 100)

Canadian-controlled private corporations throughout the taxation year

Aggregate investment income **440** 97,000 X 26 2/3 % =		25,867	A
(Amount P from Part 1 of Schedule 7)			

Foreign non-business income tax credit from line 632 on page 7

Deduct:

Foreign investment income **445** ___ X 9 1/3 % =			
(Amount O from Part 1 of Schedule 7)	(if negative, enter "0")		B
Amount A **minus** amount B (if negative, enter "0")		25,867	C

Taxable income from line 360 on page 3	1,620,000	

Deduct:

Least of amounts on lines 400, 405, 410, and 425 on page 4	200,000			
Foreign non-business income tax credit from line 632 on page 7 ___ x 25/9 =				
Foreign business income tax credit from line 636 on page 7 ___ x 10/4 =				
	200,000	200,000		
		1,420,000 X 26 2/3% =	378,667	D

Part I tax payable minus investment tax credit refund (line 700 minus line 780 on page 8)	360,593		
Deduct corporate surtax from line 600 on page 7	18,144		
Net amount	342,449 ▶	342,449	E

Refundable portion of Part I tax - the least of amounts C, D, and E	**450**	25,867	F

Refundable dividend tax on hand (item 101)

Refundable dividend tax on hand at the end of the preceding tax year	**460**			
Deduct dividend refund for the previous taxation year	**465**			
		▶		A

Add the total of:

Refundable portion of Part I tax from line 450 above	25,867		
Total Part IV tax payable from line 360 on page 2 of Schedule 3	12,000		
Net refundable dividend tax on hand transferred from a predecessor corporation on amalgamation, or from a wound-up subsidiary corporation **480**			
	37,867 ▶	37,867	B

Refundable dividend tax on hand at the end of the taxation year - Amount A plus Amount B	**485**	37,867

Dividend refund (item 102)

Private and subject corporations at the time taxable dividends were paid in the taxation year

Taxable dividends paid in the taxation year from line 460 on page 2 of Schedule 3 100,000 X 1/3		33,333	A
Refundable dividend tax on hand at the end of the taxation year from line 485 above		37,867	B
Dividend refund - Lesser of amounts A and B (enter this amount on line 784 on page 8)		33,333	

Metro Inc.   CCRA Business # 123456789   Year-end: 2001-12-31   Printed: 2001-07-14 22:27

Part I tax

Base amount of Part I tax - 38% of taxable income (line 360 or amount Z, whichever applies) from page 3 (item 103)		**550** 615,600	A

Corporate surtax calculation (item 104)

Base amount from line A above	615,600	1
Deduct:		
10% of taxable income (line 360 or amount Z, whichever applies) from page 3	162,000	2
Investment corporation deduction from line 620 below		3
Federal logging tax credit from line 640 below		4
Federal qualifying environment trust tax credit from line 648 below		5

For a mutual fund corporation or an investment corporation throughout the taxation year, enter the least of a, b and c below on line 6:

28% of taxable income from line 360 on page 3		a	
28% of taxed capital gains		b	6
Part I tax otherwise payable			
(line A **plus** line C and D **minus** line F)	335,982	c	

Total of lines 2 to 6	162,000	7
Net amount (line 1 minus line 7)	453,600	8

Corporate surtax - 4% of the amount on line 8		**600** 18,144	B
Recapture of investment tax credit from line XX in Part 16 on page 8 of Schedule 31 (item 105)		**602**	C

Calculation for the refundable tax on Canadian-controlled private corporation's investment income
(for a CCPC throughout the taxation year) (item 103)

Aggregate investment income from line 440 on page 6		97,000	i
Taxable income from line 360 on page 4	1,620,000		
Deduct:			
The least of amounts on lines 400, 405, 410, and 425 on page 3	200,000		
Net amount	1,420,000	1,420,000	ii

Refundable tax on CCPC's investment income - 6 2/3 % of the lesser of amounts i or ii		**604** 6,467	D
	Subtotal (add lines A, B, C, and D)	640,211	E

Deduct:

Small business deduction from line 430 on page 4		32,000	9
Federal tax abatement (item 107)	**608**	162,000	
Manufacturing and processing profits deduction from amount BB or VV of Schedule 27 (item 108)	**616**	84,453	
Investment corporation deduction (item 109)	**620**		
(Taxed capital gains **624**)			
Additional deduction - credit unions from Schedule 17 (item 110)	**628**		
Federal foreign non-business income tax credit from Schedule 21 (item 111)	**632**		
Federal foreign business income tax credit from Schedule 21 (item 112)	**636**		
Accelerated tax reduction from amount O of page 4 (item 113)	**637**		
General tax reduction for CCPC's from amount L of page 5 (item 114)	**638**	1,165	
General tax reduction from amount I of page 5 (item 114)	**639**		
Federal logging tax credit from Schedule 21 (item 115)	**640**		
Federal political contribution tax credit (item 116)	**644**		
Federal political contributions **646**			
Federal qualifying environmental trust tax credit (item 117)	**648**		
Investment tax credit from Schedule 31 (item 118)	**652**		
	Subtotal	279,618	279,618 F
Part I tax payable - Line E minus line F (enter amount G on line 700 on page 8) (item 119)			360,593 G

Metro Inc.   CCRA Business # 123456789   Year-end: 2001-12-31   Printed: 2001-07-14 22:27

Summary of tax and credits

Federal tax

Part I tax payable from page 5 (item 120)	**700**	360,593
Part I.3 tax payable from Schedule 33, 34, or 35 (item 121)	**704**	
Part II tax payable from Schedule 46 (item 122)	**708**	
Part IV tax payable from Schedule 3 (item 123)	**712**	12,000
Part IV.1 tax payable from Schedule 43 (item 124)	**716**	
Part VI tax payable from Schedule 38 (item 125)	**720**	
Part VI.1 tax payable from Schedule 43 (item 126)	**724**	
Part XIV tax payable from Schedule 20 (item 127)	**728**	
	Total federal tax	372,593

Add provincial and territorial tax

Provincial or territorial jurisdiction (item 128) **750** SK			
(if more than one jurisdiction, enter "multiple" and complete Schedule 5)			
Net provincial and territorial tax payable (except Quebec, Ontario and Alberta)	**760**	255,384	
Provincial tax on large corporations (New Brunswick and Nova Scotia) (item 143)	**765**		
		255,384	255,384
	Total tax payable **770**		627,977 A

Deduct other credits

Investment tax credit refund from Schedule 31 (items 144)	**780**		
Dividend refund from Page 4 (items 145)	**784**	33,333	
Federal capital gains refund from Schedule 18 (item 146)	**788**		
Federal qualifying environmental trust tax credit refund (item 147)	**792**		
Canadian film or video production tax credit refund from Form T1131 (item 148)	**796**		
Film or video production services tax credit refund from Form T1177 (item 149)	**797**		
Tax withheld at source (item 150)	**800**		
Total payments on which tax has been withheld (item 150) **801**			
Allowable refund for non-resident-owned investment corporations - Schedule 26	**804**		
Provincial and territorial capital gains refund from Schedule 18 (item 152)	**808**		
Provincial and territorial refundable tax credits from Schedule 5 (item 153)	**812**		
Royalties deductible under Syncrude Remission Order **815**			
Tax remitted under Syncrude Remission Order (item 154)	**816**		
Tax instalments paid (item 155)	**840**		
	Total credits **890**	33,333	33,333 B
	Balance (line A minus line B)		594,644 I

Refund Code   **894** ☐   Overpayment _____
(item 156)   (item 159)

If the result is negative, you have an **overpayment**.
If the result is positive, you have a **balance unpaid**.
Enter the amount on whichever line applies.
We do not charge or refund a difference of less than $2.

Balance unpaid (item 159)   594,644

Direct Deposit Request (item 160)

To have the corporation's refund deposited directly into the corporation's bank account at a financial institution in Canada, or to change banking information you already gave us, complete the information below.
☐ Start   ☐ Change information   **910** _____
                                           Branch number

914 _____   **918** _____
    Institution number   Account number

Enclosed payment   **898** _____

If the corporation is a Canadian-controlled private corporation throughout the taxation year, does it qualify for the one-month extension of the date the balance is due? (item 157)   **896** 1 Yes ☒   2 No ☐   NA ☐

Certification

950 _____   **951** _____   **954** _____
        Surname   First name   Position, office or rank

955 _____   **956** (___) _____
        Date   Telephone number

Is the contact person the same as the authorized signing officer? If *no*, complete the information below.   **957** 1 Yes ☐   2 No ☒

958 _____   **959** (___) _____
            Name   Telephone number

Language of correspondence - Langue de correspondance (item 162)

990	Language of choice/Langue de choix 1 English / Anglais ☒ 2 Français / French ☐

Metro Inc.   CCRA Business # 123456789   Year-end: 2001-12-31   Printed: 2001-07-14 22:28

 Canada Customs   Agence des douanes   **NET INCOME (LOSS) FOR INCOME TAX PURPOSES**   **Schedule 1**
and Revenue Agency   et du revenu du Canada

- The purpose of this schedule is to provide a reconciliation between the corporation's net income (loss) as reported on the financial statements and its net income (loss) for tax purposes.

Net income (loss) after taxes and extraordinary items per financial statements	**A**	1,760,000

Add:

Provision for income taxes - current	**101**	
Provision for income taxes - deferred	**102**	
Interest and penalties on taxes	**103**	2,300
Amortization of tangible assets	**104**	407,000
Amortization of natural resource assets	**105**	
Amortization of intangible assets	**106**	
Recapture of capital cost allowance - Schedule 8	**107**	150,000
Gain on sale of eligible capital property - Schedule 10	**108**	
Income/loss for tax purposes - joint ventures/partnerships	**109**	
Loss in equity of subsidiaries and affiliates	**110**	
Loss on disposal of assets	**111**	
Charitable donations - Schedule 2	**112**	15,000
Taxable capital gains - Schedule 6	**113**	14,000
Political donations	**114**	
Holdbacks	**115**	
Deferred and prepaid expenses	**116**	
Depreciation in inventory - end of year	**117**	
Scientific research expenditures deducted per financial statements	**118**	
Capitalized interest	**119**	
Non-deductible club dues and fees	**120**	
Non-deductible meals and entertainment expenses X 50%	**121**	
Non-deductible automobile expenses	**122**	
Non-deductible life insurance premiums	**123**	
Non-deductible company pension plans	**124**	
Tax reserves deducted in prior year - Schedule 13	**125**	
Reserves from financial statements - balance at the end of the year	**126**	
Soft costs on construction and renovation of buildings	**127**	
Additions from page 2, if completed	**199**	
Subtotal **500**	588,300 ▶	588,300

Deduct:

Gain on disposal of assets per financial statements	**401**	160,000
Dividends not taxable under Section 83 - Schedule 3	**402**	
Capital cost allowance - Schedule 8	**403**	441,000
Terminal loss - Schedule 8	**404**	
Cumulative eligible capital deduction - Schedule 10	**405**	6,300
Allowable business investment loss - Schedule 6	**406**	
Foreign non-business tax deduction under subsection 20(12)	**407**	
Holdbacks	**408**	
Deferred and prepaid expenses	**409**	
Depreciation in inventory - end of prior year	**410**	
Scientific research expenses claimed in year - Schedule 32	**411**	
Tax reserves claimed in current year - Schedule 13	**413**	
Reserves from financial statements - balance at the beginning of the year	**414**	
Provincial capital tax	**415**	
Patronage dividends - Schedule 16	**416**	
Contributions to deferred income plans - Schedule 15	**417**	
Deductions from page 3, if completed	**499**	
Subtotal **510**	607,300 ▶	607,300

Net income (loss) for income tax purposes (enter on line 300 of the T2 return)	1,741,000

Exercises

(The solutions for these exercises can be found following Chapter 21 of the text.)

Exercise Fifteen - 1 (Determination Of PUC And Adjusted Cost Base)
Morton Halide Ltd. issued its first 100,000 shares at a price of $1.10 each. Two years later, an additional 50,000 shares were sold for $1.35 per share. During the current year, a further 30,000 shares were issued for $1.82 per share. One of the investors in the Company acquired 2,400 shares of the first group of shares issued, and an additional 3,850 shares from the most recent issue. Determine the adjusted cost base per share, as well as the total PUC of this investor's shares.

Exercise Fifteen - 2 (Capital Dividend Account)
The following transactions involve the Knerd Corporation's capital dividend account:

- In 1987, they sold a capital asset with an adjusted cost base of $98,000 for proceeds of $123,000.

- In 1993, they sold a capital asset with an adjusted cost base of $86,000 for proceeds of $72,000.

- During the year ending December 31, 2000, the Company received a capital dividend of $8,200.

- On July 1, 2001, they sold goodwill for proceeds of $42,000. They had paid $37,000 for this goodwill in the previous year. It is the Company's policy to make maximum CCA and CEC deductions.

- On October 31, 2001, the Company paid an ITA 83(2) dividend of $16,000. The appropriate election was made.

Determine the balance in the capital dividend account at December 31, 2001.

Exercise Fifteen - 3 (Deemed Dividends)
At the beginning of the current year, Unilev Inc. has 126,000 shares of common stock outstanding. The shares were originally issued for $1,323,000, with this amount constituting the PUC. During the current year, a creditor holding $450,000 of the Company's debt agrees to accept 40,000 newly issued common shares of the Company in exchange for settlement of the debt obligation. At the time of this exchange, the shares are trading at $12.70.

1. Describe the tax consequence(s) to the shareholders of Unilev Inc. as a result of the exchange of debt for common shares.

2. Subsequent to the exchange, a shareholder with 5,000 shares that were purchased at the time of their original issue, sells the shares for $13.42. Describe the tax consequences to this shareholder resulting from the sale of Unilev Inc. shares.

Exercise Fifteen - 4 (Deemed Dividends)
When first incorporated, Tandy Ltd. issued 233,000 common shares in return for $1,922,250 in cash ($8.25 per share). All of the shares were issued to Ms. Jessy Tandy, the founder of the company. Except for 15,000 shares, she is still holding all of the originally issued shares. The 15,000 shares were sold to Ms. Tandy's brother, Jesuiah, for $10.57 per share, the estimated market value of the shares at that time. Because of ongoing difficulties between the two siblings, Ms. Tandy has arranged for Tandy Ltd. to redeem all of her brother's shares at a price of $11.75 per share. The redemption takes place on August 24, 2001. Determine the tax consequences of this redemption to Ms. Tandy's brother, Jesuiah.

Exercise Fifteen - 5 (Refundable Part I Tax)

During the current year, Debut Inc. has the following amounts of property income:

Dividends From Portfolio Investments	$22,000
Foreign Non Business Income (Net Of 5 Percent Withholding)	14,250
Capital Gains	38,250
Net Rental Income	6,500
Interest Income	9,200

The Company's Net Income For Tax Purposes is $136,700. The only deductions in the calculation of Taxable Income are the dividends on portfolio investments and a Net Capital Loss from 1991 of $13,500 [(3/4)($18,000)]. Debut Inc. is a Canadian controlled private corporation. An $8,000 small business deduction and a foreign tax credit of $750 served to reduce Taxes Payable. Assume that the Company's Taxes Payable have been correctly determined to be $21,300, including $1,183 in corporate surtax.

Required: Determine the refundable amount of Part I tax for the current year.

Exercise Fifteen - 6 (Part IV Tax)

Opal Ltd., a Canadian controlled private corporation, received the following amounts of dividends during the current year:

Dividends On Various Portfolio Investments	$14,000
Dividends From Wholly Owned Subsidiary (No Dividend Refund Received)	41,500
Dividends From Significantly Influenced Investee*	18,000

*Opal Ltd. owns 30 percent of this Company. As a result of paying this dividend, the investee received a dividend refund of $15,000.

Determine the amount of Part IV Tax Payable by Opal Ltd. as a result of receiving these dividends.

Exercise Fifteen - 7 (Dividend Refund)

Quan Imports Ltd. (QIL) is a Canadian controlled private corporation. At the end of the previous year, it had an RDTOH balance of $12,500. It paid dividends during that year of $6,000, resulting in a dividend refund of $2,000. During the current year, QIL's only income is $24,000 in taxable capital gains and $6,000 in dividends received from a temporary investment in Royal Bank shares. During the year, the company declares and pays a $15,000 dividend on its common shares. Determine the Company's dividend refund for the year.

Problems For Self Study

(The solutions for these problems can be found following Chapter 21 of the text.)

Self Study Problem Fifteen - 1

Groman Ltd. is a Canadian controlled private corporation. On December 31, 2001, the Company's condensed Balance Sheet is as follows:

Total Assets		$62,000
Liabilities		$22,000
Shareholders' Equity:		
500 Preferred Shares (Paid Up Capital)	$11,000	
600 Common Shares (Paid Up Capital)	15,600	
Retained Earnings	13,400	40,000
Total Equities		$62,000

Required: Discuss the tax consequences of each of the following *independent* transactions:

A. (i) A long term debtholder has agreed to convert $10,000 of his securities for 500 preferred shares with a Paid Up Capital of $11,000.

   (ii) After the conversion described in A(i), a different shareholder with 250 preferred shares sold them for $11,000 in an arm's length transaction. His shares cost $4,100 a number of years ago.

B. The Company declared and distributed a 5 percent stock dividend on the Common Shares. An addition of $780 was made to Paid Up Capital, with Retained Earnings reduced accordingly.

C. In return for assets with a fair market value of $17,500, the Company issued a demand note for $7,500 and 250 fully paid preferred shares having a per share Paid Up Capital equal to those currently outstanding.

D. An investor owns 100 of the Common Shares. They were purchased at a price of $15 per share. The Company redeems these shares at a price of $32 per share.

Self Study Problem Fifteen - 2

Mr. Stevens, a Canadian resident, owns 100 percent of the shares of Stevens Holdings Inc. (SHI) which owns 100 percent of Fancy Operating Ltd. (FOL). Both SHI and FOL have a December 31 year end. Neither Company paid any dividends in 2000.

The following information pertains to the year ending December 31, 2001:

Stevens Holdings Inc.

• The balance in the Refundable Dividend Tax On Hand account at December 31, 2000 was $8,000.
• The Company received a taxable dividend from FOL of $75,000.
• The Company received a taxable dividend from Dofasco of $8,000.
• The Company earned Canadian interest income of $12,000.
• The Company realized a capital gain of $47,250.
• The Company paid a capital dividend of $10,500 and a taxable dividend of $50,000 to Mr. Stevens.

Fancy Operating Ltd.

• The balance in the Refundable Dividend Tax On Hand account at December 31, 2000 was $2,000.
• The Company earned Active Business Income of $80,000 and Canadian interest income of $7,000.
• The Company paid taxable dividends to SHI of $75,000.

Required:

A. Calculate the dividend refund for FOL for 2001.

B. Calculate the Part IV Tax for SHI for 2001.

C. Calculate the dividend refund for SHI for 2001.

(OICA Adapted)

Self Study Problem Fifteen - 3

Burton Investments Ltd. is a Canadian controlled private corporation which sells office supplies. It owns 52 percent of the outstanding shares of Puligny Inc. On December 15, 2001, Puligny Inc. declared and paid a dividend of $122,000 of which Burton Investments Ltd. received $63,440 (52 percent). As a result of paying the $122,000 dividend, Puligny Inc. received a dividend refund in the amount of $12,500.

Other 2001 income that was reported by Burton Investments consisted of the following amounts:

Capital Gain	$18,000
Dividends From Bank of Montreal	13,480
Interest	2,150

The capital gain was on the sale of land which had been used as an auxiliary parking lot, but was no longer needed.

Burton's office supply business is seasonal and, as a consequence, temporary cash balances must be set aside for the purchase of inventories during the busy parts of the year. All of the $2,150 in interest was earned on such temporary cash balances.

At the end of 2000, the Company's refundable dividend tax on hand was $22,346. The 2000 dividend refund was $7,920.

The Company's taxable income for the year ending December 31, 2001 was $62,800. No foreign income was included in this total. Burton Investments paid taxable dividends of $22,500.

Required For the taxation year ending December 31, 2001, determine the Part IV and refundable Part I taxes that will be payable by Burton Investments Ltd. In addition, determine the balance in the refundable dividend tax on hand account at December 31, 2001 and any dividend refund available.

Self Study Problem Fifteen - 4

Sinzer Ltd. is a Canadian controlled private corporation. Its business operations consist of sales and consulting with respect to interior design and decoration and its head office is in Windsor, Ontario. For the taxation year ending December 31, 2001, taxable income for Sinzer Ltd. was calculated as follows:

Interest Income From Canadian Sources (Note 1)	$ 48,300
Dividends From Taxable Canadian Corporations (Note 2)	88,100
Foreign Non Business Income (Note 3)	55,000
Taxable Capital Gains On Sale Of Shares	24,500
Income From Design Consulting (Note 4)	103,000
Income From Sales (Note 4)	386,000
Net Income For Tax Purposes	$704,900
Dividends From Taxable Canadian Corporations	(88,100)
Contributions To A Registered Charity	(24,600)
Non Capital Losses	(76,400)
Net Capital Losses	(12,300)
Taxable Income	$503,500

Note 1 The Canadian interest is from the following sources:

Interest On Loan To A Majority Owned Subsidiary (The Subsidiary Has No Active Business Income)	$43,250
Term Deposit And Bank Interest Arising From Seasonal Investment Of Excess Cash From Operations	5,050
Total	$48,300

Note 2 The dividends from taxable Canadian corporations consisted of the following:

Portfolio Dividends From Non Connected Corporations	$19,600
Dividends From 75 Percent Owned Subsidiary (Total Dividend Refund Of $12,750 To The Subsidiary)	68,500
Total	$88,100

Note 3 The $55,000 is before withholding of $8,250 in foreign taxes. This $8,250 was claimed as a foreign tax credit in the calculation of Part I Tax Payable.

Note 4 The Income From Design Consulting includes $38,200 in income from operations in the U.S. The $372,000 in Income From Sales includes $98,000 in sales made in the U.S. A total of $34,000 was paid in U.S. taxes on this income. This amount was claimed as a foreign tax credit in the calculation of Part I Tax Payable.

Other Information:

1. Assume that the total federal Part I tax has been correctly computed to be $85,595, including a $5,639 federal surtax and $7,363 ITA 123.3 tax on investment income. This is after the deduction of the maximum $32,000 of small business deduction on the basis of an annual business limit of $200,000 which was allocated to Sinzer Ltd.

2. During 2001, Sinzer declared four quarterly taxable dividends in the amount of $28,000 each. The first of these dividends was paid in March, 2001, the second in June, 2001, the third in October, 2001, and the fourth was paid in January, 2002. A $25,000 taxable dividend, declared in December, 2000, was paid in January, 2001.

3. The balance in the Refundable Dividend Tax On Hand account on December 31, 2000 was $23,500 and the dividend refund for 2000 was $9,600.

Required: Determine the amount of Sinzer's dividend refund for 2001. Show all calculations, regardless of whether they are necessary for the final answer.

Self Study Problem Fifteen - 5

Acme Imports Ltd. is a Canadian controlled private company. Its basic business activity is importing a variety of consumer products for distribution to wholesalers in Canada. The before income taxes Balance Sheet and Income Statement of Acme Imports Ltd. for the year ending December 31, 2001 are as follows:

Acme Imports Ltd.
Balance Sheet Before Income Taxes
As At December 31, 2001

Assets

Accounts Receivable		$1,080,000
Inventories		940,000
Loan To Shareholder		97,000
Federal Income Tax Instalments Paid		28,000
Investment In Sarco Ltd.		695,000
Land		385,000
Equipment - Cost	$840,000	
Accumulated Depreciation	(414,000)	426,000
Goodwill		183,000
Total Assets		$3,834,000

Equities

Bank Overdraft		$ 87,000
Note To Bank		306,000
Accounts Payable		682,000
Mortgage On Land		244,000
Future Income Tax Liability		53,000
Common Stock - No Par		32,000
Retained Earnings		2,430,000
Total Equities		$3,834,000

Acme Imports Ltd.
Income Statement Before Income Taxes
Year Ending December 31, 2001

Sales	$7,387,700
Dividend Income	24,000
Interest Revenue	10,000
Gain On Sale Of Equipment	57,000
Total Revenues	**$7,478,700**
Cost Of Goods Sold	$6,071,400
Rent	118,000
Selling Expenses	283,000
Wages And Salaries	276,000
Employee Benefits	32,000
Office Expenses	158,000
Fees For Professional Services	43,000
Interest	47,000
Promotional Expenses	99,000
Amortization Expense	20,000
Charitable Donations	25,000
Vehicle Costs	74,000
Total Expenses Not Including Income Taxes	**$7,246,400**
Income Before Taxes	**$ 232,300**

Other Information: The following additional information is available with respect to the 2001 operations of Acme Imports Ltd.:

1. The goodwill consists of an amount paid for a list of potential customers. This list was acquired during December, 2001 from a competitor who had ceased doing business. The cost was not amortized for accounting purposes during the year.

2. On January 1, 2001, the Equipment, which is all in Class 8, had an undepreciated capital cost of $256,000.

3. Acme Imports Ltd. did not declare or pay any dividends during the year. On January 1, 2001 Acme Imports Ltd. had a nil balance in its refundable dividend tax on hand.

4. The gain on sale of equipment resulted from selling display fixtures and equipment with an original cost of $62,000 and a net book value of $27,500, for cash proceeds of $84,500.

5. The loan outstanding to the shareholder was made in January of 1999. It is a non interest bearing loan.

6. Included in Promotional Expenses is a $2,800 membership fee to a local golf and country club. In addition, there were charges at this club for business meals and entertainment totalling $6,720.

7. The Company provides cars for the principal shareholder and the manager of the Company. Included in vehicle costs are lease payments of $500 per month for 12 months for each car and a total of $11,000 in operating costs associated with providing these cars. While these individuals use the cars for some business purposes, it is estimated that over 80 percent of their usage is personal.

8. A small group of new shares were issued during the year. The costs of printing these shares was $950 and was included in the office expenses. In addition, $7,000 of the professional fees paid were legal and other costs associated with obtaining the supplementary letters patent required to issue these shares.

9. The dividend income of $24,000 was Acme's share of a dividend declared by Sarco Ltd., a

60 percent owned subsidiary company. As a result of declaring the dividend, Sarco received a total dividend refund of $5,000. None of the annual limit for the small business deduction was allocated to Sarco.

10. The interest income came from Canada Savings Bonds that had been held for four years and sold during the year.

11. During the year, the Company decided that it had grown to the point where additional space was needed and, rather than continue to rent space, it has decided to acquire its own premises. It paid a fee of $3,500 (included in fees for professional services) to a site consultant and, on the basis of his recommendation, acquired land at a cost of $385,000. The site was purchased on April 1, 2001 and construction of the new facility is to begin early in 2002. The Company's Other Expenses included $12,300 in interest on the mortgage used to finance this land.

Required: Calculate the minimum federal taxes payable and the closing balance in the refundable dividend tax on hand account of Acme Imports Ltd. for the year ending December 31, 2001.

Self Study Problem Fifteen - 6

Brasco Distributors is a Canadian controlled private corporation. Its primary business is the distribution of a variety of consumer products to retailers throughout Canada. Its fiscal year ends on December 31.

While its current operations are providing a reasonable rate of return on invested capital, losses have been experienced in previous years. As a result, at the beginning of the year ending December 31, 2001, it has available, a non capital loss carry forward of $25,800 and a net capital loss carry forward of $64,500 [(1/2)($129,000)] from 2000.

Other Information:

1. During the year ending December 31, 2001, the Company made contributions of $11,900 to registered Canadian charities.

2. Its net capital gains for 2001 amounted to $72,000.

3. The Company's 2001 active business income, computed in accordance with the requirements of the *Income Tax Act*, amounted to $171,000.

4. Total dividends paid to shareholders of the Company amounted to $69,500. This total was made up of $39,000 in taxable dividends and $30,500 out of the capital dividend account.

5. During 2001, the Company received $2,200 in interest from long term Canadian bonds. In addition, on common shares which represent portfolio investments in taxable Canadian companies, the Company received dividends of $15,800. The Company received foreign source investment income of $3,825. This was a net amount after the withholding of $675 in taxes by the taxation authorities in the foreign jurisdiction.

6. Brasco owns 60 percent of the outstanding voting shares of Masco, a Canadian subsidiary. During the year, Brasco received $37,800 in dividends from Masco. The total 2001 dividends paid by the subsidiary amounted to $63,000 and, as a result of paying this dividend, Masco claimed a dividend refund of $21,000. Because it is an associated Company, Brasco must share the annual limit on its small business deduction with Masco. Brasco has been allocated $125,000 and Masco has been allocated $75,000 of the annual limit.

7. The balance in the Brasco Distributors' refundable dividend tax on hand account was $7,000 on December 31, 2000. Brasco paid no dividends in 2000.

Required: Calculate, for Brasco Distributors, the total minimum federal taxes payable for the year ending December 31, 2001, net of any dividend refund and the balance in the refundable dividend tax on hand account as at December 31, 2001.

Assignment Problems

(The solutions for these problems are only available in
the solutions manual that has been provided to your instructor.)

Assignment Problem Fifteen - 1

Using the following assumptions, provide an example of how integration works:

- The corporation's business income for the year is $50,000.
- The individual's marginal federal tax rate is 29 percent and marginal provincial tax rate is 14.5 percent.
- The provincial dividend tax credit is equal to one-third of the gross up.
- The combined federal and provincial corporate tax rate is 20 percent.

Assignment Problem Fifteen - 2

During June, 2001, Hemingway Industries Ltd., a Canadian controlled private company, sold a number of its capital properties. None of the properties disposed of were depreciable capital properties. The relevant facts are as follows:

Property	Proceeds Of Disposition	Cost	Selling Expenses
1	$8,100	$4,200	$200
2	7,900	3,950	375
3	2,200	4,300	700
4	1,900	3,450	260

Required: Compute the effects of the dispositions on the capital dividend account.

Assignment Problem Fifteen - 3

Deemit Inc. is a Canadian controlled private corporation. However, it is not a qualified small business corporation. All of the shares of the Company are held by individuals resident in Canada. On December 31 of the current year, its condensed Balance Sheet is as follows:

Total Assets		$790,000
Total Liabilities		$110,000
Shareholders' Equity:		
Preferred Shares	$150,000	
Common Shares	370,000	
Retained Earnings	160,000	680,000
Total Equities		$790,000

There are 20,000 Preferred Shares outstanding and they were issued at a price of $7.50 per share. The PUC of these shares is equal to their carrying value of $150,000.

There are 185,000 Common Shares outstanding and they have been issued at various prices. The PUC of these shares is equal to their carrying value of $370,000.

Required: Indicate the tax consequences to the relevant shareholders of the transaction(s) described in each of the following **independent** cases. Tax consequences would include both the increase or decrease in the individual shareholder's Taxable Income, as well as any change in the adjusted cost base of shares that are still in the hands of the individual shareholder after the described transaction(s).

Case A   An individual owns 10,000 of the outstanding Preferred Shares. His adjusted cost base for the shares is $72,000. The Company redeems these shares, providing the individual with a payment of $78,000.

Case B   The company declares a dividend of $.50 per share on the outstanding Common Shares. The total amount of the dividend is less than the balance in the capital dividend account and the company makes the appropriate election under ITA 83(2).

Case C   In order to partially liquidate the company, a dividend of $2.10 per share is declared on the Common Shares. This dividend is accompanied by a $370,000 reduction in the PUC of the Common Shares.

Case D   A $50,000 loan, from an individual who is not a shareholder of the Company, is settled by the issuance of 8,000 Preferred Shares with a PUC of $60,000. The Preferred Shares received by this individual are immediately sold at their fair market value of $60,000.

Assignment Problem Fifteen - 4

Conrod Holdings Ltd. is a Canadian controlled private corporation which sells office supplies. It owns 70 percent of the outstanding shares of Morsal Inc. On November 1, 2001, Morsal Inc. declared and paid a dividend of $21,000 of which Conrod Holdings Ltd. received $14,700 (70 percent). As a result of paying the $21,000 dividend, Morsal Inc. received a dividend refund in the amount of $7,000.

Other income that was reported by Conrod Holdings consisted of the following amounts:

Capital gain	$9,200
Dividends From Alcan Ltd.	500
Interest	1,450

The capital gain was on the sale of land which was formerly used as a storage area for inventories. Improved inventory control procedures have eliminated the need for this land.

The interest is on deposits of temporary cash balances set aside for the purchase of inventories.

At the end of 2000, the Company's refundable dividend tax on hand was $8,950. The 2000 dividend refund was $4,000.

The Company's taxable income for the year ending December 31, 2001 was $44,700. No foreign income was included in this total. Conrod Holdings paid taxable dividends of $10,000 during the year.

Required   For the taxation year ending December 31, 2001, determine the Part IV and refundable Part I taxes that will be payable by Conrod Holdings. In addition, determine the balance in the refundable dividend tax on hand account at December 31, 2001 and any dividend refund available.

Assignment Problem Fifteen - 5

Vader Ltd. is a Canadian controlled private company involved in the distribution of domestically produced laser products. It had the following condensed Income Statement for the year ending December 31, 2001:

Active Business Income	$216,300
Dividends From Canadian Corporations:	
Wholly Owned Subsidiary	108,000
Portfolio Investments	56,000
Interest On Government Bonds	36,300
Taxable Capital Gains [(1/2)($114,600)]	57,300
Net Income For Tax Purposes	$473,900

During 2000, Vader Ltd. paid no dividends. On October 1, 2001, Vader Ltd. paid taxable dividends to its shareholders in the amount of $32,400. The dividends paid to Vader Ltd. by the wholly owned subsidiary did not entitle the subsidiary to any dividend refund.

The balance in the refundable dividend tax on hand account was zero on December 31, 2000. Vader Ltd. will claim the maximum annual small business deduction and this amount will not be shared with the wholly owned subsidiary. This is the first year that Vader Ltd. has reported any capital gains.

Required: For Vader Ltd.'s 2001 taxation year, calculate the following items:

A.   Federal Part I taxes payable.
B.   The Part IV tax.
C.   The balance of the refundable dividend tax on hand account on December 31, 2001.
D.   The dividend refund, if any.
E.   The balance in the capital dividend account.
F.   Federal taxes payable (net of any dividend refund).

Assignment Problem Fifteen - 6

The following data is for Masterson Ltd., a Canadian controlled private corporation. The data is for the taxation year ending December 31, 2001:

Canadian Source Active Business Income (Includes	
$99,000 Of Manufacturing And Processing Profits)	$133,000
Foreign Investment Income (Net Of $1,200 In Withheld Foreign Taxes)	6,800
Net Income For Tax Purposes (Division B Income)	141,000
Taxable Income	95,000

No net capital loss carry forwards were deducted during 2001.

Required: Calculate the federal Part I Tax Payable for the taxation year ending December 31, 2001. In preparing your solution, assume that the tax credit on foreign investment income is equal to the $1,200 in taxes withheld.

Assignment Problem Fifteen - 7

Gardner Distributing Company, a Canadian controlled private corporation, was established ten years ago by Mr. Hugh Gardner. Its only business activity is the distribution of specialty gardening products to retailers across Canada. Mr. Gardner is a Canadian resident and is the sole shareholder of the Company. The Company has a fiscal year which ends on December 31, and for 2001 the Company's accountant produced the following income statement:

Sales Revenue		$1,800,000
Cost Of Goods Sold		940,000
Gross Profit		$ 860,000
Operating Expenses:		
Selling And Administration		$ 318,000
Depreciation		47,000
Charitable Donations		12,000
Total Operating Expenses		$ 377,000
Operating Income		$ 483,000
Other Income And Losses:		
Dividends From Taxable Canadian Companies		27,000
Loss On Sale Of Truck	(	19,000)
Gain On Sale Of Investments		7,000
Pre Tax Accounting Income		$ 498,000

Other information:

1. The Company had depreciable assets with the following undepreciated capital cost (UCC) at the end of its 2000 taxation year:

	UCC
Class 3 (5%)	$726,000
Class 8 (20%)	472,000
Class 10 (30%)	22,000

The balance in Class 10 reflects a single truck that was used for deliveries. It had an original cost in 1999 of $38,000 and a net book value for accounting purposes of $29,000. It was sold on October 1, 2001 for $10,000 and replaced with a leased truck.

The only other transaction involving depreciable assets during the year was the acquisition of $82,000 in Class 8 assets.

2. On December 31, 2000, the Company had a balance in its refundable dividend tax on hand account of $19,000. The Company claimed a dividend refund of $5,000 in its 2000 corporate tax return.

3. The balance in the capital dividend account was $27,200 on December 31, 2000.

4. The investments that were sold during the year had been purchased for $93,000. They were sold for $100,000.

5. The Gardner Distributing Company paid $17,000 in taxable dividends to Mr. Gardner. In addition, the Company elected to pay a capital dividend of $10,000 to Mr. Gardner during the year.

Required: For the 2001 taxation year, determine the minimum federal income taxes payable for the Gardner Distributing Company. Your answer should be net of any dividend refund. In addition, calculate the end of the year balances in the refundable dividend tax on hand account and the capital dividend account.

Assignment Problem Fifteen - 8

B & C Limited is a Canadian controlled private corporation throughout its taxation year ending December 31, 2001. For that year, its Net Income For Tax Purposes and Taxable Income can be calculated as follows:

Canadian Manufacturing And Processing Profits As Per ITR 5200 Formula	$123,000
Other Canadian Active Business Income	78,000
Canadian Source Interest Income	10,000
Canadian Source Taxable Capital Gains	24,000
Foreign Non Business Income (Before $3,000 Withholding)	20,000
Foreign Business Income (Before $6,000 Withholding)	40,000
Portfolio Dividends From Taxable Canadian Corporations	26,000
Net Income For Tax Purposes	$321,000
Portfolio Dividends From Taxable Canadian Corporations	(26,000)
Charitable Contributions	(32,000)
Net Capital Loss Carried Forward From 2000	(18,000)
Taxable Income	$245,000

Other Information:

1. B & C Limited paid taxable dividends of $124,000 during the year.

2. It has been determined that 91 percent of B & C Limited's Taxable Income was earned in Canada.

3. The December 31, 2000 balance in the Refundable Dividend Tax On Hand account was

$132,000. The dividend refund for the year ending December 31, 2000 was $28,000.

4. B & C Limited is associated with another Canadian controlled private corporation. They have elected to each claim a 50 percent share of the annual business limit.

Required:

A. Determine B & C Limited's federal Part I Tax Payable for the year ending December 31, 2001. In making this calculation, assume that the Foreign Tax Credits for business and non business income are equal to the amounts withheld.

B. Determine the December 31, 2001 balance in the Refundable Dividend Tax On Hand account.

C. Determine the dividend refund for the year ending December 31, 2001.

Assignment Problem Fifteen - 9

Startop Ltd. is a Canadian controlled private corporation that was established in Manitoba in 1996. It has a December 31 year end and for the taxation year ending December 31, 2001, its accounting income before taxes, as determined using GAAP, was $462,000. Other information for the 2001 fiscal year follows.

Other Information:

1. Startop sold depreciable assets for $450,000. These assets had an original cost of $390,000 and a Net Book Value of $330,000. They were Class 8 assets and, at the beginning of 2001, the balance in this Class was $350,000. The Company has other assets left in this Class.

2. The Company's Depreciation Expense was $546,000. Maximum deductible CCA for the year was $730,000 before consideration of the Class 8 assets that were sold.

3. The Company spent $50,000 on business meals and entertainment.

4. During the year, the company begins selling a product on which they provide a five year warranty. At the end of the year, they established a warranty reserve of $20,000 to reflect the expected costs of providing warranty services.

5. It has been determined that Startop has active business income of $190,000 for the year. Manufacturing and processing profits for the year, as determined under the *Income Tax Regulations*, totalled $150,000.

6. The Company's revenues included foreign source non business income of $17,000 (Canadian dollars). This was the amount that was received after the withholding of $3,000 (15 percent of the gross) for the foreign tax authorities. Any excess of foreign tax withheld over the federal foreign tax credit will be applied against the provincial tax liability.

7. During the year, the Company had the following amounts of Canadian source investment income:

Interest On Long Term Investments	$25,000
Taxable Capital Gains	30,000
Dividends On Bell Canada Shares	11,000

8. At December 31, 2000, the Company had a Non Capital Loss carry forward of $205,000 and a Net Capital Loss carry forward of $19,000 [(1/2)($38,000)] from 2000.

9. Because of losses in previous years, no instalment payments were made for the year.

10. As a result of expenditures made during the year, the Company has available investment tax credits of $2,000.

11. As of December 31, 2000, the balance in Startop's capital dividend account was $20,000.

12. As of December 31, 2000, the balance in Startop's RDTOH account was $17,000. No dividends were paid during 2000. During the year ending December 31, 2001, the

Company used its existing cash resources to pay taxable dividends of $210,000.

Required:

A. Calculate Startop's minimum Net Income For Tax Purposes for the taxation year ending December 31, 2001.

B. Calculate Startop's minimum Taxable Income for the year ending December 31, 2001.

C. Calculate Startop's federal Part I and Part IV Taxes Payable, net of any refund resulting from the payment of dividends, for the year ending December 31, 2001. Comment on any tax planning issues that should be reviewed.

Assignment Problem Fifteen - 10 (Electronic Library Research Problem)

Provide a brief answer to the following question. Your answer should be supported by references to materials found in your Electronic Library.

A. Does the CCRA pay interest on amounts owing to a corporate taxpayer as a dividend refund? If so, how is the amount of interest calculated?

Cases - Using ProFile T2 Software For Corporate Returns

Case Fifteen - 1 (Using ProFile T2 Software For Corporate Returns)

Radion Industries Ltd. (RIL) is a Canadian controlled private corporation located at 333 Laurier Avenue West in Ottawa, Ontario K1A 0L9. Its Business Number is 111111111RC 0001 and its telephone number is (613) 598-2290. The Company has 1,000 shares of common stock issued and outstanding, all of which are held by Margaret Reid (SIN 527-000-301). Ms. Reid, the president of the company, is the person who should be contacted with respect to matters concerning the company's books and records.

RIL is a manufacturer of plastic patio furniture. All of its sales and production occur within Canada. RIL also holds some of the investments that Ms. Reid inherited from a substantial estate two years earlier.

It owns all of the 500 common shares of Reid Inc. (Business Number 222222222RC0001), which holds most of Ms. Reid's inherited investments. Reid Inc. is also involved in earning active business income through the marketing and distribution of RIL's products. Reid Inc. has a December 31 fiscal year end.

For the taxation year ending December 31, 2001, RIL's GAAP based Income Statement, before any deduction for income taxes, was as follows:

Sales Revenues	$561,000
Interest On Long Term Debt	27,500
Interest Received On Foreign Bank Account (Note 1)	18,000
Dividends On Royal Bank Shares	17,500
Dividends From Reid Inc. (Note 2)	42,000
Gain On Sale Of Class 43.1 Assets	46,000
Total Revenues	$712,000
Cost Of Goods Sold	$208,000
Depreciation And Amortization Expense	122,000
Other Operating Expenses	147,000
Total Expenses (Excluding Taxes)	$477,000
Net Income (Before Taxes)	$235,000
Dividends Declared and Paid	(92,000)
Increase In Retained Earnings	$143,000

Note 1 This interest is net of $2,000 in taxes withheld in Ireland.

Note 2 As a result of paying this $42,000 in dividends to RIL, Reid Inc. received a dividend refund of $14,000.

Other Information:

1. The opening UCC balances were $135,000 for Class 8, $90,000 for Class 10, $246,000 for Class 43 and $71,000 for Class 43.1. The Class 43.1 assets were purchased for $112,000 on February 20, 1999, had a net book value of $93,000 and were sold for $139,000. They were the only assets in Class 43.1. The only other fixed asset disposition was the sale of a delivery truck. The truck had cost $35,000 and was sold for $12,000. The only fixed asset acquisition was $52,000 in equipment to be used for manufacturing furniture.

2. During the year, RIL incurred $20,000 in landscaping costs. For accounting purposes these are being treated as a capital asset to be written off by the straight line method over 10 years.

3. At December 31, 2000, RIL had a Non Capital Loss carry forward of $64,000 and a Net Capital Loss carry forward of $33,000 [(3/4)($44,000)]. The Net Capital Loss is from a 1995 disposition.

4. As RIL had no Taxable Income in the previous year, no tax instalments were paid during the year.

5. Expenses include a deduction for charitable contributions to the Ottawa Civic Hospital in the amount of $5,000 and a donation to the federal Liberal party of $2,000 on November 11, 2001.

6. At December 31, 2000, the balance in RIL's RDTOH account was $5,200. No dividends were paid in 2000.

7. RIL's Expenses include penalties of $3,500 resulting from a judgment in the Tax Court Of Canada.

8. RIL reimbursed Ms. Reid $34,000 for business meals and entertainment for clients and suppliers during the year.

9. RIL allocates 50 percent of the annual business limit to Reid Inc.

10. RIL has total assets of $4,236,000 as at December 31, 2001.

11. Assume that RIL has no Ontario capital tax liability for 2001.

Required: Prepare the federal corporate tax return for RIL for the 2001 taxation year using the ProFile T2 corporate software program. Ignore the GIFI requirements.

Case Fifteen - 2 (Using ProFile T2 Software For Corporate Returns)

Martin Manufacturing Company (MMC, hereafter) is a Canadian controlled private corporation with its head office in Flin Flon, Manitoba at 9999 Third Avenue. Its Business Number is 111111111RC0001 and its telephone number is (204) 987-6543. The Company has 20,000 shares of common stock issued and outstanding, 96 percent of which are owned by Mr. Micky Martin (SIN 527-000-384), a Canadian resident. The remaining 4 percent are held by a U.S. company, Stars And Stripes Incorporated. Mr. Martin is the person that should be contacted with respect to matters concerning the company's books and records.

The Company is a manufacturer of small electric motors with business operations in Manitoba, British Columbia, Nova Scotia and Newfoundland. Its taxation year ends on December 31.

The Company experienced major operating and sales problems during the past two years, a situation which resulted in significant losses. There has been a dramatic turnaround in 2001. Micky Martin has signed several major contracts in the last quarter of 2001 and labour relations have improved due to personnel changes. The taxable income for 2001 is estimated to be at least $1,800,000.

Using information from the Company's GAAP based financial statements for the year ending December 31, 2001, the accounting department has prepared the following financial statements to assist in preparing the corporate tax return.

Martin Manufacturing Company
Balance Sheet
As At December 31, 2001

Assets

Cash	$ 226,500
Temporary Investments (Note 1)	1,523,000
Accounts Receivable (Note 2)	2,741,000
Inventory	6,098,000
Long Term Investments At Cost (Note 3)	260,000
Plant And Equipment (Net)	856,500
Future Income Tax Debit	7,000
Total Assets	**$11,712,000**

Equities

Accounts Payable (Note 4)	$ 812,000
Bonds Payable	387,000
Loans From Corporations	1,238,000
Common Stock	2,600,000
Retained Earnings	6,675,000
Total Equities	**$11,712,000**

Notes To The Balance Sheet

Note 1   The Temporary Investments consist entirely of term deposits that have been held for more than 120 days prior to December 31, 2001.

Note 2   The Accounts Receivable include a $147,000 loan to an unrelated corporation.

Note 3   The Long Term Investments consist of shares in other corporations.

Note 4   Included in Accounts Payable are the following:

- a $47,000 trade payable to Micky Martin that has been outstanding since November 15, 2000;

- a $27,000 trade payable to a corporation for equipment repairs that has been outstanding for 150 days; and

- a $4,000 trade payable to a supplier that has been outstanding for more than 365 days due to a disputed balance.

Martin Manufacturing Company
Income Statement
For The Year Ending December 31, 2001

Total Sales	$5,079,000
Cost Of Goods Sold	(3,287,000)
Gross Margin	$1,792,000
Other Revenues	620,000
Selling And Administrative Expenses	(1,228,000)
Income Before Taxes	$1,184,000
Provision For Income Taxes (Initial Estimate)	(260,000)
Net Income	$ 924,000

Other Information:

1. In December, 2001, a loan of $11,000 was made to the president of MMC to allow him to purchase an automobile that will be used in his work for the Company. The loan bears interest at 7 percent.

2. Due to the late payment of 2000 Part IV taxes, MMC was required to pay $420 in interest to the CCRA. This amount was charged to Selling And Administrative Expenses.

3. During 2000, MMC paid $45,000 in taxable dividends. At the end of 2000, the refundable dividend tax on hand balance was $80,000 and the capital dividend account was nil. The dividend refund for 2000 was $1,500. During 2001, MMC paid $52,000 in taxable dividends and $6,500 in capital dividends.

4. Both the Manitoba capital tax and the Nova Scotia tax on large corporations for the year have been calculated correctly and deducted in Selling and Administrative Expenses. There were no provincial tax instalments paid.

5. Included in Selling And Administrative Expenses are donations to the Flin Flon United Way (Registration #62) of $1,000, and to the United Nations (Registration #78) for $800.

6. Total 2001 salaries paid to the Company's employees were as follows:

Manufacturing and Shipping:	
Production, assembly, and line supervision	$367,000
Engineering design, quality control	53,000
Receiving and storing of raw materials	72,000
Purchasing of raw materials	22,000
Storing and shipping finished goods	28,000
Total Manufacturing and Shipping Salaries	$542,000
Selling And Administrative Salaries	87,000
Total Salaries	$629,000

Included in the $629,000 is a salary payment to Micky Martin of $38,000 for management services. In addition to the total salaries, MMC paid employee benefits of $43,000 which included the employer's share of Canada Pension Plan contributions and Employment Insurance premiums.

7. The allocation of salaries and sales for MCC, as well as the provincial tax rates on taxable income in the four provinces where it has permanent establishments are as follows:

	Salaries	Sales
Newfoundland	$ 68,000	$ 742,000
Nova Scotia	40,000	412,000
Manitoba	487,000	3,610,000
British Columbia	34,000	315,000
Totals	$629,000	$5,079,000

8. The Company has a net capital loss carry forward from 1998 of $13,500 and a non capital loss carry forward from 2000 of $1,100.

9. During 2001, MMC arranged for a long term U.S. dollar loan. The proceeds of the loan were used to acquire capital assets. Other Revenues includes unrealized exchange gains on this loan of $6,500.

10. During 2001, MMC paid $5,000 for the permanent right to manufacture a product designed by a Winnipeg company, Wastash Products Ltd. MMC also has an arrangement with Wastash Products Ltd. to pay royalties for the use of a special die. The royalties are based on the number of pressings made with the die and required 2001 payments of $13,000. Both of these payments were expensed in the accounting records.

11. On December 1, 2001, MMC made a federal tax instalment payment of $99,000.

12. Dividends received are included in Other Revenues. During 2001, dividends were received from the following companies:

- Lorn Ltd. (A Canadian Public Corporation) $2,000
- Eagle Industries (An Unrelated U.S. Corporation, Recorded In Canadian Dollars Net Of 15% Withholding) $4,250

13. Dividends were also received during 2001 from Sooner Inc. (Business Number 222222222RC0001), a connected Canadian private company with a December 31 year end. MMC owns 20 percent of this Company and received dividends of $6,000. The total 2001 dividends paid by Sooner Inc. amounted to $30,000, an amount on which a dividend refund of $10,000 was received by the Company.

14. MMC sponsors a registered pension plan (Registration No. B-14786) for four of its key employees. It is a defined contribution plan with MMC's annual contributions specified as 10 percent of each employee's annual salary. The 2001 salaries of these employees totalled $210,000, allocated as follows:

Two Production Managers At $60,000	$120,000
Two Supervisors At $45,000	90,000
Total	$210,000

This resulted in a contribution of $21,000 to the plan, the full amount of which was deducted in the accounting records. The Company also contributed $5,000 ($2,500 each) to a deferred profit sharing plan (Registration #48726) for the two managers. This amount was also deducted in the accounting records.

15. On April 18, 2001, MMC sold its 5 percent interest in the shares of Whaleback Ltd., a Canadian controlled private company which is a small business corporation. These shares were purchased in 1991 at a cost of $8,000 and were sold for $5,500. Selling costs were $200.

16. On July 1, 2001, a contribution was made to a registered federal political party (the New Liberal Conservative Bloc Reform Democrats) in the amount of $1,500. This amount is included in Selling And Administrative Expenses.

17. With respect to undepreciated capital cost, the class balances as at December 31, 2000, were as follows:

Class	Balance
3	$110,000
8	658,200
10	6,800
43	44,000
Total	$819,000

18. The accounting records contain the following analysis of the Plant And Equipment account:

	Cost	Accumulated Amortization	Net Book Value
January 1, 2001	$1,042,000	$456,000	$586,000
Additions	561,000	152,000	409,000
Disposals	(154,000)	(15,500)	(138,500)
December 31, 2001	$1,449,000	$592,500	$856,500

Individual Plant And Equipment items disposed of, including the only tract of Land in the January 1, 2001 balance, had costs as follows:

Buildings (See Item 23)	$ 44,000
Land (See Item 23)	102,000
Automobile (See Item 21)	8,000
Total Cost of Disposals	$154,000

As of December 31, 2001, the cost of Plant And Equipment, excluding Land, that was used directly in M&P activities amounted to $840,000.

19. In June, 2001, MMC moved its manufacturing operations from Thompson, Manitoba to Flin Flon upon acquiring its new factory. The costs of the factory were allocated as follows:

Land (The only tract acquired during 2001)	$402,000
Building	41,000
Total	$443,000

20. In November, 2001, MMC completed the construction of a building next to its new Flin Flon factory. The building cost $48,000. Due to mechanical problems in the ventilation system, the building cannot be used until February, 2002.

21. As of November 1, 2001, MMC began leasing both of its automobiles. In accordance with the Recommendations of Section 3065 of the *CICA Handbook*, these leases were capitalized, resulting in a $14,000 addition to the Company's Plant And Equipment. However, for tax purposes they were considered to be operating leases. Lease payments for the year totalled $900, of which $150 was charged to expense and the remainder to the liability account. Amortization on the asset balance is included in the schedule in Item 17. One of the automobiles that was previously included in Class 10 with a net book value of $5,500, was disposed of for proceeds of $3,400.

22. As indicated in Item 18, total additions to Plant And Equipment for the year were $561,000. Some of these additions were described in Items 18 through 21. The remaining additions were as follows:

Manufacturing Machinery And Equipment	$28,000
Furniture, Fixtures, And Office Equipment	12,000
Two Computer Workstations (Each complete workstation cost $8,000)	16,000

23. In late November, 2001, MMC managed to dispose of its Thompson land and factory. This property was located at 23 Broad Street and details of the transaction were as follows:

Building

Proceeds, Less Costs Of Disposition	$62,000
UCC, December 31, 2000	36,480
Net Book Value	31,000
Cost On December 1, 1987	44,000

Land

Proceeds, Less Costs Of Disposition	$520,000
Cost On December 1, 1989	102,000

The total gain recorded for accounting purposes was $449,000, allocated $418,000 to the land and $31,000 to the building. Of the total proceeds of $582,000, $130,000 is payable on December 31, 2001, with the remaining $452,000 payable on December 31, 2002.

24. MMC has not paid Part I.3 tax in any previous year.

Required: Complete a corporate tax return for the Martin Manufacturing Company for the year ending December 31, 2001 using the T2 ProFile tax software program. Ignore the GIFI requirements.

Chapter 16

Corporate Taxation And Management Decisions

The Decision To Incorporate

Introduction

16-1.   One of the more important decisions facing the owner of a business is deciding whether or not the business should be incorporated. There are, of course, a number of non tax considerations involved in this decision and these factors will be reviewed in this Chapter. At this point, however, we are concerned with the influence of corporate taxation on this decision.

16-2.   The decision to incorporate, both from a legal and a tax point of view, has the effect of separating the business from its owners. This means that, in order for incorporated business income to be made available to the owner, it must go through two levels of taxation. First, the amount of taxes payable applicable to the corporation will be determined. Then, when any remaining amounts are distributed to the owner, either as salary or as dividends, additional personal taxes will be payable on the amounts received.

16-3.   This dual system of taxation may or may not be advantageous to the owner of the business. In terms of tax advantages resulting from incorporating business income, there are three possibilities. In simplified terms, they can be described as follows:

Tax Reduction   In some situations, the total taxes that would be paid at the combined corporate and personal level will be less when the business is incorporated than would be the case if the individual had earned the business income directly as an individual proprietor.

Tax Deferral   As was noted in Paragraph 16-2, getting income from its source through a corporation and into the hands of a shareholder involves two levels of taxation. If the shareholder does not require all of the income for his personal needs, after tax funds can be left in the corporation, and the second level of taxation can be postponed until the income is needed. If the rate at which the corporation is taxed is lower than the rate at which the individual would be taxed on the direct receipt of the income, the use of a corporation provides tax deferral.

Income Splitting   Even in situations where the use of a corporation neither reduces nor defers significant amounts of taxes, the arrangement may be attractive from the point of view of income splitting. Among family members, it is not uncommon to find some individuals earning amounts far above the level required to put them in the maximum personal tax bracket, while other members are in lower brackets or earning such small amounts that they are not subject to any taxation. Because of the progressive nature of the personal tax system, the redistribution of income within such a family group will usually result in significant tax savings. A corporation can be used very effectively to achieve this goal.

16-4. Tax reduction, tax deferral, and income splitting are the basic possibilities for gaining tax advantages through the use of a corporation. Today's corporate rates are such that there is rarely any tax reduction associated with income flowed through a corporation. With respect to deferral, such provisions as the additional refundable tax on a CCPC's investment income, as well as the Part IV tax on dividends received by a private corporation, act to reduce opportunities in this area. Note, however, significant deferral is usually available on corporate income that is eligible for the small business deduction. However, to gain this advantage, the shareholder must be in a financial position to leave the income in the corporation.

16-5. Income splitting continues to be an important tax reason for using the corporate form of organization. Note, however, the 1999 budget change that was described in Chapter 13 (see "Tax On Split Income" at Paragraph 13-11) reduces the ability of an individual to undertake this type of tax planning with related individuals under 18 years of age.

16-6. It should also be noted that the integration provisions that are contained in Canadian tax legislation are based on the assumption that certain corporate and personal tax rates prevail. As the overall rates for these taxable entities vary from province to province, it is possible to find situations where the imperfections in the integration system result in certain advantages to taxpayers using the corporate form of organization.

16-7. As you probably discerned while proceeding through the previous corporate taxation Chapters, whether the presence of a corporation will provide a deferral or reduction of taxes depends on both the type of corporation and the type of income that is being earned by that business entity. In the material that follows, we will examine a variety of possible combinations with a view to determining whether opportunities for tax deferral or tax reduction are available. We will then consider the advantages, and in some cases disadvantages, that can result from imperfections in the integration system. Following this material, we will provide an illustration of the use of a corporation to split income among the members of a family group. Attention will also be given to other, largely non tax considerations, that enter into any decision related to incorporating a given source of income.

Example For Comparative Analysis

Basic Approach

16-8. In order to consider the various results that can be achieved by incorporating a source of income, we will use a simple example in which an individual, Mr. Renaud, has access to $100,000 in income that he can either receive directly or channel through a corporation. We will assume that, before any consideration of this additional $100,000, Mr. Renaud has sufficient taxable income and taxes payable to absorb all of his personal and other tax credits. Additional income will be taxed at the maximum personal rate of 29 percent.

16-9. To illustrate the effects of incorporating different types of income, several cases will be presented with varying assumptions as to the source of this income and the type of corporation that will be established. However, before turning to these cases, we will give consideration to the various personal and corporate tax rates that will be used.

Personal Tax Rates And Taxes Payable

16-10. In these examples, we will assume that Mr. Renaud lives in a province where the maximum rate on individuals is 16 percent. As all of Mr. Renaud's additional income will be subject to this maximum rate, his combined federal/provincial marginal rate will be 45 (29 + 16) percent. Referring to Chapter 13's listing of combined rates on ordinary income, this rate would be slightly below the average rate of 46.1 percent, but above the middle of the range which starts at 39 percent and extends to 48.7 percent (see the table in Paragraph 13-27).

16-11.   This 45 percent rate is applicable to the direct receipt of income. This means that, if Mr. Renaud receives the $100,000 in income without channeling it through a corporation, taxes of $45,000 will be paid and $55,000 will be retained.

16-12.   If the income is received in the form of dividends from a taxable Canadian corporation, the matter becomes more complex. The amount of the dividends received must be grossed up by 25 percent and consideration must be given to the dividend tax credit. In these examples, we will assume that Mr. Renaud's province of residence provides a dividend tax credit equal to one-third of the gross up. This, in effect, sets the combined federal/provincial dividend tax credit equal to the gross up $(2/3 + 1/3 = 1)$. Taking these items into consideration, the effective tax rate on dividends received (before the gross up) by Mr. Renaud will be 31.25 percent as shown in the following calculations:

	Percent
Dividends Received	100.00
Add: Gross Up	25.00
Equals: Personal Taxable Income	125.00
Combined Federal/Provincial Rate	45.00
Equals: Combined Federal/Provincial Tax Rate On Dividends Received	56.25
Less: Dividend Tax Credit [(2/3 + 1/3)(25%)]	(25.00)
Effective Personal Tax Rate On Dividends Received	31.25

16-13.   In the examples which follow, we will round this rate to 31 percent of dividends received. Again referring to the table in Paragraph 13-27, this rate is almost exactly the average rate applicable to dividend income in the various provinces. Once again, however, it is above the middle of the range which starts at 24.1 percent and extends to 33.8 percent.

Corporate Tax Rates

16-14.   In making the required calculations, we will use the corporate federal rates that apply for the 2001 calendar year. With respect to provincial rates, we have used 7 percent for income eligible for the small business deduction, and 14 percent for other income. These rates are similar to those that apply in Alberta and Ontario. The rates to be used are as follows:

General Part I Tax Rate	38.0%
General Rate Reduction	1.0%
Accelerated Rate Reduction For CCPCs	7.0%
Part I Tax Rate On Investment Income Of A CCPC (ART)	6-2/3%
Federal Tax Abatement	10.0%
Corporate Surtax	4.0%
Federal Manufacturing And Processing Profits Deduction	7.0%
Federal Small Business Deduction	16.0%
Provincial Tax Rates	
Income Eligible For Federal Small Business Deduction	7.0%
Income Not Eligible For Federal Small Business Deduction	14.0%
Refundable Portion of Part I Tax On Investment Income	26-2/3%
Refundable Part IV Tax	33-1/3%

16-15.   Note that the general rate reduction is not applicable to income that benefits from either the small business deduction or the M&P deduction. In addition, in the case of a CCPC, it is not applicable to aggregate investment income (taxable capital gains and property income). In addition, as the accelerated rate reduction for CCPCs is only applicable to active business income amounts between $200,000 and $300,000, our general example cannot be used to illustrate this rate. However, we will give consideration to the corporate rates which result when this reduction is applicable.

16-16.   We will apply this basic information in a number of different situations in order to examine the question of whether the incorporation of $100,000 in income will serve to either reduce or defer taxes for an individual taxpayer.

Reduction and Deferral of Taxes
Public Corporation

16-17.   With only $100,000 of income, it is not likely that Mr. Renaud would be in a position to establish a public company. However, this case does serve to illustrate a simple calculation of corporate taxes. In addition, this same tax calculation would apply to a Canadian controlled private corporation on amounts of income in excess of $300,000 (the $200,000 annual business limit, plus the additional $100,000 which benefits from the 7 percent accelerated rate reduction).

16-18.   The corporate taxes that would be paid on $100,000 in Taxable Income would depend on whether the company was eligible for the manufacturing and processing profits deduction. The results for both an eligible and ineligible company are as follows:

Public Corporation	M&P Eligible	Ineligible
Federal Tax At 38%	$38,000	$38,000
General Rate Reduction At 1%	N/A	(1,000)
Federal Tax Abatement At 10%	(10,000)	(10,000)
Corporate Surtax [(4%)(28%)]	1,120	1,120
Manufacturing and Processing Profits Deduction	(7,000)	N/A
Federal Tax Payable	$22,120	$28,120
Provincial Tax At 14%	14,000	14,000
Corporate Taxes Payable	$36,120	$42,120
Corporate Business Income	$100,000	$100,000
Corporate Taxes Payable	(36,120)	(42,120)
Maximum Dividend Payable	$ 63,880	$ 57,880
Individual Tax On Dividends At 31%	(19,803)	(17,943)
Income Retained By The Individual	$ 44,077	$ 39,937
After Tax Flow Through With Corporation	$ 44,077	$ 39,937
After Tax Flow Through Without Corporation	(55,000)	(55,000)
Advantage (Disadvantage) With Corporation	($ 10,923)	($ 15,063)

16-19.   If the $100,000 had been received directly, $55,000 [($100,000)(1 - .45)] would be retained, an amount significantly greater than the after tax retention that occurs when the $100,000 is flowed through a corporation. Clearly, in terms of total taxes paid, Mr. Renaud has not done as well with the use of a corporation. In evaluating this outcome, it should be noted that the combined rate on the M&P income would be reduced in those provinces which extend a more favourable provincial rate to this type of income. For example, Newfoundland and Saskatchewan apply the small business rate to this type of income.

16-20.   However, there is a deferral of tax on income that is left within the corporation. The corporate taxes for the two cases are $36,120 and $42,120, as compared with $45,000 in personal taxes that would be paid if the income were received directly. While it is unlikely that the modest deferral that occurs when there is no M&P deduction would be sufficient to offset the significantly higher tax cost that occurs on the flow through of income, the more generous deferral that is available when the M&P deduction is present may make incorporation attractive in those cases where income can be left in the corporation. Also note that, when the full 7 percent general rate reduction is phased in, the ineligible income will be taxed at the same rates as the M&P income.

16-21.   As we indicated at the beginning of this example, it is unlikely that Mr. Renaud would be able to form a public company on the basis of $100,000 in income. However, the analysis for those Canadian controlled private companies (CCPCs) that regularly earn more than $300,000 would be identical to the preceding results for an ineligible company. For an individual who owns a company that regularly earns more than this amount, continuing to channel income through the corporation in excess of that limit will result in a higher level of taxes payable than if the income were received directly.

16-22.   If the owner of the CCPC is in a position to leave significant amounts of earnings in the corporation, this may not be a problem. The deferral of tax at the corporate level may justify paying higher total taxes when the income is removed from the corporation. In addition, if the corporation is being used for income splitting purposes, the preceding analysis of the total taxation on flow through results may not be appropriate. That is, if the income is being directed from the corporation to a related individual in a lower tax bracket, the overall tax burden will be less than that calculated in Paragraph 16-18.

Active Business Income - Canadian Controlled Private Corporation

16-23.   In previous years, this situation was less complex in that a special rate was applicable to the first $200,000 of active business income, with amounts in excess of this limit taxed at regular corporate rates. As of 2001, the $200,000 annual business limit remains in place. However, the introduction of the 7 percent general tax reduction was accelerated for an addition $100,000 of active business income earned by a CCPC. This creates, at least until 2004 when the 7 percent rate reduction is fully phased in for all corporations, a different rate for amounts of active business income between $200,000 and $300,000 when it is earned by a CCPC. Adding further complexity is the fact that, at the time this book is being written, some provinces extend their small business or other special rate to this additional $100,000 (e.g., Prince Edward Island), while others do not (e.g., Manitoba).

16-24.   To deal with this complexity, we will first examine corporate rates using our basic example involving Mr. Renaud's $100,000 in income. This will be followed by a similar presentation based on the assumption that we are dealing with an additional $100,000 over the $200,000 annual business limit. We will look at this case both in situations where the provincial small business rate is available and for situations where this rate is not extended beyond the usual $200,000 limit.

16-25.   Assuming that Mr. Renaud's $100,000 is the only amount earned by a CCPC results in the amounts shown in the following table. We have included, for comparative purposes, the results for $100,000 of active business income that is not eligible for the small business deduction or the accelerated rate reduction (these are the same as the results for a public company that is ineligible for the M&P deduction). These results would be applicable to active business income of a CCPC in excess of its enhanced annual business limit ($300,000, or less if shared between associated corporations).

Active Business Income Of CCPC	Eligible For SBD	Ineligible For SBD
Federal Tax At 38%	$ 38,000	$ 38,000
General Rate Reduction At 1%	N/A	(1,000)
Federal Tax Abatement At 10%	(10,000)	(10,000)
Corporate Surtax [(4%)(28%)]	1,120	1,120
Small Business Deduction At 16%	(16,000)	N/A
Federal Tax Payable	$ 13,120	$ 28,120
Provincial Tax:		
At 7%	7,000	N/A
At 14%	N/A	14,000
Corporate Taxes Payable	$ 20,120	$ 42,120

Active Business Income Of CCPC	Eligible For SBD	Ineligible For SBD
Corporate Business Income	$100,000	$100,000
Corporate Taxes Payable	(20,120)	(42,120)
Maximum Dividend Payable	$ 79,880	$ 57,880
Individual Tax On Dividends At 31%	(24,763)	(17,943)
Income Retained By The Individual	$ 55,117	$ 39,937

16-26.   Again assuming a combined federal/provincial tax rate of 45 percent on income received directly, after tax retention on $100,000 of direct receipt income would be $55,000. A comparison of the corporate flow through and direct receipt results for a Canadian controlled private corporation is as follows:

Active Business Income Of CCPC	Eligible For SBD	Ineligible For SBD
After Tax Flow Through With Corporation	$ 55,117	$ 39,937
After Tax Flow Through Without Corporation	(55,000)	(55,000)
Advantage (Disadvantage) With Corporation	$ 117	($ 15,063)

16-27.   The first point to be made in this situation is that the use of a corporation provides tax deferral, whether or not the income is eligible for the small business deduction. On eligible income, the tax that is assessed at the corporate level is $20,120, well below the $45,000 that would be applicable if Mr. Renaud had received the income directly. Even on the more heavily taxed ineligible income, the corporate taxes of $42,120 are still below the $45,000 that would be applicable on direct receipt of the $100,000.

16-28.   While this situation does offer excellent opportunities for tax deferral, one point is sometimes overlooked. Any income that is left in the corporation should not be left idle. If it is not needed in the principal activities, it is likely that it will be invested in assets that will produce investment income. If this income is not eligible for the small business deduction, the amount of deferral at the corporate level is significantly smaller. This will be illustrated in the next section when we look at the taxation of investment income received by a Canadian controlled private corporation.

16-29.   If the income is eligible for the small business deduction, there is a some amount of aggregate tax reduction on the corporate flow through. As shown in Paragraph 16-26, after tax retention of $100,000 flowed through a corporation is $55,117, $117 more than the amount that would be retained without the use of a corporation. On $100,000 of income, this small savings would be unlikely to cover the costs associated with maintaining a corporation.

16-30.   In the table which follows, we do an alternative analysis, based on the assumption that Mr. Renaud's $100,000 is in addition to the $200,000 amount that is eligible for the small business deduction. To reflect the diversity in provincial practices in this area, we have prepared results using both the provincial small business rate of 7 percent, along with alternative results based on using the regular provincial rate of 14 percent. Note that these are marginal calculations applicable to the active business income of a CCPC that is between $200,000 and $300,000. Overall comparisons, based on the full amount of $300,000 would require additional calculations. However, for tax planning decisions, the marginal comparisons will be more useful.

Active Business Income Of CCPC Amounts Between $200,000 And $300,000	Eligible With 7% Rate	Eligible With 14% Rate
Federal Tax At 38%	$ 38,000	$ 38,000
General Rate Reduction At 1%	N/A	N/A
Accelerated Rate Reduction At 7%	(7,000)	(7,000)
Federal Tax Abatement At 10%	(10,000)	(10,000)
Corporate Surtax [(4%)(28%)]	1,120	1,120
Small Business Deduction At 16%	N/A	N/A
Federal Tax Payable	$ 22,120	$ 22,120
Provincial Tax:		
At 7%	7,000	N/A
At 14%	N/A	14,000
Corporate Taxes Payable	$ 29,120	$ 36,120
Corporate Business Income	$100,000	$100,000
Corporate Taxes Payable	(29,120)	(36,120)
Maximum Dividend Payable	$ 70,880	$ 63,880
Individual Tax On Dividends At 31%	(21,973)	(19,803)
Income Retained By The Individual	$ 48,907	$ 44,077
After Tax Flow Through With Corporation	$ 48,907	$ 44,077
After Tax Flow Through Without Corporation	(55,000)	(55,000)
Advantage (Disadvantage) With Corporation	($ 6,093)	($ 10,923)

16-31.　While it provides better after tax cash retention than would be the case if it were not available, it is clear that the accelerated rate reduction available to CCPCs does not result in an overall tax savings when compared to direct receipt of income without the use of a corporation. Even in the case where the province extends the small business rate to this extra $100,000 of income, the tax disadvantage exceeds $6,000.

16-32.　The accelerated rate reduction does, however, provide for improved deferral. You will recall that when corporate income is taxed at full rates, corporate taxes on $100,000 of income amounted to $42,120 (see Paragraph 16-25), very close to the $45,000 in taxes that would be paid on direct receipt of income. In contrast, the taxes on the income which benefits from the accelerated rate reduction are $29,120 when the province extends the small business rate to cover this income and $36,120 when it is taxed at full provincial rates.

Active Business Income - Bonusing Down

16-33.　For many years it has been traditional tax planning advice that owners of CCPCs should "bonus down". That is, when the income of the corporation exceeded $200,000, owner-managers were advised to pay sufficient salary to reduce income to that level. This first $200,000 of income was taxed in a manner that resulted in after tax retention that was generally higher than was the case with the direct receipt of income. In our basic example (Paragraph 16-25), after tax retention was $55,117 as compared to $55,000 on direct receipt of income. Further, there was significant tax deferral associated with any income that could be left in the corporation. Alternatively, if Taxable Income was allowed to exceed $200,000, not only would the after tax retention on flow through of the income be lower ($39,957 vs. $55,000), there would be no significant tax deferral of income retained within the corporation ($42,120 in corporate taxes vs. $45,000 in personal taxes on direct receipt of income). As a consequence, it invariably made sense to pay an amount of salary that would reduce the CCPC's Taxable Income to $200,000.

16-34.　The introduction of the accelerated rate reduction for an additional $100,000 of CCPC active business income has significantly muddied these tax planning waters. While bonusing down to $200,000 leaves only that income that is clearly taxed in a desirable manner, providing the owner-manager with both a tax deferral and tax saving, the question now arises as to whether bonusing down should stop at the $300,000 income level, rather than the $200,000 level. While there is no overall tax savings associated with leaving the extra $100,000 that benefits from the accelerated rate reduction in the corporation, there is significant tax deferral, even when provincial corporate rates are not reduced to correspond with the federal benefit. It then becomes a question of whether the owner-manager is willing to pay the extra taxes that will occur on the flow through of this income, in order to achieve the tax deferral that is available on income left in the corporation. While other factors may be influential, it would appear that the most significant variable in making this decision is the length of time that the income can be left in the corporation.

16-35. As a final point here, we would note that you may find it difficult to persuade owner-managers that bonusing down is a good idea, whether it is to the $200,000 level or the $300,000 level. The problem is that bonusing down involves paying taxes out of the owner-manager's personal funds. It is not uncommon to encounter individuals who, even in situations where there is a clear cut tax advantage to using this procedure, will simply refuse to make the required salary payments.

Investment Income - Canadian Controlled Private Corporation

16-36. Investment income, other than dividends that are deductible in the calculation of corporate taxable income, is taxed at full corporate rates with no small business deduction available. In addition, for a CCPC, there is an additional refundable tax under ITA 123.3 equal to 6-2/3 percent of such investment income. Finally, the investment income of a CCPC is not eligible for the 1 percent general rate reduction as it is ultimately taxed preferentially through the refundable tax procedures.

16-37. To offset this high level of taxation, a dividend refund is available on dividends paid at a rate of $1 for each $3 of dividends paid. Income retained on $100,000 of investment income received by a Canadian controlled private corporation, compared to the direct receipt of investment income, would be as follows:

Investment Income Of CCPC

Federal Tax At 38%	$ 38,000
General Rate Reduction	N/A
Federal Tax Abatement At 10%	(10,000)
Corporate Surtax [(4%)(28%)]	1,120
Tax On Investment Income At 6-2/3 Percent	6,667
Federal Tax Payable	$ 35,787
Provincial Tax At 14%	14,000
Corporate Taxes Payable	$ 49,787
Corporate Investment Income	$100,000
Corporate Taxes Payable	(49,787)
Net Corporate Income Before Dividend Refund	$ 50,213
Maximum Dividend Refund (See Note)	25,107
Maximum Dividend Payable	$ 75,320
Individual Tax On Dividends At 31%	(23,349)
Income Retained By The Individual	$ 51,971
After Tax Flow Through With Corporation	$ 51,971
After Tax Flow Through Without Corporation	(55,000)
Advantage (Disadvantage) With Corporation	($ 3,029)

Note   There was a $26,667 [($100,000)(26-2/3%)] addition to the RDTOH during the year. However, the amount of the refund is the lesser of this balance and one-third of dividends paid. As only $50,213 in after tax income was available for the payment of dividends, the refund is limited to $25,107 [(1/3)($75,320)] or one-half the net income before the dividend refund. In general, the refund will be less than the addition to the RDTOH whenever the combined federal/provincial tax rate exceeds 46-2/3 percent. When the combined rate is below 46-2/3 percent, the addition to the RDTOH will be less than the funds available to pay the dividends.

16-38.   In terms of either tax deferral or tax savings, there does not appear to be any advantage associated with using a Canadian controlled private corporation to receive investment income. Not only is there no deferral, there is a fairly large prepayment of taxes when a corporation is used ($49,787 vs. $45,000). In addition, the total tax bill on the flow through of the income is $3,029 higher using this approach.

Dividend Income - Canadian Controlled Private Corporation

16-39.   The analysis here will depend on whether the dividends received by the corporation are subject to the Part IV refundable tax. For example, if the taxable dividends are received from portfolio investments or from a connected company that received a dividend refund as a result of paying the dividend, they are subject to Part IV tax which can only be refunded when the dividends are distributed to shareholders. Alternatively, if they are received from a connected corporation that did not receive a dividend refund on the payment of the dividend, they will not be subject to any corporate taxation and can flow through to the shareholder in the same amounts as if the dividends were received directly. Recalling that Mr. Renaud would pay taxes on dividends at a rate of 31 percent (see Paragraph 16-13), his after tax retention of dividend income received directly would be $69,000 [($100,000)(1 - .31)]. A comparison of this retention with the after tax results using a corporation would be as follows:

Dividend Income Of CCPC	No Part IV Tax	With Part IV Tax
Corporate Dividend Income	$100,000	$100,000
Part IV Taxes Payable At 33-1/3%	N/A	(33,333)
Net Corporate Income Before Dividend Refund	$100,000	$66,667
Dividend Refund ($1/$3)	-0-	33,333
Maximum Dividend Payable	$100,000	$100,000
Individual Tax On Dividends At 31%	(31,000)	(31,000)
Income Retained By Individual	$ 69,000	$ 69,000
After Tax Flow Through With Corporation	$ 69,000	$ 69,000
After Tax Flow Through Without Corporation	(69,000)	(69,000)
Advantage (Disadvantage) With Corporation	$ -0-	$ -0-

16-40.   In both cases, the dividend that can flow through to the investor is the full $100,000. Thus, the total taxes payable on dividends are the same whether the investment is held personally or in a corporation. Note that this conclusion only applies to dividends received from taxable Canadian corporations. Foreign source dividends are included in taxable income in a similar manner to interest income, but foreign taxes paid can be claimed as a tax credit.

16-41.   The Part IV tax does, however, influence the conclusions on tax deferral. If the dividends are subject to Part IV tax, this 33-1/3 percent tax is slightly higher than the 31 percent tax the individual taxpayer would pay if the dividends were received directly. Thus, there is no deferral available through incorporating to earn dividend income that is subject to a Part IV tax. The situation is different in the absence of a Part IV tax in that no taxes will be assessed on dividends received at the corporate level. This, of course, provides for a significant deferral of taxes payable on dividends not subject to Part IV tax.

Conclusions On Tax Reduction And Deferrals

16-42. The preceding cases illustrate the effects of incorporating to earn various types of income on both the deferral of taxes payable and the reduction of total taxes paid. In the case of dividend income, there is no difference in the after tax retention if the dividends are received directly or flowed through a corporation (See Paragraph 16-39). The other results, along with the relevant Paragraph references, are as follows:

After Tax Retention If $100,000 Received As Non Dividend Income	$55,000
Public Corporation:	
With Manufacturing And Processing (Paragraph 16-18)	$44,077
Without Manufacturing And Processing (Paragraph 16-18)	39,937
Canadian Controlled Private Corporation:	
Active Business Income Eligible For SBD (Paragraph 16-25)	$55,117
Active Business Income Not Eligible For SBD (Paragraph 16-25)	39,937
Active Business Income Eligible For Accelerated Rate Reduction	
7 Percent Provincial Rate (Paragraph 16-30)	$48,907
14 Percent Provincial Rate (Paragraph 16-30)	44,077
Investment Income (Paragraph 16-36)	51,971

16-43. The conclusions reached can be summarized as follows:

Tax Reduction Available In the case of a Canadian controlled private corporation earning income that is eligible for the small business deduction, there is a small reduction in overall taxes paid ($117 on $100,000 in income). In all other cases, total taxes are either the same (dividend income of a CCPC) or higher (all income earned by a public company). In some cases, the difference in taxes is very significant (e.g., income that is not eligible for the small business deduction or M&P deduction would incur over $15,000 in additional taxes).

Tax Deferral Available Incorporating to earn business income produces some degree of tax deferral in the following cases:

- A public company, with the deferral being greater for those companies that qualify for the manufacturing and processing profits deduction.

- A Canadian controlled private corporation earning active business income or dividend income that is not subject to Part IV tax. With respect to active business income, the deferral is greatest on the first $200,000 of such income when it is eligible for the small business deduction ($24,880 on $100,000 of income). A smaller, but still significant deferral, is available on the next $100,000 of such income as it benefits from the 7 percent accelerated rate reduction ($15,880 or $8,880, depending on whether the provincial rate is 14 percent or 7 percent). Once the CCPC's active business income exceeds $300,000, a small deferral is still available ($2,880 on $100,000 of income).

  There is also deferral in the case of dividend income when it is not subject to Part IV tax. However, for dividends to not be subject to Part IV tax, they must be received from a connected corporation that did not receive a dividend refund on their payment. This would generally involve payment from a Canadian controlled private corporation earning business income. This means that deferral would have been available at the level of the paying corporation, without the use of an additional corporation to receive the dividends.

16-44. These conclusions are based on assumed provincial personal and corporate tax rates as outlined previously. These assumptions have a great deal of general applicability as the tax rates used are close to the average rates that apply in the various provinces. However, exceptions to these conclusions can be important and some attention will be given to other possibilities in the next Section of this Chapter.

Using Imperfections In The Integration System

Effect Of Provincial Taxes

16-45.   As the preceding cases illustrate, the current tax rate structure along with the various provisions to integrate personal and corporate rates, have served to limit the ability to use a corporation to reduce overall levels of taxation. However, imperfections exist in the integration system and, in particular situations, they may make the use of a corporation more effective in maximizing after tax income.

16-46.   Opportunities to reduce taxes exist because of variations in provincial tax rates on individuals (for 2001, maximum rates applied to Taxes Payable range from Alberta's 10 percent to Quebec's 25 percent, not including the surtaxes that are applicable in some provinces) or in provincial tax rates on corporations (for 2001, rates range from 5 percent on income eligible for the small business deduction to 17 percent on general corporation income). In the examples in the preceding Section, we used combined federal/provincial rates based on specific provincial rates. Both at the corporate and personal levels, provincial variations in rates, tax holidays, and the presence of provincial surtaxes can modify the results that were based on the assumed rates.

Different Provincial Rates For Individuals

16-47.   In the top bracket, combined federal/provincial tax rates on ordinary income range from a low of 39 percent (20 percent federal, plus 10 percent provincial) to a high of 49 percent (29 percent federal, plus 25 percent provincial). In terms of tax deferral, a high provincial rate on individual income clearly favours the use of a corporation. Given a CCPC with taxable income of $100,000 and subject to a tax rate of 20 percent, use of a corporation in the 25 percent province defers $29,000 in tax payable, while the corresponding deferral in the 10 percent province is only $19,000 in tax payable.

16-48.   With respect to tax savings through the use of a corporation, it is not the basic provincial rate on individuals that makes the difference. Given a CCPC with taxable income of $100,000 and paying $20,000 combined federal/provincial taxes, a total of $80,000 in dividend could be paid. If the provincial dividend tax credit is equal to one-third of the gross up, the combined federal/provincial dividend tax credit is equal to the gross up (2/3 + 1/3). Under these circumstances, it would make no difference, in terms of the comparative after tax retention, whether the income was earned in the 10 percent province or the 25 percent province — the overall tax burden would be the same with or without a corporation.

16-49.   The factor that makes the difference is the provincial dividend tax credit. If it is greater than one-third of the gross up, the after tax flow through using a corporation will be higher. Alternatively, if is less than one-third of the gross up, the after tax retention will be lower with the use of a corporation. Continuing with our CCPC with $100,000 of taxable income, $20,000 in corporate taxes, and paying dividends of $80,000, assume that these dividends are received by an individual subject to a combined federal/provincial tax rate of 45 percent. Using various provincial dividend tax credit rates, the total personal and corporate taxes on the $80,000 income stream would be as follows:

	Provincial Dividend Tax Credit		
	20% Of Gross Up	1/3 Of Gross Up	40% Of Gross Up
Dividends Received	$ 80,000	$ 80,000	$ 80,000
Gross Up	20,000	20,000	20,000
Taxable Dividends	$100,000	$100,000	$100,000
Personal Tax Rate	45%	45%	45%
Taxes Before Dividend Tax Credit	$ 45,000	$ 45,000	$ 45,000
Dividend Tax Credit [(2/3 + Provincial)(Gross Up)]	(17,333)	(20,000)	(21,333)
Total Personal Taxes	$ 27,667	$ 25,000	$ 23,667

16-50. This results in the following after tax retention in the cases under consideration:

	Provincial Dividend Tax Credit		
	20% Of Gross Up	1/3 Of Gross Up	40% Of Gross Up
Corporate Income	$100,000	$100,000	$100,000
Personal Taxes	(27,667)	(25,000)	(23,667)
Corporate Taxes	(20,000)	(20,000)	(20,000)
After Tax Retention	$ 52,333	$ 55,000	$56,333

16-51. If the $100,000 in income had been received directly, the individual in our example would have paid taxes of $45,000 and retained $55,000. This is identical to the amount retained when the provincial dividend tax credit is equal to one-third of the gross up. When the provincial credit is less than one-third of the gross up there is under integration and when the credit exceeds one-third of the gross up, there is over integration. After tax results would follow this pattern, without regard to the provincial tax rate on the individual.

Different Provincial Rates For Corporations

16-52. All other things being equal, residing in a province with higher tax rates on corporate income will make incorporation less attractive. The higher taxes reduce the amount of deferral available, as well as the amount of after tax flow through. In contrast, the availability of lower rates will make channeling income through a corporation more attractive.

16-53. Using our basic example, we will return to the assumption that the province has a 16 percent rate of tax on personal Taxable Income, resulting in a combined federal/provincial rate of 31 percent on dividend income and 45 percent on other types of income. However, we will assume that the $100,000 in corporate income is eligible for the small business deduction and that the province has a tax holiday (zero tax rate) for this type of business. The following table compares the after tax flow through for this Canadian controlled private corporation with the after tax flow through for the same corporation when the provincial rate is 10 percent. These amounts are then compared with the after tax retention on $100,000 of income by an individual subject to a combined federal/provincial rate of 45 percent.

	Corporate Provincial Tax Rate	
	10%	0%
Federal Tax At 38%	$ 38,000	$ 38,000
General Rate Reduction	N/A	N/A
Federal Tax Abatement At 10%	(10,000)	(10,000)
Corporate Surtax [(4%)(28%)]	1,120	1,120
Small Business Deduction At 16%	(16,000)	(16,000)
Federal Tax Payable	$ 13,120	$ 13,120
Provincial Tax At 10% And Nil	10,000	-0-
Corporate Taxes Payable	$ 23,120	$ 13,120
Corporate Business Income	$100,000	$100,000
Corporate Taxes Payable	(23,120)	(13,120)
Maximum Dividend Payable	$ 76,880	$ 86,880
Individual Tax On Dividends At 31%	(23,833)	(26,933)
Income Retained By The Individual	$ 53,047	$ 59,947
After Tax Flow Through With Corporation	$ 53,047	$ 59,947
After Tax Retention Without Corporation	(55,000)	(55,000)
Advantage (Disadvantage) With Corporation	($ 1,953)	$ 4,947

16-54.   The corporate taxes payable at either rate are well below the $45,000 that would be paid if the $100,000 in income were received directly. This means that there is significant tax deferral on income that can be retained in the corporation. With respect to tax savings, the results are mixed. You may recall that when we used a 7 percent provincial rate in our original example, the result was a tax savings of $117 (see Paragraph 16-25). When we increase the provincial rate on corporations to 10 percent, this small tax savings becomes a fairly significant tax cost. However, when we reduce the provincial corporate rate to nil, the $117 savings increases to nearly $5,000. The general principle here is that higher provincial rates on corporations make the use of corporations less attractive, while lower rates make using this form of business organization more attractive.

Exercises Sixteen-1 to Sixteen-4 deal with after tax retention when a corporation is used. This would be an appropriate time to attempt these exercises.

Income Splitting

16-55.   The preceding examples have served to make it fairly clear that current legislation places limits on the ability of an individual to achieve tax reduction or deferral through the use of a corporation. However, the tax savings related to income splitting continue to make incorporation a desirable alternative when an individual has a spouse or children whose incomes place them in a lower tax bracket. While the "tax on split income" (see Paragraph 13-11) has made this goal more difficult to achieve when children are under 18 years of age, there are no significant limits on the ability to share income with adult family members. The use of a corporation is often a key element in such plans.

16-56.   While there are a variety of ways a corporation could be used to accomplish income splitting, at this stage we will use a simple illustration involving the establishment of a holding company. The data for this example is as follows:

> **Example**   Mrs. Breck has an investment portfolio with a fair market value of $1,000,000. Because of Mrs. Breck's great skill in assessing stock market trends, her annual return on this portfolio has averaged 25 percent per year before taxes. All of this return has been in the form of capital gains. In addition to her investment income, Mrs. Breck has employment income sufficient to place her in a combined federal/provincial tax bracket of 48 percent. Mrs. Breck has five children over 17 years of age, none of whom have any income of their own. Although she wishes all of her children to have an equal share in the income from her investments, Mrs. Breck wants to retain control over the management of these funds.

16-57.   Mrs. Breck's wishes can be accomplished through the use of an investment company, established with two classes of shares. The preferred shares will have the right to vote and 10 of these shares will be issued to Mrs. Breck at a price of $1 per share. The common shares will not have voting rights and 20 of these shares will be issued to and will be paid for by each of her five children at a price of $10 per share. The initial capital structure of the company would be as follows:

10 Voting Preferred Shares	$ 10
100 Non Voting Common Shares	1,000
Total Equities	$1,010

16-58.   At this point, Mrs. Breck's $1,000,000 in interest bearing investments would be transferred to the corporation in return for long term debt which pays interest at a rate of 7 percent. Assuming this is the prescribed rate at the time of the transfer, there will be no corporate income attributed back to Mrs. Breck. If there are accrued but unrealized gains on any of Mrs. Breck's investments, they can be transferred to the corporation on a tax free basis using the provisions of ITA 85(1). This procedure is discussed in Chapter 17.

16-59.   The resulting initial Balance Sheet of this Canadian controlled private company would be as follows:

Assets

Cash	$ 1,010
Investments	1,000,000
Total Assets	**$1,001,010**

Equities

Long Term Debt	$1,000,000
Preferred Stock	10
Common Stock	1,000
Total Equities	**$1,001,010**

16-60.   All of the income of this Canadian controlled private corporation will be investment income and, as a result, a dividend refund will be available when dividends are paid. Continuing to use the corporate rates that were presented in Paragraph 16-13, we will base our analysis of the situation on a combined federal/provincial corporate rate of 49.8 percent. This includes the 6-2/3 percent ITA 123.3 tax on the investment income of a Canadian controlled private company. Assuming Mrs. Breck's investments earn $250,000 in capital gains (a 25 percent rate of return on the $1,000,000 of investments) during the corporation's first year, corporate taxes and maximum dividend payable are calculated as follows:

Taxable Capital Gains [(1/2)($250,000)]	$125,000
Interest On Debt [(7%)($1,000,000)]	(70,000)
Taxable Income	$ 55,000
Corporate Taxes Payable At 49.8%	(27,390)
Income Before Dividends	$ 27,610
Dividend Refund ($1/$3)	13,805
Maximum Taxable Dividend Payable	$ 41,415
Capital Dividend [(1/2)($250,000)]	125,000
Total Dividends	$166,415

16-61.   Based on the preceding calculations, each of the five children would receive a total of $31,225, $25,000 ($125,000 ÷ 5) in the form of a tax free capital dividend and $8,283 ($41,415 ÷ 5) in the form of a taxable dividend. However, as these children have no other source of income, they could receive this amount of dividends on a tax free basis in the current taxation year (the amount of dividends that can be received on a tax free basis is discussed in detail in a subsequent section of this Chapter).

16-62.   As a consequence, the only taxes that would be paid on the $250,000 of investment income would be at the corporate level, plus the personal taxes that Mrs. Breck would pay on the interest received from the corporation. A comparison of taxes payable with and without the investment company would show the following:

Tax If Income Directly Received By Mrs. Breck [(45%)(1/2)($250,000)]	$56,250
Net Taxes Paid By The Company ($27,390 - $13,805)	(13,585)
Taxes Paid By Mrs. Breck On Interest [(45%)($70,000)]	(31,500)
Tax Savings	$11,165

16-63.   This example makes a basic point clear — incorporation can significantly reduce taxes payable when it is used to split income among family members in lower tax brackets, particularly when those family members have little or no other source of income and can receive dividends on a tax free basis. Of importance is the fact that the savings illustrated in the preceding example is not a one shot improvement in Mrs. Breck's tax position. These savings will continue to be available in subsequent years, as long as the conditions which produced it remain unchanged.

Other Advantages And Disadvantages Of Incorporation

16-64.   The basic tax features associated with the incorporation of business or investment income have been covered in the preceding sections on tax reduction, tax deferral, and income splitting. Other possible advantages of incorporation include:

Limited Liability   Because a corporation is a separate legal entity, the shareholders' liabilities to creditors are limited to the amount that they have invested. That is, creditors of the corporation can look only to the assets of the corporation for satisfaction of their claims. However, for smaller corporations, obtaining significant amounts of financing will almost always require the owners to provide personal guarantees on any loans, making this advantage somewhat illusory for this type of company. Note, however, limited liability may still be important for a business that is exposed to significant product or environmental claims.

Lifetime Capital Gains Deduction   Individuals who dispose of the shares or debt of a qualified small business corporation are eligible to claim the $500,000 lifetime capital gains deduction. To qualify, a business must be a Canadian controlled private corporation with substantially all of the fair market value of its assets (at least 90 percent) used in an active business carried on primarily in Canada (at least 50 percent) at the time of disposal. In addition, no one other than the seller can own the shares or debt during the 24 months preceding the sale. During this 24 month period, more than 50 percent of the fair market value of the assets must have been used in active business primarily in Canada. For a more complete discussion of this provision, see Chapter 12.

Foreign Taxes   Foreign estate taxes can often be avoided by placing foreign property in a Canadian corporation.

Estate Planning   A corporation can be used in estate planning, particularly with respect to freezing the asset values of an estate.

16-65.   Disadvantages associated with incorporation include the following:

Loss Deductions   An individual can deduct business and farm losses against any other source of income, including employment and property income. If the business or farm is incorporated, such losses can only be deducted against past or future corporate income. The corporation's losses cannot be used to offset an individual's other sources of income. This is of particular importance to operations that are just getting started as they will frequently experience significant losses in their formative years.

Tax Credits   A corporation is not eligible for personal tax credits, such as the basic personal, tuition fee, education, age, pension and disability tax credits.

Charitable Donations   Charitable donations provide the basis for a tax credit for individuals, largely at the maximum 29 percent federal rate. In contrast, they are a deduction in calculating taxable income for a corporation. If the corporate tax rate is low, they will be of less value to a corporation than they would be to an individual.

Extra Taxation   As illustrated in the examples in this Chapter, incorporation can result in extra taxation.

Additional Maintenance Costs   The legal, accounting, and other costs associated with maintaining a business operation will be significantly higher in the case of a corporation (e.g., the cost of filing a corporate tax return on an annual basis).

Winding Up Procedures   The complications associated with the termination of an incorporated business will be greater than would usually be the case with a proprietorship or partnership. In addition, there may be adverse tax effects on winding up.

16-66.   While there may be other factors that are relevant in particular circumstances, the preceding material has dealt with the principal considerations that enter into a decision about whether income should be incorporated.

Management Compensation
General Principles
16-67. The most obvious and straightforward way to compensate managers is to pay salaries. Provided they are reasonable, the amounts are a deductible expense to the corporation. At the same time, they are fully taxable to the recipient, rendering such payments neutral in terms of tax planning. For large publicly traded corporations, where the managers are not the principal owners of the business, salary is the usual starting point in negotiating management compensation. However, we recognize that, for high income executives, stock options may be of greater importance than salary.

16-68. Even with a public corporation, however, the tax effects of various methods of compensation should not be ignored. By paying salaries, a corporation receives a deduction from taxable income in the year of accrual, while the recipient employee receives an equal addition to taxable income in the year of payment. Any form of compensation that creates an excess of the corporation's deductions over the employee's inclusions or, that delays the inclusion of the same amount in the income of the employee, can produce overall tax savings. This, in turn, can allow for some combination of improved after tax benefits to the employee or lower after tax cost to the corporation. In large corporations, these trade-offs provide the basis for management compensation policies.

16-69. Some simple examples of compensation features that can be used to defer or reduce the payment of taxes are as follows:

- **Registered Pension Plans** Within prescribed limits, a corporation can deduct contributions to registered pension plans in the year of contribution. These contributions will not become taxable to the employee until they are received as a pension benefit, resulting in an effective tax deferral arrangement.

- **Deferred Profit Sharing Plans** In a fashion similar to registered pension plans, amounts that are currently deductible to the corporation are deferred with respect to inclusion in the employee's taxable income.

- **Provision Of Private Health Care Plans** The premiums paid by the corporation for such benefits as dental plans can be deducted in full by the corporation and will not be considered a taxable benefit to the employee.

- **Stock Options** Stock options provide employees with an incentive to improve the performance of the enterprise. In addition, taxation of any benefits resulting from the options is deferred until they are exercised or sold (for a full discussion of the deferral of stock options benefits, see Chapter 12). Note, however, the corporation does not receive a deduction on issuing stock options.

Exercises Sixteen-5 and Sixteen-6 deal with shareholder loans. This would be an appropriate time to attempt these exercises.

16-70. Changes in tax legislation over the years have served to restrict the tax benefits associated with employee compensation. Perhaps most importantly, the current rules related to taxable benefits on employer provided automobiles are very unfavourable, in most cases eliminating the benefits of this type of arrangement. The rules related to employee and shareholder benefits have been covered in Chapters 5 (employee fringe benefits), 6 (deferred compensation), 11 (shareholder loans) and 12 (stock options).

Salary Vs. Dividends
16-71. For large public corporations, there is little point in considering the tax benefits related to salary/dividend trade-offs. The dividend policy of public corporations is normally based on considerations that extend well beyond the compensation that is provided to the management group of the company.

16-72. In situations where the manager of the business is also an owner, such an individual is in a position to receive compensation in the form of either salary or dividends. If other owners are not involved, the choice is completely at the discretion of the owner and tax factors will generally be an important consideration in making this decision. The choice between compensation in the form of salary and compensation in the form of dividends — the salary vs. dividend decision, will be considered in the next Section of this Chapter.

Salary Vs. Dividends For The Owner - Manager

Tax Free Dividends

16-73.   Since income earned by a corporation is subject to taxation at the corporate level, the application of full rates of taxation to its distribution in the form of dividends would result in a very high level of taxation. Given this potential problem, the receipt of dividends is subject to a gross up and tax credit procedure that results in a reduced level of taxation on dividend income. For an individual in the 29 percent federal tax bracket, subject to a 16 percent provincial tax rate on Taxable Income, and living in a province where the dividend tax credit is equal to one-third of the gross up, the combined federal/provincial rate on dividends is 31.25 percent [(29% + 16%)(1.25) - (2/3 + 1/3)(25%)] on dividends received. This rate is well above the 22.5 percent rate [(29% + 16%)(1/2)] that is applicable to capital gains, but well below the maximum 45 percent rate (29% + 16%) that would be applicable to most other types of income.

16-74.   In addition to the fact that dividends are taxed at favourable rates, the structure of the dividend tax credit system is such that a substantial amount of dividends can be received without incurring any taxation.

16-75.   For 2001, every individual has a personal credit against taxes payable based on $7,412. As the actual basic personal tax credit is based on $7,412 multiplied by the 16 percent rate applicable to the lowest federal tax bracket, it means that the first $7,412 of an individual's income can be received tax free. Extending this analysis, it can be said that, for most types of income, the amount that can be received tax free is limited to the total amount of tax credits available to the individual. That is, for every dollar of tax credit amount, one dollar of income can be received on a tax free basis. There are two exceptions to this:

> **Charitable Contributions**   The tax credit here on amounts over $200 is based on 29 percent, rather than the 16 percent applicable to other credit amounts. This means that a dollar of charitable contributions in excess of $200 will allow the individual to receive $1.81 in tax free income.

> **Dividends**   An individual with only the basic personal credit of $1,186 can receive tax free dividends of nearly four times the $7,412 base for this credit. More specifically, such an individual can receive $27,980 in dividends without incurring any liability for federal taxes (calculations in Paragraph 16-79). Note that, depending on the manner in which the provincial dividend tax credit is determined, this amount may or may not be free of provincial taxes.

16-76.   Why does this situation exist with respect to the tax free receipt of dividends? The answer lies in the dividend gross up/tax credit mechanism. For each dollar of dividends received, the individual must add a gross up of $0.25 to taxable income. For individuals in the lowest federal tax bracket, the federal taxes on this amount will be $0.20 [($1.25)(16%)]. However, there will be a federal credit against these taxes payable equal to two-thirds of the gross up or $0.1667 [(2/3)($0.25)]. This means that, as long as an individual is in the lowest tax bracket, the increase in taxes associated with one dollar of dividends can be calculated as follows:

Increase In Federal Taxes Payable	$.2000
Dividend Tax Credit	(.1667)
Increase In Basic Federal Tax	$.0333

16-77.   As compared to an increase in basic federal tax of $.1600 for each one dollar increase in non dividend income, there is only a $.0333 increase in basic federal tax for each one dollar increase in dividends. This means that dividend income uses up an individual's available tax credits at a much slower rate than other types of income. While one dollar of, for example, employment income, will use up one dollar of an individual's personal tax credit amount of $7,412, one dollar of dividends received will use up only $.2081 of this amount

[($1.00)($.0333 ÷ $.1600)]. This means that, in comparison with other types of income, a much larger amount of dividends can be received before an individual's tax credits are absorbed and taxes will have to be paid.

16-78.   The amount of tax free dividends that can be received by an individual with no other source of income is a function of the total amount of their personal tax credits and can, in fact, become a fairly large amount. You should note however, that even for an individual with only the basic personal credit, the amount of tax free dividends is such that the grossed up amount is more than $30,754, the top of the 16 percent tax bracket. As the amount of dividends received moves into the 22 percent tax bracket, the relationship described in Paragraph 16-77 becomes less favourable and the amount of tax free dividends available for each dollar of tax credits declines.

16-79.   For 2001, ignoring possible tax credits other than the basic personal and spousal, the amount of dividends that can be received free of federal taxes by a single individual, and by an individual with a dependent spouse with no other source of income, is as follows:

	Single Individual	Dependent Spouse
Dividends Received	$27,980	$37,270
Gross Up (25%)	6,995	9,318
Taxable Income	$34,975	$46,588
Federal Tax On First $30,754 At 16%	$4,921	$4,921
Federal Tax On Remainder At 22%	928	3,484
Dividend Tax Credit - 2/3 Of Gross Up	(4,663)	(6,212)
Basic Personal Tax Credit [(16%)($7,412)]	(1,186)	(1,186)
Spousal Tax Credit [(16%)($6,294)]	N/A	(1,007)
Basic Federal Tax Payable	$ -0-	$ -0-

16-80.   In the past, if the dividend tax credit eliminated basic federal tax payable, provincial taxes which were based on this number were also eliminated. Under the new TONI (Tax ON Income) approach to calculating provincial taxes, this will not be the case. It appears that since most provinces base their dividend tax credit either on the gross up or the federal dividend tax credit, this amount may or may not serve to eliminate provincial tax payable.

16-81.   The alternative minimum tax is not a factor in determining the amount of dividends that can be received on a tax free basis. As the dividend tax credit is not available in the calculation of the alternative minimum tax payable, the receipt of dividends can create problems in this area for high income individuals. However, the $40,000 basic exemption that is provided by the alternative minimum tax legislation would serve to eliminate alternative minimum tax on most of the tax free dividends as shown in Paragraph 16-79.

The Basic Tradeoff
Example
16-82.   To illustrate the basic tradeoff that is involved in salary vs. dividend decisions, assume that Ms. Olney owns all of the shares of a corporation which has $100,000 in taxable income, and that she has sufficient property income from other sources to place her in the 45 percent federal/provincial tax bracket (29% federal rate plus 16% provincial rate). If the full $100,000 of corporate income is paid to Ms. Olney in the form of salary, it can be deducted by the corporation and will reduce the corporation's taxable income to nil. This means that no taxes will be paid at the corporate level. However, the $100,000 will be taxed at Ms. Olney's marginal rate of 45 percent. This means that she will pay taxes of $45,000 and be left with after tax funds of $55,000.

16-83.   If no salary is paid to Ms. Olney, corporate taxes will be assessed and any remaining amount, after adjustments for any refundable taxes, will be paid in dividends. This will be subject to personal taxes and the resulting after tax cash flow to the individual taxpayer can be determined. These amounts, which are dependent on the type of corporation and the type of income earned, were calculated earlier in this Chapter. The results of those calculations, along with the relevant Paragraph references, are repeated here for your convenience:

After Tax Retention If $100,000 Received As Salary	$55,000
Public Corporation:	
With Manufacturing And Processing (Paragraph 16-18)	$44,077
Without Manufacturing And Processing (Paragraph 16-18)	39,937
Canadian Controlled Private Corporation:	
Active Business Income Eligible For SBD (Paragraph 16-25)	$55,117
Active Business Income Not Eligible For SBD (Paragraph 16-25)	39,937
Active Business Income Eligible For Accelerated Rate Reduction	
7 Percent Provincial Rate (Paragraph 16-30)	$48,907
14 Percent Provincial Rate (Paragraph 16-30)	44,077
Investment Income (Paragraph 16-36)	51,971

Analysis Of The Example

16-84.   In looking at the question of whether or not to incorporate an income source, we looked at the possibilities for both tax deferral and tax reduction through the use of a corporation. In salary vs. dividend decisions, we are not concerned with deferral. The question here is — "What is the most tax effective way to have a corporation provide its owner-manager with a required amount of after tax income?" There is, of course, no deferral involved on amounts that are to be removed from the corporation.

16-85.   In comparing Ms. Olney's $55,000 retained with the various results listed in Paragraph 16-83, it is very clear that, except in the case of a Canadian controlled private corporation earning active business income of less than $200,000, payment of dividends results in less after tax retention than does the payment of salary. In this case, after tax retention is only higher by $117 ($55,117 vs. $55,000). In all other cases, the use of dividends as opposed to tax deductible salary results in higher levels of taxation.

16-86.   This would suggest that, except for CCPCs with income eligible for the small business deduction, salary should be used. However, the preceding analysis is based on a number of assumptions with respect to provincial tax rates on personal and corporate income. In addition, other factors such as CPP and payroll tax costs have been ignored. These factors will be considered in the next section.

Other Considerations

Provincial Tax Rates

16-87.   The results cited in Paragraph 16-83 assumed a provincial tax rate on individuals of 16 percent, and provincial rates on corporations of 7 and 14 percent respectively for income eligible for the small business deduction and other types of income. While such rates are fairly representative, they are not the only applicable rates. In assessing the importance of these differences, you should recognize that the payment of salaries is analogous to the direct receipt of income. That is, if a corporation has $100,000 in income and pays this entire amount in salaries, there will be no corporate taxes. Further, the taxes paid by the individual on the salary will, in general, be the same as would be paid if he had received the income directly. This means that the comparison of salary payments with dividends involves the same analysis as the comparison of the after tax retention associated with direct receipt of income as opposed to the after tax retention resulting from channeling income through a corporation.

16-88.   Given this, we can discuss the effect of varying provincial rates of tax on the salary vs. dividend decision on the same basis that was used for comparing direct receipt vs. flow through decisions. Direct receipt vs. flow through decisions were considered in Paragraphs 16-45 through 16-54. Applying that analysis to salary vs. dividend decisions, the following statements can be made:

Personal Tax Rates All other things being equal, a higher provincial tax rate on individuals will favour the increased use of dividends as opposed to salaries. Lower rates will favour the use of salaries.

Corporate Tax Rates All other things being equal, higher corporate tax rates make the deductibility of salaries more desirable. Alternatively, lower corporate rates make this deductibility less valuable, making the use of dividends more attractive. For example, if a corporation can take advantage of a provincial tax holiday, dividends clearly become the better alternative in terms of overall levels of taxation.

Income Splitting

16-89. When a corporation is used for income splitting purposes, amounts may be distributed to individuals with no other source of income. As was noted in a previous section of this Chapter, almost $28,000 in dividends can be paid to such an individual without any tax liability being incurred. The fact that this is a much larger amount than can be distributed tax free in any other form clearly favours the use of dividends for distributions of corporate assets in these circumstances.

Earned Income For RRSP and CPP

16-90. One of the most attractive features of the Canadian income tax system is the ability to make contributions to an RRSP. Not only are the contributions deductible at the time that they are made, once inside the plan they enjoy the tremendous benefits associated with tax free compounding over, what may be, a period of many years. Most individuals will want to take advantage of these provisions. Although the Canada Pension Plan (CPP) does not offer the flexibility and control available from RRSPs, it is still considered an important source of retirement income.

16-91. Dividends do not constitute earned income for the purposes of determining the maximum RRSP contributions or CPP pensionable earnings. As a consequence, if the owner-manager has no other source of earned income (e.g., employment income from a source other than his corporation), it will be necessary for the corporation to pay salary so that the individual can make deductible RRSP contributions and CPP contributions.

16-92. Until 2003, the maximum annual RRSP contribution is equal to the lesser of $13,500 and 18 percent of the individual's earned income for the previous year. This means that, if the owner-manager has no other source of earned income in these years, a salary of $75,000 will be required to make the maximum annual RRSP contribution of $13,500. The maximum for CPP pensionable earnings in a year is considerably less than $75,000 ($38,300 for 2001). In order to be eligible for the maximum CPP payments at retirement, salary of at least the maximum pensionable earnings for the year should be paid.

Cumulative Net Investment Loss

16-93. An individual's cumulative net investment loss (CNIL) is the amount by which investment expenses exceed investment income (see Chapter 12 for an explanation of this amount, as well as the general provisions of the lifetime capital gains deduction). An individual's ability to make a deduction under the provisions of the lifetime capital gains deduction is reduced, on a dollar-for-dollar basis by the balance in the CNIL account. This means that, if an individual contemplates selling either a qualified farm property, or shares or debt of a qualified small business corporation, sensible tax planning would suggest the elimination of any CNIL balance.

16-94. For an individual whose income is provided by his owner-managed corporation, dividends can assist with this problem. The receipt of dividends reduces the CNIL on a dollar-for-dollar basis. In contrast, salary payments leave this balance unchanged. Another possibility, if the corporation has an amount owing to the shareholder, is to pay interest to the shareholder on the balance outstanding. This interest would also decrease any CNIL.

Taxes Payable

16-95. In a particular year, an owner-manager may wish to withdraw amounts in excess of the earnings of the corporation. If this happens, there will be no current tax savings associated with the payment of salaries, a fact that would tend to make the payment of such amounts less attractive. However, payment of salaries in this situation would serve to create a loss carry over and, if we assume that the loss carry over can be used in some past or future year, the corporate tax savings associated with the payment of salaries would not be lost. The savings, however, will be deferred in the case of a carry forward and this means that, to properly evaluate the payment of salaries in this situation, consideration would have to be given to the time value of money.

Added Costs Of Salary

16-96. In our example from Paragraph 16-82, we ignored the fact that salaries cannot be paid without contributions being made to the Canada Pension Plan (CPP). In addition, some Provinces levy a payroll tax on salaries and wages. These costs can constitute a significant reduction in the after tax cash flow associated with the payment of salaries. We have not mentioned Employment Insurance premiums in this context because, if the owner-manager owns more than 40 percent of the outstanding shares of the corporation, he cannot participate in this program.

16-97. With respect to CPP contributions, 2001 employee contributions are based on 4.3 percent of $38,300 (maximum pensionable earnings), less a basic exemption of $3,500. This results in a maximum employee contribution for 2001 of $1,496. The employer is required to withhold this contribution and, in addition, is required to make a further contribution in an amount that is equal to the contribution made by the employee. This brings the total CPP cost of paying salaries of $38,300 or more to $2,992.

16-98. While generally not relevant here, an employee's maximum employment insurance premium for 2001 is 2.25 percent of $39,000 (maximum insurable earnings), with no basic exemption. This gives a maximum employee premium of $878. In addition, the employer must contribute 1.4 times this amount or $1,229.

16-99. Depending on the province, payroll taxes can be from one to two percent of salaries and wages paid. For example, the so-called employer health tax in Ontario requires payments equal to 1.95 percent of salaries in excess of $400,000. While the federal government continues to threaten the elimination of deductibility of payroll taxes, at the present time they are still deductible and serve to reduce federal taxes payable.

16-100. Returning to our example of Ms. Olney from Paragraph 16-82, as the owner of 100 percent of the shares of the corporation, she is not eligible to participate in the Employment Insurance program. In addition, the province in which she lives assesses a 2 percent payroll tax to finance its health care program. Her corporation is Canadian controlled and all of its $100,000 in income will be eligible for the small business deduction. Given this income limitation, the maximum salary that could be paid to Ms. Olney would be $96,735, a figure which would result in no corporate taxes payable. This can be seen as follows:

Before Tax Corporate Income	$100,000
Employer's CPP Contribution	(1,496)
Salary [($100,000 - $1,496) ÷ 1.02]	(96,573)
Payroll Tax [(2%)($96,573)]	(1,931)
Corporate Taxable Income	Nil

16-101. If this amount is paid to Ms. Olney as salary, her personal taxes are as follows:

Federal Tax Before Credit [(29% + 16%)($96,573)]	$43,458
CPP Credit [(16%)($1,496)]*	(239)
Total Tax Payable	$43,219

*We have assumed that Ms. Olney has sufficient other property income to place her in the maximum federal tax bracket. This income would absorb other tax credits and, as a consequence, only the new CPP credit that results from the payment of salary is included in this analysis.

16-102.   With this amount of tax payable, Ms. Olney's after tax retention would be calculated as follows:

Salary Received	$96,573
Total Tax Payable	(43,219)
Employee's CPP Contribution	(1,496)
After Tax Cash Retained	$51,858

16-103.   This compares with after tax retention of salary when CPP and payroll taxes are ignored of $55,000 (see Paragraph 16-82). This less favourable but more realistic result makes the use of dividends from business income eligible for the small business deduction an even more desirable choice ($55,117 retained vs. $51,858). Further, when these more realistic assumptions with respect to salary payments are used, salary now provides somewhat less after tax cash than dividends paid out of the investment income of a Canadian controlled private corporation ($51,971 vs. $51,858).

Use Of Tax Credits

16-104.   Our example in this section has involved an individual with other sources of income that placed her in the maximum federal tax bracket. This amount of income would generally be sufficient to absorb any tax credits available to the individual. However, there may be situations where a salary vs. dividend decision is being made with respect to an individual with no other source of income. This would be a fairly common situation when a corporation is being used for income splitting purposes or for a corporation with only a limited amount of income to distribute.

16-105.   If the individual has no other source of income and provincial tax rates favour the use of dividends, there may be a problem with the full use of available tax credits. We noted earlier in this Chapter that dividend payments use up tax credits much more slowly than other types of income such as salary. If only limited amounts of income are being distributed, the use of dividends may leave a portion of the individual's tax credits unused. If this is the case, some combination of salary and dividends may provide the optimum solution. An added complication with the TONI system for provincial tax is that provincial personal and dividend tax credits can only be deducted against the provincial tax liability and federal tax credits can only be deducted against the federal tax liability. In our examples and problems we have not taken this into consideration and give a single figure for combined federal/provincial tax credits. In the real world, it would be possible to have a situation where an individual would have to pay some federal tax in order to use up all their provincial tax credits or vice versa. The following example illustrates the salary vs. dividend issue when the full utilization of tax credits is a consideration.

> **Example**   Mr. Eric Swenson is the sole shareholder of Swenson Sweets, a Canadian controlled private company. The Company has a December 31 year end and, at December 31, 2001, it has taxable income for the year of $29,500, all of which results from active business activities. This amount is available in cash prior to the payment of any salary or dividends. Mr. Swenson has combined federal/provincial personal tax credits of $3,920.
>
> The corporation operates in a province with a corporate tax rate on active business income of 8 percent. The provincial tax rate on personal income is 10 percent of the first $30,754 of Taxable Income, with a provincial dividend tax credit that is equal to one-third of the dividend gross up. In solving this problem, we will ignore CPP and provincial payroll taxes.

16-106.   If the full $29,500 is paid out in salary, there would be no corporate taxes and Mr. Swenson's after tax cash retention would be as follows:

Salary Payment		$29,500
Taxes At 26 Percent (16% + 10%)	$7,670	
Federal/Provincial Tax Credits	(3,920)	(3,750)
After Tax Cash Retained (Salary)		$25,750

16-107.   As dividends are not deductible, corporate taxes must be paid prior to any dividend distribution. The combined federal/provincial tax rate would be 21.12 percent {([38% - 10%][1.04]) - 16% + 8%}. This means that the maximum dividend that can be paid will be $23,270 [($29,500)(1.0000 - .2112)]. The after tax retention in this case is as follows:

Dividends Received	$23,270
Gross Up	5,818
Taxable Dividends	$29,088

Taxes At 26%	$7,563
Personal Tax Credits	(3,920)
Dividend Tax Credit [(2/3 + 1/3)($5,818)]	(5,818)
Taxes Payable*	Nil

*While Taxes Payable cannot be negative, there are $2,175 in unused credits.

Dividends Received	$23,270
Personal Taxes Payable	Nil
After Tax Cash Retained (Dividends)	$23,270

16-108.   While the provincial tax rates (low corporate and high personal rate) suggest that dividends should be the best alternative, the preceding results do not confirm this view. The problem is, as was noted previously, dividend income absorbs available tax credits at a much lower rate than other types of income. The fact that the all dividend solution leaves $2,175 of unused tax credits suggests that a better solution might be to pay a combination of dividends, plus sufficient salary to absorb these unused credits.

16-109.   To investigate this possibility, we need to determine the salary/dividend mix that will just use up all of Mr. Swenson's credits. To begin, consider what would happen when we add a $1,000 salary payment to the all dividends case. As the salary will be fully deductible, the after tax cost of making this payment is $788.80 [($1,000)(1.0000 - .2112)]. As a consequence, in this type of problem where the goal is to distribute all of the available corporate income, dividends will only have to be reduced by this $788.80 per $1,000 of salary increase.

16-110.   The resulting increase in taxes payable can be calculated as follows:

Increase In Salary	$1,000.00
Decrease In Dividends	(788.80)
Decrease In Dividend Gross Up [(25%)($788.80)]	(197.20)
Increase In Taxable Income	$ 14.00

Increase In Tax At 26%	$ 3.64
Decrease In Dividend Tax Credit [(2/3 + 1/3)($197.20)]	197.20
Increase In Personal Tax	$200.84

16-111.   This analysis demonstrates that each $1,000 increase in salary results in an increase in personal taxes payable of $200.84. Alternatively, this can be stated as a $0.20084 increase in taxes for every dollar of increase in salary. This means that to use up Mr. Swenson's $2,175 in unused tax credits, salary will have to be $10,830 ($2,175 ÷ $0.20084). This results in the following amount being available for dividends:

Pre Salary Taxable Income	$29,500
Salary	(10,830)
Corporate Taxable Income	$18,670
Corporate Taxes At 21.12%	(3,943)
Available For Dividends	$14,727

16-112. When this dividend is paid out to Mr. Swenson, his after tax retention can be calculated as follows:

Dividends Received	$14,727
Gross Up	3,682
Taxable Dividends	$18,409
Salary	10,830
Taxable Income	$29,239

Tax At 26%	$7,602
Personal Tax Credits	(3,920)
Dividend Tax Credit [(2/3 + 1/3)($3,682)]	(3,682)
Taxes Payable	Nil

Dividends Received	$14,717
Salary Received	10,830
Personal Taxes Payable	Nil
After Tax Cash Retained (Dividends And Salary)	$25,557

16-113. As shown in the preceding calculations, this mix of salary and dividends is such that it just absorbs all of Mr. Swenson's tax credits and leaves taxes payable of nil. However, it is not an optimum solution. While it improves on the all dividend solution which results in after tax retention of 23,270, it is less attractive than the all salary solution which results in after tax retention of $25,750. It would appear that the optimum solution in this example would be to pay only salary.

16-114. Before leaving this subject, we would note that the issue of using up tax credits is sometimes approached with a different objective. In the preceding example, the objective was to remove all of the corporate income in the most tax efficient manner. This meant that when we analyzed the tax effect of increasing salary payments, an increase in tax deductible salary was accompanied by a smaller reduction in dividend payments.

16-115. An alternative version of this type of problem involves a situation in which the corporation has income and funds in excess of what the owner-manager needs it to distribute and the all dividend solution does not use all the available tax credits. The objective in this situation is to leave the shareholder with a specified amount of after tax funds. In other words, the goal is to distribute an amount of salary and/or dividends that will leave the recipient with a specified amount of cash. In examining the tax effects of an increase in salary, we do not have to consider the after tax funds that will be used up at the corporate level as there are more corporate funds available than the owner-manager needs.

Exercises Sixteen-7 through Sixteen-10 deal with salary vs. dividend decisions. This would be an appropriate time to attempt these exercises.

16-116. In this latter type of problem, we are going to pay just enough salary to eliminate tax credits, so there will be no personal taxes payable. As a consequence, the after tax retention from one dollar of extra salary will be identical to the after tax retention of one dollar of dividends. This means that the increase in taxes payable resulting from a given increase in salary will be based on a decrease in dividends that is equal to the increase in salary. This is in contrast to the type of problem that we have just examined (Mr. Swenson) in which the decrease in dividends was based on the after tax cost to the corporation of the increase in salary.

Conclusion

16-117.   As the preceding discussion makes clear, the salary vs. dividend decision is complex. Determination of the total tax consequences of the two alternatives does not necessarily resolve the issue. Among other factors that are specific to individual taxpayers, consideration should be given to:

- other sources of income
- the need to provide for retirement income
- the ability to split the corporation's income among various members of a family unit
- the personal level of expenditures desired
- the need to reduce corporate income to the annual limit for the small business deduction

16-118.   The preceding material does not give you a comprehensive approach to solving these problems on a quantitative basis. In actual fact, there are problems here that are probably not subject to quantitative solutions. For example, whether or not an individual feels a need for retirement income involves many subjective considerations. With an issue such as this, a tax advisor can only outline the various possible outcomes.

16-119.   As a final point here, it appears that, at this point in time, the reduction in provincial tax rates on individuals (favours salary) has generally improved the benefits of using salary instead of dividends. While corporate tax rates have been and will continue to be reduced (favours dividends), these current and future reductions have been on corporate income other than the first $200,000 of active business income earned by a CCPC. Since these salary vs. dividend decisions are largely related to rates applicable to this block of income, it would appear that tax policy is operating in a manner that will discourage the use of dividends by the owner-managers of CCPCs.

References

16-120.   For more detailed study of the material in this Chapter, we refer you to the following:

ITA 6(1)	Amounts To Be Included As Income From Office Or Employment
ITA 15(1)	Benefit Conferred On Shareholder
ITA 18(1)	General Limitations (On Deductions)
ITA 20(1)(j)	Repayment Of Loan By Shareholder
ITA 67	General Limitation Re Expenses
ITA 80.4(2)	Loans (To Shareholders)
ITA 82(1)	Taxable Dividends Received
ITA 121	Deduction For Taxable Dividends
ITA 123 To	
125.4	Rules Applicable To Corporations
ITA 146	Registered Retirement Savings Plans
ITA 147	Deferred Profit Sharing Plans
IT-67R3	Taxable Dividends From Corporations Resident In Canada
IT-80	Interest On Money Borrowed To Redeem Shares, Or To Pay Dividends
IT-119R4	Debts To Shareholders And Certain Persons Connected With Shareholders
IT-124R6	Contributions To Registered Retirement Savings Plans
IT-307R3	Spousal Registered Retirement Savings Plans
IT-421R2	Benefits To Individuals, Corporations And Shareholders From Loans Or Debt
IT-432R2	Benefits Conferred On Shareholders
IT-470R	Employee's Fringe Benefits
IT-487	General Limitation On Deduction Of Outlays Or Expenses
IT-498	The Deductibility Of Interest On Money Borrowed To Reloan To Employees Or Shareholders

Exercises

(The solutions for these exercises can be found following Chapter 21 of the text.)

Exercise Sixteen - 1 (Incorporation Of Active Business Income)
An individual has an unincorporated business that he anticipates will have active business income of $126,000 during the coming year. This individual has employment income in excess of $100,000 and is subject to a provincial tax rate of 14 percent of taxable income. The provincial dividend tax credit is equal to one-third of the dividend gross up. Also in this province, the corporate tax rate is 7 percent on income eligible for the small business deduction, and 15.4 percent on other income. He has asked your advice as to whether he should incorporate this business. Advise the individual with respect to any tax deferral that could be available on income left in the corporation and on any tax savings that could be available if all of the income is paid out in dividends.

Exercise Sixteen - 2 (Incorporation Of Interest Income)
An individual has investments which he anticipates will earn interest income of $126,000 during the coming year. This individual has employment income in excess of $100,000 and is subject to a provincial tax rate of 14 percent of taxable income. The provincial dividend tax credit is equal to one-third of the dividend gross up. Also in this province, the corporate tax rate is 7 percent on income eligible for the small business deduction, and 15.4 percent on other income. He has asked your advice as to whether he should transfer these investments to a corporation in which he would own all of the shares. Advise the individual with respect to any tax deferral that could be available on income left in the corporation and on any tax savings that could be available if all of the income is paid out in dividends.

Exercise Sixteen - 3 (Incorporation Of Investment Income)
One of your clients has asked your advice on whether he should transfer a group of investments to a new corporation that can be established to hold them. The corporation will be a Canadian controlled private corporation and he anticipates that the transferred investments will have the following amounts of income during the current year:

Dividends On Portfolio Investments	$46,000
Dividends From 100 Percent Owned Subsidiary (A Dividend Refund of $23,000 Will Be Received by The Payor)	87,000
Interest Income	32,000

Despite having employment income of over $100,000, the client needs all of the income that is produced by these investments. The corporation will be subject to a provincial tax rate of 10 percent on income eligible for the small business deduction and 15 percent on other income. The client is subject to a provincial tax rate equal to 15 percent of taxable income. The provincial dividend tax credit is equal to one-third of the dividend gross up. Provide the advice requested.

Exercise Sixteen - 4 (Incorporation Of Investment Income)
One of your clients has asked your advice on whether she should transfer a group of investments to a new corporation that can be established to hold them. The corporation will be a Canadian controlled private corporation and she anticipates that, during the coming year, the investments will create taxable capital gains of $46,000 [(1/2)($92,000)]. No other income will be generated by the investments. Despite having employment income in excess of $125,000, the client needs all of the income that is produced by these investments. The corporation will be subject to a provincial tax rate of 8 percent on income eligible for the small business deduction and 16 percent on other income. The client is subject to a provincial tax rate equal to 16 percent of taxable income. The province has a dividend tax credit equal to one-third of the dividend gross up. Provide the advice requested.

Exercise Sixteen - 5 (Shareholder Loans)

On June 1, 2001, Generic Inc. loans $162,000 to its principal shareholder, Ms. Jan Fisk, in order to finance her gambling debts. Generic Inc. has a taxation year which ends on June 30. The loan bears interest at two percent. Assume that, during all relevant periods, the prescribed rate is five percent (not including the extra percentage points applicable to amounts owing to or from the Minister Of Revenue).

A.   What are the tax consequences to Ms. Fisk if the loan is repaid on January 1, 2002?

B.   What are the tax consequences to Ms. Fisk if the loan is repaid on December 31, 2002?

Exercise Sixteen - 6 (Shareholder Loans)

On November, 1, 2001, Hasid Ltd. loans Mr. Samual Hasid, the CEO and principal shareholder of the Company, $123,000 in order to assist in his purchase of a principal residence. The Company has a taxation year which ends on December 31. The loan does not bear interest and, during all relevant periods, assume that the prescribed rate is five percent. The loan is repaid on January 1, 2003. What are the tax consequences of this loan to Mr. Hasid? State any assumptions that you are required to make in providing your answer.

Exercise Sixteen - 7 (Salary vs. Dividends)

Broadmoor Inc. is a Canadian controlled private corporation with Net Income For Tax Purposes and Taxable Income of $233,000. All of this income is from active business activities. The Cash balance of the Company, prior to any payments on the current year's taxes, is also equal to this amount. It is subject to a provincial tax rate of 8 percent on income eligible for the small business deduction and 17 percent on other income. Its only shareholder, Ms. Sarah Broad, has no income other than dividends or salary paid by the corporation and has combined federal/provincial personal tax credits of $2,800. She lives in a Province which has a flat personal tax rate equal to 10 percent of taxable income. The provincial dividend tax credit is equal to 40 percent of the dividend gross up. Determine the amount of after tax cash that Ms. Broad will retain if the maximum salary is paid by the corporation out of the available cash of $233,000.

Exercise Sixteen - 8 (Salary vs. Dividends)

Broadmoor Inc. is a Canadian controlled private corporation with Net Income For Tax Purposes and Taxable Income of $233,000. All of this income is from active business activities. The Cash balance of the Company, prior to any payments on the current year's taxes, is also equal to this amount. It is subject to a provincial tax rate of 8 percent on the $200,000 of income eligible for the small business deduction and 17 percent on other income, including any income that qualifies for the accelerated rate reduction. Its only shareholder, Ms. Sarah Broad, has no income other than dividends or salary paid by the corporation and has combined federal/provincial personal tax credits of $2,800. She lives in a Province which has a flat personal tax rate equal to 10 percent of taxable income. The provincial dividend tax credit is equal to 40 percent of the dividend gross up. Determine the amount of after tax cash that Ms. Broad will retain if the maximum dividend is paid by the corporation out of the available cash of $233,000.

Exercise Sixteen - 9 (Salary vs. Dividends)

Fargo Ltd. has Net Income For Tax Purposes and Taxable Income for the current taxation year of $21,500. The Company's cash balance, prior to the payment of any taxes for this year is $18,500. The Company's income is subject to a combined federal/provincial tax rate, including all surtaxes, of 17.3 percent. The Company's President and sole shareholder has no other source of income, has combined federal/provincial personal tax credits of $3,950, and lives in a province which has a personal tax rate on the first $30,754 of taxable income equal to 10 percent. The President of the corporation would like to remove all of the cash from the corporation and has asked your advice as to whether it would be better to take it out in the form of dividends or, alternatively, as salary. Provide the advice requested.

Exercise Sixteen - 10 (Salary vs. Dividends)

Mortell Inc. has Net Income For Tax Purposes and Taxable Income for the current taxation year of $198,000. The Company's cash balance is over $200,000. It is subject to a combined federal/provincial tax rate, including all surtaxes, of 16.5 percent. The Company's only shareholder has employment income of over $150,000 and, in normal circumstances, does not make withdrawals from the Corporation. However, because of an increasing fondness for certain types of mood enhancing chemicals, he needs an additional $30,000 in cash. He lives in a province where the personal tax rate in his bracket is equal to 16 percent of taxable income and the provincial dividend tax credit is equal to 25 percent of the dividend gross up. He has asked your advice as to the best way to remove the required funds from the corporation. Provide the advice requested.

Problems For Self Study

(The solutions for these problems can be found following Chapter 21 of the text.)

Self Study Problem Sixteen - 1

Ms. Lusk is divorced and has no dependants. She is the sole shareholder and only employee of Lusk Esthetics, a private Canadian corporation. She does not make CPP contributions as she is 66 years old. All of the income of this Corporation is derived from active business activity.

As the result of a settlement with her former husband, she receives spousal support in an amount sufficient to result in a 2001 taxable income of $44,385.

Lusk Esthetics qualifies for the small business deduction on all of its 2001 income and, as a consequence, is subject to a combined federal and provincial tax rate, including the corporate surtax, of 21 percent on its taxable income. During 2001, the Corporation has not paid any salaries or dividends to Ms. Lusk.

The provincial tax rate applicable to Ms. Lusk's personal income is a flat rate of 10 percent applied to all taxable income. The provincial dividend tax credit is equal to one-third of the dividend gross up.

In reviewing her budget, it is clear to Ms. Lusk that by the end of 2001 she will need an additional $10,000 in after tax dollars to meet all of her personal expenditures. She expects Lusk Esthetics to be the source of this additional amount as her Company has had a successful year. She would like to acquire the funds in a manner that will minimize the combined tax cost to both herself and her Corporation.

Required: Determine whether the payment of salary by Lusk Esthetics or, alternatively the payment of dividends by the Company, would provide the required $10,000 in after tax dollars at the lowest combined tax cost to Ms. Lusk and Lusk Esthetics. Your answer should include the explicit tax cost of providing the $10,000 to Ms. Lusk under each of the two alternatives.

Self Study Problem Sixteen - 2

Ms. Ashley is a successful dentist with an established practice in a major Canadian city. On January 1, 2001, she established a new Company, Ashley Management Services, to manage her professional practice and to hold some of her investments. The Company's year end is December 31.

Ms. Ashley's husband became unemployed in 2000. She hired him to manage this Company and he is paid a salary of $18,400 per year. This salary is reasonable in view of the services that he performs for Ashley Management Services.

During its first year of operation, the Company had the following revenues:

Interest Income	$ 21,600
Dividends From Canadian Public Companies	13,900
Management Fees	82,900
Rental Revenues	34,600
Total Revenues	$153,000

In the process of earning these revenues, Ashley Management Services incurred, in addition to the salary paid to Ms. Ashley's husband, the following expenses:

Expenses On Rental Property (Including CCA)	$27,800
Office Salaries	25,400
Office Rent	8,180
CCA On Office And Dental Equipment	5,700
Other Business Expenses	2,170
Total Before Manager's Salary	$69,250
Mr. Ashley's Salary	18,400
Total Expenses	$87,650

The corporation's active business income will be taxed at a combined federal/provincial rate of 20 percent and its investment income will be taxed at a combined federal/provincial rate of 51 percent (including the ITA 123.3 tax on the investment income of Canadian controlled private corporations). These rates include the effect of the corporate surtax.

It is the intended policy of the Company to pay dividends equal to its after tax profits for each year.

Ms. Ashley's professional income, without inclusion of any income from Ashley Management Services, is sufficient to give her a combined federal/provincial marginal tax rate of 47 percent. The dividend tax credit in her province is equal to 25 percent of the dividend gross up.

Mr. Ashley owns 60 percent of the voting shares in the Company. The shares were purchased with funds that he had earned in his previous job. Mr. Ashley has no other source of income during 2001. In order to simplify calculations, assume that all of his income will be taxed at a combined federal/provincial rate of 30 percent, with a dividend tax credit equal to 25 percent of the dividend gross up.

Required:

A. Calculate the minimum total federal and provincial taxes payable by Ashley Management Services and its shareholders for 2001.

B. Calculate the minimum taxes payable by Ms. Ashley assuming she had not established a corporation and had received all of the income personally with no salary being paid to Mr. Ashley.

Ignore personal tax credits and CPP contributions in your solution.

Self Study Problem Sixteen - 3

Mr. Bedford is the only shareholder of Bedford Inc., a Canadian controlled private company. The Company has a December 31 year end and, at December 31, 2001, Mr. Bedford determines that taxable income of the Company for the year will be $27,500. The Company has this amount available in cash, prior to the payment of taxes, dividends, or salary. All of the Company's income qualifies as active business income, though none of it results from manufacturing and processing activities. The Company's activities are confined to a province in which the applicable corporate rate of taxation is 6 percent on income which is eligible for the small business deduction. The province does not levy a payroll tax for health or post secondary education.

Mr. Bedford has no other source of income and the province in which he lives taxes the first $30,754 of personal taxable income at a rate of 9 percent. The provincial dividend tax credit is equal to 30 percent of the dividend gross up. Mr. Bedford has combined federal/provincial personal tax credits for the 2001 taxation year in the amount of $3,750.

Required:

A. Determine the after tax amount of cash that Mr. Bedford will retain if all of the Company's income is paid to him in the form of salary. Ignore CPP contributions.

B. Determine the after tax amount of cash that Mr. Bedford will retain if the Company pays the maximum possible dividend.

C. Can Mr. Bedford improve his after tax cash balance by using a combination of salary and dividends? Explain your conclusion.

D. Determine the combination of salary and dividends that will produce the maximum after tax cash balance for Mr. Bedford. Calculate the amount of this after tax cash retention.

Assignment Problems

(The solutions for these problems are only available in
the solutions manual that has been provided to your instructor.)

Assignment Problem Sixteen - 1

Mrs. Martin is considering investing $200,000 in interest bearing securities at a rate of 7 percent. The pre tax interest income on this investment would be $14,000 and Mrs. Martin has no other investment income. The combined federal and provincial corporate tax rate on investment income is 50 percent (including the ITA 123.3 tax on the investment income of a Canadian controlled private corporation and the corporate surtax.) Mrs. Martin is subject to a federal marginal tax rate of 29 percent and provincial marginal tax rate of 19 percent of taxable income. The provincial dividend tax credit is equal to one-third of the dividend gross up.

Required: Prepare calculations that will compare the after tax retention of income that will accrue to Mrs. Martin if:

A. The investment in the interest bearing securities is owned by her as an individual.

B. The investment is made by a corporation in which she is the sole shareholder and which pays out all available income in dividends.

Assignment Problem Sixteen - 2

Mr. Martin is considering investing $200,000 in the preferred shares of Canadian public companies. These shares pay dividends at a rate of 7 percent. The pre tax dividend income on this investment would be $14,000 and Mr. Martin has no other investment income. The combined federal and provincial corporate tax rate on investment income is 50 percent (including the ITA 123.3 tax on the investment income of a Canadian controlled private corporation and the corporate surtax.) Mr. Martin is subject to a federal marginal tax rate of 29 percent and a provincial marginal tax rate of 19 percent of taxable income. The provincial dividend tax credit is equal to one-third of the dividend gross up.

Required: Prepare calculations that will compare the after tax retention of income that will accrue to Mr. Martin if:

A. The investment in the dividend paying securities is owned by him as an individual.

B. The investment is made by a corporation in which he is the sole shareholder and which pays out all available income in dividends.

Assignment Problem Sixteen - 3

Mr. Jerome Farr owns all of the outstanding shares of Farr Flung Ltd. (FFL), a Canadian controlled private company with an October 31 year end. The Company has been extremely successful and, as a consequence, it has accumulated over $1,500,000 in cash that is not needed in the operations of the business. Given this situation, Mr. Farr has decided to give himself loans for a variety of purposes. Because of the abundance of cash in the corporation, Mr. Farr has indicated that, with respect to loans that will be used to acquire a dwelling or an automobile to be used in the business, loans will be extended to other employees of the company on the same basis that they are extended to himself. Mr. Farr spends at least 40 hours per week working in the business and, in most years, receives a significant amount of salary from the Company.

He has been advised by his accountant that he should keep detailed records with respect to the date on which each loan was made and the purpose of the loan. During the calendar year ending December 31, 2001, his records indicate the following:

Personal Expenditures   Because of his increasing appreciation of the finer things in life, Mr. Farr experienced a need for larger amounts of cash to be used for personal expenditures. During 2001, his Company loans him three separate amounts, with the details of the loans as follows:

- June 30, 2001   The Company loans $20,000 on an interest free basis. The loan is to be repaid on June 30, 2002.

- October 31, 2001   The Company loans $40,000 with an interest rate of 2 percent per annum. The loan is to be repaid on November 1, 2002.

- December 1, 2001   The company loans $60,000 with an interest rate of 4 percent per annum. The loan is to be repaid on January 1, 2003.

Dwelling   On January 1, 2001, Mr. Farr gives himself a $100,000 loan to acquire a dwelling. The rate on the loan is 2 percent per annum and the loan agreement calls for five annual payments of $20,000 plus accrued interest, commencing January 1, 2002.

Automobile   On June 30, 2001, Mr. Farr gives himself a $50,000 loan to acquire an automobile to be used in the business . The rate on the loan is interest free. Because of his commitment to repay the other loans, Mr. Farr is not sure when he will be able to repay this loan.

All repayments are made as scheduled. In all of the years under consideration, assume the prescribed rate is six percent (not including the extra two or four percent on amounts owing to or from the CCRA).

Required   Indicate the tax consequences, in each of the years 2001, 2002, and 2003, that will accrue to Mr. Farr as a result of receiving these loans. Briefly explain your conclusions. Base your interest calculations on the number of months the loans are outstanding.

Assignment Problem Sixteen - 4

Morcan Inc. is a Canadian controlled private corporation with a single shareholder, Mrs. Nadia Litvak. During 2001, Mrs. Litvak drew an amount of salary from the Company sufficient to put her into a combined federal and provincial tax bracket of 45 percent. In her province of residence, the combined federal/provincial dividend tax credit is equal to the dividend gross up.

For the taxation year ending December 31, 2001, the Company expects to have taxable income of $310,000, all of which is active business income. The Company is subject to a combined federal/provincial tax rate of 44 percent on active business income in excess of $300,000, and 37 percent on income between $200,000 and $300,000 (this range of income qualifies for the accelerated rate reduction).

As Mrs. Litvak's tax consultant you have advised her that she should consider taking out an additional salary of at least $10,000 and possibly $110,000, in order to reduce her Company's taxable income to $200,000. She is resisting this suggestion because she feels her present salary is more than adequate to meet her current living needs.

Required: Explain to Mrs. Litvak the tax advantages that would be associated with withdrawing the additional salary.

Assignment Problem Sixteen - 5

Miss Morgan established and has operated an extremely successful retail operation in downtown Fredericton. The business is incorporated and Miss Morgan is the sole shareholder. Her company is subject to a tax rate of 19 percent on all of its income. This rate includes the corporate surtax.

Due to the excellent returns on her portfolio investments, Miss Morgan is in the 29 percent federal tax bracket and the 12 percent provincial tax bracket. In her province, the dividend tax credit is equal to 25 percent of the dividend gross up.

During the 2001 fiscal year, Miss Morgan expects the business to have Net Income For Tax Purposes of about $170,000. This figure includes a deduction for the payment of her own salary of $84,000.

As Miss Morgan wishes to take an extended holiday during January and February of next year, she is in need of an extra $20,000 in cash in December of 2001. Her company has sufficient excess cash to allow her to either pay additional salary or to declare a dividend.

Required: Determine the amount that would be required in the way of salary and in the way of dividends, in order to provide Miss Morgan with the required after tax funds of $20,000. What would you advise her to do?

Assignment Problem Sixteen - 6

Ms. Barbra Stickle is the only shareholder of Stickle Ltd., a Canadian controlled private company. The Company has a December 31 year end and, at December 31, 2001, Ms. Stickle determines that taxable income of the Company for the year will be $24,200. The Company has this amount available in cash, prior to the payment of taxes, dividends, or salary. All of the Company's income qualifies as active business income. The Company's activities are confined to a province in which the applicable corporate rate of taxation is 7 percent on income eligible for the small business deduction and which does not levy a payroll tax.

Ms. Stickle has no other source of income and the province in which she lives taxes the first $30,754 of personal income at a rate of 9 percent. The provincial dividend tax credit has been set at 30 percent of the dividend gross up. Ms. Stickle has combined personal tax credits for the 2001 taxation year in the amount of $3,423.

Required:

A. Determine the after tax amount of cash that Ms. Stickle will retain if all of the Company's income is paid to her in the form of salary. Ignore CPP contributions.

B. Determine the after tax amount of cash that Ms. Stickle will retain if the Company pays the maximum possible dividend.

C. Can Ms. Stickle improve her after tax cash balance by using a combination of salary and dividends? Explain your conclusion.

D. Determine the combination of salary and/or dividends that will produce the maximum after tax cash balance for Ms. Stickle. Calculate the amount of this after tax cash retention.

Assignment Problem Sixteen - 7

Your client, Keith Slater, is contemplating the creation of Slater Ltd. He would be the sole shareholder and he plans to transfer his accounting business and investment portfolio to the company. All of the after tax corporate income would be paid out to him in dividends to finance his passion for art collecting. He has annual pension and RRIF income of over $100,000.

Having taken tax courses in the distant past, he vaguely remembers that something called integration plays a role in whether a corporation is tax advantageous or not. After some discussion and research, you compile the following estimated income amounts and tax rates:

Taxable Income Of Accounting Business (Active Business Income)	$80,000
Portfolio Dividends	96,000
Federal Corporate Tax Rate After Federal Abatement	28%
Federal Small Business Deduction	16%
Federal Corporate Surtax	4%
Provincial Corporate Tax Rate - CCPC Rate	8%
Marginal Federal Personal Tax Rate	29%
Marginal Provincial Personal Tax Rate	13%
Provincial Dividend Tax Credit	1/3 Dividend Gross Up

Required:

A. Briefly summarize the concept of integration.

B. Assume no corporation is used and the income is received personally. Calculate Mr. Slater's personal taxes payable, showing separately the taxes payable on the active business income and the dividends.

C. Assume the income and dividends are received by Slater Ltd. Calculate corporate taxes payable, after tax income available for distribution and personal taxes that would be payable on the distribution. Your calculations should show separately the taxes payable on the active business income and the dividends.

D. Compare the total taxes payable with and without the use of Slater Ltd. and explain why the tax payable amounts are different.

Assignment Problem Sixteen - 8

Cora Yates is a contract engineer who is joining the real estate firm Glenora Developers as the firm's tenth partner. Cora can join the partnership as an individual or she can form a corporation to join the partnership. Cora knows that a corporation will not provide the benefit of limited liability for her professional actions, but she would like to know if it would be advantageous in maximizing her after tax income from the partnership.

Cora estimates that for the partnership fiscal year ended December 31 of this year, her share of the partnership income will be $65,000 (one-tenth of $650,000 net partnership income), all of which will be active business income. Cora needs all of her after tax partnership income for personal living expenses as she has no other source of income.

After researching this issue you find that:

• Contract engineers are allowed to form corporations that can carry on a professional practice and join partnerships.

• The corporation would be eligible for the small business deduction. It would not be deemed a personal services business as the work is independent and the duties can be subcontracted. The annual business limit must be allocated on a pro rata basis among all corporate and unincorporated partners.

Ms. Yates is subject to graduated provincial tax rates of 8 percent on the first $30,754 of taxable income, 12 percent on the next $30,755, and 16 percent on amounts of $61,509. She has personal tax credits of $3,342 and the province has a dividend tax credit equal to one-third of the dividend gross up.

The corporation would be subject to combined federal/provincial taxes on income eligible for the small business deduction at a rate of 19 percent, on income that is eligible for the accelerated rate reduction at a rate of 28 percent, and on other active business income at a rate of 44 percent (includes the 1 percent general rate reduction).

You are reviewing three different scenarios as follows:

Scenario 1 Cora joins the partnership as an individual, and she does not form a corporation. All partnership income is received personally.

Scenario 2 Cora forms a corporation that joins the partnership. The corporation pays corporate tax on all of the partnership income, and pays the after tax partnership income to Cora as taxable dividends.

Scenario 3 Cora forms a corporation that joins the partnership. The corporation pays corporate tax on the portion of partnership income that qualifies for the small business deduction as well as the portion that is eligible for the accelerated rate reduction. The balance of the partnership income is paid to Cora as salary.

Required:

A. Calculate the after tax personal retention of the partnership income for each of the three scenarios.

B. Which scenario would you recommend? Briefly explain why this scenario is the best.

C. Outline other factors Cora should consider in deciding whether or not she should form a corporation to join the Glenora Developers partnership.

Assignment Problem Sixteen - 9

Judith Hughes owns an investment portfolio that will generate the following Canadian source income in the year ending December 31, 2001:

Interest	$12,000
Portfolio Dividends	40,000
Capital Gains	30,000

Judith needs $15,000 of the income for personal purposes and will reinvest the remainder. She estimates that her taxable income for this year from other sources will be $100,000. Her combined marginal tax rate is 47 percent on interest and taxable capital gains and 33 percent on dividends received.

It is October 12, 2001. You are a tax consultant and Judith is meeting with you to find out how she can minimize her next year's taxes payable. Should she form a holding company and transfer some or all of the investments into the company? Alternatively, should Judith continue to hold any or all investments personally?

The federal/provincial corporate tax rate applicable to investment income is 50 percent (including the ITA 123.3 tax on the investment income of Canadian controlled private corporations and the corporate surtax).

Required:

A. For each investment, describe how the investment income earned would be taxed in a Canadian controlled private corporation.

B. For each investment, indicate whether Judith should transfer the investment to a holding company or, alternatively, continue to hold it personally. For the investment(s) you recommend she holds personally, calculate her after tax income.

Assignment Problem Sixteen - 10 (Electronic Library Research Problem)

Provide brief answers to the following questions. Your answers should be supported by references to materials found in your Electronic Library.

A. An individual has the use of a residence which is owned by a corporation. The individual is the sole shareholder of that corporation. How will the amount of the ITA 15(1) benefit to be assessed be calculated?

B. An individual acquires a capital asset from a corporation in which he is a shareholder. The acquisition price is less than the fair market value of the capital asset. What are the tax consequences to the corporation and to the individual?

C. A corporation borrows $200,000 to provide a loan to its principal shareholder. The annual rate of interest on this loan is nine percent. The money is loaned to the shareholder at an annual rate of two percent, with repayment required prior to the second corporate year end after the loan was made. What are the tax consequences of this loan to the corporation and to the shareholder?

Chapter 17

Rollovers Under Section 85

Rollovers Under Section 85

Introduction

17-1. Chapter 16 gave detailed consideration to the question of whether it would be advantageous to establish a corporation in order to reduce, defer, or redistribute the amount of taxes payable. If the results of this analysis are favourable to the use of a corporation, Section 85 of the Act provides an attractive basis for the transfer of property to the new corporation.

17-2. The problem that is involved with such a transfer is that the assets may have been owned by the transferor for some period of time. In these circumstances, it is possible that their fair market values may be well in excess of their adjusted cost base and/or their undepreciated capital cost. As a transfer by a taxpayer to a corporation would be considered a disposition by that taxpayer, the incorporation of an existing business could result in a need to include both capital gains and recapture in the transferor's taxable income. In a typical situation, where the owner of an operating business decides to transfer all of its assets to a newly formed corporation, the resulting tax liability could be significant.

17-3. Section 85 of the *Income Tax Act* is designed to provide relief in this type of situation. In somewhat simplified terms, it permits property to be transferred or rolled over into a corporation on either a tax free basis, or with a level of taxation that is determined at the discretion of the transferor. This makes ITA 85 an extremely important Section of the *Income Tax Act*.

General Rules For The Transfer

Transferor And Transferee

17-4. As indicated in the introduction, we are concerned here with transfers of property to a corporation at a value that can be elected by the transferor and the corporation. With respect to the identity of the transferor, ITA 85(1) refers to taxpayers and this could be an individual, a trust, or a corporation. As partnerships are not "taxpayers" for income tax purposes, a separate ITA 85(2) provides for transfer of assets to a corporation by a partnership.

17-5. With respect to transferees, Section 85 requires that they be taxable Canadian corporations. A Canadian corporation is defined in ITA 89(1) as a corporation that is currently resident in Canada and that was either incorporated in Canada or has been a resident continuously since June 18, 1971. ITA 89(1) also defines a taxable Canadian corporation as a Canadian corporation that was not, by virtue of a statutory provision, exempt from taxation under Part I of the *Income Tax Act*.

Eligible Property

17-6.   Only "eligible property", the components of which are defined in ITA 85(1.1), can be transferred under Section 85. Items listed in the subsection are as follows:

- both depreciable and non depreciable capital property, not including real property owned by non residents;
- eligible capital property;
- Canadian resource properties;
- foreign resource properties;
- inventories, other than inventories of real property; and
- real property owned by a non resident person and used in the year in a business carried on by that person in Canada.

17-7.   The general exclusion of real property owned by non residents reflects the fact that this type of property is taxable Canadian property and gains on its disposition are subject to Canadian taxes, without regard to the residency of the seller. The exclusion is designed to prevent a non resident who owns Canadian real estate from being able to transfer the property on a tax free basis to a corporation and subsequently selling the shares in the corporation on a tax free basis.

17-8.   The second exclusion from assets eligible for the Section 85 rollover would be Canadian resident owned real property which constitutes an inventory. That is, if a group of real property assets are being actively traded rather than being held for their income producing ability, they are not eligible for a tax free rollover under ITA 85.

17-9.   This latter exclusion of inventories of real property can be a particularly troublesome provision due to the fact that, in practice, some taxpayers may not be certain as to the status of their real estate holdings. If the taxpayer was to go through the Section 85 rollover procedures and then, after the fact, find that the transferred real estate holdings were seen by the CCRA as inventory, the tax consequences would be very severe. In this type of situation, it would be advisable that any real properties transferred, be held by the corporation for some period of time before they are sold.

Consideration To Transferor

17-10.   In return for the property transferred to the corporation, the corporation may provide various types of consideration to the transferor. The one requirement that is specified in ITA 85(1) is that some part of this consideration must consist of shares of the transferee corporation. The shares issued may be either preferred, common, or some combination of the two types. Further, the requirement for share consideration to be used can be satisfied by the issuance of as little as one share to the transferor. For reasons that will become evident later, the usual Section 85 transaction involves the use of a combination of shares and non share consideration. In this context, the non share consideration is usually referred to as "boot".

Making The Election

17-11.   Both the transferor and the transferee corporation must elect to have the Section 85 provisions apply. This joint election is accomplished by filing Form T2057 (transfers from individuals and corporations) or T2058 (transfers from partnerships) on or before the date on which the normal tax returns are due for the two taxpayers. A late election may be filed for up to three years after this date and, with the permission of the CCRA, a late election will be accepted after the end of this three year period. Whenever there is a late election, a penalty of one-quarter of one percent of any deferred gain will be assessed for each month beyond the normal filing date. The maximum penalty is $100 per month and a total amount of $8,000.

17-12.   In making the election, it is crucial that the taxpayer list all of the properties that are to be covered. If a property is omitted from the forms, the normal rules associated with dispositions will apply. This could result in the need to recognize capital gains, recapture, or business income on the transfer, an outcome that might require needless payment of taxes.

Establishing The Transfer Price

Importance

17-13.   One of the most significant features of ITA 85 is that it provides for the transfer of various properties to a corporation at values that are jointly elected by the transferor and transferee. Careful consideration must be given to the election of an appropriate transfer price in that, in general, this transfer price establishes three important values. These are:

Transferor   The deemed proceeds of disposition for the property given up, as well as the adjusted cost base of the property received from the corporation.

Transferee   The adjusted cost base of the property received.

General Rules

17-14.   While there are a number of complications associated with establishing transfer prices, the basic rules are very straightforward. The elected values cannot exceed fair market values and cannot be less than the adjusted cost base of non depreciable assets or the UCC of depreciable assets (as we will see in the next section, the floor elected value is also limited by the boot or non share consideration received). For example, assume Mr. Thompson owns non depreciable assets with a fair market value of $750,000 and an adjusted cost base of $500,000. On the transfer of these assets to a corporation, he will receive consideration with a fair market value of $750,000. However, under the provisions of ITA 85, the elected value can be any value between a floor of $500,000 and a ceiling of $750,000. In most situations, the transferor wishes to avoid recognizing income on the transfer and, in order to do this, the elected value will be the floor of $500,000. The election of this value will have the following tax consequences for the transferor and the transferee:

- The $500,000 will be the proceeds of disposition to the transferor. As this is equal to his adjusted cost base for the asset, there will be no capital gain on the transfer.

- The adjusted cost base to the corporation will be $500,000. This means that, if the corporation were to sell the asset immediately for its fair market value of $750,000, a capital gain of $250,000 ($750,000 - $500,000) would have to be recognized. This reflects the fact that the gain on the asset at the time of transfer was only deferred, not eliminated, by the use of the ITA 85 rollover.

- While we have not specified the type of consideration that will be received by the transferor, the election of $500,000 as the transfer price means that the adjusted cost base of the consideration will be this amount. This will be less than the $750,000 fair market value of the consideration.

17-15.   You should note that this scenario raises the possibility of double taxation on the $250,000 gain. The adjusted cost base of the property transferred and the consideration received by the transferor is $500,000. If the corporation sells the asset for its fair market value of $750,000, there will be a $250,000 gain at the corporate level. If the consideration received by the transferor is in the form of shares, a sale of these shares at their fair market value of $750,000 would result in the $250,000 gain being taxed a second time at the individual level. This would suggest that, if either the assets transferred or the consideration received by the transferor are to be sold, the election should be made at the fair market value of $750,000.

Non Share Consideration (Boot)

17-16.   The term, "boot" is commonly used to refer to non share consideration given to the transferor in an ITA 85 rollover. It would include cash paid to the transferor and new debt of the transferee corporation issued to the transferor. In those cases where an existing business is being transferred under these provisions, boot would include the assumption by the transferee corporation of old debt of the existing business that is being transferred.

17-17.   Boot is of considerable significance in that, if the rollover is properly structured, it constitutes an amount of cash or equivalent that will be received by the transferor on a tax free basis. Because of this, the other basic rule on establishing a transfer price is that the elected amount cannot be less than the value of non share consideration provided to the transferor.

17-18.   Returning to the basic example that was presented in Paragraph 17-14, assume Mr. Thompson receives the following from the transferee corporation:

Cash	$600,000
Shares Of Transferee Corporation	150,000
Total (Equals Fair Market Value Of Assets Transferred)	$750,000

17-19.   Because the elected value cannot be below the value of the non share consideration, the minimum elected value would be $600,000, resulting in the following tax consequences:

• The proceeds of disposition to the transferor would be $600,000, resulting in a taxable capital gain of $50,000 [(1/2)($600,000 - $500,000)].

• The adjusted cost base of the assets to the corporation would be the transfer price of $600,000. This means that if the corporation sells the assets for their fair market value of $750,000, the gain would be $150,000.

• The adjusted cost base of the consideration received by the transferor would be $600,000. As will be discussed at a later point, all of this amount must be allocated to the non share consideration, leaving the share consideration with an adjusted cost base of nil.

The Usual Scenario

17-20.   As illustrated in the preceding example, if the boot exceeds the tax values (adjusted cost base or UCC) of the assets transferred, the result is income for tax purposes. As one of the usual goals in using ITA 85 is to avoid income on the transfer of assets, the normal procedure is to set the transfer price at an amount equal to the tax values of the assets and to restrict the use of boot to this value. In the example presented, this would mean using $500,000 as the elected value and issuing non share consideration in this same amount. In addition, as the fair market value of the consideration received by the transferor must be equal to the fair market value of the assets transferred to the corporation, share consideration with a fair market value of $250,000 would be issued to the transferor. This would have the following tax consequences:

• As the proceeds of disposition would be $500,000, no capital gain would arise on the transfer to the corporation.

• The adjusted cost base to the corporation of the assets acquired will be $500,000.

• The adjusted cost base of the non share consideration to the transferor would be $500,000. This means that the adjusted cost base of the share consideration would be nil.

17-21.   There are a number of complications associated with rollovers under ITA 85 and they will be the subject of much of the remainder of this Chapter. However, the great majority of these transactions will follow the pattern illustrated in the preceding simple example. You should keep these basic concepts and procedures in mind as we examine the more detailed procedures required in ITA 85 rollovers.

Transfer Prices - Detailed Rules

Introduction

17-22.   There are a number of rules in ITA 85 that apply to all types of property. To begin, ITA 85(1)(a) establishes that the amount elected by the taxpayer and corporation shall be deemed to be the taxpayer's proceeds of disposition, as well as the cost of the property to the corporation.

17-23.   A further general rule is as follows:

ITA 85(1)(b)   ...where the amount that the taxpayer and corporation have agreed on in their election in respect of the property is less than the fair market value, at the time of the disposition, of the consideration therefor (other than any shares of the capital stock of the corporation or a right to receive any such shares) received by the taxpayer, the amount so agreed on shall, irrespective of the amount actually so agreed on by them, be deemed to be an amount equal to that fair market value;

17-24.   This establishes that the elected value cannot be less than the boot (consideration other than shares of stock of the corporation).

17-25.   Finally, a further provision limits the elected value to the fair market value of the property transferred:

> **ITA 85(1)(c)**   … where the amount that the taxpayer and the corporation have agreed on in their election in respect of the property is greater than the fair market value, at the time of the disposition, of the property so disposed of, the amount so agreed on shall, irrespective of the amount actually so agreed on, be deemed to be an amount equal to that fair market value;

17-26.   These general rules apply to all assets transferred, thereby establishing a range for the election. This range can be outlined as follows:

Ceiling Value   Fair market value of the assets transferred to the corporation.

Floor Value   The floor value will be equal to the greater of:

- the fair market value of the non share consideration (boot) given to the transferor in return for the assets transferred; and

- the tax values (adjusted cost base or UCC) of the assets transferred.

17-27.   The application of the term tax values in the preceding outline of the rules will vary with the type of asset involved. Attention will be given to these differences in the material which follows.

Accounts Receivable

17-28.   When Accounts Receivable are transferred in conjunction with all of the other assets of a business, the disposition will be treated as a capital transaction, with any resulting loss being only one-half deductible. Further, as the transferee has not included these amounts in income, no deduction can be made for bad debts. If less than the transfer amount of the Accounts Receivable is collected, the difference must be treated as a one-half deductible capital loss. The usual procedure to avoid these results is to use a joint election under ITA 22. This election allows any loss to be treated as a fully deductible business loss and permits the transferee to deduct bad debts as appropriate. This election was discussed in Chapter 7 on Business Income.

17-29.   While Accounts Receivable can be transferred under ITA 85, taxpayers are not permitted to elect under both ITA 85 and ITA 22. In general, it will be to the advantage of the taxpayer to make the ITA 22 election and, as a consequence, Accounts Receivable will usually not be one of the assets listed in the ITA 85 election. Note, however, this does not prevent these assets from being transferred to the corporation. After making the ITA 22 joint election, they can be transferred at fair market value, with any resulting loss being fully deductible to the transferor.

Inventories And Non Depreciable Capital Property

17-30.   Unlike the situation with Accounts Receivable, when Inventories are disposed of in conjunction with the sale of substantially all of the assets of a business, any difference between fair market value and cost is treated as business income or loss, not as a capital gain or loss. This is specifically provided for in ITA 23, with no election being required to bring this provision into effect.

17-31.   Non depreciable capital property of a business would include land, temporary investments, and long term investments. As capital property is involved, any gain or loss on their disposition would be treated as a capital gain or loss.

17-32. In making the election here, the highest value will be the fair market value of the assets transferred to the corporation. The minimum election cannot be below the amount of the boot received by the transferor. However, a further floor limit is specified for the inventories and non depreciable capital property in ITA 85(1)(c.1). This limit is the lesser of the fair market value of the property and its tax cost. For non depreciable capital assets, the tax cost would be the adjusted cost base of the property. For inventory, tax cost would be either cost or market, depending on how the inventory balance is carried for tax purposes.

17-33. Putting these limits together means that the minimum elected value for the floor will be the greater of:

A. The fair market value of the boot (the general floor for all assets); and

B. The lesser of:
   • the fair market value of the property; and
   • the tax cost of the property.

17-34. These rules can be illustrated using the three examples that follow:

	Example One	Example Two	Example Three
Fair Market Value Of Asset	$15,000	$10,000	$20,000
Adjusted Cost Base	12,000	12,000	14,000
Fair Market Value Of The Boot	5,000	5,000	17,000

17-35. In Example One, the maximum value is the fair market value of $15,000 and the minimum value is the cost of $12,000. The normal election value would be $12,000. Also note that up to $12,000 of boot could have been taken out without changing the minimum election or creating taxable income.

17-36. In Example Two, the $10,000 fair market value is both the floor and the ceiling. If the property is inventories, this required election will result in a fully deductible business loss of $2,000 ($12,000 - $10,000). Alternatively, if the election was made on non depreciable capital property, the result would be an allowable capital loss of $1,000 [(1/2)($12,000 - $10,000)].

17-37. In Example Three, the maximum value is again the fair market value. While the $14,000 cost is lower than the $20,000 fair market value, it is also lower than the boot. This means that, in this example, the minimum value that can be elected is the boot of $17,000. If this property is inventory, this election will result in fully taxable business income of $3,000 ($17,000 - $14,000). If the election was made on non depreciable capital property, the result will be taxable capital gain of $1,500 [(1/2)($17,000 - $14,000)].

17-38. Note that Example Three is unrealistic in that the transferor will normally structure the rollover to avoid any gain on the transfer of assets. This means that the usual procedure is to limit the non share consideration to the minimum elected value as otherwise determined.

Non Depreciable Capital Property - Disallowed Capital Losses On Transfers To Affiliated Persons
General Rules

17-39. The special rules described in this section apply only to non depreciable capital assets. They do not apply to either inventories or depreciable capital assets as it is not possible to have capital losses on these assets. While we are discussing these rules in the material related to Section 85 rollovers, you should note that they are applicable to transfers to affiliated persons, without regard to whether Section 85 is being used. The discussion is located here because, when a non depreciable capital asset is transferred under ITA 85, the recognition of a loss may be unavoidable because of the rules limiting the elected values. This was the case in Example Two in Paragraph 17-34.

17-40. The basic rule applicable to these situations is found in ITA 40(2)(g) which indicates that a taxpayer's loss, to the extent that it is a "superficial loss", is deemed to be nil. As with many other concepts related to capital assets, the definition of "superficial loss" is found in

ITA 54:

> **"superficial loss"** of a taxpayer means the taxpayer's loss from the disposition of a particular property where
>
> (a) during the period that begins 30 days before and ends 30 days after the disposition, the taxpayer or a person affiliated with the taxpayer acquires a property (in this definition referred to as the "substituted property") that is, or is identical to, the particular property, and
>
> (b) at the end of that period, the taxpayer or a person affiliated with the taxpayer owns or had a right to acquire the substituted property.

17-41.   Read together, these provisions deem to be nil any capital loss of a taxpayer arising on a transfer to an affiliated person. While the allocation of the loss will depend on whether the taxpayer is an individual or a corporation, the denial of the loss is applicable to all taxpayers. The actual allocation of the denied loss will be dealt with after our discussion of affiliated persons.

Affiliated Persons

17-42.   The term "affiliated person" is defined in ITA 251.1(1) as follows:

> A. An individual is affiliated to another individual only if that individual is his spouse or common-law partner.
>
> B. A corporation is affiliated with:
>   1. a person who controls the corporation;
>   2. each member of an affiliated group of persons who controls the corporation; and
>   3. the spouse or common-law partner of a person listed in (1) or (2).
>
> C. Two corporations are affiliated if:
>   1. each corporation is controlled by a person, and the person by whom one corporation is controlled is affiliated with the person by whom the other corporation is controlled;
>   2. one corporation is controlled by a person, the other corporation is controlled by a group of persons, and each member of that group is affiliated with that person; or
>   3. each corporation is controlled by a group of persons, and each member of each group is affiliated with at least one member of the other group.

17-43.   ITA 251.1(3) contains definitions which are required in the application of these rules. The two that are of importance here are:

> **Affiliated group of persons** means a group of persons each member of which is affiliated with every other member.
>
> **Control** means controlled, directly or indirectly in any manner whatever. [The reference here is to de facto control, which does not necessarily require majority ownership of shares.]

17-44.   As was previously noted, if a capital loss arises on a transfer to an affiliated person, it is deemed to be nil. This rule applies to all taxpayers, including both individuals and corporations.

Allocation Of Disallowed Loss

17-45.   When the transferor is a natural person (a.k.a., an individual), the disallowed loss is allocated to the adjusted cost base of the transferred property. This requirement is dictated by ITA 53(1)(f), which describes adjustments to the cost base of a transferred property.

> **Example**   Ms. Hannah Howard, the sole shareholder of HH Ltd., transfers land with an adjusted cost base of $50,000 and a fair market value of $40,000, to HH Ltd. The transfer is made under Section 85 at an elected value of $40,000.

Tax Consequences   The $10,000 loss ($40,000 - $50,000) on the transfer is disallowed. As the transferor is an individual, it will be allocated to the adjusted cost base of the land in the tax records of HH Ltd. This means that the adjusted cost base to HH Ltd. will be the same $50,000 ($40,000, plus the $10,000 loss) that was the adjusted cost base to Ms. Howard.

17-46.   When the transferor is a corporation or a partnership, the allocation of the disallowed loss is covered under ITA 40(3.4). In effect, this provision keeps the loss in the tax records of the transferor to be recognized when one of the following events occurs:

- the transferee disposes of the property to an arm's length person (includes deemed dispositions);
- if the transferor is a corporation, it is subject to an acquisition of control; or
- the transferor is subject to a wind up.

Example   HC Ltd. transfers land with an adjusted cost base of $50,000 and a fair market value of $40,000 to an affiliated person (e.g., a corporation controlled by HC Ltd.). Two years later, the affiliated person sells the land for $35,000.

Tax Consequences   The $10,000 ($40,000 - $50,000) loss on the transfer to the affiliated person will be disallowed at the time of the transfer. However, when the land is sold by the affiliated person for $35,000, the $10,000 loss that was disallowed at the time of the transfer will be recognized by HC Ltd. The affiliated person will recognize a $5,000 ($40,000 - $35,000) loss at the time of sale.

Tax Planning

17-47.   To the extent that the asset in question is necessary to the continued operations of the business, for example land on which the enterprise's factory is located, it makes no difference whether it is transferred under the provisions of ITA 85 or outside the election. In either case, the loss will be disallowed at the time of the transfer.

17-48.   If an asset is not essential to the operations of the corporation, the preferable course of action may be to sell it to an arm's length party. This will permit the immediate recognition of any loss on its disposition. However, if the asset is an integral part of the operations of the transferor (e.g., land on which the factory of the business is located), this is not a viable alternative.

17-49.   The other basic point here is, that if the asset in question has an accrued loss, there is no reason to elect to transfer it under Section 85. The objective that the taxpayer is attempting to achieve in using Section 85 is to defer the taxation of income. When losses are involved, including those assets in the Section 85 rollover complicates the election without contributing to the taxpayer's desired goals.

Depreciable Property

General Rules

17-50.   As with other assets, the ceiling for the election is the fair market value of the asset and the general floor is the fair market value of the non share consideration received by the transferor. However, as was the case with inventories and non depreciable capital property, a further lower limit is specified in the *Act*. ITA 85(1)(e) indicates that for depreciable property, the lower limit is the least of the UCC for the class, the fair market value of each individual property, and the cost of each individual property. This means that the overall lower limit for the election is the greater of:

A.   The fair market value of the boot (general floor for all assets)

B.   The least of:

- the balance of the UCC for the class;
- the fair market value of each individual property; and
- the cost to the taxpayer of each individual property.

Examples

17-51.   These rules can be illustrated by the following two examples, each involving the transfer of the only asset in a CCA Class:

	Example One	Example Two
Fair Market Value Of The Property	$50,000	$18,000
UCC Of Class (Last Asset In Class)	20,000	20,000
Cost Of The Property	27,000	30,000
Fair Market Value Of The Boot	15,000	15,000

17-52.   In Example One, the range of the election would extend from the UCC of $20,000 as the floor to the fair market value of $50,000. Note that any election in between the UCC of $20,000 and the cost of $27,000 would result in recapture of CCA. The normal election here would be the UCC of $20,000 which results in the transferor not recognizing a capital gain or recapture of CCA. In addition, the transferor would usually take out that amount in boot.

17-53.   In Example Two, the ceiling value and the floor value would be the $18,000 fair market value of the property. With the ceiling and floor at the same value, the general rules would suggest that only this $18,000 value could be elected. Since the transfer of the property removes the last asset in this CCA class, the fact that the elected value is below the UCC suggests a terminal loss. As will be discussed in a later section in this Chapter, this terminal loss may be disallowed.

Order Of Disposal

17-54.   An additional problem arises in the case of depreciable assets in situations where a number of different assets which belong to the same CCA class are being transferred. This problem can be illustrated by the following example:

Example   An individual owns two assets in a particular CCA class and the UCC for that class is $28,000. Data on the two assets is as follows:

	Asset One	Asset Two
Cost Of Asset	$15,000	$30,000
Fair Market Value	20,000	25,000

17-55.   The problem here is that the wording of the transfer price rules for depreciable assets requires the floor to be based on the least of cost for each individual asset, fair market value for each individual asset, but UCC for the class as a whole. This determination has to be with respect to each asset in the class, with the resulting figures summed for purposes of the election floor. This means that, if these general rules were applied, the floor values would be $15,000 for Asset One plus $25,000 for Asset Two. This reflects the fact that both of these individual values are less than the $28,000 UCC for the class. However, if these values are selected, a total of $40,000 would be subtracted from the class. Since the UCC balance for the class is only $28,000, this would result in recapture of $12,000.

17-56.   To alleviate this problem, ITA 85(1)(e.1) allows an assumption that the properties are transferred one at a time. This means that for the transfer of Asset One, if the floor value of $15,000 was elected (this assumes that the non share consideration provided to the transferor does not exceed this amount), this $15,000 would be subtracted from the UCC of $28,000. The resulting UCC balance would be $13,000 and when the depreciable asset rules are applied to Asset Two, this UCC balance of $13,000 would become the floor. If the taxpayer again elected to use the floor value, the $13,000 would be deducted from the UCC and this would reduce the account to zero without triggering recaptured CCA.

Terminal Losses Disallowed

General Rules

17-57.   In Paragraph 17-53, we noted that the terminal loss resulting from the required election on the asset in Example Two is likely to be disallowed. More specifically, if a depreciable property with a fair market value that is less than its UCC is transferred to an affiliated person (see Paragraph 17-42), ITA 13(21.2) indicates that:

- ITA 85 does not apply;
- the proceeds of the disposition are deemed to be the UCC amount, thereby disallowing the terminal loss; and
- the transferee's capital cost for the property is deemed to be the transferor's capital cost, with the excess of that amount over the fair market value of the asset deemed to be CCA deducted in previous periods.

17-58.   Until recently, the preceding rules did not apply to individuals. However, amendments resulting from the 2000 budget have changed ITA 13(21.2) so that it now applies to all taxpayers, including individuals.

17-59.   Returning to Example Two from Paragraph 17-51, the property would be transferred at a value that would disallow the terminal loss on the transfer. The loss, however, does not disappear.

17-60.   For the transferee corporation, the property will have a deemed capital cost of $30,000 and a UCC value of $18,000. The $2,000 disallowed loss will be deemed to be a depreciable property that is owned by the transferor. It will be allocated to the same class as the transferred property for CCA purposes and will be subject to the usual CCA procedures. However, it will be kept in a separate class so that any unamortized amount can be recognized when one of the following events occurs:

- the transferee disposes of the property to an arm's length person (includes deemed dispositions);
- the use of the property is changed from income earning to non income earning;
- if the transferor is a corporation, it is subject to an acquisition of control; or
- if the transferor is a corporation, it is subject to a wind up.

Tax Planning

17-61.   As was noted in our discussion of capital losses on transfers of non depreciable capital property, Section 85 is normally used in order to defer the taxation of various types of income. If there is a terminal loss present on a depreciable property, to the extent that the asset is necessary to the continued operations of the business, it makes no difference whether it is transferred under the provisions of ITA 85 or outside the election. In either case, the terminal loss will be disallowed at the time of the transfer. Electing to transfer the asset under Section 85 can complicate the transaction without improving the situation of the taxpayer.

Cumulative Eligible Capital

17-62.   As is the case for all other assets, the general ceiling and floor for making an election under ITA 85(1) is the fair market value of the assets transferred and the fair market value of the non share consideration received, respectively. As was the case with inventories, non depreciable property, and depreciable property, a further lower limit is specified in the *Act*. ITA 85(1)(d) limits the floor to the least of 4/3 of the taxpayer's cumulative eligible capital in respect of the business immediately before the disposition, the cost to the taxpayer of the property, and the fair market value of the property at the time of the disposition. This means that the overall lower limit for the election is the greater of:

A.   The fair market value of the boot (general floor for all assets).

B.   The least of:
- 4/3 of the cumulative eligible capital balance;
- the cost of the individual property; and
- the fair market value of the individual property.

Examples

17-63. Assuming that the corporation has only one eligible capital property, these provisions can be illustrated using the following examples:

	Example One	Example Two
Fair Market Value Of The Property	$60,000	$60,000
Cumulative Eligible Capital Balance	37,500	52,500
4/3 Cumulative Eligible Capital Balance	50,000	70,000
Cost Of The Property	55,000	80,000
Fair Market Value Of The Boot	40,000	40,000

17-64. In Example One, the range of election values would extend from a floor of $50,000 to a ceiling of $60,000. The floor value would normally be elected because its use would have no immediate tax implications. Note that additional non share consideration could be taken out in this example without creating taxable income.

17-65. In Example Two, $60,000 is both the floor and the ceiling and if this amount is elected, it would result in the reduction of the transferor's cumulative eligible capital account by $45,000 (three-quarters of $60,000). This disposition would normally produce a loss of $7,500 ($52,500 - $45,000). However, such losses may be disallowed. This point will be covered more completely in the following section.

17-66. As discussed in Chapter 8, the most important component of cumulative eligible capital is usually goodwill. An individual transferring a business to a corporation would generally not have a balance in the cumulative eligible capital account, reflecting the fact that only purchased goodwill is given accounting recognition. This means that under the general rules for transfer price elections, the goodwill could be transferred at a price of zero. The danger in this is that giving no consideration to goodwill could result in this asset being inadvertently omitted from the election. This would make the transfer a non arm's length gift and, under ITA 69, the proceeds would be deemed to be fair market value. To avoid this possibility, a value of at least $1 should be assigned to goodwill when assets which constitute a business entity are being transferred to a corporation.

Losses Disallowed On Dispositions Of Cumulative Eligible Capital Property

General Rules

17-67. When a taxpayer ceases to carry on business, three-quarters of any disposition proceeds allocated to cumulative eligible capital items will be subtracted from the balance in this account. If the result is a negative amount of cumulative eligible capital, the result will be an income inclusion under ITA 14(1). Alternatively, if a positive balance remains, it can generally be deducted under ITA 24(1). Note that these amounts are very much like recaptured CCA and terminal losses on depreciable assets. However, these latter items are included or deducted under other sections of the *Act* and, as a consequence, those terms are not applied when the analogous events occur with respect to cumulative eligible capital.

17-68. With respect to the deduction under ITA 24(1), it is dealt with in much the same fashion as terminal losses (see Paragraph 17-57). That is, the deduction related to the disposition of the cumulative eligible capital balance is disallowed.

17-69. Under ITA 14(12), when a deduction is available under ITA 24(1) as a result of a transfer of property to an affiliated person (see Paragraph 17-42), the transferor is deemed to continue to own the cumulative eligible capital. The positive balance in this account will continue to be subject to the usual rules related to cumulative eligible capital until such time as:

- the transferee disposes of the property to an arm's length person (includes deemed dispositions);
- the use of the property is changed from income earning to non income earning;
- if the transferee is a corporation, it is subject to an acquisition of control; or
- the transferor is subject to a wind up.

17-70. On the occurrence of one of these events, any remaining unamortized balance can be deducted under ITA 24(1).

17-71. With respect to Example Two from Paragraph 17-63, the $7,500 would be left as a cumulative eligible capital balance on the books of the transferor. The transferor would continue to amortize the balance (he is deemed not to have ceased carrying on business). This would continue until one of the events specified in Paragraph 17-69 occurs. At the occurrence of one of these events, the transferor can deduct the remaining balance in the cumulative eligible capital account under ITA 24(1).

Tax Planning

17-72. We have previously noted with respect to capital losses on non depreciable capital assets and terminal losses on depreciable capital assets that, in most circumstances, there is no reason to list the relevant assets under the ITA 85 election. Identical results can be obtained by simply selling the assets at their fair market value.

17-73. Implementation of this advice with respect to cumulative eligible capital may be more difficult. While some balances included in cumulative eligible capital can be sold independently of the related business (e.g., an unlimited life government licence), other components (e.g., goodwill) may have no meaningful value when measured independently of the business. This may require their inclusion in the ITA 85 election, even if it creates a disallowed deduction.

Allocation Of The Elected Value

Consideration Received By The Transferor (Shareholder)

17-74. As noted previously, the election price for the assets transferred is used to establish the adjusted cost base of all consideration received by the transferor. The rules for allocating this total to the various types of consideration that may be used are found in ITA 85(1)(f), (g), and (h). They involve a sequential process that can be outlined as follows:

Elected Value (Total Adjusted Cost Base Of All Consideration)	$xxx
Less: Adjusted Cost Base Of Non Share Consideration (Fair Market Value)	(xxx)
Adjusted Cost Base Of All Shares Issued (Usually Nil)	$xxx
Less: Adjusted Cost Base Of Preferred Stock Issued (Usually Nil But Limited To Fair Market Value)	(xxx)
Adjusted Cost Base Of Common Stock Issued (A Residual - Usually Nil)	$xxx

> Exercise Seventeen-1 deals with allocation of consideration received. This would be an appropriate time to attempt this exercise.

17-75. As noted in our description of the usual ITA 85 scenario, minimum asset values will normally be elected in order to avoid the recognition of income on the transfer. Boot will then be taken out in an amount equal to these minimum values. This means that in the usual situation, non share consideration will be equal to the elected value and, in terms of the preceding allocation process, both preferred and common shares will have an adjusted cost base of nil.

Assets Acquired By The Corporation

General Rules

17-76. With respect to the assets acquired by the transferee corporation, the basic rules are as follows:

Non Depreciable Property The elected transfer price becomes the adjusted cost base of these assets to the corporation.

Depreciable Property ITA 85(5) requires that the capital cost to the transferee be equal to the amount that was the capital cost to the transferor. In most cases, the elected value will be equal to the transferor's UCC. ITA 85(5) requires that the difference between these two values be treated as deemed CCA. To illustrate this, consider the following asset:

Cost	$100,000
UCC	67,000
Fair Market Value	105,000
Non Share Consideration	67,000
Elected Value	67,000

The capital cost of the asset to the transferee will be $100,000, there will be deemed CCA taken of $33,000, and future CCA will be based on the elected value of $67,000. The reason for requiring the transferee to retain the transferor's capital cost is to avoid having the transferor convert potential recaptured CCA into a capital gain, only one-half of which will be taxed.

You should also note that, in the usual situation where the transferor is not dealing at arm's length with the transferee corporation, the first year rules do not apply to the calculation of CCA by the transferee, as long as the transferor has owned the asset for at least 365 days prior to the transfer and used it as a capital property to earn business or property income.

17-77.   What these rules mean is that, in cases where the election has been made at a price equal to the transferor's tax cost, the corporation essentially assumes the tax position of the transferor.

Capital Gains On Transfer

17-78.   The objective of using ITA 85(1) is usually to avoid tax consequences when assets are transferred to a corporation. This means that, in general, the elected values will be equal to the transferor's tax values (adjusted cost base or UCC).

17-79.   There are, however, circumstances in which the transferor may wish to generate a capital gain through the transfer of assets to a corporation. This was very common when the general lifetime capital gains deduction was available, as the transferor could realize capital gains with no tax consequences. While less common at present, there may still be reasons to elect values that will trigger capital gains for the transferor. An example of this might be an individual with unused capital loss carryovers that he wishes to absorb.

17-80.   The problem with this type of transaction is that, under the general rules applicable to ITA 85(1) transfers, the elected value will become the basis for future CCA by the corporation. This means that an election which is in excess of the transferor's cost will convert a capital gain, of which only one-half is taxable, into UCC which will be fully deductible to the corporation. An example of an asset that is to be transferred under ITA 85(1), with the elected value equal to fair market value, will serve to make this point clear:

Cost	$ 80,000
Fair Market Value	120,000
UCC	75,000
Elected Value	120,000
Non Share Consideration	120,000

17-81.   The election at $120,000 would create the following amounts of income:

Recaptured CCA ($80,000 - $75,000)	$ 5,000
Taxable Capital Gain [(1/2)($120,000 - $80,000)]	20,000
Total Income	$25,000

17-82.   In the absence of special rules, the cost and UCC of this asset to the corporation would be $120,000. This value would create $45,000 more CCA for the corporation than would have been available to the transferor ($120,000 - $75,000). This has been accomplished through an increase in the transferor's income of only $25,000, clearly not an equitable situation.

17-83. ITA 13(7)(e) acts to correct this situation. This provision applies to all non arm's length transfers of depreciable property which result in a capital gain for the transferor. In these situations, ITA 13(7)(e) limits the capital cost of the asset for CCA purposes to the transferor's cost, plus one-half of any capital gain which results from the transfer. As applied to the example in Paragraph 17-81, the capital cost to the transferor, for CCA and recapture purposes only, under ITA 13(7)(e) would be as follows:

Transferor's Cost		$ 80,000
Transfer Price	$120,000	
Transferor's Cost	(80,000)	
Capital Gain	$ 40,000	
Taxable Portion	1/2	20,000
Capital Cost To The Transferee For CCA Purposes		$100,000

17-84. Based on this capital cost, the increased CCA to the corporation is only $25,000 ($100,000 - $75,000), the same amount the transferor recognized as income as a result of the transfer. Note, however, that for future capital gains calculations, the capital cost of the asset to the transferee is the elected value of $120,000.

Paid Up Capital Of Shares Issued

General Rules

17-85. Establishing the Paid Up Capital (PUC) for the shares received is important as it represents an amount that can be distributed to the shareholders as a tax free return of capital. In general, the amount of paid up capital for tax purposes is equal to the amount attributed to the shares under the appropriate corporate laws (legal capital).

17-86. While there are some complications in those Provinces which still permit the issuance of par value shares, the legal capital of a corporation is generally based on the fair market value of the consideration received in return for issued shares. In the case of shares issued in an ITA 85 rollover, this amount would be the fair market value of the assets transferred.

17-87. From the point of view of the taxpayer receiving the new shares, their adjusted cost base will be determined by the values elected for the transfer of assets. In the normal scenario, the taxpayer will elect minimum values for the assets transferred and these will usually be less than fair market values. With paid up capital of the shares initially based on fair market values and adjusted cost base determined using elected values, the initial paid up capital of the shares will generally be larger than the adjusted cost base of the shares.

Paid Up Capital Reduction

17-88. As you should now be aware, ITA 85 permits assets to be transferred without the recognition of the income that would normally be associated with their disposition. As the transferor's old tax values are generally flowed through to the transferee corporation, the potential income is deferred until the assets are used or disposed of by that corporation.

17-89. If the transferor had been required to recognize normal amounts of income on the transfer of assets, this income would likely have consisted of both partially taxable capital gains and fully taxable recaptured CCA. If the PUC of the shares issued is allowed to remain at their fair market value at issue, it may result in this deferred income being taxed more favourably, or not at all. To illustrate the problem that this creates, consider the following example:

Example Assets with a fair market value of $200,000, a capital cost of $180,000, and a UCC of $120,000 are transferred under ITA 85 using an elected value of $120,000. The consideration given consists of cash of $120,000 and shares with a fair market value and legal stated capital of $80,000 (total consideration equals $200,000).

17-90. If these assets had been sold to an arm's length party, the vendor would have had to pay taxes on a total of $70,000, $60,000 in recapture and $10,000 [(1/2)($200,000 -

$180,000)] in taxable capital gains. As is the intent of the legislation, these amounts of income are deferred when Section 85 is used properly. However, if the shares issued in the rollover were allowed to have a PUC equal to their $80,000 fair market value, all or part of the $70,000 in deferred income may escape taxation. Consider the following possibilities:

1. If the shares are redeemed at $80,000, the redemption proceeds would be equal to the PUC of the shares and there would be no ITA 84(3) dividends. As the adjusted cost base of the shares is nil, the $80,000 would be a capital gain. The problem with this for the CCRA is that, at best, only $40,000 [(1/2)($80,000)] of this amount would be taxable and, at worst, the lifetime capital gains deduction could eliminate all taxation.

2. If the shares were sold in an arm's length transaction, there would again be a capital gain of $80,000. Taxation would either be limited to the $40,000 [(1/2)($80,000)] taxable capital gain, or eliminated through the use of the lifetime capital gains deduction.

3. If the transferor continues to hold the shares, the $80,000 in PUC could be removed from the corporation on a tax free basis.

17-91. In view of these problems, ITA 85(2.1) requires that the paid up capital of issued shares be reduced by an amount equal to the total increase in legal stated capital, less any excess of the elected value over non share consideration given. Continuing with our example, the reduction would be as follows:

Increase In Legal Stated Capital		$80,000
Less Excess, If Any, Of:		
Total Elected Value	($120,000)	
Reduced By Non Share Consideration	120,000	-0-
Reduction In Paid Up Capital		$80,000
Balance Of Paid Up Capital ($80,000 - $80,000)		Nil

17-92. It is easy to see the conceptual basis for this reduction. Unless the non share consideration is less than the elected value, the PUC reduction will be equal to the full fair market value of the shares, and the resulting PUC will be nil. This process also sets the PUC equal to the adjusted cost based that is allocated to the shares.

17-93. In our example, the non share consideration is equal to the elected value, resulting in a PUC of nil. With respect to the first problem listed in Paragraph 17-90, it has been eliminated. If the shares were redeemed at fair market value, the excess of the $80,000 proceeds of disposition over the paid up capital of nil would be treated as a deemed dividend under ITA 84(3). For purposes of capital gains determination, this deemed dividend would be removed from the proceeds of disposition, leaving this value at nil. As the adjusted cost base of the shares is also nil, there would be no capital gain or loss that would be eligible for the lifetime capital gains deduction.

17-94. This paid up capital reduction provision does not deal with the second problem. If the shares are sold, the result will be a capital gain that is eligible for either favourable taxation or the lifetime capital gains deduction.

17-95. The third problem has been eliminated in that the PUC balance has been reduced to nil, leaving no balance to be withdrawn on a tax free basis.

More Than One Class Of Shares
17-96. In the majority of Section 85 rollovers, the ITA 85(5.1) formula will reduce the PUC of all shares issued to nil. This reflects the fact that the non share consideration taken will equal the elected value, resulting in the PUC reduction being equal to the increase in legal stated capital. This was the case in the calculation in Paragraph 17-91. If this is the case, having more than one class of shares does not create any difficulties.

17-97. If, however, the non share consideration is less than the elected value, the PUC reduction must be allocated to the various classes of shares. You will recall that, when we allocated the adjusted cost base, it was a sequential process (see Paragraph 17-74). The total adjusted cost base (i.e, the elected value) was allocated first to non share consideration, then to preferred shares to the extent of their fair market value, and finally to the common shares. This is not the case with the PUC reduction. The formula in ITA 85(5.1) is such that the reduction is allocated to different classes of shares on a pro rata basis.

Example Joan Creek transfers non depreciable assets with a fair market value of $1,600,000 to a corporation under the provisions of ITA 85(1). The elected value is equal to the $900,000 cost of the assets and, as consideration, she receives cash of $600,000, redeemable preferred shares with a fair market value of $250,000, and common shares with a fair market value of $750,000.

Tax Consequences The total adjusted cost base for the consideration would be allocated as follows:

Elected Value (Total Adjusted Cost Base Of All Consideration)	$900,000
Non Share Consideration (Fair Market Value)	(600,000)
Adjusted Cost Base Of All Shares Issued	$300,000
Less: Adjusted Cost Base Of Preferred Stock Issued (Limited To Fair Market Value)	(250,000)
Adjusted Cost Base Of Common Stock Issued	$ 50,000

The PUC reduction would be calculated as follows:

Increase In Legal Stated Capital ($250,000 + $750,000)		$1,000,000
Less Excess, If Any, Of:		
Total Elected Value	($900,000)	
Reduced By Non Share Consideration	600,000	(300,000)
Reduction In Paid Up Capital		$ 700,000

The PUC of the two classes of shares, reduced by a pro rata allocation of the $700,000 PUC reduction, would be allocated as follows:

$$\text{PUC of Preferred Stock} \left[\$250,000 - \left(\frac{\$250,000}{\$1,000,000} \right)(\$700,000) \right] = \$75,000$$

Exercise Seventeen-2 deals with the Section 85 PUC reduction. This would be an appropriate time to attempt this exercise.

$$\text{PUC of Common Stock} \left[\$750,000 - \left(\frac{\$750,000}{\$1,000,000} \right)(\$700,000) \right] = \$225,000$$

17-98. Note that the total PUC of the two classes is equal to $300,000 ($75,000 + $225,000). As you would expect, this is equal to the total adjusted cost base of the two classes ($250,000 + $50,000) as well as the difference between the elected value of $900,000 and the non share consideration of $600,000. The fact that the amounts are different reflects the difference between the sequential allocation process for the adjusted cost base amount, in contrast to the pro rata allocation of the PUC reduction.

Section 85 Rollovers — Comprehensive Example

Basic Information

17-99. John Martin has been operating an unincorporated business. The tax costs (UCC or adjusted cost base) and fair market values for its assets and liabilities are as follows:

	Tax Value	Fair Market Value
Cash	$ 20,000	$ 20,000
Accounts Receivable	50,000	49,000
Inventories	100,000	100,000
Prepaid Expenses	10,000	10,000
Land	50,000	70,000
Building (Capital Cost = $150,000)	110,000	140,000
Equipment (Capital Cost = $70,000)	40,000	35,000
Goodwill	Nil	50,000
Total Assets	$380,000	$474,000
Liabilities	$100,000	$100,000

Excluded Assets

17-100.   The rollover would involve a new corporation, the Martin Company, assuming all of Mr. Martin's liabilities and acquiring all of his business assets except the following:

Asset	Tax Value
Cash	$ 20,000
Accounts Receivable	50,000
Prepaid Expenses	10,000
Equipment	40,000
Total Tax Values For Excluded Assets	$120,000

17-101.   With respect to the Cash and Prepaid Expenses, they have fair market values that are equal to their tax values and, as a result, there is no advantage to including them in the ITA 85 election.

17-102.   The Accounts Receivable could be transferred under ITA 85. However, the $1,000 ($50,000 - $49,000) loss would have to be treated as a capital loss, only one-half of which would be deductible. Further, any additional bad debts incurred by the corporation would also have to be treated as capital losses. The alternative is a joint election under ITA 22. This allows the $1,000 current loss to be treated as a fully deductible business loss. In addition, the corporation will then be able to deduct the full amount of any additional bad debts. Taxpayers are not permitted to use both the ITA 22 and the ITA 85 elections for their Accounts Receivable and, as a consequence, we have excluded it from the ITA 85 election.

17-103.   The equipment is excluded because there is a terminal loss of $5,000 present. While the property could be transferred under ITA 85(1), it makes no sense to use ITA 85(1) for this asset. The usual reasons for using ITA 85(1) is to defer the taxation of gains. As a loss is involved with respect to the equipment, there is no tax advantage in using this provision. The equipment can simply be sold to the corporation at its fair market value, thereby avoiding the additional complications associated with listing it under the ITA 85(1) election.

Implementing The Election

17-104.   Mr. Martin is interested in deferring all of the capital gains that are present on his assets and, as a consequence, he elects tax values for most of the assets that are to be transferred under ITA 85. The one exception to this is goodwill which is transferred at a value of $1 to ensure that it is listed in the election. There would be a $.75 income inclusion under ITA 14(1) with respect to the $1.00 elected value for goodwill. Mr. Martin's total elected value of $260,001 is calculated as follows:

Tax Values Of Total Assets		$380,000
Tax Value Of Excluded Assets (Paragraph 17-100)		(120,000)
Nominal Value To Goodwill		1
Total Elected Value		**$260,001**

17-105.   With respect to the consideration to be given Mr. Martin, it must equal the fair market value of the assets transferred. This amount would be $360,000 ($474,000 total, less Cash of $20,000, Accounts Receivable of $49,000, Prepaid Expenses of $10,000, and Equipment of $35,000). The normal procedure would be to take back non share consideration with a fair market value equal to the elected value of $260,001, along with shares with a fair market value equal to the $99,999 excess of the fair market value of the assets transferred over the elected value. Assuming that the non share consideration is all in the form of debt, the analysis of the rollover would be as follows:

	Elected Value	Consideration At Fair Market Value Debt	Shares
Inventories	$100,000	$100,000	$ -0-
Land	50,000	50,000	20,000
Building (Capital Cost = $150,000)	110,000	110,000	30,000
Goodwill	1	1	49,999
Total Assets	**$260,001**	**$260,001**	**$ 99,999**

Note   This schedule relates each asset to a particular type of consideration, a process which has no basis in tax legislation. However, it does provide a matrix analysis that insures that each asset transferred is supported by an appropriate amount of consideration when measured at fair market value. The widespread use of this type of analysis in text books probably reflects the fact that it is in a form similar to that used in the T2057 form on which the ITA 85 election is made.

17-106.   The $260,001 in debt consideration is made up of $100,000 in debt of the existing business that has been assumed by the corporation, plus $160,001 in new debt issued by the corporation.

17-107.   From the point of view of the corporation, the elected values would become the tax values to be used in subsequent periods of operation. The adjusted cost base of the shares that were issued to Mr. Martin would be determined as follows:

Total Elected Value	$260,001
Non Share Consideration	(260,001)
Adjusted Cost Base Of Shares	**Nil**

17-108.   The paid up capital of these shares would initially be their legal stated capital, an amount equal to their fair market value of $99,999. However, there would be an ITA 85(2.1) reduction in this balance as follows:

Increase In PUC		$99,999
Less The Excess Of:		
Elected Value	($260,001)	
Reduced By Non Share Consideration	260,001	Nil
Reduction In Paid Up Capital		**$ 99,999**

17-109.   At this point, both the adjusted cost base and the PUC of the shares is nil. If they were redeemed at their $99,999 fair market value, Mr. Martin would have to recognize an ITA 84(3) deemed dividend of $99,999. This deemed dividend would reduce the proceeds of disposition for capital gains purposes to nil, resulting in no capital gain on the redemption. Alternatively, if he were to sell the shares at their fair market value, the result would be a capital gain of $99,999. In either case, the gain that was deferred by the use of ITA 85 would have to be recognized in order for Mr. Martin to remove his remaining investment in the Martin Company.

Exercises Seventeen-3 and Seventeen-4 deal with the tax consequences of Section 85 rollovers. This would be an appropriate time to attempt these exercises.

Gift To Related Person - Section 85

17-110.   If the transferor of the assets is the only shareholder of the transferee corporation, the indirect gift rules in ITA 85(1)(e.2) are not applicable. However, Section 85 rollovers are often used for income splitting purposes and this usually means that other members of the transferor's family will be involved as shareholders in the transferee corporation. The indirect gift rules are designed to insure that, while other family members will be permitted to share in the future growth and income of the corporation, they will not be permitted to receive a portion of the current values of the transferred assets in the form of a gift.

17-111.   The general rules are that if the fair market value of the transferred property exceeds the greater of:

1.   the fair market value of all consideration received from the corporation; and
2.   the amount elected for the transfer;

and it is reasonable to regard that excess as a gift made by the taxpayer for the benefit of any related shareholder, the elected transfer price is increased by the excess without any increase in the adjusted cost base of the shares received.

17-112.   The following example will serve to illustrate these indirect gift rules.

Example   Mr. Pohl transfers property with the following values to a new corporation.

Adjusted cost base of property	$ 30,000
Fair market value of property	180,000
Elected amount - Initial value	30,000

The new corporation issues a $30,000 note payable to Mr. Pohl. In addition, it issues common shares with a fair market value of $150,000, with one-half of these shares going to Mr. Pohl and the remaining one-half going to his 25 year old son. The total consideration received by Mr. Pohl is $105,000 [$30,000 + (1/2)($150,000)]. The adjusted cost base of the shares would be nil.

17-113.   The gift can be calculated as follows:

Fair Market Value Of Property Transferred	$180,000
Greater Of Fair Market Value Of Consideration Received And The Elected Amount	(105,000)
Gift	$ 75,000

17-114.   Under ITA 85(1)(e.2), the $75,000 gift must be added to the $30,000 elected amount to determine the cost base of the assets to the corporation and the proceeds of the disposition to Mr. Pohl. The resulting value would be $105,000. As a consequence, Mr. Pohl would have a taxable capital gain on the transfer of $37,500 [(1/2)($105,000 - $30,000)]. However, the adjusted cost base of the shares issued by the corporation is not increased by the amount of the gift and, as a consequence, would remain at nil. This creates the potential for double taxation of the $75,000 difference between the fair market value of Mr. Pohl's shares and their adjusted cost base. In addition, the shares held by his son would have a fair market value of $75,000 and an adjusted cost base of nil. This difference would be taxed on any subsequent disposition of the shares by his son. The overall result is that there will be immediate taxation on the amount of the gift, plus additional taxation of the full $150,000 of the original gain at such time as Mr. Pohl and his son sell their shares.

17-115.   The way to avoid this problem is fairly obvious. In situations where the rollover is

Exercise Seventeen-5 deals with gifts to the transferee. This would be an appropriate time to attempt this exercise.

being used for income splitting and other members of the transferor's family will be receiving shares, the transferor should always take back an amount of consideration that is equal to the fair market value of the property transferred. This will usually involve the transferor taking back a non growth security such as preferred shares for the difference between the fair market value of the property and its cost base for tax purposes. Common shares can then be issued to the other family members at a nominal value. While the initial value of these shares will be nominal, it will be these shares that enjoy future growth in the value of the corporation.

Benefit To Transferor - Section 85

17-116.   In the previous section we considered the tax consequences of using Section 85 to make a gift to a related person. A different possibility would involve a situation where the transferor takes back consideration with a fair market value that exceeds the property transferred to the corporation under Section 85.

Example   Ms. Sally Swit transfers property with an adjusted cost base of $120,000 and a fair market value of $150,000, to a corporation in which she is the sole shareholder. She takes back debt with a fair market value of $170,000 and redeemable preferred shares with a fair market value and PUC of $30,000. She elects to make the transfer at $150,000 (she cannot elect above the ceiling of fair market value) and, as a result, must recognize a capital gain of $30,000 ($150,000 - $120,000).

Tax Consequences   The $200,000 value of the consideration exceeds the $150,000 fair market value of the property transferred, by $50,000. This is clearly a benefit to Ms. Swit that is in addition to the $30,000 capital gain previously noted. However, it must be divided into two components:

Fair Market Value Of Boot	$170,000
Fair Market Value Of Property Transferred	(150,000)
ITA 15(1) Shareholder Benefit	$ 20,000

PUC Of New Shares	$30,000
Increase In Net Assets	Nil
ITA 84(1) Dividend	$30,000

Exercise Seventeen-6 deals with benefits to the transferor. This would be an appropriate time to attempt this exercise.

17-117.   If shares had not been received by Ms. Swit, the full excess of consideration received over the fair market value of the property transferred would be a shareholder benefit under ITA 15(1). This is less desirable than the receipt of ITA 84(1) dividends as this latter type of income receives favourable tax treatment.

GST And Section 85 Rollovers

17-118.   When property used in a commercial activity is rolled into a corporation under Section 85 of the *Income Tax Act*, the rollover is a taxable transaction for GST purposes. For example, if a sole proprietorship or partnership transfers property when a business is incorporated, the rollover of property will be deemed to be a taxable supply for consideration equal to the fair market value of the property. This amount will then be subject to GST. A joint election may be available to avoid any related GST liability, providing the vendor sells or transfers all or substantially all (i.e., 90 percent or more) of the assets that can reasonably be regarded as being necessary for the purchaser to carry on the business. In addition, if the vendor is a GST registrant, the purchaser must also be a GST registrant.

17-119.   If the transfer of property is a taxable supply, GST will be payable on the total share and non share consideration for the property, with the elected amount under Section 85 of the *Income Tax Act* being irrelevant. If the transferred property is subsequently used in commercial activities, an input tax credit may be claimed by the transferee for any GST paid on the transfer of the property.

17-120.   The GST implications in this area will be covered at the end of Chapter 18, after we have discussed the sale of an incorporated business.

Dividend Stripping — ITA 84.1

Background

17-121.   The term dividend stripping is applied to two types of situations, depending on when the relevant shares were issued by the corporation. In simple terms, both scenarios involve an individual who is attempting to remove assets from a corporation on a tax free basis. This goal could be accomplished in either case if the individual was simply willing to sell the shares to an arm's length party. However, the dividend stripping rules involve situations where the individual also wishes to retain ownership and control of the corporation.

17-122.   The first application of the dividend stripping rules from ITA 84.1 involves shares that have been issued after 1971 or, more importantly, after the introduction of the lifetime capital gains deduction in 1985. In this case the individual is trying to remove resources from the corporation in the form of a capital gain that will be eligible for the lifetime capital gains deduction. This could easily be accomplished by selling the shares to an arm's length party. However, this is not a desirable course of action in situations where the individual wishes to retain control of the business.

17-123.   The second situation involves an individual who has owned an operating company for some period of time prior to 1972. If the operating company has been successful, there may be significant amounts of pre 1972 earnings accumulated in the business. As these amounts are probably reflected in the valuation day (V-Day) value of the business, the individual could get these amounts out of the business on a tax free basis by selling the shares and using the valuation day value as the adjusted cost base. This, however, would not be compatible with the individual's desire to retain ownership of the corporation. In this case, the dividend stripping rules prevent this from happening by converting the pre V-Day capital gain into a dividend under ITA 84.1(1)(b).

17-124.   At one point in time, dividend stripping related to pre V-Day shares was an important topic. As we have noted at several places in this text, V-Day was nearly 30 years ago and, while a knowledge of the procedures associated with that date can be very important in particular cases, such cases are no longer common. As a consequence, you may wish to skip over the material on this application of ITA 84.1.

17-125.   The first type of situation involving post 1971 shares continues to be of importance and, in view of this, we would suggest that you concentrate your efforts in this area.

Applicability Of ITA 84.1

17-126.   Without regard to whether pre 1972 or post 1971 shares are involved, ITA 84.1(1) specifies the conditions under which the dividend stripping rules become applicable. These conditions are as follows:

- there is a disposition by a resident Canadian taxpayer of shares of a resident Canadian corporation (the subject corporation);

- the taxpayer held the shares as capital property (i.e., were held to produce income, not for resale at a profit);

- the disposition is made to a corporation with which the taxpayer does not deal at arm's length; and

- the subject corporation must be connected with the purchaser corporation (i.e., the purchaser corporation must control the subject corporation or own more than 10 percent of the voting shares and 10 percent of the fair market value of all shares).

17-127.   When these conditions are present, the provisions of ITA 84.1 will generally serve to eliminate the individual's ability to achieve their dividend stripping goals.

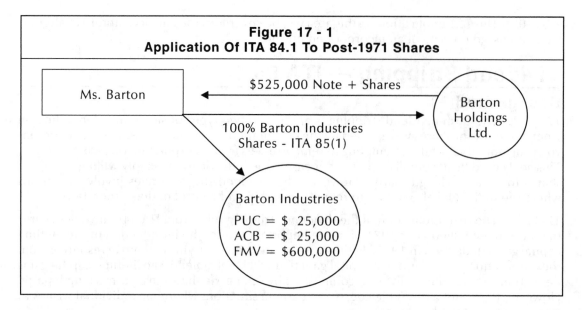

Figure 17 - 1
Application Of ITA 84.1 To Post-1971 Shares

Dividend Stripping Example - Post-1971 Shares

17-128.   A simple example will serve to illustrate the application of ITA 84.1 to post 1971 shares. As shown in Figure 17-1, Ms. Barton is the only shareholder of Barton Industries (BI), a Canadian controlled private corporation. The Company was established in 1986 with an investment of $25,000 on the part of Ms. Barton. There has been no additional investment in the Company and, as a consequence, this is the adjusted cost base of her shares as well as their PUC. The shares have a fair market value of $600,000 and Ms. Barton has made no previous use of her lifetime capital gains deduction. BI is a qualified small business corporation.

17-129.   Ms. Barton could, of course, make use of her lifetime capital gains deduction by selling the BI shares to an arm's length party and realizing a capital gain of $575,000 ($600,000 - $25,000). However, this approach would result in taxes payable as the capital gain exceeds the amount of the available lifetime capital gains deduction. In addition, Ms. Barton does not wish to lose control of the Company.

17-130.   Given these considerations, she chooses to transfer the BI shares to a new company, Barton Holdings Ltd. (BHL), using the provisions of Section 85(1). Ms. Barton uses an elected value for the transfer of $525,000 in order to limit her capital gain to $500,000. She takes back $525,000 in new debt of BHL, along with the common shares of the new Company. These shares have a fair market value of $75,000 ($600,000 - $525,000) and an adjusted cost base of nil.

17-131.   Through this procedure, Ms. Barton appears to have realized the required $500,000 of the accrued capital gain on the BI shares and, at the same time, retained control of the Company. However, Ms. Barton is a resident Canadian who has made a disposition of shares held as capital property to a corporation with which she does not deal at arm's length. In addition, BI is connected with BHL subsequent to the transaction. As a consequence, ITA 84.1 is applicable.

17-132.   The required ITA 84.1(1)(a) PUC reduction would be calculated as follows:

Increase In Legal Stated Capital Of BHL Shares		$75,000
Less Excess, If Any Of:		
PUC Of Barton Industries Shares*	($ 25,000)	
Reduced By Boot	525,000	Nil
ITA 84.1(1)(a) PUC Reduction		$75,000

*This amount is technically the greater of the PUC of the old shares and their cost. In this example, the two amounts are equal.

17-133. This would leave the PUC of the new shares at nil ($75,000 - $75,000). Given this, the ITA 84.1(1)(b) deemed dividend would be calculated as follows:

Increase In Legal Stated Capital Of BHL Shares		$ 75,000
Non Share Consideration		525,000
Total		$600,000
Less The Sum Of:		
PUC Of Barton Industries Shares	($25,000)	
PUC Reduction Under ITA 84.1(1)(a)	(75,000)	(100,000)
ITA 84.1(1)(b) Deemed Dividend		$500,000

17-134. The results from Ms. Barton's disposition of her BI shares would be as follows:

Elected Proceeds	$525,000
ITA 84.1(1)(b) Deemed Dividend	(500,000)
Proceeds Of Disposition (ITA 54)	$ 25,000
Adjusted Cost Base (Barton Industries)	(25,000)
Capital Gain	$ Nil

17-135. As the preceding example makes clear, the effect of ITA 84.1 in this situation is to convert the $500,000 of the available capital gain on the BI shares into an ITA 84.1 deemed dividend. This means that Ms. Barton will not be able to make use of her lifetime capital gains deduction and that she will be subject to taxation on the deemed dividend. ITA 84.1 has clearly served to make this type of transaction unattractive.

> Exercise Seventeen-7 deals with dividend stripping. This would be an appropriate time to attempt this exercise.

17-136. As a final point, you should note that Ms. Barton could have achieved her goal of triggering a capital gain for purposes of the lifetime capital gains deduction. Her problem was that she also wanted to remove the gain in the form of non share consideration. If, as an alternative, she had elected a transfer price of $525,000, but limited the non share consideration to the $25,000 PUC value, she would have had her $500,000 capital gain without creating an ITA 84.1 deemed dividend.

Dividend Stripping Example - Pre-1972 Shares

17-137. A simple example will serve to illustrate the application of ITA 84.1 to pre-1972 shares. As shown in Figure 17-2 (following page), Mr. Sander holds 100 percent of the outstanding voting shares of Sander Inc., an operating company which he has owned and managed since 1954. His original investment was $50,000 and this is both the PUC and the adjusted cost base of his common shares.

17-138. Mr. Sander would like to realize his tax free, pre V-Day capital gain of $400,000 ($450,000 - $50,000). This could be accomplished, of course, if he simply sold his shares in an arm's length transaction. However, he wishes to retain complete control of Sander Inc.

17-139. In order to accomplish his goal of realizing the pre V-Day capital gain while retaining control of Sander Inc., Mr. Sander uses the provisions of ITA 85 to rollover the shares of Sander Inc. into a new company, Sander Investments Ltd. The elected value for the transfer is the Valuation Day amount of $450,000 and Mr. Sander receives non share consideration of $450,000 in the form of a demand note from Sander Investments Ltd. In addition, he receives shares in Sander Investments Ltd. with a fair market value and legal stated capital of $550,000, bringing the fair market value of the total consideration received to $1,000,000, the fair market value of the Sander Inc. shares that have been given up. With the elected value at $450,000 and non share consideration equal to this amount, the adjusted cost base of the Sander Investments Ltd. shares would be nil.

17-140. Without ITA 84.1, Sander Investments Ltd. could receive tax free dividends from Sander Inc. in the amount of $450,000 and this amount could be transferred to Mr. Sander in repayment of the debt that he received in the rollover transaction. In effect, Mr. Sander would

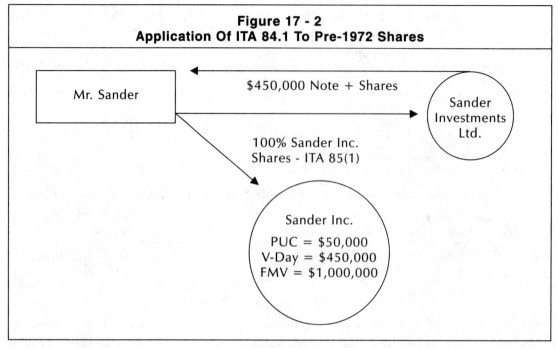

Figure 17 - 2
Application Of ITA 84.1 To Pre-1972 Shares

have received the Valuation Day value of Sander Inc. on a tax free basis. To the extent of Sander Inc.'s $50,000 PUC, there is a tax free return of capital. However, the remaining $400,000 involves the removal of accumulated earnings and, as a consequence, this type of transaction is referred to as a dividend strip. The intent of ITA 84.1 is to prevent this $400,000 amount from being received by Mr. Sander in the form of a pre V-Day tax free capital gain. In effect, it will convert such capital gains into fully taxable deemed dividends.

17-141. In our example, the conditions described in Paragraph 17-126 are met and ITA 84.1 is applicable. These provisions begin by requiring a PUC reduction under ITA 84.1(1)(a) as follows:

Increase In Legal Stated Capital Of Sander Investments Shares		$550,000
Less Excess, If Any Of:		
PUC Of Sander Inc. Shares*	($ 50,000)	
Reduced By Boot	450,000	Nil
ITA 84.1(1)(a) PUC Reduction		$550,000

   *This amount is technically the greater of the PUC of the old shares and their cost (without the use of the V-Day or median rule). In this example, the two amounts are equal.

17-142. Subsequent to this reduction, the PUC of the Sander Investments shares would be nil ($550,000 - $550,000).

17-143. At this point, ITA 84.1(1)(b) requires the calculation of a deemed dividend as follows:

Increase In Legal Stated Capital Of Sander Investments Shares		$ 550,000
Non Share Consideration		450,000
Total		$1,000,000
Less The Sum Of:		
PUC Of Sander Inc. Shares*	($ 50,000)	
PUC Reduction Under ITA 84.1(1)(a)	(550,000)	(600,000)
ITA 84.1(1)(b) Deemed Dividend		$ 400,000

*This amount is technically the greater of the PUC of the old shares and their cost (without the use of the V-Day or median rule). In this example, the two amounts are equal.

17-144. For purposes of determining the capital gain on the disposition of Sander Inc. shares, ITA 54 defines proceeds of disposition to exclude amounts that are treated as deemed dividends under ITA 84.1(1). This means that Mr. Sander would have a capital loss on the disposal of Sander Inc. shares as follows:

Proceeds Before Adjustment (From Elected Value)	$450,000
ITA 84.1(1)(b) Deemed Dividend	(400,000)
Proceeds Of Disposition (ITA 54)	$ 50,000
Adjusted Cost Base (Using Median Rule)	(450,000)
Capital Loss	($400,000)

17-145. As the sale of shares (a non depreciable capital asset) is to an affiliated person (Sander Investments Ltd. is controlled by Mr. Sander), the capital loss would be disallowed by ITA 40(2)(g). As discussed in Paragraph 17-45, when the transferor is an individual, the disallowed loss is added to the adjusted cost base of the substituted property which would be the Sander Inc. shares held by Sander Investments Ltd. This would give these shares an adjusted cost base of $850,000 ($450,000 + $400,000).

17-146. If these shares are sold by Sander Investments Ltd., the result would be a capital gain of $150,000 ($1,000,000 - $850,000). When this is added to the $400,000 deemed dividend that has been allocated to Mr. Sander, the total amount of income is $550,000, the same amount that would have been recorded by Mr. Sander if he had simply sold the Sander Inc. shares for $1,000,000.

17-147. Given this required treatment under ITA 84.1, there is no advantage in the rollover of Sander Inc. shares to Sander Investments Ltd. The taxes that Mr. Sander will pay on the deemed ITA 84.1 dividend are equal to those he would have paid if Sander Inc. had paid the dividend to him directly.

17-148. Note, however, that if the rollover had been structured so that the non share consideration received by Mr. Sander was limited to $50,000, the old Paid Up Capital of Sander Inc., no deemed dividend would have resulted from the transaction and the desired tax free capital gain would have been generated. (This would have required the Sander Investments Ltd. shares to have a fair market value of $950,000.) However, this approach would not provide for the tax free removal of the extra $400,000 from Sander Investments Ltd.

Capital Gains Stripping — ITA 55(2)

The Problem

17-149. A problem similar to that involved in dividend stripping arises when a corporation owns shares in a different corporation. If there is an accrued capital gain on these shares, a disposition of the shares will result in the recognition of that income. Further, corporations are not eligible to use the lifetime capital gains deduction. This means that a disposition of the shares will increase both the taxable income and taxes payable of the corporation.

17-150. While capital gains are subject to corporate income taxes, intercorporate dividends generally escape corporate taxes. This means that, if the investor corporation can devise some method of disposing of its investment so that the proceeds of disposition are received in the form of dividends, payment of corporate taxes could be avoided.

17-151. In the absence of an anti-avoidance provision, this could be accomplished in a variety of ways. If we assume that Investee Company is a wholly owned subsidiary of Investor Company, two ways in which Investor could dispose of Investee are as follows:

- Investee could borrow sufficient funds to pay Investor dividends equal to the accrued capital gain. This could serve to reduce the fair market value of its shares to Investor's adjusted cost base and the disposition could be made with no capital gain being recognized.

- ITA 85(1) could be used to roll the Investee shares into a purchaser corporation in return for redeemable preferred shares. Redemption of the shares would result in an ITA 84(3) deemed dividend as opposed to a capital gain.

17-152. Such procedures are referred to as capital gains stripping. ITA 55(2) is an anti-avoidance provision designed to prevent such conversions of capital gains to dividends by a corporation disposing of an investment in shares.

Application Of ITA 55(2)

17-153. The provisions of ITA 55(2) are applicable when:

- A corporation has received dividends that are deductible under ITA 112(1) as part of a transaction involving a disposition of shares.

- One of the purposes of the dividend was to effect a significant reduction in any capital gain which, in the absence of the dividend, would have been realized on the disposition of shares.

- The disposition was to an arm's length party or there has been a significant increase in the interest of an arm's length party in either corporation.

17-154. If these conditions are present, the following rules apply to the dividend:

ITA 55(2)(a) The dividend shall be deemed not to be a dividend received by the corporation.

ITA 55(2)(b) Where a corporation has disposed of the share, the dividend shall be deemed to be proceeds of disposition of the share except to the extent that it is otherwise included in computing such proceeds.

ITA 55(2)(c) Where a corporation has not disposed of the share, the dividend shall be deemed to be a gain of the corporation for the year in which the dividend was received from the disposition of a capital property.

17-155. These rules do not apply if the dividend represents a distribution of what is commonly referred to as "safe income". This "safe income" is income that has accrued after 1971 or, if the acquisition of the shares was after that date, after the date on which the shares were acquired.

Capital Gains Stripping - Example One

17-156. The first example is diagramed in Figure 17-3 (following page). In this example, Lor Inc. owns 100 percent of the shares of Lee Ltd. The shares have a fair market value of $800,000, an adjusted cost base of $200,000, and a potential capital gain of $600,000. Lee Ltd. has safe income of $250,000. An arm's length purchaser is willing to pay $800,000 for these shares. In order to sell the shares to the arm's length purchaser, Lor Inc. arranges the following:

- Lee Ltd. borrows $600,000 from a financial institution.
- The borrowed funds are used to pay a $600,000 tax free dividend to Lor Inc. This reduces the fair market value of Lee Ltd. to $200,000.
- Lor Inc. sells the shares to the arm's length purchaser for $200,000 in cash. As this is the adjusted cost base of the shares, there will be no capital gain.
- The arm's length purchaser invests $600,000 in Lee Ltd., with the funds being used to retire the $600,000 loan.

17-157. In the absence of ITA 55(2), Lor Inc. would have managed to dispose of its interest in Lee Ltd. without the recognition of a taxable capital gain. However, ITA 55(2) will prevent this from happening.

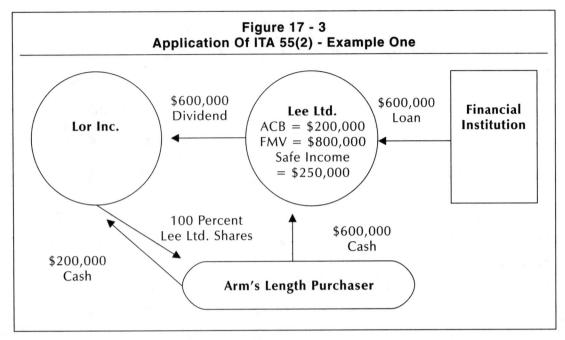

Figure 17 - 3
Application Of ITA 55(2) - Example One

17-158.   Under ITA 55(2)(a), the $600,000 dividend will be deemed not to be a dividend. Under ITA 55(2)(b), the dividend will be treated as proceeds of disposition. This results in the following capital gain calculation:

Dividends Received (Tax Free)	$600,000
Dividend Attributable To Safe Income	(250,000)
Deemed Proceeds Of Disposition	$350,000
Actual Proceeds Of Disposition	200,000
Total Proceeds Of Disposition	$550,000
Adjusted Cost Base	(200,000)
Capital Gain	$350,000

17-159.   As can be seen in the preceding calculation, ITA 55(2) has served to convert the portion of the dividend not paid from safe income into a capital gain which will be taxed. The $250,000 dividend attributable to safe income will be deducted in calculating taxable income resulting in no tax cost.

Capital Gains Stripping - Example Two

17-160.   This example is diagramed in Figure 17-4 (following page) and involves the same two Companies that were used in the previous example. The only difference is in the approach that they use in attempting to convert the taxable capital gain into a tax free dividend.

17-161.   In this case, ITA 85(1) is used to roll the Lee Ltd. shares into the purchaser corporation at an elected value equal to the $200,000 adjusted cost base of the shares. As consideration for the shares, Lor Inc. takes back $800,000 in redeemable preferred shares. These shares have a PUC and an adjusted cost base of $200,000.

17-162.   As the elected value was equal to the adjusted cost base of the shares, there will be no capital gain on the transaction. Further, in the absence of ITA 55(2), the redemption of the shares would have the following results:

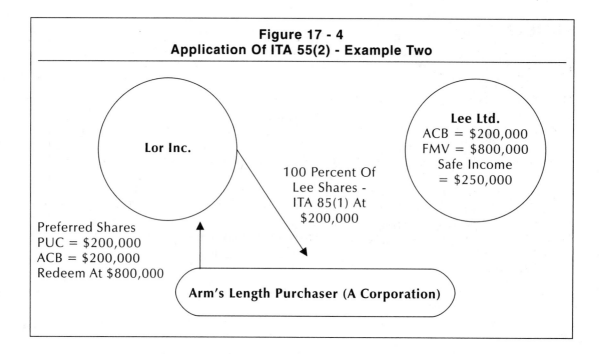

Figure 17 - 4
Application Of ITA 55(2) - Example Two

Lor Inc.

Lee Ltd.
ACB = $200,000
FMV = $800,000
Safe Income
= $250,000

100 Percent Of
Lee Shares -
ITA 85(1) At
$200,000

Preferred Shares
PUC = $200,000
ACB = $200,000
Redeem At $800,000

Arm's Length Purchaser (A Corporation)

Redemption Proceeds	$800,000
PUC Of Shares	(200,000)
ITA 84(3) Deemed Dividend [Absence of ITA 55(2)]	$600,000

Redemption Proceeds	$800,000
ITA 84(3) Deemed Dividend	(600,000)
ITA 54 Deemed Proceeds Of Disposition	$200,000
Adjusted Cost Base	(200,000)
Capital Gain [Absence of ITA 55(2)]	Nil

17-163.   In this example, ITA 55(2)(a) would deem the portion of the dividend that is not from safe income to not be a dividend. This would reduce the ITA 84(3) dividend as follows:

ITA 84(3) Deemed Dividend	$600,000
Amount Deemed Not To Be A Dividend ($600,000 - $250,000)	(350,000)
Remaining ITA 84(3) Deemed Dividend	$250,000

17-164.   Given this reduction in the ITA 84(3) dividend, the capital gain calculation is as follows:

Redemption Proceeds	$800,000
ITA 84(3) Deemed Dividend	(250,000)
ITA 54 Deemed Proceeds Of Disposition	$550,000
Adjusted Cost Base	(200,000)
Capital Gain	$350,000

> Exercise Seventeen-8 deals with capital gains stripping. This would be an appropriate time to attempt this exercise.

17-165.   In this example, ITA 55(2) has served to convert the ITA 84(3) dividend that was not paid from safe income into a capital gain which will be taxed.

References

17-166.   For more detailed study of the material in this Chapter, we would refer you to the following:

ITA 55(2)	Deemed Proceeds Or Capital Gain
ITA 84.1(1)	Non Arm's Length Sale Of Shares
ITA 85(1)	Transfer Of Property To Corporation By Shareholders
IC 76-19R3	Transfer Of Property To A Corporation Under Section 85
IT-188R	Sale of Accounts Receivable
IT-291R2	Transfer Of Property To A Corporation Under Subsection 85(1)
IT-378R	Winding-Up Of A Partnership
IT-489R	Non Arm's Length Sale Of Shares To A Corporation

Exercises

(The solutions for these exercises can be found following Chapter 21 of the text.)

Exercise Seventeen - 1 (Transfers Under Section 85 - ACB Of Consideration)

Using ITA 85, Mrs. Jennifer Lee transfers non depreciable property to a corporation at an elected value of $62,000. The property has an adjusted cost base of $62,000 and a fair market value of $176,000. As consideration she receives a note for $51,000, preferred shares with a fair market value of $53,000, and common shares with a fair market value of $72,000. Indicate the adjusted cost base of the individual items of consideration received by Mrs. Lee.

Exercise Seventeen - 2 (Transfers Under Section 85 - PUC Reduction)

Using ITA 85, Mr. Rob McCleen transfers non depreciable property to a corporation at an elected value of $114,000. The property has an adjusted cost base of $114,000 and a fair market value of $234,000. As consideration he receives a note for $83,000, preferred shares with a fair market value and legal stated capital of $97,000, and common shares with a fair market value and legal stated capital of $54,000. Indicate the PUC of the preferred and common shares that were issued to Mr. McCleen.

Exercise Seventeen - 3 (Transfers Under Section 85)

Goodwill with a cost of $42,000 and a fair market value of $86,000, is reflected in a cumulative eligible capital balance of $25,337. Using ITA 85, an individual transfers it to a corporation in return for preferred shares with a fair market value and a legal stated capital of $93,000. Indicate the minimum and maximum transfer values that can be elected, the amount of taxable capital gain that will result if the most advantageous value is elected, the amount of any benefit that will have to be included in the transferor's income under ITA 15(1) or ITA 84(1) and the adjusted cost base of the preferred shares issued if the most advantageous value is elected.

Exercise Seventeen - 4 (Transfers Under Section 85 - Tax Consequences)

John Savage owns a depreciable property with a capital cost of $120,000 and a fair market value of $180,000. It is the only asset in its CCA Class and the UCC balance for the Class is $98,000. On June 1, 2001, he uses ITA 85 to transfer this property to a corporation at an elected value of $160,000. In return for the property, he receives a note for $160,000, in addition to common shares with a fair market value of $20,000. What are the tax implications of this transaction for both John Savage and the transferee corporation?

Exercise Seventeen - 5 (Section 85 - Gift To Transferee)

Janice Bellows establishes a new corporation, arranging to have all of its common shares issued to her daughter for cash of $1,000. Ms. Bellows then transfers, using ITA 85, non depreciable property with an adjusted cost base of $50,000 and a fair market value of $110,000. The transfer is made at an elected value of $50,000. As consideration for this property, the corporation gives Ms. Bellows a note for $50,000 and preferred stock with a fair market value and a legal stated capital of $15,000. Describe the tax consequences of these transactions for both Ms. Bellows and her daughter.

Exercise Seventeen - 6 (Section 85 - Gift To Transferor)

Mr. Larry Custer uses ITA 85 to transfer non depreciable property to a corporation. The adjusted cost base of the property is $123,000 and it has a fair market value of $217,000. In consideration for this property, Mr. Custer receives a note for $248,000 and preferred stock with a fair market value and a legal stated capital of $22,000. What are the tax consequences of this transaction to Mr. Custer?

Exercise Seventeen - 7 (Dividend Strips)

Miss Sarah Cole owns 100 percent of the outstanding shares of Cole Inc., a qualified small business corporation. The shares have a PUC and an adjusted cost base of $125,000 and a fair market value of $767,000. In order to make full use of her lifetime capital gains deduction, Miss Cole uses ITA 85(1) to transfer these shares to Sarah's Holdings Ltd. at an elected value of $625,000. As consideration she receives a note for $450,000 and preferred shares with a fair market value and a legal stated capital of $317,000. Miss Cole owns all of the shares of Sarah's Holdings Ltd. What are the tax consequences of this transaction to Miss Cole?

Exercise Seventeen - 8 (Capital Gains Strips)

Markem Ltd. owns 100 percent of the outstanding common shares of Larkin Ltd. The shares of Larkin have an adjusted cost base of $75,000 and a fair market value of $840,000. Included in its Retained Earnings balance is $225,000 of income that has been earned since its acquisition by Markem Ltd. Markem Ltd. would like to sell its shares in Larkin Ltd. In order to implement this sale, Markem Ltd. has instructed Larkin Ltd. to borrow $750,000 from its bank and use all of these funds to pay a dividend on the shares held by Markem Ltd. The shares are then sold to Mr. J. Leaner for $90,000. Mr. Leaner is not related to Markem Ltd. or Larkin Ltd. What are the tax consequences to Markem Ltd. of these transactions?

Problems For Self Study

(The solutions for these problems can be found following Chapter 21 of the text.)

Self Study Problem Seventeen - 1

Ms. Audrey Flack has operated a gift shop for 15 years as a sole proprietorship. After considerable analysis, she has decided that she would experience a number of advantages if she were to incorporate. On December 1, 2001, the assets that she proposes to transfer to the new corporation are as follows:

	Tax Cost	Fair Market Value
Cash	$ 27,000	$ 27,000
Accounts Receivable	51,000	45,000
Inventories	73,000	88,000
Furniture And Fixtures	62,000	45,000
Goodwill	-0-	150,000
Totals	$213,000	$355,000

The Undepreciated Capital Cost of the Furniture And Fixtures is $38,000 at this point in time.

Ms. Flack will receive no consideration other than shares and, as she has no immediate family, she will be the only shareholder in the new company. She has used all of her lifetime capital gains deduction on other dispositions of capital assets.

Required:

A. If no elections are made by Ms. Flack and the assets are transferred at fair market value on December 31, 2001, calculate the taxable income resulting from the transfer that Ms. Flack would have to report.

B. Indicate the elections that could be used by Ms. Flack to reduce the amount of taxable income on the transfer of assets to the new corporation. Calculate the amount of taxable income that would result from the transfer being made under these elections.

Self Study Problem Seventeen - 2

For nearly 20 years Ms. Monica Speaks has operated a very successful manufacturing business. During much of this period you have constantly reminded her that there would be many advantages associated with incorporation, including the availability of the small business deduction. In the past she has indicated that she has all of the money that she requires and simply cannot be bothered with the complications associated with incorporation. However, in late 2001, you have finally convinced her that incorporation may be the wisest course of action.

She indicates that she is still concerned with respect to taxes that might arise on the transfer of her business assets to a corporation. In response, you have indicated that Section 85 of the *Income Tax Act* provides a method of transfer which will result in little or no taxation at the time of the transfer. As a consequence, she decides to proceed with incorporation, indicating that all of the shares in the new company (Speaks Inc.) will be issued to her.

On October 1, 2001, the transfer date, the business assets of Ms. Speaks have tax values as follows:

Cash		$ 36,300
Accounts Receivable		78,500
Inventories - Cost		261,000
Land - Cost		196,000
Building - Cost	$155,500	
Accumulated CCA	(51,900)	103,600
Equipment - Cost	$222,000	
Accumulated CCA	(155,000)	67,000
Total		$742,400

On October 1, 2001, the identifiable assets have the following fair market values:

Accounts Receivable	$ 78,500
Inventories	311,000
Land	282,000
Building	253,000
Equipment	32,500
Goodwill	339,000
Total	$1,296,000

Required:

A. Indicate which assets are eligible for transfer under the provisions of ITA 85 and whether they should be transferred under this provision.

B. Given that Ms. Speaks wishes to minimize the tax consequences of the incorporation transaction, calculate the minimum transfer price for each asset.

C. Describe the tax consequences for both Ms. Speaks and Speaks Inc. if she transfers the assets at the values indicated in Part B.

Self Study Problem Seventeen - 3

During 2000, Mr. Richard Dix acquired a business location consisting of land with a brick store building located on it. The total price was $1,260,000 with $315,000 of this allocated to the land and $945,000 allocated to the building.

After operating the business during 2000 and the first six months of 2001 as a proprietorship, Mr. Dix decides to incorporate. In this process he uses ITA 85 to transfer the land and building to the corporation on a tax free basis. He elects a transfer price of $1,241,100. The details of the transfer are as follows:

	Land	Building
Capital Cost Or UCC	$315,000	$ 926,100
Appraised Value	787,500	1,102,500
Elected Amount	315,000	926,100
Consideration:		
Debt*	315,000	926,100
Shares	472,500	176,400

*The debt related to the Land and Building includes the corporation's assumption of an existing mortgage of $519,750. This means that the total new debt issued by the corporation is as follows:

Debt On Land	$ 315,000
Debt On Building	926,100
Total Debt	$1,241,100
Mortgage Assumed	(519,750)
Net Debt Issued	$ 721,350

On December 1, 2001, the corporation redeems the $721,350 of new debt issued at its face value. On December 28, 2001, Mr. Dix sells his shares in the corporation for $894,000.

Required:

A. Describe the tax consequences of the transfer and compute the adjusted cost base of the consideration received by Mr. Dix.

B. Describe the tax consequences of the debt redemption and share sale for Mr. Dix.

Self Study Problem Seventeen - 4

Mr. Lardner is the owner of an unincorporated business which is involved in the distribution of various types of paper products. It is his wish that all of the assets of this business be transferred to a new corporation, Lardner Distribution Ltd. Mr. Lardner will be the only shareholder of this new corporation.

The assets of the business have "tax values" (adjusted cost base or undepreciated capital cost, as appropriate) which total $492,000. The liabilities of the business total $122,000. The total fair market value of all of the assets of the business is $746,000. Except in the case of Accounts Receivable, the fair market values of the individual assets exceed their respective tax values. The Accounts Receivable have a carrying value of $25,000 and a fair market value of $20,000. A joint election will be made under ITA 22 to transfer them to the corporation and, as a consequence, they will be excluded from the ITA 85 election.

The assets other than the Accounts Receivable will be transferred under the provisions of Section 85 using a total elected value of $467,000 ($492,000 - $25,000). The new corporation will assume the $122,000 of liabilities owed by the unincorporated business. As consideration for the net assets of the business, Mr. Lardner will receive from the corporation $128,000 in new debt securities, preferred shares with a fair market value of $150,000, and common shares with a fair market value of $326,000. The total value of the consideration, including both the old and the new debt, is equal to the $726,000 fair market value of the assets transferred under ITA 85 ($746,000 - $20,000).

Immediately after the transfer of assets to Lardner Distribution Ltd., the Company redeems both the preferred shares and the common shares at their respective fair market values. The Company borrows the funds required to make the redemption.

Required:

A. Determine the adjusted cost base for the preferred stock issued to Mr. Lardner, and for the common stock issued to Mr. Lardner.

B. Determine the paid up capital for the preferred stock issued to Mr. Lardner, and for the common shares issued to Mr. Lardner.

C. Indicate the tax consequences to Mr. Lardner that would result from the corporation redeeming the preferred and common shares.

Self Study Problem Seventeen - 5

Miss Doreen Brock owns an unincorporated business which operates out of leased premises. Her accounting records are based on the same information that has been used for tax purposes. On December 31, 2001, the business has the following assets and liabilities:

	Tax Value	Fair Market Value
Accounts Receivable	$ 78,000	$ 75,000
Inventory	174,000	208,000
Equipment (Cost = $420,000)	234,000	317,000
Goodwill	-0-	350,000
Total Assets	$486,000	$950,000
Liabilities	(95,000)	(95,000)
Net Assets	$391,000	$855,000

Miss Brock wishes to incorporate her business in a manner that minimizes or eliminates any tax effects resulting from the transaction. All of the assets of the unincorporated business will be transferred to the new corporation and the new corporation will assume the outstanding liabilities of Miss Brock's business. In addition, the corporation will issue new debt to Miss Brock in the amount of $75,000, Preferred Stock with a fair market value of $225,000, and Common Stock with a fair market value of $480,000. The joint election under ITA 22 is made on the transfer of the Accounts Receivable. Miss Brock has totally utilized her lifetime capital gains deduction.

Required:

A. Given that Miss Brock wishes to minimize or eliminate current taxes, indicate the values that should be elected for each of the assets to be transferred.

B. Determine the Adjusted Cost Base of the debt, preferred shares, and common shares that would be received by Miss Brock on the rollover.

C. Determine the paid up capital of the Common Stock and Preferred Stock that were issued by the new corporation to Miss Brock.

D. Determine the tax consequences to Miss Brock if the preferred and common shares that she received in the rollover were immediately redeemed by the new corporation at fair market value.

Self Study Problem Seventeen - 6

Ms. Doreen Chisholm owns 75 percent of the outstanding shares of Dor Manufacturing Ltd. (DML). The remaining 25 percent of this Canadian controlled private company are held by her married daughter Elaine Lee.

When the Company was founded ten years ago, all of the shares were issued to Ms. Chisholm in return for $100,000 in cash. This $100,000 amount is the paid up capital of the DML shares, as well as Ms. Chisholm's adjusted cost base.

In 1996, Ms. Chisholm sold 25 percent of the DML shares to her daughter for cash of $25,000, the fair market value of the shares at that time. There have been no other transactions in the shares since DML was founded.

On December 31, 2001, the fair market value of Ms. Chisholm's holding of DML shares is $900,000. At her direction, Ms. Chisholm's lawyer establishes a new company, Dorlaine Inc. Using the provisions of ITA 85(1), Ms. Chisholm's DML shares are transferred to this new Company at an elected value of $575,000. In return for the DML shares, Ms. Chisholm receives debt securities of the new Company with a fair market value of $500,000, along with newly issued Dorlaine Inc. common shares with a fair market value of $400,000.

Ms. Chisholm transfers various other investments she is holding personally into Dorlaine Inc. in return for debt securities equal to the investments' fair market value.

Her daughter continues to hold the remaining 25 percent of the DML shares. Ms. Chisholm has made no use of her $500,000 lifetime capital gains deduction.

Required

A. What are the tax consequences to Ms. Chisholm of transferring the DML shares to Dorlaine Inc.?

B. Ms. Chisholm dies on January 1, 2002. The terms of her will leave all of the Dorlaine Inc. shares to her daughter. What are the tax consequences arising as a result of Ms. Chisholm's death?

Your answer to both Part A and Part B should be expressed in terms of the type (e.g., dividends, taxable capital gains, or allowable capital losses) and amount of net income for tax purposes resulting from the transaction or event.

Assignment Problems

(The solutions for these problems are only available in
the solutions manual that has been provided to your instructor.)

Assignment Problem Seventeen - 1

Several years ago, Ms. Fox acquired a small apartment building for a total consideration of $950,000. This total was allocated on the basis of $225,000 for the land and $725,000 for the building.

At present, the property has a fair market value of $1,200,000 and Ms. Fox would like to transfer it to a corporation using a Section 85 rollover. At the end of the preceding year the building had an undepreciated capital cost of $582,000 and there is a mortgage against the property in the amount of $350,000. The values elected for the transfer and the consideration given to Ms. Fox are as follows:

Elected Value Of Property ($225,000 + $582,000)	$807,000
Consideration To Ms. Fox:	
Mortgage Assumed	$350,000
Preferred Shares (Market Value)	$300,000
Number of Common Shares	12,000

Shortly after the Section 85 rollover is completed, Ms. Fox sells all of the common shares received for $550,000.

Required: Describe the tax consequences for Ms. Fox of selling the shares.

Assignment Problem Seventeen - 2

The following four independent cases involve transfers of assets under ITA 85. For each of the four cases indicate:

A. the minimum and maximum transfer prices that could be used under the provisions of ITA 85;

B. the minimum amount to be included in the income of the transferor, assuming ITA 85 is used advantageously;

C. the adjusted cost base of the Preferred and Common Stock consideration, assuming ITA 85 is used advantageously; and

D. any benefits that will have to be included in the income of the shareholder as a share-holder appropriation (ITA 15[1]) or a deemed dividend (ITA 84[1]), assuming ITA 85 is used advantageously.

Case One   Inventories with a fair market value of $15,000 and a cost of $10,000 are transferred in exchange for $12,000 in non share consideration and $3,000 in Preferred Stock (fair market value and legal stated capital).

Case Two   Land with a cost of $120,000, and a fair market value of $150,000, is transferred in exchange for non share consideration of $120,000, and Preferred Stock of $30,000 (fair market value and legal stated capital).

Case Three   Equipment with a cost of $50,000, a fair market value of $35,000, and an unde-preciated capital cost of $20,000, is transferred in exchange for non share consideration of $25,000, Preferred Stock of $5,000 (fair market value and legal stated capital) and Common Stock of $5,000.

Case Four   Goodwill with a cost of $20,000, a fair market value of $40,000, and a cumula-tive eligible capital amount of $10,950, is transferred in exchange for Preferred Stock of $44,000 (fair market value and legal stated capital).

Assignment Problem Seventeen - 3

Miss Suzanne Blake intends to transfer a parcel of land to a new corporation using the provisions of Section 85. The land has an adjusted cost base of $400,000 and a fair market value of $800,000. Miss Blake will transfer the land at an elected value of $400,000.

Miss Blake is considering the following alternative consideration packages:

	Alternative		
	One	Two	Three
Debt Of The New Corporation	$300,000	$200,000	$320,000
Preferred Shares	50,000	600,000	Nil
Common Shares	450,000	Nil	480,000
Total	$800,000	$800,000	$800,000

All of the amounts in the preceding table are fair market values.

Required:

A. For each of the three alternatives, determine the adjusted cost base of the individual items of consideration received by Miss Blake.

B. For each of the three alternatives, determine the legal stated capital and the paid up capital (PUC) for the preferred and/or common shares issued.

Assignment Problem Seventeen - 4

During December, 2001, Mr. Norris Notion transferred a depreciable capital property to a new corporation. The property is the only asset in its CCA Class and Mr. Notion will own all of the shares of the new corporation. The CCA Class had a UCC of $52,000. The property had an original cost of $58,000 and a fair market value of $92,000. As Mr. Notion had a capital loss of $20,000 during 2001, he elected to transfer the property under ITA 85(1) at a value of $78,000. As consideration for the property, Mr. Notion takes back a note for $68,000, preferred shares with a fair market value of $20,000, and common shares with a fair market value of $4,000.

Required: Describe the income tax implications resulting from this transaction. Your answer should include both current tax implications and the determination of values which will have future tax implications.

Assignment Problem Seventeen - 5

Several years ago, Ms. Katrina Bond acquired a business location which included land and a building for a total of $950,000. At the time it was estimated that the value of the land was $220,000 and the value of the building was $730,000.

Ms. Bond operated the business for several years as a sole proprietorship and during this period she took capital cost allowance on the building. As there were years in which she experienced losses, she did not always take the maximum amount of capital cost allowance.

Ms. Bond has finally agreed to take your advice and incorporate the business. She will use ITA 85(1) to transfer the land and building to the new corporation. At the time of the transfer the building had an undepreciated capital cost of $625,000. Other relevant values were as follows:

Asset	Tax Cost	Appraised Value	Elected Amount
Land	$220,000	$ 510,000	$220,000
Building	625,000	980,000	730,000
Total	$845,000	$1,490,000	$950,000

There is a $400,000 mortgage on the land and building which will be assumed by the new corporation. In addition, the new corporation will issue $500,000 in new debt to Ms. Bond. The remaining consideration will be common shares with a fair market value of $590,000.

Required:

A. What are the tax consequences of making this transfer at the elected value of $950,000? Your answer should include amounts to be included in Ms. Bond's income as a result of the transfer, as well as the corporation's tax values for the assets.

B. Compute the adjusted cost base of each component of the consideration that Ms. Bond has received from the corporation.

C. Compute the PUC of the corporation's newly issued common shares.

D. What amounts would be included in Ms. Bond's Net Income For Tax Purposes if, at a later point in time, she sells her common shares for $650,000?

E. What amounts would be included in Ms. Bond's Net Income For Tax Purposes if, at a later point in time, the corporation redeems her common shares for $650,000?

Assignment Problem Seventeen - 6

Mike Danforth has, for a number of years, operated a successful proprietorship involved in retail sales of home improvement products. Mr. Danforth has decided to incorporate his business operations under the name of Danforth Inc. For tax purposes, this decision will be implemented using ITA 85(1).

At the end of 2001, the tax values (adjusted cost base or UCC) and fair market values of the assets and liabilities on his Balance Sheet are as follows:

	Tax Values	Fair Market Values
Cash	$ 2,500	$ 2,500
Temporary Investments	27,500	37,500
Accounts Receivable	13,750	12,500
Inventories	17,500	17,500
Prepayments	7,500	7,500
Land	105,000	77,500
Buildings (Cost = $113,000)	70,000	125,000
Equipment (Cost = $48,000)	20,000	7,500
Goodwill	-0-	117,500
Liabilities	(20,000)	(20,000)
Total	$243,750	$385,000

Other Information:

1. The Temporary Investments contain securities that have been purchased in order to absorb a seasonal excess of cash.

2. With respect to the Accounts Receivable, the $1,250 difference between their tax value and their fair market value reflects Mr. Danforth's estimate of potential bad debts.

3. In implementing this rollover, Mr. Danforth will take debt as his non share consideration. Additional consideration, in excess of the maximum amount of non share consideration that can be taken without incurring a tax liability, will be taken in the form of common shares.

4. In 2002, Mr. Danforth sells the shares that he receives in this rollover for $208,000.

Required:

A. Advise Mr. Danforth with respect to which assets and liabilities should be transferred under the provisions of ITA 85(1) and the values that should be elected in order to minimize his current taxes payable.

B. Indicate the maximum amount of non share consideration that Mr. Danforth can receive without being subject to additional taxation.

C. Calculate Mr. Danforth's taxable capital gain and indicate the effect of the sale of shares on his taxable income.

Assignment Problem Seventeen - 7

For the last six years, Ms. Sarah Delmor has operated Delmor Industries as a sole proprietorship. The business has been very successful and, as a consequence, has experienced rapid growth. Given this situation, Ms. Delmor has concluded that in order to enhance her ability to raise additional capital, the assets and liabilities of Delmor Industries should be transferred to a new corporation, Delmor Inc.

On July 1, 2001, the tax values (adjusted cost base or UCC) and fair market values of the assets and liabilities of Delmor Industries are as follows:

	Tax Value	Fair Market Value
Accounts Receivable	$ 120,000	$ 112,000
Temporary Investments	42,000	37,000
Inventories	220,000	231,000
Depreciable Assets - CCA Class 8 (Note One)	53,000	61,500
Machinery (Note Two)	197,000	273,000
Land	150,000	311,000
Building (Note Three)	416,000	523,500
Total Assets	$1,198,000	$1,549,000
Liabilities	(72,000)	(72,000)
Total Net Assets (Owner's Equity)	$1,126,000	$1,477,000

Note One   There are two assets in Class 8. Asset A has a cost of $27,000 and a fair market value of $32,500. Asset B has a cost of $33,000 and a fair market value of $29,000.

Note Two   The cost of the Machinery was $212,500.

Note Three   The cost of the Building was $472,000.

The transfer of the Delmor Industries assets to Delmor Inc. will take place on July 1, 2001 and an election will be made under ITA 85. Any shares issued by Delmor Inc. as part of this roll-over will be issued to Ms. Delmor who is a Canadian resident.

Required:

A. Determine whether the Accounts Receivable and Temporary Investments should be transferred under the provisions of ITA 85. Explain your conclusion and, if you recommend that ITA 85 should not be used, indicate the appropriate alternative treatment.

B. Without regard to your conclusions in Part A, assume that all of the assets are transferred to the new corporation under the provisions of ITA 85. Indicate the minimum values that can be elected for each of the assets. Include a detailed explanation of how the election would apply to Asset A and Asset B in Class 8.

C. The transfer of the assets of Delmor Industries to Delmor Inc. is going to be made using the provisions of ITA 85. Ms. Delmor intends to elect the values that you have determined in Part B and transfer all of the assets of Delmor Industries (whether or not appropriate) un-der this rollover provision. Delmor Inc. will assume the liabilities of Delmor Industries and, in addition, will issue $800,000 in new debt to Ms. Delmor. With respect to share consideration, the new Company will issue Preferred Stock with a fair market value of $200,000 and Common Stock with a fair market value of $477,000. Determine the ad-justed cost base of the non share consideration, Preferred Stock and Common Stock received by Ms. Delmor. In addition, determine the paid up capital amounts for the Pre-ferred Stock and the Common Stock.

D. Indicate the tax consequences to Ms. Delmor if the Preferred Stock and Common Stock that she received in the rollover were immediately redeemed by the new corporation at fair market value.

Assignment Problem Seventeen - 8

Note   This problem requires knowledge of ITA 84.1 (dividend stripping) provisions related to V-Day values.

Mr. Doug Johnston is the sole shareholder of Johnston Home Furnishings, a Canadian con-trolled private company involved in the sale of retail products for the home. He has operated this Company since 1967, in most years earning a satisfactory rate of return on the invested assets.

As of December 31, 2001, relevant information as to the values associated with his Company is as follows:

Initial Investment In 1967 (Paid Up Capital)	$ 478,000
December 31, 1971 Valuation Day Value	$3,985,000
Fair Market Value - December 31, 2001	$8,214,000

Mr. Johnston is nearing retirement and wishes to gradually dispose of his business. In preparation for retirement, he has enrolled in a variety of courses at a local college. One of these courses, Taxation 405, has introduced him to the concept of transferring property to a corporation under Section 85 of the *Income Tax Act*. In reviewing this Section, along with the various transitional provisions associated with assets owned prior to December 31, 1971, it has occurred to him that by transferring the shares of Johnston Home Furnishings to a new Company he could effectively escape taxation on the difference between his initial investment of $478,000 and the valuation day value of his business of $3,985,000.

In view of his analysis of this situation, he has planned to transfer all of the shares of Johnston Home Furnishings to a new company, Johnston Investments. The transfer will be made under the provisions of ITA 85(1) and an elected value of $3,985,000 will be used for the securities. In return for this transfer, Mr. Johnston will receive a non interest bearing note for $3,985,000 and 10 shares of the new Company's no par common shares. The note will be due in one year and Mr. Johnston anticipates that, as a result of dividends received from Johnston Home Furnishings, Johnston Investments will have sufficient cash to pay the entire amount at that time.

Required:

A. In the absence of ITA 84.1, indicate the tax consequences of Johnston Investments paying off the $3,985,000 loan next year.

B. Determine whether ITA 84.1 would be applicable in this case. Assuming that ITA 84.1 is applicable, calculate the deemed dividend that would arise on this transfer. In addition, indicate the net economic effect that would result from this transfer combined with a redemption of the Johnston Investments shares at their fair market value of $4,229,000 ($8,214,000 - $3,985,000).

Assignment Problem Seventeen - 9

Norton Ltd. is a Canadian controlled private corporation established six years ago with an initial investment by Ms. Nora Chadwick of $225,000. In return for her investment, Ms. Chadwick received 22,500 common shares with a paid up capital of $225,000. The corporation has a December 31 year end.

The Company has been very successful and, as a consequence, it is estimated that the current fair market value of the common shares is $2,465,000. Ms. Chadwick has a serious heart condition which has significantly reduced her life expectancy. As a consequence, she would like to transfer any future increase in value of the Norton Ltd. shares to her companion of the last 25 years, Mr. Bobby Borque. Mr. Borque cohabits with Ms. Chadwick in a conjugal relationship. In order to accomplish this goal, she intends to have Bobby establish a new Company, Borque Inc. All 100 of the common shares of Borque Inc. will be issued to Bobby in return for a cash investment of $1,000.

Once the new Company is established, Ms. Chadwick would transfer all of her common shares in Norton Ltd. to Borque Inc. She will make the transfer under the provisions of ITA 85(1), electing a value of $725,000. It is her intention to take back consideration consisting of a $725,000 interest bearing note (fair market value = $725,000), along with retractable preferred shares with a fair market value and a paid up capital of $1,740,000.

Norton Ltd. is a qualified small business corporation and Ms. Chadwick has made no use of her lifetime capital gains deduction. She believes that this rollover transaction has been structured in a manner that will allow her to utilize the full $500,000 amount of this deduction.

Required:

A. Explain the tax consequences of the proposed ITA 85(1) transfer of the Norton Ltd. shares to Borque Inc.

B. The results in Part A indicate that Ms. Chadwick did not accomplish her goal of triggering a $500,000 capital gain on her disposition of Norton Ltd. shares. Explain briefly how you would change the ITA 85(1) transaction in order to accomplish this goal. In addition, determine the tax implications that would result from this new approach.

C. As an alternative approach to using her $500,000 lifetime capital gains deduction, Ms. Chadwick proposes selling 5,022 shares of Norton Ltd. to Borque Inc. for cash. The shares would be sold for their current fair market value. Explain the tax consequences of this proposed transaction.

Assignment Problem Seventeen - 10

Gaynor Ltd. owns 100 percent of the outstanding shares of Northcote Inc. The Northcote shares have a Paid Up Capital of $250,000 and a fair market value of $1,300,000. Gaynor's Adjusted Cost Base for the Northcote shares is $250,000. Northcote Inc. has post 1971 Retained Earnings (safe income) of $450,000 and has a nil balance in the Refundable Dividend Tax On Hand account.

Required: Indicate the amount and type of income that would accrue to Gaynor Ltd. in both of the following independent situations:

A. Northcote Inc. obtains a bank loan in the amount of $1,050,000 and uses all of the acquired funds to pay a dividend to Gaynor Ltd. Subsequent to the receipt of this dividend, Gaynor Ltd. sells the Northcote shares to Mr. Jones, an arm's length party, for $250,000.

B. Using ITA 85, Gaynor transfers the Northcote shares to Jones Ltd., an unrelated corporation. The elected value is $250,000. In return for the Northcote shares, Gaynor receives Jones Ltd. Preferred Stock with a Paid Up Capital of $250,000 and a redemption value of $1,300,000. Immediately after the transfer, Jones Ltd. redeems the Preferred Stock for $1,300,000.

Assignment Problem Seventeen - 11 (Electronic Library Research Problem)

Provide brief answers to the following questions. Your answers should be supported by references to materials found in your Electronic Library.

A. A transfer of property under ITA 85(1) may involve a capital contribution. For example, an individual may give property with a fair market value of $100,000 in return for shares with a fair market value of $10,000, in circumstances such that no gift to a related party is involved. Can the amount of the capital contribution be added to the adjusted cost base of the shares received?

B. Property is sometimes omitted or misstated in the process of filing an ITA 85(1) election. Under what circumstances will the CCRA allow the filing of an amended election?

C. When the provisions of ITA 84.1 are applicable, there is usually a PUC reduction under ITA ITA 84.1(1). How is this reduction applied when more than one class of shares is involved?

Chapter 18

Other Rollovers, Business Valuation, Sale Of An Incorporated Business and Tax Shelters

Introduction

18-1.   The preceding Chapter gave detailed consideration to the Section 85 rollover provisions, which provide for a tax deferred transfer of property to a corporation. In addition, Chapter 10 dealt with rollovers involving transfers to a spouse and transfers of farm property to children. As indicated previously, there are a number of other rollover provisions in the Act which will be discussed in this Chapter.

18-2.   These additional rollover provisions cover share for share exchanges among corporations, share exchanges in the process of reorganization of a corporation, amalgamations of existing corporations, winding up of a 90 percent or more owned subsidiary, and conversions of debt to shares. The winding up of a Canadian corporation which is not a 90 percent owned subsidiary is also covered. This latter transaction does not involve a rollover, but is dealt with in the same Section of the *Income Tax Act* as the winding up of a 90 percent or more owned subsidiary.

18-3.   In the process of arranging a rollover, a valuation of business assets is often required, so alternative methods of valuation are introduced in this Chapter. Valuations are also integral to decisions involving a sale of a business. Issues associated with selling the assets and shares of a business are addressed, along with the substantially different income tax consequences of each. Finally, the concept of tax shelters is introduced, followed by a summary of methods to evaluate such investments.

Share For Share Exchanges

18-4.   ITA 85.1 provides for a rollover in which a shareholder exchanges his shares for shares of an acquiring corporation. When there are many diverse shareholders, a share for share exchange is easier to accomplish than a Section 85 rollover, because there is no need for each shareholder to file an election. Further, the provisions of Section 85.1 apply automatically unless the vendor includes any gain or loss on the transaction in his income tax return. Given these features, a Section 85.1 exchange is an important arrangement in business combination transactions.

18-5.   A brief example will serve to illustrate the basic provisions of Section 85.1:

> **Example**   Ms. Cowper is the sole shareholder of Cowper Inc., owning a total of 1,000 shares with a paid up capital and an adjusted cost base of $10,000. Mega Holdings Ltd. acquires these shares in return for 5,000 of its common shares. The Mega Holdings shares are currently trading at $25 per share, resulting in a value for the 5,000 shares of $125,000.

18-6.   In the absence of the rollover provisions in ITA 85.1, Ms. Cowper would have a capital gain of $115,000 ($125,000 - $10,000). However, under the provisions of ITA 85.1, Ms. Cowper is deemed to have disposed of her shares for an amount equal to their adjusted cost base and to have acquired the shares in Mega Holdings for the same amount. Also, the paid up capital of the Mega shares is limited to $10,000, which is the paid up capital of the Cowper shares.

18-7.   There are a number of restrictions on this rollover, as follows:

- Ms. Cowper must hold the shares of Cowper Inc. as capital property. That is, they must be held to earn investment income or capital appreciation, and cannot be held as a temporary investment or as inventory.

- Mega Holdings Ltd. must be a Canadian corporation.

- Ms. Cowper must deal at arm's length with Mega Holdings Ltd.

- Ms. Cowper, or persons with whom she does not deal at arm's length, cannot control Mega Holdings Ltd. (the purchasing corporation) immediately after the exchange. Likewise, they cannot own shares having a fair market value in excess of 50 percent of the total fair market value of the corporation's outstanding shares.

- Mega Holdings Ltd. must issue its own shares in the exchange, and it can issue only one class of shares to Ms. Cowper.

- No election can be made under ITA 85(1) or (2) with respect to the exchanged shares.

18-8.   The adjusted cost base of the Cowper shares to Mega Holdings Ltd. will be the lesser of their fair market value and paid up capital. In this case, the paid up capital figure is lower, establishing the adjusted cost base of the Cowper shares at $10,000.

18-9.   In most circumstances, the paid up capital of shares will equal the legal stated capital of the shares. The legal stated capital is the amount paid for the shares, in the legal sense, according to the appropriate corporation act (e.g., *Canada Business Corporation Act*). Paid up capital is an income tax term, and while the calculation starts with the legal stated capital amount, certain adjustments may be required in rollover situations. ITA 85.1(2.1) applies to limit the addition to the paid up capital of the purchaser corporation (in this case, Mega Holdings Ltd.) to the amount of the paid up capital of the shares acquired (in this case, Cowper Inc. shares). In this example, it is likely that the legal stated capital of the Mega Holdings Ltd. shares issued would be their fair market value of $125,000, well in excess of the paid up capital of the Cowper Inc. shares. If this is the case, there would be a paid up capital reduction or grind mechanism applied to limit the paid up capital to $10,000.

> Exercise Eighteen-1 deals with share for share exchanges. This would be an appropriate time to attempt this exercise.

Exchange Of Shares In A Reorganization

Application Of Section 86

18-10.   Under Section 86, a reorganization involves an exchange of shares within a single corporation. The Section applies to situations where a shareholder of a corporation exchanges shares held in at least one class of existing shares for authorized shares in the same company, or for authorized shares in the same company combined with non share consideration. In effect, there is a redemption of the taxpayer's current shareholding, combined with an acquisition of a new shareholding. Section 86 allows this transaction to take place without tax consequences to a taxpayer whose shares are being redeemed.

18-11.   One of the most common applications of ITA 86 is in an estate freeze, where an owner of a business wishes to pass on the growth of the business to other family members or to arrange an orderly succession to another individual or group. In a typical scenario, a father holds all of the outstanding common shares of a corporation. These shares will have a fair market value in excess of their adjusted cost base and, as a consequence, their sale or redemption would normally result in a capital gain. Further, if the father continues to hold the shares, future growth in the corporation will accrue to him.

18-12.   To avoid this situation, the father will exchange the common or growth shares of the corporation for newly issued preferred shares of the corporation. The preferred shares will have a fixed redemption value equal to the fair market value of the common shares and, the fact that their value is fixed will serve to freeze the value of the father's interest in the corporation. Common shares will then be sold to a spouse, a child, or some other related person. As the preferred shares held by the father reflect the full fair market value of the company, the new common shares can be sold to the related person at a fairly nominal value. However, any future growth in the value of the company will accrue to these common shares. Section 86 provides for the father's exchange of shares to take place on a tax free or rollover basis (see Chapter 20 for a more detailed discussion of estate freezes).

Conditions For The Reorganization

18-13.   For the provisions of ITA 86 to apply, several conditions must be met. First, the original owner's shares must be capital property to the owner. They cannot be an inventory of securities that is being held for trading purposes.

18-14.   A second condition is that the transaction must result in an exchange of all of the outstanding shares of a particular class that are owned by the transferor. For example, all Class A common shares that are owned by the transferor must be exchanged for some other type of share. Note that there is no requirement that Class A common shares that are held by other shareholders be exchanged as part of the transaction. Further, it is not necessary that other classes of shares owned by the transferor be exchanged for new shares.

18-15.   A third condition is that the share exchange must be integral to a reorganization of the capital of the corporation. This will generally require that the articles of incorporation be amended to authorize any new class of shares.

18-16.   A final condition is that the transferor must receive shares of the capital stock of the corporation. While this does not preclude the transferor from receiving non share consideration, such non share consideration should not exceed the adjusted cost base of the shares transferred. If it does, the excess will have to be taken into income, either as a taxable capital gain or as a deemed dividend.

18-17.   In the more common applications of Section 86, the new shares received by the transferor will usually be preferred shares. These shares must be designed in such a fashion as to clearly establish their fair market value. If this is not the case, a subsequent dispute with the CCRA could result in some of the benefits of using Section 86 being lost. Designing the shares with the following characteristics will serve to establish this value:

- The preferred shares must be redeemable at the option of the shareholder. The CCRA rigorously enforces this requirement to protect the fair market value of the preferred shares.

- The preferred shares should be entitled to a dividend at a reasonable rate, but the entitlement need not be cumulative. Without a reasonable dividend entitlement to the old shareholder, the incoming shareholders could benefit by receiving a disproportionate share of the corporation's future profits.

- The corporation must undertake that dividends will not be paid, on any other class of shares, that could result in the corporation having insufficient net assets to redeem the preferred shares at their redemption amount.

- The preferred shares must become cumulative if the fair value of the net assets of the corporation falls below the redemption value of the preferred shares, or if the corporation is unable to redeem the shares on a call for redemption.

- The preferred shares may or may not have normal voting rights, but they should carry votes on any matter regarding the rights attached to the preferred shares.

18-18.   The preferred shares should have preference on liquidation of the corporation. The very nature of preferred shares should guarantee preference, but the CCRA requires additional reassurance.

Procedures

18-19.   As noted previously, an ITA 86 reorganization involves a redemption of a given shareholder's holding of a particular class of shares (old shares, hereafter). In return, the shareholder receives shares of a different class (new shares, hereafter) and, in some reorganizations, non share consideration. ITA 86(1) specifies a number of rules that apply in such a reorganization of capital. These are as follows:

Non Share Consideration   ITA 86(1)(a) indicates that the cost to the taxpayer of this consideration is deemed to be its fair market value.

Cost Of New Shares   ITA 86(1)(b) indicates that the cost of the new shares is equal to the cost of the old shares, less the cost of any non share consideration.

Proceeds Of Disposition For Old Shares   There are actually two different figures that must be used here. For purposes of determining the amount of any ITA 84(3) dividend, ITA 84(5)(d) defines the proceeds of redemption of the old shares as the cost of the non share consideration, plus the PUC of the new shares (as will be discussed subsequently, the PUC of the new shares will be subject to a reduction in some reorganizations). For purposes of determining capital gains, ITA 86(1)(c) defines the proceeds of disposition as being equal to the cost of the new shares (the cost of the old shares, less non share consideration), plus any non share consideration received by the taxpayer. To avoid double counting of a portion of any gain, this latter proceeds of disposition is reduced, for purposes of determining capital gains, by any ITA 84(3) dividends. This reduction is found in ITA 54 under the definition "proceeds of disposition".

18-20.   As noted in the preceding rules, a PUC reduction may be required on the new shares. This is specified in ITA 86(2.1)(a). This reduction is calculated as follows:

Increase In Legal Stated Capital Of New Shares		$xx,xxx
Less The Excess, If Any, Of:		
PUC Of Old Shares	($x,xxx)	
Reduced By Non Share Consideration	x,xxx	(x,xxx)
ITA 86(2.1)(a) PUC Reduction		$xx,xxx

18-21.   In reviewing this PUC reduction formula, note that where the non share consideration is equal to or greater than the PUC of the old shares, the amount subtracted from the increase in the legal stated capital of the new shares will be nil. This means that the PUC reduction will be equal to the increase in legal stated capital for the new shares, thereby setting the PUC of these shares at nil.

18-22.   If there is more than one class of new shares, this PUC reduction will be allocated to the individual classes on the basis of their relative fair market values.

Example

18-23.   An example will serve to illustrate the procedures discussed in the preceding section. You might note that the example illustrates the manner in which an ITA 86 reorganization of capital can be used to freeze the value of an individual's estate.

Example   Mr. David Jones owns all of the outstanding shares of Jones Inc. These common shares have an adjusted cost base of $50,000 and a paid up capital of $75,000. Because of the successful operations of the company, the current fair market value of these common shares is $500,000.

Mr. Jones would like to have future growth in the value of the corporation accrue to his daughter, Ms. Veronica Jones. To accomplish this, Mr. Jones exchanges his common shares for a $150,000 note payable from the corporation and preferred shares with a fair market value and a legal stated capital of $350,000. Common shares are purchased by Veronica Jones for $1,000. Subsequent to these transactions, these are the only Jones Inc. common shares outstanding.

18-24.   The first step in applying the ITA 86 rules in this situation would be to calculate the required PUC reduction and the resulting PUC value for the new shares. The calculations would be as follows:

Increase In Legal Stated Capital Of New Shares		$350,000
Less The Excess, If Any, Of:		
PUC Of Old Shares	($ 75,000)	
Reduced By Non Share Consideration	150,000	Nil
ITA 86(2.1)(a) PUC Reduction		$350,000

Increase In Legal Stated Capital Of New Shares	$350,000
ITA 86(2.1)(a) PUC Reduction	(350,000)
PUC Of New Shares	$ Nil

18-25.   Other required values can be calculated as follows:

Cost Of Non Share Consideration	$150,000

Adjusted Cost Base Of Old Shares	$ 50,000
Non Share Consideration	(150,000)
Adjusted Cost Base Of New Shares	$ Nil

Non Share Consideration	$150,000
Plus PUC Of New Shares	Nil
Proceeds Of Redemption Under ITA 84(5)(d)	$150,000
PUC Of Old Shares	(75,000)
ITA 84(3) Deemed Dividend	$ 75,000

Adjusted Cost Base Of New Shares	Nil
Plus Non Share Consideration	150,000
Proceeds Of Disposition Under ITA 86(1)(c)	$150,000
ITA 84(3) Deemed Dividend	(75,000)
Adjusted Proceeds	$ 75,000
Adjusted Cost Base Of Old Shares	(50,000)
Capital Gain	$ 25,000

18-26.   The shares held by his daughter, Veronica, will have a cost of $1,000 and this will also be their current fair market value. However, if the corporation prospers, all future increases in its value will accrue to her. In other words, by taking out non growth preferred shares, Mr. Jones has frozen the value of his interest in Jones Inc.

18-27.   In reviewing this example, you should note that Mr. Jones' potential gain has not disappeared. If he had simply sold his shares without the reorganization, he would have realized a gain of $450,000 ($500,000 - $50,000). As a result of the reorganization, he has recognized $100,000 ($75,000 + $25,000) of this amount, leaving a deferred gain of $350,000. After the reorganization, his holding of preferred shares has a cost and PUC of nil. As the fair market value of the shares is $350,000, any redemption or sale of these shares will result in Mr. Jones having to take the deferred $350,000 into income.

18-28.   A final point here is that this example does not represent a typical ITA 86 estate freeze. While it does accomplish the goal of transferring future growth in the corporation to a related party, the approach used has resulted in current taxes payable for Mr. Jones. The reason for this is that he gave himself non share consideration in excess of both the PUC and the adjusted cost base of the old shares. Had he limited the non share consideration to $50,000, the estate freeze objective could have been accomplished without current taxation.

Exercises Eighteen-2 through Eighteen-4 deal with reorganizations. This would be an appropriate time to attempt these exercises.

Benefit Rule

18-29.   ITA 86(2) contains a rule designed to prevent a taxpayer from using this rollover provision to confer a benefit on a related person. This rule is applicable whenever the fair market value of the old shares exceeds the sum of the fair market value of the new shares and the fair market value of the non share consideration received, and it is reasonable to regard all or part of this excess as a gift to a related person.

18-30.   This type of situation can be illustrated by returning to our Jones Inc. example from Paragraph 18-23. If, instead of taking back the $150,000 note and preferred shares with a fair market value of $350,000, Mr. Jones exchanged his common shares for a $150,000 note and preferred shares with a fair market value of $250,000, the $100,000 difference between the fair market value of the old shares he gave up, and the fair market value of the consideration he received would accrue to the common shareholders of Jones Inc. As his daughter is the only holder of common shares, this $100,000 gift would accrue to her. As she is clearly a related person, ITA 86(2) would be applicable.

18-31.   In situations where ITA 86(2) applies, the rules for the reorganization of share capital are changed as follows:

Proceeds Of Disposition   Under ITA 86(2)(c), the proceeds of the disposition for capital gains purposes on the old shares will be equal to the lesser of:

- the fair market value of the non share consideration, plus the gift; and
- the fair market value of the old shares.

This compares to proceeds under ITA 86(1) equal to the cost of the new shares, plus the fair market value of the non share consideration.

Capital Losses   Under ITA 86(2)(d), any capital loss resulting from the disposition of the old shares will be deemed to be nil.

Cost Of New Shares   Under ITA 86(2)(e), the cost to the taxpayer of the new shares will be equal to:

- the cost of the old shares;
- less the sum of the non share consideration plus the gift.

This compares to a cost for the new shares under ITA 86(1) equal to the cost of the old shares, less non share consideration.

18-32.   To illustrate these procedures, we will use the example presented in Paragraph 18-23, as modified in Paragraph 18-30 (i.e., the fair market value of the preferred shares received is reduced from $350,000 to $250,000). The PUC reduction and PUC of the new shares is calculated as follows:

Increase In Legal Stated Capital Of New Shares		$250,000
Less The Excess, If Any, Of:		
PUC Of Old Shares	($ 75,000)	
Reduced By Non Share Consideration	150,000	Nil
ITA 86(2.1)(a) PUC Reduction		$250,000

Increase In Legal Stated Capital Of New Shares	$250,000
ITA 86(2.1)(a) PUC Reduction	(250,000)
PUC Of New Shares	$ Nil

18-33.   The remaining calculations that would be required under ITA 86(2) are as follows:

| Cost Of Non Share Consideration | $150,000 |

Adjusted Cost Base Of Old Shares	$ 50,000
Non Share Consideration	(150,000)
Gift	(100,000)
Adjusted Cost Base Of New Shares	$ Nil

Non Share Consideration	$150,000
PUC Of New Shares	Nil
Proceeds Of Redemption Under ITA 84(5)(d)	$150,000
PUC Of Old Shares	(75,000)
ITA 84(3) Deemed Dividend	$ 75,000

ITA 86(2)(c) Proceeds:	
Non Share Consideration	$150,000
Gift	100,000
Total Proceeds Of Disposition	$250,000
ITA 84(3) Deemed Dividend	(75,000)
Adjusted Proceeds	$175,000
Adjusted Cost Base Of Old Shares	(50,000)
Capital Gain	$125,000

18-34.   The final capital gain figure of $125,000 is $100,000 in excess of the gain recorded in the original version of this example. In effect, the amount of the gift has been added to the capital gain that must be included in the income of Mr. Jones.

18-35.   While there is less deferral of income, the total amount of gain that will be taxed in Mr. Jones' hands is unchanged. Mr. Jones has preferred shares with a fair market value of $250,000 and a cost of nil, reflecting the initial $450,000 gain that was present, less the $200,000 ($75,000 + $125,000) in income recognized as a result of the reorganization.

18-36.   ITA 86 does, however, involve a penalty to the taxpayer. The new common shares issued to his daughter will have a fair market value equal to $101,000, the $1,000 she paid plus the $100,000 benefit. The $100,000 additional value will not be reflected in the adjusted cost base of her shares and, as a consequence, this amount will be taxed when she disposes of the shares. In effect, the granting of the benefit has increased the amount that will be subject to taxation through his daughter by the $100,000 amount of the gift without reducing Mr. Jones' total current and deferred income on the shares. This makes it clear that Section 86 reorganizations should be structured in a manner that avoids such benefits being granted.

> Exercise Eighteen-5 deals with the benefit rule in reorganizations. This would be an appropriate time to attempt this exercise.

Practical Considerations

18-37.   Some of the practical considerations that must be given consideration in a reorganization of capital can be described as follows:

- The first step requires a valuation of the existing common shares. The valuation should be carefully documented and the assistance of professional valuators may be required.

- As a second step, it is often necessary to amend the articles of incorporation to introduce one or more new classes of shares. Depending on the wishes of the original owner, the new shares may be voting or non voting.

- The third step is the exchange of the existing shares for the new shares. As previously discussed, the preferred shares should be redeemable at their fair market value on the date of the share exchange. This requirement exists so that the past success of the corporation accrues to the existing shareholder and no benefit is bestowed on the incoming shareholders.

- The fourth step involves issuing new common shares to the incoming shareholders. Note that the incoming shareholders should provide the capital required from their own sources to avoid potential attribution problems. Often the required amounts are nominal.

- An agreement should be drawn up to document the share reorganization. To ensure future flexibility, a price adjustment clause should be included to provide for a change in the redemption amount or the number of issued shares in certain circumstances. The price adjustment clause is particularly useful if the CCRA assesses the original shares as having a higher fair market valuation. Without such a clause, the incoming shareholders could be assessed as having received a taxable benefit in the reorganization. Therefore, the price adjustment clause protects the incoming shareholders from a potential tax liability related to the reorganization.

Using Section 86

18-38.   A Section 86 share reorganization is simpler to implement than a Section 85 rollover. There are several reasons for this, but the most obvious is that by using Section 86 we can avoid the set up of a separate corporation with its ongoing administrative requirements. With a Section 86 share reorganization, there is no need to have a separate corporation. In addition, the corporate law steps are easier, only requiring shares to be exchanged, and possibly new share classes to be formed. A further positive feature of Section 86 rollovers is that no election needs to be filed with the CCRA.

18-39.   As with all rollovers, there are some disadvantages to Section 86 reorganizations. One disadvantage relates to the limitations of carrying on business through a single corporation. It is difficult to segregate investment income from active business income unless there are two corporations. Likewise, a single corporation exposes all of the assets to any operating risk, and limited liability protection is reduced. Another disadvantage relates to the need for all of the taxpayer's shares of a particular class to be exchanged in a Section 86 reorganization. To get around this complete exchange requirement in a Section 86 reorganization, common shares can be reissued to the existing shareholder after the reorganization is completed.

18-40.   In addition to its use in estate freezes, an exchange of shares can be very effective when arranging for gradual succession to a key employee. For example, consider the situation when the employee has little personal equity, but has a good work record with the company and excellent owner-manager potential. A Section 86 reorganization can be used to convert common shares owned by an existing shareholder into preferred shares. Then, the employee could purchase, for example, 20 percent of the common shares each year for five years. The annual investments in common shares will likely be modest, as most of the company's value will be reflected in the preferred shares, making the investments feasible for the incoming shareholder. The original owner can be involved in the business throughout the succession years and can continue to help the business grow. Eventually, when the original owner is ready to sell the preferred shares, the incoming shareholder will have the benefit of at least five years of management experience, and should more easily be able to obtain funding to acquire the preferred shares. A variation of this reorganization involves the incoming shareholder gradually acquiring the preferred and common shares, simultaneously.

Amalgamations

The Nature Of An Amalgamation

18-41.   ITA 87 provides for a tax deferred rollover in situations where there is an amalgamation of corporations. This may involve two independent corporations wishing to merge and continue their business affairs on a combined basis. Likewise, associated or related corporations may amalgamate to pursue common corporate goals. If the two corporations want to transfer their assets to a new corporation on a tax free basis, the rollover provisions of ITA 87 would apply. The following simple example will illustrate this kind of situation:

> **Example**   The shareholders of Company Alpha have shares with an adjusted cost base of $1,000,000 and a fair market value of $5,000,000, while the shareholders of Company Beta have shares with an adjusted cost base of $1,700,000 and a fair market value of $5,000,000. All of the assets and liabilities (except intercompany balances) of Company Alpha and Company Beta are transferred to a new Company, Alpha-Beta Ltd. The shareholders of Company Alpha and Company Beta exchange their shares for shares in Alpha-Beta Ltd.

18-42.   In the absence of ITA 87, the shareholders of Companies Alpha and Beta would be viewed as having disposed of their shares for proceeds equal to the fair market value of the shares, resulting in the realization of significant capital gains. In addition, the transfer of assets from Companies Alpha and Beta to the new Alpha-Beta Ltd. could result in additional capital gains as well as possible recapture on the dispositions of the assets transferred. The total tax liability could be sufficiently large that, in many cases, this type of transaction would not be feasible.

18-43.   To facilitate amalgamations of corporations, ITA 87 contains rollover provisions for both the transfer of assets to the new corporation and for the exchange of shares. For the ITA 87 provisions to be applicable, the following conditions must be met:

- Both of the predecessor corporations must be taxable Canadian corporations.

- With the exception of incorporated shareholders, all shareholders of the predecessor corporations must receive shares of the new corporation due to the amalgamation.

- All of the assets and liabilities of the predecessor corporations must be transferred to the new corporation in the amalgamation, with the exception of intercompany balances.

- The transfer cannot simply be a normal purchase of property or involve the distribution of assets on the wind up of a corporation.

Position Of The Amalgamated Company

18-44.   The tax values for the new corporation's assets will simply be the sum of the tax values of the assets that were present in the records of the predecessor corporations. In addition, all types of loss carry forwards (capital, non capital and farm) of the predecessor corporations flow through and become available to the new corporation. The predecessor corporations will be deemed to have a year end on the date of the amalgamation, and this extra year end will count towards the expiration of non capital and farm losses. The new corporation is deemed to have been formed on this date and may choose any year end it wishes.

18-45.   With respect to assets, reserves, loss carry forwards, and other tax accounts of the old companies, ITA 87 provides rollover provisions as follows:

Rollover Provisions In ITA 87 Amalgamations

Item	Rollover Effect
Inventories	At Cost
Depreciable Capital Property	At UCC
Non Depreciable Capital Property	At ACB
Eligible Capital Property	4/3 Of CEC
Reserves	Flowed Through
Non Capital Losses	Flowed Through
Net Capital Losses	Flowed Through
Restricted Farm Losses	Flowed Through
Capital Dividend Account (See Note)	Flowed Through
Refundable Dividend Tax On Hand (See Note)	Flowed Through

Note The capital dividend account and the refundable dividend tax on hand account are only applicable to private companies. If either of the predecessor companies is a public company, these accounts would be lost.

18-46. As can be seen in the preceding table, ITA 87 basically provides for a summing of the relevant tax values of the assets of the two companies that are amalgamating. The new corporation will be liable for recapture and capital gains on the same basis as the predecessor corporations. With respect to loss carry forwards, the limitations that were discussed in Chapter 14 are applicable if there is an acquisition of control. In addition, the deemed year end of a predecessor corporation will count as one year in any carry forward period. However, losses carried forward may qualify for deduction in the first year end of the amalgamated company.

Position Of The Shareholders
General Rules
18-47. The shareholders of the predecessor corporations are deemed to dispose of their shares for proceeds equal to the adjusted cost base of the shares, and they are deemed to acquire the shares of the amalgamated company at the same value. For these general provisions to apply, the following conditions must be met:

- The shareholders must not receive any consideration other than shares in the amalgamated company or its Canadian parent.
- The original shares must be capital property of the shareholders.
- The amalgamation must not result in a deemed gift to a person related to the shareholders.

Vertical Amalgamations (Parent And Subsidiary)
18-48. In situations where there is a desire to combine a parent and its subsidiary, a choice of rollovers may be available. The alternative to ITA 87, "Amalgamations", is the use of ITA 88(1), "Winding Up". However, ITA 88(1) is only applicable to situations where the parent company owns 90 percent or more of the shares of each class of capital stock of the subsidiary. In contrast, ITA 87 can be used without regard to the percentage of ownership.

18-49. As will be discussed more fully later in this Chapter, the cost of a subsidiary's shares often exceeds the underlying tax values in the records of the subsidiary. If the parent and subsidiary are amalgamated under ITA 87, this extra value or premium will be lost. An advantage that can be associated with ITA 88(1) is that, to a limited extent, this extra cost can be recognized in the tax records of the combined company.

Non Tax Considerations
18-50. As this form of amalgamation involves creating a new company to replace two predecessor companies, there may be many legal complications. All contracts with employees, suppliers and customers will have to be revised. In addition, all debt obligations of the predecessor corporations will have to be transferred to the new company. In fact, the approval of some creditors may be required before the amalgamation can be carried out. The negotiation

of these arrangements can add considerable complexity to this legal form for combining two companies.

Tax Planning Considerations

18-51.   A Section 87 amalgamation offers a number of opportunities for tax planning. Some of the possibilities include:

- The utilization of loss carry over amounts that the predecessor corporation(s) might not be able to absorb. Note, however, that if there is an acquisition of control, the usual restrictions on the use of loss carry forwards apply.

- Current year losses of one predecessor corporation can be utilized against taxable income of the other.

- Bringing together a profitable and an unprofitable corporation may allow for a faster write off of capital cost allowances than would otherwise be possible by the unprofitable predecessor corporation.

- The amalgamation may provide for an increase in the amount of the manufacturing and processing profits tax deduction (see discussion in Chapter 15).

18-52.   The timing of an amalgamation should be carefully considered. As the amalgamation transaction results in a deemed year end, the company may have a short fiscal year for purposes of calculating capital cost allowances. In addition, outstanding reserves may have to be brought into income sooner, and the short fiscal period will count as a full year in the eligible loss carry forward years.

18-53.   A rather onerous result of amalgamations relates to employee source deductions. Many full time employees reach the maximum annual Canada Pension Plan contribution limit a few months before the calendar year ends, at which time the employee and employer no longer need to make any further contributions. In an amalgamation, there is no look through to predecessor corporations for source deduction history. The amalgamated company must start over in calculating employee Canada Pension Plan contributions and Employment Insurance premiums and remit the full employee and employer amounts. While this results in a cash flow inconvenience for employees, they will obtain a refund of Canada Pension Plan and Employment Insurance overpayments. However, for the combined companies, it results in an additional cash outflow as no refund of excess employer premiums is available.

> Exercise Eighteen-6 deals with amalgamations. This would be an appropriate time to attempt this exercise.

18-54.   For income tax instalments there is a look through provision. While the amalgamated company does not have a previous tax year on which to base instalments of income tax, prepayments continue to be required based on the instalment history of the predecessor corporations.

Winding Up Of A 90 Percent Owned Subsidiary

The Nature Of A Winding Up
Winding Up Of Corporations In General

18-55.   This Section and the Section which follows deal with the winding up of a corporation. IT-126R2 states that a corporation is considered to have been "wound up" where:

(a) it has followed the procedures for winding up and dissolution provided by the appropriate federal or provincial companies Act or winding up Act, or

(b) it has carried out a wind up, other than by means of the statutory procedures contemplated in (a) above, and has been dissolved under the provisions of its incorporating statute.

18-56.   In general, a wind up operation requires that all outstanding creditor claims be satisfied and that all corporate property be distributed to the shareholders before the wind up is undertaken. IT-126R2 also notes that, where there is substantial evidence that dissolution procedures will be completed within a short period of time, the wind up may qualify for special tax deferrals under Section 88.

18-57.   A wind up may be undertaken for several reasons. As with amalgamations, a wind up allows for the losses of a subsidiary to be carried over to the parent corporation. Wind ups are also undertaken to simplify an organizational structure or when a subsidiary is ceasing its business operations. In either circumstance, the wind up is often promoted as a rationalization of operations.

90 Percent Owned Subsidiary

18-58.   The two major subsections of ITA 88 can be described as follows:

Subsection 88(1)   This subsection is a rollover provision, providing for the tax free combination of the assets of a 90 percent or more owned subsidiary with those of its parent.

Subsection 88(2)   This section deals with the general winding up of corporations, other than those to which ITA 88(1) is applicable. It is not a rollover provision.

18-59.   At this point we are concerned only with the provisions contained in ITA 88(1). The content of ITA 88(2) will be considered in the next Section of this Chapter.

18-60.   To use the ITA 88(1) rollover, the parent corporation must own at least 90 percent of each class of the corporation's shares. Therefore, not all wind ups of subsidiaries qualify for the treatment contemplated in ITA 88(1). A wind up involving a subsidiary where a parent corporation has control but owns less than 90 percent of the shares would be implemented on a taxable basis under the provisions of ITA 88(2).

18-61.   If the parent has the required 90 percent or more ownership, it is permitted to exchange the subsidiary shares for the assets of the subsidiary on a tax deferred basis. This transaction is very similar to an amalgamation as it allows the assets of the two companies to be combined without recognizing any accrued capital gains or recaptured CCA on the transfers required to effect the combination.

18-62.   As with other rollovers, there are two components to a wind up transaction. The first is the acquisition of the subsidiary's assets by the parent, while the second is the deemed disposition of the subsidiary's shares by the parent. We will now turn our attention to these components.

Acquisition Of Assets
General Rules

18-63.   In a Section 88(1) wind up, the subsidiary is deemed to have disposed of its assets and the parent is deemed to have acquired the assets on the following basis:

- A cost of zero in the case of resource property.
- Four-thirds of the balance in the subsidiary's cumulative eligible capital account immediately before the wind up.
- The "cost amount" to the subsidiary in the case of other property. Cost amount is defined in ITA 248(1) as UCC for depreciable property and adjusted cost base for non depreciable capital property.

18-64.   As indicated previously, this transfer is very similar to an amalgamation. However, there are two important differences:

- The first difference relates to the fact that the parent may have acquired the subsidiary's shares at a value in excess of their tax values (the tax values of a subsidiary's assets are not altered when its shares are acquired in a business combination transaction). The ITA 87 amalgamation rules make no provision for the transfer of any excess purchase premium and a substantial part of it may be lost for income tax purposes. In contrast, ITA 88(1) contains a provision which allows for a limited bump up of tax values to reflect this excess.

- The second difference is the fact that, under the ITA 88(1) procedures, the recognition of loss carry forwards is deferred until the first taxation year of the parent company ending after the wind up.

Asset Bump Up

18-65.   As noted, a wind up under ITA 88(1) may allow for the transfer of all or part of the excess of the purchase price of a subsidiary's shares over the tax values of the subsidiary's assets. The amount of this bump up in tax values is limited by two amounts:

1.   The basic amount of the bump up is found in ITA 88(1)(d)(i) and (i.1). This amount is the excess of the adjusted cost base of the subsidiary shares held by the parent, over the sum of:

    - the tax values of the subsidiary's net assets at the time of the wind up; and
    - dividends paid by the subsidiary to the parent since the time of the acquisition (including capital dividends).

2.   ITA 88(1)(d)(ii) further limits the amount that can be recognized to the excess of the fair market value of the subsidiary's non depreciable assets over their tax values at the time the parent acquired control of the subsidiary.

18-66.   A simple example will illustrate these procedures:

Example   On December 31, 1991, ParentCo acquires 100 percent of the outstanding shares of SubCo for $5,000,000. At that time, the only non depreciable asset owned by SubCo was land with a fair market value of $2,000,000 and a cost of $1,000,000. Between December 31, 1991 and December 31, 2001, Subco pays dividends of $150,000 to Parent Co. On December 31, 2001, SubCo is absorbed in a Section 88(1) wind up. At this time, the tax values of SubCo's assets total $4,200,000.

18-67.   The amount of the available asset bump up will be the lesser of the two amounts described in Paragraph 18-65:

Adjusted Cost Base Of SubCo Shares	$5,000,000
Tax Values Of SubCo Assets At Wind Up	(4,200,000)
Dividends Paid By SubCo Since Its Acquisition	(150,000)
Excess	$ 650,000
Fair Market Value Of Land At Acquisition	$2,000,000
Cost Of Land At Acquisition	(1,000,000)
Excess	$1,000,000

18-68.   In this situation, the write up of the land is restricted to the lower figure of $650,000. Fortunately, ParentCo is able to use the entire excess of the purchase premium over the tax values of the assets at the wind up date, but only because the pre acquisition appreciation on the land was greater than $650,000. Note that this bump up in the value of non depreciable assets would not be available if the combination had taken place as an amalgamation under ITA 87.

Deferral Of Loss Carry Overs

18-69.   As previously noted, the other major difference between an amalgamation under ITA 87 and the wind up of a subsidiary under ITA 88(1) involves loss carry overs. Under ITA 88(1), non capital losses and net capital losses of the subsidiary will be available to the parent company. However, they will not become available until the first taxation year of the parent beginning after the wind up is completed. For example, if a parent's fiscal year begins on February 1 and a wind up occurs on February 15, 2001, the losses of the subsidiary will not be available to the parent until its fiscal year beginning February 1, 2002.

18-70.   In those situations where the subsidiary has a different year end than the parent, subsidiary losses are deemed to have occurred in the parent's fiscal year which includes the subsidiary's year end. Consider a situation in which the parent has a June 30 year end, while its subsidiary has a September 30 year end. If the subsidiary has a non capital loss on August 31, 2000, and there is a wind up on that date, the loss will be deemed to have occurred in the parent's year ending June 30, 2001. This means that it would not expire until the parent's year ending June 30, 2008.

Disposition Of Shares

18-71. The disposition of shares component of the wind up is straightforward. The parent is deemed, in general, to have disposed of its shares of the subsidiary for proceeds equal to the adjusted cost base of the shares. As an example, assume the parent had paid $4,000,000 for the subsidiary's shares. This amount would be the deemed proceeds of the disposition and there would be no capital gain.

18-72. An exception to this general rule will arise if the subsidiary asset values transferred or the paid up capital of the subsidiary is more than the amount paid for the shares by the parent. If the subsidiary is acquired at a price that is substantially less than the tax values of the subsidiary's assets at the acquisition date, the deemed proceeds of disposition will be the lesser of the paid up capital and the tax values of the assets transferred. Therefore, a capital gain can arise in these situations.

> **Example** Prawn Ltd. owns 100 percent of the outstanding shares of Shrimp Inc. The cost of these shares was $4,000,000. This investment is being wound up under the provisions of ITA 88(1). At the time of the wind up the tax value of the subsidiary's assets equal $4,800,000 and the PUC of the subsidiary shares is equal to $4,500,000.
>
> **Tax Consequences** The proceeds would be the greater of the $4,000,000 cost of the shares and $4,500,000. This latter figure is the lesser of the $4,800,000 tax value of the subsidiary's assets and the $4,500,000 PUC of the subsidiary shares. This give proceeds of disposition of $4,500,000 and a capital gain of $500,000 ($4,500,000 - $4,000,000). It is expected that such gains situations would be fairly rare and, because the proceeds are defined using cost except when it is less than the alternative values, there is no possibility of a capital loss.

> Exercises Eighteen-7 and Eighteen-8 deal with winding up a 90 percent owned subsidiary. This would be an appropriate time to attempt these exercises.

Tax Planning Considerations — Amalgamation Vs. Wind Up

18-73. The main considerations in deciding between an amalgamation under ITA 87 and a wind up under ITA 88(1) relate to the excess of the parent company's cost over the subsidiary's tax values, the use of loss carry overs, the availability of CCA claims, and the treatment of any minority interest in the subsidiary.

18-74. With respect to the excess of subsidiary cost over its tax values, an ITA 88(1) wind up permits non depreciable asset values to be written up to the extent that the fair market values of these assets exceed their tax values at the time the subsidiary was acquired. In contrast, ITA 87 makes no provision for recognizing any part of this excess. However, under either approach, it is possible that substantial tax values will simply disappear in the transaction. This would suggest that, when the adjusted cost base of the parent's investment is significantly greater than the tax values of the subsidiary's assets, it may be better to continue to operate the subsidiary as a separate legal entity.

18-75. Under the amalgamation procedures, the predecessor corporations will have a deemed year end which will count toward the expiry of time limited non capital loss carry overs. However, the new company will be able to use the losses immediately. In contrast, the parent company that is using ITA 88(1) to absorb a 90 percent owned subsidiary will have its usual year end. However, it will not be able to use subsidiary loss carry overs until the first taxation year beginning subsequent to the wind up. The analysis of this situation may be complicated by differing year ends for the two corporations.

18-76. In considering CCA claims, ITA 87 creates a deemed year end for both predecessor corporations, allowing them to take pro rata CCA claims for what will normally be a short fiscal period. Under the ITA 88(1) procedures, the subsidiary disposes of its assets prior to its year end and, as a consequence, there will be no claim for CCA in the subsidiary's final year. However, capital cost allowances may be claimed on these assets by the parent company, subsequent to their being acquired under the wind up procedures.

18-77.   If the subsidiary is not 100 percent owned, a Section 88(1) wind up will have implications for the minority shareholders. A wind up will require reporting of capital gains and recaptured CCA on the underlying minority interest in the assets. Further, any liquidating dividend paid to the minority shareholder will be a taxable dividend.

18-78.   The following Figure 18-1 contains a comparison of the features of an amalgamation under ITA 87 and the wind up of a 90 percent owned subsidiary under ITA 88.

Figure 18 - 1 Comparison Of Amalgamation Under ITA 87 And Wind Up Under ITA 88(1)		
Effect of Rollover	**Amalgamation - ITA 87**	**Winding Up - ITA 88(1)**
Valuation of assets	Sum of tax values of assets of predecessor corporations.	Tax values of subsidiary's assets carried forward to parent.
Allocation of share purchase premium	No allocation.	Write-up allowed if excess associated with values of non depreciable capital assets.
Capital cost allowances	Claim in last year of predecessor and first year of amalgamated corporation.	Do not claim by subsidiary in year of wind up, but available to parent in year of wind up.
Loss carry forwards	Carried forward, but acquisition of control rules apply.	Carried forward, but only available to parent in taxation year after wind up.
Year end	Deemed year end before amalgamation, counts one year for loss carry forwards.	Year end of parent corporation continued.

Winding Up Of A Canadian Corporation

The Nature Of The Transaction

18-79.   The winding up procedures for a Canadian corporation, as described in ITA 88(2), are applicable where a corporation is being liquidated. If, for example, owners of a corporation decide that the business is no longer viable, wind up procedures can be used in the disposition of the corporation's assets and the distribution of the resulting proceeds to the shareholders.

18-80.   In distinguishing the wind up of a 90 percent or more owned subsidiary from a liquidating wind up, you should note that the liquidation of a business has quite different objectives. In the case of the wind up of a 90 percent or more owned subsidiary, we are usually not disposing of the business but, rather, are transferring its assets to a different legal entity which is controlled by the same individual or group of investors. This explains why a rollover is available on the wind up of a 90 percent or more owned subsidiary, and no equivalent provision is available for the wind up when a liquidation is under way.

18-81.   While a wind up can be implemented by distributing corporate assets directly to the shareholders, it is generally simpler for the corporation to liquidate its assets, pay off its creditors, pay any taxes that are applicable at the corporate level, and distribute the after tax proceeds to the shareholders. This distribution will usually result in additional taxation at the shareholder level.

18-82. The distribution to shareholders becomes a fairly complex issue when a corporation is liquidated, as the proceeds available for distribution will consist of a combination of capital being returned, earnings that can be distributed on a tax free basis and earnings that can only be distributed in the form of taxable dividends.

18-83. Later in this Chapter we will be discussing the transfer of an incorporated business to a different group of owners. This can be accomplished through a sale of shares or, alternatively, through a sale of the corporation's assets. If the sale of assets is the more advantageous approach, the provisions of ITA 88(2) apply. That is, there will be a winding up of the old corporation followed by a distribution of the after tax proceeds of the wind up to the shareholders. While the business will continue to operate, the assets will now be on the books of a different legal entity.

18-84. The ITA 88(2) procedures will be illustrated in the following example. This example involves a corporation which was established after December 31, 1971 (V-Day). As a consequence, it does not illustrate the impact of V-Day values on asset dispositions or the treatment of a pre 1972 Capital Surplus On Hand balance. We are of the opinion that this material is no longer of sufficient importance to warrant coverage in a general text such as this.

Example

18-85. The example which follows will be used to illustrate the winding up of a Canadian corporation.

> **Example**   The Marker Company has been in operation since 1983. On June 1, 2001, the following Balance Sheet based on tax values has been prepared in contemplation of liquidating the company:
>
>
>
> **The Marker Company**
> **Balance Sheet - As At June 1, 2001**
>
>
>
> | | |
> |---|---:|
> | Accounts Receivable (Net Realizable Value) | $ 12,000 |
> | Refundable Dividend Tax On Hand | 8,000 |
> | Land - At Cost (Note One) | 250,000 |
> | Building - At UCC (Note Two) | 195,000 |
> | Total Assets | $465,000 |
> | | |
> | Liabilities | $ -0- |
> | Common Stock - No Par (Note Three) | 10,000 |
> | Retained Earnings (Note Three) | 455,000 |
> | Total Equities | $465,000 |
>
> **Note One**   The current fair market value of the Land is $300,000.
>
> **Note Two**   The cost of the Building was $320,000. Its current fair market value is $350,000.
>
> **Note Three**   The Paid Up Capital and adjusted cost base of the common shares is $10,000. The Retained Earnings includes $75,000 in the capital dividend account.

The assets of the Company are sold for fair market values which total $662,000. The corporation pays tax at a combined federal and provincial rate of 20 percent on income eligible for the small business deduction and 50 percent on investment income (this includes the ITA 123.3 tax on the investment income of Canadian controlled private companies, as well as the corporate surtax).

Required: Calculate the amount available for distribution to shareholders. Determine the components of the distribution to the shareholders and their liability for tax after the distribution has been made.

18-86. At the corporate level, the proceeds from the disposition of the individual assets and the related tax effects are as follows:

Asset	Proceeds	Taxable Capital Gain	Business Income
Accounts Receivable	$ 12,000	$ -0-	$ -0-
Land	300,000	25,000	-0-
Building	350,000	15,000	125,000
Totals	$662,000	$40,000	$125,000

18-87. The balance in the refundable dividend tax on hand account, subsequent to the preceding dispositions, is calculated as follows:

Balance Before Dispositions (From Balance Sheet)	$ 8,000
Additions ([26-2/3%*][$40,000])	10,667
Balance Available	$20,667

*Given the absence of foreign non business income tax credits and large amounts of taxable income and taxes payable, we have omitted the full ITA 129(3) calculation of this amount.

18-88. The after tax amount of cash that is available for distribution to shareholders is calculated as follows:

Gross Proceeds	$662,000
Taxes On Investment Income [(50%)($40,000)]	(20,000)
Taxes On Recapture [(20%)($125,000)]	(25,000)
Refundable Dividend Tax On Hand	18,667
Available For Distribution	$635,667

18-89. The balance in the capital dividend account can be calculated as follows:

Balance Before Dispositions	$ 75,000
Disposition Of Land	25,000
Disposition Of Building	15,000
Capital Dividend Account - Ending Balance	$115,000

18-90. The taxable dividend component of the total distribution to the shareholders is calculated as follows:

Total Distribution	$635,667
Paid Up Capital	(10,000)
ITA 84(2) Dividend On Winding Up	$625,667
Capital Dividend Account	(115,000)
Taxable Dividend	$510,667

18-91. Treatment of the $115,000 as a capital dividend is conditional on the appropriate election being made under ITA 83(2). The remaining taxable dividend will be subject to the usual gross up and tax credit procedures.

18-92. In the ITA 54 definition of "proceeds of disposition", paragraph j indicates that amounts that are deemed to be a dividend under ITA 84(2) are not included in this amount. As a consequence, in determining the capital gain on the distribution to the shareholders, the ITA 84(2) dividend will be subtracted as follows:

Total Distribution to Shareholders	$635,667
ITA 84(2) Deemed Dividend	(625,667)
Deemed Proceeds	$ 10,000
Adjusted Cost Base Of Shares	(10,000)
Capital Gain	Nil

Convertible Properties

18-93.   There is one more rollover which you should be familiar with. ITA 51 contains a provision which permits a holder of shares or debt of a corporation to exchange those securities for shares of that corporation on a tax free basis. For this rollover provision to apply, the following two conditions must be met:

- The exchange must not involve any consideration other than the securities that are being exchanged.

- The exchange must not be part of a reorganization of capital or a rollover of property by shareholders to a corporation.

18-94.   In practical terms, this provision is designed to accommodate a tax deferred conversion of debt or preferred shares of a corporation into preferred or common shares of the same corporation. A simple example will clarify the application of the provision:

Example   An investor acquires convertible bonds with a par value of $10,000 at a price equal to par value. The bonds are convertible into 50 shares of the issuing company's common stock and, at the time of purchase, this common stock is trading at $180 per share (the conversion value of the bonds is $9,000).

18-95.   If we assume that when the bonds are converted, the common shares are trading at $220 per share, the shares that constitute the proceeds of disposition for the debt would have a value of $11,000 ($220 per share times 50 shares). In the absence of a special provision, the conversion would be viewed as a disposition of bonds with an adjusted cost base of $10,000. The proceeds of disposition would equal $11,000, the fair market value of the equity securities received. This would ordinarily result in the recognition of a capital gain of $1,000. ITA 51 avoids the recognition of this gain by deeming the exchange to not be a disposition. While no gain is recognized, the adjusted cost base of the common stock received is deemed to be equal to the $10,000 adjusted cost base of the bonds that were given up.

18-96.   This provision can assist corporations seeking to add an equity kicker to enhance the marketability of their debt or preferred shares. In addition, conversion arrangements can be used to facilitate income splitting within a corporation. Different classes of shares can be used to allow the redistribution of income and, with the ability to convert different classes on a tax deferred basis, an additional element of flexibility is introduced into such arrangements.

18-97.   ITA 51.1 contains a similar provision to cover situations under which bondholders of a particular company are allowed to convert their holdings into a different debt security of that company. Here again, there is a tax deferred rollover with the adjusted cost base of the old bond holding becoming the creditor's adjusted cost base for the new debt security.

18-98.   We would call your attention to the fact that the accounting rules on debt which is convertible into common or preferred shares require that the proceeds from its issuance be divided between the amount paid by investors for the liability component of the financial instrument and the amount paid for the equity option (see Section 3860 of the *CICA Handbook*). This important issue has not, at this point in time, been given recognition in tax legislation. For tax purposes, the full amount received for convertible debt must be allocated to the debt component of the security.

The Valuation Of A Business

Alternative Methods Of Valuation

18-99.   In our discussion of the various rollovers that are available to corporations, we frequently referred to the fair market value of the common shares of a corporation. In contrast to the valuation of preferred shares or non share consideration, the valuation of common shares requires that a value be placed on the business as an operating entity. This, in turn, requires a knowledge of business valuation techniques. Knowledge of this subject will also be required at a later point in this Chapter when we deal with the procedures involved in the sale of an incorporated business.

18-100.   The subject of business valuations is far too broad a subject to be dealt with in a text on taxation. In actual fact, it is not a subject that is normally given any consideration in such texts. Rather, it is usually dealt with in separate or specialized books giving exclusive coverage to the topic, or as a component of a finance text. However, because some understanding of this subject is required in considering the procedures used in the sale of a corporation, brief coverage of business valuations will be provided.

18-101.   Essentially, there are two approaches to the valuation of a business. In limited circumstances, it may be possible to arrive at an appropriate value for a business by determining the current fair values of its identifiable assets and liabilities. However, this approach does not take into consideration how successfully the assets have been combined into an operating company.

18-102.   As any accountant will know, businesses that use their assets in an effective manner (as measured by higher than normal rates of return), will tend to have a worth that exceeds the sum of their net asset values. This excess is commonly referred to as goodwill. Correspondingly, a business which has earnings that provide less than normal rates of return on the assets invested will tend to be worth less than the sum of its asset values resulting in negative goodwill.

18-103.   In the great majority of situations, the value of a business will be determined on the basis of its expected future earnings stream, rather than on the basis of its identifiable asset values. While there are many pitfalls in this approach, expected future earnings are generally based on the past earnings trend.

Asset Based Methods

General Principles

18-104.   One approach to the valuation of a business is to simply determine the current fair values of the identifiable assets and liabilities of the enterprise. Using various appraisal and estimation techniques, a value can be arrived at for each asset and liability and these values can be totaled to arrive at a value for the business. No attention will be given to estimating any goodwill values and, in most cases, other intangibles will also be ignored. As in any other appraisal process, attention should be given to the tax status of the various assets. For example, in determining the current fair value of a depreciable asset, the amount of the undepreciated capital cost of the asset is relevant in some types of acquisitions.

18-105.   As indicated in the introduction to this section, this asset by asset approach to the valuation of a business is of limited usefulness. Businesses are seldom worth the sum of their asset values, being worth more if the business generates high levels of income and less if the income returns on the assets are not adequate. Since an asset based approach to business valuations would not give any consideration to the earning power that has been generated by the particular combination of assets in a business, the results of using such a method could be seriously misleading.

Applicability Of The Approach

18-106.   There are, however, two special situations in which an asset based approach to business valuations would be appropriate. First, in situations where the business is simply a holding company for a variety of investments, the company's earning power is limited to the earnings produced by the various investments and it would be difficult to justify a price for the business which would be significantly different than the sum of the values of the individual investments. Note, however, that if the investments included the sole ownership or a controlling interest in another business, we would still be confronted with a business valuation problem requiring income based valuation techniques.

18-107.   The second situation in which asset based valuation methods could be appropriate would be for a business liquidation. Since there will be no continued operation of the business, the only relevant values here are the liquidation values of the individual assets. The value of the business would coincide with the estimated proceeds resulting from the sale of individual assets, less the funds required to extinguish any liabilities.

Income Based Methods
General Principles
18-108.   It is a well established principle in management accounting and finance that the value of an asset is determined by the present value of discounted cash flows that will be produced by that asset. This means that to place a value on a business as a going concern, an estimate is required of cash flows that the business is expected to provide. Note that these cash flows are not equal to the income of the business. Rather, in the case of an incorporated business, they would be the anticipated dividend payments and, in the case of an unincorporated business, the cash withdrawals available to the owner.

18-109.   There are of course, a number of problems in the use of discounted cash flows. First, the estimation of the undiscounted cash flows is a difficult undertaking which often produces unreliable results. There are also questions related to the choice of an appropriate risk adjusted discount rate, how to distinguish between normal and abnormal levels of earnings, and the question of what time horizon to use as the estimation period. Despite these problems, the discounted cash flow techniques provide important valuation information. As a reflection of this, they are widely used in business valuations.

18-110.   However, the predominate approach to business valuations still relies on the use of earnings (net income) or gross revenue figures, rather than cash flows. In addition, relatively primitive techniques such as earnings multipliers are often used in place of the more complex present value techniques.

18-111.   In practical terms, the reliability of the estimates used in business valuations is very weak. Further, the establishment of a price for a business is normally the result of complex negotiations in which many financial and non financial considerations enter the picture. To attempt to make this process appear more scientific by using present value factors which are accurate to five decimal places may, in fact, mislead the users of the information with respect to the accuracy that can be attached to the results. In view of these problems, there is some justification in the use of less sophisticated valuation techniques based on income streams and simple multipliers of those streams. These techniques will be described in the sections which follow.

Valuation Based On Gross Revenues
18-112.   It is possible to value a business on the basis of some multiplier of its gross revenues. However, in view of the tremendous variations in the percentage of gross revenues which reach the bottom line profit figures, this approach is of only limited use.

18-113.   The one situation in which it may be applicable would be when the purchaser of the business is in a position to service the revenues of the acquired business within the existing cost structure. For example, a practicing professional, such as a lawyer, accountant or insurance agent, might be able to absorb another professional practice without any significant increase in either the fixed or variable costs. However, when additional costs would be incurred, the basis for valuation of the business should shift to an income oriented approach. In situations where the valuation based on gross revenues approach is practical, the purchase multiple will tend to be lower than would be the case with earnings multiples. For example, a purchaser might pay 1.5 to 2 times the annualized gross revenues for a small professional practice that could be absorbed into an existing practice without a significant increase in costs.

Valuation Based On Earnings

18-114.   The usual process of business valuation is based on an examination of past net earnings and the application of an appropriate multiple to an average of these earnings to provide a capitalized value for the business. In general terms, the process can be described as follows:

Establish Normalized Earnings   This will involve an examination of the earnings of the business over some past period of time. The most usual period that is used for this purpose is five years. These earnings will be adjusted for any factors which do not have a bearing on the future earning power of the business. For example, all non recurring items, whether their effect was favourable or unfavourable, would be removed. In addition, the financial effects of any operations that are no longer a part of the business would also have to be eliminated. The earnings would be calculated on an after tax basis and, for purposes of applying a multiplier, an average for the period chosen would be used.

Establish An Appropriate Multiplier   The choice of an appropriate multiplier will be based on a number of different considerations. The most important of these would be the risk associated with the earnings stream and the potential for income growth. Risk would generally be measured by the variability of past earnings. If past earnings were highly variable, a smaller multiple would be required than would be the case with a relatively smooth stream of earnings. With respect to growth potential, in establishing normalized earnings, attention would be given to the trend of these earnings. If a pattern of growth was present, a higher multiplier would be required than would be the case with flat or declining earnings. In practical terms, these multipliers tend to range between a value of 5 (this would provide an earnings return of 20 percent on the established value) and an upper limit of 10 (this would provide an earnings return of 10 percent on the established value). Multiples in excess of 10 would require either extremely low risk or the expectation that there will be significant income growth in future years.

Other Factors   The preceding techniques will provide a rough value for the business. At this point, many other tangible and intangible factors will have to be considered. For example, the business may have redundant assets which can be sold. If this is the case, the anticipated sales price of such assets should be added to the rough initial value. Other factors would include the company's prospective competitive position, the anticipated continuity of management, specific developments related to particular products or markets, trends in the business' cost structure, and the question of whether any abnormally high profits can be maintained. Only when all of these factors have been given some kind of a quantitative weight can we arrive at a final figure for consideration as a value for the business.

18-115.   In general terms, the preceding describes a common approach to business valuations. It is a relatively unsophisticated approach, but is representative of a common solution to this problem that is found in practice. The method's lack of sophistication is simply a reflection of the subjective nature of the decision that is under consideration. However, the presentation of this approach to the problem does provide a basis for the following discussion which deals with the sale of an incorporated business.

Sale Of An Incorporated Business

Alternatives

18-116.   Assume that you are the sole owner of an incorporated business and that you have decided to dispose of your company. If the business has a value that extends beyond your personal services, it should be possible to arrange a sale of the business. In approaching the problem of selling an incorporated business, you are usually confronted with the following three alternatives:

- Sale of the individual assets of the business, on a piecemeal basis.
- Sale of the shares of the business.
- Sale of the total net assets of the business, including any unrecorded intangibles such as goodwill.

18-117.   In the next Section, consideration will be given to the advantages and disadvantages as well as to the tax effects that are associated with each of these alternatives.

Sale Of Individual Assets

18-118.   If the business has not been successful in producing an adequate rate of return on the assets invested, the most reasonable course of action may be a piece by piece liquidation of the identifiable assets of the enterprise. Another situation in which this approach might be required involves owner managed businesses where the income producing activities are so closely tied to the skills of the owner/manager that the sale of the business independent of those skills would not be feasible. In either of these situations, the asset sales would occur at the individual fair market values and could produce a combination of business income, capital gains, recapture, and terminal losses. In other words, the business would be liquidated rather than sold as a going concern.

18-119.   This type of liquidation would only occur in situations described in the preceding paragraph. In such situations, alternative approaches to disposing of the business will not be feasible. Given that the circumstances associated with the particular business will dictate whether this approach will be used, there is no need to devote any attention to the advantages or disadvantages of this alternative.

Sale Of Shares
General Procedures
18-120.   In terms of accounting, legal, and tax complications, this is the simplest way to sell a business. The calculation of the gain on the sale only requires the adjusted cost base of the shares to be subtracted from the proceeds received from their disposition. Any resulting difference will be a capital gain or loss and will be subject to the usual treatment accorded to share dispositions.

18-121.   In preparing for the sale of shares, a shareholder will generally pay out any dividends that are reflected in the capital dividend or the refundable dividend tax on hand accounts. In addition, outstanding shareholder loans, either to or from the corporation, should be settled prior to the sale.

Lifetime Capital Gains Deduction
18-122.   If the corporation is a "qualified small business corporation" as defined in ITA 110.6(1), the disposition of shares may qualify for the lifetime capital gains deduction of $500,000. The conditions associated with the designation "qualified small business corporation" were discussed in Chapter 12.

Sale Of Total Assets
18-123.   In contrast to a liquidation, where the assets are sold on an individual basis, the purchaser in this situation would acquire the firm's assets as a going concern and, in so doing, would acquire any goodwill or other intangibles which might be associated with the enterprise. In order to ensure that the purchaser does, in fact, acquire all of the intangible benefits associated with owning the business, the vendor may be required to sign a non competition agreement as part of the sale transaction.

18-124.   The disposition of an incorporated business by selling all of the assets is considerably more complex than a disposition of shares. As was the case with the piece by piece sale of individual assets, the sale of all assets may result in a combination of business income, capital gains, recapture, or terminal losses. In both types of asset sales, you should note that there are really two transactions involved. First, the business itself must absorb any tax consequences associated with the sale of its various assets. This will leave the original owner still holding the shares of the corporation and the corporation's assets should then consist entirely of the after corporate tax proceeds from the disposition of its business assets. As a consequence, in most situations the owner will choose to distribute these assets and wind up the corporation.

18-125.   The second transaction involves the distribution of the after tax proceeds of the sale of corporate assets. This will involve income tax effects at the personal level. Given this two level process, a complete analysis of the alternatives of selling the assets of the business versus disposing of the shares, will require dealing with both taxation on the corporation as a result of disposing of the assets and personal taxation as a result of distributing the after tax proceeds of this sale.

18-126.   In dealing with the sale of corporate assets, an understanding of the tax effects associated with such dispositions is required. These effects can be outlined as follows:

Cash   In most circumstances, the cash of the business will be retained in the business. If it is "sold", there will be no tax consequences associated with its disposition.

Accounts Receivable   In the absence of any special election, the sale of accounts receivable as a component of the sale of a business will be treated as a capital transaction. This means that any difference between the face value and the consideration received will be treated as a capital loss, only one-half of which will be deductible. However, ITA 22 provides for a joint election to treat the sale of receivables as an income transaction. This allows the purchaser to treat any difference between the amount paid for the receivables and the amount actually collected as a bad debt expense.

Inventories   Even when inventories are sold as part of the sale of a business, any difference between the sales price and the vendor's cost will be treated as ordinary business income. This is provided for in ITA 23 and, unlike the situation with the ITA 22 treatment of receivable, no election is required. From the point of view of the purchaser, the transfer price becomes the tax cost that will eventually be allocated to cost of goods sold.

Prepayments   There is no specific provision in the Act dealing with prepayments. However, in practice, their sale will be treated as an income transaction using the same general procedures that are applied to inventories. However, in most cases, prepayments will have a fair market value equal to their tax value. This means that they can be sold at fair market value without any tax consequences.

Non Depreciable Capital Assets   The most common non depreciable capital assets of the business are land and investments. Depending on the amount of consideration received for these assets, the transferor will either have a capital gain or a capital loss. Such capital gains are not eligible for the small business deduction as they will be considered investment income. However, if some of the consideration being paid for these assets is deferred, the corporation can use capital gains reserves to defer part of the applicable taxation. Any capital losses can only be deducted from capital gains. For the transferee, the capital cost of non depreciable capital assets will be the purchase price, which presumably is fair market value.

Depreciable Assets   The disposition of a depreciable asset can result in recapture, a terminal loss, or some combination of recapture and a capital gain. Unlike capital gains, recapture or terminal losses will be subject to 100 percent inclusion in, or deduction from active business income and will be eligible for small business deduction treatment. Capital gains and losses arising on the sale of depreciable assets will be subject to the same constraints that were discussed with respect to non depreciable capital assets. Like non depreciable capital assets, the capital cost of depreciable assets to the transferee will be the purchase price (fair market value).

Goodwill   If goodwill is present, in most cases it will not have a tax value in the records of the transferor. When the goodwill is sold, three-quarters of the consideration received will be subtracted from the cumulative eligible capital account, often creating a negative balance in this account. Any negative balance will have to be adjusted to reflect the 50 percent capital gains inclusion rate and then taken into the transferor's income under ITA 14(1). Three-quarters of the purchase price for goodwill will be added to the transferee's cumulative eligible capital account and will provide a basis for future deductions.

Evaluation Of Alternatives

Advantages Of Selling Shares

18-127.   Generally speaking, the vendor of a business will favour selling shares over selling assets. Factors favouring this alternative are as follows:

- The sale of shares offers the simplicity of a single transaction. In contrast, in a sale of assets, the transferor must deal with the legal and tax consequences arising at the corporate level. In addition, the transferor must steer the corporation through a wind up procedure and deal with the personal tax consequences of these procedures. The greater complexity will require additional personal efforts on the part of the transferor. Also, the legal and accounting fees associated with these transactions are likely to be significant.

- Any income produced by the sale of shares will usually be reported as capital gains. At worst, only one-half of such gains are taxable. At best, the taxable gains may be reduced or eliminated through the use of the $500,000 lifetime capital gains deduction. If assets are sold by the corporation, some of the resulting income could be recaptured CCA which must be included in income. In addition, if capital gains arise on the sale of assets, they will be treated as investment income to the corporation and will not be eligible for the small business deduction.

- If the enterprise has an unused non capital loss carry forward, it will still be available to the enterprise if shares are sold. Any non capital loss carry forwards are, of course, subject to the acquisition of control rules, requiring that they be applied against income earned in the same line of business in which the losses were incurred. However, if the sale of assets alternative is chosen, such loss carry forward balances will be completely unavailable to the purchaser.

- A sale of assets is likely to result in the payment of land transfer taxes which would not be applicable where shares are sold.

Advantages Of Purchasing Assets

18-128.   As just described, there are a number of advantages that can be associated with selling shares, most of them benefitting the transferor. From the point of view of the transferee, a purchase of assets is generally more desirable than a purchase of shares. Some of the advantages of purchasing assets are as follows:

- In acquiring assets, the purchaser acquires a completely new, and usually higher, set of tax values for the assets transferred. For example, consider a depreciable asset with a capital cost of $100,000, a UCC of $40,000, and a fair market value of $400,000. If shares are acquired, the CCA deductions available to the corporation will continue to be based on $40,000 and, if the assets are subsequently disposed of, capital gains will be determined from the original capital cost of $100,000. In contrast, if the asset were purchased for its fair market value of $400,000, this amount would be the capital cost and UCC to the purchaser. This bump up in asset values and the availability of higher CCA claims will significantly reduce the tax liabilities of the transferee from the level that would have prevailed if shares were purchased.

- Goodwill (cumulative eligible capital) can be recognized when assets are acquired. The CEC deductions related to these amounts are not available if shares are acquired.

- If shares are acquired, all of the assets must be acquired. If redundant assets are present, they can be left out of an acquisition of assets.

- If shares are acquired, the transferee becomes responsible for any future tax reassessments. This exposure results because the corporation continues to operate and the new owner inherits any difficulties that may be lurking in past returns. If assets are purchased, the new owner starts with a clean slate and has no responsibility for any tax problems which may arise on previous corporate tax returns. The same may also apply to potential non-tax liabilities such as those related to polluting the environment.

- Most of the preceding discussion has implicitly assumed that the corporation's assets have fair market values in excess of their related tax values. If this is not the case and unrealized losses are present, selling assets may be advantageous to the transferor as well as the transferee. This is based on the fact that the transferor would prefer to have fully deductible terminal or business losses, rather than capital losses which are only one-half deductible against taxable capital gains.

Conclusion

18-129.   While each situation needs to be evaluated on the basis of the specific assets and values involved, in general, a vendor will wish to sell shares while a purchaser will wish to acquire assets. As a result, negotiations will usually involve higher prices being offered for the assets of the business than are offered for the shares of the incorporated business. The following very simplified example illustrates the type of analysis that is required in comparing a sale of assets and a sale of shares.

Example

18-130.   To illustrate the sale of an incorporated business, we will use the following simple example.

> **Example**   Mr. O'Leary owns all of the outstanding shares of O'Leary Ltd., a Canadian controlled private company established in 1983. Mr. O'Leary has reached retirement age and wishes to dispose of the business. He has received an offer to buy the shares for $180,000 or, alternatively, the assets of the business for $200,000. All of the liabilities of the business have been settled in preparation for the sale.
>
> The cost of Mr. O'Leary's original investment was $50,000 and this is also the adjusted cost base and paid up capital of the outstanding shares. The Company has no liabilities. The corporation is taxed at a combined federal/provincial rate of 19 percent on business income and 50 percent (including the ITA 123.3 tax on investment income and the federal surtax). Mr. O'Leary is subject combined federal/provincial rate of 46 percent on non dividend income and 31 percent on dividend income. The corporation has no balance in either its RDTOH account or its capital dividend account.
>
> The relevant information on the assets of the business is as follows:

Asset	Cost	Fair Market Value
Cash	$ 5,000	$ 5,000
Receivables	10,000	10,000
Inventories	55,000	60,000
Land	20,000	40,000
Plant And Equipment (UCC = $45,000)	95,000	60,000
Goodwill	-0-	25,000
Total	$185,000	$200,000

> **Required**   Determine the tax consequences to Mr. O'Leary if he sells his shares for $180,000 and, alternatively, if he sells the assets for $200,000.

Sale Of Shares

18-131.   With respect to the sale of shares, the tax consequences are as follows:

Proceeds Of Disposition	$180,000
Adjusted Cost Base	(50,000)
Capital Gain	$130,000
Inclusion Rate	1/2
Taxable Capital Gain	$ 65,000

18-132. At a 46 percent rate, the normal taxes payable on this gain would be $29,900, leaving Mr. O'Leary with after tax funds of $150,100 ($180,000 - $29,900). However, it is likely that O'Leary Ltd. is a qualified small business corporation. If this is the case, the $500,000 lifetime capital gains deduction could be used to eliminate all of the taxes on this disposition of shares, resulting in Mr. O'Leary retaining the entire $180,000 proceeds. Alternative minimum tax might be applicable if the capital gain is sheltered through the lifetime capital gains deduction.

Sale Of Assets

18-133. The tax consequences resulting from selling the assets are calculated as follows:

Account	Taxable Income
Inventories ($60,000 - $55,000)	$ 5,000
Land [($40,000 - $20,000)(1/2)]	10,000
Plant And Equipment - Recaptured CCA ($60,000 - $45,000)	15,000
Goodwill [($25,000)(3/4)(1/2 ÷ 3/4)]	12,500
Total Taxable Income	$42,500

18-134. Except for the taxable capital gain on the disposition of Land, all of this income is business income. The resulting taxes payable would be calculated as follows:

Taxable Capital Gain [(50%)($10,000)]	$ 5,000
Business Income [(19%)($5,000 + $15,000 + $12,500)]	6,175
Total	$11,175

18-135. The taxable capital gain would result in a $2,667 [(26-2/3%)($10,000)] addition to RDTOH and an allocation to the capital dividend account calculated as follows:

Capital Gain On Land [(1/2)($20,000)]	$10,000
Goodwill [($25,000)(1/4)(1/2 ÷ 1/4)]	12,500
Capital Dividend Account	$22,500

18-136. Given the preceding analysis of the liquidation of the corporate assets, the net cash retained by Mr. O'Leary after the distribution of corporate assets can be calculated as follows:

Proceeds of Disposition - Sale Of Assets	$200,000
Dividend Refund (RDTOH balance)	2,667
Corporate Taxes	(11,175)
Net Available for Distribution	$191,492
Paid Up Capital	(50,000)
ITA 84(2) Deemed Dividend	$141,492
Capital Dividend (Sale Of Land And Goodwill)	(22,500)
Deemed Taxable Dividend	$118,992
Tax Rate On Dividends	31%
Personal Taxes Payable On Dividends	$ 36,888

18-137. There would be no capital gain on the distribution as shown in the following calculation:

Total Distribution	$191,492
ITA 84(2) Deemed Dividend	(141,492)
Deemed Proceeds Of Disposition	$ 50,000
Adjusted Cost Base Of The Shares	(50,000)
Capital Gain	Nil

18-138. Based on the preceding calculations, Mr. O'Leary's after tax retention from the sale of assets would be calculated as follows:

Amount Distributed	$191,492
Taxes On Deemed Dividend	(36,888)
Cash Retained	$154,604

18-139. This amount is larger than the $150,100 that would be retained from a sale of shares if the resulting capital gain was subject to tax. However, it is significantly smaller than the $180,000 that would be retained from a sale of shares if the lifetime capital gains deduction could be used to eliminate the entire gain on the sale.

GST Implications
Transfer of Assets
18-140. The sale of taxable assets of a business is a taxable supply under the GST. This applies regardless of the legal form in which the business is carried on. However, where "all or substantially all" of the assets that the purchaser needs to carry on a business are being acquired by the purchaser, the GST legislation allows the vendor and purchaser to elect to treat the supply as if it were zero rated. This applies to businesses that are involved in the provision of exempt supplies, as well as to businesses that are involved in providing fully taxable or zero rated supplies. The use of the election is not permitted when the vendor is a registrant and the purchaser is a non registrant. However, the election can be used when both the vendor and the purchaser are not GST registrants.

18-141. If the election is made, the vendor does not collect GST on the sale of taxable supplies and the purchaser will not subsequently claim an input tax credit. Also, no GST applies to the sale of goodwill. Therefore, a transfer of assets of a business can be made without payment of GST. When this occurs, the purchaser is required to file the joint election form with the CCRA by the due date of the GST return covering the reporting period in which the sale took place. The purpose of this election is to provide cash flow relief to the purchaser of a business who would normally have to wait for a refund from the CCRA of the GST paid on the purchase of the assets of a business.

18-142. If the election is not made, and the assets being sold were last used by the vendor primarily in commercial activities, GST will be collected on the sale. Offsetting input tax credits may be available to the purchaser through the normal input tax credit procedures. Whether or not the election is used, if the transferred business is a commercial activity, the vendor and purchaser will be able to claim input tax credits on any costs incurred to carry out the transaction.

18-143. In determining whether "all or substantially all" of the assets necessary to carry on the business are transferred, the CCRA relies on a 90 percent or more test. The CCRA has several policy papers on this election in order to provide registrants with guidance in determining compliance with the 90 percent or more test.

Amalgamations, Mergers, Winding Up of a Business
18-144. Where two corporations are merged or amalgamated into a single corporation, or the activities of one corporation are wound up through a merger with another corporation,

the new corporation is generally treated for GST purposes as a person separate from each of the predecessor corporations. If the transfer of assets involves an amalgamation under ITA 87 or a winding up under ITA 88, the transfer of assets is deemed not to be a taxable supply for GST purposes and no election is required. The asset or property transferred on the merger or amalgamation is not a taxable supply under the legislation, thus, there are no GST consequences.

18-145. For GST reporting and remittance purposes, the new corporation's threshold amounts are calculated by reference to supplies made by the predecessor corporations. The summation of the threshold amounts to become the new corporation's threshold amount may necessitate more frequent GST reporting and remitting.

Sale of Shares
18-146. As a general rule, the sale of shares in a corporation is not a taxable supply because, under the GST legislation, the sale of a financial instrument such as shares is an exempt supply. Therefore, share for share exchanges are not taxable for GST purposes. Any related costs, such as legal and accounting fees that are subject to GST, will generally be refundable, provided the business is involved in a commercial activity.

Transfers Within Corporate Groups
18-147. Transfers of goods and services between members of corporate groups will normally attract GST. However, an election can be made to have such transfers deemed to be made for nil consideration (only for GST purposes), resulting in no required payment of GST. The conditions for this election are quite strict and require either the ownership of at least 90 percent of the voting shares of one corporation by the other, or that the companies are sister corporations owned by a parent corporation. In addition, the electing corporations must be Canadian residents and the supplies involved must be used exclusively (more than 90 percent) in a commercial activity.

Holding Companies
18-148. Many holding companies only hold shares or debt and, in the past, they have not been able to register for GST and claim input tax credits because they have not been carrying on a "commercial activity." Changes to the GST legislation allow holding companies to register for the GST and claim input tax credits if they hold shares or debt in another company that owns property that is used at least 90 percent for commercial activities. These provisions allow holding companies to obtain refunds of GST paid on the purchase of property or services solely related to the holding of the shares or debt.

Ceasing To Carry On Business
18-149. When a person ceases to carry on a commercial activity or becomes a small supplier and, as a result, ceases to be a registrant, the person is deemed to have sold all assets at fair market value upon deregistration. Similar rules, discussed in Chapter 9, apply to the changes in the use of capital property used or acquired for use in a commercial activity and the cessation of use of capital property in a commercial activity. If the assets are used for commercial purposes, GST will be payable on the deemed dispositions.

Tax Shelters

Introduction
18-150. The term tax shelter is used in a variety of ways, most commonly to describe various types of investments which either defer the taxation of income to a later point in time or, alternatively, generate an absolute reduction in taxes payable. This distinction is not always a clear one in that, if a deferral results in taxable income being recognized in a period in which the taxpayer is in a lower tax bracket, the deferral process may also generate an absolute reduction in taxes payable. Examples of tax shelters which provide deferrals of taxable income include registered retirement savings plans and certified Canadian films. In contrast, absolute reductions in taxes can be generated with flow through shares.

18-151. In a practical context, the term tax shelter has two different meanings. In some cases, an investment will have a negative or nil cash flow but will produce tax deductions that can be applied against other sources of income. For example, an investment in a limited partnership might produce no cash flows during the first year after acquisition. However, the partnership losses may be applied against the investor's employment or other income. In this situation, other sources of income are being sheltered.

18-152. In other circumstances, the tax shelter investment may produce nil taxable income, despite the fact that it is generating a positive cash flow. Ordinary real estate investments, where positive operating cash flows are offset by CCA deductions, often exhibit this characteristic. In this case, the positive cash flow, rather than another source of income, is being sheltered.

18-153. ITA 237.1 provides a definition of tax shelters. It basically states that a tax shelter is any property where the purchaser will likely be entitled to deduct losses or other amounts, in the four years following the acquisition of the investment, that are in excess of the cost of the investment. This definition concentrates on shelters which protect other types of income, and would not necessarily include investments designed to shelter positive cash flows. Flow through shares are specifically excluded from the definition.

18-154. Tax changes during recent years have limited publicly available investments for sheltering income. There are not many tax shelters available and those that exist have had their tax benefits restricted.

Marketing Of Tax Shelters

18-155. It is important to stress at the outset that losing money is not a desirable tax shelter. Millions of dollars have been lost by investors attempting to reduce taxes without looking at the underlying investment characteristics that were present. A bad investment cannot be converted into a desirable one by its tax features.

18-156. Investors must use great caution in evaluating the claims made by promoters of tax shelters, with decisions being based on all of the tax and non tax features that the investment provides. At the end of this section there is a list of some important factors to consider in the evaluation of tax shelter investments.

Legal Forms
Direct Investment

18-157. The most straightforward tax shelter investment involves an individual investor making a direct investment in the relevant property. This approach is very common in real estate investments, particularly in situations involving relatively small amounts of funds. However, when films, resource properties, or significant parcels of real estate are involved, the need to accumulate larger amounts of funds will generally require that the amounts be raised from a number of investors.

Limited Partnerships

18-158. When more than one investor is needed to support a project, a common legal form is the limited partnership. The general partner in a limited partnership has unlimited liability and has control of the business. Limited partners cannot play an active role in the control of the business operations of the partnership. While the limited partners have limited liability similar to that of shareholders in a corporation, they can take advantage of tax benefits resulting from being a partner.

18-159. This approach allows the funds of several investors to be combined and, at the same time, any possibility that the limited partners' other assets are at risk is avoided.

At Risk Rules

18-160. The limited partnership form has been widely used in real estate, Canadian film, and resource property investments. In earlier years, limited partnerships were used to create investments in which the potential tax deductions exceeded the amount that the investor could lose on the investment. To limit the losses that can be deducted, the "at risk" rules were created and are applicable to losses incurred after 1986. These rules limit the amount that can be deducted for tax purposes by the partner to the at risk amount at the end of the year.

18-161.   The following simple example will serve to give you a basic understanding of how the "at risk" amount is calculated as per ITA 96(2.2). There is additional discussion of these rules in Chapter 20 which also provides general coverage of partnerships.

> **Example**   Mr. Hilary has purchased a limited partnership interest that has a cost of $100,000 with only $5,000 paid in cash. The remaining $95,000 of the cost is owed to the partnership. If Mr. Hilary's share of the limited partnership loss for the first year is $12,000, he can only deduct his $5,000 at risk amount on his current year's tax return. This is calculated as follows:

The partner's adjusted cost base	$100,000
Less - Amounts owing to the partnership by the partner	(95,000)
Less - Amounts or benefits which the partner has been promised to protect him from loss on the investment	-0-
At Risk Amount (before allocation of current loss)	$ 5,000
Less - The partner's share of the current year's undistributed loss	(12,000)
Limited Partnership Loss Carry Forward	($ 7,000)

Flow Through Shares

18-162.   Flow through shares are issued by corporations, usually in the resource industries, so that certain claims for tax deductions or credits can be transferred to the purchaser. Through such arrangements the investor is entitled to claim the company's deductions for such items as Canadian Exploration Expense and, in the case of mining exploration, Earned Depletion Allowances. After using the available deductions, the investor is left with shares which constitute capital property. In most cases, the write offs are sufficiently generous that the adjusted cost base of the shares will be nil, and all of the proceeds from any subsequent sale will be treated as capital gains. The liquidity of the shares will depend on whether they are publicly traded, which in turn will influence the entire disposition process and the ultimate return that is made on the investment.

18-163.   Prior to 1986, it was possible for the issuer to ensure the liquidity of the investment by agreeing to buy back the shares at a price specified at the time of issue. Current legislation requires that any future repurchase of shares is based on fair market value at the time of repurchase, an arrangement that can result in financial losses.

Resource Investments

18-164.   Tax shelter investments in the oil and gas, and mining industries are usually in the form of flow through shares or limited partnership interests. The basic types of tax deductions available through these investment vehicles are briefly described as follows:

> **Canadian Exploration Expenses**   Provided these costs are incurred within the appropriate time period, they are 100 percent deductible on a flow through basis.

> **Canadian Development Expenses**   These costs are fully deductible, but only on the basis of 30 percent per year, with the 30 percent applied to the declining balance amount.

18-165.   The losses that can be deducted through resource limited partnerships are limited by the previously mentioned "at risk" rules. For individuals subject to maximum rates of personal taxation, these deductions can generate tax savings in excess of the cash flows required to carry the investment. This, of course, is dependent on financing a significant portion of the investment. It hardly needs to be pointed out, however, that there are significant risks associated with investments of this type.

Certified Canadian Films
Current Rules
18-166.   At one time, certified Canadian films provided the basis for effective tax shelter arrangements. Investments in these films were eligible for CCA at a rate of 30 percent of the declining balance. Additional CCA was available to the extent of film income and the half year rule was not applicable. If losses subsequently resulted on the investment, these amounts could be deducted against any source of income.

18-167.   A variety of measures have served to eliminate the advantages of these shelters, with the most recent being a 1997 requirement that the timing of the deductions be matched with the timing of the revenues. These measures have served to shut down this type of shelter arrangement.

18-168.   In conjunction with these other changes, a Canadian film and video production tax credit was made available to qualifying corporations. Under ITA 125.4, this credit is equal to 25 percent of qualified labour expenditures. This credit is lost if any of the deductions are flowed through to an investor in the corporation.

Rental Properties
General Rules
18-169.   The general rules with respect to the taxation of rental properties were presented in Chapter 11 and will not be repeated here. As previously mentioned, three factors limit the tax advantages related to owning rental properties. These are as follows:

- Capital cost allowances cannot be used to produce a rental loss to be deducted against other income.

- Each rental property, with a building cost in excess of $50,000, must be allocated to a separate CCA class.

- At the owner's death there is a deemed disposition at fair market value, unless the property is bequeathed to a spouse or a spousal trust.

18-170.   Prior to 1972, it was possible to generate non cash flow losses on rental properties for indefinite periods of time. Older properties could be replaced as their undepreciated capital cost decreased. Further, in the absence of the separate classes requirement, the replacement process did not engender recapture. In fact, this could go on until the taxpayer died, at which point the property could be transferred to a spouse, again without creating recapture. In those "good old days", rental properties represented an almost perfect tax shelter. Unfortunately, the "good old days" are gone for investments in rental properties.

18-171.   The inability to deduct CCA to produce a rental loss has reduced the tax advantages associated with real estate investments. However, CCA can still be used to shelter a positive cash flow from real estate investments. For example, a $100,000 building might produce a net cash flow (gross rents, less interest, property taxes, and other out of pocket costs) of $3,500 per year. As the CCA rate on such a building is four percent, the $4,000 (ignoring the half-year rules) of CCA would produce a nil Net Income for Tax Purposes, despite the presence of a positive cash flow.

18-172.   In many cases, the major motivation for holding real estate is its appreciation in value, particularly in view of the fact that such increases in value are taxed at favourable capital gains rates. Very large gains have been realized during certain periods of time in particular markets. However, this is not always the case. In recent years, some real estate gains have been quite modest, while carrying and selling costs can be relatively high. Another potential problem in some areas of Canada is that real estate can be a very illiquid investment.

Evaluation Of Tax Shelter Investments
18-173.   As noted previously, the evaluation of a tax shelter investment should take into consideration all of the tax and non tax factors that are associated with the investment. This,

of course, requires a complex evaluation process and one which must be applied on an investment by investment basis. However, there are a number of general points which can be relevant in this evaluation:

- **Alternative Minimum Tax** Promoters of tax shelter investments rarely include the alternative minimum tax in their projections. As tax shelters can create an alternative minimum tax liability, it should be considered in the evaluation process. An investor who uses tax shelters to an extent that minimum tax is incurred will often find that the actual rates of return, after accounting for the alternative minimum tax cost, are not attractive.

- **Capital Gains Treatment** As the expected return on tax shelters often includes a capital gains component, it is important to examine the investor's particular circumstances to ascertain whether the expected capital gains treatment is appropriate.

- **CNIL** Many tax shelter investments will cause additions to the Cumulative Net Investment Loss (CNIL) balance. When this happens, the availability of the $500,000 lifetime capital gains deduction on qualified property is reduced.

- **Interest Deductibility** As noted in Chapter 11, care has to be exercised to ensure that interest related to investments is deductible. To be deductible, the interest must be incurred to earn property or business income. However, interest expense incurred to make investments for capital appreciation, only, does not qualify. For example, if a tax shelter involves vacant land to be held for capital appreciation, interest costs on financing associated with this land will not be deductible as they are incurred. Special rules also limit the deduction of interest related to vacant land being held for business purposes. The lack of interest deductibility can significantly change the expected rate of return on a tax shelter investment.

- **Guarantees** Tax shelter investments can provide cash flow or repurchase guarantees and, in many cases, these appear to significantly reduce the risk associated with the investment. However, such guarantees are only as good as the financial ability of the guarantor to make good on promised payments. Guarantees can also affect the calculation of an investor's at risk amount.

- **The Promoter** To a certain extent, the success of virtually all tax shelters requires a promoter with the ability and integrity to protect the interest of investors in the arrangement. Care should be taken to ascertain the reputation of the vendor of the tax shelter, both in the business community at large and in the more specific area of the tax shelter investment.

- **Filing Requirements** The tax shelter promoter must provide the CCRA with an annual information return (Form T5002) and investors with a supplementary information form T5003 each year. The investors' form contains an identification number for the tax shelter and must be filed in order to claim any shelter benefits on a tax return. The investor should ensure that the tax shelter promoter has an identification number before investing. Since many of the tax shelters require more complex tax reporting, the investor should be assured that the information form will be issued by the promoter in a timely fashion and will contain accurate and appropriate tax information. If there is a dispute over the validity of the tax shelter, the CCRA can readily identify the investors involved by using the identification number.

18-174. An additional consideration is that investments in tax shelters can significantly complicate filing the investor's personal tax return. Such investments can easily convert a simple T1 exercise into a process in which professional assistance is mandatory. It would also be prudent for an investor to discuss the tax shelter with a tax professional before investing. The costs of such assistance can significantly reduce the effective rate of return on such investments.

A Final Note

18-175. As with any area where large sums of money are involved, tax shelters are an extremely complex area of tax practice. As a reflection of this fact, we hesitated to include material on this subject in a general text on Canadian income tax such as this one.

18-176.   However, it is our experience that all sorts of taxpayers become involved in these schemes. It is difficult to advise a couple with moderate income holding a limited partnership investment that was supposed to ensure the future financial well being of their family when they have no idea of the nature of their investment and, in many cases, do not realize the cost of having to deal with its tax aspects exceeds the return on the investment. Given this problem, we have included a brief survey of tax shelters in this text.

18-177.   Our goal in including this review is not to make you an expert in this area. Rather, our hope is that we have provided enough information to give you some familiarity with the types of tax shelters that exist and to show that these investments should not be made without sound and, most importantly, independent advice.

References

18-178.   For more detailed study of the material in this Chapter, we refer you to the following:

ITA 18(2)	Limit On Certain Interest And Property Tax
ITA 22	Sale Of Accounts Receivable
ITA 23	Sale Of Inventory
ITA 39(4)	Election Concerning Disposition Of Canadian Securities
ITA 51	Convertible Property
ITA 54	Definitions (Proceeds Of Disposition)
ITA 84(2)	Distribution on Winding Up, Etc.
ITA 85	Transfer Of Property To Corporation By Shareholders
ITA 85.1	Share For Share Exchange
ITA 86	Exchange Of Shares By A Shareholder In Course Of Reorganization Of Capital
ITA 87	Amalgamations
ITA 88	Winding Up
ITA 96(2.2)	At Risk Amount
ITA 110.6	Capital Gains Exemption
ITA 237.1	Tax Shelters
ITR 1104	Division V - Interpretation [Capital Cost Allowances]
IC-89-4	Tax Shelter Reporting
IT-102R2	Conversion Of Property, Other Than Real Property, From Or To Inventory
IT-115R2	Fractional Interest In Shares
IT-126R2	Meaning Of "Winding Up"
IT-142R3	Settlement Of Debts On The Winding-up Of A Corporation
IT-146R4	Shares Entitling Shareholders To Choose Taxable Or Capital Dividends
IT-149R4	Winding Up Dividend
IT-153R3	Land Developers - Subdivision And Development Costs And Carrying Charges On Land
IT-188R	Sale Of Accounts Receivable
IT-195R4	Rental Property - Capital Cost Allowance Restrictions
IT-243R4	Dividend Refund To Private Corporations
IT-259R3	Exchanges Of Property
IT-287R2	Sale Of Inventory
IT-302R3	Losses Of A Corporation - The Effect That Acquisitions Of Control, Amalgamations, And Windings-up Have On Their Deductibility - After January 15, 1987
IT-305R4	Testamentary Spouse Trusts
IT-315	Interest Expense Incurred For The Purpose Of Winding-up Or Amalgamation
IT-367R3	Capital Cost Allowance - Multiple Unit Residential Buildings
IT-430R3	Life Insurance Proceeds Received By A Private Corporation Or A Partnership As A Consequence Of Death
IT-434R	Rental Of Real Property By Individual
IT-444R	Corporations — Involuntary Dissolutions
IT-450R	Share For Share Exchange
IT-474R	Amalgamations Of Canadian Corporations
IT-479R	Transactions In Securities
IT-488R2	Winding Up Of 90% Owned Taxable Canadian Corporations
IT-489R	Non Arm's Length Sale Of Shares To A Corporation

Exercises

(The solutions for these exercises can be found following Chapter 21 of the text.)

Exercise Eighteen - 1 (Share For Share Exchange)

Ms. Aly Alee is the sole shareholder of Aayee Ltd., a Canadian controlled private corporation. The corporation was established several years ago by Ms. Alee with an investment of $450,000. It has identifiable net assets with a fair value of $2,200,000. The shares of her company are acquired by a large publicly traded company, Global Outreach Inc., through the issuance of 50,000 new shares. At the time of this business combination, the Global Outreach Inc. shares are trading at $49 per share. Ms. Alee has fully utilized her lifetime capital gains deduction in the past. Indicate the tax consequences of this transaction to both Ms. Alee and Global Outreach Inc.

Exercise Eighteen - 2 (Exchange of Shares in Reorganization)

Mr. Sam Samson is the sole shareholder of Samdoo Ltd. It is a Canadian controlled private company and its common shares have a fair market value of $2,300,000, an adjusted cost base (ACB) of $1,000,000, and a paid up capital (PUC) of $1,000,000. Mr. Samson exchanges all of his Samdoo Ltd. shares for cash of $1,000,000 and preferred shares that are redeemable for $1,300,000. Determine the ACB and the PUC of the redeemable preferred shares. Indicate the amount and type of any income that will result from this transaction.

Exercise Eighteen - 3 (Exchange of Shares in Reorganization)

Mr. Sam Samson is the sole shareholder of Samdoo Ltd. It is a Canadian controlled private company and its common shares have a fair market value of $2,300,000, an adjusted cost base (ACB) of $1,250,000, and a paid up capital (PUC) of $1,000,000. Mr. Samson exchanges all of his Samdoo Ltd. shares for cash of $1,000,000 and preferred shares that are redeemable for $1,300,000. Determine the ACB and the PUC of the redeemable preferred shares. Indicate the amount and type of any income that will result from this transaction.

Exercise Eighteen - 4 (Exchange of Shares in Reorganization)

Mr. Sam Samson is the sole shareholder of Samdoo Ltd. It is a Canadian controlled private company and its common shares have a fair market value of $2,300,000, an adjusted cost base (ACB) of $1,250,000, and a paid up capital (PUC) of $1,000,000. Mr. Samson exchanges all of his Samdoo Ltd. shares for cash of $1,200,000 and preferred shares that are redeemable for $1,100,000. Determine the ACB and the PUC of the redeemable preferred shares. Indicate the amount and type of any income that will result from this transaction.

Exercise Eighteen - 5 (Gifts)

Ms. Jan Reviser owns 80 percent of the shares of Janrev Inc. The remaining shares are held by her 19 year old daughter. The corporation is a Canadian controlled private company and its shares have a fair market value of $1,600,000, an adjusted cost base (ACB) of $250,000, and a paid up capital (PUC) of $250,000. Ms. Reviser exchanged all of her Janrev Inc. shares for cash of $300,000 and preferred shares that are redeemable for $800,000. Indicate the amount and type of any income that will result from this transaction.

Exercise Eighteen - 6 (Losses In A Windup)

During its taxation year ending December 31, 2000, Downer Ltd. incurs a non capital loss of $93,000 and a net capital loss of $150,000. On January 1, 2001, using the provisions of ITA 87, the company is amalgamated with Upton Inc., a company which also has a December 31 year end. The combined company is named Amalgo Inc. and it elects to use a December 31, year end. The terms of the amalgamation give 20,000 Amalgo Inc. shares to the Downer Ltd. shareholders and 150,000 Amalgo Inc. shares to Upton Inc. shareholders. During the year ending December 31, 2001, Amalgo Inc. has Net Income For Tax Purposes of $1,200,000, including over $300,000 in taxable capital gains. Will Amalgo Inc. be able to deduct the losses incurred by Upton Inc. prior to the amalgamation during its 2001 taxation year? Explain your conclusion.

Exercise Eighteen-7 (Losses In An Amalgamation)

Park Inc. has a September 15 year end, while its 100 percent owned subsidiary, Side Ltd., has an October 31 year end. Side Ltd. has a non capital loss carry forward of $50,000 from its year ending October 31, 1996. On June 30, 2001, there is a wind up of Side Ltd., using the rollover provision found in ITA 88(1). What is the earliest taxation year in which the $50,000 loss can be deducted? If it is not deducted, in what taxation year will it expire?

Exercise Eighteen - 8 (Wind Up)

On December 31, 2001, the condensed Balance Sheet of Lorne Inc. was as follows:

Cash	$120,000
Land - At Cost	140,000
Depreciable Assets - At UCC	240,000
Total Assets	$500,000
Liabilities	$ 75,000
Shareholders' Equity	425,000
Total Equities	$500,000

On January 1, 1997, Procul Ltd. acquired 100 percent of the outstanding shares of Lorne Inc. at a cost of $1,200,000. At this point in time, the fair market value of Lorne's identifiable net assets was $850,000, including $270,000 for the Land. The tax value for the net assets at that time was $410,000. Lorne Inc. has paid no dividends since its acquisition by Procul Ltd.

On December 31, 2001, there is a wind up of Lorne Inc. under the provisions of ITA 88(1). Determine the tax values that will be recorded for Lorne Inc.'s assets after they have been incorporated into the records of Procul Ltd.

Problems For Self Study

(The solutions for these problems can be found following Chapter 21 of the text.)

Self Study Problem Eighteen - 1

Ricon Ltd. owns 100 percent of the outstanding shares of Lynn Inc. Ricon acquired the Lynn shares in 1999 at a total cost of $380,000. Their current fair market value is $490,000. The only asset owned by Lynn Inc. is a parcel of Land. Lynn had paid $175,000 for this land in 1994 and, at the time Ricon Ltd. acquired the shares of Lynn Inc., the fair market value of the Land was $390,000. The Land now has a fair market value of $425,000. Lynn has paid no dividends since its shares were acquired by Ricon.

Required: The two companies wish to combine using either ITA 87 or ITA 88(1). Which provision should be used in this situation? Explain your conclusion.

Self Study Problem Eighteen - 2

John Farnsworth owns 75 percent of the outstanding common shares of Farnsworth Inc. His original investment was $99,000 on December 31, 1998. On this same date, his only daughter acquires the remaining 25 percent of the common shares of Farnsworth Inc. for $33,000.

Mr. Farnsworth's original investment of $99,000 is also the amount of the paid up capital for his shares and the amount of his adjusted cost base for the shares. On December 31, 2001, the fair market value of Mr. Farnworth's shares is $450,000.

As Mr. Farnsworth is nearing retirement, he would like to freeze the value of his estate. To this end, he exchanges his common shares in Farnsworth Inc. for cash of $69,000 and preferred shares that are redeemable at his discretion for $381,000 in cash. The new shares have a legal stated capital of $99,000 and a fair market value of $381,000. The exchange takes place December 31, 2001.

Required: Determine the following:

A. The paid up capital of the newly issued redeemable preferred shares.

B. The adjusted cost base of the newly issued preferred shares.

C. The proceeds of disposition that Mr. Farnsworth would use to calculate any capital gain arising from the disposition of his old common shares of Farnsworth Inc.

D. The tax consequences for Mr. Farnsworth of this reorganization of the capital of Farnsworth Inc.

E. The tax consequences for Mr. Farnsworth if the new Farnsworth Inc. preferred shares are redeemed for $381,000.

Self Study Problem Eighteen - 3

Mr. Jerry Long owns 90 percent of the outstanding common shares of Long Industries Ltd., while his 35 year old daughter Ms. Gerri Long owns the remaining 10 percent. The Company was established in 1988 by Mr. Ian Seto, an unrelated party, with an initial investment of $100,000. No further investment was made by Mr. Seto and, during 1992, Mr. Long purchased 100 percent of the shares for their fair market value of $360,000.

During 1995, he gave 10 percent of the shares to his daughter. The fair market value of 100 percent of the shares at that time was $450,000.

It is now December 1, 2001 and the fair market value of 100 percent of the Long Industries Ltd. shares is $900,000. In order to freeze his estate, Mr. Long would like to use the provisions of ITA 86 to reorganize the capital of the corporation. He is considering two alternative approaches to structuring this reorganization as follows:

Approach One Mr. Long would exchange all of his common shares in return for a note with a fair market value of $90,000 and retractable preferred shares with a legal stated capital of $234,000 and a fair market value of $720,000.

Approach Two Mr. Long would exchange all of his common shares in return for a note with a fair market value of $50,000 and retractable preferred shares with a legal stated capital of $40,000 and a fair market value of $660,000.

Required: Indicate the tax consequences to Mr. Long with respect to the two suggested approaches to an ITA 86 reorganization.

Self Study Problem Eighteen - 4

Intertel Inc., a Canadian controlled private company, has been in operation for a number of years and in the beginning was a profitable enterprise. However, in recent years it has become apparent that its competitive position has been badly eroded and it is not likely that it will be able to earn a satisfactory return on its invested capital. As a consequence, the shareholders have agreed to a liquidation of the Company. The Company's year end is December 31.

In contemplation of the liquidation, a Balance Sheet has been prepared based on the tax values of its assets and liabilities as at December 31, 2001. This Balance Sheet is as follows:

Intertel Inc.
Balance Sheet
As At December 31, 2001

Inventories (Net Realizable Value and Tax Cost)	$	43,750
Refundable Dividend Tax On Hand		33,750
Land - Capital Cost		778,750
Building - Undepreciated Capital Cost		732,500
Total Assets		$1,588,750
Liabilities	$	-0-
Common Stock - No Par		68,750
Retained Earnings		1,520,000
Total Equities		$1,588,750

Other Information:

1. The Land has a current fair market value of $1,553,750. The Building had an original cost of $1,093,750. Its fair market value on December 31, 2001 is $1,591,250.

2. The Retained Earnings balance includes $268,750 in the capital dividend account. The Company has paid no dividends in the last two years.

3. The adjusted cost base of the shares is equal to $68,750, the original capital investment by the shareholders.

4. The corporation pays tax at a combined federal and provincial rate of 18 percent on income eligible for the small business deduction, 27 percent on income that is eligible for the accelerated rate reduction, 43 percent on other active business income, and 50-2/3 percent on other income. This latter rate includes the ITA 123.3 tax on the investment income of Canadian controlled private companies.

5. The preceding Balance Sheet reflects all of the 2001 income, as well as the applicable tax effects, prior to the sale of assets and wind up procedures.

6. All of the assets are disposed of at their fair market values on December 31, 2001.

Required:

A. Calculate the amount that will be available for distribution to the shareholders after the liquidation.

B. Determine the components of the distribution to the shareholders and the amount of taxable capital gains that will accrue to them once the proceeds of the liquidation are distributed to them. Assume that appropriate elections will be made to minimize the taxes that will be paid by the shareholders.

Self Study Problem Eighteen - 5

Mr. Donald Brock is the sole shareholder of Brock Enterprises, a Canadian controlled private company. While the business has, for the most part, operated successfully, Mr. Brock wishes to devote his attention to other matters and is considering selling the enterprise. The business has been in operation continuously since 1982 and has a December 31 year end.

To date he has received two different offers for the business. An individual has offered to pay $455,000 for all of the shares of Brock Enterprises. Alternatively, another company has offered to pay $491,000 for the assets of the business. All current liabilities would be assumed in this asset purchase.

In order to be in a better position to analyze the offers that he has received for the business, Mr. Brock has had a statement of assets prepared as at January 1, 2001. This statement provides the values included in his accounting records, values that are relevant for tax purposes and the estimated fair market values. This statement is as follows:

	Accounting Book Value	Tax Value	Fair Market Value
Cash	$ 14,000	$ 14,000	$ 14,000
Accounts Receivable	24,500	24,500	24,500
Inventories	105,000	105,000	109,500
Land	35,000	35,000	70,000
Building (Note)	122,500	35,000	136,500
Equipment (Note)	87,500	63,000	42,000
Goodwill	-0-	-0-	164,500
Totals	$388,500	$276,500	$561,000

Note The accounting value in the assets schedule equals its capital cost (the accumulated depreciation is shown with the equities).

On January 1, 2001, Brock Enterprises has no balance in its RDTOH.

The related accounting and tax figures on the equity side of the Balance Sheet, on this same date, were as follows:

	Accounting Book Value	Tax Value
Current Liabilities	$ 70,000	$ 70,000
Future Income Tax Liability	10,500	N/A
Accumulated Depreciation On Buildings and Equipment	77,000	N/A
Common Stock - No Par	52,500	52,500
Capital Dividend Account	N/A	70,000
Other Income Retained	N/A	84,000
Retained Earnings	196,000	N/A
Totals	$406,000	$276,500

The adjusted cost base of the shares of Brock Enterprises is equal to the invested capital of $52,500. The corporation is subject to a combined federal and provincial tax rate of 18 percent on income eligible for the small business deduction and 47 percent (including the ITA 123.3 tax on the investment income of Canadian controlled private corporations) on other income.

Mr. Brock is in the maximum tax bracket and is taxed at an overall combined rate of 47 percent on regular income and 31 percent on any dividend income (cash amount) that he receives. He has realized other capital gains sufficient to absorb the maximum limit for the lifetime capital gains deduction.

The sale of the business will take place early in January, 2001.

Required: Determine which of the two offers Mr. Brock should accept.

Assignment Problems

(The solutions for these problems are only available in
the solutions manual that has been provided to your instructor.)

Assignment Problem Eighteen - 1

Limbo Company currently has the following assets:

Asset	Capital Cost	Tax Value	FMV
Equipment	$ 1,000	$ 300	$ 700
Land	14,000	14,000	16,500
Goodwill	Nil	Nil	2,000

There are no liabilities and no tax loss carry forwards. Limbo is one hundred percent owned by Dunbar Holdings Ltd., who purchased the shares of Limbo Company for $20,000 in 1997. At that time, the equipment was valued at its capital cost, the land was valued at $19,000, and there was no goodwill. Limbo has paid dividends of $2,000 to Dunbar since its acquisition.

Required: Dunbar does not wish to have Limbo continue as a separate legal entity. As a consequence, it will use either ITA 87 or ITA 88(1) to absorb Limbo into its parent company. For each asset owned by Limbo, outline what the tax consequences would be if:

A. Limbo was amalgamated into Dunbar Holdings using Section 87.

B. Limbo was rolled into Dunbar Holdings using a Section 88(1) Winding Up.

Assignment Problem Eighteen - 2

In 1997, Acme Ltd. purchased all of the outstanding voting shares of Cross Industries for cash of $1,400,000. The assets of Cross Industries at the time of the acquisition had tax values of $1,250,000 and included a piece of land that was being held as a location for a possible second manufacturing facility. This land had been acquired in 1993 for $640,000 and, at the time Acme acquired the Cross shares, it had a fair market value of $705,000.

Acme currently believes that the Cross operations have become so integrated with Acme's, that it no longer makes sense to operate Cross as a separate entity. As a consequence, they are considering the possibility of absorbing Cross using an ITA 88(1) windup. At this time the tax values of the assets of Cross Industries total $1,270,000. The company is still holding the land for the additional manufacturing facility and it now has a fair market value of $790,000. Cross Industries has paid Acme Ltd. dividends totalling $20,000 since its acquisition.

Required: Explain the tax implications of the proposed windup from both Acme's point of view and from the point of view of Cross Industries.

Assignment Problem Eighteen - 3

Mr. Mark and his son Jack own, respectively, 80 percent and 20 percent of the 1,000 common shares of Markit Ltd. They acquired their shares four years ago, when the Company was incorporated, for $8,000 and $2,000 respectively. The current fair market value of the Markit shares is $2,400,000.

Mr. Mark wishes to freeze the value of his shares at their current value. To accomplish this goal, he will give up these shares for preferred shares of Markit Ltd. having a legal stated capital of $8,000 and a fair market value of $1,600,000. Subsequent to this reorganization of capital, his son Jack will own the only common shares outstanding.

Required:

A. Describe the immediate tax consequences of this transaction to Mr. Mark and his son Jack.

B. Describe the tax consequences of this transaction to Mr. Mark if the new preferred shares in Markit Ltd. were redeemed at their fair market value of $1,600,000.

Assignment Problem Eighteen - 4

Lyle Hunter started an automobile dealership, Hunter Motors Inc. in 1980. As the business is running smoothly, he is planning to turn most of the administration over to his 27 year old daughter, Pat and his 24 year old son, Alan. This will allow Lyle to concentrate on improving his golf game to prepare for retirement.

He is eventually planning to gift his shares of Hunter Motors Inc. to his children, but the immediate tax cost of the disposition might be prohibitive. Instead, Lyle would like to know how a share for share exchange can be used to transfer the business and pass on any future growth to the children. They each have available $5,000 of their own funds to invest in the company.

On November 30, 2001, the condensed balance sheet of the business is as follows:

Hunter Motors Inc.
Balance Sheet
As At November 30, 2001

Assets (book value)	$10,000,000
Bank Loan	$1,490,000
Common Stock (No Par - 100 Shares)	10,000
Retained Earnings	8,500,000
Total Debt and Shareholders' Equity	$10,000,000

An independent appraiser has valued the tangible assets at their book values and goodwill at $1,000,000.

Required: Advise Mr. Hunter. Include in your solution the shareholders' equity section of the Balance Sheet after your proposed share transactions.

Assignment Problem Eighteen - 5

Ms. Suzanne Platt founded the corporation Platt Industries Ltd. (PIL) in 1988 with an initial investment of $120,000 in cash. At that time she was issued common shares with a fair market value and paid up capital equal to her investment of $120,000.

Thanks to Ms. Platt's expertise in managing the enterprise, the fair market value of her common shares increased from their original 1988 value of $120,000, to a fair market value of $960,000 on December 31, 1998. On this date, she sells 25 percent of the common shares of PIL to her 22 year old son for $240,000. The son uses funds that he won in a lottery to pay for the shares.

In December, 2001, Ms. Platt decides to retire. She would like to transfer control of PIL to her son and, if possible, freeze the value of her interest in the company. As at December 31, 2001, her holding of PIL common shares has a fair market value of $1,350,000. It is her understanding that she can exchange her common shares in PIL for a combination of non voting preferred shares and non share consideration without incurring any immediate tax consequences. With this in mind she has proposed two alternative approaches to transferring control of PIL to her son:

Approach One   She exchanges her common shares in PIL for cash of $50,000 and preferred shares that are redeemable at her discretion for $1,300,000. The preferred shares have a legal stated capital of $90,000 and a fair market value of $1,300,000.

Approach Two   She exchanges her common shares in PIL for cash of $50,000 and preferred shares that are redeemable at her discretion for $1,270,000. The preferred shares have a legal stated capital of $1,270,000 and a fair market value of $1,270,000.

PIL is not a qualified small business corporation.

Required: For each of the two suggested approaches determine:

A. the amount of any gift to a related party resulting from the exchange of shares;

B. the paid up capital of the newly issued preferred shares;

C. the adjusted cost base of the newly issued preferred shares;

D. the proceeds of disposition that Ms. Platt received for the old common shares of PIL;

E. the immediate tax consequences for Ms. Platt of the reorganization of the capital of PIL; and

F. the tax consequences for Ms. Platt if the new PIL preferred shares are immediately redeemed for their fair market value.

Assignment Problem Eighteen - 6

For a number of years, Ms. Conrad has operated a very successful gourmet chocolate store in London, Ontario. As she is approaching retirement age, she is considering selling her unincorporated business and has sought your advice in establishing a reasonable asking price.

The business is operated in leased premises that until recently required payments of $2,000 per month. However, under the terms of a new long term lease the rent has been increased to $4,500 per month.

The current fair market values of the identifiable assets of the business are as follows:

Inventories	$206,000
Furniture And Fixtures	$ 56,000

The fair market values of the Furniture and Fixtures are equal to their UCC.

While Ms. Conrad currently manages the business herself, she has two full time sales clerks and part time help during the Christmas season. Ms. Conrad does not draw a salary from the business and she estimates that it would require a salary of about $30,000 per year to find someone to adequately replace her. The most recent income statement for the store, which is very representative of the last several years of operation, is as follows:

Sales		$962,000
Cost Of Goods Sold		747,600
Gross Margin		$214,400
Operating Expenses:		
Salaries And Wages	$31,000	
Rent	24,000	
Depreciation	11,000	
Advertising	10,500	
Other Operating Costs	9,700	86,200
Operating Income Before Taxes		$128,200

Required: Given that investors in this type of business are looking for a 25 percent rate of return before taxes on the total investment in the business, calculate the price you would recommend that Ms. Conrad ask for her business.

Assignment Problem Eighteen - 7

Kruger Ltd. is a Canadian controlled private corporation that has been in operation for over 10 years. Due to increased competition and an inability to adapt to the rapidly changing technological advancements in the industry, it appears unlikely that Kruger Ltd. will be able to earn a satisfactory return on its invested capital in the future. As a consequence, the shareholders have agreed to a liquidation of the Company.

In contemplation of this liquidation, a Balance Sheet has been prepared based on the tax values of its assets and liabilities as at December 31, 2001, the end of the Company's taxation year. This Balance Sheet is as follows:

Kruger Ltd.
Balance Sheet
As At December 31, 2001

Inventories (Net Realizable Value and Tax Cost)	$ 35,000
Refundable Dividend Tax On Hand	27,000
Land - Capital Cost	623,000
Building - Undepreciated Capital Cost	586,000
Total Assets	**$1,271,000**
Liabilities	$ -0-
Paid Up Capital	447,000
Capital Dividend Account	215,000
Other Surplus	609,000
Total Equities	**$1,271,000**

Other Information:

1. The current fair market value of the Land is $1,243,000.

2. The Building had an original cost of $775,000. Its fair market value on December 31, 2001 is $1,173,000.

3. The adjusted cost base of the common shares is equal to $447,000, their Paid Up Capital.

4. On December 31, 2001, the Company has no loss carry overs from prior taxation years. The preceding Balance Sheet reflects all of the 2001 income, as well as the applicable tax effects, prior to the sale of assets and wind up procedures.

5. All of the assets are sold on December 31, 2001 at their fair market values.

6. The corporation pays tax at a combined federal and provincial rate of 20 percent on income eligible for the small business deduction, 29 percent on income eligible for the accelerated rate reduction, and 50 percent on investment income (including the ITA 123.3 tax on the investment income of a Canadian controlled private corporation).

7. No dividends have been paid in the previous two years.

Required:

A. Calculate the amount that will be available for distribution to the shareholders after the liquidation.

B. Determine the components of the distribution to the shareholders and the amount of taxable capital gains that will accrue to the shareholders as a result of the winding up of Kruger Ltd. Assume that appropriate elections will be made to minimize the taxes that will be paid by the shareholders.

Assignment Problem Eighteen - 8

Mr. Cecil Tyrone owns 100 percent of the shares of CT Industries, a Canadian controlled private company. The Company was incorporated in 1981 with an investment of $84,000 for common share capital. The Company has a December 31 year end.

Mr. Tyrone is 73 years old and has never cared for women, children, or small animals. As a consequence, he has no heirs with an interest in taking over the operation of the business. At this point in time he would like to sell the business and devote his attention to the study of astronomy.

He has received two offers for the corporation. The first, made by Ms. Heather Greenwand, is an offer to buy the shares for $1,250,000. The second offer has been made by Mr. Barkley Charms and is an offer to acquire the assets of the business. The specific assets that he would buy and the prices that he is offering are as follows:

Accounts Receivable	$ 58,000
Inventories	185,000
Land	411,000
Building	306,000
Goodwill	351,000
Total	$1,311,000

Both offers would require the purchase to take place on January 1, 2002.

On December 31, 2001, the Balance Sheet of CT Industries is as follows:

Term Deposits	$158,000
Accounts Receivable (Face Amount = $62,000)	51,000
Marketable Securities At Cost (Equal To Fair Market Value)	173,000
Inventories At Cost	176,000
Land At Cost	102,000
Building At Net Book Value*	156,000
Total Assets	$816,000
Liabilities	$247,000
Paid Up Capital	84,000
Retained Earnings	485,000
Total Equities	$816,000

*The capital cost of the Building was $263,000, it is the only asset in its Class, and the UCC for the Class is $112,000.

The Term Deposits have been on the Company's books for over five years. They represent an investment of excess funds. Mr. Tyrone had no personal need for these funds and he wished to defer personal taxation on the earnings they were generating. All of the Company's non current assets have been acquired in the last ten years.

CT Industries is taxed at a rate of 19 percent on income eligible for the small business deduction, 28 percent on active business income that is eligible for the accelerated rate reduction, 43 percent on additional active business income, and 50-2/3 percent on investment income (includes the ITA 123.3 tax on the investment income of a Canadian controlled private corporation). Mr. Tyrone has other sources of income in excess of $100,000 and, as a consequence, his federal tax rate on all additional income is 29 percent at the federal level, plus an additional 16 percent at the provincial level. He lives in a province where the provincial dividend tax credit is equal to one-third of the gross up.

Mr. Tyrone has not used any of his lifetime capital gains deduction.

At December 31, 2001, prior to the sale of any of the listed assets, there is no balance in either the capital dividend account or the refundable dividend tax on hand account.

If Mr. Tyrone accepts Mr. Charms' offer to purchase the business assets, Mr. Tyrone will sell the term deposits and marketable securities at their carrying values. The fair market values for these assets are equal to their carrying values. With respect to the sale of Accounts Receivable, Mr. Charms and Mr. Tyrone will elect to transfer them under the provisions of ITA 22. There would be a wind up of the corporation subsequent to the sale of its assets.

Required: Determine which of the two offers will provide Mr. Tyrone with the largest amount of personal, after tax funds. Ignore the possibility that Mr. Tyrone might be subject to the alternative minimum tax.

Assignment Problem Eighteen - 9

Note This sale of an incorporated business problem involves assets with V-Day values and should only be done if you have covered this material.

Mr. David Carson is the President and only shareholder of Carson Enterprises Ltd., a Canadian controlled private company. The Company's fiscal year ends on December 31.

Mr. Carson established the Company in 1962 by investing $265,000 in cash. The valuation day value of the Company was estimated to be $1,219,000.

Mr. Carson is considering selling the Corporation and, in order to better evaluate this possibility, he prepared a special statement of assets. In this special statement, comparative disclosure is provided for the values included in his accounting records, values that are relevant for tax purposes, and fair market values. This statement is as follows:

Carson Enterprises Ltd.
Statement Of Assets
As At December 31, 2001

	Accounting Net Book Value	Tax Value	Fair Market Value
Cash	$ 54,500	$ 54,500	$ 54,500
Accounts Receivable	406,000	406,000	372,250
Inventories	869,750	869,750	976,000
Land (Note One)	201,500	201,500	405,000
Building (Note Two)	538,000	469,250	2,061,000
Equipment (Note Three)	434,000	294,000	171,250
Goodwill	-0-	-0-	811,000
Total Assets	$2,503,750	$2,295,000	$4,851,000

Note One   The valuation day value of the Land was $336,500.

Note Two   This Building cost $1,281,000 and had a valuation day value of $1,755,000.

Note Three   The Equipment had a cost of $807,500.

At the same time that this statement of assets was prepared, a similar statement of equities was drawn up. This latter statement contained the following accounting and tax values:

	Accounting Book Value	Tax Value
Current Liabilities	$ 697,000	$ 697,000
Loan From Shareholder	137,500	137,500
Future Income Tax Liability	542,000	N/A
Common Stock - No Par	265,000	265,000
Capital Dividend Account	N/A	164,500
Pre 1972 Capital Surplus On Hand	N/A	244,250
Other Income Retained	N/A	786,750
Retained Earnings	862,250	N/A
Totals	$2,503,750	$2,295,000

In addition to the information included in the preceding statements, the following other information about the Company is available:

- The Company has Net Income of nil for the year ending December 31, 2001, before consideration of any income from either offer.

- The Company has available non capital loss carry overs of $83,000.

- The Company has available a net capital loss carry over from 1998 of $194,475 [(3/4)($259,300)].

- Carson Enterprises Ltd. is subject to a combined federal and provincial tax rate of 19 percent on income eligible for the small business deduction, 28 percent on income that is eligible for the accelerated rate reduction, 43 percent on active business income in excess of $300,000, and 50-2/3 percent on investment income (this includes the ITA 123.3 tax on the investment income of Canadian controlled private companies).

- On December 31, 2000, the Company has no balance in its RDTOH.

Mr. Carson has received two offers for his Company and he plans to accept one of them on December 31, 2001. The first offer involves a cash payment of $3,508,000 in return for all of the shares of the Company. Alternatively, another investor has expressed a willingness to acquire the assets and liabilities of the business at a price equal to their fair market values. He has agreed to file an ITA 22 election with respect to the Accounts Receivable if his offer is accepted. If the assets are sold, it is Mr. Carson's intention to wind up the corporation.

Mr. Carson has about $300,000 in 2001 income from other sources and, as a consequence, any income that arises on the disposition of this business will be taxed at the maximum federal rate of 29 percent, combined with a provincial rate of 16 percent. He lives in a province where the provincial dividend tax credit is equal to one-third of the gross up. He has used the ITAR 26(7) V-Day election in the past to determine capital gains or losses on sales of pre 1972 capital assets. He has used all of his lifetime capital gains deduction in prior years.

Required: Determine which of the two offers Mr. Carson should accept. Ignore the possibility that Mr. Carson might be subject to the alternative minimum tax.

Assignment Problem Eighteen - 10 (Electronic Library Research Problem)
Provide brief answers to the following questions. Your answers should be supported by references to materials found in your Electronic Library.

A. A corporation may be dissolved on an involuntary basis. If the shareholders continue to carry on some part of the corporation's business and the corporation is later restored, how will the business income earned during the period of dissolution be taxed?

B. ITA 87(2) uses the phrase "time of amalgamation" as indicative of when the old fiscal years of the predecessor corporations end and when the new fiscal year of the amalgamated corporation begins. How is this "time" determined?

C. In the process of an ITA 88(1) wind up, a subsidiary may incur significant costs for accounting, legal, or other services necessary to implement the transactions. What is the appropriate tax treatment of these costs?

Chapter 19

Trusts and Estates

The Nature Of Trusts

What Is A Trust?

19-1. A trust is a relationship in which a person (the settlor) transfers property to another person (the trustee) for the benefit of a third person (the beneficiary). In so doing, the owner-ship and management of the transferred assets is separated from their enjoyment. Trusts can be established by a person, by a court order, or by a statute. The terms of a trust are usually spelled out in a written trust document in which the settlor of the trust indicates his or her in-structions for the property. The settlor of the trust can also be a trustee.

19-2. As described in the CCRA's *Trust Guide*, a trust has three essential characteristics. There has to be certainty of:

1. the intent on the part of the settlor to create a trust;
2. the identity of the property to be placed in the trust; and
3. the identity of the beneficiary or beneficiaries of the trust.

19-3. With respect to the third item, it is acceptable to identify a class of beneficiaries rather than specific individuals. An example of this would be specifying an individual's children as the beneficiaries. This could be structured to include both current children as well as children born subsequent to the establishment of the trust.

19-4. Despite the fact that they are treated as separate persons for income tax purposes, a trust is not a separate legal entity. It cannot enter into contracts, own properties or incur liabil-ities. Rather, such transactions can only be entered into by the trustees who are the registered owners of trust property and who should be described as the parties to any agreement.

19-5. As noted, a trust provides for the management of assets to be separated from the ben-eficial interest in the assets. This is useful when the settlor lacks confidence in the ability of the beneficiary to effectively deal with the problems associated with managing the assets. An ex-ample of this would be an individual transferring an investment portfolio to a trust in favour of a spouse in circumstances where that spouse has had no experience in managing investments. Such trust arrangements can be of particular importance when the beneficiaries are minors as, in general, minors cannot enter into binding contracts. Contracts entered into with a minor outside of a trust could be voided by that minor at their discretion. Use of a trust can avoid this type of problem.

Estates

19-6. In normal business and legal usage, the terms trust and estate are quite distinct. In contrast to the restrictive meaning of trust arrangements, the term estate is a more general term used simply to refer to the property and possessions of an individual. While we often associate the term estate with the property of a deceased person, this is clearly not a restriction that is inherent in the term. The term is also used to refer to the property owned by a living individual.

19-7. During an individual's lifetime, management of that individual's estate is a personal matter. After an individual's death, an executor normally administers the deceased's estate and makes distributions to the beneficiaries of the estate. While both executors and trustees serve as fiduciaries, the role of an executor is more limited and usually of shorter duration. Note that in Quebec, an executor is referred to as a liquidator.

19-8. In comparing the terms trust and estate, every individual has, to some degree, an estate. Further, this estate may be subject to a trust document. Estates exist which are not subject to trust documents and trusts are established to deal with assets that could not reasonably be referred to as an estate. While the two terms overlap, they should not be viewed as synonyms.

19-9. Unfortunately, the *Income Tax Act* uses the terms trust and estate interchangeably, a situation which can cause confusion. This can be seen in ITA 104(1) that refers to the terms as follows:

> In this *Act*, a reference to a trust or estate shall be read as a reference to the trustee or the executor, administrator, heir or other legal representative having ownership or control of the trust property.

19-10. While the general definition seems to confuse the terms trust and estate, and to indicate that taxation is directed at the trustee rather than the trust property, it becomes clear in reading through Subdivision k (Trusts And Their Beneficiaries) that this reference to estate in the *Act* is really referring to assets that are administered by a trustee for the benefit of beneficiaries.

19-11. The definition of trust has been clarified to exclude bare trusts. A bare trust is one in which the trustee holds property without any further duties to perform except to convey it to the beneficiaries on demand or as directed by the beneficiaries. The trustee has no independent power or responsibilities and can only take action regarding trust property with instructions from the beneficiaries. In the case of such bare trusts, the income of the assets is considered to be the income of the beneficiaries, with no recognition of the legal arrangements for their conveyence.

19-12. The CCRA normally looks to trust assets in collecting related taxes, but the responsibility for paying taxes on trust property rests with the trustees. If the assets are difficult to liquidate or have declined substantially in value, the CCRA has widened the responsibility net beyond trustees. Legal representatives have continuous joint and several liability for the taxes of trusts and estates. In addition to executors and trustees, heirs and individuals granted a power of attorney are also liable.

Types Of Trusts

General Classification

19-13. The CCRA's *Tax Guide* lists and defines over 15 different types of trusts. Included on this list are personal trusts, spousal trusts, offshore trusts, mutual fund trusts, employee benefit plans, insurance segregated fund trusts, salary deferral arrangements, and master trusts. This is made more confusing by the fact that some the defined arrangements are really not a separate type of trust but, rather, a variation on one of the other defined types of arrangements. For example, a spousal trust is, in fact a particular type of personal trust.

19-14. We have encountered some of these arrangements in earlier chapters. For example, both registered pension plans and registered retirement savings plans involve trust arrangements that were discussed in Chapter 5. Further, some attention was given to mutual fund trusts when we discussed property income in Chapter 11. These types of arrangements will not be reviewed in this Chapter, nor will we devote attention to such arrangements as insurance segregated fund trusts or master trusts.

19-15. Our focus in this Chapter will be on what can be loosely described as personal trusts. In particular, our concern will be with trusts that are arranged on a customized basis and administered to meet the particular needs of certain individuals. These arrangements constitute an important component of tax planning, particularly with respect to matters involving the estates of both living and deceased individuals.

Personal Trusts
Inter vivos and Testamentary Trusts
19-16. The CCRA *Trust Guide* indicates that a personal trust is either:

- a testamentary trust; or
- an inter vivos trust in which no beneficial interest was acquired for consideration payable either to the trust, or to a person who contributed to the trust.

The person or related persons who create an inter vivos trust may acquire all the interests in it without the trust losing its status as a personal trust.

19-17. This definition establishes the two basic types of personal trusts, but uses terms that required further definition.

- **Testamentary Trust** refers to a trust that arises upon or in consequence of the death of an individual.

- **Inter Vivos Trust** refers to any personal trust other than a testamentary trust. Stated alternatively, an inter vivos (Latin for "among the living") trust is a trust created during the lifetime of the settlor. Note that an inter vivos trust does not become a testamentary trust on the death of the contributor. These trusts are sometimes called living trusts.

19-18. These definitions establish the fact that all personal trusts can be categorized as either testamentary or inter vivos. This means that any other type of defined personal trust must also fall into either one or both of these categories. More specifically, qualified spousal trusts can be either testamentary or inter vivos. In contrast, alter ego trusts can only be established as inter vivos trusts.

Qualifying Spousal Trusts
19-19. For convenience, we will continue to use the term spouse and spousal in this section. Recognize however, that the current definition of spouse includes common-law arrangements and, in addition, those provisions of the *Act* that are directed towards spouses also cover common-law partners (same-sex couples).

19-20. As noted in the preceding paragraph, a spousal trust can be either an inter vivos trust or a testamentary trust. To be a qualifying spousal trust, the following conditions must be met:

- The transferor's spouse is entitled to receive all of the income of the trust arising before the spouse's death.

- No person other than the spouse may receive or benefit from any of the income or capital of the trust, prior to the spouse's death.

19-21. Qualification also requires that the settlor and the trust must be resident in Canada when the property is transferred. Somewhat surprisingly, the spouse can be a non resident. Further, for testamentary trusts, the property must vest indefeasibly in the spousal trust within 36 months after the death of the transferor. The meaning of "vest indefeasibly" is described in IT-449R as follows:

In the Department's view a property vests indefeasibly in a spouse or child of the deceased when such a person obtains a right to absolute ownership of that property in such a manner that such right cannot be defeated by any future event, even though that person may not be entitled to the immediate enjoyment of all the benefits arising from that right.

19-22.   The transfer of property to a qualifying spousal trust is done on a rollover basis. That is, when a settlor transfers property to a qualifying spousal trust, the spousal trust is deemed to have acquired the property at the settlor's tax cost. For non depreciable properties, this value is the transferor's adjusted cost base. If the property is depreciable property, the transfer is at the transferor's UCC amount. For purposes of determining recapture, the transferor's original cost is the transferee's cost.

19-23.   This means that the use of a qualifying spousal trust allows the settlor to defer the taxation of gains on any property that is transferred. In the case of an inter vivos trust, this is accomplished during the settlor's lifetime. Similarly, a testamentary trust established by the settlor's will will accomplish this same goal at the time of death.

19-24.   An election can be made under ITA 73(1) for the transfer to be made at fair market value, allowing for the recognition of any related capital gains or recapture of CCA that are present at the time of the transfer.

19-25.   A special rule applies to transfers of real property inventory to spousal trusts. Real property inventory may not be transferred to an inter vivos spousal trust on a tax deferred basis, but it may be rolled into a testamentary spousal trust without realizing any income or loss that has accrued.

19-26.   As discussed in Chapter 10, a rollover of assets to a spouse can be accomplished without the use of a trust. In the case of a living individual, the rollover is provided for under ITA 73(1), while for a deceased individual, the enabling provision is ITA 70(6). This makes it clear that a trust is not required to implement a tax free transfer of property to a spouse. Why then are we concerned with spousal trusts? There are essentially two important reasons:

1.   A trust can provide for the appropriate management of the transferred assets, particular when these assets include an active business. In many cases, the spouse of a settlor may have no experience in the management of assets and, in such situations, the trust document can ensure that professional management is used. If the assets were simply transferred to the spouse, the use of such management would be left to the discretion and control of the transferee.

2.   Also of importance is that the use of a trust can ensure that the assets are distributed in the manner desired by the settlor. While qualification requires that the transferred assets must "vest indefeasibly" with the spouse, the trust document can specify who the assets should be distributed to after the spouse's death. This could ensure, for example, that the assets are ultimately distributed only to the settlor's children if the spouse has remarried.

Alter Ego and Joint Partner (a.k.a. Joint Spousal) Trusts

19-27.   There are a number of reasons that an individual, or an individual and his spouse, may wish to transfer assets to a trust prior to their death (we will discuss these reasons prior to leaving this section). Until recently this was not a very practical procedure in that such transfers were dispositions and, in the absence of some special provision, any accrued income on the property would have to be recognized at the time of transfer. For trusts established after 1999, special provisions are now available that change this situation.

19-28.   The first of these provisions provides for the establishment of an inter vivos trust that is referred to as an alter ego trust. The conditions for the establishment of an alter ego trust are:

• The settlor must be 65 years of age or over.

• All of the income must be received by the settlor during their lifetime.

• No person other than the settlor can receive or make use of the capital or income of the trust during the settlor's lifetime.

19-29.   A similar arrangement is available for an individual and his spouse or common-law partner. These arrangements are referred to as joint spousal or joint partner trusts and the conditions for establishing these arrangements are:

- The settlor must be 65 years of age or over.

- All of the income must be received by the settlor and their spouse or common-law partner until the later of their deaths.

- No person other than the settlor and his spouse or common-law partner can receive or make use of the capital or income of the trust during the period until the later of their deaths.

19-30.   For trusts that qualify under either of the provisions, property can be transferred from the settlor to the trust with no tax consequences. The transfer is treated as a disposition at fair market value resulting in in no tax consequences for the transferor. As you would expect, the property is received by the trust at the same value that was used by the transferor.

19-31.   Note, however, that this does not provide for additional deferral at death. In the case of an alter ego trust, there will be a deemed disposition of the trust property at fair market value when the settlor dies. In similar fashion, for joint partner trusts there will be a deemed disposition of trust property at fair market value at the later of the settlor's death or the death of the settlor's spouse or partner.

19-32.   The basic reason for using these arrangements is that the trust property will not be included in the settlor's estate and, as a consequence will not be subject to probate procedures (probate is a court process which proves the authenticity and validity of a will). There are a number of advantages associated with avoiding probate:

- The probate fees can be high, sometimes as much as 1-1/2 percent of the total value of an estate.
- The probate process can be time consuming. This can create difficulties for the management of an active business, as well as liquidity problems for the estate.
- When assets such as real estate are held in more than one jurisdiction (e.g., Canada and the U.S.), the probate procedures must be undertaken in multiple jurisdictions.
- Once probated, a will is in the public domain. For a nominal fee, any interested individual can obtain a copy, with the possibility that this will invade the privacy of surviving family members.

19-33.   A further point here is that it is easier, from a legal point of view, to challenge the validity of a will than it is to challenge the validity of a trust. Courts can be asked to consider moral obligations to family members in distributing the assets of an estate. With a trust, there is no will to challenge.

Discretionary and Non Discretionary Trusts

19-34.   Testamentary and inter vivos trusts can be set up as discretionary or non discretionary trusts. Discretionary trusts are frequently used as financial planning vehicles to maximize future flexibility. Typically, a wealthy individual wants to create a trust for children or grandchildren in relatively low tax brackets. Which descendants are the most deserving is uncertain, and the individual wants to defer making a final decision on the distribution of property. A discretionary trust can be an excellent solution to this dilemma.

19-35.   Assets can be placed in an inter vivos discretionary trust with the settlor's various descendants as beneficiaries. This can also serve the purpose of freezing the settlor's estate (see subsequent discussion of estate freezes in this Chapter). The assets will be controlled by the trustee, yet any capital appreciation will accrue to the beneficiaries. Further, income from the trust's assets can accumulate in the trust without immediate distribution. Finally, the discretionary nature of the trust allows the trustee to defer and revise decisions as to the eventual distribution of the trust's income and assets.

19-36.   As the name implies, the trustee of a discretionary trust has the right to make one or more choices. These choices can be useful tools in tax planning and might include:

- The date on which the assets of the trust will be distributed.
- Amounts to be allocated or paid to individual beneficiaries.
- The date on which the trust is to be terminated.

19-37.   In contrast to discretionary trusts, some trust documents are very specific with respect to income and capital distributions and the shares that are to be received by individual beneficiaries. Such trusts are referred to as non discretionary trusts. Non discretionary trusts have become increasingly popular as the use of such trusts makes it easier to allocate trust income to minors while retaining it in the trust.

Creating A Personal Trust

19-38.   A trust generally comes into existence when property is transferred by the settlor to the trustees. As specified in the ITA 54 definitions, a disposition of property normally occurs when there is any transfer of property to a trust.

19-39.   When a capital asset is transferred to a personal trust, a disposition is deemed to take place at fair market value. The settlor is deemed to receive proceeds of disposition equal to fair market value and the trust is deemed to acquire the property at that same value. The fair market value disposition rule applies equally to non depreciable and depreciable capital property. However, in the case of depreciable property, ITA 13(7)(e) indicates that, when the fair market value of the asset being transferred exceeds the transferor's capital cost, the transferee's cost for purposes of calculating CCA and determining recapture is equal to the transferor's cost, plus one-half of the difference between transferor's cost and the fair market value at transfer. This prevents the transferor's capital gain, of which only one-half is included in income, from being converted to fully deductible CCA. Deemed dispositions also arise on transfers to specialized trusts, such as RRSPs, DPSPs, and RRIFs. In these specialized cases, the transfer is treated as a disposition, despite the fact that there is usually no change in the beneficial interest.

> Exercises Nineteen-1 through Nineteen-4 deal with transfers to trusts. This would be an appropriate time to attempt these exercises.

19-40.   As noted in our discussion of types of trusts, there are three important exceptions to the transfer at fair market value rules. These exceptions are (1) qualified spousal trusts, (2) alter ego trusts, and (3) joint partner trusts.

19-41.   As noted previously when a transfer of property is made to one of these types of trusts, it is recorded at the settlor's tax cost, both by the settlor and by the trust. These rollover provisions serve to defer any accrued income on the transferred property until a later point in time, usually when the property is subsequently disposed of by the trust.

Trust Tax Returns

19-42.   As was noted in Chapters 1 and 2, for income tax purposes a trust is considered to be a "person" and, as such, is required to file a return and pay taxes as an entity separate from the trustee or the beneficiaries. While the procedures used by trusts are similar to those used by individuals and corporations, there are differences. These differences will be described in this section.

19-43.   With respect to the payment of taxes, trusts are in a very favourable position. Testamentary trusts are not required to make instalment payments. While inter vivos trusts are technically required to make quarterly instalments, as an administrative practice, the CCRA does not enforce this requirement. Given this situation, trusts enjoy significant tax deferral as compared to individuals and corporations.

19-44.   With respect to taxation years, testamentary trusts can select a taxation year other than the calendar year. However, inter vivos trusts are required to use the calendar year.

19-45.   The due date for filing trust information returns and for paying taxes payable by a trust is 90 days after the year end of the trust. Note that the due date is not three months after a trust's year end. Unfortunately, many trustees are unaware of this nuance.

19-46.   Annual reporting of trust income is required on a T3 Trust Income Tax and Information Return and the corresponding information return for beneficiaries is a T3 slip. The T3 slip, "Statement of Trust Income Allocations And Designations", is issued to each beneficiary by the trustee within 90 days of the trust's year end. The T3 indicates the amount and type of income which must be reported on the beneficiary's income tax return for the year. The trust can designate the income that is allocated to the beneficiaries to ensure there is a flow through of the nature of the income. For example, amounts can be designated for:

- net taxable capital gains;
- pension income eligible for the pension income credit;
- dividends from taxable Canadian corporations;
- foreign business and foreign non-business income.

19-47. These designations allow the beneficiary to take advantage of the credits or deductions related to the designated income, such as the dividend tax credit. In general, trusts cannot allocate capital losses or non capital losses to beneficiaries.

Net and Taxable Income of Personal Trusts

Alternatives

19-48. As will be discussed more fully in the next section, trusts are generally subject to the same rules that are applicable to individuals. However, the application of these rules can be confusing in that there is discretion in the way these rules are applied to trusts. This results in what we consider to be three alternative scenarios which are briefly described as follows:

The Usual Scenario The trust Net and Taxable Income calculations will follow the usual procedures for determining net business and property income and net taxable capital gains. The one unusual feature is that, to the extent that the trust income is allocated to beneficiaries, it will be deducted in the calculation of the trust's Net and Taxable Income. This means that a trust that allocates all of its income to beneficiaries will have Taxable Income of nil and will pay no taxes at the trust level. As you would expect, this income is allocated to and taxed in the hands of the beneficiaries.

Income Retention Scenario An alternative is available under which the trust chooses not to allocate income to beneficiaries. Under this scenario, taxable income is calculated without any deductions for allocations to beneficiaries, resulting in the trust being subject to tax on these amounts. As you would expect, the beneficiaries are not taxed on these amounts when they are paid out.

Preferred Beneficiary Scenario The preferred beneficiary election is available for disabled individuals. Under this scenario, the trust can allocate income to such beneficiaries without the amounts being either paid or payable to them. The trust will be able to deduct the allocations while retaining the income in the trust, and the income will be taxed in the hands of the beneficiary.

19-49. We will devote most of our attention to the first of these scenarios. However, a brief description will be provided with respect to the other alternatives.

General Rules

19-50. ITA 104(2) indicates that, in general, trusts resident in Canada are taxed according to the rules applicable to individual taxpayers. As all references to trusts in the *Act* are to be read as references to the trustees, it is not surprising that the residence of a trust depends on the residency of the trustees. Therefore, the residence of a trust is generally not affected by the residence of the settlor or beneficiaries. However, if the trust is merely used as a conduit, and all income is flowed through to the beneficiaries, the residence of the trust is deemed to be the same as the residence of the beneficiaries.

19-51. A trust is treated as a separate person for purposes of determining net income, taxable income and taxes payable. The general rules used by individuals in computing net income for tax purposes and taxable income also apply to trusts. For example, the use of generally accepted accounting principles and accrual rules apply to the calculation of business income. Capital gains and losses are realized on the disposition of capital assets. Also, in the calculation of net income for tax purposes, taxable dividends are grossed up as they would be for individuals. Finally, deductions are allowed for non capital, net capital and certain other types of losses.

19-52. Income is reported on the trust tax return in much the same form as income is reported for individuals. That is, sources and amounts of income are identified by categories, and category totals are entered on the return. In contrast, the corporate tax return starts with net income per financial statements, and a reconciliation schedule is used to calculate net income for tax purposes.

19-53. As noted in the preceding section, a unique feature in the calculation of the Net and Taxable Income of a trust is the ability to deduct amounts that are allocated to beneficiaries. This is an extremely important feature in that, for those trusts which allocate all of their income to beneficiaries, there will be no Taxable Income or Taxes Payable. The next section gives more detailed consideration to income allocations to beneficiaries.

Income Allocations to Beneficiaries
General Rules

19-54. Since a trust is a separate taxable entity, any income that is earned by trust assets will initially accrue to the trust. However, any income that is allocated to a trust beneficiary can be deducted in the calculation of the trust's net income for tax purposes. Correspondingly, the amount deducted by the trust must be included in the net income for tax purposes of the relevant beneficiary. In effect, when trust income is allocated to a beneficiary, the obligation to pay income taxes on that income is transferred from the trust to the beneficiary.

19-55. Trusts may also make payments to third parties. Most of these payments relate to expenses incurred to earn trust income, that are deductible in calculating net income. Other third party payments relate to benefits for beneficiaries and include such expenses as daycare, tuition and medical fees. These amounts are deductible by the trust as allocations to beneficiaries, but will be considered income payable to the beneficiaries. Also, payments made to a parent as a reimbursement of eligible expenses because the beneficiary is a minor will be considered as having been paid to the beneficiary.

19-56. To be deductible by the trust, the allocated amounts must be paid or payable. While it is easy to determine whether an amount has been paid, questions often arise in determining whether or not an amount is payable to a beneficiary. ITA 104(24) provides that an amount is:

> ... deemed not to have become payable in a taxation year unless it was paid in the year to the beneficiary or the beneficiary was entitled in the year to enforce payment of the amount.

19-57. Issuing a promissory note or a cheque payable to the beneficiary for the share of the trust income will usually fulfill the payable requirement. The CCRA expands the definition of payable in IT-286R2 by stating that an amount is not considered to be payable in any of the following circumstances:

- A beneficiary can only enforce payment of an amount of income by forcing the trustee to wind up the trust.
- The beneficiary's right to income is subject to the approval of a third party.
- Payment of income is at the trustee's discretion.
- The beneficiary has the power to amend the trust deed and must do so to cause the income to be payable.

19-58. Discretionary trusts cannot be used when amounts are intended to be payable instead of being paid to beneficiaries, based on the above restrictions. To ensure that income allocations that are payable, but not paid, to beneficiaries are fully deductible at the trust level, non discretionary trusts should be used. As a result, most personal trusts are now set up as non discretionary trusts whereby the trustees can control the timing, but not the amounts or types, of income payments to respective beneficiaries.

Tax On Split Income

19-59.   Prior to 2000, trusts provided an outstanding income splitting opportunity. Parents would direct dividends or other income from businesses which they owned into the trust. This income would then be used to pay for many of the costs incurred by the children, including food, clothing, and other necessities of life. While the income would be allocated to the children, their income would be so low that the result would be either no or minimal taxes. This obviously unfair practice was significantly curtailed or, in some cases, eliminated completely with the introduction of the tax on split income or "kiddy tax" applicable to 2000 and subsequent years.

19-60.   Where minor beneficiaries (under 18 years of age) are allocated dividends from private corporations or income earned by a business carried on by a related person, the income will be subject to the tax on split income at the top federal rate of 29 percent. In addition, only the dividend tax credit can be applied against any resulting taxes payable. This special tax eliminates many of the benefits of using a trust to flow certain income through to minor children. The tax on split income will not apply to a minor who does not have a Canadian resident parent or to income from property inherited from a parent. As well, the tax is not applicable to income from property inherited from any person if the minor is either enrolled full-time at a post-secondary institution or is eligible for the disability tax credit. More detailed coverage of this tax is found in Chapter 13. This new tax will clearly have a major impact on tax planning involving income allocations to minors through inter vivos trusts.

Beneficiaries Under The Age Of 21

19-61.   Frequently, amounts can be allocated to minors, with the actual income being retained in the trust until the minor reaches a certain age, for example 18 years. When this occurs, ITA 104(18) deems the amounts to be payable to the minor beneficiaries, providing the child is less than 21 years of age at the end of the year, their right to the income has vested, and there is no other reason the income has not been paid or become payable. While this allows the trust to claim a deduction for such amounts, the child must report that amount as taxable income, pay the required income tax, and if applicable, the tax on split income. If the income is payable to a particular child, the trustees should invest it in a separate account for that child to clearly segregate allocated income from other trust assets.

> Exercise Nineteen-5 deals with personal trusts. This would be an appropriate time to attempt this exercise.

Designation to Retain Income In Trust

19-62.   Amounts allocated to a beneficiary are generally deducted by the trust and included in the income of the beneficiary. However, ITA 104(13.1) permits a trust to designate all or part of its income as "not to have been paid" or "not to have become payable in the year". The amounts so designated are not included in the beneficiaries' net income and are not deductible in computing the net income of the trust. This designation is only available to trusts that are resident in Canada throughout the taxation year and which are subject to Part I tax.

19-63.   The designation to retain income is useful when a trust will benefit from lower marginal tax rates than would apply to a beneficiary. In addition, if a trust has losses carried forward, it may be beneficial to designate income to be reported in the trust to offset these losses. An additional advantage relates to the avoidance of instalments. Trusts are not required to pay instalments of income tax, whereas individuals and corporations are required to do so. The designation to retain income, which will be taxed at the trust level, instead of being taxed personally, may avoid the need to make any tax instalments.

Preferred Beneficiary Election

19-64.   A preferred beneficiary election is available for disabled beneficiaries. The beneficiary must either be eligible for the disability tax credit or be eligible to be claimed by another individual as an infirm dependant 18 years or older. This allows any amount of trust income allocated to that beneficiary to be taxed in the beneficiary's hands while still remaining in the trust. Subsequent distributions of this income will not be taxed. The preferred beneficiary election recognizes that it may not be advisable for disabled beneficiaries to have access to annual distributions of trust income. For other beneficiaries, with the possible exception of beneficiaries under the age of 21, unless trust income is actually paid or payable to a beneficiary, the trust income will be taxed in the trust.

Other Considerations in Determining Net and Taxable Income
Flow Through Provisions
19-65.   Income accruing to a trust typically includes some combination of dividends from private or public taxable Canadian corporations, interest from Canadian sources, pensions, taxable capital gains, and management service fees. As these types of income are subject to different tax rules (e.g., only one-half of capital gains are subject to tax), it is very important that these various types of income retain their tax characteristics when they are allocated to beneficiaries. This is, in fact, what happens. More specifically:

- Dividend income received by a trust and allocated to a beneficiary can be designated as a dividend in the hands of that beneficiary. As such, it will be subject to the usual gross up and tax credit procedures and, in general, taxes at the appropriate marginal rates.

- Capital gains realized by a trust and allocated to a beneficiary can be designated as capital gains in the hands of that beneficiary. This means that only an appropriate portion (currently one-half) of the gain will be taxed and, in addition, the beneficiary can use such capital gains to offset capital losses that he has realized from non trust sources.

19-66.   As indicated previously, minor beneficiaries will be subject to the tax on split income at the top federal rate of 29 percent if they are allocated dividends from private corporations or income earned by a business carried on by a related person. Despite the tax on split income, a trust is still a useful income splitting technique to flow dividends from public corporations and income from most other passive investments to any beneficiaries.

Capital Cost Allowances and Recapture of CCA
19-67.   Under trust law, the amount of income that may be distributed to beneficiaries should be determined after providing for accounting amortization. Therefore, the income allocations are supposed to be independent of capital cost allowance claims, which may differ from accounting depreciation amounts. Trustees must account for any differences between depreciation and capital cost allowances, which can require some complicated reconciliations. To simplify bookkeeping, most trustees, and even some trust documents, simply set accounting amortization equal to capital cost allowances.

19-68.   Capital cost allowance claims are deductible in determining net income at the trust level. Like partnerships, capital cost allowance is effectively flowed through to beneficiaries through the allocation of net business or property income. Conceivably, cash allocations can be made before capital cost allowance, and therefore may differ from net income allocated for income tax purposes.

19-69.   While capital cost allowances can be effectively flowed through to beneficiaries, a similar flow through is not possible for recaptured capital cost allowance. Rather, recapture is taxable at the trust level and any related income tax must be borne by capital beneficiaries. This can create significant inequities in situations where income beneficiaries have benefitted from the related deductions for capital cost allowance.

Trustee's or Executor's Fees
19-70.   To calculate net income of a trust, deductions may be claimed for fees that are paid to a trustee or executor whose principal business is rendering investment advice or providing administrative services relating to investments.

Principal Residence Exemption
19-71.   This exemption is usually considered to be available only to individuals. However, personal trusts can also benefit from the principal residence exemption. A residence held in a trust will qualify for the exemption if the residence was ordinarily inhabited in the year by a beneficiary of the trust, or by a spouse, former spouse or child of such beneficiary. As well, the full gain on a principal residence will qualify for the exemption where the trust has more than one beneficiary, but only one of the beneficiaries occupies the residence.

RRSPs

19-72. Deductions for contributions to registered retirement savings plans (RRSPs) are not allowed to trusts. But, a qualifying spousal trust, that is also a testamentary trust, may be designated as the beneficiary of an RRSP on the death of a taxpayer. This enables a refund of premiums from the RRSP to be transferred from the trust to the surviving spouse's RRSP on a tax deferred basis.

Tax Payable of Personal Trusts

General Approach

19-73. In keeping with the previously expressed idea that trusts are to be taxed in the same manner as individuals, the taxes payable for a trust are calculated using the same rates that are applicable to individuals. However, how these rates will be applied differs, depending on whether the trust is an inter vivos trust or, alternatively, a testamentary trust. These differences will be discussed in the material which follows.

Taxation of Testamentary Trusts

19-74. Testamentary trusts are taxed using the same schedule of progressive rates that apply to individuals. The rates range from a low of 16 percent on the first $30,754 of taxable income, to a maximum of 29 percent on taxable amounts in excess of $100,000. These rates are applied to taxable income, generally determined after the amounts allocated to beneficiaries have been deducted.

19-75. The fact that the full range of progressive rates is available to each trust suggests that when an individual wishes to have several beneficiaries of his estate, a separate testamentary trust should be established for each one. In contrast to the use of a single trust for all beneficiaries, this arrangement provides for multiple applications of the low rates in the progressive rate schedule that is applicable to individuals.

19-76. While there is no general prohibition against an individual being a beneficiary of more than one testamentary trust, there is concern this type of arrangement might be used purely for income splitting purposes. To prevent multiple trusts from being created solely for this purpose, ITA 104(2) notes that where substantially all of the property of two or more trusts has been received from a single individual and the income from the trusts will ultimately accrue to the same beneficiary or group of beneficiaries, the CCRA may designate the trusts as one trust. A 1956 case, Mitchel vs. M.N.R. found that where an individual set up a separate trust for each of his four children, this provision did not apply because it could not be held that the income of the trusts accrues, or will ultimately accrue, to the same beneficiary or group of beneficiaries. To legitimize separate testamentary trusts, a will should include a clear direction as to whether distinct trusts are to be established for each beneficiary. Further, guidance should be provided stating that trust administrators can seek independent investment objectives suitable to the needs of the respective beneficiaries. Ideally, each trust should be created with separate terms and conditions.

> Exercise Nineteen-6 deals with testamentary trusts. This would be an appropriate time to attempt this exercise.

19-77. Contributions by living persons to an existing testamentary trust can cause that trust to become tainted and lose its testamentary status. If this happens, the trust will no longer benefit from the use of graduated rates and will be taxed as an inter vivos trust. As noted in the next section, this means that all of its income will be taxed at a rate of 29 percent.

Taxation of Inter Vivos Trusts

19-78. Most inter vivos trusts are subject to a flat federal tax of 29 percent on all trust income that is not distributed to beneficiaries, based on ITA 122(1). Since the top federal marginal rate for individuals is also 29 percent, the flat federal tax levy on trusts is equal to or greater than the tax that would be paid by a beneficiary receiving the income. Given this, there is little income tax incentive to allow income to accumulate in an inter vivos trust.

19-79.   Keeping in mind that the high rate used to calculate taxes payable for an inter vivos trust is only applicable to income retained in the trust, inter vivos trusts can be used very effectively in tax planning — most notably to split income among family members. Income splitting can be achieved by carefully setting up a trust, and flowing income through to low income beneficiaries. For example, a family trust can be established to hold the family investment portfolio or to own shares in family owned corporations. Provided all of the income of the trust is distributed, no taxes will be assessed at the high rate of 29 percent. The income earned by the trust will be distributed to low income family members where, depending on the amounts involved, it will be either free of tax or subject to low marginal rates. Note, however, with the introduction of the tax on split income, this type of arrangement is no longer effective for certain types of income if the beneficiaries are minors.

19-80.   Assuming that a trust is set up properly, the potential tax savings can be significant. For example, in 2001, a beneficiary with no other source of income can receive $27,980 of taxable Canadian dividends and pay no federal income tax (see Paragraph 16-79). Alternatively, if the same amount of dividends is received by a taxpayer subject to a combined federal/provincial rate of 45 percent and living in a province where the provincial dividend tax credit is equal to one-third of the gross up, marginal taxes payable on the receipt of this amount of additional dividends can be calculated as follows.

Dividends Received	$27,980
Gross Up (25%)	6,995
Taxable Dividends	$34,975
Tax At 45 Percent	$ 15,739
Dividend Tax Credit [(2/3 + 1/3)($6,995)]	(6,995)
Total Taxes Payable	$ 8,744

> Exercise Nineteen-7 deals with inter vivos trusts. This would be an appropriate time to attempt this exercise.

19-81.   This example illustrates that, by transferring dividend yielding investments to a trust and flowing the income through to beneficiaries with no other source of income, there is a potential tax savings of $8,744 per beneficiary.

Tax Credits and the Alternative Minimum Tax

19-82.   While, in principle, trusts are to be taxed in the same manner as individuals, there are obvious differences between a legally constructed entity and a living, breathing human being. These differences are reflected in the fact that trusts are not eligible for many of the tax credits that are available to individuals. To begin, ITA 122(1.1) specifically prohibits a trust from making any of the deductions listed under ITA 118 (personal tax credits). Further, most of the other credits listed in ITA 118.1 through 118.9 are clearly directed at individuals (e.g., a trust is not likely to have medical expenses). However, some tax credits are available to trusts, generally on the same basis as they are available to individuals. These include:

- Donations and gifts. As is the case with individuals, there is a credit of 16 percent on the first $200 of donations and 29 percent on additional amounts.
- Dividend tax credits
- Foreign tax credits
- Investment tax credits
- Political contributions tax credits

19-83.   As is the case with individuals, trusts are subject to the alternative minimum tax legislation. However, there is one important difference. The exemption with respect to the first $40,000 of income is only available to testamentary trusts. For inter vivos trusts, the minimum tax calculation is based on all income amounts.

Income Attribution

General Rules

19-84. The income attribution rules (see Chapter 10) may apply where property is transferred or loaned to an inter vivos trust for the benefit of a "designated person". ITA 74.5(5) defines "designated person" to mean a spouse, a person under 18 who does not deal at arm's length with the transferor (usually a child or grandchild), or the transferor's niece or nephew under the age of 18. The attribution rules also apply when there is a reversionary trust, which is a trust in which the property can revert to the transferor.

19-85. When the income attribution rules apply to spouses, both taxable capital gains, and most other types of income earned on property transferred to a trust, will be attributed back to the transferor. Where the designated person is anyone other than a spouse, the attribution rules apply only to income and do not apply to taxable capital gains.

19-86. Note that attribution does not occur when assets are simply transferred to a trust in which a designated person is a beneficiary. Rather, attribution occurs when income from those assets is allocated to a designated person. If the trust chooses to be taxed on the income before allocation, or if the income is allocated to individuals other than designated persons, income will not be attributed to the transferor.

Tax Planning

19-87. Where trustees have some discretion in the distribution of income and capital, the income attribution rules can usually be avoided by structuring the distributions appropriately. For example, distributions of capital should be made to beneficiaries who are subject to the income attribution rules, and income distributions should be made to other beneficiaries. The attribution rules may also be avoided if the trust is settled by a non resident. Ideally, to avoid the attribution rules, a non resident grandparent will settle a trust for beneficiaries that are non arm's length minors.

19-88. The income attribution rules do not apply when a transfer is made at fair market value or equivalent proceeds are received. Also of note is that income attribution only applies to property income and does not extend to business income. A further point here is that the attribution rules do not apply to compound earnings or specific types of income. Given all of these factors, effective advance tax planning should be used to avoid the effects of the income attribution rules.

Dispositions Of Trust Property

Capital Distributions To Beneficiaries

19-89. A capital distribution to one or more beneficiaries is also a disposition from a trust. ITA 107(2) provides that when a trust makes a capital distribution, it is deemed to dispose of the property for proceeds equal to the cost of the property to the trust. For non depreciable property, the cost is the adjusted cost base of the property. If depreciable property is being distributed, the cost will be its UCC. In general, this will mean that the distribution of assets from a trust to one or more beneficiaries of the trust will not result in any gains having to be reported or income taxes being incurred by the trust.

19-90. For a beneficiary, a capital disposition from a trust is simply a tax deferred receipt of the related assets. A beneficiary is deemed to acquire the assets at the trust's adjusted cost base for non depreciable assets and the trust's UCC for depreciable assets. More specifically, the capital beneficiary acquires depreciable property at its original cost to the trust and is deemed to have been allowed the CCA that the trust was allowed. In return for the property distributed, the beneficiary has a deemed disposition of a capital interest in the trust. When the beneficiary disposes the property, capital gains and/or recaptured CCA will be calculated using the adjusted cost base from the trust.

21 Year Deemed Disposition Rule

19-91.   Trust arrangements ordinarily allow capital gains on trust assets to accumulate for extended periods of time. Unless the capital assets are sold by the trust, accrued gains will not attract any taxes and the assets can be left in a trust for periods that exceed the life of the individual establishing the trust.

19-92.   In order to place limits on this deferral process, ITA 104(4)(b) requires that there be a deemed disposition and reacquisition of trust capital property every 21 years. The disposition is deemed to be at fair market value, resulting in the recognition of any accrued income on the assets. In the case of depreciable assets, if the deemed proceeds are less than the original capital cost, the original value is retained for purposes of determining recapture.

19-93.   This rule is generally applicable only to personal trusts and does not apply to trusts such as employee benefit plans or registered education plans. Further, the rules are modified in the case of qualified spousal trusts, alter ego trusts, and joint partner trusts. For qualified spousal trusts, the deemed disposition occurs with the death of the spouse. In the case of alter ego trusts, the death of the settlor is the event that triggers the deemed disposition. When a joint partner trust is used, the deemed disposition occurs at the death of the settlor or the partner, whichever is later.

19-94.   Given these rules, most inter vivos trusts should be structured so that they can be collapsed prior to the end of 21 years. As beneficiaries can receive capital distributions on a tax deferred basis, the recognition of any capital gains on assets is delayed until the beneficiaries dispose of the property. In most situations, this is better than the risk of having a deemed disposition of trust property at the end of 21 years. As a result, it is good tax planning for trust documents to allow the trustees to distribute assets to the beneficiaries to avoid the deemed disposition rule.

Purchase Or Sale Of An Interest In A Trust

Income Interest

19-95.   An income interest in a trust is the right of a beneficiary under the trust to receive all or part of the income from the trust. The purchaser of an income interest in a trust will have a cost equal to the fair market value of the consideration given for that interest. This cost can be deducted against amounts of trust income that otherwise would be included in the individual's taxable income. Any portion of the cost that is not deducted against income from the trust in the current year can be carried forward for deduction against allocated trust income in subsequent years. When income allocations have reduced the cost of the interest to nil, subsequent receipts of income will be fully taxable.

19-96.   An individual may sell his income interest in a trust to a third party. From the point of view of the vendor, the proceeds will be equal to the fair market value of the consideration received. If the cost of the income interest (often nil) is different than the proceeds received, there will be a gain or loss on the disposition. As an income interest is not a capital asset, the gain or loss on its disposal will be treated as fully taxable property income.

Capital Interest

19-97.   As defined in ITA 108(1), a capital interest is the right of a beneficiary to receive all or part of the capital of the trust or the right to enforce payment thereof. As a result, a capital interest is a capital asset and any gain or loss on its disposition will be treated as a capital gain or loss.

19-98.   When a capital interest in a trust is purchased, the adjusted cost base is equal to the fair market value of the consideration given. This amount will be reduced by future distributions of assets from the trust. The distribution of trust assets to a beneficiary results in a partial or full settlement of a capital interest. ITA 107(1) generally provides for a tax deferred rollover of trust assets from the trust to the beneficiary holding the capital interest.

19-99.   If a beneficiary sells a capital interest in a trust, the proceeds of disposition will equal the fair market value of the consideration received. The adjusted cost base of the taxpayer's capital interest will normally be nil, in which case the entire proceeds of disposition will be a capital gain. However, to determine the gain on a disposition of a capital interest in a resident trust, ITA 107(1)(a) defines the adjusted cost base to be the greater of:

- The adjusted cost base as usually determined.
- The "cost amount" to the beneficiary.

19-100.   ITA 108(1) defines this cost amount as the beneficiary's proportionate interest in the net assets of the trust. This prevents the beneficiary from being taxed on the cost amount of the trust's assets, an amount that could be received on a tax free basis as a distribution from the trust. Losses on the disposition of a capital interest in a trust are also calculated factoring in the adjusted cost base. As this amount is usually nil, losses are uncommon.

Offshore Trusts

Common Types and Uses of Offshore Trusts

19-101.   Offshore trusts have received much attention from investment advisers and the business press. While perceived abuses have been sensationalized, offshore trusts have many legitimate purposes in tax planning. As the related legal and tax issues are very complex, expert professional counsel is necessary when setting up foreign trusts. The following two types of trusts are examples of how offshore trusts are being used.

Asset Protection Trusts   This type of trust is gaining popularity as a method to protect assets from third party claims. Increasingly, taxpayers want to preserve and protect their wealth from creditors, the risks of insolvency, spousal claims and domestic inheritance laws. In addition, asset protection trusts are viewed as a means to spread risk, guard against domestic economic downturns, and maintain confidentiality of one's financial affairs. Typically, an asset protection trust is set up as a foreign discretionary trust in an offshore jurisdiction. A taxpayer will transfer assets to arm's length trustees for no consideration, and appoint a protector to watch over the trustees. While the trustees have broad discretionary power under the trust, a taxpayer usually provides guidance through a non binding "letter of wishes". Whether or not an asset protection trust is taxable in Canada depends on a variety of factors, and especially whether or not the trust is deemed to be resident in Canada. The legal relationships among the settlor, trustee and beneficiaries are overshadowed by de facto control factors. As the CCRA is very skeptical of such structures, look-through mechanisms can attribute income to Canadian residents who really control the trust affairs, no matter how sophisticated a structure is used.

Immigrant Trusts   This type of trust is often established by wealthy immigrants before they become Canadian residents. Properly structured immigrant trusts can shelter income and gains earned by the trust from Canadian tax for the first five years of the immigrant's residence in Canada. Often, a non resident relative of the immigrant becomes the settlor of the trust with a nominal amount of funds. The immigrant invests in a new company, and the trust exchanges a non interest bearing note for shares of the company. The beneficiaries typically are members of the immigrant's immediate family. To ensure independence, the immigrant should not have any legal control over the shares or over the administration of the immigrant trust. At the end of the five years, the immigrant trust will usually be deemed a resident of Canada and will become subject to Canadian tax.

19-102.   In an effort to track investments in offshore trusts, the foreign investment reporting requirements are designed to ensure comprehensive reporting of any beneficial interests in foreign trusts. (See coverage of the general requirements in Chapter 2.) All Canadian taxpayers are obliged to report annually any beneficial interest they have in a foreign trust, even if there were no distributions received from or payments to the foreign trust in the year. To encourage compliance, the penalties for non reporting are very onerous.

Estate Planning

Objectives Of Estate Planning

19-103. The subject of estate planning is complex and involves considerations that go well beyond the scope of this text. In fact, appropriate planning for a large estate will often involve lawyers, investment advisors, accountants, and tax advisors. Indeed, it may even be necessary to have religious advisors or psychological counsellors participate in order to deal with some of the moral or emotional issues that are involved.

19-104. The following points are among the more important non tax considerations in planning an estate:

Intent Of The Testator The foremost goal of estate planning is to ensure that the wishes of the testator (a person who has died leaving a will) are carried out. This will involve ensuring that the assets left by the testator are distributed at the appropriate times and to the specified beneficiaries. The primary document for ensuring that the intent of the testator is fulfilled is, of course, the will.

Preparation Of A Final Will The major document in the estate planning process is the final will. It should be carefully prepared to provide detailed instructions for the disposition of assets, investment decisions to be made, and extent to which trusts will be used. An executor should be named to administer the estate, and the will should be reviewed periodically to ensure that it reflects the testator's current wishes and family status.

Preparation Of A Living Will Equally important to the preparation of a final will, a living will provides detailed instructions regarding investments and other personal decisions in the event of physical or mental incapacity at any point in a person's lifetime. A power of attorney is similar, except that it requires an individual to be of sound mind when any action is taken on one's behalf.

Ensuring Liquidity A plan should be established to provide for liquidity at the time of death. Major expenses, often including taxes, will arise at this time. Funds needed for these payments should be set aside or adequate life insurance should be arranged in advance, to avoid the need for emergency sales of capital assets to raise the necessary cash.

Simplicity While the disposition of a large estate will rarely be simple, effective estate planning should ensure that the plan can be understood by the testator and all beneficiaries of legal age. In addition, any actions that can reduce the cost and complexity of administering the estate should be considered. This might involve disposing of investments in non public shares or repatriating assets that are located in foreign countries that might become subject to foreign taxation.

Avoidance Of Family Disputes Unfortunately, disputes among beneficiaries are a common part of estate settlement procedures. If equitable treatment of beneficiaries is a goal of the testator, efforts should be made to ensure that all beneficiaries believe that they have been treated in an equitable manner. If the testator wants to distribute assets in a fashion that could be viewed as inequitable by any of the interested parties, care should be taken to make this intention unequivocal.

Expediting The Transition The procedures required in the settlement of an estate should be designed to expedite the process. An extensive settlement period can amplify uncertainties related to the value of assets, add to the complications associated with the required distribution of such property, and protract the frustrations of beneficiaries.

19-105. In addition to the preceding non tax considerations, estate planning must also consider various tax factors. Fundamental tax planning goals for all taxpayers apply equally to estate planning. Briefly, these goals involve the legal and orderly arrangement of one's affairs, before the time of a transaction or event, to reduce and defer income taxes.

19-106.   In effective estate planning, the overriding income tax goals are to defer and minimize tax payments. Several important issues should be considered in dealing with this problem. These can be described as follows:

Prior To Death   Planning should attempt to minimize taxes for the individual in the years prior to death. If the individual earns income that is not required in these years, attempts should be made to defer the tax and transfer the before-tax income to the ultimate beneficiaries. The use of a discretionary trust can assist in achieving this goal.

Year Of Death   Planning should attempt to minimize income taxes payable in the year of death. Deemed dispositions will occur at death and, in addition, amounts in certain types of deferred income plans usually must be included in the taxpayer's final return. Relief can be achieved through tax deferred rollovers to a spouse and transfers of certain types of property, (e.g., farm property) to children or grandchildren. The will can also contain instructions to ensure the maximum RRSP contribution is made to the spouse's RRSP within the deadline.

Income Splitting   Effective planning should allow income splitting among family members who are in lower progressive tax brackets. This can be accomplished by the appropriate splitting of income (e.g., paying salaries and wages for services rendered) and distributing property among beneficiaries throughout a taxpayer's lifetime, recognizing the limitations imposed by the tax on split income.

Foreign Jurisdictions   Planning should normally attempt to minimize taxes that will be incurred in foreign jurisdictions, especially those with onerous estate taxes. To the extent that it is consistent with the individual's investment plans and the residence of intended beneficiaries, holdings of foreign assets at death or distributions to beneficiaries in foreign locations should usually be avoided by residents of Canada. Minimizing foreign investments will also simplify the administration of an estate.

Administration Period   Planning should minimize taxes payable while the estate is being administered. Discretion provided to trustees in distributing the income of an inter vivos trust may assist in achieving this goal.

19-107.   Most of the tax procedures related to accomplishing these goals have already been introduced. We have discussed spousal rollovers and deemed dispositions in previous Chapters and the use of trusts was covered earlier in this Chapter. An important aspect of estate planning that requires additional consideration is the estate freeze. Procedures to be used in these arrangements are outlined in the section which follows.

Objectives of an Estate Freeze

19-108.   The objective of an estate freeze is, as the name implies, to freeze the value of the estate for tax purposes at a particular point in time. Typically, arrangements are made for all future appreciation to accrue to related parties such as a spouse, children, or grandchildren. Transfers of income generating private company shares to minor children may be deferred to avoid the tax on split income.

Example   Mr. Chisholm is a wealthy and successful entrepreneur who owns a variety of capital assets that are producing taxable income and appreciating in value. He has several objectives in planning his estate:

- During the remainder of his life, Mr. Chisholm would like to transfer all or part of his taxable income to a group of individuals and charities who will ultimately be the beneficiaries of his estate.

- Mr. Chisholm would like to freeze the tax values of his assets and allow future growth to accrue to the intended beneficiaries.

- Since the current fair market value of his assets exceeds their tax cost, Mr. Chisholm would like to avoid any immediate taxation resulting from a disposition of these assets with accrued gains.

- Mr. Chisholm would like the transfer of future growth in asset values to accrue so that his beneficiaries will not be subject to taxation in the year of the estate freeze, in any intervening years or in the year of his death.

- Mr. Chisholm wants to retain the right to the current value of the property at the time of the estate freeze. In addition, he wishes to retain control of the use of the property until his death.

19-109.   This example will be used as a basis for discussing a variety of techniques that can be used to freeze an estate's value. Some of these techniques will achieve all of Mr. Chilsholm's goals while others will only succeed with one or two of them.

Techniques Not Involving Rollovers
Gifts
19-110.   Mr. Chisholm can freeze the value of his estate without using rollover provisions. The most straightforward technique is to simply give property to his prospective beneficiaries. While this would accomplish the goal of transferring future growth in the estate to the beneficiaries, it would have the serious drawback of attracting immediate capital gains taxation on any difference between the fair market value of the assets and Mr. Chisholm's adjusted cost base. In addition, if the person receiving the gift is a spouse or minor child, income attribution rules could apply after the gift is made. Further drawbacks are the fact that Mr. Chisholm would lose control over the assets and certain income received by minor children may be subject to the tax on split income.

19-111.   While gifts result in a loss of control, Mr. Chisholm may want to accelerate his donations to registered charities. If Mr. Chisholm owns any securities that are listed on prescribed stock exchanges, he may want to gift them to charities before the end of the year 2001 (the reduced inclusion rate for capital gains realized by making charitable contributions of publicly traded securities is scheduled to expire at the end of 2001). This will allow Mr. Chisholm to reduce the inclusion rate on these gains from one-half to one-quarter, while at the same time allowing 100 percent of the donation to be used to calculate the tax credit.

Instalment Sales
19-112.   Mr. Chisholm could freeze the value of the estate by selling the assets to the intended beneficiaries on an instalment basis. Capital gains could be deferred until payment is received, but the gains would need to be reported over the next five years based on the capital gains reserve calculations.

19-113.   To avoid income attribution and inadequate consideration problems, the sale should be made at fair market value. However, if the intended beneficiaries do not have sufficient assets to make the purchase, this may not be a feasible solution. A further problem is that Mr. Chisholm would lose control over the property.

Establishing A Trust
19-114.   An estate freeze can also be accomplished by setting up a trust in favour of one or more beneficiaries. Here again, this will transfer income and future growth from Mr. Chisholm's hands to the trust. The trust can be structured so that he retains some control over the assets. The problem with this arrangement is that, except in the case of a spousal trust, joint partner trust or alter ego trust, there is no rollover provision that provides for tax deferred transfers of assets to a trust. As a result, if the trust is set up for beneficiaries other than Mr. Chisholm or his spouse, Mr. Chisholm will incur taxation on any capital gains accrued at the time of the transfer. As well, any dividends received from a private corporation by minor beneficiaries will be subject to the tax on split income, whether the shares are held through a trust or directly.

Use Of A Holding Company
19-115.   Mr. Chisholm could transfer assets to a holding company in which intended beneficiaries have a substantial equity interest, without using a rollover provision. This will freeze the value of his estate and, if the assets transferred have fair market values that are equal to or less than their adjusted cost base, it can be an effective vehicle for realizing losses. However,

without the use of a rollover provision, such as that found in Section 85, any capital gains that have accrued to the time of the transfer will become subject to immediate taxation.

Section 86 Share Exchange

Nature Of The Exchange

19-116.   The preceding Chapter provided an overview of ITA 86 which applies to the exchange of shares by a shareholder in the course of a reorganization of capital. In certain situations, a share exchange constitutes an ideal solution to the estate freeze problem. Specifically, this rollover is most appropriate in a situation that involves an individual who is the sole owner of a successful private corporation. By exchanging common shares for preferred shares which have equal value, the owner will, in effect, eliminate any participation in the future growth of the company. At the same time, common shares can be issued to intended beneficiaries at a nominal value, and these shareholders can participate in the company's future income and any growth in the value of its assets.

Example

19-117.   The preceding Chapter contained an example of a reorganization using Section 86. The following simple example will serve to review these procedures.

Over her lifetime, Mrs. Hadley has been the sole owner and driving force behind Hadley Inc., a manufacturing business located in Alberta. On December 31, 2001, the condensed Balance Sheet of this Company was as follows:

Hadley Inc.
Balance Sheet
As At December 31, 2001

Net Identifiable Assets	$10,000,000
Common Stock (No Par - 1,000 Shares)	$ 2,000,000
Retained Earnings	8,000,000
Total Shareholders' Equity	$10,000,000

On the basis of an independent appraisal, the fair market value of this business was established at $15,000,000. Mrs. Hadley has a husband and three children and would like them to share equally in her estate.

19-118.   Under Section 86, Mrs. Hadley can exchange, on a tax deferred basis, her common shares which have an adjusted cost base of $2,000,000 (also the amount of contributed capital) for preferred shares with a redemption value of $15,000,000 (the fair market value of the business). These preferred shares would have no participation in the future growth of the company and, as a result, Mrs. Hadley has effectively frozen the value of her estate.

19-119.   If Mrs. Hadley wishes to retain control of the company, the preferred shares can be established as the only outstanding voting shares. While this share exchange will be free of any capital gains taxation, Mrs. Hadley's adjusted cost base for the new preferred shares remains at the former common share value of $2,000,000. If the preferred shares are sold, capital gains will result using $2,000,000 as the adjusted cost base. Alternatively, if the shares are redeemed by the Company, any amount that is received in excess of Mrs. Hadley's original paid up capital will be treated as a taxable dividend under ITA 84(3).

19-120.   The tax cost basis for the identifiable assets owned by the Company has not been altered by the share exchange transaction.

19-121.   At this point, the redemption value of Mrs. Hadley's preferred shares represents the entire fair market value of the business and, as a consequence, the value of any common shares issued will not exceed the amount contributed by the investors. This means that such shares can be issued for a nominal value without any appearance that the purchasers are indirectly receiving a gift from Mrs. Hadley. Thus, 1,000 common shares could be issued to Mrs. Hadley's intended beneficiaries at $10 per share as follows:

Spouse (250 Shares At $10)	$ 2,500
Child One (250 Shares At $10)	2,500
Child Two (250 Shares At $10)	2,500
Child Three (250 Shares At $10)	2,500
Total Common Stock Contributed	$10,000

19-122.   These common shares would benefit from the future income and growth in asset values that may be experienced by Hadley Inc.

19-123.   As illustrated in this example, a Section 86 rollover can provide an ideal solution to the estate freeze problem. It can be used to transfer all future growth in the estate into the hands of intended beneficiaries with no immediate tax effects on the individual making the transfer. The beneficiaries will be taxed on income earned subsequent to the estate freeze. (If any beneficiaries are minors, they will have to pay the tax on split income on any dividends received.) A Section 86 rollover is fairly straightforward to administer and does not require the formation of a separate holding corporation.

Section 85 Rollover Provisions

19-124.   A Section 85 tax deferred rollover of property to a holding corporation can also be used to implement an estate freeze. The rollover provisions of ITA 85 were given full consideration in Chapter 17, and will not be repeated here. The creation of a holding company could be combined with the use of a trust to hold the shares of the company, rather than have the intended beneficiaries hold the shares directly.

19-125.   In choosing between the use of Section 85 and Section 86, you should note that Section 85 can be used in a broader variety of circumstances than is the case with Section 86. More specifically, Section 86 deals only with exchanges of shares in the course of the reorganization of an existing corporation. This means that Section 86 can only be used in situations where the assets involved in the estate freeze are shares of a corporation controlled by the person undertaking the freeze. Section 85 would have to be used where the estate consists of other types of property.

19-126.   When Section 86 can be used, it is an easier procedure to implement. Unlike Section 85, which requires a formal election to be made and a new corporation to be formed, Section 86 only involves the existing corporation. By using a Section 86 reorganization, the savings in legal and accounting fees can be significant. In effecting a particular estate freeze using rollovers, many complications can surface and practical considerations are important. These additional complexities make it difficult to comment on the relative desirability of Sections 85 and 86.

GST and Trusts

19-127.   A trust is included in the definition of person under the *Excise Tax Act* and, as a consequence, a trust that is engaged in commercial activities is required to register and collect GST on taxable supplies. However, an interest in a trust is considered to be a financial instrument, so the sale of such an interest in a trust is an exempt financial service and is not taxable for GST purposes.

19-128.   A distribution of trust property by a trustee to the beneficiaries of a trust is treated as a supply by the trust. The consideration is the same as proceeds of disposition for purposes of the *Income Tax Act*. Distributions of non commercial property by a trust in the process of the settlement of an estate are generally not considered to be in the course of commercial activities of the trust and are thus exempt. Similarly, a distribution of financial securities is exempt as a financial service. The GST only applies to properties acquired by the trust that are used in a commercial activity.

19-129.   Where property is settled through the use of an inter vivos trust, including the new alter ego or joint spousal trust, the consideration for the property transferred is deemed to equal the amount determined under the *Income Tax Act*. The supply is considered to be made at fair market value and GST is payable on all taxable supplies. However, when an estate is settled, an election can be filed to distribute any property of a deceased registrant without the payment of GST. In this situation, the beneficiary of the deceased's estate must be a registrant and the beneficiary is deemed to have acquired the property for use exclusively in a commercial activity.

References

19-130.   For more detailed study of the material in this Chapter, we would refer you to the following:

ITA 85	Transfer Of Property To Corporation By Shareholders
ITA 86	Exchange Of Shares By A Shareholder In Course Of Reorganization Of Capital
ITA 104 to 108	Trusts And Their Beneficiaries
IC-76-19R3	Transfer Of Property To A Corporation Under Section 85
IT-201R2	Foreign Tax Credit - Trusts And Beneficiaries
IT-209R	Inter-Vivos Gifts Of Capital Property To Individuals Directly Or Through Trusts
IT-286R2	Trusts - Amount Payable
IT-291R2	Transfer Of Property To A Corporation Under Subsection 85(1)
IT-305R4	Testamentary Spouse Trusts
IT-342R	Trusts - Income Payable To Beneficiaries
IT-369R	Attribution Of Trust Income To Settlor
IT-374	Meaning Of "Settlor"
IT-381R3	Trusts - Capital Gains And Losses And The Flow-Through Of Taxable Capital Gains To Beneficiaries
IT-385R2	Disposition Of An Income Interest In A Trust
IT-394R2	Preferred Beneficiary Election
IT-406R2	Tax Payable By An Inter Vivos Trust
IT-447	Residence Of A Trust Or Estate
IT-449R	Meaning Of "Vested Indefeasibly"
IT-465R	Non Resident Beneficiaries Of Trusts
IT-511R	Interspousal And Certain Other Transfers And Loans Of Property
IT-524	Trusts - Flow Through Of Taxable Dividends To A Beneficiary After 1987

Exercises

(The solutions for these exercises can be found following Chapter 21 of the text.)

Exercise Nineteen - 1 (Spousal Trusts)

Louise died late this year, and bequeathed a non-depreciable capital asset to a spousal trust created in her will. Louise is survived by her husband. The asset, which cost $6,000 was valued at $9,000 on the date of her death. State how the gain should be reported for income tax purposes. Also, determine the adjusted cost base of the asset to the spousal trust.

Exercise Nineteen - 2 (Spousal Trusts)

Three years ago, a depreciable asset was transferred from Gerald's estate to a spousal trust created on his death. The asset, which cost $70,000, had an undepreciated capital cost of $46,000. On Gerald's death, the asset had a market value of $82,000. Since then, the trust has claimed CCA of $6,000. At the end of the current year, the trust sold the asset for $76,000. Determine the income tax effects of the transfer of the asset to the spousal trust and the disposition of the asset by the trust.

Exercise Nineteen - 3 (Family Trusts)

Last year, Trevor Carlisle transferred to a family trust, for no consideration, bonds which pay interest of $27,000 per annum. The beneficiaries of the trust are Trevor's spouse, Carmen and their two children, Mitch (16 years old) and Rhonda (22 years old). The trust income and capital gains are allocated equally and are payable to each beneficiary during the year. Total interest income earned by the trust during the year was $27,000. As well, a taxable capital gain of $3,000 was earned on the disposition of one of the bonds that Trevor Carlisle transferred into the trust last year. The trust designated $1,000 of taxable capital gains as payable to each beneficiary. Determine the taxable income allocations to each beneficiary.

Exercise Nineteen - 4 (Transfers To Trusts)

Several scenarios are presented for the transfer of property to a trust under a variety of circumstances. For each scenario, summarize the income tax effects of the transfer by the settlor to the trust and specify the adjusted cost base of the property in the trust. Also, summarize the tax effects of the transfers from the trusts to the beneficiaries.

The following assumptions apply in each scenario:

Cost of capital property to settlor	$1,000
Fair market value of capital property at date of transfer:	
• Into trust	$1,600
• To beneficiary (if applicable)	$1,900

Scenario 1: Transfer by settlor to inter vivos trust for adult child
Scenario 2: Transfer by settlor to inter vivos trust for minor child
Scenario 3: Transfer to testamentary trust for friend
Scenario 4: Transfer to inter vivos spousal trust
Scenario 5: Transfer to testamentary spousal trust
Scenario 6: Transfer to joint spousal trust
Scenario 7: Transfer to alter ego trust

Exercise Nineteen - 5 (Personal Trusts)

Is it possible to set up a personal trust and transfer assets to the trust for the benefit of, and to split income with, minor grandchildren?

Exercise Nineteen - 6 (Multiple Testamentary Trusts)

Under his will, Maxim intends to have five separate trusts created for his daughter Julie, with the intention that each trust will benefit from the lowest progressive tax rates. Can Maxim do this?

Exercise Nineteen - 7 (Inter Vivos Trust)

The income of an inter vivos trust is $20,000, made up of dividends from a private Canadian corporation. The sole beneficiary of the trust is the adult son of the settlor. The beneficiary was paid $15,000 from the dividend income, which also was his sole income for the year. Calculate the taxable income for the year for the trust and for the beneficiary.

Problems For Self Study

(The solutions for these problems can be found following Chapter 21 of the text.)

Self Study Problem Nineteen - 1

A testamentary trust was created when Mr. Rowand died in 1998. The trust provides for one-half of dividend income to be retained in the trust. Of the remaining income (net of expenses and tax deductions), 60 percent is to be paid to Mrs. Rowand and 40 percent to an adult son, Roger. For the current year ended on September 30, the following amounts are reported for the trust:

Business Income	$20,000
Interest	4,000
Dividends From Taxable Canadian Corporations	26,000
Rent Receipts	12,000
Rental Operating Expenses	6,000
CCA On Rental Property	2,000

Mrs. Rowand and Roger have no other sources of income. They have no tax credits other than their personal credits under ITA 118.

Required:

A. For each person, including the trust, calculate taxable income and federal taxes payable.

B. Assume that all dividend income will be allocated to Mrs. Rowand and Roger on the same 60 percent and 40 percent basis as the other trust income. For Mrs. Rowand and Roger, calculate taxable income and federal taxes payable.

C. Compare the total federal tax paid in Part A and Part B. Explain any difference.

Self Study Problem Nineteen - 2

Ms. Robinson is a very successful business person who has a son and a daughter and wishes to have most of her property ultimately transferred to them. Both of Ms. Robinson's children are over 30 years old. To achieve her goal, she transferred a substantial amount of property to a trust in their favor on September 1, 1988. The trust has a December 31 year end and Ms. Robinson assists with its management. However, she has no beneficial interest in either its income or its capital.

The terms of the trust call for the son to receive 30 percent of the income while the daughter receives 50 percent. The remaining income is to accumulate within the trust, to be paid to Ms. Robinson's two children at the time of her death. Trust income includes any capital gains earned in the trust. The current year's income figures for the trust are as follows:

Interest On Government Bonds	$ 65,000
Dividends From Taxable Canadian Corporations	250,000
Revenues From Rental Property	492,000
Cash Expenses On Rental Property	342,000

Prior to the current year, the capital cost allowances on the rental property were allocated to and deducted by the trust. However, late in the current year, the rental property was sold. The property consisted of an apartment building and the land on which it was located. It was transferred into the trust when the trust was first established. The relevant information related to the disposition is as follows:

	Building	Land
Proceeds Of Disposition	$4,560,000	$2,300,000
Undepreciated Capital Cost	3,380,000	N/A
Capital Cost	3,840,000	1,430,000

Required: Determine the amount of income that will be taxed in the hands of each beneficiary for the current year and the federal taxes payable for the trust for its current fiscal year.

Self Study Problem Nineteen - 3

In March of the current year, Mr. Masters died at his home in Corner Brook, Newfoundland. Under the terms of his will, all of his property was transferred to a testamentary trust. The trust document establishes December 31 as the year end for the trust and contains the following additional provisions:

1. Thirty percent of the income is to be paid to Mr. Masters' daughter, Mrs. Joan Nelson.

2. Fifty percent of the income is to be paid to Mr. Masters' son, Charles Masters.

3. The remaining income is to be retained by the trust to be distributed at the discretion of the trustees. No distributions were made prior to December 31 of this year.

From the time it was established until December 31, the trust had the following income and expenses:

Dividends Received From Taxable Canadian Public Companies		$ 87,000
Interest On British Bonds (Net Of 15 Percent Withholding Tax)		93,500
Rental Income	$123,000	
Rental Expenses (Not Including CCA)	(62,000)	61,000
Total Income		$241,500

The maximum capital cost allowance on the rental property is $45,000. The trust provides for the pro rata share of net rental income, before capital cost allowance, to be paid to the beneficiaries. The capital cost allowance deduction is also proportionately allocated.

Required: Determine the amount of income that will be taxed in the hands of each beneficiary for the current taxation year and compute the federal taxes payable for the trust for its fiscal year ending December 31 of this year.

Assignment Problems

(The solutions for these problems are only available in
the solutions manual that has been provided to your instructor.)

Assignment Problem Nineteen - 1
Each of the following independent cases involve transfers of property to trusts by way of gifts:

A. A gift of capital property to a trust. The cost of the capital property to the settlor was $1,000 and the fair market value on the date of the gift is $1,500.

B. A gift of depreciable property to a trust. The capital cost of the depreciable property to the settlor was $1,000. On the date of the gift, the UCC is $750 and the fair market value is $1,100.

C. A trust distributes capital property to a capital beneficiary. The capital property had a fair market value of $1,500 when the property was received by the trust, and the fair market value on the distribution date is $2,000.

D. A trust distributes depreciable property to a capital beneficiary. The property had a fair market value of $1,100 when it was purchased by the trust. On the date of distribution, the property has a UCC of $900 and a fair market value of $1,200.

E. A transfer of capital property is made to a spousal testamentary trust. The cost of the capital property to the deceased spouse was $1,000 and the fair market value on the date of the transfer to the trust is $1,500.

F. A gift of capital property is made to an alter ego trust. The cost of the capital property to the settlor was $800 and the fair market value on the date of the gift is $2,200.

Required: For each case, discuss the income tax effects of the transfer to the settlor and beneficiary of the various gift transactions.

Assignment Problem Nineteen - 2
In planning an estate freeze, Mrs. Dion plans to settle cash and portfolio investments in a trust. The terms of the trust will provide that:

- Sixty percent of the annual income will be paid to Mr. Dion.

- Forty percent of the annual income will be allocated to the Dion twins, who are 20 years old and in university. The income will be split equally and the timing of payments is at the discretion of the trustee.

- The trust capital will be distributed on December 31, 2012, following the same allocation as for income.

Required:

A. Identify what type of trust is being used.

B. Identify what the trust's year end date will be.

C. Outline how the trust income will be taxed in the first and second year of the trust.

D. Explain how your answer to Part C would change if Mrs. Dion formed the trust by the settlement of a nominal amount and lent money to the trust to purchase income earning investments.

(continued)

E. Explain how the taxation of the trust income will change should Mr. and Mrs. Dion divorce before the trust capital is distributed.

F. Outline the income tax effect if the trust provides for a return of capital to Mrs. Dion in the event of a marriage breakdown.

Assignment Problem Nineteen - 3

Genevieve Marcoux is a biochemist who annually earns a $125,000 salary and $40,000 in investment income from an $800,000 term deposit she inherited.

Genevieve is a single mother with two children. Her daughter, Lisa, is 21 years old and attends university in the U.S. Lisa plans to become a medical doctor and expects to attend university for another seven years. Lisa's tuition and books total $30,000 each year. Genevieve's son, Philip, is one year old, and is cared for by a nanny who is paid $14,500 a year. When Philip is five years old, Genevieve intends to send him to a private school, and the fees will be comparable to the cost of a nanny. In addition, Genevieve incurs $500 each month in direct expenses for each child, totaling $12,000 a year. Genevieve does not expect either Lisa or Philip to earn any taxable income until they complete university.

Genevieve would like to transfer the term deposit to a trust for her children, so the family can benefit from income splitting currently and in the future. While she supports her children fully, she does not want them to receive any cash directly from the trust until they are each 35 years old. Until then, she wants the trust to pay for their care, education and other direct expenses.

Required: Outline how a trust might be used to split income among Genevieve's family members.

Assignment Problem Nineteen - 4

Mr. Hyde died early in 2001, and a testamentary trust was established under his will. The trust will have a December 31 year end. The beneficiaries of the trust are Mrs. Hyde, an architect earning more than $135,000 per year, and her son Ross, a university student with no other income. Each year, payments of $25,000 and $15,000 will be made to Mrs. Hyde and Ross, respectively. While the payment to Mrs. Hyde is fixed, the trustee may pay Ross additional amounts from the trust as he considers appropriate for Ross's education and personal needs. Any remaining capital of the trust will eventually be paid to Ross.

For the years ended December 31, 2001 and 2002, the trustee projects the following trust income receipts:

Trust Income	2001	2002
Interest	$24,000	$24,000
Dividends Received From Taxable Canadian Corporations	22,000	24,000
Total	$46,000	$48,000

Payments to Mrs. Hyde and Ross are expected to be as follows:

Trust Payments	2001	2002
Mrs. Hyde	$25,000	$25,000
Ross Hyde	15,000	24,000

Required: With a view to minimizing total taxes payable by the trust and the beneficiaries, identify potential tax planning opportunities and potential tax savings.

Assignment Problem Nineteen - 5

Mr. Samuel Rosen is a successful businessman who has two sons and wishes to have most of his property ultimately wind up in their hands. In a move designed to help achieve this goal, he transferred a substantial amount of property to a trust in their favour on July 15, 1986. The fiscal year of the trust ends on December 31, and Mr. Rosen has no beneficial interest in either the income or capital of the trust.

The terms of the trust provide for the older son, Jonathan, age 38, to receive 35 percent of the income of the trust while the younger son, Robert, age 35, is to receive a 25 percent share. Trust income includes any capital gains earned in the trust. Both Jonathan and Robert Rosen are single and have no current sources of income other than the trust. The remaining income is to accumulate within the trust to be paid out to the two sons at the time of Mr. Samuel Rosen's death. The income figures for the current year ending on December 31 are as follows:

Interest Income On Government Bonds	$ 55,000
Dividends From Taxable Canadian Corporations	245,000
Revenues From Rental Property	394,000
Cash Expenses On Rental Property	247,000

On September 1 of this year, the rental property was sold. The property consisted of an apartment building and the land on which it was located, all of which was transferred into the trust when it was created. The relevant information related to the disposition is as follows:

	Building	Land
Proceeds Of Disposition	$1,857,000	$1,100,000
Undepreciated Capital Cost	1,371,000	N/A
Capital Cost	1,620,000	785,000

This is the first disposal of capital property by the trust since its establishment.

Required:

A. Calculate the taxable incomes of the trust, Jonathan and Robert Rosen for the current year.

B. Calculate the federal taxes payable for the trust for the year ending on December of this year.

Assignment Problem Nineteen - 6

On March 1 of this year, Ms. Denise Lord died at her home in Victoria. Under the terms of her will, all of her property is transferred to a testamentary trust. This trust will have a fiscal year which ends on December 31 and the trust agreement contains the following provisions:

- Forty percent of the income is to be paid to her 38 year old daughter, Joan Lord.

- Twenty percent of the income is to be paid to her 43 year old son, Richard Lord.

- The remaining income will be retained by the trust. While this income can be distributed at the discretion of the trustees, there were no distributions prior to December 31 of this year.

Neither of her children have any income other than income from the trust.

During its first fiscal year, between March 1 and December 31 of this year, the following income and expense amounts were recorded by the trust:

Canadian Dividends Received		$ 58,000
U.S. Source Interest ($13,000, Net Of		
10 Percent Withholding Tax)		11,700
Rental Income	$158,000	
Rental Expenses Other Than CCA	(31,000)	127,000
Total Income		$196,700

The rental property is in Class 1 and had an undepreciated capital cost of $3,096,000 on March 1. Net rental income, before capital cost allowance, is to be paid to the beneficiaries. Capital cost allowance is to be calculated with reference only to rental income retained by the trust.

Required:

A. Determine the amount of income that will be taxed in the hands of each beneficiary for the current taxation year.

B. Compute the total federal taxes payable for the trust for its first fiscal year.

Assignment Problem Nineteen - 7 (Electronic Library Research Problem)

Provide brief answers to the following questions. Your answers should be supported by references to materials found in your Electronic Library.

A. Answer the following True or False questions, and reference your answer to the relevant section in the *Act*.

1. A trust must have a calendar year end.
2. A trustee is treated the same as an executor in references to trusts or estates.
3. A testamentary trust can result from the conversion of an inter vivos trust.
4. All trusts are subject to the 21 year deemed disposition rule.
5. A personal trust includes an inter vivos trust for which no beneficial interest has been acquired for consideration to the trust, or to a person who contributed to the trust.
6. Under her will, Rebecca has arranged for five testamentary trusts to be created for her son rather than one. She feels the added administrative costs of the five trusts will be less than the tax savings from the increased use of the low marginal tax rate.
7. In computing taxable income for a year, a trust must deduct income amounts paid to the beneficiaries.
8. A personal trust can distribute property to the beneficiaries at no tax cost to the beneficiaries.
9. Income can be deemed paid to a 15 year old beneficiary, even if the amount is not paid or payable in the year.
10. A beneficiary can be someone that does not have an immediate interest in the income or capital of the trust.

B. Outline four important criteria that influence the residence of a trust.

C. Comment on whether a trust and its beneficiary are considered to operate at arm's length from each other.

D. Describe the term "vested indefeasibly" in the context of trusts and trust beneficiaries.

E. Generally, a trust is taxed as an individual. Cite the related provision.

F. Generally, a trust is taxed as an individual. Cite three exceptions to this generalization.

Chapter 20

Partnerships

The Nature of Partnerships

Definition of Partnership

20-1.   A partnership is usually defined as a business, carried on in common by two or more persons, with the intention of making a profit. A similar definition is included in most provincial partnership Acts and the Civil Code of Quebec. Other considerations in identifying whether a partnership exists are an express or implied agreement to share profits instead of gross revenues, and the ability of one partner to bind the partnership by negotiating contracts and signing cheques. Most partnership situations involve the co-ownership of assets used in the business, as well as joint and several liability with respect to debts incurred by the partnership.

20-2.   IT-90, *What Is A Partnership?*, sets out the CCRA's views on factors to be considered in determining whether a particular arrangement should be viewed as a partnership. This Interpretation Bulletin notes that the *Income Tax Act* does not define the term partnership, but generally speaking:

> ... a partnership is the relation that subsists between persons carrying on a business in common with a view to profit.

20-3.   For more specific guidance on what constitutes a partnership, reference should be made to relevant provincial law. Such law is viewed as persuasive by the Department Of National Revenue.

20-4.   Members of a partnership are usually individuals. However, a group of corporations can also form a partnership. In most provinces, professionals such as doctors, lawyers, and public accountants must use the partnership form of organization as they are prevented from carrying on their activities within a corporation. However, Alberta has provided for the incorporation of professionals for many years. More recently, Ontario has changed its legislation to provide similar rules for professionals in that province.

Significance Of The Classification

20-5.   Case law establishes that a partnership is not a legal entity as partners carry on the partnership business directly. IT-90 also makes it clear that a partnership is not a person and, as a consequence, no separate income tax return is required. However, ITA 96 requires net income of a partnership to be calculated as if "the partnership were a separate person resident in Canada". The partnership is envisaged as a separate person solely to measure or calculate the flow of income to individual partners. In addition, other provisions in the *Income Tax Act* deal with a partnership as a separate entity. For example, some provisions deem a partnership to own capital property and others allow for the transfer of assets to a partnership on a tax deferred basis. However, it is not the partnership, but the partners who are subject to taxation.

20-6.   Because of these taxing provisions, it is important to distinguish partnership arrangements from other relationships that can be made between two or more taxpayers to carry out a combined business undertaking. These alternative arrangements are generally referred to as joint ventures. If a business relationship is classified as a joint venture, a separate calculation of its net income is not required and the provisions that allow for a tax free rollover of assets to the business will not be available.

Joint Ventures
Legal Definition
20-7.   As with partnerships, no definition of joint ventures is provided in the *Income Tax Act*. Nonetheless, joint ventures are referenced in three important pieces of Canadian legislation, notably the *Canada-U.S. Free Trade Agreement*, the *Investment Canada Act* and the *Excise Tax Act*. In the latter, joint ventures may make certain GST/HST filing elections that are unavailable to partnerships. While little official recognition has been afforded joint ventures in Canada, there is some evidence that the courts recognize the existence of joint ventures and view joint ventures as relationships other than partnerships.

General Description
20-8.   Even though the legal definition of a joint venture is elusive, a description of this type of relationship is possible. In general terms, a joint venture will have some or all of the following characteristics:

- The joint venture is established to carry out a single business endeavour or common undertaking over a limited period of time. Examples of this would be the exploitation of a mineral deposit or the construction of a new highway.

- The co-venturers retain their ownership of individual assets, allowing the assets to be pooled for business use for the duration of the joint venture only.

- The co-venturers are entitled to a share of the gross revenues, and sometimes gross expenses, from the venture and not a share of a net income figure that may be determined separately for the joint venture. They use their own fiscal year and individually determine the amount of tax deductions to claim against their share of the joint venture revenues.

- The joint venture will not incur debts on a joint and several liability basis.

- The joint venture is conducted with a view to earning a profit.

Application In Practice
20-9.   An arrangement with all of the characteristics listed in the preceding section would, without question, be viewed as a joint venture. It is clearly not a partnership and could not use the tax rules applicable to partnerships. In practice, it would be unusual to find such a clear cut situation. Some partnership arrangements might have one or more of the joint venture characteristics. On the other hand, rarely would a joint venture agreement contain all of the items listed in the general description. This, of course, creates a considerable amount of uncertainty.

20-10.   Given this uncertainty, parties to any business relationship should determine in advance how they wish to be taxed. If their goal is to be taxed as individual participants in a joint venture, their agreement should contain most of the characteristics listed in our general description of joint ventures. The more closely the agreement complies with this list, the more likely it is that the CCRA will accept the enterprise as a joint venture.

20-11.   No specific income tax rules are directly applicable to joint venture arrangements. This means that there will be no separate calculation of the income of the joint venture and none of the rollover provisions applicable to partnerships can be used. Each participant in a

	Figure 20 - 1 Summary Of Partnership And Joint Venture Differences	
Feature	**Partnership**	**Joint Venture**
Business duration and purpose	Carrying on a particular type of business for the foreseeable future.	Carrying out a specific transaction or project over a limited period of time.
Terminology	Participants are referred to as partners and the organization is referred to as a partnership.	Participants are referred to as co-venturers or co-owners and the organization is referred to as a joint venture.
Property ownership	Property belongs to the partnership. Partners own partnership interests, which are distinct from the underlying assets.	Co-venturers retain individual ownership of the assets being used by the joint venture.
Contractual obligations	Individual partners may enter into contracts and act on behalf of the partnership.	Co-venturers may not act as an agent for other co-venturers.
Fiscal period	Deemed to have its own fiscal period under ITA 96(1)(b).	Each co-venturer uses his own fiscal period.
Income determination	Net income is calculated at the partnership level, and is allocated according to the partnership agreement.	Revenues and certain expenses are allocated to the co-venturers to be used in the determination of the co-venturer's income from the joint venture.

joint venture will be treated as a separate taxable entity. Co-venturers will be subject to the rules applicable to individuals, corporations or trusts, depending on their legal status.

> Exercise Twenty-1 deals with partnerships vs. joint ventures. This would be an appropriate time to attempt this exercise.

Summary Comparison

20-12. In general, a joint venture is regarded as a more informal and temporary relationship than a partnership, and is usually confined to a single project or undertaking of limited duration. A summary of the major differences between partnerships and joint ventures is found in Figure 20-1.

Limited Partnerships

General Rules

20-13. The definition of a partnership indicates that, in most partnerships, all of the partners will have joint and several liability for any debts incurred by the partnership. Such partners are referred to as general partners. In a general partnership, all partners are liable for the partnership liabilities.

20-14. An alternative to general partnership arrangements is the limited partnership. A limited partnership exists when the liability of certain partners is limited to their capital invested in the partnership. To qualify as a limited partnership, the relevant provincial act that governs limited partnerships must be strictly adhered to. Limited partners are restricted to passive investors that take no part in management or control of the business of the partnership. Further, the partnership agreement should specify what these restrictions are.

20-15. Regardless of whether there are two or twenty limited partners in a limited partnership, at least one general partner must have unlimited liability. The general partner is normally jointly and severally liable for partnership liabilities and may not be supported financially by other partners if a loss results. Usually this partner is the controlling or managing partner.

Reasonable Expectation Of Profit

20-16.   The limited partnership form is widely used in tax shelter arrangements (see Chapter 18), often generating large losses that can be deducted against other income. While the CCRA has no objection to this when a viable business is involved, they are concerned that this legal form not be used purely as a mechanism for avoiding tax or for creating untaxed benefits of a personal nature (e.g., ownership of a condominium that is used periodically by the investor and his family). As a consequence, it is not uncommon for the CCRA to question where a particular arrangement has a reasonable expectation of profit. In cases where they conclude that no such expectation exists, the losses may be disallowed. In fact, disputes over this issue often wind up in the courts.

Taxation Of Partnership Income

Taxation Year

1995 Stub Period Income

20-17.   Prior to 1995, there were no restrictions on the use of non calendar fiscal years by either a proprietorship or a partnership. This situation provided significant tax deferral for individuals owning such unincorporated businesses, a situation that the government found offensive. To deal with this situation, legislation was introduced which resulted in many unincorporated businesses switching to a December 31 year end. As this process resulted in two year ends in a single calendar year, a fairly complex transitional provision involving so-called stub period income was introduced. As these transitional provisions are of limited interest to most readers of this text, we have placed the material in the Appendix to this Chapter which begins at Paragraph 20-98.

Non Calendar Fiscal Years

20-18.   In general, partnerships can use a non calendar fiscal year. However, if one or more members of the partnership is (1) an individual, (2) a professional corporation, or (3) a partnership with a member as described in (1) or (2), a non calendar fiscal year can only be used if an election is made using form T1139. This election requires a special income inclusion based on an estimate of the income for the period between the end of the selected fiscal year and the end of the calendar year. The calculation of this "Additional Business Income" can be fairly complex and it is covered in the Appendix to this Chapter beginning at Paragraph 20-102.

20-19.   The following example illustrates fiscal year procedures for a partnership where all of the partners are corporations and, therefore, can use a non calendar fiscal year without making an election.

> **Example**   Seaside Partnership, a partnership with a June 30 year end, has only corporate partners. One of the partners, Sailboard Inc., has a March 31 year end.
>
> **Tax Consequences**   Sailboard Inc.'s share of the partnership income for the partnership's taxation year ending June 30, 2001, will be reported in the calculation of Sailboard Inc.'s net income for tax purposes for its taxation year ending March 31, 2002. There is no December 31 year end requirement for the Seaside Partnership.

Tax On Split Income

20-20.   The new tax on split income, described in Chapter 13, is applicable to taxable dividends on unlisted shares of corporations if paid to a minor child through a partnership or trust. Similarly, the tax on split income applies to income paid to a child out of a partnership or trust where the income is derived from providing goods or services to a business carried on by a relative.

Reporting Requirements
Partnerships

20-21.   Most partnerships are assigned a unique identification number by the CCRA and are required to file an annual Partnership Information Return which is referred to as the T5013 Summary. This Return must detail the income or loss of the partnership for the fiscal period, identify the individual partners, and indicate the amount of income and tax credits allocated to each of the identified partners. The due dates for this information return depend on the nature of the participating partners. The due dates are as follows:

- **All Partners Are Individuals**   The information return is due on or before March 31 of the calendar year following the calendar year in which the fiscal period of the partnership ended.

- **All Partners Are Corporations**   The information return is due within five months after the end of the fiscal period of the partnership.

- **Other Cases**   The information return is due on or before the earlier of the two dates above (March 31 or five months after the fiscal period end).

20-22.   The individual partners are not required to file the complete partnership information return with their tax returns. Rather, individual partners should file individual partner information (as reported on a T5013 Supplementary, which is similar to a T4 or T5) with their tax returns.

20-23.   Some partnerships are exempt from these reporting requirements, including partnerships with five or less members, limited partnerships whose only activity is restricted to investment in flow-through shares, and investment clubs that file T3 returns. While such partnerships have no obligation to file a Partnership Information Return, there are reasons why filing should be considered. By not filing a Return, the related partnership income will never become statute barred and the partnership year will remain open indefinitely for reassessment. It is also possible that events occurring during the year, for example, the addition of a sixth partner, result in the requirement to file a Return for the first time, but the partners neglect to do so. A late filing penalty, up to a maximum of $2,500, could be assessed if a required Partnership Information Return is filed late.

Joint Ventures

20-24.   Joint ventures have no official reporting requirements. As they have no specific year end for income tax purposes, revenues and expenses of each co-venturer are usually determined on a monthly basis and are reported in the appropriate fiscal period of the co-venturer. Therefore, each co-venturer's tax year determines when the joint venture revenues and expenses are reported for income tax purposes.

20-25.   As this separate reporting can be cumbersome, the CCRA has developed administrative procedures to simplify the reporting of joint venture revenues and expenses. If all co-venturers agree, a joint venture may choose a fiscal year end for reporting of revenues and expenses. If the co-venturers have different year ends, any year end may be selected for the joint venture. Where the co-venturers have the same year end, a different year end may be selected if there is a valid business reason for doing so.

Determining Partnership Income
General Rules

20-26.   As previously noted, ITA 96 requires partnership income to be calculated as though the partnership is a separate person resident in Canada. In determining this amount, most of the basic rules are identical to those used for corporations or proprietorships. As these are covered in detail in Chapter 7, they will not be reviewed here.

20-27.   There are, however, a number of special provisions that relate directly to the determination of partnership income. These will be covered in the sections which follow.

Capital Cost Allowances

20-28.   Partnerships can own capital property, so the appropriate capital cost allowances on property must be determined and claimed at the partnership level. Partnership income is allocated after the deduction of capital cost allowance. This uniformity may create conflicts among partners, as some partners may not want the maximum available capital cost allowance claimed. Therefore, the partnership agreement should specify exactly how discretionary tax deductions, such as capital cost allowance, will be determined each year.

20-29.   The short fiscal period rule applies to partnerships. This restricts capital cost allowances claimed in short fiscal periods. Also, the first year rules apply to partnership assets. This requires that only one-half of the net acquisitions for the year be included in the CCA calculation. Note, however, in situations where a non arm's length party rolls depreciable property into a partnership, the first year rules do not apply.

20-30.   The requirement to calculate capital cost allowance at the partnership level can provide an opportunity to avoid the CCA limit applicable to rental properties. As covered in Chapter 11, the deduction of CCA on a rental properties is limited to the amount that will reduce net rental income to nil. If rental properties that have a pre-CCA profit are held in a partnership and those with pre-CCA losses are held outside the partnership, the CCA claim on the profitable units will not be offset by losses on the remaining units. This means that using a partnership to hold profitable rental properties may allow greater capital cost allowance claims overall than if all rental properties are held personally or all are in a partnership.

Reserves

20-31.   As with capital cost allowance claims, reserves permitted under the *Act* must be claimed in determining income or loss at the partnership level. The reserves under Section 20 for doubtful debts, goods and services to be delivered in future periods, and proceeds of sales due in a future period must be claimed by the partnership, not by the partners individually. Likewise, the ITA 40(1)(a) reserve for capital gains, applicable where proceeds are due after the year end, should be determined at the partnership level despite the flow-through of capital gains to individual partners.

Amounts Paid to Partners

20-32.   When partners withdraw income from a partnership, the withdrawals are considered a distribution of partnership profits and are not a deductible expense of the partnership. Consequently, any salary amounts paid to partners are usually not deductible in the calculation of partnership income. Some partnership agreements specify that a fixed amount is to be paid to certain partners, after which the profits or losses are to be split among all partners according to a formula. The fixed amount may be referred to as a salary, but it is not a deductible expense. Rather, it is simply one component of allocated partnership profits.

20-33.   When a partnership leases property from a partner, any rent paid is an expense of the partnership and can be deducted in the calculation of partnership income. Also, any interest paid to a partner is deductible if the interest relates to a bona fide loan to the partnership, but not if the interest is paid on a partner's capital account. The respective partner must report corresponding rental and interest income that relate to deductible partnership expenses.

Flow Through Provisions

20-34.   ITA 96 makes it clear that various types of income retain their identity as they are allocated to partners. This means that the partnership must separately calculate income from taxable and capital dividends, capital gains and losses, rental income and foreign source income. These income amounts will be allocated to the partners in the same form as they are received by the partnership. All amounts allocated to an individual partner for each year are reported on a T5013 supplementary information slip.

20-35.   Partnership activity may generate amounts for which credits can be claimed against taxes payable. Since there is no calculation of taxes payable for the partnership, tax credits cannot be used at the partnership level. Instead, charitable contributions, dividend income, federal political contributions, foreign income and investment tax credits are allocated to the individual partners. The allocation of these amounts to the partners will usually be on the same basis that is used for profit sharing. Then, each partner calculates and claims the relevant tax credits. Note that, in the case of corporate partners, partnership charitable contributions generate a deduction rather than a tax credit as would be the case for partners who are individuals.

20-36.   When investment tax credits relate to depreciable property, the cost of the property is reduced in the year the property is acquired, regardless of when the investment tax credits are actually claimed by the partners. This reduction will reduce the future CCA claims made at the partnership level.

Scientific Research And Experimental Development Expenditures

20-37.   The deductibility of scientific research and experimental development expenses incurred by partnerships is very restricted. Any deduction must be claimed in the year incurred under ITA 96(1)(e.1). This is in sharp contrast to the generous indefinite carry forward provisions for these deductions that are normally available to other taxpayers. The forced immediate deduction often results in a partnership loss being reported. Such losses, if unused by the respective partners, can be carried forward for seven years. The deductibility of scientific research and experimental development losses is even more punitive for limited partners, with losses being denied, irrespective of how much the limited partner has invested in the partnership.

> Exercise Twenty-2 deals with partnership deductions. This would be an appropriate time to attempt this exercise.

Allocation Of Partnership Income

20-38.   The net income of the partnership must be allocated among the partners. However, the *Act* is vague about how to allocate income among partners. ITA 96(1)(f) requires the inclusion of partnership income "to the extent of the taxpayer's share thereof." Usually, income is allocated to the partners to the extent of their respective partnership interest or as specified in the allocation formula in the partnership agreement. The allocation should be reasonable in the circumstances, considering capital contributed and effort expended. Although there are no restrictions on the manner in which partners share in partnership profits and losses, typically the proportion is the same regardless of whether a profit or loss is reported.

20-39.   The fact that tax legislation does not specify a particular basis for the allocation of partnership income provides opportunities for income splitting between related parties. However, this has to be done within the general constraint of reasonableness. ITA 103(1.1) contains an anti-avoidance provision which indicates that if the allocation does not reflect "the capital invested in or work performed for the partnership", it will be considered unreasonable. In these circumstances, a different allocation will be required.

> Exercises Twenty-3 and Twenty-4 deal with allocation of partnership income and losses. This would be an appropriate time to attempt these exercises.

20-40.   One situation in which a preferential allocation may be allowed is when property that was rolled into a partnership is subsequently disposed of. Normally, such property is rolled in with an adjusted cost base that is less than fair market value at the time of the transfer. On the subsequent disposition of the property, the gain may be allocated entirely to the partner that contributed the property, up to the amount of the tax deferred gain on the rollover. Such a preferential allocation of partnership income would not be a violation of ITA 103(1.1).

At Risk Rules

20-41.   For a member of a general partnership, the allocated share of partnership active business losses can be deducted against any other source of income. Such losses are deductible in the current, seven year carry forward or three year carry back periods. As a general partner realizes the losses, there are no stop loss rules applied that are unique to partnerships.

20-42.   These generous loss deductions have been widely used in the structuring of tax shelters. Prior to the introduction of the at risk rules, it was not uncommon for the loss write-offs associated with investments in limited partnerships to exceed the amount of any current or future investment that might be made by the investor. Reflecting the view that this situation was abusive, ITA 96(2.1) and 96(2.2) were added to the *Act*. These subsections, which are frequently referred to as the "at risk" rules, limit the write-offs available to a limited partner to the amounts that the partner has "at risk" under the terms of the partnership agreement. Note that these rules only apply to limited partners. They do not apply to general partners, even those involved in partnerships where some partners' obligations have been limited.

20-43. To calculate the at risk amount, the limited partner's investment amount starts with capital originally contributed by the partner, if any. This amount is increased by allocated amounts of partnership income, and is reduced by amounts owing by the limited partner to the partnership and any guarantees provided to the limited partner to protect against a loss.

20-44. The at risk amount is calculated at the year end of the limited partnership, and any loss incurred by the limited partnership for the year is deductible up to the at risk amount. Any unutilized loss from a limited partnership loss can be carried forward indefinitely, to be deductible whenever the at risk amount is increased. However, if the limited partner becomes a general partner, or if the limited partnership interest is sold, any limited partnership loss carry forward is permanently lost.

Example Of At Risk Rules

20-45. A fairly simple example which illustrates the application of the at risk rules follows:

	1998	1999	2000	2001
At Risk Amount, Beginning Of Year (Note 1)	Nil	$ 600	($ 500)	($1,100)
New Investment During Year	$3,000	Nil	900	2,000
At Risk Amount, Pre Loss Allocation	$3,000	$ 600	$ 400	$ 900
Allocated Loss For Year	(2,400)	(1,100)	(1,500)	Nil
At Risk Amount, End Of Year	$ 600	($ 500)	($1,100)	$ 900
Loss Claim For The Year (Note 2)	($2,400)	($ 600)	($ 400)	($ 900)
Loss To Be Carried Forward From Current Year (Note 3)	Nil	($ 500)	($1,100)	Nil
Loss Carry Forward (Note 4)	Nil	($ 500)	($1,600)	($ 700)

Note 1 This example assumes that there are no amounts owing from the limited partner to the partnership and that the limited partner has no guarantees from the partnership to protect against the loss of his investment.

Exercise Twenty-5 deals with limited partnerships. This would be an appropriate time to attempt this exercise.

Note 2 The loss claim for the year is the lesser of the at risk amount, before any loss allocation, and the sum of the allocated loss for the year and the loss carry forward from the prior year end.

Note 3 The allocated loss for the year, less the loss claimed for the year, provides the amount of the loss to be carried forward from the current year.

Note 4 There was no loss allocated in 2001, therefore the $900 loss claimed for the year reduced the loss carry forward from $1,600 to $700.

Corporate Partnerships

Introduction

20-46. In recent years, partnerships where all partners are corporations have become more common. These are normally referred to as corporate partnerships. While non-tax factors usually provide the initial impetus for the formation of a corporate partnership, income tax considerations can also be very important.

20-47. Most of the rules associated with the determination of partnership income and the subsequent allocation of that income to member partners are the same, without regard to whether the partners are individuals or corporations. However, there is a unique feature that requires additional consideration. This involves the application of the limits on income eligible for the small business deduction and for the accelerated rate reduction.

Small Business Deduction Restricted

20-48.   For a Canadian controlled private corporation, the small business deduction is potentially available on the first $200,000 of Canadian active business income. To prevent this rule from being circumvented by related parties creating a group of corporations, ITA 125(3) requires associated corporations to share the $200,000 limit (see Chapter 14). The definition of specified partnership income contained in ITA 125(7) provides rules which require a similar sharing of the $200,000 limit by all members of a partnership, regardless of whether or not all partners are corporations. These rules apply irrespective of whether the incorporated members of the partnership are associated.

20-49.   The general rules for the small business deduction limit the amount eligible for this deduction to specified partnership income. For a corporate partner, the definition of specified partnership income eligible for the small business deduction is the lesser of:

- the corporate partner's share of the active business income of the partnership; and
- the corporate partner's share of the $200,000 annual business limit.

20-50.   Corporate partners can add active business income from other activities to this specified partnership income allocation to determine the total income eligible for the small business deduction. An example will serve to clarify these rules.

> **Example**   Northway Ltd. has a 25 percent interest in a partnership that, during the year ending December 31, 2001, earned active business income of $285,000. Through other independent activities during the year, Northway Ltd. earned $65,000 of active business income.

20-51.   Northway's specified partnership income for the year is equal to the lesser of:

Share Of Partnership Income [(25%)($285,000)]	$71,250
Share Of Annual Business Limit [(25%)($200,000)]	$50,000

20-52.   The lesser amount is $50,000 and, when this is added to Northway's other active business income, the total amount eligible for the small business deduction is $115,000 ($50,000 + $65,000).

Accelerated Rate Reduction

20-53.   As discussed in Chapter 14, as of 2001, a 7 percentage point reduction in the federal tax rate is available to CCPC's on amounts of Canadian active business income between $200,000 and $300,000. This is, in effect, an accelerated application of the general rate reduction for corporations which is at 1 percentage point for 2001, but will increase to the same 7 percentage point reduction by 2004. As described in Chapter 14, the extra $100,000 that is eligible for this accelerated reduction must be shared by associated companies. In the same manner, corporate members of specified partnerships will also have to share this amount.

20-54.   To illustrate the application of the accelerated rate reduction, we will extend the Northway Ltd. example. Northway's share of partnership income was $71,250, of which $50,000 was eligible for the small business deduction. The remaining allocated partnership income of $21,250 ($71,250 - $50,000) will then be eligible for the accelerated tax reduction as it is less than Northway's $25,000 share of the $100,000 that can qualify for this benefit. As was outlined in Paragraph 20-52, Northway will have $115,000 in income that is eligible for the small business deduction, with the remaining $21,250 of the Company's active business income eligible for the accelerated rate reduction.

20-55.   The small business deduction and accelerated rate reduction are not available when non residents or public companies are partners in the partnership. ITA 125(6.2) deems the specified partnership income to be nil where a corporation is a member of a partnership that was controlled directly or indirectly by one or more non resident persons or public corpora-

Exercise Twenty-6 deals with corporate partnerships. This would be an appropriate time to attempt this exercise.

tions, or by any combination thereof, at any time in the fiscal period. Therefore, if a partnership is controlled by a non resident person or a public company for even one day during the fiscal period, any active business income for the period will not qualify for the small business deduction or the accelerated rate reduction.

Partnership Vs. Incorporation

20-56.   A group of investors wishing to start a business can choose between the partnership form of organization and the use of a corporation. In addition, partnerships that have been in operation for some time may wish to consider whether it would be more appropriate to continue the business as a corporation. In either case, it is important to understand and compare the advantages and disadvantages of the partnership and corporate forms of business organization.

20-57.   Before considering these advantages and disadvantages, you should note that incorporation is not an available alternative for some professionals. For example, when doctors, lawyers, and accountants are interested in carrying on their activities as a group, they can be forced by provincial legislation to use the partnership form of organization. The basis for this type of legislation is the belief that such professionals should not have the advantages of limited liability associated with incorporation.

20-58.   In most other situations, there will be a choice with respect to the form of business organization. In making this choice, a major advantage that a partnership has over a corporation is the ability to flow losses out of the partnership to individual partners. As well, cash earnings may be distributed without the incidence of double taxation that applies when taxable dividends are received from corporations by individuals.

20-59.   Often, the overall taxes paid may be lower when a partnership is used than would be the case if the same business was incorporated. However, the tax savings will depend on the type of corporation, the nature of its income, and the corporate and personal tax rates applicable in the province in which the business operates.

20-60.   A partnership can also provide flexibility. If provided for in the partnership agreement, profit sharing ratios can be varied on an annual basis. In addition, opportunities for tax deferrals exist when corporate partnerships have year ends immediately after the year ends of the corporate partners, resulting in a potential deferral of tax payments by approximately one year. Note, however, that incorporation also provides deferral opportunities when income is left in a corporation without dividends being distributed to the owners.

20-61.   Partnerships, in general, are less costly to maintain than corporations. There is no need for such formalities as charters, by-laws, resolutions, elections, and minutes of director's meetings. Further, they do not require a separate tax return and they are not subject to incorporation fees or, in some provinces, very onerous capital taxes.

20-62.   An important disadvantage of the partnership form of business is that losses on the disposition of a partnership interest do not qualify for the allowable business investment loss provisions. A further disadvantage is the fact that gains on the disposition of a partnership interest are not eligible for the $500,000 lifetime capital gains deduction. Finally, the partnership form of business is usually less convenient for raising large amounts of capital and coping with changes in the investor group.

Disposition Of A Partnership Interest

20-63.   An interest in a partnership is treated as a capital asset under the *Act*. It is a distinct property apart from the assets of a partnership. As a consequence, the disposal of such an interest will normally result in a capital gain or loss. This gain or loss will be calculated in the usual way by subtracting the adjusted cost base along with any costs of disposal from the proceeds of disposition. In simple terms, the adjusted cost base of a partnership interest is the cumulative amount invested, plus any excess of the partner's share of earnings over withdrawals during the period of ownership. The example which follows illustrates the basic procedures required to calculate the adjusted cost base of a partnership interest.

Example   Ms. Jones acquires a 25 percent interest in a partnership by contributing $100,000 on December 1, 1993. During the period December 1, 1993 through November 30, 2001, the partnership earns $800,000 and Ms. Jones withdraws $150,000. The adjusted cost base of her partnership interest is calculated as follows:

Capital contributions	$100,000
Income share [(25%)($800,000)]	200,000
Withdrawals	(150,000)
Adjusted cost base, November 30, 2001	$150,000

20-64.   While the preceding example illustrates the calculation of the adjusted cost base of a partnership interest in a very simple situation, a number of other adjustments to the adjusted cost base are required in more realistic situations. The most common adjustments are as follows.

Additions To Adjusted Cost Base
- Amount paid for the partnership interest
- Capital contributions
- Partner's share of partnership income (Including 100 percent of capital gains and 100 percent of proceeds of disposition from eligible capital property)
- Partner's share of capital dividends received by the partnership
- Life insurance proceeds
- Non deductible interest and real estate development costs

Deductions From Adjusted Cost Base
- Partner's share of partnership losses (Including 100 percent of capital losses)
- Partner's drawings
- Distributions of capital to the partner
- Partner's share of charitable and political contributions
- Amount of any investment tax credits used by the partner

20-65.   As some of the listed adjustments are applicable throughout a year (e.g., drawings), while others are only applicable at year end (e.g., income allocation), the timing of the disposition of a partnership interest can be crucial. The adjusted cost base of a partnership interest and the resulting gain or loss on disposition can differ substantially before and after a year end. As an example of this, partnership income is deemed to be earned on the last day of the partnership year, and is normally allocated to active partners on that date. This means that income of the partnership for the current fiscal year is added to the adjusted cost base only at the end of the current fiscal year. Income earned for the year in progress is therefore ignored in calculating the adjusted cost base throughout the year.

20-66.   Consistent with the exclusion of current year income from the adjusted cost base, when a partner retires or withdraws from a partnership, the income for the stub period is usually not reported in his income. However, where this creates anomalous results (e.g., double taxation of the income due to the death of a partner), the CCRA allows the current year's income to be added to the adjusted cost base.

20-67.   Retiring partners are typically allocated and paid their share of undrawn profits for the part of the year prior to the retirement. The recipient typically treats such a payment as part of the proceeds of disposition resulting from the sale of a partnership interest. Conflicting with this is the fact that the remaining partners usually allocate the payment to the retiring partner, as a share of profits for the year. When the partnership agreement is not clear as to the nature of these payments, the courts have had a tendency to treat them as income allocations.

20-68.   A similar issue arises when a partnership agreement calls for payments to a retiring partner that is in excess of the partner's capital account balance. The extra amounts paid may be viewed as either capital payments or an allocation of profits. If the amount is viewed as a capital payment, it becomes the proceeds of disposition for the retiring partner and it is not

Exercise Twenty-7 deals with admission of a partner. This would be an appropriate time to attempt this exercise.

deductible from the partnership income allocated to the other partners. By contrast, if the payment is viewed as an allocation of profits, it is income to the retiring partner and deducted from the income of the other partners. Given this problem, a partnership agreement should be explicit as to the intent of retirement payments.

Negative Adjusted Cost Base

20-69.   One unusual feature sometimes occurs with respect to the adjusted cost base of partnership interests. A partnership interest can develop a negative adjusted cost base. This can result, for example, from substantial partnership losses or excess partner withdrawals. With other assets, this situation would result in an income inclusion. For example, when a depreciable asset has a negative UCC, recaptured CCA is added to income. Correspondingly, when non depreciable capital assets have a negative adjusted cost base, ITA 40(3) requires this negative amount to be included in income.

20-70.   This is not the case with a general partnership interest. For general partners, an exception to ITA 40(3) usually allows a negative adjusted cost base to be carried forward until there is a disposition of the partnership interest. This treatment enables partners to draw out amounts in excess of their equity accounts without immediate tax consequences. In effect, general partners can receive interest free loans from a partnership without reporting a tax benefit. In contrast, loans to individual shareholders of a corporation must generally be included in a shareholder's income if the balance is outstanding over two consecutive corporate year ends.

20-71.   When a partnership interest is deemed to be disposed of on death, any negative adjusted cost base must be taken into income and the ITA 40(3) exception does not apply, unless there is a rollover to a spouse or spousal trust. Also, a negative adjusted cost base must be recognized for all limited partnership investments as well as for any sales or transfers of partnership interests.

Rollovers Involving Partnerships

Transfers To A Partnership By A Partner
No Rollover

20-72.   A partner often transfers various business assets to a partnership. This is a fairly common transaction, particularly at the inception of a new partnership. Under ITA 97(1), this type of transfer is treated as a deemed disposition by the partner and a deemed acquisition by the partnership, with fair market value being used to record both sides of the transaction. In many situations, this transfer could result in the partner having to recognize both capital gains and recapture.

20-73.   As is the case with transfers of property to a corporation, there are some special rules associated with such transfers. The more important of these are as follows:

- For depreciable assets that have a fair market value in excess of their capital cost, the capital cost to the partnership, for purposes of determining CCA and recapture, is limited to the transferor's capital cost, plus one-half of the difference between this value and the fair market value. For capital gains purposes, the capital cost is the fair market value.

- For depreciable assets that have a fair market value that is between the capital cost and the UCC of the asset, the partnership retains the capital cost of the transferor for purposes of determining capital gains and recapture.

- Terminal losses that arise on such transfers may be denied. This will be the case when the transferor and the partnership are affiliated. While an individual is not affiliated with a partnership in which he is a member, a corporation is affiliated when it has a majority interest in the partnership.

- In similar fashion, capital losses on non depreciable assets will be denied in those situations where the transferor and the partnership are affiliated persons.

With Rollover

20-74.   In most situations, income recognition can be avoided when property is transferred to a partnership. ITA 97(2) permits inventories, capital property, and cumulative eligible capital to be rolled into a partnership on a basis very similar to that provided under ITA 85 for transfers of property to a corporation by a shareholder. To qualify for a tax deferred rollover, the partnership must be a Canadian partnership immediately after the rollover.

20-75.   Under ITA 102, a Canadian partnership is defined as one in which all of the members are Canadian residents. A retired partner, with an income participation interest only, is not considered to be a full partner. As a consequence, such a partner can be non resident without jeopardizing the Canadian partnership status or the rollover eligibility. Further, the partnership can operate outside of Canada, as the definition only refers to the residence of the active partners. If the partnership intends to have non resident partners, any transfers that will be made by resident partners should be completed before the non resident partners join the group.

20-76.   For the rollover provision to apply, all of the partners must elect under ITA 97(2). With respect to elected values, the rules are the same as those applicable to Section 85 transfers to a corporation. This means that, in general, the partners can elect to have the transfer take place at any value between an upper limit of the fair market value of the property and a lower limit of any consideration received by the partner other than a partnership interest. Also, this lower limit must be higher than the tax value of the property, meaning that a loss cannot be triggered by the rollover.

Transfers From A Partnership To A Partner

General Rule

20-77.   Under ITA 98(2), a transfer of an asset from a partnership to a partner is deemed to be a disposition at fair market value by the partnership and an acquisition at this same value by the partner. This may result in the need to recognize income at the partnership level. However, the partner's adjusted cost base will be established at fair market value at the transfer date and he will escape responsibility for any income that has accrued to that date. This rule applies as long as the partnership continues to exist and, under ITA 98(1), it continues to exist until all of its property is distributed to the partners.

ITA 98(3) Rollover

20-78.   When a partnership ceases to exist, a rollover provision allows property to be transferred to the partners without tax consequences to the partnership. For this rollover to apply, all of the property must be distributed to the partners and each partner must have an undivided interest in each property based on his interest in the former partnership. This rule is designed to prevent assets with large accrued gains from being transferred to low income partners.

20-79.   When this rollover is available, the partnership is deemed to have disposed of the assets at their tax cost, with the partners deemed to have acquired the property at his ownership percentage of this same value. This means that there are no tax consequences at the partnership level and any accrued income on the property has been deferred. When the partners dispose of this property, the accrued income will be taxed in their hands.

20-80.   The cessation of the partnership also means that each partner has had a disposition of his interest in the partnership. Under ITA 98(3)(a), their proceeds of disposition are deemed to be the greater of:

- the partner's adjusted cost base for his partnership interest, and
- the partner's proportionate share of the cost amount of partnership property distributed, plus any cash received.

20-81.   If the greater amount is the proportionate share of partnership property plus cash, the partner will have a capital gain on the disposition. Alternatively, if the adjusted cost base of the partnership interest is the larger amount, there will be no gain or loss on the disposition as the adjusted cost base will be used as the deemed proceeds of disposition. The excess of this adjusted cost base over the cost of the assets transferred will be allocated to non depreciable assets received from the partnership.

Other Types Of Transfers

Partnership Becomes A Sole Proprietorship

20-82.   Occasionally, when a partnership is dissolved, one partner remains to operate the business as a sole proprietorship. In this situation, ITA 98(5) provides a tax deferred rollover for the partnership assets that are used by the remaining partner to carry on the business. The rollover is available providing the proprietor continues to carry on the business within three months of the partnership ceasing to exist.

20-83.   To initiate this rollover, the continuing partner will acquire the interests of all of the other partners and the cost of the partnership property acquired will be added to his adjusted cost base. A deemed disposition of the proprietor's partnership interest results, with deemed proceeds being the greater of:

- the adjusted cost base of the partnership interest (including the cost of acquiring the other partnership interests) and
- the cost amount of all partnership property acquired for the business plus the fair market value of any other property distributed to the partner.

20-84.   As with the rollover under ITA 98(3), the cost and fair market value amounts of property received may exceed the adjusted cost base of the partnership interest, resulting in a capital gain. However, these values cannot be less than the adjusted cost base, and as a consequence, no capital loss can be realized on this disposition. Any implicit loss (excess of adjusted cost base over the value of property received) will be allocated to non depreciable assets.

20-85.   Note that the departing partners are not eligible for a tax deferred rollover under ITA 98(3). This rollover is only available when it is used by the continuing partner and the partnership ceases to exist. Therefore, when the partnership becomes a sole proprietorship, the other partners will receive the partnership assets at fair market value as required by ITA 98(2).

Partnership Becomes A Corporation

20-86.   As a partnership grows, it will often become advantageous to continue the business as a corporation. Normally this occurs after the business becomes profitable, and the partners have deducted start-up losses of the partnership against other personal taxable income. Some benefits of incorporation may be desired, such as limited liability and access to financing and the small business deduction.

20-87.   A partnership which incorporates can elect under ITA 85(2) to transfer its assets to a corporation on a tax deferred basis. Under this rollover provision, the partnership continues to exist, and the shares or other consideration provided by the corporation will become assets of the partnership. If an election is not made, the assets are deemed to be transferred at their fair market value.

20-88.   A more likely scenario would involve a rollover provided under ITA 85(3). This rollover requires the partnership to be wound up within 60 days of the transfer. In this situation, the shares and other consideration given in return for the partnership assets are transferred directly to the partners. The adjusted cost base for the shares received by the partners will generally equal the adjusted cost base of their former interest in the partnership plus any cash received. The only limitation is that if the corporation gives consideration other than shares, and the fair market value exceeds the adjusted cost base of the former partnership interest, the excess will be treated as a capital gain. For the Section 85(2) and 85(3) rollovers, the corporation must be a taxable Canadian corporation, but the partnership may have non Canadian partners.

20-89.   Real estate held for resale cannot normally be rolled into a corporation, as a rollover of real property inventory is excluded from the definition of eligible property that is found in ITA 85(1.1). The inability to roll real property inventory only applies to rollovers to corporations, and does not apply to rollovers of assets from a partner to a partnership under ITA 97(2). If real property inventory is held in a partnership and the partnership interest is transferred to a corporation in a rollover, the taxation authorities do not look through to the underlying assets of the partnership. Therefore, real property inventory held in a partnership can be indirectly rolled into a corporation. The real estate industry is concerned that this treatment may be challenged through the general anti-avoidance provisions.

Changes In The Partnership Group

20-90.   If one or more partners leave the partnership group with some of the partners continuing to operate the business as a partnership, ITA 98(6) provides a rollover provision for partners that continue to operate the business. This rollover avoids the general interpretation that the withdrawal of one or more partners is a dissolution of a partnership, combined with the formation of a new one. Most partnership agreements include a continuation clause anticipating partner changes. Without the rollover provision, a dissolution would require reporting of deemed dispositions of all partnership assets at their fair market values.

20-91.   Note that ITA 98(6) does not cover situations in which new partners are admitted or, alternatively, the merger of two or more partnerships. When new partners are admitted, a tax deferred rollover can be accomplished by dissolving the partnership under ITA 98(3). This must be followed by having the partners, including any new ones, transfer assets to a new partnership under ITA 97(2). In a similar fashion, these rollover provisions can be used to provide an effective rollover for mergers of old partnerships and newly formed partnerships.

20-92.   The issues associated with the retirement of a partner, death of a partner and non resident partners are more complex. Even a cursory coverage of these topic areas is beyond the scope of this book.

GST and Partnerships

20-93.   Unlike the treatment of partnerships under the *Income Tax Act*, partnerships are treated as if they are separate legal entities for GST purposes under the *Excise Tax Act*. As a result, partnerships are required to register and collect GST on taxable supplies. A partnership is entitled to claim input tax credits for GST paid on purchases of property and services used in the commercial activities of the partnership. As well, a rebate of GST may be claimed by partners for GST paid on expenses they incur personally that relate to the commercial activities of the partnership. This rebate is similar to the rebate available to employees, as discussed in Chapter 5.

20-94.   A partnership interest is considered a financial instrument. Therefore, no GST is payable on the issue or transfer of ownership of a partnership interest. When professional services, such as legal and accounting services, are provided to a partnership, the fees are taxable and input tax credits are available for GST paid on these fees if they relate to the partnership's commercial activities.

20-95.   With certain exceptions, the transfer of property to a partnership will generally be subject to GST. If a cash contribution is made to the partnership, there are no GST implications. Likewise, the transfer of debt and accounts receivable are considered to be exempt financial services, and are not subject to GST. Further, if the partners were not previously engaged in commercial activities and the capital property was not used in commercial activities, GST is not payable on the transfer. For example, GST is not payable on the transfer of property from a medical or dental practitioner to a partnership since the fees earned by doctors and dentists are generally exempt.

20-96.   On the cessation of a partnership, the transfer of property to the partners may be subject to GST. If the partnership was not a registrant because it was engaged in making exempt supplies, GST would not be payable on the transfer. If the partnership was a registrant and is transferring the business as a going concern, the general rules relating to the sale of property used in a commercial activity may apply. However, if substantially all of the business assets are transferred, an election may be available to exempt the transfer from GST.

References

20-97.   For more detailed study of the material in this Chapter, we refer you to the following:

ITA 96   General Rules (Partnerships And Their Members)
ITA 97   Contribution Of Property To Partnership
ITA 98   Disposition Of Partnership Property
ITA 99   Fiscal Period Of Terminated Partnership
ITA 100   Disposition Of An Interest in a Partnership
ITA 102   Definition Of "Canadian Partnership"
ITA 103   Agreement To Share Income

IC-89-5R   Partnership Information Return

IT-81R   Partnerships - Income Of Non Resident Partners
IT-90   What Is A Partnership?
IT-151R4   Scientific Research And Experimental Development Expenditures
IT-183   Foreign Tax Credit - Member Of A Partnership
IT-231R2   Partnerships - Partners Not Dealing At Arm's Length
IT-242R   Retired Partners
IT-278R2   Death Of A Partner Or Of A Retired Partner
IT-338R2   Partnership Interests - Effects On Adjusted Cost Base Resulting From The Admission Or Retirement Of A Partner
IT-353R2   Partnership Interest - Some Adjustments To Cost Base
IT-358   Partnerships - Deferment Of Fiscal Year End
IT-378R   Winding Up Of A Partnership
IT-413R   Election By Members Of A Partnership Under Subsection 97(2)
IT-457R   Election By Professionals To Exclude Work In Progress From Income
IT-471R   Merger Of Partnerships

P-171R   GST/HST Policy Statement, "Distinguishing Between a Joint Venture and a Partnership for the Purposes of the Section 273 Joint Venture Election", February 24, 1999.

Appendix To Chapter 20 - December 31, 1995 Income (Stub Period Income) and Additional Business Income

Rules Before 1995

20-98. Unincorporated businesses (proprietorships and partnerships) are not separate taxable entities. Rather, business income generated by these types of organizations will be allocated to the individual proprietors or partners and taxed in their hands. The rule contained in ITA 11(1) for recognizing income from such unincorporated businesses took the position that all of the income from the fiscal year of the business would be included in the individual's taxation year in which the fiscal year of the business ended.

20-99. This meant that, if a proprietorship or a partnership had a fiscal period ending on January 10, 1994, its income would be deemed to be earned on the last day of the fiscal year (January 10, 1994) and included in the proprietor's or partners' income for calendar 1994. This was the case despite the fact that most of the business income was probably earned in calendar 1993.

20-100. This created a tax planning opportunity for individuals with business income. By establishing a fiscal year for their business income that ended in January, they could have effectively deferred taxation on business income for nearly a full year. For example, for the proprietorship or partnership with a fiscal year that ended on January 10, 1994, only the business income earned between January 11, 1993 and January 10, 1994 would be included in the owner's personal tax return for the calendar year ending December 31, 1994. Under the rules which prevailed prior to the February 27, 1995 budget, the income earned between January 11, 1994 and December 31, 1994 would not be included in the individual proprietor's or partner's 1994 tax return, but would be deferred until his 1995 tax return was filed.

20-101. From the point of view of the Government, the situation described in the preceding section gave an unfair advantage to owners of proprietorships and partnerships. The conclusion was reached that the system would be fairer if these businesses were required to pay taxes on their income in the calendar year in which the income was earned. As a consequence, the 1995 budget changed the rules in this area and made non calendar fiscal periods much less desirable.

Non Calendar Year Election

20-102. There are cases in which there is a business reason for having a non calendar fiscal year. For many businesses, December is a particularly busy month and, as a consequence, having to deal with year end procedures at this time is extremely difficult. In other words, for businesses in this situation, there is a valid and non tax related reason for having a fiscal year end that is not December 31.

20-103. In view of the problem, the government concluded that unincorporated businesses should be able to have a non calendar fiscal year. An election can be made by any new business that begins operations subsequent to 1994 to have a fiscal year end other than December 31. The election can be made until June 15 of the year following the start of the business. If the election is not made in the first year of operation, it cannot be made in any subsequent year.

20-104. If this election is made, taxpayers have to include an amount of income for the period between the end of their normal fiscal year and December 31 of that year in order to eliminate the deferral advantage. This income is referred to as "Additional Business Income" and, in simple terms, it is based on the income of the fiscal period just ending, pro rated for the number of days in that period [the formula is found in ITA 34.1(1)]. An example can be used to clarify this situation:

Example   Jack Bartowski forms a new business on November 1, 2000. It has a fiscal year end of January 31 and, for the period November 1 through January 31, 2001, it has income of $25,000. The "additional business income" that must be added for 2001 is calculated as follows:

$$[(\$25,000)(334 \text{ Days}/92 \text{Days})] = \$90,761$$

The 334 days is for the period February 1, 2001 through December 31, 2001. The 92 days is for the period November 1, 2000 through January 31, 2001. The income that will be reported by Mr. Bartowski in his 2001 personal tax return is $115,761 ($25,000 + $90,761). Note that he will be taxed on estimated income for 14 months. There is an election available that would alleviate this situation by allowing him to report the November and December 2000 income in 2000 and not 2001.

In 2002, Mr. Bartowski's tax return will include his actual business income for the period February 1, 2001 through January 31, 2002, plus an "additional business income amount" similar to the preceding calculation, but based on the income for the fiscal period ending on January 31, 2002. This total is reduced by the "additional business income" included in his 2001 tax return to provide an estimate of the income earned in calendar 2002.

> Exercise Twenty-8 deals with additional business income. This would be an appropriate time to attempt this exercise.

1995 Stub Period Income

20-105.   A serious problem for businesses using a non calendar fiscal year prior to 1995 was that immediate implementation of the 1995 budget changes would require the inclusion of income of more than one fiscal period in a single taxation year. As an example of this problem, consider the previously described situation in which a taxpayer was using a January 10 year end. In his 1995 tax return, this individual would have to include his proprietorship or partnership income for the fiscal year ending January 10, 1995 and, in addition, he would also have to include the proprietorship or partnership income for the period January 11, 1995 through December 31, 1995. Given the progressive tax rates that are applicable to individuals, this would not be a very equitable situation.

20-106.   As a solution to this problem, in situations where an unincorporated business had used a non calendar fiscal year, the budget included provisions which allowed a taxpayer to deduct a reserve with respect to the income earned in the period between the normal 1995 fiscal year end (January 11, 1995 in our example) and December 31, 1995. In somewhat simplified terms, the income for this short fiscal period is referred to as "December 31, 1995 Income" or stub period income. This reserve, which is defined in ITA 33(1), allowed the income for this period to be deferred and recognized for tax purposes over a period of 10 years. The maximum amount of the reserve, along with the percentage of "December 31, 1995 Income" which will be recognized in each of the ten years is shown in Figure 20-2.

Figure 20 - 2
Maximum Reserve For
December 31, 1995
Income

Year	Deductible Reserve	Included In Income
1995	95%	5%
1996	85%	10%
1997	75%	10%
1998	65%	10%
1999	55%	10%
2000	45%	10%
2001	35%	10%
2002	25%	10%
2003	15%	10%
2004	0%	15%
Total		100%

20-107.   As you can see from the schedule in Figure 20-2, tax practitioners will have to deal with the results of this change until 2004. As a consequence, the following example of how the system works is presented:

Example   Ms. Turner has an unincorporated business with a January 31 year end. For the fiscal year ending January 31, 1995, the business earns $120,000. It has income of $110,000 in the fiscal period February 1, 1995 through December 31, 1995. The income of the business for the calendar year ending December 31, 1996 is $120,000. The calculation of the business income to be included in Ms. Turner's 1995 and 1996 tax returns is as follows:

	1995	1996
Income From Business		
Fiscal Period Ended January 31, 1995	$120,000	
Fiscal Period Ended December 31, 1996		$120,000
Inclusion Of Income That Otherwise Would Have		
Been Deferred		
5 Percent Of $110,000	5,500	
10 Percent Of $110,000		11,000
Income From Business To Be Reported	$125,500	$131,000

20-108. In the years 1997 through 2003, Ms. Turner will have to include $11,000 (10%) of deferred income in her return. In 2004, the amount will be $16,500 (15%).

Consequences Of Retirement Or Partnership Dissolution

20-109. When a partner retires or a partnership dissolves, the ten year deferral of 1995 stub period income is lost and the reserve balance must be reported as income in the following calendar year, unless the partner continues to practice in a similar business. In this case, the reserve can continue to be claimed by that partner.

20-110. We would note before leaving this subject that the preceding examples are very simple. There are many complications associated with this legislation and complete coverage of these issues goes well beyond the scope of this book.

Exercises

(The solutions for these exercises can be found following Chapter 21 of the text.)

Exercise Twenty - 1 (Partnership vs. Joint Venture)

Contrast the disposition of a partnership interest and the disposition of a joint venture interest.

Exercise Twenty - 2 (Partnership Deductions)

Determine whether the following are deductible from partnership income:

(A) Office rent paid to one partner for a building owned outside the partnership.
(B) Interest on capital accounts.
(C) Interest on a short-term loan from a partner.
(D) Salary paid to partners.

Exercise Twenty - 3 (Partnership Losses)

If a partnership realizes a tax loss, can that loss be carried forward or back to be applied against partnership income in previous or subsequent years?

Exercise Twenty - 4 (Partnership Income Allocation)

Emily Luft and Ruth Blakie formed the Emblem Partnership to provide Internet portal consulting services. Emily contributed the capital to buy servers and Ruth is doing most of the consulting work. They have agreed that Ruth will be allocated $40,000 from the partnership each year, regardless of profits realized. Emily and Ruth will share equally in the remainder of the profit or loss. In the current year, the partnership has net income of $35,000. Determine how partnership income should be allocated between Emily and Ruth.

Exercise Twenty - 5 (Limited Partnership Loss)

Stuart Jones has invested $50,000 cash in a limited partnership and has assumed a related $150,000 loan that is payable in eight years. If at any time he wants to sell the investment, the promoter will purchase the investment and assume the loan. For the current year, the limited partnership has allocated a loss of $75,000 to Stuart Jones. How much of this loss is Stuart Jones entitled to claim as a deduction on his tax return?

Exercise Twenty - 6 (Allocation Of Small Business Deduction)

Do corporate partners share the $200,000 small business deduction limit? Likewise, will corporate partners share the accelerated rate reduction for Canadian controlled private corporations?

Exercise Twenty - 7 (Admission of Partner)

Alan and Balan are equal partners in the Alban Partnership. The partnership has a November 30 year end, and at the end of this year, Alan and Balan's partnership capital account balances are $48,000 each. This is also equal to their partnership adjusted cost bases. Caitlan is admitted as an equal partner on December 1 and pays $40,000 to Alan and Balan (a total of $80,000). Calculate the tax effects of the partner admission for Alan and Balan and determine the ending capital account balances and adjusted cost base for each partner.

Exercise Twenty - 8 (Additional Business Income - Appendix)

Mr. Morgan Gelato starts a business on February 1 of this year. Because it will be a slow time of year for him, he intends to have a fiscal year which ends on June 30. During the period February 1, 2001, through June 30, 2001, his business has income of $12,300. What amount of business income will Mr. Gelato report in his personal tax return for the year ending December 31, 2001.

Problems For Self Study

(The solutions for these problems can be found following Chapter 21 of the text.)

Self Study Problem Twenty - 1

Mr. Baker and Mr. Caldwell are partners in an accounting firm. The Income Statement of the partnership for the year ending December 31 of the current year is as follows:

Fees Received In Cash		$403,000
Capital Gains On Temporary Holdings Of Canadian Securities		14,000
Dividends Received From Taxable Canadian Companies		48,000
Total Revenues		$465,000
Less: Business Expenses:		
Salaries And Wages	$197,000	
Rent On Office Space	19,200	
Interest On Bank Loans	5,800	
Depreciation - Office Furniture And Equipment	12,500	
General Office Expense	28,400	
Charitable Donations	7,200	
Costs Of Attending Convention	2,800	272,900
Net Income		$192,100

Other Information:

1. The partnership agreement calls for Net Income to be allocated equally to the two partners. In addition, the Salaries And Wages in the preceding Income Statement include a payment of $44,000 to each of the two partners.

2. The convention costs were for the two partners to attend the annual conference of the Canadian Institute Of Certified General Management Accountants.

3. Both partners use their personal vehicles for business purposes and pay their own operating expenses. At the beginning of the current year, Mr. Caldwell's car had an Undepreciated Capital Cost of $13,500. His operating expenses for the year were $4,000 for a total of 48,000 kilometers driven. Only 25 percent of these kilometers were for personal use.

4. At the beginning of the current fiscal year, the partnership had fees receivable from clients of $27,000. At the end of the year, the corresponding balance was $56,000.

5. At the beginning of the year, the Undepreciated Capital Cost of the office furniture was $26,000 and the Undepreciated Capital Cost of the computer equipment was $14,000. During the year, a computer was purchased for $8,500.

Required: Determine the Net Income For Tax Purposes which will be included in Mr. Caldwell's personal income tax return for the year ending December 31 of the current year. Describe any tax credits that will be available to Mr. Caldwell as a result of the partnership income. Ignore GST and PST considerations.

Self Study Problem Twenty - 2

On March 1, 1998, John Olson, his son Fred Olson, and Eric Beam form a partnership to provide accounting and tax services. The partners each contribute $225,000 and agree that all income and losses are to be shared equally. The fiscal year for the partnership is established to end on December 31.

For the period March 1, 1998 to December 31, 2000, the following information is available:

1. The partnership earned total income of $195,000. Included in this amount is a taxable capital gain of $33,000 [(1/2)($66,000)].

2. During this period, Eric Beam made withdrawals from the partnership totalling $43,000.

3. The partnership made a number of charitable donations during the period. The total amount involved was $12,000 and this total was allocated equally to each of the three partners.

4. Additional capital was required to expand the operations of the office and, as a consequence, each partner contributed an additional $65,000 in cash.

Eric Beam decided to withdraw from the partnership effective May 31, 2001. After some negotiations, the other partners agreed to pay him $355,000 in cash for his interest in the partnership. The payment is made on June 1, 2001. Eric Beam incurred legal and accounting fees in conjunction with this transaction totalling $1,800.

During the period January 1 to June 1, 2001, the partnership earned $36,000. Eric Beam did not make any withdrawals nor was he allocated any income for that period.

Required: Calculate Eric Beam's gain or loss on the disposition of his partnership interest. Explain how this amount and any other amounts related to the partnership will be taxed in his hands.

Self Study Problem Twenty - 3

A number of years ago, Jack Porter, Cid Quinn, and Norman Roberts established the Porter, Quinn, and Roberts partnership. At the time the partnership was formed, each of the partners invested $350,000 in cash. The partnership agreement calls for all income and losses to be shared equally. The fiscal year of the partnership ends on December 31.

On January 1 of the current year, the adjusted cost base of the interests of the three partners is as follows:

Jack Porter	$ 382,000
Cid Quinn	526,000
Norman Roberts	726,000
Total	$1,634,000

Early in the current year, the property of the partnership is transferred to a corporation under the provisions of ITA 85(2) in return for the following consideration:

Cash	$ 722,000
Preferred Shares (At Fair Market Value)	540,000
Common Shares (At Fair Market Value)	1,080,000
Total Consideration	$2,342,000

Subsequent to the ITA 85(2) transfer, the partners decide to wind up the partnership. Reflecting this decision, the consideration provided by the corporation is transferred to the individual partners. Under the terms of the partnership agreement they receive the following amounts:

	Porter	Quinn	Roberts	Total
Cash	$ 78,000	$222,000	$422,000	$ 722,000
Preferred Shares	180,000	180,000	180,000	540,000
Common Shares	360,000	360,000	360,000	1,080,000
Total	$618,000	$762,000	$962,000	$2,342,000

Required: Determine the adjusted cost base of the assets received by the partners as a result of this transfer of partnership assets to the corporation. Calculate the capital gain or loss for each partner resulting from the transfer.

Assignment Problems

(The solutions for these problems are only available in
the solutions manual that has been provided to your instructor.)

Assignment Problem Twenty - 1

Burt and Sam Jones are brothers and professional accountants. They operate a partnership that specializes in doing accounting and tax work for small to medium sized manufacturing companies. The partnership agreement calls for them to share the partnership profits equally. The partnership has a fiscal year which ends on December 31.

For the current year ending December 31, they have prepared the following income statement for the partnership:

Burt And Sam Jones
Partnership Income Statement
Current Year Ending December 31

Revenues		$707,000
Dividends From Canadian Corporations		32,000
Gain On Sale Of Shares Of Canadian Public Corporations		52,000
Total Revenues		$791,000
Expenses:		
Salaries To Staff	$286,000	
Office Rent	64,000	
Office Supplies	26,000	
Capital Cost Allowance On Office Equipment	29,000	
Charitable Donations	63,000	
Drawings By Burt	145,000	
Drawings By Sam	153,000	766,000
Net Income		$ 25,000

The Revenues include the December 31 balance of work in process of $232,000. The corresponding balance as at the previous December 31 year end was $98,000 and this amount was included in the accounting revenues for that year. While the Jones brothers have chosen to include work in process as a revenue in their accounting statements, they have elected under ITA 34 to exclude these amounts from their tax calculations.

Required: Calculate the amount of net business income from the partnership to be recorded in the tax returns of each of the brothers for the current year ending December 31 and describe any available tax credits arising from the partnership income.

Assignment Problem Twenty - 2

Two of your university friends, who became lawyers, left the firms where they were employed and set up their own practice on January 1 of this year. They started the practice by contributing $10,000 working capital each and decided to split the profits equally and pay themselves equal salaries. Their bookkeeper has prepared the following financial statements:

Friends Forever Law Practice
Balance Sheet
As At December 31

Cash	$ 2,000
Accounts Receivable	30,000
Work In Progress	25,000
Computer Hardware, At Cost	10,000
Computer Applications Software, At Cost	8,000
Total Assets	**$75,000**
Accounts Payable	$15,000
Initial Partner Capital	20,000
Income For The Period	40,000
Total Equities	**$75,000**

Friends Forever Law Practice
Income Statement
For The Current Year Ending December 31

Revenues	$230,000
Meals And Entertainment	$ 6,000
Office Supplies	4,000
Partners' Salaries	130,000
Rent	24,000
Secretary's Salary	26,000
Total Expenses	**$190,000**
Income For The Period	**$ 40,000**

The work in progress represents work done by the lawyers at their standard charge rate that has not been billed to clients at the year end.

Required: (Your answers should ignore GST and PST considerations.)

Part A Your friends have come to you to determine the minimum amount that they must include in their current year tax returns as Net Income For Tax Purposes of the Partnership.

Part B They would also like to know if there are any partnership related expenses which they may have incurred personally which they can deduct on their current tax return.

Part C Compute the adjusted cost base of each partner's partnership interest at December 31.

(ICAO Adopted)

Assignment Problem Twenty - 3

Yoho Airways became a 10 percent limited partner in the new Frontier Holidays Partnership in 1999. Yoho made capital contributions to Frontier of $30,000 in 1999, $20,000 in 2000, and $15,000 in 2001. Frontier experienced a $500,000 loss in 1999, followed by a $120,000 loss in 2000. Fortunately, the general partner guaranteed that Yoho's share of any loss in any one year would be limited to $40,000. There is no cap on income allocations. Income of $150,000 was earned in 2001.

Required: For each of 1999, 2000 and 2001, calculate the at risk amount at the end of the year, the limited partnership income (loss), and the limited partnership loss carry forward for Yoho Airways.

Assignment Problem Twenty - 4

Bohemia Ltd. is a Canadian controlled private company which holds interests in two corporate partnerships, Bonn and Mia. Bohemia has active business income from its own operations of $100,000 for the year ended January 31, 2001. Bohemia owns 20 percent of the Bonn Partnership, which reported active business income of $300,000 for its year ended February 28, 2000, and 30 percent of the Mia Partnership which reported active business income of $120,000 for its first fiscal period ended June 30, 2000. The Mia Partnership was established on January 1, 2000. The December 31 year end requirement does not apply to either partnership.

Required: Determine the amount that Bohemia Ltd. can claim as income eligible for the small business deduction in its 2001 tax return. (Ignore the accelerated rate reduction.)

Assignment Problem Twenty - 5

During 1998, Susan Field, Christine Black, and John Henderson form a partnership to provide management consulting services. The partners each contribute $350,000 and agree that all income and losses are to be shared equally. The fiscal year for the partnership is established to end on December 31.

For the period beginning when the partnership was formed and ending December 31, 2000, the following information is available:

- During 2000, the partnership made a number of charitable donations. The total amount involved was $9,000 and this total was allocated equally to each of the three partners.

- The partnership earned income of $273,000. This figure does not include a deduction for the charitable donations, but does include the taxable one-half of a $42,000 total capital gain.

- During this period, John Henderson made withdrawals from the partnership totalling $74,000.

- Additional capital was required to expand the operations of the office and, as a consequence, each partner contributed an additional $100,000 in cash.

John Henderson decided to withdraw from the partnership effective April 30, 2001. After some negotiations, the other partners agreed to pay him $550,000 in cash for his interest in the partnership. None of this amount relates to John's share of unpaid profits or work in process as at April 30, 2001. The payment is made on May 1, 2001. John incurred legal and accounting fees in conjunction with this transaction totalling $2,500.

During the period January 1 to May 1, 2001, the partnership earned $48,000 and made no charitable donations. John Henderson did not make any withdrawals during this period.

Required: Calculate John Henderson's gain or loss on the disposition of his partnership interest. Explain how this amount and any other amounts related to the partnership will be taxed in his hands.

Assignment Problem Twenty - 6

A number of years ago, Jack Howard, Bud Jones, and Dwight Delaney established the Howard, Jones, and Delaney partnership. At the time the partnership was formed, each of the partners invested $600,000 in cash. The partnership agreement calls for all income and losses to be shared equally. The fiscal year of the partnership ends on December 31.

On January 1 of the current year, the adjusted cost base of the partnership interests that are applicable to the three partners are as follows:

Jack Howard	$1,173,000
Bud Jones	930,000
Dwight Delaney	756,000
Total	$2,859,000

Early in the current year, the property of the partnership was transferred to a corporation in return for the following consideration:

Cash	$1,200,000
Preferred Shares (At Fair Market Value)	900,000
Common Shares (At Fair Market Value)	1,800,000
Total Consideration	$3,900,000

The partners elect to use the rollover provisions of ITA 85(2) and, as a result, the partnership is liquidated and the preceding consideration is transferred to the partners. Under the terms of the partnership agreement they receive the following amounts:

	Howard	Jones	Delaney	Total
Cash	$ 620,000	$ 377,000	$ 203,000	$1,200,000
Preferred Shares	300,000	300,000	300,000	900,000
Common Shares	600,000	600,000	600,000	1,800,000
Total	$1,520,000	$1,277,000	$1,103,000	$3,900,000

Required: Determine the adjusted cost base for the assets received by the partners as a result of this rollover of partnership assets to the corporation. Calculate the capital gain or loss for each partner resulting from the transfer.

Assignment Problem Twenty - 7

Mr. Marrazzo owns an undeveloped parcel of land in Suburbia. He purchased the land four years ago with the intention of developing residential lots. The land cost $400,000 and now has a fair market value of $1,200,000.

Banks are reluctant to lend for real estate development, so Mr. Marrazzo has been unsuccessful in obtaining the $1,200,000 financing that is required for site servicing costs. A heavy equipment supplier may be interested in providing interest-free financing in return for ownership of 50 percent of the property and 50 percent of the profits from the sale of the lots.

If Mr. Marrazzo proceeds with this plan, site servicing could be completed in one year and all lots could be sold in the following year for proceeds approximating $4,400,000. He is considering whether he should form a partnership with the heavy equipment supplier or proceed with the project as a joint venture.

If a partnership is created, Mr. Marrazzo would take advantage of the rollover provision to defer reporting the accrued gain on the land. The partnership agreement would specify that Mr. Marrazzo is entitled to 100 percent of the accrued gain until the property is rolled into the partnership and 50 percent of any subsequent gains.

Required: Calculate what the taxable income inclusions would be for Mr. Marrazzo in the year the land is developed, and in the subsequent year, if the project is undertaken as a:

A. Partnership. Include a calculation of the adjusted cost base of his partnership interest after all the lots are sold.

B. Joint Venture.

Assignment Problem Twenty - 8

Note This problem involves additional business income.

On April 1, 1998, Craig Cardinal and Don Kvill formed a partnership to teach small craft flying lessons. They elected to use a March 31 fiscal year end to coincide with the end of the winter aircraft maintenance program and the beginning of the summer training schedule. The two partners share equally in the profits of the partnership.

During the year ending March 31, 2000, the partnership earned taxable income of $64,000, of which $42,200 was deemed earned before December 31, 1999 for the alternative income reserve purposes. Also, the partners withdrew $56,000.

From April 1, 2000 to March 31, 2001, the partnership earned $58,000 and the partners withdrew $74,000.

Required: Determine the minimum amount of partnership income that Craig Cardinal and Don Kvill will have to include in their personal tax returns for the years 2000 and 2001.

Assignment Problem Twenty - 9

Note This problem involves 1995 stub period income.

Art Calvin and Sarah Knox have operated Calvin And Knox Enterprises as a partnership for over 10 years. When this partnership was initiated, they were advised to select January 15 as their year end in order to defer taxes on partnership income. As they had no business reason for choosing a particular year end, they took this advice and have used January 15 as their year end since the inception of the business. The two partners have equal shares in the profits of the partnership.

During the period January 16, 1995 through December 31, 1995, the partnership had taxable income of $123,000 and the partners each made a drawing of $52,000. They did not elect to retain their January 15 year end for 1995 and each year claimed the maximum reserve for 1995 stub period income.

During the calendar year ending December 31, 2000, the partnership earned taxable income of $106,000. Also during this period, each of the partners made a drawing of $48,000.

During the calendar year ending December 31, 2001, the partnership had taxable income of $147,000 and each of the partners made a drawing of $61,000.

Required: Determine the minimum amount of partnership income that Art Calvin and Sarah Knox would have to include in their personal tax returns for the years 2000 and 2001.

Assignment Problem Twenty - 10 (Electronic Library Research Problem)
Provide brief answers to the following questions. Your answers should be supported by references to materials found in your Electronic Library.

A. Answer the following True or False questions, and reference your answer to the relevant section in the *Act*.

  1. Charitable donations made by a partnership are deductible before the calculation of partnership net income allocations.
  2. When a partnership is terminated, a fiscal period is deemed to end immediately before that time.

3. When a partnership includes a husband and wife, profits can be allocated to the wife, only, and losses allocated to the husband, only.
4. A partnership is treated as a separate person for the purpose of computing income from the partnership.
5. A partnership can allocate profits and losses to partners in different proportions.
6. An allocated limited partnership loss is always deductible in computing a tax-payer's income for the year.
7. The small business deduction is available only to a specified partner if the partnership is Canadian controlled throughout the entire year.
8. When a partnership ceases to exist and property is transferred to a partner, a deemed disposition results.
9. Corporate partners are entitled to the full use of the $200,000 small business deduction for their share of partnership income.
10. A loss on the disposition of a partnership interest will qualify as an allowable business investment loss.

B. Determine which partnerships are exempt from the filing of Partnership Information Returns.

C. Determine how the following amounts should be reported at the partnership and partner levels.

1. capital cost allowance
2. dividends from taxable Canadian corporations
3. capital dispositions
4. rent paid to a partner

D. Partners can elect to exclude Work In Progress from the calculation of Net Income. Determine what types of income this election applies to, and how partners and partnerships comply with the election.

E. Merger mania has been the buzz word among Canadian accounting firms for the last few years. In most cases, the accounting firms are partnerships. Outline whether the merger of two accounting firm partnerships can occur on a tax deferred basis.

Chapter 21

Taxation Of International Income

Principles of International Taxation

21-1.   The taxation of international income is based on two fundamental principles. The first is the right of a country to tax income earned within its boundaries. The second is the right of the country of residence of the taxpayer to tax worldwide income, regardless of where the income is earned. The result is known as a dual tax regime, as most income is taxable in the country of residence as well as in the country where the income is earned.

21-2.   Canada uses a dual tax regime, in common with most democratic countries. Residents of Canada, and non resident persons that earn income in Canada, are liable to pay tax under Canada's domestic tax acts, which include the *Income Tax Act*, the *Excise Tax Act* and various provincial tax acts. As the Canadian tax base includes income earned in Canada, and income earned by residents of Canada (which may also be taxed in another country), double taxation can result.

21-3.   To prevent the same income from being double taxed, bilateral tax conventions have been negotiated between many countries to resolve international taxing dilemmas. These are a very important source of international tax law. Most international tax conventions follow the Organization for Economic Cooperation and Development (OECD) model convention, which outlines methods to eliminate double taxation. For example, most conventions specify that business profits will be taxed in the country, or countries, where the business has a permanent establishment, even if the services are performed or sales are made in other countries.

21-4.   In terms of domestic legislation, foreign tax credits can be claimed for any taxes paid on foreign source income when a resident reports the income in Canada. Foreign tax credits are allowed regardless of whether or not Canada has signed an international tax convention with the particular countries where the foreign taxes were paid.

21-5.   This Chapter will focus on taxation under the Canadian *Income Tax Act* and the *Canada/U.S. Income Tax Convention, 1980* (as amended by the Fourth revised Protocol which entered into force on December 16, 1997). Taxation of income earned in Canada by non residents (Canadian source income) and international income earned by Canadians (foreign source income) will be covered. As well, relevant provisions from the Canada/U.S. convention will be summarized to illustrate how international tax conventions relieve the incidence of double taxation and provide administrative streamlining in the taxation of international income.

Residence

Residence of Individuals

21-6.   The concept of residence is very important in the realm of international taxation. Worldwide income earned by an individual in the year is generally taxed in the individual's country of residence. The definition of residence for Canadian income tax purposes was introduced in Chapter 3, and coverage is continued in this chapter.

21-7.   Under the *Income Tax Act*, residence is the main factor influencing whether an individual is subject to Canadian tax. ITA 2(1) requires that "an income tax shall be paid on the taxable income for each taxation year of every person resident in Canada at any time in the year". The term residence is not defined in the *Act*, so we look to jurisprudence for guidance. Recall that the criteria to determine residence differ depending on whether the taxpayer is an individual, corporation or trust. For individuals, residence is determined by where a person, in the settled routine of life, regularly or customarily lives. Other factors influencing Canadian residence for individuals include:

- economic, social and family ties;
- past and current living patterns;
- regularity and length of stay(s) in Canada;
- purpose of the presence in, or the absence from, Canada;
- availability of a permanent home in Canada and in a foreign jurisdiction; and
- permanence of a stay in a foreign jurisdiction.

21-8.   These factors are discussed in IT-221R2 which outlines the administrative policies of the CCRA in this area. While this Bulletin does not have the status of law, it offers insight into how the CCRA may view an individual's residence. If a taxpayer is uncertain with respect to his residency status, he may submit to the CCRA a request for determination of residence status. This is done by using Form NR73 (leaving Canada) or NR74 (entering Canada).

21-9.   In today's world, there are situations where members of the same family may reside in different countries. A case in point is that of Mr. Shih, whose family moved to Canada in 1989 so that his children could receive a North American education. Mr. Shih came to Canada three or four times each year to stay with or visit his wife and sons, but he spent most of his time employed in Taiwan. On March 31, 2000 the Tax Court of Canada [Shih vs. H.M.Q. 97-3044(IT)G] ruled that Mr. Shih did not have enough connections to Canada to conclude that he resided here in any of the years in question. Even though the family home was in Canada, Mr. Shih was not in Canada often or long enough to establish any personal connections whether they were commercial, educational, cultural, recreational or social.

21-10.   The term residence is separate and distinct from citizenship or domicile. Canada does not impose a tax upon a person merely because he or she is a citizen of or is domiciled in Canada. On the other hand, the U.S. taxes all U.S. citizens, regardless of where they reside in the world. Citizenship is based on domestic rules, and, in most cases, more than landed immigrant status is required to be a citizen of a country. The notion of residence relates to where a person routinely lives; citizenship relates to rights and privileges granted to an individual by a specific country; and, the concept of domicile relates to where a person's physical home is. For example, Canadian residents who are also U.S. citizens must file U.S. tax returns (as U.S. citizens) as well as Canadian tax returns (as Canadian residents).

21-11.   ITA 250(1) deems certain individuals to be residents of Canada, even if they do not set foot in Canada during the year. A common example of this would be members of the armed forces. Also included under this provision would be Canadian ambassadors and other government representatives, children of deemed residents provided they are dependent for support, spouses of deemed residents that are exempt from taxation in the foreign country, and individuals who have sojourned in Canada for 183 days or more during the year.

21-12.   Deemed residence for Canadian diplomats complements a tax exemption for foreign diplomats that are employed in Canada. The foreign diplomat exemption extends to all foreign government staff that work and reside in Canada, regardless of whether the individuals are ambassadors or clerks, and to members of the foreign diplomat's family residing in Canada. Several conditions must be met for this exemption. For individuals, the exemption conditions require that they:

- reside outside of Canada before assuming the duties;
- not be concurrently engaged in any business or otherwise employed in Canada; and
- not be citizens of Canada.

21-13.　To qualify for the foreign diplomat exemption, the other country must grant reciprocal relief for officers or servants of Canada who are employed and reside in that country. In addition, employees of the United Nations are exempt from Canadian income tax.

21-14.　As you can see, the definition of residence is very broad. Both individuals residing in Canada and Canadian diplomats living abroad are subject to Canadian income tax. The tax base for Taxable Income is also very broad, with almost all worldwide income earned by residents being taxed in Canada, along with most income earned in Canada by non residents.

Residence of Corporations

21-15.　The determination of residence of corporations is simpler than it is for individuals. Two tests are used to decide whether or not a corporation is deemed resident in Canada. The first test deems that all corporations incorporated in Canada after April 26, 1965 are resident in Canada. The second test deems corporations that carried on business in Canada after April 26, 1965 to be resident under ITA 250(4).

21-16.　Whether a corporation has carried on business or is carrying on business in Canada is based on a central management and control test. A corporation is deemed to be resident if the directors meet and carry out their responsibilities in Canada. Even if only some central management and control is located here, residence in Canada is assumed.

21-17.　An important exemption from Canadian income tax applies to certain shipping corporations. To qualify for this exemption, the corporation must:

- be incorporated outside of Canada,

- operate ships used primarily (more than 50 percent) in transporting passengers or goods in international traffic throughout the year (principal business), and

- earn all or substantially all (more than 90 percent) of the corporation's gross revenue from the operation of ships.

21-18.　When a corporation ceases to be a resident of Canada, all property owned by the corporation is deemed to be disposed of at its fair market value. In addition, ITA 219.1 imposes a 25 percent Part XIV tax on the accumulated retained earnings of the corporation at the same date.

Residence of Trusts

21-19.　As with individuals and corporations, the residence of a trust is also a question of fact. Under ITA 104(1), any reference to a trust shall be read as a reference to the trustee or the executor, administrator, heir or other legal representative having ownership or control of the trust property. Thus, a trustee's residence can be considered to be a trust's residence. If several trustees exist, residence is deemed to be where the trustees generally meet to administer the trust's affairs. This would include the place where all trust properties are administered and where the trust property is located. Guidelines on the determination of a trust's residence are provided in IT-447.

Residence of Partnerships

21-20.　The *Income Tax Act* acknowledges partnerships for income computation and foreign investment reporting purposes. Worldwide income of partnerships is pooled at the partnership level. But, as partnerships are not taxpaying entities, they are treated as conduits. Partnership income is allocated to partners, whether individuals, corporations or trusts, with the income retaining its character (e.g., business income, capital gains). The important residence issues associated with partnerships are that partnership income is taxed in Canada if it is allocated to a Canadian resident partner, or if Canadian-source business income is earned in which case the partner must report the income in Canada. Therefore, as partnerships are not specifically taxed under the *Act*, the determination of residence of a partnership is largely irrelevant.

International Tax Conventions

21-21.   A main goal of international tax conventions is to eliminate double taxation for taxpayers that reside in one jurisdiction and earn income in another. An example will illustrate the potential for double taxation. Residents of Canada are taxed on income earned worldwide. The U.S. income tax net is broader than just residents of the U.S., as it applies to all U.S. citizens regardless of where they live. With many U.S. citizens being resident and earning income in Canada, and worldwide income being the tax base in both tax jurisdictions, the income earned by these individuals is generally taxable in Canada and in the U.S. Hence, the possibility for double taxation.

21-22.   In common with most international tax conventions, the Canada/U.S. convention provides relief from double taxation. Usually this relief is provided by taxing income in the country in which the income is earned, regardless of citizenship or residence. For example, where a U.S. citizen earns employment income and is resident in Canada, the individual will pay tax on that income only in Canada. While the income needs to be reported on a U.S. tax return, most, if not all, of the U.S. taxes payable are offset by a foreign tax credit for Canadian taxes paid. As Canadian taxes usually exceed the U.S. amounts, the U.S. tax liability will be eliminated, except for any U.S. alternative minimum tax that may be payable.

21-23.   International tax conventions always have priority over domestic tax legislation, thus avoiding potential conflicts with the domestic laws of countries. However, tax conventions are not designed to allow tax advantages to residents. Taxpayers will not avoid paying income taxes simply because an international tax convention applies to their situation.

Resolution of Dual Residence

21-24.   Some individuals may be considered resident in two or more countries, perhaps because they live in one country and work in another. Also, some individuals have homes and spend considerable time in more than one country. These situations are not anticipated in domestic tax laws, and without special tax relief, double taxation can result if worldwide income earned by these individuals is taxed in more than one country.

21-25.   To determine the residence of an individual, the domestic tax laws of each country should first be referred to. When a taxpayer's residence status is unclear, or if an individual is considered to be resident in more than one country, then the respective international tax convention must be relied upon to decide which country has preference in income taxation. The relevant rules are typically referred to as the tie-breaker rules. To provide an example of tie-breaker rules, Article IV from the Canada/U.S. convention is summarized.

21-26.   The Canada/U.S. tie-breaker rules consist of five rules, to be applied sequentially. These rules deem an individual's attachment to one country to supersede that of another country, as follows:

1. Preference is given to the country in which the individual has a "permanent home available to him".

2. If there is a permanent home available in both countries, an individual is deemed resident in the country in which "personal and economic relations are closer". This is referred to as the center of vital interests.

3. If the country in which there is a center of vital interests cannot be determined, the individual is deemed resident in the country where there is an habitual abode. To have an habitual abode implies being physically present in a normal and customary manner through repeated stays. Generally, habitual abode covers a period of more than one

year.

4. If an individual has an habitual abode in both countries or in neither, the individual is considered a resident of the country "of which he is a citizen".

5. If an individual is a citizen of both countries or of neither of them, then competent authorities from both countries will meet and settle the question by mutual agreement. The competent authorities are representatives from the Minister of National Revenue in Canada and the Secretary of the Treasury in the U.S.

21-27.   As a result of the preceding tie-breaking procedures, the taxpayer is considered a resident of one of the countries, and will be assessed accordingly. Therefore, worldwide income will be aggregated and taxed in the country of residence, and foreign tax credits will be available in that country for any income taxes paid in other countries.

21-28.   The resolution of dual residence questions for corporations and trusts is less problematic than it is for individuals. For corporations, the country of incorporation is the most significant determinant. More questions arise regarding the residence of trusts which is affected by the residence of trustees, and in some cases, by the residence of beneficiaries if all the trust income is allocated to the beneficiaries. When an estate or trust is a resident of more than one country, the competent authorities endeavor to settle the question of principal residence.

21-29.   In recent years, the U.S. Internal Revenue Service (IRS) has been actively pursuing potential U.S. taxpayers. In this regard, Canadians who spend considerable amounts of time in the U.S. need to closely review their residency status. If they have a closer connection to Canada, whether under the domestic residence or the tax convention tie-breaker rules, they should file a "Closer Connection Exception Statement for Aliens" in the U.S. which documents the individual's close ties to Canada. This applies to individuals who have a substantial presence (e.g., spend more than four months a year) in the U.S., a permanent home in Canada and a closer connection to Canada than to the U.S. Filing of the closer connection statement will usually ensure adherence with U.S. law, protection from U.S. tax exposure for certain types of income that might not be protected by international tax conventions, and access to U.S. tax deductions should the individual later be assessed as a U.S. resident.

21-30.   Canadian taxpayers doing business in the U.S. should also review potential exposure to U.S. taxes. The Internal Revenue Service is aggressively searching for corporations that conduct a trade or business in the U.S., even if no permanent establishment is maintained there. To be on the safe side, any affected Canadian corporations should file a tax return in the U.S., in most cases reporting no income attributable to a U.S. permanent establishment, to which is appended a closer connection statement (treaty exemption). As with individuals, this precautionary filing simply protects tax deductions in the event of a future unfavourable federal U.S. assessment.

21-31.   Greater uncertainty surrounds potential exposure to U.S. state taxes. The states are not bound by the Canada/U.S. convention. Therefore, a Canadian business may be subject to U.S. state income taxes, but not U.S. federal income taxes, even if the business has no permanent establishment in the U.S. While the calculation of income tax is usually based on federal taxable income adjusted for certain state additions and deductions, stringent filing requirements often apply when business is conducted in a state. Further, most states impose a sales tax on the sale of tangible personal property that is delivered to customers located in the state. Each state has its own income and sales tax rules which must be reviewed carefully to ensure the tax reporting requirements are met.

Foreign Tax Credits

21-32.   Worldwide income earned by Canadian residents must be reported for income tax purposes in Canada. When income taxes have been withheld from income earned in another country, the income should be reported in Canada gross of any foreign income taxes paid, whether federal, state or civil taxes. Then, a foreign tax credit for the foreign income taxes paid may usually be claimed. This foreign tax credit offsets most double taxation that would otherwise result.

21-33.   The concept of foreign tax credits is illustrated in the following scenario. Assume that a Canadian resident earns employment income in the U.S. This situation is especially common when individuals live near the Canada/U.S. border. The employment income will usually be subject to U.S. federal and state taxes, above certain minimum income amounts. When the individual reports the employment income in Canada, any U.S. income taxes paid can be claimed as a foreign tax credit and will reduce the Canadian taxes otherwise payable on that income. The net effect is that the employment income is taxed at the higher of the applicable cumulative U.S. or Canadian personal taxes. The U.S. has the first opportunity to tax U.S. employment income, and Canada will only receive incremental tax on the income if the relevant Canadian taxes are higher than those in the U.S.

21-34.   In Canada, foreign tax credits are calculated separately for business and non-business income, and on a country by country basis. Further, foreign tax credits are generally limited to the lesser of foreign income tax paid (not payable) and Canadian income tax payable on the foreign source income. The intended effect is relatively straightforward, however the tax credit calculations are rather complicated. The calculations were described in Chapter 13 for individuals, with further elaboration for corporations in Chapter 14.

21-35.   In simplified form, the calculation for the allowable foreign tax credit for investment (non business) income is the lesser of:

- foreign income tax paid on foreign investment income, and

$$\bullet \left[\frac{\text{Foreign Investment Income}}{\text{Adjusted Net Income}}\right]\left[\begin{array}{c}\text{Canadian Income Tax}\\ \text{Otherwise Payable}\end{array}\right]$$

21-36.   If the foreign income tax paid exceeds the foreign tax credit allowed by this formula, any excess may usually be claimed either as a credit against provincial income tax payable or as a deduction in calculating net income. The calculation of a foreign tax credit for foreign business income is similar, but unabsorbed foreign business taxes may be carried back for three years and forward for seven years. IT-270R2, IT-395R and IT-520 contain further information on foreign tax credits.

Exercises Twenty-One-1 and 2 deal with taxation of foreign income. This would be an appropriate time to attempt these exercises.

21-37.   Foreign tax credits can be claimed by individuals, corporations and trusts. However, non taxable entities cannot claim foreign tax credits and normally must absorb foreign withholding taxes. This was particularly burdensome for non taxable trusts, such as Canadian RRSP and pension funds that could not claim foreign tax credits and also could not flow the benefit of foreign tax credits through to fund holders. To alleviate this problem, an exemption is now included in the Canada/U.S. convention. Dividends and income paid to a Canadian pension or retirement savings plan from a U.S. payer are exempt from U.S. withholding taxes.

U.S. Estate Taxes

21-38.   U.S. estate taxes are of concern to Canadian residents who are U.S. citizens, as well as to Canadian citizens with large property holdings in the U.S. These taxes are levied as a percentage of the fair market value of assets held at death. The amount is payable, without regard to whether the subject assets have increased or decreased in value since their acquisition. Further, the payment of these taxes does not change the adjusted cost base of such assets.

21-39.   While there are no estate taxes in Canada, tax legislation requires a deemed disposition at death of all property held by an individual. In general, this disposition is deemed to take place at fair market value and will usually result in the recognition of some amount of income (as noted in Chapter 10, there are exceptions to these rules for transfers to a spouse and certain intergenerational transfers of farm property). The fact that these deemed disposition rules do not make any allowance for U.S. estate taxes, when combined with the fact that U.S. estate taxes do not take into consideration taxes resulting from the Canadian deemed disposition rules, create a situation where the taxes arising at death can be very onerous.

21-40.   U.S. estate taxes are levied on the worldwide assets owned by U.S. citizens on death, as well as on U.S. situated property owned by non U.S. citizens. The U.S. estate tax is payable at graduated rates from 18 to 55 percent on amounts above the exemption limits. For 2001, Canadian residents and U.S. citizens alike, are exempt from the U.S. estate tax on the first $675,000 U.S. of an estate. The exemption effectively eliminates the U.S. estate tax for U.S. citizens who have worldwide estates of less than $675,000 U.S., providing that there were no prior taxable U.S. gifts. This exemption, which is officially referred to as the Unified Credit Exclusion Equivalent, is gradually increasing to $1,000,000 U.S. by 2006, as follows:

Year	Exemption (U.S. Dollars)
2000 - 2001	$675,000
2002 - 2003	700,000
2004	850,000
2005	950,000
2006 and later	1,000,000

21-41.   The application of this exemption to individuals who are not U.S. citizens, but have estates in excess of $675,000 U.S. involves a pro rata calculation. In this circumstance, the U.S. estate tax exemption is pro rated based on the ratio of an individual's U.S. assets to worldwide assets. Certificates of deposit with U.S. banks are not included in the taxable estate for non U.S. citizens.

21-42.   An additional estate tax exemption is available where property passes to a spouse on death. Further, a U.S. citizen can transfer up to $100,000 U.S. of assets each year to his non U.S. citizen spouse without any gift tax liability or erosion of the estate tax exemption. Similarly, a U.S. gift tax exclusion allows U.S. citizens to make annual gifts of up to $10,000 each to other family members. These transfers allow a U.S. citizen to significantly reduce eventual U.S. estate tax. Effective estate planning, sometimes involving transfers to corporations and trusts, in addition to transfers to family members, can minimize or defer U.S. federal estate tax.

21-43.   U.S. estate tax can be claimed as a foreign tax credit in Canada to reduce tax otherwise payable on the deemed disposition of assets on death. However, for U.S. citizens, the credit is not based on the U.S. estate tax assessed by the IRS. Rather, it is based on what would have been paid if the deceased taxpayer were not a U.S. citizen. This is usually much lower that the amount assessed by the IRS. As the foreign tax credit limitation can result in double taxation, the competent authorities from both jurisdictions need to review this policy with a view to eliminating double taxation prospectively.

> Exercise Twenty-One-3 deals with U.S. estate taxes. This would be an appropriate time to attempt this exercise.

Becoming a Non Resident

General Rules

21-44.   There are many factors that must be considered when an individual becomes a non resident, a determination that is crucial for income tax purposes. It will have an influence on the amount of income to be included in the individual's Canadian tax return and, in many cases, becoming a non resident will trigger a number of deemed dispositions.

21-45.   A Canadian resident generally becomes a non resident on the latest of the following days:

- on leaving Canada
- when a spouse and/or dependants leave Canada
- on becoming a resident of another country

21-46.   For the individual who leaves Canada and does not return, the preceding rules represent the end of the story. However, as was discussed in Chapter 2, if the absence is temporary, there may be a presumption that the individual did not cease to be a resident, leaving him subject to Canadian taxation during his absence. IT-221R2 indicates that, if the absence from Canada is for less than two years, the individual is deemed to retain Canadian residence status. If the absence is for longer than two years, the individual will be treated as a non resident, provided he severs all social and economic ties with Canada. To be considered a non resident in these circumstances, an individual should ensure that:

- a spouse and minor children also become non residents;
- if minor children remain in Canada, they should do so only for educational purposes;
- all assets in Canada are sold or otherwise disposed of, including any residences, other real property and automobiles;
- all economic ties (e.g., bank and investment accounts, credit cards) in Canada are severed;
- social and professional ties (e.g., club memberships, professional associations, athletic clubs) in Canada are severed;
- no contributions are made to pension plans in Canada;
- director and other management functions in Canada are discontinued and declined; and
- all personal and family representations to friends, business associates and government agencies should be as non residents.

Deemed Disposition at Departure

21-47.   The most significant tax event resulting from becoming a non resident is the application of the deemed disposition rules under ITA 128.1. These are often referred to as Canada's departure tax. Emigrants from Canada are deemed to have disposed of almost all property owned, including taxable Canadian property, immediately before their departure.

21-48.   The deemed disposition rules on departure exclude certain capital property such as Canadian real estate, Canadian business assets, stock options, property of short-term residents, pensions and certain other entitlements (e.g., RRSPs, annuities and future benefits). When the property is eventually disposed of, any gains will be taxed under Part I (personal or corporate income tax), and any pension and other entitlements paid will be subject to withholding taxes under Part XIII.

21-49.   In effect, every emigrant has to determine his Canadian tax liability on accrued capital gains on most assets held upon departure from Canada. The departure tax can be paid immediately, or emigrants have the option of giving the CCRA security and paying the tax later, without interest charges, when the property is actually sold. Different or less security than would normally be required, may be accepted in circumstances of undue hardship. Individual emigrants do not need to provide security on the first $50,000 of taxable income.

21-50.   Fortunately, post-emigration losses can be applied against deemed departure gains, and Canada will also allow foreign tax credits for post emigration taxes paid on the gains in another country. Special provisions allow for the unwinding of deemed disposition gains when an individual departs from Canada and later returns. Finally, short-term residents (less than five years of residence in the preceding ten years) are exempt from the departure tax rules for assets owned upon arrival in Canada and inherited foreign assets.

21-51.   In anticipation of a taxpayer becoming a non resident, anti avoidance measures prevent a tax deferred transfer to a trust that is made to avoid the departure tax rules. The deemed disposition rules will apply when the individual ceases to reside in Canada, irrespective of the trust transfer. In this way, the departure tax rules cannot be avoided. Likewise, an individual cannot convert what would be a capital gain, which would ordinarily be subject to Part I tax, to a trust distribution that is subject to Part XIII tax.

21-52.   Foreign reporting obligations extend to all individuals who leave Canada and who own property with a value of more than $25,000 on the departure date. All property holdings at that date must be reported on an information return (Form T1161) as per ITA 128.1(8). This information is attached to the personal income tax return for the year they leave Canada. An exception is made for any personal use property, for example, clothing, household goods and vehicles, with a value of less than $10,000.

Tax Planning When Becoming A Non Resident

21-53.   Aside from careful attention to factors influencing residency status, the following tax planning opportunities exist when an individual is becoming a non resident:

- **Employment income**   Employment income is taxed only when the income is received. If there is some flexibility regarding when employment income is received, consider deferring the income until a subsequent calendar year. Employment income earned in Canada might be the only income to be reported that year for Canadian income tax purposes. If so, the benefit of low marginal Canadian tax rates can be obtained in the new year when the individual is a non resident.

- **Moving expenses**   Expenses associated with a move to a foreign country are not deductible in Canada. It may be advantageous to have a foreign employer reimburse moving expenses rather than pay an equivalent salary amount or signing bonus. The reimbursement of reasonable moving expenses is not taxable, but an equivalent salary would be taxable in Canada.

- **Stock options**   Non residents who exercise stock options for both private and public corporations granted prior to departure will be subject to tax in Canada upon exercise or sale, even if the option is exercised after becoming a non resident. (For a more detailed discussion of the tax implications of stock options for non residents, refer to Paragraph 12-36.)

- **Business income**   A non resident is subject to tax on all income from a business carried on in Canada. If the business is carried on after departure, the part year residence provisions will not apply to the business income.

- **Capital gains**   Before becoming a non resident, capital gains, in some situations, should be triggered, even though the asset may not be disposed of. For example, where there are accrued capital gains on Canadian real estate, realizing the gains can be useful to offset any loss carry forwards. As well, a bumped up cost base may be beneficial to avoid eventual tax on the accrued gain in the foreign country. For individuals holding either qualified farm property or shares of a qualified small business corporation, any unrealized gains should be triggered in order to use the $500,000 lifetime capital gains deduction. This planning point is very important as the capital gains deduction is not available once an individual becomes a non resident.

- **Dispositions of Taxable Canadian Property**   Another consideration when becoming a non resident is the potential tax that will apply to subsequent dispositions of taxable Canadian property. Purchasers of taxable Canadian property from non residents are required to withhold tax based on the purchase price of the property further to ITA 116(5). The required federal tax withholding is 25 percent of the gross purchase price, and applicable provincial taxes must also be withheld. For example, if an asset is sold for $100,000, federal withholdings of $25,000 would be required and, assuming a 15 percent provincial tax rate, another $15,000 would be withheld. In total, $40,000 would be withheld, regardless of what the cost base of the asset is. These remittances, based on gross proceeds, can be particularly burdensome when the inherent gain is small. In such instances, requests can be made under ITA 116 to base the withholding tax on the estimated gain instead of the gross proceeds. If in the above example, the cost base of the asset is $80,000 and the resulting $20,000 gain is a business gain, an ITA 116 certificate should be requested in advance of the disposition. Then, the required withholdings would be federal taxes of $5,000 [($20,000)(25%)] and provincial taxes of $3,000 [($20,000)(15%)]. The resulting cash flow savings of $32,000 ($40,000 - $5,000 - $3,000) makes obtaining an ITA 116 certificate very worthwhile.

- **Principal residence**   An important consideration is whether or not to sell a principal residence located in Canada. As a principal residence is Canadian real estate, the deemed disposition rules will not apply. Instead, the decision may influence residency status. Also, it is important to consider what will happen when the residence is eventually sold, and how any rental income will be taxed in the intervening period. If the home was designated as a principal residence, no income taxes are payable on the appreciation during the years the individual was resident in Canada. If an individual becomes a resident of the U.S., under the Canada/U.S. convention there is a deemed disposition and reacquisition of a principal residence at fair market value on the date residency changes. When the home is eventually sold, only the gain earned after becoming a resident of the U.S. will be taxable in the U.S. This is the only case where the U.S. recognizes a bumped up cost base without an actual disposition of a capital asset.

- **Rental income**   Where property in Canada is rented from a non resident, a Part XIII tax of 25 percent of the gross rent will apply. This tax is a fixed rate tax and is not a withholding tax to be credited against taxes that will become payable when a tax return is filed. The tax rate may be reduced by relevant international tax conventions. As the Part XIII tax can be burdensome when there are substantial related costs like interest and property taxes, non residents can elect under ITA 216(1) to have a withholding tax apply to net rents (after expenses). When this election is made, the estimated rental income must be reported on a Form NR6, "An Undertaking to File an Income Tax Return by a Non Resident Receiving Rent from Real Property or Receiving a Timber Royalty". A separate Section 216 tax return (T1 or T2, depending on whether the non resident is an individual or a corporation) is also required to report actual net income and Part I tax payable. Where the non resident is an individual, or a corporation with a December 31 year end, the due date for filing a return under ITA 216 is generally June 30 of the following year.

- **Investment income**   A general Part XIII tax of 25 percent applies to passive income payments to non residents. However, this rate is reduced under most of Canada's international tax treaties. For example, under the revised Canada/U.S. convention, the withholding tax rates are as follows:

Dividends (Article X)	15%
Intercorporate dividends (Note 1)	5%
Interest (Article XI)	10%
Interest on government and foreign securities (Note 2)	0%
Royalties (Note 3)	0 or 10%

Note 1   Intercorporate dividends, where at least 10 percent of the voting shares are owned by a Canadian company, are subject to a reduced withholding rate of 5 percent pursuant to Article X.

Note 2   Interest payments may be exempted from withholding tax in Article XI. Exemptions apply to interest earned on government and foreign investments, including government bonds, Canada Savings Bonds, municipal bonds, Treasury Bills, Canadian dollar deposits in foreign branches of Canadian banks, and foreign currency deposits in Canadian banks. Before becoming a non resident, an individual may want to invest in these types of investments to avoid withholding taxes on income earned subsequently.

Note 3   Royalties may be exempt from withholding under Article XII. Exemptions for royalties include most copyright royalties, payments for use of computer software, fees for patent information and broadcasting fees. However, payments for information connected with a rental or franchise agreement are subject to Part XIII taxes.

- **RRSPs and RRIFs**   If an RRSP is collapsed before departure, the entire RRSP amount will be taxable in Canada at the individual's marginal income tax rates. Whereas, if an RRSP is collapsed after departure, a tax of 25 percent applies to the amounts withdrawn. The withholding tax is reduced to 15 percent on periodic payments from an RRSP (or RRIF). When a Canadian becomes a resident of the U.S., the current value of an RRSP is considered capital and may be received tax-free for U.S. purposes. However, the RRSP is considered a grantor trust in the U.S. and income earned in the RRSP is taxable as the income accrues unless an election to defer tax on income is made under the Canada/U.S. convention. For RRSP contributions by non residents and new residents of Canada, the regular RRSP deduction limits apply as do the deadlines for contributions to plans. In the year of entry, an RRSP deduction is not normally available as the allowable deduction is limited by the prior year's Canadian-source earned income. Some amounts received from foreign retirement arrangements, such as Individual Retirement Accounts (IRAs) in the U.S., can be rolled into RRSPs on a tax deferred basis.

- **Old Age Security**   Non residents of Canada who are OAS recipients must file a statement of worldwide income to continue to receive OAS benefits. Non residents with worldwide incomes above $55,309 are subject to the social benefits recovery (clawback) requirements for OAS. The recovery amounts are withheld monthly, based on the previous year's income. If no statement of worldwide income is filed, the full amount of OAS will be withheld. Under the Canada/U.S. tax convention, social security benefits are taxed in the country of residence, only. OAS, Canada Pension Plan and Quebec Pension Plan payments to U.S. residents are taxable only in the U.S. U.S. residents who receive OAS benefits are not subject to the OAS clawback. To adjust for differences between U.S. and Canadian tax rates, Canadian residents include in taxable income only 85 percent of U.S. social security that is received in a year. The other 15 percent is exempt from tax.

- **Election to report income in Canada**   A special election is available under ITA 217 for non residents relating to income received from OAS, Canada Pension Plan (Quebec Pension Plan), RRSPs, RRIFs, Deferred Profit Sharing Plans and other pension plans, along with retiring allowances, death benefits and employment insurance. The election allows a non resident individual to report receipts from the above sources in Canada, and to apply Part I tax to the reported income. Further, personal tax credits may be claimed if more than 90 percent of the individual's income is taxable or is elected to be taxable in Canada. This election is only available to individuals who are non residents for the entire calendar year. The election may be advantageous if the effective tax rate on the income in Canada will be less than the Part XIII withholding tax that would otherwise apply to the amounts paid. Generally, the election is only beneficial to a taxpayer with no other income.

> Exercises Twenty-One-4 and 5 deal with departures from Canada. This would be an appropriate time to attempt these exercises.

Foreign Investments

Foreign Investment Reporting

21-54.   As noted in Chapter 2, Procedures and Administration, reporting requirements apply to foreign investments totalling more than $100,000 held by Canadian residents. These reporting obligations are intended to discourage Canadians from concealing assets offshore in foreign trusts, corporations or other investments.

21-55.   Canadian taxpayers and partnerships are required to file an information return to report specified assets situated outside Canada, if the total cost exceeds $100,000 at any time in the year. A "check-the-box" reporting format requires taxpayers to indicate the range and location of different categories of foreign property investments, and the total income earned in the year from the investments. Most foreign assets, including passive investments like bank accounts, real property and shares must be disclosed. Related debt cannot be deducted from the cost of assets in determining the total cost. However, several types of property need not be disclosed, including personal-use property that is used primarily for the enjoyment of the taxpayer or the taxpayer's family, RRSPs, and assets used in an active business.

21-56.   The information return for reporting foreign investments, the Foreign Income Verification Statement (T1135), confirms that the principal purposes of the form are to encourage reporting of foreign income and provide information to enable the CCRA to audit the income sources.

21-57.   Beneficiaries of non resident trusts are required to file an information return for each year. Taxpayers that have a beneficial interest in a non resident trust, or that receive a distribution from the trust, must file an annual return in respect of the trust. In addition, taxpayers that have transferred or loaned property to a non resident trust need to file an annual information return.

21-58.   Taxpayers with investments in foreign affiliates must provide detailed information for each affiliate, regardless of the amount of the investment. A foreign affiliate is a non resident corporation in which a Canadian taxpayer or partnership owns more than 1 percent of the shares of any class and, together with a related group, owns more than 10 percent of the

Exercise Twenty-One-6 deals with foreign investment reporting. This would be an appropriate time to attempt this exercise.

shares of any class. All foreign affiliate investments held must be reported within 18 months of the taxpayer's year end.

21-59.   Substantial penalties, starting at $500 per month to a maximum of $24,000, plus five percent of the cost of unreported foreign property, will result if the foreign investment reporting requirements for foreign assets and trust transactions are not complied with.

Income From Foreign Affiliates

21-60.   A rather complex area of taxation is the foreign affiliate system which addresses income earned by Canadian residents that invest in foreign corporations. The basic policy objectives of the foreign affiliate rules are twofold. The first objective is to allow Canadian corporations to compete internationally, by alleviating the double taxation of foreign corporate earnings paid as dividends to Canadian corporations. The second objective is to tax Canadian taxpayers currently on passive income earned by investing in foreign corporations, typically in an offshore tax haven. Whether the foreign affiliate's income is active or passive is the main factor in determining when the income is taxable in Canada. The foreign affiliate rules apply regardless of whether the investments are made by individuals, trusts or corporations.

21-61.   First, we will summarize the tax treatment of dividends received from foreign corporations, which differs depending on whether or not the non resident corporation is a foreign affiliate. Next, we will review the taxation of passive income earned through a foreign corporation. Integral to this section is whether the non resident corporation is a "controlled" foreign affiliate.

21-62.   A foreign affiliate is defined in ITA 95(1) as a non resident corporation in which a Canadian taxpayer has an equity percentage of at least 1 percent. As well, the aggregate equity percentages of the taxpayer and each person related to the taxpayer must be at least 10 percent. The ownership percentage can be established either on a direct or indirect basis, and is defined as the greatest percentage holding in any class of the non resident corporation's capital stock.

21-63.   Consider a Canadian corporation (CanCo) that owns 70 percent of the only class of shares of a non resident corporation (OffshoreCo-1). In turn, OffshoreCo-1 owns 20 percent of the only class of shares of another non resident corporation (OffshoreCo-2). OffshoreCo-1 is a foreign affiliate of CanCo because of the 70 percent direct ownership. OffshoreCo-2 is also a foreign affiliate of CanCo as the indirect ownership is 14 percent [(20%)(70%)], which exceeds the required 10 percent ownership.

21-64.   Most dividends received from foreign affiliates are included in net income and deducted in computing taxable income under ITA 113. This effectively exempts them from tax. However, a full dividend deduction is not automatic and can only be claimed if:

- the dividend is received from a foreign affiliate;
- the dividend is paid out of active business income; or
- the business was conducted in country with which Canada has an international tax convention (known as a designated treaty country).

21-65.   The above dividend deduction is similar to the ITA 112(1) deduction for taxable dividends received by Canadian corporations. This deduction is allowed as a recognition that dividends are an after-tax distribution of corporate profits, and ensures that no further corporate tax is assessed on such earnings. The rationale for not taxing active business earnings of foreign affiliates also relates to a need for Canadian firms to be competitive in the international business environment. If a Canadian firm is burdened with a Canadian tax liability over and above any applicable domestic tax liability, the Canadian firm may not be competitive and may be unable to take advantage of potential international business opportunities.

21-66.   Dividends received from corporations that are not foreign affiliates are taxable in Canada when received. Similarly, dividends received out of the active business earnings of foreign affiliates are taxable if the business is not conducted in a designated treaty country. In both cases, the income is taxable in Canada not as it is earned (accrued), but rather when it is repatriated as dividends. As the dividends are not exempt from Canadian tax, foreign tax credits are allowed to reduce any related Canadian corporate tax.

Controlled Foreign Affiliates and Foreign Accrual Property Income (FAPI)

General Rules

21-67.   The preceding approach to the taxation of foreign affiliates could allow income on passive investments to be sheltered in tax haven parts of the world, where the level of taxation is either minimal or nonexistent. If a foreign affiliate is controlled by Canadian residents, the shareholders can easily shift the passive income of a foreign affiliate, for example interest, to a tax haven, to avoid current taxation on the property income. For this reason, the Foreign Accrual Property Income (FAPI, hereafter) rules ensure that passive income of controlled foreign affiliates is taxed in Canada as the income is earned or accrued, not when it is distributed.

21-68.   In simplified terms, FAPI is the passive income of a controlled foreign affiliate. FAPI includes income from property and taxable capital gains. With the exception of rental income, income from property is usually distinguished by the fact that its geographic source is easily moved from one tax jurisdiction to another.

21-69.   The FAPI rules prevent a controlled foreign affiliate from using the mobility of property income to reduce Canadian taxes payable. Control of a foreign affiliate is defined in ITA 95(1). A foreign affiliate is deemed to be controlled by the taxpayer if that taxpayer and not more than four other persons, or a related group of which the taxpayer is a member, has voting control. Evidence of control is the direct or indirect ownership of more than 50 percent of the outstanding voting shares of the affiliate. Where a foreign affiliate is controlled by Canadian residents, investments in tax havens cannot be used to avoid or defer Canadian taxes.

21-70.   The property income definition for FAPI includes income from a foreign investment business. This income is comparable to income earned from a specified investment business, (see Chapter 14). The principal purpose of a specified investment business is to derive income from property, including interest, dividends, rent or royalties. Earnings from a specified investment business are excluded from the definition of active business in calculating the small business deduction for corporations. The specified investment business concept has been extended to include businesses operating outside of Canada. Income from a foreign investment business is taxable in Canada as it is earned and is not exempt as is the case with foreign active business income. However, under rules similar to the specified investment business rules, a foreign affiliate that employs more than the equivalent of five employees full-time in earning income from property is deemed to earn active business income. This "five-employee" exception is especially important in deciding whether foreign rental income is active (exempt from the FAPI rules) or passive (to be reported as FAPI).

21-71.   In determining whether the FAPI rules apply, three questions need to be asked. First, is the foreign corporation a foreign affiliate? To be a foreign affiliate, the taxpayer must own more than 1 percent of any class of shares of the foreign corporation and the total of the equity percentages of the taxpayer and related persons cannot be less than 10 percent. Second, is the corporation a controlled foreign affiliate? To be so classified, the taxpayer and not more than four other persons, or a related group of which the taxpayer is a member, must control the voting shares of the foreign affiliate. Third, is income from an investment business or other passive income earned by the controlled foreign affiliate? Affirmative answers to each question lead to the conclusion that FAPI is earned.

21-72.   Canadian residents are required to report FAPI of controlled foreign affiliates in excess of $5,000. The $5,000 exemption figure recognizes that the computation of FAPI is quite complex and should not be required when the amount of income is small. As FAPI income is taxed as it accrues, dividends paid out of such income are not taxable.

	Figure 21 - 1	
	Summary of Tax Treatment of Foreign Affiliate Income	
Type of Underlying Foreign Affiliate Income	**Canadian Tax Effect**	**Surplus Account**
Passive income	FAPI Accrue (flow through) undistributed income. Taxable in Canada when earned. Claim foreign tax credit.	Taxable surplus
Active business income not earned in a designated treaty country.	Not FAPI Taxable in Canada when dividend received. Claim foreign tax credit.	Taxable surplus
Active business income earned in a designated treaty country.	Not FAPI Exempt from Canadian tax as earned. Also, exempt when repatriated to Canada.	Exempt surplus

21-73. A summary of the Canadian tax effects of earning various types of income by a foreign affiliate is found in Figure 21-1. As you will see in the next section, surplus accounts are used to track income earned in foreign affiliates.

FAPI Calculations

21-74. To calculate FAPI, the surplus accounts (retained earnings) of foreign affiliates are segregated into three categories. Each surplus calculation is separate for each shareholder in a foreign affiliate, as there are different starting points based on different investment dates. The amounts should initially be calculated in the foreign currency of the affiliate. Further, the surplus amounts can be positive or negative. The three surplus categories for foreign affiliates, described in simplified terms, are as follows:

Exempt Surplus This balance includes net income earned between 1972 and 1975, plus post 1975 active business income and the tax exempt portion of net capital gains. The active business income of the foreign affiliate does not include investment income and losses (FAPI), and the related foreign income taxes. Taxpayers may elect to use book rather than tax depreciation to calculate active business income. Note that the earnings must be from an active business carried on in a designated treaty country, but the foreign affiliate may be resident in any country.

The exempt income, which is the annual addition to exempt surplus, includes active business income and the tax exempt portion of net capital gains. However, if a capital gain is realized from the disposition of shares of a foreign affiliate, and the underlying gain relates to assets used in an active business, the capital gain is left in exempt income and is not considered FAPI. Exempt income is not taxable in Canada. Generally, dividends are deemed to be paid from this surplus category, first. While dividends paid out of exempt surplus are included in income of Canadian residents under ITA 90, they are also fully deductible under ITA 113. As a result, the dividends are not taxed.

Taxable Surplus This balance includes post 1975 passive income (earlier described as FAPI). To FAPI is added active business income from a business not carried on in a designated treaty country (not included in Exempt Surplus). Finally, the taxable portion (one-half) of net capital gains earned on investment assets is included in taxable surplus. Dividends paid out of the non FAPI portion of Taxable Surplus will be included in income under ITA 90 but will give rise to a deduction based on foreign taxes paid. This generally has the effect of eliminating all such dividends from taxable income where foreign taxes are equal to or greater than the relevant Canadian taxes. Any portion of the dividend that was previously taxed as FAPI is not taxable when the dividend is finally received to avoid double taxation of the underlying income.

Figure 21 - 2
FAPI Example

| | Amounts In Canadian Dollars | | |
| | Taxable | Foreign | Net |
Sources Of Income For OffshoreCo.	Income	Tax Payable	Earnings
Passive investment income	$ 325	$ 75	$ 250
Capital gain on passive asset	260	50	210
Capital gain on shares of foreign affiliate (active business)	400	90	310
Active business income	550	100	450
Totals	$1,535	$315	$1,220

FAPI (taxable income in Canada when earned)		Exempt Income (not taxable in Canada when earned or received)	
		Active business income	$450
Passive investment income	$250	Capital gain - passive (1/2)	105
Capital gain - passive (1/2)	105	Capital gain - foreign affiliate	310
Addition to taxable surplus	$390	Addition to exempt surplus	$865

Pre-acquisition Surplus   This balance consists of amounts of both active and passive income earned before the foreign investee qualified as a foreign affiliate.   The pre-acquisition surplus amount is not taxable in Canada. Dividends paid out of pre-acquisition surplus are included in income under ITA 90 but are fully deductible under ITA 113. Also, any dividends reduce the adjusted cost base of the investment.

21-75.   The example in Figure 21-2 shows how the surplus categories are used in the calculation of FAPI. The example assumes that the foreign taxes are deducted from each source of income and that the net amounts are added to the surplus pools. Technically, the allocation of foreign taxes is formula-based, and is more complex than in the example.

21-76.   While the FAPI procedures are complex, they accomplish the desired goal. They avoid double taxation and eliminate Canadian taxation on dividends received from foreign affiliates out of income taxed at rates which would have prevailed in Canada. In cases where a foreign affiliate's passive income has attracted abnormally low rates of taxation, the rules provide for additional taxation on amounts earned by Canadian investors. The additional taxes are payable as the income is earned, not when it is repatriated to Canada at a later date.

21-77.   The Canadian public perceives that foreign affiliates are used to avoid Canadian income taxes. While this perception is questionable, and some say unfounded, the determination of FAPI is gradually expanding to include all types of property income, so that active business income (exempt income) is reduced. As well, the countries in which foreign affiliates can earn exempt earnings are restricted to countries with which Canada has signed international tax conventions.

Transfer Pricing

21-78.   As business is increasingly conducted on a global scale, an understanding of the subject of transfer pricing becomes more important. Transfer pricing relates to the prices at which services and property are traded across international borders between non arm's length parties. The procedures used to set these prices can have a tremendous impact on the amount of income that is allocated to particular business entities, as well as to individual countries. There are obvious incentives to use these procedures in a manner that will allocate income to jurisdictions where tax rates are low.

21-79. We will focus on intercorporate transactions between resident and non resident parties that are non arm's length, including foreign affiliates. In setting transfer prices for intercorporate transactions, Canada embodies the internationally accepted "arm's length principle". Stated simply, this principle states that the prices used for transfers between non arm's length parties should be based on the best indication of the prices that would be used for transfers between unrelated parties.

21-80. Transfer pricing methods used must be noted on the T106 information return that reports non arm's length transactions with non resident persons. This return is required by corporations, partnerships, trusts and individuals if the capital and income related transactions with all non arm's length entities, in total, exceed $1 million. If reporting is required, a T106 form should be completed for every non arm's length entity with which the Canadian taxpayer transacts, regardless of the dollar volume of the transactions with each entity.

21-81. Three transfer pricing methods are commonly used, as outlined on the T106 form. The comparable, uncontrolled price (CUP) method is preferred as it establishes the price as it would be set in the same market and circumstances by arm's length parties. The cost plus method relies on GAAP to determine the cost of goods, to which an appropriate markup is added. This method is most relevant where semi-finished goods are sold or services are provided. The resale price method is often used when there are no comparable prices available and little value is added to the product. In determining the transfer price, the nominal costs and a reasonable profit margin should be deducted from the resale price. Other acceptable methods include the cost of materials, full production cost and replacement value. However, these methods are likely to be more carefully scrutinized by the CCRA.

21-82. Following the lead of the U.S. and other OECD countries, important changes to transfer pricing policies were introduced in Canada in 1997. While detailed transfer pricing rules have not been legislated, the arm's length standard is vigorously adopted in ITA 247(2) and IC 87-2R. As well, new requirements were introduced for taxpayers to create and maintain appropriate documentation on the determination of and methods used for transfer prices. Substantial penalties will be levied where proper documentation is not maintained and where taxpayers do not diligently establish transfer prices.

21-83. A survey conducted by Ernst & Young in 1999 reported that 61 percent of multi-national enterprises indicated that transfer pricing was the most important international tax issue facing them. This survey demonstrates how significant the move toward arm's length transfer pricing is for businesses. Complying with the new pricing requirements and preparing the detailed documentation involves a major worldwide coordination of teams of economists, accountants and tax specialists. In many businesses, the transfer pricing conversion and compliance costs are very significant. Relatively small multi-national enterprises are expected to spend more than $500,000 each in this process.

Taxation of Non Residents

21-84. While a Canadian resident is subject to Canadian income tax on worldwide income, a non resident is subject to Canadian tax only on Canadian source income. Specifically, ITA 2(3) requires Part I income tax to be payable in Canada by a non resident person who:

(a) was employed in Canada
(b) carried on a business in Canada, or
(c) disposed of a Taxable Canadian Property.

21-85. For non residents earning any of the above sources of income, great potential exists for double taxation. This results from the two fundamental principles of international taxation — the right of a country to tax income earned within its boundaries combined with the right of a country to tax worldwide income of its residents, regardless of where the income is earned. Fortunately, any Canadian tax paid on such income can usually be claimed as a foreign tax credit in the individual's country of residence.

Employment in Canada

21-86. Where a non resident individual is employed and reports to work in Canada, regular withholding of income tax at source will apply to the wages or salary. The withholdings represent instalment payments towards an estimated Canadian tax liability to be established later. If the ultimate liability does not equal the instalments paid, refunds will be available or additional payments will be required.

21-87. An individual is required to report employment income in a Canadian personal tax return, and pay Canadian income tax at the standard progressive personal tax rates. Personal tax credits under ITA 118 through 118.9 can be claimed if substantially all (more than 90 percent) of worldwide income is reported in Canada. These include credits for the basic personal amount, disability amount, Employment Insurance premiums, Canada Pension Plan contributions, medical expenses, tuition fees and the education amount.

21-88. Contemporary employment arrangements are now being arranged where, for example, employees work from their homes in the U.S. for Canadian employers. A shortage of specially trained employees in Canada and widespread access to telecommunications make it possible for employees to never physically report to work in Canada. Canadian tax law did not anticipate these employment situations and considerable uncertainty surrounds where such individuals are employed and whether or not Canadian taxation applies to the employment income.

21-89. Where a U.S. resident is employed in Canada, the Canada/U.S. convention (Article XV) states that the employee will not be taxable in Canada if:

- remuneration from employment in Canada does not exceed $10,000 Canadian in a year, or
- the individual is present in Canada for 183 days or less, and the remuneration is not borne by a Canadian employer or by a fixed base or permanent establishment of a non resident employer. However, this treaty exemption does not apply where a non resident corporation charges back the remuneration to a Canadian subsidiary. The CCRA also takes the position that the treaty exemption does not apply if the Canadian subsidiary directs the employee on a day-to-day basis.

21-90. U.S. resident artists and athletes that perform or compete in Canada may be exempt from Canadian income tax under the employment income exemption, as outlined above, or if their gross proceeds in a calendar year do not exceed $15,000 Canadian. This rule does not apply to athletes employed by a team which participates in a league with regularly scheduled games in both countries.

21-91. An additional exemption applies to inducement payments. If a Canadian resident pays a U.S. resident an "inducement to sign an agreement relating to the performance of the services of an athlete," the amount will be taxed at a maximum rate of 15 percent in Canada. This means that if the Part I taxes that would otherwise be payable in Canada on the inducement result in less than a 15 percent effective tax rate, then the lower amount will be payable. These rules for artists and athletes are contained in Article XVI of the Canada/U.S. convention.

21-92. Reciprocal rules apply when a Canadian resident is employed, or performs as an artist or athlete, in the U.S. However, the exemptions are stated in U.S. rather than Canadian dollars.

Disposition of Taxable Canadian Property

21-93. Where a non resident disposes of Taxable Canadian Property, any gain or loss must be reported in Canada in the year of disposition. Part I tax will apply to the net gain which may be a capital gain or business income. As well, personal credits can only be claimed if substantially all (more than 90 percent) of worldwide income is reported in Canada.

Carrying On A Business In Canada
General Rules
21-94.   When non residents begin carrying on a business in Canada, they often enter the market in a small and piecemeal way. Then, if successful, the level of activity expands and, with expansion, the organization becomes more formal. Typically, business activity moves from the simple form of travelling salespersons, to the more complex form of a subsidiary, in the following order:

1.   Direct sales activity through advertising and travelling salespersons.
2.   Independent agents contracted to make sales.
3.   Dependent agents, usually as employees.
4.   Branch of foreign corporation.
5.   Independent subsidiary.

21-95.   The preference for a particular form of organization is dependent on many tax and non tax factors, such as access to capital, market intensity, type of income earned and existence of losses. A comprehensive discussion of the tax issues associated with carrying on business in Canada under these various forms of organization is beyond the scope of this book. Reflecting this, we will limit our review to the taxation issues associated with the general concept of carrying on a business in Canada.

21-96.   A non resident is liable for Canadian income tax on business income earned while "carrying on a business in Canada" or which is attributable to a "permanent establishment" in Canada under Canada's international tax conventions. We will begin by discussing the issue of carrying on a business in Canada, followed by a review what constitutes a permanent establishment.

Meaning of "Carrying On A Business"
21-97.   In order to determine whether a non resident is carrying on a business in Canada, the first question that must be answered is whether the non resident is carrying on a business. Business includes ongoing commercial activities and adventures in the nature of trade. Generally, a reasonable expectation of earning a profit must exist. There is a presumption that corporations are carrying on a business, particularly if the business activities fall within the objects for the corporation. Making passive investments, which earn property income or capital gains, and earning employment income are excluded from the definition of carrying on a business.

21-98.   Amounts earned in Canada by a non resident from carrying on a business must be distinguished from income from property. This differentiation is important for determining whether Part I income tax or Part XIII withholding tax applies. In this respect, the CCRA has issued the following guideline in IT-420R3:

> Where doubt exists as to the nature of the income earned in Canada, a determination
> will have to be made based on the facts of the case. Generally, the degree of activity,
> i.e., the time, attention and labour expended by the non resident in earning the in-
> come, is the major factor. Little or no related activity indicates income from property,
> whereas significant activity indicates that a business is being carried on.

Meaning of "In Canada"
21-99.   If the activity is considered to be a business activity, the second question then becomes whether the business is being carried on in Canada. To be taxable, the business must be carried on within the geographical boundaries of Canada. This comprises the land mass of Canada, and all water and air space within a twelve nautical mile limit of Canada's coasts. As well, under ITA 255, a business relating to the exploration or drilling for any minerals, petroleum, natural gas or hydrocarbons is taxable if carried on in the sea bed, subsoil, seas, and airspace related to the continental shelf of Canada.

21-100.   A particular business can be connected to several places or countries. The courts have determined that the most important factor in assessing where a business is carried on is where contracts are made, in particular those related to sales.

21-101.   A business may also be carried on in the place where:

- the operations are located and profits arise;
- central management and control is located;
- goods are delivered;
- payments or purchases are made;
- goods are manufactured or produced;
- inventory is stored;
- branch office or agency is located;
- bank accounts are located;
- business is listed in a telephone directory; or
- agents or employees are located.

21-102.   The rendering of services in Canada usually indicates that a business is being carried on. However, the provision of technical services in Canada, which are ancillary to sales by a non resident firm, do not normally constitute the carrying on of business in Canada. This would occur, for example, when machinery or equipment is purchased outside of Canada from a non resident, but start up and technical support is provided in Canada.

21-103.   In referring back to the forms of organizations used to carry on business in a foreign country, we can conclude that even the activities of travelling salespersons and independent agents may be considered to be carrying on a business using the preceding guidelines. The most important criterion in assessing whether an individual is carrying on a business is if there is authority to approve sales contracts, further to points raised in the next section. However, to simplify administration of tax systems, the concept of permanent establishment is used to narrow the scope of taxable business activities.

Permanent Establishments

21-104.   To be taxable, most international tax conventions also require a business to be carried on in a "permanent establishment" in a particular country. The OECD Model Convention defines permanent establishment as a "fixed place of business through which the business of an enterprise is wholly or partly carried on". Accordingly, a place of business is located where premises, facilities, or machinery and equipment used for carrying on the business of the enterprise are located. The word "permanent" implies that a temporary place of business would not qualify.

21-105.   The OECD Model Convention specifies that a permanent establishment includes a place of management, a branch, an office, a factory, a workshop, a mine, an oil or gas well, a quarry or any other place of extraction of natural resources. As further clarification, it specifies that a "building site or construction project or installation project constitutes a permanent establishment only if it lasts more than twelve months."

21-106.   Notwithstanding the above, the term permanent establishment is deemed not to include:

- use of facilities solely for storage, display or delivery of goods;
- maintenance of a stock of goods or merchandise for storage, display or delivery;
- maintenance of a fixed place of business solely for purchasing goods or merchandise or of collecting information; or
- maintenance of a fixed place of business solely for the purpose of carrying on any other activity of a preparatory or auxiliary character.

21-107.   E-business is challenging conventional thinking about permanent establishments. Can a non resident that sells goods and services to Canadian customers through a website be considered to be carrying on business through a permanent establishment in Canada? This decision impacts income, GST and provincial sales tax decisions. At this point, informal CCRA rulings conclude that a non resident conducting business on the Internet, but with no physical presence in Canada, is not conducting business in Canada, even if the web site is housed on a server in Canada that is owned by the non resident. This position is controversial, and the question of whether or not a server can constitute a permanent establishment will continue to be shrouded in uncertainty for some time yet. Relevant questions include whether or not human intervention is required before a server can constitute a fixed place of business, and, if so, does the intervention have to physically take place at the server's location or can it be remote? Is an employer-employee relationship critical? At this point, a case by case analysis of all of the relevant facts is necessary to make an informed decision.

21-108. Where Canada has an international tax convention with a country, reference should be made to the particular convention for specifics of what constitutes a permanent establishment. In the Canada/U.S. convention, the definition of permanent establishment is included in Article V, which follows the OECD model definition, as outlined previously.

Non Resident Corporations Carrying On Business In Canada

21-109. Non residents that earn profits from carrying on business in Canada, employment income and the disposition of taxable Canadian property are taxable under Part I of the *Act*. These sources of income are also reported by individuals, corporations or trusts that are resident in Canada. For individuals, whether resident or non resident, Part I personal taxes are the final income tax on any income earned. However, when corporate profits are paid to shareholders as dividends, the payments are subject to Part I corporate tax if the shareholders are resident in Canada and to Part XIII tax if the shareholders are non residents.

21-110. Non residents usually carry on business in Canada through a subsidiary established as a separate corporation, but they can also use the more informal arrangement of a branch operation. If the non resident's operations are conducted using a branch, the profits will be taxable under Part I, assuming the business is carried on through a permanent establishment. But, unlike dividends paid to non residents, the after-tax profits could be repatriated in their entirety to non resident shareholders were it not for a special branch profits tax. To compensate, all net branch profits earned in Canada by foreign corporations are taxable under Part XIV, unless the profits are reinvested in Canada.

21-111. A tax is levied under Part XIV (ITA 219 through ITA 219.3) on the net income of the branch. While the computation of branch income is a fairly complex matter, the Part XIV tax is levied at a rate of 25 percent of net branch profits. This tax is designed to tax the non resident owned branch on approximately the same basis as a non resident owned subsidiary that distributes dividends.

Passive Income Earned in Canada by Non Residents

The Nature Of Part XIII Tax

21-112. Passive income earned by non residents is taxable under Part XIII of the *Income Tax Act*. These payments include dividends, interest, management fees and rents. A tax of 25 percent applies to the gross amount of most passive income payments to non residents, but the rate is often reduced in international tax conventions. For a complete list of rates for various countries, see IC-76-12R4 and the related Addendum.

21-113. The Part XIII tax is withheld from payments to non residents and constitutes a tax levied immediately and completely at the time of withholding. This tax can be contrasted to the tax withheld from employment income, which is an interim tax levy with the final tax liability to be established separately. The Part XIII tax is levied at a flat rate on the gross amount of income and, except for a few special cases, no provision can be made for any expenses that have been incurred by the taxpayer.

21-114. With the exception of OAS receipts, the non resident is not required to file a Canadian tax return to report this income and, in normal circumstances, no additional payment is required nor any refund available in Canada. However, additional taxes may be payable in the country of residence depending on the domestic tax rates and the foreign tax credits allowed for Canadian taxes paid under Part XIII.

Liability for Part XIII Tax

21-115. Liability for Part XIII tax arises when a person resident in Canada pays or credits, to a non resident of Canada, an amount for one or more of the following types of income. While the following material gives detailed attention to various payments that are subject to Part XIII tax, the major items covered by this tax include:

- Interest, rents, and royalties;
- Dividends from corporations resident in Canada;
- Pension benefits and retiring allowances;
- Management or administration fees;
- Estate and trust income;
- Taxable portions of annuity payments; and
- Payments out of RRSPs, Registered Education Savings Plans and Deferred Profit Sharing Plans.

Interest

21-116. To be considered interest, a payment must be related to an obligation to pay a principal amount of money or a debt. Part XIII withholding applies to interest payments made to non residents. However, ITA 212(1)(b) exempts certain interest payments from Part XIII taxes. Some examples of these exemptions relate to interest payable to a non resident:

- by a resident corporation on an obligation issued after June 23, 1975, provided that the corporation may not be obliged to repay more than 25 percent of the principal amount within five years from the date of issue;

- on certain government and government guaranteed bonds;

- on a mortgage secured by real property located outside of Canada; or

- on certain payments in a currency other than Canadian currency to a person with whom the payer is dealing at arm's length.

21-117. Several other exemptions apply to the withholding of Part XIII tax on interest income. They are usually designed to encourage non residents to make certain types of investments in Canada.

Rents And Royalties

21-118. The general rule is that rents and royalties paid to non residents are subject to Part XIII withholding. Under ITA 212(1)(d), rents and royalties are deemed to include payments for the use, or the right to use in Canada, any property, invention, trade name, patent, trade mark, design or model, plan, secret formula, process, or other similar item. Also included in the definition are payments for information or services concerning industrial, commercial or scientific experience where the amount payable is at least partly dependent on the use of the information or the benefit to be derived from its use.

21-119. Rents, royalties or similar payments do not include payments for copyright use, bona fide cost-sharing arrangements or use of railway or common carriers. Similarly, payments for the use of capital property outside of Canada are excluded. As mentioned in the tax planning points when becoming a non resident, the Canada/U.S. convention exempts many types of royalty payments from withholding taxes.

21-120. In our discussion of the nature of Part XIII taxes, we noted that these taxes apply to gross payments with no general provision for the deduction of expenses related to the payment. This can be particularly onerous in the case of rental payments where the non resident lessor may be incurring substantial outflows for property taxes, maintenance, and financing charges on the rental property. To deal with this problem, ITA 216 provides for taxation on a net basis.

21-121. Under this alternative, the non resident may elect to file a Canadian tax return under Part I of the *Income Tax Act*. This return will be filed as though the taxpayer were a resident of Canada and the only income from Canada is rental income from real property and timber royalties. The taxpayer will be allowed to deduct all of the usual expenses available to a resident, including capital cost allowance on the rental property. However, no other deductions can be made in the calculation of taxable income and no personal tax credits can be used in determining taxes payable. To be valid, the tax return should be filed within six months of the end of the relevant taxation year. As well, if capital cost allowance is claimed, a taxpayer may be required to file an additional tax return in the year the rental property is disposed of. This return is separate from the return reporting any capital gain or loss on the disposition of taxable Canadian property.

21-122. In many situations, this alternative will reduce the Canadian tax liability on rental income earned by the non resident. However, since the tax rate under Part XIII is limited to a flat 25 percent, each situation requires careful examination of the complete tax consequences of the alternatives before a decision can be made. If the ITA 216 election is chosen, the taxpayer can claim a refund of Part XIII taxes withheld at the time the relevant tax return is filed. If the taxpayer will be making this election, a request may be filed for a reduction in the amount of Part XIII tax to be withheld.

Dividends
21-123. A Part XIII tax is generally applicable to dividends paid to non residents. In addition to regular dividends paid out of retained earnings, capital dividends, life insurance capital dividends and some stock dividends are also subject to the Part XIII tax. Note that capital dividends would not be subject to taxation if they were paid to a resident of Canada. Also, withholding is required in those situations where there is a deemed dividend on redemption of shares under ITA 84(3).

Pension Benefits
21-124. Most pension and superannuation payments to non residents are subject to Part XIII tax. In particular, Canada Pension Plan and Quebec Pension Plan payments are subject to a 25 percent withholding tax, as discussed in the planning points for becoming a non resident. The Canada/U.S. tax convention eliminated withholding tax for cross border payments of social security. As OAS payments to U.S. residents and U.S. social security payments to Canadian residents are only taxed in the recipient's country of residence, no withholding taxes are applied to such payments. Also, the following pensions are exempt from the withholding tax requirements:

- Pension benefit payments which are the result of services rendered in years during which the person was not resident or employed in Canada;

- Any portion of such payments that would be exempt from taxation if the recipient were a resident of Canada; and

- Pension benefits transferred to an RRSP or a Registered Pension Fund for the non resident.

21-125. As Part XIII taxes on pension payments may exceed the amount that would be paid if the taxpayer received the same amount as a resident of Canada, ITA 217 allows non resident taxpayers who receive Canadian pension benefits to elect to file as if they are Canadian residents. If this reporting results in a lower amount of taxes payable, a refund of Part XIII taxes is available.

Management And Administration Fees
21-126. The term management or administration fee generally includes payments or credits for the functions of planning, direction, control, coordination, systems or other functions at a managerial level. However, ITA 212(4) points out that the term management fee does not include either:

- payments for services performed in the ordinary course of business by a non resident under circumstances where the non resident and the Canadian payer deal with each other at arm's length, or

- reimbursements to a non resident for specific expenses incurred for the benefit of the Canadian resident.

21-127. Payments to a non resident parent company by a Canadian subsidiary in the form of general administrative fees will be subject to the Part XIII withholding. However, such fees reduce the profits of the Canadian subsidiary and, if the subsidiary is subject to a tax rate above the withholding rate, an overall reduction in Canadian taxes can result. Because of this potential leakage of Canadian tax, such fees must be reasonable in the circumstances and must meet transfer pricing standards or they may be disallowed as expense deductions.

21-128.   In addition to the required Part XIII tax, Regulation 105 requires that 15 percent of any fee paid to a non resident for services rendered (e.g., consulting fees) in Canada should be withheld and remitted for application to any Part I tax which may be payable. If no Part I tax is eventually payable, a full refund of the amount withheld may be received. To avoid Part I tax on services rendered, an individual or firm needs to prove that the services are not provided from a permanent establishment in Canada. This is a situation where Part I and Part XIII tax may apply to the same payment. As well, stringent GST collection procedures apply to non resident service providers. For instance, non resident performers who are GST registrants are required to remit GST collections and file a GST return before departing from Canada.

21-129.   Where an individual U.S. resident renders independent personal services in Canada, the income will be taxed in Canada if the income is attributable to a fixed base here. The income will be taxed as business income under Part I. The U.S. will also tax the income, but should allow a foreign tax credit for any Canadian tax paid on the income.

> Exercises Twenty-One-7 through 9 deal with taxation of non residents. This would be an appropriate time to attempt these exercises.

Support Payments

21-130.   Payments of spousal and child support to non residents are no longer subject to Part XIII tax. You may recall from Chapter 11, in 1997, payments for child support were made non deductible to the payer and non taxable to the recipient. While spousal support continues to be deductible to the payer and taxable to the recipient, ITA 212(1) was amended to remove both of these items from the list of taxable items.

Non Resident Owned Investment Corporations (NROC)

21-131.   The non resident owned investment corporation (NROC, hereafter) was used by non residents who wished to invest in Canada. Under ITA 133(1), income could be accumulated in these corporations at a relatively low rate of tax and could be reinvested without distribution to the shareholders of the NROC. The goal was to approximate the tax treatment that would apply to the non resident shareholders if, instead of using a NROC, they had owned the investments directly. However, the government concluded that these organizations were being used to avoid Canadian taxes and, as a consequence, they are being phased out over a three year period, beginning February 27, 2000. Existing NROCs will not be able to increase their overall assets or debt during the three-year phase out period. However, as NROCs will exist until 2003, we will provide a brief review of their tax features.

21-132.   To qualify as a NROC before February 27, 2000, the corporation must have been beneficially owned by non resident persons. In addition, its income must have been derived from owning or trading in securities, rents, interest, dividends, estate or trust income, and capital gains. Not more than 10 percent of its gross revenues could be from rents and its principal business must not have been the making of loans or trading in securities.

21-133.   If a corporation met the preceding conditions and elected to be taxed as an NROC, its income will include the full amount of capital gains, net of capital losses, on the disposition of Taxable Canadian Property, plus any capital dividends received. Other capital gains and losses are not included, for example gains and losses on the trading in shares of Canadian public corporations, as a reflection of the fact that such gains and losses are not normally taxable in the hands of non residents.

21-134.   An NROC is taxed at a basic rate of 25 percent. Then, any dividends paid to non residents from the NROC are subject to Part XIII tax. While interest is not deductible in the computation of an NROC's income, no tax is assessed on distributions of interest to non residents. However, an NROC is eligible for refunds which are based on the tax paid on its income and on tax paid in respect of disallowed interest expense. The net effect is much the same as if the shareholder had received the income directly.

21-135.   All residents of Canada must include dividends received from a non resident corporation in income under ITA 90. Where the dividend is not received from a foreign affiliate, no real tax relief in the form of dividend tax credits is available.

References

21-136.　For more detailed study of the material in this Chapter, we refer you to the following:

ITA 2	Tax Payable By Persons Resident In Canada
ITA 90	Dividends Received From Non Resident Corporation
ITA 95	[Foreign Accrual Property Income]
ITA 113	Deduction In Respect Of Dividend Received From Foreign Affiliate
ITA 115	Non Resident's Taxable Income (Earned) In Canada (and Taxable Canadian Property)
ITA 116	Disposition By Non Resident Person Of Certain Property
ITA 118	Personal Credits
ITA 128.1	Immigration
ITA 133	Non Resident Owned Investment Corporations
ITA 149	Miscellaneous Exemptions
ITA 212	Tax On Income From Canada Of Non Resident Persons (This is the principal section in ITA Part XIII which deals with Canadian income of non resident persons.)
ITA 216	Alternatives Re Rents And Timber Royalties
ITA 217	Alternative Re Canadian Benefits
ITA 219	Additional Tax on Non Resident Corporations [Branch Tax]
ITA 233	Information Returns with respect to Certain Non Resident Persons and Foreign Property
ITA 247	Transfer Pricing
ITA 250	Person Deemed Resident
ITA 255	Canada
IC 72-17R4	Procedures Concerning The Disposition Of Taxable Canadian Property By Non Residents Of Canada - Section 116
IC 75-6R	Required Withholding from Amounts Paid to Non Resident Persons Performing Services in Canada
IC 76-12R4	Applicable Rate Of Part XIII Tax On Amounts Paid Or Credited To Persons In Treaty Countries
IC 77-16R4	Non Resident Income Tax
IC 87-2R	International Transfer Pricing
IC 94-4R	International Transfer Pricing: Advance Pricing Agreements (APA)
IT-163R2	Election By Non Resident Individuals On Certain Canadian Source Income
IT-171R2	Non Resident Individuals - Computation of Taxable Income Earned in Canada and Non Refundable Tax Credits (1999 and subsequent taxation years)
IT-176R2	Taxable Canadian Property - Interests In And Options On Real Property And Shares
IT-221R2	Determination Of An Individual's Residence Status
IT-270R2	Foreign Tax Credit
IT-361R3	Exemption From Part XIII Tax On Interest Payments To Non Residents
IT-393R2	Election Re Tax On Rents And Timber Royalties - Non Residents
IT-395R	Foreign Tax Credit - Foreign-Source Capital Gains And Losses
IT-420R3	Non Residents - Income Earned In Canada
IT-447	Residence Of A Trust or Estate
IT-520	Unused Foreign Tax Credits - Carryforward And Carryback

Exercises

(The solutions for these exercises can be found following Chapter 21 of the text.)

Exercise Twenty-One - 1 (Taxation Of Foreign Income)

Does a Canadian resident who is also a U.S. citizen have an obligation to pay Canadian income tax if that person's only source of income is U.S. interest income?

Exercise Twenty-One - 2 (Taxation Of Foreign Income)

Bob Benson is a Canadian resident working year round in Tacoma, Washington. Explain how Bob will be taxed in Canada on his U.S. employment income, if at all.

Exercise Twenty-One - 3 (U.S. Estate Taxes)

Morrie Udetsky is a bachelor who lives in Regina. He owns approximately $2 million in U.S. rental property with no debt. The accrued gain is low as the property has a high cost base. Briefly explain how Morrie will be taxed on the real estate when he dies.

Exercise Twenty-One - 4 (Departure From Canada)

Helena Pinsky lived and worked in Canada from January to the end of April. After having a Canadian tax fit at the end of April, she moved to the U.S. on May 1 and worked there from July to December. Where does Helena have to file tax returns for the year of the move?

Exercise Twenty-One - 5 (Departure From Canada)

Charmaine emigrated from Canada in May 2001. When she left, she owned shares of a public corporation that were valued at $2,000,000. These shares are her only substantive capital asset. She inherited the shares from her late husband, who had acquired the shares on an Initial Public Offering several years ago at a cost of $200,000. No capital gains have been reported related to the shares. What will be the tax effect of Charmaine's departure from Canada?

Exercise Twenty-One - 6 (Foreign Investment Reporting)

Simon Taylor, a Canadian resident, has a UK bank account with a balance of £30,000 UK. He has also made an interest free loan of £35,000 UK to his brother-in-law in Scotland. No formal loan agreement is involved. Does Simon have any foreign investment reporting obligations? Assume £1 = $2.4.

Exercise Twenty-One - 7 (Taxation Of Non Residents)

Wen Long is a resident of Hong Kong. He has a brokerage account in Vancouver and trades in Canadian mutual funds and penny mining stocks. Is he subject to any Canadian tax on capital gains, dividends and interest income?

Exercise Twenty-One - 8 (Taxation Of Non Residents)

Timothy is a resident of the U.S. and received the following income amounts in 2001:

- $15,000 from a pension plan in Canada
- $700 interest from a Savings & Loan branch in Nevada
- $300 interest from the Bank of Montreal in B.C.

Timothy elects to file a tax return under Section 217. Determine which income should be reported on the return and whether or not any personal tax credits can be claimed.

Exercise Twenty-One - 9 (Taxation Of Non Residents - Rental Income)

Maya emigrated to Africa in 1999, but she retained her cottage in northern Ontario. She plans to rent the cottage for all of 2002, and expects to receive $15,000 of rental income and to have $12,000 of related expenses. Maya is visiting in Canada for her 2001 holidays, and requests your advice on how she should report her rental income in Canada in 2002.

Problems For Self Study

(The solutions for these problems can be found following Chapter 21 of the text.)

Self Study Problem Twenty-One - 1

Paul Brossard accepts an offer to move to the U.S. from Canada to become a manager for a revitalized Black Hills Gold Savings and Loan branch in South Dakota. Paul has resigned from his federal government position, and severed his professional association ties. Further, he purchased a home in South Dakota. However, his daughter is nearing completion of an elite French Immersion secondary school program in Ottawa, so Paul's wife and daughter intend to remain in Canada for two years. They continue to live in the family home in Ottawa.

After six months in South Dakota, the Savings and Loan branch closed. Paul then sold the U.S. home and moved back to Canada.

Required: Assess whether or not Paul became a non resident of Canada and if Paul will be taxed in Canada for the period during which he was living and working in the U.S.

Self Study Problem Twenty-One - 2

Debbie Maari is the vice-president of communications for an international advertising agency. Having risen to the pinnacle of success in Canada, she is enroute to Hong Kong to rebuild the firm's base in the Pacific Rim. The transfer will be for an indefinite duration, and Debbie has already obtained approval for immigration that does not restrict the length of her family's stay in Hong Kong. Debbie's family includes her husband and the family pets.

Debbie's husband is a sales representative in a pharmaceutical firm, and he plans to develop a client base in Asia over the next six months. Meanwhile, he plans to service his North American clients from Toronto and will commute monthly to Hong Kong.

On November 1, 2001, Debbie owned the following assets:

Description	Date Acquired	Original Cost	Fair Market Value
Interest in CCPC (10 percent)	1993	$ 90,000	$ 140,000
House (Note 1)	1992	150,000	225,000
Whistler ski chalet (Note)	1999	125,000	185,000
Sports car	1996	18,000	15,000
Paintings	1987	50,000	175,000
RRSP	1991-2000	66,000	86,000
10 percent interest in Sorrento Co., a Canadian public company	1991	180,000	110,000

Note The reported amounts for the house reflect Debbie's 50 percent ownership share. The other 50 percent is owned by her husband. Debbie owns 100 percent of the ski chalet.

Debbie plans to sell all of the assets except for the house and ski chalet, which she plans to rent out. She has used all of the $500,000 capital gains deduction in previous years.

Debbie's firm is prepared to pay her a $50,000 allowance to cover moving costs, with no requirement to provide supporting receipts.

Debbie has enquired about the Hong Kong tax regime and has been informed that the personal tax rates are lower than the rates in Canada. Further, the Hong Kong tax system is expected to continue as a "source" system rather than a "residence" system, meaning that only income arising in or derived from Hong Kong will be taxable there. Any additional income that Debbie earns in 2001 will be taxed at a combined federal/provincial rate of 45 percent.

Required: Debbie would like to know the Canadian tax implications of moving to Hong Kong, and whether there are any tax planning opportunities to minimize taxes payable for the current and future years.

Self Study Problem Twenty-One - 3
The following assets are owned by different Canadian taxpayers, who hold no other foreign investments at any time during the year.

A. Term deposits totalling $23,000 in a bank account in Missoula, Montana.

B. Florida condominium, purchased for $127,000 in August, 1998.

C. Arizona condominium, purchased for $25,000 cash down and assumption of a $77,000 mortgage.

D. Shares of an operating company in the U.S., costing $45,000 and representing 50% of the votes and value of the company.

E. A small manufacturing plant and machinery in Boise, Idaho owned by a Canadian company.

Required: For each investment, evaluate whether or not the foreign investment reporting rules apply and explain why.

Self Study Problem Twenty-One - 4
Tritec Enterprises is a Canadian controlled private company with its only offices in Vancouver. It is involved in providing consulting and real estate management services to a wide variety of clients. As it has been very successful in its operations in British Columbia, it is considering opening operations in various cities on the west coast of the United States. While it would expect to initially lose money on these operations, there is little doubt in management's mind that such an operation will eventually be profitable. Management intends to invest the eventual U.S. profits in various real estate developments in Southern California. In considering this possible foreign venture, the Company has sought your advice as to whether they should carry out their operations as a branch or as a wholly owned subsidiary incorporated in the United States.

Required: Prepare a memorandum contrasting the tax treatment of a branch operation to that of a subsidiary incorporated in the United States.

Self Study Problem Twenty-One - 5
A. A Canadian resident hockey player is recruited in the off-season to lead one hockey school in Florida and another in Ontario. The hockey schools are run by a Florida promoter, and the hockey player is paid US$2,000 per day for each 7 day school, for a total of US$28,000 for 14 days.

B. A Montreal theatre production firm employs a Winnipeg computer wizard to prepare special three-dimensional animation effects. The computer wizard works in the Silicon Valley in California for three periods, each of which is for two months (60 days). In California, the work involves using special animation equipment unavailable in Canada.

C. A San Francisco manufacturer pays a Vancouver roller blader US$12,000 to sign a contract to demonstrate the latest roller blades in daring demonstrations on the hills of San Francisco. The roller blader will also receive royalties, based on subsequent sales.

Required: For each of the above situations and evaluate whether or not the individual will be taxed in the U.S.

Assignment Problems

(The solutions for these problems are only available in
the solutions manual that has been provided to your instructor.)

Assignment Problem Twenty-One - 1

Holly Rancher, a Canadian resident, has been asked by the Brazilian government to start a
strip farming operation in the Brazilian rain forest. Holly and her husband own equal shares in
the following assets:

	FMV	ACB
Home in Cochrane, Alberta	$500,000	$200,000
Land Rover 4x4 truck	15,000	20,000
Cash	10,000	

In addition, Holly owns the following assets personally:

	FMV	ACB
Cottage on Lake Manitou	$ 65,000	$ 45,000
RRSP	55,000	
Shares in IOU Ranch Ltd, CCPC	40,000	25,000
Shares in public companies	40,000	30,000

Holly is seriously considering the Brazilian government's offer, and would like to know what
the tax effect of a move would be. Holly has claimed the full $500,000 capital gains deduction
previously.

Required:

A. Analyze the Canadian income tax effect if Holly becomes a non resident of Canada.

B. Identify important factors that could influence Holly's residence status.

C. If Holly decides to move to Brazil, and in so doing becomes a non resident of Canada,
identify effective tax planning opportunities to be considered.

Assignment Problem Twenty-One - 2

The following assets are owned by different Canadian taxpayers, who hold no other foreign
investments at any time during the year.

A. A warehouse in Miami with a cost of $568,000, owned by a Canadian corporation and
used to store its products for distribution.

B. Units in a U.S. special growth mutual fund purchased in a self-directed RRSP, where the
cost of the units is $113,000.

C. An Hawaiian cottage, purchased for $56,000 cash down and assumption of a $200,000
mortgage.

D. Shares of a U.S. operating company, costing $10,000 and representing 100% of the votes
and value of the company.

E. An individual owns a 5 percent share of a U.S. company with a cost of $32,000 and a bank
account in Vermont with $95,000 on deposit.

Required: For each investment, evaluate whether or not the foreign investment reporting
rules apply and explain why.

Assignment Problem Twenty-One - 3

Amy Borody works and resides in Winnipeg, Manitoba. Amy has been discreetly saving for her retirement by investing in the U.S. In the current year, she earned the following investment income. The dividends and interest are net of any U.S. withholding taxes.

Dividends from a U.S. Savings & Loan portfolio	U.S. $ 5,100
Interest on U.S. term deposits (in New York)	U.S. $19,800
Net rent from Palm Beach apartment	U.S. $18,000

Required: Describe how the investment income should be reported in Canada, and discuss any related foreign investment reporting requirements.

Assignment Problem Twenty-One - 4

A Canadian gun cabinet manufacturer is considering entering the buoyant U.S. market by following a gradual business expansion strategy. The market entry will be staged, using the following approaches:

A. Advertising in gun magazines.

B. Selling cabinets to U.S. distributors, with cabinets shipped FOB to the closest Canadian port or border crossing.

C. Direct sales to wholesalers by non-exclusive agents. The agents will represent other suppliers.

D. Direct sales to wholesalers by full-time salespeople in each of three regions of the U.S. No sales offices will be opened, and the cabinets will be shipped from a warehouse in Canada but only after a customer's credit and contract are approved by the Canadian head office.

E. The salespeople will report to a sales office in each region. The sales offices will coordinate marketing and shipping of products from warehouses located in the U.S. However, formal approval of contracts will be administered in the Canadian head office.

F. The sales offices become independent profit centres, with regional credit managers, and warehouses will be stocked nearby from which orders are filled.

Required: For each market expansion approach, assess whether or not the Canadian manufacturer will be deemed to have a permanent establishment in the U.S. Support your assessment, and identify any other information required to back up your position.

Assignment Problem Twenty-One - 5

A California company, Generation Inc., distributes a Seventh Generation software package in Canada through a Canadian subsidiary. Generation Inc. also distributes Millennium Nexus software directly through a sales representative who works in Canada and is an employee of Generation Inc. To ensure the sales of the Millennium Nexus software are administered efficiently, the Canadian subsidiary provides the Millennium Nexus sales representative with an office, pays the salary and withholds appropriate source deductions. The related expenses are reimbursed by Generation Inc.

Required: Determine if Generation Inc. is subject to tax in Canada on profits from its direct sales of the Millennium Nexus software and its indirect sales of the Seventh Generation software.

Assignment Problem Twenty-One - 6

Case A   The Maple Company, a public company resident in Canada, has 2,400,000 shares of its no par common stock outstanding. Sixty percent of these shares are owned by its American parent, the Condor Company. The remaining shares are owned by Canadian residents. In addition to the common shares, the Condor Company holds all of an outstanding issue of Maple Company debenture bonds. Two of the five directors of the Maple Company are Canadian residents while the remaining three are residents of the United States. During the current year, the Maple Company paid a dividend of $1 per share on its common stock and interest of $900,000 on its outstanding debenture bonds.

Required: Calculate the amount of Part XIII taxes to be withheld by the Maple Company with respect to the interest and dividend payments to its American parent.

Case B   Mr. John McQueen was for many years a resident of Ontario. On his retirement in 1981 he returned to his native Scotland and has not since returned to Canada. However, he has retained considerable investments in Canada, as follows:

- **Common Stocks**   He has a large portfolio of common stocks that are registered in the name of his Toronto broker. The broker receives all dividends and periodically sends a cheque to Mr. McQueen in Scotland.

- **Mortgage Portfolio**   He has a large portfolio of second mortgages. All collections on these mortgages are made by a Toronto law firm and are deposited into a Toronto bank account in the name of Mr. McQueen.

  Required: Who is responsible for tax withholdings under Part XIII of the *Income Tax Act* and on which amounts must withholdings be made?

Case C   Hotels International is a U.S. corporation with hotel properties throughout the world. It has recently developed a property in Nova Scotia which will open during the current year. A long term management lease has been signed with Hotel Operators Ltd., a Canadian company specializing in the management of hotels. Under the terms of the lease, Hotel Operators Ltd. will pay all of the operating expenses of the hotel and, in addition, make an annual payment of $1,250,000 to the American owners of the new hotel.

Required: Will the American company, Hotels International, be subject to Canadian income taxes on the management fee or rental income, and, if so, to what extent?

Case D   Mr. Jack Holt is an employee of Stillwell Industries, an American manufacturing Company. During the period June 15 through December 6 of the current year, Mr. Holt worked in Canada providing technical assistance to a Canadian subsidiary of Stillwell Industries. His salary was U.S. $5,500 per month. During the period that Mr. Holt was in Canada, Stillwell Industries continued to deposit his salary into his normal U.S. bank account. Both his salary for this period and all of his related travelling expenses were billed to the Canadian subsidiary.

Required: Explain Mr. Holt's tax position, including the question of whether any withholdings should have been made with respect to Canadian taxes owing.

Assignment Problem Twenty-One - 7 (Electronic Library Research Problem)

Provide brief answers to the following questions. Your answers should be supported by references to materials found in your Electronic Library.

A. Answer the following True or False questions, and reference your answer to the relevant section in the *Act*.

1. Estate or trust income paid to a non resident is subject to withholding tax.
2. Following the disposition of a Canadian rental property by a non resident, the taxable capital gain is subject to Part XIII withholding tax.
3. A controlled foreign affiliate can be controlled by five persons resident in Canada.
4. A foreign affiliate means a non resident corporation that is owned at least one percent by the taxpayer or at least 10 percent by the taxpayer and related persons.
5. A non resident person that disposes of taxable Canadian property can request the CCRA to provide a waiver of income tax withholdings relating to the purchase.
6. Where an Italian art collector immigrates to Canada, the adjusted cost base of his art collection that migrates with him does not change.
7. A Canadian citizen that is employed by the government of Switzerland and works in Ottawa is not subject to tax in Canada on employment earnings.
8. A non resident owner of rental property in Canada can be taxed on the rental income as a resident would be taxed.
9. Contemporaneous documentation for transfer pricing purposes means that the documentation is prepared and provided extemporaneously to the CCRA.
10. A corporation is deemed resident of Canada is it was incorporated before April 9, 1959.

B. Contrast the comparable uncontrolled price (CUP) method, which is the preferred method to use for transfer pricing, and the resale price method.

C. Outline the tax treatment of social security payments from the U.S. that are received by a resident of Canada.

D. The notion of permanent establishment is increasing in importance, particularly in the context of e-businesses. Describe how business profits are to be allocated to permanent establishments.

E. Foreign income taxes paid form the basis for foreign tax credits. Provide examples of taxes that are excluded from the calculation of total foreign business and foreign non-business incomes taxes paid or payable.

F. Foreign tax credits are calculated on a country-by-country basis. If a taxpayer earns taxable capital gains in one country and incurs an allowable capital loss in another country, how should the allowable capital losses be allocated for purposes of calculating the foreign non business income for each respective country?

Appendix

Solutions To Exercises and

Self Study Problems

The following pages contain detailed solutions to the exercises and self study problems found at the end of Chapters 2 through 21.

Solution to Chapter Two Exercises

Exercise Two - 1

Ms. Sally Cheung's 2001 tax return must be filed by the later of six months after the date of her death and her normal filing date. As she has business income, her normal filing date is June 15. The later of the two dates would be August 15, 2002, six months after the date of her death.

Exercise Two - 2

While Mr. Katarski's 2001 tax return does not have to be filed until June 15, 2001, his tax liability must be paid by April 30, 2001 in order to avoid the assessment of interest.

Exercise Two - 3

She is not required to make instalment payments as long as her actual 2001 net tax owing is less than $2,000.

Exercise Two - 4

As his net tax owing in the current year and one of the two preceding years is in excess of $2,000, he is required to make instalment payments. The minimum amount would be based on the preceding taxation year net tax owing of $1,500 and would be $375 per quarter.

Exercise Two - 5

For the first two quarters, the minimum instalments would be based on the second preceding year net tax owing of $25,000. The two payments would be $6,250 each. For the third and fourth quarters his minimum instalments would be based on the estimated net tax owing for the current year of $32,000, less the $12,500 paid in the first two quarters. These payments would be $9,750 each.

Exercise Two - 6

Given the size of her net tax owing, ITA 163.1 will not be applicable and there will be no penalties for late instalments. However, a penalty of 7 percent of taxes payable will be assessed for filing two months late (5 percent, plus 1 percent per month). If, in one of the three preceding taxation years she has committed a similar offence, the penalty would be 14 percent (10 percent, plus 2 percent per month).

Exercise Two - 7

Radco Inc.'s tax return is due six months after their year end, on July 31, 2001. Unless Radco is able to claim the small business deduction, the final payment on their taxes must be made two months after their year end on March 31, 2001. If they are eligible for the small business deduction, they can defer the final payment for an additional month, to April 30, 2001.

Exercise Two - 8

The first two instalments would be based on the second preceding year and would be $4,333 each ($52,000 ÷ 12). The remaining 10 instalments would be based on the preceding year, less the $8,666 paid in the first two instalments. The amount would be $8,033 [($89,000 - $8,666) ÷ 10].

Exercise Two - 9

The minimum instalments would be based on the estimated tax payable for the current year. The amount would be $5,583 ($67,000 ÷ 12). Note that, if the estimate for 2001 is too low, interest will be assessed on the deficiency.

Exercise Two - 10

The notice of objection must be filed by the later of:

- 90 days after the date of mailing of the reassessment (August 13, 2002); or
- one year after the due date for filing the return that is being reassessed (April 30, 2002).

The later of these two dates is August 13, 2002.

Solution to Self Study Problem Two - 1

Need For Instalments   Instalments are required when an individual's "net tax owing" exceeds $2,000 in the current year and in either of the two preceding years. In somewhat simplified terms, "net tax owing" is defined as the combined federal and provincial tax liability, less amounts withheld under ITA 153. Mr. Gore's net tax owing for 2001 is $4,000 ($17,000 - $13,000). In addition, the amount for 1999 is $2,500. As both of these amounts are in excess of $2,000, Mr. Gore would be required to pay instalments.

Amounts   The amount of the instalments could be based on the net tax owing for 2000 or 2001. In addition, the first two 2001 instalments could be based on the net tax owing for 1999. However, since net tax owing for 2000 is nil, the best solution for Mr. Gore is to use that year. This means that, even though Mr. Gore meets the requirements for making instalment payments, the minimum amount of the required instalments would be nil.

If Mr. Gore did have to pay instalments, the due dates would have been March 15, June 15, September 15 and December 15.

Solution to Self Study Problem Two - 2

There are three possible payment schedules that could be used by the Amalmor Company in this situation. The amounts involved are calculated as follows:

Current Year Base   The payments could be 1/12th of the estimated taxes payable for the current year. This amount would be $7,917 ($95,000/12).

Previous Year Base   The payments could be 1/12th of the taxes that were paid in the immediately preceding year. This amount would be $6,667 ($80,000/12).

Previous And Second Previous Years   A final alternative would be to base the first two payments on one twelfth of the taxes paid in the second previous year with the remaining ten payments based on the previous year total, less the amounts paid in the first two instalments. The first two amounts would be $5,208 ($62,500/12), or a total of $10,416. In the remaining 10 months of the year, the payments would be $6,958 [($80,000 - $10,416)/10].

The last alternative involves the greatest amount of tax payment deferral and would be the schedule chosen by the taxpayer. Note that any remaining taxes payable must be paid within two months of the Company's year end (three months for companies that qualify for the small business deduction).

Solution to Self Study Problem Two - 3

Case One

A.   The net tax owing in the current year is nil and, as a consequence, no instalments are required for 2001.

B.   Given that instalments are not required, this part of the question is not applicable.

Case Two

A.   The net tax owing for the current year is $2,885. In addition, the net tax owing in 2000 was $5,216. As the net tax owing for the current year and one of the two preceding years exceeds $2,000, instalment payments are required.

B.   One choice for instalment payments would be to use the current year. This would result in required instalment payments of $721 ($2,885 ÷ 4) to be paid on March 15, June 15, September 15, and December 15.

The alternative that will be used by the CCRA in its instalment notices will be based on the net tax owing for 1999 of $1,820 for the first two instalments. These instalment payments would be $455 per quarter, $266 lower than the $721 required using the current year as the instalment base. However, the third and fourth payments would be $2,153 {[$5,216 - (2)($455)] ÷ 2}. As this is $1,432 higher than the $721 required using the current year's net tax owing, the small savings in the first two quarters would quickly be wiped out and the taxpayer would wind up paying a much larger total ($5,216 vs. $2,885).

The best alternative would be to base the first two instalments on the net tax owing for 1999 which would be $455 payable on March 15 and June 15. The third and fourth instalments would be based on the actual 2001 net tax, less the first two instalments. This would equal $988 {[$2,885 - (2)($455)] ÷ 2} for September 15 and December 15.

Case Three

A. Corporations are required to make instalment payments unless the taxes paid in the preceding taxation year or the estimated taxes payable for the current year are less than $1,000.

B. The best choice would be to use the previous year. This would result in instalment payments of $956 ($11,466 ÷ 12) to be paid at the end of each month beginning January 31.

Case Four

A. Corporations are required to make instalment payments unless the taxes paid in the preceding taxation year or the estimated taxes payable for the current year are less than $1,000.

B. If the current year is used as the base, this would result in instalment payments of $2,060 ($24,718 ÷ 12) to be paid at the end of each month beginning January 31. If 1999 is used as the base, the first two instalments would be $1,962, somewhat less than the $2,060 amount required using the current year. However, the remaining 10 instalments would be a much higher $2,864 {[$32,560 - (2)($1,962)] ÷ 10]}.

The best alternative would probably be to base the first two instalments on 1999 and the remaining 10 instalments on the current year, less the first two instalments. This would equal $2,079 {[$24,718 - (2)($1,962)] ÷ 10}. Although there is not much difference in the amounts for this method and the current year method, this would allow an extra two months to calculate the current year's estimate.

Solution to Self Study Problem Two - 4

Tax Evasion   One of the best explanations of the differences involved here was found in IC 73-10R2 (subsequently replaced by IC 73-10R3). It described tax evasion as follows:

> The commission or omission of an act knowingly with the intent to deceive so that the tax reported by the taxpayer is less than the tax payable under the law, or a conspiracy to commit such an offence. This may be accomplished by the deliberate omission of revenue, the fraudulent claiming of expenses or allowances and the deliberate misrepresentation, concealment or withholding of material fact.

IC 73-10R3 has revised this description as follows:

> Tax evasion is the *commission* or *omission* of an act knowingly, the conspiracy to commit such an act or involvement in the accommodation of such an act, which can result in a charge being laid in the Criminal Court under subsection 239(1) of the *Income Tax Act*.

An example of a common type of tax evasion would be a failure to report cash sales as part of Net Income For Tax Purposes.

Tax Planning   At the other end of the spectrum, the superseded Information Circular 73-10R2 described tax planning as follows:

> A taxpayer, in seeking a beneficial tax result, has merely selected a certain course of action that is either clearly provided for or not specifically prohibited in the law and has implemented that decision in a real way. Such planning consists of a genuine arranging of one's affairs openly and within the framework of the law so as to keep one's taxes to a minimum.

An example of tax planning would be the establishment of an investment company in order to split income among members of a family.

Tax Avoidance   The Circular described tax avoidance as follows:

> The taxpayer has apparently circumvented the law, without giving rise to a criminal offence, by the use of a scheme, arrangement or device, often of a complex nature, whose main or sole purpose is to defer, reduce or completely avoid the tax payable under the law.

Prior to 1986, this latter description supported a very broad provision in ITA 246 as follows:

> Where the Treasury Board has decided that one of the main purposes for a transaction or transactions effected before or after the coming into force of this Act was improper avoidance or reduction of taxes that might otherwise have become payable under this Act, the Treasury Board may give such directions as it considers appropriate to counteract the avoidance or reduction.

It is very difficult to provide a clear cut example of what was meant by avoidance under these general provisions. ITA 246 has never been applied and it was eliminated in 1984. In addition, an important Supreme Court decision (Stubart Investments Ltd. Vs. The Queen - 84 DTC 6305) ruled that the fact that a transaction was undertaken purely to avoid taxes did not make it unacceptable for purposes of determining taxable income and taxes payable. This leaves the question of what avoidance in general terms really means somewhat up in the air. However, there remain several more specific anti avoidance provisions which could be cited here. These would include ITA 69 on inadequate considerations as well as a number of provisions that were instituted to prevent other types of income from being artificially converted to capital gains in order to take advantage of the lifetime capital gains deduction.

Adding to the confusion in this area is Section 245 which contains a general anti-avoidance rule (GAAR). This broadly based provision indicates that any transaction or series of transactions that has no other purpose than to reduce taxes payable may be considered tax avoidance. As a result of this provision, the decision of whether a particular tax reduction arrangement is tax avoidance or tax planning is one which depends largely on the administrative discretion of the CCRA.

Solution to Self Study Problem Two - 5

With respect to resolving the dispute, a first step may involve nothing more than a call to the CCRA to discuss the matter. If Mr. Coffee feels that there has been a misunderstanding that can be resolved by providing a more detailed explanation of the relevant facts, this may be the only step required. However, in some cases more formal steps will be necessary and they can be outlined as follows:

> **Notice Of Objection**   As the reassessment relates to the previous year's tax return, it is within the three year time limit and, therefore, a legitimate procedure for the Minister. This means that within 90 days of the mailing date on the notice of reassessment

or (as Mr. Coffee is an individual) one year from the due date for the return under reassessment, a notice of objection can be filed. This objection or Form T400A should be sent by registered mail and should explain the facts and reasons why Mr. Coffee does not agree with the reassessment.

Tax Court Of Canada   If there is an adverse decision on the notice of objection, Mr. Coffee has up to 90 days after the mailing date of the response to the notice of objection to appeal to the Tax Court of Canada. Alternatively, if he does not receive a response to his notice of objection within 90 days, he will then be able to appeal to the Tax Court of Canada. As the amount involved is only $5,000, it would probably be advisable for Mr. Coffee to choose the informal procedure.

Federal Courts   If Mr. Coffee has elected the informal Tax Court of Canada procedure, no appeal of an adverse decision is possible. An appeal to the Federal Court - Appeals Division would, however, be possible if an adverse decision was rendered under the general procedure. In theory, an adverse decision by the Federal Court could be appealed to the Supreme Court of Canada. However, this can only happen if the Federal Court recommends it or the Supreme Court authorizes such action. This would be extremely unlikely given the amount involved.

If you are to become involved in representing Mr. Coffee's interest in this matter, a signed Consent Form, T1013 which would give you authorization to discuss the case with the CCRA would have to be on file with the CCRA.

Solution to Self Study Problem Two - 6

The three taxable entities are individuals, corporations, and trusts. The required information for each is as follows:

Individuals   For individuals without business income, the taxation year is the calendar year and the filing deadline is April 30 of the following year. Individuals with business income and their spouses have an extended filing deadline of June 15. Instalment payments for all individuals, if required, are to be made quarterly on March 15, June 15, September 15, and December 15.

Corporations   Corporations can choose any fiscal year that does not exceed 53 weeks. The filing deadline is six months after the year end and instalments, when required, must be made on a monthly basis.

Trusts   Testamentary trusts can choose any fiscal year not exceeding 12 months. Their filing deadline is 90 days after the year end and they are not required to make instalments. Other trusts must use a calendar year. They are also required to file within 90 days of the end of the year and quarterly instalment payments are required under the same rules as those used by individuals.

Solution to Chapter Three Exercises

Exercise Three - 1

Mr. Kirsh will be a part year resident and liable for Canadian taxes on his worldwide income, including any income on the U.S. bank accounts, for the period September 1 through December 31 of the current year.

Exercise Three - 2

While Ms. Blakey is the child of a Canadian High Commissioner, it appears that she is no longer a dependant of this individual. As a consequence, she would not be considered a deemed resident under ITA 250(1).

Exercise Three - 3

Roswell Ltd. would be considered to be a resident of Canada for tax purposes because the "mind and management" of the company appear to be located in Kemptville, Ontario.

Exercise Three - 4

As the Company was incorporated in Canada after April 26, 1965, it would be deemed to be a Canadian resident under ITA 250(4).

Exercise Three - 5

Her belief is not correct. Under ITA 2(3) she would be subject to Canadian taxes on employment income earned in Canada.

Exercise Three - 6

His Net Income For Tax Purposes would be $38,000 ($42,000 - $15,000 + $24,000 - $13,000).

Exercise Three - 7

Her Net Income For Tax Purposes would be Nil. She would have a non capital loss carry over of $10,480 ($33,240 + $24,750 - $19,500 - $48,970).

Exercise Three - 8

Her Net Income For Tax Purposes would be $7,894 ($42,680 + Nil - $8,460 - $26,326). She would have an allowable capital loss carry over of $5,880 ($27,400 - $33,280).

Exercise Three - 9

Mr. Chung is clearly involved in income splitting. He is getting the deduction from taxable income now and his wife will be taxed on the income in the future. All RRSP contributions normally create a tax deferral. The contribution will be deductible and the earnings on the contribution will accumulate on a tax free basis. However, all of these amounts will be taxable when they are withdrawn from the plan. There may also be tax avoidance. This will happen if his spouse is taxed at a lower rate than is currently applicable to Mr. Chung when the funds become taxable to her.

Exercise Three - 10

As the dental plan is a benefit that can be received by Mr. Green without being taxed (private health care), tax avoidance is illustrated.

Solution to Self Study Problem Three - 1

A. Jane Smith would be deemed a Canadian resident because she is a dependent child of a Canadian Ambassador [ITA 250(1)(f)].

B. Marvin Black would not be considered a resident of Canada as he does not live in Canada. However, he would be subject to Canadian taxation on the employment income earned in Canada. [ITA 2(3)]

C. John Leather would be considered a resident of Canada for the part of the year until September 12. As his presence in Canada during the first part of the year was not on a part time basis, he would not fall under the sojourning rules.

D. Members of the Canadian armed forces are deemed to be Canadian residents without regard to where they actually live. As Francine Donaire is exempt from French taxation due to her relationship to a deemed resident, she is a deemed resident of Canada. [ITA 250(1)(g)]

E.   More information would be required here. Robert would either be a part year resident of Canada or, alternatively, a non resident employed in Canada depending on the nature of his stay in the country.

F.   The fact that Susan Allen is a Canadian citizen is irrelevant to the determination of residency. Since she appears to have no residential ties with Canada, she would not be considered a Canadian resident.

Solution to Self Study Problem Three - 2

A.   As AMT Ltd. was incorporated prior to April 27, 1965, it is not automatically considered to be a resident of Canada under ITA 250(4)(a). However, it was a resident of Canada subsequent to April 26, 1965 and, as a consequence, it would still be deemed a Canadian resident under ITA 250(4)(c).

B.   UIF Inc. was not incorporated in Canada and its central control and management are not currently within Canada. Therefore, UIF Inc. would not be considered a Canadian resident.

C.   BDT Ltd. would be deemed a Canadian resident under ITA 250(4)(a). This is because it was incorporated in Canada subsequent to April 26, 1965.

D.   While QRS Inc. was not incorporated in Canada, it would appear that central control and management are located in Ontario. This would result in QRS Inc. being treated as a Canadian resident.

Solution to Self Study Problem Three - 3

A.   Molly London would be considered a part year resident of Canada until October 31, the date of her departure. As her presence in Canada during the first part of the year was on a full time basis, she would not fall under the sojourning rules.

B.   Daryl Bennett would not be considered a Canadian resident. He was present in Canada for less than 183 days so he would not be a sojourner. As his principal residence is in the U.S., he would be a U.S. resident. His Canadian citizenship would not affect his residency status.

C.   While Tweeks Inc. was not incorporated in Canada, it would appear that central control and management are located in Quebec. This would result in Tweeks Inc. being treated as a Canadian resident.

D.   Bordot Industries would be deemed a Canadian resident under ITA 250(4)(a). This is because it was incorporated in Canada subsequent to April 26, 1965.

Solution to Self Study Problem Three - 4

Mr. Aiken And Mr. Baker   Assuming that their respective moves were permanent in nature, both Mr. Aiken and Mr. Baker would be treated as part year residents. This means that they would be considered residents of Canada only for that portion of the year that they were actually in Canada. As a result, they will be liable for Canadian taxes only for a part of the current year (see ITA 114 and ITA 118.91 for the procedures required to prorate income and tax credits in this situation).

Mr. Chase   While Mr. Chase was in Canada for the same number of days as the other individuals, the fact that he was present only on a temporary basis makes him subject to the sojourning rule. Under this rule [see ITA 250(1)], he will be considered a resident for the full year if he sojourns in Canada for 183 days or more during any calendar year. As Mr. Chase was present for 192 days, he would be viewed as a Canadian resident throughout the year and subject to Canadian income taxes on his world income. The U.S. tax treaty would have to be taken into consideration in this case.

Solution to Self Study Problem Three - 5

Case A   The Case A solution would be calculated as follows:

Income Under ITA 3(a):		
Employment Income	$34,000	
Income From Property	21,000	$55,000
Income Under ITA 3(b):		
Taxable Capital Gains	$42,000	
Allowable Capital Losses	(57,000)	$ NIL
Income Under ITA 3(c):		
Balance From 3(a)	$55,000	
Subdivision e Deductions	(5,500)	$49,500
Income Under ITA 3(d):		
Balance From 3(c)	$49,500	
Business Loss	(36,000)	$13,500

In this Case Miss Bain would have Division B income of $13,500 and a carryover of allowable capital losses in the amount of $15,000 ($57,000 - $42,000).

Case B   The Case B solution would be calculated as follows:

Income Under ITA 3(a):		
Employment Income	$18,500	
Income From Property	12,000	$30,500
Income Under ITA 3(b):		
Taxable Capital Gains	$ 9,000	
Allowable Capital Losses	(12,000)	$ NIL
Income Under ITA 3(c):		
Balance From 3(a)	$30,500	
Subdivision e Deductions	(10,500)	$20,000
Income Under ITA 3(d):		
Balance From 3(c)	$20,000	
Business Loss	(28,200)	$ NIL

As Miss Bain's Business Loss exceeds the amount carried forward from ITA 3(c), her Division B income is nil. This means there would be a carryover of noncapital losses in the amount of $8,200 ($28,200 - $20,000) and of allowable capital losses in the amount of $3,000 ($12,000 - $9,000).

Solution to Self Study Problem Three - 6

Case A   The Case A solution would be calculated as follows:

Income Under ITA 3(a):		
Employment Income	$45,000	
Income From Property	15,000	$60,000
Income Under ITA 3(b):		
Taxable Capital Gains	$25,000	
Allowable Capital Losses	(10,000)	$15,000
Income Under ITA 3(c):		
Totals From 3(a) And 3(b)	$75,000	
Subdivision e Deductions	(5,000)	$70,000
Income Under ITA 3(d):		
Balance From 3(c)	$70,000	
Business Loss	(20,000)	$50,000

In this Case Mr. Haynes' Division B income is $50,000.

Case B   The Case B solution would be calculated as follows:

Income Under ITA 3(a):		
Employment Income	$17,000	
Income From Property	12,000	$29,000
Income Under ITA 3(b):		
Taxable Capital Gains	$22,000	
Allowable Capital Losses	(8,000)	$14,000
Income Under ITA 3(c):		
Totals From 3(a) And 3(b)	$43,000	
Subdivision e Deductions	(6,000)	$37,000
Income Under ITA 3(d):		
Balance From 3(c)	$37,000	
Business Loss	(42,000)	$ NIL

In this Case Mr. Haynes' Division B income is nil and he will have a non capital loss carry over of $5,000.

Case C   The Case C solution would be calculated as follows:

Income Under ITA 3(a):		
Employment Income	$24,000	
Income From Property	47,000	$71,000
Income Under ITA 3(b):		
Taxable Capital Gains	$22,000	
Allowable Capital Losses	(73,000)	$ NIL
Income Under ITA 3(c):		
Balance From 3(a)	$71,000	
Subdivision e Deductions	(4,000)	$67,000
Income Under ITA 3(d):		
Balance From 3(c)	$67,000	
Business Loss	(48,000)	$19,000

In this Case Mr. Haynes would have Division B income of $19,000 and a carry over of allowable capital losses in the amount of $51,000.

Case D   The Case D solution would be calculated as follows:

Income Under ITA 3(a):
Employment Income	$18,000	
Income From Property	7,000	$25,000

Income Under ITA 3(b):
Taxable Capital Gains	$13,000	
Allowable Capital Losses	(18,000)	$ NIL

Income Under ITA 3(c):
Balance From 3(a)	$25,000	
Subdivision e Deductions	(12,000)	$13,000

Income Under ITA 3(d):
Balance From 3(c)	$13,000	
Business Loss	(20,000)	$ NIL

As Mr. Haynes' Business Loss exceeds the amount carried forward from 3(c), his Division B income is nil. This means there would be a carry over of non capital losses in the amount of $7,000 and of allowable capital losses in the amount of $5,000.

Solution to Chapter Four Exercises

Exercise Four - 1
Under a VAT system, the five percent would be applied to the value added, resulting in a tax of $7,600 [(5%)($416,000 - $264,000)]. Alternatively, under a GST system $20,800 [(5%)($416,000)] would be owing on sales, but would be offset by an input tax credit of $11,650 [(5%)($233,000)] on purchases. The net tax owing in this case would be $9,150.

Exercise Four - 2
As her sales exceed $30,000 in the third quarter, she will be required to begin collecting GST on the first sale in that quarter that exceeds the $30,000 threshold. This means she will have to begin collecting GST sometime between July 1 and September 30.

Exercise Four - 3
As Mr. Laughton's sales accumulate to more than $30,000 by the end of the second quarter, he will have to begin collecting GST on August 1, the first day of the second month of the third quarter.

Exercise Four - 4
The GST payable would be calculated as follows:

Sales [(7%)($1,223,000)]	$85,610
Input Tax Credits:	
Purchases [(7%)($843,000 + $126,000)]	(67,830)
Salaries, Interest, And Depreciation	Nil
GST Payable For Quarter	$17,780

Exercise Four - 5
The GST payable would be calculated as follows:

Sales [(7%)($124,000)]	$8,680
Input Tax Credits:	
Capital Expenditures [(7%)($36,000 + $20,000)]	(3,920)
Assistant's Salary	Nil
Rent [(7%)($25,800)]	(1,806)
GST Payable For The Year	$2,954

Exercise Four - 6

The renovations would be considered part of the acquisition cost of the building, and therefore would be subject to the normal input tax credit rules for real property acquisitions. The pro rata input tax credit for the land and building acquisition would be $39,928 [(7%)(40%)($1,200,000 + $226,000)].

Exercise Four - 7

The total GST included sales for the quarter would be $45,475. The purchases made do not affect the quick method calculation. The GST payable under the quick method would be calculated as follows:

First $30,000 At 1.5%	$450
Remaining $15,475 At 2.5%	387
Total GST Payable For Quarter	$837

Exercise Four - 8

If the quick method is not used, the GST payable (refund) would be calculated as follows:

Sales [(7%)($56,100)]	$3,927
Input Tax Credits:	
Current Costs [(7%)($23,400]	(1,638)
Capital Expenditures [(7%)($42,000)]	(2,940)
GST Payable (Refund) For Quarter	($ 651)

Alternatively, under the quick method, the calculation would be as follows:

First $30,000 At 1.5%	$450
Remaining $30,027* At 2.5%	751
Subtotal	$1,201
Input Tax Credit On Capital Expenditures	(2,940)
GST Payable (Refund) For Quarter	($1,739)

*GST included sales would be $60,027 [(1.07)($56,100)].

As the quick method produces a larger refund, it would be the preferable method. Note that input tax credits on capital expenditures are available, even when the quick method is used.

Solution to Self Study Problem Four - 1

Businesses are required to register for the GST if taxable revenues for the current calendar quarter or previous four quarters exceed $30,000. As revenues for the four quarters ending September 30, 2001 were under the $30,000 threshold, the business was not required to collect GST in the quarter ending December 31, or in the month of January, 2002.

However, the small supplier threshold was exceeded at the end of December, 2001 with revenues for the four quarters then ending totalling $36,500 ($29,000 - $4,000 + $11,500). Therefore, Chantelle Chance is required to start collecting GST on February 1, 2002 and should register within 30 days.

Solution to Self Study Problem Four - 2

First, determine the selling price at each turnover.

Vendor	Cost	Value Added	Selling Price
Manufacturer	$100	$ 50	$150
Wholesaler	150	75	225
Distributor	225	112	337
Retailer	337	168	505

Under the normal GST system, a 7 percent tax is applied on the selling price at each stage and the business gets an input tax credit for the tax paid on purchased inputs. The net result is that all payments of GST by vendors are refunded as input tax credits, so there is no net out-of-pocket cost (other than administration) to vendors from the GST. The consumer bears the full cost of the tax by paying $35 [($505)(7%)] with no opportunity to get an input tax credit.

Turnover Tax Calculation

The turnover tax is similar to the GST as it applies to revenue. However, the turnover tax is significantly different as there is no input tax credit for tax paid at each stage on purchased goods (inputs). So the tax is passed on to the purchasers in the chain, resulting in pyramidding of the tax. Because of the multiple times goods get taxed, to raise the same amount of tax revenue, the turnover tax rate of 2.88 percent (as shown in the following calculation) is much lower than the 7 percent GST rate.

$$[(\$150)(X\%)] + [(\$225)(X\%)] + [(\$337)(X\%)] + [(\$505)(X\%)] = \$35$$
$$[(\$150 + \$225 + \$337 + \$505)(X\%)] = \$35$$
$$[(\$1,217)(X\%)] = \$35$$
$$X\% = \$35/\$1,217$$
$$X\% = 2.88\%$$

Solution to Self Study Problem Four - 3

Input tax credits can be claimed for periods starting when a business registers or is required to be registered for the GST. Just-In-Time Consulting was required to start collecting the GST in September, as soon as sales passed the $30,000 small supplier threshold. Input tax credits could be claimed for expenses incurred from that point on. It follows that registration and the collection of GST was required in each of October and November, and input tax credits can be claimed for those months as well.

While input tax credits will be calculated from September, they will only be credited to the account of Just-In-Time Consulting once they are actually claimed. Therefore, interest will not be paid on unclaimed input tax credits. If we assume that Just-In-Time's annual revenues will be more than $500,000, but less than $6 million, Just-In-Time will be required to file quarterly GST returns. The return for the quarter ended September 30 of the current year would be due October 31 of the current year. This return is late and interest and penalties will apply. The return for the quarter ended December 31 of the current year will not be late if it is filed by January 31 of the following year.

Solution to Self Study Problem Four - 4

GST is due on the earliest of:

- the invoice date
- the date the invoice should have been issued, but for undue delay
- the date the consideration is due, pursuant to written agreement

GST payment due dates for Quint Technics are:

Fees	Invoice Date	Reporting Period	GST Due
August	September 10	September	October 31
September	October 10	October	November 30
October	December 10	December	January 31
November	January 10	January	February 28
December	January 10	January	February 28

The CCRA could claim that there were unreasonable delays in rendering the October and November invoices, and that the amounts were actually due when the invoices would normally have been issued. That is, the October fees were due on November 10 and the November fees were due on December 10. Therefore, the following due dates could be enforced for these invoices:

Fees	Normal Invoice Date	Reporting Period	GST Due
October	November 10	November	December 31
November	December 10	December	January 31

If the CCRA's claims are legitimate, Quint Technics could be penalized for deficient payments. Normal interest charges would also apply.

Solution to Self Study Problem Four - 5

The required GST remittance for Bombardeaux is based on Canadian GST included sales, and is calculated as follows:

First $30,000 at 4%	$1,200
Remaining $44,900 At 5%	2,245
Subtotal	$3,445
Input Tax Credit (GST Paid On Capital Expenditures) [(7%)($20,000)]	(1,400)
GST Remittance	$2,045

Solution to Self Study Problem Four - 6

The GST refund for Lassen Ltd. for the year would be calculated as follows:

GST Collected ([7%][$5,700,000 - $1,200,000 - $2,400,000 - $1,000,000])	$ 77,000
HST Collected ([15%][$1,000,000])	150,000
Input Tax Credits:	
Purchases ([7%][$2,600,000 - $200,000])	(168,000)
Depreciation And Amortization	Nil
Salaries And Wages	Nil
Building ([7%][$3,000,000][40%])	(84,000)
Other Capital Expenditures	Nil
Nova Scotia Operating Expenses ([15%][$100,000])	(15,000)
Other Operating Expenses ([7%][$370,000 - $100,000])	(18,900)
Accrued Interest	Nil
GST Payable (Refund)	($ 58,900)

Notes:

- The fact that purchases on which GST was paid ($2,400,000) exceed fully taxable sales ($2,100,000) could be the result of zero rated sales. Some zero rated supplies involve

selling items on which GST is paid. An example of this would be export sales.
- There is no need to depreciate or amortize capital expenditures for GST purposes.
- Input tax credits on real property are available based on a pro rata portion of their usage in providing taxable supplies.
- No input tax credits are available on capital expenditures other than real property if less than 50 percent of their usage is for fully taxable and zero rated supplies.
- No GST is paid on salaries or wages and, therefore, no input tax credits are available.
- No GST is paid on accrued interest and, therefore, no input tax credits are available.
- HST at a rate of 15 percent applies to sales and purchases of taxable supplies in Nova Scotia.

Solution to Chapter Five Exercises

Exercise Five - 1

The bonus will be taxed in Mr. Neelson's hands in the year of receipt. This means that it will be included in his 2002 tax return. With respect to Neelson Inc., the bonus is not payable until more that 180 days after the year end. As a consequence, they will not be able to deduct the bonus in the year ending September 30, 2001. It will be deducted in their year ending September 30, 2002.

Exercise Five - 2

Ms. Correli's taxable benefit would be $4,815, the $4,500 cost of the trip, plus the additional $315 in GST.

Exercise Five - 3

The standby charge would be $6,900 [($28,750)(2%)(12)] and the operating cost benefit would be $640 [($0.16)(4,000)], a total of $7,540. As her employment driving is less than 90 percent of the total, she cannot use the reduced standby charge calculation. While she could use the alternative calculation of the operating cost benefit, it would produce a higher taxable benefit.

Exercise Five - 4

The basic standby charge would be $4,428 [(2/3)($7,245)(11/12)]. The 11 is 325/30 rounded to the nearest whole number and represents the months available for use. As his employment related driving exceeds 90 percent of the total, this standby charge can be reduced. The reduced amount would be $1,208 [($4,428)(3,000/11,000)]. The 11,000 is based on multiplying 1,000 kilometers per month by the 11 months the car is available. Mr. Forthwith's operating cost benefit would be $480 [($0.16)(3,000)], resulting in a total taxable benefit of $1,688.

Exercise Five - 5

She will have to include the $3,600 allowance that was received from her employer. She can deduct the employment related portion of her actual automobile costs against this amount. This would be $1,936 [($7,150)(6,500/24,000)]. The net inclusion would be $1,664 ($3,600 - $1,936).

Exercise Five - 6

As his employer contributes to the plan, the $5,250 in benefits received during the year will be included in his Employment Income. This can be offset by the $600 in non deductible contributions that he made during 2000 and 2001, leaving a net inclusion of $4,650.

Exercise Five - 7

The benefit would be $625 [($25,000)(4%)(1/4) + ($25,000)(4%)(1/4) + ($25,000)(3%)(2/4) - ($25,000)(1%)]. Since this is a home purchase, the interest rate used to impute interest will not exceed the prescribed rate at the time the loan was granted (during the first five years of the loan). If the rate decreases, the imputed interest will be calculated using the lower rate. In this case, the second quarter rate is greater than the 4 percent rate on January 1 and the interest rate for the second quarter is limited to 4 percent.

Exercise Five - 8

The employment income inclusion is $22,000 [(1,000)($45 - $23)]. Although she could have deferred this inclusion, she did not choose to make the election to do so.

Exercise Five - 9

For options to buy shares of a private company, no employment income benefit is included until the shares are sold. No election is required to defer the income. As a result, the exercise of the stock options does not affect her employment income for 2001.

Exercise Five - 10

The potential deduction is $27,100 [$8,000 + (1/2)($12,000) + $13,100]. However, this total exceeds his commission income and cannot be deducted under ITA 8(1)(f). If he deducts under ITA 8(1)(h), there is no limit on the total. However, he cannot deduct the advertising or the entertainment. As the travel costs that are deductible under ITA 8(1)(h) exceed the $12,200 limited deduction under ITA 8(1)(f), his maximum deduction is the $13,100 in travel costs.

Solution to Self Study Problem Five - 1

Toyota Camry   The taxable benefit on this vehicle would be calculated as follows:

Full Standby Charge [(5 Months)(2%)($39,000 + $3,120 + $2,730)]	$4,485
Reduced Standby Charge [($4,485)(3,400/5,000)]	$3,050
Operating Cost Benefit ([3,400][$0.16])	544
Total Benefit On Toyota Camry	$3,594

With employment related usage at over 90 percent of the total, Ms. Vines is eligible for the reduced standby charge calculation. With employment related usage at over 50 percent of total usage, Ms. Vines could have calculated the operating cost benefit as one-half of the standby charge or $1,525. The use of the alternative $0.16 per kilometer results in a lower operating cost benefit.

Ford Taurus   The taxable benefit on this vehicle is calculated as follows:

Full Standby Charge ([6 Months][2/3][$625 + $42 + $37 - $100])	$2,416
Operating Cost Benefit ([1/2][$2,416])	1,208
Total Benefit On Ford Taurus	$3,624

As the car was driven less than 90 percent for employment related purposes, no reduction in the standby charge is available. The $100 insurance included in the monthly lease payment is removed from the standby charge calculation as it is an operating cost.

As the car was driven more than 50 percent for employment related purposes, Ms. Vines can calculate the operating cost benefit as either 50 percent of the standby charge or $0.16 per kilometer of personal use. As the $0.16 per kilometer calculation results in a benefit of $2,336 ([14,600 Km][$0.16]), the one-half standby charge approach is preferable. To use this approach, Ms. Vines must notify her employer before the end of the year.

Total Benefit   The total taxable benefit would be calculated as follows:

Total Benefit - Toyota	$3,594
Total Benefit - Ford	3,624
Reimbursement To Company ([$0.10][3,400 Km + 14,600 Km])	(1,800)
Total Taxable Benefit	$5,418

Notes:

- The taxable benefit calculation is not influenced by restrictions on the amount that the Company can deduct with respect to the Camry.
- Calculation of the operating cost benefit is not influenced by the employer's actual operating costs.

Solution to Self Study Problem Five - 2

Mr. Sam Stern   The taxable benefit for the President of the Company would be calculated as follows:

Standby Charge [(2%)(8)($78,000)]	$12,480
Operating Cost Benefit [($0.16)(32,000)]	5,120
Taxable Benefit	$17,600

As Mr. Stern drove the car less than 90 percent for employment related purposes, no reduction in the standby charge is available. Since his employment related use was less than 50 percent, he cannot use the alternative calculation of the operating cost benefit. In this case, it would have produced a higher benefit.

Ms. Sarah Blue   The taxable benefit for the marketing vice president would be as follows:

Standby Charge [(2/3)(12)($900)(5,000/12,000)]	$3,000
Operating Cost Benefit [($0.16)(5,000)]	800
Taxable Benefit	$3,800

As employment related driving was over 90 percent, Ms. Blue can reduce the standby charge on the basis of actual personal usage. While she could have also used the alternative calculation of the operating cost benefit ([1/2][$3,000] = $1,500), it would have produced a higher benefit.

Mr. John Stack   The taxable benefit for the finance vice president would be as follows:

Standby Charge [(2%)(12)($48,000)]	$11,520
Operating Cost Benefit [($0.16)(10,000)]	1,600
Payment For Use of Company Car	(8,000)
Taxable Benefit	$ 5,120

Mr. Stack's employment related driving was less than 90 percent of the total and, as a consequence, he cannot reduce his standby charge on the basis of actual personal milage. While he could use the alternative calculation of the operating cost benefit he would not do so as the result would be $5,760 ([1/2][$11,520]).

Mr. Alex Decker   The taxable benefit for the industrial relations vice president would be calculated as follows:

Standby Charge [(2/3)(10)($500)(8,500/10,000)]	$2,833
Operating Cost Benefit [($0.16)(8,500)]	1,360
Taxable Benefit	$4,193

As Mr. Decker's employment related driving exceeds 90 percent of the total, he can reduce his standby charge on the basis of actual personal milage. He could have used the alternative calculation of the operating cost benefit, but it would have produced a higher benefit. While the $10,000 deposit will affect the deductibility of the lease payments by the employer, it does not influence the calculation of the taxable benefit to Mr. Decker.

Tax Planning   With respect to the tax planning of management compensation, two points can be made. First, the question of providing company cars as a method of compensation should be examined on a case by case basis. In situations where a car is owned by the company and provided to an executive for a fairly long period of time, the taxable benefit assessed may exceed the value of the benefit. For example, over five years the taxable benefit without regard for operating costs on Mr. Stern's Mercedes could total $93,600 [(2%)(60)($78,000)].

This is more than $15,000 in excess of the cost of the car. In addition, with the limitations on the deductibility of CCA and leasing costs on cars, the after tax cost to the company of owning and leasing luxury cars can be very high. While a complete analysis of this issue will depend on a number of variables, it is possible that some of these executives would be better off receiving additional amounts of salary and billing the Company for employment related mileage driven in their own cars.

The second point to be made here is that, except in situations where the car is kept for very short periods of time, the employee will be allocated a smaller taxable benefit if the Company were to lease cars rather than buy them. In general, monthly lease payments on a three year lease will tend to be between 2 percent and 2.5 percent of the capital cost of the car. As the leasing standby charge is based on two-thirds of the monthly lease payment, it is clear that the standby charge under this type of arrangement will be less than the 2 percent per month that is assessed when the Company owns the car. However, for shorter lease terms, the lease payment will be a greater percentage of the capital cost and this relationship may reverse.

Other tax planning techniques would involve any procedure that would reduce the capital cost of purchased cars or the lease payments on leased cars. Such procedures would include high residual values on leasing arrangements and low trade in values assigned to old cars when new ones are purchased. In addition, it might be possible to reduce a taxable benefit such as the one being allocated to Mr. Stern by selling his car to a leasing company with an immediate leaseback arrangement. Although large refundable deposits on leasing arrangements would reduce the lease payment and therefore the standby charge, there would be a tax cost to the employer (see Chapter 7).

Solution to Self Study Problem Five - 3

Approach   The appropriate comparison in evaluating the interest free loan arrangement would be to determine the cost to the Company of providing the loan and then compare this amount with the cost of providing an equivalent benefit in the form of straight salary.

Cost Of Providing Interest Payments On Mortgage   As the problem indicates, Mr. Malone can borrow on a regular mortgage at a rate of interest of 9 percent. This means that the annual interest payments on $200,000 would amount to $18,000. However, Mr. Malone is in the 45 percent tax bracket and, as a consequence, $32,727 ($18,000 ÷ .55) of before tax salary would be required to provide the necessary $18,000 in after tax funds. The annual cost to the Company of this alternative would be as follows:

Gross Salary Increase		$32,727
Reduction In Corporate Taxes (At 40 Percent)		(13,091)
Net Cost To Company		$19,636

Cost Of Providing Interest Free Loan   Mr. Malone would be assessed a taxable benefit on the loan in the amount of imputed interest at the Regulation 4301 rate. The benefit would amount to $14,000 [(7%)($200,000)] for one year. In order to make the two alternatives comparable, it is necessary to recognize that Mr. Malone would pay an additional $6,300 [(45%)($14,000)] in taxes on this benefit and, as a consequence, the Company would have to pay him an additional $11,455 ($6,300 ÷ .55) in salary to provide for this outflow of funds. Given this, the annual cost to the Company of the loan alternative can be calculated as follows:

Gross Salary Increase	$11,455
Reduction In Corporate Taxes (At 40 Percent)	(4,582)
Lost Earnings On Funds Loaned (At 18 Percent)	36,000
Corporate Taxes On Imputed Earnings (At 40 Percent)	(14,400)
Net Cost To Company	$28,473

Conclusion   On the basis of the preceding analysis, it can be concluded that the Company should provide an additional $32,727 in salary rather than providing Mr. Malone with an interest free loan of $200,000. This alternative results in a net annual cost to the Company which is $8,837 lower.

Alternative Calculation   An alternative solution to the question involves calculating the cost to the Company using the value of the interest free loan to Mr. Malone. The annual cost of the mortgage to Mr. Malone is $18,000 (9% of $200,000) and the cost of the taxable benefit on the interest free loan is $6,300 (45% of 7% of $200,000). This means the value of the interest free loan to Mr. Malone is $11,700 ($18,000 - $6,300). He would require $21,273 in before tax salary to make up this difference. To the Company, the after tax cost of the additional $21,273 is $12,764. The cost of the interest free loan to the company after taxes is $21,600 ([18% of $200,000][1 - .4]). The difference in cost is $8,836 ($21,600 - $12,764) in favour of the increased salary. Ignoring the $1 rounding difference, this is the same result that we arrived at under the first calculation.

Solution to Self Study Problem Five - 4

Salary From Maritime Trust [(6/12)($65,000)]		$32,500
Salary From Bolten [(6/12)9$50,000)]		25,000
Total Salaries		$57,500
Maritime Trust Stock Options: (Note 1)		
Market Price Of Shares (5,000 @ $16)	$80,000	
Option Price (5,000 @ $15)	(75,000)	5,000
Bolton Financial Services Stock Options (Note 2)		Nil
Taxable Benefit - Car:		
Standby Charge [(2%)(4 Months)($25,000)]	$2,000	
Operating Costs - The Lesser Of:		
• $1,600 [($0.16)(10,000)]		
• $1,000 [(1/2)($2,000)]	1,000	3,000
Taxable Benefit - Loan [(6%)($100,000)(6/12)]		3,000
Income From Employment		$68,500

Notes:

1. The 2000 budget introduced a provision which allows the deferral of the employment income inclusion on the exercise of publicly traded company stock until the acquired shares are sold. However, Mr. Jurgens did not make this election.

2. As Bolten Financial Services is a Canadian controlled private company, the exercise of the options to purchase its common stock does not result in a taxable benefit at the time of exercise. When the shares are sold, he will have to include the difference between the option price and the fair market value at the time of exercise in employment income.

3. As Mr. Jurgens' employment related milage is less than 90 percent of the total milage, he cannot make use of the reduced standby charge formula. However, his employment related milage is more than 50 percent of the total and, as a consequence, he can elect to calculate the operating cost benefit as 50 percent of the standby charge. Since this amount of $1,000 [(50%)(2,000)] is less than the $1,600 [($0.16)(10,000)] determined through the usual calculation, the $1,000 would be included in Mr. Jurgens' employment income.

4. The imputed interest on the interest free loan must be included in employment income under the requirements of ITA 6(9), a benefit which is defined in ITA 80.4(1). Note, however, there is a deduction under ITA 110(1)(j) for the amount of this benefit which relates to an interest free home relocation loan of $25,000. However, this is a deduction in the calculation of Taxable Income and will not affect the amount of employment income.

5. The interest and dividend income is not included in the calculation of employment income.

Solution to Self Study Problem Five - 5

Mr. Barth's net employment income for the year would be calculated as follows:

Gross Salary	$ 82,500
Bonus (Note One)	20,000
Registered Pension Plan Contributions	(3,200)
Other Withholdings (Note Two)	Nil
Professional Dues	(1,800)
Automobile Benefit (Note Three)	2,860
Counselling Benefit (Note Four)	1,500
Imputed Interest Benefit (Note Five)	750
Net Employment Income	$102,610

Note One   As the bonus is not payable until more than three years after the end of the employer's taxation year, it is a salary deferral arrangement and must be included in income under ITA 6(11).

Note Two   Income taxes withheld are not deductible. United Way donations create a credit against taxes payable, but are not deductible in the determination of employment income. The payments for personal use of the company car are used in the calculation of the taxable benefit associated with this automobile.

Note Three   Since Mr. Barth's employment related usage is less than 90 percent, there is no reduction of the full standby charge. The automobile benefit is calculated as follows:

Standby Charge [(2%)(10)($27,500)]	$5,500
Operating Cost Benefit [($0.16)(6,000 Km)]	960
Total Before Payments	$6,460
Payments Withheld	(3,600)
Taxable Benefit	$2,860

Note Four   IT-470R indicates that counselling services, with the exception of those items specified under ITA 6(1), are considered taxable benefits. The items specified under ITA 6(1) are counselling with respect to mental or physical health or with respect to re-employment. As a consequence, the counselling on personal finances is a taxable benefit.

Note Five   The imputed interest benefit is calculated as follows:

Basic Benefit [($75,000)(6%)(3/12)]	$1,125
Interest Paid	(375)
Taxable Benefit	$ 750

Since the loan was used to invest in income producing assets, Mr. Barth has deductible interest expense of $1,125 related to this loan. However, the interest is not deductible from employment income.

Solution to Self Study Problem Five - 6

Ms. Firth's net employment income for the year would be calculated as follows:

Gross Salary	$ 72,000
Commission Income	14,000
Registered Pension Plan Contributions (Note One)	(3,200)
Disability Insurance Receipts Less Employee's Premium ($2,000 - $250)	1,750
Automobile Benefit (Note Two)	12,920
Automobile Expenses (Note Two)	(5,728)
Term Life Insurance Benefit [($1,350)(2/3)]	900
Low Interest Loan Benefit [($200,000)(6%) - $3,000]	9,000
Christmas Gift (Included Because Employer Deducts)	200
Stock Option Benefit [(1,000)($7 - $5)]	2,000
Entertainment Expenses ([50%][$6,500])	(3,250)
Travel Meals ([50%][$1,300])	(650)
Lodging	(3,500)
Travel Allowance	3,600
Net Employment Income	$100,042

Note One   Contributions made to a registered pension plan under the terms of the plan are deductible. The matching contributions made by the employer are not a taxable benefit.

Note Two   The personal benefit on the company car, taking into consideration the month she was in the hospital and unable to make use of the car, would be calculated as follows:

Reduced Standby Charge [(7,000 ÷ 11,000)(2%)($58,000)(11)]	$ 8,120
Car Allowance	7,200
Operating Costs Benefit	-0-
Total Benefit	$15,320
Less: Payments Withheld By Employer	(2,400)
Taxable Benefit	$12,920

The deductible car expenses would be $5,728 [($6,200)(85,000 Km/92,000 Km)].

Excluded Items   Items not included and the reason for their exclusion:

- Federal and provincial income taxes withheld are not deductible.

- The purchase of Canada savings bonds is a non deductible capital expenditure. Any interest charged on the payroll deduction purchase is deductible from Net Income For Tax Purposes, but does not affect employment income.

Solution to Chapter Six Exercises

Exercise Six - 1

The basic mechanism here is the Pension Adjustment (PA). Individuals who belong to an RPP or a DPSP have their RRSP deduction limit reduced by the amount of their PA for the previous year. PAs are designed to reflect the amount of contributions or benefits that have been accumulated in employer sponsored RPPs and DPSPs.

Exercise Six - 2

The addition to deduction room for 2001 is $6,840 [(18%)($38,000)]. At the end of the year, his Unused RRSP Deduction Room would be $7,140 ($4,800 + $6,840 - $4,500).

Exercise Six - 3

His Earned Income for RRSP purposes would be $70,500 ($56,000 + $2,500 + $12,000).

Exercise Six - 4

Her Earned Income for RRSP purposes would be $54,500 ($82,000 + $3,000 - $12,500 - $18,000).

Exercise Six - 5

The Pension Adjustment will be $6,400 ($2,300 + $1,800 + $2,300).

Exercise Six - 6

Given Ms. Brownell's level of income, she will have a $13,500 addition to her deduction room in both 2000 and 2001 (this is the RRSP dollar limit for both years). As her 2000 contribution is $14,500, she will only be in excess of her deduction room by $1,000 and no penalty will be assessed. However, when she makes the May 1, 2001 contribution, she will be over her deduction room by $4,000 [$14,500 + $16,500 - (2)($13,500)]. A one percent per month penalty is applicable to amounts above $2,000. As a consequence, there will be a 2001 penalty of $160 [(1%)($4,000 - $2,000)(8)].

Exercise Six - 7

As the withdrawal is before January 1, 2002, Mrs. Garveau will be responsible for the taxes on $5,000 of the withdrawal, the amount of her contribution. The remaining $4,000 will be taxed in the hands of her husband.

Exercise Six - 8

Ms. DeBoo will have to repay $867 [(1/15)($18,000 - $5,000)] during 2001. Note that the voluntary payment that was made during 2000 did not reduce the fraction of the remaining balance that must be paid in 2001.

Exercise Six - 9

There are no tax consequences associated with the withdrawal of $5,000. As he will have no education tax credit in either 2002 or 2003, his repayment period begins in 2003. As he makes the required payments of $500 in each of the years 2004 through 2013, there are no tax consequences associated with his repayments. This is true despite the fact that the payments are made in the first 60 days of the year following their due date.

Exercise Six - 10

He has no required minimum withdrawal for 2001, the year the RRIF is established. His minimum withdrawal for 2002 will be $26,042 [$625,000 ÷ (90 - 66)].

Exercise Six - 11

Mr. Bartoli can rollover a total of $59,500 [($2,000)(20 Years Before 1996) + ($1,500)(13 Years Before 1989)] to his RRSP. The remainder of the retiring allowance will be taxed in 2001.

Solution to Self Study Problem Six - 1

Mr. Barnes' 2000 Earned Income for RRSP purposes would be calculated as follows:

Salary	$40,175
Taxable Benefits	1,150
Union Dues	(175)
Net Employment Income	$41,150
Business Income	4,150
Rental Loss	(11,875)
Spousal Support Received	2,400
Earned Income	$35,825

Part A - Not A Member Of RPP Or DPSP　Under the assumption that Mr. Barnes is not a member of a Registered Pension Plan or a Deferred Profit Sharing Plan, the increase in his RRSP Deduction Limit for 2001 is the lesser of $13,500 or $6,449 (18 percent of 2000 Earned Income). In this case, $6,449 would be the smaller amount.

Also note that Canada Pension Plan contributions do not reduce Earned Income for purposes of maximum allowable contributions to a Registered Retirement Savings Plan.

Based on the preceding, Mr. Barnes' maximum deductible RRSP contribution for 2001 is calculated as follows:

2000 Unused RRSP Deduction Room	$ 700
2001 Earned Income Limit (18% Of $35,825)	6,449
RRSP Deduction Limit	$7,149

Part B - Member Of RPP　In this case, the maximum 2001 deduction would be the amount calculated in Part A, reduced by his 2000 pension adjustment of $4,200. This would leave a maximum deductible RRSP contribution of only $2,949 ($7,149 - $4,200). Note that while Mr. Barnes' actual net employment income for 2000 would be reduced by any RPP contributions made for that year, the employment income amount used in the RRSP Earned Income calculation does not reflect this reduction.

Solution to Self Study Problem Six - 2

The most desirable solution would be to find benefits that would be fully deductible to the Company and free of taxation for Mr. Jones. The only items that fall into this category would be payments for private health care plans, and discounts on Company merchandise. Discounts on industrial engines are not likely to be of any value to Mr. Jones. However, Mr. Jones should arrange to have the Company provide private health care coverage including a dental plan. The Company could also pay the premiums on a disability insurance plan without it becoming a taxable benefit to Mr. Jones at the time of payment. Any benefits received under such a plan would have to be taken into income when received.

In terms of tax deferral, Mr. Jones should be included in the Company's registered pension plan. Once he is admitted to the plan, both he and the company should make the maximum contributions that are permitted under the terms of the plan. The limiting factor here is that these contributions cannot result in a pension adjustment that is in excess of the lesser of 18 percent of Mr. Jones' employment income for the year or the money purchase limit for the year under consideration ($13,500 for 2001).

While there is no indication that the Company has such an arrangement, a deferred profit sharing plan might also be useful. Whether or not Mr. Jones would be able to use such an arrangement would depend on the total employee/employer contributions to the Company's registered pension plan. Contributions to a deferred profit sharing plan are included in the calculation of Mr. Jones' pension adjustment and, when combined with the registered pension plan contributions, the total is subject to the limitation described in the preceding paragraph.

It would also be advisable for Mr. Jones to arrange for some of the compensation to be received in the form of a retiring allowance to be paid to a Registered Retirement Savings Plan at the end of the three years. As he will have been employed a total of 14 years by Martin, 11 of them prior to 1996, a total of $22,000 ($2,000 per year of pre-1996 service) could be rolled over in this form. In addition, an additional amount of $1,500 per year of pre-1989 service while not a member of the registered pension plan could also be rolled over on a tax free basis to this Registered Retirement Savings Plan.

The Company could provide a loan to Mr. Jones to purchase his new residence. As Mr. Jones is moving, he is eligible for a deduction of the benefit associated with a $25,000 interest free "home relocation" loan. Any additional low interest or interest free loan will result in imputed interest being added to Mr. Jones' taxable income without an offsetting deduction. Whether or not this will be beneficial will depend on a number of factors including whether he is able to raise the funds at a rate lower than that specified under Regulation 4301 for assessing imputed interest. As the Regulation 4301 rate changes on a quarterly basis, some attention would also have to be given to expected future movements of this rate. However, Mr. Jones can use the rate in effect at the time the loan is made for the first five years.

The Company could provide Mr. Jones with an automobile. In this case Mr. Jones will be assessed for a personal benefit of a standby charge (24 percent per year of the capital cost or two-thirds of the lease payments) and for operating costs (one-half of the standby charge or $0.16 per kilometer of personal use). Whether or not this will be desirable depends on an analysis of how Mr. Jones would actually use the car. In some cases, especially if the car has a list price of more than $30,000, the taxable benefit may exceed the actual benefit, making this an undesirable form of compensation.

The Company could pay the dues for any recreational facilities that Mr. Jones might wish to use. While these amounts will not be treated as a taxable benefit to Mr. Jones, the payments will not be deductible to the Company. Given that both the Company and Mr. Jones will be in the 50 percent tax bracket, there would appear to be no significant advantage to this type of arrangement.

The Company could provide assistance with the costs that will be incurred by Mr. Jones in moving to Hamilton. With respect to costs that Mr. Jones would be permitted to deduct, it makes little difference whether the Company pays the costs or simply pays an equivalent amount in salary and lets Mr. Jones pay the costs and deduct them. However, certain types of moving costs that would not be deductible by Mr. Jones can be paid by the Company without creating a taxable benefit. An example of this would be compensation for a loss on a personal residence owned by Mr. Jones in Vancouver. (See Chapter 11)

If Martin Manufacturing has a year end after July 6, it can declare a bonus in the third year, but not pay it until the following calendar year. This will defer Mr. Jones' taxation of the bonus by one year without deferring Martin's deduction.

Since Mr. Jones has been operating as a consultant for the last seven years, it may be possible to structure the project so that he will be considered an independent contractor rather than an employee. This would considerably increase the amount and type of expenditures that would be deductible by him and also create an opportunity to income split with his wife if she could assist him in the project in some way. In considering this alternative it should be kept in mind that, if Mr. Jones is not an employee, some of the possibilities that have been previously discussed would no longer be feasible. For example, unless Mr. Jones is an employee, it would not be possible for him to be a member of the Company's registered pension plan.

Another possibility would be for Mr. Jones to provide his services through a corporation. However, this would probably not be helpful. Given his relationship with Martin Manufacturing Company, any corporation would likely be viewed as a personal services business and taxed at full corporate rates.

As an incentive, the Company could grant Mr. Jones options to purchase its stock. This would have no cost to the Company. The timing of the tax cost of the options for Mr. Jones could be delayed until after retirement.

Solution to Self Study Problem Six - 3

Part A Mr. Beasley's net employment income for 2000 would be $22,700, his gross salary of $24,000 reduced by RPP contributions of $1,300.

Part B Mr. Beasley's maximum deductible 2001 RRSP contribution would be equal to the lesser of $13,500 and 18 percent of his 2000 earned income, reduced by his 2000 pension adjustment. His earned income would be calculated as follows:

Net Employment Income	$22,700
RPP Contributions	1,300
Spousal Support	9,000
Net Rental Loss	(5,000)
Earned Income	$28,000

Eighteen percent of this amount is $5,040, which is less than the limit of $13,500. Therefore his maximum deductible 2001 RRSP contribution would be $2,440, $5,040 less the 2000 pension adjustment of $2,600. Note that the damage award, royalties, interest, dividends, and gift are not included in earned income.

Part C As Mr. Beasley has made no contributions prior to 2001, he has no undeducted contributions. In addition, he has substantial savings which are earning interest and dividends that are subject to current taxes payable. This would suggest that Mr. Beasley should contribute the maximum deductible amount of $2,440 in 2001. In addition, he should make a further 2001 contribution of $2,000, the maximum over contribution that would not subject him to the one percent per month penalty on such amounts. While he could not currently deduct this over contribution, it will enjoy the benefit of having any income compounded on a tax free basis. Further, this amount can be deducted in any future year, subject to the usual RRSP deduction limits.

Note that this $4,440 contribution should be made, whether or not Mr. Beasley decides to make the maximum deduction of $2,440 in 2001. Since he will not be in the maximum federal tax bracket until 2002, it could be advantageous to defer taking the $2,440 available deduction until 2002.

Solution to Self Study Problem Six - 4

Part A   Ms. Stratton's employment income would be calculated as follows:

Gross Salary	$72,000
Additions:	
Employer Contribution To Provincial Health Insurance Plan	482
Employer's Contributions For Life Insurance	96
Trip To Bermuda	4,500
Deductions:	
RPP Contributions	(2,390)
Professional Dues	(225)
Net Employment Income	$74,463

The reasons for not including the other items in the problem in the preceding calculation are as follows:

1. Income taxes cannot be deducted in the calculation of net income for tax purposes or taxable income.

2. Contributions to registered charities create a credit against taxes payable, but cannot be deducted in the calculation of employment income.

3. Employer payments to employee dental plans and private health care plans are not a taxable benefit.

4. Employer payments to employee group income protection plans are not a taxable benefit.

5. The EI and CPP contributions are eligible for tax credit treatment.

6. Employer payments for membership fees in social or recreational clubs are generally not a taxable benefit to the employee, provided the facilities are used for business purposes.

7. As the travel allowance is based on actual milage and costs, it does not have to be included in the employee's income.

8. Contributions to the Registered Retirement Savings Plan can be deducted under Subdivision e but not in the calculation of employment income.

Part B   Ms. Stratton's maximum deductible 2001 RRSP contribution is the lesser of 18 percent of 2000 earned income of $76,853 ($74,463 + $2,390) and $13,500, reduced by her 2000 pension adjustment of $5,560. The lesser figure is $13,500, resulting in a maximum deductible contribution of $7,940 ($13,500 - $5,560). This means that $1,060 ($9,000 - $7,940) of the contribution will not be deductible in 2001.

However, the $9,000 contribution is still a good idea. Funds invested in an RRSP accumulate earnings on a tax free basis and, unless non deductible contributions accumulate to $2,000 or more, no penalty is applied. Further, contributions which are not deducted can be carried over and are available for deduction in any subsequent year. This means that Ms. Stratton will enjoy the benefits of tax free compounding without experiencing any unfavourable tax consequences.

Solution to Self Study Problem Six - 5

Part A   With respect to the retiring allowance, ITA 56(1)(a)(ii) requires that the entire $125,000 must be included in income. Then, to the extent that such amounts are transferred or contributed to an RRSP for which the taxpayer is the annuitant, the taxpayer is entitled to a deduction under ITA 60(j.1) equal to $2,000 for each year of service prior to 1996 with the employer, plus an additional $1,500 for each year of service before 1989 for which the employee was not a member of an RPP. This provides for the following maximum deduction under ITA 60(j.1):

19 Years At $2,000 Per Year	$38,000
12 Years At $1,500 Per Year	18,000
Total	$56,000

Given this calculation, the maximum RRSP deduction that Mr. Colt would be allowed for 2001 would be calculated as follows:

Retiring Allowance Rollover (See Preceding)	$56,000
Opening RRSP Deduction Room	32,000
Addition For Year [(18%)(46,000)]	8,280
Pension Adjustment	(8,000)
Maximum Deduction	$88,280

Part B   Mr. Colt will be able to deduct the full $50,000 of the retiring allowance that was transferred to his own RRSP. While another $38,280 could have been deducted under ITA 60(j.1), the amounts transferred to a spousal RRSP are not eligible for this deduction. However, contributions to the spousal RRSP can be deducted under ITA 60(i). Using the assumed maximum ITA 60(i) deduction calculated in the preceding paragraph, we can calculate the following amount of non deductible contributions:

Total Contributions	$125,000
Maximum Deduction Under ITA 60(j.1)	(50,000)
Maximum Regular Deduction ($88,280 - $56,000)	(32,280)
Non Deductible Contributions	$ 42,720

To the extent that non deductible contributions exceed $2,000, they are subject to a heavy penalty of one percent per month. As a consequence, Mr. Colt should immediately withdraw $40,720 ($42,720 - $2,000) from the spousal RRSP. If this occurs before March 2, 2002, he can contribute and deduct an additional $6,000 ($56,000 - $50,000) to his own RRSP.

Unless he is in need of the funds, he should leave the $2,000 non deductible contribution in the spousal plan and contribute $2,000 more to his own RRSP in order to enjoy the advantages of tax free accumulation of earnings on the $2,000 cushion that is available.

Solution to Chapter Seven Exercises

Exercise Seven - 1
Provided that she can demonstrate that her intent was to operate the building as a rental property, the gain should qualify as a capital gain.

Exercise Seven - 2
The net amount to be included in business income for tax purposes would be $73,675 ($53,400 + $26,300 - $5,600 - $425).

Exercise Seven - 3

For tax purposes, the lease would be treated as an operating lease, with the deduction being based only on the lease payments. Under GAAP, the lease would have to be treated as a purchase (capitalized). This is because the lease term is more than 75 percent of the asset's expected useful life, and the lease payments are more than 90 percent of the asset's fair value at the inception of the lease. This means that the accounting deductions would be for amortization on the capitalized asset and interest costs on the associated liability.

Exercise Seven - 4

The net decrease for the year will be $19,600 ($16,000 - $17,200 - $18,400).

Exercise Seven - 5

The actual daily interest cost on the car loan is $11.11 ($1,200/108 days). This is greater than the daily allowable limit of $10.00. As a result, she will only be able to deduct $10.00 ($300/30) per day for the 108 days the financing was in place, a total of $1,080.

Exercise Seven - 6

The amount he can deduct is limited to $2,229, the lesser of:

- $4,080 [($800)(153/30)]; and
- $2,229 {[$4,925][$30,000 ÷ (85%)($78,000)]}.

Exercise Seven - 7

The required adjustment will be an addition of $2,300 ($13,500 - $11,200) to cost of sales, with a corresponding reduction in net income for tax purposes.

Exercise Seven - 8

Ms. Morph appears to be a part time farmer and, as a consequence, her farm losses will be restricted. The amount she can deduct for 2001 will be $8,750 [$2,500 + (1/2)($12,500)]. The remaining restricted farm loss is available for carry over.

Exercise Seven - 9

The tax effect would be a net deduction of $1,450 [$3,800 - ($53,450 - $48,200)].

Solution to Self Study Problem Seven - 1

Part A   In Part A(i), Ms. Wise is an employee and, because her income includes commissions, she can deduct expenses related to the production of employment income under ITA 8(1)(f), provided no deduction is made for traveling expenses (including automobile costs other than capital costs) under ITA 8(1)(h) or ITA 8(1)(h.1). Deductions under ITA 8(1)(f) are limited to the amount of commissions earned. Alternatively, traveling costs can be deducted under ITA 8(1)(h) and ITA 8(1)(h.1) without being limited to commission income. A further limitation, which is not illustrated in this problem, prevents the deduction of home office costs from creating an employment loss. The deduction of dues and other expenses under ITA 8(1)(i) and automobile capital costs under ITA 8(1)(j) is permitted without regard to other provisions used.

The first column of the solution which follows calculates the available deduction using ITA 8(1)(h), (h.1), (i), and (j). Note that when this approach is used, home office costs are limited to utilities and maintenance. Further, there is no deduction for entertainment costs. This provides for a total deduction of $32,390.

The second and third columns calculate the available deductions under ITA 8(1)(i) and (j), as well as separately under ITA 8(1)(f). As the ITA 8(1)(f) amount is limited to the $15,000 in commission income, the total deduction is $28,390 ($13,390 + $15,000), $4,000 less than the amount available using ITA 8(1)(h), (h.1), (i), and (j). Of the non deductible costs arising under this approach, the $2,260 ($380 + $1,880) in home office costs can be carried forward to be deducted under ITA 8(1)(f) in a subsequent year.

	Part A(i) ITA 8(1)(h), (h.1), (i), and (j)	Part A(i) ITA 8(1) (i) and (j)	Part A(i) ITA 8(1)(f)	Part A(ii)
Professional Dues	$ 600	$ 600		$ 600
Automobile Costs:				
Operating Costs [(35,000/50,000)($8,500)]	5,950	5,950		5,950
CCA (Note One)	4,820	4,820		4,820
Home Office Costs:				
Utilities [(40%)($3,550)]	1,420	1,420		1,420
Maintenance [(40%)($1,500)]	600	600		600
Insurance [(40%)($950)]			$ 380	380
Property Taxes [(40%)($4,700)]			1,880	1,880
Interest [(40%)($13,500)]				5,400
CCA [($120,000)(4%)(40%)]				1,920
Travel Costs	23,000		23,000	23,000
Non Deductible Meals (50% of $8,000)	(4,000)		(4,000)	(4,000)
Entertainment Expenses			12,000	12,000
Non Deductible (Note Two)			(7,250)	(7,250)
Total	$32,390	$13,390	$26,010	$46,720

Note One The car will be allocated to Class 10.1 at a value of $27,000, the 2000 limit. The excess of $3,000 will not be deductible. Maximum CCA for 2000 would have been $4,050 [(30%)(1/2)($27,000)]. The January 1, 2001 UCC would be $22,950 ($27,000 - $4,050) and 2001 CCA equals $4,820 [(30%)($22,950)(70%)]. Her 2000 business usage would not be relevant as the maximum CCA would be deducted from the UCC, but only the portion of CCA related to her business use of the car would be deducted from employment or business income.

Note Two The non deductible costs charged by the local country club are as follows:

Membership Dues	$2,500
Entertainment Costs ([50%][$9,500])	4,750
Total Non Deductible	$7,250

Comparing Case A (i) and A (ii), there is a difference of $14,330 ($46,720 - $32,390) between the maximum employee and self employed calculations, illustrating the importance of the difference between being an employee and being self employed. The example is, of course, somewhat unrealistic in that, if Ms. Wise was an employee, it is likely that she would be compensated or reimbursed for at least part of her employment related expenses.

Part B The deduction of capital cost allowance would be virtually certain to trigger recapture and capital gains on a proportionate part of her personal residence when it is eventually sold. While taxation on capital gains might occur even if no capital cost allowance is taken, the deduction of capital cost allowance makes taxes on a proportionate part of recapture and capital gains virtually certain.

Solution to Self Study Problem Seven - 2

The required calculations would be as follows:

Accounting Net Income		$298,000
Additions:		
LIFO Excess ($296,000 - $271,000)	$ 25,000	
Increase In Warranty Reserve	14,500	
Income Tax Expense	158,000	
Depreciation Expense	53,750	
Contributions To Registered Charity	4,300	
Life Insurance Premium	3,100	
Golf Club Membership	1,400	
50% of Business Meals (50% of $3,400)	1,700	
Cost Of Amending Articles (Note One)	14,300	
Appraisal Costs (Note One)	7,400	
Stock Issue Costs (Note Two)	12,480	295,930
Subtotal		$593,930
Deduction:		
Bond Premium Amortization		(5,900)
Business Income		$588,030

Note One   The cost of amending the Company's articles would be considered an eligible capital expenditure, three-quarters of which would be added to cumulative eligible capital. The fees paid to appraise certain of the Company's assets for sale would be added to the adjusted cost base of these assets.

Note Two   ITA 20(1)(e) requires the deduction of stock issue costs over a five year period at a rate of 20 percent per year. For the current year, 80% of the total stock issue costs of $15,600 are nondeductible and added to Accounting Net Income.

Note Three   In general, contributions to RPPs and DPSPs are deductible as long as they are made under the provisions of registered plans. Continued registration of the plan requires that they not create a pension adjustment that exceeds the lesser of 18% of the employee's income and the money purchase limit for the year. This is clearly not a problem here. There is a further restriction on DPSP contributions in that they cannot exceed one-half of the money purchase limit for the year. Again, this is not a problem here.

Note Four   While interest on late income tax instalments is clearly not deductible, there does not appear to be a similar prohibition against interest on late property taxes.

Note Five   As the landscaping costs have already been deducted in accounting Net Income, they do not require adjustment for tax purposes.

Solution to Self Study Problem Seven - 3

The minimum Income From Business Or Property for Barnes Industries would be as follows:

Accounting Income Before Taxes		$426,000
Additions:		
Contributions To Charities (Item 2)	$ 2,500	
Contributions To Political Parties (Item 2)	1,000	
LIFO/FIFO Adjustment (Item 3 - Note One)	4,000	
Depreciation Expense	241,000	
Director's Fees (Item 5 - Note Two)	25,000	
Warranty Reserve (Item 8 - Note Three)	9,000	
Non Deductible Meals And		
Entertainment (50% of $13,500) (Item 12)	6,750	
Amortization Of Bond Discount	1,800	
Non Deductible Lease Payments		
(Item 14 - Note Four)	13,037	304,087
Deductions:		
Capital Cost Allowance (Item 6)	(389,000)	
Issue Costs (Item 10 - Note Five)	(1,600)	
Landscaping Costs (Item 11)	(11,000)	(401,600)
Minimum Income From Business Or Property		$328,487

Note One As LIFO cannot be used for tax purposes, the tax figures will have to be adjusted to a FIFO basis. This will require a $20,000 ($366,000 - $346,000) increase in the opening Inventory and a $24,000 ($447,000 -$423,000) increase in the closing inventory. This will reduce Cost Of Goods Sold by $4,000 and increase tax income by a corresponding amount.

Note Two Under ITA 67, these fees would be disallowed as not being reasonable in the circumstances.

Note Three For tax purposes, warranty costs can only be deducted as incurred. Therefore, the $9,000 ($27,000 - $18,000) increase in the warranty reserve must be added back to accounting income.

Note Four Under ITA 67.3, the deductible amount of the lease payments is limited to the lesser of:

- $[(\$800)(365/30)] = \$9,733$
- $\{[\$18,000][\$30,000 \div (85\%)(\$128,000)]\} = \$4,963$

The non deductible portion of the lease payments is $13,037 ($18,000 - $4,963).

Note Five Under ITA 20(1)(e), issue costs must be amortized at the rate of 20 percent per year. As the full amount was treated as an asset in the accounting records, the required adjustment is a deduction of $1,600 [(20%)($8,000)].

Several of the items described in the problem did not require any adjustment. The explanations for these omissions are as follows:

Item 1 As the accounting income figure is before taxes, no adjustment is required for the estimate of income tax expense.

Item 7 As the advertising was not directed at the Canadian market, it can be deducted for tax purposes and no adjustment is required.

Item 9 As the same bad debt estimates were used for tax purposes and accounting purposes, no adjustment is required with respect to bad debts.

Solution to Self Study Problem Seven - 4

The income from business and property of Darby Inc. would be calculated as follows:

Accounting Income (Loss) Before Taxes	($113,000)
Additions:	
Item 2 - Property Taxes On Recreational Facility	1,100
Item 3 - Donations (Note One)	13,700
Item 9 - Lease Cancellation Payment (Note Two)	17,000
Item 11 - Insurance Premium (Note Three)	9,500
Item 12 - Excess Of FIFO Inventory Value Over LIFO Value	37,200
Item 16 - Bad Debt On Supplier Loan (Note Four)	4,500
Item 17 - Renovation Costs (Note Five)	153,000
Item 18 - Wife's Convention Expenses	1,900
Item 19 - Bond Discount Amortization	950
Item 20 - Cost Of Amending Articles (Note Six)	3,600
Item 21 - Non Deductible Portion Of	
Meals and Entertainment ([50%][$12,500])	6,250
Income From Business Or Property	**$135,700**

Note One   The contributions to registered charities will be deductible in the computation of taxable income but not in the computation of income from a business or property. Charitable contributions are still a deduction for corporations, although they are eligible for tax credit treatment for individuals. The political contributions are not deductible at any stage but will generate a credit in determining the amount of taxes payable.

Note Two   ITA 20(1)(z) requires that lease cancellation payments be amortized over the term of the lease remaining immediately before cancellation. The amount to be deducted is a pro rata calculation based on the number of days remaining subsequent to the calculation. As the cancellation occurred on December 31, 2001, none of the amount would be deductible during the current year. The $17,000 would be deducted over the seven years that would have remained of the lease term at the rate of $2,429 per year.

Note Three   Life insurance premiums are not paid to produce income and are not deductible when not required by a creditor.

Note Four   For an amount to be deductible as a bad debt in the computation of business income, it must have been included in the business income of some prior period. As this loan has not been included in income, the write off cannot be deducted as a bad debt expense. It will, however, give rise to an allowable capital loss of $2,250 ([1/2][$4,500]). As this problem asks only for the calculation of income from business or property, this allowable capital loss has not been considered in the solution.

Note Five   These amounts serve to extend the life of the relevant asset and should be treated as capital expenditures.

Note Six   The payment to amend the articles of incorporation would be an eligible capital expenditure and three-quarters of the $3,600 would be added to the cumulative eligible capital amount. The Company would be able to deduct amortization of this amount. However, you have been instructed to ignore such amortization in this problem.

Other Items   Further explanation related to the items not included in the preceding calculation of income from a business or property are as follows:

Item 1   If the damages relate to a transaction that produces business income, they are considered a business expense.

Item 4   Landscaping costs are fully deductible under ITA 20(1)(aa).

Item 5   As the subsidiary is likely to produce dividend income, the interest on funds borrowed to acquire the shares is deductible.

Item 6   Contributions to RPPs are deductible to the extent that they are made in accordance with the provisions of the plan. To maintain its registration, the plan cannot be structured in a manner that will produce pension adjustments that exceed the lesser of the money purchase limit for the year ($13,500 for 2001) and 18 percent of the employee's compensation for the year. Given the compensation of the employees under consideration, that would not appear to be the case here and, as a consequence, all of the RPP contributions would be deductible for tax purposes in 2001.

Item 7   To be deductible, DPSP contributions cannot exceed the lesser of one-half the money purchase limit for the year ($6,750 for 2001) and 18 percent of the employee's compensation for the year. All of the contributions here are within this limit and, as a consequence, can be deducted for tax purposes in 2001.

Item 8   Losses of this type, unless they result from the activity of senior officers or shareholders, are considered to be deductible as a normal cost of doing business.

Item 10   The bonus to the President would be deductible in 2001.

Item 13   Such appraisal costs are considered to be deductible as a normal cost of doing business.

Item 14   The dividends are included in the calculation of income from a business or property. They are deducted from taxable income.

Item 15   The $51,000 in management bonuses would be deductible in 2001. The forfeited bonuses would be given the same treatment for tax purposes as they were in the accounting records.

Item 16   The bad debts, other than those related to the loan to a shareholder of a supplier, would be fully deductible.

Item 18   The $3,300 in costs associated with the President attending the convention would be deductible.

Item 20   Both the costs of defending against the breach of contract action, as well as the costs related to the income tax reassessment, would be fully deductible.

Solution to Self Study Problem Seven - 5

The solution provides a detailed analysis of each of the items described in the problem after the following calculation of Division B, Subdivision b income from business or property.

Accounting Income	$ 780,000
Life Insurance Premiums (Item 1)	19,000
Convention Costs (Item 3)	4,500
Legal Costs (Item 6)	3,600
Excess of CCA over Depreciation (Item 7)	(135,000)
Contributions (Item 8)	21,500
Bad Debts Adjustment (Item 10)	8,500
Dividend Paid (Item 11)	17,000
Bond Discount (Item 13)	14,000
Lease Cancellation (Item 14)	24,989
LIFO Adjustment (Item 16)	72,000
Remodelling Costs (Item 17)	225,000
Subdivision b Income From Business or Property	$1,055,089

Notes:

Item 1   When the proceeds of a life insurance policy are payable to the company, the cost is not directed towards producing income and the premiums are not deductible. This amount must be added back to income.

Item 3   The cost of taking Mr. Norton's family to the convention would be a living expense, specifically prohibited under ITA 18. This amount must be added back to income.

Item 6   With respect to the legal costs, both the $8,000 cost of defending against an action by a customer and the $10,500 cost of disputing an income tax assessment would be deductible and would require no adjustment. However, the cost of issuing new shares must be amortized over five years. This means that $3,600 [(4/5)($4,500)] must be added to income.

Item 7   The accounting depreciation expense of $275,000 would have to be added back and the maximum capital cost allowance of $410,000 would be deducted. The net adjustment would be a deduction of $135,000.

Item 8   Neither of these amounts can be deducted in the computation of Division B, subdivision b income. The charitable contributions will be deductible in the computation of Division C taxable income and the political contributions will provide a credit against taxes payable. At this level, however, the entire $21,500 must be added back to income.

Item 10   ITA 20(1)(p) requires that an amount must be previously included in income before it can be written off as a bad debt. The loan described here does not fall into that category and is, therefore, not deductible as a bad debt expense. However, one-half of the amount can be deducted as an allowable capital loss, provided the Company has capital gains that it can be applied against. As the problem only asks for subdivision b income, this loss is not reflected in the solution.

Item 11   No adjustment is required for the bonus. The $17,000 dividend paid is not deductible and must be added back to income.

Item 13   The amortization of bond discount is not deductible during the life of the bond. As a consequence, the full $14,000 must be added back to income.

Item 14   Under ITA 20(1)(z), the lessor's costs of cancelling a lease are deductible over the term of the lease remaining immediately before its cancellation. This means that for the year ending December 31, 2001, only $3,011 of the total is deductible. This amount is calculated by taking the 275 days remaining in 2001 after the cancellation fee was paid and dividing it by the 2,557 days [(7 Years)(365 Days) + 2 Days for the leap years in 2004 and 2008) which would have remained in the term of the lease after March 31, 2001. This fraction is then multiplied by the fee of $28,000 to give $3,011. With only $3,011 being deductible during the current year, $24,989 must be added back to income.

Item 16   The last in, first out method is not allowed by the CCRA, a position that has been supported by litigation (see Anaconda American Brass Ltd. 55 DTC 1220). As a consequence, the difference between the first in, first out and the last in, first out values will have to be added back to income.

Item 17   Under ITA 18(1)(b), any expenditure which prolongs the life of an asset must be treated as an addition to the capital cost of that asset. This means that the $225,000 must be added back to income. The effect of this addition should be reflected in the maximum capital cost allowance calculation in Item 7.

Other items that do not require adjustments to Net Income are as follows:

Item 2   Since the interest expense was incurred to acquire an income producing investment, it will be deductible and no adjustment is required.

Item 4   ITA 20(1)(aa) specifically provides for the deduction of landscaping costs, even though they might be considered a capital expenditure. No adjustment is required.

Item 5   Appraisal costs required for the maintenance of normal insurance coverage is a deductible expense. No adjustment is required.

Item 9   The dividend received would be included under income from property. The dividend would then be deducted in the calculation of taxable income. No adjustment is required.

Item 12   As long as the theft was not committed by a senior officer it will be considered deductible. Assuming that this is the case, no adjustment is required.

Item 15   Employer contributions to a RPP are deductible as long as they are made under the normal terms of a registered plan. To retain its registration, the plan must be designed in such a fashion that it does not produce pension adjustments that exceed the lesser of the money purchase limit for the year ($13,500 for 2001) and 18 percent of the employee's compensation for the year. As the plan is registered, it can be assumed that the contributions are within the limits.

Solution to Chapter Eight Exercises

Exercise Eight - 1
CCA should have been $48,900 [($326,000)(1/2)(30%)]. The amount recorded was $6,520 [($326,000)(1/2)(4%)]. This error understated deductions and overstated income by $42,380 ($48,900 - $6,520).

Exercise Eight - 2
Computers would be included in Class 10, a 30 percent declining balance class. If no election is made, there will be a deduction for CCA of $17,850 [($100,000 - $3,000 + $22,000)(1/2)(30%)]. Alternatively, if each machine is allocated to a separate class, there will be a deduction for CCA of $15,300 {[(8)($10,000) + (2)($11,000)][1/2][30%]}. In addition, there will be a terminal loss of $17,000 [($10,000 - $1,500)(2)]. The use of the election increases the total deduction by $14,450.

Exercise Eight - 3
The CCA on the 1996 capital costs would be $3,467 [($52,000 ÷ 15)]. The CCA on the 2001 capital costs, after taking into consideration the half year rules, would be $1,550 [($31,000 ÷ 10)(1/2)]. The total for the year would be $5,017 ($3,467 + $1,550).

Exercise Eight - 4
The required information would be calculated as follows:

December 31, 2000 UCC Balance	$212,000
Additions	37,400
Proceeds Of Disposal	(18,300)
One-Half Net Additions [(50%)($37,400 - $18,300)]	(9,550)
CCA Base	$221,550
2001 CCA @ 20 Percent	(44,310)
One-Half Net Additions	9,550
December 31, 2001 UCC Balance	$186,790

Exercise Eight - 5
The maximum CCA for the year is $4,821 [(20%)($115,000)(1/2)(153/365)].

Exercise Eight - 6

The effect would be an addition of $2,117 ($24,883 - $27,000) in recaptured CCA. While there would also be a taxable capital gain of $750 [($28,500 - $27,000)(1/2)], this would not be included in Net Business Income.

Exercise Eight - 7

As there is a positive balance in the Class at the end of the year, but no remaining assets, there would be a terminal loss of $6,883 ($24,883 - $18,000).

Exercise Eight - 8

The Company would have to record recapture of $750,000 ($650,000 - $1,400,000) during 2000. This is reversed during 2001 by electing under ITA 13(4). The result is that the UCC of the new building would be limited to $1,600,000 ($2,350,000 - $750,000).

Exercise Eight - 9

The amount that will be added to the UCC balance is $147,000 [$111,000 + (1/2)($183,000 - $111,000)]. The maximum CCA of $7,400 [(15%)($147,000)(1/2)(245/365)] involves both the half year rule and the short fiscal period procedures.

Exercise Eight - 10

The required income inclusion can be calculated as follows:

	CEC Balance	CEC Deductions
1999 CEC Addition [(3/4)($85,600)]	$64,200	
1999 Deduction At 7 Percent	(4,494)	$4,494
Balance January 1, 2000	$59,706	
2000 Deduction At 7 Percent	(4,179)	4,179
Balance January 1, 2001	$55,527	
Proceeds From Sale [(3/4)($93,400)]	(70,050)	
Balance After Sale	($14,523)	$8,673

The negative balance in the CEC account after the sale is more than the total of the CEC deductions in the past two years ($8,673). Given this, the income inclusion will be as follows:

- $8,673 (the CEC deducted), plus
- $3,900 [(2/3)($14,523 - $8,673)].

As a result, $12,573 ($8,673 + $3,900) will be included in income in 2001.

Exercise Eight-11

A total of $385,500 [($514,000)(3/4)] will be added to Que's CEC balance during the taxation year ending December 31, 2001. The deduction for amortization of this amount will be $26,985 [($385,500))(7%)], leaving a balance of $358,515. If no election is made, there would be no income inclusion as the proceeds of disposition for the customer list of $296,000 is less than the $358,515 CEC balance. If the election is made, the CEC balance will be reduced by the $223,000 cost of the customer list, leaving a positive balance of $135,515. With the election, there would be a capital gain of $73,000 ($296,000 - $223,000) resulting in an income inclusion of $36,500 [(1/2)($73,000)].

Solution to Self Study Problem Eight - 1

The maximum deduction for Capital Cost Allowance and the ending Undepreciated Capital Cost can be calculated as follows:

	Class 8	Class 10	Class 3
Opening Balance	$ 96,000	$ 6,700	$115,000
Additions	52,000	8,000	-0-
Disposals	(35,000)	(20,000)	(110,000)
One-Half Net Additions	(8,500)	N/A	N/A
CCA Base	$104,500	($ 5,300)	$ 5,000
CCA	(20,900)		
One-Half Net Additions	8,500		
Recapture		5,300	
Terminal Loss			(5,000)
Ending UCC	$ 92,100	Nil	Nil

Class 8 The CCA for Class 8 is $20,900 [(20%)($104,500)].

Class 10 As the cost of the used car is less than $30,000, its cost is added to Class 10. With respect to the retirement, only the capital cost of the truck sold is deducted from Class 10. The excess of the $25,000 proceeds over the capital cost of $20,000 is a $5,000 capital gain, one-half of which would be taxable. The $12,000 net deduction creates a negative balance in the class and, as a consequence, no CCA will be taken for 2001. However, the negative balance of $5,300 will have to be taken into income as recapture.

Class 3 In Class 3, since the building sold is the last asset in the class, there is a terminal loss of $5,000. Since the land which the building was situated on was leased, the special rules on disposal of buildings at a loss do not apply.

Summary Results The preceding results can be summarized as follows:

CCA - Class 8	($20,900)
Recapture - Class 10	5,300
Terminal Loss - Class 3	(5,000)
Subtotal	($20,600)
Taxable Capital Gain - Class 10 [(1/2)($25,000 - $20,000)]	2,500
Decrease In Net Income for Tax Purposes	($18,100)

Solution to Self Study Problem Eight - 2

Class 3 - Building There were no additions or disposals in this class. As a consequence, the maximum capital cost allowance would be $31,250 [(5%)($625,000)]. The ending undepreciated capital cost of Class 3 would be $593,750.

Class 8 - Office Furniture And Equipment The required calculations for this Class would be as follows:

Opening Balance	$155,000
Additions During Fiscal Year	27,000
Disposals During Fiscal Year	(22,000)
One-Half Net Additions	(2,500)
CCA Base	$157,500
Capital Cost Allowance (20%)	(31,500)
One-Half Net Additions	2,500
Ending UCC Balance	$128,500

With respect to the disposal during the year, there would be a capital gain of $13,000 ($35,000 - $22,000), one-half of which is taxable. Only the capital cost of $22,000 is deducted from the undepreciated capital cost of the class.

Class 10 - Vehicles   The required calculations for this class would be as follows:

Opening Balance	$118,000
Additions During Fiscal Year	33,000
Disposals During Fiscal Year ($8,500 + $8,000)	(16,500)
One-Half Net Additions	(8,250)
CCA Base	$126,250
Capital Cost Allowance (30%)	(37,875)
One-Half Net Additions	8,250
Ending UCC Balance	$ 96,625

Note that the amount received from the insurance on the destroyed vehicle is treated as proceeds from a disposal.

Class 12 - Tools   The tools are eligible for a writeoff rate of 100 percent and they are not subject to the half year rules on net additions. As a consequence, the entire $34,000 can be deducted as capital cost allowance for the current year leaving no balance in the account.

Class 13 - Leasehold Improvements   In general, leasehold improvements will be written off over the term of the lease on a straight line basis. For purposes of applying this calculation, the term of the lease would include the first renewal option beginning in a period after the improvements were made. In the case of the original improvements, the period to be used is 12 years. With respect to the improvements during the current year, the writeoff period will be nine years. Also note that Class 13 assets are subject to the half year rules on net additions. The required calculations are as follows:

Opening Balance	$ 61,750
Additions	45,000
CCA Base	$106,750
Capital Cost Allowance:	
First Improvements ($78,000 ÷ 12)	(6,500)
Current Improvements [($45,000 ÷ 9)(1/2)]	(2,500)
Ending UCC Balance	$ 97,750

Class 43 - Manufacturing Equipment   Manufacturing equipment is allocated to Class 43, a 30 percent declining balance class. As this class is subject to the half year rules, the CCA would be $32,550 [($217,000)(30%)(1/2)]. The remaining UCC balance for the Class would be $184,450 ($217,000 - $32,550).

Cumulative Eligible Capital   The required calculations for the sale of the licence would be as follows:

Opening Balance, Cumulative Eligible Capital	$ -0-
Proceeds Of Disposal [($87,000)(3/4)]	(65,250)
Balance	($65,250)
Addition to Balance	65,250
Ending Balance	$ - 0 -

The proceeds are based on 75 percent of the amount received. Therefore, 75 percent of the proceeds of $87,000 would be deducted, thereby creating a negative balance for cumulative eligible capital in the amount of $65,250. As no CEC has been deducted in previous years, the entire negative balance in the cumulative eligible capital account would be multiplied by two-thirds, resulting in an income inclusion of $43,500. In effect, the entire $87,000 proceeds is being given capital gains treatment, with only one-half of this amount being included in income. The $65,250 will also be added back to the CEC balance, restoring the balance to nil.

Summary Of The Results The maximum capital cost allowances for the year and the ending undepreciated capital cost balances can be summarized as follows:

	Maximum Capital Cost Allowance	Undepreciated Capital Cost
Class 3	$ 31,250	$593,750
Class 8	31,500	128,500
Class 10	37,875	96,625
Class 12	34,000	-0-
Class 13	9,000	97,750
Class 43	32,550	184,450

In addition, the following income effects resulted from the information provided in the problem:

Taxable Capital Gain on Class 8 Assets [(1/2)($13,000)]	$ 6,500
Income From License Sale [(2/3)($65,250)]	43,500
Total	$50,000

Solution to Self Study Problem Eight - 3

1996 Solution The required calculations are as follows:

Additions To Class (20 Cars @ $12,000)	$240,000
One-Half Net Additions [(1/2)($240,000)]	(120,000)
CCA Base	$120,000
CCA [($120,000)(30%)(122/365)]	(12,033)
One-Half Net Additions	120,000
Ending UCC Balance	$227,967

Note that one-half of the net additions for the year is deducted to provide the basis for calculating the 1996 Capital Cost Allowance and then added back to establish the opening Undepreciated Capital Cost base for the next period. The other point that is illustrated in this first year is application of the short fiscal period rules. As the business was established on September 1, 1996, its operations were carried out for only 122 of the 365 days in that year. This means that only a proportionate share of the annual Capital Cost Allowance charge may be taken. Note that it is the period of operation, not the period of ownership of the assets, that establishes the fraction of the year for which capital cost allowance is to be recorded.

1997 Solution The required calculations are as follows:

Opening Balance For The Class	$227,967
Additions (5 Units @ $12,500)	62,500
Disposals (Proceeds)	(27,500)
One-Half Net Additions [(1/2)(($62,500 - $27,500)]	(17,500)
CCA Base	$245,467
CCA At 30 Percent	(73,640)
One-Half Net Additions	17,500
Ending UCC Balance	$189,327

Here again, one-half of the net additions for the year are deducted in establishing the base for calculating Capital Cost Allowance, with the same amount being added back to determine the opening Undepreciated Capital Cost for the next period.

1998 Solution   The required calculations are as follows:

Opening Balance For The Class	$189,327
Disposals (Proceeds)	(38,000)
CCA Base	$151,327
CCA At 30 Percent	(45,398)
Ending UCC Balance	$105,929

The calculations are simplified by the absence of additions to the delivery car fleet. To establish the Capital Cost Allowance base, it is only necessary to deduct the proceeds of the disposals. The new Undepreciated Capital Cost is that Capital Cost Allowance base, less the Capital Cost Allowance for the period.

1999 Solution   The required calculations are as follows:

Opening Balance For The Class	$105,929
Dispositions (Proceeds)	(128,000)
Negative Balance	($ 22,071)
Recapture	22,071
Ending UCC Balance	$ -0-

The inability to replace the fleet cars in a timely fashion was a costly mistake in that the $22,071 in recapture will be included in the 1999 net income. In a more realistic situation, it is likely that actions would have been taken to delay the retirement of the older cars and, thereby, avoid the tax implications of recapture. Note also that when recapture occurs, the balance in the class for the next period is reduced to zero.

2000 Solution   The required calculations are as follows:

Opening Balance For The Class	$ -0-
Acquisitions (25 Cars @ $16,000)	400,000
One-Half Net Additions [(1/2)($400,000)]	(200,000)
CCA Base	$200,000
CCA At 30 Percent	(60,000)
One-Half Net Additions	200,000
Ending UCC Balance	$340,000

As was the case in 1996 and 1997, one-half of the net additions must be deducted in establishing the base for Capital Cost Allowance and then added back to determine the opening Undepreciated Capital Cost balance for the next period.

2001 Solution   The required calculations are as follows:

Opening Balance For The Class	$340,000
Disposals (Proceeds)	(268,000)
Terminal Loss	$ 72,000

At this point, all of the assets in Class 10 have been retired and there is still a $72,000 balance in the Undepreciated Capital Cost. This results in a terminal loss which will be deducted in full from the net income of Golden Dragon Ltd.

Solution to Self Study Problem Eight - 4

Part A   The required calculation of the maximum Capital Cost Allowance is as follows:

	Class 1	Class 8	Class 10
Opening Balance	$876,000	$220,000	$163,000
Additions	-0-	-0-	122,000
Proceeds Of Disposal	-0-	-0-	(87,000)
One-Half Net Additions	-0-	-0-	(17,500)
CCA Base	$876,000	$220,000	$180,500
CCA Rate	4%	20%	30%
Maximum CCA	$ 35,040	$ 44,000	$ 54,150

This gives a maximum amount for CCA of $133,190 for the taxation year.

Part B   Since Marion Enterprises only has 2001 Net and Taxable Income before CCA of $53,000, the business may wish to deduct less than the maximum CCA that is available to them. However, there is no question that the business will wish to deduct the $53,000 that is required to reduce the current year's Taxable Income to nil. Further, it would be advisable to deduct an additional $46,000. This would create a Taxable Loss in 2001 of $46,000 which could then be carried back to claim refunds of taxes paid in the three preceding years.

Beyond the deduction of $99,000 ($53,000 + $46,000), the solution to the problem becomes less clear cut. If additional CCA is taken it will serve to create a taxable loss which can only be deducted as a carry forward over the next seven years. If there is not sufficient taxable income in the next seven years to absorb this carry over, the benefit of the loss will not be realized. Given the uncertainty expressed about profits for the next eight to ten years, the prudent course of action may be to only deduct 2001 CCA of $99,000. However, the alternatives here should be explained and discussed with management.

Assuming the 2001 CCA deduction is limited to $99,000, it would normally be deducted in the class or classes with the lowest rates. This would leave the unused amounts in classes with higher rates which, in turn, would maximize the amount that could be deducted in the first profitable years. Taking this approach, the $99,000 would be deducted as follows:

Class 1 (Maximum Available)	$35,040
Class 8 (Maximum Available)	44,000
Class 10 (Required Balance)	19,960
Total CCA	$99,000

This CCA deduction would reduce 2001 Taxable Income to nil and would create a loss carry back of $46,000.

Solution to Self Study Problem Eight - 5

The required schedule showing the relevant balances in the cumulative eligible capital account would be as follows:

	CEC Balance	CEC Deductions
Balance, January 1, 1998	$ -0-	
1998 Addition ([3/4][$500,000])	375,000	
1998 Amortization At 7 Percent	(26,250)	$26,250
CEC Balance, January 1, 1999	$348,750	
1999 Amortization At 7 Percent	(24,413)	24,413
CEC Balance, January 1, 2000	$324,337	
2000 Amortization At 7 Percent	(22,704)	22,704
CEC Balance, January 1, 2001	$301,633	
Proceeds From Sale ([3/4][$780,000])	(585,000)	
Balance After Sale	($283,367)	$73,367

As can be seen in the preceding table, $73,367 of the negative balance reflects CEC deductions that have been made in previous years. This full amount will have to be included in the 2001 income. The remaining $210,000 ($283,367 - $73,367) reflects three-quarters of the $280,000 ($780,000 - $500,000) gain on the disposition. This will have to converted to the 2001 capital gains inclusion rate by multiplying by two-thirds. This will result in a further income in 2001 income of $140,000 [(2/3)($210,000)]. This give a total 2001 income inclusion of $213,367 ($73,367 + $140,000).

Solution to Self Study Problem Eight - 6

The calculation of Markham Ltd.'s business income would be as follows:

Accounting Net Income		$140,000
Additions:		
Depreciation Expense (Income Statement)	$156,000	
Amortization Of Goodwill (Income Statement)	7,000	
Income Tax Expense (Income Statement)	129,000	
Non Deductible Meals and Entertainment (50% of $15,000) (Item 3)	7,500	
Contributions To Registered Charities (Item 4)	2,500	
Contributions To Federal Political Parties (Item 4)	1,200	
Articles Of Incorporation Amendment Costs (Item 5)	6,000	
Bond Discount Amortization (Item 7)	2,500	
Golf Club Membership Fees (Item 8)	3,400	
Accounting Loss On Class 10 Assets (Item 9)	15,000	
Interest On Late Income Tax Instalments (Item 10)	500	330,600
Deductions:		
Landscaping Costs (Item 1)	($ 6,000)	
Net Adjustment From LIFO To FIFO (Item 2)	(1,000)	
Gain On Sale Of Building (Item 9)	(105,000)	
Terminal Loss (Note One) (Item 9))	(8,000)	
Capital Cost Allowance (Note One)	(154,060)	
Amortization Of Eligible Capital Expenditures (Note Two)	(3,733)	(277,793)
Net Business Income		$192,807

Note One   Maximum CCA and other related inclusions and deductions can be calculated as follows:

Opening Class 1 Balance	$400,000
Addition (Capital Cost)	623,000
Disposal (Capital Cost)	(500,000)
One-Half Net Additions [(1/2)($623,000 - $500,000)]	(61,500)
CCA Base	$461,500
CCA At 4 Percent	(18,460)
One-Half Net Additions	61,500
Closing Balance	$504,540

Opening Class 8 Balance	$575,000
Additions	126,000
One-Half Net Additions	(63,000)
CCA Base	$638,000
CCA At 20 Percent	(127,600)
One-Half Net Additions	63,000
Closing Balance	$573,400

Opening Class 10 Balance	$ 45,000
Disposal Proceeds	(37,000)
Balance After Disposition	$ 8,000
Terminal Loss	(8,000)
Closing Balance	$ -0-

Opening Class 13 Balance	$68,000
Amortization:	
1999 Expenditures ($50,000 ÷ 10 Years)	(5,000)
2000 Expenditures ($27,000 ÷ 9 Years)	(3,000)
Closing Balance	$60,000

The preceding calculations result in a total CCA of $154,060 ($18,460 + $127,600 + $5,000 + $3,000).

Note Two   The amortization of the Cumulative Eligible Capital account can be calculated as follows:

2000 Additions [(3/4)($70,000)]	$52,500
2000 Amortization At 7 Percent	(3,675)
Opening Balance, 2001	$48,825
Current Year Additions [(3/4)($6,000 Legal Costs)]	4,500
Balance Before Amortization	$53,325
Amortization At 7 Percent	(3,733)
Closing Balance	$49,592

Other Notes

- While there is a specific prohibition against the deduction of interest on late income tax instalments, there is no equivalent restriction on interest due to late municipal taxes and it would appear that these amounts are deductible.

- The Class 1 disposal results in a capital gain of $62,000. This amount, however, would not be included as a component of business income. Also note that, as the old building is not a rental property, the new building can be added to the same Class 1 which contained the old building. If this were not the case, this transaction would have resulted in recapture of CCA on the disposal of the old building.

Solution to Chapter Nine Exercises

Exercise Nine - 1

The total loss on the sale of 1,000 shares would be $8,500 [(1,000)($14.50 - $23.00)]. As she acquires 500 shares of identical property within 30 days of the sale, one-half of the loss would be disallowed. This $4,250 disallowed loss would be added to the adjusted cost base of the new shares. The remaining capital loss of $4,250 will create an allowable capital loss of $2,125 [(1/2)($4,250)].

Exercise Nine - 2

The capital gain will be $48,750 [(1,000 Shares)($92.25 - $43.50)]. The taxable capital gain will be $24,375 [(1/2)($48,750)].

Exercise Nine - 3

The average cost of the shares purchased in 2000 is $23.76 {[(650)($23.50) + (345)($24.25)] ÷ 995}. Given this, Ms. Montrose's taxable capital gain for 2000 is $243.60 {[2/3][(210)($25.50 - $23.76)]}. At the end of 2000, she has 785 shares with an average cost of $23.76.

When her 2001 purchase is added to this balance, her average cost becomes $25.34 {[(785)($23.76) + (875)($26.75)] ÷ 1,660}. Given this, Ms. Montrose's taxable capital gain for 2001 is $707.20 {[1/2][(340)($29.50 - $25.34])}

Exercise Nine - 4

For 2000, there will be a taxable capital gain of $27,500 [(1/2)($292,000 - $237,000)]. During 2001, there will be an allowable capital loss of $2,400 [(1/2)($4,800)].

Exercise Nine - 5

Mr. Goodson's capital gain on this transaction is $71,800 ($382,000 - $293,000 - $17,200). The maximum reserve for 2000 is $56,387, the lesser of:

- $56,387 [($71,800)($300,000 ÷ $382,000)]
- $57,440 [($71,800)(20%)(4 - 0)]

For 2001, the maximum is $43,080, the lesser of :

- $45,110 [($71,800)($240,000 ÷ $382,000)]
- $43,080 [($71,800)(20%)(4 - 1)]

Exercise Nine - 6

As the adjusted cost base of the shares sold does not exceed $2,000,000, the entire gain would be qualifying. In addition, all of the $1,350,000 proceeds of disposition would be qualifying. As the qualifying cost of the replacement shares was equal to the qualifying proceeds of dispositions, all of the $600,000 capital gain can be deferred. The resulting adjusted cost base of the replacement shares will be $750,000 ($1,350,000 - $600,000).

Exercise Nine - 7

As the replacement did not occur until 2002, Hadfeld's 2001 tax return will include a taxable capital gain of $112,500 [(1/2)($950,000 - $725,000)], and recapture of $101,850 ($725,000 - $623,150). In 2002 these amounts can be removed from income and asset values through an amended return. The capital cost of the new building will be $755,000 [$980,000 - ($950,000 - $725,000)]. Its UCC will be $653,150 ($755,000 - $101,850).

Exercise Nine - 8

This change in use will be a deemed disposition and re-acquisition of the property. For capital gains purposes, the transaction will take place at the fair market value of $111,000, resulting in a taxable capital gain for Ms. Larson of $44,000 [(1/2)($111,000 - $23,000)]. The new adjusted cost base for the property will be $111,000. As the change is from personal to business use and the fair market value is greater than the cost, the new UCC for the property will be its cost, plus one-half of the difference between the fair market value and the cost. This amount is $67,000 [$23,000 + (1/2)($111,000 - $23,000)].

Exercise Nine - 9

There would be no tax consequences due to the sales. There would be a capital gain on the first sale of $20,500 ($109,500 - $89,000). This gain could be eliminated by designating the first property as his principal residence for the six years 1992 through 1997. The gain reduction would be calculated as follows:

$$\left(\$20{,}500 \times \frac{6}{6}\right) = \underline{\underline{\$20{,}500}}$$

The $26,000 ($178,000 - $152,000) capital gain on the second home could be eliminated by designating the second property as his principal residence for the years 1998 through 2001 and adding the plus one in the numerator. The gain reduction would be calculated as follows:

$$\left(\$26{,}000 \times \frac{(4+1)}{5}\right) = \underline{\underline{\$26{,}000}}$$

Exercise Nine - 10

The annual gain on the house is $6,000 [($198,000 - $126,000) ÷ 12 Years], while the annual gain on the cottage is $6,500 [($143,500 - $85,000) ÷ 9 Years]. Given this, the years 1994 through 2001 should allocated to the cottage. When these eight years are combined with the plus one in the numerator of the reduction formula, the $58,500 gain on the cottage will be completely eliminated. This leaves the years 1990 through 1993 for the Ottawa house, resulting in the following gain reduction:

$$\left(\$72{,}000 \times \frac{(4+1)}{12}\right) = \underline{\underline{\$30{,}000}}$$

This will leave a total capital gain on the sale of the two properties of $42,000 ($72,000 + $58,500 - $58,500 - $30,000).

Exercise Nine - 11

There will be a capital gain of $4,644 {[($0.32)(450)(FF96) - [($0.30)(450)(FF68)]} on the sale. As this gain includes a foreign currency gain of $612 [(FF68)(450)($0.32 - $0.30)], $200 of this amount is exempt from tax. One-half of the net total or $2,222 [(1/2)($4,644 - $200)] will be included in his 2001 Net Income For Tax Purposes.

Solution to Self Study Problem Nine - 1

Part A   The taxable capital gain resulting from the May 8, 1979 sale of shares would be calculated as follows:

Proceeds Of Disposition [(1,500)($52)]	$78,000
Adjusted Cost Base [(1,500)($40)]	(60,000)
Capital Gain	$18,000
Non Taxable One-Half (Pre 1988 Inclusion Rate)	(9,000)
Taxable Capital Gain	$ 9,000

The taxable capital gain resulting from the February 3, 1984 sale of shares would be calculated as follows:

Proceeds [(2,600)($94)]	$244,400
Adjusted Cost Base [(2,600)($57.3333)]*	(149,067)
Capital Gain	$ 95,333
Non Taxable One-Half (Pre 1988 Inclusion Rate)	(47,667)
Taxable Capital Gain	$ 47,666

*The average cost of these shares would be calculated as follows:

October 15, 1977 Purchase [(5,500 - 1,500)($40)]	$160,000
December 12, 1983 Purchase [(3,200)($79)]	252,800
Total Cost	$412,800
Average Cost ($412,800 ÷ 7,200)	$57.3333

Part B   The adjusted cost base of the shares on hand on March 15, 2001 can be calculated as follows:

	Addition To Number Of Shares	Addition To Adjusted Cost Base
Balance After 1984 Sale	4,600	$263,733
January 15, 1988 Stock Dividend	460	45,540
June 15, 1992 Purchase	3,800	395,200
December 23, 1994 Stock Dividend	886	110,750
Totals	9,746	$815,223

The taxable capital gain would be calculated as follows:

Proceeds Of Disposition [(9,746)($174)]	$1,695,804
Adjusted Cost Base	(815,223)
Capital Gain	$ 880,581
Non Taxable One-Half	(440,291)
Taxable Capital Gain	$440,290

Solution to Self Study Problem Nine - 2

Total Gain   The total amount of the taxable capital gain can be calculated as follows:

Proceeds Of Disposition		$500,000
Less:		
Adjusted Cost Base	$230,000	
Disposition Costs	20,000	250,000
Total Capital Gain		$250,000
Inclusion Rate		1/2
Total Taxable Capital Gain		$125,000

Reserve Limits   As Miss Stevens has not received the entire proceeds in the year of sale, she is entitled under ITA 40(1) to establish a reserve. The reserve that would be available at the end of each year would be the lesser of:

- [(Capital Gain)(Proceeds Not Yet Due ÷ Total Proceeds)]
- {[(20%)(Capital Gain)](4 - Number Of Preceding Years Ending After Disposition)}

2001 Gain   As the cash proceeds during 2001 are well in excess of 20 percent of the total proceeds, the maximum reserve at the end of 2001 would be calculated as follows:

   [($250,000)($300,000 ÷ $500,000)] = $150,000

With a reserve of $150,000, the capital gain to be recognized for 2001 would be $100,000 ($250,000 - $150,000). This would result in a taxable capital gain of $50,000.

2002 Gain   At the end of 2002, the two calculations provide equal results as follows:

- [($250,000)($300,000 ÷ $500,000)] = $150,000
- [(20%)($250,000)(Four Years - One Year)] = $150,000

This means the 2002 taxable capital gain would be calculated as follows:

Addition Of The 2001 Reserve	$ 150,000
Deduction Of The 2002 Reserve	(150,000)
2002 Capital Gain	$ -0-

2003, 2004 And 2005 Gains   In these three years no further proceeds are receivable and, as a consequence, the reserve calculation based on proceeds not receivable until after December 31 would remain unchanged at $150,000. However, the alternative calculations would decline to:

- $100,000 at the end of 2003 [(20%)($250,000)(Four Years - Two Years)],
- $50,000 at the end of 2004 [(20%)($250,000)(Four Years - Three Years)],
- nil at the end of 2005 [(20%)($250,000)(Four Years - Four Years)].

This means that a gain of $50,000 would be recognized in each of the three years and would require the inclusion of a taxable capital gain of $25,000 in each year's Net Income For Tax Purposes. At this point, the entire taxable capital gain of $125,000 would have been taken into income as per the following schedule:

Year	Capital Gain	Taxable Capital Gain
2001	$100,000	$50,000
2002	-0-	-0-
2003	50,000	25,000
2004	50,000	25,000
2005	50,000	25,000
Total	$250,000	$125,000

2006 And 2007 Gains   As the entire taxable capital gain was taken into net income for tax purposes by the end of 2005, no further gains will be recognized in either 2006 or 2007.

Solution to Self Study Problem Nine - 3

Part A - With respect to Net Income For Tax Purposes, the 2001 tax effects related to the involuntary dispositions would be as follows:

   Land   In the absence of the ITA 44(1) election, the taxable capital gain on the Land would be as follows:

Proceeds Of Disposition	$723,000
Adjusted Cost Base	(256,000)
Capital Gain	$467,000
Inclusion Rate	1/2
Taxable Capital Gain	$233,500

Building   In the absence of the ITA 44(1) election, the taxable capital gain on the building would be as follows:

Proceeds Of Disposition	$4,800,000
Adjusted Cost Base	(3,700,000)
Capital Gain	$1,100,000
Inclusion Rate	1/2
Taxable Capital Gain	$ 550,000

If the ITA 13(4) election is not used, the disposal of the building would result in recapture as per the following calculation:

Adjusted Cost Base	$3,700,000
Undepreciated Capital Cost	(1,856,000)
Recaptured CCA	$1,844,000

Building Contents   In the absence of the ITA 44(1) election, the taxable capital gain on the building contents would be as follows:

Proceeds Of Disposition	$1,256,000
Adjusted Cost Base	(972,000)
Capital Gain	$ 284,000
Inclusion Rate	1/2
Taxable Capital Gain	$ 142,000

If the ITA 13(4) election is not used, the disposal of the building contents would result in recapture as per the following calculation:

Adjusted Cost Base	$972,000
Undepreciated Capital Cost	(72,000)
Recaptured CCA	$900,000

Part B   The effects of using the ITA 13(4) and ITA 44(1) elections can be calculated as follows:

Land   The taxable capital gain can be reduced to the following under the ITA 44(1) election:

Proceeds Of Disposition	$723,000
Cost Of Replacement Property	(500,000)
Capital Gain	$223,000
Inclusion Rate	1/2
Taxable Capital Gain	$111,500

If the election is used, the adjusted cost base of the replacement property (which is equal to the adjusted cost base of the expropriated land) would be calculated as follows:

Actual Cost	$500,000
Capital Gain Removed By Election ($467,000 - $223,000)	(244,000)
Adjusted Cost Base	$256,000

Building   The taxable capital gain can be reduced to the following under the ITA 44(1) election:

Proceeds Of Disposition	$4,800,000
Cost Of Replacement Property	(5,700,000)
Capital Gain	$ -0-

The adjusted cost base of the replacement property (which is equal to the adjusted cost base of the old building plus the $900,000 excess of the cost of the new building over the insurance proceeds) would be calculated as follows:

Actual Cost	$5,700,000
Capital Gain Removed By Election ($1,100,000 - Nil)	(1,100,000)
Adjusted Cost Base	$4,600,000

Use of the ITA 13(4) election would eliminate the recapture and leave the following undepreciated capital cost for the new property:

Adjusted Cost Base	$4,600,000
CCA Removed By Election ($1,844,000 - Nil)	(1,844,000)
Adjusted Undepreciated Capital Cost	$2,756,000

Building Contents   If this were a voluntary disposition, the building contents would not be "former business property" and would not qualify for either the ITA 13(4) election or the ITA 44(1) election. However, as this is an involuntary disposition, both elections are available. Use of the ITA 44(1) election would reduce the capital gain on the building contents to the amount shown in the following calculation:

Proceeds Of Disposition	$1,256,000
Cost Of Replacement Property	(1,233,000)
Capital Gain	$ 23,000
Inclusion Rate	1/2
Taxable Capital Gain	$ 11,500

The adjusted cost base of the new building contents would be as follows:

Actual Cost	$1,233,000
Capital Gain Removed By Election ($284,000 - $23,000)	(261,000)
Adjusted Cost Base	$ 972,000

Use of the ITA 13(4) election would eliminate the recapture and leave the following undepreciated capital cost for the new property:

Adjusted Cost Base	$972,000
CCA Removed By Election ($900,000 - Nil)	(900,000)
Adjusted Undepreciated Capital Cost	$ 72,000

Part C   As there was a $223,000 capital gain remaining on the land and no gain remaining on the building, a reduction of Net Income For Tax Purposes can be achieved under the ITA 44(6) election. In fact, the excess of replacement cost over the old cost for the Building is sufficient that all of the gain can be eliminated on the Land without creating a gain on the Building. This is accomplished by electing under ITA 44(6) to transfer $223,000 of the Land proceeds to the Building proceeds. This will completely eliminate the $223,000 capital gain on the Land and will increase the capital gain removed by election on the Building by $223,000. In turn, the adjusted cost base of the Building will now be $4,377,000 ($4,600,000 - $223,000) and the undepreciated capital cost will be $2,533,000 ($4,600,000 - $223,000 - $1,844,000). The adjusted cost base of the land will remain at $256,000.

Note that this election is not made without a cost. Had the $223,000 been left as a capital gain, tax would have applied on only one-half of the total. While we have eliminated this $111,500 in income, we have given up future capital cost allowance for the full amount of the $223,000. In other words we have given up $223,000 in future deductions in return for eliminating $111,500 of income in 2001. This makes the use of this election somewhat questionable. Factors that should be considered include whether capital gains are taxed at different rates than business income (corporations) and the anticipated future tax rates and timing of taxable income.

Solution to Self Study Problem Nine - 4

Part A   With respect to net income for tax purposes, the sale of the Toronto properties would have the following tax effects:

Land   In the absence of the ITA 44(1) election, the capital gain on the land is as follows:

Proceeds Of Disposition	$772,000
Adjusted Cost Base	(137,000)
Capital Gain - No ITA 44(1) Election	$635,000

However, this can be reduced as follows under the ITA 44(1) election:

Proceeds Of Disposition	$772,000
Cost Of Replacement Property	(253,000)
Capital Gain Using ITA 44(1) Election	$519,000

This will result in a $259,500 [(1/2)($519,000)] taxable capital gain being included in the 2001 net income for tax purposes. The adjusted cost base of the replacement property, which is equal to the adjusted cost base of the land sold, would be calculated as follows:

Actual Cost	$253,000
Capital Gain Removed By Election ($635,000 - $519,000)	(116,000)
Adjusted Cost Base	$137,000

Building   In the absence of the ITA 44(1) election, the capital gain on the building would be as follows:

Proceeds Of Disposition	$989,000
Adjusted Cost Base	(605,000)
Capital Gain - No ITA 44(1) Election	$384,000

This gain can be eliminated as follows by using the election:

Proceeds Of Disposition	$ 989,000
Cost Of Replacement Property	(1,042,000)
Capital Gain Using ITA 44(1) Election	$ -0-

No capital gain would be included in the 2001 net income for tax purposes and the adjusted cost base of the new building, which is equal to the adjusted cost base of the building that was sold plus the $53,000 excess of the cost of the new building over the proceeds from the old building, would be calculated as follows:

Actual Cost	$1,042,000
Capital Gain Removed By Election	(384,000)
Adjusted Cost Base	$ 658,000

If the ITA 13(4) election is not used, the disposal of the building results in recapture as follows:

Adjusted Cost Base	$605,000
Undepreciated Capital Cost	(342,000)
Recapture - No ITA 13(4) Election	$263,000

Use of the ITA 13(4) election would eliminate the recapture and leave the following undepreciated capital cost for the new property:

Adjusted Cost Base	$658,000
CCA Removed By Election	263,000
Adjusted Undepreciated Capital Cost	$395,000

Note that the UCC for the new building is equal to the UCC of the old building ($342,000), plus additional $53,000 in funds required for its acquisition.

Equipment   As this is a voluntary disposition, the equipment does not qualify as "former business property" and, as a consequence, neither the ITA 44(1) nor the ITA 13(4) election can be used. However, as there were no other assets in the class at the end of 2001, there will be a terminal loss of $13,000 ($127,000 - $114,000). The new equipment has an adjusted cost base equal to its undepreciated capital cost and equal to its actual cost of $205,000.

Part B   As calculated in Part A, there was a $519,000 capital gain on the land and no gain on the building, some reduction of net income for tax purposes can be achieved under the ITA 44(6) election. However, the reduction is limited to the $53,000 difference between the $989,000 fair market value of the old building and the $1,042,000 cost of the replacement building. This would reduce the capital gain on the land by $53,000. The adjusted cost base of the replacement land would remain at $137,000. This would still leave the capital gain on the building at nil. This can be shown as follows:

Deemed Proceeds Of Disposition ($989,000 + $53,000)	$1,042,000
Less: Cost Of Replacement Property	1,042,000
Capital Gain	$ -0-

Using this election, net income for tax purposes would be reduced by $26,500 [(1/2)($53,000)]. It would be possible to further reduce the gain on the land by transferring more of the proceeds to the building. The result, however, would be a new gain on the building that would be equal to the loss reduction on the land.

Also note that there is a cost involved with this election. While the Company has reduced its 2001 net income for tax purposes by one-half of the $53,000 capital gain, it has forgone future capital cost allowances for the full amount of $53,000.

With the use of this election, the adjusted cost base of the new building would be $605,000 ($1,042,000 - [$989,000 + $53,000 - $605,000]) and the undepreciated capital cost would be reduced to $342,000 ($605,000 - $263,000).

Solution to Self Study Problem Nine - 5

Part A - Use Of ITA 40(2)(b)   The calculations here begin with the calculation of the gain per year of ownership for the entire period 1972 through 2001, the amounts would be as follows:

English Bay = ([$515,000 - $125,000] ÷ 30) = $13,000

Cottage = ([$320,000 - $40,000] ÷ 25) = $11,200

As the annual gain is greater on the English Bay property, this should be the designated principal residence for most of the years. The gain on this property can be completely eliminated by designating 29 years and adding the one additional year that is available in the exemption formula. This will leave one year to be used on the cottage and the exemption here would be calculated as follows:

$$([1 + 1] ÷ 25)($280,000) = $22,400$$

Under this approach, the total capital gain to be recognized in 2001 would be as follows:

Gain On English Bay	$390,000
Exemption On English Bay	(390,000)
Gain On Cottage	280,000
Exemption On Cottage	(22,400)
Total Capital Gain	$257,600

Part B - Use Of ITA 40(6)   Under this approach, there would be separate calculations of the annual gains on the two properties for both the pre 1982 period and the post 1981 period. These calculations are as follows:

Annual Gains, 1972 Through 1981

English Bay = ([$335,000 - $125,000] ÷ 10) = $21,000

Cottage = ([$205,000 - $40,000] ÷ 5) = $33,000

Total Gains, 1982 Through 2001

English Bay = ($515,000 - $335,000) = $180,000

Cottage = ($320,000 - $205,000) = $115,000

Under this alternative approach, it would be appropriate to maximize the exemption for the cottage during the 1972 through 1981 period as the per year amount for the cottage is $33,000, vs. $21,000 for the English Bay property. To completely eliminate the gain for this period on the cottage would require the use of four designated years plus the one additional year. This would leave six years for the English Bay property and the exemption would be calculated as follows:

[(6 + 1) ÷ 10][$335,000 - $125,000] = $147,000

For the period 1982 through 2001, the larger gain would be on the English Bay property and, as a consequence, the exemption on this property should be maximized. As the plus one rule does not apply in this period, the entire 20 years will be required to eliminate the gain on this property and no years can be allocated to the cottage. Summarizing the results under this dual approach, we would use the following calculations:

Cottage Gain - 1972-1981	$165,000
Exemption	(165,000)
English Bay Gain - 1972-1981	210,000
Exemption	(147,000)
English Bay Gain - 1982-2001	180,000
Exemption	(180,000)
Cottage Gain - 1982-2001	115,000
Exemption	(-0-)
Total Capital Gain	$178,000

Note that the use of ITA 40(6) results in a significantly lower gain than was the case using ITA 40(2)(b).

Solution to Self Study Problem Nine - 6

GST paid on the expensed costs cannot be claimed as input tax credits, unless the corporation was registered or was required to be registered when the costs were incurred. Quincy Corporation is required to be registered if taxable supplies were greater than $30,000 in the current calendar quarter or in the previous four quarters (twelve months). As the corporation's business is in the start-up phase, it appears that registration was not required and no input tax credit can be claimed on operating expenses.

However, GST paid on the capital costs (building and professional fees) should qualify for input tax credits when Quincy registers for GST. This results from the deemed acquisition of the capital assets and deemed payment of GST at the time of registration. The allowable input tax credit will be based on GST applicable to the lower of the original cost and the fair market value of the capital assets.

Solution to Self Study Problem Nine - 7

The GST and total cost of each purchase would be:

Shuswap Cedar A-Frame

GST = Nil
Total Cost = $120,000

Millcreek Bi-Level

GST = [($90,000+$14,000)(7%)] - [($90,000+$14,000)(2.52%)] + [($10,000)(7%)]
= $7,280 - $2,621 + $700
= $5,359

Total Cost = $90,000 + $24,000 + $5,359 = $119,359

Sunset Beach Cottage

The renovations are considered substantial. If the renovations were carried out by the vendor prior to the sale, the purchase would be deemed to be that of a "new" home. Therefore, the purchase price would be subject to the full GST and a new housing rebate could be claimed on the total, as follows:

GST = [($116,000)(7%)] - [($116,000)(2.52%)]
= $8,120 - $2,923
= $5,197

Total Cost = $116,000 + $5,197 = $121,197

Solution to Self Study Problem Nine - 8

A. The purchase of the commercial property will be taxable at 7 percent. Therefore, GST of $700,000 ([$10,000,000][7%]) will be payable by Tiffany.

B. As Tiffany is a GST registrant, the company is responsible for remitting the GST on the purchase. No election is required. When Tiffany's GST return is filed for the period including the purchase date, the required remittance of $700,000 should be reported. At the same time, Tiffany can also claim any available input tax credit. The input tax credit is $476,000 {([$700,000][60%]) + ([$700,000][40%][20%])}.

Therefore, the required GST remittance will be $700,000, for the GST on the purchase, from which a $476,000 input tax credit can be deducted, for a net cash outlay of $224,000. In the calculation of the input tax credit, we assume that the 20 percent general administrative expense allocation is also a reasonable allocation for Tiffany's commercial use of the space.

C. The lease to commercial tenants is a commercial activity, so Tiffany will have to charge GST on the lease.

Solution to Chapter Ten Exercises

Exercise Ten - 1

Mr. Lipky's proceeds of disposition will be the amount received of $95,000, resulting in a capital loss of $5,000 ($95,000 - $100,000). His brother's adjusted cost base will be the fair market value of the land or $75,000. There will be double taxation on a subsequent sale by his brother on the difference between $95,000 and $75,000.

Exercise Ten - 2

As the transfer was to a related party for an amount less than the fair market value of the asset, Ms. Lee will be deemed to have received the fair market value of $56,600. This will result in a taxable capital gain of $1,800 [(1/2)($56,600 - $53,000) and recapture of CCA of $15,800 ($53,000 - $37,200). The capital cost of the property to her father will be $37,200, the amount paid for the asset. There will be double taxation on a subsequent sale by her father on the difference between $56,600 and $37,200.

Exercise Ten - 3

Under ITA 69(1.2), the proceeds of disposition in this case will be the greater of the $33,000 actual proceeds, and the $211,000 fair market value of the property without considering the lease. The greater amount would be $211,000, resulting in a capital gain for Mr. Bates of $178,000 ($211,000 - $33,000). The adjusted cost base to the corporation would be the actual transfer price of $33,000. This would lead to double taxation on a subsequent sale of the property of the difference between $211,000 and $33,000.

Exercise Ten - 4

As ITA 73(1) provides for a tax free rollover of capital property to a spouse, there would be no tax consequences for either Mr. or Mrs. Moreau in 2000. For 2001, both the dividends and the capital gain would be attributed to Mrs. Moreau. The taxable amount of the dividends would be $3,125 [(1.25)($2,500)] and the taxable capital gain would be $9,500 [(1/2)($42,000 - $23,000)].

Exercise Ten - 5

As there is no provision for a tax free transfer of shares to a child, Mrs. Moreau will have a taxable capital gain in 2000 of $7,000 [(1/2)($37,000 - $23,000)]. The taxable amount of the dividends of $3,125 [(1.25)($2,500)] would be attributed back to Mrs. Moreau. However, the 2001 taxable gain of $2,500 [(1/2)($42,000 - $37,000)] would be taxed in Nicki's hands.

Exercise Ten - 6

Unless Mr. Bronski elects out of ITA 73(1) by including a gain in his 2000 tax return, there will be no tax consequences to either Mr. or Mrs. Bronski in 2000. In addition, because the transfer is a tax free rollover, the adjusted cost base of the bonds to Mrs. Bronski will be $115,000. As the loan did not bear interest at market rates, all of the 2001 interest income on the bonds will be attributed back to Mr. Bronski. In addition to the interest of $6,100, there would be a taxable capital gain of $7,000 [(1/2)($129,000 - $115,000)], a total of $13,100.

Exercise Ten - 7

There would be a deemed disposition on her departure, leaving her liable for the taxes on a $10,500 [(1/2)($49,000 - $28,000)] taxable capital gain.

Exercise Ten - 8

As real property is exempt from the deemed disposition provision contained in ITA 128.1(1)(b), there would be no tax consequences with respect to the rental property at the time of Mr. Chrysler's departure. However, real property is Taxable Canadian Property and, as a consequence, he would be liable for Canadian taxes on both recapture and capital gains resulting from a subsequent sale of the property even though he is a non resident.

Exercise Ten - 9

With respect to truck A, it would be transferred to her husband at its UCC value of $25,500 [($51,000)($33,000/$66,000)]. No income would be included in Ms. Lardner's final tax return and, while the UCC value for the truck in Michel's hands would be the $25,500 transfer value, it would retain its original capital cost of $42,000. Truck B would be transferred to Melinda at its fair market value of $33,000. This would result in $7,500 ($33,000 - $25,500) in recapture being included in Ms. Lardner's final tax return. The $33,000 transfer price would be the UCC value to Melinda. Since Ms. Lardner's original capital cost exceeds the $33,000 fair market value, Melinda would retain Ms. Lardner's $42,000 capital cost.

Exercise Ten - 10

The carry forward must be applied on an adjusted basis to eliminate the 2001 taxable capital gain. To implement this, the $7,500 amount (three-quarter basis) must be adjusted to $5,000 (one-half basis). The $2,000 taxable capital gain will use $2,000 of the adjusted 1990 carry forward, leaving $3,000. This amount must be adjusted back to the 3/4 inclusion rate. The resulting $4,500 [(3/4)(($3,000)] can be applied against any other type of income in 2001 or, if there is not sufficient other income in that year, against any other type of income in 2000 (amended return).

Solution to Self Study Problem Ten - 1

Case A   In this Case, the shares were transferred at a price that was below market value. However, John Bolton will have deemed proceeds under ITA 69(1)(b) equal to the fair market value of $525,000 [(5,000)($105)]. With his cost base at $225,000 [(5,000)($45)], this will result in a capital gain of $300,000, one-half of which would be included in John's Taxable Income. From the point of view of Alex Bolton, his cost base for the shares will be the actual price paid of $375,000 [(5,000)($75)]. This means that, if Alex Bolton sells these shares at some later point in time for a price in excess of $75, the difference between his sales price and the price per share he paid of $75 would be taxed in his hands. In effect, any gain arising from a sales price of up to $105 will be subject to double taxation.

Case B   In this situation, the gain to be recorded by John Bolton would be based on $625,000, the actual amount received. This would result in a capital gain of $400,000 ($625,000 - $225,000), one-half of which would be included in John's

Taxable Income. From the point of view of Alex Bolton, ITA 69(1)(a) would limit his adjusted cost base to $525,000, the fair market value of the shares at the time of purchase. In a manner similar to Case A, there is the likelihood of double taxation being assessed on the difference between the $625,000 price paid and the $525,000 fair market value at the time of the sale.

Case C In this Case, both the proceeds to John Bolton and the adjusted cost base to Alex Bolton will be equal to the amount paid for the shares. This will result in John recording a capital gain of $300,000 as calculated in Case A, one-half of which would be included in John's Taxable Income. However, in this Case, the adjusted cost base to Alex Bolton will be $525,000 and no double taxation will arise.

Case D In this Case Mr. John Bolton will be deemed to have received proceeds equal to the fair market value of $525,000. This will result in the same $300,000 capital gain that was calculated in Case A and C. As in Case C, the adjusted cost base to Alex Bolton will be $525,000 and no double taxation will arise.

Solution to Self Study Problem Ten - 2

Mr. Langdon would be assessed for income attribution of $10,000, $5,000 each for his spouse and minor child. As Heather did not use the funds to produce income, there would be no tax consequences of making the loan to her.

Solution to Self Study Problem Ten - 3

Case A With ITA 73(1) in effect, the December 31, 2001 transfer would be a deemed disposition at the adjusted cost base of $185,000. This means that Dr. Bolt would not record a capital gain at the time of the transfer and the adjusted cost base of the securities to Mr. Bolt would be $185,000. In 2002, the $23,125 in taxable dividends would be attributed back to Dr. Bolt and included in her Net Income for that year. When Mr. Bolt sells the securities, the 2003 taxable capital gain of $37,500 [(1/2)($260,000 - $185,000)] would also be attributed back to Dr. Bolt. This transfer would not affect Mr. Bolt's Net Income in any of the three years under consideration.

Case B With ITA 73(1) in effect, the December 31, 2001 transfer would still take place at the adjusted cost base of $185,000 and the resulting 2001, 2002 and 2003 results for both Dr. Bolt and Mr. Bolt would be identical to Case A.

Case C With the decision to elect out of ITA 73(1) and payment of consideration equal to fair market value, the transfer will be recorded as a disposition at fair market value. This will result in a 2001 taxable capital gain for Dr. Bolt of $20,000 [(1/2)($225,000 - $185,000)] and an adjusted cost base to Mr. Bolt of $225,000. Given that the transfer was at fair market value and Dr. Bolt chose to elect out of ITA 73(1), there would be no attribution of either income or capital gains. The taxable dividends of $23,125 will be included in Mr. Bolt's 2002 Net Income, and the 2003 taxable capital gain of $17,500 [(1/2)($260,000 - $225,000)] will be included in his 2003 Net Income. The transfer would not affect Dr. Bolt's Net Income in either 2002 or 2003.

Case D As ITA 73(1) continues to be applicable in this Case, the transfer would take place at the adjusted cost base of $185,000 and both dividends and capital gains would be attributed back to Dr. Bolt. For both Dr. and Mr. Bolt the results for all three years would be identical to those described in Case A.

Case E When a taxpayer elects out of ITA 73(1) and a transfer is made for consideration that is less than fair market value, the provisions of ITA 69(1) are applicable to the transferor. Under these provisions, if a taxpayer disposes of a property for less than its fair market value, the proceeds of disposition are deemed to be the fair market value amount. This will result in Dr.

Bolt recording a 2001 taxable capital gain of $20,000 [(1/2)($225,000 - $185,000)]. As the transfer is for consideration that is less than the fair market value of the securities, the income attribution rules will be applicable, resulting in the 2002 taxable dividends of $23,125 being included in Dr. Bolt's 2002 Net Income. In addition, the 2003 taxable capital gain of $60,000 [(1/2)($260,000 - $140,000)] would also be attributed back to her and included in her 2003 Net Income.

Note that the adjusted cost base for the securities is based on the actual price paid by Mr. Bolt, subjecting the $40,000 ($225,000 - $185,000) difference between the transfer price and the adjusted cost base to double taxation. In addition, Dr. Bolt's $45,000 ($185,000 - $140,000) loss on the sale would not be deductible. Dr. Bolt's total taxable capital gain on these shares is $80,000 ($20,000 + $60,000). This is $42,500 more than the taxable capital gain in Case A and represents [(1/2)($225,000 - $140,000)]. The transfer would not affect Mr. Bolt's Net Income in any of the three years under consideration.

Case F   Under ITA 69, a non arm's length gift is deemed to be a disposition and acquisition to be recorded by both parties at fair market value. This means that Dr. Bolt would have to record a 2001 taxable capital gain of $20,000 [(1/2)($225,000 - $185,000)]. As a gift to a minor was involved, income attribution rules will apply and the 2002 taxable dividends of $23,125 will have to be included in the 2002 Net Income of Dr. Bolt. However, the attribution rules do not apply to capital gains when the attribution results from a transfer to someone under 18 years of age. As a consequence, Dolly Bolt will include a taxable capital gain of $17,500 [(1/2)($260,000 - $225,000)] in her 2003 Net Income. The transfer will have no effect on the 2001 and 2002 Net Income of Dolly Bolt, nor on the 2003 Net Income of Dr. Bolt.

Case G   The transfer at fair market value will result in Dr. Bolt recording a taxable capital gain of $20,000 [(1/2)($225,000 - $185,000)] in 2001. As the transfer is at fair market and the related loan requires interest at commercial rates, the income attribution rules are not applicable. This means that Dolly will include taxable dividends of $23,125 in her 2002 Net Income and a taxable capital gain of $17,500 [(1/2)($260,000 - $225,000)] in her 2003 Net Income. The transaction will have no effect on the 2002 and 2003 Net Income of Dr. Bolt, nor on the 2001 Net Income of Dolly Bolt.

Case H   As the transfer is at fair market value, Dr. Bolt will have a taxable capital gain of $20,000 [(1/2)($225,000 - $185,000)] included in her 2001 Net Income. Dirk's adjusted cost base for the securities will be $225,000 and the transfer will not affect his 2001 Net Income. As Dirk is not under 18 years of age, the attribution rules found in ITA 74.1(2) do not apply. However, ITA 56(4.1) indicates that income attribution applies in situations where an interest free or low interest loan has been given to a non arm's length individual and one of the main purposes of the loan is to reduce or avoid taxes. As Dirk has only limited income and would be in a lower tax bracket than Dr. Bolt, it is likely that this condition would apply in this Case. As a result, the 2002 taxable dividends of $23,125 would be included in the 2002 Net Income of Dr. Bolt, rather than in the Net Income of her son. However, the 2003 taxable capital gain of $17,500 [(1/2)($260,000 - $225,000)] would not be attributed back to Dr. Bolt. Rather, it would be included in the 2003 Net Income of Dirk Bolt.

Solution to Self Study Problem Ten - 4

Note   As the farm would be considered qualified farm property, any capital gains arising from a transfer would be eligible for the $500,000 lifetime capital gains deduction. If Long Consulting Ltd. is a qualified small business corporation, capital gains on the disposition of these shares would also be eligible for the $500,000 deduction.

Long Consulting Ltd. - Gift To Spouse   ITA 73(1) permits transfers of a capital property to a spouse at its tax value (adjusted cost base or UCC). This means that the shares in Long Consulting Ltd. could be gifted to Mr. Long with no immediate tax consequences. However, the tax basis for these shares would remain at the adjusted cost base of $210,000 and income attribution would apply.

Any dividends paid on the shares would be attributed to Mrs. Long. In addition, should Mr. Long subsequently sell these shares for $475,000, the resulting taxable capital gain of $132,500, as calculated below, would also be attributed to Mrs. Long.

Proceeds (Fair Market Value)	$475,000
Adjusted Cost Base	(210,000)
Capital Gain	$265,000
Inclusion Rate	1/2
Taxable Capital Gain	$132,500

As an alternative, Mrs. Long could elect out of the provisions of ITA 73(1). Under ITA 69, the gift would be recorded as a disposition at the $475,000 fair market value. Mrs. Long would have an immediate taxable capital gain of $132,500 (as calculated in the preceding paragraph) and Mr. Long's adjusted cost base would be $475,000. However, if the transfer is a gift, and Mr. Long does not use his own funds to purchase the shares, income attribution would apply both to any dividends received by Mr. Long and to any capital gain arising from a later sale at an amount in excess of $475,000.

Long Consulting Ltd. - Gift To Children   Under ITA 69, a gift to a related party is deemed to be a transfer at fair market value. Given this, the taxable capital gain of $132,500 (as calculated for Mr. Long) would result from the transfer to either child.

The adjusted cost base to the children would be the fair market value of $475,000. The effect of the gift on Mrs. Long's immediate tax situation would be the same, regardless of which child receives the gift.

As Mary is under 18 year of age, a transfer to her would result in all dividend income received by Mary prior to her reaching age 18 being attributed back to Mrs. Long. However, if Mary sells the shares for more or less than her adjusted cost base of $475,000, the resulting capital gain or loss would not be attributed back to Mrs. Long. This would be the case whether or not Mary was 18 or older at the time of the sale. As Barry is over 18, the gift would not result in attribution of either dividends or capital gains.

Rental Property - Gift To Spouse   Here again, ITA 73(1) would permit a transfer to Mr. Long at tax values with no immediate tax consequences. The tax basis of the property would not be changed. However, as the transfer is a gift, income attribution rules would apply. This means that any net rental income would be attributed to Mrs. Long. In addition, if Mr. Long were to later sell the property for its current fair market value of $275,000, the following amounts would be attributed to Mrs. Long:

Capital Cost	$190,000
Undepreciated Capital Cost	(125,000)
Recaptured CCA	$ 65,000
Proceeds Of Disposition	$275,000
Capital Cost	(190,000)
Capital Gain	$ 85,000
Inclusion Rate	1/2
Taxable Capital Gain	$ 42,500

Mrs. Long could also elect out of the provisions of ITA 73(1) and transfer the rental property at its fair market value. However, if she does, she would immediately be taxed on the recapture as well as the taxable capital gain. Electing out of ITA 73(1) would not change the fact that the transfer is a gift to a spouse and, as a consequence, future rental income, capital gains, and recapture would be attributed to Mrs. Long.

Rental Property - Gift To Children   There is no exemption from the general rules of ITA 69 for transfers of depreciable property to children. As a consequence, Mrs. Long would be subject to taxation based on a disposition of the property at its fair market value of $275,000. This would result in immediate taxation on a $42,500 taxable capital gain and recapture in the amount of $65,000 (see preceding calculations).

The tax base to either of the children would be $275,000 and a sale at this price would have no tax consequences for either Mrs. Long or the children. Here again, however, if this property were given to Mary, the income attribution rules of ITA 74.1 would apply to any amount of property income subsequently earned. This would mean that until Mary reached 18 years of age, all property income would be allocated to Mrs. Long. Alternatively, if the property were gifted to her son Barry, all subsequent income would be allocated to him. There would be no attribution of further capital gains on a gift to either child.

Dynamics Inc. - Gift To Spouse   As with the other properties, these shares could be given to Mr. Long and, under the provisions of ITA 73(1), no immediate tax consequences would arise. However, any dividend income on the shares would be attributed to Mrs. Long and, if Mr. Long were to sell them for their fair market value of $384,000, the income attribution rules of ITA 74.1 would require that the following taxable capital gain be allocated to the income of Mrs. Long:

Proceeds Of Disposition	$384,000
Adjusted Cost Base	(212,000)
Capital Gain	$172,000
Inclusion Rate	1/2
Taxable Capital Gain	$ 86,000

Mrs. Long could elect out of ITA 73(1) by recording the $86,000 taxable capital gain at the time of the transfer to her spouse. However, as long as the property was transferred as a gift, attribution would apply to both dividend income received by Mr. Long and to any further capital gains realized on a subsequent sale.

Dynamics Inc. - Gift To Children   In the case of a transfer to either of her children, ITA 69 would require that the gift be treated as a deemed disposition with the proceeds at the fair market value of $384,000. This would result in an immediate taxable capital gain of $86,000 as was calculated in the preceding paragraph. However, the tax base to the children would be the fair market value of $384,000 and there would be no tax consequences for any of the parties if a sale took place at that price.

As was the case with the other properties considered, a transfer to Mary would result in the application of the income attribution rules of ITA 74.1. This would mean that subsequent dividend income on these shares would be allocated to Mrs. Long until Mary reaches 18 years of age. If Mary were to sell the property for more than $384,000, there would be no attribution of the capital gain. If the shares were transferred to Barry, there would be no attribution of either dividends or capital gains.

Farm Land - Gift To Spouse   As with all of the other properties, Mrs. Long could make a tax free transfer of the farm land to her husband under ITA 73(1). The transfer would take place at the adjusted cost base of $80,000 and, in the event of a subsequent sale, the following taxable capital gain would be attributed to Mrs. Long under ITA 74.1:

Proceeds Of Disposition	$175,000
Adjusted Cost Base	(80,000)
Capital Gain	$ 95,000
Inclusion Rate	1/2
Taxable Capital Gain	$ 47,500

Alternatively, Mrs. Long could elect out of ITA 73(1) and transfer the property at its fair market value of $175,000, resulting in the taxable capital gain of $47,500 being recognized at the time of transfer.

As farm income is considered to be business income rather than property income, there would be no attribution of any farm income that arises while Mr. Long is holding the property.

Farm Land - Gift To Children   ITA 73(3) permits the inter vivos transfer of farm property used by the taxpayer or her family to a child on a tax free basis. The deemed proceeds would be Mrs. Long's adjusted cost base, which means that Mrs. Long would incur no taxation at the time of the gift to either child. The adjusted cost base to either child would be the same $80,000 that was deemed to be the proceeds of the disposition.

As noted in our discussion of the transfer of this property to Mr. Long, because farm income is business rather than property income, there will be no attribution of farm income in the case of a transfer to either child.

On most transfers to related minors, there is no attribution of capital gains. This is a reflection of the fact that, unlike the rules for transfers to a spouse, there is no general rollover provision for transfers to related minors on a tax free basis. However, when a transfer is made to a related minor under the provisions of ITA 73(3) and the transfer value is below fair market value, ITA 75.1 requires that any subsequent gain resulting a disposition by the transferee before they reach age 18 be attributed back to the transferor.

This means that, if the farm property is transferred to Mary and she sells the property for $175,000 before she reaches age 18, a taxable capital gain of $47,500 (see preceding calculations for Mr. Long) will be attributed to Mrs. Long.

Solution to Self Study Problem Ten - 5

Note   As the farm would be considered qualified farm property, any capital gains would be eligible for the $500,000 lifetime capital gains deduction. Further, if Caswell Enterprises is a qualified small business corporation, capital gains on the disposition of these shares would also be eligible for the $500,000 deduction.

Case A   Whenever a taxpayer dies, there is a deemed disposition of all of his property. If the transfer is to a spouse, the disposition is deemed to have taken place at the adjusted cost base of capital property other than depreciable property, or at the undepreciated capital cost of depreciable property. This would mean that there would be no immediate tax consequences associated with Mr. Caswell's death in this Case where all of the property is transferred to his spouse. Note, however, that on a subsequent disposition by Mr. Caswell's spouse, her tax base would be the same as Mr. Caswell's. These values would be as follows:

Rental Property - Undepreciated Capital Cost	$ 67,000
Rental Property - Capital Cost	95,000
General Industries Ltd. - Adjusted Cost Base	200,000
Farm Land - Adjusted Cost Base	325,000
Caswell Enterprises - Adjusted Cost Base	275,000

It is possible, after Mr. Caswell's death, for his legal representative to elect to have assets transferred to his spouse at fair market values. This would result in taxable capital gains and other income being included in his final tax return. However, this would not be a reasonable alternative unless Mr. Caswell has unused loss carry forwards at the time of his death or the lifetime capital gains deduction can be utilized on his final return.

Case B   This case is more complex and would follow the general rules applicable to transfers made at death to anyone other than a spouse. For both depreciable and non depreciable property, other than farm property, the transfer will be deemed to have taken place at fair market value.

In the case of the rental property, the deemed proceeds would be $133,000, resulting in taxable income of $47,000 for Mr. Caswell's estate. This would be calculated as follows:

Deemed Proceeds Of Disposition	$133,000
Capital Cost	(95,000)
Capital Gain	$ 38,000
Inclusion Rate	1/2
Taxable Capital Gain	$ 19,000

Capital Cost	$ 95,000
Undepreciated Capital Cost	(67,000)
Recaptured CCA	$ 28,000

The capital cost and UCC for his son, John, is the fair market value of $133,000.

In the case of the General Industries shares, the deemed proceeds would be $350,000 and the tax consequences to Mr. Caswell's estate would be as follows:

Deemed Proceeds Of Disposition	$350,000
Adjusted Cost Base	(200,000)
Capital Gain	$150,000
Inclusion Rate	1/2
Taxable Capital Gain	$ 75,000

In the case of the farm land which is being used by the taxpayer or a member of his family, ITA 70(9) permits a tax free transfer of such property to a child, at the time of death. The deemed proceeds would be Mr. Caswell's adjusted cost base, resulting in no tax consequences for his estate. As you would expect, the adjusted cost base to Mr. Caswell's son John would be the same $325,000 that was deemed to be the proceeds of the disposition on Mr. Caswell's death.

With respect to the shares of a Canadian controlled private company, the tax consequences to Mr. Caswell's estate would be as follows:

Deemed Proceeds Of Disposition	$426,000
Adjusted Cost Base	(275,000)
Capital Gain	$151,000
Inclusion Rate	1/2
Taxable Capital Gain	$ 75,500

This gives a total increase in Net Income of $197,500.

Case C   With respect to the departure from Canada, ITA 128.1(4)(b) requires a deemed disposition of all property except real property, property used in a Canadian business, and excluded personal property [i.e., a variety of items specified under ITA 128.1(9)]. This means there would be a deemed disposition for Mr. Caswell of both the General Industries Ltd. shares and the Caswell Enterprises shares. The tax consequences of the two dispositions would be as follows:

Deemed Proceeds (General Industries))	$350,000
Adjusted Cost Base	(200,000)
Capital Gain	$150,000
Inclusion Rate	1/2
Taxable Capital Gain	$ 75,000

Deemed Proceeds (Caswell Enterprises)	$426,000
Adjusted Cost Base	(275,000)
Capital Gain	$151,000
Inclusion Rate	1/2
Taxable Capital Gain	$ 75,500

This gives a total increase in Net Income of $150,500.

Two additional facts might be noted here. First, Mr. Caswell could elect under ITA 128.1(4)(d) to have a deemed disposition of the other properties at the time of his departure. Given the amounts already added to his income, this would not appear to be a desirable alternative unless he can utilize the lifetime capital gains deduction on the farm land. Also of importance is the fact that Mr. Caswell can defer the taxation on these amounts. Provided adequate security is provided, ITA 220(4.5) allows an emigrant to defer the taxation on deemed dispositions created by ITA 128.1(4)(b) until such time as the assets are sold. This would likely be an attractive alternative to Mr. Caswell.

Solution to Chapter Eleven Exercises

Exercise Eleven - 1

The total interest to be recorded on the investment is $28,800 [($60,000)(8%)(6 years)]. It will be allocated as follows: 2001 - $0, 2002 - $4,800, 2003 - $4,800, 2004 - $6,000, 2005 - $3,600, 2006 - $4,800 and 2007 - $4,800.

As no anniversary date occurred and no interest was received during 2001, no interest will have to be included in Ms. Dumont's 2001 tax return. In 2002, the first anniversary date occurs and this requires the recognition of $4,800 [(8%)($60,000)] of interest. In 2003, the second anniversary date occurs and this requires the recognition of an additional $4,800 of interest. In 2004, the third anniversary date requires the recognition of $4,800 and, in addition, a $15,600 [(8%)($60,000)(3.25)] payment is received. As $14,400 [(3)($4,800)] of this amount has been accrued on the three anniversary dates, only $1,200 of this amount will be added to income. This gives a total for the year 2004 of $6,000. In 2005, the anniversary date will require recognition of $4,800. However, only $3,600 of this amount will be included as $1,200 was recognized in 2004. In 2006, $4,800 will be recognized on the anniversary date. In 2007, a payment of $13,200 [(2.75)($4,800)] will be received. As $8,400 ($3,600 + $4,800) of the amount received has been recorded on the 2005 and 2006 anniversary dates, the total for 2007 will be $4,800 ($13,200 - $8,400).

Exercise Eleven - 2

With respect to the maturity amount, the interest to be included in the purchaser's tax return would be calculated as follows:

Year	Initial Balance	Interest At 7%	Closing Balance
2001	$204,075	$14,285	$218,360
2002	218,360	15,285	233,645
2003	233,645	16,355	250,000

Calculations with respect to the coupon payments are as follows:

Year	Initial Balance	Interest At 7%	Interest Received	Closing Balance
2001	$45,925	$3,215	($17,500)	$31,640
2002	31,640	2,215	(17,500)	16,355
2003	16,355	1,145	(17,500)	Nil

Exercise Eleven - 3

Mr. Milford will have to include the full $6,000 received. However, under ITA 20(14) he is eligible for a deduction of $2,000 [($3,000)(4/6)], reflecting the interest that was accrued on the bonds at the time of his purchase. The net amount that will be included in his tax return is $4,000.

Exercise Eleven - 4

The total annual interest will be R8,000,000. The deductible component will be limited to 8 percent in each of the three years. However, the extra 12 percent must be tracked as it can be applied against the exchange gain at maturity. The translated amounts are as follows:

	Deductible	Non Deductible	Total
2001 (R8,000,000 @$0.35)	$1,120,000	$1,680,000	$2,800,000
2002 (R8,000,000 @$0.25)	800,000	1,200,000	2,000,000
2003 (R8,000,000 @$0.18)	576,000	864,000	1,440,000
Total	$2,496,000	$3,744,000	$6,240,000

When the debt is repaid, there will be an exchange gain of $8,800,000 [(R40,000,000)($0.40 - $0.18)]. ITA 20.3 requires this to be treated as business income, regardless of whether the proceeds of the debt were invested in capital assets or inventory. However, this amount can be reduced by the non deductible interest of $3,744,000, leaving a net gain for 2003 of $5,056,000.

Exercise Eleven - 5

As the improvements will have to be added to her CCA base, her maximum available CCA on the rental property is $3,560 [(4%)(1/2)($185,000 - $42,000 + $35,000)]. However, the maximum CCA that she can deduct will be limited by her net rental income before CCA. This amount is $2,100 ($7,200 - $5,100).

Exercise Eleven - 6

The taxes payable by Mr. Johns would be calculated as follows:

Dividends Received	$17,000.00
Gross Up At 25%	4,250.00
Taxable Dividends [(1.25)($17,000)]	$21,250.00
Taxes at 41% (29% + 12%)	$8,712.50
Dividend Tax Credit [(2/3 + 40%)($4,250)]	(4,108.33)
Total Federal And Provincial Tax	$ 4,604.17

Exercise Eleven - 7

It is likely that Ms. Rourke will have to include the $50,000 principal amount of the loan in her Net Income For Tax Purposes for the current year. She owns more than 10 percent of the shares, making her a specified employee. While she is an employee, it is unlikely that this type of loan would be generally available to all employees and, as a consequence, it is likely that she received the loan because of her shareholder's status as opposed to her employee status. In the unlikely event that the loan is not included in income, she will have to include imputed interest based on the six percent prescribed rate for the period of the loan.

Exercise Eleven - 8

The total required child support is $9,000 [(6 Months)($1,500)] and Sandra's payments will be allocated to this requirement first. This means that $9,000 of her payment will not be deductible to her or taxable to Jerry. The remaining $2,000 will be considered a payment towards spousal support and will be deductible to Sandra and taxable to Jerry.

Exercise Eleven - 9

The $15,873 will be included in his annual tax return. However, the net taxable amount is $2,123 ($15,873 - $13,750), because the annuity was purchased with tax paid funds and he is eligible for a deduction equal to:

$$\left(\frac{\$55,000}{\$63,492}\right)(\$15,873) = \$13,750$$

Exercise Eleven - 10

Her potentially deductible costs are $7,600 ($6,400 + $1,200). While she cannot personally deduct the $1,300 related to the visit to Regina, her employer can pay for these costs without creating a taxable benefit. This leaves $4,700 ($6,000 - $1,300) of her employer's contribution that must be applied to her deductible costs. In turn, this leaves $2,900 that she can potentially deduct in 2001. However, the 2001 deduction is limited to the $2,000 that she earned at the new work location, leaving $900 to be carried forward and deducted in 2002.

Exercise Eleven - 11

The deduction will have to be made by the lower income spouse, Mr. Sampras. The deduction will be the least of the following amounts:

- The actual costs of $10,500.

- Annual expense amount of $15,000 [(1)($7,000) + (2)($4,000)]

- 2/3 of Mr. Sampras' Earned Income, an amount of $24,000 [(2/3)($36,000)].

The least of these three amounts is $10,500.

Solution to Self Study Problem Eleven - 1

After Tax Return On The Bonds   This amount would be calculated as follows:

Interest Received [(7.75%)($20,000)]	$1,550.00
Taxes At 38% (26% + 12%)	(589.00)
After Tax Return	$ 961.00

After Tax Return On Preferred Shares   This amount would be calculated as follows:

Dividends Received [(5%)($20,000)]	$1,000.00
Gross Up Of 25 Percent	250.00
Taxable Dividends	$1,250.00
Taxes At 38% (26% + 12%)	$475.00
Dividend Tax Credit [(2/3 + 30%)($250.00)]	(241.67)
Total Taxes Payable	$233.33
Dividends Received	$1,000.00
Total Taxes Payable	(233.33)
After Tax Return	$ 766.67

Conclusion   Based on after tax returns, the investment in bonds is the better alternative.

Solution to Self Study Problem Eleven - 2

Part A   As the amount is a lump sum rather than a periodic payment, it would not be taxed in the hands of Ms. Holmes or deductible by her former husband.

Part B   The after tax cash flows associated with the alternative investments would be as follows:

Guaranteed Investment Certificate   The before tax return here would be $5,500 and this would result in an after tax return calculated as follows:

Interest	$5,500
Federal/Provincial Taxes Payable [($5,500)(29% + 15%)]	(2,420)
After Tax Cash Flow	$3,080

Rental Property   The net rental income from the property would be calculated as follows:

Gross Rents	$13,200
Cash Expenses	(9,600)
CCA (Property Sold Prior To Year End)	-0-
Net Rental Income	$ 3,600

In addition to this Net Rental Income, Ms. Holmes anticipates a capital gain of $10,000 ($175,000 - $165,000), of which one-half or $5,000 would be included in her income. The total after tax cash flow would be as follows:

Net Rental Income	$ 3,600
Capital Gain	10,000
Taxes Payable [($3,600 + $5,000)(29% + 15%)]	(3,784)
After Tax Cash Flow	$ 9,816

Norton Ltd. Shares   The calculations here would be as follows:

Dividends Received	$5,000	
Gross Up (25 Percent)	1,250	
Taxable Dividends		$6,250
Capital Gain	$6,000	
Inclusion Rate	1/2	
Taxable Capital Gain		3,000
Net Income		$9,250
Tax At 44% (29% + $15%)		$4,070
Dividend Tax Credit [($1,250)(2/3 + 35%)]		(1,270)
Total Taxes Payable		$2,800
Before Tax Cash Flow ($5,000 + $6,000)		$11,000
Total Taxes Payable		(2,800)
After Tax Cash Flow		$ 8,200

Based on cash flow considerations only, it would appear that Ms. Holmes should acquire the rental property. However, this alternative probably involves the highest degree of risk and can require significant personal involvement if there are problems with the tenant or repairs become necessary. In addition, the real estate investment is the least liquid of the three alternatives and Ms. Holmes might encounter difficulties in the disposal of this investment. While you were asked not to consider transaction costs, we would also point out that they would be much higher on this investment than on either of the other two.

In choosing between the guaranteed investment certificate and the shares of Norton Ltd., the after tax cash flows from the shares are considerably higher. However, the return on the shares is made up of dividends and a potential capital gain, both of which are more uncertain than the interest on the guaranteed investment certificate. Given this, the possibility of greater than anticipated dividends and/or capital gains must be weighed against the additional risk of lower than anticipated returns.

You might also wish to note that the interest and principal on guaranteed investment certificates is only covered by government insurance to a maximum of $60,000 with any one issuer. This would suggest the use of two different certificates with different financial institutions.

Solution to Self Study Problem Eleven - 3

The allowable moving expenses can be calculated as follows:

First Trip Hotel and Food After Acquiring New Residence (4 Days At $150)		$ 600
Selling Costs Of Old Residence ($9,500 + $1,400)		10,900
Acquisition Cost Of New Residence ($1,850 + $600)		2,450
Halifax Hotel And Food		420
Expenses Of Travel To Regina:		
Gasoline	$350	
Hotels (7 Days At $95)	665	
Food (7 Days At $45)	315	1,330
Moving Company Fees		3,800
Hotel And Food In Regina (8 Days At $140)		1,120
Total Allowable Expenses		$20,620
Employment Income In New Location		(10,500)
Carryover To Next Year		$10,120

Notes:

1. With respect to the first trip, only the cost of meals and lodging which occurred after the acquisition of the new residence would be allowed. The airfare, the cost of car rentals, and the cost of meals and lodging prior to acquisition of the new residence would not be deductible.

2. The taxes on the old home to date of sale would not be an allowable moving expense.

3. Food and lodging costs near the old or new residences are limited to 15 days in total. For Ms. Fox this would include 4 days on her first trip to Regina, the 3 days in Halifax, but only 8 of the 16 days during which she lived in a hotel on arriving in Regina. Note that the seven days spent travelling to Regina are not included in the 15 day total.

4. The storage costs are deductible.

5. The unused moving cost balance of $10,120 can be carried over and applied against employment income in the following year only.

Solution to Self Study Problem Eleven - 4

Generally the spouse with the lower income must claim the deduction for child care expenses. However, under certain circumstances, for example if this spouse is hospitalized, the spouse with the higher income can claim the deduction for the period of hospitalization. Thus Mr. Pleasant can claim the least of the following:

Actual Payments (48 weeks at $100)	$ 4,800
Annual Amount [(3)($4,000)]	12,000
2/3 Of Earned Income [(2/3)($33,000)]	22,000
Periodic Amount [($100)(3)(6 weeks)]	1,800

There does not appear to be any requirement that actual child care costs claimed by the higher income spouse need be limited to the specific amounts paid during the six week period of eligibility. This means that the lowest of the preceding figures would be $100 per child for six weeks which would result in a deduction of $1,800 for Mr. Pleasant.

Mrs. Pleasant's deduction will be based on the least of:

Actual Payments	$ 4,800
Annual Amount	12,000
2/3 Of Earned Income ([2/3] [$18,000])	12,000

Here the lowest figure is the actual costs of $4,800. This amount will be reduced by the $1,800 that was deducted by Mr. Pleasant. This results in a $1,320 deduction for Mrs. Pleasant.

Solution to Chapter Twelve Exercises

Exercise Twelve - 1
At time of exercise, he will have an employment income benefit of $21,250 [($31.50 - $23.00)(2,500 Shares)]. As he sells the shares immediately at the exercise date fair market value, there will be no deferral of the employment income benefit and no capital gain or loss on the sale. As the option price at issue exceeded the fair market value at issue, Mr. Guise will be able to deduct $10,625 [(1/2)($21,250)] in the determination of Taxable Income. The net effect on Taxable Income will be $10,625 ($21,250 - $10,625).

Exercise Twelve - 2
At the time the shares are sold, there will be an employment income benefit of $58,500 [($75.00 - $42.50)(1,800 Shares)]. As she did not hold the shares for the required two years, there is no deduction under ITA 110(1)(d.1). Further, as the option price was below fair market value at the time the options were issued, there is no deduction under ITA 110(1)(d). When she sells the shares, she will have an allowable capital loss of $23,400 [(1/2)($49.00 - $75.00)(1,800 Shares)]. The net addition to Taxable Income is $35,100 ($58,500 - $31,200).

Exercise Twelve - 3
The specified value of the shares involved with these options is $20,000 [(1,000)($20)]. As this is well below the $100,000 annual limit under ITA 7(8), she can defer all of the $22,000 [(1,000)($45 - $23)] employment benefit that is measured at the time of exercise. This means that the 2001 Taxable Income inclusion will be nil. As the shares are sold in 2002, the $22,000 employment income benefit will be recognized in that year. There will also be a 2002 deduction of $11,000 [(1/2)($22,000)] under ITA 110(1)(d) and a 2002 allowable capital loss of $1,500 [(1,000)($42 - $45)(1/2)]. Assuming she has taxable capital gains against which she can net the allowable capital loss, the 2002 increase in Taxable Income is $9,500 ($22,000 - $11,000 - $1,500).

Exercise Twelve - 4

The Taxable Income amounts for 2001 and 2002 would be identical to those in Exercise Twelve-3. The only difference is that no election is required to defer the 2001 employment income inclusion.

Exercise Twelve - 5

The specified value of the shares that vested in 2002 is $120,000 [(10,000)($12)]. This means that the ITA 7(8) election can only be made on 8,333 of the shares [(8,333)($12) = $99,996]. This results in a deferral of $166,660 [(8,333)($32 - $12)] and an income inclusion of $33,340 [(1,667)($32 - $12)]. The specified value of the shares that vested in 2003 is $180,000 [(15,000)($12)]. As was the case in 2002, the ITA 7(8) election can only be made on 8,333 of the shares, resulting in a deferral of $166,660 [(8,333)($32 - $12)] and an income inclusion of $133,340 [(6,667)($32 - $12)]. This information will be reflected in Mr. Traverse's 2004 T4 as a special item of deferred income of $333,320 ($166,660 + $166,660) and an employment income inclusion of $166,680 ($33,340 + $133,340).

Exercise Twelve - 6

Mr. Smothers will have a net capital loss carry over from 2000 of $5,500 [(1/2)($89,000 - $100,000)]. This can only be applied against the taxable gain of $2,000 [(1/2)($53,000 - $49,000)]. As this is a listed personal property loss carry over, it will be deducted in the calculation of Net Income For Tax Purposes, leaving this balance at the amount of his employment income, $62,000. This will also be his 2001 Taxable Income. In addition, he will have an allowable listed personal property loss carry forward of $3,500 [$5,500 - $2,000)].

Exercise Twelve - 7

Her Net Income For Tax Purposes for 2001 will be $10,000 ($40,000 - $30,000). As she has taxable capital gains in excess of her net capital loss carry forward, she can use this carry forward instead of the net rental loss. This will leave her net capital loss carry over at nil and her non capital loss carry over at $5,000 [$30,000 + (2/3)($22,500) - $40,000].

Exercise Twelve - 8

Of the total BIL, $26,000 will be disallowed because of the previous use of the lifetime capital gains deduction. The remaining $24,000 can be deducted against $12,000 [(1/2)($24,000)] of his employment income. The disallowed $26,000 becomes an ordinary capital loss, of which $18,000 can be deducted against the capital gains on publicly traded securities. This leaves a net capital loss carry over of $4,000 [(1/2)($26,000 - $18,000)].

Exercise Twelve - 9

During 2000, her farm loss was restricted to $8,750 [$2,500 + (1/2)($12,500)]. The remaining $7,250 can be carried forward to 2001. In 2001, $3,500 of this carry forward can be deducted against the 2001 farm income. The remaining $3,750 will be carried forward to future years. Ms. Bodkin's 2001 Net Income For Tax Purposes is $88,500 ($85,000 + $3,500) and her 2001 Taxable Income is $85,000 ($88,500 - $3,500).

Exercise Twelve - 10

For 2001, his maximum lifetime capital gains deduction is $223,500, the least of the following three items:

Available Deduction His remaining deduction would be $232,000 [(1/2)($500,000 - $10,000 - $26,000)].

Annual Gains Limit This would be the 2001 taxable capital gain of $255,000 [(1/2)($510,000)], reduced by the net capital loss deducted of $31,500 [(1/2)($63,000)]. This leaves a net amount of $223,500 ($255,000 - $31,500).

Cumulative Gains Limit This amount would be calculated as follows:

Sum Of Capital Gains ($5,000 + $17,333 + $255,000)	$277,333
Previous Years' Capital Gains Deduction ($5,000 + $17,333)	(22,333)
Net Capital Losses Deducted	(31,500)
Cumulative Gains Limit	$223,500

Exercise Twelve - 11

The net effect of this home relocation loan on Taxable Income would be as follows:

Taxable Benefit [(5% - 2%)($82,000)]	$2,460
ITA 110(1)(j) Deduction [(5%)($25,000)]	(1,250)
Net Addition To Taxable Income	$1,210

Solution to Self Study Problem Twelve - 1

Case A   In 2001, the year in which the options are issued, there would be no tax consequences for Ms. Wu. The tax consequences in 2002 would be as follows:

Fair Market Value [(12,000)($31)]	$372,000
Option Price [(12,000)($22)]	(264,000)
Employment Income Inclusion	$108,000
Deduction Under ITA 110(1)(d) (One-Half)	(54,000)
Increase In Taxable Income	$ 54,000

As Ms. Wu is a specified shareholder, none of this amount can be deferred until the shares are sold.

When the shares are sold in 2003, the tax consequences would be as follows:

Proceeds Of Disposition [(12,000)($28)]	$336,000
Adjusted Cost Base [(12,000)($31)]	(372,000)
Capital Loss	($ 36,000)
Inclusion Rate	1/2
Allowable Capital Loss	($ 18,000)

Case B   In this Case we have a public company. However, the results are different than in Case A as we are assuming that Ms. Wu is not a specified shareholder. This means that a portion of the gain at the time of exercise can be deferred until the shares are sold. This is limited to the first $100,000 of fair market value of shares at the time the options are granted. As the fair market value of the shares at the time the options are granted is $20 per share, this applies to the gain on 5,000 of the 12,000 shares acquired by Ms. Wu.

As in the previous case, there would be no tax consequence associated with the issuance of the options in 2001. The 2002 tax consequences would be calculated as follows:

Fair Market Value [(12,000)($31)]	$372,000
Option Price [(12,000)($22)]	(264,000)
Employment Income	$108,000
Available Deferral [(5,000/12,000)($108,000)]	(45,000)
Employment Income Inclusion For 2002	$ 63,000
Deduction Under ITA 110(1)(d) (One-Half)	(31,500)
Increase In Taxable Income	$ 31,500

When the shares are sold in 2003, there would be an increase in taxable income of $22,500. This is made up of the deferred employment income inclusion of $45,000, less the one-half deduction under ITA 110(1)(d). In addition, there would be an $18,000 allowable capital loss, calculated as in Case A.

Case C   In this Case, because Imports Ltd. is a Canadian controlled private company, there are no consequences either in 2001 when the options are issued, or in 2002 when they are exercised. When the shares are sold in 2003, there would be an increase in Taxable Income of $54,000 and an allowable capital loss of $18,000. The calculation of these amounts is as in Case A.

Note that in all three cases the increase in Taxable Income due to the stock options for 2002 and 2003 totals $54,000.

Solution to Self Study Problem Twelve - 2

1998 Analysis   Mr. Fox's net and taxable income would be calculated as follows:

Paragraph 3(a)		
Employment Income	$18,000	
Business Income	14,500	
Grossed Up Dividends [($5,000)(125%)]	6,250	$38,750
Paragraph 3(b)		
Taxable Capital Gains	$ Nil	
Allowable Capital Losses [(3/4)($3,600)]	(2,700)	Nil
Paragraph 3(c)		$38,750
Paragraph 3(d)		
Farming Income (Loss)*		(4,250)
Net And Taxable Income		$34,500

*Given that Mr. Fox is only a part time farmer, his deductible farm loss would be restricted as follows:

Total Farm Loss		$6,000
Deductible Amount:		
First $2,500	($2,500)	
One-Half of $3,500	(1,750)	(4,250)
Farm Loss Carry Over		$1,750

In addition to the preceding farm loss carry over, Mr. Fox would have a net capital loss carry over of $2,700 [(3/4)($3,600)]

1999 Analysis   Mr. Fox's net and taxable income would be calculated as follows:

Paragraph 3(a)

Employment Income	$15,000	
Farming Income	1,000	
Grossed Up Dividends [($6,525)(125%)]	8,156	$24,156

Paragraph 3(b)

Taxable Capital Gains [(3/4)($7,400)]	$ 5,550	
Allowable Capital Losses	Nil	5,550

Paragraph 3(c)	$29,706
Paragraph 3(d)	
Business Income (Loss)	(39,000)
Net Income	$ Nil
Net Capital Loss Carried Forward	(2,700)
Taxable Income	$ Nil

Since there are taxable capital gains this year, the net capital loss carry forward of $2,700 is added to the balance of the non capital loss. The non capital loss for the year would be calculated as follows:

Business Loss	$39,000
Net Capital Loss Deducted	2,700
Paragraph 3(c) Income	(29,706)
Non Capital Loss For 1999	$11,994

This non capital loss will be carried back to 1998, resulting in the following amended Taxable Income for that year:

1998 Taxable Income (As Reported)	$34,500
Non Capital Loss Carry Back From 1999	(11,994)
1998 Amended Taxable Income	$22,506

Given this carry back, the only remaining loss carry forward at the end of 1999 would be the $1,750 restricted farm loss from 1998.

2000 Analysis   Mr. Fox's net and taxable income would be calculated as follows:

Paragraph 3(a)

Employment Income	$19,000	
Business Income	34,000	
Farming Income	8,000	
Grossed Up Dividends [($8,000)(125%)]	10,000	$71,000

Paragraph 3(b)

Taxable Capital Gains [(1/2)($6,300)]	$ 3,150	
Allowable Capital Losses	Nil	3,150

Paragraph 3(c)	$74,150
Paragraph 3(d)	Nil
Net Income	$74,150
Farm Loss Carry Forward	(1,750)
Taxable Income	$72,400

Given the deduction of the farm loss carry forward, there are no loss carry overs remaining at the end of 2000.

2001 Analysis   Mr. Fox's net and taxable income would be calculated as follows:

Paragraph 3(a)		
Employment Income	$12,000	
Grossed Up Dividends [($10,125)(125%)]	12,656	$24,656
Paragraph 3(b)		
Taxable Capital Gains	$ Nil	
Allowable Capital Losses [(1/2)($15,000)]	(7,500)	Nil
Paragraph 3(c)		$24,656
Paragraph 3(d)		
Business Income (Loss)		(52,000)
Farm Income (Loss)		(2,000)
Net And Taxable Income		$ Nil

The non capital loss for the year would be calculated as follows:

Business Loss	$52,000
Farm Loss	2,000
Paragraph 3(c) Income	(24,656)
Non Capital Loss For 2001	$29,344

In addition to the non capital loss carry over, there would be a $7,500 net capital loss carry over for the year. The entire non capital loss carry over can be carried back to 2000. In addition, $3,150 [(1/2)($6,300)] of the net capital loss carry over can be carried back to that year (the carry back is limited to the taxable capital gains recorded in 2000). This will result in the following amended taxable income for that year:

2000 Taxable Income (As Reported)	$72,400
Non Capital Loss Carry Back From 2001	(29,344)
Net Capital Loss Carry Back From 2001	(3,150)
2000 Amended Taxable Income	$39,906

It will also be possible to carry back a further amount of the net capital loss to 1999. In that year, a taxable capital gain was recorded in the amount of $5,550 (3/4 inclusion rate). Of this amount, $2,700 was eliminated by the carry forward of the 1998 net capital loss, leaving a balance of $2,850. This means that $1,900 [(2/3)($2,850)] of the 2001 net capital loss can be carried back to that year, resulting in the following amended non capital loss for 1999:

Business Loss	$39,000
Net Capital Loss Deducted - 1998	2,700
Net Capital Loss Deducted - 2001 [(3/2)($1,900)]	2,850
Paragraph 3(c) Income	(29,706)
Non Capital Loss For 1999	$14,844

As $11,994 of the 1999 non capital loss was carried back to 1998, the revision of this amount will require another amendment of the 1998 return as follows:

1998 Taxable Income (As Previously Amended)	$22,506
Additional Non Capital Loss Carry Back From 1999	(2,850)
1998 Amended Taxable Income	$19,656

At the end of 2001, the only remaining loss carry forward will be a net capital loss calculated as follows:

2001 Allowable Capital Loss	$ 7,500
Carried Back To 2000	(3,150)
Carried Back To 1999	(1,900)
Remaining Carry Forward	$ 2,450

Solution to Self Study Problem Twelve - 3

Mr. Borgen's minimum Taxable Income would be calculated as follows:

Net Employment Income	$36,000
Net Taxable Capital Gains ($37,500 - $9,000)	28,500
Interest Expense	(17,000)
Net Income For Tax Purposes	$47,500
Lifetime Capital Gains Deduction (See Note)	(11,500)
Taxable Income	$36,000

Note The lifetime capital gains deduction is the least of:

Capital Gains Deduction Available	$250,000
Annual Gains Limit	$ 28,500
Cumulative Net Taxable Capital Gains	$ 28,500
Cumulative Net Investment Loss	(17,000)
Cumulative Gains Limit	$ 11,500

It would have been possible for Mr. Borgen to deduct the $9,900 [(75%)($19,800)(2/3)] net capital loss carry forward instead of $9,900 of the lifetime capital gains deduction. In view of the uncertainty associated with the continuing availability of this deduction on the sale of shares of a qualified small business corporation, and the fact there is an unlimited carry forward period on net capital losses, use of the lifetime capital gains deduction is probably the better alternative.

Solution to Self Study Problem Twelve - 4

The Taxable Income of Mr. Shipley can be calculated as follows:

Employment Income (Note One)		$44,000
Income From Business And Property:		
Grossed Up Cash Dividends [(460)($1.10)(125%)]		633
Grossed Up Stock Dividends [(69)($10.00)(125%)]		863
Taxable Capital Gains:		
On CDC Shares (Note Two)	$ 843	
On Partnership Disposition (Note Three)	1,250	2,093
Profits From Illegal Business (Note Four)		18,000
Partnership Income [(25%)($4,500)]		1,125
Spousal Support Payments (Note Five)		Nil
RRSP Deduction (Note Six)		(7,500)
Net Income And Taxable Income		$59,214

Note One As the Urban Construction Company is a Canadian controlled private company, the stock options will not constitute a taxable benefit when they are exercised.

When the shares are sold, a capital gain or loss will be recognized using the $15 fair market value at time of exercise as the adjusted cost base. In addition, the difference between this $15 fair market value and the $10.50 option price paid for the shares will be included as employment income in the year of sale. Since the option price for the shares exceeded the fair market value of the shares at the time the options were issued, this employment income inclusion will be offset by a deduction in the calculation of Taxable Income equal to one-half of the included amount.

Note Two   The taxable capital gain on the CDC shares will be based on the proceeds of selling the 529 shares [(460)(1.15)] that are available after the stock dividend at a price of $12.75 per share. The $10.00 per share increase in paid up capital due to the stock dividend must be included in income and be added to the adjusted cost base. The total adjusted cost base of the shares is $9.50 per purchased share, plus the $690.00 increase in paid up capital which accompanied the stock dividend. This gives a taxable capital gain as follows:

Proceeds [(529)($12.75)]	$6,745
Adjusted Cost Base {[(460)($9.50)] + $690.00}	(5,060)
Capital Gain	$1,685
Inclusion Rate	1/2
Taxable Capital Gain	$ 843

Note Three   The taxable capital gain resulting from the partnership disposition would be calculated as follows:

Proceeds Of Disposition ([25%][$32,000])	$8,000
Adjusted Cost Base	(5,500)
Capital Gain	$2,500
Inclusion Rate	1/2
Taxable Capital Gain	$1,250

Note Four   There have been several cases in which profits from an illegal business have been held to be taxable. It is not clear, however, whether losses would be deductible.

Note Five The $25,000 lump sum payment would not be deductible. It is neither periodic nor paid in accordance with the divorce decree. Although certain lump sum payments are deductible, such payments must be directed towards maintenance or support, not towards a property settlement as is the case for Mr. Shipley's payment. Therefore, the $25,000 payment would not qualify as a spousal support payment. As Mr. Shipley did not make the monthly support payments during 2001, he has no deduction for spousal support.

Note Six   Mr. Shipley's maximum RRSP deduction would be the lesser of $13,500, his actual RRSP contributions and 18 percent of 2000 Earned Income (assumed to be equal to 2001 Earned Income). His 2001 Earned Income of $63,125 would include his employment income, his income from illegal activities and his partnership income ($44,000 + $18,000 + $1,125). His deduction room for the year is $11,363. However, his deduction would be limited to his actual contribution of $7,500.

Solution to Self Study Problem Twelve - 5

Mr. Bubel's Net and Taxable Income would be calculated as follows:

Employment Income:		
Commissions	$61,200	
Stock Option Benefit [(1,000)($28 - $22)] (Note 1)	6,000	
Hotels And Deductible Portion of Meals	(4,100)	
Airline Tickets	(3,800)	
Automobile Operating Costs [(60%)($4,700)]	(2,820)	
Automobile CCA (See Note 2)	(2,718)	
Telephone Answering Service	(2,400)	$51,362
Income From Property:		
Dividends Received	$1,800	
One-Quarter Gross Up	450	
Interest On Foreign Bonds ($945 ÷ 75%)	1,260	
Withholding On Foreign Interest In Excess of		
15 Percent [(85%)($1,260) - $945]	(126)	
Interest Earned On Gifts To Children	800	4,184
Taxable Capital Gains (Losses):		
Wife's Sale Of Shares [(1/2)($10,800)]	$5,400	
Loss On Sale of Stock Option Shares (Note 1)	(5,000)	
Sale Of Common Shares (Note 3)	(350)	50
Workers' Compensation Board Payment (Note 4)		10,000
RRSP Deduction (See Note 5)		(9,245)
Net Income For Tax Purposes		$56,351
Deduction For Stock Option Benefit - ITA 110(1)(d) [(1/2)($6,000)]		(3,000)
Workers' Compensation Board Payment		(10,000)
Taxable Income		$43,351

Note 1   While Mr. Bubel could have filed the election to defer the stock option income inclusion with his employer, the fact that he sold the shares during the year means that the deferral would end during the year. There is, however, an allowable capital loss of $5,000 [(1,000)($28 - $18)(1/2)].

Note 2   Whether the car is in Class 10 or Class 10.1, it is subject to declining balance CCA at a 30 percent rate. This would amount to $4,530 [(30%)($15,100)] if the automobile was used entirely for business. However, as the usage is only 60 percent business, the deduction is $2,718 [(60%)([$4,530)].

Note 3   Mr. Bubel's loss on the 50 common shares which he reacquired would be considered a superficial loss and, therefore, not deductible. This means his allowable capital loss would be calculated as follows:

Proceeds Of Disposition ([$75][100 Shares])	$7,500
Adjusted Cost Base ([$89][100 Shares])	(8,900)
Capital Loss	($1,400)
Disallowed As Superficial (50/100)	700
Balance	($ 700)
Inclusion Rate	1/2
Allowable Capital Loss	($ 350)

Note that the $700 loss on the 50 shares that were sold and repurchased would be added to the adjusted cost base of the replacement shares.

Note 4   The Workers' Compensation Board Payment is not subject to income taxes. However, to accomplish this result, it is included in Net Income and deducted in arriving at Taxable Income.

Note 5   Since Mr. Bubel has no unused RRSP deduction room from the preceding year nor a PA, his maximum RRSP deduction for 2001 is the lesser of $13,500 and 18% of his 2000 Earned Income. His 2001 Earned Income is his Employment Income of $51,362 and the problem asks you to assume that it was the same for 2000. Eighteen percent of this amount is $9,245, less than the 2001 RRSP Dollar Limit of $13,500. As Mr. Bubel is not a member of an RPP, there is no need to reduce the $9,245 for a Pension Adjustment.

Contributions eligible for deduction in 2001 total $9,500 ($5,500 + $4,000). This means he can deduct the maximum amount of $9,245, leaving a carry over of $255 to be deducted in future years. There is no time limit on this carry over.

Note 6   The convention expenses are not deductible as Mr. Bubel is not self employed.

Note 7   The demonstration software is a Class 12 capital asset (100%) which is subject to the one-half first year rule. However as Mr. Bubel is an employee, he can only deduct CCA related to the use of a car or airplane and the software cost is non deductible.

Note 8   Race track winnings are not subject to income taxes as long as Mr. Bubel is not a professional gambler.

Solution to Chapter Thirteen Exercises

Exercise Thirteen - 1

Without the transfer, Mr. Ho would have no spousal tax credit, while with the transfer he would be eligible for the full $1,007. Given this, the analysis of his position at the federal level would be as follows:

Spousal Tax Credit	($1,007)
Additional Taxes On Dividends [(1.25)($5,700)(29% + 14.5%)]	3,099
Dividend Tax Credit [(2/3 + 1/3)(25%)($5,700)]	(1,425)
Tax Increase (Decrease)	$ 667

As there is an increase in taxes, the election would not be desirable.

Exercise Thirteen - 2

The required amount would be calculated as follows:

Basic Personal Amount	$ 7,412
Spousal Amount [$6,294 - ($2,600 - $629)]	4,323
Credit Base	$11,735
Rate	16%
Credit	$1,878

Exercise Thirteen - 3

Her tax credits would be determined as follows:

Basic Personal Amount	$ 7,412
Equivalent To Spouse [$6,294 - ($1,800 - $629)]	5,123
Infirm Dependant Over 18	3,500
Credit Base	$16,035
Rate	16%
Total Credits	$ 2,566

Although she could have claimed the equivalent to spouse credit for her son, the credit would only have been worth $1,007 [(16%)($6,294)]. She is better off claiming the infirm dependant credit plus the decreased equivalent to spouse credit. Ms. Forest could have also considered claiming the caregiver credit, instead of the infirm dependant over 18 credit, for her son. However, the caregiver credit is $560 [(16%)($3,500)], the same amount as the infirm dependant over 18 credit. Therefore, the caregiver credit is of no extra value to Ms. Forest.

Exercise Thirteen - 4

With the inclusion of the taxable capital gain resulting from the contribution, Mr. Radeem's Taxable Income for 2001 would be $90,000 [$70,000 + (1/4)($110,000 - $30,000)]. In determining his charitable donations tax credit, the maximum base for this credit would be $67,500 [(75%)($90,000)], plus $5,000 [(25%)(1/4)($110,000 - $30,000)], a total of $72,500. However, he does not need all of this credit to reduce his Taxes Payable to nil:

Tax On First $61,509	$11,687
Tax At 26 Percent On Remaining $28,491	7,408
Tax Before Credits	$19,095
Tax Credits	(4,000)
Taxes Payable Before Contributions Credit	$15,095

Given this amount of Taxes Payable, the use of $52,141 of his contribution will produce the $15,095 [(16%)($200) + (29%)($52,141 - $200)] credit that will reduce his Basic Federal Tax to nil. This leaves a carry over of $57,859 ($110,000 - $52,141).

Exercise Thirteen - 5

Her medical expense tax credit would be calculated as follows:

Total Medical Expenses (Includes Spouse And Son)	$12,755
Threshold Amount (Maximum)	(1,678)
Eligible For Credit	$11,077
Rate	16%
Credit Before Reduction	$ 1,772
Reduction [(68%)($7,460 - $7,412)]	(33)
Medical Expense Credit	$ 1,739

It is beneficial for Ms. Davies to claim her son's medical expenses. They increase her credit by $1,315 [(16%)($8,425) - $33]. Although her son will pay taxes on $48 ($7,460 - $7,412) in Net Income if he has no credits other than the basic personal credit, the family unit is better off.

Exercise Thirteen - 6

His tax credits would be calculated as follows:

Basic Personal Amount	$ 7,412
Spousal Amount	6,294
Age [$3,619 - (15%)($42,000 - $26,941)]	1,360
Pension Income	1,000
Spousal Age Transfer	3,619
Spousal Tuition Fee And Education Transfer [$2,200 + (4 Months)($400)]	3,800
Credit Base	$23,485
Rate	16%
Total Credits	$ 3,758

Exercise Thirteen - 7

Ms. Unger's credit would be calculated as follows:

First $200 (75%)	$150
Next $350 (50%)	175
Remaining $235 (1/3)	78
Total Political Contributions Tax Credit	$403

Exercise Thirteen - 8

The credit will be $450 [(15%)($3,000)]. As his acquisition is less than the $5,000 maximum, the full cost is eligible for the 15 percent credit.

Exercise Thirteen - 9

She will have to repay $3,002 [(15%)($75,400 - $55,390)].

Exercise Thirteen - 10

Mr. Blouson's regular taxes payable would be calculated as follows:

Tax Before Credits:	
First $61,509	$11,687
Next $23,491 At 26 Percent	6,108
Total	$17,795
Basic Personal Credit	(1,186)
Dividend Tax Credit [(2/3)($5,000)]	(3,333)
Basic Federal Tax	$13,276

For alternative minimum tax purposes, his adjusted taxable income would be calculated as follows:

Regular Taxable Income	$85,000
Non Taxable Half Of Capital Gains	22,500
Dividend Gross Up	(5,000)
Adjusted Taxable Income	$102,500

Calculation of the alternative minimum tax would be as follows:

Adjusted Taxable Income	$102,500
Basic Exemption	(40,000)
Amount Subject To Tax	$62,500
Rate	16%
Minimum Tax Before Credit	$10,000
Basic Personal Credit	(1,186)
Alternative Minimum Tax Payable	$ 8,814

Mr. Blouson would not be liable for the alternative minimum tax as $8,814 is less than the regular tax of $13,276.

Solution to Self Study Problem Thirteen - 1

Mr. and Mrs. Bahry's Taxable Income would be calculated as follows:

	Mr. Bahry	Mrs. Bahry
Old Age Security Pension	$ 5,200	$5,200
Registered Pension Plan Receipts	12,340	820
Registered Retirement Income Fund	N/A	700
Canada Pension Plan	3,690	830
Taxable Dividends (125%)	2,000	420
Interest On Savings Accounts	1,239	443
Net Taxable Capital Gain:		
Mr. Bahry	Nil	
Mrs. Bahry		Nil
Taxable Income	$24,469	$ 8,413

Neither Mr. Bahry's capital loss nor Mrs. Bahry's net capital loss can be deducted in 2001. They can be carried back three years and carried forward indefinitely to be applied against capital gains.

Mrs. Bahry's Personal Credit is equal to $1,186 [(16%)($7,412)].

Mr. Bahry's maximum tax credits would be as follows:

Base Amount	$ 7,412
Age (No Reduction Required)	3,619
Pension	1,000
Transfers From Mrs. Bahry (See Note)	3,618
Credit Base	$15,649
Rate	16%
Total	$ 2,504
Charitable Donations ([16%][$200] + [29%][$1,510 - $200])	412
Dividend Tax Credit ([2/3][25%][$1,600])	267
Total Credits	$ 3,183

Note   Mr. Bahry cannot take the spousal credit because Mrs. Bahry's income is too high. Mrs. Bahry's age credit and pension income credit are eligible for transfer under ITA 118.8. Mrs. Bahry's taxes payable before any credits would be $1,346 [(16%)($8,413)], of which $1,186 would be eliminated by her basic personal credit. Mr. Bahry is not eligible for the ITA 82(3) election to include his wife's dividends in his income as the transfer would not increase or create a spousal credit. Mrs. Bahry must include the $84 gross up on her dividends in her taxable income which decreases the amount of tax credits she can transfer. Because she will not claim the dividend tax credit due to the ordering rules for claiming credits (her age and pension credits must be claimed first) and it is not a credit that can be transferred, her dividend tax credit will be lost. The total credit base (the credits will be 16 percent of this amount) that can be transferred are as follows:

Age	$3,619
Pension	1,000
Less Excess Of Taxable Income Over Basic Personal	
Credit ($8,413 - $7,412)	(1,001)
Credit Base Transferred To Spouse	$3,618

Solution to Self Study Problem Thirteen - 2

Case A The solution to this first case can be completed as follows:

Net and Taxable Income		$41,000
Gross Federal Tax [$4,921 + (22%)($41,000 - $30,754)]		$ 7,175
Basic Personal Amount	$ 7,412	
Caregiver	3,500	
Interest On Student Loans	375	
Credit Base	$11,287	
Rate	16%	(1,806)
Basic Federal Tax		$ 5,369

Since Mr. Murphy's father's Net Income is greater than $6,923, the equivalent to spouse credit is not available. If it had been available due to his father's infirmity, the infirm dependant over 18 credit would have been partially eroded as Stanley's father has Net Income greater than $4,966. Therefore, the use of the caregiver credit will minimize taxes payable.

Case B The solution for this case is as follows:

Net and Taxable Income		$41,000
Gross Federal Tax [$4,921 + (22%)($41,000 - $30,754)]		$ 7,175
Basic Personal Amount	$ 7,412	
Spousal [$6,294 - ($4,650 - $629)]	2,273	
Medical Expenses [$3,150 - (3%)($41,000)]	1,920	
Credit Base	$11,605	
Rate	16%	(1,857)
Basic Federal Tax		$ 5,318

As family Net Income is greater than $28,506, Stanley Murphy is not eligible for the refundable medical expense supplement [($28,506 - $18,106)(5%) = $520, the amount of the refundable medical expense supplement].

Case C The solution for this case is as follows:

Net and Taxable Income		$41,000
Gross Federal Tax [$4,921 + (22%)($41,000 - $30,754)]		$ 7,175
Basic Personal Amount	$ 7,412	
Spousal [$6,294 - ($5,050 - $629)]	1,873	
Albert's Education And Tuition: Lesser Of:		
• $5,000; and		
• $6,600 [($400)(8 Months) + $3,400)]	5,000	
Credit Base	$14,285	
Rate	16%	(2,286)
Basic Federal Tax		$ 4,889

The transfer of Albert's education and tuition credits is limited to $5,000. Alternatively, Albert can carry forward his tuition and education tax credits to be applied against his future income taxes payable.

Case D   Given that the Murphys will use the ITA 82(3) election to include Helen's dividends in Stanley's income so that he can claim the resulting dividend tax credit, the solution for this case is as follows:

Stanley's Net and Taxable Income ($41,250 + $150)		$41,400
Gross Federal Tax [$4,921 + (22%)($41,400 - $30,754)]		$ 7,263
Basic Personal Amount	$ 7,412	
Spousal [$6,294 - ($6,100 - $150 - $629)]	973	
Age [$3,619 - (15%)($41,400 - $26,941)]	1,450	
Pension	1,000	
Spouse's Age	3,619	
Spouse's Disability	6,000	
Spouse's Pension	500	
Credit Base	$20,954	
Rate	16%	(3,353)
Dividend Tax Credit ([13-1/3%][$600 + $150])		(100)
Basic Federal Tax		$ 3,810

The Old Age Security and Canada Pension Plan receipts are not eligible for the pension income credit. As a result, Helen's pension income credit is limited to 16 percent of her Registered Pension Plan receipt. As Helen Murphy's income is below $26,941, there is no reduction in her age credit.

Case E   The solution for this case would be as follows:

Net and Taxable Income	$41,000
Gross Federal Tax [$4,921 + (22%)($41,000 - $30,754)]	$ 7,175
Basic Personal Credit [(16%)($7,412)]	(1,186)
Dividend Tax Credit [(13-1/3%)($3,600)	(480)
Basic Federal Tax	$ 5,509
Political Contributions Tax Credit (Note)	(475)
Federal Taxes Payable	$ 5,034

Note   The political contributions tax credit would be calculated as follows:

75 Percent Of $200	$150
50 Percent Of $350	175
1/3 Of $450	150
Total Credit	$475

Solution to Self Study Problem Thirteen - 3

Taxable Income   Mr. Slater's Net and Taxable Income would be calculated as follows:

Employment Income - Salary (Note One)		$ 35,000
Proprietorship Income (Note Two)		26,000
Income From Investments:		
Interest On Savings Account	$ 4,600	
Interest On Loans To Friends	12,000	
Canadian Dividends (125 Percent)	55,000	
Dividends From U.S Companies		
(Before Withholding)	10,000	
	$81,600	
Safety Deposit Box Rental	(150)	81,450
Taxable Capital Gain [(1/2)($111,500 - $23,000)]		44,250
Farm Loss (Note Three):		
Revenues	$36,000	
Expenses	(45,000)	
Total Loss	($ 9,000)	
Carry Over [(1/2)($9,000 - $2,500)]	3,250	(5,750)
CPP Benefits		5,100
Old Age Security		5,200
Net Income Before OAS Repayment		$191,250
OAS Repayment - Lesser Of:		
• $5,200		
• $20,391 [(15%)($191,250 - $55,309)]		(5,200)
Net and Taxable Income		$186,050

Note One   Since Mr. Slater is over 70 years old, he does not have deductions from salary for EI or CPP.

Note Two   The drawings from the proprietorship have no effect on the Net Income for tax purposes of Mr. Slater. The proprietorship income of $28,300 is reduced by the interest of $2,300 on the proprietorship bank loan.

Note Three   Since Mr. Slater is not a full time farmer, his farm loss would be restricted to $2,500 plus 50 percent of the next $6,500, a total of $5,750. The $3,250 balance could be carried back to the preceding three years and forward for 10 years to be deducted against farming income.

Taxes Payable   Mr. Slater's taxes payable would be calculated as follows:

Tax On First $100,000		$21,695
Tax On Next $86,050 ($186,050 - $100,000) At 29 Percent		24,955
Gross Federal Tax		$46,650
Tax Credits:		
Basic Personal Amount	$ 7,412	
Mr. Slater's Age ($3,619 - $3,619)	Nil	
Spousal	6,294	
Spouse's Disability	6,000	
Credit Base	$19,706	
Rate	16%	(3,153)
Charitable Donations		
{([16%][$200]) + ([29%][$2,700 - $200])}		(757)
Dividend Tax Credit ([2/3][25%][$44,000])		(7,333)
Basic Federal Taxes Payable		$35,407
Foreign Tax Credit (Note One)		(1,500)
Federal Political Contributions Tax Credit (Note Two)		(300)
Federal Taxes Payable		$33,607
Credits:		
Employer Withholding	($9,000)	
Instalments	(2,500)	(11,500)
Balance Before Interest And Penalties		$22,107
Late Filing Penalty (Note Three)		1,326
Interest (Note Four)		414
Amount Owing On June 30		$23,847

Note One   The federal foreign tax credit will be the lesser of the foreign taxes actually paid of $1,500 and an amount determined by the following formula:

$$\left[\frac{\text{Foreign Non Business Income}}{\text{Adjusted Net Income}} \right] [\text{Federal Tax*}]$$

*Basic Federal Tax before the dividend tax credit is deducted.

This amount would be ($35,407 + $7,333) multiplied by ($10,000 ÷ $186,050). This equals $2,298, leaving the actual taxes of $1,500 as the lesser amount.

Note Two   The political contributions tax credit can be calculated as follows:

75 Percent Of First $200	$150
50 Percent Of The Next $300	150
Total Credit	$300

Note Three   The due date for Mr. Slater's return is June 15 as he has business income. The penalty for the late filing of a return is 5 percent plus 1 percent per month for each complete month after the filing deadline. By filing on July 15, 2002, Mr. Slater's penalty will be 6 percent of $22,107, or $1,326.

Note Four   Although interest calculations are based on daily compounding, this is difficult to compute. Simple interest on late taxes at a rate of 9 percent from April 30, 2002 as required in the problem is as follows:

$$([\$22,107][9\%][76/365]) = \$414$$

Other Notes   Other points that should be noted are as follows:

- The gambling income would not be taxable unless Mr. Slater's activity was extensive enough to be considered a business.
- Inheritances are capital receipts and do not constitute Taxable Income.
- Drawings from the proprietorship are not taxable income and funds invested are capital and not deductible.
- The life insurance premiums are not deductible.
- The mortgage payments on his personal residence are not deductible.

Solution to Self Study Problem Thirteen - 4

Taxable Income   Ms. Worthmore's minimum Taxable Income is calculated as follows:

Employment Income		
Gross Salary - Intra Graphics	$72,476	
Gross Salary - Lindworth Inc.	2,500	
RPP Contributions	(1,233)	
Premium For Provincial Health Care	413	$74,156
Income From Property		
Dividend Attribution (Note One)	$ 228	
Dividends From Lindworth (Note Two)	5,406	
Loan Principal (Note Two)	5,000	10,634
Taxable Capital Gains		
Attribution From Husband (Note Three)	$ 1,144	
Transfer To Jayne (Note Four)	122	
Lackmere Shares (Note Five)	394	
Agricultural Land (Note Six)	9,000	10,660
Other Income And Deductions		
RRSP Deduction (Note Seven)	($ 6,923)	
Spousal Support Payments	(2,700)	(9,623)
Net Income For Tax Purposes And Taxable Income		$85,827

Note One   There would be income attribution for the dividends received by Mr. Dalton on the shares received as a gift. The amount would be $228 [($3.50)(52 Shares)(1.25 Gross Up)].

Note Two   The dividends from Lindworth Inc. would be included in the amount of $5,406 [($4,325)(1.25 Gross Up)]. With respect to the loan principal, it will be outstanding on more than two consecutive corporate year ends and, as a consequence, it must be included in Ms. Worthmore's Net Income. However, there will be no imputed interest on the loan and, when it is repaid, it can be deducted by Ms. Worthmore.

Note Three   In the case of transfers to a spouse, unless an election is made not to have Section 73 apply, the property is transferred at the adjusted cost base of the transferor. There is no recognition of capital gains at the time of transfer. However, when Mr. Dalton sells the shares on August 31, 2001, there would be attribution of taxable capital gains in the amount of $1,144 [($56 - $12)(52)(1/2)].

Note Four   In the case of a gift to a minor child, it is treated as a deemed disposition at fair market value. This results in a taxable capital gain at the time of transfer in the amount of $122 [($27 - $18)(27)(1/2)].

Note Five   The taxable capital gain on the Lackmere Ltd. shares would be computed using the average value for the shares. The average value would be calculated as follows:

122 Shares At $92	$11,224
178 Shares At $71	12,638
Total Cost	$23,862
Average Cost ($23,862 ÷ 300 Shares)	$ 79.54

This results in a taxable capital gain of $394 [($86 - $79.54)(122)(1/2)].

Note Six   When there is a non arms' length transfer of property for consideration of less than fair market value, ITA 69 deems that, for the transferor, the transfer takes place at fair market value.   This will result in a taxable capital gain of $9,000 [($28,000 - $10,000)(1/2)]. Note that for the transferee, the adjusted cost base will only be the transfer price of $10,000. This could result in double taxation of some or all of the $18,000 capital gain if the transferee subsequently sells the land for more than $10,000.

Note Seven   Ms. Worthmore's 2000 Earned Income (assumed to be equal to the 2001 figure) is as follows:

Gross Salary - Intra	$72,476
Gross Salary - Lindworth	2,500
Employment Benefit - Provincial Health Care	413
Spousal Support Paid And Deducted	(2,700)
Earned Income	$72,689

Eighteen percent of this is $13,084, which is less than the 2001 RRSP Dollar Limit of $13,500. Therefore Ms. Worthmore's deduction limit is $6,923 ($13,084, less the 2000 pension adjustment of $6,161). The excess contribution of $577 ($7,500 - $6,923) can be carried forward and deducted in future years.

Taxes Payable   Ms. Worthmore's Taxes Payable can be calculated as follows:

Tax On First $61,509		$11,687
Tax On Next $24,318 ($85,827 - $61,509) At 26 Percent		6,323
Gross Federal Tax Payable		$18,010
Basic Personal Amount	$ 7,412	
Spousal [$6,294 - ($750 + $2,475 - $629)]}	3,698	
CPP	1,496	
EI	878	
Transfer Of Spouse's Tuition	2,300	
Transfer Of Spouse's Education [(4 Months)($400)]	1,600	
Credit Base	$17,384	
Rate	16%	(2,781)
Dividend Tax Credit [(2/3)(25%)($182 + $4,325)]		(751)
Charitable Donations {[(16%)($200)] + [(29%)($342 - $200)]}		(73)
Medical Expenses (Note Eight)		(1,666)
Basic Federal Tax		$12,739
Political Contributions ([75%][$100])		(75)
Federal Tax Payable		$12,664

Note Eight   Provided she reduces her total medical expenses tax credit by 68 percent of their Net Income in excess of $7,412 (basic personal credit) Ms. Worthmore can use all of the medical expenses of her daughters Joyce and June. The credit is calculated as follows:

Medical Expenses of Children ($2,200 + $9,850)	$12,050
Provincial Health Care Premiums	413
Total Medical Expenses	$12,463
Threshold Amount (Maximum)	(1,678)
Eligible For Credit	$10,785
Rate	16%
Credit Before Reduction	$ 1,726
Reduction for June [(68%)($7,500 - $7,412)]	(60)
Medical Expense Credit	$ 1,666

Solution to Self Study Problem Thirteen - 5

Regular Taxes Payable   The minimum regular taxable income and taxes payable calculations would be as follows:

	Cheryl	Alma	Irene
Employment And Business Income	$ 60,800	$36,000	$ 22,900
Dividends Received	26,300	-0-	29,400
Dividend Gross Up (25%)	6,575	-0-	7,350
Taxable Capital Gains	9,100	-0-	300,000
Retiring Allowance	-0-	58,000	-0-
RRSP Deductions (Note 1)	(2,344)	(58,000)	-0-
Net Income For Tax Purposes	$100,431	$36,000	$359,650
Lifetime Capital Gains Deduction	(9,100)	-0-	(250,000)
Taxable Income	$ 91,331	$36,000	$109,650
Federal Taxes (Note 2)	$ 19,441	$ 6,075	$ 24,494
Basic Personal Credit	(1,186)	(1,186)	(1,186)
Dividend Tax Credit (2/3 of Gross Up)	(4,383)	-0-	(4,900)
Regular Federal Tax Payable	$ 13,872	$ 4,889	$ 18,408

Note 1   Cheryl's maximum 2001 RRSP Deduction of $2,344 is the least of:

- $3,500, her actual contribution
- $4,900, the 2001 RRSP dollar limit of $13,500 reduced by her 2000 Pension Adjustment of $8,600
- $2,344, 18% of 2000 Earned Income of $60,800 (assumed to be equal to her 2001 Earned Income) reduced by her 2000 Pension Adjustment of $8,600

Note 2   The federal taxes payable, before the dividend tax credit, were calculated as follows:

	Taxable Income	Federal Tax Calculations	Federal Tax
Cheryl	$ 91,331	$11,687 + (26%)($29,822)	$19,441
Alma	$ 36,000	$ 4,921 + (22%)($ 5,246)	$ 6,075
Irene	$109,650	$21,695 + (29%)($ 9,650)	$24,494

Alternative Minimum Tax Payable   The Alternative Minimum Tax (AMT) calculations would be as follows:

	Cheryl	Alma	Irene
Regular Taxable Income	$91,331	$36,000	$109,650
Non Taxable Half Of Capital Gains			
(Equal To The Taxable Amount)	9,100	-0-	300,000
Dividend Gross Up	(6,575)	-0-	(7,350)
Adjusted Taxable Income	$93,856	$36,000	$402,300
AMT Exemption	(40,000)	(40,000)	(40,000)
AMT Base	$53,856	$ Nil	$362,300
Rate	16%	16%	16%
Federal AMT Before Credit	$ 8,617	$ Nil	$ 57,968
Basic Personal Credit	(1,186)	(1,186)	(1,186)
Federal AMT	$ 7,431	$ Nil	$ 56,782
Regular Federal Taxes Payable	(13,872)	(4,889)	(18,408)
Additional Taxes Required	$ Nil	$ -0-	$ 38,374

The excess of AMT over regular taxes payable for Irene can be carried forward for seven years and applied against any future excess of regular taxes payable over the alternative minimum tax.

Solution to Chapter Fourteen Exercises

Exercise Fourteen - 1

Item 1   You would add the accounting loss of $5,600 ($48,300 - $53,900). You would also add the recapture of CCA of $13,700 ($34,600 - $48,300) for a total addition of $19,300.

Item 2   You would add the accounting amortization of $18,000 ($180,000 ÷ 10). You would subtract the CEC amortization of $9,450 [($180,000)(3/4)(7%)] for a net addition of $8,550.

Item 3   You would add the estimated warranty costs of $15,000.

Item 4   You would deduct the premium amortization of $4,500.

Exercise Fourteen - 2

Net Income For Tax Purposes	$263,000
Dividends	(14,200)
Contributions	(8,600)
Non Capital Loss Carry Over	(82,000)
Net Capital Loss*	(14,250)
Taxable Income	$143,950

*Limited to current year's taxable capital gains of $14,250.

Exercise Fourteen - 3

As this transaction would be subject to the stop loss rules, the deductible loss would be calculated as follows:

Proceeds Of Disposition [($21.15)(1,000)]	$21,150
Adjusted Cost Base [($25.30)(1,000)]	(25,300)
Total Loss	($ 4,150)
Disallowed Portion [($2.16)(1,000)]	2,160
Capital Loss	($ 1,990)
Inclusion Rate	1/2
Allowable Capital Loss	($ 995)

Exercise Fourteen - 4

No Acquisition Of Control   Taxable Income for 2000 would be nil, with a non capital loss carry over of $135,000 ($57,000 - $192,000). Net Income for 2001 would be $289,000 ($42,000 + $247,000) and, if there was no acquisition of control, the $135,000 loss carry forward could be deducted, resulting in a Taxable Income for 2001 of $154,000 ($289,000 - $135,000).

Exercise Fourteen - 5

The non capital loss balance at the end of the year would be calculated as follows:

Amount E	
ABIL	$ 5,250
Dividends Received	48,000
Business Loss	273,000
Net Capital Loss	13,500
Total	$339,750
Amount F ($13,500 + $48,000 + $27,200)	(88,700)
Non Capital Loss At End Of Year	$251,050

*Limited to taxable capital gains of $13,500 [($111,000 - $84,000)(1/2)].

Exercise Fourteen - 6

The net capital loss would be $7,650 [($23,100 - $38,400)(1/2)]. The allowable portion of the business investment loss would be $75,750 [(1/2)($151,500)]. As only $63,500 of this amount can be deducted against current income, the remainder would be a non capital loss carry over of $12,250 ($75,750 - $63,500).

Acquisition Of Control   The acquisition of control would not change the 2000 results. However, there would be a deemed year end and, in the following taxation year, the 2000 non capital loss carry forward could only be deducted to the extent of the profits in the pen division. This would result in 2001 Taxable Income of $247,000 ($289,000 - $42,000) and a non capital loss carry forward of $93,000 ($135,000 - $42,000).

Exercise Fourteen - 7

The percentage of Taxable Income earned in each Province would be calculated as follows:

	Gross Revenues		Wages And Salaries	
	Amount	Percent	Amount	Percent
Ontario	$1,303,000	44.6%	$ 52,000	31.5%
Manitoba	896,000	30.7%	94,000	57.0%
Not Related To A Province	724,000	24.7%	19,000	11.5%
Total	$2,923,000	100.0%	$165,000	100.0%

The average of the two percentages applicable for income not related to a province is 18.1%, leaving an average for income related to a province of 81.9%. Given this, federal taxes payable can be calculated as follows:

Base Amount of Part I Tax [(38%)($226,000)]	$85,880
Surtax [(4%)(28%)($226,000)]	2,531
Federal Tax Abatement [(10%)(81.9%)($226,000)]	(18,509)
General Rate Reduction [(1%)($226,000)]	(2,260)
Total Federal Tax Payable	$67,642

Exercise Fourteen - 8

Taxable Capital	$27,900,000
Percentage Employed In Canada	78%
Taxable Capital Employed In Canada	$21,762,000
Capital Deduction	(10,000,000)
Amount Subject To Tax	$11,762,000
Part I.3 Rate	.00225
Large Corporations Tax Before Surtax	$ 26,465
Canadian Surtax Paid*	(5,443)
Large Corporations Tax Payable	$ 21,022

The Canadian surtax paid would be $5,443 [($623,000)(4%)(28%)(78%)]. Note that only the surtax related to income earned in a Canadian jurisdiction is available as a credit against the Part I.3 tax on large corporations.

Exercise Fourteen - 9

The components of the M&P formula would be as follows:

• Adjusted Active Business Income		$ 333,000
• Cost Of Capital:		
Owned Assets [(10%)($1,432,000)]	$143,200	
Leased Assets	26,000	$ 169,200
• Cost Of M&P Capital		
Total Capital	$169,200	
Non Qualifying:		
Storing Finished Goods [(12%)($143,200)]	(17,184)	
Purchasing Operations [(10%)($143,200)]	(14,320)	
Employee Facilities [(10%)($143,200)]	(14,320)	$ 123,376
Fraction		100/85
Total		$ 145,148
• Cost Of Labour ($987,000 + $45,000)		$1,032,000
• Cost Of M&P Labour		
Cost Before Adjustment		$ 987,000
Fraction		100/75
Total		$1,316,000

As $1,316,000 is larger than the cost of labour figure, we will use the $1,032,000 cost of labour figure.

Using these numbers in the M&P formula provides the following M&P profits:

$$(\$333,000)\left(\frac{\$145,148 + \$1,032,000}{\$169,200 + \$1,032,000}\right) = \$326,332$$

S - 90 Solution to Chapter Fourteen Exercises

Exercise Fourteen - 10

Top And Middle   Top and Middle are associated under ITA 256(1)(a) as Top controls Middle.

Top And Bottom   Top and Bottom are associated under ITA 256(1)(b) as they are both controlled by the same person, Mr. Top. He controls Top directly. In addition, he controls Bottom through a combination of indirect ownership (Middle's 22 percent) and direct ownership {his own 5 percent, his minor son's 15 percent [deemed his by ITA 256(1.3)], and a further 10 percent through options [deemed his by ITA 256(1.4)]}.

Middle And Bottom   Middle and Bottom are associated under ITA 256(1)(b) as they are both controlled by the same person, Mr. Top. Mr. Top controls Middle indirectly through Top. He controls Bottom through a combination of direct and indirect control as described in the discussion of Top and Bottom.

Exercise Fourteen - 11

The small business deduction for Largely Small Inc. is equal to 16 percent of the least of:

• Active Business Income ($1,233,000 - $36,000)		$1,197,000
• Taxable Income ($1,233,000 - $914,000)	$319,000	
10/3 FTC On Non Business Income ($5,400)	(18,000)	$301,000
• Annual Business Limit*		$148,000

*As Largely Small Inc. has Taxable Capital Employed In Canada in excess of $10 million, its annual business limit will be eroded by the Part I.3 tax payable for the preceding year. This amount was $2,925 [(.00225)($11,300,000 - $10,000,000)]. Note that, for this purpose, it is not reduced for any surtax paid during the year. As specified in ITA 125(5.1), the reduction in the annual business limit would be calculated as follows:

$$(\$200,000)\left(\frac{\$2,925}{\$11,250}\right) = \$52,000$$

This reduction leaves the annual business limit at $148,000 ($200,000 - $52,000). As this is the least of the three figures, the small business deduction is equal to $23,680 [(16%)($148,000)].

Exercise Fourteen - 12

The small business deduction for Marion Manufacturing would be equal to 16 percent of the least of:

• Active Business Income		$311,000
• Taxable Income ($362,000 - $210,000)	$152,000	
10/4 Of Business FTC ($3,150)	(7,875)	$144,125
• Annual Business Limit		$200,000

Based on this, the small business deduction would be $23,060 [(16%)($144,125)].

The manufacturing and processing deduction is equal to seven percent of the lesser of:

• M&P Profits	$311,000	
Amount Eligible For Small Business Deduction	(144,125)	$166,875
• Taxable Income	$152,000	
Amount Eligible For Small Business Deduction	(144,125)	
10/4 Of Business FTC ($3,150)	(7,875)	
Aggregate Investment Income	(30,000)	$ Nil

The M&P profits deduction would be equal to Nil.

It would have been possible to deduct only $154,125 of the charitable donations and carry forward, for up to five years, the remaining $55,875. This would have increased the small business deduction available to the annual maximum, while increasing Taxable Income and the total taxes payable for the year. However, there could still be an ultimate tax savings with this approach as the small business deduction cannot be carried over, while charitable donations can be.

Exercise Fourteen - 13

The total amount of investment tax credits available can be calculated as follows:

Qualified Property [(10%)($123,000)]	$ 12,300
SR&ED - 1st $2,000,000 At 35%	700,000
SR&ED - Remaining $700,000 At 20%	140,000
Total Available Amount	$852,300

The refund available would be as follows:

Qualified Property [(40%)($12,300)]	$ 4,920
SR&ED Current Expenditures [(100%)(35%)($1,200,000)]	420,000
SR&ED Capital:	
1st $800,000 [(40%)(35%)($800,000)]	112,000
Remainder [(40%)(20%)($700,000)]	56,000
Total Refund Available	$592,920

The non refunded investment tax credit of $259,380 can be carried over to other years.

Solution to Self Study Problem Fourteen - 1

The minimum Net Income For Tax Purposes and Taxable Income of Margo Ltd. would be calculated as follows:

Pre Tax Accounting Income		$ 31,940
Additions:		
Inventory Reserve	$15,000	
Property Taxes On Vacant Land	1,200	
Depreciation Expense	35,600	
Goodwill Amortization	1,700	
Charitable Contributions	19,800	
Taxable Capital Gain [(1/2)($30,500 - $21,000)]	4,750	
Warranty Provision	5,500	
Social Club Membership Fees	7,210	
Interest On Late Income Tax Instalments	1,020	
Foreign Taxes Withheld	270	
Premium On Share Redemption	480	92,530
Deductions:		
Capital Cost Allowance	($78,000)	
Amortization Of Cumulative		
Eligible Capital (Note)	(1,785)	
Accounting Gain On Sale of Investments	(9,500)	(89,285)
Net Income For Tax Purposes		$ 35,185
Deductions:		
Charitable Contributions	($19,800)	
Dividends	(3,000)	(22,800)
Taxable Income		$ 12,385

Note The cumulative eligible capital account has an addition of $25,500 [(3/4)($34,000)] for the goodwill acquired. Amortization for the year is $1,785 [(7%)($25,500)].

Solution to Self Study Problem Fourteen - 2

Net Income And Taxable Income Before Carry Overs The income calculations for the four years, before any consideration of loss carry overs, would be as follows:

	1998	1999	2000	2001
Business Income (Loss)	$ 95,000	($205,000)	$ 69,500	$ 90,000
Taxable Capital Gain	-0-	-0-	4,500	5,000
Dividends	12,000	42,000	28,000	32,000
Net Income (Loss)*	$107,000	($163,000)	$102,000	$127,000
Dividends	(12,000)	(42,000)	(28,000)	(32,000)
Charitable Donations	(21,400)	-0-	(8,000)	(22,000)
Taxable Income (Loss)* Before Carry Overs	$ 73,600	($205,000)	$ 66,000	$ 73,000

*There is, of course, no concept of a negative Net or Taxable Income. However, showing the 1999 loss amount as negative is useful in problems involving loss carry overs.

1998 Analysis The Taxable Income as reported in the 1998 tax return would be $73,600, as in the preceding schedule. There would be a carry forward at the end of the year as follows:

- Net Capital Loss [($10,000)(3/4)] $7,500

1999 Analysis For 1999, Net and Taxable Income are nil. This would leave a non capital loss carry over of $205,000, a portion of which could be carried back to 1998. This would result in the following amended 1998 Taxable Income:

1998 Taxable Income As Reported In 1998	$73,600
Non Capital Loss Carry Back From 1999	(73,600)
Amended 1998 Taxable Income	$ Nil

This would leave the following carry over balances at the end of 1999:

- Non Capital Loss ($205,000 - $73,600) $131,400

- Charitable Donations $ 4,600

- Net Capital Loss From 1998 [($10,000)(3/4)] $ 7,500
  Addition From 1999 [($14,000)(3/4)]   10,500 $18,000

2000 Analysis As shown in the preceding schedule, 2000 Taxable Income before the application of carry overs was $66,000. The various balances carried forward from 1999 could be used in any order that the taxpayer chooses. The following calculation uses the losses in inverse order to their time limits. As charitable donations expire after five years, we have deducted those first. This is followed by non capital losses which expire after seven years. As shown in the following calculation, this leaves no room for the deduction of capital loss carry overs:

2000 Taxable Income Before Carry Overs	$66,000
Carry Over Of Charitable Donations	(4,600)
Carry Over Of 1999 Non Capital Loss (Maximum)	(61,400)
2000 Taxable Income After Carry Overs	$ -0-

The order that we have used in deducting losses will generally be preferable as long as the tax-payer anticipates future taxable capital gains. Note, however, that while capital loss carry overs have an unlimited life, they can only be deducted against capital gains. If Linden does not anticipate future capital gains, they would probably deduct the maximum $4,500 of net capital loss and make a corresponding reduction in the non capital loss deduction.

After the preceding allocation of losses, the following balances remain:

- Charitable Donations ($4,600 - $4,600)   Nil
- Non Capital Loss ($131,400 - $61,400) $70,000
- Net Capital Loss (Unchanged) $18,000

2001 Analysis   Using the same order as in 2000, the 2001 Taxable Income after the application of carry forward provisions would be as follows:

2001 Taxable Income Before Carry Overs	$73,000
Remaining 1999 Non Capital Loss Carry Over	(70,000)
Balance Available	$ 3,000
Net Capital Loss Carry Over (Maximum)	(3,000)
Taxable Income After Carry Overs	$ -0-

The amount of the net capital loss carry forward used in this period is limited to the balance of income available after deducting the 1999 non capital loss carryover. Note, however, if 2001 taxable capital gains had been less than $3,000, they would have been the limiting factor for recognition of the net capital loss.

At the end of 2001, the only remaining carry forward is the balance of the Net Capital Loss:

- Net Capital Loss [$18,000 - (3/4 ÷ 1/2)($3,000)] $13,500

Solution to Self Study Problem Fourteen - 3

Deemed Year End   As a result of the acquisition of control, LF will have a deemed taxation year end on April 30, 2001. This results in a short January 1, 2001 through April 30, 2001 taxation year for LF. The effects of this include:

- An additional year will be counted towards the expiry of the non capital losses.
- If CCA is to be taken, it will have to be calculated for a portion of the year.
- Any Net Capital Loss balance that can't be used will expire.
- All of the usual year end procedures (timing of bonuses, inclusion of reserves, etc.) will have to be carried out.

For the first year after the acquisition of control, LF can choose a new fiscal year end on any date up to 53 weeks after the deemed year end.

Non Capital Loss Balance   The non capital loss balance at April 30, 2001 is calculated as follows:

1999 And 2000 Losses		$320,000
Short Fiscal Period Loss:		
Operating Loss To April 30, 2001	$55,000	
Class 43 - Excess Of UCC Over FMV		
(Required write down to FMV under ITA 111[5.1])	90,000	145,000
Total Non Capital Loss		$465,000

If the non capital loss cannot be used in the year ending April 30, 2001, it will be carried forward and can be deducted against income earned in the same or a similar line of business in future years. However, if there is doubt about LF's ability to use the non capital loss carry forward balance before it expires, an election can be made to have one or more deemed dispositions (ITA 111[4][e]) in order to trigger capital gains or recapture, either of which can be used to absorb the non capital loss.

Net Capital Loss Balance   If the net capital loss balance of $75,000 cannot be used in the year ending April 30, 2001, it will expire on the acquisition of control. However, as noted in the preceding paragraph, LF can make an election to have one or more deemed dispositions in order to trigger capital gains against which the capital loss balance can be applied.

Possible Elections   Assets with potential capital gains or recapture are as follows:

Asset	Cost	UCC	FMV
Land	$450,000	N/A	$925,000
Class 3	675,000	$515,000	650,000
Class 8	25,000	10,000	15,000

Asset	Maximum Recapture	Maximum Capital Gain
Land	N/A	$475,000
Class 3	$135,000	Nil
Class 8	5,000	Nil
Total Income	$140,000	$475,000

Note that when the fair market value of the asset exceeds its adjusted cost base, the election can be made for any value between these two values. This means that, in the case of LF's Land, all or part of the accrued capital gain can be recognized.

If the election is made on the Land, its adjusted cost base will be increased to the elected value. If the election is made on the depreciable assets, their UCC will be increased to the elected value. However, for purposes of determining future recapture or capital gains, the cost of the depreciable assets will be unchanged. The difference between their original cost and their new UCC is deemed to have been claimed as CCA.

Recommendation - Uncertainty As To Future Income   At a minimum, elections should be made to insure use of the net capital loss carry forward as it will not survive the acquisition of control. Further, if there is uncertainty with respect to the ability of OLC and LF to generate income in the same or similar line of business in amounts sufficient to absorb the non capital loss carry forward, additional elections should be made to absorb as much of this balance as possible. This would require elections on all of the assets listed in the preceding table. The resulting Taxable Income would be as follows:

Land - Taxable Capital Gain [(1/2)($475,000)]	$237,500
Class 3 - Recapture	135,000
Class 8 - Recapture	5,000
Total Income From ITA 111(4)(e) Election	$377,500
Short Fiscal Period Loss	(145,000)
Net Income For Tax Purposes	$232,500
Net Capital Loss Carry Forward [(1/2 ÷ 3/4)($75,000)]	(50,000)
Balance	$182,500
Non Capital Loss Carry Forward (Maximum)	(182,500)
Taxable Income	Nil

This leaves a non capital loss carry forward of $137,500 ($320,000 - $182,500).

Recommendation - Expected Future Income   If the Companies believe that they will be able to generate sufficient income to use the non capital loss carry forward in future periods, they will not want to make elections that will result in maximum pre acquisition income. If the elections are made, the losses are converted to Cost or UCC balances. In the case of land, the increased cost will not be of benefit until the land is sold. In the case of the depreciable assets, the increased UCC will only be deductible at the applicable rates of 5 or 20 percent. Alternatively, a non capital loss carry forward can be deducted in full as soon as the Companies have sufficient income to absorb it.

In certain circumstances, companies can effectively use a net capital loss balance even when non capital losses have reduced Net Income For Tax Purposes to nil. More specifically, if an enterprise has net taxable capital gains for the year, they are permitted to deduct a net capital loss carry over from a nil net income, with the amount of the deduction being added to the non capital loss balance.

In the case at hand, it would be necessary to elect a value of $550,000 on the Land in order to trigger the required taxable capital gain of $50,000 [(1/2)($550,000 - $450,000)]. The results would be as follows:

ITA 3(a)	Nil
Plus ITA 3(b)	$ 50,000
Equals ITA 3(c)	$ 50,000
Less ITA 3(d)	(145,000)
Net Income For Tax Purposes	Nil
Less ITA 111(1)(b) - [(1/2 ÷ 3/4)($75,000)]	($ 50,000)
Taxable Income	Nil

This would leave a non capital loss carry forward from the short fiscal period of $145,000, calculated as follows:

Short Fiscal Period Loss	$145,000
Addition Of Net Capital Loss Deducted	50,000
Balance	$195,000
Less ITA 3(c) Balance	(50,000)
Non Capital Loss Balance	$145,000

The total non capital loss carry forward of $465,000 is the $320,000 carry forward from 1999 and 2000, plus the preceding short fiscal period loss of $145,000. There is no net capital loss carry forward.

Using LF's Losses   Without changing the structure of the two Companies, it may be possible to generate income for LF through transfer pricing between the Companies, or by selling some of OLC's profitable assets to LF. Alternatively, to directly apply LF's losses against OCL's profits, it will be necessary to have a wind-up, amalgamation, or other form of corporate reorganization.

Solution to Self Study Problem Fourteen - 4

From the descriptions in the problem, it would appear that each of the provincial offices of the Sundean Company would qualify as a permanent establishment. As a consequence, the allocation would be to each of these provinces on the basis of the following calculations:

Province	Gross Revenues Amount	Gross Revenues Percent	Salaries And Wages Amount	Salaries And Wages Percent
Alberta	$ 1,873,000	18%	$ 264,000	21%
British Columbia	2,246,000	22%	273,000	22%
Nova Scotia	1,397,000	13%	179,000	14%
Saskatchewan	1,298,000	12%	104,000	8%
Ontario	3,669,000	35%	427,000	35%
Total	$10,483,000	100%	$1,247,000	100%

The Province by Province average of the two percentages calculated above and the allocation of the total taxable income of $1,546,000 would be as follows:

Province	Revenues	Wages	Average	Taxable Income
Alberta	18%	21%	19.5%	$ 301,470
British Columbia	22%	22%	22.0%	340,120
Nova Scotia	13%	14%	13.5%	208,710
Saskatchewan	12%	8%	10.0%	154,600
Ontario	35%	35%	35.0%	541,100
Total	100%	100%	100.0%	$1,546,000

Solution to Self Study Problem Fourteen - 5

Total Capital The total capital would be calculated as follows:

Mortgage Payable	$ 97,000,000
Bank Debt (Due On Demand)	106,000,000
Future Income Taxes	242,000,000
Common Stock - No Par	60,000,000
Retained Earnings (Note)	192,000,000
Total Capital	$697,000,000

Note The use of the equity method for the Investment In Mini Ltd. has resulted in $4,000,000 ($63,000,000 - $59,000,000) being added to both the investment account and to Max Inc.'s Retained Earnings. As ITA 181(3) makes clear, the equity method is not acceptable in the calculation of Total Capital. As a consequence, the $4,000,000 difference between the equity value of the investment and its cost must be removed from both the Investment In Mini Ltd. and Max Inc.'s Retained Earnings.

Investment Allowance The investment allowance includes both the cost of the Investment In Mini Ltd. ($59,000,000) and the Loan To Mini Ltd. ($14,000,000), a total of $73,000,000. Note that the loan to the President of Mini Ltd. does not add to this allowance as it is not a loan to a corporate entity.

Part I.3 Tax Payable This amount would be calculated as follows:

Total Capital	$697,000,000
Investment Allowance	(73,000,000)
Taxable Capital	$624,000,000
Percentage Employed In Canada	73%
Taxable Capital Employed In Canada	$455,520,000
Capital Deduction (As Allocated Within Group)	(6,500,000)
Amount Subject To Part I.3 Tax	$449,020,000
Rate	.00225
Part I.3 Tax Payable Before Surtax	$ 1,010,295
Canadian Surtax (Note)	(343,392)
Part I.3 Tax Payable	$ 666,903

Note   This amount would be calculated as follows:

Total Corporate Surtax [(4%)(28%)($42,000,000)]	$470,400
Portion Of Income Earned In A Province	73%
Canadian Surtax	$343,392

As the Part I.3 tax exceeds the surtax, there will no carry over of the surtax credit to previous or subsequent years.

Solution to Self Study Problem Fourteen - 6

Only the Canadian active business income would have any eligibility for the manufacturing and processing profits deduction. Neither the investment income nor the income of the U.S. subsidiary would fall within the definition of adjusted active business income. As the Gladstone Company is a public company, none of its income is eligible for the small business deduction.

The formula for computing the amount of income that is eligible for the manufacturing and processing profits tax deduction is found in Income Tax Regulation 5200 as follows:

$$\begin{bmatrix} \text{Adjusted} \\ \text{Active} \\ \text{Business} \\ \text{Income} \end{bmatrix} \left[\frac{\left(\frac{100}{75} \text{ of Canadian} \atop \text{M\&P Labour Costs} \right) + \left(\frac{100}{85} \text{ of Canadian} \atop \text{M\&P Capital Costs} \right)}{\left(\text{Total Canadian} \atop \text{Labour Costs} \right) + \left(\text{Total Canadian Active Business} \atop \text{Income Capital Costs} \right)} \right]$$

Applying this formula to the information for the Gladstone Company provides the following result:

$$[\$2,353,000] \left[\frac{(\frac{100}{75})(\$2,986,000) + (\frac{100}{85})(\$4,127,000)}{(\$4,618,000 + \$4,923,000)} \right]$$

$$= [\$2,353,000] \left[\frac{\$8,836,627}{\$9,541,000} \right]$$

$$= \underline{\$2,179,288}$$

Solution to Self Study Problem Fourteen - 7

Assuming the rental income is considered property income, the components to be used in the calculation of the manufacturing and processing profits deduction for Mason Industries are as follows:

Adjusted Active Business Income ($1,556,000 - $106,000)	$1,450,000
Cost Of Labour	$1,940,000
Cost Of Manufacturing Labour	$1,270,000
Cost Of Capital:	
Rent Paid [(75%)($325,000)]	$ 243,750
Depreciable Assets [(10%)($6,850,000)]	685,000
Total Cost Of Capital	$ 928,750
Cost Of Manufacturing Capital:	
Rent [(55%)($325,000)]	$ 178,750
Depreciable Assets [(10%)($5,560,000)]	556,000
Total Cost Of Manufacturing Capital	$ 734,750

Given the preceding, the base for the manufacturing and processing profits deduction is calculated as follows:

$$[\$1,450,000]\left[\frac{(^{100}\!/_{75})(\$1,270,000)+(^{100}\!/_{85})(\$734,750)}{(\$1,940,000+\$928,750)}\right]$$

$$= \ \underline{\$1,292,804}$$

The manufacturing and processing profits deduction rate is 7 percent. The federal taxes payable for Mason Industries Ltd. would be calculated as follows:

Taxable Income As Given	$1,556,000
Base Amount of Part I Tax [(38%)($1,556,000)]	$ 591,280
Surtax [(4%)(28%)($1,556,000)]	17,427
Federal Tax Abatement [(10%)($1,556,000)]	(155,600)
M&P Deduction [(7%)($1,292,804)]	(90,496)
General Rate Reduction [1%][$1,556,000 - (100/7)($90,496)]	(2,632)
Federal Taxes Payable	$ 359,979

Solution to Self Study Problem Fourteen - 8

Taxable Income   The Company's Taxable Income would be calculated as follows:

Accounting Income Before Taxes	$523,000
Non Taxable Portion Of Capital Gain [(1/2)($22,900)]	(11,450)
Donations To Registered Canadian Charity	18,700
Contributions To Registered Political Party	7,400
Net Income For Tax Purposes	$537,650
Donations To Registered Canadian Charity	(18,700)
Dividends From Taxable Canadian Corporations	(9,400)
Non Capital Loss Carry Over	(21,950)
Net Capital Loss Carry Over*	(11,450)
Taxable Income	$476,150

*Lesser of $11,450 [(1/2)($22,900)] and $13,500 [(1/2)($27,000)].

Part I Tax Payable   The Company's Part I Tax Payable would be calculated as follows:

Base Amount of Part I Tax [(38%)($476,150)]	$180,937
Surtax [(4%)(28%)($476,150)]	5,333
General Rate Reduction {[1%][$476,150 - (100/7)($28,728)]}	(658)
Federal Tax Abatement (Note One)	(42,854)
Subtotal	$142,758
Foreign Non Business Tax Credit (Note Two)	(4,845)
Foreign Business Tax Credit (Note Three)	(20,700)
M&P Deduction (Note Four)	(28,728)
Political Contributions Tax Credit (Note Five)	(500)
Part I Tax Payable	$ 87,985

Note One   No income would be allocated to Manitoba as there are no permanent establishments in that Province. However, the Manitoba sales would be included in the Ontario total as the Manitoba customers are serviced through that Province. Based on this, the allocation would be as follows:

Gross Revenues	Amount	Percent
Ontario (Including Manitoba)	$5,725,000	91.0
New York	565,000	9.0
Total	$6,290,000	100.0

Salaries And Wages	Amount	Percent
Ontario	$3,540,000	89.0
New York	438,000	11.0
Total	$3,978,000	100.0

Average Ontario Percent [(91.0% + 89.0%) ÷ 2]	90.0%
Average New York Percent [(9.0% + 11.0%) ÷ 2]	10.0%
Total	100.0%

Based on the preceding calculations, the Federal Tax Abatement would be $42,854 [(10%)(90%)($476,150)].

Note Two   The foreign non business tax credit would be the lesser of:

- The Amount Withheld $4,845

- An Amount Calculated As Follows:

$$\left(\frac{\text{Net Foreign Non Business Income}}{\text{Adjusted Net Income}} \right)(\text{Part I Tax Otherwise Payable})$$

$$= \left(\frac{\$32,300}{\$537,650 - \$11,450 - \$9,400} \right)(\$142,758) \qquad \$8,922$$

The lesser figure would be the actual withholding of $4,845.

Note Three   The foreign business tax credit would be the least of:

- The Amount Withheld

$20,700

- An Amount Calculated As Follows:

$$\left(\frac{\text{Net Foreign Business Income}}{\text{Adjusted Net Income}} \right)(\text{Part I Tax Otherwise Payable})$$

$$= \left(\frac{\$64,200}{\$537,650 - \$11,450 - \$9,400} \right)(\$142,758 + \$42,854)$$

$23,058

- Tax Otherwise Payable Less The Foreign Non
     Business Tax Credit ($142,758 + $42,854 - $4,845)

$180,767

The least of these three figures would be the U.S. taxes withheld of $20,700.

Note Four   There is no small business deduction in the calculation of Part I tax as Mercury Manufacturing Company is not Canadian controlled. The M&P Deduction (see following calculations) would be equal to $28,728. This amount is seven percent of $410,406 which is the lesser of:

• M & P Profits		$410,406
• Taxable Income	$476,150	
Less, 10/4 Of the Foreign Business Tax Credit [(10/4)($20,700)]*	(51,750)	$424,400

Technically, a second calculation of the foreign tax credit, made without regard to the general rate reduction is required here. However, the result would be unchanged as the credit is based on the actual withholding.

The components used in the M & P profits formula would be calculated as follows:

Adjusted Business Income (ADJUBI)

Net Income For Tax Purposes	$537,650
Taxable Capital Gains [(1/2)($22,900)]	(11,450)
Dividends From Taxable Canadian Corporations	(9,400)
Interest Income From Canadian Sources	(7,800)
Dividends From U.S. Corporations	(32,300)
Foreign Business Income	(64,200)
Income From An Active Business In Canada	$412,500

Cost Of Capital (C)

Gross Cost Of Business Property In Canada	$2,680,000
Applicable Percent	10%
Cost Of Capital Owned	$ 268,000
Canadian Rental Costs	67,200
Total Cost Of Capital	$ 335,200

Cost Of M & P Capital (MC)

Gross Cost Of Business Property Used In M & P [(75%)($2,680,000)]	$2,010,000
Applicable Percent	10%
Cost Of Capital Used In M & P	$ 201,000
M & P Rental Costs	67,200
Total Cost Of M & P Capital	$ 268,200
Gross Up Factor	100/85
Cost Of M & P Capital	$ 315,529

Cost Of Labour (L)

Canadian Salaries And Wages (Total Cost of Labour)	$3,540,000

Cost Of M & P Labour (ML)

Canadian Salaries And Wages Used In M & P	$3,250,000
Gross Up Factor	100/75
Cost Of M & P Labour*	$4,333,333

*As this grossed up amount exceeds the actual total cost of Canadian labour, the actual total cost of labour of $3,540,000 will be used in the formula.

Application Of The M & P Formula

$$\begin{bmatrix} \text{Adjusted} \\ \text{Active} \\ \text{Business} \\ \text{Income} \end{bmatrix} \left[\dfrac{\left(\left[^{100}/_{75}\right] \text{ of Canadian M\&P Labour Costs} \right) + \left(\left[^{100}/_{85}\right] \text{ of Canadian M\&P Capital Costs} \right)}{\left(\begin{array}{c}\text{Total Canadian} \\ \text{Labour Costs}\end{array} \right) + \left(\begin{array}{c}\text{Total Canadian Active} \\ \text{Business Income Capital Costs}\end{array} \right)} \right]$$

$$= [\$412,500] \left[\frac{(\$3,540,000 + \$315,529)}{(\$3,540,000 + \$335,200)} \right]$$

$$= \ \underline{\$410,406}$$

Note Five The political contributions tax credit would be calculated as follows:

75% Of First $200	$150
50% Of Next $350	175
One-Third Of Next $525	175
Maximum Contribution	$500

Solution to Self Study Problem Fourteen - 9

Part A By virtue of ITA 251(6)(b), John Fleming and Eric Flame are related by the fact that they are married to persons who are connected by a blood relationship (their wives). Further, under ITA 256(1.5), a person who holds shares in two or more corporations shall be, as a shareholder of one of the corporations, deemed to be related to himself as a shareholder of the other corporations. Therefore, Fleming Ltd. and Lartch Inc. are associated under ITA 256(1)(d) because John Fleming controls Fleming Ltd., is a member of a related group (John Fleming and Eric Flame) that controls Lartch Inc., and owns more than 25 percent of the voting shares of Lartch Inc. In a similar fashion, Flame Ltd. is associated with Lartch Inc. under ITA 256(1)(d) as Eric Flame controls Flame Ltd., is a member of a related group (John Fleming and

Eric Flame) that controls Lartch Inc., and owns more than 25 percent of Lartch Inc. Fleming Ltd. and Flame Ltd. are associated under ITA 256(2) as they are both associated with a third corporation, Lartch Inc.

Part B Mr. and Mrs. Cuso are a group with respect to both Male Ltd. and Female Inc. (ITA 256[1.2][a] - two or more persons holding shares in the same corporation). As a group, they control both Male Ltd. and Female Inc. Therefore, the two Companies are associated under ITA 256 (1)(b). The fact that Mr. and Mrs. Cuso are related is not relevant.

Part C Ms. Jones and Miss Lange are a group that controls Alliance Ltd. However, they do not control Breaker Inc. as Mrs. Kelly (not a member of the group that controls Alliance Ltd.) owns 50 percent of the shares. Therefore, Alliance Ltd. and Breaker Inc. are not associated.

Part D Mr. Martin and Mr. Oakley constitute a group (ITA 256[1.2][a]) with respect to both Martin Inc. and Oakley Ltd. ITA 256(1.2)(b)(i) indicates that where one person in a group controls a corporation, the group is considered to control that corporation. As the group Mr. Martin and Mr. Oakley control both corporations, the two companies are associated under ITA 256(1)(b).

Solution to Self Study Problem Fourteen - 10

The Taxable Income and Taxes Payable for the Serendipity Shop Corp. for the year would be calculated as follows:

Net Income for Tax Purposes		$240,000
Deductions:		
Dividends	($20,000)	
Donations (Note One)	(48,000)	(68,000)
Taxable Income		$172,000

Base Amount of Part I Tax [(38%)($172,000)]	$ 65,360
Federal Surtax [(4%)(28%)($172,000)]	1,926
Federal Tax Abatement [(10%)($172,000)]	(17,200)
Small Business Deduction (Note Two)	(21,600)
Accelerated Rate Reduction (Note Three)	(2,590)
General Rate Reduction	Nil
Part I Federal Tax Payable	$ 25,896

Note One The $48,000 charitable donation would have been added to income for financial statement purposes to calculate the Net Income For Tax Purposes given in the problem.

Note Two The small business deduction is based on the least of the following:

Active business income	$220,000
Taxable income	172,000
Annual business limit	135,000

The small business deduction is equal to $21,600 [($135,000)(16%)].

Note Three The base for Serendipity's accelerated rate reduction would be the least of:

3/2 of the annual business limit of $135,000	$202,500
Active business income	220,000
Taxable income	172,000

This gives an accelerated reduction of $2,590 {[7%][$172,000 - (100/16)($21,600)]}

Note Four The general rate reduction is nil {[1%][$172,000 - (100/16)($21,600)] - (100/7)($2,590)}.

Solution to Self Study Problem Fourteen - 11

Part A   The minimum Net Income for Borscan Inc. would be calculated as follows:

Accounting Income Before Taxes		$1,375,000
Additions:		
Amortization Expense	$255,000	
Taxable Capital Gain [(1/2)($525,000 - $500,000)]	12,500	
Recaptured CCA ($500,000 - $350,000)	150,000	
Political Contributions	1,500	
Interest And Penalties - Late Return	500	
Charitable Contributions	12,000	431,500
		$1,806,500
Deductions:		
Capital Cost Allowance	($287,000)	
Extraordinary Gain	(125,000)	
Amortization Of Cumulative Eligible Capital [(7% of $85,000)]	(5,950)	(417,950)
Net Income		$1,388,550

Part B   The minimum Taxable Income for Borscan Inc. would be calculated as follows:

Net Income	$1,388,550
Charitable Contributions	(12,000)
Non Capital Loss Carry Over	(35,000)
Net Capital Loss Carry Over (Note)	(12,500)
Dividends Received	(25,000)
Taxable Income	$1,304,050

Note   The net capital loss carry forward can be used only to the extent of the taxable capital gain for the year, resulting in a deduction of $12,500. This leaves a remaining carry forward of $11,250 [$30,000 - (3/4 ÷ 1/2)($12,500)].

Part C   The minimum Federal Taxes Payable for Borscan Inc. are as follows:

Base Amount of Part I Tax [(38%)($1,304,350)]	$495,539
Surtax [(4%)(28%)($1,304,050)]	14,605
Federal Tax Abatement [(10%)($1,304,050)]	(130,405)
General Rate Reduction [(1%)($1,304,050)]	(13,041)
Political Contributions Credit (Maximum)	(500)
Federal Taxes Payable	$366,198

Solution to Chapter Fifteen Exercises

Exercise Fifteen - 1

The adjusted cost base of the shares would be determined as follows:

Cost Of Shares:	
1st Purchase [(2,400)($1.10)]	$2,640
2nd Purchase [(3,850)($1.82)]	7,007
Total Cost	$9,647

The adjusted cost base per share would be $1.54 ($9,647 ÷ 6,250).

The PUC for the investor's shares would be calculated as follows:

PUC:

1st Sale [(100,000)($1.10)]	$110,000
2nd Sale [(50,000)($1.35)]	67,500
3rd Sale [(30,000)($1.82)]	54,600
Total PUC	$232,100

Number Of Shares (2,400 + 3,850)	6,250
PUC Per Share [$232,100 ÷ 180,000 Shares]	$ 1.29
PUC For Investor's Shares	$8,063

Exercise Fifteen - 2

The balance in the capital dividend account as at December 31, 2001 would be as follows:

1987 Capital Gain [(1/2)($123,000 - $98,000)]	$12,500
1993 Capital Loss [(1/4)($72,000 - $86,000)]	(3,500)
Capital Dividend Received - 2000	8,200
2001 Sale Of Goodwill [(3/4)($42,000 - $37,000)(2/3)]	2,500
Capital Dividend Paid - 2001	(16,000)
Balance - End Of 2001	$ 3,700

Exercise Fifteen - 3

This transaction will result in an ITA 84(1) deemed dividend, calculated as follows:

PUC Of New Shares [(40,000)($12.70)]	$508,000
Increase In Net Assets	(450,000)
ITA 84(1) Deemed Dividend	$ 58,000

This would be allocated to all 166,000 shares outstanding, on the basis of $0.35 per share. This would be a taxable dividend, subject to the usual gross up and tax credit procedures. This amount would be added to the adjusted cost base of all 166,000 shares.

The original issue of shares sold for $10.50 per share ($1,323,000 ÷ 126,000). With the addition of $0.35 resulting from the ITA 84(1) deemed dividend, the adjusted cost base of these shares is now $10.85. The sale of 5,000 shares at $13.42 per share would result in a taxable capital gain of $6,425 [(1/2)(5,000)($13.42 - $10.85)].

Exercise Fifteen - 4

The tax consequences to Jesuiah Tandy resulting from the redemption of his shares would be as follows:

Proceeds Of Redemption [(15,000)($11.75)]	$176,250
PUC [(15,000)($8.25)]	(123,750)
ITA 84(3) Deemed Dividend	$ 52,500

Proceeds Of Redemption [(15,000)($11.75)]	$176,250
ITA 84(3) Deemed Dividend	(52,500)
Proceeds Of Disposition	$123,750
Adjusted Cost Base [(15,000)($10.57)]	(158,550)
Capital Loss	($ 34,800)
Inclusion Rate	1/2
Allowable Capital Loss	($ 17,400)

The deemed dividend of $52,500 would be subject to the usual gross up and dividend tax credit treatment. The allowable capital loss can be used in the current period, only to the extent of taxable capital gains in the current period.

Exercise Fifteen - 5

The refundable amount of Debut Inc.'s Part I tax for the current year would be the least of the following three figures:

Foreign Non Business Income (100 Percent)		$15,000
Taxable Capital Gains [(1/2)($38,250)]		19,125
Net Rental Income		6,500
Interest Income		9,200
Net Capital Losses Deducted [(1/2 ÷ 3/4)($13,500)]		(9,000)
Aggregate Investment Income Under ITA 129(4)		$40,825
Rate		26-2/3%
Amount Before Foreign Income Adjustment		$10,887
Less The Excess, If Any, Of:		
Foreign Non Business Tax Credit	$ 750	
Over 9-1/3 Percent Of $15,000	1,400	Nil
ITA 129(3)(a)(i) Amount		$10,887
Taxable Income ($136,700 - $22,000 - $9,000)		$105,700
Amount Eligible For The Small Business		
Deduction ($8,000 ÷ 16%)	($50,000)	
25/9 Foreign Non Business Tax Credit	(2,083)	(52,083)
Adjusted Taxable Income		$ 53,617
Rate		26-2/3%
ITA 129(3)(a)(ii) Amount		$ 14,298
ITA 129(3)(a)(iii) Amount ($21,300 - $1,183)		$ 20,117

The least of these three amounts is $10,887 and this would be the refundable portion of Part I tax for the year.

Exercise Fifteen - 6

The amount of Part IV tax would be calculated as follows:

Tax On Portfolio Investments [(1/3)($14,000)]	$4,667
Tax On Subsidiary Dividends	Nil
Tax On SI Investee [(30%)($15,000)]	4,500
Total Part IV Tax Payable	$9,167

Exercise Fifteen - 7

The balance in the RDTOH account of QIL would be as follows:

Opening Balance ($12,500 - $2,000)	$10,500
Part I Refundable Addition [(26-2/3%)($24,000)]	6,400
Part IV Tax On Portfolio Dividends [(1/3)($6,000)]	2,000
Balance - RDTOH	$18,900

The dividend refund would be $5,000, the lesser of one-third of the dividends paid and the $18,900 balance in the RDTOH account.

Solution to Self Study Problem Fifteen - 1

Part A(i)   There would be an ITA 84(1) deemed dividend calculated as follows:

Increase In PUC - Preferred Shares	$11,000
Increase In Net Assets (Decrease In Liabilities)	(10,000)
ITA 84(1) Deemed Dividend	$ 1,000

This $1,000 deemed dividend is applicable to all 1,000 of the Preferred Shares that are now outstanding. A pro rata share of the dividend, $1 per share, will be added to the adjusted cost base of all of the Preferred Shares that are outstanding. All of the Preferred Stock investors will be taxed on the deemed dividend of $1 per share.

Part A(ii)   This investor's taxable capital gain would be calculated as follows:

Proceeds Of Disposition		$11,000
Adjusted Cost Base:		
Original Cost	($4,100)	
ITA 84(1) Dividend (250 @ $1)	(250)	(4,350)
Capital Gain		$ 6,650
Inclusion Rate		1/2
Taxable Capital Gain		$ 3,325

Part B   As noted in ITA 84(1)(a), a stock dividend is not considered to be a deemed dividend under ITA 84. However, the $780 addition to Paid Up Capital will be considered to be a regular dividend under the definition in ITA 248(1). The holders of the Common Shares will have a dividend of $1.30 per share and this will be grossed up to a taxable dividend of $1.63 per share.

Part C   As the increase in Paid Up Capital was less than the increase in net assets, there is no deemed dividend or any other tax consequences in this case. This is verified in the following calculation:

Increase In Paid Up Capital [(250/500)($11,000)]		$ 5,500
Increase In Net Assets:		
New Assets Acquired	$17,500	
Increase In Liabilities	(7,500)	(10,000)
ITA 84(1) Deemed Dividend		Nil

Part D   The ITA 84(3) deemed dividend would be calculated as follows:

Redemption Price [(100 Shares)($32)]	$3,200
Paid Up Capital [(100 Shares)($26)]	(2,600)
ITA 84(3) Deemed Dividend	$ 600

In addition there would be a taxable capital gain calculated as follows:

Redemption Price	$3,200
ITA 84(3) Deemed Dividend	(600)
Deemed Proceeds Of Disposition	$2,600
Adjusted Cost Base	(1,500)
Capital Gain	$1,100
Inclusion Rate	1/2
Taxable Capital Gain	$ 550

Solution to Self Study Problem Fifteen - 2

Part A   The ending RDTOH balance for FOL would be as follows:

Refundable Dividend Tax On Hand - Beginning	$2,000
Refundable Portion Of Part I Tax [(26-2/3%)($7,000)]	1,867
Refundable Dividend Tax On Hand - Ending	$3,867

As FOL has no foreign investment income or deductions for loss carry overs, the calculation of the addition to the RDTOH for the refundable portion of Part I tax is based solely on the interest income.

The dividend refund would be $3,867, the lesser of:

- One-Third Of Taxable Dividends Paid [(1/3)($75,000)] $25,000
- Refundable Dividend Tax On Hand - Ending $ 3,867

Part B   The Part IV tax for SHI would be calculated as follows:

Portfolio Dividends [(1/3)($8,000)]	$2,667
SHI's Share Of FOL's Dividend Refund (100%)	3,867
Part IV Tax Payable	$6,534

Part C   SHI's Aggregate Investment Income totals $35,625, the sum of $12,000 in interest income and $23,625 [(1/2)($47,250)] in Taxable Capital Gains. This means that the ending RDTOH balance for SHI would be as follows:

Refundable Dividend Tax On Hand - Beginning	$ 8,000
Refundable Portion Of Part I Tax [(26-2/3%)($35,625)]	9,500
Part IV Tax Payable (Part B)	6,534
Refundable Dividend Tax On Hand - Ending	$24,034

The dividend refund would be $16,667, the lesser of:

- One-Third Of Taxable Dividends Paid [(1/3)($50,000)] $16,667
- Refundable Dividend Tax On Hand - Ending $24,034

Solution to Self Study Problem Fifteen - 3

The Part IV tax payable for Burton Investments Ltd. would be calculated as follows:

Portfolio Dividends From Bank of Montreal [(1/3)($13,480)]	$ 4,493
Burton's Share Of Puligny's Dividend Refund [(52%)($12,500)]	6,500
Total Part IV Tax Payable	$10,993

The end of year balance in the refundable dividend tax on hand account and refundable Part I tax can be calculated as follows:

Balance - End Of Preceding Year	$22,346
Dividend Refund For The Preceding Year	(7,920)
Opening Balance	$14,426
Part IV Tax	10,993
Refundable Part I Tax On Capital Gain [(1/2)($18,000)(26-2/3%)]	2,400
Balance - End Of The Year	$27,819

As the interest received appears to be related to temporary balances resulting from the Company's normal business activities, it would be viewed as active business income and would not influence the preceding calculations.

The dividends paid of $22,500 will generate a $7,500 [(1/3)($22,500)] dividend refund, as this is less than the $27,819 balance in the refundable dividend tax on hand account.

Solution to Self Study Problem Fifteen - 4

Refundable Part I Tax   The refundable portion of Part I tax would be the least of three amounts which would be calculated as follows:

ITA 129(3)(a)(i)

Interest On Loan To Subsidiary		$ 43,250
Taxable Capital Gains		24,500
Foreign Investment Income		55,000
Net Capital Losses Claimed		(12,300)
Aggregate Investment Income (Note One)		$110,450
Rate		26-2/3%
Total		$ 29,453
Foreign Non Business Income Tax Credit	($8,250)	
9-1/3 Percent Foreign Non Business Income	5,133	(3,117)
Amount Under ITA 129(3)(a)(i)		$ 26,336

Note One   The definition contained in ITA 129(4.1) excludes income from property that is incident to carrying on an active business and, as a consequence, we have left out the $5,050 of term deposit interest. With respect to the interest on the loan to the subsidiary, if the subsidiary had deducted the $43,250 in computing active business income eligible for the small business deduction, ITA 129(6) would have deemed this interest to be active business income rather than investment income. However, the subsidiary was not involved in the production of active business income and, as a consequence, the interest from the subsidiary is included in the above aggregate investment income calculation.

ITA 129(3)(a)(ii)

Taxable Income		$503,500
Amount Eligible For Small Business Deduction		(200,000)
25/9 Foreign Non Business Tax Credit [(25/9)($8,250)]		(22,917)
10/4 Foreign Business Tax Credit [(10/4)($34,000)]		(85,000)
		$195,583
Rate		26-2/3%
Amount Under ITA 129(3)(a)(ii)		$ 52,155

ITA 129(3)(a)(iii)

Part I Tax Payable Excluding Surtax ($85,595 - $5,639)	$ 79,956

The least of these three amounts is $26,336, the amount calculated under ITA 129(3)(a)(i).

Part IV Refundable Tax Payable   The Part IV refundable tax payable would be calculated as follows:

One-Third Of Portfolio Dividends Received [(1/3)($19,600)]	$ 6,533
Share Of Dividend Refund Included In	
Dividends From Subsidiary [(75%)($12,750)]	9,563
Part IV Tax Payable	$16,096

Refundable Dividend Tax On Hand Balance   This balance would be calculated as follows:

RDTOH Balance - End Of The Preceding Year	$23,500	
Dividend Refund For The Preceding Year	(9,600)	$13,900
Refundable Portion Of Part I Tax		26,336
Part IV Tax Payable		16,096
RDTOH Balance - End Of The Year		$56,332

Dividend Refund   The dividend refund would be $36,333, the lesser of:

Dividends Paid During Year [$25,000 + (3)($28,000)]	$109,000
Rate	1/3
Total	$ 36,333

RDTOH Balance - End Of The Year	$ 56,332

Solution to Self Study Problem Fifteen - 5

Calculation Of Net And Taxable Income   The calculation of Acme Imports' net income for tax purposes and taxable income for the year would be as follows:

Accounting Income Before Taxes		$232,300
Additions For Tax Purposes:		
Amortization Expense	$20,000	
Charitable Donations	25,000	
Taxable Capital Gain On Sale Of Equipment		
[(1/2)($84,500 - $62,000)]	11,250	
Golf Club Membership	2,800	
50 Percent Of Business Meals And Entertainment	3,360	
Share Issue Costs [(80%)($950)]	760	
Costs Of Supplementary Letters Patent	7,000	
Interest On Mortgage For The Land	12,300	82,470
Deductions For Tax Purposes:		
CCA For The Year (Note 1)	($38,800)	
Gain On Sale Of Equipment ($84,500 - $27,500)	(57,000)	
Cumulative Eligible Capital:		
Goodwill [($183,000)(3/4)(7%)]	(9,608)	
Letters Patent [($7,000)(3/4)(7%)]	(368)	(105,776)
Net Income For Tax Purposes		$208,994
Charitable Donations (All)		(25,000)
Dividends (All)		(24,000)
Taxable Income		$159,994

Note One   The maximum CCA on the equipment would be calculated as follows:

Opening UCC	$256,000
Disposal (Capital Cost)	(62,000)
Ending UCC	$194,000
Rate - Class 8	20%
CCA for the year	$ 38,800

Several of the items in this problem need further comment. These are as follows:

- **Item 5**   As the loan to the shareholder has been included in two consecutive Balance Sheets, it will become income to the shareholder. However, this does not affect the Company's calculations.

- **Item 6**   Only 50 percent of the $6,720 in charges at the local golf and country club are deductible.

- **Item 7**   The cars provided to the principal shareholder and to the manager of the Company will result in their being assessed for a substantial taxable benefit. However, the costs are fully deductible to the Company.

- **Item 8**   With respect to the costs of issuing shares, IT-341R indicates that these amounts are deductible under ITA 20(1)(e). However, such amounts have to be deducted over at least five years at a maximum rate of 20 percent per year. With respect to the costs of acquiring supplementary letters patent, they are considered to be an eligible capital expenditure, three-quarters of which must be added to the cumulative eligible capital account and amortized at seven percent.

- **Item 11**   The fees paid to the site consultant are deductible as indicated in ITA 20(1)(dd). ITA 18(3.1) disallows the deduction of interest on financing related to land during construction. The $12,300 interest on the $244,000 mortgage on the land would be capitalized and is not deductible.

Taxes Payable   The calculation of Acme Ltd.'s taxes payable would be as follows:

Base Amount of Part I Tax [(38%)($159,994)]	$ 60,798
Corporate Surtax [(4%)(28%)($159,994)]	1,792
ART On Investment Income (Note One)	Nil
Federal Tax Abatement [(10%)($159,994)]	(15,999)
Small Business Deduction (Note One)	(25,599)
General Rate Reduction (Note Two)	Nil
Part I Tax Payable	$ 20,992
Part IV Tax Payable (Note Three)	3,000
Total Federal Taxes Payable	$ 23,992
Instalments Paid (From Balance Sheet)	(28,000)
Balance Due From CCRA	$ 4,008

Note One   The active business income of Acme is as follows:

Net Income For Tax Purposes		$208,994
Dividends		(24,000)
Aggregate Investment Income:		
Interest Revenue	(10,000)	
Taxable Capital Gain	(11,250)	(21,250)
Active Business Income		$163,744

Since none of the annual business limit has been allocated to Sarco, the small business deduction is equal to 16 percent of the least of the following amounts:

• Active Business Income	$163,744
• Taxable Income (no foreign tax credit adjustment)	159,994
• Annual Business Limit	200,000

Taxable income is the lowest of the three figures and the small business deduction would be $25,599 [(16%)($159,994)]. Since the income eligible for the small business deduction is equal to taxable income, there is no ITA 123.3 tax on investment income payable.

Note Two   The base for the accelerated rate reduction under ITA 123.4(3) would be the least of:

• 3/2 the annual business limit of $200,000	$300,000
• Active business income	163,744
• Taxable income for small business deduction, less aggregate investment income ($159,994 - $21,250)	138,744

Use of the $138,744 would provide an accelerated rate reduction of nil {[7%][$138,744 - (100/16)($25,599)]}.

The general rate reduction under ITA 123.4(2) would also be nil {[1%][$159,994 - (100/16)($25,599) - $21,250]}.

Note Three   Acme would have to pay a Part IV tax equal to its share of the dividend refund received from Sarco Ltd. This amount would be $3,000 [(60%)($5,000)].

Refundable Part I Tax   The amount of refundable Part I tax will be the least of three amounts. In this problem, the calculation of these amounts is greatly simplified by the absence of foreign non business income. The calculations are as follows:

ITA 129(3)(a)(i)   This amount would be $5,667, 26-2/3 percent of Aggregate Investment income of $21,250 ($10,000 + $11,250).

ITA 129(3)(a)(ii)   This amount would be nil, 26-2/3 percent of Taxable Income, reduced by the amount of income that is eligible for the small business deduction [(26-2/3%)($159,994 - $159,994)].

ITA 129(3)(a)(iii)   This amount would be Part I Tax Payable, less the corporate surtax ($20,992 - $1,792) = $19,200.

The least of these amounts is nil, so there would be no refundable portion of Part I tax.

Refundable Dividend Tax On Hand   The ending balance in this account would be calculated as follows:

Opening Balance	$ -0-
Part I Refundable Tax	-0-
Part IV Refundable Tax	3,000
Closing Balance	$3,000

Solution to Self Study Problem Fifteen - 6

Taxable Income The taxable income for the year is calculated as follows:

Active Business Income	$171,000
Taxable Capital Gains [($72,000)(1/2)]	36,000
Canadian Source Interest Income	2,200
Portfolio Dividends	15,800
Foreign Source Investment Income (Gross Amount)	4,500
Dividends From Subsidiary	37,800
Net Income For Tax Purposes	$267,300
Dividends Received:	
Portfolio ($15,800)	
Subsidiary (37,800)	(53,600)
Charitable Contributions	(11,900)
Non Capital Loss Carry Over	(25,800)
Net Capital Loss Carry Over *	(36,000)
Taxable Income	$140,000

*Note that the net capital loss carry over is limited to the taxable capital gains. This will leave a carry over of $28,500 ($64,500 - $36,000) for subsequent periods.

Part I Taxes Payable The calculation of Part I taxes payable would be as follows:

Base Amount of Part I Tax [(38%)($140,000)]	$53,200
Corporate Surtax [(4%)(28%)($140,000)]	1,568
Federal Tax Abatement [(10%)($140,000)]	(14,000)
Small Business Deduction (Note One)	(20,000)
Additional Refundable Tax On Investment Income (Note Two)	447
Foreign Non Business Tax Credit (Note Three)	(675)
General Rate Reduction (Note Four)	(446)
Part I Tax Payable	$20,094

Note One The use of foreign taxes paid as credits against Canadian taxes payable is limited by a formula that includes the "tax otherwise payable". In the case of foreign taxes paid on non business income, the "tax otherwise payable" in the formula includes the ART that is assessed under ITA 123.3. This creates a problem in that the calculation of ART includes the amount eligible for the small business deduction [ITA 123.3(b)]. In turn, the determination of the amount eligible for the small business deduction requires the use of the foreign tax credits for foreign taxes paid on non business and business income [ITA 125(b)(i) and (ii)].

To solve this circular calculation, for the purpose of calculating the small business deduction, the foreign tax credit for taxes paid on non business income is calculated using a "tax otherwise payable" figure that does not include the ART under ITA 123.3. This means that in situations where foreign non business income, the small business deduction and the ART are involved, the following procedures should be used:

1. Calculate the foreign non business tax credit using a "tax otherwise payable" that excludes the ART. This initial version of the foreign non business tax credit will be used only for determining the small business deduction, with the actual credit to be applied calculated after the ART has been determined.

2. Calculate the amount eligible for the small business deduction using the numbers determined in step 1.

3. Calculate the ART, using the amount eligible for the small business deduction determined in step 2.

4. Calculate the actual foreign non business tax credit using a "tax otherwise payable" figure which includes the ART.

The initial version of the foreign non business tax credit will be the lesser of the actual tax paid of $675 and an amount determined by the following formula:

$$\left(\frac{\text{Net Foreign Non Business Income}}{\text{Adjusted Net Income}} \right) (\text{Part I Tax Otherwise Payable})$$

$$= \left(\frac{\$4,500}{\$267,300 - \$53,600 - \$36,000} \right) (\$53,200 - \$14,000 + \$1,568)$$

$$= \underline{\$1,032}$$

Part I Tax Otherwise Payable in the preceding formula does not include the ART under ITA 123.3 or the general rate reduction under ITA 123.4. The ITA 123.4 reduction will also be excluded in the calculation of the regular foreign tax credit as the definition of Tax Otherwise Payable excludes this amount for CCPCs. Adjusted Net Income in the formula is Net Income minus deductible dividends and net capital losses. In this case, the actual tax paid of $675 will be the credit.

The small business deduction is 16 percent of the least of the following three amounts:

- Active Business Income $171,000
- Taxable Income, Less 10/3 of the Foreign Non Business Tax Credit
      calculated without the ART ($140,000 - $2,250)   137,750
- Annual Business Limit (Brasco's Allocation)   125,000

The lowest of these figures is the allocated annual limit of $125,000 and this gives a small business deduction of $20,000 [(16%)($125,000)].

Note Two   The ITA 123.3 tax on aggregate investment income of $447 (6-2/3% of $6,700) is 6-2/3 percent of the lesser of:

Canadian Interest	$ 2,200
Taxable Capital Gains	36,000
Foreign Interest	4,500
Capital Loss Carry Forward Deducted	(36,000)
Aggregate Investment Income	$ 6,700

Taxable Income	$140,000
Income Eligible For The Small Business Deduction	(125,000)
Excess	$ 15,000

Note Three   The actual foreign non business tax credit which takes into consideration the ART will be the lesser of the actual tax paid of $675 and an amount determined by the following formula:

$$\left(\frac{\text{Net Foreign Non Business Income}}{\text{Adjusted Net Income}} \right) (\text{Part I Tax Otherwise Payable})$$

$$= \left(\frac{\$4,500}{\$267,300 - \$53,600 - \$36,000} \right) (\$53,200 - \$14,000 + \$1,568 + \$447)$$

$$= \underline{\$1,044}$$

In this calculation, the actual tax paid of $675 will again be the credit.

Note Four   The base for the accelerated rate reduction under ITA 123.4(3) would be the least of:

• 3/2 the annual business limit of $125,000	$187,500
• Active business income	171,000
• Taxable income used for small business deduction, less	
aggregate investment income ($137,750 - $6,700)	131,050

This would provide an accelerated rate reduction of $424 {[7%][$131,050 - (100/16)($20,000)]}.

Given this, the general rate reduction under ITA 123.4(2) would be $22 {[1%][$140,000 - (100/16)($20,000) - $6,700 - (100/7)($424)]}. This gives a total reduction of $446.

Refundable Part I Tax   The amount of refundable Part I tax will be the least of three amounts, calculated as follows:

ITA 129(3)(a)(i)

Canadian Interest		$ 2,200
Taxable Capital Gains		36,000
Foreign Interest		4,500
Capital Loss Carry Forward Claimed		(36,000)
Aggregate Investment Income		$ 6,700
Rate		26-2/3%
		$ 1,787
Foreign Non Business Tax Credit	($675)	
9-1/3% Of Foreign Non Business Income	420	(255)
Amount Under ITA 129(3)(a)(i)		$ 1,532

ITA 129(3)(a)(ii)

Taxable Income	$140,000
Income Eligible For The Small Business Deduction	(125,000)
25/9 Of Foreign Non-Business Tax Credit [(25/9)($675)]	(1,875)
Total	$ 13,125
Rate	26-2/3%
Amount Under ITA 129(3)(a)(ii)	$ 3,500

ITA 129(3)(a)(iii)

Part I Tax Payable Excluding Surtax ($20,094 - $1,568)	$ 18,526

The least of these three amounts would be $1,526, the amount calculated under ITA 129(3)(a)(i).

Part IV Tax   The calculation of Part IV tax would be as follows:

Part IV Tax Transfer From Masco [(60%)($21,000)]	$12,600
On Portfolio Dividends [(1/3)($15,800)]	5,267
Total Part IV Tax	$17,867

Refundable Dividend Tax On Hand   The ending balance in this account would be calculated as follows:

Balance - End Of The Preceding Year	$ 7,000
Dividend Refund For The Preceding Year	Nil
Part I Refundable Tax	1,526
Part IV Refundable Tax	17,867
Balance - End Of The Year	$26,393

Dividend Refund   The refund will be the lesser of:

- The $26,393 balance in the refundable dividend tax on hand account.

- One-third of taxable dividends paid. This would be $13,000 [(1/3)($39,000)]. Capital dividends are not taxable and do not generate a tax refund.

The lesser of these two amounts would be $13,000.

Total Of Taxes Payable   The total taxes payable for Brasco Distributors, net of the dividend refund, equals $24,961 ($20,094 + $17,867 - $13,000).

Solution to Chapter Sixteen Exercises

Exercise Sixteen - 1

The individual's combined tax rate on income earned by the unincorporated business is 43 percent (29% + 14%). If he does incorporate, all of the $126,000 will be eligible for the small business deduction. This means it will be taxed at a rate of 20.12 percent [(38% - 10%)(1.04) - 16% + 7.0%)]. There is clearly a significant amount of tax deferral with respect to income left in the corporation.

The individual's tax rate is 28.75 percent [(1.25)(43%) - (2/3 + 1/3)(25%)] on dividend income. This means that the overall tax rate on income that is paid out in dividends is 43 percent [20.12% + (100% - 20.12%)(28.75%)]. This is equal to the 43 percent rate applicable to income from the unincorporated business. As a consequence, there is no tax savings available on income that is paid out in dividends.

Exercise Sixteen - 2

The individual's tax rate on interest income earned outside the corporation is 43 percent (29% + 14%). If he does incorporate, the interest income will not be eligible for the small business deduction and it will be subject to the ART. This means that, if the investments are transferred to a corporation, the interest will be taxed at a rate of 51.2 percent [(38% - 10%)(1.04) + 6-2/3% + 15.4%]. As this is higher than the 43 percent rate applicable to the direct receipt of interest income, the corporation does not provide any deferral on amounts left within the corporation. In this case, incorporation requires prepayment of taxes.

After being taxed at 51.2 percent, the corporation would have $61,488 in after tax funds available. With the available refund, this would allow the payment of a dividend of $92,232 [(3/2)($61,488)]. The individual's tax rate on dividend income is 28.75 percent [(1.25)(43%) - (2/3 + 1/3)(25%)]. After payment of taxes at this rate, the individual would be left with $65,715 in after tax funds. If he does not incorporate, the $126,000 in interest income would be taxed at 43 percent, leaving an after tax amount of $71,820. There is clearly a tax cost as a result of transferring the investments to a corporation.

Exercise Sixteen - 3

Direct Receipt   If the income is received directly, the total tax payable will be as follows:

Dividends Received ($46,000 + $87,000)	$133,000
Gross Up (25%)	33,250
Taxable Dividends	$166,250
Interest Income	32,000
Taxable Income	$198,250
Personal Tax Rate (29% + 15%)	44%
Tax Payable Before Dividend Tax Credit	$ 87,230
Dividend Tax Credit [(2/3 + 1/3)($33,250)]	(33,250)
Total Personal Tax Payable	$ 53,980

The after tax retention can be calculated as follows:

Cash Received ($46,000 + $87,000 + $32,000)	$165,000
Total Tax Payable	(53,980)
After Tax Retention	$111,020

Transfer To Corporation   If the investments are transferred to a corporation, the corporate taxes will be as follows:

Part IV Tax On Dividends Received [(1/3)($46,000) + $23,000]	$38,333
Part I Tax On Interest Income	
[$32,000][(38% - 10%)(1.04) + 6-2/3% + 15%]	16,252
Corporate Tax Payable Before Refund	$54,585

The RDTOH balance prior to the dividend refund would be calculated as follows:

Part IV Addition	$38,333
Part I Addition [(26-2/3%)($32,000)]	8,533
RDTOH Balance	$46,866

The cash available for paying dividends would be $110,415 ($165,000 - $54,585). This represents two-thirds of $165,623, a dividend that would generate a dividend refund of $55,208. However, as the balance in the RDTOH is only $46,866, the maximum dividend that can be paid is $157,281 ($110,415 + $46,866). This would result in personal taxes as follows:

Dividends Received	$157,281
Gross Up (25%)	39,320
Taxable Dividends	$196,601
Personal Tax Rate	44%
Tax Before Dividend Tax Credit	$ 86,504
Dividend Tax Credit [(2/3 + 1/3)($39,320)]	(39,320)
Total Tax Payable	$ 47,184

After tax retention with the use of a corporation would be $110,097 ($165,000 - $54,585 + $46,866 - $47,184). This is $923 less than the $111,020 that would be retained through direct receipt of this income.

Exercise Sixteen - 4

The client's combined tax rate on direct receipt of income is 45 percent (29% + 16%). If she receives the capital gains directly, the Taxes Payable will be $20,700 [($46,000)(45%)]. This will leave her with after tax cash of $71,300 ($92,000 - $20,700).

If the investments are transferred to a CCPC, the aggregate investment income will be $46,000. The applicable tax rate will be 51.8% [(38% - 10%)(1.04) + 6-2/3% + 16%]. Corporate Taxes Payable will be $23,828 [(51.8%)($46,000)], leaving cash of $68,172 ($92,000 - $23,828). Of this total, $46,000 [(1/2)($92,000)] can be distributed as a tax free capital dividend. The remaining $22,172 ($68,172 - $46,000) must be distributed as a taxable dividend. This represents two-thirds of $33,258, a dividend that would generate a dividend refund of $11,086. As the balance in the RDTOH is $12,267 [(26-2/3%)($46,000)], a taxable dividend of $33,258 can be paid.

The client's tax rate on dividend income is 31.25 percent [(1.25)(45%) - (2/3 + 1/3)(25%)], resulting in Taxes Payable on the dividend received of $10,393 [(31.25%)($33,258)]. The overall after tax retention when a corporation is used would be as follows:

Capital Dividend Received	$46,000
Taxable Dividend Received	33,258
Tax Payable On Dividend Received	(10,393)
After Tax Cash Retained	$68,865

As this is less than the after tax cash retained on the direct receipt of the income, the use of a corporation to hold these investments is not an appropriate choice.

Exercise Sixteen - 5

Part A   If the loan is repaid by January 1, 2002, it will not be included in two consecutive Generic Inc. Balance Sheets. As a consequence, the principal amount will not have to be included in Ms. Fisk's income. However, as it is a low interest loan, she will be assessed with a taxable benefit on the loan. The amount would be $2,835 [($162,000)(5% - 2%)(7/12)].

Part B   If the loan is not repaid until December 31, 2002, it will appear in two consecutive Generic Inc. Balance Sheets. This means the $162,000 in principal will have to be included in Ms. Fisk's income for the taxation year ending December 31, 2001. However, there will be no imputed interest benefit based on the loan's low rate of interest. In addition, when the loan is repaid, the payment can be deducted from Net Income For Tax Purposes.

Exercise Sixteen - 6

Provided Mr. Hasid receives the loan in his capacity as an employee of Hasid Ltd., the loan is one of the exceptions listed under ITA 15(2). This means that the principal amount will not have to be included in income. However, as the loan is interest free, a taxable benefit will arise. It will be calculated by applying the prescribed rate of five percent to the principal of the loan for all periods that it is outstanding. The amount would be $1,025 [($123,000)(5%)(2/12)] for 2001 and $6,150 [($123,000)(5%)] for 2002.

If Mr. Hasid cannot claim that he received the loan in his capacity as an employee of Hasid Ltd., the $123,000 principal amount will have to be included in income in 2001. However, no taxable benefit will be assessed for the fact that it is an interest free loan. When the loan is repaid, Mr. Hasid will be able to deduct it from his income. It was assumed that this loan did not qualify as a home relocation loan.

Exercise Sixteen - 7

If the full $233,000 is paid out as salary, it will be deductible and will reduce the Company's Taxable Income to nil. This means that no corporate taxes will be paid. This salary payment will result in Ms. Broad having Taxable Income of $233,000. Given this, her Taxes Payable will be calculated as follows:

Federal Tax On First $100,000	$21,695
Federal Tax On Remaining $133,000 At 29%	38,570
Provincial Tax At 10 Percent Of $233,000	23,300
Tax Payable Before Credits	$83,565
Personal Tax Credits	(2,800)
Total Tax Payable	$80,765

Based on the preceding Taxes Payable, Ms. Broad's after tax retention would be $152,235 ($233,000 - $80,765).

Exercise Sixteen - 8

As dividends are not deductible for tax purposes, corporate taxes will have to be paid prior to the payment of any dividends. While the $33,000 of income in excess of the annual business limit of $200,000 would not get the small business deduction, it would be eligible for the accelerated rate reduction of 7 percent. Given this, the corporate rate on this income would be 39.12% [(38% - 10%)(1.04) - 7% + 17%]. On income eligible for the small business deduction, the rate would be 21.12% [(38% - 10%)(1.04) - 16% + 8%]. Using these rates, corporate taxes would be calculated as follows:

Income Not Eligible For SBD [(39.12%)($33,000)]	$12,910
Income Eligible For SBD [(21.12%)($200,000)]	42,240
Total Corporate Taxes Payable	$55,150

After payment of these taxes, the maximum dividend that could be paid would be $177,850 ($233,000 - $55,150). Personal taxes on this dividend would be calculated as follows:

Dividends Received	$177,850
Gross Up	44,463
Taxable Dividends	$222,313

Federal Tax On First $100,000	$ 21,695
Federal Tax On Remaining $122,313 At 29%	35,471
Provincial Tax At 10 Percent Of $222,313	22,231
Taxes Payable Before Credits	$ 79,397
Personal Tax Credits	(2,800)
Dividend Tax Credit [(2/3 + 40%)($44,463)]	(47,427)
Total Taxes Payable	$29,170

The after tax retention would be equal to $148,680 ($177,850 - $29,170).

Exercise Sixteen - 9

As the available cash is less than Taxable Income, some taxes will have to be paid since there is not sufficient cash to pay a salary equivalent to Taxable Income. To determine the maximum salary that can be paid (X), it is necessary to solve the following equation:

$$X = \$18,500 - [(\$21,500 - X)(17.3\%)]$$

$$X = \underline{\$17,873}$$

Given this salary, the shareholder would be subject to the following personal Taxes Payable:

Taxes Payable Before Credits [(16% + 10%)($17,873)]	$4,647
Available Tax Credits	(3,950)
Total Taxes Payable	$ 697

Given the preceding Taxes Payable, the shareholder's after tax retention on salary would be $17,176 ($17,873 - $697).

As dividends are not deductible, corporate taxes would have to be paid on the full $21,500. These taxes would be $3,720 [(17.3%)($21,500)], leaving an amount available for dividends of $14,780 ($18,500 - $3,720). As no individual taxes would be payable on this amount of dividends, the full $14,780 would be retained.

Given these calculations, it is clear that the preferred approach is to pay the maximum salary. Note, however, some combination of dividends and salary may provide an even better result.

Exercise Sixteen - 10

The shareholder's combined tax rate on additional salary is 45 percent (29% + 16%). In order to have $30,000 in after tax funds, he would have to receive salary of $54,545 [$30,000 ÷ (1 - .45)]. If the corporation pays this amount in deductible salary, it will pay taxes at a rate of 16.5 percent on $143,455 ($198,000 - $54,545), an amount of $23,670. The combined cash outflow for salary and taxes would be $78,215.

The shareholder's tax rate on dividends is 33.3 percent [(1.25)(45%) - (2/3 + 25%)(25%)]. In order to have $30,000 in after tax funds, he would have to receive dividends of $44,978 [$30,000 ÷ (1 - .333)]. As none of this amount would be deductible, the corporation will pay taxes at 16.5 percent on the full $198,000 of Taxable Income, an amount of $32,670. The combined cash outflow for dividends and taxes would be $77,648.

As the cash outflows associated with the payment of salary are larger, the dividend alternative would be preferable.

Solution to Self Study Problem Sixteen - 1

Salary Alternative   In order to determine the amount of salary that would be required to produce $10,000 in after tax income, we need to know Ms. Lusk's effective tax rate on additional income. In this regard, her taxable income of $44,385 puts her in approximately the middle of the 22 percent federal tax bracket. She will stay in this bracket for the next $17,124 ($61,509 - $44,385) of income. Any income in excess of $61,509 would be taxed at a 26 percent federal rate.

When the federal rates of 22 and 26 percent are combined with an additional 10 percent at the provincial level, Ms. Lusk's combined rates are 32 percent on the next $17,124 of income and 36 percent on any additional amounts. As $10,000 in after tax cash would only require $14,706 in additional salary [$10,000 ÷ (1 - .32)], the higher bracket does not have to be considered. With the additional salary of $14,706 being fully deductible to the corporation, the only tax cost associated with this alternative would be an additional $4,706 ($14,706 - $10,000) in personal taxes for Ms. Lusk.

Dividend Alternative   The dividend alternative involves a more complex analysis. The approximate relevant tax rates on dividends would be as follows:

[(125%)(32%) - (2/3 + 1/3)(25%)] = 15%
[(125%)(36%) - (2/3 + 1/3)(25%)] = 20%

With a tax rate of of 15 percent on dividends, a dividend of $11,764 would be required to provide an after tax amount of $10,000 [$10,000 ÷ (1 - .15)]. This would create a taxable dividend of $14,705 and a total taxable income of $59,090. As this is below the threshold for the next bracket, the 20 percent rate on dividends can be ignored.

As dividends are not deductible for the corporation, any pre tax corporate income that is used for the payment of dividends will be subject to the Company's Part I tax rate of 21 percent. This means that, in order to pay $11,764 in dividends to Ms. Lusk, $14,891 [$11,764 ÷ (1 - .21)] of pre tax corporate income will be required.

The total personal and corporate tax cost of the dividend alternative can be calculated as follows:

Personal Taxes On Dividends ($11,764 - $10,000)	$ 1,764
Corporate Taxes ($14,891 - $11,764)	3,127
Total Tax Cost	$4,891

Conclusion   Since the salary alternative would require tax payments of only $4,706 while the dividend alternative would require tax payments of $4,891, the salary alternative is better.

Solution to Self Study Problem Sixteen - 2

Calculation Of Corporate Business Income   The business income of the corporation would be calculated as follows:

Management Fees		$82,900
Expenses:		
Mr. Ashley's Salary	($18,400)	
Office Salaries	(25,400)	
Office Rent	(8,180)	
CCA On Office And Dental Equipment	(5,700)	
Other Business Expenses	(2,170)	(59,850)
Business Income		$23,050
Rate On Active Business Income		20%
Tax On Active Business Income		$ 4,610

Taxes payable on the dividends and investment income would be calculated as follows:

Interest Income [(51%)($21,600)]	$11,016
Net Rental Income [(51%)($34,600 - $27,800)]	3,468
Part IV Tax On Dividends Received [(1/3)($13,900)]	4,633
Tax On Property Income	$19,117

Payment of the preceding taxes on property income would create an RDTOH balance as follows:

Part I Refundable Amount [(26.67%)($21,600 + $6,800)]	$ 7,574
Part IV Refundable Amount [(1/3)($13,900)]	4,633
RDTOH Balance	$12,207

Given the preceding calculations, the maximum dividend that could be paid is as follows:

Business Income	$23,050
Interest Income	21,600
Net Rental Income	6,800
Dividends	13,900
Taxes On Business Income	(4,610)
Taxes On Property Income	(19,117)
Balance Before Refund	$41,623
Refundable Taxes (RDTOH Balance)	12,207
Available For Dividends	$53,830

On the basis of their relative shareholdings, this payment would go $32,298 to Mr. Ashley (60 percent) and $21,532 to Ms. Ashley (40 percent). This would result in the following taxes payable:

	Ms. Ashley	Mr. Ashley
Salary	$ -0-	$18,400
Dividends	21,532	32,298
Gross Up	5,383	8,075
Taxable Income	$26,915	$58,773
Tax Rate	47%	30%
Tax Payable	$12,650	$17,632
Dividend Tax Credit [(2/3 + 25%)(Gross Up)]	(4,934)	(7,402)
Net Tax Payable	$ 7,716	$10,230

This would leave after tax balances available to Ms. and Mr. Ashley as follows:

Ms. Ashley ($21,532 - $7,716)	$13,816
Mr. Ashley ($18,400 + $32,298 - $10,230)	40,468
Total Available	$54,284

Balances With No Corporation   If Ms. Ashley had received all of the amounts involved directly, her taxes payable and net retention could be calculated as follows:

Business Income (No Salary To Husband)	$41,450
Interest Income	21,600
Rental Income (Net)	6,800
Dividends	13,900
Gross Up (25%)	3,475
Taxable Income	$87,225
Tax Rate	47%
Tax Before Dividend Credit	$40,996
Dividend Tax Credit [(2/3 + 25%)(Gross Up)]	(3,185)
Tax Payable	$37,811
Income Received ($41,450 + $21,600 + $6,800 + $13,900)	$83,750
Tax Payable	(37,811)
Net Retention	$45,939

It is clear from these calculations that the use of the management company has had a positive effect on after tax retention of income. Without the corporation, Ms. Ashley would have ended up with only $45,939. This compares to a total of $54,284 for Mr. and Ms. Ashley when the corporation is used, an improvement of over $8,000. Although personal tax credits were not taken into consideration, they would have made only a small difference as Ms. Ashley would be able to claim the spousal credit in full if Mr. Ashley had no income.

Solution to Self Study Problem Sixteen - 3

Part A   As salary payments can be deducted by the corporation, the entire $27,500 can be paid as salary. Given this deduction, no taxes would be paid by the Company. With a salary payment of $27,500, Mr. Bedford's after tax cash balance would be as follows:

Salary Payment		$27,500
Tax Before Credits [(16% + 9%)($27,500)]	($ 6,875)	
Personal Tax Credits	3,750	(3,125)
After Tax Cash Retained		$24,375

Part B   The tax rate for Bedford Inc., taking into consideration the corporate surtax, would be 19.12% {[(38% - 10%)(1.04)] - 16% + 6%}. As dividend payments are not deductible to the Company, taxes of $5,258 [(19.12%)($27,500)] will have to be paid, leaving a maximum of $22,242 to be used for the payment of dividends. When this is paid, the retention by Mr. Bedford will be as follows:

Dividends Received	$22,242
Gross Up	5,561
Taxable Dividends	$27,803

Taxes At 25 Percent (16% + 9%)	$ 6,951
Personal Tax Credits	(3,750)
Dividend Tax Credit [(2/3 + 30%)($5,561)]	(5,376)
Taxes Payable	$ Nil

Dividends Received	$22,242
Taxes Payable	Nil
After Tax Cash Retained	$22,242

Part C   While Mr. Bedford's Taxes Payable are nil, subtracting personal and dividend tax credits from the tax balance gives a negative $2,175. This means that the all dividend approach leaves unused tax credits. While not conclusive, this suggests that there may be a better solution than either all salary or all dividends.

Part D   To examine the possibility of an optimum solution using both salary and dividends, consider the result that occurs when $1,000 in salary is paid in lieu of some dividends. Because the deductible salary payment would reduce corporate taxes, dividends would only have to be decreased by $808.80 [($1,000)(1 - .1912)]. The tax effects of this switch can be calculated as follows:

Increase In Salary	$1,000.00
Decrease In Dividend	(808.80)
Decrease In Dividend Gross Up	(202.20)
Decrease In Mr. Bedford's Taxable Income	($ 11.00)

Decrease In Tax At 25% (16% + 9%)	($ 2.75)
Decrease In Dividend Tax Credit [(2/3 + 30%)($202.20)]	195.46
Increase In Personal Tax	$ 192.71

The rate on a $1,000 increase in salary is 19.271% ($192.71 ÷ $1,000). Applying this rate to the unused credits of $2,175 (see Part C), gives a required increase in salary of $11,286 ($2,175 ÷ .19271).

Based on this payment of salary, corporate taxes and funds available for dividend payments would be calculated as follows:

Pre Salary Corporate Taxable Income	$27,500
Salary	(11,286)
Corporate Taxable Income	$16,214
Corporate Tax At 19.12 Percent	(3,100)
Available For Dividends	$13,114

After tax retention at the personal level would be calculated as follows:

Dividends Received	$13,114
Gross Up	3,279
Taxable Dividends	$16,393
Salary	11,286
Mr. Bedford's Taxable Income	$27,679

Tax At 25 Percent (16% + 9%)	$ 6,920
Personal Tax Credits	(3,750)
Dividend Tax Credit [(2/3 + 30%))($3,279)]	(3,170)
Taxes Payable	$ Nil

Amounts Received ($11,286 + $13,114)	$24,400
Personal Taxes Payable	Nil
After Tax Cash Retained	$24,400

This combination of salary and dividends will produce the maximum after tax cash balance for Mr. Bedford. While it is a significant improvement over the all dividend after tax retention of $22,242, it is only a very marginal improvement over the all salary after tax retention of $24,375.

Solution to Chapter Seventeen Exercises

Exercise Seventeen - 1

The adjusted cost base amounts would be calculated as follows:

Elected Value	$62,000
ACB Of Note (Fair Market Value)	(51,000)
Available For Shares	$11,000
ACB Of Preferred Shares (Limited To $11,000)	(11,000)
ACB Of Common Shares (Residual)	$ Nil

Exercise Seventeen - 2

The total PUC reduction would be calculated as follows:

Increase In Legal Stated Capital ($97,000 + $54,000)		$151,000
Less Excess Of:		
Total Elected Value	($114,000)	
Reduced By Total Non Share Consideration	83,000	(31,000)
PUC Reduction		$120,000

This PUC reduction would be split between the preferred and common shares on the basis of their fair market values, resulting in the following PUC values:

- Preferred Shares = $97,000 - [(97/151)($120,000)] = $19,914
- Common Shares = $54,000 - [(54/151)($120,000)] = $11,086

Exercise Seventeen - 3

The required information is as follows:

- Minimum and maximum transfer value = $33,783 ($25,337 ÷ .75) to $86,000.
- If the minimum value of $33,783 is elected, there would be no income resulting from the transfer.
- As the PUC of the shares issued ($93,000) exceeds the fair market value of the net assets acquired ($86,000), there would be an ITA 84(1) deemed dividend of $7,000. The taxable dividend of $$8,750 [(125%)($7,000)] would be eligible for federal and provincial dividend tax credits.
- The adjusted cost base of the preferred shares will be $40,783, the elected value of $33,783, plus the $7,000 ITA 84(1) benefit.

Exercise Seventeen - 4

The tax consequences to Mr. Savage and the corporation can be described as follows:

- Mr. Savage will have a taxable capital gain of $20,000 [(1/2)($160,000 - $120,000)].
- Mr. Savage will have recapture of CCA of $22,000 ($120,000 - $98,000).
- Mr. Savage will be holding shares with an adjusted cost base of nil and a PUC of nil.
- The corporation will have a depreciable asset with a capital cost of $160,000 and a value for CCA and recapture purposes of $140,000 [$120,000 + (1/2)($160,000 - $120,000)].

Exercise Seventeen - 5

As Ms. Bellows transferred property with a fair market value of $110,000 and received consideration with a fair market value of $65,000 ($50,000 + $15,000), she has made a gift to her daughter of $45,000 ($110,000 - $65,000). The tax consequences for Ms. Bellows and her daughter are as follows:

- The $45,000 gift will be added to the $50,000 elected value, giving Ms. Bellows a total proceeds of disposition of $95,000. This will result in a taxable capital gain of $22,500 [(1/2)($95,000 - $50,000)].
- The preferred shares issued to Ms. Bellows will have an adjusted cost base and a PUC of nil.
- The shares acquired by the daughter will have an adjusted cost base and a PUC of $1,000. However, because of the gift, they will have a fair market value of $46,000 ($1,000 + $45,000). This means that on a subsequent sale for fair market value, the daughter would have a capital gain of $45,000 with a taxable amount of $22,500 [(1/2)($45,000)].

Exercise Seventeen - 6

The tax consequences to Mr. Custer can be described as follows:

- Mr. Custer's minimum election value will be the fair market value of $217,000. This election will result in a taxable capital gain of $47,000 [(1/2)($217,000 - $123,000)].
- As his non share consideration ($248,000) exceeds the fair market value of the transferred property ($217,000), there is an ITA 15(1) benefit of $31,000.
- In addition to the ITA 15(1) benefit, there is an ITA 84(1) deemed dividend of $22,000, the excess of the increase in PUC of the preferred shares ($22,000) over the related increase in net assets (Nil). The taxable dividend of $$27,500 [(125%)($22,000)] would be eligible for federal and provincial dividend tax credits.

- The $22,000 ITA 84(1) deemed dividend will be added to the adjusted cost base of the shares.

Exercise Seventeen - 7

Miss Cole (an individual) has sold shares of a subject corporation to a purchasing corporation, both corporations are not at arm's length with Miss Cole, and the two corporations are connected subsequent to the sale. As a consequence, ITA 84.1 is applicable. Given this, the tax consequences of this transaction to Miss Cole are as follows:

Increase In Legal Stated Capital		$317,000
PUC And ACB Of Old Shares	($125,000)	
Non Share Consideration	450,000	Nil
PUC Reduction		$317,000
PUC Of New Shares ($317,000 - $317,000)		Nil
Increase In Legal Stated Capital		$317,000
Non Share Consideration		450,000
		$767,000
PUC And ACB Of Old Shares	($125,000)	
PUC Reduction	(317,000)	(442,000)
ITA 84.1 Deemed Dividend		$325,000
Proceeds For Old Shares		$625,000
ITA 84.1 Deemed Dividend		(325,000)
Proceeds For Capital Gains Purposes		$300,000
ACB Of Old Shares		(125,000)
Capital Gain		$175,000
Inclusion Rate		1/2
Taxable Capital Gain		$ 87,500
ACB Of New Shares ($625,000 - $450,000)		$175,000

Exercise Seventeen - 8

A deductible dividend has been paid in conjunction with an arm's length sale of shares, and it would appear that the dividend payment served to eliminate the potential capital gain on the transaction. As a consequence, ITA 55 is applicable and the tax consequences of the transaction are as follows:

Dividend Payment (Tax Free)	$750,000
Safe Income	(225,000)
Deemed Proceeds Of Disposition	$525,000
Actual Proceeds Of Disposition	90,000
Total Proceeds Of Disposition	$615,000
Adjusted Cost Base Of Shares	(75,000)
Capital Gain	$540,000
Inclusion Rate	1/2
Taxable Capital Gain	$270,000

Solution to Self Study Problem Seventeen - 1

Part A   The disposition of a business is a capital transaction and, in the absence of special provisions, any resulting gain or loss must be treated as a capital gain or loss. With respect to Inventories, a special provision in ITA 23 indicates that, when such assets are sold as part of the disposition of a business, the sale is deemed to be in the ordinary course of carrying on business and any resulting gain or loss is business income. ITA 23 automatically applies in the disposition of a business and no election is required on the part of the vendor. ITA 22 provides for a similar treatment of Accounts Receivable. However, a joint election by the vendor and purchaser is required before this business income treatment is applicable. In the absence of this election, losses on Accounts Receivable are treated as capital losses.

If the assets are transferred at fair market values, the taxable income resulting from the transfer can be calculated as follows:

Inventories - Business Income ($88,000 - $73,000)	$15,000
Furniture And Fixtures - Recaptured CCA ($45,000 -$38,000)	7,000
Goodwill [(3/4)($150,000)(1/2 ÷ 3/4)]	75,000
Taxable Income	$97,000

When the $112,500 [(3/4)($150,000)] proceeds for the goodwill is subtracted from cumulative eligible capital balance, a business income inclusion is created. As no amounts have been deducted under ITA 20(1)(b), this amount is reduced from a three-quarters inclusion to a one-half inclusion by multiplying the negative balance by (1/2 ÷ 3/4).

There is also an allowable capital loss of $3,000 [(1/2)($51,000 - $45,000)] on the disposition of the Accounts Receivable. However, ITA 40(2)(g) would disallow this loss as the accounts are being transferred to a corporation that is controlled by the transferor. This loss would be added to the tax cost of the Accounts Receivable on the corporation's books.

Part B   The cash can, of course, be transferred to the corporation with no tax consequences. All of the other assets can be transferred at elected values under ITA 85. Under the provisions of this section, the tax consequences would be as follows:

Accounts Receivable   If the Accounts Receivable are transferred under ITA 85, the maximum value that can be elected is the fair market value of $45,000. This will result in a capital loss of $6,000 (allowable amount $4,500). However, this loss will be disallowed under ITA 40(2)(g) because the transfer is to a corporation which will be controlled by Ms. Flack.

Inventories   The inventories can be transferred at an elected value of $73,000, resulting in no taxable income on the transfer.

Furniture And Fixtures   The Furniture And Fixtures can be transferred at their UCC of $38,000, resulting in no taxable income on the transfer.

Goodwill   The Goodwill can be transferred at a nominal value of $1, resulting in no significant taxable income on the transfer.

An alternative with respect to the Accounts Receivable would be to transfer these assets under the provisions of ITA 22. If Ms. Flack and her corporation were to make this joint election, the $6,000 loss resulting from transferring these assets to the corporation would be fully deductible as a business loss. As it is not a capital loss, it would not be disallowed and Ms. Flack would be able to deduct the full $6,000 against any other source of income in the year of transfer. Using the ITA 22 election is the preferable approach to the transfer of these Accounts Receivable.

Solution to Self Study Problem Seventeen - 2

Part A   All of the assets except cash would be eligible for the transfer. However, it is normal to transfer Accounts Receivable under ITA 22 rather than ITA 85 in order to protect the full deductibility of future bad debts. The Equipment has a terminal loss which will be disallowed on the transfer. We have assumed that the Equipment will be included in the rollover, though there is no tax advantage for doing so.

Part B   The transfer values for the assets to be included in the rollover would be as follows:

Inventories (Cost)	$261,000
Land (Adjusted Cost Base)	196,000
Building (Undepreciated Capital Cost)	103,600
Equipment (Fair Market Value)	32,500
Goodwill (Nominal Value)	1

Note   The goodwill has been given a nominal elected value to insure that it is specifically included in the transfer. A failure to do this could result in the goodwill being assessed on the basis of a transfer at fair market value.

Part C   The tax consequences of the Section 85 transfers with respect to both Ms. Speaks and Speaks Inc. can be described as follows:

Inventories   The cost of the Inventories to Speaks Inc. would be the transfer price of $261,000. As this was the cost of the Inventories, there would be no tax consequence to Ms. Speaks.

Land   The cost of the Land to Speaks Inc. would be the transfer price of $196,000. As this was the adjusted cost base of the Land, there would be no tax consequence to Ms. Speaks.

Building   The capital cost of the Building to Speaks Inc. would be $155,500 and Speaks Inc. would be deemed to have taken CCA in the amount of $51,900. As the net value of the transfer is equal to UCC, there would be no tax consequence to Ms. Speaks.

Equipment   The capital cost of the Equipment to Speaks Inc. will be its fair market value of $32,500. Ms. Speaks will have a terminal loss of $34,500 ($67,000 - $32,500) which she will not be able to deduct. The $34,500 loss will be placed the same CCA class as the Equipment was and Ms. Speaks will continue to take CCA on this class until the Equipment is disposed of by Speaks Inc. or there is no balance left in the class.

Goodwill   The cost of the Goodwill to Speaks Inc. will be $1 and three quarters of this amount will be added to the Company's Cumulative Eligible Capital balance. There would be no material tax consequence to Ms. Speaks resulting from this transfer.

Solution to Self Study Problem Seventeen - 3

Part A   As the $1,241,100 elected price was equal to the sum of the capital cost of the land and the undepreciated capital cost of the building ($315,000 + $926,100), there would be no tax consequences associated with the transfer of the assets. However, the corporation will be deemed to have acquired these assets at their old tax values to Mr. Dix, not at their fair market values at the time of transfer.

Under ITA 85(1)(f), the adjusted cost base of the non share consideration is equal to its fair market value which is $1,241,100. The problem does not specify whether preferred shares, common shares or a combination of both were issued. Under ITA 85(1)(g), the adjusted cost base of any preferred shares received is the lesser of their fair market value and the total elected value reduced by the non share consideration. As the $1,241,100 elected value is equal to the non share consideration provided by the corporation, the adjusted cost base of any preferred shares would be nil. Under ITA 85(1)(h), the adjusted cost base of any common shares issued would be the elected value, reduced by non share consideration and amounts allocated to preferred stock. This value would also be nil.

Part B As the debt was redeemed at face value, this amount would be equal to Mr. Dix's adjusted cost base and he would have no gain or loss. However, the shares have an adjusted cost base of nil and, as a consequence, he would have a capital gain equal to the entire proceeds of $894,000. This would result in a taxable capital gain of $447,000 [(1/2)($894,000)].

It is likely that the corporation is a "qualified small business corporation". If this is the case, Mr. Dix would be eligible for the $500,000 ($250,000 taxable amount) lifetime capital gains deduction. To qualify, the corporation must be a Canadian controlled private corporation with at least 90 percent of the fair market value of its assets being used in an active business primarily operating in Canada. The 24 month holding period requirement would be met as no other taxpayer has owned the business in the preceding 24 months.

Even if Mr. Dix is eligible for the full lifetime capital gains deduction, he would still have to pay taxes on a $197,000 ($447,000 - $250,000) taxable capital gain. Whether or not he can use the lifetime capital gains deduction, he may need to pay alternative minimum tax.

Solution to Self Study Problem Seventeen - 4

Part A The adjusted cost base (ACB) of the shares would be as follows:

Total Elected Value	$467,000
Non Share Consideration ($122,000 + $128,000)	(250,000)
Adjusted Cost Base Preferred And Common Shares	$217,000
Allocated To Preferred Shares (FMV)	(150,000)
Adjusted Cost Base Common Shares (Residual)	$ 67,000

Part B The legal stated capital of the preferred and common shares would be their respective fair market values of $150,000 and $326,000. The PUC reduction required under ITA 85(2.1) would be calculated as follows:

Increase In Legal Stated Capital ($150,000 + $326,000)		$476,000
Less Excess Of:		
Total Elected Value	($467,000)	
Reduced By Total Non Share Consideration	250,000	(217,000)
Reduction In Paid Up Capital		$259,000

Note that this total reduction is equal to the deferred gain on the election ($726,000 - $467,000). This total will be allocated to the two classes of shares on the basis of their relative fair market values. The relevant calculations are as follows:

Preferred Shares = ($150,000 ÷ $476,000)($259,000) = $81,618

Common Shares = ($326,000 ÷ $476,000)($259,000) = $177,382

The PUC of the two classes of shares after the ITA 85(2.1) reduction is as follows:

	Preferred Shares	Common Shares
Legal Stated Capital	$150,000	$326,000
PUC Reduction	(81,618)	(177,382)
PUC	$ 68,382	$148,618

Part C   The tax consequences to Mr. Lardner if the corporation redeemed both classes of shares at their respective fair market values would be calculated as follows:

	Preferred Shares	Common Shares
Redemption Proceeds	$150,000	$326,000
PUC (See Preceding Calculations)	(68,382)	(148,618)
ITA 84(3) Deemed Dividend	$ 81,618	$177,382
Actual Redemption Proceeds	$150,000	$326,000
ITA 84(3) Deemed Dividend	(81,618)	(177,382)
Proceeds Of Disposition	$ 68,382	$148,618
Adjusted Cost Base	(150,000)	(67,000)
Capital Gain (Loss)	($ 81,618)	$ 81,618

Mr. Lardner would have a deemed dividend of $259,000 ($81,618 + $177,382) which would be subject to the usual gross up and tax credit procedures. He has a net capital gain of nil ($81,618 - $81,618).

Solution to Self Study Problem Seventeen - 5

Part A   With the Accounts Receivable transferred using ITA 22, the values that should be elected on the other assets in order to eliminate any current taxes payable on the transfer are as follows:

Inventory	$174,000
Equipment	234,000
Goodwill	1
Total	$408,001

Part B   The total elected value would become the Adjusted Cost Base of the consideration received by Miss Brock. It would be allocated to the individual items as follows:

Total Elected Value	$408,001
Debt ($95,000 + $75,000)	(170,000)
Available For Preferred And Common Stock	$238,001
Adjusted Cost Base - Preferred Stock (Maximum Of $225,000)	(225,000)
Adjusted Cost Base - Common Stock	$ 13,001

Part C   The calculation of Paid Up Capital would begin with the legal stated capital associated with the two classes of shares which is their fair market value. This would be $225,000 for the Preferred Stock and $480,000 for the Common Stock, a total of $705,000. ITA 85(2.1) would require a reduction in this total as follows:

Increase In Legal Stated Capital		$705,000
Less Excess Of:		
Total Elected Value	($408,001)	
Reduced By Total Non Share Consideration	170,000	(238,001)
Reduction In Paid Up Capital		$466,999

This reduction in Paid Up Capital would be allocated to the two classes of shares on the basis of their fair market values. The calculations would be as follows:

Preferred Stock = ($225,000 ÷ $705,000) ($466,999) = $149,042

Common Stock = ($480,000 ÷ $705,000) ($466,999) = $317,957

Using this allocation, the Paid Up Capital of the two classes of shares would be as follows:

Preferred Stock = $225,000 - $149,042 = $ 75,958

Common Stock = $480,000 - $317,957 = $162,043

Note that the total Paid Up Capital of $238,001 ($75,958 + $162,043) is equal to the difference between the elected values for the assets ($408,001) and the non share consideration received by Miss Brock ($170,000).

Part D   The tax consequences for Miss Brock on the redemption of the preferred and common shares would be calculated as follows:

	Preferred Stock	Common Stock
Redemption Proceeds	$225,000	$480,000
Paid Up Capital	(75,958)	(162,043)
ITA 84(3) Deemed Dividend	$149,042	$317,957
Actual Redemption Proceeds	$225,000	$480,000
ITA 84(3) Deemed Dividend	(149,042)	(317,957)
Deemed Proceeds Of Disposition - ITA 54(h)(x)	$ 75,958	$162,043
Adjusted Cost Base	(225,000)	(13,001)
Capital Gain (Loss)	($149,042)	$149,042

Miss Brock would have a deemed dividend of $466,999 ($149,042 + $317,957) which would be subject to the usual gross up and tax credit procedures. This is also the amount of the gain that was deferred through the use of Section 85 ($875,000 - $408,001). There would be a net taxable capital gain of nil ($149,042 - $149,042).

Solution to Self Study Problem Seventeen - 6

Part A   In the absence of ITA 84.1, the Section 85 rollover would have resulted in a capital gain of $500,000. This is based on the elected value of $575,000, less the adjusted cost base of $75,000 [(75%)($100,000)]. However:

- There has been a sale by a Canadian resident (Ms. Chisholm) of shares in a subject corporation (DML).

- The purchaser of the subject corporation (Dorlaine Inc.) does not deal at arm's length with the Canadian resident (Ms. Chisholm).

- Immediately after the disposition, the subject corporation (DML) and the purchaser corporation (Dorlaine Inc.) are connected (Dorlaine Inc. controls DML).

As a consequence, the provisions of ITA 84.1 are applicable. This means that there will be a reduction of paid up capital under ITA 84.1(1)(a) as follows:

Increase In Legal Stated Capital Of Dorlaine Inc.		$400,000
Less Excess Of:		
PUC and ACB Of DML Shares	($ 75,000)	
Reduced By Non Share Consideration	500,000	Nil
PUC Reduction		$400,000

The PUC of the Dorlaine Inc. shares would be nil ($400,000 - $400,000).

The transfer would result in an ITA 84.1(1)(b) deemed dividend that would be calculated as follows:

Increase In Legal Stated Capital Of Dorlaine Inc.		$400,000
Non Share Consideration		500,000
Total		$900,000
PUC and ACB Of DML Shares	($ 75,000)	
PUC Reduction Under ITA 84.1(1)(a)	(400,000)	(475,000)
ITA 84.1(1)(b) Deemed Dividend		$425,000

The capital gain on the disposition of the DML shares would be calculated as follows:

Proceeds Before Adjustment of DML Shares (Elected Value)	$575,000
Deemed ITA 84.1(1)(b) Dividend	(425,000)
Adjusted Proceeds Of Disposition (ITA 54)	$150,000
Adjusted Cost Base Of DML Shares	(75,000)
Capital Gain	$ 75,000
Inclusion Rate	1/2
Taxable Capital Gain	$ 37,500

The tax consequences of transferring the DML shares are:

- a deemed dividend of $425,000 which would be subject to the usual gross up and tax credit procedures; and

- a taxable capital gain of $37,500 which would be eligible for the lifetime capital gains deduction as long as DML is a qualified small business corporation.

Note that, if Ms. Chisholm had elected the same $575,000 value, but limited her non share consideration to $75,000 (the PUC and ACB of the DML shares), there would have been no deemed dividend. Under this approach she would have realized the desired $500,000 capital gain and still retained control of her Company.

Part B At Ms. Chisholm's death, there would be a deemed disposition of all of her capital property at its fair market value, $400,000 in the case of the Dorlaine Inc. shares. The adjusted cost base of these shares would be $75,000, calculated as follows:

Value Elected In Section 85 Rollover	$575,000
Fair Market Value Of Non Share Consideration	(500,000)
Adjusted Cost Base Of Dorlaine Inc. Shares	$ 75,000

Given this, the taxable capital gain on the deemed disposition would be calculated as follows:

Deemed Proceeds Of Disposition (Fair Market Value)	$400,000
Adjusted Cost Base	(75,000)
Capital Gain	$325,000
Inclusion Rate	1/2
Taxable Capital Gain	$162,500

Since Dorlaine Inc. is holding various investments, it would not be a qualified small business corporation. As a result, none of the taxable capital gain would be eligible for the lifetime capital gains deduction.

Solution to Chapter Eighteen Exercises

Exercise Eighteen - 1

It would appear that, in this example, there is a share for share exchange which meets the conditions of ITA 85.1. Unless Ms. Alee elects out of this rollover provision in her income tax return, the tax consequences of this transaction for Ms. Alee would be as follows:

- Ms. Alee would be deemed to have disposed of her Aayee Ltd. shares at a value equal to their adjusted cost base of $450,000. As a consequence, there would be no capital gain on the disposition.
- Ms. Alee would be deemed to have acquired her Global Outreach Inc. shares at a cost equal to the adjusted cost base of the Aayee Ltd. shares or $450,000.

With respect to Global Outreach Inc., they would be deemed to have acquired the Aayee Ltd. shares at the lesser of their fair market value and the paid up capital. In this case, the $450,000 paid up capital amount is the lower figure.

Exercise Eighteen - 2

The required PUC reduction on the redeemable preferred shares would be calculated as follows:

Increase In Legal Stated Capital		$1,300,000
Less The Excess, If Any, Of:		
PUC Of Common Shares	($1,000,000)	
Reduced By Non Share Consideration	1,000,000	Nil
PUC Reduction		$1,300,000

This means that the redeemable preferred shares would have a PUC of nil ($1,300,000 - $1,300,000).

The adjusted cost base of the redeemable preferred shares would be calculated as follows:

Adjusted Cost Base Of Common Shares	$1,000,000
Non Share Consideration	(1,000,000)
Adjusted Cost Base Of Redeemable Preferred Shares	Nil

The proceeds of redemption of the common shares would be $1,000,000 ($1,000,000 + Nil), resulting in an ITA 84(3) deemed dividend of nil ($1,000,000 - $1,000,000). The proceeds of disposition would also be $1,000,000 ($1,000,000 + Nil), resulting in a capital gain of nil ($1,000,000 - $1,000,000).

Exercise Eighteen - 3

The required PUC reduction on the redeemable preferred shares would be calculated as follows:

Increase In Legal Stated Capital		$1,300,000
Less The Excess, If Any, Of:		
PUC Of Common Shares	($1,000,000)	
Reduced By Non Share Consideration	1,000,000	Nil
PUC Reduction		$1,300,000

This means that the redeemable preferred shares would have a PUC of nil ($1,300,000 - $1,300,000).

The adjusted cost base of the redeemable preferred shares would be calculated as follows:

Adjusted Cost Base Of Common Shares	$1,250,000
Non Share Consideration	(1,000,000)
Adjusted Cost Base Of Redeemable Preferred Shares	$ 250,000

The proceeds of redemption of the common shares would be $1,000,000 ($1,000,000 + Nil), resulting in an ITA 84(3) deemed dividend of nil ($1,000,000 - $1,000,000). The proceeds of disposition would be $1,250,000 ($1,000,000 + $250,000), resulting in a capital gain of nil ($1,250,000 - $1,250,000).

Exercise Eighteen - 4

The required PUC reduction on the redeemable preferred shares would be calculated as follows:

Increase In Legal Stated Capital		$1,100,000
Less The Excess, If Any, Of:		
PUC Of Common Shares	($1,000,000)	
Reduced By Non Share Consideration	1,200,000	Nil
PUC Reduction		$1,100,000

This means that the redeemable preferred shares would have a PUC of nil ($1,100,000 - $1,100,000).

The adjusted cost base of the redeemable preferred shares would be calculated as follows:

Adjusted Cost Base Of Common Shares	$1,250,000
Non Share Consideration	(1,200,000)
Adjusted Cost Base Of Redeemable Preferred Shares	$ 50,000

The proceeds of redemption of the common shares would be $1,200,000 ($1,200,000 + Nil), resulting in an ITA 84(3) deemed dividend of $200,000 ($1,200,000 - $1,000,000). The proceeds of disposition would be $1,050,000 ($50,000 + $1,200,000 - $200,000), resulting in a capital loss of $200,000 ($1,050,000 - $1,250,000). The taxable dividend would be $250,000 [(125%)($200,000)] and the allowable capital loss would be $100,000 [(1/2)($200,000)].

Exercise Eighteen - 5

Ms. Reviser gave up shares with a fair market value of $1,280,000, [(80%)($1,600,000)] in return for consideration of $1,100,000 ($300,000 + $800,000). As her daughter holds common shares, it would appear that there is a gift to the daughter of $180,000. This means that ITA 86(2) is applicable.

The PUC reduction on the new shares would be calculated as follows:

Increase In Legal Stated Capital		$800,000
Less The Excess, If Any, Of:		
PUC Of Common Shares		
[(80%)($250,000)]	($200,000)	
Reduced By Non Share Consideration	300,000	Nil
PUC Reduction		$800,000

This means that the redeemable preferred shares would have a PUC of nil ($800,000 - $800,000).

Under ITA 86(2)(e) the adjusted cost base of the redeemable preferred shares would be calculated as follows:

Adjusted Cost Base Of Common Shares		
[(80%)($250,000)]		$200,000
Non Share Consideration	($300,000)	
Gift	(180,000)	(480,000)
Adjusted Cost Base Of Preferred Shares		Nil

The proceeds of redemption of the common shares would be $300,000 ($300,000 + Nil), resulting in an ITA 84(3) deemed dividend of $100,000 ($300,000 - $200,000). Under ITA 86(2)(c), the proceeds of disposition would be $480,000 ($300,000 + $180,000). This would be reduced to $380,000 by the deduction of the ITA 84(3) deemed dividend of $100,000, resulting in a capital gain of $180,000 ($380,000 - $200,000). The taxable dividend would be $125,000 [(125%)($100,000)] and the taxable capital gain would be $90,000 [(1/2)($180,000)].

Exercise Eighteen - 6

As Upton Inc. has a clear majority of the shares in Amalgo Inc., it would appear that they have acquired control of Downer Ltd. As the acquisition of control rules would be applicable, there would be deemed year end (the amalgamation also creates a deemed year end of Downer Ltd.) and the net capital loss would expire at that time. With respect to the non capital loss, it would still be available. However for it to be used by the amalgamated company, Amalgo Inc. would have to continue the line of business in which the loss occurred. Further, the loss carry forward could only be applied against profits in that line of business.

Exercise Eighteen - 7

Subsequent to an ITA 88(1) wind up, the parent company can deduct subsidiary losses in its first taxation year beginning after the wind up. This would be the year ending September 15, 2002.

Side's loss is deemed to occur in Park's fiscal year which includes Side's year end. This would be the year ending September 15, 1997. This means that it will expire at the end of Park's taxation year ending September 15, 2004.

Exercise Eighteen - 8

Under ITA 88(1), a limited bump up of non depreciable assets is available. The basic limit would be calculated as follows:

Adjusted Cost Base Of Lorne Inc. Shares		$1,200,000
Tax Values Of Lorne Inc.'s Net Assets		
At Wind Up ($500,000 - $75,000)		(425,000)
Dividends Paid By Lorne Since Acquisition		Nil
Excess		$ 775,000

However, this basic amount cannot exceed the difference between the fair market value of non depreciable assets at the time of the share acquisition, and their tax cost at that time. This amount would be $130,000 ($270,000 - $140,000). The bump up in the land value is limited to that amount, resulting in the following tax values for Lorne's assets at the time of the ITA 88(1) wind up:

Cash	$120,000
Land ($140,000 + $130,000)	270,000
Depreciable Assets - At UCC	240,000
Total Assets	$630,000

Solution to Self Study Problem Eighteen - 1

Section 87   If ITA 87 is used, the tax consequences are as follows:

- Lynn will have proceeds of disposition equal to the adjusted cost base of the Land of $175,000. No capital gain or loss will be recorded.

- Ricon Ltd. will be deemed to have acquired the Land at its adjusted cost base of $175,000.

Section 88(1)   If ITA 88(1) is used, the tax consequences are as follows:

- Lynn will have proceeds of disposition equal to the adjusted cost base of the Land of $175,000. No capital gain or loss will be recorded.

- Ricon Ltd. will have a "bump" in the tax value of the Land that is the lesser of:

Adjusted Cost Base Of Lynn Shares		$380,000
Less:		
Cost Of Lynn's Assets	$175,000	
Dividends Paid By Lynn	Nil	(175,000)
Maximum Bump		$205,000

Fair Market Value Of Land When Lynn Shares Acquired	$390,000
Adjusted Cost Base Of Land	(175,000)
Maximum Increase In Land Value	$215,000

The amount of the bump will be limited to $205,000, resulting in an adjusted cost base of the Land of $380,000 ($175,000 + $205,000).

Conclusion   ITA 88(1) is the preferable approach as it adds $205,000 to Ricon's adjusted cost base for the Land. This will serve to reduce any future capital gain on an arm's length disposition of the Land.

Solution to Self Study Problem Eighteen - 2

Part A   The paid up capital of the new shares would be reduced under ITA 86(2.1) as follows:

Increase In Legal Stated Capital Of New Shares		$99,000
Paid Up Capital - Old Shares	($99,000)	
Non Share Consideration	69,000	(30,000)
Reduction In Paid Up Capital		$69,000

Given this reduction, the resulting paid up capital of the new preferred shares would be as follows:

Increase In Legal Stated Capital Of New Shares	$99,000
Reduction In Paid Up Capital	(69,000)
Paid Up Capital - New Shares	$30,000

Part B The adjusted cost base of the new preferred shares would be calculated as follows:

Adjusted Cost Base - Old Shares	$99,000
Non Share Consideration	(69,000)
Adjusted Cost Base - New Shares	$30,000

Part C The proceeds of disposition for the old common shares would be calculated as follows:

Adjusted Cost Base And PUC - New Shares	$30,000
Non Share Consideration	69,000
Proceeds Of Disposition - Old Shares	$99,000

This would be the proceeds of disposition under both ITA 86(1)(b) and ITA 84(5)(d).

Part D As the proceeds of disposition is equal to both the adjusted cost base and PUC of the old shares, there would be no ITA 84(3) dividend and no capital gain for Mr. Farnsworth at the time of the reorganization transaction.

Part E If the preferred shares were redeemed for $381,000, the tax consequences would be as follows:

Redemption Proceeds	$381,000
Paid Up Capital - Preferred Shares	(30,000)
ITA 84(3) Deemed Dividend	$351,000
Proceeds Of Disposition	$381,000
ITA 84(3) Deemed Dividend	(351,000)
Adjusted Proceeds Of Disposition	$ 30,000
Adjusted Cost Base - Preferred Shares	(30,000)
Capital Gain	Nil

There would be a taxable dividend of $438,750 [(125%)($351,000)] which would be eligible for a dividend tax credit of $58,500 [(2/3)(25%)($351,000)].

Solution to Self Study Problem Eighteen - 3

Approach One

Gift The fair market value of the common shares given up is $810,000 [(90%)($900,000)] and this is equal to the fair market value of the consideration received ($90,000 + $720,000). Given this, no gift is involved in the rollover and ITA 86(1) applies.

Cost Of New Preferred Shares The adjusted cost base of these shares is calculated as follows:

Adjusted Cost Base Of Old Common Shares [($360,000)(90%)]	$324,000
Fair Market Value Of Boot	(90,000)
Cost Of Preferred Shares	$234,000

PUC Reduction - New Shares   The PUC reduction on the new shares would be calculated as follows:

Increase In Legal Stated Capital Of New Shares		$234,000
PUC Of Common Shares [(90%)($100,000)]	($90,000)	
Fair Market Value Of Boot	90,000	Nil
PUC Reduction		$234,000

PUC Of New Preferred Shares   Giving the preceding PUC reduction, the PUC of the new shares would be nil ($234,000 - $234,000).

Redemption Of Common Shares   For purposes of determining any ITA 84(3) dividend, the calculation would be as follows:

Non Share Consideration	$90,000
PUC Of New Shares	Nil
Proceeds Of Redemption - ITA 84(5)(d)	$90,000
PUC Of Common Shares Redeemed [(90%)($100,000)]	(90,000)
ITA 84(3) Deemed Dividend	$ Nil

For purposes of determining any capital gain or loss, the calculation would be as follows:

Proceeds of Disposition - ITA 86(1)(c) ($90,000 + $234,000)	$324,000
Less: ITA 84(3) Deemed Dividend	Nil
Adjusted Proceeds Of Disposition - ITA 54	$324,000
Adjusted Cost Base [(90%)($360,000)]	(324,000)
Capital Gain	$ Nil

Net Economic Effect   No current income would be assessed to Mr. Long as a result of this reorganization transaction. He would retain the $90,000 note along with the preferred stock with a fair market value of $720,000. The $486,000 ($720,000 - $234,000) deferred capital gain on these shares would be the same as the deferred capital gain that was present on his previous holding of common shares ($810,000 - $324,000). He has accomplished the goal of freezing the value of his estate with no immediate tax consequences.

Approach Two

Gift   There is a gift involved in this approach, calculated as follows:

FMV Of Common Shares [(90%)($900,000)]		$810,000
FMV Of Boot	($ 50,000)	
FMV Of Preferred Shares	(660,000)	(710,000)
Gift		$100,000

As Mr. Long's daughter holds the remaining common shares, it is reasonable to assume that this $100,000 in value accrues to her. This means that the provisions of ITA 86(2) will be applicable if this approach is used.

Cost Of New Preferred Shares   Under the provisions of ITA 86(2), the adjusted cost base of the new preferred shares would be calculated as follows:

Adjusted Cost Base Of Old Common		
Shares [(90%)($360,000)]		$324,000
Fair Market Value Of Boot	($ 50,000)	
Amount Of Gift	(100,000)	(150,000)
Cost Of Preferred Shares		$174,000

PUC Reduction - New Shares   The PUC reduction on the new shares would be calculated as follows:

Increase In Legal Stated Capital		
Of New Shares		$40,000
PUC Of Common Shares	($90,000)	
Fair Market Value Of Boot	50,000	(40,000)
PUC Reduction		$ Nil

PUC Of New Preferred Shares   As there is no PUC reduction, the PUC of the new shares would be $40,000.

Redemption Of Common Shares   For purposes of determining any ITA 84(3) deemed dividend, the calculation would be as follows:

Fair Market Value Of The Boot	$50,000
PUC Of Preferred Shares	40,000
Proceeds Of Redemption - ITA 84(5)(d)	$90,000
PUC Of Common Shares Redeemed	(90,000)
ITA 84(3) Deemed Dividend	$ Nil

For purposes of determining any capital gain or loss, the calculation would be as follows:

Fair Market Value Of The Boot	$ 50,000
Gift	100,000
Proceeds Of Disposition - ITA 86(2)(c)	$150,000
ITA 84(3) Deemed Dividend	Nil
Adjusted Proceeds Of Disposition - ITA 54	$150,000
Adjusted Cost Base [(90%)($360,000)]	(324,000)
Capital Loss [Disallowed By ITA 86(2)(b)]	$ Nil

Net Economic Result   No current income would be assessed to Mr. Long as a result of this reorganization transaction. He would retain the $50,000 note along with the preferred stock with a fair market value of $660,000. The $486,000 ($660,000 - $174,000) deferred capital gain on these shares would be same as the deferred capital gain that was present on his previous holding of common shares. However, the value of his investment has been reduced by $150,000 ($810,000 - $660,000). While he has received $50,000 of this reduction in non share consideration, there is no corresponding reduction in tax values for the remaining $100,000. In addition, the fair market value of his daughter's shares have increased by $100,000 with no corresponding increase in their tax value. In effect, this approach will result in the amount of the $100,000 gift being subject to tax in his daughter's hands, with no compensating benefit available to either his daughter or himself.

Solution to Self Study Problem Eighteen - 4

The proceeds from the disposition and the taxable capital gains at the corporate level can be calculated as follows:

Asset	Proceeds	Taxable Capital Gains	Business Income (Recapture)
Inventories	$ 43,750	$ -0-	$ -0-
Land	1,553,750	387,500	-0-
Building	1,591,250	248,750	361,250
Totals	$3,188,750	$636,250	$361,250

The taxable capital gains will result in an addition to the refundable dividend tax on hand account. This will leave a balance in this account as follows:

RDTOH Balance Prior To Asset Dispositions	$ 33,750
Additions [(26-2/3%)($636,250)]	169,667
Ending RDTOH Balance	$203,417

The amount available for distribution to the shareholders after the payment of all taxes at the corporate level can be calculated as follows:

Gross Proceeds ($43,750 + $1,553,750 + $1,591,250)	$3,188,750
Tax On Income Eligible For Small Business Deduction [(18%)($200,000)]	(36,000)
Tax On Income Eligible For Accelerated Rate Reduction [(27%)($100,000)]	(27,000)
Tax On Remaining Active Business Income ([43%][$361,250 - $300,000])	(26,338)
Tax On Taxable Capital Gains [(50-2/3%)($636,250)]	(322,367)
Dividend Refund (Note)	203,417
Available For Distribution	$2,980,462

Note The dividend refund is equal to the balance in the RDTOH account. As will be shown in a subsequent calculation, the taxable dividends paid on the wind up are well in excess of the amount needed to trigger the refund of the balance in the RDTOH account.

With respect to the capital dividend account, the final balance is calculated as follows:

Balance Before Dispositions	$268,750
Disposition Of Land	387,500
Disposition Of Building	248,750
Ending Balance	$905,000

The taxable dividend component of the total distribution to the shareholders can be calculated as follows:

Distribution To Shareholders	$2,980,462
Paid Up Capital	(68,750)
ITA 84(2) Deemed Dividend	$2,911,712
ITA 83(2) Capital Dividend (Election Required)	(905,000)
Deemed Taxable Dividend	$2,006,712

ITA 54 indicates that the proceeds of disposition for purposes of determining any capital gain on the disposition of shares does not include any amount paid out as ITA 84(2) deemed dividends. Given the preceding calculation, the capital gain to the shareholders would be calculated as follows:

Distribution To Shareholders	$2,980,462
ITA 84(2) Deemed Dividend	(2,911,712)
Deemed Proceeds	$ 68,750
Adjusted Cost Base Of Shares	(68,750)
Capital Gain	$ Nil

Solution to Self Study Problem Eighteen - 5

Sale Of Shares   If the shares are sold for $455,000, the after tax results are as follows:

Proceeds Of Disposition	$455,000
Adjusted Cost Base	(52,500)
Capital Gain	$402,500
Inclusion Rate	1/2
Taxable Capital Gain	$201,250
Tax Rate For Mr. Brock	47%
Tax Payable	$ 94,588

Proceeds Of Disposition	$455,000
Tax Payable	(94,588)
After Tax Proceeds	$360,412

Sale Of Assets   This more complex transaction begins with a calculation of the taxes payable at the corporate level, subsequent to the sale of assets:

	Business Income	Taxable Capital Gains
Inventory ($109,500 - $105,000)	$ 4,500	$ -0-
Land	-0-	17,500
Building	87,500	7,000
Equipment (Note One)	(21,000)	-0-
Goodwill (Note Two)	82,250	-0-
Taxable Amounts	$153,250	$24,500
Tax Rate	18%	47%
Tax Payable	$ 27,585	$11,515

Note One   There is a terminal loss of $21,000 ($63,000 - $42,000).

Note Two   Business income in the amount of $82,250 [(3/4)($164,500)(1/2 ÷ 3/4)] will have to be recognized on the disposition of business assets.

Given the preceding calculations, the amount that would be available for distribution to Mr. Brock would be as follows:

Gross Proceeds ($561,000 - $70,000)	$491,000
Tax Payable ($27,585 + $11,515)	(39,100)
Dividend Refund (Note)	6,533
Available For Distribution	$458,433

Note   The dividend refund would be the lesser of the balance in the RDTOH and an amount equal to $1 for every $3 in taxable dividends paid. As the Part I Refundable Tax would only be equal to $6,533 [(26-2/3%)($24,500)], it would be the limiting factor.

Before proceeding to the calculation of the after tax proceeds to Mr. Brock, one other amount must be determined at the corporate level:

Capital Dividend Account   The pre sale balance in this account was $70,000. The disposition of the land added $17,500 [(1/2)($70,000 - $35,000)], the disposition of the building added $7,000 [(1/2)($136,500 - $122,500)], and the disposition of the goodwill added $82,250 [(1/4)($164,500)(1/2 ÷ 1/4)]. This leaves a balance of $176,750.

The calculation of the taxable dividend to Mr. Brock would be as follows:

Funds Available For Distribution	$458,433
Paid Up Capital	(52,500)
ITA 84(2) Deemed Dividend	$405,933
ITA 83(2) Capital Dividend (Election Required)	(176,750)
Deemed Taxable Dividend	$229,183

The gain or loss resulting from the disposition of shares on winding up the corporation is calculated as follows:

Funds Distributed	$458,433
ITA 84(2) Deemed Dividend	(405,933)
Deemed Proceeds Of Disposition For Shares	$ 52,500
Adjusted Cost Base	(52,500)
Capital Gain	$ -0-

The total cash retained after the deemed dividends and winding up of the corporation can be calculated as follows:

Funds Distributed	$458,933
Tax On Deemed Taxable Dividend [(31%)($229,183)]	(71,047)
After Tax Proceeds	$387,886

As this result is more favourable than the $360,912 in after tax proceeds resulting from the sale of shares, Mr. Brock should sell the assets rather than the shares.

Solution to Chapter Nineteen Exercises

Exercise Nineteen - 1

As there is a rollover available on transfers to a spousal trust, the accrued $3,000 gain ($9,000 - $6,000) will not be recognized until the surviving spouse eventually disposes of the asset. The spousal trust acquires the asset at an adjusted cost base of $6,000.

Exercise Nineteen - 2

The trust acquired the depreciable asset at a capital cost of $70,000 and was deemed to have claimed $24,000 of CCA, so that the trust's opening UCC was $46,000 after the transfer. At the end of the current year, the UCC is $40,000 ($46,000 - $6,000). The disposition of the asset by the trust results in a capital gain of $6,000 ($76,000 - $70,000), of which 1/2 or $3,000 is a taxable capital gain. Also, recaptured CCA of $30,000 ($70,000 - $40,000) will need to be reported by the trust.

Exercise Nineteen - 3

Income on the term deposits is subject to the attribution rules to the extent that the income is allocated to Trevor's spouse, Carmen and to their son Mitch as he is a minor. Therefore, one-third of the term deposit interest income needs to be attributed back to Trevor from each of Carmen's and Mitch's trust income allocations. As well, Carmen's share of the taxable capital gain is attributed back to Trevor. The income allocations are as follows:

	Carmen	Mitch	Rhonda
Interest income ($27,000/3)	$9,000	$9,000	$ 9,000
Interest attribution to Trevor	(9,000)	(9,000)	Nil
Taxable capital gain	1,000	1,000	1,000
Capital gain attribution to Trevor ($3,000/3)	(1,000)	Nil	Nil
Allocated trust income	Nil	$1,000	$10,000

In summary, Trevor is allocated $18,000 of the interest income and $1,000 of the taxable capital gains. Carmen, Mitch and Rhonda are allocated $11,000 (nil + $1,000 + $10,000), for an overall reported total of $30,000 ($19,000 + $11,000).

Exercise Nineteen - 4

Scenario	Settlor Taxable Capital Gain (1/2)	Adjusted Cost Base In Trust	Trust Taxable Capital Gain On Transfer To Beneficiary (1/2)
1. Inter vivos trust for adult child	$200	$1,600	$150
2. Inter vivos trust for minor child	200	1,600	150
3. Testamentary trust for friend	200	1,600	150
4. Inter vivos spousal trust (Note 1)	Nil	1,000	Nil
5. Testamentary spousal trust (Note 2)	Nil	1,000	Nil
6. Joint spousal trust (Note 2)	Nil	1,000	Nil
7. Alter ego trust	Nil	1,000	450

Note 1   The taxable capital gain will be attributed to the settlor if the capital asset is sold to another individual (other than the spouse) or otherwise disposed of. No gain will be realized by the trust if the asset is transferred to the surviving spouse.

Note 2   The eventual taxable capital gain will be reported by the trust if the capital asset is disposed of, or by the surviving spouse if the asset is transferred.

Exercise Nineteen - 5

It is possible to set up the trust, but income splitting may not be achievable, depending on what type of assets would be transferred to the trust. In general, the income attribution rules will require income on property transferred, but not capital gains, to be taxed in the transferor's hands. However, this result can be avoided if the distributions are structured appropriately, or if the property is transferred at fair market value and equivalent proceeds are received. If the property transferred is shares of a private corporation, the minor grandchildren will be subject to the tax on split income on any related dividends received until they are 18 years old. The dividend income will be taxed at the highest marginal rate, thus negating any potential income splitting benefits.

Exercise Nineteen - 6

Yes, however the five trusts will be designated as a single taxpayer, so that only one consolidated trust can benefit from the low progressive tax rates.

Exercise Nineteen - 7

Taxable Income for the trust, for the year, would be calculated as follows:

Income from dividends	$20,000
Deduction for distribution to beneficiary	(15,000)
Net dividend income	$ 5,000
Dividend gross up (25 percent)	1,250
Taxable Income For The Trust	$ 6,250

Taxable Income for the son, for the year, would be calculated as follows:

Income from the trust	$15,000
Dividend gross up (25 percent)	3,750
Taxable Income For The Son	$18,750

Solution to Self Study Problem Nineteen - 1

A. The following schedule allocates income as per the trust agreement:

Income Allocation	Trust	Spouse	Son
Business Income	$ -0-	$12,000	$ 8,000
Interest	-0-	2,400	1,600
Dividends	13,000	7,800	5,200
Dividend Gross Up (25%)	3,250	1,950	1,300
Net Rental Income (Note)	-0-	2,400	1,600
Net And Taxable Income	$16,250	$26,550	$17,700
Federal Income Tax (16%)	$2,600	$4,248	$2,832
Basic Personal Credit	N/A	(1,186)	(1,186)
Dividend Tax Credit	(2,167)	(1,300)	(867)
Basic Federal Tax	$ 433	$1,762	$ 779

Note   The $4,000 net rental income is calculated as the rent receipts of $12,000, less the operating expenses of $6,000 and CCA of $2,000. The CCA is claimed at the trust level, and is flowed through as a deduction in calculating the income of the beneficiaries.

B. The following income allocation assumes that all dividend income will be allocated to Mrs. Rowand and Roger.

Income Allocation	Spouse	Son
Business Income	$12,000	$ 8,000
Interest	2,400	1,600
Dividends	15,600	10,400
Dividend Gross Up (25%)	3,900	2,600
Net Rental Income	2,400	1,600
Net And Taxable Income	$36,300	$24,200
Federal Income Tax		
On 1st $30,754 At 16 Percent	$4,921	$3,872
On Remaining $5,546 At 22 Percent	1,220	Nil
Basic Personal Credit	(1,186)	(1,186)
Dividend Tax Credit	(2,600)	(1,733)
Basic Federal Tax	$2,355	$ 953

C. The total basic federal tax in Part B is $3,308, which is $334 higher than the total of $2,974 in Part A. This excess tax bill of $334 results because $5,546 of Mrs. Rowand's income is taxed at 22 percent instead of 16 percent (there is a $2 rounding error in this calculation).

Solution to Self Study Problem Nineteen - 2

Calculation Of Taxable Incomes   The taxable income of the two beneficiaries and the trust would be calculated as shown in the following table. With the exception of the recapture on the sale of rental property, all amounts are allocated 30 percent to Ms. Robinson's son, 50 percent to her daughter, and 20 percent to the trust.

	Son	Daughter	Trust
Interest On Government Bonds	$ 19,500	$ 32,500	$ 13,000
Dividends On Canadian Stocks	75,000	125,000	50,000
Gross Up Of 25 Percent	18,750	31,250	12,500
Rental Revenues	147,600	246,000	98,400
Rental Expenses	(102,600)	(171,000)	(68,400)
Taxable Capital Gain On Land [(1/2)($2,300,000 - $1,430,000)]	130,500	217,500	87,000
Taxable Capital Gain - Building [(1/2)($4,560,000 - $3,840,000)]	108,000	180,000	72,000
Recaptured CCA On Building (Note)	-0-	-0-	460,000
Net And Taxable Income	$396,750	$661,250	$724,500

Note   The recapture of CCA on the building is calculated as follows:

Capital Cost	$3,840,000
Undepreciated Capital Cost	(3,380,000)
Recaptured CCA	$ 460,000

There is no provision for allocating recaptured capital cost allowance to the beneficiaries of the trust. As a consequence, the entire amount is allocated to and taxed in the hands of the trust.

Calculation Of Taxes Payable   Based on the preceding taxable income, the federal taxes payable of the trust can be calculated as follows:

Federal Tax (29 Percent Of $724,500)	$210,105
Dividend Tax Credit [(2/3)($12,500)]	(8,333)
Federal Taxes Payable	$201,772

Solution to Self Study Problem Nineteen - 3

The various components of the trust's income would be allocated as follows:

	Daughter	Son	Trust
Net Rental Income	$18,300	$ 30,500	$12,200
Capital Cost Allowance	(13,500)	(22,500)	(9,000)
Taxable Canadian Dividends	26,100	43,500	17,400
Gross Up Of 25 Percent	6,525	10,875	4,350
British Interest (Gross Amount Of $110,000)	33,000	55,000	22,000
Net And Taxable Income	$70,425	$117,375	$46,950
British Taxes Paid ($16,500)	$ 4,950	$ 8,250	$ 3,300

The CCA is claimed at the trust level, and is flowed through as a deduction in calculating the taxable income of the beneficiaries. Except for the fact that the ITA 118 personal tax credits are not available, income which remains in a testamentary trust is taxed in the same general manner as would apply to an individual. Given this, Taxes Payable for the trust would be calculated as follows:

Federal Income Tax	
On First $30,754 At 16 Percent	$4,921
On Remaining $16,196 At 22 Percent	3,563
	$8,484
Dividend Tax Credit [(2/3)($4,350)]	(2,900)
Basic Federal Tax	$5,584
Foreign Tax Credit (See Note)	(3,300)
Total Taxes Payable	$2,284

Note   The amount that can be deducted for the foreign tax credit is the lesser of the amount of foreign taxes withheld and an amount determined by the following formula:

$$\left(\frac{\text{Foreign Non Business Income}}{\text{Net Income}}\right)(\text{Tax Payable Before Credits})$$

$$= (\$22,000 \div \$46,950)\,(\$8,484)$$
$$= \$3,975$$

As this amount is more than the actual foreign taxes of $3,300 allocated to the trust, the actual foreign taxes paid would be the lesser amount and would be deductible.

Solution to Chapter Twenty Exercises

Exercise Twenty - 1

A partnership interest has an adjusted cost base (ACB) whereas a joint venture interest does not. When a partnership interest is disposed of, a gain or loss results. The disposition of a joint venture interest results in a disposition of a pro-rata share of all assets and liabilities of the joint venture. Hence, the joint venture assets and liabilities are disposed of in contrast to a partnership interest or single asset disposition. In both situations, a capital gain or loss may be realized, however a disposition of joint venture assets can also result in recaptured CCA, terminal losses, or business income (loss).

Exercise Twenty - 2

A) Deductible - Office rent expense is allowed if incurred to earn property or business income.
B) Not deductible - Interest on capital accounts is considered a form of income allocation.
C) Deductible - Interest can be deducted if the loan is bona fide.
D) Not deductible - Salary paid to partners is a form of income allocation.

Exercise Twenty - 3

No, a partnership cannot carryover losses. If a partnership loss is realized, the entire net loss is shared among the partners and is used by each partner in the current year to offset other income. Any unutilized loss by the partners can be carried forward or back depending on each partner's tax situation.

Exercise Twenty - 4

The required first $40,000 of partnership income should first be allocated to Ruth. The remaining $5,000 loss should be allocated equally between Emily and Ruth, as follows:

	Emily	Ruth	Total
Guaranteed income allocation	Nil	$40,000	$40,000
Share of remainder	($2,500)	(2,500)	(5,000)
Net allocations	($2,500)	$37,500	$35,000

This solution follows the recommendation in IT-138R, "Computation And Flow Through Of Partnership Income" for when salaries are deemed to be paid to partners.

Exercise Twenty - 5

Stuart Jones is allowed to deduct the limited partnership loss up to his at risk amount. The at risk amount will include the $50,000 cash investment, but not the loan, as Stuart Jones is not at risk for the loan due to the promoter buy back and loan assumption option. Therefore, $50,000 of the loss is deductible in the current year and the remaining $25,000 will become a limited partnership loss carry forward.

Exercise Twenty - 6

All partners must pro-rate the small business deduction limit based on each partner's income allocation, regardless of whether the partner is a corporation, individual or trust. All partners will also be required to pro-rate the extra $100,000 ($300,000 - $200,000) of active business income that is subject to the accelerated rate reduction for small business corporations.

Exercise Twenty - 7

Alan and Balan will each have a disposition of one-third of their partnership interests for $40,000. The adjusted cost base of each third is $16,000 [(1/3)($48,000)], so Alan and Balan will each have a $24,000 capital gain, of which one-half, or $12,000, will be a taxable capital gain.

The partner capital account transactions and ending balances will be:

	Alan	Balan	Caitlin
Opening capital accounts	$48,000	$48,000	Nil
Adjustment for Caitlin's admission	(16,000)	(16,000)	32,000
Ending capital accounts	$32,000	$32,000	$32,000
Adjusted cost base of partnership interest	$32,000	$32,000	$80,000

Exercise Twenty - 8

Mr. Gelato's additional business income for the current year will be $15,088 [($12,300)(184 Days ÷ 150 Days)]. The 184 days is for the period July 1 through December 31, while the 150 days is for the period February 1 through June 30. The total business income for the year will be $27,388 ($15,088 + $12,300).

Solution to Self Study Problem Twenty - 1

Partnership Net Income　To determine the amount that will be allocated to the incomes of the partners, we must calculate the income of the partnership as if the partnership were a separate person resident in Canada. The calculation is as follows:

Net Income As Per Statement		$192,100
Additions:		
Partners' Salaries [(2)($44,000)]	$88,000	
Depreciation Deducted	12,500	
Charitable Donations	7,200	
Closing Accounts Receivable (Note One)	56,000	163,700
Deductions:		
Opening Accounts Receivable (Note One)	($27,000)	
Capital Gains On Securities (Note Two)	(14,000)	
Dividends (Note Two)	(48,000)	
Capital Cost Allowance:		
Class 8 [(20%)($26,000)]	(5,200)	
Class 10 [30%][$14,000 + ($8,500)(50%)]	(5,475)	(99,675)
Net Business Income		$256,125

Note One　The addition of closing Accounts Receivable and the deduction of the opening Accounts Receivable are required to adjust the cash based income figure to an accrual based income figure.

Note Two　The total capital gain is added back to the partnership income figure so that the taxable one-half of these gains can be included on a flow through basis in the income of the individual partners. In corresponding fashion, the dividends are removed so that they can be flowed through as taxable Canadian dividends in the income of the individual partners.

Mr. Caldwell's Personal Income　The amount to be included in Mr. Caldwell's personal tax return would be calculated as follows:

Partnership Income [(1/2)($256,125)]	$128,063
Automobile Costs:	
CCA [($13,500)(30%)(75%)]	(3,038)
Operating Costs [($4,000)(75%)]	(3,000)
Net Income From Professional Practice	$122,025
Taxable Capital Gains [(1/2)($14,000)(1/2)]	3,500
Dividends From Taxable Canadian Corporations [($48,000)(125%)(1/2)]	30,000
Net Income For Tax Purposes	$155,525

Mr. Caldwell's $3,600 [(1/2)($7,200)] share of the charitable donations can be used as the basis for a credit against his personal taxes payable. The amount of the credit would be $1,018 [(16%)($200) + (29%)($3,400)].

He is also entitled to a federal dividend tax credit of $4,000 [(2/3)($48,000)(25%)(1/2)].

Solution to Self Study Problem Twenty - 2

The adjusted cost base of Eric Beam's partnership interest on the date he withdrew from the partnership is calculated as follows:

Initial Investment	$225,000
Share Of Partnership Income Prior To The Current Year [(1/3)($195,000)]	65,000
Non Taxable One-Half Of Capital Gain (Note One) [(1/3)(1/2)($66,000)]	11,000
Drawings From The Partnership	(43,000)
Share Of Charitable Donations (Note Two) [(1/3)($12,000)]	(4,000)
Additional Capital Contributions	65,000
Adjusted Cost Base On June 1, 2001	$319,000

Note One   As with individuals, only one-half of capital gains will be included in computing the income of a partnership. However, the remaining one-half is included in the assets of the partnership and, in the absence of a special provision to deal with this situation, the realization of this amount would be added to any capital gain realized on the disposition of the partnership interest. ITA 53(1)(e)(i) provides such a provision, indicating that the full amount of any capital gains must be added to the adjusted cost base of a partnership interest.

Note Two   Charitable donations cannot be deducted in the calculation of partnership income. Instead, they are allocated to the individual partners to be used by them as the basis for credits against their personal taxes payable. Given this, ITA 53(2)(c)(iii) requires that these amounts be deducted from the adjusted cost base of the partnership interest.

Given the preceding calculation, the gain on the disposal of the partnership interest can be calculated as follows:

Proceeds Of Disposition		$355,000
Adjusted Cost Base:		
From Preceding Calculation	($319,000)	
Legal And Accounting Fees	(1,800)	(320,800)
Capital Gain		$ 34,200
Inclusion Rate		1/2
Taxable Capital Gain		$ 17,100

This amount would be included in Eric Beam's income for the current year as a taxable capital gain. He would not include any partnership income for the period January 1 to June 1, 2001 as he was not allocated any income. However, it is likely that Eric's share of income for the period from January 1 to June 1, 2001, would have been factored into the proceeds for the partnership interest. This can result in converting business income into capital gain, depending on how much income is credited to him in the final settlement.

On the other hand, if any proceeds relate directly to the income from January 1 to June 1, 2001, and especially if the financial statements report an income allocation to Eric, they should be reported as partnership income. This would serve to reduce the proceeds of disposition of the partnership interest with a corresponding reduction in the capital gain.

Solution to Self Study Problem Twenty - 3

Preferred Shares With respect to the preferred shares received by each partner, ITA 85(3)(e) indicates that their adjusted cost base will be the lesser of:

- Their fair market value which would be $180,000 for each of the three partners; and

- The adjusted cost base of each partnership interest, reduced by the amount of non share consideration received by the partner.

This latter value would be calculated as follows for each of the three partners:

	Porter	Quinn	Roberts
Adjusted Cost Base	$382,000	$526,000	$726,000
Cash Received	(78,000)	(222,000)	(422,000)
Balance	$304,000	$304,000	$304,000

For each of the three partners, the lower figure would be the fair market value of $180,000 and, as a consequence, this would be the adjusted cost base of their preferred shares.

Common Shares Under ITA 85(3)(f), the adjusted cost base of the common shares received by each partner would be the adjusted cost base of their partnership interest, less the sum of the value of the non share consideration received and the value assigned to the preferred shares received. These amounts would be calculated as follows:

	Porter	Quinn	Roberts
Adjusted Cost Base - Partnership Interest	$382,000	$526,000	$726,000
Cash Received	(78,000)	(222,000)	(422,000)
Adjusted Cost Base - Preferred Shares	(180,000)	(180,000)	(180,000)
Adjusted Cost Base - Common Shares	$124,000	$124,000	$124,000

Capital Gain Or Loss As the non share consideration had a value that was less than the value of the assets transferred, there will be no immediate gain or loss on this rollover. This can be demonstrated with the following calculation:

	Porter	Quinn	Roberts
Proceeds Of Disposition:			
Cash	$ 78,000	$222,000	$422,000
Preferred Shares	180,000	180,000	180,000
Common Shares	124,000	124,000	124,000
Total Proceeds	$382,000	$526,000	$726,000
Adjusted Cost Base	(382,000)	(526,000)	(726,000)
Gain Or Loss	$ -0-	$ -0-	$ -0-

From an economic point of view the gain is still present. We have simply deferred recording it for tax purposes by placing a value on the common shares of $372,000 [(3)($124,000)]. This is significantly below their current fair market value of $1,080,000.

Solution to Chapter Twenty-One Exercises

Exercise Twenty-One - 1

Canada taxes individuals on the basis of residency. As such, all residents are required to report worldwide income regardless of where it is earned. U.S. citizens are also obliged to report worldwide income in the U.S. Therefore, Canadian residents who are U.S. citizens report essentially the same income in each country. Relief from potential double taxation is provided by way of foreign tax credits. In Canada, a foreign tax credit can be claimed for any U.S. tax paid on the interest income.

Exercise Twenty-One - 2

Bob will be taxed in Canada, on his worldwide income, including all employment income as he is a Canadian resident. If his annual U.S. employment income exceeds U.S. $10,000 it will also be taxable in the U.S. However, he can claim a foreign tax credit in Canada for the lesser of U.S. tax paid and Canadian taxes payable on U.S. source income.

Exercise Twenty-One - 3

U.S. estate tax will apply to the rental property, as the estate exceeds the 2001 $675,000 estate tax exemption and U.S. situated property is owned. The U.S. estate tax rates vary between 18% and 55%. Canadian income tax will apply to the accrued capital gain and recaptured CCA, if any, from the deemed disposition on death. The U.S. estate tax can be claimed as a foreign tax credit in Canada, up to the amount of any Canadian tax payable on the capital gain and recaptured CCA.

Exercise Twenty-One - 4

If Helena broke her residential ties with Canada when she moved to the U.S., she will be considered a resident in Canada from January to April, and a resident in the U.S. for the remainder of the year. Helena must file tax returns in both countries to report worldwide income that was earned for the period of the year she was resident in each country.

Exercise Twenty-One - 5

The shares will have an adjusted cost base of $200,000 and an unrealized gain of $1,800,000. A disposition will be deemed to occur on the date Charmaine emigrated. One-half of the gain will be taxable, resulting in a taxable capital gain of $900,000. This needs to be reported on Charmaine's 2001 tax return. The related tax payable can be paid or appropriate security can be provided. Very likely, the CCRA will accept the shares as security for the tax payable.

Exercise Twenty-One - 6

Simon's total foreign investments of £65,000 push him over the $100,000 Canadian reporting limit [(£65,000)($2.4) = $156,000]. Therefore, he should report foreign investments held during the year by filing form T1135. He is also required to report any foreign interest income that he earns.

Exercise Twenty-One - 7

Non residents are required to pay Canadian tax on capital gains realized on the disposition of taxable Canadian property. As mutual funds and shares traded on a stock exchange are not considered taxable Canadian property, any resulting capital gains are not subject to Canadian taxation. Dividends and interest, on the other hand, are taxed under Part XIII. A 25% withholding tax applies to dividends unless the relevant international tax convention reduces the tax rate.

Exercise Twenty-One - 8

Timothy should report only the pension plan income on the tax return. The U.S. interest is not taxable in Canada and the Canadian interest is not taxable under Part I as Timothy is a U.S. resident. Instead, Canadian interest is taxable under Part XIII.

Timothy can claim the full personal tax credits as 93.75% [$15,000/($15,000 + $700 + $300)], which is more than 90%, of his worldwide income is elected to be taxable in Canada. Timothy must determine whether or not the $15,000 is net of withholding tax or gross. The gross pension should be reported, and any withholding tax can be claimed as a Canadian tax prepayment.

Exercise Twenty-One - 9

If Maya submits a Form NR6 by December 31, 2000, the withholding requirements on her rental income will be 25% of the expected net rental income of $3,000 ($15,000 - $12,000), instead of 25% of the gross rent. As the former is $750 rather than $3,750 [(25%)($15,000)], Maya is advised to complete and submit an NR6. As well, she must submit a calendar year 2001 Section 216 tax return by June 30, 2002.

Solution to Self Study Problem Twenty-One - 1

For Canadian residency purposes, Paul will still be considered a resident of Canada as his family ties (wife and daughter) are in Canada. For U.S. tax purposes, Paul is likely considered a U.S. resident because he has moved to the U.S., has bought a home there and is working there. As this is a possible case of dual residence, we need to refer to the tie-breaker rules.

As Paul has a permanent home available in both locations, we need to apply the center of vital interests criterion. The personal ties appear to be stronger in Canada, so we would conclude that the center of vital interests is Canada, and Paul would be considered a resident of Canada for the entire period.

Paul should report his worldwide income in Canada and claim a foreign tax credit for any U.S. tax paid on his employment income while he was living and working in the U.S.

Solution to Self Study Problem Twenty-One - 2

Debbie will have a deemed disposition of all property except Canadian real estate and RRSPs. The deemed dispositions should result in the following gains, which will likely be capital gains.

Gains on dispositions of capital assets

Description	ACB	FMV	Gain (Loss)
Interest in CCPC (10 percent)	$ 90,000	$140,000	$ 50,000
Sports car (Note 1)	18,000	15,000	-0-
Paintings	50,000	175,000	125,000
10 percent interest in Sorrento Co., a Canadian public company	180,000	110,000	(70,000)
Total capital gains			$105,000
Inclusion rate			1/2
Taxable capital gains			$ 52,500
Personal tax rate			45%
Personal taxes payable (Note 2)			$ 23,625

Note 1   No loss is available on personal use property.

Note 2   If Debbie continues to own the above assets, the CCRA will accept security in lieu of cash for the related personal taxes payable. The unpaid tax is due when the assets are eventually disposed of.

Deferred gains on real estate

Description	ACB	FMV	Gain
House	$150,000	$225,000	$75,000
Whistler ski chalet	125,000	185,000	60,000

As the $20,000 ($60,000/3) annual gain on the Whistler ski chalet is much greater than the $7,500 ($75,000/10) annual gain on her 50 percent portion of the house, Debbie should elect the family's principal residence to be the ski chalet for 2000 and 2001 thereby avoiding reporting the entire gain as a taxable capital gain (due to the plus one year rule for principal residences). Then, the house will be deemed the principal residence from 1992 to 1999. This results in the gain on the house for just 2001 being taxable (due to the plus one year rule for principal residences), but only when the property is eventually sold. Debbie should obtain professional advice on how Hong Kong tax laws will affect the eventual sale of the house.

Report of assets held

As Debbie owns assets exceeding $25,000, she is obliged to provide a list to the CCRA of all assets owned on her departure date and their related costs. Personal use property up to $10,000 can be excluded. The list of assets owned (Form T1161) should be attached to her tax return for the year of departure.

Other planning points   The following factors should also be considered.

Non resident date   As Debbie's husband may defer his move for six months, the deemed date of non residence will be when he finally moves to Hong Kong. To minimize taxes payable, this may be undesirable for Debbie as the Hong Kong tax rates are less than Canadian rates. Until Debbie is officially non resident, all of her income will have to be reported in Canada and will be subject to the relatively high Canadian tax rates. As Debbie's husband will be commuting anyway, it could be more advantageous for him to work from his Hong Kong base to wind up his Canadian client affairs. In this way, the non resident date could be advanced and tax savings would be realized.

Moving expenses   The $50,000 moving allowance may be taxable in Canada, particularly if the date of cessation of residence is delayed for a few months. It would be preferable for Debbie to be reimbursed for specific moving costs as a reimbursement for reasonable moving expenses is not taxable.

RRSP   Debbie will have relatively high income in 2001, so she should not collapse her RRSP while resident in Canada in 2001. If the departure from Canada is deferred to 2002, she could collapse some of the RRSP early that year, to be taxed at the low personal tax rates. This assumes that Debbie has no other Canadian income in 2002. It may be more advantageous for Debbie to collapse the RRSP after becoming a non resident. At that time, a 25 percent Part XIII tax would apply in Canada, and there would likely not be any applicable Hong Kong income tax. Alternatively, Debbie can leave the RRSP invested in Canada and withdraw amounts, after withholding taxes are applied, in later years.

Rental income   If the house and ski chalet are rented, a 25 percent Part XIII tax will apply to the gross rents received. Debbie can also elect to have the rental income taxed as regular Canadian income so that expenses can be deducted and withholding taxes reduced. She should compare which alternative will be more advantageous.

Solution to Self Study Problem Twenty-One - 3

A. The term deposits do not need to be reported because the total amount is less than $100,000.

B. If the Florida condominium is primarily for personal use, then reporting of the asset is not required. On the other hand, if it is rented out to third parties, it would need to be reported, as the total cost amount is greater than $100,000.

C. As the total cost of the Arizona condominium is $102,000, reporting is required if the condominium is not personal use property.

D. Foreign investment reporting is required for all foreign affiliates, regardless of the cost of the shares. The operating company is a foreign affiliate as more than 10 percent of the shares are owned by the taxpayer.

E. No foreign investment reporting is required when assets are used in an active business.

Solution to Self Study Problem Twenty-One - 4

Operation As A Branch   As a branch, any profits will be taxed in the United States. In addition, they will be taxed in Canada as part of worldwide income earned by the Canadian company. However, any Canadian taxes payable will be reduced by foreign tax credits for U.S. taxes paid on branch profits.

As the earnings of the branch will not be active business income earned in Canada, no small business deduction will be available to Tritec. However, any loss suffered in the U.S. operation will be deductible in arriving at taxable income for Canadian tax purposes.

Operation As A Subsidiary   A subsidiary will be subject to U.S. taxes on its worldwide income and, if the subsidiary earns investment income, the foreign accrual property rules will result in this income being taxed in Canada as the investment income is earned. Subsidiary losses will not be deductible in Canada and, in addition, the U.S. taxation authorities will assess a withholding tax on any management fees, interest or dividends paid to the Canadian parent.

Solution to Self Study Problem Twenty-One - 5

A. With respect to the Florida School, the US$14,000 fee exceeds the US$10,000 that would provide a general exemption from U.S. taxation. However, it is less than the US$15,000 limit that is applicable to artists and athletes. Assuming that the individual is considered to be an athlete, he would not be subject to U.S. tax. However, as the individual is a Canadian resident, all of the earnings will be taxable in Canada.

B. While we do not know the amount of remuneration, presumably it exceeds the US$10,000 limit. Regardless, the employment is exempt as the total number of days employed in the U.S. is 180 days [(60 days)(3 periods)] which is less than the cut-off of 183 days. Also, the wages are borne by a Canadian employer and the computer wizard is likely not considered an artist. Therefore, the earnings would not be subject to U.S. tax, but would be taxable in Canada.

C. First, we determine that the remuneration is not exempt under Article XV as it exceeds US$10,000. Next, we must consider whether the roller blader is an athlete. This is debatable, but assuming roller blading is considered an athletic activity, the answer is likely yes. Although the contract is for promotional purposes, the payment is for the services of an athlete. We next need to assess whether the amount can be considered an inducement to sign an agreement relating to the performance of an athlete. Again, the answer appears to be yes. Therefore, we conclude that the $12,000 signing bonus is subject to U.S. tax at a maximum rate of 15 percent. No withholding tax will apply to the royalties. The signing bonus and subsequent royalties would be reported as Canadian income, and any amounts paid for U.S. taxes can likely be claimed as foreign tax credits in Canada.

Index

G

M